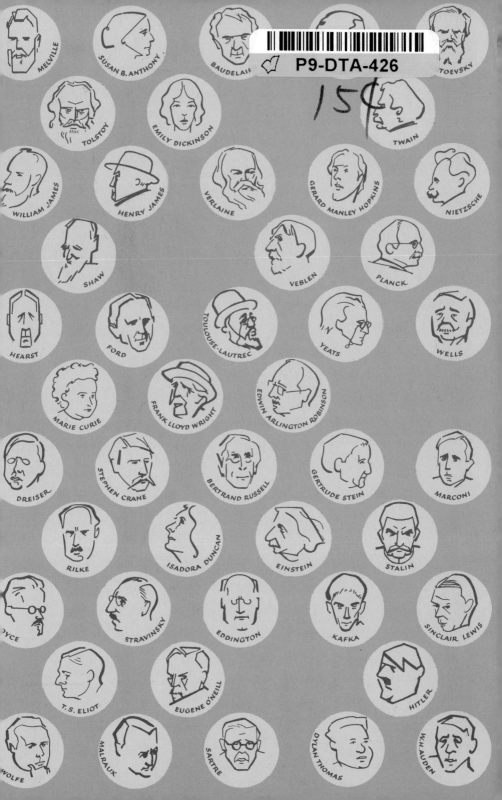

15¢

MAKERS
of the
MODERN WORLD

*The Lives of Ninety-two Writers, Artists,
Scientists, Statesmen, Inventors, Philosophers,
Composers, and Other Creators Who Formed
the Pattern of Our Century*

BY

Louis Untermeyer

19 — 55

SIMON AND SCHUSTER · NEW YORK

FOURTH PRINTING
LIBRARY OF CONGRESS CATALOG CARD NUMBER: 54–12364
DEWEY DECIMAL CLASSIFICATION NUMBER: 920
MANUFACTURED IN THE UNITED STATES OF AMERICA

For Bryna

WITHOUT WHOM, NOTHING

Foreword

MAKERS OF THE MODERN WORLD *does not begin to include all the important figures of our times. It is limited to ninety-two men and women whose creative contribution during the last one hundred years has broken new ground, altered our cultural patterns, and changed our way of living. These are seminal beings, "movers and shakers," whose influence upon those who followed has been profound and unmistakable. Their ideas, revolutionary in thought and expression, have made the modern world what it is.*

Writing critical and biographical studies of these guiding—and in some instances, misguided—spirits, I was constantly reminded of the role of experimenters and pioneers, the inevitable nonconformers. Innovators in art have consistently been deplored and condemned; trail-blazing inventors and scientists have had to battle against a barrage of savage ridicule. Every departure from the norm has been accomplished only by indomitable faith, menaced by disbelief, interference, and almost universal opposition. Society, devoted to preserving the status quo, is suspicious of those who disturb it; it is a platitude of progress that a new way of thinking invariably provokes personal hostility and general antagonism. It is, furthermore, a continuing paradox that, in the end, the world worships those whom, in the beginning, it persecuted.

Among the ninety-two portraits, I have included several to whom the world cannot be grateful. However, their impact upon our era has been so violent and so dominant that they could not be omitted.

—2—

THE SELECTION *of the ninety-two personalities was determined partly by what seemed to me the imperatives, partly by preference.*

It has been said that history is not only written but continually re-written. Some of the estimates in this book may be sharply revised ten years from now, but the great majority are not subject to dimin-ishing evaluations. The work of a Darwin, a Van Gogh, a Proust, an Einstein, an Edison will maintain its authority and be appreciated at least for its relation to our time. A Chaplin, an Isadora Duncan, a Gerard Manley Hopkins may not seem as imperative, but their in-fluence on their art forms have been as distinctive.

Some of the omissions may be questioned more sharply than the inclusions. I have not, for example, included Richard Strauss, whose derivation from Richard Wagner is so obvious that he was nick-named Richard the Second, or such superb melody-makers as Grieg and Tchaikowsky; although greatly gifted and highly popular, none of the three discovered a new musical vocabulary. On the other hand, such innovators as Schönberg and Bartók have been left out since their influence, though not negligible, has been extremely spe-cial. Among the poets, I have not included Carl Sandburg, Wallace Stevens, and Marianne Moore (to name three of the more eminent omissions) for, although their work is remarkable, it is sui generis, self-enclosed and self-complete. Certain pioneers have been omitted whose work was anticipated by others; the accomplishments of Lister, for example, are foreshadowed in the chapter on Pasteur.

These pages purport to suggest the essential qualities of the men and women included in them. Such an aim is interpretive rather than merely factual, and interpretation can never be free of the predilections of the interpreter. Nevertheless, although the writer cannot assume impersonality, he can try for impartiality. Since I am not a disciple of any school of thought, having (as someone must have said) no axiom to grind, I have been scrupulous about the facts and not, I hope, arbitrary about their final value.

–3–

THERE ARE *several reasons why the book has not been arranged in a series of convenient categories—Poets, Painters, Philosophers, Physi-*

*cists, Political Leaders, et cetera. For one thing, many of the per-
sonalities do not easily fit in any one class. Bertrand Russell is no
less a mathematician for being a philosopher. T. S. Eliot is not only
a poet but a playwright and an essayist. It would be misleading to
limit the scope of Gandhi's activities by placing him in a division
marked "Politicians," although Gandhi unquestionably was one; just
as it would put the wrong emphasis on Albert Schweitzer to make
him the sole representative of a section marked "Saints," although
Schweitzer may well merit sainthood.*

*For another thing, the arrangement adopted here makes for a
better balance as well as a sharper contrast; it furnishes a less academic and more interesting presentation of the fluctuating forces of
change. Moreover, the chronological order places events in their
proper sequence and gives a gradually unfolding picture of the pattern of historical development.*

*Throughout the work, independent of cross-references, the reader
may trace the course of many influences. Such interrelations can be
found in the connecting ideas of Nietzsche, Wagner, and Hitler, or,
to take a somewhat more special example, those of Kierkegaard,
Kafka, and Sartre.*

–4–

THIS BOOK *is not for the specialist or the critical scholar, to whom
the estimates will seem obvious and sketchy. On the contrary, it
presupposes little previous knowledge of scientific technicalities and
literary techniques. It does presume, however, to define the contributions of ninety-two men and women and relate them to our time.
In an effort to distill the essence of their work, some six hundred
volumes have been consulted, and I am deeply indebted to a host
of preceding biographers, critics, and analyzers, many of whom are
listed in* A SELECTED BIBLIOGRAPHY, *at the end of this volume.*

*A few passages in these pages originally appeared in my previous
writings. For permission to reprint such excerpts I am obligated to
the following publishers: Harcourt Brace and Company for* MOD-

ERN AMERICAN AND BRITISH POETRY *and* THE COLLEGE SURVEY OF ENGLISH LITERATURE; *Henry Holt and Company for* THE ROAD NOT TAKEN; *The George Macy Companies for* SELECTED POEMS OF EMILY DICKINSON; *Simon and Schuster, Inc. for* THE INNER SANCTUM EDITION OF WALT WHITMAN.

For many suggestions during the progress of the work, I am happy to make acknowledgment to Jack Goodman, Philip Van Doren Stern, Merrill Moore, and Stanley Burnshaw. For aid in research, I owe thanks to Ulric Kaskell, Elaine Lorber, Beatrice Braude, and my daughter-in-law, Norma Anchin Untermeyer.

For checking many details, particularly those in connection with scientific data, I am happily indebted to my son, John Moore, who also supplied the chapters on Planck and Eddington.

Finally, for constant collaboration, to say nothing of her editorial acumen, I am, first and last, grateful to my wife, Bryna Ivens.

LOUIS UNTERMEYER

Newtown, Connecticut, 1955

Contents

FOREWORD   *vii*

Charles Darwin   [1809–1882]
"The reaction was immediate and sensational."   *1*

Søren Kierkegaard   [1813–1855]
"He offered provocations instead of panaceas."   *7*

Richard Wagner   [1813–1883]
*"I am much better qualified to squander 60,000 francs than to earn
them."*   *12*

Karl Marx   [1818–1883]
"It was unlikely to find many readers among the general public."   *26*

Walt Whitman   [1819–1892]
*"A great urgency, an onward-going movement, the tempo and forward
thrust of a half-idealistic, half-materialistic, but ever-expanding America."*   *34*

Herman Melville   [1819–1891]
"The tragic and challenging No."   *47*

Susan B. Anthony   [1820–1906]
"That women might own and possess their own souls."   *60*

Charles Baudelaire   [1821–1867]
"Dante merely visited Hell; Baudelaire came from there."   *66*

xi

Mary Baker Eddy   [1821–1910]
". . . the error of giving intelligence to matter . . ."   73

Fyodor Dostoevsky   [1821–1881]
"He put flesh upon abstractions and turned ideas into greatly suffering
men and women."   82

Gustave Flaubert   [1821–1880]
"He created the modern realistic novel and, directly or indirectly,
influenced all writers of fiction since his day."   91

Louis Pasteur   [1822–1895]
"The greatest disorder of the mind is to allow the will to direct the
belief."   102

Henrik Ibsen   [1828–1906]
"That man is right who has allied himself most closely with the
future."   113

Leo Tolstoy   [1828–1910]
"Whatever he was—and he was almost everything—he was also its
opposite."   121

Emily Dickinson   [1830–1886]
". . . scribbled on the backs of recipes, on brown paper bags from the
grocer, inside envelopes, and across small scraps of paper . . ."   132

Mark Twain   [1835–1910]
"He kept digging into the reader's ribs until they were sore."   139

Paul Cézanne   [1839–1906]
"He labored furiously to achieve an effect of quiet."   149

Emile Zola   [1840–1902]
"Physician to the body politic."   156

Thomas Hardy   [1840–1928]
"He could not regard a pitiless universe without pity."   165

Auguste Rodin [1840–1917]
"When the artist follows nature, he gets everything." *170*

Auguste Renoir [1841–1919]
"It must be indescribable and it must be inimitable." *177*

William James [1842–1910]
". . . concreteness, facts, action and power . . ." *182*

Henry James [1843–1916]
"His readers are divided into two unalterably opposed camps." *190*

Paul Verlaine [1844–1896]
"Take rhetoric and wring its neck." *198*

Gerard Manley Hopkins [1844–1889]
"A spasmodic cry of joy, a passionate glorification of God's world." *204*

Friedrich Nietzsche [1844–1900]
"How to Philosophize with a Hammer." *209*

Thomas Alva Edison [1847–1931]
"His brain had the highest cash value in history." *218*

Vincent Van Gogh [1853–1890]
"Not trees, but growth; not blossoms, but bloom." *228*

Sigmund Freud [1856–1939]
"Life is a problem for everybody." *238*

George Bernard Shaw [1856–1950]
"It is not only good for people to be shocked occasionally, but absolutely necessary to the progress of society that they should be shocked pretty often." *247*

Thorstein Veblen   [1857–1929]

"... *compounded of wit and ferocity, slowly accumulating clauses
and quickly stabbing thoughts.*"   262

Max Planck   [1858–1947]

"*A startling but balanced philosophy.*"   270

A. E. Housman   [1859–1936]

"*And malt does more than Milton can
To justify God's ways to man ...*"   275

Henri Bergson   [1859–1941]

"*His speculations spread from salon to salon almost as fast as the latest
gossip.*"   281

John Dewey   [1859–1952]

"*Not perfection as a final goal, but the ever-enduring process of perfecting, maturing, refining, is the aim of living.*"   287

Anton Chekhov   [1860–1904]

"*Medicine is my lawful wife and literature my mistress.*"   294

Claude Achille Debussy   [1862–1918]

"*He delighted in confessing his fondness for every kind of gluttony.*" 302

William Randolph Hearst   [1863–1951]

"*When you looked at the first page you said, 'Gee Whiz.' When you
saw the second page, you gasped, 'Holy Moses!' And when
you glimpsed the third page, you exclaimed 'Good God Al-
mighty!' *"   311

Henry Ford   [1863–1947]

"*The little man's little man.*"   321

Henri de Toulouse-Lautrec   [1864–1901]

"... *And everywhere, ugliness has its beautiful aspects ...*"   329

William Butler Yeats [1865–1939]
"The mystical life is the center of all that I do and all that I think and all that I write." 336

H. G. Wells [1866–1946]
"He claimed an unlimited right to think, criticize, discuss and suggest." 345

Sun Yat-sen [1866–1925]
"The Earth, the Universe, belongs to Everyone." 352

Wilbur Wright [1867–1912]
and Orville Wright [1871–1948]
"Human flight is not only impossible but illogical." 360

Marie Curie [1867–1934]
"Pierre's first gift was a copy of his latest pamphlet, 'On Symmetry in Physical Phenomena: Symmetry of an Electric Field and of a Magnetic Field.'" 368

Frank Lloyd Wright [1869–]
"I intend to be the greatest architect that ever lived." 379

Mohandas Karamchand Gandhi [1869–1948]
"He had the might of a dictator and the mind of a democrat." 389

Edwin Arlington Robinson [1869–1935]
"The world frightens me." 399

Henri Matisse [1869–1954]
"He does more harm than alcohol." 405

Nikolai Lenin [1870–1924]
"From Spark to Flame." 410

Georges Rouault [1871–]
"The brutal and the breath-taking, the vulgar and the pitiful." 420

Contents

Marcel Proust   [1871–1922]
"Little boy lost . . . torn between integrity and expediency."   424

Theodore Dreiser   [1871–1945]
"He had no talent, but a great deal of genius."   434

Stephen Crane   [1871–1900]
". . . all inside—he had no surface."   444

Bertrand Russell   [1872–   ]
*"The wish to discover whether we possess anything that can be called
knowledge."*   450

Gertrude Stein   [1874–1946]
"Simplify! Simplify!"   458

Robert Frost   [1874–   ]
"His poems are people talking."   468

Guglielmo Marconi   [1874–1937]
"There are no limits in science."   478

Winston Churchill   [1874–   ]
" 'I am finished,' he wrote in 1915."   484

Albert Schweitzer   [1875–   ]
"Reverence for life."   500

Thomas Mann   [1875–1955]
"Artist with a bad conscience."   506

Rainer Maria Rilke   [1875–1926]
" 'The Santa Claus of loneliness.' "   514

Isadora Duncan   [1878–1927]
"Born under a dancing star."   522

Albert Einstein   [1879–1955]
"I cannot believe that God plays dice with the cosmos."   533

Joseph Stalin   [1879–1953]
"Genghis Khan with a telephone."   542

Lytton Strachey   [1880–1932]
"Clean brevity; dispassionate truth; free spirit of inquiry."   550

Oswald Spengler   [1880–1936]
"Without reason, without hope."   553

Alexander Fleming   [1881–1955]
"A triumph of accident."   559

Pablo Picasso   [1881–   ]
"Painting is not done to decorate apartments . . . It is an instrument of war against brutality and darkness."   565

Franklin Delano Roosevelt   [1882–1945]
"There is nothing I love so much as a good fight."   575

James Joyce   [1882–1941]
"To achieve a multi-dimensional effect . . . a multi-dimensional language."   586

Igor Stravinsky   [1882–   ]
"Beauty is the essence and glory of order."   597

Arthur Eddington   [1882–1944]
"Man's logic is his best instrument."   605

Franz Kafka   [1883–1924]
"I have none of the qualities needed for a successful life."   612

Sinclair Lewis   [1885–1951]
"He lodged a piece of the continent in the world's imagination."   619

Ring Lardner   [1885–1933]
*"He had the habit of catching human beings when they think no one
is looking at them."*   626

D. H. Lawrence   [1885–1930]
"He was sure that instinct was superior to intelligence."   632

Ezra Pound   [1885–   ]
*"It is easy to belittle the eccentric theorist, but the poet must not be
deprecated."*   643

T. S. Eliot   [1888–   ]
"The boredom, and the horror, and the glory."   650

Eugene O'Neill   [1888–1953]
"The world drives men to assume characters which are not their own."   662

Charles Chaplin   [1889–   ]
"Pan, too, had been much assailed . . ."   669

Adolf Hitler   [1889–1945]
"The gutter had come to power."   678

F. Scott Fitzgerald   [1896–1940]
"I wish I were twenty-two again."   691

William Faulkner   [1897–   ]
"His work celebrates the dark grandeur of destruction."   702

George Gershwin [1898–1937]
"He lived in a kind of fitful radiance." 712

Ernest Hemingway [1899–   ]
"Half the young writers tried to imitate him and half tried not to." 717

Thomas Wolfe [1900–1938]
". . . the fierce energy that will not be beaten into form . . ." 726

André Malraux [1901–   ]
". . . the story of art is the story of man." 736

Jean-Paul Sartre [1905–   ]
". . . the hectic and impossible existence that is known as the lot of man." 741

W. H. Auden [1907–   ]
"People do not understand that it is possible to believe in a thing and ridicule it at the same time." 747

Dylan Thomas [1914–1953]
". . . whirling images, wild metaphors, and a high eldritch music . . ." 753

A SELECTED BIBLIOGRAPHY 758

INDEX 779

Charles Darwin

[1 8 o 9 - 1 8 8 2]

*"The reaction was immediate and
sensational."*

IT IS a scant century since man's estimate of himself and his entire
thinking habits have been changed by a once revolutionary
and, to many, repugnant concept: the concept of evolution. The
theory, hailed by one group of scientists as a liberating cultural force
and reviled by another as a degrading heresy, swiftly grew into an
increasingly bitter controversy after Darwin published *The Origin of Species* in 1859. The conception of a continually developing process of creation did not originate with Darwin. The
ancient Greek philosopher, Heraclitus, had suggested that all life
"evolved," that everything was growing in a constant state of flux,
and the Roman poet, Lucretius, had suggested a scientific account
of evolution in his far-reaching *De Rerum Natura.* More than twenty
centuries after Heraclitus and a few years before Darwin, Herbert Spencer published *Principles of Psychology,* which related the
doctrine of evolution to various areas of research. But it was Darwin who applied the theory to life itself and presented it as a challenge to a startled world.

Born February 12, 1809, at Shrewsbury, England, Charles Darwin was brought up in a world which clung to doctrine and rarely
questioned religious dogma. All but a few rebellious spirits believed
that the Bible was not only the literal word of God but a record of
unquestionable facts. According to most of Darwin's contemporaries, the Creator made the universe in a precise order with a multitude of separate creations, each form of life distinct from the other.
Even the scientists regarded special creation as an established truth,
an article of faith.

In only one member of the Darwin family was there a strain of
dissent. Darwin's father was a country doctor, an adherent of plain
living and not too much thinking, Church of England to the bone.
One grandfather, Erasmus Darwin, was a botanist, philosopher,
physician, and a minor poet by avocation. Another grandfather,
Josiah Wedgwood, was a craftsman, manufacturer of the delicate

pottery which was so much sought after that the family attained so-cial eminence as well as financial security. Darwin's mother was the nonconformer; unable to accept revealed religion, she became a Unitarian.

As a boy, Darwin was always glad to visit his mother's tolerant family and be among her fellow liberals. He was less happy at home, where he was guarded by an apprehensive father and closely watched by a dominating sister and a jealous older brother. Unfortunately, his mother died when he was six, and his stern father agonized over him. "You will never amount to anything," complained Dr. Darwin. "You care for nothing except animals!" Packed off to school, young Charles loathed the classroom with its routine questions and prescribed answers. After eight years of grammar school, he was sent to Edinburgh University to follow his father's profession. But he hated the sight of blood, and two years of medicine was as much as he could stand. When it was evident that Charles would never be a doctor, his father decided he should become a divine. At eighteen young Darwin was sent to Cambridge to study for the ministry.

Formal training at Cambridge almost broke Darwin's spirit, but he gravitated toward the sciences, developed a habit of inquiry, and, in 1831, managed to get a B.A. degree. He was then twenty-two, curious about everything and certain of nothing except that he would never be a dogmatist. It was at this time that there occurred a kind of accident which determined Darwin's future. A government vessel, the *Beagle,* was sailing to South America on a scientific exploring cruise. Darwin was offered a position as naturalist of the expedition. His father at first refused to let his son accept, insisting that such a junket was poor preparation for the pulpit. The commander, Captain Fitzroy, a confirmed phrenologist who fancied he could read a person's character from his features, did not like the shape of Darwin's nose. But his instructor in botany and mineralogy spoke up for the young man in search of a career, and, at the last minute, Darwin went aboard ship. The cruise was planned to take two years; instead, it lasted five, from 1831 to 1836.

During the long trip Darwin continually succumbed to seasickness. His quarters were cramped; the diet was bad; the conditions were primitive. The long voyage ruined his health, and he remained something of an invalid the rest of his life. But the things he learned, the specimens he collected, the opportunities for observation while charting a shoreline or on field trips inland were as unusual as they were invaluable. Darwin himself realized that his years on the *Beagle* formed "by far the most important event of my life . . . I have always felt that I owed the voyage the first real training or education of my mind." At the age of twenty-seven Darwin's career was determined. The untrained, reluctant minister vanished and the searching biologist appeared.

At thirty Darwin married his first cousin, Emma Wedgwood, by whom he had five sons and two daughters, and whose fortune and patience enabled him to carry on his work for more than forty years in spite of severe astigmatism, nausea, because of stomach trouble, and long periods of general illness. For a while the couple resided in London, but after three years, they moved to Sussex, to the countryside Darwin loved and which was the background for his best work. In his forties he compensated for his baldness by growing a long beard which gave him a half-grotesque, half-patriarchal appearance. In his thirties, however, his hair was a lively nut-brown and his clear blue eyes snapped under broad, beetling eyebrows. He was a tall, pink man, but when he held back an infrequent mounting temper, his face acquired the copper color of an Indian chief. Despite the attacks he had to endure in later life, he maintained a dignified and pervasive calm until he died at seventy-three, April 19, 1882.

As soon as the five-year voyage of the *Beagle* was ended Darwin collated his facts. Three years later he issued his first book, *Journal of Researches into the Geology and Natural History of the Various Countries visited by H.M.S. Beagle.* This was followed by several other studies and monographs based on the cruise, but for a score of years Darwin was a name occasionally mentioned in scientific circles and unknown anywhere else. Meanwhile, he began to compare his findings with everything even remotely related to them. He absorbed Lamarck's *Natural History of Invertebrates* and, later, Chambers' *The Vestiges of Creation.* Malthus' treatise on population acted not only as a key but as a catalytic agent. It clarified his thinking and crystallized his conclusions about the adaptation of organisms to their environment. "Being well prepared to appreciate the struggle for existence which everywhere goes on," wrote Darwin, "from long-continued observation of the habits of plants and animals, it at once struck me that under these circumstances favorable variations would tend to be preserved, and unfavorable ones destroyed. The result of this would be the formulation of new species." It was, however, twenty-two years before Darwin was ready to submit his thesis to the public. Darwin would have postponed publication still further, but another naturalist, Alfred Russel Wallace, had also been inspired by Malthus to work out a theory virtually identical with Darwin's. Convinced by his friends that he should delay no longer, Darwin, at fifty, published his epoch-making book. The first edition was sold out in one day. It bore a long and, at first glance, intimidating title: *On the Origin of Species By Means of Natural Selection, or the Preservation of Favored Races in the Struggle for Life.* The title was a challenge in itself, a masterpiece of language-making. The reader was immediately arrested by such provocative phrases as "Origin of Species," "Natural Selection," "Favored Races," "Struggle for Life." Their impact on social sciences, philosophy, and, most of all, religion, was as violent as it was unforeseen. Darwin was hailed as the "Newton of biology" and denounced as "the man who banished God from the universe." The scientist Thomas Huxley, who became Darwin's enthusiastic supporter and disciple, remarked that "The publication of the *Origin of Species* marks the Hegira of Science from the idolatries of special creation to the purer faith of evolution." In essence Darwin enlarged the old theory of a developing creation and added to it the stark concept of natural selection—the law which permits only the fit to survive. Moreover, he insisted that the species which survive, not only reproduce but transmit and change their characteristics according to the conditions around them.

The reaction was immediate and sensational. Critics found it hard to consider the book without a sense of shock; the newspapers were cautious and even apprehensive. In a somewhat ponderous and puzzled essay the reviewer in *The New York Times* (March 28, 1860) concluded: "The doctrine that has long prevailed is that each species has been independently created. The idea of the permanence of species is embodied in one shape or another in every definition of the term which has been framed. No article of scientific faith is of more canonical authority . . . and is commonly regarded as one of those doctrines which no man altogether in his right senses would set himself seriously to oppose. Mr. Darwin, as the fruit of a quarter of a century of patient observation and experiment, throws out a series of arguments and inferences so revolutionary as, if established, to necessitate a radical reconstruction of the fundamental doctrine of natural history . . . He ascends with the swoop and force of analogy to the august and audacious statement that 'All the organic beings which have ever lived on this earth have descended from some one primordial form.' " This statement seemed far more audacious than august to the greater part of an outraged generation. It was reinforced by *The Descent of Man,* a work published twelve years after *The Origin of Species.* In his contention that "Man is descended from some less highly organized form," Darwin maintained that man shared a common ancestry with the monkeys. To many biologists and to almost all ministers that was the last straw. The book was not only condemned but publicly banned. In the state of Tennessee a statute made it unlawful to teach the theory of evolution in any public school. The edict was enforced as late as 1925, in which year a high school teacher, John Thomas Scopes, was arrested for violating the law. The resulting trial was a worldwide sensation. Scopes and modern science were defended by the "radical" attorney Clarence Darrow, while the prosecution was strengthened by the "fundamentalist" orator William Jennings Bryan who, after two failures to win the presidency of the United States, had been appointed Secretary of State under Woodrow Wilson and was considered the country's leading spellbinder. Although the trial ended in the conviction of Scopes it also resulted in an ignominious cross-examination of Bryan which, complicated by his violent rhetorical exertions in the midsummer heat, caused his death.

The furor caused by Darwin's two books did not drive him into a stubborn set of defensive dogmas. On the contrary he began to revise, amend, and enlarge. He modified his views to include a greater frequency of mutations or "jumps" in the process of evolution; he conceded the direct action of environment and of use and disuse as factors of change. But, although controversy can no longer be said to rage about Darwin, echoes of dispute are still heard. In 1941 Jacques Barzun published a savage critique entitled *Darwin, Marx, Wagner,* the theme of which was indicated by the jacket's subtitle "The Fatal Legacy of 'Progress.'" Barzun was not alone in asserting that Darwin was greatly responsible for "the idea of mechanical materialism which prevails in our thinking" and the end result of "a world which is alien, cold, and uncomfortable." Others considered the influence of Darwin not only an enduring part of our civilization but an incalculable cultural force. In his brilliantly analytical account of the great naturalist, *Charles Darwin* (1950), Paul B. Sears wrote: "The immediate effect of Darwin on science was one of magnificent release. It was not, properly speaking, a stimulus—the vast unexplored world of the unknown was stimulus enough, and curiosity was straining to understand it. Darwin cut the leash, and the human mind leaped ahead . . . He wrought mightily, and others with him, for a newer and greater faith—faith in universal order, whose secrets open themselves to men truly free to question."

Vigorously upheld and virtuously attacked, the theory of evolution accomplished not only the separation of biology and religion, but compelled a completely new interpretation of the universe. Everything underwent a rigorous reappraisal: ethics, economics, sociology. History itself was rewritten, objectively, dispassionately, freed of supernatural factors. The man conceded even by his enemies to be a gently modest human being, a quiet investigator opposed to vehemence, proclaimed an idea whose violence still reverberates throughout the world.

Søren Kierkegaard

[1813-1855]

*"He offered provocations instead of
panaceas."*

APASSIONATE NINETEENTH-CENTURY DANISH THEOLOGIAN, condemned in his day as an inimical critic of Christianity, Søren Aabye Kierkegaard was forgotten for three generations. He then was rediscovered as a great Christian mystic who inspired a new faith and founded the controversial philosophy of Existentialism. As late as 1937, one hundred and twenty-four years after his birth, no English translation of his work had been undertaken, and nothing about him was available to the general public. In the 1940's he was acclaimed as "the profoundest interpreter of the psychology of the religious life since St. Augustine," a prophet who foretold the crisis that was to follow the tyranny of regimentation, the dictator's scorn of the individual, the cruelty of the fearful herdmind, and the "total bankruptcy toward which the whole of Europe seems to be heading."

Søren Kierkegaard was born May 5, 1813, in Copenhagen. He was the seventh and last child of Michael Pedersen Kierkegaard and his second wife, who had been a servant in the house. Søren's father, fifty-six years older than his youngest son, was a prosperous and outwardly pious merchant. A sinner in private, he grimly quoted dogmas which promised eternal damnation and dragged Søren to sermons which breathed bigotry and brought the fear of hell-fire upon the unthinking young, "the children of Satan himself." An atmosphere of gloom and a sense of sin pervaded the household. So strict and coldly severe was young Søren's upbringing that, many years later, he declared: "I was already an old man when I was born; I leapt completely over childhood and youth." In spite of unsocial tendencies Søren graduated from the university in 1840 and, except for a brief sojourn abroad, remained in his native city the rest of his short and uneventful life.

At twenty-four he fell in love with Regine Olsen, who was a little more than fourteen. Two years later they were engaged, and a date for the wedding was set. As the day drew nearer, and Regine ("light as a bird and bold as thought") grew more ardent, Kierkegaard began to have misgivings; his doubts grew into a panic of fear and, with a brutal suddenness, he broke the engagement. Regine begged him in the name of Christ and by the memory of his father not to desert her. But the adjuration only strengthened his determination. He shook off his frantic fiancée and, leaving her to face the scandal, headed for Berlin. "If I had to explain myself," he wrote in his diary, "I should have been compelled to initiate her into dreadful thoughts, my relation to my father, my abysmal melancholy, the eternal night which broods in my innermost being."

However Kierkegaard may have rationalized his motives, it is apparent that they were strangely mixed. It was one thing for a spiritual young man to idealize a child of fourteen, but fulfilling the expectations of a full-blooded young woman was something quite different. It has been conjectured that, having listened to countless sermons about the evils of the flesh, Kierkegaard had imposed sexual taboos upon himself, and he was probably incapable of lovemaking. The very idea of marital obligations may have been repugnant to him; for marriage implied happiness and, to the spirit which exalted suffering, earthly happiness was a sin. Revolted by the knowledge of his father's secret excesses—a shocking contrast to his pietistic attitude—Kierkegaard was preoccupied with the purity of his own soul. It has also been argued that, realizing his psychological and perhaps physical incapacity for marriage, Kierkegaard freed Regine for the life of the body while he freed himself for a life of the spirit. Nevertheless, Kierkegaard was greatly depressed when Regine married another, and the thought of her remained with him not only as a plaguing memory, but also as the embodiment of his dream, a devout and dehumanized vision that was a continual creative stimulus. His greatest work, *Enten-Eller* (*Either-Or*) was written for her; "I owe everything to the wisdom of an old man and the simplicity of a young girl."

Returning to Copenhagen, Kierkegaard devoted himself to religious philosophy and wrote a series of books under various transparent pseudonyms. *The Concept of Irony,* his dissertation for a master's degree, was followed by *Either-Or,* which was signed "Victor Eremitus." *Fear and Trembling,* which he called "a dialectical lyric," was purported to be by "Johannes de Silentio." The author of *Prefaces* was given as "Nicholas Notabene," that of *The Concept of Dread* as "Virgilius Haufniensis," that of *Stages on Life's Road* as "Hilarius Bookbinder." Other books were written under the disguise of "Johannes Climacus," "Inter et Inter," "Frater Taciturnus," "H. H.," "Constantin Constantius." *Either-Or* is a prologue as well as an announcement of his program. Published when Kierkegaard was barely thirty, it presents two points of view: that of the esthete, to whom the world is a pleasure-ground of sensations, and that of the man devoted to ethics and moral law. The alternatives are presented, and Kierkegaard points out that every decision is a risk. Moreover, since man is impelled by the infinite, his decision must be to choose between All or Nothing—a concept which Ibsen powerfully dramatized in *Brand*.

In his thirties Kierkegaard began shaping a theology which, through its impassioned and often conflicting interpreters, has influenced and disturbed the Western mind. Writing in a curious blend of irony, ingenuity, and sheer ingenuousness, Kierkegaard turned against all system-making institutions and all systems of thought with driving sarcasm and serene assurance. Lost in a labyrinth of mechanical progress, man, said Kierkegaard, is not only helpless but almost hopeless. His one hope is an understanding of his own existence, the only finite reality. Such an understanding, however, cannot be attained by the intellect but by pure faith, not by reason but by rapport with God. This rapport is not possible through dogmas, churchliness, or any ecclesiastical standards; it is achieved only by direct personal relationship between God and man. The intellect must not only be humbled but, in a sense, crucified before it can be resurrected and "leap to God." The existent individual is not a Being but a Becoming. Christianity, too, is a Becoming—an endless progress through anxiety, insecurity, and suffering; it ceases to be Christianity when it sinks complacently into peace of mind.

Kierkegaard objected to the Church as a haven for timid and self-indulgent men; he scorned the ministers of his day for refusing to believe in the Church Militant and for being false "seekers," seeking placidity and influential positions in the community rather than salvation through suffering. Christ's teachings, said Kierkegaard, have been so diluted and debased that the Church has practically abolished Christianity in the name of Christ. "Why do we no longer see the contradiction between Christianity's nature as polemical and the State's essence as a quantitative entity? Why do we not see that the State is paying its officers [the ministers] to destroy Christianity?" His antagonism to the clergy was concentrated in such writings as his *Attack Upon Christendom:* "One hears often, and especially from the priests, that one cannot live on nothing. But the priests manage to do precisely that. For them Christianity does not exist—and yet they live on it . . . One can be a Christian only in opposition." As Walter Lowrie wrote in the first comprehensive study of Kierkegaard, "He is quite capable of convincing you that you are not a Christian, and perhaps making it clear to you that you do not wish to become such. He may even persuade you not to pretend any longer to be a Christian."

An unsparing critic of the society in which he lived, Kierkegaard was belabored and lampooned by his contemporaries. Schoolmen jeered at his learning; preachers railed at his declaration that the self-assured believer was a greater sinner in the eyes of God than the troubled disbeliever. Newspapers attacked him; cartoonists found him an easy target, caricaturing his long, thin legs and cranelike body, his bony cranium extending into a towering top hat. Because of the sneers, Kierkegaard redoubled his attacks. His later work is a mounting denunciation of the Church as an organized theological monopoly, attempting to dispense publicly that which is the private concern of the individual soul: religion. Continually inveighing against intellectualism, Kierkegaard pleaded for simplicity as well as humility. Man, he stated, is the eternal paradox: he is his own reason for being, and yet he is nothing without the transcendent power of God. Man exists in time, but he must learn to live in timelessness and partake of transcendence: a life which is beyond the limits of experience and the limitations of human knowledge.

Fighting for what he felt to be revealed truth, he saw himself as one who was meant to offer provocations instead of panaceas; his function was not to utter comforting platitudes but to hurl violent blasts in the face of a decadent church and a corrupt civilization. "What I require," he wrote, "is a voice as piercing as a lynx's eye, as terrible as the sigh of a giant, as persistent as a cry of nature, with a range extending from the deepest bass to the highest and most melting treble, with a modulation capable of the lightest sacred whisper and the fire-spouting fury of madness. That is what I need in order to deliver myself of what is in my mind, to shake the bowels of anger, sympathy, and understanding." "Things have become too easy; it is time to make them difficult again."

In his forty-third year, Kierkegaard fell to the street in a fainting spell. When he was taken to the hospital, it was found that he was paralyzed from the waist down. A little more than a month later, he suffered another stroke and died November 11, 1855. On his deathbed, when asked whether he was angry with his critics and bitter toward the world for not accepting his doctrine, he replied, "No, not bitter—but afflicted, grieved, and indignant in the highest degree."

Unappreciated in his day, he has become a belated force and an admonitory influence in our times. His questioning of "reality" echoes in the strikingly different work of Franz Kafka and Thomas Mann. He stands out, said William Hubben in *Four Prophets of Our Destiny,* as one "whose incisive truths and courageous personal fight have . . . opened our eyes to the shallowness of much of our pseudo-Christian life and to the outright deception in politics which Christianity has been made to serve." Kierkegaard's insistence on transcendence and God's immanence stimulated a revival of fundamentalism; the present-day Protestant Neo-Orthodoxy of Karl Barth and Reinhold Niebuhr owes much to Kierkegaard's opposition to modern science and modern civilization and to his contention that man's affirming existence is greater than all the concepts of his intellect. On the other hand, Kierkegaard's assertion that man cannot escape from subjectivity and is his own meaning and measure gave rise to the esthetic-atheistic aspect of Existentialism expounded by Sartre and his followers. Thus Kierkegaard's refusals to countenance self-deceit and his condemnations of the superficial life bridge the years. They excite, wrote E. W. F. Tomlin in *The Great Philosophers,* "the respect and sympathy of a generation—our own—which, in consequence of the upheavals of war and postwar disorganization, experiences a similar revulsion from the traditional values of western civilization . . . For Kierkegaard, modern man, cut off from the natural world by his pursuit of techniques and removed from God, is a 'displaced person': an individual with whom the world is having to reckon and whose psychology it does not yet wholly understand."

Richard Wagner

[1813-1883]

*"I am much better qualified to squander
60,000 francs than to earn them."*

A SELF-PAMPERED VOLUPTUARY who preached the gospel of self-denial and renunciation, an unscrupulous opportunist who, deceiving his wife, assured her that "your suffering will be rewarded by my fame," an importunate cadger who was also an accomplished cad, Richard Wagner not only changed the whole course of modern music but built a monumental edifice which has withstood the controversial assaults of battering animosity, critical scorn, and wildly changing taste.

The controversy began with his birth. The youngest of nine children, he was born May 22, 1813, in Leipzig, and christened Wilhelm Richard Wagner—he discarded the first name before he was twenty—but there has always been a nagging doubt about his paternity. According to the record, his father was Karl Friedrich Wagner, a police clerk, who died a few months after the boy was born. But the widowed mother had been extremely fond of an intimate friend of the family, Ludwig Geyer, a gifted painter-playwright-actor, reputedly of Jewish blood, and, following her husband's death, she married him. Six months after the marriage, she bore him a daughter, Cäcilie, and, although there were now eight children to support—two of Karl Wagner's children had failed to survive infancy—Geyer became a devoted stepfather as well as an indulgent father. He was especially protective of Richard. When the boy was two, the family moved to Dresden and Geyer, wrote Wagner in *My Life,* "undertook my education with the greatest care and love. He made it obvious that he wished to adopt me as his own son. When I went to my first school, he gave me his name, so that, until my fourteenth year, my schoolfellows knew me as Richard Geyer." It was some years after Geyer's death, and after Geyer's brother had assumed the responsibility for the boy, that, at fifteen, gossip persisting, Richard Geyer became Richard Wagner. It is more than probable that the mere possibility of being "tainted" with Jewish blood so disturbed the later apostle of pure Teutonism that it developed into an anti-Semitism of spectacular virulence.

No disturbances of any kind were apparent in the developing youth. From the beginning he gravitated to the arts but, strangely enough, his talent seemed to be less musical—his piano teacher said that nothing would ever come of him—than literary. At fourteen he learned English; at fifteen he fell in love with Shakespeare and promptly wrote a play. In his bloodcurdling variation of *Hamlet,* entitled *Leubald und Adelaide,* he killed off (so he said) forty-two characters in the early acts and had to make them reappear as ghosts in order to end the tragedy. He was fascinated by the Greek poets, but his teacher made him learn simple Greek prose after he had translated (according to later and equally dubious claims) twelve books of Homer. Music meant little to him until he heard Weber's *Freischütz,* after which he applied himself to the piano, determined to be a composer as well as a dramatist. Listening to Beethoven's *Fidelio* overture he was led to *Egmont* and, in a rapid crescendo of enthusiasm, to the sonatas and symphonies. He was transported: "In ecstatic dreams I met Beethoven and Shakespeare. I talked with them, and I awoke bathed in tears."

At sixteen young Wagner, too rapt to bother with the rules of composition, began to compose. He picked up harmony by instinct, counterpoint from Beethoven, and orchestration from the scores of Mozart. His family was not displeased that he had turned to music —an older sister, Clara, was an opera singer—but they hoped he would give up this fantasy of being a composer and become a performer, a man assured of a steady position. At his mother's insistence, he practiced piano and the violin but one of his teachers declared Wagner was his worst pupil—"intelligent but lazy"—and he never learned to play any instrument with a degree of competence. At eighteen he entered Leipzig University and studied briefly with Theodor Weinlig, a successor of Bach as cantor of St. Thomas' Church, and Weinlig persuaded the famous firm of Breitkopf and Härtel to publish two of his compositions: a piano sonata and a polonaise. (An overture, which, to indicate the progress of the themes, Wagner had penned in three different-colored inks, had been performed without provoking anything more than amusement.) He alternated his studies with bouts of drinking and other dissipations; he squandered his mother's pension as well as his own property to the last thaler in the local gambling house.

One of his early compositions, a symphony in C major, was given in Prague and, during a visit to that city, Wagner started work on his first opera, *Die Hochzeit* (*The Wedding*), which was never completed, and threw himself into his first venture in love, which was not reciprocated. He was barely twenty-one when he set to work on his second opera, *Die Feen* (*The Fairies*), which he never saw performed, and a set of compositions for Goethe's *Faust*. By this time he was a practicing professional. His brother Albert, who was stage manager at a theater in Würzburg, procured a position for him there as chorus master. The company was small but large enough to give him a livelihood, sufficient means to conduct a few casual amours, and time to begin his third opera, *Das Liebesverbot* (*The Love Ban*), in which Shakespeare's *Measure for Measure* was turned into a celebration of promiscuity and general licentiousness set to Donizetti-like fripperies. An offer to assume the post of musical director of another small theater company brought him to Magdeburg, but neither the place nor the people pleased him and he was about to return to Leipzig when he met Minna Planer.

Minna Planer was the juvenile lead of the company, a few years older than Wagner. Although uncultured, she was experienced in the life of the theater and, unmarried with a six-year-old daughter, skilled in the ways of the world. When it was obvious that Wagner had become infatuated, she grew cool and reticent; when they became lovers she proved so stimulating to his ego and so helpful to his ambitions that, after almost two years of romantically illicit relations, they were married.

Wagner was now twenty-three. The years of bohemianism had encouraged a life of recklessness and extravagance, a general irresponsibility which was to become a fixed pattern. He got into debt and quarreled with Minna. When it became evident that the practical Minna, impatient with his experiments, wanted him to write to please the public, the quarrels increased and the debts mounted. Six months after their marriage, she left him. Wagner followed her to her mother's home and patched up their differences. The reconciliation was brief; there were fresh recriminations, another flight and, this time, acknowledged mutual infidelity. Yet when Wagner became music director at the new and sumptuous theater in Riga, Minna rejoined him and settled down to the difficult role of being the wife of a genius.

At Riga, where the Wagners spent two years, he wrote most of the florid *Rienzi*, which was intended to challenge the brassy popularity of Meyerbeer. The debts piled up. Wagner had already written to his friend Theodor Apel, "I must have money or I shall go mad." Money, continually melting away, became an obsession with him. He turned his charm shamelessly upon strangers as well as friends; he borrowed without a thought of repaying. He looked upon any sacrifice made for him as a duty; contributions were not regarded as loans to be petitioned but tributes demanded to sustain his art. At last things became so bad in Riga that he was discharged and, with a little borrowed money and no prospects, the Wagners left Russia in desperate haste and headed for Paris.

To escape the creditors in East Prussia, they made a circuitous journey to France by way of the Norwegian fiords and an ocean voyage to England. The boat trip was normally eight days but, due to incessant storms, it was more than three weeks before the Wagners landed in London. The ill winds blew some good in the shaping of Wagner's third opera, *The Flying Dutchman*. Wagner had already read the legend in Heine's *Memoirs of Schnabelewopski*, which took hold of his imagination and, against a background of black skies and howling seas, the tale "gained a distinct poetic-musical coloring from these new impressions." From London Wagner crossed to the Continent, met the popular and powerful Meyerbeer, who praised *Rienzi*, spent a month in Boulogne, and went on to Paris. A modern critic, Gerald Abraham, calls attention to the fact that, six years after meeting Meyerbeer, Wagner wrote to him that "it is a great happiness to be indebted to you," signed himself "your everlastingly indebted Richard Wagner," and, five years later, vilified his debtor and all other Jews in "Das Judenthum in der Musik" ("Judaism in Music").

Wagner's life in Paris was a hell of failures. "He arrived full of high hopes, with letters of introduction from Meyerbeer himself," writes Abraham. "Within a year or so he and Minna were faced with poverty worse than any they had experienced in their fifth-rate German theatrical world. In retrospect that world must even have seemed one of security and plenty. The almost incredible bitterness of these Paris years left an indelible mark, as large as it was ugly, on Wagner's soul." A lodger occupied one room of their tiny quarters, and Minna not only had to wait upon him but had to clean his shoes. On one occasion Wagner had to beg Minna to pawn her few remaining trinkets only to learn that she had already disposed of everything except the clothes she was wearing. He took on all sorts of drudgery to buy bread. He read proof, arranged currently popular melodies for piano solo, transcribed operatic arias for the cornet and other instruments, composed romances to French verses, translated librettos, turned out novelettes, sketches, essays, and hackwork reviews—he even tried to get a job in the chorus of a shabby boulevard theater, "but the leader of the orchestra discovered that I could not sing at all and had no use for me."

In spite of these humiliations and a general sense of isolation—a starving artist in an apathetic foreign country—Wagner managed to complete *Rienzi,* which was accepted by the opera house in Dresden, as well as *The Flying Dutchman,* which also found favor in Berlin. Of Wagner's early works *The Flying Dutchman* is the only one which has remained in the repertoire of every major opera house. It still harks back to the old-fashioned formula cherished by his contemporaries—the division into separate scenes, the set pieces, the bravura songs—but the opera furnishes a clue to a leading characteristic of the later composer: the blend of self-identification and cosmic symbolism. He breathed his own self-pity into the fustian of a doom-driven soul and the image of a bride who asks nothing more than the right to sacrifice herself. Ten years later, in *A Communication to My Friends,* he acknowledged that the Dutchman's eternal quest for salvation was like his desperate "yearning for the German homeland" in the midst of "the utter homelessness of Paris," and his feeling for the sacrificial heroine was "like the longing of my Flying Dutchman for the Redeeming Woman . . . the element of Womanhood in general—the Woman of the Future."

After almost three dismal years, the darkness began to recede and Wagner had a place in the sun. Borrowing the price of the fare, Wagner set out for Dresden, where *Rienzi* was to be heard. The opera was such a success that the Dresden company put on *The Flying Dutchman* and, in 1843, the coveted position of *Hofkapellmeister* (Royal Conductor) was offered to the thirty-year-old composer who, less than a year before, had been sunk in poverty and surrounded by hostility. The position should have kept him happy, but Wagner was never one to enjoy content. Although he remained in Dresden six years, he could not adjust to the routine of rehearsals and performances. He met Mendelssohn, Schumann, and Berlioz, but he was never able to be friendly with or generous to other composers since he regarded his colleagues as competitors. Although the salary he received was more than enough for his needs, it was insufficient for his tastes and, demanding to live in luxury, Wagner went more deeply than ever in debt. He planned two music-dramas, *Jesus of Nazareth* and *Frederick Barbarossa,* and abandoned both. Nevertheless, at Dresden he completed *Tannhäuser* in his thirty-first year and, two years later, *Lohengrin.*

Tannhäuser was a long step from *Rienzi.* It was not yet the music-drama which Wagner finally evolved—it had the formal overture, the traditional march, the prescribed solo numbers and static choruses typical of the prevailing Italian-style opera which Wagner derided as "a concert in costume"—but, like the true Wagnerian productions which followed, the music, words, and action were inseparably integrated. Moreover, Wagner's prowess as a dramatic poet had begun to manifest itself. "An ardent and penetrating imagination, the imagination of the born dramatist, seeing all his characters as creatures of flesh and blood, is now playing upon the material offered to the musician by the poet," wrote Ernest Newman in *Wagner As Man and Artist.* "The Wagner of this period reaches the height of his powers in *Lohengrin.*"

There is a young exuberance in *Tannhäuser* and a serenity in *Lohengrin* which is lacking in much of the later Wagner. But the Wagner of the period was anything but serene. He went into debt on an ever-widening scale; his creditors included even his hard-pressed assistant and Minna's doctor. He proposed drastic changes in the Dresden orchestra and, when his suggestions were unheeded, turned from reform to revolution. A disgruntled liberal, he foregathered with Bakunin, the Russian anarchist, and conceived the outline of an epic poem (*Siegfried's Death*), in which the Norse hero appeared to be a German socialist. A naïve politician, he delivered an inflammatory speech before the Vaterlandsverein (The Fatherland Association) calling for the end of the aristocracy, the abolishment of the standing army, and an overnight change of Saxony from a monarchy to a republic. Less than a year later, in May, 1849, an insurrection broke out. The streets were barricaded; the royal troops tried to disperse the crowds and, when shots were fired, Wagner joined the rebels. The extent of his participation has always been a matter of conjecture, but, when the revolutionists were defeated and the ringleaders captured, Wagner, disguised as a coachman, fled to Weimar. In Weimar he expected to find asylum with Franz Liszt, whom he knew slightly and who had conducted his *Tannhäuser.* But he was not permitted a haven anywhere in Germany; a police warrant was issued for his arrest as "a politically dangerous individual" and, with Liszt's help, he escaped to Zürich where he was joined by Minna and where, except for occasional journeys, he remained in exile for ten years.

A graphic portrait of Wagner at thirty-six was furnished by the Dresden police department. The warrant described him as a man "of medium stature, brown hair, open forehead; brown eyebrows, gray-blue eyes; nose prominent and mouth proportionate; chin round, and [*sic!*] wears spectacles. Special characteristics: rapid in movements and speech." The description to the contrary, Wagner's movements in Switzerland were anything but rapid. Resentful at fate, he dragged his chains. His ordinarily dynamic tempo slowed down in sullen retreat; instead of composing, he wrote vain and dogmatic papers on "The Art-Work of the Future," the self-glorifying "Art and Revolution," the almost pathological "Judaism in Music," and a 407-page treatise, "Opera and Drama." Since he felt guilty about substituting criticism for creation and since he knew, moreover, (as he wrote to Liszt) that he was preaching to deaf ears, he took it out on Minna, who still believed in him but, a well-meaning Philistine, also hoped that he would turn his undeniable talents to something generally acceptable and pleasantly profitable.

Wagnerian commentators, considering that he abandoned composition from early 1848 to late 1853, speak of this period as his "six wasted years." Wagner did not waste himself only on long defensive tracts and pompous essays: he engaged in love affairs that were sometimes furtive but more often unconcealed and blandly self-righteous. At thirty-seven he "yielded to a passion" for an English girl of twenty-two, Jessie Laussot, who, admiring the composer's music, fell in love with the man. Married to a Bordeaux merchant, wealthy in her own right, she planned to endow Wagner with a considerable subsidy, and he, with increased ardor, proposed an elopement to Greece. When her mother persuaded Jessie not to do anything rash, and when her husband threatened to shoot the adventurer, Wagner was more affronted than fearful. He shrugged off the affair with a remark about the girl's "weakness of character . . . The woman who was to have brought me salvation has proved herself a child," he told a mutual friend. "Forgive me if I regard her merely as something pitiable."

Salvation, at least inspiration, was brought to him by another married woman—Wagner had an incurable predilection for other men's wives. At forty he had met Otto Wesendonck and his beautiful twenty-eight-year-old wife, Mathilde, and the pair of music-lovers contributed to Wagner's support. In 1857 Wesendonck, who had amassed a fortune in the silk industry, was building a new villa in Zürich. Wagner, now forty-three, was at work on the *Ring,* and the Wesendoncks installed him in an adjoining cottage. "Then began a new phase in my relations with this family," Wagner remarks with delightful ingenuousness in *My Life*. "The proximity strengthened our ties through daily intercourse." Mathilde was not only gentle and lovable but undoubtedly one of the most profound influences on his work. She and Wagner were deeply in love; her husband was magnanimous and devoted to her. There was great rapport and even greater ecstasy, but there could be no happy ending. Putting aside the *Ring* for the time being, Wagner sublimated the poignant situation into *Tristan und Isolde*, a prolonged and overwhelming outcry of mingled delight and despair in which the voices of the leading characters were immediately recognizable. The understanding Otto Wesendonck was the noble King Mark, Mathilde was the devoted Isolde, and Wagner the tortured Tristan. Minna had seemed to accept the situation. There was little that she would not do to keep her husband in physical comfort and, recognizing that she was not his intellectual equal, she did not complain too much when he was mentally stimulated by others. But the reading of an intercepted love letter to Mathilde provoked a new fury of recriminations. Only the arrival of Liszt and his daughter Cosima prevented an ugly dénouement. There was a temporary separation but, in 1859, there was a reunion and matters were smoothed over for a few more years.

At forty-six, Wagner's attitude to Minna was that of hard-won resignation. A martyred air seeps into his letters as he writes, "May Heaven grant that I shall always feel able to carry out my firm but cordial determination to treat her in the most considerate manner. I confess that my relation to this poor woman, who has had so many trials, and is now suffering so much, has always spurred me on to preserve and develop my moral powers." In the meantime, while Wagner ran off to Venice to finish the mountingly sensual second act of *Tristan*, Minna went to Dresden, trying to obtain an amnesty which would allow her husband to re-enter Germany. Shortly after receiving a promise that a pardon might be granted, she rejoined Wagner in Paris.

Although Wagner had put aside the *Ring* to complete *Tristan*, he had been working intermittently on his major work for six years. He had completed the libretto of *Siegfried's Death* as early as 1848. He now resumed the gigantic task of creating something which would be part drama, part opera, and all epic, an epitome of the ancient German spirit. He conceived the work backwards. He began with Siegfried's death, which became the concluding *Götter-dämmerung* (*Dusk of the Gods*), and proceeded with *Siegfried, Die Walküre* (*The Valkyrie*), and *Das Rheingold* (*The Rhinegold*). The entire text was privately printed in 1853, the year in which Wagner, reversing the order in which he had written the texts, started to compose *Das Rheingold*. Never had there been music of this nature, amazingly sonorous, orchestrally turbulent, but always melodic. The Wagnerian melody is a unique phenomenon. It does not follow the rules of meter; it is not confined within a specified number of bars; and, frequently using tonal suspensions to achieve a feeling of psychological suspense, it does not always end with a perfect cadence. But it is a melody which is all the more potent for being free, rising and falling, flowing into still another melody, until the listener has a sense of infinite play, endless fluency. The melodic current streams through the orchestra which becomes one of the drama's leading protagonists, while the voice, instead of being merely a solo instrument—exhibiting its coloratura flourishes with the orchestra accompanying it like a monstrous guitar—is able to supply a countermelody and stress the import of each word.

Another vital feature of the endless melodic texture is the *Leit-motiv* (the leading motive), which is a characterizing theme. Woven into the orchestral fabric, the *Leitmotiv* is the embodiment of a person or an idea. It identifies each figure, comments upon his actions, and explains his fluctuating emotions and state of mind. Extraordinarily flexible, it is sometimes distorted for emphasis or inverted to express ridicule. "Therein," wrote Albert Lavignac in *The Music Dramas of Richard Wagner*, "lies its power. With a few notes it calls up a whole throng of ideas without any more effort on the part of the listener than in having a well-known image pass before his eyes. It is (in short) a musical portrait, but one which changes with mood and situation and is a living presentment."

Wagner hoped to present *Tristan* in Paris; he was surprised, not too pleasantly, when *Tannhäuser* was chosen. He was still more surprised when he learned that no opera could be put on at the Grand Opera House without a ballet. Since *Tannhäuser* lacked this feature, Wagner set about writing one. Fifteen years had passed since its first production in Dresden and, having achieved a much ampler style, Wagner enriched the polyphony and elaborated the first act in the Venusberg with a voluptuous and almost orgiastic bacchanale. But this did not satisfy the members of the Jockey Club, the arbiters of Parisian high society, whose mistresses were the ballet girls who traditionally appeared in the *second* act. The opening was a nightmare of interruptions, derisive comments, and catcalls. The second night was much worse. The gentlemen of the Jockey Club enlarged their number with "guests," all of whom were equipped with penny whistles, and the whistling, reinforced by stamping and shrieking, drowned out everything except the drums. The third performance was held on a Sunday, when the aristocratic clique customarily stayed away from the opera. But the opposition was not to be cheated out of its sport; the demonstration was noisier than ever, and Wagner was forced to withdraw his score. Thoroughly disillusioned with Paris, Wagner welcomed the amnesty which Minna had finally procured and, after a twelve-year absence from his fatherland, took up residence in Biebrich on the Rhine.

Wagner was now in his fiftieth year, a harassed man and an unsuccessful composer, ready to begin work on the score of the just-completed text of *Die Meistersinger,* his most human creation and the one most redolent of native soil. He was more emotionally disturbed than ever. Still married to Minna and still attached to Mathilde, he had fallen in love with Cosima Liszt, now married to the musician, Hans von Bülow, who had been Wagner's pupil. He also had two alternate mistresses, the clever Mathilde Maier and the young actress, Friederike Meyer. Unable to concentrate on any one place or person, he dashed about, giving concerts in various cities—Berlin, Prague, Moscow—slipping in and out of casual affairs and, obeying an old compulsion, getting deeper into debt.

He was rescued by a miracle. He was called to Munich, to the court of the King of Bavaria, the nineteen-year-old Ludwig II, a monarch who was something of a madman. The royal patron, who could not do enough for his favorite, regarded him with adoration and planned to have all his works performed with the most famous singers. Wagner appreciated the young King's enthusiasm—"never before have I seen such unrestrained eagerness, comprehension, ardor, and loving care"—but he was passionately involved with Cosima. It was easy for Wagner to induce the King to appoint Bülow court pianist, and thus Cosima became part of the entourage. The King was not cognizant of the intimacy between the lovers and Bülow refused to face the facts, but the scandalmongers began to whisper. Wagner's extravagances caused more trouble than his indiscretions. He insisted on luxurious surroundings; he filled his rooms with priceless rugs, velvets and satin hangings; it was said that, in order to create the cave-dwelling Nibelungs and the savage Siegfried, Wagner had to swathe himself in heavy silk dressing gowns, of which he had twenty-four. The King notwithstanding, the populace was solidly against Wagner. The man in the streets resented his misuse of money—"I am much better qualified to squander 60,000 francs than to earn them," he confessed to Liszt—; the political parties distrusted his recantation of revolutionary "errors"; and the clergy condemned him as a profligate. The King's advisors told the ruler that Wagner's life was in danger and Ludwig, with tears in his eyes, advised him to leave Munich. Wagner was in his fifty-third year when he returned to Switzerland and, thanks to the King's generous pension, secured a home at Triebschen on the picturesque lake of Lucerne.

Even during this period of fulfillment and patronage, critics continued to say what they had been saying: that Wagner's music was the negation not only of art and beauty but of common sense. The *London Times* announced that *Tannhäuser* was "a commonplace display of noise"; *Tristan* sounded as if "a bomb had exploded and scattered all the notes"; an eminent German critic predicted that "not a single one of Wagner's compositions will survive." "Charlatan," "humbug," "concocter of poisoned counterpoint," "vandal," "melody-hating maniac," were a few of the hurled epithets. The noted Viennese critic, Dr. Eduard Hanslick, whom Wagner caricatured in Beckmesser, found that Wagner could not write a tune, lacked humor as well as humility, and reduced everything to a "deliberate dissolution of form into a formless, sensually intoxicating mass of sound," while the English expert, H. H. Statham, after hearing *Götterdämmerung*, concluded that "it would be cruel to judge such trash by any known literary standard."

In Munich, Cosima had borne Wagner a child, which Bülow accepted as his own. After following him to Triebschen, where she lived openly with the composer, Cosima had a second daughter—"if it had been anyone but Wagner," said Bülow, "I would have shot him." Minna died of a heart attack in 1866 and, after Cosima had given Wagner a third child, a son, the complaisant Bülow consented to a divorce. Married in 1870, Wagner found Cosima the ideal, self-effacing, worshipful wife—it is a small sign of her homage that the children were named after three of Wagner's own characters: Isolde, Eva, and Siegfried.

At this time there began a remarkable friendship which later exploded into irreconcilable enmity. A young and inflammatory philosopher, Friedrich Nietzsche, hailed Wagner's contempt for convention, declaring "Wagner is a simplifier of the universe." For a while the fifty-six-year-old libertarian and the twenty-four-year-old agnostic were inseparable. But Wagner's growing concern with religious values distressed the iconoclast: Nietzsche had turned his back on Christianity and thought that Wagner had done the same. With the years his distrust increased. Nietzsche admired Wagner the failure but he loathed the later success. Success in the theater, Nietzsche held, was decadent. Wagner's music was the opiate of the people, and Wagner had committed a crime against culture by administering the drug. "My objections to Wagner are physiological," Nietzsche wrote in *Nietzsche Contra Wagner.* "I breathe with difficulty as soon as Wagner's music begins to act on me . . . Even my stomach is in revolt."

Success came late to Wagner, but it gathered momentum with the years. Germany was entering an epoch of imperialism, and it decided to honor a native son. Wagner's tetralogy, *The Ring of the Nibelungs* was nearing completion and Bayreuth was chosen as the site for its première. Wagner was fifty-nine when he laid the foundation stone of the Bayreuth *Festspielhaus.* He was sixty-three when the first Bayreuth festival made history and the first Ring cycle was given before two emperors, a king, three grand dukes, and a scattering of princes and lesser nobles. In spite of the triumph there was a great deficit, and Wagner once more went on a concert tour to clear the debt. He was exhausted, but full of plans for a religious festival-play, *Parsifal,* a turning away from heathen myth to Christian theology. He finished the versification in 1877, but the score was not completed until five years later. Although Wagner believed he approached the subject of redemption in a spirit of reverence, it is obvious that he was fascinated by its combination of purity and theatricalism. As a result *Parsifal,* for all its hushed, sacramental atmosphere, is a self-divided work, a paradox of austerity and sensuality.

Wagner was a sick man at sixty-five when the Prelude to *Parsifal* was performed as a present for Cosima's birthday. He had been complaining of rheumatic twinges and heart trouble, but he suffered most from erysipelas. When attacks of the skin disease became agonizingly acute, he sought relief in the soft climate of Italy. After some months in Naples he went to Palermo, where he completed the orchestration of *Parsifal.* There were heart attacks upon his return to Germany—one of them struck during an ovation in Berlin—but he supervised performances of his last work in Bayreuth and, still weak, went to Venice to recuperate. There, in the Vendramini Palace, at seventy he worked over his youthful *Symphony in C* and wrote a pamphlet "On the Feminine in Human Nature." He was deep in the latter when, on February 13th, 1883, the final attack stopped his heart. The last words he wrote were "Liebe-Tragik" (intermingled love and tragedy) an unpremeditated but fairly accurate summary of a problem which occupied Wagner most of his life.

Although it is hard to separate Wagner the writer from Wagner the musician, it is obvious that the poet is a poor second-best. The "books" of the music-dramas are, with the exception of *Meistersinger,* stilted and pompous; the text of the *Ring* is particularly tiresome, a long-drawn-out horror of alliteration, feebly imitating the verse of old northern sagas, drenched in the fatalism of Schopenhauer. The critical writings are egocentric and spiteful. Written in thick and turgid sentences—Wagnerian German is a language of its own—they are the despair of the most fanatic devotees. "The Art-Work of the Future" is a blatant piece of exhibitionism and the scurrilous "Judaism in Music" is, as Wagner himself admitted to Liszt, "a long-repressed resentment," prompted largely by the outstanding successes of Mendelssohn and Meyerbeer. His personal rancor mounted on a wave of "instinctive antipathy," and his anti-Semitism, coupled with his glorification of primitive Teutonism, was elevated to a national slogan under Hitler, who hailed Wagner as his only predecessor. His autobiography is even more misleading: wallowing in self-deception, Wagner not only presents himself in the most favorable light but, a master of stagecraft, rearranges the lighting. Wagner's explanations, wrote Bernard Shaw in *The Perfect Wagnerite,* "explain nothing but the mood in which he happened to be on the day he advanced them."

As a poet Wagner suffers from a fondness for mystification on varying levels of ambiguity. His penchant for symbolism has led commentators into a quagmire of interpretations. The *Ring* is an almost endless source of possible allegories. Some consider it a Nietzschean parable concerning the dusk of old faiths and the decay of modern civilization, with the barbaric Siegfried as the herald of a "master race." Others regard it as a social treatise on the relations between Capital, symbolized by the ruthless gods, and Labor, represented by the exploited, earth-bound workers who must do their will. Still others find moral parallels in the suggestion that the lure of gold is proverbially evil and that humanity can rise above its temptations (to which even the gods are subject) only by renunciation. In the twentieth century it was fashionable to find the Oedipus complex in the motivations of the music-dramas; in 1951 Wieland Wagner, the composer's eldest grandson, staged a Bayreuth production of the *Ring* which consciously employed Freudian symbols as a foundation.

Wagner confused his followers as well as himself by a peculiarly ambivalent attitude toward Woman. The composer and the man were obsessed by the *Ewig-weibliche,* Goethe's eternal feminine that draws man on either to paradise or perdition. Wagner, however, went further than Goethe; he symbolized his feminine creations to such an extent that they cease to be human. They are either superlatively good or irrevocably bad, creatures of supernal innocence or unbelievable malevolence. Sometimes, as in *Parsifal,* the sacred and profane are combined, and we have the split personality of a Kundry. Sometimes purity and wicked purpose are arrayed against each other, as in the suffering Elsa and the evil Ortrud in *Lohengrin,* or the blithely trusting Brünnhilde and the relentless Fricka in *The Valkyrie.* Wagner presents his heroines not only as personifications of virtue but as instruments of redemption. The holy Elizabeth saves Tannhäuser from the spell of the pagan Venus, and the rapt Senta dooms herself in order to rescue the Dutchman from his lifelong curse. In his dramas as in his life, Wagner's heroines are embodiments of a love which is not only redeeming but compulsively self-sacrificial.

There remains the music. After Wagner's death his music swept the world, reforming—literally re-forming—the opera into a medium of unprecedented grandeur and eloquence. Its very popularity caused the inevitable reaction. Such modern composers as Debussy and Stravinsky rebelled against what they considered the over-luxuriant orchestration, the drugged sensuality, the orgies of impure romanticism. But there is no gainsaying the power of the Wagnerian style. It enormously enlarged the resources of the orchestra and gave new scope to the creative artist. If it is rhetorical and grandiose, it is also subtle and attains a depth of psychological penetration far beyond the reach of the music of the past. Time has already disposed of the shoddy and merely showy components in Wagner. But the establishment of a new musical form, the invention of a vast musical language, and the total splendor of his achievement have the assurance of timelessness.

Karl Marx

[1 8 1 8 - 1 8 8 3]

*"It was unlikely to find many readers among
the general public."*

THE LIFE AND WORKS of Karl Marx centered about a long series
of contradictions. A man whose whole creed was one of action,
he spent practically all his time in libraries. An iconoclast
whose entire philosophy was uncompromisingly realistic as opposed
to the romantic, his own love story was an uninterrupted romance.
Loving and tender to his family, loyal to his intimate friends, he
was heartless and intolerant to anyone who did not immediately
accept all his ideas. A middle class writer and thinker who never
engaged in day labor, he was elected the first president of the first
international association of workers. A German who lived the
greater part of his life in England, his fiercely revolutionary influence has been most apparent in Russia and the Far East. He wrote
a treatise which has had a cataclysmic effect on modern history, yet
almost no one seems to have read it.

His full name was Heinrich Karl Marx and he was born May 5,
1818, in Trier in the German Rhineland. On both sides of his family, his ancestors were deeply religious; his paternal grandfather was
a rabbi; his mother, a Dutch Jewess, was descended from a long
line of rabbis. His father was an intellectual liberal as well as a distinguished advocate who, since Jews were not permitted to practice
in the higher courts, had adopted Christianity when the boy was six
years old. Karl—the oldest son and the second child of a large family—had a happy childhood. His parents showed no partiality
among their children, but, even when he was a youth, Karl's gifted
mind was recognized and encouraged, although his predisposition
for versifying made his father worry that he might become "a common poetaster."

At seventeen he entered the University of Bonn. His idol, the
philosopher, Georg Wilhelm Hegel, had chosen theology as his
chief study and Marx, more interested in law than in religion, decided to study jurisprudence. Marx soon found that he was as mistaken as was his mentor in his first choice. His notes were disor-

ganized; he seemed incapable of balancing a budget; his small allowance was scattered on a few undergraduate wild oats. Two years before he attained his majority, he became engaged to a childhood playmate, Jenny, daughter of Baron von Westphalen. She was a girl of extraordinary beauty, character, and spirit. Her ancestry was distinguished—she was a lineal descendant of the Earl of Argyle; four years Karl's senior, she gave up many suitors for him. The engagement was opposed by her father and, although consent was subsequently given, it was seven years before the young couple were able to get married.

After a year at Bonn, during which he disappointed his father by failing to distinguish himself in any field, Karl was sent to the University of Berlin. For a while he continued his courses in jurisprudence, but a growing conviction that the practice of law was a parasitic profession drove him to history and philosophy. More and more he was fascinated by Hegel's cool rationalism. Hegel maintained that reason (or pure logic) not only conceives things but generates them, compelling action; that there is no line between philosophic theory and its extension into scientific fact; that life incessantly changes as a result of a dialectical struggle of opposing ideas in which the opposites achieve synthesis, only to give rise to their own contradictions. Marx carried the Hegelian philosophy still further. Marx's dialectical materialism, emphasizing the rationale of reality, contended that the existing system was not rational and should, therefore, be changed into a system that was. In Hegel's world of incessant flux, all life contains within itself its own death. Marx conceived this as applying to the economic institutions, as well as to philosophic ideas, and believed that even the most sacrosanct were dying of their excesses and would be supplanted by a society that would not be subject to the contradictions of capitalism. He did not underestimate the importance of ideas or their effects, but he saw them as resulting from the economic society which, then, they tended to change. Marx had not yet formulated his speculations into a system, but, even at twenty, he was getting ready to challenge conventions by questioning the inviolability of the status quo.

Meanwhile, at the University of Berlin, he applied himself with a new access of vigor and an unsuspected capacity for work. Yet, even as he coldly analyzed approaches toward an abstract truth, he filled three exercise books with romantically yearning poems to Jenny. Still following Hegel's example, he confined himself to academic circles and had every intention of becoming a teacher. But

by the time he received his degree of doctor of philosophy, his reputation for dangerous thinking was so widespread that no school
wanted him on its faculty. He was twenty-three when he discovered that a philosopher out of a job might make a living as a journalist. He began by writing for the advance guard of the "little magazines"; then, as his pieces grew bolder, he was published by the
radical journals. At twenty-five he joined the staff of the *Rheinische*
Zeitung and, in order to examine its ideas in a climate more con-
ducive to experiment, went to Paris. With him went Jenny who, in
spite of family objections and no financial aid, had become his
bride.

In Paris Marx became acquainted with Friedrich Engels who,
two years younger than Marx, became his disciple, his collaborator,
and eventually editor of his posthumous work. Son of a Calvinist
German cotton manufacturer, Engels was a student of economics
who, born in Westphalia, had rebelled against his own class, a class
that lived on inherited wealth, and had espoused the part of the
poor. A gifted scholar and brilliant writer, Engels followed Marx's
lead in developing the theory of historical materialism. As E. W. F.
Tomlin summarized in *The Great Philosophers of the Western*
World: "That section of mankind which was most completely enslaved to the machine, and whose lives were most heavily oppressed with material cares, was the proletariat, the workers of the
world . . . Society was composed of a ruling class which held down
the workers whose labor they ruthlessly exploited, but the basis of
society was this very class of manual workers. In the same way, the
universe of the philosophers was composed of a stratum of spiritual
entities, but matter was the supreme reality. Hence materialism and
proletarianism went hand in hand. The struggles of the working
class throughout history were paralleled by the dialectical evolution
of matter: or, to speak more accurately, the historical manifestation
of the dialectical evolution of matter was the struggle of the working class towards freedom." Marx put it in a succinct sentence
when, in the *Communist Manifesto,* he asserted: "All history is the
history of class struggle."

In spite of favoring hopes, the atmosphere of Paris grew politically sultry and culturally oppressive. There were a few compensa-
tions—Marx's first child, a daughter, was born—but a tightening cen-
sorship and other pressures forced him to move to Brussels, where
he was joined by Engels. In Brussels he assisted in organizing the
German Workingmen's Association and, with Engels, issued the

Communist Manifesto, the first public declaration of international socialism. In the same year Marx published his first important volume, a reply to a heavily rhetorical work by the French economist Proudhon. Proudhon called his book *The Philosophy of Poverty;* Marx's volume, also written in French, was mordantly entitled *The Poverty of Philosophy.*

After the defeat of the French Revolution in 1848 political conditions on the Continent grew worse. All socialist groups inevitably became secret societies and were driven underground. The all-powerful Prussian police were everywhere; Marx was among others who were arrested and put on trial in Cologne. He was charged with high treason and, although he was acquitted, was expelled from all territory controlled by Prussia. He returned to Paris. His stay there was brief. Paris was just recovering from a bloody insurrection, and it was not disposed to welcome any inciter of the masses, especially the author of a manifesto which heralded a class struggle destined, wrote Engels, "to do for history what Darwin's theory had done for biology." Marx was given the option of settling in some small provincial county or leaving France entirely. He chose the latter course and, with his family, moved to London, where he stayed the rest of his life. Although Engels, who was engaged in business in England, helped him from time to time, Marx lived in extreme poverty in one of the shabbiest parts of Bloomsbury. His lodgings had only one advantage: they were near the British Museum, where he went daily and worked hour after hour reading, comparing, and collating the material for the seemingly dull work which was to startle and shake the world. His circumstances were so poor and money was so scarce that the family suffered great privations. Three of his six children died in youth.

At thirty Marx was a thick-set man with a fixed and almost forbidding expression. His broad forehead was already lined and his dark eyes were distressed. His hair, worn long, was a jet-black turbulence, and even when Marx sat quietly at his desk in the reading room of the Museum, it seemed that the wind was blowing through it. He looked a little like a Norse god in a frock coat, a shrunken, beetle-browed Wotan. Not a talkative man, he spoke in short, sharp sentences; he did not enjoy the give-and-take of casual conversation but delivered his opinions as though they were conclusive verdicts. Except with his family, he never had the inclination or time for the pleasant trivialities of everyday.

In the *Communist Manifesto* Marx applied Hegel's dialectic to history and economics. Briefly summarized, the *Manifesto* maintained that the ownership of the means, or tools, of production is the significant factor in historical materialism. The key difference between classes is the distinction between which class owns the means of production and which class does not. By the very nature of its position, the class which owns the tools exploits the class which it employs to use the tools. The exploited class is bound to struggle in opposition. All history—from early primitive communism, through feudalism, to capitalism and on—is the result of these class struggles. The class that controls the means of production creates ever stronger and more bitter opposition until, by the contradictions inherent in its nature, it is overthrown. This is what Marx meant by the inevitability of the advent of socialism: not that it will come without anyone doing anything about it, for capitalist injustice forces the proletariat to overthrow it. Socialism is an attempt to put an end to this cycle by eliminating the exploited and the exploiter, by creating a classless society. Thus capitalism, by its very character, by mass production, grouping of workers, socializing production, et cetera, lays the foundations for socialism and carries its own death within itself. Following the collapse of capitalism there would be a "dictatorship of the proletariat." But this, Marx insisted, would be a transitional phase. Ultimately, the world would no longer be divided between the exploiters and the exploited, and class antagonisms would therefore vanish. Governments would control products and property rather than people, and the State as we know it (the embodiment of national rivalries, power politics, and military aggressions) would wither away. An era of busily constructive peace, not the utopia of a dreamer's Never-Never-Land, would ensue and bring about a world of creative brotherhood.

While Marx's concept of materialist history is not specifically outlined or systematically developed, it underlies all his writing. Twenty years after the *Communist Manifesto* (which is an application of that concept) Marx amplified the conception in *Capital* (*Das Kapital*). The first volume of what is unquestionably his major work appeared in 1867; two posthumous volumes, edited by Engels, were published in 1885 and 1894. *Capital,* which was eighteen years in the writing and never, in Marx's opinion, finished to his satisfaction, meticulously analyzes the capitalist system, its functioning, tendencies, dialectics, and eventual destruction. As Robert L. Heilbroner points out in *The Worldly Philosophers,* "the Marxist model of how capitalism worked was extraordinarily prophetic." The cycles of depressions and recoveries, the growth of monopolies, the need for ever new labor-saving techniques, the decline in the percentage of profits were charted by Marx as necessary symptoms of even an enlightened capitalist structure, long before they manifested themselves in fact. The cornerstone of his argument, examined in many turgid chapters of *Capital,* is the doctrine of surplus value. Highly simplified, the doctrine contends that it is the labor put into a product which gives it its value. The laborer is paid enough money to maintain him—sometimes a little more, sometimes a little less—but, since he produces far more than that for which he is paid, he receives only a small and inadequate recompense. The capitalist thus takes, in the form of profit, the disproportionately greater share, the surplus value which the workers' labor has added to the product. This theory of surplus value has been disputed by statisticians and repudiated by countless economists, and, since no pragmatic testing seems possible, it remains a contentious theory that has neither been proved nor disproved.

Another feature of *Capital* was more generally recognized: the author's fusion of theory and practice. It was quickly apparent that the chapters were not mere propositions but a cumulative call to action. Marx was a polemicist and political economist, perhaps even a prophet, rather than a philosopher; yet the logic of his work put a set of abstract and tortuous ideas into sudden, violent performance.

At sixty Marx's health began to fail rapidly. His shaggy white hair and thick white beard gave him the air of a distracted patriarch. The income he had been receiving from Engels was barely enough to support himself and his family with the most stringent necessities. Jenny, with whose encouragement he had fought "exhausting and unnecessary battles," developed cancer and died in 1881 while Marx was suffering from pleurisy. Although he recovered, he was so weakened by illness and the shock of his wife's death that he never regained health. Fifteen months after losing Jenny he succumbed and died in London, March 14, 1883, at the age of sixty-five.

During his life Marx admitted no halfway measures and, even today, his followers are unable to compromise. He has been hailed as a Revealer of Truth and condemned as the Father of Lies. His very name has evoked the extremes of unreserved adulation and violent objurgation; he has been considered both the workers' Messiah and the Antichrist. Marxists regard *Capital* as a modern Testament; Tomlin refers to it as an apocalyptic Gospel in which the Chosen

People become the Chosen Class. In an acrid chapter in Jacques Barzun's *Darwin, Marx, Wagner,* the author castigates Marx for being a disagreeable character—apart from tenacity of purpose and domestic devotion—self-centered and insensitive to the point of cruelty, a dogmatist who deceived his readers into thinking that economic facts produce ideas, a plagiarist whose premises are borrowed without acknowledgment from his betters, a polemicist with a thirst for blood. Yet, continues Barzun, "it was surely out of a passionate hatred of injustice that Marx spoke of exploitation . . . His own moral indignation at the lot of the poor, his passion for the good life, his quotations from the poets and his idealization of Greek art—these must have been true learning and right thinking . . . The first volume of *Capital* is badly written, ill put together, lacking in order, logic, and homogeneity of material." Yet, "though candid Marxists reject all pretense that it is intrinsically a great book," Barzun says, "extrinsically considered it has been a powerful source of emotion, discussion, and controversy; it has in a measure become the 'Bible of the working classes' and the oracle of a great nation; and its name and associations will not soon be erased from men's minds." Heilbroner adds: "The real and lasting impact of Marx and Engels is not their revolutionary activity, none of which bore too much fruit during their own lifetimes. It is with Marx the economist that capitalism must finally come to grips. For the final imprint he made on history was his prediction that capitalism must inevitably and necessarily collapse. On that prediction, on that 'scientific' prognostication, communism has built its edifice."

The contradictions implicit in Marx's life persisted in the estimates of his work. In 1887, four years after Marx's death, *The New York Times* reviewed the third edition of *Capital* as the work of a man in "a towering rage," in which the paragraphs "are replete with kicks and cuffs . . . He may not encourage the spilling of blood to effect the ends he desires; but the means he proposes point to that inevitable conclusion." Nevertheless, the *Times* conceded that "if much is bad in this remarkable book, it is most powerful in the brilliant manner in which the actual wrongs of the laboring classes are exposed . . . To understand the whole working of the factory acts in England, its entire progress cannot be better studied than in this work. Marx has mastered the whole subject in its most minute details. That horrible system of serfdom which wrecked human lives, that made beasts of men, brutes of women, that kept thousands in a condition worse tenfold than slaves, is ruthlessly exposed. Here

Karl Marx rises to his highest pitch. He does not indulge in sarcasm. He is conscious that no word of his could make the picture he draws so clearly more hideous." George Bernard Shaw was convinced of Marx's prophetic role; he stated unequivocally that Marx looked toward the future. "He never condescends to cast a glance of useless longing at the past." To this he added a typical Shavian commentary: "Marx's *Capital* is not a treatise on Socialism; it is a jeremiad against the bourgeoisie, supported by such a mass of evidence and such a relentless genius for denunciation as had never been brought to bear before."

It was not until half a century after the publication of *Capital* that its full effect was manifest. It caused a revolution that split the faithful into a dozen camps consisting of old line socialists who advocated collective ownership and democratic management of the production and distribution of goods; communists who favored the abolition of property as well as profit; bolshevists who abandoned Marx's theory of value as impractical; irreconcilable Stalinists; Trotskyites; and other "deviationists." Strangely enough, the revolution did not occur, as Marx predicted, in America, the richest and, presumably, most susceptible capitalist country, but in Russia, the nation least affected by capitalist development. The influence of a harassed German journalist had spread so far that in 1953 the Soviet Communists controlled the destinies of eight hundred million people, one-third of the inhabitants of the globe. It is a crowning historical irony that when *Capital* was first published the Russian censor, alertly suspicious of any work which might be considered politically subversive, permitted the book to be circulated because "it was unlikely to find many readers among the general public."

Walt Whitman

[1819-1892]

"A great urgency, an onward-going movement, the tempo and forward thrust of a half-idealistic, half-materialistic, but ever-⁀xpanding America."

THE UNHERALDED APPEARANCE of a thin volume of twelve untitled poems in 1855 marked the close of one cultural order and the beginning of another. That the book was published on the Fourth of July seemed to symbolize another declaration of independence from foreign influences, for with *Leaves of Grass* modern American poetry broke with tradition and established an indisputably native idiom. Its author was born at West Hills, Huntington, Long Island, May 31, 1819, and was christened Walter Whitman, Jr., the second son in a family of nine children. His father was a country carpenter and at best an indifferent worker, who moved from Long Island to Brooklyn, where the boy was brought up among Quakers. His life at home was none too happy. All of the youngster's affection was centered in his mother, who was an ailing illiterate. His father was a defeated, uncommunicative, and almost inarticulate man. One sister, Hannah, was a neurotic slattern. Jesse, the oldest brother, was a ne'er-do-well who contracted syphilis and died in an insane asylum. Another brother, Andrew, was shifty as well as shiftless. Edward, the youngest, was a half-wit. Jeff, like his father, was a barely competent boy who, later, became an engineer in St. Louis. George (named after George Washington) was the most successful; he became inspector of iron pipes on the Board of Water Works. Long after *Leaves of Grass* had been acclaimed as a pioneering work, George acknowledged that he cared nothing about his brother's work. "I saw the book," he said, "but I didn't read it at all—didn't think it worth reading. Mother thought as I did."

Whitman's schooling was over at eleven. At that age he ran errands for a firm of lawyers; at twelve he became a printer's apprentice and learned to set type; at thirteen he worked at the press of the *Long Island Star*. His adolescence was marked by a restlessness which became a habit and drove him from one place to another. He had to work, but he hated to be tied down; he wanted, he said, "to just live." At sixteen he earned a living as a compositor in New York, but at seventeen he felt he had had enough of journalism and decided to be a schoolteacher. During the next three years young Whitman taught at seven different country schools while he boarded with families of his pupils.

At twenty, the youth changed his mind again; he determined to be an editor. He bought a small press and founded the *Long Islander* in his home town of Huntington; he did practically all the work of getting out the paper, including the presswork. Nevertheless, a year after starting zealously to publish his own paper he abandoned it and got employment elsewhere. For six years he worked on half a dozen dailies and semi-weeklies; at twenty-seven he was editor of the *Brooklyn Eagle*. He had already been writing prose and verse, some of which had been published. The pieces of fiction were turgid and wallowed in rhetoric; the short stories bore such lurid titles as "One Wicked Impulse," "Death in the School-room," "Revenge and Requital: A Tale of a Murderer Escaped," "Wild Frank's Return." The poems were worse. Composed in conventional rhythms and dogged rhyme, the verse (chiefly devoted to lugubrious subjects) was platitudinous in sentiment, stilted in expression and, even for a beginner, absurd in tone and technique.

Whitman remained on the *Eagle* until he was almost thirty. During this two-year tenure he helped his father build houses, wrote dutifully dull articles and breezy causeries, attended the theater, went to the opera—his favorite composer seems to have been Donizetti—reviewed books, and wrote *Franklin Evans, or The Inebriate,* a temperance tract disguised as a novel. He also turned out sentimental fillers and other hackwork, promenaded Broadway, and flirted alternately with low politics and high society. At this period, Whitman conducted himself like a dandy; he sported a frock coat and high hat, carried a small cane, and wore a flower in his lapel. A chance acquaintance told him about a position open on the *New Orleans Daily Crescent* and in February, 1848, Whitman, taking his fifteen-year-old brother Jeff with him, traveled South over the Alleghenies, across Ohio, and down the Mississippi. His journalism struck a new low in New Orleans and his connection with the *Crescent* lasted less than three months. By June Whitman was back again in Brooklyn, where he became editor of the *Freeman,* a liberal weekly, which he left with a bitter valedictory at the end of a year.

More than forty years later, to protect himself from imputations of homosexuality, Whitman referred loosely to an illicit affair in the South and to mysterious unnamed children. The utterance was unsupported by the smallest scrap of evidence. Nevertheless, some commentators accepted Whitman's vague and obviously defensive remarks as facts and agreed upon New Orleans as the scene of furtive romance. One biographer unearthed a photograph of a dusky beauty who, she contended, was Whitman's "dark lady." The statistical record reveals nothing nearly so colorful; there is not the slightest indication of a passionate, or even a platonic, attachment.

In his late twenties and early thirties Whitman began to experiment in a poetic style which, if not wholly new in literature, was new for him. It was altogether different from the crude and clumsy verse he had published in the newspapers. The form was free; the rhythms were flexible; the rhymes had all but vanished. The combination of strong stresses and irregular beat suggested the sonority of the King James version of the Bible; the balanced repetitions, parallelisms and cadences, in common with those of the Hebrew psalmists, compensated for the lack of strict metrical measures. In his thirty-fifth year the experiments became an extraordinary accomplishment. In 1855 Walter Whitman, Jr., signed himself Walt Whitman, partly to distinguish himself from his father and partly to mark an emancipation from everything that had gone before. He set a little book of his polyrhythmical poems in a small Brooklyn printshop, called it *Leaves of Grass* as a glorification of the "democratic herbage" which he identified with the American spirit.

The portrait facing the title page was significant of the change which had occurred. The well-groomed dilettante had disappeared; the slick cane and the tailored frock coat had vanished in favor of rough workman's clothes, belted trousers, and hip boots. The poet, slouching deliberately, was shown in a careless pose, coatless, the shirt open at the throat, revealing a colored undershirt, and felt hat rakishly tilted across the forehead. The Whitman legend had begun. It was a legend which Whitman cultivated assiduously; he worked at the book and the legend the rest of his life. With the first publication of *Leaves of Grass* Whitman advertised himself as a fellow laborer, "beloved by the illiterate." It was a time of self-puffery (Barnum was its genius) and Whitman did not disdain to write his own unsigned reviews. Hoping for a mass audience and wanting to make sure that the reader recognized the new democratic person as well as the new poet of democracy, he wrote: "Of pure American breed, large and lusty—age thirty-six years—never once using medicine—never dressed in black, always dressed freshly and cleanly in strong clothes—neck open, shirt-collar flat and broad, countenance tawny transparent red, beard well-mottled with white, hair like hay after it has been mowed in the fields—a person singularly beloved and looked toward, especially by young men and the illiterate—one who does not associate with literary people—never on platforms, amid the crowds of clergymen or aldermen or professors —rather down in the bay with fishers in their fishing-smacks, or riding on a Broadway omnibus, side by side with the driver, or with a band of loungers over the open grounds of the country . . . one in whom you will see the singularity which consists in no singularity —whose contact is no dazzle, but has the easy fascination of what is homely and accustomed, as of something you knew before and were waiting for—there you have Walt Whitman, the begetter of a new offspring in literature."

Whitman was obviously protesting too much, pushing exaggeration to the point of mendacity, especially when, for the sake of popular appeal, he posed as a man in the street, "one of the roughs," attempting to sell his singular quality as the illiterate talk of pilots, bus drivers, and loungers. Yet there was excuse, even need, for some of the puffery. Whitman had to blow his own florid trumpet to drown out the jeers which issued from the critics in a chorus of blaring scorn. "The book is an impertinence toward the English language; in sentiment it is an affront upon the recognized morality of respectable people," wrote the *Christian Examiner* in one of the more restrained reviews. "We leave this gathering of muck to the laws which, certainly, if they fulfill their intent, must have power to suppress such obscenity," declared the *New York Criterion*. "We do not believe there is a newspaper so vile that it would print extracts." The *Boston Intelligencer* outdid the *Criterion* in viciousness: ". . . this heterogeneous mass of bombast, egotism, vulgarity, and nonsense. The beastliness of the author is set forth in his own description of himself, and we can conceive no better reward than the lash for such a violation of decency as we have before us . . . The author should be kicked from all decent society as below the level of the brute. There is no wit or method in his disjointed babbling, and it seems to us he must be some escaped lunatic raving in pitiable delirium."

The English reviewers were only a little less savage. The *London Critic* sneered: "Is it possible that the most prudish nation in the world will accept a poet whose indecencies stink in the nostrils? . . . Walt Whitman is as unacquainted with art as a hog is with mathematics." The last phrase seemed an echo of a column in *The New York Times* which held that the author of *Leaves of Grass* was "a centaur, half man, half beast . . . who roots like a pig among the rotten garbage of licentious thoughts."

By a paradoxical act of poetic justice, the first signs of recognition came from puritan and proverbially tight-lipped New England. Charles Eliot Norton gave the book a sensitively balanced review which began: "A curious and lawless collection . . . neither in rhyme nor in blank verse, but in a sort of excited prose broken into lines without any attempt at measure or regularity . . . But the writer," continued Norton, "is a new light in poetry." An even more favorable notice was written by Edward Everett Hale, the famous Boston clergyman and, later, author of *The Man Without a Country*. Conceding that the book was "odd and out of the way," Hale contended that "one reads and enjoys the freshness, simplicity, and reality of what he reads, just as the tired man, lying on the hillside in summer, enjoys the leaves of grass about him . . . There are, in this curious book, little thumbnail sketches of life—which, as they are unfolded one after another, strike us as real, so real that we wonder how they came on paper." But the most unexpected word of commendation came from Ralph Waldo Emerson. The poorly printed book of twelve effusions by an unknown poet printed by an unheard-of publisher was acknowledged with unreserved generosity by Emerson a few days after it was received. Emerson did not write to Whitman as a master craftsman to an untried apprentice, but as one member of the fraternity of poets to another. "Dear Sir," wrote Emerson, "I am not blind to the worth of the wonderful gift of *Leaves of Grass*. I find it the most extraordinary piece of wit and wisdom that America has yet contributed. I am very happy in reading it, as great power makes us happy . . . I give you joy of your free and brave thought . . . I find incomparable things said incomparably well. I find the courage of treatment which so delights us, and which large perception only can inspire. I greet you at the beginning of a great career."

Emerson's salutation had prophetic overtones, but it was a prophecy that was not fulfilled for many years. The career was questioned, derided, interrupted, assailed, and all but destroyed. Whitman himself was responsible for some of the assaults, especially those which belabored the sexual implications of his work, for Whitman was not above provoking the conservatives and outraging the orthodox with an aggressive frankness that was close to exhibitionism. "Sex will not be put aside," he wrote in one of his thumping estimates of *Leaves of Grass,* "it is the great ordination of the universe. He [Whitman] works the muscle of the male and the teeming fiber of the female throughout his writings as wholesome realities . . . Right and left he flings his arms, drawing men and women with undeniable love to his close embrace, loving the clasp of their hands, the touch of their necks and breasts and the sound of their voices. All else seems to burn up under his fierce affection for persons."

The affection was not only fierce but all-inclusive. A protagonist of the common man, "the divine average," he celebrated humanity —large, proud, affectionate, sensual, garrulous, and imperious—by celebrating himself. He declared the unity at the very beginning of his challenging and, in many ways, his most important poem, "Song of Myself":

> I celebrate myself, and sing myself,
> And what I assume you shall assume,
> For every atom belonging to me as good belongs to you.

The identification of one man, himself, and all men continued to grow as the poems grew in number. The second edition of *Leaves of Grass* ran to 384 pages; the original twelve poems had increased to thirty-two. The third edition, published five years after the first, contained 456 pages and 124 new poems as well as drastic revisions of the old ones. Subsequent editions added other poems and groups of poems, but nothing of great significance. Several posthumous and "rejected" poems were published in the Inclusive Edition printed in 1926. The ninth edition, completed in 1891, was the last to be supervised by Whitman himself.

Although the book on which Whitman worked all his life enlarged his reputation, it scarcely enhanced his income. Two years after its publication, Whitman, on the verge of starvation, had to fall back on journalism. In the spring of 1857, when he was thirty-eight, he became editor of the *Brooklyn Daily Times* and lashed out against the legalized chicanery, organized prostitution, and social abuses accepted by the complacent majority. He was in the midst of his most searching prose writing when the war between the states uprooted him. His brother George was wounded at Fredericksburg, and Whitman left Brooklyn to attend him in a hospital camp in Virginia.

Various explanations have been offered to account for Whitman's failure to enlist and actively fight for the Union which he had magnified so vehemently in prose and verse. It has been suggested that Whitman considered himself too old to become a soldier at forty-two, and also that he refused to take up arms because of his Quaker upbringing. It is more likely, however, that his temperamental resistance to enforced discipline, his lifelong habit of loafing and "inviting his soul," unfitted him for a routine of regimentation. Whitman found out that George had not been seriously hurt; he learned to dress wounds, and remained in Washington twelve years. He had already had some experience with wounded men in Brooklyn prisons and New York hospitals; now he devoted himself to nursing disabled soldiers. Washington was one vast hospital, and Whitman gave every moment to his work of mercy. Most of all, he gave himself. "There is something in personal love, caresses, and the magnetic flood of sympathy," he wrote in *Hospital Visits*, "that does, in its way, more good than all the medicine in the world." Whitman had no income, but he did enough hackwork, copying official documents and writing occasional articles, to keep himself going and supplying his charges with gifts of tobacco, stamps, small sums of money for knickknacks, sugar for lemonade, an apple or orange, or even an occasional book. Whitman talked intimately with the bedridden men, wrote letters for them, and was inspired to compose the deeply moving series *Drum-Taps*, in which the poet's emotion is controlled and clarified by saddening experience. From a persistent self-study Whitman was moved to a deep concern for others; instead of inditing abstract patriotic paeans to democracy, he framed lines which revealed the beauty and terror of life, "immense in passion, pulse, and power" and a practical sharing with humanity.

Whitman's services as a wound-dresser mollified those who had vilified him as a writer. As late as 1865, ten years after the publication of *Leaves of Grass*, *The New York Times* reviewed *Drum-Taps* and found that Whitman was deficient on all counts as a poet and that his product, whatever it might be called, showed "a poverty of thought paraded forth with a hubbub of stray words." But, continued the *Times*, "Mr. Whitman has better claims on the gratitude of his countrymen than he will ever derive from his vocation as a poet

. . . His devotion to the most painful of duties in the hospitals at Washington during the war will confer honor on his memory when *Leaves of Grass* are withered and when *Drum-Taps* have ceased to vibrate."

The gratitude of Whitman's countrymen expressed itself through a member of Lincoln's cabinet and the poet was given a clerkship in the Indian Bureau of the Department of the Interior. A few months after his position seemed secure, James Harland, Secretary of the Interior, discovered Whitman's book in a private drawer, read it with horror, and discharged Whitman in haste. The poet's friends were indignant. William Douglas O'Connor produced a fiery pamphlet entitled "The Good Gray Poet," and Whitman was "transferred" to the office of the Attorney General, where he remained until he was fifty-three. At that age he still had to struggle to survive; he not only had to print but peddle his own books. A notice attached to the fifth edition of *Leaves of Grass* informed the reader that Whitman's books (including *Passage to India* at one dollar and the panoramic *Democratic Vistas* at seventy-five cents) could be obtained from the author.

Nevertheless, although he complained of pains in his head, which he attributed to germs contracted during his work as wound-dresser, and spells of alarming faintness, Whitman liked Washington. He made several friends besides the faithful O'Connor. He continued to see many of the soldiers he had attended in the wards and attracted young men by his curiously masculine motherliness. "I think to be a woman is greater than to be a man," he said. He visualized "intense and loving comradeship, the personal and passionate attachment of man to man," as the key to a richer democracy. He formed a close attachment with an eighteen-year-old Irish-American boy, Peter Doyle, who had been a Confederate prisoner of war and was a streetcar conductor. Whitman wrote him long motherly letters and their correspondence lasted more than twelve years.

Meanwhile the pains increased and Whitman began to feel homeless and alone. The hushed preoccupation with death which had haunted him for years was now outspoken. Past fifty-four, Whitman paid a visit to his mother who was living with his brother George in Camden, New Jersey. A few days later Whitman's mother died and Whitman suffered a complete breakdown. He could not be moved. George gave him a room on the upper floor of the house and he remained in Camden. His circle of friends had broken and his life changed visibly. He grew suddenly old; spasmodic pains made him look much feebler than he was. Short bursts of energy were followed by long fits of depression. "If you write about my books," he wrote Edward Dowden, the English critic who had unreservedly praised him abroad, "I think it would be proper and even essential to include the important facts that they and their author are contemptuously ignored by the recognized organs here in the United States, rejected by the publishing houses, and the author deprived of his means of support." Hoping to support himself, he delivered books from a basket in the streets of Camden. Although he got out of doors a little he could not walk any distance.

Whitman never recovered from the stroke suffered in his mid-fifties, although it took him twenty years to die. For a while in his early sixties, his health seemed to improve. He undertook a journey as far as Colorado and delivered a lecture on Lincoln—his poem "When Lilacs Last in the Dooryard Bloom'd" was beginning to be recognized as a native classic. At sixty-five he lived in a dingy place on Mickle Street near a railway crossing, in a room littered with old newspapers. Trains shrieked by and the smells from a fertilizer factory were almost overpowering. A sailor's widow kept house for him, cooked his meals, and patched his shirts. Admirers collected sums of money and sent them to him. To provide him with a means of transportation, he was presented with a horse and buggy by thirty-two well-wishers, among whom were Oliver Wendell Holmes and Samuel L. Clemens. At sixty-nine he suffered a new series of paralytic shocks. Besides being crippled, he was tortured with kidney trouble. Yet he was able to rouse himself sufficiently to attend a celebration on his seventieth birthday and, a year later, deliver his Lincoln lecture at a dinner in nearby Philadelphia. Most of the time, however, he lay in his room on the top floor of the little house on Mickle Street in Camden, dying but not defeated. After a spell of talking there would be long silences; he would sit for hours in front of the stove, aimlessly stirring (or, as Edmund Gosse put it, "irritating") the fire. He thought much about the end, planned his tomb, and prepared a series of final valedictories.

At seventy-two he put together the 1891 (or Deathbed) edition of *Leaves of Grass,* which had grown from the initial twelve poems to more than three hundred. He described himself as a "hardcased, dilapidated, grim, ancient shellfish or time-banged conch—no legs, utterly nonlocomotive—cast up high and dry on the shore sands." Toward the end of December, 1891, Whitman contracted pneumonia; the autopsy showed widespread tuberculosis. Somehow, he hung on through the winter. Then, on March 26, 1892, two months before his seventy-third birthday, he died.

The large and lusty sexuality integrated in *Leaves of Grass,* and particularly in "Song of Myself" and the "Children of Adam" poems, contrast strangely with Whitman's celibate life. The poet never married, and the only record of anything like a love affair is a correspondence with Mrs. Anne Gilchrist, an English reviewer who nominated herself as a mate for the middle-aged bachelor. But Whitman's side of the correspondence is a shrewd campaign of evasion, caution, fear, and final retreat. Peter Doyle, who became Whitman's companion when the poet was forty-seven, told one of Whitman's executors that he "never knew of Walt's being bothered up by a woman," while Whitman's brother George insisted that Walt never showed females any attention; "he did not seem to affect the girls." Whitman was cognizant of his peculiarity; he made a sharp distinction between "amativeness," physical love between the sexes, and "adhesiveness," which meant the capacity for friendship and "a personal attraction between men which is stronger than friendship." The "Calamus" poems celebrate this "adhesiveness" with a combination of recklessness and naïveté—reckless because Whitman was more than half aware of the implications and ambiguities which lie in the poems; naïve because he equated the "robust love" of men kissing each other with the natural and nonchalant salute of American friends. Part of his program, he told Emerson, was to glorify manly friendship as well as heterosexual love. Fortunately, the poet surpassed the prophet. Whitman's dual nature led him to misread the meaning of comradeship, but it equipped him with extra sensitivities. It added an intensified awareness of the multiform complexities of being, the infinite variations of suffering and, above all, an elemental pity and participation.

Castigated by his adversaries, Whitman suffered almost as much from his idolators. For those whom Bliss Perry called "the hot little disciples," Whitman could do no wrong. Those who accepted him without reservation considered Whitman a revealer whose books were a new gospel. His book was "The Word," the latter-day "Bible of Democracy." Suspending criticism entirely and soaring into the upper reaches of obscurantism, such men as O'Connor, Burroughs, and Bucke concluded that Whitman was Nature itself, a Creation apart, an originator without antecedents. Actually, Whitman's philosophy is an amalgam of countless sources. Everything he read was funneled and filtered through his absorptive personality. His prime debt, insufficiently acknowledged, was to Emerson; many passages in the prose of the older poet are paralleled in the poetry of the younger. For example, in "The American Scholar," Emerson concluded: "We have listened too long to the courtly muses of Europe. The spirit of the American free man is already suspected to be timid, imitative, tame . . . Not so, brothers and friends, please God, ours shall not be so. We will walk on our own feet; we will work with our own hands; we will speak with our own minds." Some twenty years after this was written, it became Whitman's theme song. Its message—America's independence of an outworn past—was explicitly restated in Whitman's challenging "Song of the Exposition":

> Come Muse migrate from Greece and Ionia,
> Cross out please those immensely overpaid accounts,
> That matter of Troy and Achilles' wrath, and Aeneas',
>   Odysseus' wanderings,
> Placard "Removed" and "To Let" on the rocks of your
>   snowy Parnassus,
> For know a better, fresher, busier sphere, a wide, untried
>   domain awaits, demands you.

Such lines reflect the poet's program and indicate his influence. Whitman fathered free verse, but he did much more; he also widened the gamut, extended the subject matter, and liberated the spirit of modern poetry. Yet it is not only because of his technical innovations that Whitman became the resonant voice of a rapidly developing civilization. In almost everything he wrote there is a great urgency, an onward-going movement, the tempo and forward thrust of a half-idealistic, half-materialistic, but ever-expanding America.

Whitman committed himself, at least in theory, to a speech which was indigenous, recognizably American rather than English; he sometimes spoke of the *Leaves* as a language experiment. Poetry, he asserted, should be founded on the colloquial tone with "its bases broad and low, close to the ground." In *An American Primer* he urged more freedom in the use of the voice of the people. "Ten thousand native idiomatic words are growing, or are already grown, out of which vast numbers could be used by American writers— words that would be welcome, being of the national blood . . . What is the fitness, what the strange charm of aboriginal names?

Monongahela—it rolls with venison richness upon the palate! . . .
A perfect user of words uses things—they exude in power and
beauty from him—miracles from his hands—miracles from his mouth
. . . We need limber, lasting fierce words. Do you suppose the liberties and brawn of These States have to do only with delicate lady
words? With gloved gentlemen words?" In practice, however, Whitman's vocabulary was a queer mixture of living speech and literary
patches, an incongruous blend of freshness and affectation. He championed the vitality of the casual word and praised the creative
gusto of slang, yet he allowed himself such polyglot phrasing as "the
tangl'd long-deferred éclaircissement" and "See my cantabile—you
Libertad!" as well as such absurd coinages as "Me imperturbe,"
"philosophs," and "exalté, the mighty earth-eidolon." Whitman was
not afraid of inconsistencies. "Do I contradict myself?" he shrugged.
"Very well, I contradict myself. I am large; I contain multitudes."
His credo opened doors and windows, dissolved forms, and forced
the reader out of shrouded libraries into the coarse sunlight and the
buoyant air. To Whitman the cosmic and the commonplace were
synonymous:

> I believe a leaf of grass is no less than the journeywork of
>   the stars,
> And the pismire is equally perfect, and a grain of sand, and
>   the egg of the wren,
> And the tree-toad is a chef-d'oeuvre for the highest,
> And the running blackberry would adorn the parlors of
>   heaven,
> And the narrowest hinge in my hand puts to scorn all
>   machinery,
> And the cow crunching with depress'd head surpasses any
>   statue,
> And a mouse is miracle enough to stagger sextillions of
>   infidels.

Whitman repels many readers not only by his lack of taste but
by an unrestrained garrulousness and a lumping together of the significant and the trivial in sprawling catalogs—"I expected him to
make the songs of the nation," wrote Emerson in a later rueful estimate, "but he seems content to make the inventories." Nevertheless,
the autobiographical shirt-sleeve prose of *Specimen Days* and the
sharply savage indictments of *Democratic Vistas,* to say nothing of
the best of the poems, shake themselves free of bombast and rise
into an atmosphere which has the amplitude of time. The lines are
gross and sensual and poignantly tender. They are explosive as a

vehement oath and as grave as the Psalms which shaped their measures. Everything in Whitman alternately reveals and reconciles his contradictions; his spirit is uncritically all-embracing and over-vigorously optimistic. But Whitman's indiscriminate acceptance is the very core of his faith, enclosing beauty and ugliness, good and evil, in the mystic's circle of complete affirmation.

Leaves of Grass is admittedly uneven, ungainly, even shapeless; but it is monumental, a mountainous book. It is not a single towering eminence but a series of uneven ranges. If some of the depths seem to descend below sea level, the heights are dazzling with peaks whose altitudinous grandeur has seldom been surpassed. Moreover, the book is the man. From it Whitman emerges a challenging and controversial figure, enigmatic, roughhewn and lopsided, but a titan in his times and in our own.

Herman Melville

[1 8 1 9 - 1 8 9 1]

"The tragic and challenging No."

AUTHOR OF THE GREATEST NOVEL ever produced in America, a seer and a poet who was also a successful writer of popular fiction, Herman Melville was practically unknown at the time of his death, remembered vaguely as the man who ran away from home to live with cannibals. He was born in New York City, August 1, 1819, of proud American stock; both sides of the family had ancestors who had participated heroically in the Revolutionary War. Herman's paternal grandfather was a major who helped organize the Boston Tea Party; his maternal grandfather, General Peter Gansevoort, was the hero who had stubbornly held Fort Stanwix against the attacks of the British and their Indian allies. The home site of his mother's family was Gansevoort, the little Dutch-settled town near Albany, and his mother, Maria Gansevoort, maintained the stern Dutch-American tradition. The background was stubbornly Calvinist, the church was the Dutch Reform Church; but the children—Herman was the third of eight—were brought up in comfortable and cultivated if not convivial circumstances. The house in which the Melvilles lived had more than a few evidences of luxury; there were objets d'art and fine furnishings which Herman's father, Allen Melville, a well-to-do importer and commission merchant, brought back from his various trips abroad. Herman was sent to a good school, visited his upstate relatives, and enjoyed his vacations in the Saratoga countryside. Petted though not pampered by his mother, taken about New York by his attentive father, Herman Melville enjoyed an easy and untroubled childhood.

All this changed by 1830, at which time the boy was eleven. As a result of a general business depression, his father was forced into bankruptcy, and the family moved to Albany, close to his mother's people. Allen Melville was induced to go into the fur business, but he was overburdened with debts and shaken by a sense of failure. Defeated before he could organize his affairs, he was so damaged by the struggle that he grew physically ill. Worse, his mind was affected; he became violently deranged and, a few weeks after the

47

first attack, died of a stroke, while still in his forties. Melville's old-est brother, Gansevoort, was only sixteen, but he assumed support of the family by trying to save the remnants of his father's business. For a while things seemed to prosper. Herman attended the Al-bany Academy, the Albany Classical School, and joined a debating society. The period of semi-security was brief. Gansevoort's business enterprise began to fail; Herman took small clerking jobs from time to time; the Melvilles came to depend more and more on "loans" from the Gansevoort family.

At eighteen Herman was able to obtain a teaching job in Pittsfield in the Berkshires, but he could not hold it. Further economies were necessary, and the family moved to Lansingburg, where Melville, thinking to become an engineer, took a course in surveying, but nothing came of it. A few little pieces of fugitive prose ("Frag-ments From a Writing Desk") appeared in the local newspaper.

In June, 1839, when he was in his twentieth year, Melville signed up as a cabin boy on the *St. Lawrence* bound for Liverpool. His companions were rough and riotous, but the stinging spray, the huge tides, and the lurching chaos of the sea got into his blood. "I was conscious of a wonderful thing in me, that responded to all the wild commotion of the outer world and went reeling on and on with the planets in their orbits and was lost in one delirious throb at the center of the All. A wild bubbling and bursting at my heart, as if a hidden spring gushed out there . . . But how soon these rap-tures abated, when after a brief interval, we were again set to work, and I had a vile commission to clean out the chicken-coops, and make up the beds of the pigs in the long boats. Miserable dog's life is this of the sea: commanded like a slave and set to work like an ass; vulgar and brutal men lording it over me, as if I were an Afri-can in Alabama." Nevertheless, Melville's journals make it clear that, although work aboard ship was hard, he did not disdain it enough to abjure further sea-going. On the contrary, it whetted his desire for ocean voyages, the more so since they became the ever-varying and propulsive backgrounds for his major novels.

On this first trip he was away four months, six weeks of which were spent in the sordid strangeness of a grimy Liverpool, and when he returned to New York on October 1, he faced a future more uncertain than before. During the winter he taught in another country school, tried to adapt himself to rural life, flirted aimlessly with the village favorites, and wrote fragments which were, at the best, apprentice work. In 1841, unable to find work, he sailed as a member of the whaling ship *Acushnet*. It was a long journey. During dull days, the young seaman wove mats; the exciting ones were spent hunting the whale, cutting up the carcass, and learning the hundred details recaptured and brilliantly illuminated in *Moby Dick*. Though the conditions were such that Melville was forced to jump ship, the artist in him realized the value of the rigorous training. "If I shall ever deserve any real repute in that small but high hushed world which I might not unreasonably be ambitious of; if hereafter I shall do anything that, upon the whole, a man might rather have done than left undone; if, at my death, my executors or more properly my creditors find any precious mss. in my desk, then I prospectively ascribe all the honor and glory to whaling; for a whale-ship was my Yale College and my Harvard."

The *Acushnet* sailed from New Bedford, Massachusetts, with a mixed crew on January 3, 1841. The ship was crowded and uncomfortable; the captain was a tyrant; the men were moody and almost mutinous; the voyage seemed interminable. Melville found the routine worse than the hardships and, a year and a half later when they reached the Marquesas, he and another sailor deserted the ship and escaped to the interior of Nuku-Hiva. While there Melville and his comrade were entertained by the Typees (or Taipis), a tribe of cannibals who treated him both as an honored guest and a captive. He learned to wear the native costume, to swim naked in a dusky Eden with the original of the childlike Fayaway depicted in *Typee*. Although the savages concealed their cannibalism, he was initiated into the other rituals and shared the ceremonials with which the handsome Marquesans celebrated their delight in beauty and sexual pleasure. It was a dream world that Melville inhabited for a while, a world of bronze-gold people in a Golden Age far from the commerce-ridden centers of trade and the difficulties of earning a living in what Melville called "snivelization." But he was too young and too modern to go native and remain a primitive for long. Besides, he was homesick and, worse, he had a painful leg injury and an infection which the Typees, for all their medicine men, could not heal. Somehow, in spite of the possessive watchfulness of his captors, he managed to get away and, with the help of a friendly tribesman, paddle out to an Australian whaling bark, the *Lucy Ann*.

Life aboard the *Lucy Ann* was as bad as on the *Acushnet*. The captain was a bully and a drunkard, and when the ship reached Papeete the crew mutinied. They were imprisoned; but their chains were light, the natives were amiable. When Melville was released, he was happily footloose. But it was not long before he discovered that, in spite of the opportunities for endless leisure, he could not idle his life away. Unable to become a beachcomber, or *omoo,* he made one more attempt to become a whaling hand; he persuaded the skipper of the *Charles and Henry* to sign him up. It was his third whaler. In April, 1843, he found himself ashore in Hawaii, where he clerked for an English storekeeper, did odd jobs as a handyman, and when he was without funds and food, set up pins in a bowling alley in Honolulu. Tired of drifting, but equally weary of whaling, he determined to return to his own country and, four months after landing in Hawaii, enlisted as an ordinary seaman on the American frigate, the *United States.*

Melville spent fourteen months in the Navy as a sailor, revisited the Marquesas, and journeyed to South America, where he saw the strange, sad city of Lima, a corrupt ruin he was never to forget. He made friends aboard ship; the most lasting was the "matchless and unmatchable" Jack Chase to whom, many years later, Melville dedicated *Billy Budd.* He also witnessed floggings, which were then common in the Navy, and was revolted by their sadistic brutality. On October 3, 1844, the *United States* sailed into Boston and, ten days later, Melville received his discharge from the Navy. He had packed a lot of hazardous living into his twenty-five years and two months, and he was not reluctant to go home to his mother and sisters in Lansingburg.

Now he began to write, the ideas rushing and the words tumbling out in a gathering crescendo of power. Out of the experiences on Nuku-Hiva came *Typee,* published in 1846. Melville's transcripts of the events, as well as his illumination of Polynesian customs, were accurate—the sailor who escaped with him testified to their truth—but everything is so heightened and tightly integrated that it is hard to tell where biography ends and fantasy begins. "*Typee,*" said Lewis Mumford in his rich and subtle *Herman Melville,* "belongs to the morning of the imagination. It is direct, fresh, free from self-consciousness." Comparing Melville and Thoreau, Mumford went on: "Melville had found in the Marquesas the simplicity and directness of livelihood that Thoreau sought nearer at hand . . . Both Melville and Thoreau had found out what it meant to throw off the impedimenta of civilization; and, though both of them returned to the society of their own kind, they carried back to everyday American life a little contempt."

Readers ignored the contempt and relished the picture of a simple, carefree, and almost prehistoric society; they enjoyed *Typee* because it was, to them, a picaresque series of adventures in an exotic and glamorous tradition. As a result, *Typee* was a sensational success; the demand for it was increased by charges of immorality brought by a few prurient critics offended at the "lewdness" of the native customs described. Encouraged and a little apprehensive, Melville started work on *Omoo,* a sort of sequel to *Typee. Omoo* is a narration of what happened to Melville after he escaped from the Typees until the time he signed up on the next whaling ship. It was published in 1847, when Melville was twenty-eight, and it, too, was a popular success. Melville began to have literary friends; he enjoyed the novelty of being lionized. The troubles of the past were forgotten and he looked forward to the future with some confidence. He married Elizabeth Shaw, daughter of Lemuel Shaw, Chief Justice of Massachusetts, an outstanding liberal and a distinguished jurist who had been a close friend of Melville's father. Melville had known her since childhood and, though their marriage was not passionately romantic, it was solid. Elizabeth was a not particularly pretty girl nor was she a woman of more than average mind or limited imagination. But she was a sympathetic wife, devoted to a husband she took literally and never understood. Without comprehending the quality of his work, she knew that his writing was vital to him, and when it was necessary—and it was necessary much of his later life—she borrowed, scraped, and made every sacrifice for it. On his side, Melville appreciated his wife without condescension; he confided in her, took long walks with her, and read to her almost every evening. Before he settled down to work and domesticity, there was a hurried honeymoon through Vermont, after which he went back to his old desk, newly furbished by his wife who teasingly admonished him not to work too late and not, in the fury of creation, to upset the inkpot.

At twenty-nine Melville wrote his third book, *Mardi,* and discovered Shakespeare. "Dolt and ass that I am," he groaned, "I have lived more than twenty-nine years and, until a few days ago, never made acquaintance with the divine William. Ah, he's full of sermons-on-the-mount, and gentle almost as Jesus. I fancy this Shakespeare in heaven ranks with Gabriel, Raphael, and Michael. And if another Messiah ever comes, he will be in Shakespeare's person." The accent and eloquence of Shakespeare began to show in Melville's writing. It fused with Melville's tumultuous rhetoric in *Moby*

Dick, but it manifested itself as early as *Mardi,* a book which is not so much a novel as an attempt to write in several manners, a mixture of satire, philosophy, poetry and allegory. The setting seems to be Melville's favorite South Seas; but the mythical Dominora is England, Propheero is Europe, Franko is France, and Vivenza is the United States.

Mardi puzzled the critics and discouraged the readers. It did not sell, and Melville, hurrying to repair the possible damage to his reputation as a writer of salt sea fiction, turned once more to his own adventures. He wrote a book about his first voyage to Europe as a cabin boy, his experiences on board ship and abroad, and his return. He called it *Redburn.* It was not what his readers might have expected—there is bitterness in it, a protest against the fate that pitted an unprepared boy against the cruelty of a ruthless world—but, in spite of its excesses and apparent inconsistencies, *Redburn* is a rousing sea story. Melville belittled the book; he complained that it was a beggarly work, written to pay his bills—his first son, Malcolm, had been born in 1849—and buy a little tobacco. But he was gratified to learn (a) that its truthfulness was recognized and (b) that it sold twice as well as *Mardi.* He turned immediately to his fifth book, *White-Jacket, or The World in a Man-of-War.* In a little more than one year (1848-9) Melville had composed the greater part of three volumes.

White-Jacket, which was completed in two and a half months, is based on Melville's life on the Navy frigate, the *United States.* It is a mature successor to *Redburn* and, although there are evidences of haste in the writing, it is anything but a potboiler. Besides the exciting story element, it contains a Hogarthian gallery of nautical types: the magnificent Jack Chase, the scoundrelly Master-at-Arms, the more-than-rational Mad Jack, the shrewd Jermin, Mr. Pert, and other sharply recorded individuals. *White-Jacket* was also a critical work; as a result of its exposures of shipboard brutality, flogging was abolished by the Navy. It was, moreover, a symbolical work. The white-jacket symbolized the "outsider," the young man with a protective but vulnerable difference, "the white sheep in the black flock of a man-of-war," says Mumford, who adds: "Melville, who had found the world was something of a man-of-war, discovered also that a man-of-war's crew was a pretty good representation of the world."

At thirty-one Melville began his magnum opus, *Moby Dick,* and met Nathaniel Hawthorne, whose companionship he sought with almost painful eagerness. Longing for understanding which no one seemed able to give him, he seized upon Hawthorne as the idealized friend, the person whose art he admired and whose mind was attuned to the grave philosophical problems as well as the delicate nuances which concerned Melville. For a while the friendship flourished. Sophia Hawthorne left a memorable impression of the young author: "I am not quite sure that I do not think him a very great man . . . A man with a true, warm heart, and a soul and an intellect—with life to his finger-tips; earnest, sincere and reverent; very tender and modest. He has very keen perceptive power; but what astonishes me is, that his eyes are not large and deep. He seems to me to see everything accurately; and how he can do so with his small eyes, I cannot tell. His nose is straight and handsome, his mouth expressive of sensibility and emotion. He is tall and erect, with an air free, brave and manly. When conversing, he is full of gesture and force, and loses himself in his subject . . . Once in a while, his animation gives place to a singularly quiet expression out of those eyes to which I have objected: an indrawn, dim look, but which at the same time makes you feel that he is at that moment taking deepest note of what is before him. It is a strange, lazy glance, but with a power in it quite unique. It does not seem to penetrate through you, but to take you into itself." Newton Arvin quotes a vivid family scene in his interpretive biography, *Herman Melville:* "There was one evening when 'Mr. Omoo' related to Sophia and her husband the story of a fight he had once witnessed between two Polynesian braves, in which one of them had performed prodigies of valor with a heavy club. When their guest had gone, Hawthorne and Sophia looked high and low for the club with which Melville had been 'laying about him so,' and gradually became aware that it had existed only in his imagination and theirs."

What Melville found in Hawthorne was a confirmation of his own dark magic and his darker misgivings about the world. "It is the blackness in Hawthorne that so fixes and fascinates me . . . I feel that he has dropped germinous seeds into my soul." What Melville failed to find was a reciprocal understanding, a response to his affection. After a promising beginning, the intimacy began to fade; Hawthorne was a little wary of the impetuous and sometimes importunate Melville. The meetings grew fewer and the friendship fell quietly apart.

In 1851 *Moby Dick* appeared, synthesizing the varied themes which Melville had sounded in his preceding books, and adding a series of astounding variations on the main motif. Here, in one overwhelming volume, is the luxuriance of *Typee,* the tropical air of *Omoo,* the poetic allusiveness of *Mardi,* the narrative strength of *Redburn,* the sharp character delineation of *White-Jacket. Moby Dick* not only combined the best elements of all these, it transformed them. Nothing like it had ever come out of America. *Moby Dick* has something of the rhapsodies of Koheleth, the wild imagery of Job, and the swelling catalogs of Rabelais. One is inevitably reminded of the Bible—the first words of *Moby Dick* are "Call me Ishmael"—and the book's monstrous symbol is the white whale, glorious and terror-striking Leviathan. Ahab's tempestuous soliloquies recall the Shakespeare that Melville discovered only a little more than a year before he began his colossal work. Like the preceding volumes, this, too, is the story of a voyage: the saga of a young man (Ishmael) who sails to get away from his unhappiness. His desire to escape is mixed with a self-destructive impulse; he says, "With a philosophical flourish Cato throws himself upon his sword; I quietly take to the ship." Companion to Ishmael is the Polynesian savage, Queequeg, whom the narrator comes to love, much as Melville came to love the primitive South Sea Islanders. The captain of the ship is Ahab (another reminiscence of the Bible), whose leg has been bitten off by a white whale, and who has vowed to kill the monster as an act of pure vengeance. Instead, the whale eventually kills Ahab, the ship is destroyed, and Ishmael alone lives to tell the heavily weighted tale.

Though the setting is not unfamiliar, *Moby Dick* differs from anything Melville ever attempted. He called for Vesuvius' crater for an inkstand so that he could include "the whole circle of the sciences, and all the generations of whales and men and mastodons, past, present, and to come, with all the revolving panoramas of empire on earth, and throughout the whole universe, not excluding its suburbs." Although he half-mocked the magnitude, he scarcely exaggerated. The structure of *Moby Dick* is so vast and complicated that the pattern is often twisted askew. Technically, the book has many defects—it was said of Melville, as it had been said of others, that he had great genius but little talent—yet no one has questioned the epic quality of the work. It stands in superb isolation, a literary monolith.

Moby Dick failed to impress the critics and the uncritical readers. Melville's admirers wanted another *Typee,* which he now despised;

they were bewildered by the rhetorical apostrophes, suspicious of the heroic pessimism, antipathetic to a novel that turned into a parable, especially a parable unaccompanied by a comfortable explanation. The reviews ranged from perfunctory applause to prolonged disapproval; *The New Monthly Magazine* ridiculed the book as "mad as a March hare; gibbering, screaming, like an incurable Bedlamite, reckless of keeper or strait-jacket." In short, the book was a critical failure and a financial disaster.

The writing of *Moby Dick* seems to have exhausted Melville's energy, and its reception completely dispirited him. Even before he finished the book, he was worried by debts and harassed by the thought that he could no longer write the kind of fiction that would sell. In a letter written to Hawthorne in 1851 he voiced his fears: "I am so pulled hither and thither by circumstances. The calm, the coolness, the silent grass-growing mood in which a man *ought* always to compose—that, I fear, can seldom be mine. Dollars damn me; and the malicious Devil is forever grinning in upon me, holding the door ajar. . . . What I feel most moved to write, that is banned—it will not pay. Yet write the other way, I cannot. So the product is a final hash, and all my books are botches . . . What's the use of elaborating! Though I wrote the Gospels in this century, I should die in the gutter. What reputation H. M. has is horrible. Think of it! To go down to posterity as the man who lived among the cannibals!"

Notwithstanding the lack of appreciation and goaded by the ever-pressing need of funds—his second son, Stanwix, had just been born—Melville plunged into his seventh novel, *Pierre, or The Ambiguities.* Its subtitle was well chosen: the story concerned a young man and his widowed mother, the relation between them being more like that of brother and sister, with incestuous overtones. Attempting to rid himself of any connection with the sea or sea stories, Melville was, literally, out of his element. The style of *Pierre* is mawkishly ornate, the tone is dismally sad, and the chief effect is that of desperate strain. On money borrowed from his father-in-law he had bought a farm near Pittsfield, in the foothills of the Berkshires, where he lived for sixteen years. But he could not sustain himself without continued assistance. *Pierre* was no help. A headlong descent after the towering heights of *Moby Dick,* it was even more of a commercial failure. Melville's heyday was over before he was thirty-two.

The next forty years were unhappy ones. Though by no means

sunk in isolation, as implied by early commentators, Melville was neglected by all but his family and a few friends, usually impoverished and subject to ill health. He suffered from sciatica, rheumatism, and a definite touch of neurasthenia. His first daughter was born when he was thirty-three, another daughter was born two years later. His oldest son, Malcolm, committed suicide or was accidentally killed at eighteen, and his second son, predeceasing him, died of tuberculosis. Although Melville never withdrew from the world, he developed a disdain for it. It was apparent that he had spent his creative energies too prodigally in the short span between his twenty-sixth and thirty-first years, but he had not written himself out. At thirty-seven he published *Benito Cereno,* a long short story, which is a brilliant retelling of an old yarn; at thirty-eight he brought out another novel, *The Confidence-Man,* and a collection of small pieces of fiction, *The Piazza Tales.*

Suddenly Melville found himself without either the desire or the ability to write. His health became so bad that a breakdown was indicated and, on money given to him by his father-in-law, Melville set sail for England and the East. He visited Greece, Turkey, and Egypt, returning home by way of Italy and England. Back in America he tried lecturing, but he derived little profit and no pleasure from public appearances. At fifty, he gave up all thought of earning a living by his pen and turned from prose to poetry.

Melville's poetry has been greatly underrated. Its surface faults are obvious; the meter is rough and the syllables are often as gnarled as the verse of Thomas Hardy who, in his fifties, also turned from prose to poetry. Three volumes containing more than two hundred poems showed his devotion to the compact intensity of the medium. The best are unquestionably the *Battle-Pieces.* Inspired by the Civil War, the lines are full of strong, percussive music and sultry lightning flashes. *Clarel* is a two-volume narrative poem with Melville's visit to the Holy Land as a background. Obviously written to please himself (the publication costs were paid by his uncle Peter Gansevoort), Melville was a little hurt though not surprised when it failed to please others; *Clarel,* Melville wrote to a friend, "is a work eminently adapted for unpopularity."

Struggling with sickness and poverty, Melville attempted to get a consular post, a naval appointment, or any position which would give him a measure of security. He waited for years and was fortyseven before he was made Inspector of Customs for the Port of New York, and moved his family from Pittsfield to New York City.

The work was monotonous, but Melville did not complain. "Herman's position is in the Surveyor's Department," Elizabeth Melville wrote to her cousin Catherine. "Apart from everything else, the occupation is a great thing for him—he could not take any other post that required head work and sitting at a desk." Melville held the position for twenty years until he was sixty-seven, when a legacy received by his wife allowed him to leave his job and go back to his study.

The last five years of his life were spent in contemplative solitude; only his wife and his two small granddaughters could penetrate the barrier of reserve. New Yorkers occasionally saw a tall, commanding figure with an Olympian brow and an amazing beard striding down the street. One of his granchildren recalled how she often saw him "don his heavy ulster and plush cap and set forth for several weeks on the ocean—all without a word of warning. Even when he was pacing his narrow porch at home, there was something in his gait and manner which I could associate only with a rolling ship in a heavy sea."

At sixty-nine he made his last voyage—to Bermuda—and privately printed *John Marr and Other Sailors,* a book of poems. At seventy-one he had a severe attack of erysipelas and almost succumbed. He lived long enough to bring out one more book of poetry and the powerful story, *Billy Budd, Foretopman,* a drama of spiritual innocence and technical guilt. This story, the clash and reconciliation of uncompromising duty and pure virtue, was the final epitome of the novelist as philosopher; it brought Melville's career to a close. The erysipelas attacks caused an enlargement of the heart, and Melville died September 28, 1891. The obituary notice in the *Press* brought him out of obscurity to announce: "Death of a Once Popular Author."

For more than a quarter of a century after his death Melville remained unknown except to a few devotees of *Moby Dick*. At last Raymond M. Weaver persuaded a publisher to print his *Herman Melville: Mariner and Mystic* in 1921. The following year a definitive edition of Melville's works was undertaken—not in America, but in London—and by 1924 the set of sixteen volumes was complete. This was the beginning of the Melville renaissance. Within the next three decades there were a hundred treatises, countless analytical essays, and a dozen full-length studies and biographies.

The biographers differed widely in the matter of interpretation; they outdid themselves in their search for symbols. *Moby Dick* was the favorite hunting ground, so trampled that the pages became a morass of double meanings. Mumford maintained that "no other fable, except perhaps Dante's, demands that we open so many doors and turn so many keys; for, finally, *Moby Dick* is a labyrinth, and that labyrinth is the universe . . . It is one of the first great mythologies to be created in the modern world . . . The white whale stands for the brute energies of existence, blind, fatal, overpowering; while Ahab is the spirit of man, small and feeble but purposive, that pits its puniness against this might, and its purpose against the black senselessness of power." John Freeman saw the work as a parable of an eternal strife; he paralleled it to Milton's Lucifer and the Archangels. On the other hand, Richard Chase argued that "Ahab is the American cultural image: the captain of industry and his soul . . . Moby Dick is God incarnate in the whale." D. H. Lawrence, finding a great deal of Lawrence in Melville, declared that the whale, Moby Dick, "is the deepest blood-being of the white race, our deepest blood-nature. And he is hunted, hunted, hunted by the maniacal fanaticism of our white mental consciousness . . . We get dark races and pale to help us, red, yellow, and black [Lawrence was thinking of the mixed crew of the whaling ship]: we get them to help us in this ghastly hunt which is our doom and our suicide."

Melville had a dread that his work might be regarded as "a monstrous fable or, still worse and more detestable, a hideous and intolerable allegory." In *Great Novelists and their Novels,* W. Somerset Maugham objected to the assumption that Melville set out to write such an allegory; any interpretation in symbolical terms, he contended, would have to be arbitrary and misleading. "According to Ellery Sedgwick," said Maugham, "Ahab is Man—man sentient, speculative, religious, standing his full stature against the immense mystery of creation. I find this hard to believe. A more plausible interpretation is Mumford's. He takes Moby Dick as a symbol of Evil, and Ahab's conflict with him as the conflict of Good and Evil in which Good is finally vanquished . . . Why have the commentators assumed that Moby Dick is a symbol of evil? Why should the White Whale not represent goodness rather than evil? Splendid in beauty, vast in size, great in strength! Captain Ahab with his insane pride is pitiless, harsh, cruel and revengeful; *he* is Evil . . . Or, if you want another interpretation, you might take Ahab with his dark wickedness for Satan and the White Whale for his Creator . . . Fortunately, *Moby Dick* may be read, and read with passionate interest, without a thought of what allegorical significance it may or may not have."

The grandeur of Melville's conceptions and the sheer splendor of his accomplishment loom larger as the body of Melville criticism grows greater. It is now apparent that Melville's ironies are as characteristic as his rhapsodies, that he matched myth and humor, that he did not shrink from the despised pun in the extension of his major themes: the clash of reality and irresponsibility, the wastefulness of life, and the inextricability of good and evil.

Melville's values were not the values of his generation. He never strove for fame, "the triumph of the insincere mediocrity." He was not sure of anything, including mankind, never unreservedly affirmative. Unable to accept the sweeping optimism of Longfellow, Emerson, and Whitman, he adds his skepticism to the troubling doubts of Hawthorne and Poe. Against the happy yea-sayers he pits his tragic and challenging No. Instead of Emerson's peaceful rainbow he presents thunderheads; instead of Whitman's splendid sun he calls up heroic blackness. His stature constantly increasing, Melville not only measures up to the American giants but towers darkly above them.

Susan B. Anthony

[1820-1906]

*"That women might own and possess their
own souls."*

WHAT IS PERHAPS the most radical alteration of social relation-ships in the last century is already so taken for granted that its newness is generally overlooked. Yet less than one hundred years ago women had no rights. The first organized demand occurred as late as 1848 and asked for such essentials as the right "to have personal freedom, to acquire an education, to earn a living, to claim her wages, to own property, to make contracts, to bring suit, to testify in court, to obtain a divorce for just cause, to possess her children, to claim a fair share of the accumulations during marriage." Only one college in the United States admitted women; there were no women doctors or lawyers in the country. Married women literally "belonged" to their husbands as slaves or chattels. If they earned money or inherited it, legally it was not theirs but their husbands'. Single women had to be represented by male guardians. Obviously, no woman was entitled to vote. Except in ancient Egypt and under Roman law, this approximately had been the status of women from the beginnings of time.

The dogged seventy-five-year campaign of prodding, petitioning, and pleading that emancipated modern woman owed its strength and its strategy to Susan Brownell Anthony, sometimes called "the Napoleon of Feminism." She was born February 15, 1820, in Adams, Massachusetts, the second child in a family of eight. Her father, Daniel Anthony, was a man of strong intellect and liberal in-clinations. Though a Quaker, he was not a conformist. For his wife, he picked Lucy Read, who was not only a Baptist but a young woman of lively disposition. However, when she became Mrs. An-thony she observed all the Quaker customs. Susan was brought up in a household that, in her childhood, wore Quaker clothes, spoke in Quaker terms, and proscribed frivolity. Though Daniel was a prosperous mill owner, it was incumbent on his wife to do all her own work, including farm chores, as well as board and serve the mill hands who lived with them from time to time. The children, particularly the older girls, were trained early in household accomplishments. But their education was far from neglected. Before she was five, precocious Susan could read and write. As her schooling progressed, whenever she came to a subject in which she was interested (such as more and more advanced arithmetic) she insisted on being taught it—even though it was nothing that girls were supposed to know. The early learning was obtained at home from a governess. In her teens, Susan was sent to an inexpensive finishing school near Philadelphia, Miss Deborah Moulson's Select Seminary for Females. Miss Moulson's task, as she saw it, was to mold her pupils in the prevailing forms, rather than direct an inquisitive spirit, and Susan's inquiring mind was bound to rebel.

Daniel Anthony went bankrupt in the panic of 1838. He was forced to move his family from Battenville, New York, where they had been living for more than ten years, to the aptly named town of Hardscrabble, where he had a farm. All other means of surviving failed; Daniel found employment with the New York Life Insurance Company and was a salaried worker for them for the rest of his life.

Susan was not unhappy to be taken out of Miss Moulson's Seminary; her main concern was to help in the financial emergency. Due to the depression, probably for the first time numbers of young women from formerly well-to-do homes were thinking the same thing, and the more courageous—or more desperate—were moving into the world of men's concerns. Susan's first step, however, was in a field where women had been tolerated for some time: the teaching profession. She served as assistant principal of a boarding school in New Rochelle, and received thirty dollars for fifteen weeks of work. Her next appointment was in a country school, succeeding a man who had been paid $10 a week. Not being a man, Susan was given a salary of $2.50 a week.

Better teaching posts followed, culminating in a position as the principal of the girls' department in the Canajoharie Academy. Living away from home, in a free environment, with money of her own to spend on a few indulgences, Susan broke away from her Quaker ways and repressions. Tall, broad-shouldered, vigorous, she attracted suitors, but none suited her. She was conceded to be "the smartest woman in Canajoharie"; her sympathies were with the extreme Abolitionists; she had become interested in the temperance movement, a genuine social problem during that hard-drinking period. For some time she had questioned the inequalities in em-

ployment of women, not only in the teaching field but from what
she had seen in her own father's mills. She waited only for the opportunity to help right the prevailing wrongs.

It was through her own family that in 1848, she heard about the
Seneca Falls Convention, derided as "The Hen Convention," called
by Elizabeth Cady Stanton and Lucretia Mott to discuss the social,
civil, and religious rights of women. Preferring to throw her now
impatient energy into the temperance fight, Susan joined the
Daughters of Temperance, sparked her local Canajoharie branch,
spread out as an organizer up to state level, finally gave up her
teaching position and devoted herself to the Woman's State Temperance Society. Not an eloquent speaker, she learned to be a
forceful one. Not a graceful writer, she became a convincing one.
Her main gift was for organization. It was dismaying to find that
her work was being blocked, not by an indifferent public, but by
the opposition of the men's temperance society. The men would not
allow the women to work with them—at that time women might be
seen but not heard at a public meeting—and were afraid they would
do disservice to the whole temperance cause by raising the divert-
ing question of women's rights. Susan, who had embarked on her
fifty-year friendship with Elizabeth Stanton, was beginning to be
swayed by her friend's reiteration that the fight for women's rights
was really the main fight. She shifted her focus of attention for the
last time. Susan carried one of her earliest bids for recognition into
the New York State Teachers' Association and succeeded in forcing
through a vote that permitted female teachers to "share in all the
privileges and deliberations" of the organization.

By 1853, the women's rights cause had become her main absorbing interest. At first she was junior to Elizabeth Stanton in age and
leadership; gradually she became the guiding mind of the crusade.
Much of the time, Susan lived with Elizabeth and her lawyer husband, so that the two friends could write speeches, organize groups,
draft petitions, and agitate the country between household chores.
Susan was already termed an old maid, but Mrs. Stanton mothered
seven children. Since Mrs. Stanton was the better speaker, Susan
frequently minded the home so that Elizabeth could campaign.

For several years, the leaders in the movement dramatized their
protest against the stifling constraint of corsets and other oppressive
clothing by appearing in public in "bloomers," loose trousers that
were gathered at the ankles. Susan cut off her lustrous brown hair
for further effect. Soon it became evident that the sensationalism

of the costumes drew attention away from basic issues, and the feminists, more publicized than they had ever been, went back to layers and layers of floor-sweeping skirts.

Still the work lagged, mainly through lack of funds. The root of the difficulty, Susan saw, was that few women had money to call their own. A radical remedy was needed: a campaign to force the New York State legislature to alter the status of women. Susan threatened to bring the matter up again year after year after year until the laws were changed. It took ten years, ten years wearing the same old clothes, slogging away at tedious details, traveling about in all weathers under adverse conditions, in all kinds of conveyances, carrying arguments into other states where word about her had spread. In 1860, the first great change was accomplished. By New York State law, a married woman thenceforward could control her own property, her own earnings, would have joint guardianship over her children, and be granted many of the economic demands raised by Susan and her co-workers. Several other states were forced by strong women's rights groups to take similar action.

In between the victories were many defeats and bitter, merciless opposition. The onslaughts were vicious; a typical volume, written by a noted minister, was entitled *Woman Suffrage: the Reform Against Nature*. Many of the attacks were spiteful and personally wounding. The *New York World* reported gleefully that "Susan is lean, cadaverous, and intellectual, with the proportions of a file, and the voice of a hurdy-gurdy."

Meanwhile, the Civil War was embroiling the nation. Immediately upon Lincoln's election the extreme Abolitionists, with whom Susan had always identified herself, had campaigned—at first against Lincoln who was trying to prevent the war—for immediate emancipation. During the war the women's rights fight was suspended. The New York State legislature took advantage of the situation by repealing that part of the law they had passed two years earlier covering women's rights over children. Susan was immobilized on her father's farm. In her journal she noted: "Tried to interest myself in a sewing society; but little intelligence among them." Besides the farm work, she passed the time reading Elizabeth Barrett Browning and George Eliot, storing up energy towards the next battle. The call for it sounded in the clanging notes of the Emancipation Proclamation. Free the women as well as the slaves, Susan demanded. Let this be a government of the people, by the people, including women, she insisted—assuming that women are people.

Arguing that women's rights could be tied in with Negro rights, Elizabeth Stanton and Susan organized large numbers of women to campaign for a constitutional amendment abolishing slavery; the signatures they succeeded in getting to a petition helped effect the passage of the Thirteenth Amendment. It was with dismay, then, that they read the proposed Fourteenth Amendment and learned that civil rights were reserved for previously disenfranchised *male* citizens only. If they could have that one word struck out of the amendment, then all women, white as well as Negro, would win the vote at one stroke. The amendment, however, was passed as written.

Susan retired to home ground, concentrating on the votes-for-women issue in Albany. It was at this time that the famous exchange of discourtesies took place between her and Horace Greeley.

"Miss Anthony," said Greeley with deadly suavity, "you are aware that the ballot and the bullet go together. If you vote, are you also prepared to fight?"

"Certainly, Mr. Greeley," Susan retorted. "Just as you fought in the last war—at the point of a goose-quill."

Greeley and other opponents blocked the drive for votes for women in the New York State legislature. Discouraging years followed. Susan briefly edited a newspaper, called *Revolution.* Its motto was: "Men, their rights, and nothing more; Women, their rights, and nothing less." The paper was finally forced to suspend, and although it took years for her to do it, Susan personally paid off the newspaper's debt of ten thousand dollars. During all this time, she lived on a bit of money left her by her father and on lecture earnings. She often spent her last cent to enable women with no money at all to attend conventions and participate in the work. She was a party to a suit in 1872 to test the Fourteenth and Fifteenth Amendments. She cast a vote in the Presidential election of that year, was tried for violating the constitution, was fined $100 and costs. She refused to pay. On and off she worked on the monumental *History of Woman Suffrage,* the first three volumes with the collaboration of Mrs. Stanton and Matilda Joslyn Gage, the last two with Ida Husted Harper.

By now, the organization which she headed was called the National American Woman Suffrage Association. As Mrs. Rheta Childe Dorr explained in *Susan B. Anthony: The Woman Who Changed the Mind of a Nation,* "To her the whole object of the woman suf frage movement was sex equality, the wiping out of every arbitrary distinction in law and custom, that women, as she phrased it, might own and possess their own souls." In 1883, she took the first vacation she ever had, went to Europe, and found herself famous, particularly in England, where the feminist movement was just gaining momentum.

When she was seventy, her sister Mary, retiring as a school-teacher, urged her to make a home with her in Rochester. Neither had enough money to furnish the house they had inherited there. As a tribute to her, the Political Equality League of Rochester furnished the house. But Susan was too busy to stay in it. Not before she was eighty did she retire as president of the Woman Suffrage Association. Completing the *History of Woman Suffrage,* she emphasized her final demand that American women must get the vote through an amendment to the federal constitution, not through state laws.

In 1904, when the International Woman Suffrage Alliance was formed, she was automatically acknowledged by the women of the world as their undisputed leader. Early in 1906, she attended what she suspected would be her last convention and told the delegates: "The fight must not stop. You must see it does not stop!" On her eighty-sixth birthday, she insisted on going to Washington to attend a dinner in her honor and ended her remarks by insisting, "Failure is impossible."

It was success, however, that seemed impossible. When, as the result of a cold caught on the trip to Washington, she died on March 13, 1906, though the country flew its flags at half-mast in grief at her passing, she was eulogized as "The Champion of a Lost Cause."

Thirteen years later, on May 21, 1919, the lost cause was won; an amendment giving women the full rights of citizenship was added to the United States Constitution. It was called the Susan B. Anthony Amendment.

Charles Baudelaire

[1 8 2 1 - 1 8 6 7]

*"Dante merely visited Hell; Baudelaire
came from there."*

SURFEITED WITH THE SWEETS of romanticism, suffering from a prolonged attack of *mal du siècle,* many nineteenth-century French writers lashed themselves and their readers. They turned their irritations and depressions into private sensationalism and public exhibitionism. Barbey d'Aurevilly led a lobster down the Bois de Boulogne because "it knew the secrets of the sea and its soul was pure"; Baudelaire appeared on the street wearing a red feather boa and dyed green hair; Rimbaud scrawled his blasphemy on a park bench: "Merde à Dieu." Baudelaire suffered most. More than any writer of his generation he was tortured equally by a cultivated diabolism and an anxiety goaded by a sense of guilt. It was not without a long contemplation of evil that he called his great book *Fleurs du Mal,* and it was not without justice that d'Aurevilly said, "Dante merely visited Hell; Baudelaire came from there."

He was born April 9, 1821, in Paris, and was christened Charles Pierre Baudelaire. His father was sixty-two; his mother twenty-six. The boy, the only child of the marriage, had a great love for his father who, a wealthy art lover, stirred the fascinated child with stories he told on their rounds of the museums. He was not quite seven when the adored parent died and his mother married a young soldier, Commandant Aupick, whom the boy hated as much as Hamlet hated the man whom his "seeming-virtuous" mother had married in such unseemly haste. His love for his mother was embittered by the feeling that she had betrayed him. He was too young, of course, to recognize the sensual nature of his affection, but more than thirty years later, he wrote, in an otherwise factual letter to his publisher, this strange revelation: "What is it that the child loves so passionately in his mother? Is it merely the being who feeds, combs, bathes, and rocks him? It is also the caresses and the sensuous voluptuousness that he loves. He loves his mother for the enticing tickling of silk and fur, for the perfume of her breast and hair, for the clicking of her jewels." Baudelaire's obsession with the smell of woman's hair, the seduction of his mistress' breast, and his insistence on the erotic excitement of jewels and perfumes were obviously acquired in his mother's arms.

Charles was a satisfactory but not an outstanding pupil; he showed little interest in any subject except literature. He won a prize for some Latin verses, was expelled for insubordination, was reinstated, passed his "baccalauréat," and began writing or, as Commandant Aupick felt, wasting his time. In the summer of 1841, to save him from drifting into bad company, his stepfather sent him on a long sea voyage to Calcutta. But although the youth was complimented for his bravery when the ship was disabled during a terrific storm, he refused to continue the journey. The vessel had to put in for repairs at Mauritius, and Charles remained for a while, in love with the tropical scenery and the exotic women who stimulated many of the later languorous and musky poems. He was twenty-one when he returned to Paris and, having come into his inheritance, began to live like the other young bloods who constituted themselves a bohemian aristocracy. Baudelaire became a dandy, joined Barbey d'Aurevilly and other eccentrics, and indulged in one extravagance after another. He saw a young mulatto girl who, when she was not being a prostitute, played small parts in the theater, and made her his mistress. He wrote poetry more sensual, more satanic, and more shocking than the fashionable immoralities of the moment. Although he indited occasional verses to various women, most of the poems were inspired by Jeanne Duval, his "dark Venus," the "brown-skinned enchantress" with "ebony thighs." An ignorant octoroon, with whom Baudelaire continually quarreled, whom he loved and hated and was often on the point of leaving, she was his *femme,* the consuming passion of his life. Sometimes it was Jeanne who determined to leave Baudelaire. "My liaison, my affair of fourteen years with Jeanne, is broken," he wrote his mother in 1856. "I did all that was humanly possible to prevent the rupture. This tearing apart, this prolonged struggle, has lasted more than two weeks. Jeanne replies imperturbably that nothing can be done with my character, and that, anyhow, I shall thank her some day for her resolution. There you have the gross wisdom of women. I only know that whatever good things happen to me—money, joy, vanity—I shall always regret this woman." The break did not occur. For twenty years Jeanne remained his "dancing serpent," his "pitiless demon," his "bizarre deity," his inexorable and insatiable Beauty. He could never decide whether Beauty came from heaven or the deepest pit of hell—*Viens-tu du ciel profond ou sors-tu de* *l'abîme*—and, unable to reconcile the endless conflict of concupis-cence and revulsion, he wrote poetry which burned with love and loathing, with feverish brilliance and brooding darkness.

Living too lavishly, careless of expenditures, Baudelaire ran through half his inherited fortune. His family, hoping to save the rest of the capital, obtained a decree to entrust it to the notary M. Ancelle, who became the poet's financial guardian. Suddenly life was changed for Baudelaire. He had to plead and haggle for anything more than the barest expenses; he borrowed and was al-ways in debt; he became the prey of moneylenders. His whole appearance altered. His round mobile face hardened; the laughing mouth tightened; lines deepened between his nostrils and cheeks; the bland brow grew more and more furrowed. He discarded his flashy clothes for dark ones; he wore nothing but black broadcloth. Abandoning bohemianism, he turned farther away from the bour-geoisie. In the June Revolution of 1848 he threw in his lot with the revolutionaries and actually helped man the barricades. It is said that he waved a banner stating "We must shoot General Aupick!" But the object of Baudelaire's hatred—the soldier who had risen to the rank of general and was to become an ambassador as well as a senator—had been identified in Baudelaire's mind with much more than his personal life. He personified, wrote Joseph M. Bernstein, "all the bourgeois attributes he detested: careerism, opportunism, smugness, vulgar materialism, and toadying to the great. Moreover, throughout his writings, particularly in his vividly realistic descrip-tions of Paris and his insight into the life of a big city, Baudelaire never failed to manifest a profound sympathy for the poor and lowly." He became one of a group which started a revolutionary journal, *Salut Public,* associated with Gustave Courbet, the un-compromisingly realistic painter, with Honoré Daumier, the savage critic of society, whose victims were not merely drawn in savage blacks and whites, but drawn and quartered. Disheartened when the revolution failed and was succeeded by the dictatorship of the Second Empire, Baudelaire turned his back on politics, distrusted the easily cajoled mob, and sank into a state of apathy.

He was twenty-seven when he was roused from his depression by the pull of another distressed spirit, Edgar Allan Poe, whom he had discovered two years before. Baudelaire determined to put into French the work of the American poet-storyteller, who was, he felt, his spiritual kin. "Do you know why I so patiently translated Poe?

Because he resembled me! The first time I opened one of his books, I saw, with awe and ecstasy, not only subjects dreamed by me, but whole sentences thought by me and written by him!" As a Catholic, Baudelaire believed in original sin; moreover, like Poe, he felt that evil was implicit in the nature of man. He worked intermittently for sixteen years, almost half of his creative life, on five volumes of translations of Poe's tales. Strangely enough, Baudelaire never translated any of Poe's poetry—the only American poem he presented in French was part of Longfellow's "Hiawatha"! However, after immersing himself in Poe, Baudelaire widened the gamut of his own subject matter. His style varied; the tone grew less salacious and more melancholy. For example, the title of "Un Voyage à Cythère" promises a romantic and possibly lascivious episode. The poem, however, is one of the most morbid expostulations ever written by a writer of love lyrics; it proceeds from a picture of "demented infatuation" through the ruin of a rock-strewn desert to infamous desecration and final horror. This is the concluding quatrain, as translated by Arthur Symons:

> In thine isle, O Venus, I found only upthrust
> A Calvary symbol whereon my image hung . . .
> Give me, Lord God, to look upon that dung,
> My body and my heart, without disgust!

"There is his perversity," wrote P. Mansell Jones in his study of the poet, "and he knows it not as a literary affectation, but as *sin*, an attitude of the soul. His plight is abject and not without complicity, but there is no shade of falsehood in his clairvoyance." In his early thirties Baudelaire balanced the expression of reckless sensuality with increasingly somber and self-critical meditations. In 1857, when he was thirty-six, he published *Les Fleurs du Mal*.

As soon as *Les Fleurs du Mal* was offered for sale it was condemned by the public prosecutor and copies were seized by the police. Baudelaire and his publisher were charged with blasphemy as well as indecency. Both men resented the insinuations and determined to fight the case. "The book," Baudelaire wrote to his mother, "is clothed in cold and sinister beauty, and it was created with rage and patience." "I have put all my tenderness, my hate, and my religion into the book," he informed his financial guardian. "I cannot feel guilty in any sense," he wrote to the Secretary of State. "On the contrary, I am proud of having written a book that inspired nothing but fear and horror of evil." He guided the defense. "The book must be judged as a whole," he insisted in a statement he prepared for his attorney. "If it is so judged, its essential and terrifying morality will be apparent." The trial judge dismissed the charge of blasphemy, but declared the work obscene and refused to permit it to be circulated unless six of the poems (two of them dealing with Lesbianism) were deleted. Baudelaire consented, and the second edition, published in 1861, appeared without them. To compensate for the omission Baudelaire added thirty-five new poems, but the "architecture" which he claimed for the book had been damaged. Baudelaire maintained that the work "grew" from desire to disillusion, from considerations of the poet's joys and miseries to the sinner's anguish. As for the poet's function, Baudelaire believed that the very "goal" of poetry was twofold: "the distinction between the Good and the Beautiful; the discerning of Beauty in Evil." True to his program, he coaxed a resisting beauty not only out of ugliness but out of sensual decay, the degradation of the body, even out of the blossoming putrescence of a rotting carcass. Nowhere in literature has there been found a more astonishing mixture of radiance and what Baudelaire called "spleen," of the macabre and the magnificent.

Differing from most poets, Baudelaire denied that poetry and criticism were antithetical. Holding quite the opposite view, he contended that the poet was the best of critics and that, moreover, unless he were a critic he would be only half a poet. The poet, said Baudelaire, is not only a translator of ideas and experiences into words and images, he is also a transformer who fuses all the arts into a set of immortal sounds. Baudelaire's critical articles on literature, art, music, and esthetics were important creations as well as discoveries (he was one of Wagner's earliest champions); they transformed "delight into knowledge." "He believed," wrote Enid Starkie, "that material objects exist in this world only because they have their origin in the world of the spirit . . . Everything in this world is merely the symbol of a hieroglyphic language, and he claimed that it was the function of the artist to decipher the hidden writings of nature and to interpret the mysteries of the universe . . . Beauty was essentially a spiritual reality, and he was convinced that art was the greatest and perhaps the only means of effecting beauty in this world . . . Beauty for him did not lie in the subject itself, but in what the artist brought to it . . . In his poetry he endeavored to use the idiom of all the arts, to render what his eye saw not merely in line and color, not what his ear perceived only in harmony, but to glide imperceptibly from one mode of expression to another."

The suppression and failure of *Les Fleurs du Mal* caused, or came at the same time as, a breakdown in Baudelaire's health. The second edition, amplified with some of his best but most despairing poems, was no more successful than the first. Baudelaire had barely adjusted himself to the poor reception when he received another blow: his publisher went bankrupt and slipped into Belgium to evade his creditors. Hoping to retrieve some of the loss, Baudelaire set out on a lecture tour, but the results were unfortunate. His audiences were small, unappreciative, even hostile; travel conditions were poor; the entire trip was disastrous. He was ill—sicker than he knew. In Namur, Belgium, he suffered his first attack of paralysis.

Baudelaire had been fighting a venereal disease for some years. He had taken drugs to dull the physical pain and lift himself from the depths of acute depressions. He had toyed with suicide; he often thought himself on the edge of insanity and felt "the wind of the wings of madness." He was only forty-three when, in 1864, he collapsed; he remained in Belgium in a pitiable state for two years. In 1866 he was able to be moved to Paris, where, in the final stages of paresis, aphasia set in. He could not talk; he lost all bodily controls. If his mind was still alive, it must have been grateful when death relieved the helpless paralytic on August 31, 1867.

His funeral was a shabby affair. There were only a few mourners; no society of arts and letters sent any of its representatives; even such friends as the critics Sainte-Beuve and the poet-novelist, Théophile Gautier, to whom Baudelaire had dedicated *Fleurs du Mal,* failed to attend. His passing was scarcely noticed by the literary journals. During his lifetime the only comprehensive review of his work was a laudatory article which appeared in three numbers of an inconspicuous magazine, *L'Art;* it was written by a twenty-one-year-old poet, Paul Verlaine.

Ignored while he was alive, after his death Baudelaire became all things to all readers. Swinburne saw him as a fire-scarred spirit "who feeds our hearts with flame." In the elegiac eulogy, "Ave Atque Vale," Baudelaire was hailed in a prolonged burst of pure Swinburnese:

> Thou sawest, in thine old singing season, brother,
>   Secrets and sorrows unbeheld of us:
>   Fierce loves, and lovely leaf-buds poisonous,
> Bare to thy subtler eye, but for none other

Blowing by night in some unbreathed-in clime;
The hidden harvest of luxurious time,
Sin without shape, and pleasure without speech;
And where strange dreams in a tumultuous sleep
Make the shut eyes of stricken spirits weep;
And with each face thou sawest the shadow on each,
Seeing as men sow men reap.

The symbolists regarded Baudelaire as their prime progenitor. They paid tribute to him as the pioneer who enriched poetry with the techniques of music, and who used clustered images, agglomerating metaphors, and curiously commonplace objects as symbols to communicate complicated states of emotion. The revolutionists, forgetting his revulsions and disillusions, remembered his scorn of middle class morality. The analytical modernists acclaimed him as one of the first men of the nineteenth century to make a double art of creation and dissection. The religionists lauded him as one who transformed a seemingly insatiable appetite for sin into a hunger for spiritual sustenance.

Today Baudelaire is no longer looked upon as an instigator or even a member of any one school. His influence, widespread and devious, has penetrated modern literature; his modern spirit is apparent in its freedom from restraints, its mixture of sexuality and cynicism, and its refusal to find any subject matter too sordid or too sacrosanct. "Heaven or Hell, what does it matter," cried Baudelaire in the last lines of "Le Voyage." "Let us plunge into the depths. In the very pit of the Unknown we will find the New."

Mary Baker Eddy

[1821-1910]

". . . the error of giving intelligence to
matter . . ."

ALTHOUGH MARY BAKER EDDY, the only woman ever to found a religion, lived in the twentieth century, it is almost impossible to find any account of her life which is unassailable. The facts have been variously interpreted, denied, or entirely omitted; instead of honest differences of opinion the accounts are rife with charges of prejudice, fanaticism, and fraud. The writings by her followers are surrounded by an aura of devotion and an absence of documentation. So effectively have the true believers been able to control anything written about her that the articles on Christian Science and its founder in both the *Encyclopaedia Britannica* and the *Encyclopedia Americana* were written by Clifford P. Smith, formerly Reader of the First Church, its president, and the editor of its periodicals. In *Mary Baker Eddy In a New Light* Fernand E. d'Humy ends his estimate with: "As we look over history we can note many parallels between the life of Jesus and that of Mary Baker Eddy"—a statement typical of those who have treated her either as a divinity or as one who will, in time, become one. Any work which depicts her as anything less than a sanctified spirit is attacked as dishonest and vicious; whatever facts have been brought forward that might reflect against her, or even "humanize" her, are virtuously ignored.

On the other hand, the few authors who have gone to original sources, in order to get at the truth, have failed to attain objectivity. The contrast between their subject's all-too-human existence and her deification have roused them to a sarcasm which, in its very exasperation, distorts the picture. Mark Twain devoted an entire book to an unusually savage exposure, part ridicule and part rage. Edwin Franden Dakin's biography grants Mrs. Eddy a certain grandeur, and concedes her extraordinary accomplishments, but Dakin writes with such disparaging irony that his portrait is blurred. There is a small library of anti-Christian Science, including such titles as *Is Christian Science a Humbug? The Church of St.*

Bunco, Mental Assassination or Christian Science: A Physical, In-
tellectual, Moral and Spiritual Peril.

The ascertainable and published facts are these: Mary Ann
Morse Baker, was born July 16, 1821, in the little town of Bow,
New Hampshire. The Baker family, originally from Scotland and
England, were pioneers who had been in New England for six
generations. Mary's mother, Abigail, was a woman of upright and
enduring spirit, hardworking as any man. Her father Mark was
harshly pious, a Congregationalist, who imposed his rigorous standards of religion on his family of three boys and three girls, of whom
Mary was the youngest.

Mary was an indisputably ailing child. Her followers speak of her
as "delicate" and refer to her illnesses as the result of a highstrung
nature. Less devout research mentions "fits"; her family doctor
stated that she manifested hysteria mingled with bad temper. Because of these attacks, her attendance at school was irregular and
most of her education consisted of what she absorbed from books at
home. She was a pretty girl, dainty and intensely feminine, but she
was preoccupied with religion at an unusually early age. "When I
was about eight years old," she recorded in *Retrospection and In-*
trospection, "I repeatedly heard a voice, calling me by name, three
times, in an ascending scale." It has been suggested that this was a
later fantasy, something which she imagined which gave her a
kinship with Joan of Arc, or a memory that grew out of her love for
self-dramatization and the Bible story of Samuel. She also claimed
that at twelve, like the child Jesus, she argued effectively with the
church elders, but her refusal to accept the doctrine of predestina-
tion apparently occurred at a later date.

When she was fifteen the Bakers moved to Tilton, later called
Sanbornton Bridge, where Mary's health seemed to improve. Some
of her schoolmates remember her as somewhat supercilious and disdainful of her companions. She fancied herself a poet and began
to write verse in the stilted tone and hymn-tune rhythms of the
period. In her nineteenth year she suffered a severe depression
when her brother Albert died. He had been a lawyer and state
legislator, sensitive and sickly like his sister, and his death deprived
her of her closest and most enriching relationship. Two years later
her emotional needs found an outlet in a neighbor who was a friend
of her brother Samuel, and in 1843 she married George Washington Glover.

Glover was a stone mason. He had established a small contracting business in Charleston, South Carolina, and took his bride with him. She accompanied him on several of his business trips, on one of which he contracted yellow fever and died after nine wretched days. The young widow, penniless, went back to her parents' home a few months after her marriage. In September, 1844, she bore a son who was named after his father.

The strain of childbirth following the shock of her loss caused a severe setback. Even before the baby's birth, she was in such a state that her survival was doubtful. The attacks continued with such force that she was unable to nurse her son, who was wetnursed by a neighbor's wife. The members of her family devoted much of their time to the alleviation of her distress. Between periods of crippling nervousness, she continued to write poetry, and at two separate intervals tried to support herself by teaching school. At no time, however, was she strong enough to cope with raising her son, and the boy was taken care of by a Mrs. Sanborn, wife of the village blacksmith.

When Mary was in her late twenties her mother died, her father remarried, and she continued to live with him. Semi-invalided in her father's house she led a lonely life, and when she was squired by John Bartlett she responded to the courtship. She was, however, unlucky in her relations with men. Bartlett migrated to California and when, after three years, word of his death was received in New Hampshire, Mary Glover went into mourning as his fiancée.

Her son's foster-mother moved to the Far West, and young George Glover was taken along. Mary did nothing to reclaim him. In later years she said that she had no control over the situation because she was not self-supporting. She also related that she did not know the boy's whereabouts, nor was she in contact with him until he was a man of thirty-four with a wife and two children. As a proof of her emotion when he was permanently removed from her, she wrote a poem entitled "Mother's Darling," which wallowed in such stereotyped bathos as:

> Thy smile through tears, as sunshine o'er the sea,
> Awoke new beauty in the surge's roll.
> Oh, life is dead, bereft of all, with thee—
> Star of my earthly hope, babe of my soul.

At thirty-two Mary tried matrimony again and married Daniel Patterson, a dentist. He knew of her precarious health but he was a hearty man, full of bouncing energy, and hoped to infect her with his own vigor. He was disappointed by her failure to enjoy his vitality; she, repelled by his animal spirits, felt defeated. They moved to North Groton in the White Mountains where she became isolated. There was no companionship with her husband when he was home, and when, as a traveling practitioner he left her, she was bored. She made no effort to form friendships. A North Groton resident wrote that the townspeople recalled her "as one who carried herself above her fellows. With no stretch of imagination they remember her ungovernable temper and hysterical ways." Dr. Patterson eventually proved unfaithful to her; his finances worsened; one of Mary's married sisters came and took her to her own home.

She was forty when she heard of Phineas P. Quimby, of Portland, Maine, a man who was reputed to effect marvelous healings through the use of mesmerism. She was suddenly convinced that Quimby would be her salvation and determined to get him to help her. Secretly and alone she set off for Maine. Her very first session with Quimby changed not only her physical life but her spiritual direction. She had found something in which she could believe. Impressed with her zeal, Quimby gave her his time and, in countless talks, imparted everything he knew. On her part Mary Baker became his champion. She read all his writings and wrote letters to the newspapers extolling his work. She denied that he accomplished his results by hypnotism or "animal magnetism," but that he was able to cure by a "science not understood." "I can see dimly the great principle which underlies Dr. Quimby's faith and works . . . the truth which he opposed to the error of giving intelligence to matter."

Quimby's favorite patient subscribed to his kind of thinking so passionately that she devoted her whole life to it. The first written version of her beliefs, entitled *Science and Health,* embodies much of Quimby, almost verbatim. Controversy was to rage violently concerning her debt to her teacher. It is possible that she convinced herself later that her "science" was her own and that what was similar in Quimby's writings and hers was material she had given him when he was "only a mesmerist."

After her healing by Quimby, Mary's way of life was suddenly and completely transformed. No longer a sheltered and ailing creature, she now was daunted by nothing. She pursued her "call," upheld by convictions that were unarguable and a self-assurance that was unassailable. She began to proselytize, then to lecture, then to attempt mental healing. In January, 1866, Quimby died and Mary

Baker wrote a commemorative poem, "Lines on the Death of Dr. P. P. Quimby, Who Healed with the Truth that Christ Taught in Contradistinction to All Isms." A few weeks later she fell on the sidewalk, injured herself severely, and was told (so she wrote to another Quimby patient) that she had taken her last step. However, remembering the adage, "Physician, heal thyself," she repudiated the doctors and "in two days I got out of bed alone and walked."

Afterwards Mary Baker traced the beginning of Christian Science to this near-miracle. Although her later narration of the event does not altogether jibe with factual data she wrote: "It was in Massachusetts, in February, 1866 . . . that I discovered the science of divine metaphysical healing, which I named Christian Science . . . During twenty years prior to my discovery, I had been trying to trace all physical effects to a mental cause; and in the latter part of 1866 I gained the scientific certainty that all causation was Mind, and every effect a mental phenomenon. My immediate recovery from the effects of an injury caused by an accident . . . an injury that neither medicine nor surgery could reach . . . was the falling apple that led me to the discovery how to be well myself, and how to make others so."

There were many hard years before Mary was to establish her religion. She had no income except a short-lived allowance of two hundred dollars a year from Dr. Patterson; she had no place of her own. She began a series of pride-trying visits from the home of one more or less tolerant housewife to another, offering instruction and mental healing in return for room and board. Her nervous tensions frequently created antagonisms, and she was asked to move on. Her "text" during these years was a manuscript labeled "Extracts from Doctor P. P. Quimby's Writings." Shortly afterward, Mary denied using anything of Quimby's. The disavowal was natural enough, for she was writing her own book. She was in her fiftieth year, when after four years of pain, poverty, and lonely struggle, she finished the first draft of the volume which gave her life its eminence. The book was not only a document of deliverance from pain, but an escape from the self which found reality too distressing to bear. During the next decade the outlines of the practice of Christian Science began to emerge, literally through trial and error.

The documentary material on her life from contemporaries other than disciples yields little evidence of saintliness or even unselfishness. She was, someone observed, a spiritual person with a sharp

sense of bookkeeping. She had the gift of experiencing and imparting exaltation, but she herself was preoccupied with petty concerns. She preached a philosophy of love, but she distrusted and
actually feared people so much that she was incapable of sustained
affection.

Her first triumphs were with pupils who became successful
healers, efficient in helping their patients and earning a livelihood.
Mary Baker charged for the lessons she gave; in the case of the
more promising she entered into a sort of partnership. Several associations ended unpleasantly. There were inevitable rivalries, differences of method, questions of autonomy. Some of the backsliders
complained that the founder of the faith was growing arbitrary
and demanded unquestioning agreement along with unswerving
obedience. Despite occasional ruptures and defections, the momentum of her work carried her along and, for the first time in her life,
she was affluent, independent, and secure.

She divorced Dr. Patterson and, at fifty-seven, married Gilbert
Eddy, a gentle bachelor who was one of her pupils. It was her third
marriage and it was no more fortunate than the others. Eddy died
five years later.

Two years before her last marriage, Mary Baker Eddy completed
the book on which she had worked during the five long migratory
years and had taken three more years to revise. The manuscript
ran to 456 pages and it was published in 1875. Quimby had called
his method "The Science of Health"; she called her book *Science
and Health,* adding a later subtitle, "With Key to the Scriptures."
Fifteen years after its publication the various editions had sold
more than 150,000 copies—every member of her church had to buy
a copy of each new revision—and the author received a royalty of
one dollar on every copy.

Science and Health is based on Quimby's axiomatic assumption
of "mind over matter," but it also contains utterances, aphorisms,
and ideas gathered from widely divergent sources. These were
filtered through Mrs. Eddy's mind and fused in her philosophy.
Like Quimby, she denied the existence of evil—evil was a thing
thought to exist only because fear-conscious man gave it credence.
All is Mind. Matter, however, is not Mind, but its opposite—an
error, an unreality, a misapprehension of *mortal* mind. The one
reality is God, or Good, pure spirit, the Mind which is divine and
flawless. Since man is God's child he, too, can be flawless, free of
sin and sickness, perfect as his Father in Heaven is perfect . . . It

was a theology built on symbols and syllogisms—and the universal wish to be rid of pain with a minimum of effort. The founder of Christian Science buttressed her own particular Gospel with fragments from the Scriptures. She made theology act as a therapy, substituting the application of thoughts for the laying on of hands. She believed that she had unearthed or, better still, invented a hitherto unknown means of Divine Healing. "People had healed the sick with mesmerism long before," summarized Edwin Franden Dakin in *Mrs. Eddy,* "but no one had ever healed them with Mrs. Eddy's theories of theology. Ergo, she had discovered a new principle . . . how to use God. Viewed in this light, much of Eddyism now looms up not as consummate humbuggery, but as sincere belief that she had really harnessed a previously unknown Principle to serve man's needs. And to the extent that she realized the importance of religious emotionalism as an aid to applied psychology, she should have recognition for this contribution to modern thought. . . . The main thesis of *Science and Health,* stripped of its contradictions, develops the conviction that Christ came to redeem men not merely from sin but also from sickness and death; that his methods are applicable to a modern age; that all men can heal both themselves and others if they develop the correct Christ consciousness, and this long lost Christ-art was again revealed to mankind in the instructions from Mary Baker Eddy."

Mrs. Eddy's perfectibility was revealed only to those elect. The unenlightened found her not only arrogant but unscrupulous. There were many distasteful episodes, some of which ended in the law courts. Actions were brought against her for payment of unappreciated services and by her for unpaid tuition. She was party to a suit against a one-time pupil and former favorite, Daniel H. Spofford, for—incredible though it seems—witchcraft. She firmly believed in the power of suggestion and insisted that evil thoughts, even when propelled from great distances, could harm people. She called such power M. A. M., "malicious animal magnetism," and, when she felt it directed against her, would combat it by having her adherents maintain a round-the-clock watch, a cordon of mental strength, as a protective barrier.

At fifty-five she tentatively organized her students into a "Christian Science Association"; three years later a charter was issued for the establishment of "The Church of Christ, Scientist." Within two more years, eight of the charter members resigned, stating that they perceived "with sorrow a departure from the straight and narrow road (which alone leads to growth of Christ-like virtue) made manifest by frequent ebullitions of temper, love of money, and the appearance of hypocrisy," and that, therefore, they could "no longer submit to such leadership."

At sixty-one Mary Baker Eddy moved her church to Boston. It was a shrewd maneuver. In a huge city her personal idiosyncracies were less a matter of concern than her public personality. She was "news"; she learned to capitalize on the uses of adversity by the use of publicity. She started various church publications, culminating in the influential newspaper, the *Christian Science Monitor*. She guided the institution she had created with such foresight that it was reported her real genius was not for illumination but administration. Mrs. Eddy had no such conception of herself. Her sense of being "chosen" was unfaltering; she even let a much-quoted passage from the Apocalypse be considered a prescient reference to her: "And there appeared a great wonder in heaven; a woman clothed with the sun, and the moon under her feet, and upon her head a crown of twelve stars." The fact that their leader's name was Mary was too tempting for her devotees to resist; although she disapproved the appellation, they began to call her Mother.

The growth of Christian Science was so rapid that Mark Twain wrote, in all seriousness, he feared that by 1920 there would be ten million Christian Scientists in America alone; that in 1930 they would be politically formidable; and that by 1940 they would be "the governing power in the Republic—to remain that, permanently." Twain's alarm was obviously exaggerated and unjustified. Nevertheless, although the church by-laws prohibit any estimate of number of members, there were in 1950, according to the *Encyclopaedia Britannica,* more than three thousand branches of the Mother Church, of which some twenty-two hundred were in the United States and Canada.

As she grew older, Mrs. Eddy's power grew greater. With the help of a retired Unitarian minister, she improved the clarity and polished the style of the book which was regarded by her followers as a necessary counterpart of the Bible. She lectured and made converts whenever she spoke. She was a wealthy woman in absolute control of an elaborate organization. But if she had security, she lacked serenity. Although her relations with men had been unhappy, she could not do without their company. Nearing seventy she legally adopted a forty-one-year-old doctor of homeopathy; at seventy-five she could not bear to have him around. The pattern repeated itself. She found other favorites and, after a short interval, dismissed them. Attempts were made to discredit her; deaths were attributed to her teachings; she was compelled to soften her dicta against consulting medical authorities and had to permit the help of doctors and surgeons in certain circumstances. In 1907 a suit was brought, to which her son had been persuaded to become a party. It was not only against her but against her immediate circle of advisers, and it petitioned the court that Mrs. Eddy was incompetent to handle her affairs and that she was being used by a designing clique. The action, played up throughout the nation by every newspaper as the test of her sanity, broke through the privacy with which she had been surrounded and almost succeeded in driving her mad. The suit was eventually withdrawn, but not before the eighty-six-year-old woman had proved to the Masters appointed to examine her that she was completely in charge of all her intricate affairs.

She was in her ninetieth year when she died of natural causes, on December 3, 1910. The daughter of an impoverished farmer had managed to accumulate an estate of three million dollars. Practically all of it was left to the church dedicated to expose the error of materialism and the nonexistence of matter.

Fyodor Dostoevsky

[1 8 2 1 - 1 8 8 1]

*"He put flesh upon abstractions and turned
ideas into greatly suffering men and
women."*

THE WORLD OF Fyodor Mikhailovich Dostoevsky was a battle-ground of violent events and internal torments, of prophetic visions and pathological nightmares, but it was primarily a world torn between intolerable suffering and desperate salvation. The suffering was burned into Dostoevsky at the very beginning. He was born October 30, 1821, one of seven children, in the dingy flat of a Moscow public hospital where his father was staff physician; poverty, sickness, and sudden death were the everyday topics of his boyhood. Conditions grew more sordid when his father, whose habit of drinking degenerated into alcoholism, was discharged and could barely support himself by private practice. A precocious reader, Fyodor found the Book of Job when he was eight years old; even at that age, he identified himself with the afflicted soul and plagued himself with the problem of undeserved misery. The problem, as well as the Biblical parable, remained with him the rest of his years. At fifty-four he wrote to his wife: "I am reading the Book of Job, and it has reawakened in me a dark and almost morbid ecstasy. I put the book aside and pace back and forth for hours on end, scarcely able to keep back my tears. This book was one of the first to take hold of me for life."

At sixteen Fyodor, with his elder brother Mikhail, was sent to the Military Engineers' School in St. Petersburg, where he remained four years. Engineering bored him and military drills sickened him; he devoted every available hour to reading. He was particularly enthusiastic about the poetry of Pushkin and the prose of Balzac, whose *Eugénie Grandet* he translated. At twenty he obtained a commission in the army, but he stayed at school for one more year. Compelled to serve two years as an army engineer, he returned to civilian life the moment he could leave the army. His father had been murdered, and Fyodor, with a talent for improvidence which increased with the years, soon squandered the small amount of money left to him. His reading of Balzac made him dream of writing a Russian Human Comedy, and he spent six months working on a novel which he called *Poor Folk*.

Dostoevsky was an inexperienced writer, only twenty-three years old, and since *Poor Folk* was his first book, it should have been a failure. It was, on the contrary, a popular success. The poet, Nekrasov compared the young author to the great Gogol, and Belinsky, the critical god of the intelligentsia, greeted Dostoevsky on publication day with an astonished "But can you understand what you have written?" (Thirty years later Dostoevsky declared that the happiness of that day surpassed anything in his life.) He had written *Poor Folk,* in which the characters reveal themselves through their letters, on a starvation diet—milk and bread were only occasional luxuries—but now he settled down to what was to be the pleasant and apparently profitable career of a favorite author. He wrote another book, *The Double,* a dozen short stories, and could consider himself a success. He had not yet produced anything of permanent importance, but there was already evident the strong feeling for the despised and the downtrodden, a feeling which was to become a passion in the later works.

Suddenly, at twenty-seven, while halfway through a new novel, he found himself a tragic character in an incredible melodrama. A few years before, he had joined a group of young radicals who read Fourier and discussed socialism. The Russian Revolution of 1848 made such discussions not merely dangerous but treasonable. Along with other suspects, Dostoevsky was taken to the Peter and Paul Fortress. For eight months he suffered and sickened while awaiting trial. In December, 1849, he learned that he had been condemned to death. He and other members of the group were marched to the place of execution, bound to the stake, and given the crucifix to kiss while the death sentence was read. Instead of ending in a shooting, the affair turned into a piece of theatrical sadism. The muskets were raised and Dostoevsky, sixth in line, closed his eyes. "I had no more than a minute to live," he wrote. "Then a white cloth was waved; the troops sounded retreat; and we were informed that His Majesty the Czar was graciously sparing our lives." The sentence of death was commuted to four years at hard labor in Siberia to be followed by six more years of Siberian penal servitude. Most of the prisoners collapsed; one of them went mad. Dostoevsky never forgot that moment; he carried mental scars until his death.

He was twenty-eight when he was sent to Siberia, thirty-eight when he returned to St. Petersburg; one-third of his creative life was spent in destructive exile. In the Katorga, the convict prison at Omsk, he was compelled to break rocks and carry stones, never permitted to write or to read any book except the Bible. For four seemingly interminable years he was "eternally in chains, eternally under guard, eternally behind bolts and bars—and never alone! Total suppression of the mind—that was life in the fortress." Ideas seethed within him, but ideas were forbidden; he pleaded to transcribe some of his thoughts, but paper was prohibited. His health broke down; there were attacks of epilepsy.

Transferred from prison, he was stationed in the garrison of the Siberian town of Semipalatinsk, and underwent a complete change. The four years of hard labor had thrown him into daily contact with pitiful but hopeful common people; the Bible had brought him close to God. He forswore his radical associations and repudiated all social organizations as futile efforts to transform the world —"no sort of scientific teaching," he had Father Zossima declare in *The Brothers Karamazov,* "no kind of common interest will ever teach man to share property and privilege with equal consideration for all." Rejecting the progressive principles of his youth, he accepted the New Testament doctrine of salvation by suffering without question. As D. S. Mirsky said in *A History of Russian Literature,* "he became converted to the religion of the Russian people in the sense that he began not only to believe in what the people believed, but to believe in it *because* the people believed."

It was during the latter part of his military drilling at Semipalatinsk that Dostoevsky began to write again, and it was there that he met and fell in love with Maria Dmitrievna Isayeva. She was the mother of a young boy, wife of an itinerant official with whom she was forced to go from town to town. In spite of the separation, Dostoevsky remained faithful, and when her husband died, he was chagrined to learn that Maria had formed an attachment with another. Nevertheless, Dostoevsky married her, and discovered that he not only had to support Maria and her child but also her lover. He was a burdened thirty-nine when he received an amnesty and was allowed to resume life in St. Petersburg.

A reform movement was affecting all Russia and, with the collaboration of his brother, Mikhail, Dostoevsky entered the journalistic field with a periodical, *Vremya (Time)*. In its pages appeared two of the most important books of his "middle period": *The Insulted and Injured* and *The House of the Dead,* a shattering transcript of his life in prison, which Tolstoy considered his greatest work. All was going well. Even his domestic difficulties did not depress him; he seemed to thrive on the struggle. In a release of energy pent up for ten years, he flung himself into a whirlpool of productivity; he traveled to Germany, France, and England; he attacked the West for its materialistic civilization and its impious society in *Winter Notes on Summer Impressions.* Just when his periodical seemed to have established itself, it was suppressed. An article on the Polish question had been not only misunderstood but actually misread by the censor, and although resumption of the publication was finally permitted, great damage had been done. It was many years before Dostoevsky recovered from the accumulation of debts caused by the suspension of the magazine.

He was forty-two when he became involved in fresh misfortunes. His epileptic attacks increased to such an extent that his memory became impaired; his situation was so desperate that his doctor recommended a trip abroad. Dostoevsky was glad to take the advice, chiefly as an excuse to exchange his marital troubles for a violent love affair with an emancipated and reckless twenty-one-year-old girl, Polina Suslova. He had met her in connection with work on his magazine; she was now in Paris, and he determined to join her there. He was practically penniless, but news of a wealthy rival goaded him into immediate departure. Realizing the bitter need of funds and lured by dreams of winning at roulette, he stopped off at Wiesbaden, a famous German gambling resort, and went straight to the roulette table. The rapid alternation of winning and losing excited him to such an extent that he thought of nothing else. As he plunged deeper and deeper into a mania for gambling, he forgot the very reason for his journey. He remembered it in time to find that he had barely enough money left for the trip to Paris. There he learned that Polina's lover had deserted her, that she was starving, and that he would have to take care of her. Frantically he returned to Wiesbaden, accompanied by Polina, and wasted himself on the turn of the wheel. A very few days after he had won enough to travel through Italy with his mistress—they got as far as Turin—news that his wife was desperately ill brought him back to Russia. At home, he watched Maria Dmitrievna grow worse, sink into madness, and die. A few months later the death of his beloved brother depressed him almost beyond endurance. Moreover, he had to assume the burden of Mikhail's overwhelming debts. He drove himself to exhaustion, writing furiously and gambling feverishly. When the proprietor of the inn where he was lodged refused to extend credit, he pawned his remaining possessions as well as Polina's trinkets. He could not read after dark because he could not afford candles. "I am living like a beggar," he wrote, "often forced to run around for three days in order to borrow a single ruble somewhere."

Relief came from a most unexpected source. He began to write *The Gambler* and *Crime and Punishment* almost simultaneously. Compelled to meet a publisher's deadline, he engaged a stenographer, Anna Grigorievna Snitkin, and what began as a purely business relationship developed into the solidest as well as the most romantic attachment in his life. Four months after engaging his secretary, he married her. He was forty-six years old.

His grim, semi-autobiographical *Notes from Underground* (also translated as *Letters from the Underworld*) prepared the way for his major novels, of which the first, *Crime and Punishment,* was both magnificently imaginative and commercially successful. The success, however, had an unfortunate and immediate result. Apprised of the sales, Dostoevsky's creditors dunned him so relentlessly that, soon after the wedding, he and his new wife had to leave Russia. This exile lasted four years, and though the time was spent in the most picturesque parts of Germany, Switzerland, and Italy, Dostoevsky was never happy, never able to feel at ease. "I need to be home in order to work again. I need the air of Russia; I feel that, uprooted from Russian soil, all my talent, as well as all my strength, is drying up." The lust for gambling and the epileptic fits grew alarmingly worse. Yet, though the epilepsy, Dostoevsky's "little death," prostrated him for days and would have undermined stronger constitutions, it seemed only to increase the artist's sensibilities. He capitalized on it by making such characters as Kirilov and Prince Myshkin describe the sensation before the attack—"the sensation of life, of being, multiplied tenfold at that moment: all passion, all doubt, all unrest resolved as in a higher peace." Dostoevsky actually glorified what he called his "holy disease." René Fueloep-Miller's scholarly study, *Fyodor Dostoevsky,* quotes him as saying: "What do I care whether it is normal or abnormal, if in retrospect and in a healthy state I still feel that moment as one of perfect harmony and beauty, and if it rouses in me hitherto unsuspected emotions, gives me feelings of magnificence, abundance, and eternity. It is like a glorious, heavenly merging with the highest synthesis of life. . . . I do not know whether the rapture lasts for hours or seconds. But, believe me, I would not exchange it for all the joys of life. I would be prepared to give my whole existence for it."

The gambling was worse. What began as a desperate desire for money developed into an obsession. The craving became so great a compulsion that, even while he was trying to work on *The Idiot* and *The Possessed,* two of his most complicated novels, he was deserting his desk for the gambling casino, pawning his clothes, begging his wife to spare a coin from the scant household money. In Geneva, when his wife was pregnant, there were exactly five francs left. Anna lost her first child; she bore her second in Dresden under the most depressing conditions. "If you only knew how things are with us," Dostoevsky wrote to a friend. "My wife is nursing a child, and I am destitute. How can I work when I am always hungry, and have been forced to pawn my trousers . . . The devil with me and my hunger! But my wife is different—she, who is now nursing the child, has had to go to the pawnshop and pawn her last warm coat . . . If you only knew what torments make it almost impossible for me to write!"

Nevertheless, he wrote. Struggling with an overwhelming sense of sin, he subjected himself to a succession of fierce dogmas and angry revolts; he was, by turns, orthodox and irresponsible. A Slavophile, he equated Christianity's compassionate humility with Russia's historic mission to unite humanity by freeing it from "the godless West." In this he was by no means a political radical. On the contrary, he was a reactionary who had learned disillusion in prison. In a chapter entitled "Dostoevsky's Prophecies" Fueloep-Miller shows how he rejected libertarian ideals and predicted that the socialist movement would lead to an intensification of the crisis of humanity and to a complete loss of freedom. "The time is approaching when the loftiest aims of humanity will be betrayed for temporal advantages, humane feeling and striving for truth and justice will be surrendered, and a savage avidity for personal enrichment will take hold of men." But Dostoevsky was not a pamphleteer. Instead of writing polemics, he put flesh upon abstractions and turned ideas into greatly suffering men and women.

In 1871, at the age of fifty, Dostoevsky forswore gambling, ended his European exile, and returned to Russia. He was producing his largest works, and a compromise with his creditors made it possible for him to complete such majestic books as *The Possessed, The Eternal Husband,* and *The Brothers Karamazov.* He was not only

working steadily, but overworking, atoning for the years of gambling, overcompensating and killing himself. His long face was
lined and sallow; the muscles of his cheek twitched ominously; the
straggling beard was that of an unkempt fanatic monk; his gray eyes
had the look of death. He was no longer sanguine about his epilepsy. "My work progresses too slowly. I fear that the falling sickness
has robbed me not only of my memory, but also of my imaginative
powers."

The end came three months after his sixtieth birthday. He had
suffered a lung hemorrhage, but he refused to stop work; he insisted
he needed ten more years to write the books he had in mind, including a sequel to *The Brothers Karamazov.* The pen fell from
his hand on January 28, 1881. His last piece of writing was an appeal for money.

A life as lurid and disorganized as Dostoevsky's was bound to be
reflected in writings that are tense and exacerbated, high-pitched to
the point of hysteria. In one of the early American reviews of *The
Brothers Karamazov, The New York Times* (June 30, 1912) suggested that many readers believe Russian novels to be "inhabited
chiefly by escaped lunatics and uncaught candidates for Bedlam
. . . And yet the reader will not be able to deny that everybody—
every man, woman, and child—introduced into these pages is convincingly, horribly human. They are insane merely because they
live each mood as if it were the whole of life . . . They pour out
the content of their souls in talk—talk to everybody . . . Each and
all insist on making a clean breast till you are fairly overwhelmed
with the indecency of so much truth-telling."

It is "the indecency of truth-telling" that the uncongenial, inconsistent, and intolerant Dostoevsky exhibits in all his tortured and
often formless works. The passion of unburdening talk, the need of
confession, results in some of the most agitating passages in all literature. "The novels of Dostoevsky," wrote Virginia Woolf, an English novelist deeply influenced by him, "are seething whirlpools,
gyrating sandstorms, waterspouts which hiss and boil and suck us in.
They are composed purely and wholly of the stuff of the soul . . .
The elements of the soul are seen not separately but streaked, involved, inextricably confused: a new panorama of the human mind
is revealed!"

Dostoevsky's conversion and his preoccupation with the soul led
him to plunge into humanity's underworld, a limbo as murky and
terrible as any conceived by Dante. It is obvious that Dostoevsky's

fixed concern with criminals, sinners, and renegades is an extension of his own sense of guilt. It has been suggested that, since Dostoevsky hated his father and subconsciously wished his death, he felt doubly guilty when his father was killed by his own serfs; Freud interprets Dostoevsky's epilepsy and his secret passion for gambling as revealing symptoms of a desperate desire to escape. Tracing the novelist's shifting moods of disorder, darkness, and exalted mysticism, his inability to decide between good and evil, William Phillips wrote in an introduction to *The Short Stories of Dostoevsky*, "Dostoevsky seems to have been engaged in a constant—and fruitless—search for authority; that is, for some representative of the father principle . . . Hence Dostoevsky, if he were to stay within the bounds of sanity, had to find a surrogate: first in the Czar, then in morality, finally in God." Yet a great problem remains, for the confusion of Dostoevsky's woefully divided personality, the split between the pathologically driven creature and the pure creator, has never been convincingly clarified. Even Freud had to beg the question when he composed his probing essay on the author's theme of parricide: "Dostoevsky's place is not far behind Shakespeare. *The Brothers Karamazov* is the most magnificent novel ever written . . . Unfortunately," Freud concluded lamely, "before the problem of the creative artist analysis must lay down its arms."

The comparison to Shakespeare may be farfetched, but it is not without point. Dostoevsky's characters, like Shakespeare's, are neither wholly reasonable nor "real." They are larger than life and, therefore, apart from it. It is their wild thoughts and wilder acts, their agonies of doubt and anxieties of belief, which are revealed, not the little touches of "realism" which give surface verisimilitude. They are passion personified, as unconventional and shocking and irrational as passion itself. "What most people call fantastic and eccentric is for me often the true essence of reality," said Dostoevsky. If Dostoevsky did nothing else, he pushed back the borders of realism and gave the writing of fiction a new amplitude. But he did more. He created another world, peopled with men who are strange and equivocal but as authentically alive as the passion-driven Othello and the idea-tortured Hamlet. He created the saintlike Alyosha ("perhaps," said Somerset Maugham, "the most charming, sweet, and gentle creature in all fiction"); the soulless and unscrupulous Stavrogin, a monster of disinterested evil, and his opposite, the fanatic atheist, Kirillov, who killed himself to escape from God; the amoral, power-hungry Raskolnikov; the cynical murderer,

Smerdyakov; the dialectical Grand Inquisitor; the drunken old Karamazov, a battered clown of a father, and his reckless, spendthrift son, Dmitri, who might well be Dostoevsky's own self-caricature. Dostoevsky's inner conflicts, his tortured seeking for God and his acceptance of universal guilt—"everyone shares the guilt of every crime, of everything that happens on earth"—his clashes of intellectual disbelief and frantic faith are the stuff on which his sagas are built. But it is the burning revelations of his pain-racked people that compel our response. It is their convulsive lives and their twisted characters, rather than their author's credo, which we remember and cannot possibly forget.

Gustave Flaubert

[1821-1880]

*"He created the modern realistic novel and,
directly or indirectly, influenced all writers
of fiction since his day."*

GUSTAVE FLAUBERT's legendary passion for the precise word has overshadowed what he accomplished with *le mot juste*. He insisted that subject matter did not count. There are, he said, "neither good nor bad subjects. One might almost say that there is no such thing as subject and that style is, in itself, an independent and absolute manner of seeing things." Nevertheless, it was the subject matter which made Flaubert famous or, as his opponents tried to make him appear, infamous.

He was born December 12, 1821 at Rouen, Normandy, in the wing of the municipal infirmary, at which his father was resident physician and chief surgeon. There were physicians also on his mother's side—his maternal grandfather had been a country doctor —and it is conjectured that he inherited an ability to diagnose and dissect his characters with almost clinical precision. There were three children: a brother, Achille, nine years older than Gustave, and a sister, Caroline, three years younger. Achille succeeded his father at the hospital, but, even as a child, Gustave was a writer. At the age of nine he sent a letter to another boy proposing collaboration. "If you wish us to join, I will write comedy, and you shall write your dreams and, as there is a lady who comes to our house, and who always talks silly things to us, I will write them." He made friends easily. His youth was bound up with three intimate associates: Alfred Le Poittevin, whose death at twenty-seven caused him unutterable grief; Louis Bouilhet, who was a poet; and Maxime Du Camp, who became a well-known editor and journalist. All three were, at various times, his valued literary counselors.

At nineteen he studied law in Paris and hated the textbooks; he thought the Code Civil was "raving nonsense." A young bon vivant, he set himself up as something of a gourmet, went regularly to the theater, spent his allowance freely, and enjoyed everything except women. Handsome and strong, Flaubert attracted girls of every sort, but he remained chaste. A not ordinarily susceptible woman remembered him looking "like a young Greek . . . tall and slender, graceful as an athlete, unconscious of the gifts which he possessed." Maxime Du Camp's first sight aroused an even more rhapsodic response. "He was of heroic beauty. With his white skin slightly flushed upon the cheeks, his long, fine, floating hair, his tall broad-shouldered figure, his enormous eyes—the color of the green of the sea—veiled under black eyelashes, with his voice as sonorous as the blast of a trumpet . . . he was like one of those young Gallic chiefs who fought against the Roman armies."

Flaubert had already experienced love, but it was an adolescent passion, idealized and unconsummated. When he was fifteen his family spent the summer at Trouville, and there the boy fell hopelessly in love with Elisa Schlesinger, who was twenty-six, married, and nursing a baby. She and her husband were fond of the boy, took him sailing, and made much of him. Gustave was so madly in love with his goddess of "the magnificent black hair that fell to her shoulders" that he could barely speak to her and, although her voice was beautifully modulated, he could not recall anything she said. Six years later, when he was studying in Paris, he called upon the Schlesingers and was invited to their Wednesday evenings. But he was shy as ever. Elisa was gracious, sympathetic, and even touched by his obvious devotion, but nothing happened. Desirable and unattainable, she remained the great love of his life. "I loved one woman from the time I was fifteen until I was twenty without ever touching her," he wrote later, "and for three years afterward I never gave sex a thought. At that time I believed it would be so till I died, and I thanked God for it." In spite of his physical appeal, Flaubert remained a virgin until he was almost twenty-three, at which time, according to one story, he was seduced by a servant, or, if a more romantic version is to be believed, he got into conversation with a young woman who, like himself, was stopping off at a hotel, and spent the night with her.

Meanwhile, he plowed reluctantly through his studies, bogged down in the midst of them, failed in his examinations, and was stricken with the first of his seizures. The attacks were peculiar. Although he could do nothing to prevent them, he could always tell when they were coming. Before he became unconscious, he would fall into a trance, hear roaring sounds, and see golden lights accompanied by bizarre images whirling about him. He recalled that the visions combined the fantasies of Edgar Allan Poe, Saint

Theresa, and E. T. A. Hoffmann, often called the Poe of Germany. The doctors, reluctant to consider the youth a victim of epilepsy, said that he had too much energy and diagnosed his condition as "a plethora of vitality," which manifested itself in "hysterico-epileptic" attacks. His father's treatments were drastic; Flaubert was bled, starved, given constant baths, and the seizures left him until near the end of his life. The threat of attack, however, was almost worse than the attack itself. His already devoted mother watched over him more anxiously than ever, and Flaubert became increasingly apprehensive, nervous, and depressed. The pessimism, which was a concomitant of an excess of romanticism, grew more pronounced; he was, he told George Sand many years later, afraid of life.

Flaubert's father, who had acquired a moderate fortune, bought a house in Croisset, and moved his family to the picturesque village on the Seine, a little below Rouen. There, except for two journeys to the East and a few other excursions, Flaubert spent the rest of his days. His life, said one of his biographers, may be summed up in a single sentence: He lived at home and wrote. The life was not without constant troubles and intermittent tragedies. In January, 1846, less than a year after establishing the family in Croisset, Flaubert's father died of cancer. Three months later, his sister Caroline gave birth to a daughter and succumbed to puerperal fever at twenty-two. Flaubert was devastated. "It seems that Misfortune is upon us, and she will not go until she has glutted herself," he wrote. "Once again I see the black cloth and hear the sordid sound of the nailed boots of the undertaker's men descending the stairs . . . They put her wedding dress on her, with bunches of roses, immortelles, and violets. With the long white veil that went down to her feet, she seemed taller and more beautiful than in life . . . I shall beg Pradier to make a bust of her and I shall keep it in my room."

It was at Pradier's studio, during one of Flaubert's infrequent visits to Paris, that he met Louise Colet. She was in her middle thirties, married, the mother of a six-year-old daughter; Flaubert was twenty-four. His unfulfilled passion for Elisa Schlesinger had conditioned him to the allure of older married women. Besides, Louise Colet was something of a celebrity. Separated from her husband, she was the mistress of the philosopher and academician, Victor Cousin, through whose influence she had won several of the Academy's poetry prizes. Clever, striking looking and voluptuous, she thought of herself sometimes as Sappho, sometimes as the Tenth Muse, and never as anything less than the Great Inspirer of Great

Men. Cousin, many years her senior, was cooling in his ardor and Louise, infatuated with the brawny youth from Normandy, invited Flaubert to her apartment. The following evening she received him in her boudoir, read him some of her verses, and the same night the gauche novice and the accomplished opportunist became lovers. It was a curious relationship. Louise Colet was possessive and peremptory; she wanted Flaubert to move to Paris and live with her. Flaubert, devoted to his home and his mother, had no intention of leaving either. Accustomed to adoration, he was far more eager to be loved than to make love. He was content to see Louise occasionally, and she had to be satisfied with his promise to write her constantly.

His friends wondered what attracted him to a woman who, according to Maxime Du Camp, "had a genius for self-advertisement and who shrank from nothing which might awake attention," and who, said Louis Bouilhet, was so affected that she had "a natural lack of naturalness." Flaubert, knowing nothing of her pretensions, was aware only of her fascinations, and at the time he was particularly susceptible. He had lost his father, on whom he depended, and his sister, who had been his confidante; he was only beginning to rely on the counsels of Louis Bouilhet, who impressed Flaubert, the embryonic writer, with the importance of form and objectivity. Yet, although he was sexually aroused—Louis spoke of him as "an untamed buffalo from the wilds of America"—he was cautious; he seemed to be planning his retreat at the very outset. Upon his return to Croisset, a few days after their first love-making, he was warning Louise: "For me physical love is always secondary. You are the only woman to whom I have dared to give pleasure, the only one, perhaps, to whom I have given it . . . But will you understand me to the end? Will you be able to bear the burden of my spleen, my manias, my whims? You tell me, for example, to write you every day and if I do not, I know you will reproach me. But the very idea that you expect a letter every morning will prevent me from writing it. Let me love you in my own way, in the way that my nature dictates . . . force me to do nothing, and I will do everything."

It is doubtful that Flaubert would have done "everything" had Louise let him do as little as his nature demanded, but she was never to find out. She forced and Flaubert flinched; she advanced and he withdrew. He made it plain that he did not want to worry his mother, who was suspicious of the flood of letters that came from

Paris and which he said were written by "a literary friend"; she complained he should resent being "watched over like a young girl." When Flaubert visited Paris and did not appear at her apartment often enough, she invaded his hotel; when he was home she bombarded him with importunate letters and was exasperated when he refused to let her come to Croisset.

Flaubert's written avowals of love were a queer mixture of protestation and evasion. "You would like to turn me into a pagan. But try as I might, any effort in that direction would be futile. The mists of the north are in the depths of my spirit—they are the cold airs I have breathed since birth. I am infected with the melancholy of the barbarians, with their lust for wandering and their distrust of life." The truth of the matter was something less grandiose. Flaubert loved his solitude. A normal, everyday relation with a woman, either as wife or mistress, was impossible for him. He surrendered himself only to the books he wanted to read and the books he wanted to write. He said it explicitly: "I can think of nothing in the world I enjoy more than a pleasant room, well heated, with lots of leisure and the right books." Louise could not believe that anyone would prefer life in a dull, provincial village to the brilliant atmosphere of the Paris salons and her own intellectual as well as physical charms. Impatience was accompanied by petulance and followed by jealousy.

Realizing that the first passion had gone out of his letters, and fearing that it might also have gone out of his life, Louise embarrassed Flaubert with endearments, gifts, and remembrances—her bedroom slippers, locks of hair, self-portraits, passionate love poems. He gave her nothing. At New Year's he was reminded that it was customary to make a present to those one loves. "I look about to find something to send you, something which is mine . . . So, my dear Louise, accept this—a kiss." She was too smitten to be angry; she kept and labeled all the little bouquets he had given her as souvenirs of their trysts.

Although he had not yet published a volume, even in his twenties Flaubert was, first of all, a writer and only incidentally a lover. Moreover, he was not merely a writer, but a writer obsessed with writing, a man who valued events, experiences, and even emotions only insofar as they suggested material to be molded into a page, a chapter, and, if he worked hard enough, a book. As Francis Steegmuller wrote in *Flaubert and Madame Bovary,* "After a day of study, he enjoyed nothing more than putting down more or less haphazardly on paper some of the thousand ideas that swarmed in his head—literary ideas, mostly—and it was of these ideas (in addition to stormy discussions of the difficulties between them) that the letters to Louise were compounded."

Gradually the fire of the romance waned. Louise prated of virtue and her sacrifice; Flaubert was offended by her moralizing even more than by her importunities. He turned brusque; he refused to consider coming to Paris for months. "I lack the time, the money, the excuse." Yet he could not break off the correspondence. There were continual recriminations, countless adieus; but his vanity—and his compulsion to write—made him want to say the last word . . . then one more word . . . and then another. So the letter writing went on, reminiscently, reproachfully, bitterly, and often incoherently, for eight years.

Meanwhile, Flaubert had been struggling with two books, *Sentimental Education* and *Temptation of St. Anthony*. He had also gone with Du Camp on a tour of the East. The tour began in October, 1849, and was to last two to three years. The young travelers visited Alexandria, the Nile, Nazareth, Syria, Constantinople, and Rome. His mother had reluctantly permitted the journey—the doctors had advised it, and she thought it might cure him of his depressions as well as the perpetual letter-writing—but it was not long before she urged him to return. Since, in spite of the pleasures of sightseeing, Flaubert was homesick, he acceded. The moment he agreed, he regretted it, but he recognized his ambivalence. In Normandy, he had dreamed of the Nile; on the Nile, he longed for Normandy. He turned his steps west and went back home. The much-planned long tour had lasted less than five months.

Before he left for the East, Flaubert summoned Du Camp and Bouilhet and, in eight-hour sessions lasting four days, read them the first draft of the *Temptation of St. Anthony*. In it, he had pushed romanticism to its furthest limits and had composed a phantasmagoria of myths, fables, and macabre fantasies. The legend of the devil and the saint was an old one; but, to embellish the wiles of the satanic tempter, Flaubert assembled not only the powers of hell, but the gods of Olympus, the deities of Egypt, and the Hindu divinities, as well as Chaldean priests, assorted soothsayers, illusionists, snakeworshipers, martyrs, miracles, and apparitions, including the Sphinx, the Gryphon, the Basilisk, the Chimera, the Unicorn, the Catoblepas, and other even less familiar monsters. The result was a long incantation—Flaubert was obviously playing with names for their sounds—but he did not realize he had written a grotesque prose poem rather than a novel. He fully expected his friends to be enthusiastic—"If you do not howl with delight, it will prove that nothing can move you"—and he was dumbfounded when, at the end of the reading, they were silent. Finally, Du Camp shook his head and murmured, "You wanted to make music, but you have produced only noise." Bouilhet agreed. "We think you should throw it in the fire and never speak of it again." Flaubert was indignant. Crestfallen but not convinced, he put the manuscript away and, following Bouilhet's harsh advice, never spoke of it for twenty years. In 1869 he rewrote the *Temptation* and put it aside for another seven years; a third and final version was published in 1876.

At thirty Flaubert was not the blond demigod who had inflamed Louise Colet six years before. The slender youth had gained a great deal of weight and lost much of his hair; the fine features had coarsened and his cheeks were criss-crossed with red veins; the sensitive mouth was half-hidden by a drooping mustache. Yet, though he was no longer "very handsome, very winning, very vigorous," Louise tried to recapture him. She ignored his rebuffs—"You live in the backroom of my heart"—and determined to win favor with Madame Flaubert. Going to Croisset she boldly invaded his home; but it was the son, not the mother, who was affronted and turned her away from the door. In spite of this, the correspondence was resumed, although Flaubert's part of it was chiefly about his new project.

The project was another novel, the complete antithesis of the *Temptation of St. Anthony.* It was Bouilhet who suggested that Flaubert write about Dr. Delaunay, who, after studying under Flaubert's father, had practiced in a small town, and, having discovered his wife's infidelities, had committed suicide. With these facts as a framework, Flaubert spent over four painful years on *Madame Bovary.* Retiring and escapist by nature, he made himself over into a realist and wrote not only one of the greatest works of serious narration but, as W. Somerset Maugham said, "created the modern realistic novel and, directly or indirectly, influenced all writers of fiction since his day . . . The characters are drawn with consummate skill. It never occurs to us that they are figures in a novel. Homais [an apothecary], to mention one, is a creature as humorous as Mr. Micawber, as familiar to the French as Micawber is to the English."

Although Flaubert used the actual story of the discontented wife who fed on the swooning romances of Eugène Sue and George Sand, and fancied herself the heroine of assignations in appropriately operatic settings, he was thinking of Louise when he wrote that Emma found in adultery "all the platitudes of marriage." The character of Emma Bovary, however, was not patterned upon that of the unfortunate doctor's erring wife. When asked who the model for the restless, wavering, dream-deluded woman might have been, Flaubert replied, "Madame Bovary is me." Flaubert had discovered that "the grand style" did not have to concern itself only with epic events but could be created by dealing with the small but tragic realities of everyday.

It cannot be said that Flaubert enjoyed the immense labor that went into his work. Detail after detail was sought for, ascertained, and registered with the most minute exactness. He went to great lengths to avoid the least suspicion of obscurity; he fought abstractions and insisted that there was only one correct way to express true meaning. "His life," wrote Henry James, "was that of a pearl diver, breathless in the thick element while he groped for the priceless word. He passed that life in reconstructing sentences, exterminating repetitions, calculating and comparing cadences . . . The horror that haunted all his years was the horror of the cliché, the stereotyped, the things usually said." He complained that his greatest trouble was the difficulty of finding the inevitable phrase and the one perfect word rather than the merely satisfactory or even suitable word. "I have spent three days in making two corrections," he wrote. "The whole of Monday, and Tuesday also, were spent in a search for two lines that would not come."

Although *Madame Bovary* was the latest of his books to be written, it was the first to be published. It appeared on April 15, 1856, when Flaubert was a few months more than thirty-four, and he and his publisher were haled into court. The government accused the author of immorality, and the public prosecutor read aloud with great gusto the sections which he considered pornographic. The defending attorney declared that the passages were necessary to show the heroine's misconduct and, since she punished herself with death, the book was a moral preachment. The judges dismissed the charges, which included irreverence. The scene at Emma's deathbed involved a description of extreme unction, which was denounced as an outrageous parody, but which was, said Flaubert, "only a page of the Latin ritual put into French, but the good folk who watch over the maintenance of religion are not strong in catechism." Almost at the same time he shared the obloquy of a court trial with another author, Charles Baudelaire, born in the same year as Flaubert. Baudelaire's *Fleurs du Mal,* published three months later than *Madame Bovary,* was condemned and pilloried by the same public prosecutor.

The style of *Madame Bovary* may not have impressed the casual reader, but the scandal did. The trial, and the publicity given to the incriminating pages, made Flaubert a celebrity. His face appeared everywhere; one cartoon showed him with a bag of surgical instruments, a magnifying glass in one hand and, in the other, a bleeding heart impaled on a scalpel. Instead of staying in Paris to be interviewed, harangued, and lionized, Flaubert hurried back to Croisset to finish work on his next novel, *Salammbô.*

Salammbô, in preparation for which Flaubert revisited Africa, is a regression to the early "lyric" manner. A story of the First Punic War, it takes place in ancient Carthage, with Hamilcar, father of the great Hannibal, as its intrepid hero. Flaubert's research on the subject was enormous—he read hundreds of books, including all of Pliny, Diodorus, Herodotus, Pausanias, Philostratus, and other classical authorities—but, like his reading, the book is too diffuse and far too melodramatic. It is not, as Flaubert's admirers contend, a failure in the grand manner but a failure in the grand opera manner. It cries out for footlights, costumes, and music by Verdi—at twenty Moussorgsky tried to make an opera of it, but was defeated by its apparatus. Sensitive though he was to criticism, Flaubert was aware of the defects of the work. "By natural disposition," he confessed, "I love what is vague and misty, and it is only patience and study that have rid me of the white fat that clogged my muscles."

The white fat was completely eliminated in *Sentimental Education,* a book Flaubert had conceived more than twenty years before, and which was published in his late forties, just before the outbreak of the Franco-Prussian War. A return to the almost scientific realism which he had taught himself to practice, the *Education* centers about three young men (patently Flaubert's three youthful associates) and a woman who is modeled upon the never-forgotten Elisa Schlesinger. Delicately drawn, Madame Arnoux is Madame Bovary's antithesis: a virtuous, unimaginative, but unforgettable person. "The book," says Tarver, "is an elaborate analysis of Parisian upper and lower middle class society—a historical study, not a romance . . . The individual through whom we see it all is a man devoid of vice and virtue, unstable, heartless, whose chief impelling motive of action is a flickering vanity . . . And yet how appallingly true he is!" There also emerges the characteristic sense of "spleen," which Flaubert shared with Baudelaire, and his hatred of middle-class smugness, a lifelong resentment of those who will not allow their little comforts to be disturbed by any large or troublesome issue.

Misfortunes descended upon Flaubert in his fifties. With the despised Prussians invading the homeland, his semi-epileptic attacks returned. The downfall of France was to him "the coming of the end of the world . . . Paganism, Christianity, Complacency —these are the three great evolutions of humanity." Bouilhet had died in 1869; Flaubert had not recovered from the loss of "the man who saw more clearly into my own thoughts than I saw myself" when his mother died. "It is as if my very bowels have been torn from me," he wrote in anguish. "This impetuous, imperious giant," commented Maxime Du Camp, "flying out at the least contradiction, was the most respectful, the gentlest, and the most attentive son that a mother could dream of." Elisa Schlesinger was confined to an asylum for the insane, and although Flaubert was cared for by his niece, Caroline's daughter, was visited by Zola, Turgenev, and the young Guy de Maupassant, he retreated into a desolate pessimism.

He comforted himself with his books and his undiminishing correspondence—the correspondence alone, when published, filled nine large volumes. At fifty-five he wrote his most touching short story, "A Simple Heart," the history of a good-hearted, loyal, and loving servant who lives for others and is completely disregarded by them. Aging prematurely, Flaubert did not live long enough to complete his most ambitious work, *Bouvard and Pécuchet,* the half-farcical, half-satirical saga of a pair of ignorant oddities. Nothing could have served as a greater contrast to the exotic trappings and barbaric orgies of *The Temptation of St. Anthony* and *Salammbô* than this gigantic comedy of ideas which traces the spasmodic and absurd quest for culture on the part of two middle-aged clerks against the background of a humdrum village. The course of the narrative scarcely conceals Flaubert's detestation of bourgeois apathy, his anger at mankind's disdain of beauty, and his scorn of its poor taste, bad habits, and aggressive stupidity.

At fifty-six the seizures returned with new malevolence. Flaubert suffered almost continually; writing became more and more difficult. Still torturing himself with the problem of style, Flaubert had not quite finished the first half of *Bouvard and Pécuchet* when he was struck by an attack of apoplexy. One day when the servant brought his lunch to the library, she found him gasping on the couch, incoherent and helpless. An hour later he stopped breathing. He was in his fifty-ninth year when, on May 8, 1880, he died.

Louis Pasteur

[1 8 2 2 - 1 8 9 5]

*"The greatest disorder of the mind is to
allow the will to direct the belief."*

INDOMITABLE PERSISTENCE matched with almost infinite patience
changed the mild nature of Louis Pasteur into a driving force.
Before he had attained maturity he had decided that the three
words which held the deepest meanings were: *Will, Work, Wait.* He
was born December 27, 1822, at Dôle, in the Jura region of
France. His father had been a soldier under Napoleon and had
fought through the Peninsular War, but he had returned to his
trade, which was that of a tanner. His mother, Jeanne Etiennette
Roqui, came of a family of gardeners in the suburb of Salins. Although two daughters were born of the marriage, Louis was the
only son. From Dôle the Pasteurs moved to Marnoz and then to the
neighboring town of Arbois, where the intersection of the road
and the river made an ideal spot for a tannery. At Arbois, Louis was
a competent but careless pupil; he liked to fish in the Cuisance, explore the country lanes, and search for "hidden treasure" in the
junk-piles of the tannery yard. He preferred drawing to all other
studies, and his hard-working parents were worried that their son
might grow up to be an artist.

At sixteen he attended the Lycée St. Louis, a secondary school, in
Paris, and was acutely homesick. A month later he appeared to be
genuinely ill, but he said, "If I could only get one whiff of the tannery I feel I should be cured." Without a reproach, his father withdrew him from the school, and Louis went back to his crayons, fishing, and exploring. The Pasteurs were a happy, close-knit family.
"Your sisters were counting the days, they said," his father wrote
when Louis left to return to school. "It is a great joy to me to note
your attachment to each other." At a later date Louis's father reiterated his gratification when acknowledging a gift from his son.
"The presents you sent have arrived. I should prefer a thousand
times that this money should still be in your purse, and thence to a
good restaurant, spent in some good meals that you might have enjoyed with your friends. There are not many parents, my dearest

boy, who have to write such things to their son. My satisfaction in you is indeed deeper than I can express."

At nineteen, Pasteur was a student-teacher. He was no longer the country boy, dreamily sketching. He was already determined to *will* his way to success. "To will is a great thing," he wrote his sisters, "for Action and Work follow Will, and almost always Work is accompanied by Success. Will opens the doors; Work passes them; and Success is waiting to crown one's efforts." At twenty Pasteur attended lectures at the Sorbonne and was fascinated by the discourses of the celebrated chemist, J. B. Dumas. He became assistant mathematical instructor at the Royal College of Besançon, where he took his degree of Bachelor of Science. Curiously enough his studies in chemistry were classified as "barely adequate." At twenty-five Pasteur graduated from the Ecole Normale in Paris and in 1848 became Professor of Physics at Dijon, a position which he left to teach chemistry at Strasbourg University.

It was at Strasbourg that he was welcomed into the family circle of the rector, M. Laurent, and there he promptly fell in love with the younger daughter, Marie. Two weeks after his first meeting, Pasteur made a formal offer of marriage in a letter which conceals its impetuosity in a forthrightness that is as passionless as a clinical report. "I feel it my duty," wrote Pasteur, after a somewhat self-conscious beginning, "to put you in possession of the following facts which may have some weight in determining your acceptance or refusal. My father is a tanner in the small town of Arbois in the Jura. My sisters keep house for him, and assist him with his books, taking the place of my mother whom we had the misfortune to lose last May . . . My family is in easy circumstances, but with no fortune. I value what we possess at not more than 50,000 francs, and as for me, I have long ago decided to hand over to my sisters the whole of what should be my share. I have therefore no fortune. My only means are good health, some courage, and my position in the University . . . This, Sir, is all my present position. As to the future, unless my tastes should completely change, I shall give myself up entirely to chemical research. I hope to return to Paris when I have acquired some reputation through my scientific labors . . . My father will himself come to Strasbourg to make the proposal of marriage."

The twenty-six-year-old teacher was more certain of the rector's regard than of his daughter's. "There is nothing in me to attract a young girl's fancy," he wrote Madame Laurent. After he had been permitted to correspond with Marie, he pleaded in a tone of self-deprecation: "I beg you, Mademoiselle, not to judge me hastily, and, so doing, misjudge me. Time will prove that, beneath this cold, shy, and scarcely pleasing exterior, there is a heart full of affection." As became a well-brought up young lady, Marie did not demand emotional extravagances or even the rhetoric of love. Her father accepted the proposal for her and the wedding was arranged for May 29, 1848. Legend has it that Pasteur was late for the ceremony because he could not bear to leave a half-finished experiment.

The experiments were to become not only the center of his life but the reason for it. Crystals and minute active organisms, "ferments," fascinated him. At twenty-nine he devoted himself to a study of tartar and racemic acid. "I shall go to Trieste," he declared. "I shall go to the end of the world! I *must* discover the source of racemic acid! I *must* follow up the tartars to their origin!" Experiments with acids led to a growing concern with fermentation and when, in 1854, he was made Professor of the new Faculty of Sciences at Lille, Pasteur plunged into the studies which were to change the entire course of chemistry. Before and during his time, it was believed that life could originate by "spontaneous generation," and that dead substances produced living matter. All the early naturalists and philosophers—Ovid, Pliny, Lucretius, and Virgil—accepted spontaneous generation as an unquestionable fact. Virgil had told of bees swarming to life from the body of a dead bull. An Italian, Buonanni, claimed that rotting timberwood engendered butterflies, while Van Helmont said that anyone could create mice by filling a jar with dirty rags, a quantity of wheat, and pieces of cheese. Pasteur bought a small building, transformed it into a laboratory, built a stove under a staircase, and spent his days and most of his nights looking for germs, collecting specimens of dust, hermetically sealing glass flasks, searching for agents of fermentation. He climbed the Alps to prove that the greater the altitude, the fewer the germs, and that "the dusts suspended in our atmospheric air are the exclusive origin, the necessary condition of life in solution." He was forty-two before he was able, by a series of exhaustive experiments, to negate the theory of spontaneous generation and show that life is a germ, and that only a living thing can produce life. The traditionalists refused to be convinced; they disputed his findings with academic mockery. Pasteur's patience did not falter; his persistence drove him to the next step. "A man of science," he shrugged, "may hope for what may be said of him in the future, but he cannot stop to think of the insults—or the compliments—of his own day."

The next step was a further exploration of the minute organisms which determine life. The silk industry of France was in a state of panic because of a mysterious disease which had attacked the silkworms. More than three thousand sericulturists had importuned the authorities to do something about the epidemic and a senator, who had been one of Pasteur's teachers, urged him to study the situation. "Your proposition," Pasteur replied, "throws me into a great perplexity. The objective is great, but your request embarrasses me. Remember that I have never even seen a silkworm!" Nevertheless, he went to Alais, interviewed the cultivators, compared their sick worms and their futile remedies, and began to collect eggs, larvae, and moths. When he did not immediately produce a cure-all, he was harshly handled. At first there were sneers at the "mere chemist." Then, when Pasteur suggested drastic extermination of the diseased eggs, or seeds, to preserve the healthy ones, the seed-merchants slanderously attacked Pasteur's character, and some of them threw stones. When his friends asked him what he intended to do, he replied "Remain patient—and remain here." It took him four years to diagnose the disease, chart the symptoms, eliminate the trouble, breed a new crop of healthy eggs and bring the epidemic to an end. The result of Pasteur's "seeding" process was a harvest of faultless cocoons which earned the first profit shown in over ten years.

All this was accomplished during a time of pain and personal tragedy. He had lost his eldest daughter, Jeanne, in 1859, after an attack of typhus germs. His youngest child, Camille, succumbed to a fever in 1865, at the age of two. Eight months later the twelve-year-old Cécile became ill with typhoid fever and died within a few days. Already overworked and weakened by shock, Pasteur suffered a temporary paralysis. A cerebral hemorrhage affected his speech and prevented movement of his left arm. "It is like lead," complained Pasteur. "If someone would only cut it off!" But his discipline of patience re-established itself. He strengthened himself with Smiles's *Self-Help* and Bossuet's *Of The Knowledge of God and of Self*. He recovered and found wry comfort in the thought that "The greatest aberration of the mind consists in believing a thing because it is desirable."

In his late forties Pasteur was a man whose appearance projected power. His features were stern and simple, suggesting his country origin. The nose was broad and emphasized by a high forehead; the mouth tended to be tight; the beard was clipped in the conventional style of the savant. But the eyes, gray-green as a beryl, were a contradiction, being both quietly contemplative and burning with energy.

The calm as well as the energy were heavily drawn upon and almost drained during the next few years. Pasteur had discovered the microscopic vegetations which turned good wine acid, sour, and generally unfit to drink. Moreover, he had found that he could free wine from all germs of disease and deterioration by heating it, then keeping it for a few minutes at a temperature of fifty to sixty degrees centigrade—a process that became known as "pasteurization." He now turned to the development of harmful micro-organisms in beer and their relation to human ailments. His notebooks reflect the widened scope of his researches. For example: "When we see beer and wine subjected to deep alterations because they have given refuge to micro-organisms invisibly introduced and now swarming within them, it is impossible not to be driven by the thought that similar facts may—*must*—take place in animals and in man. But," he added with the caution of the true scientist, "if we are inclined to believe that it is so because we think it likely, let us remember, before we affirm it, that the greatest disorder of the mind is to allow the will to direct the belief."

Before he could extend his studies of fermentation from the germs in wine and beer to the virus in human beings, Pasteur was interrupted by the disastrous war of 1870. His only son was with the Army Corps, and when weeks passed without news, Pasteur set out to find him. The roads were full of the defeated, soldiers and stragglers—"the retreat from Moscow could not have been worse," said Pasteur—and when he located a staff officer of his son's corps he was informed that of the original twelve hundred men of the battalion fewer than three hundred had survived. Disheartened and desperate, Pasteur went on through a nightmare of winding roads choked with dead horses and men suffering from freezing cold and gangrenous wounds. Finally, Pasteur recognized a gaunt soldier, weak with hunger, wrapped to his eyes in a greatcoat, and father and son, too moved for words, embraced in silence.

The hideous consequences of the war spurred Pasteur on to an even more determined pursuit of the destructive germs, for the casualties in the hospitals were greater than those on the battlefields. "A pin-prick is an open door to Death," said an eminent French surgeon, quoted by René Vallery-Radot, Pasteur's son-in-law, in his *Life of Pasteur.* "That open door widened before the smallest operation; the mere lancing of an abscess sometimes had such serious results that surgeons hesitated before the slightest use of the scalpel . . . The very art of the surgeon was arrested and disconcerted by the fatal failures which supervened after almost every operation." Another surgeon told his pupils, "Think ten times before you perform an amputation, even when it seems imperative; for only too often, when we decide upon an operation, we sign the patient's death warrant." Pasteur maintained that, contrary to the current belief, purulent infection was not a necessary disease, not "a divinely instituted consequence of any important operation." Insisting on the control and the elimination of fast-spreading germs, Pasteur advocated not only the most scrupulous care in the dressing of wounds, but the sterilization of instruments, bandages, and all points of contact.

One of those who had taken the precaution to purify all articles used for dressing in a strong solution of carbolic acid was the eminent English surgeon, Joseph Lister, who wrote to Pasteur: "Allow me to beg your acceptance of a pamphlet, which I send by the same post, containing an account of some investigations into the subject which you have done so much to elucidate: the germ theory of fermentative changes . . . Allow me to take this opportunity to tender you my most cordial thanks for having, by your brilliant researches, demonstrated the truth of the germ theory of putrefaction, and thus furnished me with the principle upon which alone the antiseptic system can be carried out." Some years earlier, in the *Lancet* of 1867, Lister had written: "Turning now to the question how the atmosphere produces decomposition of organic substances, we find that a flood of light has been thrown upon this most important subject by the philosophic researches of M. Pasteur, who has demonstrated by thoroughly convincing evidence that it is not to its oxygen or to any of its gaseous constituents that the air owes this property, but to minute particles suspended in it, which are the germs of various low forms of life, long since revealed by the microscope, and regarded as merely accidental concomitants of putrescence, but now shown by Pasteur to be its essential cause." To which Sir William Osler, in his introduction to Vallery-Radot's *Life of Pasteur,* added, "From these beginnings modern surgery took its rise, and the whole subject of wound infection, not only in relation to surgical diseases, but to childbed fever, forms now one of the most brilliant chapters in the history of Preventive Medicine."

At fifty-five Pasteur was a famous man, but he was too busy to rest on his fame. He said, "Do not think too much about things which have already been accomplished," knowing there were still many things for him to do. He had been drawn more and more to bacteriology, and his concern was heightened by what seemed to be a plague among sheep in almost all the French provinces. In Beauce twenty sheep out of every hundred died of the disease known as splenic fever or anthrax; in the Auvergne district the mortality rate varied between thirty and fifty per cent. Not only sheep, but cows, and even human beings succumbed. Pasteur went to work in a slaughterhouse near Chartres, examining the carcasses of animals who had died of the fever, collecting diseased blood, and injecting the infectious fluid into guinea pigs and mice. Again the medical profession raged. The doctors attacked the germ theory with renewed violence and ridiculed Pasteur's claim that he could isolate bacteria, with their infinitesimal "rods," and use them to cure the very disease they had engendered. They repeated the old argument: if an idea was new it could not be good; if it was good it was not new. Even the clergy were roused to protest; one minister contended that the plague was sent as a warning, and, harking back to Biblical times, was one of those sent by the Lord to punish the Egyptians. Nevertheless, Pasteur persisted. He surmised that a bacterial attack induced the formation in the blood of "antibodies" which attacked the germs; in fatal diseases the invading germs multiplied so quickly as to cause death before enough antibodies could form. He experimented with the deadly, filament-shaped bacteria and subjected them to endless tests and counter-tests. Finally, he evolved a culture which was a mild form of the disease itself and, instead of killing, would build up a protection against the fever. The weak infection mobilized the body's defenses without injury, and when the attack was over, left those defenses ready to ambush, any time, similar but virulent infections. The virus was thus transformed into a vaccine, and Pasteur announced that he now had "a positive preventive to one of the most terrible diseases with which animals and men could be attacked."

In 1881 Pasteur arranged a demonstration which would be conclusive. He inoculated twenty-five sheep with his serum and placed them with twenty-five sheep which showed symptoms of anthrax. "The twenty-five vaccinated ones will survive." After a short period of waiting, he wrote further details: "We inoculated all the sheep, vaccinated and non-vaccinated, with very virulent splenetic fever. It is not forty-eight hours ago . . . This afternoon all the non-vaccinated subjects will be dead—eighteen are already dead this morning and the others are dying. As to the vaccinated ones, all are well."

Pasteur's triumph was not only complete but overwhelming. Those who had condemned him rushed to become his disciples. The government offered him the ribbon of the Legion of Honor; he was elected to the small circle of "immortals" in the French Academy. When Pasteur, following the custom of new Academy members calling on the older ones, suggested visiting Alexandre Dumas, Dumas replied, "I will not allow Pasteur to come and see me. Instead, I will call upon him to thank him for consenting to become one of us." Pasteur was naturally gratified, but he had neither the time nor the inclination to bask in the artificial sunlight of publicity. There was a new problem waiting for him in the laboratory.

The new challenge was actually an old one: the prevention of hydrophobia, a disease more terrible than anthrax. Unlike anthrax, hydrophobia did not manifest itself at once. A person bitten by a mad dog might show no trace of poisoning for a week or more, but after that, the symptoms were pitiful: a horrible restlessness, inability to swallow, shuddering, spasms, convulsions, choking, and almost inevitable death. Pasteur determined to isolate the germ and find a culture that would be as effective against hydrophobia as his sheep serum was against anthrax. His first experiments were with two mad dogs brought to him by an old army veterinarian whose "remedy" was the filing down of the teeth of all dogs so that their bite could not penetrate the skin. Pasteur was fearless. He handled the mad animals himself and inoculated guinea pigs and rabbits with rabies—the name given to the disease among animals as distinguished from hydrophobia, contracted by humans. Vallery-Radot graphically describes one of the experiments. "One day, Pasteur wanting to collect a little saliva from the jaws of a rabid dog, so as to obtain it directly, two of his assistants undertook to drag a mad bulldog, foaming at the mouth, from its cage. They seized it by means of a lasso, and stretched it on a table. Then, by means of a tube held between his lips, Pasteur sucked the deadly saliva into the glass."

A year later Pasteur was still uncertain about his findings concerning hydrophobia. Could the vaccinal substance associated with the rabic virus be isolated? Would the serum which neutralized the rabic virus in dogs be effective in men? In July, 1885, a nine-year-old Alsatian boy, Joseph Meister, was brought into his laboratory. He had been savagely attacked by a frothing dog and he was bleeding from fourteen wounds. Pasteur was shaken by the boy's condition and by the necessity of making a decision. He had never operated on a human being; he was unsure about the preventive treatment which, so far, had been successful only with dogs; he could only guess at the required strength of the serum; he feared the after-results. But the very hopelessness of the child's case decided him. Into the boy's side he injected a few drops, and every day for ten days Pasteur inoculated the boy with serums of increasing strength. Young Meister improved, but when there was a slight relapse, Pasteur could not sleep; he had prolonged nightmares, saw the child suffocating, and felt he had killed him. It was not until a month had passed that he knew he had saved the child and effected a universal cure.

If Pasteur had been lauded before, now he was eulogized with every superlative in the language. He was a savior; he had conquered the worst of diseases; he had fought back death. People thronged to him from all over the world. Foreign scientists and leading physicians acknowledged him as Master and begged to be his apostles. The *New York Herald* opened its columns to a subscription which sent a group of workingmen's children to Paris to be treated by Pasteur. His house was invaded by sufferers from England, Hungary, Spain, Holland. Nineteen Russians, who had been terribly torn by rabid wolves, came from Smolensk clamoring for help—the only French word they knew was "Pasteur."

On November 14, 1887, the Pasteur Institute opened its doors. It had been made possible not only by wealthy sponsors and munificent gifts from Russia, Turkey, Brazil, and other countries, but by countless contributions from the poor. Five years later, Pasteur's seventieth birthday was the occasion of international tributes. At a great gathering in Paris, the huge theater of the Sorbonne was crowded with delegates from scientific societies, members of the French Academy, eminent native professors and foreign notables. There were many addresses, but the high note was Lister's. "You have raised the veil which for centuries had covered infectious diseases," said Lister, as a representative of the Royal Societies of London and Edinburgh. "You have changed the treatment of wounds from an uncertain and too often disastrous business into a scientific and certainly beneficial art. Your relentless researches have thrown a powerful light which has illuminated the dark places in surgery." When Lister turned to embrace the deeply moved Pasteur, the grave academicians burst into cheers like schoolboys.

Two years later, while Pasteur was busy with toxins and anti-toxins, hoping to find a remedy for diphtheria, he was struck down by an attack of uremic poisoning. For almost two months he was in gasping pain, close to death. When he felt somewhat recovered, he insisted on going back to the laboratory, if only to check the results of his pupils' experiments. But his working days were over. Sitting under a canopy in the garden of the Pasteur Institute, he was too often tempted to investigate what was going on inside, and he was persuaded to retire to his country place in Villeneuve l'Etang. Here he was allowed to have a kennel so that he could pursue the study of rabies, and he spent much time in the stables which were little laboratories for the preparation of diphtheria antitoxin. No one saw him deteriorate—his mind was active as ever—but in his seventy-third year he began to die. Day by day he faded. He found it increasingly difficult to speak. Toward the end of September he was too weak to lift his head; when offered a cup of milk, he barely whispered, "I cannot," and lay back on the pillow. He re-mained in a coma for twenty-four hours, and died September 28, 1895.

Some years later, a poll was taken to find out which hero the French people considered the greatest of their countrymen. Napo-leon, the mighty war-maker, was fifth; Pasteur, whose invisible bat-tles had been fought under a microscope, was first. His contribu-tions to the world had been properly assessed and his characteristics had been acclaimed as the national character. He affected every subsequent scientist and inspired every experimenter with his phi-losophy. "Chance favors only the mind which is prepared." "Too many people transform a question of fact into a question of faith." "Exhaust every combination until the mind can conceive no others possible." "The more I contemplate the mysteries of Nature, the more my faith becomes that of a Breton peasant. Perhaps, when I learn more, I shall have the faith of a Breton peasant's wife." "Worship the spirit of criticism. Without it, everything is fallible. It always has the last word." "Two contrary laws seem to be forever wrestling for the soul of man. The one is a law of blood and death, always planning new methods of destruction, forcing nations to be constantly ready for the battlefield. The other is a law of peace, work, and health, always creating new means of delivering man from the scourges which beset him. The one seeks violent conquests; the other the relief of humanity. . . . Which of the two will ultimately prevail, God alone knows. But we may assert that science will have tried, by obeying the law of humanity, to extend the frontiers of life."

Henrik Ibsen

[1828-1906]

*"That man is right who has allied himself
most closely with the future."*

IT IS HARD for modern readers to find in Ibsen the sensational elements which shocked his contemporaries and shook the very pillars of society. His characters are flat when compared to those of Shaw, Chekhov, and Pirandello, all of whom he influenced, and his central situations seem traditional and often trite expositions of accepted facts. Yet the facts, as well as the characters, were not only startling but revolutionary when Ibsen presented them in the last quarter of the nineteenth century.

Henrik Ibsen was born March 20, 1828, in the town of Skien in the southern part of Norway. His lineage was a mixture of Scandinavian, Teutonic and Gaelic strains. One paternal ancestor, a sea captain, was a Dane; another forerunner had Scottish blood; his mother was of German descent. The Ibsens were prosperous; Henrik's father was an important member of the community, and his position seemed secure. But when Henrik was eight, his father went bankrupt, the grandiose plans for the future collapsed, and the family had to move from the handsomely furnished town home to a shabby farmhouse. Young though he was, the boy was so affected by the social and financial reverses that repercussions of the shock made themselves felt many years later in such plays as *A Doll's House, John Gabriel Borkman,* and *The Wild Duck.*

One of Ibsen's biographers speaks of his apparent aversion for his family, and it seems likely that he was ashamed of his father's failure, for he left home as early as he could and, except for a single visit, never returned. At sixteen the young Ibsen went to Grimstad, a small seaport on the south coast of Norway, where he apprenticed himself to an apothecary. There he stayed for five years, writing poetry in his spare time—chiefly satirical verses about the villagers —and dreaming of restoring the family fortunes. An affair with a servant girl ten years his senior resulted in a child, and Ibsen became a father at the age of eighteen. His family was outraged; correspondence was broken off and, except for a few letters to his younger sister, never resumed; the boy was made to feel he was a social outcast while still in his teens. Even at this age the tenet of crime and punishment was driven home, and although he contributed to the maintenance of his illegitimate son, he was already burdened with a sense of guilt—a guilt which, with its consequent retribution, constitutes a leading theme in many of his relentless dramas.

Since organized society had made Ibsen a rebel before he had attained his majority, it is not a mere coincidence that his first sustained literary effort was the glorification of a rebel. This was a verse play, *Catiline,* which, although rhetorically immature, portrayed the fight and defeat of an insurgent spirit. No publisher was interested. A friend of Ibsen's printed it at his own expense, but the publication was so complete a failure that all the unbound sheets were sold to a grocer for wrapping paper. This was the first time, Ibsen remarked later, that the mere paper on which a work was printed enabled the author to buy enough bread to keep himself alive for his next work. The publication of *Catiline* gave him the excuse to go to Christiania, where he hoped to enter the university. Failing to pass the examination, Ibsen tried journalism, and at twenty-three, was rescued from utter poverty by an appointment as stage manager at the Norwegian theater which had just been established in Bergen. Six years later he was given the post of director for the larger national theater at Christiania. He remained there until he was thirty-four, at which time the theater had to close its doors for lack of receptive audiences.

In the meanwhile, Ibsen had married, at twenty-nine, Susanna Thoresen, stepdaughter of a popular author, and had been busy as an experimental playwright. Between twenty-five and thirty-four he wrote half a dozen plays. Founded on folklore, the dramas purported to suggest the revival of a native literature, but they were youthfully romantic and even more youthfully imitative of the "heroic" plays, with their stilted dialog and shallow characterizations, popular at the time. The only one which shows traces of the mature craftsman is *Love's Comedy,* an ironic examination of love and marriage which, in its mechanical motivation, fails to be either a serious study of sacrifice or a satire on the compatibility of pure theory and ordinary living. Living itself was difficult for Ibsen who, at thirty-six, was a theatrical director without a theater, a father with a young son to support, and a writer whose plays no one wanted to see. The intellectual as well as the physical climate depressed him; another move was imperative. This time Ibsen radically changed his locale; he paid a curt farewell to the narrow-minded communities which inhibited his critical and creative spirit, and went to Rome.

He stayed in Rome five years, eking out an existence and working on a series of plays which would combine the form of the dramatic poem with the poetic drama. Although he was a reticent foreigner, his appearance was remarkable to the point of being freakish. His hair, falling below his ears when he was relaxed, flew wildly about his head whenever he argued. His eyes burned with excitement even when his mouth tightened in silence. He wore an enormous cloak and, if suddenly addressed, would retreat into that cloak "like a snail into its shell." When he broadened the side whiskers that framed his cheeks, he looked more and more like an apprehensive owl in the hollow of a dark tree.

A few years after arriving in Rome Ibsen made his first significant impact upon the theater with a strangely contrasting pair of masterpieces, *Brand* and *Peer Gynt*. Both are written in verse, and both deal with failures on a heroic scale. Brand is a saintly priest who is also a fanatic. His uncompromising "All or Nothing" is an exaggeration of Kierkegaard's "Either-Or," a summons to live not only dangerously but desperately, beyond good and evil.

> Be passion's slave, be pleasure's thrall;
> But be it utterly, all in all!

Some of Ibsen's contemporaries thought that Brand was intended to be a portrait of Kierkegaard, but Ibsen, the willful and implacable idealist, insisted that "Brand is myself in my best moments." Like Brand, Ibsen held stubbornly to his purpose, but unlike his unflinching hero, Ibsen did not allow his pride to harden into inflexible will and drag all his associates—and himself—to an idealistic doom. Peer Gynt is Brand's opposite. Brand is a moral perfectionist, an ascetic puritan; Peer Gynt is a complete creature of impulse, an apostle of lawlessness. As a sinner, however, Peer Gynt does far less harm that Brand does as a saint. "Brand would force his ideal on all men and women," Shaw wrote in *The Quintessence of Ibsenism.* "Peer Gynt keeps his ideal for himself alone: it is indeed implicit in the ideal itself that it should be unique—that he alone should have the force to realize it. For Peer's first boyish notion of the self-realized man is not the saint, but the demigod whose indomitable will is stronger than destiny: the fighter, the master, the man whom no woman can resist, the mighty hunter, the knight of a thousand adventures—the model, in short, of the lover in a lady's novel, or the hero in a boy's romance." A scoffer at all that is sacrosanct, Peer, the village outcast, flies in the face of the proprieties by becoming a vagabond to the utmost—a swaggering adventurer, a slave trader, a fake missionary, a crooked financier, a spurious scientist, a false prophet, the great lover, the fantasy-driven egotist, "Emperor of Himself," a clownish Ulysses who is saved (somewhat speciously) by the Penelope-sweetheart whose simple faith has kept his image pure throughout the years.

In his early forties Ibsen moved to Germany and lived chiefly in Munich, with occasional sojourns in Italy. In Dresden he completed a third massive poetic work. Begun in Rome, *Emperor and Galilean* has as its background the conflict of paganism and Christianity in the fourth century. Since it deals with the struggle between two irreconcilable powers in the life of the world, Ibsen called it a "world-historical drama." Beneath its historical trappings, *Emperor and Galilean* is a passionate sermon which is also a personal plea for moral unity. Ibsen seems to say that a man cannot believe in others until he believes in himself—and Ibsen's leading characters were all victims of self-deception. Depicting varying sides of himself in his various creations, Ibsen was a self-divided person, an idealist who distrusted abstract ideals, an iconoclastic truth-teller who forced himself to see the destructive power of the truth. At fifty he abandoned the rhetorical-romantic dramas in verse and concentrated on the realistic prose plays of modern life which would expose what Shaw called "the mischief of idealism."

The first of his realistic dramas is characterized by its ironic title, *Pillars of Society,* for the play is an ugly exhibit of hypocrisy. Its assortment of unctuous sermonizers, shady businessmen, time-servers, liars and lickspittles shows Ibsen's scorn of middle class "respectability." The community, to which the average citizen has to conform, was Ibsen's chief target; it was a small replica of the State, and the State was the enemy of the individual. Without proclaiming himself a philosophical anarchist, Ibsen confessed that he lacked "the gift of orthodoxy"; liberty was his first and highest consideration. "Destroy that false ideal—the State—make willingness and spiritual kinship the only essentials of unity—and you have the beginning of a liberty that has some value."

A Doll's House and *Ghosts* challenged the conventions still more

aggressively than *Pillars of Society.* They outraged the mores by
exploding the notion that marriage was a sacred institution. In
A Doll's House the Helmers seem to be happily mated. He is an
honest lawyer and a good humdrum family man; she appears to be
the ideal wife, sweet, simple, and a little silly. A slight complication
leads to a sudden crisis, and the wife, Nora, is made to realize that
her husband will always side with the conventions rather than with
her. No longer content to be merely a submissive "womanly
woman," Nora insists that she be regarded as an individual, a responsible human being. She leaves home, husband, and children,
refusing to return until the "miracle of miracles," the possibility of
a transformation of their (to her) dishonorable and degrading life
into a true companionship. *Ghosts* is the tragedy of a wife and
mother who sacrifices herself for the conventions which she knows
cannot uphold the rotting structure of her marriage. Mrs. Alving
fears the power of "what people will say" and protects her home
and husband, an unscrupulous lecher, from scandal; but she fails
to save her son, the one thing she hoped to rescue, from the curse
of an evil inheritance—clearly syphilis, the very mention of which
was taboo. In common with certain Greek tragedies, there are overtones of incest (not consummated), a crippling disease, and madness; the dread of unmerited retribution merges into the terror of
an intolerable but inexorable fate.

Both plays were condemned by an indignant press and a mortally offended public. *A Doll's House* was branded "immoral," "an
affront to all the decencies," "full of sophistries tending to domestic
misunderstandings and open insurrection." In Germany a happy
ending had to be substituted. "The morality of the period was
shocked by even such a comparatively mild catastrophe of married
life as Nora's flight," wrote Janko Lavrin in *Ibsen: An Approach.*
"The theatergoers in Berlin, Hamburg, and Vienna actually prevailed upon Ibsen to alter, for the benefit of their tender feelings,
such a dénouement. In this version Nora, when about to depart,
throws a last glance at her sleeping children, and remains, with the
remark, 'Oh, I sin before myself, but I cannot leave them!' Fortunately Ibsen discarded this idyllic finale in all the printed editions of the play." The reviewers reserved their most poisonous
invectives for *Ghosts.* William Archer, the dramatic critic and
Ibsen's official English translator, preserved many of these for a
"Dictionary of Abuse" and quoted them in an article entitled
"Ghosts and Gibberings," which appeared in the *Pall Mall Gazette*

in 1891, and which Shaw reprinted with obvious relish in his *Quintessence of Ibsenism*. Here are a few of the more pointed barbs: "An open drain; a loathsome sore unbandaged . . . Gross, almost putrid indecorum . . . Literary carrion . . . Unutterably offensive; should be prosecuted . . . Revoltingly suggestive and blasphemous . . . A piece to bring the stage into disrepute and dishonor with every right-thinking man and woman . . . Garbage and offal." Ibsen was described as "an egotist and a bungler, nasty, consistently dirty, discordant and dull," and his admirers were castigated as "lovers of prurience, dabblers in impropriety who are eager to gratify their illicit tastes under the pretence of art . . . sexless, educated and muck-ferreting dogs." It was reserved for a publication called *Truth* to utter the most obvious lie: "There is not the slightest interest in the Scandinavian humbug."

Ibsen answered his critics by turning from an attack on conventional ideas of marriage to an assault on political principles. The play was *An Enemy of the People,* a disclosure of other types of "idealists," those who announce high aims and stick to them— until they interfere with their financial interests. Ibsen planned it as a comedy, but it turned into an angry satire, the downfall of the one honest man in a community of pretenders, smooth speculators, and furtive scoundrels, aided by a venal press which organizes the uncertain elements into a "compact majority." The title, *An Enemy of the People,* is a sad as well as an ironic commentary, for the defeated Dr. Stockman, the one true idealist, is the only friend the people have . . . and he is the one who is booed, beaten, and left standing alone. Ibsen was fifty-four when, working on *An Enemy of the People,* he wrote to the Danish critic, Georg Brandes, "It will never be possible for me to join a party which has the majority on its side. Björnson says: 'The majority is always right,' and, as a practical politician, he is bound, I suppose, to say so. I, on the other hand, must of necessity say: 'The minority is always right.' Naturally I am not thinking of that minority of stagnationists who are left behind in the great middle party which we call liberal; but I mean that minority which leads the van, and pushes on to the points which the majority has not yet reached. I mean: That man is right who has allied himself most closely with the future."

It was the future which occupied Ibsen's thoughts as he entered his mid-fifties. His plays took a different turn and acquired a new tone. They had passed from the romantic to the realistic; now they became symbolic, full of dark implications and cryptic images. A central theme persisted: beware of the ideals by which man cannot live; fear the truth which only martyrs crave. "Rob the average man of his illusions," says Doctor Relling in *The Wild Duck,* "and you rob him of his happiness. . . . Life would be quite tolerable if we could only get rid of the confounded duns that, in our poverty, keep pestering us with the claims of the ideal." It is the interfering zealot who, in *The Wild Duck,* insists that a well-adjusted couple must "free themselves" by digging up the "truth" of their pasts, and wrecks a hitherto happy household. *Rosmersholm* returns to the double theme of crime and punishment and the danger of imposing a set of ideals upon those who are better off without them. It also introduces one of Ibsen's most impassioned, purposeful, and enigmatic women, Rebecca West. *The Lady from the Sea* is one of Ibsen's few plays with a happy ending, an ending brought about by the heroine's ability to give up neurotic fantasy for everyday reality. *Hedda Gabler,* another of Ibsen's powerful portraits, is a woman condemned to her own sickness, irritated by boredom, goaded by jealousy, driven by power, a Norwegian Lady Macbeth. With it Ibsen reached the depths of bitterness.

At sixty-one Ibsen became enamored of a seventeen-year-old Viennese, Emilie Bardach, whom he called "the May sun of my September life," and though Ibsen later denied it, he mentioned divorce, marriage, and a subsequent tour of the world. Nothing happened, but the impulsive girl was transformed into the danger-loving Hilda Wangel who, in *The Master Builder,* inspired Solness, the visionary architect, to his most daring achievement and his death. More cautious than his too easily tempted hero, Ibsen did not pursue the young Valkyrie, but looked homeward. He was sixty-three when he returned to Christiania, where he remained the rest of his life.

Although he had fifteen more years to live, Ibsen wrote only three more plays: *Little Eyolf, John Gabriel Borkman, When We Dead Awaken.* All are tragedies. The first is a study of desolate resignation; the second is a foreboding dance of death; the third seems to promise a resurrection but ends in a bleak doomsday. By now, Ibsen, internationally famous, could count on an eager reception for his plays, not only in his own country, but everywhere. His work was translated into a dozen languages, even into Japanese. As already indicated, the plays caused an angry furore in London, and Shaw sprang to Ibsen's aid with a brilliant, book-length defense. Echoes of irate disapproval were still heard, but

Ibsen lived long enough to realize that his position as one of the world's leading dramatists was unassailable.

At seventy-two Ibsen suffered a stroke; a second crippled his brain as well as his body. He lost the ability to concentrate; he could not read more than a few pages of a book; writing was out of the question. His will made him struggle to regain something of himself; he began laboriously to learn the letters of the alphabet. A third stroke stopped even this, and he died, at the age of seventy-eight, May 23, 1906.

In addition to the denunciations of the vituperative reviewers, Ibsen has had his more temperate detractors—the Norwegian novelist, Knut Hamsun, spoke of Ibsen as "a bookkeeper of dramatic art." But after his death, no one questioned Ibsen's position as a pioneer in the drama of social problems. His plays went straight to the basic questions of human conscience. He disturbed the accepted concepts of conduct, proposed new moral values, and, in his very dramas of disaster and defeat, suggested the imperative need as well as the inevitable triumph of truth.

Leo Tolstoy

[1 8 2 8 - 1 9 1 0]

*"Whatever he was—and he was almost
everything—he was also its opposite."*

T
HAT MAN whose purpose is his own happiness is bad; he whose
purpose is the opinion of others is weak; he whose purpose is
the happiness of others is virtuous; he whose purpose is God
is great." Tolstoy was only twenty-five when he wrote these apo-
thegms, but they were already indicative of his moral attitude.
Moreover, they characterized the man. In his gambling, lustfulness,
and domineering temper he was bad; he was weak in that he desired fame and continually did what he knew was wrong to do; his
love for his fellow men made him humble and virtuous; his love of
God, expressed in a wide variety of works and deeds, made him
great. Whatever he was—and he was almost everything—he was also
its opposite. Contradictions were woven into his fibers. He loved
life with an almost pagan responsiveness to his appetites, yet he
practiced self-denial and considered complete asceticism his goal.
His devotion to truth illuminates his writings, yet he was not above
twisting logic to suit his needs. Spiritual to the point of exaltation,
he was also a worldly story-teller. Gutter-coarse in his dismissal of
women, he was shockingly offensive. Yet his moral authority is ex-
ceeded only by the elevation of his creative spirit. "While he lives,"
wrote Chekhov in 1899, when Tolstoy was dangerously ill, "bad
taste in literature, every vulgarity, insolent or tearful, all crude and
exasperating ambitions will be kept at a distance, deep in the
shadow . . . When there is a Tolstoy, then it is pleasant and easy
to be a writer; even to recognize that one has not done or will not
do anything is not so terrible, for Tolstoy does it for all."

He was born Count Leo (Lyov) Nikolayevich Tolstoy, August
28, 1828 (according to the old style Russian calendar), at the
magnificent family estate of Yasnaya Polyana ("Clear Glade"), one
hundred and thirty miles south of Moscow. The Tolstoy family line
could be traced back twenty generations. In the seventeenth century Peter Andreyevich Tolstoy was a favorite of Peter the Great.
Leo's father was brought up in the pattern of the landed gentry of

the time, served in the army which defeated Napoleon, was captured and interned in Paris. After his return and the subsequent death of his father, the inheritance was so debt-burdened that he refused to accept it. Since he was responsible for the support of his mother and sister, he did what other young Russian noblemen were expected to do: he married a wealthy woman. His bride was not only rich but royal. She was Princess Marya Nikolayevna Volkonski, an unattractive spinster, five years his senior—thirty-two at the time of her marriage—but an unusually high-minded blue-stocking who spoke five languages and ably managed the eight hundred serfs and tenants on the vast acres of Yasnaya Polyana. She bore her husband five children: Leo was the fourth son, and there was a younger daughter.

Leo lost both parents in his childhood. His mother died when he was two, his father seven years later. He was raised by female relatives and educated by private tutors; he impressed them all as a bright and outgoing boy. As he grew older, other traits became apparent: stubbornness, intense pride, and equally intense introspection. He became sensitive about his lack of good looks—he resembled his mother rather than his handsome father—and, as a result, developed a shyness which made him self-conscious and graceless. A sense of being different made it hard for him to have friends and, because of his ability to see through people, he preserved the affection of only a few admiring intimates.

He was thirteen when his guardian-aunt Alexandra died and her sister, his aunt Pelageya, moved the family to her native city of Kazan. In due course Leo entered Kazan University and, at seventeen, was a much-demanded young man about town. He failed, however, to play up to his role. Although he showed the proper concern about clothes and other niceties and tried to act the snob, he had a congenital incapacity for social trivialities. Unlike the other young blades, he could not manage light romances with married women or flirtations with the unmarried; since he was a highly sexed young male, he frequented the brothels. The first entry in his diary, begun when he was nineteen, records an attack of gonorrhea "from that source whence it is customarily obtained." Before the end of his second year's studies, he decided to give up the university; his marks were low and his estimate of what he had learned was even lower. Besides, he felt that his place was at Yasnaya Polyana, which had been his share of the family property; he resolved to become an efficient and enlightened landowner. His determination was prompted by philosophical as well as utilitarian reasons. "I would be the unhappiest of mortals if I could not find a purpose in life—a common and useful purpose, useful because my immortal soul by virtue of its development will pass naturally into an existence superior and more suitable to it."

During the following four years, Tolstoy's life alternated between practical studies at Yasnaya Polyana and the gay life of Moscow. In the country he planned to improve the lot of the serfs; in the city he caroused and went into debt. He made resolutions for a better life, broke them, tortured himself because of his backslidings, made new resolutions, broke them again, and so on in an unhappy cycle of uprightness and dereliction, of guilt and distress. His diaries began to deepen in tone and bare the complexities of his inner life.

At twenty-three he became a "gentleman-volunteer" and, following his brother Nikolai who was already in the army, went to the Caucasus as a cadet. The irregular pattern of his life continued even in camp. He gambled and had to sell a piece of his estate to pay his debts; he had wild affairs with the beautiful Caucasian girls and had to be treated for venereal illness. The cycle of anxiety and anguish was re-established; he confessed that he had to struggle with his "three evil passions": gambling, sensuality, and vanity. Nevertheless, he saw action at the front, was almost killed when an enemy shell hit the cannon he was aiming, and in another engagement was commended for bravery. He was to receive the coveted Cross of St. George; but on the morning of the award he overslept and, instead of being presented with the honor, was sent to the guardhouse. His very "commonness" made him popular with the soldiers. Though short and slight, he was fabulously strong; he startled onlookers by lying on the floor and lifting two men who stood on his outstretched hands. His features were unprepossessing—his nose was too broad, his lips too thick, his eyes too small—but whenever he told stories or spoke intimately, the eyes were so expressive, the lips so full of smiles, that he was altogether captivating.

Although Tolstoy had never before thought seriously of being a writer, his diary was filled with pages that were far more than mere jottings and exercises. As he had written to his aunt Tatyana, "You recall the advice you once gave me: to write novels. Well, I've followed it . . . I don't know whether what I write will ever see the light of day, but it is work that amuses me, and I have persevered too long to abandon it now." In July, 1852, he sent his first piece of sustained writing, *Childhood*, to the editor of *Contemporary*, a leading literary magazine, hoping to obtain an opinion of its merit. The story was immediately bought and, when it appeared in print, caught the attention of critics who applauded the twenty-four-year-old author as "an unknown and remarkable talent." *Childhood* is an autobiography with a few fictional touches. This was typical of Tolstoy. Everything he wrote was to a great extent autobiographical, a transfer and heightening of experiences and feelings. In his earliest work he already achieved a style; there is no awkwardness or immaturity; everything is recalled with an understanding that is not affected and with emotions which are never maudlin.

Tired of his excesses, bored with life as a cadet, disdaining a future as a military man, Tolstoy spent his time reading, writing, and learning. A rapid assimilator, he acquired several languages, wrote fluently in French, and taught himself Greek so well that his translations surpassed those of a Greek professor. He was both relieved and shocked when he was transferred during the Russo-Turkish war and took part in the defense of Sevastopol. His experiences from his youth through his mid-twenties crystallized into an unyielding hatred of armies and a passionate opposition to war.

He was twenty-seven when he resigned from the army and, on the basis of his first success and a series of "Sevastopol Tales," found he had already achieved a reputation. For a short while he allowed himself to be lionized; but the precious and pretentious world of Bohemia was neither aristocratic nor coarse enough for his tastes, and he withdrew to Yasnaya Polyana. He was, however, too young to resign himself to a completely quiet life. Restless, unsure of what he wanted, he undertook the Grand Tour of Europe, returned, determined to marry, but failed to find the kind of wife he needed. He spent several hours each day at his desk, but when there were difficulties with the written word he believed that the afflatus had died and he thought of giving up writing. The critics conjectured that his early promise was never to be fulfilled, and Tolstoy did nothing to change their opinion.

At thirty-one he became enthralled with a new project; he determined to open a school for the children of his serfs. Previous sporadic attempts to educate the illiterate workers had failed, but Tolstoy felt he had been insufficiently experienced. He now undertook another trip to European countries and made a thorough study of their educational systems. He believed, first of all, that education should be free and voluntary. He also held that, contrary to the current conviction that education should improve morals, it should shape character by self-development; he sought (like John Dewey and the experimental schools which, two generations later, he strongly influenced) to further the individual's capacities by developing each pupil's self-expressiveness. Classes were conducted in an atmosphere of unhampered activity; originality was encouraged. Russian pedagogical circles strenuously disapproved of the innovations, but Tolstoy insisted that the progressive classroom might become a place of liberation as well as a laboratory.

In 1862 Tolstoy's life underwent a complete change. He had known the Bers family for years; the father was a physician, the mother a charming hostess, and the children delightful. At eighteen Sonya Bers, the "middle" daughter, had developed into a bewitching girl; at thirty-four, Tolstoy suddenly discovered he was in love with her. After a period of anxious ambivalance, doubt of the permanence of his feelings and fear that she might not reciprocate them, he proposed and was accepted. Sonya, swept off her feet by the writer who was her favorite author, worshiped him. They exchanged diaries; there were to be no secrets between them. Their family life promised to be ideal.

For the next sixteen years the promise was almost fulfilled. Sonya stimulated his writing, copied his voluminous manuscripts and, chore by chore, relieved him of the taxing managerial duties of the estate. She also bore him thirteen children. Yet, although Sonya was continually pregnant, she disliked the physical act of love and her obvious lack of response was bitter to Tolstoy's warm sexual nature. Nevertheless, the whole direction of Tolstoy's drives was changed with his marriage, and he began to write with a confident sweep. After several false starts, he devised a satisfactory plan for a novel he entitled *War and Peace*. In the book Tolstoy pictures himself as both Pierre and Prince Andrei; but the supreme feminine character, Natasha, with whom every male reader falls in love, was based not on Sonya, but on her younger sister, Tanya.

It took seven years before *War and Peace* was completed; as soon as it was published it was recognized as a gigantic masterpiece, an epic in prose. In *A History of Russian Literature*, D. S. Mirsky writes, "*War and Peace* is an advanced pioneering work, a work which widened, as few novels have done, the province and the horizon of fiction . . . [It excels in] the presentation of war as an unromantic and sordid reality, the glorification of 'natural man' . . . the satirical representation of society and of diplomacy . . . Tolstoy's personages are not classified with other characters in fic tion but with men and women of actual experience." Written on two levels, *War and Peace* is a combination of panoramic spectacle and social drama. The horror of battle, the death-throe struggle of great armies, the accidents of war and the sense of fatality are depicted on the largest scale ever attempted by a novelist; but here also are superbly detailed domestic situations, illuminations of a society which is both effete and barbarous, and the intricately tangled lives of human beings who are unforgettable. One of Tolstoy's principal aims, said Isaiah Berlin in *The Hedgehog and the Fox,* was "to contrast the 'real' texture of life, both of individuals and communities, with the 'unreal' picture presented by historians." In his monumental study, *Leo Tolstoy,* Ernest J. Simmons discloses the depth of Tolstoy's philosophy of history: "The great events in history in no sense depend upon the will of any individual, such as Napoleon; rather, they are predetermined. History, he explained, is not the slave of kings, but kings are the slaves of history. Behind a historical event is never one reason but a whole series of reasons, and all of them beyond the control of a single individual."

During the years of laboring on *War and Peace,* Tolstoy interrupted the progress of the book by writing short stories and articles. He also compiled a primer, an ABC book for the first grades, which, because it retold Russian folk tales and departed from the traditional method of instruction, was attacked. In 1873 Tolstoy began *Anna Karenina,* which appeared serially in the *Russian Messenger.* The entire novel came out in book form five years later, when Tolstoy was fifty.

Lacking the huge canvas of *War and Peace,* but as brilliantly detailed, *Anna Karenina* concentrates on a comparatively few characters and a contrast between the spiritually debilitating effects of the city and the primal sanities of the countryside. Essentially *Anna Karenina* is a study of conflicting passion and morality, the tragic story of a Russian noblewoman, young, beautiful, and sensitive, who is married to a much older man, and who falls irretrievably in love with an ardent young officer. In her struggle and surrender, her maternal tenderness and importunate desire, her doubt, defiance, and despair, Tolstoy drew one of the most memorable women in fiction. A realistic study of character, *Anna Karenina* is all-encompassing, stern and compassionate, understanding yet merciless, one of the supreme novels of the century.

All his life Tolstoy had been undergoing an inner conflict; he was beset with a plaguing sense of sin and a morbid, torturing fear of death. After he finished *Anna Karenina* his apprehensions grew too strong to be suppressed, and life as he was living it became insupportable. He felt the need of integration, a basic justification, a conversion to some moral stability. He observed that, in religion, the simple peasant found not only assurance but comfort and a calming preparation for death. Nothing else, he felt, met this deep spiritual need. At first he sought his salvation in the orthodox church; but his super-rational mind could not accept its dogmas and rituals. Finally, he "created" his own religion. He explained it in *A Confession,* drafted in 1879, which has been compared to the *Confessions of St. Augustine* and Ecclesiastes. Tolstoy's religion consisted of the imperative acceptance of God—a universal God common to all faiths —but a denial of the divinity of Christ. He believed, however, that Jesus, as man or legendary figure, was the greatest teacher of all time, the repository of all wisdom; he maintained that the Gospels and the Sermon on the Mount contained all the directives for good (or godly) living. As an implacable opponent of war, the commandment "Resist not him that is evil" seemed, if taken literally, to hold the key to peace on earth. "Tolstoy and Rousseau," wrote Janko Lavrin in *Tolstoy: An Approach,* "were at variance with their respective times largely because they were at variance with themselves . . . Unable to organize his complicated inner life, Tolstoy had only one course left: to force it into a simplified mold." He determined to combine all his talents to the service of God in man. "Individuality is weakness," he wrote to a friend. "In order to get rid of it we must find some purpose outside of ourselves. We must forget ourselves in work—as one does when making boots or plowing—in the work of a whole life." Opposed to art as mere self-expression or an esthetic for its own sake, Tolstoy insisted that art must be a medium for spreading the gospel of brotherhood and selflessness. He measured everything—art, education, personal emotion, public sentiment, government—with the yardstick of his credo. Such plays as *The Living Corpse* (known in America as *Redemption*), *The Power of Darkness,* and *The Light Shines in Darkness,* such moving stories as *The Death of Ivan Ilyich* and *The Kreutzer Sonata,* the novel *Resurrection,* and the controversial *What Is Art?* are deliberately, undeviatingly moralistic.

Tolstoy's conversion completely changed his personal life. The effects were as unforeseen as they were limitless. He wore muzhiks' trousers, coarse shirts, and often went barefoot. Since he considered it wrong to live idly on the labor of others, he waited on himself. He

controlled his passions and all his appetites; he became more continent, gave up smoking and meat-eating, wrote tracts on vegetarianism, capital punishment, and self-perfection. He began making
plans to release himself from the evil of money and the bondage of
property. All of these principles were distasteful to Sonya; the last,
in particular, was too horrifying to contemplate. She was an orthodox church follower and could not understand, much less sympa-
thize with, Tolstoy's spiritual dilemmas. Moreover, he had molded
her in the shape of the perfect mother figure, concerned only for
the family and its well-being. It was only natural for her, who was
not a peasant but a Countess, to want to enlarge the property, en-
rich the estate, and increase its wealth for the sake of the children.
Confronted by the logic of her demands, Tolstoy compromised his
convictions again and again. Instead of giving away the property,
as he had planned, he deeded it to her; instead of rescinding the
copyright on his books and presenting his works to the public, he
put them in her name. Sonya set up her own publishing firm,
brought out special editions of her husband's books and, being a capable business woman, profited handsomely.

The situation was grotesque. Tolstoy preached austerity and lived
in the midst of luxury. Undoubtedly he was tortured by his demon
of ambivalence, torn by rending weaknesses, but he did nothing to
check the resulting incongruities. Pilgrims, who were beginning to
seek out Tolstoy as their spiritual leader, were usually admitted by
a butler, who ushered them into the presence of a Count in a
peasant smock, making a pair of boots at a cobbler's bench. In
spite of the ridiculous inconsistencies, the influence of Tolstoy's
doctrines reached out beyond the divided family circle in ever-
widening radiations. Colonies were established that attempted to
put into practice all of Tolstoy's teachings. Young Russians, calling
themselves Tolstoyans, refused army conscription. His writings
were translated and circulated throughout Europe and America.
During the long famine that began in 1891 Tolstoy devoted himself
entirely to relief work, feeding whole villages with funds he collected from every country. In his sixties and seventies he was not
only the best known but the most venerated man in the world.

During the last twenty years of his life Tolstoy was considered a
menace by the Russian autocracy. The censor banned many of his
writings; many of them were illegally printed and sold under cover.
Tolstoyan conscientious objectors were imprisoned and exiled; Tolstoy himself was kept under police surveillance. At the age of sev-

enty-three he was excommunicated by the church. According to Simmons, this was not, as has been claimed, merely a public acknowledgment that Tolstoy had renounced orthodox religion, but the one public act by which the government could attack Tolstoy in an effort to weaken the esteem in which he was held. Although Tolstoy's doctrine of nonresistance was, per se, anti-revolutionary, his voice, continually raised in protest against prevailing injustices and iniquities, was inimical to the despotic state. "It was in this capacity," wrote Lavrin, "that he became not only a kind of 'conscience of his age,' but also a revolutionary stimulus . . . In spite of his negative attitude towards revolutionary activities, he cleared much of the ground for the last revolution which took place only seven years after his death."

In South Africa, half a world away from Yasnaya Polyana, a young Hindu seeker, Mohandas Gandhi, discovered *The Kingdom of God Is Within You,* and wrote to Tolstoy as his "humble follower." A correspondence ensued, and toward the end of 1910, Tolstoy sent a long letter to Gandhi, voicing his despair because Christianity refused to practice the teachings of Christ. "The longer I live," wrote Tolstoy, "and especially now when I vividly feel the nearness of death, I want to tell others what I feel so very clearly and what to my mind is of great importance—namely, that which is called passive resistance, but which in reality is nothing less than the teaching of love, uncorrupted by false interpretations . . . As soon as force was admitted into love, love was no longer the law of life. And as there was no law of love, there was no law at all, except violence—that is, the power of the strongest. Thus Christian mankind has lived for nineteen centuries!"

In his old age Tolstoy was visited by people of every faith. Humble devotees, as well as famous poets, politicians, and heads of state came to pay homage to the nobleman who had renounced earthly possessions to prove that "the kingdom of God is attained only by sacrificing outward circumstances for the sake of truth." At the same time, the discordant atmosphere in the Tolstoy home worsened in inverse ratio to his increasing prestige. Though he had been a domineering parent and an irritatingly obstinate husband earlier in life, he had also been a high-spirited companion, instigator of games and entertainments; all his children had respected and loved him. Now, however, their self-interests came into conflict with their father's peculiar, anti-worldly ideas. Communication dwindled and sympathy was withdrawn. Only his youngest daughter, Alexandra, allied herself with him; the rest presented a solid opposition with their mother.

The closing years of a man's life should be attended by a relaxing of marital tensions, an end of inquietude, and a gradually enveloping peace. It was not so with Tolstoy. On the contrary, he was perpetually harrowed and harassed. The situation resolved itself into what amounted to a venal tug-of-war between Sonya and Tolstoy's chief disciple, V. G. Chertkov, owner of a huge estate and, like Tolstoy, devoted to improving the lives of the peasants. The main points at issue were two. The first was the eventual disposition of the Tolstoy copyrights. Chertkov encouraged the aging master in his desire to make a provision in his will putting the copyrights in the public domain—which meant that Sonya and the heirs would be deprived of continuing royalties. Sonya was equally worried about a set of diaries which Tolstoy had kept secret from her and which were in Chertkov's possession. All Tolstoy's exasperations and all his wife's resentments had gone into the diaries they had been keeping for years. Now, in the final period of his unblest life, he was surrounded by diarists. Simmons states that "eight daily records were being kept simultaneously of the events taking place in this unhappy household. No family quarrel has ever been so fully documented." Sonya's mental condition, aggravated by long-suppressed hostilities and menopausal complications, bordered on the insanely hysterical. She was sure that the concealed diaries contained unfavorable references to her—besides, and this thought was most disturbing, who would have the publication rights to them after her husband's death? She wept and raved, frequently attempted suicide (never where she could successfully accomplish it), spied on Tolstoy, and charged him with unspeakable crimes. She even accused the eighty-two-year-old man of unnatural relations with Chertkov.

For thirty years Tolstoy had yielded to compromise. He could yield no longer. One cold October dawn—the hour was six in the morning, the day was October 28, 1910—Tolstoy left Yasnaya Polyana. He had no idea where he was going; he only knew he could not remain in the house another hour. His favorite daughter, Alexandra, caught up with him when he stopped at a convent where his sister liyed. The next day, as they continued their flight to an unknown destination, Tolstoy complained of a chill. He was running a high fever when the train stopped at the town of Astapovo and the stationmaster gave up his little house for the sufferer. It was soon evident that Tolstoy had pneumonia. By this time everyone knew of Tolstoy's escape and, thanks to a statement from Chertkov, the reasons for it. The world seemed to hold its breath at Tolstoy's bedside. Astapovo was crowded with reporters, photographers, officials, secret police, disciples, sons, daughters, and other relatives, the faithful and the merely curious. Sonya came but, at Tolstoy's request, was barred from the room. Not until the morning of November 7, when he was unconscious, was she permitted to see him. A few hours later he groaned, breathed heavily, and died. He was, perhaps, not the most flawless artist nor the loftiest soul ever produced by his country but, as has been indicated, he was the largest figure and the greatest moral force in Russian literary history.

Emily Dickinson

[1830-1886]

*". . . scribbled on the backs of recipes, on
brown paper bags from the grocer, inside
envelopes, and across small scraps of
paper . . ."*

THE POET who composed about eighteen hundred poems,
only seven of which were printed during her lifetime, was
almost overshadowed by the mystery surrounding her. The
legends grew into conflicting biographies and wild speculations;
even the undisputed facts were puzzling; and Emily Dickinson continues to haunt the literary world as an unaccountable ghost, imp-
ish and tragic by turns, perverse and puritan. As a girl she was said
to have had many beaux. Although she was not frivolous, she
was gay and quick-witted; her earliest writings—a teasing valen-
tine, a school composition, a few random notes—disclose an irrepressible love of banter. Her face was a contradiction, a contrast
of blandness and severity. Without being pretty, she was striking.
She had dark, bronze-color eyes, white skin, and hair that was
nearly Titian in brilliance. Declining a request for a photograph,
she portrayed herself modestly but memorably: "I have no picture,
but am small, like the wren; my hair is bold, like the chestnut
burr; and my eyes, like the sherry in the glass that the guest leaves.
Would this do just as well?"

Such self-references are rare. The physical events of her career
were similarly few and plain. Emily Dickinson was born in Amherst, Massachusetts, December 10, 1830. She lived and died in
the house in which she was born and, except for a few short trips,
never left it. She had a happy childhood with an older brother,
William Austin, and a younger sister, Lavinia. Yet, after her mid-
twenties, she isolated herself, wrote countless poems but refused to
publish them, saw practically nothing of the outside world, and
luxuriated in being anonymous. Her scorn of public notice was announced in the lines which open the second collection of her verses:

> I'm nobody! Who are you?
> Are you nobody, too?
> Then there's a pair of us—don't tell!
> They'd banish us, you know.
>
> How dreary to be somebody!
> How public, like a frog,
> To tell your name the livelong day
> To an admiring bog.

Emily Dickinson's father was a country lawyer, a legislator, and member of the Governor's Council. His children literally adored him. Emily's playful, irreverent, but always intimate references to God are full of father images, so much so that certain biographers have seen a parallel between Edward Dickinson and Edward Moulton Barrett, the possessive father of Elizabeth Barrett Browning. Unlike the English poet, however, Emily Dickinson maintained a quietly rebellious personality from the beginning. She attended Amherst Academy and Mount Holyoke Female Seminary, but she was a nonconforming student. Although she passed the routine examinations in rhetoric, geometry, chemistry, and astronomy, her attitude to religious instruction was strikingly unorthodox. She would not subscribe to the sanctimonious platitudes, nor could she echo the penitential expressions which were expected of her. "Fun is a word no lady should use," insisted Mary Lyon, first principal of the Seminary. "A young lady should be so educated that she can go as a missionary at a fortnight's notice." Emily wrote that she had "no particular objection to becoming a Christian," but she added in mock self-condemnation, "I am one of the bad ones." She persuaded her father that one year at Mount Holyoke was enough, and at eighteen Emily Dickinson faced a future with the speculative mind of a woman who would never willingly resign herself to the austerities.

Resignation, nevertheless, was forced upon her before she was thirty. Something occurred in her twenties which made the woman withdraw from the world. Poetry became her single solace, her confidential diary, and her concealed defeat. Written in secret, it was, as she paradoxically called it, her "letter to the world." Her immolation was explained by various biographers with scanty evidence and contradictory theories ranging from the plausible to the incredible. In 1930, in *The Life and Mind of Emily Dickinson,* Genevieve Taggard "discovered" two men who were involved in a vital way with Emily's broken romantic life. The first was Leonard Humphrey, who died when she was twenty. The second was George Gould, frowned upon by her father, and for whom Emily ostensibly abjured love forever, refused to go outside her garden, and became "the nun of Amherst." In the same year, in *Emily Dickinson: The Human Background,* Josephine Pollitt identified another and far more surprising candidate as the man responsible for the crisis in Emily Dickinson's life and the inspiration of her love poems: Edward Hunt, a dashing lieutenant, husband of the author of *Ramona,* Helen Hunt (Jackson), who was one of Emily's few close friends. Two years later, in *Emily Dickinson Face to Face,* Martha Dickinson Bianchi (Emily's niece, the only daughter of her brother Austin) expanded the local gossip and, in stage whispers, hinted at an abortive affair with a married man, enlarged upon Emily's refusal to ruin another woman's home, imagined a wild flight, a sudden pursuit, a violent scene of suppressed passion, and a melodramatic abnegation. In 1938 a book was published which should have ended the controversies: *This Was a Poet* by George Frisbie Whicher. This analytical biography examined the facts as well as the legends and traced the outlines of a straightforward and simple set of events. Whicher showed that Emily Dickinson had suffered two great losses before she had reached her mid-twenties. Her first "dear friend and teacher" was Benjamin Franklin Newton, an ardent reader of unusual literature and a thinker out of tune with his times. He was twenty-seven and Emily was barely eighteen when she came under his influence. Three years after meeting her, Newton married a woman twelve years older than himself; two years later he died of tuberculosis. "When I was a little girl," Emily wrote to Thomas Wentworth Higginson, an influential man of letters who had become interested in her work, "I had a friend who taught me Immortality; but, venturing too near, himself, he never returned. Soon after, my tutor died and for several years my lexicon was my only companion. Then I found one more, but he was not contented I be his scholar, so he left the land." The double loss was concentrated in her poetry, explicitly stated several times, notably in the lines beginning "I never lost as much but twice" and in two quatrains as poignant as they are famous:

> My life closed twice before its close;
>   It yet remains to see
> If Immortality unveil
>   A third event to me

So huge, so hopeless to conceive,
    As these that twice befell.
Parting is all we know of heaven,
    And all we need of hell.

The second parting was the more crippling. About a year after
Newton's death, Emily visited with her father in Washington. She
was midway between twenty-three and twenty-four. In Philadelphia
she heard a sermon delivered by the Reverend Charles Wadsworth,
admired the preacher, met him, and fell in love with him. He was
forty, married, pastor of the Arch Street Presbyterian Church. Devoted to his work, he was probably unaware of the emotion he
had roused in the heart of his listener. Emily returned to Amherst,
unable to shake off the spell woven by the minister and, unconsciously, by the man. There were two or three subsequent meetings
—chance visits rather than the clandestine trysts darkly suggested
by the townspeople—and an intermittent correspondence. Emily's
hopes for greater intimacy must have been faint; nevertheless, they
persisted. She dramatized them in her poetry; the woman and the
craftsman united to find an outlet for the secret dream, the cherished moment of recognition, the always deferred delight and final
disappointment. It is more than likely that the poet increased the
tension and heightened the pitch of grief, but it is hard for the
reader to draw a line between what was a fact, a wish, and its fulfillment in art rather than in actuality. The unrealized ecstasy is
sounded in dozens of lyrical outcries, most memorably in those beginning "I gave myself to him," "Mine by the right of the white
election," "God gave a loaf to every bird, but just a crumb to me,"
"The heart asks pleasure first," "I cannot live with you," "Pain has
an element of blank," "At leisure is the soul that gets a staggering
blow." The "element of blank" grew wider; Emily did not see Wadsworth, "the fugitive, whom to know was life," for twenty years.
He came to see her one day during the summer of 1880. Two years
later he was dead. His picture and a privately printed book of
his sermons were found among her few guarded possessions.

For twenty-five years Emily Dickinson had kept herself to herself. She had loved music, but declining to join with others in the
music-room, remained seated outside in the hall. She had sent little
verses along with jellies and flowers to neighbors and their children, but she never visited them. After Wadsworth's death she was
more alone than ever: "I do not yet fathom that he has died, and
hope I may not till he assist me in another world." Eight months

later she suffered a nervous breakdown. During her last years she seems to have been closely attached to Judge Lord, an old friend of her father; but he, too, predeceased her. She contracted Bright's disease in her fifty-fifth year and died May 15, 1886.

She had always declined to consider a publisher, and posthumous publication presented an unusually difficult problem. Over a thousand pieces of verse were unearthed in various places; they had been scribbled on the backs of recipes, on brown paper bags from the grocer, inside envelopes, and across small scraps of paper. There were often different versions of a stanza, and many alternate words were jotted down with no indication of a final choice. Lavinia Dickinson turned to Mabel Loomis Todd, a neighbor who had known Emily during the latter part of her life, and to Thomas Wentworth Higginson, the editor who had been consulted by Emily and who had been fascinated (and somewhat shocked) by her extraordinary images and verbal daring. Their first edited volume, entitled *Poems of Emily Dickinson,* contained 115 verses and appeared in 1890. Since that time a small library of Dickinsoniana has been published: seven volumes of her verses, including an omnibus *Complete Poems;* three different collections of her letters; a dozen varied biographies, memoirs, studies, introductions, and interpretations. There was even a novel (*Emily* by MacGregor Jenkins) which pretended to be "founded" on the poet's life and character, and, in 1951, a "shocker" (*The Riddle of Emily Dickinson* by Rebecca Patterson) which, based on a mass of misreadings and irrelevant surmises, sought to prove that the poet was a Lesbian. In 1950 all the Emily Dickinson letters, poems, and other papers were purchased and presented to the manuscript collection of Harvard University. There had been constant complaints about the careless editing and collating of the writings and an authentic edition had often been demanded. The critical task of sorting, arranging, and editing the disorganized manuscripts was assigned to the eminent scholar, Thomas H. Johnson, who in 1939 had discovered and edited the poems of the first important American poet, the eighteenth-century metaphysical Edward Taylor.

No one can determine how much of Emily Dickinson's poetry is a transcript of experience and how much is an extension or sublimation of it. In *The Bewitched Parsonage* (1950) William Stanley Braithwaite wrote: "Emily is the proof positive that what we call necessary experience pales to insignificance when placed in contrast to inner knowledge. She was a spirit that emerged independent of the material event." Braithwaite was writing about Emily Brontë, but the sentences apply with equal aptness to Emily Dickinson. Nowhere has "inner knowledge" so transcended the fact and so surrounded the experience with a magic which, surpassing the event, is an inexplicable creation. Emily Dickinson's characteristic is not a single quality but a contradiction of styles. It is, for one thing, a paradox of reticence and flamboyance. Emily Dickinson made no innovation in the physical form of her poems, yet she was an indubitable innovator. She used the simple four-line stanza—the strict measure of the New England hymn-tunes—to sound a new and independent note in American poetry, a note which many other poets have attempted to echo. She startled her contemporaries and fascinated her admirers two generations later with a condensed, almost conversational, idiom: a sharp poetic speech which was an unrecognized rebuke to the loose rhetoric of her times. Her odd, "suspended" rhymes and her wry assonances, like the purposeful suspensions and dissonances of modern music, were forerunners of the "slant rhymes" and "half-rhymes" characteristic of twentieth-century poetry. Her sudden shifts from rich to lean phrases, her rapid juxtaposition of the trivial and the tremendous suggested a new poetic vocabulary, and the audacious leaping images continue to delight readers attuned to the dazzling radiance of William Blake and the breathless vision of Gerard Manley Hopkins. It is no mean magic that can translate a dog's padding into "belated feet, like intermittent plush," that can watch a storm incite "a strange mob of panting trees," that can depict frost as "the blond assassin" and music as "the silver strife," that can see a train, like some catlike monster, "lap the miles and lick the valleys up," and observe evening sweep the sky "with many-colored brooms and leave the shreds behind." No other poet has accomplished more dazzling compressions; emotional tension is tightened in "death's stiff stare," in the word "zero" to describe the feeling of horror upon encountering a snake: "zero at the bone."

She wrote both as a bereaved woman and a happy, irresponsible child. Often, indeed, her writing is almost too coy for comfort. There is, at times, an embarrassing affectation, a willful naïveté, as though she were determined to be not only a child but a spoiled child—a child who patronizes the universe and is arch with its Creator. But the pertness suddenly turns to pure perception, and the teasing is forgotten in revelation. There is no way of analyzing her unique blend of whimsicality and wisdom, of solving her trick of turning what seem to be cryptic non sequiturs into crystal epigrams, no way of measuring her deceptive simplicity and her startling depths. The mystery of Emily Dickinson is not the way she lived but the way she wrote, a mystery which enabled a New England recluse to charge the literature of her country with poems she never cared to publish.

Mark Twain

[1 8 3 5 - 1 9 1 0]

*"He kept digging into the reader's ribs
until they were sore."*

THE SO-CALLED classic period of American literature (the period of Emerson, Whittier, Longfellow, Thoreau, and Hawthorne) seemed solidly established by the middle of the nineteenth century. After the advent of the Civil War, however, the genteel tradition was suddenly assailed and the dominance of New England culture rudely challenged by two barbarian voices: the high-pitched exhortations of New York's Walt Whitman and the broad, vernacular-twisted drawl of Missouri's Samuel Langhorne Clemens, known to the world as Mark Twain.

Samuel Clemens, the sixth child of John Marshall Clemens, a Virginian, and Jane Lampton Clemens, a Kentuckian, was born November 30, 1835, in the Missouri hamlet of Florida, which numbered about one hundred inhabitants. His father was a stern, self-righteous lawyer-merchant whose wildcat ventures and inevitable failures were notorious and whose headlong impracticality was inherited by his youngest son. The lineage was mixed, chiefly British and Irish, and although there was a later legend of aristocratic ancestors, the stock consisted of insecure migrants, restless trailblazers, itinerant Quakers, hardscrabble folk. The family was again on the move—this time from Tennessee—a few months before Samuel was born and, after settling in the cluster of log cabins and shabby clapboard houses that constituted Florida, John Clemens' prospects were so poor that they had to move once more. Sam was not yet four when the Clemenses established themselves in Hannibal, Missouri, where Samuel remained until he was eighteen and where, in memory and desire, he lived the rest of his life. The population of Hannibal was scarcely five hundred, but it was a world compared to Samuel's birthplace; he lovingly preserved its character, its climate, and its people. They appear, almost without transformation, in his backward-yearning books. Tom Blankenship, the vagabond river-rat, son of the town drunkard, turned into America's favorite ragamuffin, Huckleberry Finn, the boy who could not bear to be "sivilized." Samuel's mother is the Aunt Polly of the novels; his brother Henry is the model Sid. A long-suffering Negro, know in the slave quarters as Uncle Dan'l, became Jim, Huck's half-savage, half-noble companion; a widow, Mrs. Holiday, unconsciously sat for the portrait of the Widow Douglas; some strolling players entered literature as the fabulous Duke and the Dauphin. The farm where young Sam spent his summers is immortalized in various volumes—it was easily transported to paper because, he remarked, it was not a large farm.

When his father died, leaving the family more down-at-heels and out-at-elbows than ever, Sam was twelve. His schooling, elementary and haphazard at the best, ceased and the boy was apprenticed as printer's devil to his oldest brother, the well-meaning, fumbling, and vaguely idealistic Orion. Sam learned to set type, correct copy, and read any book that he came across. By the time he was twenty, he had found and absorbed most of the English classics and was an experienced journeyman printer. After having worked his way as far east as New York and Philadelphia, he rejoined Orion, who was publishing a paper in Keokuk, Iowa. Journalism was a career which both delighted and disillusioned him; it educated him beyond his expectations. "I was a newspaper reporter four years in cities," he wrote to a correspondent when he was in his fifties, "and I saw the inside of many things; and was a reporter in a legislature two sessions and the same in Congress one session— and thus learned to know personally three sample-bodies of the smallest minds and the selfishest souls and the cowardliest hearts that God makes." It was either an early sense of disillusion or an escape into adventure that made him think of trying his fortune in South America. He abandoned the fantasy, and apprenticed himself to a Mississippi pilot.

Sam was twenty-two when he began piloting. He got to know all the different kinds of steamboatmen, "a race apart and not like other folk," men who were close to his restless heart. "When I was a boy"—thus he began a series of articles entitled "Old Times on the Mississippi," which, in an enlarged form, became *Life on the Mississippi*—"there was but one permanent ambition among my comrades in our village on the west bank of the Mississippi River That was to be a steamboatman. We had transient ambitions of other sorts, but they were only transient. When a circus came and went, it left us all burning to become clowns; the first Negro minstrel show that ever came to our section left us all suffering to try that kind of life; now and then we had a hope that, if we lived and were good, God would permit us to be pirates. These ambitions faded out, each in its turn; but the ambition to be a steamboatman always remained." The book, said Bernard De Voto, "is a study in pure ecstasy . . . It records a supreme experience about whose delight there can be no doubt whatever, and it testifies to Mark's admiration of all skills and his mastery of one of the most difficult . . . Those years vastly widened his knowledge of America and fed his insatiable enjoyment of men, his absorbed observation of man's depravity, and his delight in spectacle." He might well have remained a river pilot, contented and completely fulfilled, but after four rich years, the Civil War began and all piloting ended.

The displaced pilot became a soldier—and a Confederate soldier —by accident. His pilot mate was a New Yorker who was outraged when the news came that South Carolina had seceded. "He was strong for the Union; so was I," he relates in the half-grim, half-farcical "The Private History of a Campaign that Failed." "But he would not listen to me with any patience because my father had owned slaves. I said in palliation of this dark fact that I had heard my father say that slavery was a great wrong and that he would free the solitary Negro he then owned if he could think it right to give away the property of the family when he was so straitened in means. My mate retorted that a mere impulse was nothing—anybody could pretend to a good impulse . . . A month later the secession atmosphere had considerably thickened on the Lower Mississippi and I became a rebel; so did he . . . He did his full share of the rebel shouting but was bitterly opposed to letting me do mine. He said that I came of bad stock—of a father who had been willing to see slaves free."

The light tone which characterizes the beginning of "The Private History of a Campaign that Failed" changes to horror when, after a succession of absurdities, the writer encounters death. The sight and thought of a dead man "got to preying upon me every night; I could not get rid of it. I could not drive it away; the taking of that unoffending life seemed such a wanton thing. And it seemed an epitome of war, that all war must be just the killing of strangers against whom you feel no personal animosity, strangers whom in other circumstances you would help if you found them in trouble, and who would help you if you needed it."

After Sam Clemens was mustered out of the army for "disabilities," he went west. His brother, Orion, had somehow become Secretary of the Territory of Nevada, and Sam went along as his brother's secretary. Once in Nevada, he learned that there were neither duties nor salary connected with his office and, at twenty-seven, he became a prospector, a feverish but highly unsuccessful miner. He claimed that he could tell pay rock from poor, "just with a touch of the tongue," but he was reduced to shoveling silver tailings in a quartz mill, and finally gave up speculation in favor of his old trade as newspaperman. It was while on the *Territorial Enterprise* in Virginia City, Nevada, that he wrote a series of humorous pieces and took the river pilot's call, "Mark Twain," for his pseudonym.

It is only recently that American humorists have been willing to write under their own names. In the middle of the nineteenth century, most of the professional fun-makers went to great lengths to get a laugh and, at the same time, conceal their true selves. They hid under such gaudy and unbelievable pseudonyms as "Petroleum Vesuvius Nasby," who was a serious printer named David Ross Locke, and "Orpheus C. Kerr," a bad pun ("Office Seeker") adopted by Robert H. Newell, magazine editor and amateur politician. Henry Wheeler Shaw, farmer, coal operator, real estate agent, and auctioneer, wrote comic almanacs as "Josh Billings," and Charles Farrar Browne, a reputable journeyman printer and lecturer, won national acclaim as "Artemus Ward." When Sam Clemens became Mark Twain, he did not scruple to imitate them. After becoming acquainted with Ward, he surpassed his predecessor in the use of anonymous anecdotes, contemporary backwoods humor, crude hoaxes, and wildly stretched tall tales. Twain was pleased when he was compared to the journalist-funnymen, flattered when he read that "his drolleries have the same air of innocence and surprise as Artemus Ward's." He did not reprove the later critics who rated such cheap, synthetic products as *A Tramp Abroad* and *Roughing It* above *Tom Sawyer* and *Huckleberry Finn*. There are unquestionable affinities with the easy exaggerations and grotesque clowning of the period throughout all of Twain. He strained for the laugh, worked hard to pile the guffaw on top of the chuckle, and depended too often on caricature and incongruity. But, although he used the same yarn as his fellows, he strengthened it with tougher strands, reweaving the old material into a new and longer wearing homespun. Moreover, he began to add twists of political irony and mordant commentary as, imperceptibly, the newspaper humorist grew into the social satirist.

Twain was twenty-nine when he left the *Enterprise* and went to San Francisco, where he got a position on the *Morning Call,* met Bret Harte, Charles Warren Stoddard, and other members of the West Coast intelligentsia. It was his first personal contact with purely literary people. Between his reportorial chores, he wrote humorous pieces for various California papers and, at the suggestion of Artemus Ward, sent some of his sketches East. When "Jim Smiley and His Jumping Frog" (later to become "The Notorious Jumping Frog of Calaveras County") was published in the New York *Saturday Press* toward the end of 1865, it became an overnight sensation. Suddenly he found himself a much-quoted author who had become a national favorite. He was sent to Hawaii (then called the Sandwich Islands) as a newspaper correspondent; he toured Europe, traveled to the Mediterranean and Palestine, and assembled his alternately shrewd and absurd observations in the hilarious *Innocents Abroad,* published when he was thirty-four.

The pattern of success seemed established. His following was greatly increased when he became an outstanding figure on the lecture platform. He fell in love with a picture of Olivia Langdon, daughter of a wealthy and important citizen of Elmira, New York, met her, and almost immediately after, married her. He moved to the East, pampered himself briefly as part owner of the *Buffalo Express,* and at thirty-seven, settled in Hartford, Connecticut. Here he devoted himself to a resuscitation of the past in a series of books which were sometimes sentimental, sometimes recklessly irreverent, and as he grew older, angrily misanthropic; but they were always characteristically his own, buoyant, bitter, eccentric, honest, and native to the core.

The impoverished small-town boy had come a long way. One success followed another as he, now one of the greatest of the great, mingled with the country's notables. The speculative tendency reasserted itself and, with a fortune in sight, the author became a publisher. He published not only his own volumes but the *Memoirs of U. S. Grant,* the best selling book of the period. He foolishly overexpanded; worse, he put all his money in a mechanical typesetter which, had it functioned, would have earned millions but which, failing to work, made him a bankrupt. Calamity trod close upon misfortune. At sixty, in order to pay off his debts, he undertook a world lecture tour. It was a financial triumph, but it ruined his health. His only son had failed to survive infancy, and while Twain was abroad his oldest and most cherished daughter, Susie, died. He was in Vienna when he learned of the death of his brother, Orion. Public honors furnished a poor counterpoint to personal tragedies. He continued to collect honorary degrees from various colleges in the United States as well as a Lit.D. from Oxford, but the rest of his life was a grim adjustment to unhappiness. His wife died when he was sixty-nine; another daughter Jean, stricken with epilepsy, died a few years later.

These catastrophes, according to De Voto, Twain's most penetrating interpreter, "brought Mark's misanthropy out of equilibrium . . . During this period [his last fifteen years] he wrote as much as any similar time in his life, perhaps more, but most of it is fragmentary, unfinished. Almost all of it deals with the nature of man, man's fate, and man's conceptions of honor and morality. There are fables, dialogs, diatribes—sometimes cold, sometimes passionate, derisive, withering, savage. Mark sees the American republic perishing, like republics before it, through the ineradicable cowardice, corruption, and mere baseness of mankind . . . Yet *What Is Man?* (published anonymously in 1906, but written before the turn of the century), the fullest of many developments of these themes, cannot be seen solely as a document in anthrophobia . . . Its fixed universe, with an endless chain of cause and effect from the beginning of time, permits Mark to compose many variations on the theme of human pettiness, but it also serves to free man of blame—and thus satisfies a need deeply buried in Mark's personal remorse." He castigated humanity, but he loved people, especially the people of his time and place. He made excursions into early English pageantry in *The Prince and the Pauper* and French history in *Joan of Arc*—two books which he considered his best—but the results were unconvincing; he was not at ease in any country except his own.

In his sixties Mark Twain still retained his hawklike manner—seemingly drifting but always ready to strike—his quick-darting eyes and his alert, beaked profile. The dark red hair and deep, drooping mustache had changed to a mass of white, and Twain accentuated the dazzling effect by wearing nothing but white clothes. He relinquished the white ensemble when his only surviving daughter, Clara, married the pianist, Ossip Gabrilówitsch, and for that occasion he put on the scarlet robe conferred upon him as Doctor of Literature at Oxford. He built an imposing house in Redding, Connecticut, but he did not live long enough to enjoy it. He always believed that his life was connected with Halley's comet, whose appearance coincided with his birth and when, seventy-five years later, the comet reappeared, he succumbed to angina pectoris and died April 21, 1910.

Twain's prime importance lies in his exploration of the American literary frontier. Pioneering in style and subject matter, Twain discovered and charted an entirely new domain. What he accomplished is not only expressed in the broadly democratic character of his books—books which palpitate with the vigor, customs, fears, dreams and appetites of These States—but is reflected in the native works of others following him. "All modern American literature comes out of one book by Mark Twain called *Huckleberry Finn,*" said Ernest Hemingway in a conversational aside in *The Green Hills of Africa.* "All American writing comes from that. There is nothing before. There has been nothing as good since."

Equally great was his liberating effect upon language. He exploited the infinite contrasts between the written idiom and the spoken word. More consciously than any previous writer, he relished and recreated the live vigor of talk, the color of spontaneous speech, the vivacity of the common tongue. His ease both with rhetoric and the vernacular made his writing unusually flexible, lucid, brisk, and often brilliant. An English reviewer said that Twain's chief trait was "an almost preternatural shrewdness thinly veiled under the assumption of simplicity." His wit was both bland and biting. He enjoyed the surprise of unexpected anticlimax—it was more than a trick when he referred to "the calm confidence of a Christian with four aces." Humorist and satirist joined forces in wide-sweeping aphorisms which run from sad little barbs to the extremes of cynicism, from tolerant mockeries to savage onslaughts on pretension, privilege, injustice, and man's generally cruel stupidities. Even a few examples reveal the range and quality.

> To be good is noble; but to show others how to be good is nobler and no trouble.

> Good breeding consists in concealing how much we think of ourselves and how little we think of the other person.

> Of all God's creatures there is only one that cannot be made the slave of the lash. That one is the cat. If man could be crossed with the cat it would improve man, but it would deteriorate the cat.

> Training is everything. The peach was once a bitter almond; cauliflower is nothing but cabbage with a college education.

If you pick up a starving dog and make him prosperous, he will not bite you. This is the principal difference between a dog and a man.

There is a Moral Sense and there is an Immoral Sense. History shows us that the Moral Sense enables us to perceive morality and how to avoid it, and that the Immoral Sense enables us to perceive immorality and how to enjoy it.

It is by the goodness of God that in our country we have those three unspeakably precious things: freedom of speech, freedom of conscience, and the prudence never to practice either of them.

Man is the Only Animal that blushes. Or needs to.

Prosperity is the best protector of principle.

If the desire to kill and the opportunity to kill came always together, who would escape hanging?

Each person is born to one possession which outvalues all his others—his last breath.

In the first place God made idiots. This was for practice. Then He made School Boards.

When in doubt, tell the truth.

It is difficult for us to realize the strength of Twain's impact upon his times. Today's readers regard *The Adventures of Tom Sawyer* as a perennial juvenile, a cornerstone in the literature of childhood; but when the book was reviewed in *The New York Times* on January 13, 1877, it was considered "unnecessarily sinister." "In the books to be placed into children's hands for purposes of recreation," concluded the reviewer, "we have a preference for those of a milder type than *Tom Sawyer*. Excitements derived from reading should be administered with a certain degree of circumspection." Nevertheless, the critic indicated that there was a reality about the characters and that, although Tom was "a preternaturally precocious urchin," he was to be preferred to the Sanfords and Mertons and other precious little paragons who were so superlatively and unbearably good. *The Adventures of Huckleberry Finn,* published when Mark Twain was fifty, caused less of a shock. It appeared nine years after *Tom Sawyer,* and readers had time to get used to the rough saga of sprawling life and casual death seen through the eyes of childhood. Like its predecessor, *Huckleberry Finn*—the only sequel in literature which is greater than the original—plumbed deep into the past and brought to light a longing which was not only a revelation of the writer but a page from the biography of America. In it Twain packed the windy exuberance, the fantastic bluff and bluster which, as an artist, Twain mocked but which, at the same time, he recognized and frankly enjoyed as an inseparable part of himself. From a technical standpoint, *Huckleberry Finn* is a triumph of linguistics, a mingling of literary locutions and the swaggering vernacular. Twain was by no means unaware of this. In an explanatory foreword, he listed seven different dialects which were used in the book, adding that "the shadings have not been done in a haphazard fashion or by guesswork . . . I make this explanation for the reason that without it my readers would suppose that all the characters were trying to talk alike and not succeeding." On one level *Huckleberry Finn* is an ignorant village youth's meandering account of his misadventures while helping a runaway slave to escape; on another level, it is a half-comic, half-perilous saga, a boy's odyssey which has become a national myth.

Nevertheless, even the most enthusiastic reader must admit Twain's imperfections; all the books are flawed to some extent and some of them are fatally marred. The frankly humorous books suffer from an excess of horseplay and, although Twain refined the substance while retaining the spirit, making a painful situation seem natural if not pleasant, he was unable to let fun enough alone. Instead he kept digging into the reader's ribs until they were sore. *A Connecticut Yankee in King Arthur's Court* starts as a charming and ironic fantasy but sinks into a welter of objurgations, violent attacks on the clergy as well as the aristocracy, burlesque mumbo-jumbo, and a constant intrusion of bad jokes. *The Mysterious Stranger,* Twain's most startling book, is spoiled by long lectures full of heavy-handed ridicule. The course of *Tom Sawyer* is too often deflected; it veers between an idyl of adolescence and shoals of mawkishness. Even *Huckleberry Finn,* that treasury of irresponsible adventures, raw wisdom, and rich superstitions, trails into a supposedly comic but dully protracted distortion of *The Count of Monte Cristo* and other lurid extravaganzas.

Twain was, in fact, so in love with adolescence that he indulged in a lifelong nostalgia for the vanished heaven that lay about him in his infancy. His idealization of immaturity is apparent in countless details, perhaps most revealingly in the treatment of his feminine characters. He was too timid to declare himself a misogynist, but he could not contemplate woman as candidly as he regarded man. There are no credible women, no flesh-and-blood females, in any of his books, only simpering, lace-valentine little girls, picture-book mothers, admonitory old maids, and strait-laced, persecuting widows. There are no love stories—Sandy's devotion to the Boss in *A Connecticut Yankee* is a mere dream contrivance—and, although Twain deals with plenty of rugged and presumably virile males, sex never raises its dangerous head. In a little known but significant short story, "My Platonic Sweetheart," the author describes his boyhood love for a fifteen-year-old girl, a love which was "not the affection of brother and sister and not the love of sweethearts, but something between the two and finer than either." The writer grows old but the girl to whom he always returns in dreams never ages. "It is forty-four years since I have known my dreamland sweetheart," he concludes. "I saw her again a week ago. She was fifteen, as usual, and I was still seventeen instead of going on sixty-three." It is also interesting to note that he was delighted with his wife's pet name for him; she called him "Youth."

The mawkishness and the misanthropy—sententiousness in reverse—have been forgotten. The honesty, the pleas for a decent world, the protests against meanness and cruelty and hypocrisy, keep Twain's pages radiantly alive. The soil—and the soul—are in the words. He forgot nothing and cherished every detail of his early life: the strange dialects and stranger incidents that developed into vivid characters, so that what often began as an anecdote ended as the portrait of a man and his times; the pigeon seasons, when the birds would come in millions and cover the trees until their weight broke down the branches; the prize watermelon "sunning its fat rotundity among the pumpkin vines"; the look of green apples, the wild 'coon and 'possum hunts, the raging of the rain on the roof and the white splendor of the lightning—"I can call it all back and make it as real as it ever was, and as blessed."

In spite of Twain's protestations, it is not a simple personality that is presented by the author. The reader must reconcile himself to a contradiction of brusquely sardonic disposals and garrulous affability, of chivalry masked as folly, of ingenuousness paired with ingenuity. Paradox is the very key to the conflicts which, while they made Mark Twain creatively mature, kept him from growing up emotionally. A self-confessed, self-divided spirit, holding all the contradictions together, there remains the rude but loving skeptic, the free and unflinching chronicler who was also the innocently swaggering, endlessly resourceful, and eternally irrepressible boy.

Paul Cézanne

[1 8 3 9 - 1 9 0 6]

*"He labored furiously to achieve an
effect of quiet."*

WHEN, IN 1952, one hundred and twenty-five paintings and drawings of Paul Cézanne were exhibited at New York's Metropolitan Museum of Art, the most ridiculed "dauber" of the nineteenth century was hailed as the most influential if not the most important painter of the past hundred years. Critics argued about the various aspects of his art—its revolutionary color concepts, its strangely plastic forms, its purposeful distortions, its emphasis on cubes and cones—but no one disputed its greatness.

The man who, more than any painter of his time, freed the artist from a dependence on the story element and encouraged him to take liberties with reality for the sake of a composition, was born January 19, 1839, in Aix-en-Provence, a little town in the south of France, so quiet that it seemed untouched by the busily progressive centuries. Most of the houses were built of the same soft stone which the Romans had cut from the nearby quarries; the faces of the townspeople had the carved look of antique cameos. The family, of Italian origin, got its name from the village of Cesena. Cézanne's mother was of Creole ancestry; she had been in the employ of his father who married her five years after Paul was born and two years after the birth of a daughter, Marie. Louis-Auguste Cézanne, a prosperous hat dealer who had become the town's leading banker, was a hard parent, harsh in manner and stern in judgment, and Cézanne feared him not only in childhood but until the day his father died. A few months after his death, when Cézanne was in his mid-forties and had inherited a fortune, the painter paid his father a rare tribute. "He was a man of genius," said Cézanne. "He left me an income of twenty-five thousand francs!"

Cézanne was an awkward and ill-mannered youth whose frequent rudeness was an overcompensation for an unnatural shyness; he never got rid of country manners and he seems to have cultivated a peasant's accent throughout life. His head full of drawing, he suffered twelve years of resentful schooling. When it became obvious that young Paul would not follow a business career, his father decided he should become a lawyer.

Meanwhile, the boy had formed his first and deepest friendship with another southerner of Italian descent, a youth named Emile Zola. At sixteen he, Zola, and another lad, Baptistin Baille, who became a celebrated engineer, were constantly together. They loved to hunt—or pretended to hunt—in the fields surrounding Aix. Besides game bags and guns, the trio took along books and spent most of the time reading to each other. "Sometimes," Zola recalled, "when an inquisitive bird perched not too far away we felt obliged to shoot at it. We were, however, such bad marksmen that we shot wide of the mark; the bird merely ruffled its feathers and leisurely flew off. This never bothered whoever was reading aloud and he continued without noticing the interruption." Their record as scholars is a curious one: Cézanne excelled in literature while Zola won prizes in drawing.

At twenty Cézanne hoped to be a painter, but he doubted his talent to such a degree that he continually wavered between the dangerous life of an artist and the dogged pursuit of law. His indecisions annoyed Zola who had gone to Paris to be a writer. In a particularly exasperated letter Zola reproached his friend: "You speak of throwing away your brushes . . . Regain your courage; take up the brush again; give your imagination full play . . . Is painting only a whim which took possession of you one day when you were bored? Is it nothing but a diversion, an excuse for not working? . . . Do one thing or another. Be a lawyer or really be an artist. Do not remain a nameless thing: a creature in a paint-smeared smock." Prodded by Zola, Cézanne roused himself sufficiently to face his father and, after many postponements, was finally permitted to join his companion in Paris.

In the metropolis, Cézanne was far from happy. Never at ease in company, he adopted a self-defensive surliness, a rustic's unyielding obstinacy. Proving anything to Cézanne, said Zola, was as easy "as persuading the towers of Notre Dame to dance a quadrille . . . He is stiff, stubborn, unwilling to change an idea. Nevertheless, he can be the nicest fellow in the world."

Unsocial though he was, Cézanne attended the Swiss Academy, an inexpensive atelier where impecunious young artists foregathered and where Cézanne met Pissaro, who was to become famous as one of the leading Impressionists. The young student was plagued with ambivalence. He was fascinated by the new techniques which broke up light into little blocks of wavering color, but he also wanted to paint like the Great Masters, and he spent much of his time at the Louvre making copies of Ingres and other traditionalists. He remained uncertain of his aim as well as his ability; when the Beaux Arts rejected him he retreated into his father's banking business and painted by stealth. Unfitted to lead a double life, Cézanne returned to Paris where, for almost ten years, he worked deliberately, without distinction and without the slightest augury of success.

In 1870 the Franco-Prussian war threatened to put everyone in the army. Cézanne ran off to Estaque, a little town which Cézanne not only dramatized but immortalized in paint. He lived there with Hortense Fiquet, a model who had become his mistress. Her people were farmers from the Jura district; she was nineteen, eleven years Cézanne's junior, when he met her. Two years later she gave birth to a boy. Cézanne registered him as his son and gave him his own name, Paul. Fearing his father's disapproval, he attempted to keep the affair secret; he denied the liaison and the existence of a child. The father, shrewd as he was suspicious, was not fooled. When Cézanne's deception was confirmed, he showed his indignation by a violent outburst and, worse, by cutting down Cézanne's allowance. In 1886, partly to appease the family, partly to legitimize the boy, Cézanne married Hortense—seventeen years after their first intimacy. By this time he had ceased to love her. He was rarely with Hortense, who preferred city life and travel to provincial seclusion. "My wife," Cézanne commented, "cares only for Switzerland and lemonade."

Long before his marriage Cézanne had cut himself off from the amenities of ordinary life. Like his habits, his studio was, even for an unsocial bohemian, disorderly; he distrusted his neighbors and regarded the world with unconcealed morbidity. In his thirties he was a tall man with stooped shoulders and knotty joints; the nose was thin and beaked, the eyes were deceptively soft; strangers were always surprised to hear an unusually loud voice issuing from the depths of a wild black beard. By the time he was forty his expression was cynical and, at times, sinister. He liked to paint himself with a gloomy expression, the mouth morose, the smoldering eyes peering sardonically from under a slouch hat, in the manner of a particularly crusty pirate.

He favored the Impressionists and was flagellated by the press. His paintings were despised and singled out for scorn as the fantasies of the village idiot, the diversions of "a butcher whose method reminds us of the patterns schoolchildren make by squeezing the heads of flies between the folds of a sheet of paper." Contempt was bred without familiarity. At the third exhibition of the Impressionists the critics hooted and the curiosity-seeking public cackled. "The laughs," wrote Zola, "were no longer smothered by the handkerchiefs of the ladies, and the men unbuttoned their vests to give greater vent to their guffaws." One of Cézanne's chief offenses was his intensification of the flesh color with green and yellow reflections instead of smoothing down all the skin tones into the soft-satin pinkness popularized by Bouguereau's prettified peasants and Cabanel's unblemished nudes—which led one critic to assert that Cézanne painted only in delirium tremens, while another critic warned pregnant women not to look at Cézanne's portraits lest their babies be born blotched. Even Whistler, whose experiments in color and design should have made him appreciative of what Cézanne was trying to do, declared: "If a six-year-old had drawn that [a portrait of Cézanne's sister] on his slate, his mother, if she were a good mother, would have whipped him." Landscapes which, fifty years later, sold for one hundred thousand dollars were offered at forty to eighty francs. But no one wanted to look at them, and those who were cajoled into looking turned away in disdain.

Nevertheless, Cézanne worked on doggedly, bitterly. He often used the technique of Impressionism and, although later he repudiated the Impressionists, he agreed with many of their tenets. "There are no lines in nature," he maintained. Everything was an arrangement of light and shade, a composition of shifting tones and colors. "The main thing is the modeling—and a better word for modeling is modulation." Sick of the critics' gibes, he turned against studio jargon as well as the taste of his compatriots; he condemned all mythological, historical, and legend-telling canvases as "bad literature." In 1882, when Cézanne was forty-three, one of his paintings was finally accepted by the Salon. The acceptance was accomplished by a subterfuge. A friend, Antoine Guillemet, a member of the Salon jury, exercised his prerogative to exhibit the work of a student; when the painting was shown, the catalog listed Cézanne as "pupil of Guillemet."

As he grew older, he became the victim of increasing inner conflicts. In a recent summary, Winthrop Sargeant wrote: "He painted women both as portraits and as nudes, yet he was so frightened by women that he often could not bear to remain in the same room with his female models. He was violently contemptuous of the conservative Salon painters of his time, yet he was pathetically anxious to have his own work accepted and praised by the very people he affected to despise. He was a deeply religious Catholic, yet he hated priests and had a habit of chanting the French blasphemy *Nom de Dieu* over and over again to a tune of the vesper service. A confirmed misanthrope, he lived in constant fear that fellow human beings were eager to 'get their hooks' into him." Nature was reassuring, but it was loveliest when it was inanimate. Humanity was horrible. He depended on the loyalty of Zola, but he broke with him when he suspected that the hero of Zola's novel, *L'Oeuvre*, an unsuccessful painter and a failure as a man, was based on his life and work. A naturally timid man, he tried to hearten himself by insisting that he was not only universal but unique. "There are," he said with transparently false aggressiveness, "two thousand politicians in every legislature, but there is a Cézanne only once in two centuries."

He exhibited only four times in twenty years and it was not until 1895, when he was fifty-six, that the dealer Vollard showed a large collection of his work. The public still reacted unfavorably, and the Salon, crowded with mediocrities, continued to reject him derisively. Cézanne abandoned Paris and retired to his birthplace in old Provence. He immured himself in the family home with his aged mother. Shying away from friends, he developed a phobia of persecution. "The world does not understand me," he protested. "And I do not understand the world. That is why I have withdrawn from it." "The meanness of people is so great that I could never cope with it," he wrote to his son. "Life," he shuddered, "is frightening." Nevertheless, he fought against depression and the diabetes which was exhausting him. The very light which he so loved hurt; the heat caused such a "cerebral tension" that any work was torture. Yet he continued to attack the problems of form and color. "I cannot achieve the intensity which is revealed to my senses," he groaned. "I am old and ill—but I am determined to die painting."

The death of his father in 1886 had given him financial security; he was now rich, but he lived like a day laborer. He refused to keep a horse and carriage but, suffering from fatigue, hired a man to take him to the places he wanted to paint. Even this he considered a luxury. One day he quarreled with the driver over the fare and, although he was an ailing sixty-seven, stubbornly insisted on walking. Overtaken by a storm, he fell in the road and was thoroughly drenched. A laundry wagon carried him home; he was delirious when put to bed. Next morning he insisted on getting up to retouch a portrait. A week later, on October 22, 1906, he died. His last act was a letter of complaint about some paints.

Cézanne's inner turmoils were not reflected in his work. He labored furiously to achieve an effect of quiet. Paintings that failed to satisfy him were left on the ground, pitched into bushes, or torn with the palette knife. Unlike Van Gogh's ferments, however, the turbulence never showed on the finished canvas. The keynote was serenity.

Cézanne's range was not great. He painted the same subjects—a hill, a vase with flowers, a group of card players—again and again. His gamut of colors was equally limited. He remembered that his one idol, Pissarro, had advised the elimination of black, bitumen, burnt sienna, and the ochres: "Never paint except with the three primary colors and their immediate derivatives." Cézanne did not go this far, but he held his color range to a few bright harmonies. He particularly liked arrangements of three hues: blue, green, and a pink tan. He used these colors not as mere accents in a design or as decorative units but as blocks of pure form, basic elements of structure. Using the small brush strokes of the Impressionists, scorning the classical conventions of light and shade, he "modulated" his pigments and defined his objects not by outlines but by subtly contrasting planes and patches of color, a continual change and "decomposition" of light. Although he strove for simplification in his landscapes, Cézanne abjured theories and refused to paint according to any formula. He would have been dismayed to learn that some of his conical and cube-shaped patterns would inspire a group of painters to call themselves Cubists and declare that Nature was essentially geometrical.

Cézanne glorified the inconsequential in everyday life with as much worship as he devoted to the colossal; his still lifes are as full of love as his towering landscapes. He never tired of arranging apples and oranges to express the wonder of common objects and intimate associations. For him an ordinary jug, a napkin, and a piece of fruit assumed importance and became as momentous as a mountain. He sought to communicate a tactile emotion by modeling in color alone; he spurned talks on art as literary nonsense. "Literature expresses itself by abstractions, whereas painting, by means of drawing and color, gives concrete shape not only to perceptions but sensations."

It was the unique "sensation" he was after. To that end he humbled himself before the majesty and mystery of nature. His paintings were more than pioneering arrangements of broken color; they were a happy escape from a world he did not care to understand. They became the epitome of peace. Theirs is no wild ecstasy but an orderly radiance, a purity which has the feel of permanence. The serenity was paid for with constant struggle and frustration. He painted Vollard, the first dealer to believe in him, but after one hundred and fifteen sittings, Cézanne was still dissatisfied with the portrait. He had failed to "realize his sensations" and could not coalesce his color planes into a solidly perfected form. "Still," he conceded, "the shirt-front isn't bad."

Emile Zola

[1 8 4 0 - 1 9 0 2]

"Physician to the body politic."

THE MAN who made heredity the basic theme of his epochal twenty-volume contribution to the literature of realism was a prime example of mixed heredity. His father, Francesco Zola, was a half-Italian, half-Greek engineer-adventurer, whose mother had come from the island of Corfu and whose father's family were Venetian. His mother, Françoise-Emilie Aubert, was a methodically thrifty Frenchwoman, born in the village of Dourdan, near Paris. It was in Paris that their only child was born, April 2, 1840, and was christened Emile-Edouard-Charles-Antoine.

The boy barely survived his second year. Although he recovered from a violent attack of brain fever, he was left with an extreme myopia; his features became slightly deformed and his left eye was raised somewhat higher than his right. It was at this time that his fairly prosperous father brought the family to southern France, where he had lived before his marriage and where he planned to construct a canal. There he contracted a cold which developed into pleurisy, and there he died, leaving his family no other provision than a lawsuit against the city of Aix. A complicated settlement dragged on, during which time all the Zola possessions were sold and the household was reduced to penury. Although Emile's youth as well as his childhood was spent in an atmosphere of depressed spirits and financial anxiety—frequent moves were made from one cheap lodging to another—Zola's mother managed to send him to the school at Aix as a full-time boarder.

Older than his classmates, he was not popular. His schoolfellows found him "affected," mocked his "Parisian" accent, and drove him into a self-protective timidity. He made two close friends, a gifted boy born at Aix, Paul Cézanne, and Baille, Cézanne's companion. Together, the three fifteen-year-old boys explored the wild countryside, swam in the turbulent waters of the Arc, and lay on its banks reading the romantic poetry of Victor Hugo, Alphonse de Lamartine, and Alfred de Musset. Zola imitated them all. During the next five years, while Cézanne was making his color sketches,

Zola was writing poems, ballads, and a three-act play in verse. His school work suffered while he held forth about the future of modern literature to his comrades and theorized about the function of art.

Meanwhile, things were going worse for his mother. Increasing poverty had been accompanied by periods of hunger; the Auberts, who had been supporting them, could no longer take care of their daughter and grandchild. There was practically nothing left to salvage. Mme. Zola was desperate. She borrowed a few francs and went to Paris, determined to get help from her late husband's relatives, and instructed her son to sell the remaining four sticks of furniture, buy a third-class ticket, and join her in the metropolis.

Zola was eighteen when he arrived in Paris. It was a garish city, rebuilt under Napoleon III, a hive of profiteers and parasites, of ready-made magnificence and amorality, a milieu which was the complete antithesis of the pastoral background of his earlier years. He was both shocked and delighted; "I had," he said, "a sense of profound stupefaction." A scholarship was obtained at the Lycée St. Louis, but he was an unenthusiastic, even unwilling, student. Once again he was ridiculed for his accent, this time, ironically enough, because he sounded provincial. But if he cared little for his studies, he cared even less about his classmates' derision. He devoted himself to two passions: reading and writing. The muse of poetry was his mentor and his mistress—even after he had become famous as the leader of the Naturalists, he considered himself primarily a poet. At this time, in his early twenties, he was not only a poet but a romantic one. Life was so ugly and reality so repulsive that he refused "to contemplate the dungheap" unless it was topped with a rose. "Let us eat, drink, and satisfy our coarse appetites," the dreamer declared, "but let us keep our souls sacred and apart."

At nineteen, Zola was near death again. An attack of typhoid fever was so severe that he spent more than two months in bed, and during his convalescence, his mouth was so inflamed with ulcers that he could not bear to speak. The psychological effects went deep; they were at the root of his later hypochondria and his preoccupation, as novelist, with disease. Another aftermath of his illness was the beginning of a change in the character of his writing; it was still illusory but not quite so recklessly romantic. Cézanne, it seems, had also been composing poems and Zola wrote to him: "You, old friend, are more of a poet than I. My verse may be 'truer' than yours, but yours is certainly the more poetical. You write with the heart; I with the mind." Set back by his illness, he found school worse than ever. He had vague ideas of becoming a lawyer but, unable to pass the examinations, failed to get the diploma which was "the open sesame to all the professions." He shrugged his shoulders, wrote a long and lugubrious poem, and decided to earn his living as a failure, an inglorious and unknown businessman. "My intention," he wrote to Baille, "is to enter as a clerk in the office of some organization. It is an absurd but desperate resolution! My future will be broken; I will rot on the straw of an office chair, become demoralized, and remain in the shade . . ." He was twenty when he got a job as a kind of bookkeeper on the Napoleon Docks. He had to walk two miles to work; the place was filthy; the salary was sixty francs a month. Unable to endure the conditions and live on the miserable pay, at the end of sixty days Zola was again looking for employment.

He did not look for it long. Abandoning himself to destitution, he borrowed to keep himself from starving, rented a drafty room built on a roof—a climb of six steep flights—begged a few pieces of furniture, pawned them from time to time, and became a drifter, a professional bohemian. "Laziness," he philosophized, "is a fine thing. You don't die of it sooner than of anything else." He urged his two childhood friends to join him in the "unmaterial freedom" of the Latin Quarter, and finally Cézanne, after a three-year battle with his father, was persuaded to come. The two shared not only the meager room on the roof but Cézanne's small allowance, until frequent quarrels, often stemming from Zola's dependence on Cézanne for virtual support, caused the friends to find separate lodgings. When Cézanne, restless for Aix, returned home, Zola was poorer and lonelier than ever. He still tried to hold on to the last pretty-colored remnants of romanticism, but they were being shredded by tearing gusts of disillusion. "In the city you see nothing but debauchery; in the country nothing but brutality." He looked everywhere for love, but the search was hopeless. "Everywhere sex; nowhere woman." He not only tasted despair but fed on it. "I have felt the cold horror of which Job speaks. Let them bury me and speak no more."

Sometimes he stirred himself to find work. But he was not a prepossessing applicant. His pinched face, queer eyes squinting behind spectacles, and an expression of poorly concealed bitterness scarcely recommended him to potential employers; his soiled linen and sleazy black coat, shiny at the elbows and frayed at the cuffs, were enough to terminate an interview as soon as it was begun.

Zola became ridiculous in his own eyes: a poet, a dweller in free-loving Bohemia—still a virgin at twenty-one. He found a prostitute, lived with her for a few months, and the sordid union was one more unhappy experience in a life that was rapidly being stripped of all illusions. The affair, wrote Angus Wilson in *Emile Zola,* "added to his hatred of poverty and the lives of the poor, but it also increased both his bitterness against a society which tolerated it and his compassion for the submerged." He was always scantily clothed, always hungry, too cold and almost too wretched to write. Guy de Maupassant said that Zola set traps on the roof for sparrows and roasted them at the end of a curtain rod. When the birds grew wary, he lived on stale bread dipped in a little olive oil sent from southern France. He had reached the depths of degradation when a friend of his father procured a position for him with a publishing house.

"Faith has returned," he wrote to his friends in Aix. "I believe and hope . . . I laugh a great deal." The steady wages from the firm of Hachette and Company rescued him from a past which "almost annihilated the future." His well-being increased when Monsieur Hachette, learning that Zola was a writer, promoted him to the advertising department at a higher salary. It was with a new point of view that Zola regarded his old writings. "I shall be able to draw certain details of life much better than a year ago," he wrote to Cézanne. "I hear better and see better. Senses which were lacking in me have come . . . There is a great source of poetry in Nature—*as she is.*" He gathered together the romantic stories he had already written and, after they had been printed in magazines, added others and saw his first book, *Contes à Ninon (Stories for Ninon)* published in his twenty-fifth year. A year later he turned his unhappy affair with the prostitute into his first novel, the half-rhapsodic, half-realistic *Confessions de Claude.* He dedicated it to Cézanne and Baille, and was as surprised as he was delighted when the book was attacked as indecent and, consequently, became a success. The portrait which Cézanne made of the Zola of this period shows a man in whom dream and determination are evenly balanced. There is purpose in the square forehead, firm chin, and small but aggressively tilted nose, but the broad lower lip seems to be tremulous and the eyes are dark with indecision.

Zola had discovered the outspoken naturalism of Flaubert, and his own work seemed thin and lifeless in comparison. He was overwhelmed by the honesty of *Madame Bovary,* for which Flaubert had

been brought to trial on the charge of immorality, and he envied
the exactness of observation, the cool objectivity, the living portraiture, and the relentless piling up of small but revealing details. He resolved to outdo Flaubert in accuracy and impersonality,
to achieve an expression unhampered by "good taste" and undeterred by tradition and the necessity to conform. This was the basic
tenet of what was to become known as "naturalism." Zola envisioned a kind of writing which would shock the world by its power
and range, a series of books from which nothing could be excluded.
"When I attack a subject," he said after he had realized his métier,
"I want to force the whole universe into it." Hachette and Company were of two minds about Zola. On the one hand, they were
proud that the young author was in their employ; on the other hand,
they were disturbed by the notoriety caused by the obviously autobiographical *Confessions de Claude*. After having been with them
for three years, Zola resigned and was immediately engaged by the
outstanding Paris newspaper, *L'Evénement* (*The Issue*) to write a
literary column. The publisher announced the addition of the
twenty-six-year-old Zola as "a young man versed in all the arts . . .
whose books, few but excellent, have already produced a sensation."

Two years before this, Zola had fallen strangely and violently in
love. In 1864 he had moved to new lodgings on the Left Bank.
There he met, and immediately became infatuated with, Alexandrine Mesley, whose parents had rented the rooms to him. She was a
comely young woman, recently the mistress of a medical student
who had left her, presumably for the summer, but who had not yet
returned. Though Alexandrine stormily requited Zola's passion, he
could not but contemplate apprehensively what would happen if
her former lover should return. Zola felt that the young man had a
prior claim over Alexandrine, having been her first lover. His happiest nights were troubled by the thought of losing her; he envisioned an outburst of melodrama, perhaps a duel, if the man ever
came back. Oddly enough, the medical student returned after several months and, upon surveying the situation, magnanimously
"gave" Alexandrine to Zola. Zola, relieved and grateful for so
placid a denouement, accepted the gift. After a while, Zola and
Alexandrine moved to a large, comfortable apartment. There, Zola's mother joined them, and the three lived in perfect harmony.
Six years later the couple were legally married.

In the next few years Zola greatly enlarged his field. He planned a new novel which would be both sensational and truthful; published a collection of essays entitled *Mes Haines* (*My Hates*), in which he declared his final repudiation of romanticism; championed the young painters he had met through Cézanne, fought for the Impressionists who had been denied recognition by the jury of the Salon, wrote a rapt tribute to Manet, whose "Déjeuner sur l'Herbe" ("Picnic on the Grass") had been attacked as lewd exhibitionism, and declared that "a work of art is a corner of creation seen through a temperament." He was twenty-seven when his novel, *Thérèse Raquin,* was published. He called this study of adultery, murder, and remorse, "an objective study of the passions." It was his first important work, a clinical piece of fiction not unworthy of Flaubert and justifying the much-quoted sentences of Taine: "It matters little whether the facts be physical or moral—they always have their causes. There are causes for bravery, pride and veracity, just as there are causes for digestion, muscular motions, and animal heat. Virtue and vice are [chemical] products like sugar and vitriol." Zola knew that he had "arrived" when the work was condemned as pornographic and the book went into a second printing.

Captivated by the theory of "determinism," Zola conceived a series of books which would not only show the influence of environment and heredity, but prove that such influence could be ascertained with almost mathematical certainty. He expected to chart the actions of fictional characters in relation to their background, upbringing, and "blood" as accurately as a scientist could determine the reactions of chemical agents in a laboratory. Hoping to create a major work on the order of Balzac's *Comédie Humaine,* Zola ransacked the libraries for actual monographs, case histories, psychological studies, dossiers, and interpreted them in the light of his own personality. The result of his researches, together with his detestation of a society which he felt had wronged him and debased countless other victims, was the twenty-volume Rougon-Macquart novels. It took Zola twenty-five years to complete the work, which filled ninety manuscript volumes. In order to fully document the thirty-two members of the Rougon and Macquart families, Zola frequented many milieus, from the grand houses to the underworld of the slums, pored over police records, and found no subject too unpleasant for his epical achievement. Each book was carefully planned as a separate unit, yet the volumes fitted together like stones in a massive many-buttressed structure. "In the entire history of intellectual creation," wrote Henri Barbusse, "there is scarcely another example of a man seeing so far in advance with such precision the concrete contours of a multiform work."

The first few novels of the series achieved nothing remarkable either in prestige or profit, but the seventh, *L'Assommoir* (translated as *The Dramshop* and *The Barroom*) caused a furor. Zola was accused of concentrating on filth, of wallowing on the dungheap that he once took such pains to avoid. "Literary street-cleaner," "poet of the disgusting," "purveyor of muck," were some of the invectives thrown at him, while the sales mounted and Zola became the most discussed author in France. The poverty-stricken youth was metamorphosed into the rich bourgeois who luxuriated in a summer villa, which he filled with his disciples and objets d'art in the worst taste of the nouveau riche. Because he had always been hungry, he gorged himself with rich foods and rare wines; he grew fat and pompous; his conversations attempted to be oracular but were only portly. His writing became long winded; his style coarsened.

Success, however, piled on success until, in *Germinal,* the thirteenth in the series, Zola became the social reformer. With its pictures of the hideous conditions in the coal mines, its mass upheavals and frenzied strikes, it inspired a whole school of writing which culminated in the modern proletarian novel. *Germinal* revealed an affinity with the philosophy of Karl Marx, and according to the *Encyclopedia of Social Sciences,* "implanted in its readers a faith in the revolution as an inevitable catastrophe which must precede the happier era when rival classes will be supplanted by a society of free individuals bound only by ties of cooperative labor and love." Other outstanding novels in the Rougon-Macquart saga are *Nana,* not the best but the most sensational and still the most popular of the series; *La Terre,* a raw study of the peasantry, a brutal work considered both his most indignant and most repulsive, one time characterized as "the irremediable, marked depravity of a chaste man"; and *La Débâcle,* a grisly account of the break-up of the Second Empire and the despair of a defeated army. The outcry against the unashamed picture of the workers' fierce struggles and absorption in the earth was particularly loud; it rose to such a pitch that the translator of the first English edition of *La Terre* was sent to prison, and the book remained inaccessible to English readers for more than half a century. Reproached for his excesses, Zola contended that an artist must learn to be lavish and "live at top pitch." Answering those who charged him with a fondness for prurience and moral disease, Zola insisted that his purpose was educational and, therefore, moral. He considered himself a physician to the body politic and regarded his most devastating disclosures as cultural autopsies.

In 1888 Zola, nearing the end of his huge chronicle, fell recklessly in love with Jeanne Rozerot, a maid at his summer estate. He was forty-eight; she was not yet twenty. In *Zola and His Time* Matthew Josephson describes her as possessing "a severe and uncommon beauty. Tall, gray-eyed, white complexion, it was with a certain innocence and freshness that she had come up from the provinces; having but recently learned her vocation, to serve in the household of the great author . . . Zola, dominated in his ripened years by such an emotion as he had resisted in the past, flung himself upon the young girl, tremulous with his inhibitions and desires." Jeanne bore him two children, both of whom his wife Alexandrine, at first furious but finally resigned, openly recognized. After Zola's death, Jeanne received permission from Mme. Zola to give the children their father's name and make them his legal descendants.

Zola was in his late fifties when "the Dreyfus affair" convulsed France and reverberated around the world. In 1895 Captain Alfred Dreyfus had been condemned for treason, degraded before his company, and sentenced to Devil's Island. The case had riddled French politics, shamelessly corrupt, but it had almost been forgotten when, two years later, Zola came across documents which pointed to Dreyfus' complete innocence. Zola was convinced that the real traitors were the heads of the army who were trying to explain certain "leakages" to the German military staff, and had seized upon Dreyfus as a scapegoat. Up to that moment, public sentiment had been against Dreyfus but Zola, stubborn and intrepid, came to his defense. The climax of his efforts was an open letter to Félix Faure, President of France. It was a terrible and moving document, ringing with denunciations and concluding with a series of irrefutable charges. Each paragraph began "J'Accuse!" as Zola went on to accuse the generals, the handwriting experts, the officers of the courts martial, and all those implicated in violating "human rights in condemning a prisoner on testimony kept secret from him . . . I have one passion only," he ended his peroration, "for light—in the name of humanity which has borne so much and which has a right to happiness."

For this Zola was arrested, charged with "insulting the Army," tried, and found guilty of libel. Although he was fined three thousand francs and sentenced to a year in prison, the verdict was annulled on appeal. By this time Zola had become a martyr to his supporters but a "dirty Dreyfusard" to the masses inflamed by the scurrilous, anti-Semitic, army-controlled press. When his case was reopened, Zola was forced to leave the country and, in July, 1898, landed secretly in England, where he lived for a year in exile under a pseudonym. Later, thanks to Zola's constant haranguing, Dreyfus was granted a new trial, his condemnation was set aside, and he was "pardoned," while his maligned defender returned to Paris. Zola refrained from acting either heroic or hurt; he was purged of rancor; he was above recriminations. "Truth having vanquished," he wrote, "justice reigning at last, I am reborn, and take my place again upon French soil."

While in England, Zola had begun a new series which he called *Les Quatre Evangiles* (*The Four Gospels*), consisting of *Fécondité*, a novel "about a humanity enlarged for the needs of tomorrow," *Travail* (*Labor*), a Utopia of social harmony, *Vérité*, a dramatization of the Dreyfus case, and *Justice*, which he never completed. He retired early one autumn night; the servants had made an unusually warm fire to ward off the chill. There was a defective flue; the chimney was stopped up, and all night long Zola breathed in the coal gas which filled the room. When the servants broke in the door, he was dead, asphyxiated by the carbon monoxide fumes, September 29, 1902.

Thirty thousand people followed the funeral carriages. There were orations by a minister and the president of the Society of Men of Letters. But it was the speech of a fellow novelist which was remembered. Ending a tribute to Zola as a fighter for justice as well as an author, Anatole France said, "He has honored his country and the world with an immense work and a magnificent action. Envy him his destiny and his heart, which made his lot that of the greatest: He was a moment's embodiment of humanity's conscience."

Thomas Hardy

[1840-1928]

*"He could not regard a pitiless universe
without pity."*

THE WORK of Thomas Hardy bridged the nineteenth and twentieth centuries; his half-romantic, half-realistic novels were the last expression of Victorianism, while his characteristically sharp and compact verses are among the first manifestations of modern poetry. Hardy was born June 2, 1840, in Dorset; the native landscape, which he renamed Wessex, remained his beloved background. Hardy's family tree was deeply rooted in the soil; his mother's people were farmers and his father was a rural stone mason. Hardy inherited little of his parents' rustic vigor. At birth he seemed stillborn; his nurse claimed to have brought him to life. An ailing child, he was kept from school, protected and taught by his mother. It is one of life's little ironies, the kind which Hardy himself would have appreciated, that the boy who was not expected to survive his sixth year lived to be almost eighty-eight.

At eight he was reluctantly sent to school, for his mother had taught him all she knew, and at sixteen he was finished with formal education. His father apprenticed him to an ecclesiastical architect for whom he had worked; later he sent him to study with a more famous architectural expert. At twenty-two Hardy won a prize offered by the Royal Institute of British Architects, although it seems that the award was given for literary merit rather than for any profound knowledge of the subject. Books interested him more than building, but in his twenty-seventh year he became a practicing architect. At thirty he went to Cornwall to restore a church, met the vicar's sister-in-law, Emma Gifford, fell in love, and married her.

He had already been writing poetry, but no one would publish it. He was, nevertheless, determined to give up architecture; though there were sermons in stones, there was no money in them, at least not for him. He hoped to earn a living by writing. Since poetry was obviously unprofitable, he turned to fiction. He wrote a novel, *The Poor Man and the Lady,* but George Meredith, another novelist who was also a publisher's reader, rejected it because it did not have

enough plot. Hardy immediately destroyed the manuscript and
wrote another novel, *Desperate Remedies,* in which the plot overwhelmed the characters. The book was published, although Hardy
had to pay practically all the costs; his only reward was a couple of
derogatory reviews. Two more novels, *Under the Greenwood Tree*
and *A Pair of Blue Eyes,* helped him to believe that he was essentially a writer; he was convinced of it when a magazine commissioned him to write a serial. The result was *Far from the Madding
Crowd.* It was his first financial success as well as a literary triumph
—to his discomfiture, one critic declared that Thomas Hardy was
another pseudonym for George Eliot. Full of the smells and colors of
the Wessex countryside, Hardy's fiction was both powerful and dramatic, but the power was often too strained and the drama without
distinction. Hardy had not yet achieved full control of his material.

In his mid-thirties Hardy was an interesting but far from arresting looking figure. He was slight, less than average size—barely five
feet six inches—and generally inconspicuous. His hair was thatch-
colored; his blue eyes had the sharp gaze of a farmer; a Roman
nose gave his face its chief strength. For a while Hardy and his bride
lived in London. At forty a series of internal hemorrhages threatened to end his life. Between the attacks he worked feverishly on his
next novel, hoping he would live long enough to forget fiction and
resume the only writing he genuinely loved: the writing of poetry.
Two years later he left London for his native Dorchester and again
became an architect in order to build his home, Max Gate, a landmark for sightseers. He was said to be abnormally shy and reclusive,
but Hardy mildly protested that he returned to Dorchester not because he was antisocial but because he enjoyed a private life more
than a public one.

Between 1874 and 1890 Hardy wrote eight novels and more than
thirty short stories, most of which were popular and profitable; it
was not until he published *Tess of the D'Urbervilles* at fifty that the
critics turned upon him. A tragic and outspoken narrative of
"maiden virtue rudely strumpeted," it was toned down for magazine
publication, but this did not save it from abuse. Vituperatively
called to account, Hardy replied with an even more uncompromising *Jude the Obscure.* Concerned with nature's laws as opposed to
man's decrees, upheld in preachment and violated in practice,
Hardy stressed an amoral earthiness and a grim fatalism that had
little regard for polite society. The critics shrieked at Hardy's
flaunting of taboos; they were vicious about his way of exposing the

tragedy of character and environment, of a man ruined by inner conflict and external cruelty, and dubbed the book "Jude the Obscene." When the work was published in the United States, the American editor changed the hero's illicitly conceived children to his young brothers and sisters. The book was, at the worst, lurid rather than lewd, yet it was not only denounced but defamed—one reader sent Hardy the ashes after burning the "filthy" novel. Hardy said that "the shrill crescendo of invective" completely cured him of further interest in novel writing. This was scarcely a hardship for him. Hardy said that he had been "compelled" to give up verse for prose in order to make a living—in later life he referred to his novels as "potboilers" and "wretched stuff"—and he returned with joy as well as relief to poetry.

He was almost sixty before his first book of verse, *Wessex Poems,* appeared. Containing lyrics and ballads written over thirty years, it was received without enthusiasm. *Poems of the Past and Present,* published four years later, fared little better. At sixty-four, after the critics had decided that nothing of any consequence could be expected from him, Hardy startled the world with the first part of *The Dynasts.* Four years later it was completed, a huge drama of the Napoleonic wars in three books, nineteen acts, and one hundred and thirty scenes. Critical opinion reversed itself; the *London Times* concluded that *The Dynasts* "combines, as only a work of genius could combine, a poetic philosophy with minute historical knowledge and a shrewd eye for the tragical and comical ways of men and women." Lascelles Abercrombie called it "the biggest and most consistent exhibition of fatalism in literature."

Honors suddenly descended on Hardy after he turned seventy. He received the Order of Merit, the gold medal of the Royal Society of Literature, honorary degrees from Oxford, Cambridge, Bristol, St. Andrew's; he was made a fellow of the Royal Institute of British Architects and—a gesture which touched him most deeply —was given the freedom of his own town of Dorchester. When he was seventy-two his wife died; two years later he married a writer who had been his secretary for years. It has been assumed that Somerset Maugham's much-debated *Cakes and Ale* is a disguised picture of Hardy's domestic life, but the retired author would not have recognized himself in the amusing but cruel lampoon.

Having held back the poetic drive most of his life, Hardy released it with renewed energy in his last years. His three richest books of verse appeared after he was eighty; he continued to write his characteristically knotted, delicately acrid, and clean-stripped verse until he was almost ninety. In his eighty-eighth year his throat became seriously inflamed and he succumbed to a cold, January 11, 1928. His ashes were placed in Westminster Abbey, but as requested in his will, his heart was buried near Dorchester in the countryside he loved so well.

Hardy never compromised between the truth as he saw it and the complacently unctuous taste of his times. He refused to concede that the Victorian virtues, the happily hymned "sweetness and light," prevailed. Even on his deathbed he declined to be comforted with what he felt were sanctimonious illusions. On the contrary, he asked his wife to read his favorite stanza from the *Rubáiyát:*

> Oh, Thou, who Man of baser Earth didst make,
> And who with Eden didst devise the Snake;
> For all the Sin wherewith the Face of Man
> Is blacken'd, Man's Forgiveness give—and take!

Expressing the revolutionary ideas of Darwin, Hardy rejected the concept of man as center of the universe and turned the lessons of modern science into literature. He believed that the elements are neither man's friends nor his enemies, they are supremely indifferent to him. Indifference is, according to Hardy, at the heart of creation. Fatalism was Hardy's reply to the pastoral idealism of Wordsworth, the indomitable optimism of Browning, and the unthinking pantheism of Swinburne. Hardy knew nature too intimately to believe it was benign. He saw the grim warfare of the farmer, the triumphs of drought and disease, the lifelong struggle and inevitable defeat of beast and man. If the universe was governed at all, it was governed by accident. God, according to Hardy, had ceased to be interested in humanity; if He thought of this world at all, He thought of it as one of His failures. It was not cruelty or kindness that ruled, only chance. "Crass casualty," said Hardy, "obstructs the sun and rain."

Skeptical of moralistic certainties and antagonistic to popular conventions, Hardy accepted the stern realities without joy. Recording a period of transition, belonging to the new century rather than to the old, he depicted a world of shrinking values but took no pleasure in the human dilemma. On the other hand, it did not embitter him. He could not regard a pitiless universe without pity; man's fight against all the odds gave the doomed victim tragic dignity. "He realized," wrote Siegfried Sassoon, "that the true satisfaction of life lies in imaginative conflict. Whatever their ultimate purpose, men are alive only while they struggle. When they grow aware of the futility of their effort, and yet strive to fashion something from it, they become noble." Another modern poet, W. H. Auden, praised Hardy's breadth, "his hawk's vision, his way of looking at life from a great height."

At first glance Hardy's prose is ungainly and his poetry seems clumsy and involved. But his resources are seemingly endless; he gives the lyric a curious astringency, creates narratives which are as gnarled and natural as an apple tree, and packs an epic in a dozen quiet lines. Such a ballad as "The Dark-Eyed Gentleman" is as racy and spontaneous as a folk tune, while "Satires of Circumstance" are complicated domestic dramas condensed in epigrammatic vignettes. In the end the very crudities win the reader; the most ungainly lines have an appealing awkwardness. Hardy brought a tart, talk-flavored idiom to modern poetry; he gave it not only fresh blood but tough sinews. Even his pessimism was relieved by fitful hope and offered its own kind of spiritual strength. In "The Darkling Thrush" Hardy took a storm-tossed bird, "frail, gaunt and small," as the symbol of courage. Lifted above despair, he saw the "blast-beruffled" creature as a spirit that could fling his song and his soul against the growing gloom.

> So little cause for carolings
>   Of such ecstatic sound
> Was written on terrestrial things
>   Afar or nigh around,
> That I could think there trembled through
>   His happy good-night air
> Some blessèd Hope, whereof he knew
>   And I was unaware.

Auguste Rodin

[1 8 4 0 - 1 9 1 7]

*"When the artist follows nature, he gets
everything."*

RARELY have there been more fluctuating estimates of a man's
work than the varied appraisals to which Auguste Rodin was
subjected. After Rodin's first efforts were scorned, he was
recognized as a pioneer. There followed a period in which he was
alternately honored, assailed, and worse, belittled. For a quarter of
a century his creations, regarded with faint approval, were largely
neglected. Then, a few years ago, Rodin was rediscovered and
ranked as the outstanding sculptor of the nineteenth century, perhaps one of the greatest of all times.

He was born November 12, 1840, in a squalid part of Paris which
preserved many of its ancient Gothic characteristics. His mother was
from Lorraine and his father, a workingman, was of Norman stock.
The Rodins were among the poorest in the district, and Auguste
had no organized schooling after he was thirteen. His gift for drawing was apparent while he was still a child. His mother brought
home the groceries in bags which had been made out of illustrated
comic papers and the boy copied the illustrations. Soon he began
to improve upon them and change the character of his tawdry models. By the time he was fourteen, his ability was so pronounced that
his parents hoped he might make a career as a commercial artist.
Unable to provide him with special teachers, they managed to get
him into the Petite Ecole, which concentrated on the decorative
arts. Although he was adept at pencil drawing, Rodin fell in love
with clay modeling and decided that this was to be his métier.

At eighteen he tried to enter the Ecole des Beaux-Arts, but the results of his examinations were unsatisfactory. He failed three times,
and his anxious parents were disconsolate. It was now obvious that
his father, who could barely support the family, could not continue
to send him to art classes, and Auguste had to support himself. He
became an apprentice, got a job as a journeyman ornament-
worker in clay, and was kept busy copying capitals for columns,
spiral scrolls, volutes, and occasional figurines, while he made

sketches of the foliage everywhere about him. He also tried his hand at animals, met the son of Antoine Louis Barye, the great animal sculptor, and Barye helped him to such an extent that he sometimes referred to himself as a pupil of Barye's. He next worked as a molder, then in a stone mason's yard and, at twenty-two, entered the atelier of Carrier-Belleuse who made designs for the porcelain factory at Sèvres. Here Rodin turned out statuettes, centerpieces, terra cotta busts, decorative knickknacks, and, incidentally, learned the mechanical processes of casting. He remained with Carrier-Belleuse about five years, and at the end of the time, rented a stable for the equivalent of two dollars a month. It was cavernous and, like all caverns, damp—there was a well at one end of it—but it was large, and Rodin, released for the work he wanted to do, soon filled it.

He was twenty-three when he came upon an old peasant with a work-furrowed brow, hard features, and a flat nose. He made a bust, called it "Man with a Broken Nose," and sent it to the Salon of 1864. It was not only rejected but reviled. The sculptor who was trying to carve the truth, the ardent lover of nature, was told he was far too naturalistic and that he had mistaken his medium. He returned to Carrier-Belleuse for a few more years and fed himself, physically at least, by manufacturing smooth and imitative trifles. During the siege of Paris in 1870 he served with the National Guard, and when the Franco-Prussian war was over, went to Belgium. In Brussels he worked with the Belgian sculptor Van Rasbourg, chiefly on figures for the exterior of the Stock Exchange.

Rodin was finishing a caryatid on the outside of a Paris building when he noticed a handsome girl with loose thick hair and frankly challenging eyes. She was nineteen; her name was Rose Beuret; her people were peasants in Champagne; she was earning a living in Paris as a seamstress. They became lovers. She posed for him whenever he was free and bore him a son. His parents liked her so well that she came to live with them, supporting herself and the child on the few daily sous which she earned by sewing shirts for soldiers. There were quarrels—she was possessive, Rodin was irresponsibly neglectful—and his parents usually took her side. It was, however, a solid and long-lasting union. As they grew older together, she considered herself fortunate, happy to be the "shadow of the sun." He described her to Malvina Hoffman, one of his pupils, teasingly but affectionately as a woman with "a violent nature, jealous, suspicious, but able to discriminate between falsehood and truth, like

the primitives, and possessed of the power of eternal devotion."
In 1877 the Salon permitted him for the first time to exhibit a
statue, one on which he had spent eighteen months. It was an evocation of pagan male beauty, and although he referred to it later as
"Man Awakening to Nature," he called it "The Age of Bronze." The
authorities were dumbfounded; it was so unlike the smooth and
prettified nudes to which they had given their approval that they
were shocked into dismissing it as *too* precise, *too* realistic. They
did worse; they leveled the charge that the statue must have been
cast from life and was, therefore, not an original work of art. This
type of "faking" was not uncommon, and Rodin set out to prove '
the baseness of the accusation. He designed a heroic figure and
made it larger than life; it was to be called simply "Man Walking,"
but the writer Octave Mirabeau saw in it an ideal representation
of St. John. Known today as "St. John the Baptist" it is, in its miraculous modeling, a sleeping stone that has been roused to sudden
and confident activity.

Like Whitman, Rodin believed that there was no part of the human body that was not beautiful. He not only accepted life in all
its manifestations but seized upon it with passionate avidity. "He
grasped life in its smallest details," wrote the poet Rainer Maria
Rilke, who at one time was Rodin's secretary. "He observed it and
it followed him; he awaited it at the crossroads where it lingered;
he overtook it as it ran before him; he found it in all places
equally great, equally powerful and overwhelming . . . Rodin's
'St. John' steps forth with excited, speaking arms and with the
splendid step of one who feels Another follow him. The body of
this man is not untested. Deserts have glowed through it, hunger has
made it ache, and all thirsts have tried it. He has endured and has
become hard. His lean, ascetic body is like a forked piece of wood
that encloses, as it were, the wide angle of his stride. He walks . . .
He walks as though all distances of the world were within him and
he distributed them through his mighty step. He strides . . . His
arms speak of this step, his fingers spread and seem to make the sign
of striding in the air."

As he progressed Rodin increasingly modulated his surfaces with
sharp contrasts. He set off deliberately polished surfaces against
equally deliberate areas of rough chiseling. The texture attained so
remarkable a degree of luminosity that Rodin was linked with the
Impressionist painters. "The edges of certain parts were amplified,
deformed, and falsified," wrote the American critic James Huneker,

"to ensnare the undulating appearance of life." Rodin's intensely lifelike and yet spiritually abstracted "Thought," a projection of pure meditation, is a celebrated example of his method. "It was Rodin's love of marble itself which led to this new development," wrote the English artist, Sir William Orpen. "He would leave rough the matrix from which his sculpture was hewn, so that the delicate heads and figures seem to grow like flowers out of the marble of their origin."

At forty Rodin presented a physical appearance to match his creations. Although short, his figure was impressive. Judith Cladel, his friend and official biographer, emphasizes his "medium height, large shoulders, and heavy limbs; placid and deliberate, he resembled a block of stone. Above the thick base his countenance, with its broadly designed features and steel-blue eyes, expressed an extraordinarily quick intelligence." The most characteristic feature, however, was Rodin's sweeping beard. As it turned gray, it made him look a little like an Old Testament prophet and even more like a Gallic Hans Sachs. He planned monumental projects and began "The Gate of Hell," on which he was to work for twenty years. Rodin's two favorite authors were Baudelaire and Dante, and "The Gate," thanks to its Dantesque inspiration, is an elaborate visual poem, an epic in stone. "He conjured all the forms of Dante's dreams," said Rilke, "as though from the stirring depths of personal remembrance, and gave them one after another the silent deliverance of material existence." From "The Gate" came so many of his famous figures—Adam and Eve, Paolo and Francesca, Ugolino, the group known as "The Kiss," among others—that he called it his Noah's Ark. Some have considered it a terrifying conception of the Last Judgment with the damned writhing in anguish; others have compared it to the unfinished tombs which Michelangelo designed for the Medici.

Rodin's fifties were his most fecund years. He received orders for portraits, bronze busts and statues, as well as groups for monuments. Cities commissioned him to glorify their native sons and local legends: for the town of Nancy he made a monument celebrating Claude Lorrain; for Damvillers a statue of Bastien-Lepage; for Calais "The Burghers of Calais," a group of the town's noblest citizens who, in the fourteenth century, saved the besieged city from starvation by offering themselves to Edward the Third. Rodin re-created the martyred six, individualized each of them. Instead of arranging them in a conventional group, he separated the figures in two dramatic rows, so that each man moved in a solemn procession and stood out surrounded by his own atmosphere.

It was the surrounding atmosphere that Rodin used as a vital part of his sculptures. "Sculpture," declared Rodin, "is the art of the hole and the lump." From his disposal of the "holes" Rodin shaped a conception of sculpture which instigated new schools led by such experimenters in "lumps" and "holes" as Henry Moore and Jacques Lipchitz. ("The names of Rodin and Cézanne will live forever in the glory of eternal light," wrote Lipchitz, "as the two geniuses to whom we owe our completely renewed vision.") Rodin also stressed the importance of "the cubic truth," the mathematical dignity, the supreme balance of volume and space. It might be said that he carved the air as well as the surface of the stone to bring out "the latent heroic in every natural movement."

Artists understood his power as well as his program. Critics came to respect him, but there were many reservations. Even while the savants extolled his vigor, they deprecated his "literary tendencies," his *"sentiment de l'homme,"* and spoke patronizingly of his "earnestness and enterprise." In *The Story of Art* S. Reinach rendered the judgment that "in addition to single figures and groups that Donatello might have signed, and groups of feeling or vibrant passion, he has expressed in marble all the visions of a heated fancy, often tending towards the monstrous and abnormal."

The charge of abnormality was brought up again when Rodin was fifty-six and his statue of Victor Hugo was exhibited. It had been ordered for the Pantheon and, to indicate the poet-novelist's native strength, Rodin had created a massive figure, nude, loosely wrapped in a great cloak. The academicians, who expected a properly frock-coated celebrity, were outraged. Rodin was accused of bad taste, bad form, and a fondness for erotic sensationalism. Another violent controversy erupted two years later when Rodin showed his huge statue of Balzac at the New Salon in 1898. This had been commissioned by the Society of Men of Letters who, after seeing the rough sketch for the head (now at the Metropolitan Museum of New York), rejected it. It represented the ultimate in sculptural impressionism—its monolithic rigidity reminded some critics of archaic Greek figures, some of the primitive Gothic, while others saw a resemblance to prehistoric menhirs. Rodin had not tried to reproduce the actual Balzac, who was notoriously short and fat, but the lion-headed spirit, the natural force, the tempestuous Balzac whom Lamartine called "the figure of an element." The newspapers stormed; a group of the municipal council considered the statue "an inexcusable disgrace." It was caricatured and condemned; the very critics who had accused Rodin of being too realistic now claimed he did not know how to be natural. The adverse publicity not only distressed Rodin but affected his health.

There were still many things to be done, many memorable portraits, such as the heads of George Bernard Shaw, Gustav Mahler, Charles Baudelaire, Joseph Pulitzer, and, one of the last and one of the greatest, Pope Benedict XV, as well as sensuous-symbolical figures. The small bronze jugglers and dancers which he made in 1909 and 1911 are as daring as anything he ever attempted; roughly surfaced, wrote Emily Genauer in a *New York Herald Tribune* review of an American retrospective exhibit in May, 1954, "they reach far out into space, so they delineate not so much a specific dance in motion or a pair of acrobats as they do a flowing-out of dynamic energy expressed through the metal forms and the space they measure."

At sixty Rodin was honored at the Great Exhibition in Paris when his still unfinished "Gate of Hell," the rejected bust of Balzac, and other notable works, including hundreds of his drawings which have the uninterrupted fluidity of the sculptures, were housed in a special building, the Rodin Pavilion. He began to lay down laws about his medium, and in the midst of heavy and rather regrettable pontifications, he made it clear that the true sculptor is not satisfied with appearance but with the penetration of substance. "I have invented nothing; I only rediscover," he declared. "Everything is contained in Nature. When the artist follows Nature he gets everything . . . The human body is like a temple marching. Like a temple, it has a central point around which volume is placed and spreads . . . The greatest genius of modern times has celebrated the epic of shadow, while the ancients celebrated that of light. If we now seek the spiritual significance of the technique of Michelangelo, as we did that of the Greeks, we shall find that his sculpture expressed restless energy, the will to act without the hope of success—in short, the martyrdom of the creature tormented by unrealizable aspirations."

Most of Rodin's aspirations had been realized before he was too old and feeble to be tormented by them. He knew that his work was not only the emanation of an unusually perceptive creator but an expression of the spirit of his times. The coming of the First World War dismayed him; it caused him endless doubts and may have caused his death. The fuel shortage in France was acute, and both Rose and Rodin continually suffered from the cold. On July 10, 1916, Rodin had a spell of dizziness and fell down a flight of stairs. He was put to bed, while various women, some designing and some merely sycophantic, flocked about and insisted on taking care of him. Rose was beside herself. She suffered more than ever from her habitual jealousy, but she was helpless; she was afraid to say anything which might offend the Master. The women quarreled among themselves to the extent of spite, slander, and hair-pulling; Judith Cladel had to be called in to establish peace. In September Rodin received a pension from the State. When he realized that Rose would not benefit from the pension unless she were legally his heir, he decided to make her his wife. He was not one for doing things in a hurry, but in January, 1917, he married the sixty-eight-year-old woman with whom he had lived for almost fifty years. Immediately after the ceremony Rose developed a violent cough—there was no coal available and the rooms were unheated. A few weeks later she was dead. Rodin survived her by only eight months. He, too, was weakened by the severe weather and spells of coughing. The cold grew worse, and on one of the bitterest days of a freezing autumn, he died, November 17, 1917. He and Rose were buried side by side in his garden at Meudon. The bronze statue of "The Thinker" sits in contemplation over their tomb.

Auguste Renoir

[1 8 4 1 - 1 9 1 9]

*"It must be indescribable and it must be
inimitable."*

AT TWENTY Auguste Renoir brought a few of his canvases to
Gleyre, one of the most eminent Parisian teachers, who
glanced at the work and said, "You are, I presume, dabbling
in paint to amuse yourself." "Of course," replied Renoir. "When
it ceases to amuse me, I will stop painting." It was, in the highest
sense, amusement which Renoir found in his world, an ever-
changing, unpredictable amusement which was also amazement.
Everything he painted delighted him—and he painted everything.
He worked in an unusually wide range of styles, from a slashing
palette knife technique to precise academic drawings, and was at
home in all of them. His subjects ranged from simple floral designs to complicated compositions crowded with nudes, from candid figure studies to elaborate family groups, rich and exuberant.
Never has pigment communicated a greater sense of pure pleasure.
Renoir's sun-drenched landscapes, his full-bodied bathers, his warm-
fleshed children glow with happiness and almost voluptuous health.

Renoir's first painting was not done on canvas but on porcelain.
He was born in Limoges, center of France's china industry, on February 24, 1841, and christened Pierre Auguste Renoir. When his
working-class parents moved to Paris, it was hoped that the boy
would become a musician; his teacher was the composer, Charles
Gounod. But even in grammar school his facility with pen and ink
was far greater than his dexterity at the piano, and at fourteen he
started work as an apprentice in a Paris china factory. When
machine-printing of pottery took the place of hand-painting, Renoir was out of work, but not at a loss for long. He turned his
talents to other commercial designs; he decorated fans and embellished trays so industriously that he saved enough money to pay for
tuition in Gleyre's art classes. Here he met Sisley, Monet, who was
to become his close friend, and others who were to attract and outrage the arbiters of the art world. His tastes were catholic; he
seemed to love everything that had the faintest spark of vitality. He

studied in the studios and salons—he sometimes boasted that he had lived "right in the middle of the Louvre"—but he loved the forest of Fontainebleau and the sprawling stretches of the countryside. Much to the surprise of his friends, two of his pictures were accepted by the Salon when he was only twenty-four; however, as soon as he began to work in his own idiom, his canvases were summarily rejected. Nevertheless, he was not a failure. He received commissions for portraits, gave up his shabby quarters on the Left Bank, and moved to a commodious studio on the Rue Saint-George. He was now thirty-three, a recognized painter so well established that he could afford to associate himself with the insurgents who had organized the "Societé Anonyme des Artistes, Peintres, Sculpteurs et Graveurs." The group consisted of more than twenty experimenters, including Degas, Pissarro, Monet, Cézanne, and Renoir. Their first exhibition was received with critical catcalls and general cries of derision. The second exhibition roused an equally violent press. Cézanne and Renoir were singled out for special reprobation; Renoir was told that a woman's torso is not, as the critic Albert Wolff said he had painted it, "a mass of flesh in the process of decomposition with green and violet spots which denote the state of complete putrefaction of a corpse." Even Manet ruefully whispered to Monet, "Renoir has no talent at all. You, who are his friend, should tell him kindly to give up painting."

Meanwhile the new group had been marked with a contemptuous label. Monet had contributed a canvas which he called "Impression: Sunrise" and the critics, ridiculing its vagueness, spoke of the whole group as "Impressionists." The young painters did not scorn the word; in spite of the aversion of Renoir and one or two others to forming a "school," they accepted the term. They even agreed that "treating a subject in terms of the tone and not of the subject itself is what distinguishes the Impressionists from other painters." Theirs was not so much a repudiation of reality as a reinterpretation of it. Placing the emphasis on sensibility, they established a new iridescent palette; they captured a shimmering, constantly shifting play of light "by applying their paint in perceptible strokes," wrote John Rewald in *The History of Impressionism*. "They succeeded in blurring the outlines of objects and merging them with the surroundings. This method permitted the introduction of one color into the area of another without degrading or losing it, thus enriching the color effects . . . Moreover, this technique of vivid strokes seemed best suited to their efforts at retaining rapidly changing aspects." The necessity of observing the infinite changes of light and shade, and the hope of translating the scintillations into a new vocabulary of pigment, took the artist out of the city studios into the fields and forests, to the edges of lakes and winding streams—Monet even had a room built on a small boat, a floating outdoor studio, so that he could watch the effects of light on the water from one twilight to the next. Like Cézanne, Renoir was quick to appreciate the art of "the immediate," the sensitive first impression. He was convinced that more could be expressed by the spontaneous vision of a leaf or a landscape than by an analytical study of its details.

In his thirties Renoir painted with ever-increasing vigor and brilliance. Even the antagonistic critics began to concede the radiance of his color. He surpassed his colleagues in the manipulation of light, giving his forms an amplitude and roundness which the other Impressionists rarely attained. In his forties, however, Renoir no longer considered himself one of the group. In common with Cézanne, Renoir found Impressionism too improvised, too uncertain in contours and too careless in composition. He began to distrust his own facility; he felt his colors were too soft, his designs too placid; he wanted stronger structures which would be "solid and enduring." In his quest for bolder designs and hotter colors he traveled south. He explored the semi-tropical settings around Algeria; he studied the pre-Christian Roman frescoes at Pompeii; he bathed in the glory of Michelangelo and Raphael in Rome and Florence. He never stopped observing, learning, and loving the multiple variety of nature. "Nothing can be taken for granted; nothing is stereotyped," he said. "The sections of an orange, the leaves of a tree, the petals of a flower are never identical. It would seem that beauty derives its charm from this very diversity."

As a young man Renoir looked frail; his brows were wide and pale; he waved the hair back from his forehead and nursed a delicate mustache. But he was bearded and sinewy by the time he was thirty. Unlike most of his fellow-painters, he was a mild man for whom every prospect was pleasant. He was not fussy or even fastidious about his models. "I am not hard to please," he said. "I can get along with the first slovenly scamp who comes my way as long as her skin does not repel the light."

Renoir grew old with grace and dignity. He had married the prettiest of his models, Aline Charigot, whose young charm is tenderly depicted in the large canvas, "The Boating Party Luncheon," and their life together was calm and harmonious. His wife bore him three sons, one of whom, Jean, became famous as a sensitive and successful film director. An idyllic existence was disturbed in Renoir's mid-fifties when attacks of rheumatism began. They grew worse in his sixties, and Renoir became an arthritic cripple. He could barely walk and finally had to be trundled about in a wheelchair. His hands were terribly affected; it was impossible for him to bring thumb and forefinger together. But he never stopped working, and though the spasms were often excruciating, the character of his painting was as bright and joyful as ever. It was said that his model had to fasten the brush to his impotent fingers with a kind of clamp. His son disputes this. "The truth is," wrote Jean Renoir, "that his deformed hands were still strong enough to hold a brush and were as precise as a compass. But the rubbing of the handle affected his parchment-like skin, and he had to protect it with a piece of linen. These skin irritations, added to his muscular pains, were an ordeal. His nights were worse than the days. He hated his bed—'this ridiculous invention'—and he wondered why modern science was so interested in preserving patriarchs 'like pickles in jars.' "

In his later years Renoir's canvases grew stronger and more opulent. He grew fonder of deep pinks, burgundy reds, rose-purples. At sixty-five he was questioned about his method by the American painter and critic, Walter Pach. Renoir replied: "I want a red to be sonorous, to sound like a bell. If it does not turn out that way, I put on more reds or other colors till I get it . . . I have no rules and no methods . . . I look at a nude; there are myriads of tiny tints. I must find the ones that will make the flesh on my canvas live and quiver . . . Shall I tell you what I think are the two qualities of art? It must be indescribable, and it must be inimitable."

As the pains increased the work expanded; with the help of an assistant Renoir turned sculptor. He even attempted—and accomplished—work of heroic proportions. There were no complaints. He refused to grow careless or complacent. In 1919 Renoir was still learning, still wrestling with his infirmities and the problems of paint. "I am still making progress," he said one day at seventy-eight. The next day, December 3, 1919, he was dead.

Controversy no longer rages about Renoir, although in the recent *Men of Art,* reprinted in 1950, Thomas Craven wrote: "Renoir's sentiment is commonplace; his color, especially in his earlier work, disagreeably sweet and vulgar; the huge nudes of his last years look as if they had bathed in warm strawberry juice." Other critics, stressing Renoir's discriminating taste, emphasize the quiet but none the less energetic joy of living. Renoir's women, for example, are warm and lush and, at the same time, childishly innocent; they have the fleshy luxuriance of Rubens' nudes without the Flemish painter's sensuality. Whatever Renoir touched took on a freshness, an abundance which was a kind of continual affirmation. Because of its ingratiating and happy appeal his style won a popular acceptance for Impressionism and helped to make that deprecated movement part of our everyday culture. His personal observation was not far from pure vision: lyrical, youthful, lifted with a gentle yet seemingly endless joy. When Matisse visited the aging painter, he saw that every stroke was causing renewed pain. "Why do you still have to work? Why continue to torture yourself?" inquired Matisse. "The pain passes," replied Renoir. "But the pleasure—the creation of beauty—remains."

William James

[1 8 4 2 - 1 9 1 0]

*". . . concreteness, facts, action and
power . . ."*

GENIUS was at home in the James family; theology, philosophy,
and literature were immeasurably enriched by Henry James,
Sr., William James, and Henry James, Jr. They were all independently wealthy—the grandfather, a merchant-financier, had
left an estate valued at three million dollars—and all of them turned
away from the prevailing mores and money-making careers. Henry,
Sr., whom Bernard Shaw considered the most interesting member of
the family, was a follower of Swedenborg and devoted himself to a
lifelong study of religious problems, particularly the metaphysics of
creation. William James believed that had his father been born in
a genuinely theological age, "with the best minds about him fermenting with the mystery of the Divinity, and God's relations to
mankind," he would have been one of the world's mentors. "Floated
on such a congenial tide, furthered by sympathetic comrades, and
opposed no longer by blank silence but by passionate and definite
resistance, he would infallibly have developed his resources . . .
and he would have played a prominent, perhaps a critical, part in
the struggles of our time, for he was a religious prophet and genius." Emerson attested that he was not only wise and gentle but a
"true comfort, with heroic manners and a serenity like the sun."

The family of Henry James, Sr. and Mary Robertson Walsh
James consisted of four sons and a daughter. William James, born
in New York City, January 11, 1842, was the eldest. His education
was begun in New York private schools, but when he was thirteen these were judged inadequate, and the family moved to Europe. There the children received kaleidoscopic and continually
interrupted instructions from governesses and tutors in London,
Paris, and Boulogne, as well as schools in Switzerland and Germany. William had a fair command of German and Italian, as well
as a smattering of Latin and Greek when, at eighteen, he came back
to the United States. Europe had not made him soft or effete; he
once had refused to join a gathering planned by his more sedate

younger brother because, he told Henry, Jr., "I play with boys who curse and swear." Nevertheless, he spent much of his time drawing and, at seventeen, decided to be a painter. His father objected to his choice of a career—he hated the thought that one of his sons should grow up to be an artist and, later, that another should become a novelist. Such pursuits, he announced, were not only unbecoming but "narrowing"; Henry Sr. wrote that he wanted his sons "to *be* something unconnected with specific doing, something free and uncommitted." But he yielded when William abjured the bohemian ateliers of Paris for the fashionable houses of Newport, Rhode Island, where he studied with society's favorite painter, William Hunt.

William's passion for painting lasted little more than a year—"there's nothing in the world so despicable as a bad artist," he concluded—and at nineteen, veering from anatomy to biology, natural history and physics, he abandoned art and entered the Lawrence Scientific School at Harvard. At the end of three years he thought that doctoring might be both distinguished and "practical" and went to Harvard Medical School, but a year was enough to convince him that he was a theorist rather than a practitioner. Louis Agassiz, the great Swiss-American naturalist, had been one of his teachers at the Lawrence Scientific School and when Agassiz organized an expedition to Brazil, William went along. He soon discovered that he disliked collecting and cataloguing, and reluctantly resumed his medical studies. The reluctance was so great that it precipitated a psychological block and a physical breakdown. In spite of a splendid physique James had always been subject to spells of nervousness; now it became imperative to save himself from what was an increasing neuroticism. At twenty-five he went to Germany to regain his health, complete his studies and, if possible, find out what he was best fitted to do.

He tried Berlin first, but he continued to suffer from insomnia, digestive disorders, backache, and general depression. Confinement to his room and inability to indulge in diversions drove him into an excess of reading, which, he wrote to his father, "in my half-starved and weak condition was very bad for me, making me irritable and tremulous in a way I have never before experienced . . . Although I cannot exactly say that I got low-spirited, yet thoughts of the pistol, the dagger, and the bowl began to usurp an unduly large part of my attention, and I began to think that some change, even if a hazardous one, was necessary." A doctor advised the baths at Teplitz, but the patient's condition did not improve. He traveled to Switzerland and France, sporadically listening to lectures and studying physiological works, but none of the "cures" were effective, and after eighteen months abroad, he returned to America as unstrung as when he had left it. At twenty-seven he took his medical degree at Harvard and stayed in Cambridge, ill and despondent, for almost four years.

It was during this period that James sank so low that he understood the morbid feelings of all sufferers, and as a result of something like revelation, suddenly recovered. He had been reading an essay of Renouvier on "Free Will"—Renouvier defined it as "the sustaining of a thought because one actively chooses to sustain it rather than any other thought"—and in 1870, William James declared in one of his notebooks: "I think that yesterday was a crisis in my life . . . My first act of free will shall be to believe in free will. I will abstain from mere speculation . . . and voluntarily cultivate the feeling of moral freedom . . . Hitherto, when I have felt like taking a free initiative, like daring to act originally, suicide seemed the most manly form to put my daring into; now, I will go a step further with my will, not only act with it, but believe as well —believe in my individual reality and creative power."

An act of will, the application of a drastic philosophy, had cleared his mind and healed his body. He no longer suffered from the fear of life and the fascination of death—"I take it that no man is educated who has never dallied with the thought of suicide," he wrote twenty years later. At thirty-one he was appointed instructor in anatomy and physiology at Harvard; three years later he became assistant professor. He was thirty-seven before he began teaching philosophy, and forty-three before he attained full professorship. He had married, at thirty-six, Alice Howe Gibbens, who "gave me back to myself all in one piece," and his happy wedded life was enriched by five children, four of whom survived their father. His acceptance of life as a hazard, a perilous and therefore spiritual adventure, was expressed as a basic philosophy to his wife shortly before their marriage. His attitude, he wrote, "always involves an element of active tension, of holding my own and trusting outward things to perform their part so as to make it a full harmony, but without any guaranty that they will. Make it a guaranty—and the attitude becomes stagnant and stingless. Take away the guaranty—and I feel a sort of deep enthusiastic bliss, of utter willingness to do and suffer anything."

As a teacher James was immediately popular; "his students," wrote his father, "are elated with their luck in having him." Inspired by Darwin, he inaugurated a course on the philosophy of evolution and followed this up by introducing the first course in America on the relation between physiology and psychology. His straightforward speech, as well as his bronzed skin, quick gestures, and sense of vigor, broke down the usual barrier between teacher and pupil; his loose tweeds made him look more like a sportsman than a professor. One of his students who became a distinguished philosopher, Dickinson Miller, recalled "his absolutely unfettered and untrammeled mind, ready to do sympathetic justice to the most unaccredited or despised hypotheses, yet always keeping his own sense of proportion and the evidence of balance . . . The very tendency to *feel* ideas lent a kind of emotional or esthetic color which deepened the interest . . . We *felt* his mind at work."

It was a mind which was subtle and keen, warm and witty. James disdained to rely on technical jargon and used colloquial speech to make the world of the mind as familiar as the physical world. "This universe will never be completely good as long as one being is unhappy," he said, and then casually added, with deceptive seriousness, "or as long as one poor cockroach suffers the pangs of unrequited love." When a class seemed inclined to take his logic for granted, James shook it with a flicker of philosophic raillery. "What is mind?" he once prodded a routine reciter. "No matter . . . What is matter?" he went on. "Never mind."

James was forty-eight before he published his first book, *Principles of Psychology,* and the volume has been considered not only his chief work but the central work of modern psychology. Seven years passed before his next important publication, *The Will to Believe;* but after that the books came with impressive frequency: *Human Immortality: The Varieties of Religious Experience,* an illuminated examination of man's power of vision; *Pragmatism,* which James subtitled "A New Name for Some Old Ways of Thinking"; *The Meaning of Truth,* which he called "A Sequel to Pragmatism"; *A Pluralistic Universe,* and various posthumous collections. The contents may have been recondite but the style was direct and audacious. Moreover, it was American to the core; the idioms were native and often as "down to earth" as the ordinary man's vocabulary. A much-quoted platitude ran to the effect that Henry wrote fiction as though it were philosophy while William wrote philosophy as though it were fiction. A definition of William's is memorable for its simplicity: "Philosophy is thinking about things in the most comprehensive possible way."

James's "thinking about things" may be grouped under three headings whose key words are meliorism, pragmatism, and pluralism. As a meliorist, James believed that although life is full of cruelty and injustice, it tends to get better and, what is more important, it can be improved by dogged human effort. He went further. He insisted that the world could be made better by changing the conditions under which most men live. This striving for improvement made him a stubborn crusader. He spoke up against the inequitable distribution of property, the martyrdom of Dreyfus, and the ruthless imperialism which was engulfing the world. A champion of unpopular causes, he disturbed some of his good friends by defending faith healers and opposing the Spanish-American War. He urged men to find a "moral equivalent" for war, entreating them to drain marshes, dig canals, combat disease, and fight drought and pestilence with the same passion which drives men to fight each other. "Man wants to be stretched to his utmost—if not in one way, then in another."

It was James's feeling for what was actual, attainable as well as ascertainable, which led him away from abstractions, fixed principles, and closed systems toward concreteness, facts, action and power. This was pragmatism, and it was pragmatism which made him challenge ready-made "pure reason" and the search for absolute certainty with his violent "Damn the absolute!" James discovered the seminal idea in Charles Peirce's "How to Make Our Ideas Clear," but he enlarged it and gave it a new direction. "Pragmatism represents a perfectly familiar attitude in philosophy, the empiricist attitude [the doctrine that truth is based on observation and experience], but it represents it, as it seems to me, both in a more radical and in a less objectionable form than it has ever yet assumed . . . Pragmatism is uncomfortable away from facts. Rationalism is comfortable only in the presence of abstractions. This pragmatist talk about truths in the plural, about their utility and satisfactoriness, about the success with which they 'work,' suggests to the typical intellectualist mind a sort of coarse, lame, second-rate makeshift article of truth. Such truths are not real truth. Such tests are merely subjective. As against this, objective truth must be something non-utilitarian, haughty, refined, remote, august, exalted. It must be an absolute correspondence of our thoughts with an equally absolute reality. It must be what we ought to think unconditionally. The conditioned ways in which we do think are so much irrelevance and matter for psychology. Down with psychology, up with logic, in all this question.

"See the exquisite contrast of the types of mind! The pragmatist clings to facts and concreteness, observes truth at its work in particular cases, and generalizes. Truth, for him, becomes a class-name for all sorts of definite working-values in experience. For the rationalist it remains a pure abstraction. When the pragmatist undertakes to show in detail just why we must defer, the rationalist is unable to recognize the concretes from which his own abstraction is taken. He accuses us of denying truth; whereas we have only sought to trace exactly why people follow it and always ought to follow it."

Pragmatism was, therefore, not only an attack on dogmas, the dead hand of unalterable rules, but upon the concept of fixed truths. James agreed with Keats that beauty was truth, truth beauty, but he added that both were relative. Goodness also was neither primary nor absolute; goodness, too, was consequential, dependent upon conditions and the individual point of view. "Neither the whole of truth nor the whole of good is revealed to any single observer, although each observer gains a partial superiority of insight from the peculiar position in which he stands." Truth, to be true to its promise, must be efficacious and successful; it might almost be said that truth is manifest in consequences. The true, said James, "is only the expedient in the way of our thinking, just as 'the right' is only the expedient in the way of our behaving . . . Truth is one species of good and not, as is usually supposed, a category distinct from good, and coordinate with it. The true is the name of whatever proves itself to be good in the way of belief, and good, too, for definite, assignable reasons."

Pluralism was James's answer to monism, the doctrine that there is only one kind of substance or ultimate reality. James mocked the monists: " 'The world is One!'—the formula becomes a sort of number-worship. 'Three' and 'Seven' have, it is true, been reckoned as sacred numbers. But abstractly taken, why is 'one' more excellent than 'forty-three' or than 'two million and ten'?" James was in favor of unlimited possibilities, of wide ranging contradictions and conflicts; instead of a universe he offered a multiverse. Even God, to James, was not a solitary supreme deity, immutable and imperturbable. He was *primus inter pares,* first among equals, but He was only one of the elemental forces, "one helper in the midst of all the shapers of the great world's fate." The appeal of such a God is that

He, too, is involved with the struggles of His creatures. "Suppose," wrote James, "that the world's author put the case to you before creation, saying: 'I am going to make a world not certain to be saved, a world the perfection of which shall be conditioned merely, the condition being that each agent does his level best. I offer you the chance of taking part in such a world. Its safety, you see, is unwarranted. It is a real adventure, with real danger, yet it may win through' . . . Will you trust yourself and trust the other agents enough to face the risk?" It is man's spiritual strength, his essential courage, which is being tested in a dynamic multiverse. "A monistic world is for us a dead world," wrote Will Durant in *The Story of Philosophy.* "In a finished universe individuality is a delusion; the monist assures us that we are all bits of one mosaic substance. But in an unfinished world . . . we can be free; it is a world of chance and not of fate, and what we are or do may alter everything." It is a man's privilege that he can choose. "If there be any life that is really better that we should lead," James added, "and if there be any idea which, if believed in, would help us to lead that life, then it would be really better for us to believe in that idea, unless, indeed, belief in it incidentally clashed with other greater vital benefits."

At fifty-eight James went abroad to deliver the Gifford Lectures at Edinburgh; they were the basis for his *Varieties of Religious Experience,* which the critics handled warily. *The New York Times* conceded that "writing more fresh and vivid cannot easily be imagined," but went on to warn that "the whole tribe of mind-curers, theosophists, and the like will take great comfort in his concessions; the more steady-going will insist that his data are too pathological to furnish a sound basis for a theory of religion." Unperturbed and open-minded, curious as well as tolerant, James joined the Society for Psychical Research and became its president. He retired from his Harvard professorship at sixty-five and, a year later, delivered the Hibbert Lectures at Oxford. He was sixty-eight, back in America, when he learned that his brother Henry was seriously ill in England, and went over to bring him back to America. It was William who, having suffered an earlier heart injury, succumbed. He had hardly reached his country home in Chocorua, New Hampshire, when his heart gave out and he died, August 26, 1910.

To the last, James refused to suggest metaphysical shortcuts or proffer comforting finalities. "There is no conclusion," he put down in the last sentences he ever wrote. "What has concluded that we might conclude in regard to it? There are no fortunes to be told and there is no advice to be given. Farewell." It was not abstruse theorizing but activity which stimulated his spirit, a spirit that was both "tough-minded" and "tender-minded." Instead of accepting the old duel, or dualism, between mind and matter, James saw life as a continuous experience, a progress in which things and thoughts, objects and their relations, were equally integrated. His concept of pragmatism was assailed as a yielding to the time-spirit of an expanding industrialism, to efficiency, to truth only insofar as it worked; the critic James Huneker called it "a philosophy for philistines." But although James was prone to appraise an idea in terms of its "cash value," and he conceived pragmatism chiefly as "a method for getting at the practical consequences," he opposed a literal application of expediency. He fought for inarticulate and misused humanity against the smugness, apathy, and easy triumphs of materialism. He implored his fellows to stop idolizing "the bitch goddess, Success." In a time of complacent conventions, he railed at the worship of genteel security, missing "the element of precipitousness, of strength and strenuousness, intensity and danger . . . of human nature strained to its uttermost, yet getting through alive and then turning its back on its success to pursue another rarer and more arduous still."

The influence of William James is as definite as it is demonstrable. It affected not only the political thinking of men like President Woodrow Wilson and both Roosevelts, but the juridical opinions of such great jurists as Oliver Wendell Holmes and Louis D. Brandeis, the social theories of Jane Addams, and the spiritual convictions of incalculably large groups of people. "James broke new ground," wrote Lloyd Morris, "in making religious mysticism scientifically respectable. This enabled the spiritually adrift to yield to their intuitions without violating their intelligence."

It was to the intelligence that James ultimately appealed. He was sad but never cynical about human disinclination to discard old prejudices and entertain a new perception of truth. Healthy-minded and hopeful, he never failed to believe in the perfectibility of this imperfect world and, in spite of every limitation, the limitless capacities of man.

Henry James

[1843-1916]

*"His readers are divided into two
unalterably opposed camps."*

EW AUTHORS have had so colorless a private history as Henry
James, but no modern novelist ever produced anything more
subtly colored than his *The Portrait of a Lady, The Wings of
the Dove, The Ambassadors,* and *The Golden Bowl.* There was no
lack of color in James's ancestry. His grandfather, who had emigrated from Ireland, left one of the three greatest fortunes of his
day; his father, who had turned his back on business, became a
mystic, a follower of Fourier and an apostle of Swedenborg. From
his grandfather, Henry James inherited an appreciation of wealth;
from his father, he acquired a scorn of it.

He was born April 15, 1843, in New York City, the second son of
Henry James, Sr., and Mary Robertson Walsh James. His brother
William was a little more than a year older; there were two
younger brothers (Garth Wilkinson and Robertson), both of whom
he survived, and a sister, Alice, the youngest of the children. Since
his father continually oscillated between America and Europe,
Henry was practically born a cosmopolite—he was barely a year old
when he was taken on the first of many trips abroad. With his
brother he was educated in private schools at home and in Paris,
Boulogne, London, and Geneva. He was not at ease with his schoolfellows in America. "I remember well," wrote Henry, in characteristically stylistic sentences, "how when we were all young together
we had, under the pressure of the American ideal in that matter,
then so rigid, felt it tasteless and even humiliating that the head of
our little family was *not* in business . . . Such had never been the
case with the father of any boy of our acquaintance; the business in
which the boy's father gloriously *was* stood forth inveterately as the
very first note of our comrade's impressiveness. Business alone was
respectable . . . 'What shall we tell them that you are,' could but
become on our lips at home a more constant appeal. 'Say I'm a
philosopher,' replied the father. 'Say I'm a lover of my kind; say I'm

an author of books, if you like; or, best of all, just say I'm a student.' " But these answers were neither comforting nor convincing; Henry James, Sr., was not in business, and the boys had to suffer a loss of prestige as well as a lowered self-esteem.

Henry began writing in his boyhood; when he was fourteen he was, his father wrote to his mother, "an immense writer of novels and dramas." At eighteen, helping to put out a fire in Newport, he suffered an injury which he spoke of as "a horrid even if an obscure hurt." The guarded reference gave rise to a great deal of speculation. Some critics assumed that, because of the disablement, James was accidentally castrated or rendered impotent, and it was said that this might account for James's predilection for death as an ending to many of his stories—"castration, or the fear of castration, is supposed to preoccupy the mind with ideas of suicide and death," explained one of the commentators. It remained for Leon Edel to prove, in *Henry James: The Untried Years*, that the damage was not at all sexual, but merely a severe strain, a bad backache, and that James gave it a psychological as well as a physiological persistence. He seems to have "adopted" lameness from his father who, at fifteen, had lost one of his legs—also as the result of a fire. At any rate, the trauma remained with him the rest of his life, increasing as his brother William seemed to surpass him in achievement and disappearing when the sense of rivalry was overcome. Nevertheless, the impairment was enough to keep him from accompanying his younger brothers when they joined the Union Army during the Civil War.

James was nineteen, a handsome, slightly effeminate youth, with great dark eyes and a shock of hair falling over one side of his forehead, when he entered Harvard Law School. He stayed there less than a year. He had always felt that what he wanted to be was a man of letters; after he met the Massachusetts literati—James Russell Lowell, William Dean Howells, Charles Eliot Norton—he was sure of it. His first piece of professional writing (a book review) appeared in the *North American Review* when he was twenty-one; a year later his first story was published in the *Atlantic Monthly*. He was twenty-six when he made the first of his adult transatlantic journeys. Two things happened. He realized that, instead of utilizing the material of his own milieu, he was imitating Hawthorne and Balzac; at the same time he fell in love with Europe. He stood at the "gate of expectation" and gasped at the "picturesque." Overcome with "the sense of glory" he could not sufficiently extol all that was "immemorial, complex, accumulated" and regarded himself as a fortunate "heir of all the ages."

Two years later, after a return to Cambridge, where the family had made their home, James toured extensively through Europe, sent back travel sketches, studied the French theater in Paris, met Turgenev, Zola, and Flaubert, who commended his stories and, recrossing the Channel, felt a great attachment to London. "I must be a born Londoner for the place to stand the very severe test I am putting it," he wrote to his mother. "Leaving Paris and its brilliances and familiarities, its easy resources and the abundant society I had there, to plunge into darkness, solitude and sleet, in midwinter, to say nothing of the sooty, woolly desolation of a London lodging—to do that, and to like this murky Babylon really all the better, is to feel that one is likely to get on here . . . It is interesting, inspiring, even exhilarating." England was to become his home until the end. He chose the "denser, richer, warmer European spectacle" because of its "accumulation of history and custom" as well as its complexity.

James settled down in England to write novels of "the international situation," to act as a kind of literary liaison between the Old and the New World. He not only desired but determined to be considered an "international" writer. Ten years after his first novel, *Roderick Hudson,* appeared in 1876, he wrote to his brother William, "I aspire to write in such a way that it would be impossible to an outsider to say whether I am at a given moment an American writing about England or an Englishman writing about America . . . and so far from being ashamed of such an ambiguity, I should be exceedingly proud of it." In his early period James, an inexperienced and rather naïve observer, regarded Europe as an earthly but wicked Paradise. It was all the more alluring—and more dramatic—for the young writer, wrote Michael Swan, "as a place for the moral destruction of the innocent New Worlders who visited it, the returning Puritans who had no idea of the world from which their ancestors had departed."

It is a critical cliché to divide James's writings into three periods: the work of James the First, James the Second, and James The Old Pretender. The classification is flippant but not altogether unfair. The early work betrays uncertainties in technique, weaknesses of relations between characters, inappropriate reticences, a reliance on a too delicate and too profuse verbal embroidery. The work of James's "middle period," exemplified by *The Portrait of a Lady,* is marked by a new and startling sense of life, an intellectual play and subtlety unique in English fiction. The later novels—such as *The Wings of the Dove,* published when he was sixty, and *The Golden Bowl,* which appeared two years after—are difficult, extraordinarily complex, confusing at first glance, but built with an architectonic grandeur. At thirty-six James achieved a brief spell of public approval with a novel, *Daisy Miller;* at forty his following, although limited, was so devoted that a fourteen-volume set of his books was published in England.

In 1882, after the death of his mother and father, James returned to America, but he was back in England within the shortest possible time. He did not revisit the United States for another twenty-one years. Sojourning in Italy he dreamed of a new career in a new medium. James had always wanted to be a dramatist and, what is more, a popular one. But the plays, most of which he wrote in his late forties and fifties, were failures. One of them, *Guy Domville,* was booed, and James relinquished the dream of the theater. Disappointed as a dramatist, he had learned something from play writing; he realized that the plan of a book must be "as straight as a play." He had acquired, he believed, "a mastery of fundamental statement and scenic presentation"; his future novels would be constructed according to "a really detailed scenario, with an intensely structural, intensely hinged and jointed preliminary frame." Nevertheless, it was with real regret that, rebuffed by the humiliating fiasco, James left London and the world of the theater for a house in Rye, Sussex, where he lived in "impenetrable respectability." His face grew fleshy; the nose sharpened; the features, matching his clothes, became those of a bank president. He was fond of attending "functions," to which he always wore a dark afternoon suit with silk lapels, light-colored waistcoat, stiff collar with wide wings, and a formal top hat.

He never married, but marriage was a subject of which he never tired. He made many friends, but he had few intimates. There was a rumor that, as a youth, he had been strongly attracted to his cousin, Mary ("Minny") Temple, but nothing happened. James heard of her death when he was twenty-six, in England, and she became the prototype of most of his heroines, "a disengaged and dancing flame of thought," a symbol of the virtues he cherished as American.

In his sixties he seemed to feel that life had passed him by, that he had devoted too much of his work to "special cases," too much to contemplation and not enough to the world of action. He brooded on frustration and failure. In *The Ambassadors,* one of his most autobiographical studies, his *alter ego,* Strether, advises a young man: "Live all you can. It's a mistake not to. It doesn't so much matter what you do in particular, as long as you have your life . . . Live!"

As James grew older, his plots became more implausible, his style more tortuous, his sentences increasingly involuted. Although he was still devoted to the "civilized" people of the world and the slenderness of their existence, he developed an obsession for the supernatural. Some of the stories in this vein are whimsical and nostalgic, but others, such as "The Jolly Corner," are not only spectral but enigmatically oblique, while "The Turn of the Screw" communicates a horror all the more horrible for being suggested rather than told. "The Figure in the Carpet" is an extension of James's suggestive method. The story concerns the search for the meaning hidden in the writing of a certain novelist. The "figure" (or meaning) remains obscure, and James's critics were quick to seize upon the story as a symbol of his work.

James seems to have been fretting, with a probable sense of guilt, about his expatriation and loneliness. In his sixty-third year he returned to the United States, stayed during the fall with his brother, William James, in New Hampshire, revisited Cambridge and New York, traveled into the Deep South and Far West, lecturing as he went. He did not like what he saw. "I found my native land, after so many years, interesting, formidable, fearsome, and fatiguing, and much more difficult to see and deal with in any extended way than I had supposed . . . It is an extraordinary world . . . but almost cruelly charmless, in effect, and calculated to make one crouch ever afterwards, as cravenly as possible, at Lamb House, Rye." He was disturbed by what he considered the "dauntless power" of America, the "aggressive gregariousness" of its citizens, and the civilization which bred vulgarity and corruption. "So much taste," he said to one of his hosts, "and all of it bad." He congratulated himself on having escaped all of this years ago and, after twelve months, was glad to return to Rye.

In 1907, the New York edition of his *Novels and Tales* began appearing. The rest of the twenty-six volumes was issued two years later, and James furnished extensive textual revisions and special prefaces for each. A James cult was already beginning to form but, because the set was not immediately snapped up, James considered the venture a complete failure and complained he was left "high and dry—at my age—and, after my long career, utterly, insurmountably, unsalable." "How I envy you!" he exclaimed wistfully to W. W. Jacobs, a writer of humorous stories. "Your admirable work is appreciated by a wide circle of readers; it has achieved popularity. Mine—never goes into a second edition. I should so much have loved to be popular!" Popularity of a sort eventually came, but not until after the posthumous publication of *The Novels and Stories of Henry James,* which were issued in thirty-six volumes between 1921 and 1923.

At sixty-four James resumed play-writing after abstaining from it for twelve years, but he could not sustain the strain of working simultaneously in two media. At sixty-six, there was a breakdown, aggravated by the illness of his brother William, with whom he went to Bad Nauheim, Germany, for a possible cure, and back to New Hampshire, where William died. Honorary degrees from Harvard and Oxford scarcely alleviated his suffering. The outbreak of the First World War distressed him immeasurably. His general dislike of Germany and his intense love of England roused him to an almost violent patriotism and in June, 1915, he became a naturalized British subject. Six months later, on January 1, 1916, he was given the Order of Merit, but he did not have long to cherish the award as a "lover and interpreter of the fine amenities, of brave decisions and generous loyalties." Like his brother, he had been struck with a heart attack. This was followed by pneumonia, and on February 8, 1916, he died. In two more months he would have been seventy-three.

Posthumous volumes continued to appear for years: collections of early stories; compilations of critical essays; *The Middle Years,* the third (unfinished) volume of his autobiography, which had been preceded by *A Small Boy and Others* and *Notes of a Son and Brother;* two major novels (also unfinished), one of which, *The Sense of the Past,* expresses a longing for a more ordered world than that of the present and is based on a device not unlike the time-travels of later fantasy-fiction. Altogether James left a corpus of some twenty-three novels, more than one hundred short stories and "novellas," eight full-length dramas, eight short plays and sketches, to say nothing of his important prefaces, literary reviews, memoirs, biographical silhouettes, dramatic and art criticisms, travel sketches, public journalism, personal journals, and countless letters.

Readers of Henry James are divided into two unalterably opposed camps. Those who dislike him have condemned both his style and his subject matter as rootless, perverse, unnecessarily exhaustive and infinitely exhausting. He was, they say, simultaneously fascinated and repelled by high society and, as a result, his pictures of the leisure class are both snobbish and satirical. They object to his "attenuated elegance," his rigid (or frigid) formalism, his prudish lack of passion, the thinness of his emotions, and the narrowness of his range. Newton Arvin in *Henry James and the Almighty Dollar* spoke of "the deadly lucidity" with which James observed things that he encountered without quite comprehending them. "He made out no historic meaning in the corrupt life of the great bourgeoisie or the philistine morals of the small bourgeoisie of his time, but he saw that corruption, that philistinism, as few of his contemporaries saw them." "Thank God, I've no opinions," he wrote to his nephew. "I'm more and more aware of things as a mere mad panorama, phantasmagoria and dime museum." On the other hand, T. S. Eliot praised James for "his mastery over, his baffling escape from, ideas . . . a mind so fine that no idea could violate it."

It was James's style which provoked the bitterest attacks. His detractors were willing to concede his skill but belittled it as a coldly scientific exhibit, a display of preciosity. Van Wyck Brooks accused him of "magnificent pretensions and petty performances—the fruits of an irresponsible imagination, of a deranged sense of values, of a mind working in the void, uncorrected by any clear consciousness of human cause and effect." Thomas Hardy said that he had "a ponderously warm manner of saying nothing in infinite sentences." Hugh Walpole saw him as "a sort of stuffed waxwork from whose mouth a stream of colored sentences, like rolls of green and pink paper, are forever issuing." H. G. Wells burlesqued James's style in *Boon* and described the author as "a hippopotamus rolling a pea."

It is true that many readers have been puzzled by the complex imagery, reminiscent of the more difficult figures in modern poetry, and repelled by the intricate comma-strewn sentences with interjections, modifying phrases, and qualifying clauses within clauses, like endless nests of Chinese boxes. But in spite of his difficulties, many modern critics have discovered James to be one of the first-ranking English novelists, a pioneer of the art of telling stories on two levels: that of the straightforward narrative and that of the sensitive, understanding commentator. James makes constant demands upon the reader. He must be read—and reread—with strict attention, with alertness. James would have substituted his favorite word "awareness," for, as he wrote to Howells, "the faculty of attention has utterly vanished from the general Anglo-Saxon mind." On another occasion he spoke of "the bastard vernacular of communities disinherited of the felt difference between the speech of the soil and the speech of the newspaper, and capable thereby, accordingly, of taking slang for simplicity, the composite for the quaint, and the vulgar for the natural." It is probably unwise never to assume apathy or something less than literacy on the part of the reader, but James always wrote as if he were addressing an ideal audience of agile intelligences.

Although James's interest seems to be confined to a class which is cultured, nonproductive, and parasitic, it is the decay of that class which concerns him most. His chief theme is the artist in search of himself and the individual in conflict with society. "Destiny in James's books," wrote Stephen Spender in *The Destructive Element,* "is closely linked to the decadence of the people he is describing, and to their social conditions. The decadence makes them, to a great extent, victims of their environment and of their tradition; they are limited in their very range of action." If the thoughts of James's characters are circumspect to the point of seeming censored, and the texture of their talk is thicker and more esoteric than speech has ever been, the quality of language as well as the thought is acutely, even painfully, precise and probing. The highest as well as the most "suggestive" and "nutritive" truth, according to James, was "the perfect dependence of the 'moral' sense of a work of art on the amount of felt life concerned in producing it."

Rediscovery of James places new emphasis on his search for moral significance at a time when life often lacks both significance and morality. James was not only one of America's few great novelists but one of the very first to use a fine sensibility as a weapon against the blunt insensibilities of the age. He anticipated the searching fastidiousness of Proust and the social-autobiographical intricacies of Joyce. Disdaining the meretricious, he went to such lengths to avoid anything obvious that he frequently seems precious, overelaborate and rococo. But the design, "the figure in the carpet," emerges, richer because of the infinitesimal, accurately interwoven details. The scenes are transfixed, the characters are inviolable as James makes his readers turn from outer confusion to the clear if difficult precisions of the analytical mind.

Paul Verlaine

[1 8 4 4 - 1 8 9 6]

"Take rhetoric and wring its neck."

ONE OF THE MOST dissolute of men who was also one of the purest of poets, Paul Verlaine, was born March 30, 1844, in Metz, France. His father, Nicolas Auguste Verlaine, was an infantry captain who served under Napoleon, a *chevalier* of the Legion of Honor, who envisioned a great diplomatic career for his son. For a while it seemed that his hopes might be fulfilled. In 1851 the family moved to Paris, and young Paul excelled in his studies; he took honors in rhetoric, literature, and the dead languages. After graduating from the Lycée Bonaparte, he obtained a comfortable clerkship in the city administration's accounting department, but although he retained his position, the only books in which he was interested were those of poetry. He had discovered Baudelaire at thirteen, and at the same time, found out that he could express himself better in allusive verse than in direct speech.

At twenty he joined a group of young bohemians, which included Théodore de Banville and the half-Spanish José María de Heredia, under the leadership of Leconte de Lisle. They called themselves Parnassians, indicating that they were opposed to uncontrolled romanticism and favored a return to a classicism which would be objective in attitude and precise in technique. Verlaine contributed to their miscellany, *Le Parnasse Contemporain,* and at twenty-two, published his first book, *Poèmes Saturniens.* The poems are scarcely as saturnine as the title promised. On the contrary, instead of being morose or ominous, they are extraordinarily light in texture and delicate in tone. A visual impressionism is enhanced by a fluctuating music, sensuous but serene. The violin-like sounds of long, low-sobbing winds which hurt the remembering heart are not only suggested but heard in the strange assonances of:

> *Les sanglots longs*
> *Des violons*
> *De l'automne*

Blessent mon coeur
D'une langueur
Monotone.

Verlaine was badly spoiled before he attained his majority. He had exhibited homosexual tendencies in his early teens; at eighteen he started to drink excessively. His father died when he was twenty and his mother pampered him more than ever. He challenged middle class respectability, mocked the priesthood, and flaunted the banner of atheism. A mixture of resentment and experiment shows through Verlaine's second volume *Fêtes Galantes* (*Gallant Festivals*), but only faintly. The poems, which have been compared to the nimble melodies of Mozart and the naughty delicacies of Watteau, are lightly cynical, spiced with the badinage of "Colloque Sentimental," "Sur l'Herbe," "L'Allée," the Pierrotic raillery of "A la Promenade," "Mandoline," and the pseudo-archaic loveliness of "Clair de Lune."

In the same year that Verlaine published *Fêtes Galantes,* he met and fell in love with Mathilde Mauté de Fleurville, half-sister of a family friend. The marriage, auspicious in every way, seemed to change him. Verlaine was twenty-five, an ardent husband; Mathilde was several years younger, a beautiful and adoring bride. The radiance of the betrothal and the simple delight of marriage— the sweetness of evening, the rosy hearth, the "dear fatigue," the benignly approving stars—glow through *La Bonne Chanson* (*The Good Song*) which, in contradistinction to the preceding "Parnassian" verse, is warm, intimate, and romantically unsophisticated.

This idyllic period was shortlived. During the Franco-Prussian War of 1870, a year after his marriage, Verlaine resumed his heavy drinking, fell into the old bad habits, and lost his clerkship. To make matters more difficult, his mother had invested the family securities in ill-advised speculations; there was barely enough left for her to live on, and Verlaine was given a home with Mathilde's parents. Much worse was to follow. One day Verlaine received a letter enclosing some poems from an unknown admirer. The letter was gratifying in its effusiveness, and the poems were startling, the more so since they were the work of a precocious boy. Arthur Rimbaud was seventeen when he received an invitation to visit Verlaine. Rimbaud immediately moved in and Verlaine immediately succumbed to him.

Arthur Rimbaud was born in 1854, in Charleville, in the northeastern part of France. His father, like Verlaine's, was an army officer; his mother, unlike Verlaine's, was a harshly aggressive disciplinarian. Rimbaud had nothing in common with either. He was conscious of his errant genius even as a child. At fifteen he informed Banville that he considered himself a superior Parnassian; at sixteen he ran away from school and home. During the Paris Commune, after the capitulation to the Germans in 1871, Rimbaud joined the radicals, left them abruptly, and announced that he intended "to become a seer." It was at this time that he came to Verlaine with a copy of his hundred-stanza, pagan, image-crammed *Le Bateau Ivre* (*The Drunken Boat*) and, at seventeen, making himself at home in Verlaine's crowded quarters, wrote the series of *Illuminations* in what was purported to be a state of "simple hallucination." Rimbaud believed that it was not enough for a poet to have visions; he must *make* himself a visionary and apprehend things "through a long, immense, and *reasoned derangement* of *all* the senses." Since he sought images which, instead of proceeding from recognizable associations, rose from violent disassociation, Rimbaud cultivated magic and occultism in order to attain "a new and divine disorder." Most people saw only the disorder—Rimbaud ignored the social amenities, never changed his dirty clothes, and seldom washed—but Verlaine recognized what he thought was divinity. He worshiped the youth, neglected his wife, and when her family expressed their outrage, Verlaine left the house and took Rimbaud with him.

The liaison was as noxious as it was notorious. Calling themselves "children of the sun," the couple went to London, where Verlaine supported both of them by teaching French and lecturing in English. Later they went to Belgium. The alliance lasted little more than a year. Drunken orgies were followed by violent quarrels; bitter scenes were intensified by Verlaine's fierce possessiveness and the fact that, although Rimbaud had entered into an abnormal association, he was not by nature homosexual. In a hotel room in Brussels Verlaine shot him. The wound was superficial, but Verlaine collapsed. His wife and mother were summoned and persuaded him to sever the relationship; yet on the way to the train before they parted, Verlaine fired once more at Rimbaud. This time the assault was public and Verlaine was sentenced to two years in prison.

During the months of emotional upheaval, Rimbaud had been at work on the ruthless and horrifying *Une Saison en Enfer* (*A Season in Hell*). This disjointed and disorganized autobiographical outburst which was to become the Bible of the Surrealists is, beneath its evocation of delirium, one of the wildest yet starkest documents ever written. "I believe myself in hell," wrote Rimbaud, "hence I am there." It was Rimbaud's valedictory; at nineteen he stopped writing altogether. After *A Season in Hell,* which lay forgotten in a cellar and was not published for another twenty years, Rimbaud engaged in one occupation after another. Sick of the printed word and all its past associations, he became a teacher, an attendant in a circus, a dock worker, a soldier in the Dutch Army, a laborer in the Cyprus quarries. In his mid-twenties he went to Africa, was an employee of a French exporting house, traded in gold and ivory, explored the back country of the Web River and the Ogaden region of Abyssinia, smuggled arms to the natives; it was rumored that he traded in slaves. Established as a semi-official plenipotentiary, he lived in a fabulous house in Harrar with an Abyssinian girl. He seemed to be prospering when the syphilis which he had contracted reached a critical stage. A wound in his leg festered and would not heal; he was forced to return to Europe to have the leg amputated. He survived the operation, but the inroads of the disease were too great, and Rimbaud died in a Marseilles hospital at the age of thirty-seven.

Verlaine was thirty-one when he was released from prison. During his incarceration he had renounced atheism and returned to the faith of his boyhood. Full of the ardor of the reformed sinner, he urged his wife to take him back. But she had divorced him during his prison term, and she could not be persuaded to a reconciliation. Baffled, Verlaine sought out Rimbaud who, at twenty-one, was living in Germany. But Rimbaud had no idea of renewing the disastrous connection. "Verlaine arrived here [in Stuttgart], pawing a rosary," he wrote to a friend. "Three hours later he had denied his God and started the 98 wounds of Our Lord bleeding again." While he was a prisoner Verlaine had written some of the tenderest lyrics in the language. Assembled in *Romances Sans Paroles* (*Romances Without Words*) they are unsurpassably moving, naïve yet full of subtle nuances, superficially as simple as a nursery rhyme yet, beneath their placid surfaces, darkly troubled—a poetry of the nerves but also a poetry which sounded like the songs of the people. Such plangent lines as "Il pleure dans mon coeur" ("It weeps in my heart"), with its subtitle from Rimbaud, had the same appeal for readers (and composers) as the bittersweet stanzas of Heine. Their subsequent popularity was due not only to the sentiment but to the almost colloquial idiom in which they were couched; Verlaine inspired an entire school of poets with his famous adjuration: "Take rhetoric and wring its neck."

The last eighteen years of Verlaine's life were tortured and tragic. Conscious of his sins, he lashed himself with repentance, only to return to his sinning; he continually alternated between his devotion to the Virgin Queen of Heaven and to "the green goddess," absinthe. He taught for a while; but the story of his scandal crept into the classrooms and he had to resign. He tried living close to the earth hoping to derive support from it; but he was unfitted to be a farmer. On one occasion, in a drunken fit, he beat his mother, was arrested, and sentenced to a month in jail. After he was freed he drifted from bar to bar, and whenever the absinthe haze dissipated, from one confessional to another. *Sagesse* (*Wisdom*) breathes a religious fervor which is ardent, reverential, and unquestionably sincere. At the same time Verlaine sank deeper in debauchery and wrote poems which no publisher would print. He hung about the most disreputable cafés, begging a drink or a postage stamp so he could write to friends begging for the price of another drink or a few more stamps.

In his forties he suffered increasingly frequent attacks of gout and rheumatism; he grew bald and flabby. Anatole France described him as "an old vagabond . . . a faun, a satyr, half brute and half demigod" and, indicating the contradiction of the sordid aspects of his life and the loveliness of his songs, compared him to Villon. The comparison was neither new nor welcome; it annoyed Verlaine every time it was made. Later, when he made a forlorn bid for respectability and attempted to be admitted to the French Academy, Verlaine abased himself and wrote: "Unhappily the idea came to Huysmans, in his curious book, *A Rebours,* to compare me to Villon. From that moment others began to improvise upon the theme and, because I was poor and had looked misery in the face, they presumed to speak of me as one whose temperament was like that of our great poet of another century. They dragged into their analogy everything, the jails, the hazy assassinations, the nameless hovels, even the 'Grosse Margot' poems . . ." The ultra-conservative members of the Academy did not even consider his application.

Rejected, Verlaine was more disbalanced then ever; he swung ambivalently from excessive sensuality to the extremes of mysticism. Although his books had received little praise and small recompense, he continued to write and publish poems rich with the utmost refinements of poetic form, studded with lines that were sometimes tenuous, sometimes turbulent, but always characterized by the piquant oddities and delicate dissonances which began to be echoed in the altered tone of modern poetry. He was contemplating the nineteenth book of poems when he succumbed to a complicated disease of the kidneys and stomach. He was penniless and, in spite of his eighteen volumes, almost forgotten when he died on January 8, 1896.

Gerard Manley Hopkins

[1844-1889]

*"A spasmodic cry of joy, a passionate
glorification of God's world."*

ALMOST A CENTURY after his birth, a Jesuit teacher, practically
unknown in his day, proved to be one of the greatest influences on the radical poets of the 1930's and 1940's. It was not
until thirty years after his death that poems of Gerard Manley
Hopkins were first published, and the collection, bristling with
difficulties for the casual reader, made the serious scrutinizer aware
of a mind which was provocatively plunging and a style quivering
with sensibility. Hopkins' combination of onrushing syllables and
far-reaching associations was admired, analyzed, and imitated by
W. H. Auden, Stephen Spender, Dylan Thomas, and other
twentieth-century poets. What, at first glance, seemed a willful
imprecision of language was revealed to be a vocabulary of
strangely stimulating metaphors and extraordinarily precise meanings.

Hopkins was born at Stratford, Essex (now a part of London),
June 11, 1844. At sixteen he wrote a poem which won a school
prize; at eighteen he won another prize with a more ambitious
poem written in strict heroic couplets. At nineteen he entered Bal-
liol College, where he was encouraged to write in Walter Pater's
paste-jewel manner by Pater himself. Although he was a gifted musician and painter as well as a poet, Hopkins was already preoccupied with religion. He observed the holy days with devout strin-
gencies, and in his twenty-third year was converted to Catholicism
by another convert who later became Cardinal Newman. From
that time on, Hopkins was a dedicated priest. He burned his poems and for the next ten years denied himself the luxury of verse.
He preached zealously in Chesterfield, Oxford, and Dublin. Part of
this time—after his fortieth year—he taught Greek at the Royal
University of Dublin, but continued to subject himself to ever-
stricter rituals of discipline. Increasingly conscious of the struggles
of the working people, he spent much of his time in the slums,

and it is likely that it was there he contracted the typhoid fever which caused his death, June 8, 1889.

When Hopkins turned to poetry again, he wrote with a sudden access of radiance and unshaken worship. It was not man's world he loved, but God's. Man's world filled him with fear, even with dreadful doubt. In a letter to his friend, the teacher-poet Richard Watson Dixon, he wrote: "My Liverpool experience laid upon my mind a conviction, a truly crushing conviction, of the misery of town life to the poor, and even more than to the poor . . . of the degradation of our race, of the hollowness of the century's civilization." In a letter to Robert Bridges, another and far more conservative poet who became poet laureate, Hopkins mixed despondency and anxiety with prophecy: "I am afraid some great revolution is not far off. Horrible to say, in a manner I am a Communist . . . It is a dreadful thing for the greatest and most necessary part of a very rich nation to live a hard life without dignity, knowledge, comforts, delights or hopes, in the midst of plenty —which plenty they make . . . But as the working classes have not been educated, they know nothing of all this and cannot be expected to care if they destroy it." These misgivings rarely appear in the poems. Except for a few sonnets, Hopkins' poetry is a spasmodic cry of joy, a passionate glorification of God's world. Another fear, the fear of rejection, kept him from offering his verses for publication, and none of the poems which subsequently were so triumphantly anthologized was printed during his lifetime.

An ascetic, meditating on the growing gap between religious idealism and realistic materialism, Hopkins looked the spiritual personality he was. His was a scholar's face, concentrated and composed; but a nervously quick perception shone in his eyes and his mouth was framed for startling improvisations. His closest friendship was with Robert Bridges, to whom he entrusted his manuscripts; yet it was not until 1918 that Bridges, puzzled by many of the lines, issued *Poems of Gerard Manley Hopkins* with cautious and sometimes embarrassed notes. Hopkins' theory of "sprung rhythm" and his peculiar metrical structures aroused some comments, but there was little to show that the poet had won an audience. Thirteen years later, when the experimental writers were beginning to reach an interested public, Hopkins' work was reappraised and, for the first time, his total impact was felt. With the second edition, published in 1931, Hopkins was enthusiastically "discovered."

The headlong fluency and oddity of Hopkins' verse was not altogether the result of unconscious inspiration. "The poetical language of an age," wrote Hopkins, "should be the current language heightened to any degree and unlike itself but not an obsolete one." It is obvious that Hopkins recognized his limitations but, without priding himself on his originality, knew it for what it was. "No doubt my poetry errs on the side of oddness," he wrote to Bridges. "I hope in time to have a more balanced and Miltonic style. But as air, melody, is what strikes me most of all in music, and design in painting, so design, pattern, or what I am in the habit of calling 'inscape' is what above all I aim at in poetry. Now it is the virtue of design, pattern, or 'inscape' to be distinctive, and it is the vice of distinctiveness to become queer. This vice I cannot have escaped." Surrendering himself to a delight in "all things counter, original, spare, strange," Hopkins was not only God-intoxicated but image-drunken. His poems reel with metaphors which leap recklessly from one association to another. His lines, crowded with more than they can bear, project a universe which is "charged with the grandeur of God." This rapturous celebration is implicit in everything Hopkins wrote. Sometimes it is explicit, as in the opening of "Pied Beauty":

> Glory be to God for dappled things—
> For skies of couple-color as a brinded cow;
> For rose-moles all in stipple upon trout that swim;
> Fresh-firecoal chestnut-falls; finches' wings;
> Landscape plotted and pieced—fold, fallow, and plough;
> And all trades, their gear and tackle and trim.

Such a sestet might serve as an exemplar of Hopkins' crowded lines, his hazardous love of alliteration, and the very breathlessness' of his ecstasy. His radiant affirmations were impulsive replies to himself and to the discomforting skepticism of his time, a skepticism which two contemporary poets, Thomas Hardy and, later, A. E. Housman proclaimed. Hardy, scoffing at God's concern for man, insisted that

> Man must begin, know this, where Nature ends;
> Nature and man can never be fast friends.

Housman, declaring that man was "a stranger and afraid in a world he never made," added that

> . . . malt does more than Milton can
> To justify God's ways to man.

Hopkins maintained that God's ways to man were not only justified but radiantly revealed by overwhelming displays of beauty. It
did not take anything as rare as a rainbow to make Hopkins' heart
leap up. He was all amazement at the common miracle of a nest-
ful of thrush's eggs like "little low heavens," of ordinary stars, the
"fire-folk sitting in the air," of wayside weeds "in wheels, long and
lovely and lush"; even an old horseshoe was to him a "bright and
battering sandal"!

Often indeed Hopkins stretched his metaphors to the breaking
point. Yet there was always a logic in his comparisons, however
remote they seem at first reading. Bridges was one of many who
complained that Hopkins' way with words was too daring, too
whimsical to make sense. If some of his poems, commented
Bridges, "were to be arraigned for errors of taste, they might be
convicted of occasional affectation in metaphor, as where the hills
are 'as a stallion, very-violet-sweet.' " Yet even such an apparently
wanton image is not without its logic. It can be appreciated, as
Robert Graves and Laura Riding wrote in *A Survey of Modern
Poetry,* "as a phrase reconciling the two seemingly opposed qualities of mountains: their male animal-like roughness and, at the
same time, their ethereal quality under soft light, for which the
violet in the gentle eye of the horse makes the proper association."

Nevertheless, Hopkins' excesses are indisputable. The very poet
who could mock at Swinburne for his "delirium-tremendous imagination" could surpass Swinburne in verbal riotousness and out-
alliterate him in lines like:

> I caught this morning morning's minion, king-
> Dom of daylight's Dauphin, dapple-dawn-drawn Falcon, in
>   his riding.

By 1935 Hopkins' importance was established. A new edition of
his poems, collating his smallest fragments, was followed by two
collections of his letters, a biography by G. F. Lahey, and a volume
of reminiscences by three friends. In *A Hope for Poetry* (1935) his
influence was brilliantly traced by C. Day Lewis, an English poet,
who concluded that "no poet since Donne had drawn his material
from so wide a radius . . . By him the language of poetry is removed almost as far as possible from ordinary language, while his
prosody swings to the other extreme, for it is based on the rhythms
of common speech . . . He is a true revolutionary poet, for his
imagination was always breaking up and melting down the inher

ited forms of language, fusing them into new possibilities, hammering them into new shapes." Although Hopkins' was a liberating voice, it was a limited one. He directly affected only the more determinedly experimental poets; but they, in turn, charged modern poetry with his subtle idiom and creative vigor. It was thus that Hopkins was acknowledged one of this generation's "ancestors"; his energetic innovations answered the need for a wider exploration of techniques and a more flexible poetic speech. What, on the printed page, often seems a hurlyburly of blurred sound and sense, when read aloud becomes a set of musical cadences, an incantation which brings the words into focus and gives them the power of a magic spell. With all his abrupt assonances, his bizarre rhythms, and tough textures, Hopkins' extravagances are now seen to be just and inevitable. The opulence first disturbs but eventually compels the reader, even if he can never quite catch up with Hopkins' racing lines. To Hopkins everything was a rush of overmastering emotion. The world was prodigal with vision; Nature was a divine turmoil; and God was an eternal exuberance.

Friedrich Nietzsche

[1844-1900]

"How to Philosophize with a Hammer."

A LTHOUGH Nietzsche is established in the textbooks as a philosopher, his effect upon the world was that of a terrifying prophet, an oracle who, predicting the end of the common man, was an apostle of the Superman, the aristocratic and ruthless *homo superior* who was to dominate the world. A frightening portent, he regarded life with a pessimism that was both tragic and heroic—tragedy being to Nietzsche the source not only of nobility but of power, endowing man with moments of heroism in his furious persistence to live.

The household in which Friedrich Wilhelm Nietzsche was reared was not only respectably middle class but deeply religious, the most unlikely background for the future preacher of atheism and the presager of doom. The oldest child of a Lutheran pastor, he was born October 15, 1844, in Röcken, a little town in the Prussian province of Saxony. It seemed a happy augury that the boy was born on the King's birthday, and his father made a patriotic speech when he christened his son with the name of the monarch, Friedrich Wilhelm. The Nietzsche family included two other children: a boy, Josef, who died in infancy, and a girl, Therese Elisabeth, who became her famous brother's biographer and took care of him during his latter unfortunate days.

When Friedrich was five years old, his father died as the result of a fall, and the rest of the family moved to Naumburg. Here the boy was surrounded, protected, and idolized by a group of pious women: his mother, his grandmother, his sister, and two adoring maiden aunts. Except for his dark, deep-set eyes, he was a commonplace looking, fair-haired boy, but he liked to believe that his ancestors were anything but ordinary. He claimed to be descended from the Nietskys, Polish aristocrats. "Germany is a great nation," he said, "only because its people have so much Polish blood in their veins." It was not only in youth that he fancied himself an exotic; in middle age he compared himself to those Poles who, because of their stern convictions, had suffered for their Protestantism in a Catholic country.

A pampered prodigy, he could read at four, write at five, and play Beethoven at six. Before he was ten he wrote poems, chiefly religious in character, and composed music for the voice and piano. When he went to the village school he was so prim—his aunts saw to that—that his fellow students nicknamed him "The Little Pastor"; when he precociously argued about certain passages in the Bible, one of his teachers was reminded of the twelve-year-old child Jesus in the Temple. Softened by feminine adulation and aware of his own superiority, young Nietzsche found his school-fellows both too childish and too rough for companionship. His sister remembered him as "a serious introspective child, whose dignified politeness seemed so strange to other boys that friendly advances from either side were out of the question."

At fourteen he entered the Pforta Boarding School, where he fell in love with philology and Wagner's music, both of which influenced him profoundly. Future historians relished the irony that he excelled in a devout study of religion. After six years at Pforta he entered Bonn University and, for a brief period, threw himself into the convivial pleasures of college life. He smoked and drank with a sudden excess of abandon; he affected a light and frivolous mustache which contrasted strangely with his beetling brows; he indulged in trivial "affairs," and seems to have fallen unhappily in love at least once. Defending him from the lightest breath of scandal, his sister sanctified him beyond recognition when she stated that her brother remained throughout his life "completely apart from either violent passions or vulgar pleasures; all his desires lay in the realm of knowledge, and he had only tempered emotions for anything else." Elisabeth's sententiousness to the contrary, Nietzsche disported himself as recklessly as any of his fellow students. He visited the brothels as well as the bars, and an experience in a house of prostitution may well have changed his entire life physically as well as psychologically. It is on record that when he was twenty-five an examination showed that he had contracted syphilis two or three years earlier and had done little about the infection.

Previously Nietzsche had suffered from weak eyes. He could never bear strong light; sunshine made him dizzy, and he worked best in a darkened dormitory. Now his pains increased. Everything he did was a strain. He resolved to abjure all diversions and lead the life of a monk. He gave up smoking and drinking—and suffered nervous cramps. He devoted himself entirely to books—and reading gave him continual headaches. He was an afflicted creature at twenty-two when he transferred to the University of Leipzig, and discovered Schopenhauer. His mind underwent a complete change as he read the misanthropic philosopher's *The World As Will and Idea*. He questioned everything he had once believed. "I took the book to my lodgings," Nietzsche remembered years afterward, "and flung myself on a sofa and read and read and read. It seemed as if Schopenhauer were addressing me personally. I felt his vigor and power; I seemed to see him before me. Every line of the book cried aloud for revaluation and renunciation." Schopenhauer maintained that the will to exist was the primary instinct of life, the first cause of all human ideas, motives, and actions. Instinct was at the base of every function of all living things; intelligence was the effect of will, not its source. Moreover, since will is a blind force, it has neither aim nor end; insistent and insatiable, it compels an existence which drives man from one unhappiness to another. But if will is unappeasable it is ever-active; in a world inhibited by placidity, torpor, and countless negations, it is a positive and creative force.

Nietzsche saw in the will-to-live not only a way out for himself but a philosophy which would lift the ascetic to the plane of the hero, the suffering man above pain and pleasure. Believing with Schopenhauer that human behavior was nonrational, instinctive rather than intelligent, and that its code of ethics was mere rationalizing after the fact, he began to find himself in rebellion against the current mores in all their manifestations. At twenty-four he met Wagner, who seemed to him an embodiment of Schopenhauer's dreams, and was inspired by the composer's repudiation not only of the traditional musical forms but the very ethics of his time. The young philosopher became the much older composer's disciple; the two were constantly together in Switzerland after Nietzsche was offered the chair of classical languages at Basel in 1867. His first book was dedicated to Wagner. The original title was *The Birth of Tragedy from the Spirit of Music*. Some years later, when Nietzsche's philosophy had fully evolved, he added a significant subtitle: "Hellenism and Pessimism."

In *The Birth of Tragedy* Nietzsche applied Schopenhauer's theory of the supremacy of the compulsive will to mythology. Greek thought was originally calm, classically balanced, and serene; its god was the tranquil Apollo. Opposed to him was the troubling but inspiriting figure of Dionysus, the symbol of wildness, intoxication, and ecstasy. The conflict between the two created the unsurpassed accomplishments of Greek art, song, sculpture, and the tragic drama. The power of tragedy was weakened by Socrates who believed that will and its lawlessness was not so much an evil as an error, the result of ignorance. Socrates sounded the pre-Christian hope of salvation, "the more knowledge, the more virtue." To Nietzsche this was a softening of stern ideals and the denial of the great Dionysian spirit to which he now made obeisance. Christianity was merely a sentimentalizing of Socrates, a specious escape from the rigorous demands of a dangerous but continually reanimating existence. In Wagner's music dramas Nietzsche saw a return to pure tragedy, a revivifying of the pagan power which would triumph over the disintegrating weakness of the meek Christian tradition. "To insure the eternal pleasure of creation, the eternal affirmation of the will to live," wrote Nietzsche, "the eternity of birth-pangs is absolutely required. All this is signified by the word Dionysus. I know of no higher symbolism than this Greek Dionysiac symbolism. In it the deepest instinct of life, the future of life, the eternity of life, is experienced religiously; in it generation, the way of life, is regarded as a sacred way. Christianity alone, with its fundamental horror of life, has made sexuality an impure thing, casting filth on the beginning, the very condition, of our life." The originators, concluded Nietzsche, are always the rebels, nobly daring and tragically defeated. The life-bringers, like Adam, and the light-bringers, like Prometheus, always incur the wrath of the gods. They are struck down, chained to rocks, expelled and exiled, because they hope to free men from darkness and denial.

Nietzsche's glorification of resurgent "heathenism," accompanied by what seemed a wanton attack on the religion of his fathers, caused a furor in academic circles, frightened his friends, and threatened to end his professorship. When his classes dwindled to a few apprehensive but fascinated pupils, he held on to his position by sheer obstinacy. At thirty, Nietzsche's personality began to change. He spoke with incontrovertible conviction and unarguable aggressiveness. His appearance was equally altered. The tentative thatch on his upper lip became a black and bristling mass, the thick and wiry mustache of a walrus. The coarse hair was brushed back defiantly from a stony forehead. The eyes, burning beneath the hugely jutting brows, blazed with resolution, intolerance, and a hint of the madness which later was to overwhelm him. There arose in him, said H. L. Mencken in *The Philosophy of Friedrich Nietzsche*, "a fiery loathing for all authority, and a firm belief that his own opinion regarding any matter to which he had given thought was as sound, at the least, as any other man's. Thenceforth the assertive *'Ich'* began to besprinkle his discourse and his pages. *'I* condemn Christianity . . . *I* have given to mankind . . . *I* was never modest . . . *I* think . . . *I* say . . . *I* do . . .' "

His illness was intensified by his experiences on the battle-fields during the Franco-Prussian War of 1870. Although he served only a few months on ambulance duty, he developed a chronic catarrh of the intestines, complicated by an attack of pneumonia and continual nausea, and was sent back from the front. In order to resume teaching, he resorted to narcotics and became a drug addict the rest of his life. Refusing to believe that he might be suffering the first crippling effects of syphilis, he survived one physical disturbance after another and rationalized his disease as a harsh but necessary stimulant. "It is a crucial fact," he wrote, "that the creative spirit prefers to descend upon the sick and suffering." Nevertheless, the suffering increased to such an extent that, for all his stoicism, he was forced to retire from teaching when he was only thirty-five.

A pension from the university, supplemented by a small private income, permitted him to accomplish what he wanted most to do: write and travel. He made one more forlorn bid for happiness. In Rome the author Paul Rée introduced him to a young, talented Russian-Finnish girl who bore the improbable name of Lou Salomé. Nietzsche was looking for an amanuensis; she was more than willing to help him, and Nietzsche immediately fell in love with her. Although she admired the intransigent philosopher she was repelled by the importunate man. Nietzsche offered marriage; then, when that was refused, he proposed a free relationship which would not bind her in any way. Realizing that Nietzsche was tempera-mentally unable to accept a negative from anyone, she ran away. Nietzsche pursued her halfway across Europe, from Rome to Leip-zig, and when it became obvious that he could not persuade her to live with him on any terms, he said cynically, "After all, I did not create either the world or Lou Salomé. Had I done so, both would have been more nearly perfect."

Even more unfortunate was the end of Nietzsche's friendship with Wagner. At the beginning of their attachment Nietzsche honored the composer of *The Ring of the Nibelung* because of the tradition-breaking character of his music. His regard turned to reverence when he felt that Wagner was creating a new mythology, rejecting Christianity for the old Teutonic paganism, substituting the warring Wotan and his savagely heroic Siegfried for the outworn Judaic-Christian god and his mild, self-sacrificing Jesus. The later Wagner's mysticism troubled Nietzsche. He regarded the religious trend of the music dramas with mounting distrust; the spectacle of *Parsifal*, a "sinking down at the floor of the Cross," seemed sheer apostasy. Nietzsche's disillusion found angry outlets in *The Case of Wagner, The Twilight of the Gods,* and *Nietzsche Contra Wagner,* books which spewed a stream of charges that are as vituperative as they are ridiculous. Denouncing Wagner as a miserable product of his times, a democrat and therefore decadent, Nietzsche proclaimed that the truly aristocratic art of the opera was that of Bizet's *Carmen!*

By the time Nietzsche was forty he had published such challenging works as *Untimely Thoughts; Human, All-too Human; The Dawn of Day; The Joyful Science; Thus Spake Zarathustra.* A few years after the publication of the last-named masterpiece of brilliant writing and distorted vision, signs of serious neurasthenia were evident, but Nietzsche's will drove him to produce the disputatious *Beyond Good and Evil, The Genealogy of Morals,* the autobiographical *Ecce Homo,* and the posthumously published *The Antichrist* and *The Will to Power,* which he subtitled "How to Philosophize with a Hammer" and which he said would constitute "the history of the next two centuries." His megalomania reached a pitch of insanity; symptoms of mental and emotional instability indicated the presence of paresis. He worked in a fury of inchoate energy and tension; spurts of clairvoyant wisdom were followed by pitiful exhibitionisms, delusions of grandeur. He called himself "Dionysus," "Successor to the Dead God," and inconsistently signed his letters "Antichrist" and "The Crucified One." He had hallucinations. He demanded that the Emperor be executed. He planned a letter to the heads of all the European nations advising them to form an anti-German league—then, Nietzsche explained with a great show of cunning, once surrounded, Germany would have to declare war and would conquer the world.

Nietzsche was forty-five, living in Turin, when the impending breakdown came. He collapsed in the street and was taken to a hospital in Basel and, later, to an asylum in Jena. Though his brain was damaged, he remained alive another twelve years. When he was brought home to Naumburg, his mother and sister watched over him with the pathetic hope that the once fearless mind might manifest itself again. But the controversy-rousing assailant had become a contented child. Once, when he observed his sister weeping, he put his finger on her cheek and said, " 'Lisbeth, why do you cry? Aren't we happy?" He shrank into silence and died on August 25th, 1900, in the fifty-sixth year of his life. A few days later, the most prominent heretic in Europe, "atheist by instinct," was buried with Christian ceremony in the churchyard at Röcken, where his father had taught him the Gospel.

Nietzsche's views are in violent opposition to those of the majority. "They are," wrote H. L. Mencken, one of Nietzsche's most ardent adherents, "preëminently for the man who is not of the mass, but for the man whose head is lifted, however little, above the common level. They justify the success of that man, the man above, as Christianity justifies the failure of the man below." Those views range from the philosophically rebellious to the politically repulsive. Many of them, such as Nietzsche's characterization of man, especially Nordic man, as "the blond beast," gave an impetus to the storm-troopers, cutthroats, and gangsters of a bellicose Germany. His idealization of the *Herrenvolk* was translated as a justification of a merciless Master Race. His glorification of the "will to power" helped Hitler bring on World War II. The war itself was prophesied by Nietzsche who shouted, "Within fifty years the governments will clash in a gigantic war for the markets of the world . . . The blond beasts, the race of conquerors and masters, shall rise again from the ashes of men—they shall rise in a mightier, more deadly form."

As a writer, Nietzsche has been considered by some critics as the greatest German prose stylist of his generation, the finest coiner of aphorisms since Rochefoucauld. Others have decried his speech as infinitely self-assured, brutal, full of contempt, hostile and complacent. His ideas are not presented in orderly progression but are dazzling fragments, shot out in illuminating flashes. "We are close to a fire when we listen to him," wrote William Hubben in *Four Prophets of Our Destiny,* "sensing both the consuming heat and the blinding light of his spirit. Like Kierkegaard, he demands of us a state of passion . . . He creates a mood rather than a rational conviction, and it is no surprise that he has been favorably quoted by believers as well as atheists, by conservatives as well as rebels. For almost every one of his truths there can be found another truth contradicting the first."

Proof of his self-contradictions, his major opus, *Thus Spake Zarathustra,* is a set of metaphysical and cryptic meditations, an anti-Biblical but semi-scriptural work, which Nietzsche subtitled: "A Book for Everyone and No One." Its power is that of cumulative incantation; but its flavor, its very spasmodic force, is felt in severed paragraphs. There is, for example, Zarathustra's colloquy with the hermit-saint:

> "And what doeth the saint in the forest?" asked Zarathustra.
>
> The saint answered: "I make hymns and sing them; and in making hymns I laugh and weep and mumble: thus do I praise God.
>
> "With singing, weeping, laughing, and mumbling do I praise the God who is my God. But what dost thou bring us as a gift?"
>
> When Zarathustra had heard these words, he bowed to the saint and said: "What should I have to give thee! Let me rather hurry hence lest I take aught away from thee!"— And thus they parted from one another, the old man and Zarathustra, laughing like schoolboys.
>
> When Zarathustra was alone, however, he said to his heart: "Could it be possible! This old saint in the forest hath not yet heard of it, that *God is dead!*"

Another passage, which depicts the lonely prophet addressing a crowd engrossed in the performance of a rope dancer, discloses Zarathustra-Nietzsche's scorn of the mob:

> *I teach you the Superman.* Man is something that is to be surpassed. What have you done to surpass man?
>
> All beings hitherto have created something beyond themselves: and ye want to be the ebb of that great tide, and would rather go back to the beast than surpass man?
>
> What is the ape to man? A laughing stock, a thing of shame. And just the same shall man be to the Superman: a laughing stock, a thing of shame.
>
> Ye have made your way from the worm to man, and much within you is still worm. Once were ye apes, and even yet man is more of an ape than any of the apes.
>
> Even the wisest among you is only a disharmony and hybrid of plant and phantom. But do I bid you become phantoms or plants?
>
> Lo, I teach you the Superman!
>
> The Superman is the meaning of the earth. Let your will say: The Superman *shall* be the meaning of the earth!

When the crowd laughs at Zarathustra, it is Nietzsche's voice that rebukes them: "The people and the herd are angry with me . . . They are herdsmen, but they call themselves the good and just! Herdsmen, I say; but they call themselves true believers in orthodox faith. Behold these good and just! Whom do they hate most? The one who breaketh up their old table of values, the idol-breaker, the law-breaker. He, however, is the creator . . . I tell you: one must have chaos within one to give birth to a dancing star!"

Nietzsche's star declined toward the end of his life, but it rose again after his death. A sick man's theories spread through an ailing Europe. They infected the arts as well as politics. They were greatly responsible for Hitler's attacks on culture as well as his attempt to establish an "elite" leadership, a so-called master race which, fortunately, failed to rule common and "subservient humanity." They prompted the verdict of doom which Spengler pronounced in *The Decline of the West*. They inspired the grandiose tone poems of Richard Strauss. They infiltrated the widely differing philosophies of Bergson and Sartre as well as the novels of Thomas Mann and André Gide.

Nietzsche thought of himself as a cruel but needed corrective of Christianity's "slave morality," a prophet who urged man to repudiate his dependence on "Thou shalt not" and cry "I will!" A destroyer who had to wreck before he could rebuild, Nietzsche claimed he was constructing a race of strong and triumphant individuals. "Blood is the spirit of man. Of all that is written, I love only that which is written in blood." "Be not ashamed of the hatred and envy within your hearts. It is good to hate and glorious to be envied." "Is it the good cause which halloweth even war? I say it is the good war which halloweth every cause." Looking toward a murky future, Nietzsche predicted an eternal recurrence of a "pure" and savage culture, a new dispensation which was nothing but the old barbarism with modern machinery and without control. Following his dancing star in an agony of Dionysian abandon, he abandoned the world.

Thomas Alva Edison

[1847-1931]

*"His brain had the highest cash value in
history."*

THE GENIUS of Thomas Alva Edison was not ahead of his time,
but perfectly attuned to it. To an era of tremendous industrial
expansion his inventions contributed not only extraordinary
mechanical means but totally new fields for development. He literally illuminated his world with unsuspected light and made it vibrate with the miracle of recorded sound. However, unlike most
innovators, he did not have to wait to get his reward in heaven; he
received it munificently on this gratified and grateful earth. At the
time of his death, it was estimated that the business interests based
on or largely due to his multiple inventions amounted to the staggering sum of $25,683,544,343. This, as a *New York Times* analyst
estimated it, gave Edison's brain the highest cash value in history.

The Edisons had been in America before the Revolution. Samuel
Edison came of Dutch stock and his forebears had emigrated from
Holland to the Colonial States in the early part of the eighteenth
century and had subsequently moved to Canada. Samuel was a ho-
telkeeper in the little town of Vienna, on the northern shore of
Lake Erie, when he met and married a pretty eighteen-year-old
schoolteacher, Nancy Elliott, of Scottish descent, daughter of a
Baptist minister. Samuel was not only a publican but a public-
minded citizen, and it was inevitable that he should be drawn into
politics. Unfortunately for him, he was an extremist and took part
in a radical reform movement that turned into an insurrection
against the Canadian government. When the authorities began
rounding up the reformers, Samuel slipped out of town and fled
across the border. In 1842 he settled in the small Ohio city of
Milan, got into the shingle business, prospered, and sent for his
wife.

The youngest child in the Edison house in Milan was Thomas
Alva, born February 11, 1847. He was named Thomas after a great-
grandfather who had fought in the Revolutionary War, and Alva
after Captain Alva Bradley, who had brought his mother on a lake

boat from Canada to join her fugitive husband. The superstition that older parents produce precocious children seems to have had some justification in Edison's case; at the time of his birth his father was forty-three and his mother thirty-seven.

No one could have had a more untroubled childhood. The family was close knit, the home was comfortable, the living was always agreeable if not particularly gracious. Thomas' mother made much of her youngest son's fancied frailty and delighted to pamper him. When he was seven, the household moved to Port Huron, Michigan, where the lumber business flourished. As a result the Edisons were installed in a new and spacious house. Tom was sent proudly to school; his mother expected him to outshine all the other pupils. But his habit of "dreaming" struck the teacher as mere inattention, and she complained about it. Worse, she let it be known that she considered the youngster to be slightly "addled." Whereupon Tom's mother withdrew her son indignantly from the classroom. He had been subjected to "studies" for exactly three months, which is all the formal schooling Edison ever received. Instead, he had the kind of training that almost any child would choose: a combination of loving education and prolonged incubation. His mother kept him close to her and taught him herself. That she was an excellent teacher is proved not only by her early career but by the fact that, by the time he was twelve, Tom had absorbed such classics as Gibbon's *Decline and Fall of the Roman Empire* and Burton's *Anatomy of Melancholy,* to say nothing of the *Dictionary of Sciences* and other technical works. He was not only a voracious but a rapid reader; he seized the sense of a page in the time it takes the average reader to get the sense of a line. He forgot nothing; he seems to have had the gift of total recall.

Reading prompted experimenting, and experimenting led to queer results. One story has it that Tom gave a playmate a triple dose of seidlitz powders, hoping that enough gas would be generated to enable the boy to fly. Before he was in his teens he had arranged a shelf of boxes and bottles in the cellar—he called it his laboratory—and devoted himself to "tests" and "research." This brought out an unsuspected and extraordinarily early talent for commercial enterprise. Tom wanted more books and more materials and, since he needed money to buy them, he informed his parents that he was "going into business." Overriding their objections, he entered into a number of moneymaking activities. At thirteen he went to work as a newsboy and "candy butcher"; he hawked nuts and peppermints on the train between Port Huron and Detroit. He heard of a second-hand printing press, bought it at a bargain, wrote and edited a sheet of local news, and after printing it, sold the issue to a sizable subscription list. He opened truck garden outlets in Port Huron and, with the aplomb of an experienced entrepreneur, got other boys to work for him. Already it was evident that Edison's life was to be a Success Story, an almost fictional narrative, rivaling the Fame and Fortune series of Horatio Alger. Alger was Edison's contemporary, and it is a teasing thought that Alger might well have picked Edison for his model young hero.

Edison's first coup was accomplished while he was still a newsboy and, to quote his own words, he "had a chance to learn that money can be made out of a little careful thought." It happened during the Civil War when the demand for front line news made newspapers especially valuable. The day that the Battle of Shiloh screamed across the headlines, Edison ran to the office of the *Detroit Free Press* and asked to be trusted for a thousand papers. When the amazing request was unexpectedly granted, Edison got to work. He sent word ahead to telegrapher friends at all the stations along the route, asking them to post notices to the effect that the newspapers he was bringing carried the very first bulletins of the crucial battle. Crowds came out all along the way. Edison raised the price of his papers from a nickel to ten cents, then to fifteen, and then to a quarter. He sold the remaining copies for thirty-five cents each. The day's profits totaled about one hundred dollars, a small fortune for a fifteen-year-old boy.

Edison said, "Out of this one idea I made enough money to give me a chance to learn telegraphy." Most biographers, however, tell a more typically Algeresque story about Tom, The Young Telegrapher. According to the legend, Edison was at the Mount Clemens station, talking to the station master and telegrapher, Jim Mackenzie, when Mackenzie's small son wandered across the railroad track in front of an oncoming boxcar. Edison jumped from the platform to the track, grasped the boy in his arms, and had such a narrow escape that the car brushed his sleeve as it rushed by. Mackenzie was grateful, and following the formula, was willing to do anything for the rescuer, who asked nothing more than a knowledge of the Morse code and a few other essentials of telegraph operation. Before this rewarding experience, the youthful scientist had suffered a setback. Although he returned every night to the Port Huron household, the train had become his second home. He was allowed to set up a laboratory in the baggage car, and whenever he had a half hour of leisure, he experimented with wires, test tubes, and acids. One day, while mixing some chemicals, he accidentally set fire to the car. The conductor's patience had been almost exhausted several times before; now it exploded. He extinguished the fire, threw out Tom's equipment, and boxed his ears. This was the first of the ear injuries Edison was to sustain. The next damage also occurred on the railroad. Tom was selling papers in a station when the whistle blew, the train started, and he raced to get aboard. A baggage car attendant, trying to help him, pulled him up literally by the ears. There was a clap of pain, and when the agony had eased the youngster found he had lost a good part of his hearing. From then on he grew increasingly deaf.

With a number of successful ventures behind him, Edison was independent and strangely mature at sixteen. Qualifying as a telegraph operator, he got his first salaried position in Canada. He was hard-working, but he combined industry with restlessness; his next five years were wander-years. He lost jobs not only because he refused to stay in one place, but because of the scientific experiments which he conducted to the detriment of his daily work. His extra-curricular activities kept him awake far into the night; he claimed that people slept away far too much of their lives.

At twenty-one he felt he had roamed enough, and taking a deliberate turn in his career, found a place in Boston. There began the astonishing performances which lasted as long as he lived. He was given the night shift at a Western Union telegraph office, but during the day he worked on his own ideas in a rented laboratory. He managed to get some sleep during the time left over—usually four hours. He made several devices for telegraphic equipment, but no one was interested. Then he invented a mechanism for recording votes and with this, in 1868, he took out his first patent. In the hope that Congress would adopt his recorder, he journeyed to Washington, managed somehow to get an interview with a committee, but was frankly told that his machine was "undesirable" since it would make obsolete the minority's standard weapons of delay and filibustering. This convinced Edison. Determined henceforth to work only on things that people wanted and would be willing to buy, he went to New York.

Not even Alger could have written anything more fictional than Edison's first days in the metropolis. The young man arrived absolutely penniless, but there was a masonic feeling among telegraph men and an operator loaned him a dollar and arranged for him to bed down temporarily in the battery room of a concern known as the Gold Indicator Company. This firm had the monopoly of a wire system connecting tickers in the office of stockbrokers with a central keyboard over which the fluctuating prices of gold were quoted. After three days of futile job hunting, with his borrowed dollar gone, Tom was in the Gold Indicator offices when the mechanism suddenly stopped working. The place went frantic. No one could locate the difficulty. Tom went to the president of the company and said he thought he knew what the trouble was. "Fix it, then," he was curtly told. Tom had seen what the company engineers had not: that a spring had broken and fallen down, wedging two gear wheels. Correction was quickly made and the tickers were in operation again. As a result, Tom was instantly hired as foreman of the company, at a salary of $300 a month.

As before, Tom's salary went into a workshop and materials. In a short while, with an idea for an improvement of the entire ticker system, Tom resigned his job and gave all his time to the new invention. When completed—much the same ticker equipment used by Wall Street today—he offered it to his former employer. Asked his price, he hesitated, considering whether $5000 would be prohibitive or $3000 too modest. He suggested that the firm make him an offer. "Would forty thousand dollars satisfy you?" was the answer. He was not twenty-two.

With his wealth, Edison opened a plant to manufacture the stock tickers; he had to run day and night shifts to keep up with his orders, serving as a foreman on both shifts. No matter how hard he worked or how little he slept, the inventions kept coming. By 1876, he had taken out 122 patents. According to H. Gordon Garbedian's easy-reading biography, *Thomas Alva Edison,* at one time he worked simultaneously on forty-five different inventions, most of them being further improvements on telegraphy operation.

At twenty-four Edison married Mary Stillwell, who had been helping him in the laboratory. Three children were born in the next six years: a daughter, Marion, and two sons, Thomas Alva, Jr., and William. Before 1878 Edison had moved to Menlo Park, a small town in New Jersey, where he built a workshop near his home. Visions of wider and more personal communication led him from the telegraph, with the words written in code, to another use of the wire, a wire which would transmit not only the word direct but the human voice itself. This was the telephone, which Alexander Graham Bell had already patented; but Bell's instrument was better in theory than in practice. Discovering the factor that would make for clarity as well as general practicality, Edison invented a carbon transmitter, and for its use, Western Union paid him $100,-000. Realizing that any large sum of money would be spent too quickly and on too many experiments, Edison asked to have the money paid to him over seventeen years at the rate of $6,000. Bitter legislation grew out of disputes between Western Union and the Bell Telephone Company over the Edison and Bell patents; there were seemingly endless claims and counterclaims. Finally, Western Union surrendered the Edison inventions, as well as their telephone business, in exchange for twenty per cent royalty, to the Bell system.

It is idle to speculate how much Edison's deafness was responsible for his preoccupation with sound; but even before he was thirty, he was planning new methods which would propel the human voice and record it. Something occurred to Edison while working on the telephone transmitter; a year after it was finished, he thought of a way of capturing vibrations of the air so that they could not only be recorded but reproduced. He attached an electromagnetic pickup to a revolving turntable, and ran through it a strip of paper which had been coated with paraffin. As the paper passed through the instrument, Edison shouted, "Whooooo!" When he ran the paper back through the apparatus, he could hear a ghostly but unmistakable echo of his shout. His laboratory note of July 18, 1877, reads as follows: "Tried experiment with diaphragm and embossing point held against paraffin paper moved rapidly. The speaking vibrations indented nicely; there is no doubt that I shall be able to store up and reproduce automatically at any future time the human voice perfectly." The future came more quickly than even Edison expected. A month later, he handed a drawing for an odd but simple model to one of his mechanics, John Kreusi, and said, "Here's an eighteen-dollar job for you." When the puzzled Kreusi fashioned it, Edison wound a sheet of tinfoil around the cylinder, or drum, and affixed a metal point. Then, turning the crank which revolved the cylinder, Edison recited a nursery rhyme into a mouthpiece. After he had pronounced the last syllable, he readjusted the needle to the reproducing diaphragm, and turning the cylinder again, listened intently. Squeakily but clearly the machine announced, "Mary had a little lamb; its fleece was white as snow

. . ." Although he did not expect anything as gratifying, Edison controlled his satisfaction; but the astonished Kreusi muttered "God in heaven!" and crossed himself.

Most of Edison's inventions were the result of painstaking tests involving slow, deliberate, and protracted elimination of things that would not work in order to find the one thing that would. The immediate impact of the phonograph with the suddenness of its accomplishment was spectacular. In his *Thomas A. Edison; Benefactor of Mankind,* Francis Trevelyan Miller quotes the inventor as saying, "I was never so taken aback in my life. I was always afraid of anything which worked the first time." Edison's diary shows that he considered the phonograph his greatest invention; he spent years improving the recording as well as the reproducing apparatus. He claimed that his deafness was not a liability but an asset, that it aided his concentration and enabled him to hear overtones missed by the average ear. It is interesting to note that the "ten main uses" given in 1878, when Edison applied for the patent, begin with "Letter Writing and all kinds of dictation without the aid of a stenographer," followed by "Phonograph books, which will speak to blind people without effort on their part," while "The teaching of elocution" is listed as the third use, and "Reproduction of music" is fourth.

No sooner was the phonograph invented than Edison decided to answer the challenge of electric light. That electricity could produce light was by no means unknown, but the scientists had been unable to find a material which would not burn out and instantly consume itself. Edison read everything that had been written on the subject of lighting; he filled two hundred notebooks and forty thousand pages with jottings and diagrams. He then engaged to solve the problem by doing the very opposite of what had been tried; instead of reducing resistance to the electric current, he increased it. After testing countless materials, he finally narrowed the field down to a carbonized element and discovered the effectiveness of the vacuum bulb. On December 31, 1879—appropriately on the eve of the New Year—an expectant but still doubting crowd was invited to view Edison's latest triumph, the first public exhibit of electric lighting which maintained its brilliance. The amazement was unbounded. Nicknamed "The Wizard of Menlo Park," Edison became a national figure at the age of thirty-two.

Good though it was, Edison was determined to make his electric light bulb better. He had not yet found the ideal material for the filament. Bamboo was the most promising, and Edison had to find out which variety of bamboo was the best. Expeditions which cost him over one hundred thousand dollars were sent out all over the world. Out of six thousand specimens obtained, three proved satisfactory. (Eventually Edison utilized an artificial filament, but in the early years of electric lighting, carbonized bamboo burned in every bulb.) It was now necessary to create a hitherto unknown electric lighting system, including the sources of power, the wiring, the entire elaborate apparatus. Edison invented a new dynamo as well as new types of machinery, and set up the organization which was the forerunner of such gigantic utilities as today's Consolidated Edison Company. Electric lighting, however, was not his sole interest. In his mid-thirties Edison also perfected a magnetic ore separator and an electric railway with a third rail, the type which was later adopted by the New York City subway.

At thirty-seven Edison found himself alone. His wife died of typhoid fever in 1884, the three children went to live with their maternal grandmother, and Edison spent most of his time at his New York offices. The tremendous growth of his far-reaching enterprises made an additional move necessary, and his factories were soon operating in Schenectady, transforming it from a small town, the home of Union College, to one of the great manufacturing centers of the country. Although Edison did not scorn success and public acclaim, he was a domestic person; he missed the casual comforts of a household. A year and a half after the loss of his wife he met Mina Miller, whose father, Lewis Miller, was not only an inventor of agricultural machinery but a philanthropist and educator. Mina was young, lovely, and cultivated; a rapid though shy courtship followed. He taught his sweetheart the Morse code, and after she had learned it, tested her with a message tapped out with a coin. The "message" was a proposal of marriage, and in reply Mina tapped out her acceptance. After their marriage in 1886, Edison installed the whole family on an estate in New Jersey's Orange Mountains. By his second wife Edison had three children; a daughter, Madeline, a son, Theodore, and another son, Charles, who became Secretary of the Navy and Governor of New Jersey.

By his forties Edison had attained international fame. He carried his distinction lightly. His face, according to George S. Bryan's *Edison: The Man and His Work,* "was large, calm, candid, friendly, strong. From it looked uncommonly liquid and brilliant gray eyes. The chin was firm; the mouth large, finely-molded, and sensitive; the nose prominent. Above the generous but closely-set ears, the head rose dome-like. Dark hair, already grizzled, was parted at the right, and usually a lock or two of it hung loosely over the left side of the high forehead. It was a face in which what is conventionally called the dreamer was blended with the man of action." Mina Edison furnished another description: "If you will think of one who is living in the highest state of exhilaration, seeing nothing, hearing nothing, thinking nothing, doing nothing, except what has a vital bearing on the task in hand, then you will have a perfect photograph of Mr. Edison at such times when he is working." He delighted in odd and pithy expressions. He was responsible for the often quoted epigram that genius was "one per cent inspiration and ninety-nine per cent perspiration." Asked why a certain workman was no longer in his employ, Edison replied, "He was so slow that it would take him half an hour to get out of the field of a microscope." He remarked in his diary: "Weather blasphemingly hot . . . This would be a good day to adopt Sydney Smith's plan of taking off your flesh and sitting down in your bones. *Memo*—Go to a print cloth mill and have yourself run through the calico printing machine. This would be the Ultima Thule of thin clothing."

After the phonograph and the electric light became commonplace, Edison turned to another invention which was to have an enormous influence. This was the motion picture camera, which he hoped would be a great factor in spreading education. When he saw that the production of moving pictures was almost wholly for entertainment, he ceased his original and experimental film making. Although the phonograph, the electric light, and the motion picture camera overshadowed most of his other work, Edison continued to make important contributions until the day of his death. Among other things, he radically improved the operation of the first typewriter, designed a new type of mimeograph machine, invented the long kiln for the making of Portland cement and a perfect alkaline storage battery. During the First World War, there was a shortage of carbolic acid, formerly imported from Germany. Told by American chemists that a synthetic substitute was impossible, Edison had a plant turning it out in eighteen days. One of his main preoccupations was the finding of a native source of rubber; late in life he actually succeeded in vulcanizing rubber made from goldenrod. He had only one hobby: work. "Work heals and ennobles," he said on his seventy-seventh birthday, when asked for his philosophy of life. "Work brings out the secrets of nature and applies them for the happiness of men."

In 1928 Edison was awarded the Congressional Medal of Honor. A year later Henry Ford, one of Edison's closest friends, commemorated the fiftieth anniversary of the electric light by a celebration at Dearborn, Michigan, where Ford had recreated the original laboratory at Menlo Park. Active to the end, Edison died October 18, 1931, at the age of eighty-four. Before his death the United States Patent Office had granted him 1098 separate patents.

Edison was mainly concerned with the improvement of humanity's physical well-being rather than with its spiritual advancement. He repeatedly made it clear that his first thought was the commercial potentiality of an invention. Nevertheless, he was not a money-making machine. He read widely—he was particularly fond of Shakespeare and Tom Paine—and played the violin creditably. His critics charged that Edison was an improver rather than an originator, with which Edison was disposed to agree. "Through all the years of experimenting and research, I never once made a discovery," he said modestly. "I start where the last man left off . . . All my work was deductive, and the results I achieved were those of invention pure and simple." John Tyndall put it somewhat differently: "Edison had the penetration to seize the relationship of facts and principles and the art to reduce them to novel and concrete combinations." The "novel and concrete combinations" may not have enlarged man's spiritual stature but it made his world more comfortable, more communicative, and more colorful than it had ever been.

Vincent Van Gogh

[1853-1890]

*"Not trees, but growth; not blossoms, but
bloom."*

VINCENT VAN GOGH was only thirty-seven when he killed himself and he had been a painter less than ten years. Yet in that decade he had crowded the time with some of the most passionate and personal canvases ever conceived. His spirit struggling with agonized love and fear of life is shown as explicitly in those canvases as in his revealing correspondence. Painting with him was a vehement confession, a tortured sacrament rather than a source of pleasure. He combined beauty and squalor, exaltation and misery, to turn despair into affirmative creation. "I want," he cried, "to paint humanity, humanity, and again humanity."

He was born March 30, 1853, in the village of Groot Zundert, in the province of Brabant, Holland. His father was a pastor, and Vincent, the oldest of six children, hoped to follow his example as a devout churchman. But since his parents were even poorer than most ministers' families, it was decided that the boy should have a business career. Three of his father's brothers were art dealers, and his Uncle Vincent, after whom he had been named, procured a position for him when he was sixteen with the firm of Goupil and Company, which had branches not only on the Continent but in England and, subsequently, in America. The combination of timidity, which he inherited from his father, and obstinacy, which he owed to his mother, scarcely made him a successful art salesman. Nevertheless, he was competent enough, and his uncle was sufficiently important, for him to be transferred from the Hague branch to the Paris office and, at twenty, to London. He made few friends. The only person with whom he was completely at home was his brother Theo, three years younger than himself. Theo was to become an art dealer, Vincent's sole support, and the recipient of frank and probing letters from Vincent, a correspondence constituting a virtual autobiography—one of the great human documents of our time.

It was in London that Vincent received his first shock of rejection. He fell in love with his landlady's daughter and assumed that she was similarly drawn to him. She was, however, repelled rather than attracted. Vincent was an awkward youth, whose huge head bristled with flaming red hair; his eyebrows bulged over sharply protruding cheekbones, and his small glittering blue eyes frightened her. Besides, she was already engaged. Deeply hurt, he took out his humiliation on Goupil's customers, told them they were buying trash, and insulted them. He was transferred back to Paris and only his uncle's influence kept him with the firm. His manner continued to be so offensive and his contempt for the commercial side of art was so evident that Goupil's managers finally gave him notice.

Van Gogh was twenty-three when he went back to England to teach languages in a small school at Ramsgate. He had, however, not lost the hope of being a servant of God, and he began studying and preaching Methodism in Islesworth. Although he failed in his examinations for the ministry, his purpose remained unshaken. Since he could not become a pastor, he went as a lay preacher to the Borinage in Belgium. It was a dismal district of impoverished coal miners, men who lived literally underground. Van Gogh shared their life, not only in their homes but in the pits. He suffered with them; dressed, lived and ate as poorly as they did; nursed the sick, and tried to teach the children. He gave away his meager salary, then most of his clothes, then his few possessions, including his bed. When the miners went on strike, he sided with them. This was too much for the authorities in Brussels. They disapproved of his excessive zeal; he was, in the eyes of the well-bred and well-dressed committee, a bad example. When his term came to an end, they refused to renew the appointment, and he was forbidden to preach.

He tried to pick up the threads of his past existence in his father's parsonage, but his father was sententious and reproved his son for failing to uphold the dignity of the Church. Vincent went on foot many miles to ask the advice of Jules Breton, who had painted the lowly at their simple tasks, but Breton's brilliantly lighted mansion intimidated him and he did not even knock at the door. Disillusioned and disconsolate, he returned to the Borinage.

He rented a small room from a miner and gave himself up to melancholy. "I have chosen active despair," he wrote to Theo, "insofar as I have any opportunity for action. I have found a despair that hopes and strives . . . For perhaps five years I have been straying about without an occupation . . . I confess that my studies are wretched and desperate, and I lack incomparably more than I possess . . . You may ask why I didn't stay at the university. I can only answer that I prefer to die a natural death than to prepare myself for it at a university . . . My real, my inner self, has not changed. If anything has changed at all, it is that I now think, love, and believe much more profoundly than I ever did." Love was becoming a fixed idea with him. It was not a personal love that he pursued but an understanding love of the intelligence which creates and communicates. "You must love with a high and intense determination, with your will and your intellect," he wrote, "and seek always to deepen, expand, and improve your knowledge, for that way lies God. If a man loves Rembrandt profoundly, then in his heart of hearts he knows he knows God."

He read the Bible and Michelet's *French Revolution*. He immersed himself in the novels of Hugo, Zola, Dickens, and Harriet Beecher Stowe, writers who glorified the oppressed and the enslaved. Love of creation drove him to make drawings of what he saw around him in the Borinage. The miners were his models. He taught himself to draw by copying other draftsmen. He urged Theo to send him reproductions of paintings from Paris, where Theo was beginning to prosper. Delighted that Vincent was trying to "find himself," Theo offered to send an allowance of one hundred francs a month and persuaded him to leave the black hole of the Borinage, where he had starved for two years, and study painting in Brussels.

At twenty-seven Van Gogh considered himself a failure. He had been unable to make a living, much less a career, as an art dealer, a teacher, or a missionary. Since he had no hope of succeeding in any field approved by a society dedicated to success, he chose what seemed the most eccentric and hopeless form of unemployment: he decided to be an artist. In spite of adversities, he sought a medium which would spread courage; he wanted to show gratitude for life itself. He had not begun to paint, but he hoped some day "to say something comforting as music is comforting. I want to paint men and women with that something of the eternal which the halo used to symbolize and which we seek to give by the actual radiance and vibration of coloring." As yet he did nothing but draw, and his drawings were awkward, childish in line and faulty in execution. He bought a *Manual of Design,* studied the science of anatomy, and learned perspective from a commercial illustrator. He copied and recopied Millet, whom he worshiped for his "Sower," the "Man with the Hoe," the "Gleaners," and other portrayals of the laboring peasant. Van Gogh did not aim to be a great artist; he merely hoped to record the faces and hardships of the painfully poor, of whom he was one of the humblest.

At the end of a long winter in Brussels, he went to see his parents. A cousin of his was visiting in Etten, where his father now had a parish. She was several years older than Vincent, a widow with a four-year-old son. Van Gogh declared his love and, although she discouraged him, he followed her to Amsterdam. Her parents were not even civil; they refused to let him talk to her. Van Gogh stretched his hand over an oil lamp and pleaded to be allowed to see her only as long as he could hold his hand in the flame. They turned their backs. Rejected for the second time, Van Gogh felt abandoned and alone. He no longer had anything in common with his father, whom he regarded as a sanctimonious hypocrite; the rest of his family was against him. Only Theo remained faithful and believed in him, whatever he might become.

He went to the Hague and was grateful to find that Mauve, who had married one of his cousins, was willing to teach him. Mauve was a conventional painter, popular for the reposeful atmosphere of his prettily limpid landscapes, but it was Mauve who helped Van Gogh to undertake his first efforts in oils—still life studies of potatoes, shoes, household objects. Theo continued to support him, and he was occasionally able to engage a model for a few pennies: day laborers out of work, derelicts, beggars, and prostitutes.

It was with a prostitute that he fell in love. This time he was not rejected. Christina, nicknamed Sien, had one child and was pregnant with another. She was coarse, ill, and smoked cigars, but the thirty-year-old Van Gogh took her from the gutter and proposed to marry her. For a while, he seemed to be happy, at least at peace; but although he cared for her, he could not talk to her. They had nothing in common except a background of misery. She was almost illiterate and when his fellow artists sometimes spent an evening with them she felt herself excluded. Her mother made things worse; she persuaded her daughter that her former life in a pleasantly crowded brothel was gayer than isolation in a painter's garret. Gradually Sien slipped back into her old profession and, after two years, once more Van Gogh was alone.

To Shakespeare's "Ripeness is all" Van Gogh might have added "Emotion is everything." He put emotion into every object he saw, every person he met, every thing he touched. He worked with such penetration that he plunged through the surface of appearance to the reality of being. He began to paint with a conviction which startled Mauve and which he himself did not know he possessed. He had not yet solved the mystery of color, but he was already uncovering some of its secrets. He described to Theo the way he painted an autumn sunset: "The main thing is to get the depth of color, the enormous force and solidity of the ground. I did not realize until I came to paint how much light there is even in the dark parts. I had to catch the light and yet convey the depths of solid, fat, glowing color . . . Young beech trees grow in the soil, and one side of them sucks the light and reflects a green radiance, while the other casts warm black-green shadows. Behind their slender trunks and the brown-red soil, the sky is a very tender, warm blue-gray . . . I had to paint quickly as the light was changing, and was surprised to see how solid the slim trunks were in the background. I began then with the brush, but as the ground was already covered with heavy color, the strokes simply disappeared; so I squeezed the trees and the roots straight out of the tubes and then modeled them a little with my brush. Now my little trees stand quite solidly in the earth and their roots support them."

When his parents moved to the Brabant village of Neunen, Vincent persuaded them to let him live and paint in the washhouse. It was farming country and he soaked himself in the soil. He drew and painted plowed fields, mud-colored cottages, men and women digging, a weaver at his loom, laborers at their evening meal—his first important canvas—in which the peasants look as brown and homely and earthy as the potatoes they are eating. He painted not only the workers themselves but, saturated in their clothes and in their bodies, the essence of all work. He met a woman who, like the others toward whom he had been impelled, was older than Vincent, and she seemed to care for him. But her family, having heard nothing good about the unkempt idler who refused to do an honest day's work, ridiculed him and nagged at her until she attempted to kill herself with strychnine. Once again he had been shut out, and since no one but Theo showed the slightest interest in his sketches, he was again made to realize he had nothing to offer anyone. He had to get away from everything and everybody he knew except Theo. Theo was living in Paris and in February, 1886, Vincent joined him there.

In Paris he discovered a world he never could have imagined. It was not the giddy world of the French capital but the more splendid world of the French Impressionists. He stood in front of the canvases of Pissarro, Seurat, Signac, Gauguin, Toulouse-Lautrec, and reveled in every new attempt to get rid of conventional subject matter, break down barriers, clear the palette of its somber tones, and break up color to suggest the play of light. He came upon a showing of Japanese prints and fell in love with the boldness of design, the irregular compositions, and the large areas of flat color. Without copying them he combined the discoveries and surpassed them. Although he retained the heavy rhythms and northern solidity which gave his work so powerful an impact—the very opposite of Dutch stolidity—his palette became lighter, his compositions more delicate. His brush strokes were alternately broad and broken; dots, dashes, and dancing points fused into units that not only glowed but developed luminous small designs within the major pattern. His pictures seemed to be alive, said someone, with little wriggling snakes of color. His pent-up nature erupted into one explosive canvas after another. Even his quietest and most orderly arrangements—a table, a chair, a bedroom, a young girl "arranged" to look Japanese, a seated postman—vibrate with an unconscious energy that the conscious craftsman could not repress.

There was practically no response to the work. His fellow artists, especially Gauguin, were pleasant to him, but he did not want their patronizing encouragement. Theo peddled a few of his drawings, but no dealer would look at his paintings.

Suddenly he sickened of Paris. He was tired of all the talk about styles and technique, and he had a queer feeling that he did not have long to complete the work which he had barely begun. "I must start all over again," he wrote to Theo. "I must go down into the earth, naked, once more. Three or four years, that is all I have, but I must make one more effort. Somewhere, beneath an open sky, I must find at last what I am seeking. There is wind down there—I must feel it on my skin. In Paris I have lost my sense for the wind altogether; in fact I am losing my very skin by degrees." He dreamed of a community of artists somewhere in the south, cleaned up the apartment he had shared with Theo, hung his pictures on the walls to remind Theo of him, and went to Arles.

At Arles he bathed himself and his canvases in the riotous hues of the south. He had never been so excited and so energetic. He painted everything he saw: washerwomen by a stream, the bridge above it, spring orchards bursting into bloom, a sidewalk café at night, sunflowers in every conceivable tone of yellow, portraits of himself, people of all kinds—each day for ten days he painted another picture of the flower garden. At first glance, many of the pictures appear to be improvisations, collections of rapid notes and abrupt rhythms which seem to give his forms more life than his subjects possessed. In *Vincent: A Life of Vincent Van Gogh,* Julius Meier-Graefe speaks of the "demoniacal pitch" of Van Gogh, the romanticist, who had "a hurricane in his bosom . . . His eyes bit into every object, into trees and soil, like an axe. He kneaded the ephemeral air into a solid mass . . . As everything was yellow, he had to paint yellow, but he painted it so that you could taste, hear, smell, and touch it. He painted until he made the stones talk . . . He ceased to paint trees, but painted growth, tree-like existence; not blossoms but bloom . . . The stroke of his brush, which had hitherto been a skilful instrument mastered by sheer determination, now became an organic entity with a life of its own, and the palette he had wearily acquired burst into flame." He drenched his paintings with almost blinding light, as if to make up for the dark days of the past and hold the sun for the darker days to come. He explained his method and reason for heightening his color schemes: "Blond hair is raised to orange, then to chrome, or even pale lemon. Then the stupid wall behind the head is taken away and a simple background of rich blue extends to infinity. With a simple combination of two rich colors it is possible to give luminosity to a head, as mysterious as a star in the azure sky."

He developed a sense of color symbolism in "The Night Café." He said he wanted "to express the terrible passions of humanity by means of red and green. I have tried to express the idea that the café is a place where one can ruin one's self, run mad, or commit a crime. So I have attempted, as it were, to show the powers of darkness in a low drink-shop by soft Louis XV green and malachite, contrasting with yellow green and hard blue greens—and all this in an atmosphere like a devil's furnace, of pale sulphur."

He was happy when Gauguin decided to join him at Arles. Although his art colony consisted of only two, he believed that there were no limits to what a brotherhood could produce. At first the association was rewarding, the more so since the insecure Van Gogh was fascinated by Gauguin's assertive confidence and, obviously unaware that Gauguin was his inferior, was willing to be Gauguin's pupil. It was some time before the differences in the two men made it impossible for them to work together.

Gauguin had been a financier, a successful stockbroker, who had given up a life of affluence and had begun painting as a hobby. Van Gogh, who had been reared in poverty, found it hard to adjust himself to Gauguin's expansive manners and erratic tastes. Gauguin was a large, striking-looking, swaggering bohemian, irresistible to women. Van Gogh was conscious of his own unattractive, even frightening, appearance which alienated everyone. Gauguin was sophisticated and cynical; his rough disposals of the things Van Gogh held sacred were a continual affront. Gauguin, who made fun of most of the contemporaries, was frank about his prejudices. Van Gogh's preferences were a collection of contradictions; he spoke of the sentimental landscapes of Breton and the picture-book battle pictures of Meissonier in the same breath as his adulation of Rembrandt.

Quarrels were inevitable. Van Gogh always winced at Gauguin's quick-witted, casual bitterness; after each new argument he would feel more frustrated than after the previous one. One day when Gauguin's cleverness seemed particularly cruel, Van Gogh threw a glass of absinthe at his tormentor. Gauguin picked him up and carried him out of the café. A few days later, Gauguin heard someone pattering behind him, turned, and saw Van Gogh with a knife. Van Gogh fled, and the next morning was found unconscious in his room, his head bandaged in a bloody towel. He had cut off an ear and sent it to one of the prostitutes he and Gauguin had visited. It was a Christmas present, a return for being teased about his oversized ears.

There was no question now about Van Gogh's abnormality. Theo was summoned and arranged to have Vincent sent to a hospital where, after spells of delirium, the painter seemed to recover. But when he returned to the little yellow house that had become his symbol of home, the townspeople feared it might be dangerous to have him at large. They spied upon him; the children mocked, and the grownups peered through the windows. When a crowd collected in front of the house, Van Gogh opened a window and started to preach to the people. Then he began to scream, and had to be locked in a padded cell and strapped to a metal bed. When they let him out of the isolation chamber, he begged to be taken to a quiet place, an asylum where he might get over his hallucinations. In early May, 1889, he was received in the institution for the insane at the cloister of Saint-Rémy.

It was at Saint-Rémy, between fits of what was probably epilepsy rather than (as some have speculated) schizophrenia, that Van Gogh achieved some of his greatest work. The paintings of this period are often overwrought but, in their very surcharged emotion, tremendously moving. When confined to his room with its iron-barred windows, he made colored copies of reproductions, woodcuts and lithographs, which Theo sent him; but his paintings were so much stronger, so much more aware of the essence of the originals that, as Meier-Graefe remarks, "in a few centuries his copies may be regarded as the originals and Millet's originals as weak imitations." During the many lucid intervals when he was allowed to paint in the open—he considered his art the "lightning rod" of his illness—he was completely sane and joyfully painted iris in high-keyed blues, wheat fields gay with red poppies, intricately limbed olive orchards, flame-like trees, the expanse of widening horizons. Sometimes a touch of dementia took hold of his brush and swept the canvas free of reality. "The Starry Night," for example, is not so much a painting as a riot of ecstasy. This is the way the heavens must appear to a man who is mad with wonder and apprehension. The stars are not fixed; they do not shine or sparkle in their proper place or proportions; instead, they burn and swell and spin like gigantic, fiery pinwheels spewed into space. The entire sky rushes along with them. The clouds are swirling streams of luminous matter; the cypresses shoot their green fountains into the agitated air, while all the unseen energies of night become visible and whirl by at inconceivable speed.

The attacks continued, and the fits increased in duration. Vincent believed, and Theo hoped, that he might get well in some place less prison-like, more humanely supervised, and after a year at Saint-Rémy, he was brought to Auvers on the river Oise. Things promised well. He was only twenty miles away from Theo in Paris. His doctor, the understanding Dr. Gachet, was a connoisseur of art and an accomplished etcher, sympathetic with his patient's aberrations and enthusiastic about his every creative effort. Van Gogh painted him—a sad, pale face against a deeply animated background—with an expression not unlike his own, "the heartbroken expression of our time." Afterwards the colors became wilder and the brushwork more agitated as his mood darkened to render sorrow and extreme solitude. The melancholy grew worse as he thought of the possibility that further seizures would prevent his working altogether. Rather than be doomed to a life of incurable madness and remain a never-ending burden to Theo, who had suffered so much with him, he determined to stop being a liability to himself and others. Saying he was going to shoot crows, he borrowed a revolver and shot himself in the stomach. When Theo arrived, he said, "I did it for the good of all," and died July 29, 1890, at the age of thirty-seven. Theo never recovered from the tragedy. Six months later he, too, went insane, died in Holland, and was buried in the churchyard at Auvers-sur-Oise, next to his beloved brother.

Van Gogh lived to see only one favorable article about his work; he sold only two paintings for which he was paid a few hundred francs. Sixty years after his death it was estimated that the drawings and canvases he had done in ten years were worth thirty million dollars. His very departures from academic painting showed others how to put into pigments the full force of "those terrible things, men's passions." His intensities of feeling compel not only the onlooker's attention but his participation. He lifts emotion to a pitch of almost unbearable excitement and communicates the intensity which brought him to the breaking point. "Instead of trying to reproduce exactly what I have before my eyes, I use color more arbitrarily so as to express myself more forcibly," he wrote. "I should be in despair if my figures were 'correct' . . . My great longing is to learn to make those very incorrections, those deviations, remodelings, changes of reality, that may become, yes, untruth—but more true than the literal truth." Something never before accomplished was achieved by Van Gogh's exaggerated perspectives, his strange radiations which distinguished common objects, his fused splinters of light. "Part of his continuing appeal," wrote Daniel Catton Rich, director of the Chicago Art Institute, "may lie in his unique ability to suggest those tensions and dislocations under which man lives today . . . A period that idolizes Dostoevsky and makes a prophet out of Kafka will continue to react to such intense emotions . . . To a confused world his vital images have what he desired above all else: the power to reveal and to console."

With the exceptions of Rembrandt and El Greco, Van Gogh was the most dramatic painter who ever lived. Rembrandt achieved drama by a continual play of extraordinary lighting; El Greco attained it by the suppressed violence of his distortions. But there is drama in Van Gogh's very touch, the packed lines and turbulent colors mounting to a blaze of rapture. Frenzied and tormented, Van Gogh never ceased to be concerned with the troubled human comedy; even in his paroxysms he responded to its moral force. Everything he did was another attempt to add mortal passion and pity to the immortal humanity of art.

Sigmund Freud

[1856-1939]

"Life is a problem for everybody."

A VIENNESE PSYCHOLOGIST, exploring the relation of man's emotions to his everyday environment, profoundly influenced every field of creativeness, caused a controversy whose vehemence is still unabated, and altered the thinking of an entire generation. Followed by a few disciples and dissidents, he challenged humanity's estimate of itself, changed the course of its literature, and even expanded the language to such an extent that not merely neurotic individuals, the prime source of his studies, but ordinary workmen, businessmen, and stolid mechanics, talk casually of an "inferiority complex" and other "inhibitions." People who have never heard of the *Psychopathology of Everyday Life* and who know Freud only as a name, have no hesitation in speaking of "maladjustment," "repression," "fixation," "transference," "defense mechanism," "overcompensation," "suppressed desire," "libido," and "free association," unaware that they are echoing the clinical vocabulary of the Austrian doctor and his warring interpreters.

Sigmund Freud, father of psychoanalysis, was born May 6, 1856, in Freiberg, Moravia, formerly Austria, now part of Czechoslovakia. His father was a Jewish tradesman, and when the child was four, the Freuds moved to Vienna. The eldest of eight children by his father's second marriage, the boy became the pride of the family. As a schoolboy he was unusually adept in the study of chemistry and botany. Fascinated by Darwin's then heretical theories, he developed an unusually speculative habit of inquiry, but it was the reading of Goethe's essay on Nature which made him decide to devote himself to the pursuit of human knowledge. Later he learned English in order to enjoy its literature in the original tongue, and for ten years he read only English books; he was particularly devoted to the noble rhetoric of Shakespeare and the puritan power of Milton.

Freud entered medical school at seventeen, and although he encountered a distinct display of anti-Semitism, he was not embittered by it. "I could never grasp why I should be ashamed of my origin or, as they began to say, of my 'race' . . . Nevertheless," he wrote in his *Self-Portrait,* "the first impressions produced one important result. At a rather early date, I became aware of my destiny: to belong to the critical minority as opposed to the unquestioning majority. A certain independence of judgment was therefore developed." At the university he made researches in the histology of the nervous system, and worked in the Institute of Cerebral Anatomy from his twentieth to his twenty-sixth year. Convinced that he would never be a general practitioner, yet compelled to earn a living, he entered Vienna's famous *Allgemeine Krankenhaus* (General Hospital) and worked as a clinical neurologist. He was already disturbed by the split between the fantasy and reality of his patients' symptoms, and although his orthodox reports on diseases of the nervous system were praised by his colleagues, he was searching for a method which would permit a deeper penetration into the patient's mind. In his twenty-ninth year he found a clue. A Viennese physician claimed he had cured patients of hysteria by hypnotizing them and then getting them to recall the circumstances preceding the attacks. Believing that hypnosis was one way of uncovering the source of mental disorders, Freud went to Paris, studied under Jean Marie Charcot, who was exciting the medical world by his use of hypnotism at his neurological clinic, and remained a year with the specialist as student and translator.

At thirty Freud returned to Vienna, married Martha Bernays, who had waited four years for him, and entered private practice. For a while Freud practiced what Charcot had preached. The antagonism to his method was intense; Freud was derided as an "unbalanced faddist," a "charlatan," and other opprobrious terms which, no matter how carefully he examined and revised his findings, followed him the rest of his life. "It was the age of physical therapy," wrote Dr. A. A. Brill in an introduction to *The Basic Writings of Sigmund Freud.* "Physicians knew nothing about the psychic factors in disease; everything was judged by the formula, *Mens sana in corpore sano.* Every symptom was explained on the basis of some organic lesion; if nothing physical was discovered, it was assumed that there must be something in the brain to account for the disturbance. The treatment was based on this same deficient understanding: drugs, hydrotherapy, and electrotherapy were the only agents that physicians could use." Recognizing the failure of pills, potions, cold baths, and electricity to accomplish more than temporary alleviation of deep malaises, Freud continued to experiment in hypnotic therapy. However, working on cases of amnesia and aphasia, Freud had a theory that suggestion alone might achieve the same results as suggestion under hypnotism. He tried this new and hazardous approach and discovered that by inducing the patient to recall his past through "free associations" he could revive the patient's hidden memories. The consequent release of psychic force became the nucleus of the method Freud called psychoanalysis. Those who disbelieved in the method contended it was a cruel mockery as well as a vicious fraud; those who were won over by it claimed that Freud had pioneered in a new science and had discovered a new world.

The first steps in the establishment of psychoanalysis were simple enough. Freud maintained that hysteria, and perhaps other neurotic manifestations, had their roots in some unhappy occurrence which the patient had forgotten or repressed. Since the patient was no longer conscious of the incident which had originally affected him, Freud developed a way of reaching the buried or unconscious mind. He concluded that the repression had harmed the patient more than the original hurt or shock, for what should have expressed itself in a natural psychic reaction had been blocked or "censored" and was manifesting itself in physical ailments. Recognition of the repression was not only an acknowledgment of the origin of the trouble but a purging, and the catharsis led to a cure.

Having resolved that many physical disturbances were self-induced, Freud devoted more and more time to a study of the psyche, or the mind as an organic system reaching all parts of the body. Here he had to overcome several difficulties: the patient's reluctance to probe into a painful past, his consequent resistance to the physician—an effort to evade and escape, a kind of defense mechanism—and finally, after a rapport had been established, the patient's attachment to and almost crippling dependence upon his helper. The conflict between a repressive conscious mentality and the dynamic but untapped unconscious mind—the clash between will and instinct—was disclosed primarily by Freud's analysis of the patient's dreams as symbols, distortions, frustrated desires, and wish-fulfillments. The apparent irrationality of dreams, the wild sequences and wilder non sequiturs, furnished the key to their meaning. It was in their very disorderliness that Freud found keys to the patient's locked confusions (a sort of protective dishonesty) and which led him to write: "A dream frequently has the profoundest meaning in the very places where it seems most absurd . . .

Dreams behave in real life like the prince who, in the play, pretends to be a madman. Hence we may say of dreams what Hamlet said of himself, substituting an unintelligible jest for the actual truth: 'I am but mad north-north-west; when the wind is southerly I know a hawk from a handsaw.'" After working alone for ten years Freud finished *The Interpretation of Dreams,* his first, and according to many scholars, his most important contribution to the science of psychology. "There is little doubt today," wrote Franz Alexander reviewing the work in 1953, "that the publication of *The Interpretation of Dreams* was a milestone in the advancement of human knowledge . . . Every person is capable of dreaming, and this is an unassailable proof that the human mind embraces more than rational, conscious thought processes and feelings. Understanding dreams is equivalent to learning a new language which, unlike conscious thought, primarily uses pictures instead of words."

Even those who disagreed that Freud had introduced a wholly new concept into the treatment of psychic disorders were willing to accept the theory that ungratified wishes festering in the mind might cause serious mental illnesses, and that the complex of thoughts in the subconscious, pressing upon the brain, could counteract normal functions. But they were unprepared for Freud's next deduction: that the emotional shock or wound which gave rise to the disorder was almost invariably of a sexual nature: "In a normal sex life no neurosis is possible." It was this emphasis on the sexual element, and particularly on the existence of sexuality in infants, which roused Freud's critics to furies of invective. "Seducing all manner of men from the simplest to the most enlightened," wrote Emil Ludwig in one of the hostile attacks, "Freud's opium endangers our generation."

Freud insisted that every boy had a deeply rooted attachment to his mother and a rival's hostility to his father, commonly known as an Oedipus complex, and that every girl had to contend with an Electra complex, a tendency to worship her father. The preservation of the idealized ever-loving, fully-understanding, never-censuring mother (the umbilical attachment poeticized as "the silver cord") and the devotion to the all-wise, protecting, perfect father made it difficult not only for the child but for the adult to adjust to an imperfect, critical, and cruel world. As a result, the disappointed adult mind tended to cling to its infantile dreams, dreaded the disillusions of maturity and, since it feared to grow up, refused to face normal responsibilities. Contrary to the charge of some of his antagonists,

Freud did not confine his diagnoses to the abnormalities of the sexual instinct, but studied the importance of sex in its relation to the total human personality. In an introduction to the first translation of Freud's epoch-startling *Three Contributions to the Theory of Sex*, Professor James Putnam wrote: "He has worked out, with incredible penetration, the part which instinct plays in every phase of human life and in the development of human character. Thus he has been able to establish on a firm footing the remarkable thesis that psychoneurotic illnesses never occur with a perfectly normal sexual life."

Although Freud's achievements were belittled—the University of Vienna scornfully refused him a chair—publication of his books began to attract and excite other specialists. He was a storm center in his mid-forties. Among those who came to study with him were Carl Jung, Alfred Adler, Otto Rank, Theodore Reik, A. A. Brill, Ernest Jones, Wilhelm Stekel, and Hanns Sachs, all of whom became famous in their own right. Although many of the disciples quarreled with Freud—proving his contention about the necessity of destroying the godlike father image—they merely added modifications and refinements to Freud's own revisions. Jung refused to accept the preponderance of Freud's sexual-psychological implications, amplified his teacher's theory of "sublimation" (the deflection of sexual interest from human objects to cultural, social, and nonhuman objectives), and added the concept of the "collective unconscious" whose memories go back to man's primal past, as well as the concept of the "persona," the image which a person has of himself and presents to others as his essential being. Adler stressed the danger of the sense of inadequacy developing into a damaging "inferiority complex" and consequent "overcompensation" in a drive for power. Rank professed to find prime significance in the "trauma of birth," the physical shock of the birth process as a cause of later anxieties —the struggle of being born necessitating a separation from security and a painful progress into a world in which struggle is the norm. Even those who deviated most drastically acknowledged the originality and unprecedented significance of Freud's explorations.

At fifty Freud looked like the traditional zealous teacher—thin frame, small beard, piercing eyes—with a touch of the meditative, Talmud-quoting rabbi. His devoted wife and his six children (three boys and three girls) made the household seem tribally Judaic, and although Freud's writings declared that religion was at best an illusion and at worst a neurotic obsession, the children were reared as

Jews. Reminded of the difficulties of bringing up a Jewish child in the midst of anti-Semitism, he replied, "Life is a problem for everybody. Besides, you can't expect to be a Jew for nothing!"

Nearing sixty, the Jewish scientist faced a gathering climax of physical and psychological horror. To Freud the First World War was not only a psychological setback, the victory of insane ruin over reason, but a personal devastation. Two of his sons were fighting for Germany; most of his friends and disciples were engaged in a combat alien to everything in which they believed. Cold and hunger made things harder for the saddened philosopher. He aged noticeably. "Now that his beard has thinned," wrote Stefan Zweig in his *Autobiography,* "until it no longer covers the firm chin nor conceals the sharp outlines of his lips, there is revealed something hard, even militant—the expression of an indomitable will. . . . For the first time we are aware that a mighty impetus, the severity of a formidable nature, is manifest in the face, and we murmur to ourselves: 'This is not a good, gray man mellowed by the years, but a rigorous examiner who will neither try to deceive nor allow himself to be deceived' . . . It is not the face of a superficial observer but of one who sees pitilessly into the depths."

Freud saw deeper into the depths when, at sixty-seven, he had to undergo the first of several operations for cancer of the jaw. He continued his studies of man's psyche but grew more concerned with man's cultural prowess and his creative possibilities. "My interest, after making a lifelong detour through the natural sciences, medicine, and psychotherapy," he concluded in the *Autobiography* he wrote in 1925, "has returned to the cultural problems which had fascinated me long before, when I was a youth." The old scientist and the young seeker had joined forces.

Some years after writing his *Autobiography,* Freud added a postscript in which he reviewed his studies of the "id," the inchoate mass of instinctual energy; the "ego," which translates and channels that unregulated force into reality; and the "super-ego," which controls the ego's aggressively dynamic drives. The postscript went on to say "I have made no further decisive contributions to psychoanalysis. What I have written on the subject since then has been either unessential or would soon have been supplied by someone else." However, in spite of the modest understatement, Freud at seventy-one published *The Future of an Illusion,* an amplification of *Totem and Taboo,* written fifteen years earlier, and, at seventy-four, the painfully probing *Civilization and Its Discontents.* The

world he knew was beginning to collapse; to Jung and other seces-
sionists were being added more formidable enemies, the enemies of
mankind. But Freud remained in the increasingly dangerous atmosphere of Vienna.

Freud's works were among the first to be thrown into the public
bonfire on the occasion of the burning of the books of non-Aryans
in 1933. "At least I have been burned in good company," he remarked. Freud was seventy-seven; disaster was coming closer; yet
he stayed. He was eighty-one when Hitler invaded Austria and
took over the country as part of the German empire. A little later,
Freud's passport was taken by the Nazis, his money was seized, and
his publishing house destroyed. Friends helped him to escape to London, and there, at eighty-two, he completed an extraordinarily succinct outline of psychoanalysis, with an ironic afterthought that its
intention was "naturally not to compel belief or to establish conviction." In his eighty-third year renewed attacks of pain suddenly
crippled the exile. He weakened gradually and, four months after
his eighty-third birthday, collapsed in his Hampstead home. He
died there, September 23rd, 1939.

After his death there was little doubt that Freud's sweeping theories had touched almost every shore of human thought. Only two
other contemporary revolutionaries—Karl Marx and Albert Einstein
—had produced so profound an effect upon the character of the
world they lived in. Freud's exploration of the furthest territories of
the mind resulted in a prodigious literature. In 1927 a bibliographer
listed 4739 works dealing entirely with psychoanalysis; by 1950
there were twice that many. Psychoanalytical journals were published not only in England and America but in places as widely
separated as France and India, Argentina and Japan. Freud's influence on the most varied fields of human endeavor was dissected,
disputed, and finally acknowledged. His *Totem and Taboo* started a
new psychoanalytical approach to anthropology; *Civilization and
Its Discontents,* an underscoring of the battle between man's moral
training and his inherent amorality, caused radical reappraisals in
social psychology; *The Future of an Illusion* and *Moses and Monotheism* opened, wrote Gregory Zilboorg, "one of the most passionate and revealing and instructive debates on the problem of religious faith." The persistence of Freud's purpose—to free man from
his infantile impulses and strengthen him for a mature realization of
his responsibilities—was attested by the spate of novels, plays,
poems, and essays which emphasized man's growing awareness of

the conflict between his aggressively lawless instincts and the demands of a civilization based on social order. The emancipating influence was found in the free associations of James Joyce's "stream of consciousness," in D. H. Lawrence's psychically disturbed and sex-agitated works celebrating "the hot blood's blindfold art," in Eugene O'Neill's "interior monolog" dramas, in Thomas Mann's flexible use of the penetrating power of the unconscious. Mann saw in Freud's analyses an augury of a future literature uniting psychology and myth, poetry and analysis. "I hold that we shall one day recognize in Freud's life-work the cornerstone for the building of a new anthropology," Mann maintained, "the future dwelling of a free and conscious humanity." In an examination of the increased intimacy of literature and science, the educator F. S. C. Northrop declared that modern science had not only altered man's conception of himself but the faculties necessary for such comprehension. "Darwin has been supplemented by Freud. It was Freud who replaced Locke's essentially blank, esthetically and emotionally empty soul and Darwin's merely biological behavioristic man, with an emotional being, a being of whom passion is the essence. This is the kind of scientifically conceived person with whom the arts, and their emotional and vivid esthetic materials, can best function."

On the other side, there were many voices of angry dissent. The Communists railed at psychoanalysis as a proof of bourgeois decadence and refused to permit its practice in Russia. The Catholic Church assailed it as a vicious teaching based on sordid materialism and warned that Catholics who had recourse to it committed a mortal sin. Psychiatrists united with former disciples of Freud to attack Freud's conclusions. In *The Case Against Psychoanalysis* Andrew Salter considered "Freud's map of the mind as inaccurate and widely fanciful as the pre-Columbus maps of the New World" and summarized Freud's position as "ridiculous," "utterly unscientific," and "moronic." Emil Ludwig, in a particularly vitriolic onslaught, claimed that humanity had been robbed of all decency by the sexual preoccupations of a man who, "groping in unknown regions, has set himself up as Dictator." Many of the charges had been anticipated by Freud. He himself had always been the scientific visionary, experimenting, testing, revising, equally amused and annoyed by the dogmatisms of many of his followers. "The trouble with psychoanalysis," he once said, "is the psychoanalyst."

In spite of detractors, Freud's researches went far beyond their original field; they extended to every form of intellectual activity.

The plodding spirits resented his relentless prodding; he frightened but, in the end, freed the reticent and repressed nature with his disturbing but clairvoyant questions. To accumulated and often confusing experience he added a bitter but liberating wisdom. Allowing for all the divagations and differences, it is almost impossible to overestimate Freud's contribution: the extension of the imaginative recognition of a human being of himself and his sympathetic understanding of another.

George Bernard Shaw

[1856-1950]

"It is not only good for people to be shocked occasionally, but absolutely necessary to the progress of society that they should be shocked pretty often."

WHEN GEORGE BERNARD SHAW died on November 2, 1950, he was ninety-four years old. But until the day of his death his admirers considered the nonagenarian the liveliest and, in many ways, the youngest intellect of the century. He was, wrote J. B. Priestley, playwright and novelist, "not only the last of the giants but perhaps the first of the truly civilized men." World-famous for his dramas, Shaw was primarily a critic, a "mover and shaker," an implacable foe of cant, the dedicated enemy of all accepted hypocrisies piously veiled in well-worn platitudes. He was not a satirist or a special pleader bent on a particular reform, but an incorruptible (or incorrigible) nonconformer, part teacher, part castigator, who took nothing for granted. His field—his battlefield—was the universe of ideas where, with the crusading zeal of a Don Quixote and the charm of a Don Juan, he challenged the entire morale of the western world.

He was born July 26, 1856, in Dublin, the third child and only son of George Carr Shaw, an incompetent civil servant, and Lucinda Elizabeth Gurley Shaw, daughter of a landowner. From his father, Shaw inherited the traditional Irish wit and gayety and nothing else except, by revulsion, an abhorrence of alcohol and all other dissipations. "A convivial drunkard," Shaw once told a biographer, "may be exhilarating in convivial company. Even a quarrelsome or boastful drunkard may be found entertaining by people who are not particular. But a miserable and conscience-stricken drunkard—and my father, in theory a teetotaler, was racked with shame and remorse even in his cups—is unbearable." It was Shaw's mother, a singer and student of the arts, who infected the young boy with a craving for culture, especially for music, painting, and the drama. His formal education was as negligible as it was short. He attended Wesleyan Connexional School and, at thirteen, the Central Model

Boys' School in Dublin. This institution he hated so much that for eighty years he never mentioned the place to anyone, not even to his wife. "It was to me," he recalled, "what the blacking warehouse was to Dickens." The episode ended in less than a year and his academic career closed in a Commercial Day School in 1871. His father had ceased to support the family, his mother had become a music teacher and, at fifteen, Shaw was apprenticed to a Dublin land agent. Irksome though it was, Shaw remained in the office as cashier until he was twenty, at which time he closed his desk, joined his mother who had left her alcoholic husband and, with her encouragement, determined to become a writer. "I made a man of myself—at my mother's expense," he said, and proceeded to make a career with his pen which, even at that age, was sharpened to a point so fine that it stabbed whatever it touched. He wrote five novels which were rejected as soon as submitted (and which, when Shaw became famous, were pirated by American publishers), did occasional hackwork and during nine grim years managed to earn the equivalent of thirty-five dollars, of which five pounds (about twenty-five dollars) came from an advertisement written for a patent medicine.

The poverty in which Shaw lived during his twenties was no less cramping and humiliating for being genteel. His boots were broken, his clothes were shabby, his cuffs were so ragged that they had to be continually trimmed with scissors. A seedy-looking specter, usually clad in a Norfolk jacket and knickerbockers, he haunted the British Museum, spending most of his hours alternately reading Marx's *Das Kapital* and the orchestral score of Wagner's *Tristan und Isolde*. He met William Archer, the dramatic critic and translator of Ibsen's plays, and a young civil servant, Sidney Webb, with whom Shaw shyly exchanged utopian ideas. He turned Socialist after hearing Henry George, and vegetarian after reading Shelley. He contracted smallpox and, unable to shave, grew a beard. In his twenties the beard was a mere tawny fringe framing a face which, with a head of hair smoothly parted in the middle, was that of a somewhat uncomfortable curate. In his thirties the beard grew ruddier and more aggressive; Shaw brushed it fiercely back and acquired the look of a badly-dressed Machiavelli. As his reputation spread, Shaw began to pride himself upon his pseudo-Mephistophelian appearance; after the beard was completely white he looked something like a lean and angry Santa Claus and something like a cherubic Satan.

In his late twenties, thanks to Archer, Shaw got a job reviewing books for one paper and art exhibits for another. At twenty-nine he became a music critic. Adopting the pseudonym of "Corno di Bassetto" (a kind of horn that was discarded after Mozart's time) Shaw spent six years writing about concerts and operas with a penetration, pugnacity, and gusto which are vibrant today. He knew music from the inside—he said that, before he was fifteen, he had learned thoroughly "at least one important work by Mozart, Handel, Beethoven, Mendelssohn, Rossini, and Verdi"—and reacted violently against academic and overrefined criticism, "the pretentious twaddle and spiteful cliquishness" which was currently carried to the point of being unreadable and often nonsensical. He educated a resisting public to Mozart and Wagner—his *The Perfect Wagnerite* is still the best exposition of the philosophy and implications of the massive *Ring of the Nibelungs*—and called attention to the neglected works of Gluck and the later Verdi.

He was still embarrassingly poor (his salary was a meager two guineas a week), an embarrassment sometimes saved by Shaw's mordant humor. Once, when a street musician held out his cap for a coin, Shaw said "Press!" and went on. In 1894 Shaw resigned as music critic and became drama critic for Frank Harris' *Saturday Review*. Strongly influenced by Ibsen, Shaw had already begun to write problem plays of his own, and for four years he wrote articles belaboring the so-called "well-made" play, exposing the contrived situations and illogical happy endings, ridiculing professional heroes (a ridicule which he dramatized in *Arms and the Man*), and mocking the vogue of mechanical playwriting popularized by Sardou—plays for live puppets with sawdust in their veins—as Sardoodledom. Despising coldly "impersonal criticism," he laid about him with an impetuosity which was as honest as it was compelling. "It is the capacity for making good or bad art a personal matter that makes a man a critic," he insisted. "The plain working truth is that it is not only good for people to be shocked occasionally but absolutely necessary to the progress of society that they should be shocked pretty often." At a time when Ibsen was considered dangerous, Shaw's championship of the Norwegian playwright (later expressed in *The Quintessence of Ibsenism*) was so eloquent that it altered the course of contemporary drama and affected the entire history of the theater.

Meanwhile, in 1884, after writing his fifth and last novel—"fifty or sixty refusals without a single acceptance forced me into a fierce self-sufficiency"—Shaw, already a Socialist, had joined the just-founded Fabian Society, named after Fabius, the Roman general whose strategy of avoiding open conflict finally defeated Hannibal. Like their namesake the Fabians proceeded from a cautious uto-pianism to a scientific socialism, but their motto was unequivocal from the beginning: "Educate; agitate; organize!" Shaw furnished the Society with a constitution and a manifesto which ended with the defiant statement: "We had rather face a Civil War than such another century of suffering as the present one has been." He worked incessantly for the cause, composed dozens of tracts (later incorporated in *Fabian Essays*), advocated the transfer of all un-earned income to the people, urged that the state should annex "socially created values," and, adding his coruscating wit to the concepts of liberty and utility, he translated, said William Irvine in *The Universe of G.B.S.,* "utilitarian dullness into epigram and para-dox." A born pamphleteer but a hesitant speaker, he taught him-self to talk in public, and for a dozen years lectured three times a week in parks, on street corners, and in any available hall. He schooled himself not only to address audiences on every level but to fascinate them. He conducted many of his harangues under po-lice surveillance and his forensic powers were so great that once, when a half-dozen policemen were sent to stop him from uttering affronts to the conventions, the guardians of the law applauded with unconcealed admiration. On two different occasions Shaw vol-unteered to go to prison on the issue of free speech, but the sacri-fice was not permitted. Fearing to be a bohemian and fighting against an inherited middle class Philistinism, Shaw found he could talk savagely and effectively; "because I persisted in socialistic propaganda I never once lost touch with the real world."

The playwright did not emerge until 1892. But in 1885, when Shaw was twenty-nine, he was induced to collaborate with his friend and fellow-critic, William Archer, on "a romantic 'well-made' play of the Parisian type then in vogue." It was intended to be a light piece of entertainment, but the propagandizing Shaw could not resist implanting upon it a plea for social reform, and Archer withdrew from the "revolting incongruity." Nevertheless, Shaw could not let the idea drop. Seven years later it appeared as *Widowers' Houses,* the first of his *Plays Unpleasant,* a curious mixture of comedy and controversy. Not disdaining farce, Shaw em-ployed a new type of clown and made him an instrument for un-expected sociological discussions. Although *Widowers' Houses* was

an exposure of "middle class respectability and younger son gentility fattening on the poverty of the slums," it was anything but a
one-dimensional tract. From the very beginning of his career Shaw
realized that, to survive, characters in a play must exist as people
after the fall of the curtain, and people refused to be "typed." Shaw
grasped the fact, wrote A. C. Ward in a balanced appreciation,
"that every human being, whether scoundrel or saint, has a point
of view which makes it possible for him to justify himself to himself—and at need, he hopes, to others also. The scoundrel is a man
of principle in his own eyes, and society cannot go far towards up-
rooting scoundrelism until it sees the scoundrel as he sees himself.
This is what Shaw set out to do for society, by an act of the imagination: not simply to preach against and vilify scoundrels, not
simply to praise and magnify non-scoundrels; but to create scoundrels as well as non-scoundrels three-dimensionally, in the round, so
that they live and move and have their being in the sight and sound
of the audience, exposing themselves in the penetrating light of
their own self-justification."

Within three years after *Widowers' Houses* Shaw produced six
more amazingly varied dramas. Two were "unpleasant" plays: *The
Philanderer,* a harsh satire, and *Mrs. Warren's Profession,* in which
commercialized prostitution was shown up as a vice of capitalistic
society and a social crime in which the whole community participated. Because the subject matter was an offense to Victorian
England and because the implications were too appalling, the attack on puritan virtue and philistine greed was prohibited by the
censor in England and later banned in America as "revolting, indecent and nauseating." The four succeeding works (*Arms and the
Man, Candida, The Man of Destiny,* and *You Never Can Tell*) included two of Shaw's most "pleasant" and most popular comedies,
one purely bravura piece, and in the last of the four, the first projection of the duel of the sexes which was to be treated with
greater brilliance and more caustic detail in *Man and Superman.*
Yet when the seven plays appeared in book form most of the English critics decided that the plays were absurd conglomerations of
reckless generalizations and cynical extravagances. The American
reviewers outdid themselves in vituperation. The review in *The
New York Times* (June 18, 1898) blasted away at the worthlessness
of Shaw's "barren philosophy and unbounded self-esteem. This voluble jack-of-all-trades, this so-called Socialist, this vociferous advocate of plain fare and industrial reform . . . who devotes all his

time to word-juggling about the arts of music and the drama . . .
this carnivorous vegetarian cannot be judged by his own standards
when he puts his wares in the open market. The fault of Shaw as
a dramatist is his lack of poetry . . . and the critic or satirist who
is not a bit of a poet cannot hope to win renown as a dramatist."
The *Times* not only assailed the mind which created *Widowers'*
Houses (asserting that good actors could not be persuaded to accept the roles), but attacked the portrait of the author which
served as a frontispiece for Volume I. "His face is long and narrow,
the eyes shifty, the nose large, broad and blunt at the tip, the hair
and beard scant—one who, except for the oddity of his dress and
views, would never have attracted much notice."

Such invidious comments were not rare. On the contrary they
were all too common during the next twenty years. Shaw was denounced as "an Irish Punchinello," "a pantaloon of paradox," "a
conceited jackanapes who announces the obvious in terms of the outrageous." Winston Churchill dismissed him as "the chatterbox of
Socialism." As late as 1919 the critic John Corbin asserted that
Shaw's "portrayal of the elemental instincts is shallow and perverse," while the dramatist Maxwell Anderson concluded that "Shaw
is a ready philosopher but no dramatist. His characters are exaggerations, his situations farcical." Two years later, reviewing the
monumental *Back to Methuselah,* Gilbert Seldes put it even more
curtly: "His creation does not live because he is not an artist."

With few exceptions the critics were provoked by Shaw's aggressive and contrary estimates of himself. At various times he
wrote: "I am a natural-born mountebank . . . I really cannot respond to a demand for mock-modesty. I am ashamed neither of my
work nor the way it is done. I like explaining its merits to the huge
majority who don't know good work from bad. It does them good;
and it does me good, curing me of nervousness, laziness, and snob-
bishness. I write prefaces as Dryden did, and treatises as Wagner
did, because I *can;* and I would give half a dozen of Shakespeare's
plays for one of the prefaces he ought to have written. I leave the
delicacies of retirement to those who are gentlemen first and literary
workmen afterwards. The cart and trumpet for me." "I must recognize, as even the Ancient Mariner did, that I must tell my story en-
tertainingly if I am to hold the wedding guest spellbound in spite of
the siren sounds of the loud bassoon . . . My specialty is being right
when other people are wrong. If you agreed with me I should be no
use here." "Nobody likes me. Capable persons are never liked. I am

not likable; but I am indispensable." To the repeated charge of egregious self-esteem and flagrant self-advertising Shaw replied with what one of his biographers, Maurice Colburne, has called a twinkle of the tongue: "The spontaneous recognition of really original work begins with a mere handful of people, and propagates itself so slowly that it has become a commonplace to say that genius, demanding bread, is given a stone until after its possessor's death. The remedy for this is sedulous advertisement. Accordingly, I advertised myself so well that I found myself whilst still in middle life almost as legendary as the Flying Dutchman." To the even more constant complaint that Shaw, playing the role of his own clown, turned profundities into buffooneries, he replied: "My way of joking is to tell the truth—which is the greatest joke in the world," adding that "the truth is the one thing that nobody will believe . . . In order to gain a hearing it was necessary for me to attain the footing of a privileged lunatic with the license of a jester. My method was to take the utmost trouble to find the right thing to say and then to say it with the utmost levity."

As the self-instigated Shaw legend grew, his impishness increased. Since his thrusts were aimed against orthodoxy, his raillery was equated with immorality and the name "Shaw" became a synonym for the scandalous. Actually, Shaw led not only a highly moral but almost ascetic life. His celebrated "affairs" were platonic and cerebrally emotional, passionate only on paper. He remained chaste— a sexless walking brain, said Frank Harris—until he was nearly thirty. He mooned over May Morris, daughter of the poet-designer William Morris, and attempted a spiritually ambiguous union with Mrs. Annie Besant, a Fabian who, searching for a more exciting religion, became the high priestess of Theosophy. At twenty-nine he was seduced by one Jenny Paterson, but he found the romantic side of the intercourse tedious as well as unreasonable, and since she was (said Shaw) "sexually insatiable" he seems to have been shocked into continence. Captivated by actresses, he wrote long and eloquent letters to three of them. The first was Florence Farr, a more than ordinarily cultured woman who was an amateur writer, musician, and Egyptologist, a restless groper who, attracted by the mysticism of the East, left England and died in India. His passion for the regal Ellen Terry was greater but it, too, was epistolary; there were almost nine years of intimately breathless correspondence before he overcame his fear of meeting her. He ended his Preface to the Shaw-Terry letters with these defensive words: "Let those who may complain that it [meaning their affair] was all on paper remember that only on paper has humanity yet achieved glory, beauty, truth, knowledge, virtue, and abiding love." His devotion to the beautiful Mrs. Patrick Campbell, daughter of an Italian revolutionary, was equally intense; it lasted twenty-eight years. Both playwright and actress were content to keep their relations strangely but definitely innocent. Shaw observed that "the ideal love affair is one conducted entirely by post"; Mrs. Campbell, reminded of Shaw's vegetarianism during a rehearsal of his *Pygmalion*, exclaimed, "One of these days Shaw will eat a beefsteak, and then God help all women!" He was forty before he contemplated marriage, and even then he flirted, philandered, and hesitated. He had met an Irish heiress, Charlotte Payne-Townshend, "who had cleverness and character enough to decline the station of life to which it pleased God to call her, and whom we have incorporated into our Fabian family with great success." Her money and his misgivings about matrimony brought Shaw to an aggravating state of ambivalence. There was an "understanding"; Charlotte learned to type and decipher the Shavian shorthand; there were quarrels and conflicts of personality; the engagement was broken off, and Charlotte decided to accompany the Webbs on a trip around the world. Overworked and definitely overwrought, Shaw suffered a breakdown; Charlotte returned to London, moved him out of his dingy flat, and nursed him back to health. The American success of *The Devil's Disciple* in 1897 helped Shaw overcome his scruples about Charlotte's wealth; the couple were married June 1, 1898, and lived contentedly together until Mrs. Shaw's death forty-five years later. Shaw spent most of the honeymoon composing *Caesar and Cleopatra*, one of the most anti-romantic plays ever written.

As an artist Shaw made a fetish of perfection; as a man he had an impassioned belief in the power of unfulfillment. He contended that human relations were improved by postponed delight and the unconsummated ecstasy. "What can I be to any woman," he wrote to Ellen Terry at the very time he was courting his future wife, "except to a wise Ellen who can cope with me in insight, and who knows how to clothe herself in that most blessed of all things— unsatisfied desire." Unsatisfied desire was the highest desideratum. In *The Apple Cart* Magnus speaks proudly about his asexual relations with his mistress Orinthia: "Do not let us fall into the common mistake of expecting to become one flesh and one spirit. Every star has its own orbit, and between it and its nearest neighbor there is not only a powerful attraction but an infinite distance. When the attraction becomes stronger than the distance, the two do not embrace: they crash together in ruins."

Before he had reached the half-century mark, Shaw was the author of some seventeen plays with elaborately argumentative prefaces to match, countless pamphlets, controversial essays, and collections of wide-ranging criticism. Alternately respected and reviled, a disputatious but firmly established figure, he was a dialectician who was a dynamo, a storm center in the theater and a rudely energizing force in all contemporary culture. At forty-three, preternaturally wise, he wrote the brilliant historical reappraisal, *Caesar and Cleopatra,* in which reason reproached passion, a dryly realistic answer to Shakespeare's romantically headlong *Antony and Cleopatra.* At forty-four he finished *Captain Brassbound's Conversion,* a civilized reproof to British imperialism, and at forty-five *Man and Superman.* Mispraised as a witty tour de force, *Man and Superman* is one of Shaw's most probingly serious plays, a masterpiece of intellectual dramaturgy which broke not only with the English drama but with English thinking. The hero, John Tanner (Anglicized from Don Juan Tenorio), is a rebel against all social conventions, especially against marriage, while the heroine, Ann Whitefield (Doña Ana) is an embodiment of the "Life Force," the eternal woman whose function it is to create a new—and better —generation. Reversing the roles of hunter and hunted, Shaw portrays man as the retreating quarry and woman as the disguised but remorseless pursuer, crying to the universe: "A father for the superman!" Shaw, determined to give more than good measure, was not content with a preface and a play, as well as a play within a play. John Tanner is credited with being the author of "The Revolutionist's Handbook and Pocket Companion," a work which in Act One, the philistine Ramsden describes as "the most infamous, the most scandalous, the most mischievous, the most blackguardly book that ever escaped burning at the hands of the common hangman." The audience may forget this seemingly irrelevant detail, but Shaw does not. To make good Tanner's claim to authorship, and to point the iconoclastic direction of the play, Shaw adds the entire "Handbook" complete with a Preface, ten chapters, and about two hundred maxims on education, liberty, democracy, royalty, idolatry, marriage, religion, fairplay, reason, discipline, civilization, the perfect gentleman, good intentions, and how to beat

children. Some of the maxims were so often quoted that they attained the quotability of Pope's epigrams. For example: "He who
can, does. He who cannot, teaches." "Do not do unto others as
you would that they should do unto you. Their tastes may not be
the same." "The savage bows down to idols of wood and stone;
the civilized man to idols of flesh and blood." "Democracy substitutes election by the incompetent many for appointment by the
corrupt few." "Liberty means responsibility. That is why most men
dread it." "Marriage is popular because it combines the maximum
of temptation with the maximum of opportunity." "Property, said
Proudhon, is theft. This is the only perfect truism that has ever
been uttered on the subject." "The love of fairplay is a spectator's
virtue, not a principal's." "Life levels all men; death reveals the
eminent." "We are told that when Jehovah created the world he
saw that it was good. What would he say now?" "Those who understand evil pardon it; those who resent it destroy it."

One part of *Man and Superman* was always considered unplayable, and for half a century it was practically never performed:
the extraordinary scene of Don Juan in Hell (actually the third
act) was omitted as the longest "aside" in theatrical history. But
scarcely a year after Shaw's death, a quartet of actors toured America and charmed more than a million people to listen for two hours
to a discourse on science, sex, religion, music, procreation, politics,
war, salvation, the life-force, humanity's criminal stupidity and
(conversely) the high potential destiny of man. Only Shaw could
have made unprepared listeners not merely follow his argument
but chuckle at what seemed to be a set of wicked aphorisms which
turned into one of the most profound moral preachments of the
times. As an extended piece of bravura writing, the scene has no
equal in literature, particularly the resonant speeches (or arias) of
Don Juan, culminating in the burst of twenty-seven antitheses
against those who are friends of the devil. For example: "They are
not dignified; they are only fashionably dressed . . . They are not
moral; they are only conventional. They are not virtuous; they are
only cowardly. They are not prosperous; they are only rich. They
are not loyal, they are only servile; not dutiful, only sheepish; not
public spirited only patriotic; not courageous, only quarrelsome;
not determined, only obstinate; not masterful, only domineering . . ."

Two other plays of Shaw's forties (*Major Barbara* and *The Doctor's Dilemma*) again proved Shaw's inexhaustible power of sur-

prise. The first was a tract for the Salvation Army and, although a comedy written by a supposedly irreligious scoffer, is a sermon on the essential goodness of humanity, a goodness which makes all men vital expressions of a divine purpose. "I have got rid of the bribe of bread," cries Barbara, daughter of the millionaire munitions manufacturer. "I have got rid of the bribe of heaven. Let God's work be done for its own sake: the work he had to create us to do because it cannot be done except by living men and women." *The Doctor's Dilemma* is another Shaw incongruity, a tragic farce, containing one of the longest and most amusing discussions of human ills on record and revolving about the problems of saving either a disreputable genius or a decent mediocrity. Part of the surprise was that Shaw allowed the nonentity to live and the artist to die.

In his fifties Shaw wrote eighteen plays, including *Misalliance,* a wildly comic set of situations framing an acrid treatise on the unhappy relations between children and parents; *The Shewing Up of Blanco Posnet,* another dramatized tract subtitled "A Sermon in Pure Melodrama"; *Fanny's First Play,* a whimsical gibe at the critics which, when it was first presented anonymously, led some of the critical profession to conclude it was written by James M. Barrie; *Androcles and the Lion,* a winning fable about a guileless, simple-minded, and good-hearted Greek tailor, a fairy tale prefaced by a major essay on Christ and Christianity; and *Pygmalion,* an unexpectedly popular success when it reached the motion picture screen. *Pygmalion,* inspired by Shaw's passion for phonetics, started as a plea for better speech—Shaw never ceased to agitate for a forty-two letter alphabet in which each letter should represent one precise sound—but the play got out of hand, the characters took over, and what began as a thesis that speech was the barrier between classes turned into the liveliest and most literate comedy of the century.

Shaw did not lose his strength or his stubborn insurgence as he aged; he continued to grow more inquiring, more tolerant and more troublesome with every fresh departure from accepted patterns of thought. The sixties was his richest decade. At sixty-three Shaw completed *Heartbreak House,* which some critics rated as his most important play, an impressive study of pre-war European society depicted as a rudderless ship in desperate waters, a Continental drama which showed another facet of the playwright's technical resources: Chekhov in terms of Shaw. Two years (1918-

1920) were devoted to the five plays which form the majestic parable entitled *Back to Methuselah,* which its author considered "a second legend of Creative Evolution and the knowledge by which men will live for ever." In this far-reaching fantasy, Shaw combined myth and moralizing, flippancy and piety, to argue that if man is not worthy of his part in creation and refuses to be conscious of his destiny the Life Force (or God) will discard him. But Shaw also implied that the Life Force is, like man, an imperfect power striving for perfection. Men, in short, are on probation and, like nature's prehistoric monsters, will be obsolete if they do not grow beyond themselves and progress toward pure thought and life eternal. *Back to Methuselah* was so massive a work that it was rumored that Shaw had more than fulfilled himself and, being sixty-five, was finished. Then, at sixty-seven, he wrote *Saint Joan,* his most poetic and deeply moving play, a drama that has every virtue, being tender to the protagonist, just to the antagonists, intensely human and triumphantly spiritual. Following the earnestness of *Back to Methuselah,* the philosophic beauty of *Saint Joan* made it plain that Shaw had ceased to be a mere challenger of social pretensions and had become a champion of man's soul; the contumacious propagandist was transformed into the commanding prophet. Two years later Shaw received the Nobel Prize for Literature.

After *Saint Joan,* Shaw's genius as a playwright began to decline, but he remained a powerful pamphleteer and a provocative writer of prefaces to the end. (Shaw's detractors liked to say that his prefaces were not only more exciting but more dramatic than the plays, and that the dramas were merely theatricalized prefaces.) Nevertheless, he wrote *The Apple Cart,* an unquestionably important play, at seventy-three. And though the later plays, more than a dozen, lack the eruptive brilliance of the works of his maturity, they never lack viability. As late as 1952 a popular motion picture actress, Katherine Hepburn, made a rousing success in London in *The Millionairess,* written when Shaw was almost eighty.

The two world wars confirmed Shaw's conviction that new faiths must be found for outworn beliefs. It also made him affirm his innate pacifism. When Mrs. Patrick Campbell wrote to him that her only son had been killed in action and that the chaplain had written a letter full of praise, Shaw replied in an outburst of protest and sympathy: "It is no use: I can't be sympathetic. These things simply make me furious. I want to swear. I *do* swear. Killed just because people are blasted fools! A chaplain, too, to say nice things about it. It is not his business to say nice things about it, but to shout that 'the voice of thy son's blood crieth unto God from the ground!' " At seventy-five the unsocial Socialist visited Russia; at seventy-seven Shaw made a trip around the world, and although he had always refused invitations to come to America, made two American stops. The first was on the Pacific Coast, where he visited the San Simeon ranch of William Randolph Hearst, who had syndicated some of his writings. The second was in New York, where he stayed just long enough to make a one-day tour of the city and deliver a talk at the Metropolitan Opera House, where he advised the United States to nationalize its banks, get rid of its financiers, and cancel all war debts. Upon his return to his home in the village of Ayot Saint Lawrence, Shaw reiterated his intransigent complaints against the government and, maintaining his love for democratic methods, declared that democracy, as practiced, was a fraud upon the people. During the Second World War he called himself "general consultant to mankind," was fatalistic about destruction ("we must live dangerously whether we like it or not—the worst is yet to come"), was doubtful about a permanent peace and pessimistic concerning the chances that "the iron-fisted allies" would stick together.

Uninterruptedly creative he wrote his fiftieth play, *Geneva,* at eighty-two, and after finishing *Buoyant Billions* at ninety-one, began another comedy at ninety-two. His workshop, "The Shelter," was mounted on a swivel; the one-room hut was rotated to let in as much sunlight as possible, and there, at ninety-three, Shaw prepared a *Rhyming Picture Guide to Ayot Saint Lawrence,* having taken all the photographs himself and letting his high spirits romp in swift and skylarking rhymes. It seemed that he would live alertly until he was one hundred and probably more; but Shaw suffered a fall ("a fall from grace" he grimaced) while trimming a fruit tree on September 10, 1950. However, it was not the thigh fracture which caused his death. Although Shaw was past ninety-four, the bones knit perfectly, but the shock of his fall stirred into activity a dormant kidney infection. Two operations followed; he failed to survive the second and died November 2, 1950. In spite of his sneers at capitalism—possibly because of his early privations—he

was not only shrewd but grasping in money matters and he became
extremely wealthy long before he died. His estate was valued at
considerably more than a million dollars.

Even after his death, his ghost was voluble. Speaking through
his Will, Shaw protested that he did not wish to be buried in Westminster, that he wanted his and his wife's ashes to be scattered in
their garden, and declared that he had died, as he had lived, "a believer in creative evolution . . . I desire that no public monument
or work of art or inscription or sermon or ritual service commem-
orating me shall suggest that I accepted the tenets peculiar to any
established church or denomination, nor take the form of a cross or
any other symbol of torture or symbol of blood sacrifice." Shaw derided official estimates, but Prime Minister Attlee spoke for more
than England when he concluded: "He was not only our greatest
entertainer but our greatest teacher." Sean O'Casey considered
Shaw "a fighting idealist" and concluded with a Gaelic flourish:
"Shaw will shine forth in the cathedral of man's mind a sage standing in God's holy fire as in the gold mosaic of a wall."

Hearing a Shaw play in the theater, or even reading the text
with an attentive mind, is enough to disprove the often-repeated
contention that Shaw's plays are nothing but garrulous conversations in which ventriloquizing dummies mouth elusive ideas without action or emotion. Believing that thinking and feeling people
were not occasional freaks but individuals to be found in everyday
life, Shaw, like his most illustrious predecessor, held the mirror up
to nature and created characters who not only thought widely but
felt deeply. Indefatigable and undeviating, he thundered at man's
stupidity and his failure to will himself into something better. A
mocker but a magnanimous one—someone called him "the good
man's Voltaire"—he thought of the community as a living whole
and dared to predict a millennium of cooperative faith, hope, and
work. A prophet who continually disturbed the orthodox with his
dissenting heresies and distressed them with his insistence on saying the first and having the last word, Shaw was the embodiment
of man's unpredictability. Irresistible to his devotees, his enemies
found him merely irrepressible. His method called for impertinence
and paradox, but his purpose was serious and uncompromising.
He did not aim solely to surprise and shock, though he delighted
to do both, but to change men's thinking. He looked askance at
institutions, attacked current mores, and combated the status quo
all along the line. He queried everything and, without waiting for

a reply, supplied answers that were more embarrassing than the questions. His intention was that of Aristophanes, and the words spoken by the chorus in *The Acharnians* might have been addressed by Shaw to his twentieth-century audiences: "As for you, never lose him who will always fight for the cause of justice in his comedies; he promises you that his precepts will lead you to happiness, though he uses neither flattery, nor intrigue, nor bribery, nor deceit. Instead of loading you with praise, he will point you to the better way."

Thorstein Veblen

[1857-1929]

*". . . compounded of wit and ferocity,
slowly accumulating clauses and quickly
stabbing thoughts."*

ONE OF the interpolated psychographs in John Dos Passos'
The Big Money synthesizes the tragic history of Thorstein
Veblen. Veblen spent his life, wrote Dos Passos, "dissecting
the century with a scalpel so keen, so comical, so exact that the
professors and students ninetenths of the time didn't know it was
there, and the magnates and the respected windbags and the applauded loudspeakers never knew it was there . . . Socrates asked
questions, drank down the bitter drink one night when the first
cock crowed; but Veblen drank it in little sips through a long life
in the stuffiness of classrooms, the dust of libraries, the staleness of
cheap flats . . . He fought the *boyg* all right, pedantry, routine,
timeservers at office desks, trustees, collegepresidents, the plump
flunkies of the ruling businessmen, all the good jobs kept for yes-
men, never enough money, every broadening hope thwarted. Veblen drank the bitter drink all right."

Thorstein Bunde Veblen was born July 30, 1857, on a farm in Wisconsin, the sixth of twelve children. Both parents were Norwegian
immigrants. His father was a carpenter who was also a farmer and,
although he would have scorned the term, an intellectual; unlike
the other farmers in the region, he sent his daughters as well as
his sons to college. When the family moved to Minnesota, Thorstein
was still bilingual at the age of eight—English, not Norwegian, was
the "foreign" language. Although all the Veblens were brought up
on a farm, sharing the traditional feuds between exploited country
folk and city businessmen, they were not bound to the soil. When
Thorstein was seventeen, his father sent him to Carleton, a small
institution in Northfield, Minnesota, which specialized in theology. He spent three years in the preparatory school and three in
the college. Although he majored in philosophy, he was deeply interested in philology, biology, and economics. When he was graduated at twenty-three, he went to Johns Hopkins for post-graduate

work, transferred to Yale, where he received his Ph.D. at twenty-seven.

After working his way through Yale, where his nonconformity set the pattern for future unpopularity, Veblen hoped to get a teaching appointment. But there were no jobs available for a perverse, irreverent, and probably agnostic midwesterner with a Norwegian accent. He went back to the Minnesota farm, married Ellen Rolfe, niece of the president of Carleton College, and grimly cultivated his garden. For seven years he waited and worried, his only intellectual consolation being his books and long talks with his father, whose mind he considered the best he ever encountered. The family was even more worried than Veblen. Many councils were held and, hoping that he might "find himself," it was decided that he should have one more chance in the academic world. Persuaded to become an economist rather than a philosopher, Veblen went to Cornell.

He was thirty-four years old when, wearing a workman's coat, corduroy trousers, and a coonskin cap, he entered the office of J. Laurence Laughlin, Professor of Economics, and said: "I am Thorstein Veblen." In spite of the brusque announcement—or perhaps because of it—Laughlin was impressed and amused, procured a fellowship for him at Cornell and, when Laughlin moved west to the newly opened University of Chicago, took Veblen with him. In Chicago, Veblen became a teaching-fellow at a salary of $520 a year, an even ten dollars a week; it was not until he was forty-six that he made as much as an annual $1000. Chicago was full of ferment and Veblen might well have enjoyed knowing such provocative pioneers as Albert Michelson, the physicist, and Jacques Loeb, the physiologist, but he withdrew from his colleagues. He also kept himself aloof from his students, who found his lectures dull to the point of obscurity, gave them all the same passing grade, ridiculed the protocol of faculty life, and shunned the rest of the world with objective disregard. He wrote papers on the worthiness of material labor, on the economic basis of dress, on the hope of substituting evolutionary economic science for the classroom dogmas of economics—essays that, seemingly technical, were actually full of sardonic wit—but he remained unknown until he was forty-two. In 1899 he published his first book, *The Theory of the Leisure Class.*

Although he was to be the author of another dozen books, Veblen never wrote anything which had the impact of *The Theory of the Leisure Class.* It is a mordant examination of social conduct, a criticism of the misuse of wealth and middle class imitation (Veblen called it "emulation") of the wealthy. Although Veblen's language is involved—he liked to use forbidding, thickly worded sentences and what Lewis Mumford called "desperately accurate circumlocutions"—the thesis of the book is fairly simple. Stuart Chase sums it up in a few lines: "People above the line of bare subsistence, in this age and all earlier ages, do not use the surplus which society has given them primarily for useful purposes. They do not seek to expand their own lives, to live more wisely, intelligently, understandingly, but to impress other people with the fact that they *have* a surplus. Ways and means for creating that impression are called by Veblen 'conspicuous consumption.' This consists in spending money, time, and effort quite uselessly in the pleasurable business of inflating the ego . . . Superior people lord it over their pecuniary inferiors by wasteful expenditures, whereupon the inferiors move heaven and earth to improve their status by spending to the limit themselves."

Never before had any American so savagely mocked the prevailing canons of taste and culture or castigated the pleasure of spending money by labeling it a foolish way of purchasing prestige. Veblen insisted that the leisure class made property synonymous with proficiency and even potency, felt it vitally important to advertise its expenditures, to glorify its ostentatious waste, and to encourage all classes, even the least affluent, to do the same. Moreover, he made the point that, whereas in primitive civilization everyone worked without feeling debased by his labor, modern man has ceased to take joy in his work and finds it merely necessitous and irksome. He delighted to expose the ridiculous formalities of enforced leisure and, in the midst of involuted passages, would shock the reader with a sudden shaft of barbed satire. "A certain King of France," he remarked with quiet sarcasm, "is said to have lost his life through an excess of moral stamina in the observance of good form. In the absence of the functionary whose office it was to shift his master's seat, the King sat uncomplaining before the fire and suffered his royal person to be toasted beyond recovery. But in so doing, he saved His Most Christian Majesty from menial contamination."

Veblen followed his first book five years later with a sequel, *The Theory of Business Enterprise*, "a topic," Veblen wrote to a friend, "on which I am free to theorize with the abandon that comes of immunity to the facts." The book was a triumph of paradox. Veblen made the point that the big businessman, uninterested in anything except the amassing of money and the accumulation of power, was actually the enemy of his enterprise. He was concerned with earnings not with values, with prices rather than with goods. Profit-hungry moguls sabotaged production and held the common man down by the harsh law of diminishing returns. Veblen appealed for a new set of controls, for a society of engineers who recognized the social use of the machine.

Not only Big Business but the trustees of the university found Veblen's views potentially dangerous. His private life was equally disconcerting. He was manifestly hard to live with—his wife had left him several times because of his philanderings—and the trustees were only too glad for an excuse to get rid of him. One summer he undertook what the newspapers described as "an unchaperoned crossing of the Atlantic with a lady," and when he returned, his resignation was demanded. He was forty-nine when he was able to get a position elsewhere; then he lasted less than three years at Leland Stanford. In spite of an unprepossessing face and a shambling figure, women found him attractive; there was scandal wherever he went. He had no gift for evasion—"What is one to do when a woman moves in on you?" he asked. He did not even try to be discreet. When a tactful associate referred to a young lady staying with Veblen as his niece, Veblen corrected him. "That is not my niece," he said. He wrote to a perturbed friend, "The president does not approve of my domestic arrangements, nor do I." He lived irregularly, retreating to a mountain cabin, where he built his own crude furniture. He grew more and more careless in the way he dressed; his suits were never pressed; when he lost a button he used a safety pin. Although his roughly parted hair was brown, it seemed colorless; the straggling mustache and short unkempt beard were ashy, and the pale wrinkled face accentuated the effect of an unnatural grayness. He was old at fifty-four when, through the efforts of Herbert Davenport, a friend who taught economics, he moved on to the University of Missouri.

Alone for a while—his wife had finally divorced him in 1911—he stayed in Missouri for seven years, going to his classes reluctantly but regularly, spending most of his time writing in Davenport's cellar. His unhappy experience in the educational world was the goad which prodded him to write *The Higher Learning in America,* a book that he narrowly prevented himself from subtitling "A Study in Total Depravity." Contrasting the timid college presidents, cautious trustees, and cowardly teachers with the bold and resourceful American inventors, the courageous and efficient American engineers, the intrepid and tenacious American explorers, Veblen compared the governing boards of the universities to American businessmen who, "as a class, are of a notably conservative habit of mind. In a degree scarcely equaled in any community that can lay claim to a modicum of intelligence and enterprise, the spirit of American business is a spirit of quietism, caution, compromise, collusion, and chicane." One suspects that, in challenging the institutions of learning ("the higher ignorance") Veblen was attacking the whole established, inflexible, and inviolate idea of institutions.

Other books were written during Veblen's Missouri period, notably *The Instinct of Workmanship, Imperial Germany and the Industrial Revolution, An Inquiry into the Nature of Peace and the Terms of Its Perpetuation, The Vested Interests and the State of the Industrial Arts,* books compounded of wit and ferocity, slowly accumulating clauses and quickly stabbing thoughts. At fifty-seven he married again; but his second wife, who at first seemed merely eccentric, went insane, and had to be placed in an institution. There were fresh episodes and further setbacks. *An Inquiry into the Nature of Peace,* published during the First World War, expressed a universal hope for peace; its earnestness as well as its timeliness made many consider it his clearest and most important book. In it Veblen analyzes national aspirations and shows how true patriotism is exploited by professional politicians and profiteering patrioteers. Although it became an internationally discussed work, no publisher wanted to risk anything on it, and Veblen had to pay $700 to get it published. He translated the *Laxdaela Saga,* an Icelandic epic of the Middle Ages, and retreated further into himself.

No longer welcome in Missouri, Veblen went on to New York. He became an editor of a liberal magazine, *The Dial,* but his heavily weighted pieces did not stop the circulation from sagging. He got an exceedingly minor post in wartime Washington, but his ideas were too progressive and he was soon let go. He lectured at the New School for Social Research, but he had always been a rambling speaker, and his audiences dwindled with every talk—it is said that one of his classes shrank to a single student. His *Inquiry into the Nature of Peace* had been denounced because of "subversive" tendencies; teaching was impossible, and there were no other positions which he could fill. Nearing seventy, sick with more than physical illness—there were tubercular symptoms—he went back to California, to his cabin in the woods, and after a year of melancholy detachment from the world he had failed to interest, died, August 3rd, 1929. Instead of a Will, he left a frustrated man's testament in the form of a bitter note: "It is my wish . . . that no tombstone, slab, epitaph, effigy, tablet, inscription, or monument of any name or nature, be set up to my memory or name in any place or at any time; that no obituary, memorial, portrait, or biography of me, nor any letters written to me or by me be printed or published, or in any way reproduced, copied or circulated."

According to his own lights Veblen was a failure, unable to unite the forces for good against what he believed to be the forces of evil. He was unable even to unite himself. He expected man to live up to his highest potentialities, and regarded all compromises with angry disillusion. "But," wrote Max Lerner in a long and illuminating introduction to *The Portable Veblen,* "he was a skeptic only about institutions, not about man himself. His faith was that the instinctive core of man is sound, and only the institutional husks are rotten. He seemed to have an almost Rousseauist belief in man's natural goodness. Like the creator of the noble savage, who believed that man is born free yet is everywhere in chains, Veblen believed that man is born peaceful yet is everywhere in turmoil, that he is born with the instinct to shape things for human ends, yet is everywhere surrounded by waste and futility. However much as he wished to believe that the instincts would triumph, he was too honest an observer not to give the historical odds to the institutions."

In such a conclusion Veblen differed directly with Karl Marx. He shared many of Marx's views, his dislike of private ownership, his economic interpretation of history, his conviction that capitalism and war went hand in hand; but he differed with him on many other grounds. He refused to believe in the theory of surplus value and the inevitable struggle between Capital and Labor. Veblen contended that there can be no class war because the workers emulate the owners; they do not want to eliminate the upper, or leisure, class; on the contrary, they want to *become* that class. He was likewise opposed to Marx's assumption that prolonged deprivation, fear, and suffering must end in revolution. "The experience of history," said Veblen, "teaches that abject misery carries with it deterioration and abject subjection." Veblen's revolution was to come, he hoped, with a new order of intellectual mechanics, high-minded technocrats, an aristocracy of engineers. He seemed wholly unaware that an elite of engineers might be as dangerous as a military elite when he argued for the hierarchy of technicians to take over the economic affairs of the country "and to allow and disallow what they may agree on . . . This revolutionary posture of the present state of the industrial arts may be undesirable, in some respects, but there is nothing to be gained by denying the fact. So soon—but only so soon—as the engineers draw together, take common counsel, work out a plan of action, and decide to disallow absentee ownership out of hand, that move will have been made. The obvious and simple means of doing it is a conscientious withdrawal of efficiency; that is to say the general strike, to include so much of the country's staff of technicians as will suffice to incapacitate the industrial system at large by their withdrawal, for such time as may be required to enforce their argument."

When Veblen died he was given the scantiest of obituaries; he was the unforgiven economist, the false prophet, the forgotten man. Since that time Veblen has remained in semi-obscurity. His humanitarian impulses have not been panegyrized on memorial tablets or honored by institutions devoted to the social sciences; only a few reappraisals have accorded him cautious praise. Nevertheless, *The Theory of the Leisure Class* is reprinted again and again and remains a powerful warning, demonstrating that Veblen is still a critical force in the intellectual world.

Veblen's style has been volubly praised and violently deprecated. It has been called "swift and fine-edged" by one critic and "unbearably sesquipedalian" by another; it has been termed "clinically surgical," "willfully obscurantist," contradictorily "icy" and "sultry." Sometimes Veblen writes as though he were not transcribing his thoughts but translating them from one dead language to another. Sometimes, as Lerner said, "one gets the sense of endlessly chugging polysyllables, as if the sentences were a long string of freight cars rolling on forever." But at his best Veblen is as incisive as he is corrective. The language is richer for such keen disposals as "trained incapacity," "higher learning," "conspicuous waste," "absentee ownership," "the price system," "conscientious withdrawal of efficiency," as well as his remarkable and apt incongruities: "captains of erudition" (an ironic thrust at "captains of industry" in the academic world), "reputable notoriety," "the performance of leisure," "a ready versatility of convictions and a stanch devotion to their bread."

Even small segments reveal the astringent flavor of his wit. Rarely has there been a more falsely humble or slyly malicious opening than

Veblen's Preface to *The Theory of the Leisure Class:* "Partly for reasons of convenience, and partly because there is less chance of misapprehending the sense of phenomena that are familiar to all men, the data employed to illustrate or enforce the argument have by preference been drawn from everyday life, by direct observation or through common notoriety, rather than from more recondite sources at a further remove. It is hoped that no one will find his sense of literary or scientific fitness offended by this recourse to homely facts, or by what may at times appear to be a callous freedom in handling vulgar phenomena or phenomena whose intimate place in men's lives has sometimes shielded them from the impact of economic discussion."

The faults in Veblen's thinking are obvious. Veblen failed to allow for radical alterations in a changing world. He overrated the separateness as well as the superior status of the technicians; he underrated a democratic planned economy and its ability to check errors as well as its excesses. Much of his social criticism was topical and is, therefore, outmoded. Industrial civilization did not "evolve" according to his preconceived patterns; today many of his most dramatic observations seem nothing more than aberrations. His manner was undoubtedly overemphatic, his voice too often shrill, but what he said cannot be said too often. He was not only a mocker of our snobberies and a disturber of our complacencies, but a liberator who challenged placidly accepted ways of thinking and strengthened the often suppressed but inherently stubborn power of the questioning mind.

Max Planck

[1858-1947]

"A startling but balanced philosophy."

THE "QUANTUM THEORY" may strike the ear of the layman as a faintly recognizable phrase; as a subject, however, it suggests nothing more to his mind than an elaborate artificiality, a complexity so great as to be incomprehensible. Yet its impact on physics may be said to exceed even that of Relativity. Although many scientists have achieved fame by applying quantum mechanics to different phenomena, one man alone was the source of its revolutionary doctrine.

Max Planck was born on April 23, 1858, in the German city of Kiel. His life spanned the birth and death of the German Empire from its meteoric rise to its total eclipse. His father, Professor of Constitutional Law, impressed his son with respect for the human responsibilities of science and schooled him to sift the essential truths from masses of experimental evidence.

Young Planck studied at the *Maximilian-Gymnasium* in Munich, where he specialized in mathematics. He had decided to devote himself to science ever since his early youth when he discovered "that the outside world is something independent from man, something absolute, and the quest for the laws which apply to this absolute seemed to me the most sublime scientific pursuit in life." He was encouraged not only by his father but by Hermann Müller, his high school teacher, who, with constant imagery and humor, was able to make his pupils not only understand but visualize the meaning of the laws of physics. Planck never forgot the way Müller illustrated the principle of the conservation of energy. "He told us," said Planck, "of the strength and power which a bricklayer needs to lift a huge stone to the roof of a building. The energy is never lost. It remains stored up, possibly for years, latent in the block of stone—until one day it is somehow loosened and, perhaps, drops on the head of some passerby."

After graduating from high school, Planck attended the university, first in Munich for three years and then, for another year, in Berlin. In Berlin he applied himself under Helmholtz, the physiologist and physicist; but Helmholtz was a poor lecturer, and Planck had the impression that the class bored him as much as it did his pupils. It was Kirchhoff, the physical chemist, who stimulated his interest in thermodynamics, and "The Second Law of Thermodynamics" was the subject of Planck's doctoral thesis in 1879 as well as the central point of his subsequent researches. In these he exhibited such brilliance that he became an associate professor at Kiel University when only twenty-eight. When Kirchoff died three years later, Planck was invited to take his place and became Professor Extraordinarius at the University in Berlin.

The one problem in thermodynamics which Planck attacked most strongly from 1879 to 1899 was that of thermal radiation. It was known that hot bodies emitted heat and, if hot enough, also emitted light. As an object became hotter this light went from the invisible infra-red, through dull red, scarlet, and yellow, until it reached the extreme temperatures of "white-hot." At each temperature, the radiation could be analyzed (by means of a prism) into a combination of many colors of light, each with a different wave length. For example, an iron ingot hot enough to appear yel-low actually emits a combination of red, orange, yellow, green, and blue, with the green and blue weakest and the yellow strongest.

Kirchhoff had shown that not only the apparent color, but also the distribution of different colors, depended only on the temperature and was independent of the radiating material. Such an independence indicated that a new law of nature, involving only temperature and wave length, must exist. Many experimental and theoretical efforts had been made to find the formula describing the color distribution, but even the most successful efforts could only predict the distribution over a very limited part of the spectrum.

It remained for Planck to discover the new law by uncovering a new principle. He investigated the radiation in a "black box": a hollow body whose heated inside walls emitted radiation themselves and also absorbed radiation from the other inside walls. Planck studied this "black body" or "cavity" radiation, and eventually decided to use the "method of limits." This method is a powerful tool in physics and mathematics whenever conditions cannot be computed directly. It involves the creation of an artificial condition to make computation possible, and a formula is derived that includes the untrue assumption. The artificiality is then gradually reduced in size until it becomes zero, when the derived formula will no longer include it, but should still be a valid answer.

Planck believed that black body radiation was emitted continuously, and that each color could be emitted with any energy. However, his "false" assumption (made, he thought, for purposes of calculation only) was that the apparently continuous stream of radiation consisted of many small bursts of energy, and that each burst must have a fixed amount of energy. Planck expected to derive the formula for the spectral distribution and then to let the bursts become continuous by making them smaller and smaller, and more and more numerous. Instead, his formula agreed exactly with experimental measurements before the expected smoothness was reached.

At this point, some scientists might have considered their method erroneous, or might have postulated other theoretical aberrations—anything except believe that their artificial "false" assumption could actually be true. Planck was not so timid. He had sufficient faith in the validity of his work, and sufficient recognition of its meaning, so that he confidently asserted that all radiant energy must travel in bursts, each containing an energy that was fixed. Actually, the energy was fixed separately for each color, being equal to hc/λ, when c is the speed of light, λ is the wave length corresponding to the given color, and h is a new universal constant of nature, now named Planck's Constant. This means that a heated atom, such as in a neon tube, needs more energy to emit a burst of blue light than of red light, since blue light has a shorter wave length. Consequently, an atom that had a certain amount of energy available, would emit light of one particular color.

It had long been known that excited atoms did emit colors that depended on the type of material: the strong yellow of sodium vapor, the red of pure neon, the purple-white of mercury vapor. Now, these colors could be related to the energies in different elements, and from a study of the spectra of electric sparks and arcs, the inner structure of atoms could be visualized. The relation between wave lengths and energy enabled Einstein to formulate his law of the photoelectric effect; it permitted the calculation of the heat-absorbing capacity of solids; it led to accurate control of X-rays; and it provided accurate descriptions of chemical reaction times.

Eventually, the discrete nature of energy, "quantization," was applied to matter as well as radiation. Out of this came wave mechanics, which recognized that, just as the waves of light can have some of the discrete properties of particles, so can atomic particles have some of the properties of waves. This new viewpoint led eventually to a fuller knowledge of radioactivity, to prediction of nuclear reactions, and to the design of transistors. It also led to Heisenberg's "Uncertainty Principle." Since each particle of matter has some of the properties of waves, it is not possible to locate its position exactly, any more than one can "locate" with any exactness a train of ripples on a lake. The "Uncertainty Principle" defines this inaccuracy; though it shows that uncertainty is appreciable only in sub-atomic particles, its philosophical significance is far more widespread.

The notion of "causality" had existed since Greek times, and had been tremendously reinforced by Newton's work. Causality accepted the strictness of physical laws as indicating that, if enough data were known, any event could be predicted on the basis of its contributing causes. Everyone accepted as predictable eclipses (once the motion of the earth and moon were known) or the fall of an artillery shell (knowing powder charge, gun angle, and wind). But causality went further. We could, it implied, predict the throw of dice if all the motions of one's hand were known; the seemingly "unpredictable" actions of a human being were predestined by his physical and mental past. Eventually, though, strict causality had to defend the existence of laws within the atom as rigorous as in the stars; for might not one errant atom start or stop an avalanche, or one deviant electric current in a brain-cell start or stop a new human thought?

The "Uncertainty Principle" thus removed the bedrock basis from causality. Philosophical thought was plunged into argument and speculation. Some scientists felt the whole concept of an orderly universe was outmoded by the chance motion of atoms; others (notably Albert Einstein) could not believe "that God plays dice with the universe."

Planck took a middle ground. He felt that the conflict between causality and the newer Positivism was of great importance not only in philosophical thought, but also in relation to the social responsibility of science. He did not wish the value of the Quantum Theory to become adulterated or obscured by metaphysical principles. In his words: "There is no doubt whatsoever that the stage at which theoretical physics has now arrived is beyond the average human faculties, even beyond the faculties of the great discoverers themselves. What, however, you must remember is that even if we progressed rapidly in the development of our powers of perception we could not finally unravel nature's mystery . . . Where the discrepancy comes in today is not between nature and the principle of causality but rather between the picture which we have made of nature and the realities in nature itself."

His contributions to science and the honesty of his beliefs made Planck a "scientist's scientist," respected by colleagues in all fields and of all nationalities. When he was awarded the Nobel Physics Prize in 1918, the occasion was marked by unanimous affirmation from Einstein, Niels Bohr, Lord Rutherford, and Heisenberg—each of whom might have deserved the honor—but who unreservedly agreed that it belonged to Planck.

In spite of his honors, Planck was a sad and lonely figure as he approached sixty. The First World War was a private as well as a general tragedy for him. He lost his eldest son, Karl, in 1916 during the fighting at Verdun. The Second World War affected him even more terribly. His second son, Erwin, was killed during the German terrorism in early 1945. Planck's home was struck by a bomb during an air raid, and his library, which had taken an entire lifetime to amass, was destroyed by flames. Lecturing in Kassel, he was buried in an air raid shelter for hours. In May, 1945, an American jeep rescued him from further disaster and brought him to Göttingen, in the American zone of occupation. It was there he died, on October 4, 1947. In a few more months he would have been ninety. He had not only had an extraordinarily long but a rich life. He had the double satisfaction of seeing his quantum mechanics embodied throughout physical science and knowing that his startling but balanced philosophy had been accepted throughout the world of thought.

A. E. Housman

[1859-1936]

"And malt does more than Milton can
To justify God's ways to man . . ."

IT IS A HISTORIC IRONY that during a period of solid faith, commercial expansiveness and triumphant well-being, the two most popular books in England and America were two volumes of pessimistic poetry. The first, a translation from the Persian poet Omar Khayyám, was the work of a retired English country gentleman, Edward Fitzgerald; the second, *A Shropshire Lad*, was composed by a professor of Latin, Alfred Edward Housman, who wrote about murder and suicide, man's brutality and God's malevolence. Both volumes were cherished not only by young lovers, who regarded the unorthodox sentiments as their credo, but by men and women resentful of the rigidity and moral earnestness of the period. The *Rubáiyát* and *A Shropshire Lad* were small but concentrated voices of revolt against Victorian conventions; they lured readers from disciplined imperialism with the promise of a reckless hedonism. The sustaining food and drink, Omar's loaf of bread and jug of wine, even the presence of the beloved, were not sufficient without a romantic book of verses underneath the bough. The book was almost inevitably *A Shropshire Lad*.

Although Shropshire was the scene of practically all A. E. Housman's verse, the poet never lived there. He was born May 26, 1859, in Worcestershire; the nearby Shropshire hills were the background of his early years. Oldest of a family of seven, he attended the village school at Bromsgrove and, at eighteen, entered St. John's College in Oxford. A happy, even sprightly youth, he was judiciously praised by his parents and adored by his younger brothers and sisters—one of his brothers, the playwright Laurence Housman, wrote that he had the greatest admiration for the work of A. E., "who, however, did not return the compliment." The native gayety vanished completely before he left Oxford. It has never been discovered what private grief caused a complete alteration of his nature—a tragic love affair has been conjectured, without proof, as a possible cause—but at twenty Housman was already the unsocial, laconic, and repressed recluse that he remained the rest of his life. A fellow poet, Wilfrid Scawen Blunt, wrote of him, "He does not smoke, drinks little, and would be quite silent if he were allowed to be." (When the description was repeated, Housman said that it seemed accurate enough except that Blunt offered him precious little to drink.) A member of one of his classes remarked, "He was the only person I have known who so habitually and ominously looked down his nose." He, who had made friends easily, formed no further friendships; he never married; he hugged his detachment and loved his loneliness. He was, he said later, a deist at thirteen and an atheist before he was twenty-one.

It has also been suggested that a failure to pass an examination for honors was the calamity that changed him from a blithe spirit to a bitter one. This is scarcely likely. But there is evidence that it hurt his abnormally sensitive pride, and although he graduated without trouble, he never obtained his formal degree until he received an appointment to University College at thirty-two. Before he became a teacher he spent ten years as a Higher Division clerk in the British Patent Office, during which time he lived in seclusion in London, out of touch with his family and, seemingly, the world. In 1892 he left the Office, where he said he "did as little as possible," to become professor of Latin at University College.

Nineteen years later, when he was fifty-two, he moved from University College to Trinity College, where he remained the rest of his uneventful life, teaching the classics, criticizing other Latinists, and writing a small group of short but imperishable poems. He struck his own note with absolute precision from the very first. He never "developed"; "he somehow managed," wrote Edmund Wilson, "to grow old without in a sense ever having come to maturity." He spent most of the last twenty-five years of his life preparing an analytical edition of Manilius, a crabbed and discomfiting poet of the Augustan Age. A year after the completion of the work, a strange weakness began to affect Housman. He recognized the symptoms as a heart condition and foresaw the end. Nevertheless, he continued to conduct his classes with stern regularity. He had convinced himself that teaching was a pleasure as well as a duty, and he prepared a set of lectures on Horace, one of his favorite poets, during the Lent term in 1936. He never completed the course. Suffering a second attack, he died in his seventy-eighth year, April 30, 1936.

Except for a few essays—one of which, *The Name and Nature of*

Poetry, is as tart as it is idiosyncratic—Housman published only two volumes during his long lifetime. Poetry with him was a kind of seizure. He wrote *A Shropshire Lad* during one of his rare spasms. Twenty-six years after its publication, he had produced enough poems for another volume. He made it clear that he never again expected to write poetry: with grim determination he called the book *Last Poems.* A posthumous gathering of stray verses was issued three years after his death by his brother, Laurence, as *More Poems.*

A Shropshire Lad was perhaps the most reprinted, variously pirated, and most widely imitated book of poems of the last century. Its continuing popularity is not due primarily to its philosophy, an acrid expression of despair, but to its captivating music and quotable phrases. Its countless devotees have been less concerned with the content of the book than with the pungent lines, the singing strength, and the unconventional turns Housman gave to the traditional forms. The book is limited in range and ideas. In nimble measures Housman assures us that men cheat and girls betray; that Nature is only a little less inhuman than human nature; that the countryside riots in haphazard cruelty; that, faced with cosmic injustice, man is "a stranger and afraid in a world he never made"; that the sensible person, prepared for adversity, trains for ill and not for good. There is no hope in heaven since "high heaven and earth ail from the prime foundation."

> The troubles of our proud and angry dust
> Are from eternity, and shall not fail.

Yet, continues Housman, with a resolute stoicism that recalls Hardy, although evil is a constant, it can be borne. The world is full of suffering which, if absorbed gradually, creates an immunity against pain. The "Epilogue" ends with the story of an Oriental king, Mithridates, who gathered all the poisons "from the many-venomed earth," sampled them little by little, and immune to their killing power, survived his enemies.

> They poured strychnine in his cup
> And shook to see him drink it up;
> They shook, they stared, as white's their shirt:
> Them it was their poison hurt.
> —I tell the tale that I heard told.
> Mithridates, he died old.

Sometimes the stoic joins hands with the hedonist to tell us that, though "luck's a chance but trouble's sure," the universal iniquities need not overwhelm us.

> Bear them we can, and if we can we must.
> Shoulder the sky, my lad, and drink your ale.

Last Poems is no less disillusioned. Here again the Shropshire lad pipes his merry-mournful note; here the rose-lipt maidens kiss carelessly as ever, and the heart out of the bosom is given in vain. The doomed young men still face the hills whose brief comfort cannot delay "the beautiful and death-struck year," and the hopelessness assumes a blasphemous bravado as the bitter spirit cries:

> We of a certainty are not the first
> Have sat in taverns while the tempest hurled
> Their hopeful plans to emptiness, and cursed
> Whatever brute or blackguard made the world.

Meanwhile, says Housman with mock cheerfulness, we need not despair; there is, for the moment, love and laughter and enough liquor to go around. These, insists the English poet, echoing the Persian pleasure-seeker of the *Rubáiyát,* are almost enough. Drinking is better than thinking—

> And malt does more than Milton can
> To justify God's ways to man . . .
> 'Tis true, the stuff I bring for sale
> Is not so brisk a brew as ale:
> Out of a stem that scored the hand
> I wrung it in a weary land.
> But take it: if the smack is sour,
> The better for the embittered hour.

The poetic stuff which Housman brought for sale is a peculiar blend. The philosophy is hard but it is meant to be heartening; the judgments are heavy but the tone is light. The stanzas are miracles of incongruity; the most horrendous happenings shape themselves into measures which are a cross between a jig and a hymn tune. The best of them have a purity which English poetry has rarely excelled. Anthologists have rifled Housman's two little books for such clean-cut and classical rhymes as those beginning "When I was one-and-twenty," "With rue my heart is laden," "Is my team ploughing," "On Wenlock Edge the wood's in trouble," "In summertime on Bredon," "The chestnut casts his flambeaux," "Be still, my soul, be still; the arms you bear are brittle," "Farewell to barn and stack and tree," and the twelve lines which many have considered the most memorable short lyric in the language:

> Loveliest of trees, the cherry now
> Is hung with bloom along the bough,
> And stands about the woodland ride
> Wearing white for Eastertide.   .

> Now, of my threescore years and ten,
> Twenty will not come again,
> And take from seventy springs a score,
> It only leaves me fifty more.

> And since to look at things in bloom
> Fifty springs are little room,
> About the woodlands I will go
> To see the cherry hung with snow.

Housman's prose was as sharp and severe as his poetry. His criticisms were controversies about literature and, in particular, about the process of creation. Asked to explain the quality of poetry, Housman replied, "I could no more define poetry than a terrier could define a rat; but I thought we both recognized the object by the symptoms which it provoked in us." His scholarly papers are edged with sarcasm and bristle with cold contempt. He wrote of a certain teacher, "When X has acquired a scrap of misinformation he cannot rest till he has imparted it." Another of his victims drew this devastating sentence: "Nature, not content with denying to Professor Y the faculty of thinking, has endowed him with the faculty of writing." He epitomized Swinburne's verbosity by declaring: "Swinburne has now said not only all he has to say about everything, but all he has to say about nothing." Contemptuous of careless work, he was a fanatic about his own. His notebooks show how carefully he worked for the exact word. Laurence Housman discloses that, in the superb description of the clock striking the quarters in "Eight O'Clock," the word "tossed" was arrived at only after Housman had tried and rejected "loosed," "spilt," "cast," "told," "dealt," and "pitched."

> He stood, and heard the steeple
> Sprinkle the quarters on the morning town.
> One, two, three, four, to market-place and people
> It tossed them down.

Strapped, noosed, nighing his hour,
He stood and counted them and cursed his luck.
And then the clock collected in the tower
Its strength, and struck.[1]

The limitations of Housman's poems are self-revealing. The quatrains are overfastidious; the ironies are repetitive; the manipulation is restricted and so disciplined that it is inflexible—Louis Kronenberger said that Housman was "plainly a perfect poet and just as plainly not a great one." But dozens of the poems haunt the mind, and many of them will live as long as the language. Critics never failed to celebrate the classic restraint of the terse disposals, the taut and almost epigrammatic lines. Accepting the most desolating tragedy with the most disarming urbanity, Housman was the finest Latin poet who ever wrote in English.

[1] From *Last Poems* by A. E. Housman. Copyright, 1922, by Henry Holt and Company, Inc. Copyright, 1950, by Barclays Bank, Ltd. By permission of the publishers.

Henri Bergson

[1859-1941]

"His speculations spread from salon to salon
almost as fast as the latest gossip."

CHAUVINISTS prone to detect recognizable national characteristics were discomfited to learn that the most famous as well as the most obviously French philosopher of modern times had a Polish father, an English mother, and that none of his ancestors had a trace of Gallic blood in their systems. Descended from a line of well-to-do Jewish tradesmen, Henri Bergson's father turned to the arts. An accomplished musician, he left his native Warsaw, traveled across the continent, became a British citizen, and married an English Jewess of Irish inheritance, Kátherine Levinson. Although their son was born in Paris, October 18, 1859, Henri did not become a naturalized Frenchman until he was twenty-one, and his fellow-students always regarded him as a typical Englishman. Studying at the Ecole Normale Supérieure, he devoted himself to biology and psychology, admired John Stuart Mill's emphasis on free thought and the importance of induction, and praised Herbert Spencer's *First Principles,* although he was already doubtful that "reality" could be explained in the terms used by the chief exponent of scientific evolution.

At eighteen his solution of a mathematical problem had been published in the *Annales de Mathématique* and it seemed indicated that he should pursue a career as a mathematician. Finding it hard to choose between the precision of an exact science and the speculations of an imaginative literature, young Bergson decided not to reject either but to combine both. He decided to be a writer of philosophy. He was particularly attracted to the early Greek philosophers. Zeno's suggestions of "being" and "becoming" and Heraclitus' arguments for a fluid universe continually in a state of flux captivated the young student and, years later, were richly amplified by the mature writer. Realizing that man cannot live by philosophy alone, Bergson also realized that a living can be obtained from the teaching of philosophy. Therefore, after graduating, he taught at the Lycée of Clermont-Ferrand, inspiring his pupils by

the eloquence with which he turned an academic study into provoking impassioned inquiries. His personality matched his mind.
The asceticism of his lean face and thin lips was denied by the quick
play of his gestures, the mobile mouth, and the restless eyes which
darted suddenly as he thrust home some dialectical point.

At thirty Bergson produced two theses, one of which was entitled *Les Données Immédiates de la Conscience,* his first important
work, translated into English as *Time and Free Will.* Eight years
later he was appointed to the staff of his old school, the Ecole
Normale Supérieure, and published his deeply probing *Matter and
Memory.* In 1900 Bergson received a professorship at the Collège de
France, a position which he held for forty years. His lectures were so
well attended that he became that rare and almost unprecedented
thing: a philosopher who was a popular success. His speculations
spread from salon to salon almost as fast as the latest gossip; he was
praised, imitated, and invited everywhere. Unsolicited visitors
were so frequent and so importunate that he was forced to move
from one dwelling to another; one of his admirers nicknamed him
"The Wandering Jew." His feminine audiences grew so large that
hundreds were turned away from the lecture halls. His epigrams and
illuminating phrases—"creative evolution," *"élan, vital,"* "the
stream of consciousness," "philosophy is the turning of the mind
homeward"—were quoted everywhere. At the age of fifty he had
taken the place of Taine and Renan as the most original thinker in
France and one of the most stimulating writers in the world of
ideas. At fifty-two three of his books (*Time and Free Will, Matter
and Memory,* and *Creative Evolution*) appeared simultaneously in
English translations and made new disciples in America as well as
England. Men delighted in his affable forthrightness; women idolized him. His marriage was an uninterrupted happiness.

During his fifties Bergson became a peregrinating lecturer; he
spoke at Oxford, London, Birmingham, Bologna, and New York. He
was always at ease and his audiences were increasingly enthusiastic.
At fifty-five he was elected to the French Academy. At sixty-
two he resigned from the Collège de France, but was retained as
honorary professor. At sixty-eight he was awarded the Nobel Prize
"in recognition of his rich and life-giving ideas and the resplendent
art with which they are presented." He grew increasingly religious
with age; in his seventies he was drawn to Catholicism which he saw
as "the complete fulfillment of Judaism." But the anti-Semitic
movements in France and Germany convinced him that a change

in religion would seem the act of a renegade. Besides, he wrote grimly, "I wanted to remain among those who tomorrow will be persecuted."

Persecution came with the fall of France in 1940. When the Vichy government discharged all Jews from their posts an exception was made in the case of Bergson, but he refused to take advantage of it. Feeble at eighty, he lived in uncompromising retirement. When all Jews in France were forced to register and Bergson was excused, he again ignored the exemption and took his place in line at the Registration Office, although he was eighty-one, bedridden, and barely able to stand. The strain was too much for him. "That last silent protest in the inclement weather," wrote E. W. F. Tomlin, "unnoticed and almost anonymous in its humble dignity, hastened the end." His lungs became inflamed, pulmonary congestion followed, and he died January 4th, 1941.

Considered separately, Bergson's ideas are not revolutionary, but their presentation is full of surprises and even the restatements are startling. Besides, they are so skillfully interwoven and so vividly embodied that people who protest that they cannot understand a single abstract concept find themselves reading philosophy with ease and even with excitement. Bergson offers the ordinary man an essentially positive approach in a time of confusing negatives. He assures the individual that he is a free agent because every individual is a new and creative self; every moment in his life has a new possibility, an adventure in free will. Evolution itself, says Bergson, improving upon Darwin, is freshly creative, not predetermined, and man himself can change its course. It is guided by the *élan vital,* the procreant urge, the source of energy which Bernard Shaw liked to call "the life force." This vital force, continually growing and expanding into new forms, is opposed to everything which is torpid, apathetic, and passive. Resisting the pull of inertia, infusing even seemingly inert matter with the will to live, it is bold and experimental, progressing from hard-won security to the dangers of the liberated body and the freed spirit. "So the heavy Greek hoplite was supplanted by the light Roman legionary; the knight, clad in armor, had to give way to the free-moving infantryman; and in a general way, in the evolution of life, just as in the evolution of human societies and of individual destinies, the greatest successes have been for those who accepted the greatest risks." Life is an irresistible activity, a never-hesitating, struggling, and triumphant growth. Even God is not a fixed and static power, for God also grows with his mounting creation, a swelling and ever-developing force. "God, thus defined, has nothing of the ready-made. He is unceasing life, action, freedom. Creation, so conceived, is not a mystery; we experience it in ourselves when we act freely . . . The animal leaves its source, the plant; man surmounts the world of animals; and the whole of humanity is one vast army fighting beside and before and behind each of us in an overwhelming charge to beat down every barrier, every resistance, and clear the most formidable obstacles, perhaps even the last obstacle, death."

Following such a line of thought Bergson gave matter not only a new vitality but something close to spirituality. Bergson saw beyond the shape of solid forms, even beyond the construction of the molecule. He compared the potential energy held in the atom to the release of nuclear thought within the mind. Furthermore, Bergson made a distinction between the brain, which is the calculating and measuring machine, and the mind which remembers everything and manifests itself in intuition, the source of all knowledge. The brain, said Bergson, is a wholly rational instrument; it can enumerate, assess, and analyze, but it cannot feel. The ability to respond to emotion, to suffer and sustain, in short to feel, is an intuitive process, something which had been derided by most philosophers. But intuition, Bergson claimed, was "the legitimate and noble province of the mind; indeed, it is the only means for perceiving the heart of things." The past of every individual is a dominating part of his present, never absent from his subconsciousness, he maintained in *Matter and Memory,* and it is this stream of memories that feeds the continuous flow of intuitions.

Bergson drew a further distinction between "time" and "duration." What Bergson calls "clocked time" is not real time. Real time coincides with the swing of the pendulum but, unlike clock time, it has no limits and is not restricted to precise, short-lived beats. Reality, which is an aggregation of rapidly changing experiences, cannot be defined in terms of evanescent seconds for, as Heraclitus discovered, everything moves, flows, and changes. Something more personal, more durable and permanent than measured time is needed, and this Bergson calls "duration." "Duration," he writes, "is the continuous progress of the past which gnaws into the future and which swells as it advances," for "the past in its entirety is prolonged into the present and abides there actual and acting." "Duration" is the essential pulse of our being; it *is,* as Tomlin summarized it in *The Great Philosophers of the Western World,* "our very being, for we ourselves are the conscious expression of the life-flow from which the whole universe has ultimately been derived. Matter, then, is congealed, lifeless Spirit, the hardened lava thrown up by the volcanic discharge of the creative principle or *élan vital.* The ultimate reality is Duration." Thinking in terms of the clock, we limit ourselves; we confuse that which is inert, like matter, a measurement of space, with that which is alive, intensive, and a measure of the spirit. The intuitive self, Bergson concludes, is the true self, the soul, the infinitely creative intellect. It is not the coolly calculating brain but the daring and delicately perceptive mind, the inner inextinguishable spark, which has conceived every branch of science and created every form of art.

One reason for Bergson's continuing appeal is his flexible and almost limpid style. His paragraphs are packed with kaleidoscopic but never confusing allusions; the sentences are fluid and, even when they are intricate, lucid to the point of transparence. A nimble wit plays over the most serious thoughts; Bergson does not even disdain the pun. One of his refutations of the mechanistic hypothesis is typical: "The eye is composed of distinct parts, such as the sclerotic, the cornea, the retina, the crystalline lens, etc. In each of these parts the detail is infinite. The retina alone comprises three layers of nervous elements—multipolar cells, bipolar cells, visual cells—each of which has its individuality and is undoubtedly a very complicated organism: so complicated, indeed, is the retinal membrane in its intimate structure that no simple description can give an adequate idea of it. The mechanism of the eye is, in short, composed of an infinity of mechanisms, all of extreme complexity. Yet vision is one simple fact. As soon as the eye opens, the visual act is effected . . . This contrast between the infinite complexity of the organ and the extreme simplicity of the function is what should open our eyes."

Bergson is, first of all, a writer who teases, stirs, and finally rouses the imagination; he is the poet among the philosophers. He persuades the reader that intuition surpasses reason, that the swiftly illuminating figure of speech is more powerful than precise logic. This is true—or he almost convinces us that it must be true—because imagination precedes discovery. He makes it plain that science itself is a succession of dazzling intuitions, and its miracles are merely the relating of the like and the unlike, the common and the extraordinary, in a series of breathless metaphors.

The influence of Bergson was far-reaching. In literature it quickened the mysticism of Péguy and the memory-charged revelations of Proust (whose cousin, Mlle. Neuberger, he had married); it even affected the social-syndicalism of Sorel, who applied Bergson's advocacy of the instinctive life to his own anti-intellectual revolutionary theories. At a time when men were growing fearful of their own materialistic creation, Bergson gave them back their religion and revived their drooping faith. He reaffirmed the function of philosophy, maintaining that it was a guide to the spiritual potentialities of mankind rather than to man's brain and its mechanisms. He re-established the innate sense of wonder in a world where even the machine takes on mystical powers. "Machinery will find its true vocation again; it will render services in proportion to its power if mankind, which it has bowed still lower to the earth, can succeed, through it, in standing erect and looking heavenwards." Intuition and creation, life and memory, perception and religion, are one; the immediate moment contains the entire past; everything—the accumulation of all the ages—is now.

John Dewey

[1 8 5 9 - 1 9 5 2]

*"Not perfection as a final goal, but the ever-
enduring process of perfecting, maturing,
refining, is the aim in living."*

PHILOSOPHER who combined the stubborn perseverance of a
New England farmer with the zeal of a reckless liberal, John
Dewey helped alter latter day American politics and culture
and, in particular, modern schooling. The public knew him as
"the founder of progressive education." An ardent follower of
Darwin and a disciple of William James, Dewey was not only a clari-
fier but a crusader. Like Darwin, he believed that knowledge was
not based upon abstruse, preconceived ideas but on biological
facts; like William James, he continued to thrust the pragmatic
method against authoritarianism and dogma. Disdainful of the old
logic-splitting problems, he was not intimidated by questions which
he considered obsolete. He knew that thought as well as matter
is a dynamic process, that logic is a developing discipline, and that
philosophy is not an accumulation of abstractions originating in
pure objectivity, but has a social foundation and is, therefore, a
social force.

John Dewey was born in Burlington, Vermont, on October 20th,
1859, in the same year that Darwin published his *Origin of Species*
and four days after John Brown raided Harper's Ferry. The family had been in America since the early 1600's. Dewey's father ran
a small general store; his mother was the daughter of a Vermonter
whose ancestors had farmed around Cape Cod. He buried himself in
books even as a boy; his studies were his play, and he was barely
twenty when he graduated from the University of Vermont. He
began teaching at once. His first position was in Oil City, Pennsylvania, after which he taught in the country schools of his native
state. A few years later he decided to specialize in philosophy.
Entering Johns Hopkins, he took his Ph.D. at twenty-five and married Alice Chipman, one of his students, at twenty-seven. Beginning his college teaching career as an instructor at the University

of Michigan, in 1888 he went to the University of Minnesota as Professor of Philosophy. At thirty-five he was head of the department of philosophy at the University of Chicago; two years later he became director of that institution's Laboratory School of Education.

It was a frankly experimental school, devoted to the then-revolutionary and still debatable principle that facts, figures, and even ideas should not be thrust upon children until they are curious about them. Dewey was more concerned with extending and enriching the child's present experiences than with a haphazard training for some remote and uncertain future. The emphasis was on immediacy, spontaneity, and individualism; Dewey's motto was "learning by doing." "If I were asked to name the most needed of all reforms in the spirit of education," he wrote, "I should say: 'Cease conceiving of education as mere preparation for later life, and make of it the full meaning of the present life.' And to add that only in this case does it become truly a preparation for later life is not as much a paradox as it seems. An activity which does not have worth enough to be carried out for its own sake cannot be very effective as a preparation for something else . . . The new spirit in education forms the habit of requiring that every act be an outlet of the whole self." These and other unorthodox views were expanded in his first book, *The School and Society,* published when he was forty years old.

At forty-five Dewey resigned from the University of Chicago faculty to accept a professorship at Columbia University, where he occupied a monumental position the rest of his life. Max Eastman, who was one of his pupils and assistants, recalled in the *Saturday Review of Literature* that Dewey looked like the portraits of Robert Louis Stevenson, "with the same flat hair and black mustache, and the same luminous eyes . . . I remember how he frequently used to come into class with his necktie out of contact with his collar, or a pants leg caught up on his garter. Once he came for a whole week with a rent in his coat which caused a flap of cloth to stick out near his shoulder like a cherub's wing. His hair always looked combed with a towel. He would come in through a side door, very promptly and with a brisk step. The briskness would last until he reached his chair, and then he would sag. With an elbow on the desk he would rub his hand over his face, push back his hair, and begin to purse his mouth and look vaguely off over the heads of the class, as though he might find an idea up there along the crack between the wall and the ceiling. He always would find one."

He was not an exciting speaker. His lectures were delivered in a monotonous down-East drawl without eloquence or emphasis. Irwin Edman, who became head of the department of philosophy at Columbia, listened to Dewey for the first time not only with disappointment, but with a shock of dullness and confusion. "I had not found Dewey's prose easy," wrote Edman in *Philosopher's Holiday*, "but I had learned that its difficulty lay for the most part in its intellectual honesty, which led him to qualify an idea in one sentence half a page long. In part also it lay in the fact that this profoundly original philosopher was struggling to find a vocabulary to say what had never been said in philosophy before, to find a diction that would express with exactness the reality of change and novelty, philosophical words having been used for centuries to express the absolute and the fixed. Once one had got used to the long sentences, with their string of qualifying clauses, to the sobriety, to the lack of image and of color, one sensed the liberating force of this philosophy. Here was not an answer but a quest for light in the living movement of human experience; in the very precariousness of experience there lay open to the perplexed human creature the possibilities that peril itself provocatively suggested. I had found here, as have so many of my generation, a philosophy that, instead of laying down a diagram of an ideal universe that had nothing to do with the one of actual human doings and sufferings, opened a vision of conscious control of life, of a democracy operating through creative intelligence in the liberation of human capacities and natural goods."

Dewey began to propound an enlargement of pragmatic concepts which would express the democratic spirit in philosophy as Whitman had expressed it in poetry. A new philosophic vitality was revealed in such books as *How We Think*, written at fifty; *Schools of Tomorrow*, a collaboration with his daughter, Evelyn; *Democracy and Education*, which many consider his most important book; and, at sixty-one, *Reconstruction in Philosophy*, which has been recommended as the single work of Dewey's which those unable to follow most philosophical discussions could read with comprehension.

It was not only comprehension but an active awareness that Dewey sought and hoped to communicate. He believed that the democratic system was not a static thing, but he feared that its progress was in danger of being arrested; democracy, he insisted, "cannot go forward unless the intelligence of the mass of people is educated to understand the social realities of their own times." He claimed to be shock-proof, but he was continually disturbed by the challenge to personal liberties, the underestimation of human intelligence, and the distortion of his own theories. He encountered the last again and again with a little anger but more amusement. Misapplying Dewey's idea that children should be encouraged to follow their natural interests, many progressive schools, intent upon allowing the children to "express themselves," carried unlimited freedom to absurd extremes. Once when Dewey visited a nursery school, he found his son helpless on the floor while a larger boy pummeled him. "That is part of our progressive education," said the teacher smugly. "There is so much cruelty in the world, that he might as well begin to learn it now." Another story relates that Dewey once entered a classroom where, in the midst of general clamor, one boy was quietly reading a book. "You must excuse him," the teacher apologized. "He's only been with us a week."

Dewey seemed to gather energy with the years. In his fifties and sixties he became increasingly active. He helped organize the original union of teachers in New York City, found himself in politics, and became the center of a gathering of devoted liberals who campaigned against political chicanery. Their slogan was "Vote for the man rather than for the party." He went to Japan and delivered a series of lectures at the Imperial University at Tokyo. A group of his former Chinese students persuaded him to come to China, where he stayed two years, lecturing at Peking and Nanking. Between his sixty-fifth and seventieth years he went to Turkey, Mexico, and Russia, noting and helping to direct the educational experiments in these countries.

At seventy-eight Dewey became involved in a bitterly controversial episode. He headed a commission which went to Mexico to investigate the accusations made by the Soviet Government against Leon Trotsky, who was living in exile. The Soviets had condemned to death many of Stalin's old comrades in arms; Trotsky had succeeded in escaping to Mexico where, later, he was brutally murdered. Dewey, strictly neutral, said "I am neither a Trotskyite nor a Stalinist. However, I do not accept the Moscow evidence as conclusive until I hear the other side." When the commission decided that Trotsky was completely innocent of the terrorism and fascist conspiracy with which he had been charged, Dewey became an anti-communist. In spite of attacks by Communists, he was not provoked into becoming a red-baiter. His main concern was to preserve the democracy for which he fought so doggedly all along the line. Later in his long life he became a prey to fears, as William H. Shirer wrote in *Midcentury Journey*, "that the mass of citizens of America had needlessly surrendered their liberties to a few, that rugged individualism had become ragged individualism. . . . Millions of Americans, he felt, were forced to lead lives that were personally frustrated, economically precarious, and socially sterile. In a corporate age they did not have the means or the opportunity to achieve economic success."

In his eighties Dewey never stopped agitating for the faith to which he was devoted. At eighty-five he was still a vigorous combatant. In 1946 he joined labor leaders in Chicago and Detroit, planning a People's Party. He became president of the People's Lobby, spoke of the two leading political parties as "the errand boys of big business," and announced that "the control of government must be redeemed from the special interests which have usurped it, and must be restored to the people." Reviewing his *Problems of Men*, published in 1946, Alvin Johnson, president of the New School for Social Research, declared that Dewey had struck straight at reaction in philosophy as well as in politics. "Philosophy," said Johnson, summarizing Dewey, "needs a thorough housecleaning and the final, definitive abandonment of most of its traditional values. Those values are class values. They were established in a time when the masses of mankind lived in slavery, or near-slavery, and when a little body of the elect could occupy themselves with speculations on the absolute. The present world belongs to a democracy. And democracy cannot waste time on recondite speculations that have nothing to do with life."

At eighty-seven, Dewey was still clear-eyed and clear-headed; his hair, although white, was still thick and his step was firm. In his eighty-eighth year, after twenty years of being a widower, he married Roberta L. Grant, a widow not quite half his age. By his first marriage, he had had six children, two of whom had died in childhood. A seventh child had been adopted, and in his eighties he had adopted two other children, brother and sister war refugees. His ninetieth birthday was marked by many honors, testimonial dinners, and world-wide tributes. Admirers presented him with ninety thousand dollars which went to some of his favorite educational projects. At ninety-one he fell and broke a hip, but he recovered sufficiently to accept an honorary degree from Yale. In the late spring of 1952 he was stricken with pneumonia, and although he seemed to be overcoming the disease, he failed to survive it and died in his ninety-third year, June 2, 1952.

Dewey's writings are a triumph of sense over style. His statements are complex and repetitious, the sentences are cumbersome, the idiom is dry and wooden. In his 38 books and more than 800 articles there is rarely a brilliant sentence, scarcely a quotable phrase. But underneath the unpromising exterior, there is not only a wealth of radical thinking but passionate conviction. Dewey calls for intellectual pioneering toward wider horizons. "Not everyone will understand his philosophy," concluded *The New York Times* (May 3, 1925) in a review of Dewey's *Experience and Nature,* "but nearly everyone must to some extent practice it. A sufficiently optimistic prophet might read in it the history of the next half century of American art, literature, education and, one might even hope, politics . . . His philosophy grows out of common experience and can be tested by it. It is applicable not only to college professors, but to traveling salesmen, plumbers, farmers, clerks . . . His pulse-beat quickens to the drums of humanity's blundering march toward freedom."

Dewey had little patience with traditional metaphysical problems, with word-twisting efforts to determine whether man's conception of good is "truth" and whether what he considers bad is "false." He disliked to draw a hard line between potential good and possible evil, but sometimes he drew a dividing line which infuriated the dogmatists. "The bad man is the man who, no matter how good he has been, is beginning to deteriorate, to grow less good. The good man is the man who, no matter how morally unworthy he *has* been, is moving to become better . . ." Dewey urged his readers to examine closely "the things that force us to labor, that satisfy needs, that surprise us with beauty, that compel obedience under penalty." In spite of all that has been accomplished by science —and, by implication, religion and philosophy—"the fundamentally hazardous character of the world is not seriously modified, much less eliminated." Like William James, he loved the hazards; the test of life was in the risks. If he defined life at all, it was never as a finality but always in terms of growth. "Not perfection as a final goal, but the ever-enduring process of perfecting, maturing, refining, is the aim of living," he maintained in *Reconstruction in Philosophy.* "The optimism that says the world is already the best possible of all worlds might be regarded as the most cynical of pessimisms. If this is the best possible world, what would a world which is fundamentally bad be like?" Dewey preferred meliorism (the belief that existing conditions may be bettered) or even pessimism to an optimism which is likely to become the self-satisfied creed "of those who live at ease, in comfort, and of those who have been successful in obtaining this world's rewards. Too readily optimism makes the men who hold it callous and blind to the sufferings of the less fortunate."

Art to Dewey was also pragmatic in purpose as well as origin. Far from being a cultural abstraction, art was something which "actually improves the quality of human life and experience." Even in an industrial age, art is not something apart from daily living; on the contrary, it is a vitally progressive part of it. Dewey rejects the elaborate and merely ornamental forms which show that "their owner has achieved an economic standard which makes possible the cultivation of leisure" in favor of that which meets "the characteristic human need for possession and appreciation of things."

It was, however, by his insistence that philosophers must be concerned with and, if possible, participants in contemporary social struggles that Dewey reconstructed philosophy. Art, politics, moral systems are the instruments by which man can achieve community or anarchy. "To have things in common instead of being had by them," wrote Jerome Nathanson in *John Dewey: The Reconstruction of the Democratic Life,* "is to have that freedom of expression of which words are only the tools, and the creative relation of one individuality to another is the end. To achieve this is to pursue the intelligent path of satisfying needs and life-interests. To have this is community. To have this is also to have democracy."

Democracy and community were Dewey's main preoccupations. His basic Yankee persistence made him engage in battles to liberate mankind from the slavery of authoritarian concepts. "The task of future philosophy," he declared in a tone of challenge, "is to clarify men's ideas as to the social and moral strifes of their own day. Its aim is to become, so far as humanly possible, an organ for dealing with these conflicts." For, as he wrote in one of his few epigrammatic disposals, philosophy is "a catholic and farsighted theory of the adjustment of the conflicting factors of life."

Anton Chekhov

[1 8 6 0 - 1 9 0 4]

*"Medicine is my lawful wife and literature
my mistress."*

I T IS one of literature's paradoxes that Anton Pavlovich Chekhov, who loved the comic element in life and who was known
to most of his countrymen as the author of countless humorous
stories, is celebrated today as a writer who founded a new literature of unresolved suspensions, subdued in tone and minor in key,
expressive of man's sense of unhappy isolation and his failure to
understand his fellow man.

Chekhov was born January 16, 1860, in the town of Taganrog on
the Sea of Azov. His ancestry was a little lower than plebeian. His
paternal grandfather was a slave who, through shrewd management, had been able to purchase his freedom. Chekhov's father,
Pavel, was an impecunious shopkeeper, vain, small-minded, and as
a parent, tyrannical; his mother was the daughter of a cloth-
merchant. There were six children in the family; Anton, the third
son, had two younger as well as older brothers and a sister. It was
not a happy household. "Despotism and lies so disfigured our childhood," he recalled, "that it makes me sick and horrified to think of
it." A fanatic about religious observances, the father beat the children for any infraction of the rules until they grew wary of any
close human relationship. "As a little boy," Chekhov wrote at
twenty-nine, "I was treated with so little kindness that I accept
kindness as something altogether unusual . . . I would like to be
kind to people, but I don't know how." Before they were adult,
the older brothers, Alexander and Nicholas, drank, gambled, and
ran away from all obligations. Anton, however, was destined to
be the one with responsibilities; at eight he was already at work in
the family store. Nevertheless, he was, by nature, light-hearted,
pleasure-loving, and unassuming. A handsome child, he attracted
people—especially women—without playing up to them. He was, he
said, "initiated into the secrets of love at the age of thirteen."

By the time he was sixteen his father, whose business had failed,
ran away to escape the creditors. The family followed Pavel to

Moscow—all except Anton who stayed in Taganrog to finish school, living with a family friend, whose child he tutored in exchange for board and lodging. Although he was not an outstanding student—failing in an examination, he went briefly to a trade school to learn tailoring—he managed to get enough extra tutoring to save a little money, most of which he sent to his nearly starving family. At about seventeen he suffered a serious illness and, as a result, became interested in medicine and determined to become a doctor. Through all of this, his natural gayety remained unquenched; it bubbled forth in jokes, anecdotes, and playful sketches, which he sent to his brother Alexander, who was working for comic papers in Moscow. Some of his skits were published and brought in a few more rubles for the Chekhovs.

He was nineteen when he was able to pass the examinations, obtain a scholarship for medical school, and persuade two other students from Taganrog to board with his people, whom he joined in Moscow. The two older sons had moved out and the rest of the family, crowded into a slum flat, were struggling to stay alive. Chekhov took charge; "His will," said Michael, a younger brother, "became the dominant one." He was not only the financial but the moral supporter; he admonished the erring Nicholas and signed himself "your stern but just brother." He applied himself ambivalently to his medical studies and the writing of light satires, parodies and potboilers. He was only twenty when he sold the first of his vignettes, but he realized they had no literary value and signed them with a pen-name, "Antoshe Chekhonte."

Gradually the stories were colored with a more serious tinge; they began to be critical; protest became more important than plot. By the time he was twenty-seven, while becoming an intern and getting in and out of various small amatory entanglements, Chekhov had written some six hundred short tales. Although he was a strong looking six-footer, the cumulative strains undermined his health and he was still in his mid-twenties when he contracted tuberculosis. He recognized the symptoms from the onset, but he concealed the true nature of the disease from his family. He also minimized its seriousness to himself, knowing he could not afford the necessary care and that proper prolonged treatment would mean giving up both medicine and writing.

He had started private practice at twenty-four. Well adjusted, responsive to art and science, and possessing a great zest for life, he considered himself richly "used." Contrary to the conclusions of some critics, there was no conflict between his two main pursuits. He liked to say that medicine was his lawful wife and literature his mistress. "When I get tired of one I spend a night with the other," he wrote to Suvorin, the publisher. "This may not be respectable, but it saves me from boredom—and, besides, neither of them loses anything by my alternating unfaithfulness." Suvorin, Chekhov's senior by more than twenty-five years, became the proverbial friend, philosopher, and guide. Under his influence the tone of Chekhov's writing began to change. His first collection of short stories, published when he was twenty-six, had made him aware of an audience; Suvorin made him aware of his responsibility as an artist. He tried a novel which, in the Russian tradition, would enlighten rather than entertain; but he was not fitted for a work which would be a sweeping culmination of history, philosophy, and sociology. It has been thought that his failure to become a novelist assumed tragic proportions in Chekhov's life, but he did not waste himself in self-doubts. Instead, he wrote a play, *Ivanov*, which was a complete success. He was awarded the Pushkin Prize—a rare honor for a writer still in his twenties—for his short stories, but Chekhov was too modest to believe that he deserved a place in enduring literature. He hoped no one would remember his early work: "Chekhonte wrote a great deal," he remarked dryly, "which Chekhov finds hard to accept."

Like most writers of his day, Chekhov sunned himself in the radiance of Tolstoy. Actually, he was more moved by Tolstoy's moral spirit than won over by his mystical faith. "Chekhov was a radical and an agnostic," wrote David Magarshack in *Chekhov: A Life,* "and he remained a radical and an agnostic all his life. His temporary acceptance of Tolstoy's philosophy did not affect his attitude to religion, for it was not the religious but the moral views of Tolstoy, and most of all his dogma of nonresistance to evil, that for a time exercised a powerful influence on him." Chekhov loved the man and reverenced the artist but, differing with the philosopher, distrusted the dogmatist. Finally he had to repudiate the Tolstoy who considered sex incompatible with Christian love— "the most important thing in family life," said Chekhov, "is love, sexual desire, one flesh."

Before he was thirty he was so well established that Suvorin urged him to give up his medical practice. But although his health was steadily deteriorating, he felt he needed both outlets. He was so harassed by the ever-present financial problem that he had no rest. Taking care of his mother and the younger children drained what energy he had left—he once referred to them as his "benignant tumor," but he never thought of having it cut out. For a while it seemed that his emotional burdens would be alleviated if not lifted when he met Lidiya Avelova. But she was married, a mother, and virtuous; and what might have been a light romantic episode turned into a desperate and hopeless passion. To escape it, and to discipline himself, Chekhov made a long and tedious journey to the notorious penal colony on Sakhalin Island, where he remained three months. It was as a scientist rather than an artist that he wrote his account of life among the prisoners. "The Lord's earth is so full of beauty," he concluded. "There is one thing, however, that is not beautiful—that's us."

He drove himself harder and harder. The joy of writing was lost in the continual pressures and the growing menace of time. The speech of the author Trigorin in *The Sea Gull* is a mirror of Chekhov's own mind: "Day and night I am in the grip of one besetting need to write, write, write. Hardly have I finished one book than something urges me to write another, and then a third, and then a fourth! I write ceaselessly . . . I cannot escape myself, though I feel that I am consuming my life . . . No sooner does a book leave the press than it becomes odious to me; it is not what I meant it to be; I made a mistake to write it at all; I am provoked and discouraged . . . Then the public reads it and says: 'Yes, it is very clever, very pretty, but it is not nearly as good as Tolstoy.' . . . I too, love my country and her people. I feel that, as a writer, it is my duty to speak of their sorrows, of their future, of science, and the rights of man. So I write on every subject, and the public hounds me on all sides, sometimes in anger, and I race and dodge like a fox with a pack of hounds on his trail."

Chekhov could not stop. Although he had suffered attacks of what seemed to be heart trouble, he refused to take the symptoms too seriously. He was, however, no longer at ease in the company of any but his intimates. "It would be awkward," he said with a grimace, "to fall down and die in the presence of strangers." Recalling the success of his first play, he hopefully wrote another, *The Wood Demon*. It was a failure. Discouraged but still determined to be a dramatist, he worked feverishly on the third, *The Sea Gull*. When he read it to his friends, the response was feeble, and when it was produced the audience booed and hissed. Chekhov, whose ideas had been misunderstood by the producer and who had sat through the performance in agony, fled the theater. For a while he abjured the stage, but he came back to it and was drawn into plans for the formation of a national organization which was to become known as the Moscow Art Theater. Though he disliked the director, he agreed to let him revive *The Sea Gull,* and with Stanislavsky's sensitive staging, the play was an unexpected and unqualified success.

Chekhov's dramas resist being fitted into the usual convenient categories. "Tenuous, muted, in every way fragile, they capture the heat-lightning atmosphere of a desultory and dying world," wrote Walter F. Kerr in the *New York Herald-Tribune,* reviewing a revival of *The Sea Gull.* "The traditional dramatist thrusts his events into the foreground, roughing in only so much background as is necessary for local color. Chekhov reverses the process. The local color, the loose movement of preoccupied people, takes over the center and sides of the stage, becomes the texture of the play itself. The event is heard as a whisper in the wings." Kerr was echoed by *The New York Times* critic Brooks Atkinson: "Beyond and behind the surface Chekhov has caught the great truths of life—the carelessness, selfishness, and weariness of civilized existence—the candid truth of human society, comic in its inadequate grasp on the fundamentals of social living, tragic in the consequences." *The Sea Gull* is a particularly good example of a play which is both entertaining and touching, a comedy with painful overtones and a tragic ending. It is also a refutation of the charge that "nothing happens" in a Chekhov play. Beneath the casual and seemingly aimless conversations there develop intolerable situations and violent crises. The theme, implied but never stated, is a reversal of the accepted sentimental tribute to the healing magic of love; it is, on the contrary, an exposure of love's ruinous power. A yearning, celebrity-struck country girl runs away from home, is seduced, bears a baby that dies, is cast off by the novelist at whom she has flung herself, becomes an outcast road-company actress, and loses her mind. Another young woman, hopelessly in love with the wrong man, marries a schoolteacher she despises, and thus ruins his life as well as her own. A young writer, overshadowed by his mother, a celebrated star in love with herself, is rejected by the girl to whom he has dedicated himself and his work, destroys his manuscripts and commits suicide. Chekhov does not beat his breast about the plight of his characters. He regards them with a half-amused, half-mocking detachment. The neurotic lovers, the narcissistic

mother, the defeated experimental poet, the famous but wornout
author, and the general purposelessness of their society evoke more
irony than pity. Chekhov shows a certain fondness for his maladjusted people, but he is by no means infatuated with the self-
indulgent, self-deceived, and "useless" individuals who blunder
through the world. Chekhov asserted that the time had come for
writers to admit that they were neither arbiters nor assessors. "The
artist should be," he was quoted as saying in *The Personal Papers of
Anton Chekhov,* "not the judge of his characters, but only an unbiased witness . . . My business is merely to report . . . to be able
to distinguish important and unimportant statements, to be able to
illuminate the characters and speak their language . . . to transmit
the conversation exactly as I hear it and let the jury—that is, the
readers—estimate its value."

Chekhov's voice is heard in Constantine Treplev's querulous protest against conventions in *The Sea Gull:* "Let us have new forms,
or none at all." With the new form in mind, Chekhov rewrote *The
Wood Demon,* rechristened it *Uncle Vanya,* and heard it rapturously acclaimed. He had penetrated to the agitated interior life
quivering underneath the superficially smooth aspects of reality. By
this time he was committed to the theater by personal as well as
literary bonds.

He had fallen in love with a member of the Moscow Art Theater
group, Olga Knipper, an Alsatian actress, ten years his junior, and it
was obvious that she was in love with him. But he could not speak
of marriage. Driven abroad by his failing health, trying one climate
after another, most of the love affair was conducted en route and
by mail. He felt tied to a family he had allowed to possess him;
he was desperately ill; he knew that, at best, dying could only be
delayed. But if Chekhov was doomed to suffer, Olga refused to let
him suffer alone. It took over two years to convince him—Olga had
to do the proposing—and on May 25, 1901, they were married.
Chekhov was still so morbidly timid and fearful that the marriage
was kept secret. Most of those who, like Tolstoy, knew him but did
not know him well, considered Chekhov a simple, good fellow. But
David Magarshack points out that "not even his wife who, during the
last years of his life released the deep fount of tenderness and affection in him, was able to break the impenetrable wall which he had
erected between himself and the outside world."

There were only three years left, and they were to be both rewarding and agonizing. He had been made a member of the Rus-

sian Academy at thirty-nine; two years later he was instrumental in getting his friend Maxim Gorky elected to the Academy. Soon after, the authorities objected to Gorky's political views, and the Academy cravenly invalidated his election. Chekhov confirmed his opposition to autocratic rule by resigning in protest. Two more plays were written which proved to be his most popular—the inexhaustible, endlessly vibrating *The Three Sisters* and *The Cherry Orchard.* The latter was composed in such a state of physical pain that he could write only a few lines a day. What gave him even more distress was the way in which *The Cherry Orchard* was produced. Chekhov had intended the play to be a gentle though ironic comedy about old standards and new values, but Stanislavsky presented it as a bitter conflict, the defeat of a dying aristocracy by a rising, ruthless materialism, a tragedy of futile elegance and helpless attrition.

Shortly after the opening of *The Cherry Orchard* it became obvious that Chekhov's condition was hopeless. "Growing weaker in body but stronger in spirit," wrote his wife, "he took a perfectly simple, wise, and beautiful attitude to his bodily dissolution, because he said, 'God has put a bacillus in me.' " In the forlorn hope that the pine-fresh air of the Black Forest might delay the inevitable end, he was taken to the sanitarium at Badenweiler. As he lay on his deathbed one of the physicians attempted to encourage him with specious assurances, but Chekhov was too good a doctor to be deceived. "I am dying," he said quietly, and died. The date was July 2, 1904. In six more months he would have been forty-five.

Without ever drawing up a manifesto or announcing a program, without even being aware of the part he was playing, Chekhov instituted a one-man revolution against the artificial, highly polished play and the slick short story. His followers stressed and localized his aim: to tell "the absolute and honest truth" rather than spin a plausible piece of fiction. His first English disciple, Katharine Mansfield, gave the short story new overtones; in America the voice of Chekhov is heard in practically every other piece of fiction printed in *The New Yorker,* as well as every annual compilation of prize-winning short stories. Chekhov was concerned with people rather than with plots; his plays and stories plunge immediately into a living and usually complicated situation. The author is primarily involved in a projection of actuality, in a state of almost painfully sensitive awareness, in the creation of character, not just *a* character.

It is a question whether Chekhov refused to follow the patterns of the well-made play and the carefully contrived tale because of a conscious reaction against them or merely because he was too pressed by time and too aware of the incalculability of life to supply factitious explanations. Instead of the favored formula—the teasing beginning, the dramatic middle, and the neat or surprising end —Chekhov began in the middle and usually let the reader imagine the ending. He rejected artifice, despised pretension, and achieved his most dramatic effects with the mildest and most colloquial vocabulary. His climaxes came to a head in commonplaces like "It does not matter" or "If we could know"—phrases whose very flatness suggest that the poignance is so deep as to be inexpressible. His plays and such short stories as "A Day in the Country," "The Duel," "Ward Number Six," "The Doctor," "My Life," and "Kashtanka"— to name only six of the thousand he wrote in less than twenty years —reveal, says D. S. Mirsky in *A History of Russian Literature,* "the essentials of a mature style . . . the biography of a mood—a mood developing under the trivial pinpricks of life, but owing in substance to a deep-lying, physiological and psychological cause."

That the cause is hidden makes even more mysterious Chekhov's triumphs in seemingly insignificant details, the indirect dramas, the way in which a teacup is lifted or a gesture withheld. He accomplished small but continual miracles in tremendous trifles, in the merging of the inane and the inexplicable, the lost humor, the suppressed trepidation and the unspoken anguish. His was the genius of a style, the "biography of a mood," the "slice of life" which gave rise to a new and enlarging literature of sensibility.

Claude Achille Debussy

[1 8 6 2 - 1 9 1 8]

"He delighted in confessing his fondness
for every kind of gluttony."

ALTHOUGH many musicians decry the value and even the validity of national music, modern music shows four distinct
national strains. There is the strong Germanic influence
stemming from the heavy and overelaborate orchestrations of Richard Wagner, further weighted by the baroque adornments of Richard Strauss and the intricate twelve-tone system of Arnold
Schoenberg. The Russian rejection of "bourgeois" sentimentality is
expressed in the intellectualized concepts of Igor Stravinsky and the
curious combination of the primitive and the classical in the symphonies of Dmitri Shostakovich and Sergei Prokofiev. American music has come of age in its recognition of indigenous folkstuff, country
dances, Negro spirituals, regional jazz, and other native elements.
The rarefied estheticism sounded by Erik Satie and Maurice Ravel
and perfected by Claude Achille Debussy supplied new tone colors
and a new set of subtleties not only to French compositions but to
music throughout the world.

The impact of Debussy was not as dramatic as that of most innovators, but the appreciation of his importance was no less great
for being gradual. He was born August 22, 1862, at Saint Germain-
en-Laye, not far from Paris, and was christened Claude Achille.
During his youth he signed himself "De Bussy," hoping to give the
impression that his lineage was noble, and he retained the elegant
"Achille" until he was near thirty. But there was nothing aristocratic
about the Debussys. The family had been farmers and small town
merchants for generations, and Claude Achille, the eldest of five
children, was ushered into life in a musty room above a china shop
run not too successfully by his parents.

His father liked to believe that his son inherited his taste, for although Manuel Debussy cared for nothing more serious than operettas, he affected a wide acquaintance with contemporary music.
As soon as the boy evinced talent at the piano, he neglected the
child's education, taking him to theaters and concerts instead of

sending him to school, in the hope of producing a prodigy. As a result, the composer was an uneven performer, an undisciplined artist for years, and an erratic speller all his life. Claude Achille's first piano lessons were paid for by a banker friend of the family, Achille Antoine Arosa, who was the boy's godfather as well as his aunt's lover, but when Arosa discarded his mistress, the Debussys had to look elsewhere for a sponsor. Fortunately, the boy attracted the attention of Madame Mauté de Fleurville, a pupil of Chopin as well as the mother-in-law of Paul Verlaine, who became Debussy's favorite poet. Without any sort of recompense she gave him lessons for three years, and taught him so well that he was able to enter the Paris Conservatoire at the age of eleven.

At the Conservatoire, where Debussy spent the next eleven years, he was alternately conscientious and contentious. He took liberties with harmonic progressions and he made light of the conventions; he insisted on writing compositions which violated the rules of musical grammar. "Everything he does is wrong," said one of his teachers, "but he is wrong in a talented way." He disputed the accepted principles governing the production of sound, and basic "theory." As a pianist he was both adept and eccentric. A fellow-student, the composer Gabriel Pierné, recalled that he astounded everyone by his brilliant but bizarre playing. "Either because of natural awkwardness or a fear of being thought timid, he literally charged at the piano. He seemed enraged with the instrument, treating it not only impulsively but roughly, and breathing violently whenever he came to a difficult passage." Beethoven eluded him, but he was considered a "bewitching" Chopin-player at fourteen, and at fifteen he began composing songs which, though slight, were more than conventional salon pieces.

At seventeen his studies were temporarily interrupted when, recommended by his piano teacher, he was invited to Moscow by the wealthy widow, Nadejda von Meck, who had supported Tchaikovsky for years without ever meeting him. Madame von Meck maintained her own trio and took the ensemble with her wherever she went. Debussy's musical horizons were suddenly widened. In Moscow he listened to the wild dance tunes of Borodin, the glittering, exotic palette of Rimsky-Korsakov, the poignant, self-pitying agonies of Tchaikovsky, as well as the less sophisticated music of the East: weird unaccompanied strains from the Orient, the seemingly unbroken line of Chinese melody, the sparse Greek scale with its six fundamental tones. In Venice, thanks to Madame von Meck, an ardent Wagnerite, he met Richard Wagner, and in Vienna he fell under the spell of *Tristan und Isolde.*

When he returned to the Conservatoire he was composing with one ear on experimental harmonies and the other on the *Prix de Rome.* Still praised as a performer—he won a first prize as an accompanist—he was again berated for his departures as a creator. One of the instructors discovered a dozen "errors" in a harmony examination, but far from being dismayed, Debussy remonstrated that the mistakes were made on purpose. "Why must dissonant chords always be resolved?" he asked, mildly dropping a small bombshell in the academic halls. When, somewhat later, the judges examined two of his manuscripts and concluded that they were unworthy of a man of talent, Debussy was greatly pleased. "At last," he cried exultantly, "I have written something original." As accompanist to Madame Moreau-Sainti, to whom he dedicated his first published composition, *Nuits d'Étoiles,* he was brought into a circle of artists and bohemians. Prominent among them was Madame Vasnier, the young wife of a well-known Parisian architect. Besides being beautiful, she had an unusually brilliant soprano voice and the nineteen-year-old boy immediately fell in love with her. He left his parents' home and domiciled himself near the Vasniers.

Meanwhile Debussy was having trouble reaching his immediate goal. At twenty, he failed in the preliminary test for the *Prix de Rome,* but at twenty-two he finished the cantata, *L'Enfant Prodigue,* and with it won the coveted prize.

Debussy disliked Rome intensely. The Italian temperament disturbed him; he was barely civil to his colleagues; the sumptuous Villa Medici seemed a prison. He longed to be back in the Vasnier library, repairing the gaps in his education, improvising at the piano with his Egeria, for whom he wrote the famous *Mandoline* and other early works, giving lessons to her little daughter Marguerite. After a wasted year, he fled to Paris, and only the earnest persuasion of the Vasniers reconciled him to another trial of Rome. One more year of "exile" was as much as he could stand—"if I stayed I should completely cease to exist. Since I have been in Rome, my mind has been dead." Nevertheless, during the two "waste" years Debussy managed to compose the idyllic *Printemps*—which aroused indignant protests for being written in F sharp, a key "forbidden" for an orchestral work—several poignant songs, and the pre-Raphaelite *La Damoiselle Elue,* based on Rossetti's poem, "The Blessed Damozel."

At twenty-five Debussy looked as if he had stepped out of the pages of Murger's *La Vie de Bohème*. His movements were relaxed to the point of lassitude; even when he walked he seemed to be lounging. His hair was black and unruly except where thick bangs flattened down over a bulging forehead. The nose was sharp; the heavy-lidded eyes were small but intense; the ears were disproportionately large. A thin mustache accentuated a somewhat pouting mouth; the elongated chin ended in a tentative beard. He justified the "artistic temperament" by following fits of anger with purring cajolery, "wheedling as a cat." He liked the feeling of importance in things and people, but he despised pretension; a fellow-student remembered that "he had a horror of grandiloquence."

Two changes marked his return to Paris. He became increasingly concerned, almost obsessed, with the color and eloquence of the chord during its wavering fluctuations; and he broke with the Vasniers. He found a jealous mistress in Gabrielle Dupont, known as Gaby of the Green Eyes, and discovered the strange new worlds of Mallarmé, Pierre Louys, Henri de Régnier, Paul Claudel, and André Gide. An interested student, although not a disciple of Wagner, Debussy ceased to be an admirer after his second visit to Bayreuth in 1889. Beneath the orchestral grandeur he detected an arrogance which repelled him. He was not yet able to pack his repugnance into a pointed phrase, but years later when he varied composing with criticism, he spoke of "the goose-stepping, iron-helmeted music of the Wagner . . . the fortissimo chords of the trumpets . . . the beastlike cries . . . the inhuman grandiloquence . . . the bluster and blare which constantly shout: 'I am the greatest of composers!' " He grew more and more appreciative of the Russians, especially Moussorgsky, and the extraordinary effects achieved by the glassy gamelan orchestra of the Javanese, as well as the Annamite groups which he heard at the Paris Exposition of 1889. Echoes of these influences are heard in the *Suite Bergamasque* (which includes *Clair de Lune,* possibly his most popular single piece) composed at twenty-eight, the first set of *Fêtes Galantes,* finished when he was thirty, and the *Proses Lyriques,* a set of songs with Debussy's own words. In his late twenties he had wrestled with an opera, *Rodrigue et Chimène,* trying to shake off the heavy hand of Wagner, but he never finished it. Instead he turned to what proved to be his two most characteristic and most memorable works, *Prélude à l'Après-midi d'un Faune* and *Pelléas et Mélisande.*

The title of the first is exact, for it was originally written as a prelude. It was to be followed by an interlude and a final "paraphrase," all of which was to serve as a background, a musical tapestry for Mallarmé's pagan poem. Debussy evidently realized that the *Prélude* expressed the essence of the work and, as far as is known, never began the other two sections. A personality as well as creative originality is immediately apparent in the orchestration. It is the very opposite of Wagner's solid and almost turbid scoring. Instead of massed sonorities and a piling up of mixed choirs, Debussy went to the other extreme. He emphasized the single and individualized voices of the various instruments. The *Prélude* begins with an evocative theme played by a solo flute—an effect which caused something of a sensation when it was first heard, for until then the flute was used in the orchestra almost entirely as a supporting or "doubling" instrument. "It has been well said of Debussy," wrote Oscar Thompson, in *The International Cyclopedia of Music and Musicians,* "that he gave back its original quality to each instrument, freeing it from the enormous servitude into which Wagner had forced them all in limning the scenes and portraits of his music dramas. Debussy's scorings aim at a transparency, a vaporosity, in which basic timbres do not lose their individuality by virtue of group timbre . . . Debussy thought of different parts of the compass of a given instrument as if these parts were different instruments. He was particularly drawn to the woodwinds, and wrote for them with the acme of taste and sensibility. He rescued the harp from its latter-day employment as merely a contributor to sonorous climaxes and gave it back a role of its own." His use of pure color and his method of juxtaposing tone against tone in unexpected gradations caused the critics to make the inevitable comparison to painting, and Debussy became known as a musical "impressionist."

Debussy was thirty-one when he began *Pelléas et Mélisande,* based on Maurice Maeterlinck's play. It took two years for him to finish the first draft, but he continued to polish and refine the work until the very moment of the first performance, which took place, seven years later, when Debussy was forty. He had to perform an almost impossible task: he had to preserve and even accentuate the vagueness of the text and yet bring out the emotion almost submerged in Maeterlinck's cloudy symbolism, a bodiless retelling of the story of *Paolo and Francesca.* Debussy sought for a music that would "seem to have issued from a shadowy background and should at moments return there"—a long and rippling recitative, a barely perceptible flow of nebulous, translucent melody. The score distilled the mood of twilight, an atmosphere achieved by a mixture of dissolving harmonies, kaleidoscopic dissonances, and suspended, unrelated chords.

In his mid-thirties Debussy married Rosalie Texier, a seamstress, whom he called Lily. She was tall, blonde, and "spirituelle," a living replica of the ethereal Mélisande. A few years later, Debussy became involved with Madame Emma Bardac, a singer of his songs, the mother of one of his pupils, and the wife of an eminent financier. His friends, most of whom sided with the unhappy Lily, were shocked to learn from Debussy that he was "in misery" and that he was "compelled" to desert his wife. There ensued months of melodrama, during which Lily shot herself, recovered from the wound, and instituted divorce proceedings. Debussy meanwhile had eloped with Emma Bardac. She bore him a daughter, and after Sigismond Bardac consented to a divorce, Debussy legalized his union with the mother of his child, Claude-Emma (Claudette or "Chou-chou"), to whom he dedicated the whimsical *Children's Corner*.

There was another scandal when *Pelléas et Mélisande* was produced. At the dress rehearsal an abusive pamphlet was circulated, whereupon some of the musicians expressed their hostility to the composer. It was assumed that the anonymous author of the document was the original author of the play, Maeterlinck himself, who was outraged that the part of Mélisande was not to be sung by his wife, Georgette Leblanc, but by an American, Mary Garden. That Maeterlinck either inspired or wrote the attack seems certain, for he published a signed letter expressing his detestation of the opera, concluding "I can only wish its immediate and emphatic failure." Maeterlinck was destined to be disappointed. Although the first-night audience was bewildered by the lack of arias and the sinuous windings of Debussy's phrases, and there was hissing at the end of every act, the work was a success, if only a *succès de scandale* —or curiosity.

Troubled though he was by the clamor, Debussy could not help but be stimulated by it. He was flattered by imitation, and his adulators, the *debussystes* or, as a punster once called them, Debussy-bodies, amused him as much as they annoyed him. He grew literally fat on the combination of idolatry and envy; the reticent fringe of hair on his chin became a full and assertively flourishing beard. At forty he was, according to André Suarès, "rather fleshy, almost corpulent . . . Round-featured, plump cheeks; bantering in manner; his shrewdness well concealed. He was ironical and, at the same time, sensual, melancholy and voluptuous; master of his nerves, though not of his emotions. His irony, like his love of pleasure, was natural; witty and mischievous, he delighted in confessing his fondness for every kind of gluttony . . . He had in his makeup something of the cat, something of the recluse."

Debussy had made a generally favorable impression with his *Trois Nocturnes* for orchestra, three pieces which range from the lightly flashing to the completely impalpable; but after *Pelléas et Mélisande* he planned to write operas of a far different sort, works with full-bodied themes and wider scope. He considered Poe's *Fall of the House of Usher* and *The Devil in the Belfry* as well as Shakespeare's *As You Like It* and *King Lear;* but, except for a scene from *Lear,* nothing ever came of the projects. Instead, he poured all his enriched energies into the most dramatic of his tone poems, *La Mer.* A dazzling picture of wild sea and tossing sunlight, a battle of winds and waves, *La Mer* seems painted on a large-scale canvas rather than written with small black symbols on ruled paper. The three movements are a set of climaxes and anticlimaxes, vivid contrasts to the dream-heavy indefiniteness of the earlier work. The orchestration is full of surprises—Debussy delights in giving one of the loveliest of his melodies to the strange pairing of an English horn and a solo 'cello. He was also pleased when he could indulge his fancy by presenting his piano pieces with such poetically alluring titles as "La Cathédrale Engloutie" ("The Sunken Cathedral"), "Poissons d'Or" ("Goldfish"), "Jardins sous la Pluie" ("Gardens in the Rain"), and "La Fille aux Cheveux de Lin" ("The Girl with Flaxen Hair"), in which the subjects were described in gossamer sounds, set off by drifting, bell-like echoes.

During his forties Debussy acted as music critic for several periodicals. He was an epigrammatic, somewhat crotchety appraiser rather than an aloof philosopher or musicologist; when his critical articles were posthumously assembled, they were published under the title of *Monsieur Croche: Anti-Dilettante.* Many of his aphorisms were unjust, but equally many were witty and penetrating. He mocked "Schubert's inoffensive *Lieder,* smelling of the chests-of-drawers of nice provincial old maids." He compared Massenet to a perfume manufacturer whose product "has a pleasant odor which is wholly artificial." When Cortot wielded the baton he seemed to be "a toreador teasing a bull." After a rather derogatory estimate of Wagner, he concluded that "had Wagner been a little more human, he would have been divine." An example of his humor appears in one of the pieces in *Children's Corner*. In the middle section of "Golliwog's Cake-Walk" Debussy inserts the agonized chromatic theme of longing from Wagner's *Tristan und Isolde* and, to emphasize the incongruity of the quotation, Debussy directs that the phrase should be played "with great emotion!"

When *Ibéria* was heard the public accepted Debussy ungrudgingly and the critics stopped complaining about his "orgies of modulation." Although Debussy had never spent more than part of a day in Spain, the Spanish atmosphere of *Ibéria* was not only recognizable but authentic. "Without knowing Spain," said the composer Manuel de Falla, "Debussy wrote better and truer Spanish music than Spanish composers who knew their native land only too well." Success, however, came at a time when Debussy was spiritually disturbed and physically distressed. He was fifty-two when he wrote two glittering sets of *Préludes* and the twelve extraordinary *Etudes*, with their brilliant and deliberate distortions, a startling polyphony of dissonances and block sonorities. He was fifty-three when the First World War made it almost impossible for him to continue to compose. Nevertheless, he wrote a few pieces as a protest against military Germany's scorn of culture, "trying to react by creating a little of that beauty against which the enemy rages." He signed himself "Claude Debussy, musicien français." After 1916 he ceased to write. For a while he tried to hide his suffering, but when he became "a walking corpse" it was only too apparent that he was dying of cancer. When the Germans bombarded Paris by air he was too weak to walk to the safety of the cellar. As a last emergency he underwent an operation for cancer of the rectum, but he did not recover. On March 25, 1918, as the air raids and long-range bombardment reached their screaming and thundering height, he died.

Debussy's music is both a protest and a miracle of musical pioneering. It is a protest against the overdecorated and superfluously ornamented music which was prevalent in his day and which Debussy considered not only too forensic but inexcusably inflated. Against these massive effects Debussy pitted a slender and almost unsupported purity of sound. The melodies are delicate, transparent to the vanishing point and fine-spun as a silver filament, but the gliding chords and sliding harmonies maintain the fragility without the possibility of a break. Others before him had occasionally used "the organ-tuner's scale," which consisted of six whole tones, but Debussy was the first to use the whole tone scale as a consistent and sustaining device. His innovations in technique set another milestone in the history of music, and his exquisite airs and filmy textures have become accepted as part of our popular taste. His curious harmonic progressions never cease to stir the half-attentive listener, and the subtle melodies are buoyant as a glass ball on a thin jet of water. To discard one metaphor for another, Debussy has been, in the words of Oscar Thompson, "the determining factor in the music of at least the first third of the twentieth century because of the doors he opened and the restraints he cast aside."

With Debussy the vogue of the grand manner declined. The weighty fabric of complex polyphony was exchanged for a tissue of iridescence, and the excesses of romanticism were rebuked by an impressionism which was daring in its very discipline. Germany was no longer the music-lovers' Mecca. Debussy and the impressionist-composers influenced by him—Ravel, Dukas, Roussel, among others—augmented by a chorus of poets and painters, spoke for a rejuvenated France; and, for a few stirring years, Paris seemed the center of the world.

William Randolph Hearst

[1863-1951]

*"When you looked at the first page you said,
'Gee whiz!' When you saw the second page,
you gasped, 'Holy Moses!' And when you
glimpsed the third page, you exclaimed,
'Good God Almighty!' "*

T HE STORY of William Randolph Hearst is the story of the most
inglorious success in American journalism and the gaudiest
failure in American politics. His career furnishes the greatest
possible contrast to that of his leading rival Lord of the Press,
Joseph Pulitzer. Pulitzer, starting as a specialist in sensational reporting, brought his newspaper and the whole journalistic world
to a new level of liberalism; Hearst, beginning as a vociferous
champion of the underprivileged, ended as an enemy of social reform and an instigator of the most reckless sensationalism ever
printed. Devoted to the flamboyant, Hearst lived spectacularly in
person and irresponsibly in print. If there were not enough sensations around, Hearst manufactured them. He turned current
events into daily crises, created a constantly increasing appetite for
excitement and, endowed with enormous wealth and unlimited
sense of power, became not only a director of a huge network of
newspapers but dictator of the printed word.

He was born April 29, 1863, in San Francisco, California, son of
a millionaire publisher-senator, George Hearst, and Phoebe Apperson Hearst, a cultured southerner twenty-two years her husband's junior. Born a twin (the other infant died at birth), he
grew up an only child devoted to his mother who, in turn, centered
everything upon the boy with a passionate and possessive love. Although the grown man was addicted to platitudes, believing that if
a platitude was repeated often enough it became a profundity, it
was not a commonplace but an Eternal Verity when he frequently
repeated, "A boy's best friend is his mother." Hearst's mother
brought "Sonny" up in luxury, took him on an extensive tour of
Europe when he was ten, and when they returned to California,
sent him to school in the family carriage. He had to plead with his

mother to let him walk instead, and even to sew patches on his fine clothes so that the poorer boys would not jeer at him. Meanwhile he lived at San Simeon, which at that time was a mere forty-five thousand acres, and it was a severe strain for both mother and son when at seventeen he was sent east, to St. Paul's in New Hampshire, where he prepared for Harvard.

He hated every moment of his exile at St. Paul's, neglected his studies, and longed desperately for the maternal warmth of home. At Harvard he was equally maladjusted. Unhappy and resentful, he spent his lavish allowance on pranks and parties, provided brass bands and fireworks to celebrate any occasion or merely to stir up the citizenry of Cambridge, and invented a series of practical jokes. His father's reputation and his own penchant for levity had won him the post of business manager of the *Lampoon,* the university's humorous publication, but his uncontrollable love of mischief ended his formal education. He had been often cautioned that one more offense against discipline would result in his dismissal, but he paid no attention to the warnings; he dropped most of his scholastic subjects and, according to his semi-official biographer, Mrs. Fremont Older, "majored in jokes and sociability." A few months after a short suspension, during which he had been rusticated in care of his mother, he planned one more prank which made expulsion imperative. Messenger boys hired by Hearst delivered elaborately wrapped Christmas packages to various members of the faculty, and when the staid academics opened their gifts they found antique chamber-pots with their portraits pasted on the inside. His career as a Harvard undergraduate lasted barely two years.

At twenty-one, Hearst was a pale and gangling young fellow. His hair, parted in the middle, was sandy; his eyes were pale blue and, in spite of Hearst's love of fun, not merry but cold. Determination was in the eyes, and before he was twenty-two, Hearst had determined to dominate. In 1885, when he was a junior about to be dismissed from Harvard, he wrote an extraordinary letter to his father, suggesting that he could run the *San Francisco Examiner* far better than the present owner, who happened to be his father. He urged that the *Examiner* be turned over to him with enough money to carry out his schemes. His plans included a Californian imitation of Pulitzer's *New York World* and an acceleration of that paper's "startling originality." When his father refused, young Hearst did not abandon the campaign. On the contrary, he sent another letter telling his father exactly what was wrong with his journal and showing how to improve it. "It has been conclusively proven that poor wages and mediocre talent will not do, and the only thing that remains to be tried is first-class talent and corresponding wages." In the hope of dissuading his son, Senator Hearst offered him an almost royal ranch and more than enough funds to run it luxuriously. Young Hearst declined, and his father tempted him with a vast estate in Montana including the fabulous Anaconda Copper Mine. Hearst's answer was to go to New York and get a position on the *World*. The Senator knew when he was beaten. He wired his son that he could have the *Examiner,* and before he was twenty-four years old, William Randolph Hearst became proprietor, sole owner, and editor of the foremost Democratic newspaper on the West Coast. He arrived in San Francisco, having embodied his articles of faith in another letter to his father. "We must be alarmingly enterprising and we must be startlingly original. . . . There are some things that I intend to do new and striking which will constitute a revolution in the sleepy journalism of the Pacific slope and will focus the eyes of all that section on the *Examiner*. . . . In a year we will have increased at least ten thousand in circulation. In two years we will be paying. And in five years we will be the biggest paper on the Pacific slope."

Hearst was not only prophetic but precise. His slogan was, "There Is No Substitute for Circulation," and he proved it. He called for bigger if not better headlines, doubled the space devoted to cartoons and comic strips, changed the "personals" from cold collations of tidbits to electrifyingly hot gossip columns, and not only anticipated public opinion but, by adroit and often gaudy tricks, changed it. He directed one of his staff to faint in the streets so that she would be taken to the City Receiving Hospital. In less than two days, the *Examiner* shrieked with the crudities of hospitalization in San Francisco, an exposé which accomplished a reform of conditions and, not accidentally, an increase of circulation. Nor did Hearst's reforms stop there. He risked political as well as physical attacks by challenging the bipartisan bosses who controlled the city, fought the Southern Pacific Railroad ("Public Plunder by Private Privilege"), and, thanks to an instinctive gift for disturbing the peace and exciting the mind of the reader, built up a mass medium of communication in which news and agitation were cannily combined.

For his next objective Hearst cast his line and his millions across the continent. Eight years after he took over the *San Francisco Examiner* he bought the feeble *New York Morning Journal*. His goal was to exceed the formidable *New York World* in spectacular effect and surpass it in sales. In 1895 Pulitzer's *World* sold for two cents; Hearst arbitrarily brought the price of the *Journal* down to a penny. In spite of huge initial losses Hearst went further into capital; he advertised the fact that money had no meaning beyond the betterment of his paper and, when he needed the best brains of his rival, lured Pulitzer's editors and artists away by doubling their salaries. His staff included such notable literary figures as Stephen Crane, Edgar Saltus, James L. Ford, Richard Harding Davis, who was sent to St. Petersburg for the coronation of the Czar, and Mark Twain, who was despatched to London to describe Queen Victoria's Jubilee. To offset any suspicion that the *Journal* might be too literate, Hearst installed the first newspaper color press capable of printing sixteen pages of cartoons, fashions, and lurid feature stories in full color. He added an eight-page colored comic supplement—"eight pages of iridescent polychromous effulgence that makes the rainbow look like a lead pipe"—and gave prominence to the cartoon antics of a ragamuffin in a yellow dress, known as "The Yellow Kid," the counterpart of a comic character in the *World*. It was these clowning characters and the excesses of their proprietors that gave rise to the derogatory phrase "yellow journalism." Hearst solidified his position by adding an *Evening Journal* and capturing Pultizer's editor, Arthur Brisbane, who made an international reputation by writing staccato editorials, arresting but usually commonplace statements which looked important because they stood alone as single sentences in portentous paragraphs. It became a legend that the first three pages of Hearst's newspapers were planned to elicit a rising response of ejaculations. It was remarked that when you looked at the first page you said, "Gee whiz!" When you saw the second page, you gasped, "Holy Moses!" And when you glimpsed the third page you exclaimed, "Good God Almighty!"

Perhaps Hearst's greatest journalistic coup d'état was the Spanish-American War, a war which Hearst cherished and fomented if he did not actually create it. Two years before the United States had decided to intervene on behalf of the Cuban patriots who were trying to liberate the island from Spanish oppression, Hearst had filled his papers with inflammatory articles and blood-curdling despatches; he also sent telegrams to the governors of all the states asking how many volunteers their states would furnish for sea and land forces. He had shipped the artist Frederic Remington to Havana, and when Remington wrote that he wished to return because things were quiet and that there would be no war, Hearst wired back, "Stay there. You furnish the pictures. I'll furnish the war." Many years later Hearst denied sending the message, but as John K. Winkler concluded in *Hearst: An American Phenomenon,* "The Spanish-American War came as close to being a 'one man war' as any conflict in our history." John Tebel, in *The Life and Good Times of William Randolph Hearst,* disputes this. "The viewpoint of the professional historian contradicts the standard thesis that Hearst started the war. . . . Hearst and Pulitzer sounded the emotional keynote on which the war was fought—the liberation of Cuba. Both probably knew that the real reason was the serious disruption of America's hundred million dollar trade with Cuba, caused by the collapse of the country's sugar economy. . . . But to Hearst and his fellow jingoist editors and the effervescent patriots in Congress, Spain the cruel, Spain the exploiter, was the sole cause of it all." Hearst undertook to bring on the conflict by provocative pictures and screaming headlines; after the declaration of hostilities, he carried on what he called "our pet war" practically in person. He arranged for the rescue of the daughter of a revolutionary leader from a penal colony on Isle of Pines. The fact that Evangelina Cisneros was comfortably domiciled in a suite of rooms did not deter the Hearst papers from depicting a beautiful heroine repulsing the lecherous advances of a brutal general in a loathsome, rat-infested jail. When she was smuggled out of prison, the Hearst papers almost burst their linotypewriters with pride. "Evangelina Cosio y Cisneros is at last at liberty, and the *Journal* can place to its credit the greatest journalistic coup of this age. It is an illustration of the methods of the new journalism, and it will find an indorsement in the heart of every woman who has read of the horrible sufferings of the poor girl who had been confined for fifteen long months in Rocojidas Prison. . . . The monster (Weyler) could not build a jail that would hold against *Journal* enterprise when properly set to work." Hearst spurred on the war effort. His agents intercepted diplomats' letters. When the battleship *Maine* was destroyed in Havana harbor by a mysterious explosion, Hearst offered a reward of fifty thousand dollars "for the detection of the perpetrator of the outrage." He sent his own war fleet to cover the battlefront, and on one occasion, he himself went on shore to capture a few stranded Spanish sailors. He made plans (fortunately never carried out) to obstruct Spanish vessels from taking the short route to the Pacific by sinking a large steamship in the Suez Canal—a clear violation of international law.

Meanwhile, the Hearst papers thrived, circulation leaped, and Hearst the man became a Power. He began to think in terms of empire, to reach out for greater goals and wider horizons to consolidate his victories. He established the *American* in Chicago in thirty days and issued it on the Fourth of July, 1900, just in time to stampede the Democratic Convention for Hearst's candidate, William Jennings Bryan. He solidified his gains by acquiring the *Chicago Record-Herald.* Then he branched out to other cities not yet blessed by Hearst; he bought, took over, or founded newspapers in Boston, Atlanta, Washington, Detroit, Seattle, Rochester, Oakland, Los Angeles, Syracuse, Baltimore, Pittsburgh, Omaha. . . . By 1929, in his mid-sixties, Hearst owned twenty-five major journals in eighteen key cities. His policies were both rigid and retrogressive. He began as a radical, a supporter of labor and an outspoken foe of "capitalistic arrogance," but as he progressed in power he moved further and further to the reactionary right. He became the apostle of Big Business and equated corporate welfare with public welfare. In 1919 he upheld the rights of law-abiding and law-enforcing citizens—even policemen—to strike: "every thinking human being admits the right of ordinary employees to organize and to quit work when conditions are unsatisfactory and to be taken back when conditions are amended." But fifteen years later he fought the unions, opposing the Newspaper Guild with the dictum that a man should do his work "for the romance of it," and in 1941 he was hailed by the very interests he had formerly attacked when he reversed himself on the right to strike: "strikes should be outlawed and complete machinery to enforce their suppression should be fully established and fearlessly operated."

Powerful though his dailies were, newspapers were not enough. Hearst longed for a wider, more lasting, and possibly more literate audience. He invaded the magazine field and, at one time, had a string of thirteen glossy periodicals, of which *Good Housekeeping* and *Cosmopolitan* were enormously successful. His acquisitive habits mushroomed incredibly. He became the world's largest, most untiring, and least discriminating collector. He seemed to specialize in tapestries, armor, silver, English furniture, and Moorish pottery, but he purchased worthless knickknacks and a Cellini ostrich-egg cup for $35,000 with equal zest. His agents bought things

—Benjamin Franklin's spectacles, Egyptian statues, Greek marbles, second-rate genre paintings—all over the world, and as a result, his warehouses were full of unpacked boxes loaded with objects he never saw. On one occasion he bought a Spanish monastery and built a railroad to transport the building, stone by stone. The operation cost almost half a million dollars, but it satisfied Hearst's craving to amass and it fulfilled his compulsion to possess. He bought a castle in Wales and built a gaudier one on Long Island. He enlarged the California "ranch" at San Simeon to a fabulous domain of 75,000 acres, complete with gardens of exotic flowers, a zoo, a game preserve, a Moorish palace—half monument, half mausoleum—and a ducal main building which included a vast banquet hall and more rooms than an average hotel. He also collected real estate, including Lincoln's farm homestead, theaters, hotels, apartment houses, and skyscrapers. He plunged into the motion picture business, started with news and feature films, went on to serials and "super" productions, chiefly starring Marion Davies, and ended by losing more than seven million dollars. The venture gave his talent for inconsistency free play. While his newspapers were splashing the most lurid sin-slaughter-and-sex stories across their pages, Hearst concluded that Mae West's rowdy pictures were indecent and issued a ukase that her name was not to be mentioned in any Hearst paper.

The theater exercised a fascination which went deep into Hearst's private life. At eighteen he fell in love with the beautiful and gifted Sybil Sanderson, daughter of a California judge, and an engagement followed. But when Hearst went to Harvard, Sybil Sanderson went to Paris, studied at the Conservatoire and emerged as an operatic star. Massenet wrote *Manon* and *Thaïs* for her, and she forgot all about the pale embryonic journalist. He, however, never got over it; and when two years later he fell in love again, it was with another California beauty bound for a similar career. A descendant of John Calhoun, Eleanor Calhoun accepted Hearst's attentions but warned him that she intended to become a great actress. The pattern repeated itself. There was an engagement which was terminated when Eleanor Calhoun went on the stage, traveled abroad, and became London's favorite actress. Once more he turned to his mother for comfort and security, and so strong was his dependence upon her that he did not consider marriage for another twenty years. At forty the allure of the theater recaptured him; the day before his fortieth birthday he married Millicent Willson, a chorus girl, half of "The Dancing Willson Sisters." The marriage seemed successful, resulting in five sons, all of whom worshiped their father. Millicent Hearst indulged in various charities, particularly those centering about the theater. It was one of her efforts to help young girls to get a start that brought Marion Davies (born Marion Douras) to the Hearst household. Hearst was fifty-five, Miss Davies was twenty. The consequences were dramatically sudden. The unknown blonde dancer from Brooklyn became a national celebrity overnight; "When you looked at the Hollywood sky," said Dorothy Parker, "the stars seemed to rush together to spell 'Marion Davies.'" She was cast as the romantic heroine in extravagant productions but, in spite of Hearst's money and his properly adulating press, she never became an idol of the screen. She did, however, become a loyal as well as a lovable companion who, during a financial crisis, gave him back a million dollars along with her devotion. Hearst, after separating from his wife who refused to divorce him, lavished more than material things and properties upon Miss Davies; he gave her an affection which he never knew he had.

In his forties Hearst waded boldly but foolhardily into politics. The war-maker decided to be a king-maker, perhaps even a king. In 1902 he got himself elected to Congress, his only successful foray into the political jungle. He was not a popular representative; his fellow-members mistrusted his motives and even the leader of his own party refused to confer with him. Undaunted by rebuffs, Hearst, no tactician, grew more ambitious; his eye was on the Presidency. He saw to it that his name was presented to the Democratic Convention of 1904 with a great flourish of oratory, but the stolid Judge Alton B. Parker was nominated. A year later Hearst ran for the mayoralty of New York on an independent ticket, but he was badly beaten by the Tammany machine—fraudulently, Hearst claimed. Undeterred, Hearst primed himself for the governorship of New York. A year after his defeat by the machine bosses, he formed an alliance with Tammany and made innumerable speeches up and down the state. He was forty-three, a big-boned, loose-jointed figure, with a long face and equine features. His tawny hair was sleeked over his forehead, one lock reaching his left eyebrow. To accentuate his western pride he usually wore a broad-brimmed hat and he spoke his short sentences in a voice that was drawling but high and thin. Somehow, his countless rural appearances and back-platform talks backfired. Although Hearst had spent five hundred thousand dollars on the campaign, all the Democratic candidates except Hearst were elected and his opponent, Charles Evans Hughes, who had spent $619, was elected governor by a huge majority.

Still believing in his manifest destiny, Hearst decided to be an influence behind the scene and a power to be felt not only in the White House but throughout the world. In 1908, William Howard Taft was the Republican candidate and Bryan was once more the Democrats' choice for President. Hearst, nominally a Democrat, had quarreled with Bryan, so he threw his weight behind an Independence League ticket, headed by the hitherto unheard-of Thomas L. Hisgen and John Temple Graves, one of Hearst's writers. Hearst managed to throw a bombshell into the campaign by producing stolen letters which showed that the Standard Oil Company controlled legislation through certain Senators who were virtually on the industry's payroll. Nevertheless, Taft won a resounding victory and Hisgen finished last in a field of five; he failed to get a single vote in his home county. If Hearst was discouraged he was not too disheartened to stop trying. In 1909 Hearst persuaded himself that this time he could be elected Mayor of New York. Once more he waged a vigorous and even vituperative campaign, and once again he was disastrously defeated. In 1912 he attempted to have his candidate (Champ Clark) named as the Democratic nominee for President, but Woodrow Wilson, whom he bitterly opposed, was nominated and elected.

Repudiated by both parties at home, Hearst turned to foreign affairs. Twenty years before he had brought on a war; now, in 1914, he decided to prevent one. America, facing a world war, was bound to be on the side of the Allies, but Hearst became a scornful isolationist. Worse, he declared himself against any measure that might help England and France, warned his countrymen of "the furious and terrible onslaught of a victorious Germany," dwelt on the charge (strangely resembling that of the Communists) that the war was being waged for the benefit of Wall Street and the munitions makers, and after the United States became embroiled, urged a separate peace with the enemy. After the armistice, Hearst deserted the Democrats and made friends with the Republicans. But when the Second World War loomed, Hearst spoke up for National Socialism (at least in Germany), consorted with Fascists and anti-Semites, interviewed Hitler and pictured him as a liberating force devoted to peace and economic stability. Only the entrance of Japan, Hearst's old "Oriental menace," reconciled him to the conflict.

After World War II Hearst's power waned and his health began to fail. He had been assailed often before by rival editors, politicians and presidents, but he was more vulnerable now. With the lessening of his prestige he seemed to shrink physically. Early in 1947 he suffered a heart attack and left his mountain retreat to spend the rest of his days in Marion Davies' Beverly Hills mansion. The woman who had been his companion for thirty years tended him constantly, watching him weaken, rally, grow temporarily animated, and weaken again. Hearst's persistent will to survive kept him alive for four more years. He died August 14, 1951, at the age of eighty-eight.

Long before his death Hearst had been glorified and reviled with unparalleled extremes of opinion. In an introduction to Ferdinand Lundberg's *Imperial Hearst,* Charles A. Beard, the historian, predicted that Hearst's fate would be "ostracism by decency in life and oblivion in death." William Allen White, who made the *Emporia Gazette* a symbol of small-town liberal journalism, declared: "I believe that Hearst as an ally of any politician is a form of political suicide." Beard was half wrong, for Hearst continues to live as a legend, but White was right. Hearst's appreciations and enthusiasms—from his forgotten candidates of the early 1900's through the ignominiously defeated Landon in 1936 to his last hysterical hurrah for General MacArthur in 1948—became the proverbial kiss of death. Convinced that his very contradictions were logical, Hearst impartially supported and denounced men for the very politics he alternately advocated and discarded. Yet Hearst's failures as a world-shaker and international oracle overshadowed his accomplishments as the man who forged the greatest chain of newspapers in history. Pathetically enough, Hearst complained that the public preferred to consider him as an austere power "instead of the 'human' person I earnestly strive to be." His enemies found that the single quotes around the word 'human' were significant and renewed their attacks upon the man's ruthless inconsistencies. Hearst had his answer ready. With his eyes fixed on posterity, Hearst replied: "It is not as important to be consistent as it is to be correct. A man who is completely consistent never learns anything. Conditions change, and he does not." Even his biographers have been content to let Hearst lie in his own contradictions.

Henry Ford

[1863-1947]

"The little man's little man."

HENRY FORD, the power-driven mechanic who put America on wheels, was born July 30, 1863, on a small farm near Dearborn, Michigan. His father intended the boy to be a farmer; before and after school hours he was kept busy with the country chores. But although later in life he occasionally went back to the soil, he never loved the land. "Our dairy farm," he wrote after he had become the Messiah of mass production, "is managed exactly like a factory." Even as a youth he knew he could never work with such slow-moving machines as horses and cows. "I have followed many a weary mile behind a plow and I know all the drudgery of it." There are legends that he made drawings of tractors before he ever saw one, that he hammered his mother's darning needles into screwdrivers, and that behind a protective textbook he was always tinkering with mechanical toys. Before he was fourteen he had taught himself to take a watch apart and put it together again. At sixteen, in Detroit, he spent his days as an apprentice in a machine shop at $2.50 a week and his evenings with a jeweler at a similar salary. Two years later he got a job in an engine shop; at nineteen he was back on the farm, building a single-cylinder steam farm tractor by himself. Although it worked, young Henry was not able to construct a boiler with sufficient pressure to make the tractor turn the sods over. His father, hoping to coax him back to farming, gave him forty acres of woodland, and the youngster promptly set up a sawmill, cut down the trees, and sold off the lumber. He was just twenty-one.

At twenty-four Ford married and moved to Detroit where he was employed by the Edison Illuminating Company. At twenty-six he was chief engineer of the company, joined the Detroit Automobile Club, and there, during his spare time, he put together his first automobile. He was tall and thin; his features were sharp and his face looked pinched. He resembled Washington Irving's gawky Ichabod Crane, whose "whole frame most loosely hung together." Like Crane, Ford was "in fact, an odd mixture of small shrewdness

and simple credulity." The shrewdness was evident from the beginning; it grew to vast proportions until it gave way, with surprising suddenness, to unbelievable "simple credulity."

He was already in love with the machine—one biographer says
that any moving part fascinated him. He devoted himself to it with
the fixed passion of the dedicated worshiper. He had experimented
with a combustion engine, cluttering the kitchen with queer parts
and trying out ungainly models in the woodshed, but he was thirty-
three before he rode out in a contraption jeered at as a particularly
awkward horseless carriage. Following this gasoline buggy, he built
several other cars and had a series of disheartening experiences.
Finally he constructed a racing car and entered it in a crucial contest. "I drove it myself over a surveyed mile straightaway on the
ice," he wrote in *My Life and Work*. "I shall never forget that race
. . . The ice was seamed with fissures, and at every fissure the car
leaped into the air. I never knew how it was coming down. When
I wasn't in the air I was skidding; but somehow I stayed top side
up and on the course, making a record that went all over the
world."

The record did not spur the mechanic into becoming the world's
greatest daredevil driver; on the contrary, he regarded it coldly as
an advertisement. So far he had got nowhere. He was forty when,
in 1903, he formed his own company. Among the stockholders
were a couple of lawyers, a coal dealer and his bookkeeper, two
owners of a machine shop, a clerk, a man who ran a notion shop,
a manufacturer of windmills. The cash capital totaled exactly
twenty-eight thousand dollars. Five years later Ford put the Model
T on the road and changed his countrymen from a nation of pedes-
trians to a race of riders.

The profits were fabulous beyond belief. A single example must
suffice: One of the organizers, James Couzens, had a sister, Rosetta,
a hard-pressed and cautious schoolteacher who had managed to
save up two hundred dollars. After much hesitation, she was persuaded to risk half of it in the new company. By the time the "outsiders" had been bought out in 1919 her hundred dollars had
brought her, in dividends and payment for the stock, a pyramiding
fortune of more than a third of a million—or, to be exact, three
hundred and fifty-five thousand dollars.

Everyone joked about Ford and his Tin Lizzie—they said that a
farmer sent a broken boiler and a rusted washtub to the factory
and, two days later, Ford shipped back a new automobile and a

check for $20 for the surplus metal. Everyone told half-derisive, half-affectionate Ford stories and everyone (well, nearly everyone) rode. Ford saw to it. He was not a great inventor, not an originator of new engines or new principles; he was a coordinator of other men's ideas, a hit-or-miss experimenter, an assembler. But it was his invention of the assembly line, a revolutionary method of production, that changed a generation's way of life. He made cars fast, and he made cars cheap. They were no longer the sole possessions of the rich: expensive toys for a special class. He made them for more and more people—ordinary people, working people, people who never before had been able to own cars. He raised wages and reduced prices, and he was handsomely rewarded. Fifteen million Model T cars were sold, many of them for as little as $290. Ford's theory of price reduction was sound. A low price meant an increasing market. A wide market meant a larger business. A larger business meant a lower cost. A lower cost meant a greater market . . . and so on ad infinitum. Soon every other car on the landscape was a Ford. The evils were yet to be reckoned, but there was no question about the extent of the influence. The Ford brought communities closer together, quickened contacts, and speeded up communications all over the land. It changed not only the tempo but the temper of the nation.

The Model T, no thing of beauty but a tough if cranky utility, gave place to the Model A, a smooth-lined, four-cylinder car with a more modern sliding-gear transmission and a correspondingly attractive price. The price, Ford maintained, was an integral part of the design. One month after the debut of Model A, the Ford plant was putting out six thousand a day. The assembly line, the conveyor belt, and the speedup system had come into their own.

The speed of production called for a continual acceleration of never-relaxing machinery and a consequent deterioration of human factors. During Ford's life more than thirty million motor-propelled vehicles were produced, most of them at a rate of one every minute, not including amphibian jeeps, tank destroyers, bombers, ships, Bren gun carriers, and other weapons of war. Ford's factories became immense and impersonal temples to the one god, Efficiency, a time-and-labor-saving deity, ruthless and unsparing, interested in men only insofar as they could serve the machine. To Ford the machine was paramount, a palpitating fact, a self-generating force, an element. It was the glory of creation, while man was a second-rate piece of manufacture, an essentially faulty creature, shambling and shiftless. At best he was an irresponsible child. "The average man won't really do a day's work unless he is caught and can't get out of it," said Ford. He extended his paternalism into the workers' private lives, regulated their goings and comings, spied on their homes and habits, censored their small pleasures—cigarette smoking was not only a culpable vice but grounds for dismissal. If anyone objected that a man's life could not be run like an unemotional, unerring, and inhuman assembly plant, so much the worse for the objector. Paternalistic supervision increased until the Ford domain began to resemble a dictatorship, a police state and a spy system, honeycombed with stoolpigeons, informers, and strong-arm guards, with an ex-sailor in charge of the Gestapo.

Out of the Ford factories there emerged the Ford empire. The plant at River Rouge covered over a thousand acres and employed more than one hundred thousand men. The company took over coal and iron mines, timberlands, a rubber plantation in Brazil embracing six million acres, glass factories, and smaller manufacturing outfits. There were subsidiary companies in every part of Europe and South America; in 1923 about 200,000 men were on various payrolls in the United States alone. The consequence was an incredible performance of production. A load of iron would be delivered on the docks near the River Rouge factory where it would be smelted, made into steel, then into parts that were assembled into an automobile which was shipped and sold four days later. Everything Ford touched was made over, and made money, at an astonishing rate. He bought a broken-down railroad, and a few years later, sold it at a profit of nine million dollars. By 1940 it was no longer possible to compute his wealth, but in that year it was estimated that the Ford family was worth well over 600 million dollars, and William C. Richards was not too inaccurate when he entitled his "informal portrait" of Ford, *The Last Billionaire.*

He was a man of small eccentricities and large prejudices. A personal foible often grew overnight into a full-scale campaign involving universal (and usually false) issues. He lived on contradictions; he took up "causes" and abandoned them with equal suddenness. He fought the labor unions with unprecedented savagery, but when he capitulated, he gave labor more than it had asked. Going on the warpath against tobacco—"Study the history of almost any criminal and you will find an inveterate cigarette-smoker," he said—he took on the American Tobacco Company in what looked like the battle of the century, and then forgot about it.

For art and culture as living expressions of mankind he cared nothing; he rarely read a book. He had pronounced "views" rather than a philosophy, but his egotism convinced him that at least one philosopher, Emerson, was right when he said that an institution was the lengthened shadow of one man.

During the turmoil of the First World War he suddenly appeared as a savior, the world's leading protagonist of peace. He sailed for Europe on a specially chartered ship, heading one hundred sympathizers determined to make the warring nations agree to arbitration. His slogan went around the world: "Get the boys out of the trenches by Christmas." But the zealots quarreled on the way over; the leader, confronted with the grim realities of the situation, remained aloof; and when the ship docked in Norway, Ford hurriedly left the embattled pacifists and took the next ship home.

A year after the war ended, Ford organized another and less peace-loving crusade. He declared war on the Jews. It was said that his anti-Semitism stemmed from his unhappy experience with Rozika Schwimmer, the Budapest Jewess who had inspired the peace ship misadventure; but the origins of his storm-trooping tendencies have never been authenticated. Nevertheless, Ford published a magazine, the *Dearborn Independent,* and for seven years drenched its pages with a downpour of racial defamations. He quoted discredited documents, such as the so-called "Protocols of Zion," as though they were Gospel and, in an unparalleled set of vituperative articles, held the Jews responsible for everything which was bad in world government, art, finance, illicit liquor, music, baseball, and women's use of lipstick. However, when he was sued for a million dollars by Aaron Sapiro, a Chicago attorney and organizer of co-operatives, Ford suddenly backed down. His apology was complete and abject. He blamed everything on his subordinates, admitted that the "Protocols of Zion" were gross forgeries, implied that he had been too busy to read what had been published in the *Independent,* and ordered the paper discontinued.

As Ford's kingdom grew he took on regal prerogatives: the king could do no wrong. Everything that went wrong was blamed on his supernumeraries, and Ford became expert at playing one man against another. The more important the man became with Ford, the more his career was in danger. Ford dropped top men as summarily as he fired incompetent sweepers. Some of the more important casualties were James Couzens, the organizing genius who had been with Ford from the beginning and shared a kind of working brotherhood with him; Charles Sorenson, the production superintendent who had built and equipped the huge war plant at Willow Run; Ernest Liebold, Ford's business secretary and private confidant. Of the four men closest to Ford, Harry Bennett, bodyguard and screening agent, was the only one who was with the company when Ford died. Yet Bennett, whose relations to Ford were possibly the most intimate of any, subsequently revealed that he took over an already organized "Ford Service," a hated system of plant policing, that "everyone was checking on everyone else," that every fifth employee was a spy or Serviceman, that the men were followed even to the toilets, and that nothing ever happened at the Ford Motor Company without Ford's complete knowledge and consent.

For years Ford had no doubts that he could supply all the answers to the most intricate problems. The uneducated pragmatist, who was also the world's richest manufacturer and most powerful industrialist, assumed that omniscience was another form of omnipotence. Politics was merely a kind of industry; so Ford ran for Senator from Michigan. Although he was a Republican, he failed to get the Republican party nomination; so he ran on the Democratic ticket. He was beaten, but his head was unbowed. He put his agents to work on his opponent, unearthed evidences of corruption, and forced the victor's resignation. Thereupon Ford decided to run for President. The journal he owned declared: "The next President of the United States will be a man who can read a blueprint and who understands the problems of production and how to keep men employed." The Hearst papers came out for him; straw ballots showed he stood high as "the little man's little man." Wiseacres predicted that, if Ford were not nominated by either of the two big political parties, he could win on an independent ticket. Everyone seemed to be for him—farmers who used his tractors, prohibitionists, pacifists, workers, Ford-users, in themselves a large part of the nation. Yet, when the boom was at its height, Ford unpredictably but characteristically announced that he was not a politician and that he could not be considered a candidate.

If the Ford mind was incalculable it was also canny. But it could make mistakes, and it made them on a colossal scale. Ford's basic idea was to make cars cheaper by running his assembly line faster and faster; but the bottom dropped out of the idea when the unions came in and regulated the speed of the line. As a private individual, his errors were more flagrant and far more publicized. Notoriously careless of facts outside of a factory, ignorant of history and culture, Ford sued the *Chicago Tribune* for a million dollars for calling him an ignoramus. Fighting the charge of libel by proving the truth of its assertion, the *Tribune* during the trial showed that Ford did not know who Benedict Arnold was, thought that the War of 1812 was a Revolution, and said that "history is bunk." Although Ford won the verdict—he was awarded six cents as damages —he had been ridiculed, disparaged, and for the first time in his life, browbeaten. He had not only been hurt but humbled. He had to find something to offset his humiliation, some compensation for the cruel reality of the present. He found it in the past.

He went to the past to find himself, back to his boyhood, to the time of old-fashioned tools, hand labor, and a slow-paced, simple life, to villages unlit by electricity and roads uncluttered by automobiles. He became a collector of pieces from a forgotten era, bringing the ghosts of an earlier generation to live with him. He revived the polka, the quadrille, the varsovienne, the mazurka, and other dances of a courtlier day. He instituted dancing parties at the factory and issued a booklet explaining the steps. He sought out old-time fiddlers and went on to assemble one of the largest collections of violins in America, including fabulous instruments made by Amati, Stradivari, and Guarnieri, as well as Tourte bows, some of which cost him three to five thousand dollars. He put up a museum to house every type of vehicle—everything that moved on wheels— Egyptian chariots, Japanese jinrikishas, velocipedes, bicycles, buggies, buses, bandwagons, trains, engines, autos. He built imposing replicas of American shrines, such as Philadelphia's landmark, Independence Hall. In admiration of the spectacular achievements of his friend, Thomas A. Edison, he had Edison's experimental shops taken from Menlo Park, New Jersey, and moved intact to Michigan Museum. Turning from superhuman success to homely sentiment, he bought, restored, and refurnished the Wayside Inn immortalized by Longfellow and had the speedway rerouted away from the door; reconstructed the Massachusetts schoolhouse to which a mythical Mary had presumably led a mirth-provoking lamb; transplanted the conjectured birthplace of Stephen C. Foster; planned a kind of temple for the moralizing McGuffey *Readers* and brought to Dearborn the Pennsylvania cabin where McGuffey was born; acquired a crude cupboard fashioned by Lincoln as well as the theater chair in which he was shot—and only at the last moment was persuaded not to buy a mummy purported to be the remains of the man who murdered Lincoln. History was avenged, but

Ford's nostalgia was unsatisfied. Ford dedicated Greenfield Village, some ninety structures, to the memory of his school days—and every building stressed the legendry, beauty, and purpose of a better way of life than the industrialist had made. Here, said Greenfield Village, in these reconstructed walls and quiet streets—streets undefiled by exhaust gases and the roar of motors—is not only our heritage but the hope for America. Ambivalence could go no further.

The contradiction of Ford's devotion to the present and his yearning for the past was never resolved. The Ford legend has had many interpreters. Besides his understandably biased autobiography and John Dos Passos' memorably etched "Tin Lizzie" in *U. S. A.*, there are the other books which assess the man and attempt to balance his power drives and his frustrations: William C. Richard's large and carefully measured *The Last Billionaire* and, more impressionistically and vividly, Garet Garrett's *The Wild Wheel*. Another and less pleasing picture of the Ford dynasty is presented in Harry Bennett's roughshod *We Never Called Him Henry*.

The paradox persisted to the end. At eighty Ford's memory began to fail. His mind was still alert, but it functioned only in flashes. Long after Sorenson had been forced out of the company, Ford, who could not tolerate a genius too close to him but who had always relied on his steel-hard superintendent, would say plaintively, "Let's go over and ask Charlie about this." At eighty-two he retired. It was said that the retirement had been "arranged," that Ford's goings and comings were carefully guarded, that no one outside of the family ever saw him. On April 7, 1947, nearing eighty-four, he died of a cerebral hemorrhage. A River Rouge flood had cut off all electric power in his home. It was the final paradox. The man who symbolized the power of the machine age left life as he had entered it, in a room dimly lit with a flickering oil lamp and the flame of a few candles.

Henri de Toulouse-Lautrec

[1864-1901]

*". . . And everywhere, ugliness has its
beautiful aspects . . ."*

A DEFORMED ARISTOCRAT who found himself at home with the
outcasts, sports and mutations of a malformed society, Henri
de Toulouse-Lautrec was born November 24, 1864, at Albi,
and was descended from the rulers of the Albigensian region of
France. His father, Count Alphonse de Toulouse-Lautrec-Monfa,
had married his cousin Adèle and was an unblushing eccentric who
rode a white mare on the bridle paths of Parisian parks, dis-
mounted, milked the mare, and nonchalantly drank the milk. A
proud anachronism, he went about the countryside in medieval
doublet and hose, carrying a trained hawk which he fed with the
raw meat of animals killed along the way. He lived in a fanciful
past and, except for racing, hated the modern world and especially modern art. His wife was his opposite: a quiet, plain-living
religious woman, well educated and responsive to cultural progress. The Count and Countess lived apart most of their married life
and the Count believed that the close ties of blood between him
and his wife may have been the cause of their son's physical weakness.

Like his mother, whom he adored, Henri was delicate, gently
bred and gently mannered. His only brother died in infancy and
Henri was three when the younger son was christened. Legend has
it that at the ceremony Henri asked to sign the registry book as all
the adults were doing. "But you can't write," he was told. "I know
I can't," he replied. "But I can draw an ox."

Henri's boyhood was spent between the family chateau at Albi
and a home in Paris where he attended the Lycée Condorcet. He
learned quickly, was bright and eager in his studies, made schoolboy friends, and continually drew pictures. He watched horses and
animals with delight and made countless sketches of them. Though
frail, he was expected by his father to develop into a horseman and
sportsman like himself.

At fourteen Henri fell on the polished floor of the chateau library and broke his thigh. It took a peculiarly long while for the fracture to heal. One day, when he was hobbling on crutches, he went walking with his mother. A crutch slipped, and he fell into a gully, breaking the other leg. He was fifteen. There followed almost two years of invalidism, filled with pain and illness, at the end of which time it was apparent that his legs had ceased to grow and would remain shrunken. The rest of him matured. His torso developed normally—his head in relationship to his full proportions seemed abnormally large—but the legs were a dwarf's. In maturity the fair child became a gargoyle with a bulbous nose, lips that were too thick and too red, and a mouth brusquely accentuated by a short but heavy black beard. Stunted he was—his height was a little more than four feet—and the grown man's heavy torso on the spindly little legs made him look both ridiculous and repulsive. His eyes, in contradiction to his other features, were soft, warm and friendly, but they were hidden behind large lenses. One portrait of him is not unpleasing, but Lautrec's self-portraits always emphasize his grotesque head and monkey-like disproportions.

The elegant Count Alphonse, who apparently felt betrayed by the monstrosity who was his son, turned Henri's future over to the boy's sympathetic and now more than ever protective mother. She encouraged the boy to finish his schooling and apply himself seriously to the study of art. Henri had already received some instruction from a family friend, René Princeteau, who specialized in racing and hunting scenes and who recommended the atelier of Bonnat for further studies. But Bonnat, an opinionated academician, had no use for originality and declared that Lautrec would never learn how to draw. His next instructor, Fernand Cormon, was a routine painter but a more tolerant disciplinarian, and it was at Cormon's studio that Lautrec met Van Gogh and other young experimenters. From that time on, although there were other influences, he had no other instructors.

At twenty Lautrec began living in Montmartre. This was a section of Paris which had always been filled with notorious dives and taverns, a section which originally was not only outside the city walls but outside the law. However, its vitality had dwindled until the eighteen-eighties when artists, writers, and musicians began to leave the Latin Quarter and seek out the advantages of Montmartre. Night life bloomed again. Known as *cabarets artistiques,* the night clubs and dance halls were gathering places for the literati, artists, and models. Lautrec made friends quickly among the denizens of the district. He persuaded his mother to let him move into Montmartre and, for most of the rest of his brief life, he lived in rooms there, sharing apartments with friends. He never wan^ed to be alone. He grew particularly fond of Aristide Bruant, proprietor of *Le Mirliton,* and painted many portraits and posters for him. Besides being owner of a cabaret, Bruant was a singer who wrote ballads about sots and dope fiends, the dissolute and degenerate of Montmartre. He was humorous, ribald, and intensely interested in people. Soon Lautrec became a habitué of the Montmartre dens and dance halls, bars and brothels. The dance halls served drinks and food and provided dances that were spectacular. At the Elysée-Montmartre there was introduced a particular version of the quadrille which became so wild that only professionals could dance it and patrons of the club came just to watch the dancing. The Moulin Rouge was Lautrec's favorite dance hall. All the famous dancers of Montmartre came here: the bawdy La Goulue (the Glutton), the abandoned Valentin le Désossé (by day a café owner, at night a dancer for the love of dancing), the serious, sad-faced Jane Avril. Lautrec painted all of them with a unique blend of devotion and detachment. Another cabaret proprietor, manager of the *Divan Japonais,* wrote poetry and introduced Lautrec to the diseuse, Yvette Guilbert, who roused audiences with her exciting versions of old folk songs and whose angular features fascinated the painter. One day when Guilbert was looking over some of the drawings Lautrec had made of her, she grew annoyed at the unflattering delineations. "Really," she exclaimed, "you have a genius for deformity." Lautrec made a grimace. "Naturally," he said.

Critics differ diametrically about Lautrec's reaction to Montmartre as painter and person. In *Steeplejack* James Huneker wrote: "He loathed the crew of repulsive nightbirds which he penciled and painted in old Montmartre before the foreign invasion diluted its native spontaneous wickedness . . . (His) brutality is contemptuous." And in *Modern Art* Thomas Craven adds: "The misfortune of physical deformity converted (him) to a sadistic philosophy. This sinister figure believed in the innate depravity of the human race . . . His mature life and art were confined to the cabarets of Montmartre, and the depravity of that small, convulsive world which he loved with satanic conviction, he transferred to all mankind . . . His art excludes the noble in man, and it excludes the tragic. It deals only with the decayed." To these strictures Gerstle Mack, Lautrec's best biographer, supplies a wholesome corrective.

Lautrec was, writes Mack, "an extremely hardworking, intelligent painter, observant and eager, to whom the shifting kaleidoscope of Montmartre offered a wealth of material for his brush and pen —material that was exactly suited to his temperament. It was not so much the viciousness of the tawdry night life that appealed to him as its color and movement, its animation, its gaiety, its wit and high spirits, its exuberant vitality. For there was a side to this life in which the sinister undercurrents played only a minor part. Many of the entertainers who lifted their voices or their skirts in the brightly lighted cabarets and dance halls were true artists, supreme in their own fields . . . bringing to the Montmartre of the 'gay nineties' a rare distinction, a glamour that has never been equaled in any other center of amusement."

It is, nevertheless, obvious that Lautrec felt a kinship with whatever was different, especially if it was ugly, grotesque, and a caricature of the commonplace. He would have been wretched in the aristocratic world into which he was born or, for that matter, in any world in which manners and a good appearance counted. In a world of escapists, freaks and farouches, he could be himself. If he was self-conscious about himself and his surroundings, he carried it off with a show of brashness. He consorted with clowns, equestrians, and other circus folk; he devoted himself to jockeys and bicycle riders; he never tired of sketching horsemen, dancers, acrobats, trapeze performers, experts in daring—all those who could achieve casually what he never could hope to do. He accepted everything without surprise or resentment. In *Moulin Rouge,* a fictionalized biography, Pierre Le Mure wove a romance about a lovely Jewess who, out of pity, became Lautrec's mistress. However, the unromantic facts disclose that women were repelled by "the little monster" (Yvette Guilbert's phrase) and that all his amatory fulfillments were sordid affairs with prostitutes. Despite his deformity, he was sexually normal, but his physical hideousness made him aware that he could never have a true love relationship in or out of marriage. Therefore he turned to the women of the brothels, and then, as friend and artist, he painted them in intimate aspects of their hopeless lives. Sometimes he lived in the brothels for a week or two. He even delighted, during such periods, in telling conservative friends to come to see him at these addresses, and chuckled at their dismay when they learned what the addresses were. "Everywhere there is ugliness," he said, defending the choice of his settings. "And everywhere ugliness has its beautiful aspects. It is thrilling to discover them where nobody has noticed their existence."

His studios were cluttered with important projects and accumulated odds and ends; he scarcely knew what they contained. Once when he moved he left more than eighty canvasses standing against the walls and the incoming tenant let most of them be ripped for scrub-rags. He gave fantastic parties at which he served his guests roast kangaroo (it was actually mutton) and mixed weird cocktails from the heeltaps of all the bottles—sauterne, burgundy, brandy, liqueurs—he happened to have on his shelves.

Meanwhile, he worked furiously. In his mid-twenties and early thirties, he made countless visits to music-halls, race tracks, circuses, hospitals (he was fascinated by the operating theaters), courtrooms (he was influenced by the legalistic satires of Forain and Daumier), bistros, brothels, resorts of Lesbians and other queer characters. Somehow he found time to turn out more than a thousand drawings, lithographs, and paintings. Living for the moment and not for posterity, he designed song sheets, menus, advertisements, theater programs, placards, illustrations, and commercial sketches. But he also finished canvases of great depth, notably the tender profile of his mother, and memorable portraits of Van Gogh and Oscar Wilde. A sporadic traveler, he journeyed to England, Spain, Holland, and Belgium, where he almost fought a duel with a man who had derided Van Gogh. He visited the coast of France, but instead of preserving its beauties in seascapes he brought back paintings of the local barmaids. His world was Montmartre; it was only there that he felt at home.

Lautrec had been drinking for years without appreciable harm, but he did not use liquor as an anodyne until his late twenties. By the time he was thirty-three, he was a confirmed alcoholic. Drink and other excesses, as well as unremitting work, brought about a breakdown in 1899. At his mother's request he was taken to a nursing home at Neuilly. While he was in the sanatorium it was discovered that the absence of alcohol and dissipation restored his health, and it was feared that a return to liquor would be doubly harmful. He was permitted to go out for walks, but always with an attendant. This appealed to Lautrec's sense of the incongruous. He delighted in luring the attendant to bars, where he would buy him drinks, and then would bring his custodian reeling back to the sanatorium while he, the alcoholic patient, remained coldly sober. To get through the long confinement, Lautrec drew, entirely from memory, the now-famous series "The Circus." This convinced the doctors of his mental health and he was released. Once more at liberty, zealously watched over, he attempted to live circumspectly. But within a few months he was again drinking immoderately. In the summer of 1901 he was stricken with paralysis. His mother took him to the family chateau at Malromé, but he grew rapidly worse and died September 9, 1901. He was not quite thirty-seven.

Lautrec's one concern was with dynamics, with the movements of men, women, and animals. Literature and music barely touched him. He regarded nature without interest; he thought arrangements of fruits and flowers were for spinsters, not for men. The quick visual impression was everything. "Nothing exists but the figure," he maintained. "Landscape is nothing and should remain nothing but an accessory; the painter of pure landscape is an idiot. Landscape should be used only to make the character of the figure more intelligible." From Forain he learned how to fix a character in a few strokes; but where Forain flayed humanity for its faults, Lautrec was content merely to present its oddities, pathetic and absurd. His technique owed something to Japanese prints, especially their asymmetrical compositions; he liked their spatial diagonals, broad flat areas of color, strong silhouettes, cutting off a figure with seeming arbitrariness but actually with sharp discrimination and great effect. His work was done within the short span of fifteen years and he sold practically no paintings during his lifetime. Yet though he painted for himself and his friends, his work spoke for an active if circumscribed world. "What his weak body lacked," wrote Paul de Lapparent in his biography, "his mind received in abundance. Some inner strength, which had no power over his legs, made his brain rich in creation." It was Lautrec who brought form and dignity to the poster and advertising art; modern illustration bears his imprint in every line. "He succeeded," Mack affirms, "in raising design to the level of a fine art . . . He allowed no distinction, no snobbish arbitrary barrier between commercial and pure art." A gentle and suffering soul, he repressed sentiment and abhorred sentimentality. He was neither a moralist nor a misanthrope. He was, said Francis Jourdain, "a witness. He had sworn to speak without hatred and without fear . . . He ignored society and viewed the individual with a terrible sangfroid . . . He examined with never-failing curiosity; he contemplated without reservations the collection of human types offered him in those public places which are neither Heaven nor Hell but simply places where he liked to be."

The result was a masterfully straightforward line, severe and almost naked. A rapt onlooker, he found nothing amusing in humanity's effort to escape pain and boredom. His models were dancers, drinkers, clowns, so-called daughters of joy. But there is no joy —not even the joy of color—in his work. The dancers are grave, the clowns are tired, the drinkers are dull, the whores are horrible. But the psychological insight is profound; the creator and the cripple are transcended by the realist who is beyond happiness and misery. The art of Toulouse-Lautrec is the art of an intense observer who does not render verdicts but whose reports are clear, uncritically candid, and not without compassion.

William Butler Yeats

[1865-1939]

*"The mystical life is the center of all that I
do and all that I think and all that I write."*

I T WAS Shelley who remarked that "poets are the unacknowledged
legislators of the world," a statement that is commonly regarded
as nothing more than a flight of youthful rhetoric. But William
Butler Yeats justified Shelley. Besides being a poet and a poetic
playwright, Yeats was a senator who served the Irish Free State
from 1922 to 1928. He was born at Sandymount, near Dublin, on
June 13, 1865. The family were Protestant; both Yeats's paternal
grandfather and his great-grandfather had been Anglican ministers.
His father, John Butler Yeats, was a well-known artist, his brother
Jack was also a painter, and for a while it seemed that William
might adopt their medium. At nineteen he attended the Metropolitan School of Art in Dublin, but although he made some pastels
influenced by Turner, he took more pleasure in writing and it soon
became apparent that his means of expression was not the brush
but the pen.

His youth was divided between Ireland and England. As a boy of
eleven he had studied at the Godolphin School in Hammersmith,
then a suburb of London, but he longed to be back home in County
Sligo. Although his later years were spent abroad he remained in
love with Ireland all his life. At twenty-two Yeats went to London.
There, with Ernest Rhys, he founded the Rhymers' Club, which
specialized in the latest estheticism and imitated the stained glass
attitudes of the Pre-Raphaelites. At this period he was, according
to Rhys, "extremely pale and exceedingly thin, a raven lock over
his forehead, his face so narrow that there was hardly room in it for
his luminous black eyes." Winter was coming on, and Yeats was
glad to attend the club meetings not only for intellectual companionship but for physical warmth. His autobiography recalls how he
was forced to go about London on foot because he could not afford
to ride, and he remembered that afternoon tea with hospitable
friends was not merely a social function but a meal that stayed him
during days when he went without other nourishment. He kept his

mind fixed on the delights of the imagination and turned enforced asceticism into a discipline. He had been deprived of the simple-minded religion of his youth by the materialism of Huxley and Tyndall and so, he related in his *Autobiography,* "I made a new religion, almost an infallible church of poetic tradition, of a fardel of stories and of personages, and of emotions passed on from generation to generation by poets and painters with some help from philosophers and theologians. I wished for a world where I could discover this tradition perpetually. I had even created a dogma: 'Because those imaginary people are created out of the deepest instinct of man, to be his measure and his norm, whatever I can imagine those mouths speaking may be the nearest I can go to truth.' "

Yeats's search for a new religion, part myth and part magic, led him to join the Theosophists. In 1887 he became a disciple of Madame Blavatsky, the Russian "mistress of the occult," and although she had been exposed as a fraud, Yeats remained faithful, one of the most devoted members of the Esoteric Section of the cult. He was, in fact, so overzealous—he persuaded his associates to try to summon the ghost of a flower and to induce definite dreams by putting certain objects under their pillows—that he was asked to resign. Nevertheless, he never repudiated the philosophy which stressed the value of intuitions and a "reality" beyond that of the five senses. "He had been brought into contact," wrote Richard Ellmann in his skilfully analytical *Yeats: The Man and the Masks,* "with a system based on opposition to materialism and on support of secret and ancient wisdom, and was encouraged to believe that he would be able to bring together all the fairy tales and folklore he had heard in childhood, the poetry he had read in adolescence, the dreams he had been dreaming all his life."

Preternaturally shy, his self-consciousness was increased by an awareness of his self-division; he had difficulty uniting the self which demanded energetic activities and the self that longed to remain passive, content with dreams. Before he achieved integration he joined another group of initiates, the Hermetic Students of the Golden Dawn. The rituals of this cabalistic order intensified his concern with magic, especially since they seemed to furnish a counter-movement to the increasing materialism of the age. His father and several of his friends were alarmed; but he was not to be deterred from the study which, next to his poetry, he considered the most important pursuit of his life. With the enthusiasm of a twenty-seven-year-old adept, he reiterated his conviction to John

O'Leary: "If I had not made magic my constant study I could not have written a single word of my Blake book, nor would 'The Countess Kathleen' ever have come to exist. The mystical life is the center of all that I do and all that I think and all that I write. It holds to my work the same relation that the philosophy of Godwin holds to the work of Shelley, and I have always considered myself a voice of what I believe to be a greater renascence—the revolt of the soul against the intellect—now beginning in the world."

Spiritist and nationalist were united when Yeats became a prime mover in the Celtic Revival. Two movements had sprung to life in Ireland. The first, the Gaelic League, founded in 1893, had as its object the study of ancient Irish literature and the preservation of Gaelic as the racial language. The second, organized a few years later, was a cooperative movement for "better farming, better business, better living." The social economy implicit in both movements promised a survival of the national culture. Poets, folklorists, and scholars joined forces with economists, sociologists, and agronomists. George Russell, who wrote poetry under the pseudonym "Æ," combined agrarianism with visions; Yeats dealt simultaneously with politics and clairvoyance. As the movements became more active, they grew more radical. The insurrections, suddenly rising and severely put down, were violent; rebellion flamed everywhere; the hope of a handful of dreamers became the battlecry of an embittered nation. The Irish renaissance ended in revolution; Eire was born of the blood of its poets. A poet, Douglas Hyde, founder of the Gaelic League, became Eire's first President.

Much of the activity centered about the Irish Literary Theater, with which Yeats became deeply identified. He had met and fallen in love with a beautifully regal insurrectionary, Maude Gonne; he saw her as "the fiery hand of the intellectual movement." With Maude Gonne in mind he wrote his atmospheric but fervid plays, the best of which communicated, as in a trance, a depth beyond ordinary feeling. *Cathleen ni Houlihan* lifted allegory to a plane of high patriotism. Even the most literal-minded members of the audience could not fail to see in the harried woman who had lost her fields and for whom men gladly died—a woman who never aged and who had "the walk of a queen"—the figure of Ireland. Yeats gradually became the acknowledged literary leader of the movement. He found the playwright J. M. Synge in Paris and made him return to Aran and the people of the primitive islands. "Express a life," said Yeats, "which has never found expression . . . Listen to the language which takes its vocabulary from the time of Malory and of the translators of the Bible, but its idiom and vivid metaphor from Irish."

Before his fusion was accomplished, Yeats had become a poet whose development was threatened by a style that was both precious and precocious. By the time Yeats was thirty he had already published six volumes of verse. In format the books were conventionally slim, as was the fashion of the day, but their contents were strange. The lines were lit with a pale fire; the music was misty as well as mystical, dream-heavy, drenched in the colors of "the Celtic twilight." The whole evoked a vaguely romantic yet highly individualized spell which, in its very excess of melodic effects, sacrificed strength of thought and sharpness of utterance to sheer limpidity. During this period Yeats depended on a limited set of symbols and the very rhetoric he condemned. The maturing poet, however, was not content to capitalize on his charming but restricted gamut of shadowy loveliness. He ceased to depend on sentiment and to rely on a facile rhetoric. "Sentimentality," he declared, "is deceiving one's self; rhetoric is deceiving other people."

The change is sounded tentatively in *The Wind Among the Reeds,* published when Yeats was thirty-four. The mood is still that of a trance, but the symbols take on clearer definition and the incantation is both hypnotic and moving.

> All things uncomely and broken, all things worn out and
>   old,
> The cry of a child by the roadway, the creak of a lumbering
>   cart,
> The heavy steps of the ploughman, splashing the wintry
>   mold,
> Are wronging your image that blossoms a rose in the deeps
>   of my heart.

Yeats still casts himself in the role of the narrator of supernatural lore, but the accent is new. "The Song of Wandering Aengus" is a ballad that is characteristically his own.

> I went out to the hazel wood,
> Because a fire was in my head,
> And cut and peeled a hazel wand,
> And hooked a berry to a thread;
> And when white moths were on the wing,
> And moth-like stars were flickering out,
> I dropped the berry in a stream
> And caught a little silver trout.

When I had laid it on the floor
I went to blow the fire a-flame,
But something rustled on the floor,
And someone called me by my name:
It had become a glimmering girl
With apple blossom in her hair
Who called me by my name and ran
And faded through the brightening air.

Though I am old with wandering
Through hollow lands and hilly lands,
I will find out where she has gone,
And kiss her lips and take her hands;
And walk among long dappled grass,
And pluck till time and times are done,
The silver apples of the moon,
The golden apples of the sun.[1]

A still greater change is inherent in *Responsibilities*, published in Yeats's late forties, and *The Wild Swans at Coole*, which appeared five years later. The poetry is sparser in imagery, tighter in style. The incantation has almost disappeared; the phrasing is direct rather than decorative; richly rounded cadences are accentuated by the contrast of purposely flat but highly effective lines. Even more significant is the poet's attitude to his subject matter. Emerging from his "labyrinth of images," he acknowledges the change implicitly in one of the later poems:

I made my song a coat
Covered with embroideries
Out of old mythologies
From heel to throat . . .

But, he continues, "the fools caught it,/Wore it in the world's eyes/As though they'd wrought it." He put the same thought somewhat differently in a dedication to his *Essays:* "My friends and I loved symbols, popular beliefs, and old scraps of verse that made Ireland romantic to herself; but the new Ireland, overwhelmed by responsibility, begins to long for psychological truth."

Psychological truth, however, was not enough. Yeats also wanted spiritual assurance. A return of his youthful infatuation with the occult led him to another offshoot of supernaturalism. From his mid-forties to his mid-fifties, Yeats attended spiritualist séances,

---

[1] From *Collected Poems* by William Butler Yeats. Copyright 1903, 1933, by The Macmillan Company and reprinted with permission of the publisher.

gazed into crystal balls, called up departed souls, asked about the afterlife, looked for miracles, and acquired an attendant spirit by the name of Leo Africanus. When questioned by Yeats whether he was an image or a phantom, a poet evoked from the past or something "created" by a living person, Leo Africanus replied that he, like other spirits, was "the unconscious, as you say, or, as I prefer to say, your animal spirits formed from the will and molded by the images of Spiritus Mundi." During his psychical researches, Yeats had met Georgie Hyde-Lees. He had previously proposed to Maude Gonne and had been touchingly rejected; he now turned to Miss Hyde-Lees not only as a kindred spirit but as a helpmate. He had known her for six years when, on October 21, 1917, they were married. A week after their marriage Mrs. Yeats discovered that she had a strange gift: she could suspend her conscious self and become a medium for automatic writing.

The writings "dictated" by the "communicators" made untiring collaborators of Yeats and his bride. "Since husband and wife would discuss the communications afterward," wrote Ellmann, "their conscious minds no doubt had considerable effect upon the direction which the automatic writing would take, but this effect was never sufficient to prevent the revelations from being exceedingly cryptic." The result was *A Vision,* begun in Yeats's fifty-second year and first published when he turned sixty. *A Vision* is the private code of a mystic planning a universal theology. In it, humanity is divided into twenty-eight types, twenty-eight phases of the moon, through which the soul passes in a mounting cycle of incarnations. The symbols are so intricate and the style so arcane that the work is comprehensible only to an initiate or a determined student. But when a revised edition was issued in 1937 Yeats, aware of the general skepticism, wrote, "I do not know what my book will be to others—nothing, perhaps. To me it means a last act of defense against the chaos of the world."

Before the second edition of *A Vision* appeared, Yeats was a much-honored man. He had served the Irish Free State as a senator for six years; his esoteric inclinations had not affected either his politics or his poetry; in 1923 he received the Nobel Prize for Literature. A citizen not only of the world but of two worlds, the seen and the unseen, Yeats was now at the height of his fecund powers. The poetry of his late fifties and sixties reaches a richness, a precision, and authority never previously attained. The languid, luxurious fairylands and the dim allegorical gods of his youth are dis-

carded in favor of real people and immediate experiences. In his
early Pre-Raphaelite days Yeats "hid his face amid a crowd of
stars"; now he expressed his frank delight "in the whole man—
blood, imagination, intellect, running together." "I am content to
follow to its source every event in action or in thought," Yeats
wrote in "A Dialogue of Self and Soul," a poem which he concluded with this Blake-like divination:

> When such as I cast out remorse
> So great a sweetness flows into the breast
> We must laugh and we must sing,
> We are blest by everything;
> Everything we look upon is blest.

Such a poem as "Among Schoolchildren" is more plain-spoken
yet more profound than any of the earlier work. In candid and yet
complex stanzas, the "sixty-year-old-smiling public man" remembers his own youth and the woman he loved in young manhood,
the magnificent and unattainable Maude Gonne. In a musing self-
mockery, he questions the power of all philosophies—"old clothes
upon old sticks to scare a bird"—and the figure reminds him of
himself in age, "a comfortable kind of scarecrow." Other poems in
The Tower and *The Winding Stair* contain the utterances of a
man not afraid to taste unpleasant truths and even less afraid to
say that they are unpalatable. Many of the lines are weighted with
a sense of isolation, with the disillusionments of the age—and more
particularly, of old age—with defeated dreams, with the death of
friends and the decay of beauty. Yeats had lost faith in the ordinary man he once championed. He was revolted by the middle
classes who "fumble in the greasy till, and add the halfpence to the
pence." He had given up his dream of a culturally awakened Ireland—

> Romantic Ireland's dead and gone;
> It's with O'Leary in the grave.

He began to express a yearning for "an aristocratic order"; he
overstressed the loss of decorum and courtesy; spasms of anger and
impotence alternated with Rabelaisian coarseness. Lashed by the
forces that threatened from without and frustrated by the loss of
power within, his poetry fell back upon itself with a grim "apology":

You think it horrible that Lust and Rage
Should dance attendance upon my old age;
They were not such a plague when I was young.
What else have I to spur me into song?

The ladder of fantasy was broken; he was loath to begin the long ascent again:

I must lie down where all the ladders start,
In the foul rag-and-bone shop of the heart.

Away from Ireland, living in Rapallo, a small town on the Italian Riviera, and in small towns in southern France, Yeats saw Europe degenerate and "things fall apart. The center cannot hold," he wrote in a startling poem, "The Second Coming":

Mere anarchy is loosed upon the world,
The blood-dimmed tide is loosed, and everywhere
The ceremony of innocence is drowned;
The best lack all conviction, while the worst
Are full of passionate intensity.

Although he continued to write until the very end, his last important work was "Byzantium," an extraordinary description of the process of creating a poem, a set of dazzling images concluding with "that dolphin-torn, that gong-tormented sea." After seventy he suddenly grew weak; breathing became difficult, pain was constant, and he told his wife that it was harder for him to live than to die. Toward the end of 1938 he could not endure the winter, although it was an unusually mild season. In January he suffered what was obviously a fatal breakdown, sank into a coma, and died of heart failure at Roquebrune, near Nice, January 28, 1939.

During the following decade various biographies and critical estimates attempted to appraise Yeats's complicated and often questionable symbolism, the lucidity of his thought, the strength, the suppleness and technical mastery of his verse. *The Permanence of Yeats,* composed of twenty-four essays by as many critics, served as a tentative canon of criticism, especially in John Crowe Ransom's "Yeats and His Symbols" and the contrasting pages on Yeats's "A Vision" by Cleanth Brooks and Edmund Wilson. The plays, having served their prime purpose as poetic propaganda, barely survived their era and were rarely performed. The poetry, however, continued to grow in importance. The early lyrics were perennially anthologized, while the later poems, with their new diction and multiple allusiveness, were an incalculable if unacknowledged influence on the younger poets. In his very changes of style and emphasis, Yeats enriched contemporary poetry and bro ght to it a sometimes casual, sometimes oracular tone, but always an enduring magnificence.

H. G. Wells

[1866-1946]

"He claimed an unlimited right to think, criticize, discuss and suggest."

THE MOST CANDID, if not the most critical, summary of H. G. Wells was written by Wells himself. In 1936, when he was seventy, the *Living Age* printed his "auto-obituary" under the title "The Late H. G. Wells." At the time Wells was very much alive, but he wrote what he hoped might be said of him when the time came for a post-mortem estimate. The characteristic Wellsian blend of fact and fantasy was discernible in the first paragraphs: "The name of Mr. H. G. Wells, who died yesterday afternoon of heart failure at the age of 97, will have few associations for the younger generation. But those whose adult memories stretch back to the opening decades of the present century may recall a number of titles of books he wrote and may even find in some odd attic an actual volume or so of his works. He was, indeed, one of the most prolific 'literary hacks' of that time. He not only wrote books himself but critical studies and even short volumes were written about him; the number of entries under his name in the catalogue of that mighty mausoleum, the Reading Room (long since deserted by readers) of the British Museum, amount to nearly six hundred . . . It was his vanity to compare himself to Roger Bacon . . . His origins were common . . . His father was a gardener who became a small shopkeeper and professional cricketer; his mother was the daughter of an innkeeper and, before her marriage, a 'lady's maid.' The most interesting thing about Wells was his refusal to accept the social inferiority to which he seemed to have been born, and the tenacity with which he insisted upon his role as the free citizen of a new world that was arising out of the debacle of the warring national states of the nineteenth and early twentieth centuries. He had a flair for what is coming. He was a liberal democrat in that he claimed an unlimited right to think, criticize, discuss and suggest, and he was a socialist in his antagonism to personal, racial or national monopolization."

The facts of his life are explicit in Wells's *Experiment in Autobi-*

ography, modestly subtitled "Discoveries and Conclusions of a Very Ordinary Brain," and (partly concealed, partly elaborated) in such works of fiction as *Kipps* and *Tono-Bungay.* Youngest of three sons, he was born September 21, 1866, in Bromley, Kent, and christened Herbert George Wells. As has already been indicated, he never deprecated his origins; on the contrary, he was most concerned with the lives of the lower middle class—even his fantastic scientific romances are about ordinary people confronted by extraordinary happenings. He never lost a slight Cockney accent. Toward the end of his life he said, "I may be a scientific aristocrat, but I am no gentleman."

Young Bertie, as he was called, had little early schooling. The family was extremely poor; the resentment of poverty remained with Wells all his life. It was assumed that he would follow his father's trade and become a shopkeeper. However, when he was eight he broke his leg; while recuperating, he discovered books and began to read voraciously. He devoured Dickens and Washington Irving; the novels of Scott bored him, but he learned Scott's *Marmion* and *The Lady of the Lake* by heart. "Probably I am alive today and writing this autobiography instead of being a worn-out, dismissed and already dead shop assistant, because my leg was broken . . . The reading habit got me securely." At thirteen he was briefly apprenticed to a chemist and, for two dismal years, to a draper. Between jobs and during free time, he managed to attend classes and, at fifteen, was able to continue his education when he became an usher at the Midhurst Grammar School. At eighteen he was offered a scholarship at the College of Science in South Kensington, London, studied under the great biologist, Thomas Huxley, worked after school hours, earned his way by making digests of assignments for his backward classmates, and prepared to be a teacher. At twenty-one he received a degree of Bachelor of Science at London University. During his undergraduate days he was always hungry and undernourished. He looked like the comic weekly conception of the poet, hollow-eyed, emaciated, with "a scandalously skinny body," utterly unlike the familiar pictures of the later ruddy and rotund Wells.

After his graduation, he taught privately and at Holt Academy, wrote a biology textbook, and applied himself so strenuously that his health was impaired. A more serious mishap occurred on the playing field when one of his kidneys was crushed. It was also believed that he had tuberculosis; he spat blood, but he recovered—

he said that he always had "an essential healthiness"—and, during convalescence, began to write fiction. He had already tried himself out on scientific papers and academic articles. Now he began to see a few of his personal observations in print. An account dated 1888 shows that Wells had burnt two novels, destroyed reams of poetry ("much of it comic"), sent away some whimsical prose which never was returned, and sold exactly one short story. "Net profit: One Pound." In 1893, however, he began to support himself by selling some journalistic writings and, in 1895, his first book, *Select Conversations with an Uncle,* was published. A scientific paper on time as a dimension became a series of articles on "The Time Traveler," which grew into a romance, then a serial for which he was paid one hundred pounds, and finally a volume, *The Time Machine,* a pioneering work in what was to become known as Science Fiction. It was the success of this story that led him to give up teaching at twenty-nine.

He was already in the midst of a troubled emotional life. At twenty-five he had married his cousin, Isabel Mary Wells, with whom he had fallen romantically in love during his student days in London. She was beautiful, mysteriously quiet, and vaguely sympathetic. After their marriage, Wells discovered that her silence was nothing more mysterious than a lack of anything to say and that her languid sympathy was completely without understanding. His ardor appalled her, and her resistance to pleasurable love-making instilled in Wells an intensely neurotic need to prove his masculinity and test his attractiveness elsewhere. "After six 'engagement' years of monogamic sincerity and essential faithfulness," he wrote in his autobiography, "I embarked upon an enterprising promiscuity. The old love wasn't at all dead, but I meant to get in all the minor and incidental love affairs I could."

Few people have had their extra-marital involvements as widely publicized as Wells. The entanglements were discussed not only by friends and casual commentators, but by Wells himself. He wrote of them not only honestly but analytically; he did not expose them in a spirit of exhibitionism but in an attempt to understand his sexual appetites and their compulsive drives. Two years after his marriage, Wells and his wife separated; after two more years they were divorced. He had met Amy Catherine Robbins, in whom he found the mental and spiritual companionship, as well as the stimulation and enjoyment, which Isabel had not been able to afford him. Disliking her real name, he called her Jane, a name by which she was known the rest of her life. He wrote of her as a loving friend and a playful companion. "We were allies who were not and never had been passionate lovers . . . In the absence of a real sexual fixation, we contrived a binding net of fantasy and affection that proved in the end as effective as the very closest sexual sympathy could have been in keeping us together." There were two sons, one of whom became professor of biology, and Jane made a difficult but remarkably controlled adjustment to Wells's marital irregularities.

"I was now to have *passades,*" Wells remarks guilelessly, "frequent escapades of a Don Juan among the intelligentsia." Antonina Vallentin in *H. G. Wells: Prophet of Our Day,* said he was called "the Fabian Casanova," and she goes on to describe a woman who had come into his life, "a woman who would complete him. But the meeting with her came too late. His new love affair was particularly unfitted for secrecy. The young girl was fiercely independent . . . Wells's life was split into two parts." Jane recognized the seriousness of the liaison, but did not allow it to sever the bonds which held Wells to her. They held until her death in 1927.

By this time Wells was no longer the slender young dreamer. In his middle years he had grown thick and somewhat stocky, a short man with a round face and "a drum of a chest." But he had not ceased being a dreamer. He had a concept of a changing society, a society that would evolve into a brotherhood of peoples because of the good will and "infinite perfectibility of man." A product of the English liberal-rationalist movement, he filled his work with social ideals, envisioning a better world than the world in which he lived. Wells was always plagued by the puzzle of man's reason for being and the problem of his future. His growing worry about mankind's dubious title of *Homo Sapiens* underlines even the early fantasies, such as *The Invisible Man, The War of the Worlds, When the Sleeper Wakes,* and *Tales of Space and Time.* He projected the rapid acceleration of technological progress and, with imaginative daring, foretold man's conquest of the laws which had kept him earthbound; he charted the first voyage to the moon and anticipated distance-defying adventures in outer space. Others had been attracted to such explorations, but Wells wrote about them with authoritative understanding and gave them the dignity of a literature.

In his forties Wells created what many consider his greatest works. *Kipps* and *Tono-Bungay,* realistic and semi-autobiographical novels, recalling the struggles of his youth, were vibrant with actual people as well as living ideas. *Ann Veronica* championed the revolt of emancipated women and shocked Wells's contemporaries. *Joan and Peter* was an interweaving of poignant human situations and an unsparing criticism of prevailing social methods. Discursive but passionately honest, Wells gave fantasy the persuasive power of reality and strengthened fiction with the unquestionable conviction of facts. Long before the First World War, his novels accurately predicted the use of tanks (hitherto unknown) in warfare, the coming of the airplane as a destructive weapon, and the development of rockets. He foresaw the war with Germany thirteen years before it happened and, in *The World Set Free,* written thirty-one years before Hiroshima, pictured the horror of the atom bomb. His comprehensive review of humanity, *The Outline of History,* is a miracle of condensation and a model of perspective. It sold some two million copies in English, acquired new values when it was translated into practically every modern language, and was followed by the equally astonishing *The Science of Life,* which he wrote in collaboration with his son and Julian Huxley. Equipped with incredible energy, Wells was always at work on three books simultaneously: one about to be published, one in galley proof, and one on which he was writing. There was no subject too large or too small for him; he wrote with equal enthusiasm on the salvaging of civilization, the anatomy of frustration, the World Brain, and floor games for children.

As Wells grew older, he became increasingly alarmed at the changes taking place at such dangerous speed and with such disastrous effect. As early as 1926, in *The World of William Clissold,* he deplored the complacency of people adrift and unconcerned. Comparing the apathy of those who were comfortably unaware of trouble with passengers on an ocean-going vessel, he pictured boats battling the angry seas, ships that were "mere particles upon the homeless wilderness of the waters . . . and I think of grave engineers watching oiling and pressure, of officers in the chart-room, of stokers, excessively minute because they are so remote, sweating before their furnaces, and passengers—again those passengers!—congratulating themselves upon the calmness of the night and anticipating dinner."

Many of Wells's admirers regretted what they considered too great an interest in social reconstruction. They deprecated his speculations on the wealth and worth of mankind, his ideological probings, and such prognostications as *The Shape of Things to Come.* They complained that his natural creative power had been weakened by his penchant for prophetic warnings; it was facetiously but stubbornly charged that he had "sold his birthright for a pot of message." Although in his mid-sixties he could still write such a vigorous satire as *The Bulpington of Blup,* he was decidedly less interested in the fictional play of circumstance and clash of characters than in propounding questions for which he felt mankind should (and could) learn the answers.

The reviewers began to treat Wells as an aging and repetitive oracle. *The Fate of Man,* which was published when he was seventy-three, proved to be a forceful and even frightening examination of the democratic crisis, and *The New World Order,* which followed a year later, emphasized an almost forgotten but illuminated rationalism. The critics who had scoffed at his prophecies and were annoyed that many of them had come true belittled his achievement. He was mocked for being too versatile and scolded for still being excessively fertile. By the time he was seventy-five he was the author of some ninety published volumes plus more than thirty pamphlets, and it seemed natural to refer to him as "the impure but inexhaustible Wells." Undaunted, Wells, always the student of mankind, earned his doctorate in science at the age of seventy-six; his thesis, which dissected personality, was called "Quality of Illusion in the Continuity of the Individual Life in the Higher Metazoa, with Particular Reference to Homo Sapiens."

In spite of his almost superhuman vitality Wells was no superman. Two world wars made him doubtful of his old faith: the good will and infinite perfectibility of man. After Hiroshima he said, "This can wipe out everything bad—or good—in the world. It is up to the people to decide which." In November, 1945, at seventy-nine, he issued *Mind at the End of Its Tether,* a sort of sociological testament, in which he questioned the persistence of the human animal. In it he despaired that man no longer cared enough about himself to survive, and he predicted that man "will have to give place to some other animal better adapted to the fate that closes in."

Spiritual exhaustion was accompanied by physical debilitation. For years Wells had coped successfully with diabetes. In his eightieth year his condition deteriorated and he recognized that he was nearing the end. But he refused to take it tragically or even seriously. A few weeks before his death he described himself as "having one foot in the grave and the other waving about." When a friend chided him for seeming inattentive during a conversation, Wells replied, "Don't interrupt. Can't you see I'm busy dying?" In another month he would have been eighty; he died on August 14th, 1946.

The *Encyclopaedia Britannica* listed Wells as a "novelist, sociologist, historian, and Utopian." In the light of the last characterization, *The New York Times's* obituary declared: "He dreamed of a Utopia with no Parliament, no politics, no private wealth, no business competition, no police nor prisons, no lunatics, no defectives nor cripples. He longed for a world under a world government for, he argued, in no other fashion is a secure world peace conceivable." Without political power, Wells helped change the course of English politics; he not only predicted a socialist England but, more than any other one individual, was responsible for bringing it into being. Conceding his importance as a polemicist, critics still hesitate to commit themselves about Wells's final literary evaluation, but the appraisal has been generally in his favor. *Time* spoke of his novels of sex as notable liberating forces, considered three of his other novels as the best pieces of genre comedy since Dickens, and concluded that Wells "was possibly the greatest British journalist since Defoe." Hundreds of young writers have been, consciously or unconsciously, influenced by Wells's candid naturalism, his uncompromising integrity and, despite a lifetime of disillusions, his enormous zest for life. Millions of readers have been lifted by the stubborn power of his belief and the irresistible sweep of his imagination. Our intellectual climate is clearer and our horizons are wider because of him.

Sun Yat-sen

[1866-1925]

*"The Earth, the Universe, belongs to
Everyone."*

WHEN Sun Yat-sen (or, as he is commonly known in China,
Sun Wen) was born, November 2nd, 1866, in the village
of Choy Hung, "the town of Blue Valley," China was riddled with corruption and conspiracy. The fabulously tyrannical
Ch'ing dynasty was disintegrating; the foreigners were not only at
the gates but had blown them apart. Annam was becoming a
French protectorate, Hong Kong had been ceded to the British, and
five other ports had been opened to the western traders. The Taiping rebels had been defeated, but they were still harassing the
imperial troops.

Chinese clan or family names are always placed first; the family
name of Sun literally means "a descendant." Yat indicates "leisure"
—a mother's wish for a son who was never to enjoy that luxury. Sen
is another wish-fulfillment: it means immortal. The boy's "school
name," Wen, means learned. The Chinese, however, regard the
names casually and do not think of them as symbols, any more than
an American pictures a Mr. Wheelwright as a repairer of wagons
or a German thinks of the Peace of God when he hears the name
Gottfried. Sen's father, Sun Tat-sung, was an illiterate rice farmer
who rented the land he cultivated. His house was made of mud and
crushed limestone; the floor was beaten earth. Sen was the youngest
of three sons—his father was fifty-four and his mother forty at the
time of his birth—and besides two daughters there were also a couple of widowed aunts in the crowded dwelling. In spite of the
hard work his childhood was happy, filled with the universal pleasures which every boy manages to snatch between chores: fishing,
kite-flying, playing leapfrog, setting off firecrackers to usher in the
holidays. He differed from the other boys in the village in only one
respect: he wanted something wild and strange, something prohibited by "custom" to plowboys—he wanted a bird, a bird that could
sing of freedom and faraway places. He never asked for it, but his
heart beat wildly whenever he heard one. He also dreamed of un-

known distances as he listened to an old soldier, a village derelict, tell about the battles of the strange Taipings who, daring to oppose the warlords, were monogamous, frowned on slavery, believed in a fair distribution of land, and bowed down to nothing except a cross.

As a child, Sun Yat-sen went through the customary strict schooling, stood with his face to the wall of the temple school and, flicked by the schoolmaster's bamboo rod, recited the Chinese child's primer, the "three-syllable classic." Sen's little village was particularly backward, and even as a growing child he looked forward to leaving it.

His chance came at fifteen. His brother Ah Mei, older by fifteen years, had gone to Hawaii and had prospered. After a visit back home he persuaded the family to let him have his younger brother for an assistant. When Sen arrived in Honolulu he was a stocky fourteen-year-old boy with a firm chin and a sensitive mouth. Besides owning a farm, Ah Mei had a general store and there the lad waited on customers, picked up the rudiments of Hawaiian and Japanese, and developed a craving for more knowledge. Ah Mei sent him to one of the Church of England schools, where he learned mathematics, history, and the Bible. (His father had been a convert to Christianity and his young son always considered himself a Christian.) The classes were conducted in English, and Sun Yat-sen was so adept that his brother complained he was growing more western than the westerners. He was seventeen when, having won a prize in English grammar, his brother concluded that he was no longer a boy and shipped him back to China to assume his place in the community.

The young Sun Yat-sen brought trouble as well as learning home with him. He soon manifested his refusal to accept "custom." He rebelled against idolatry, ancestor worship, and family fetishism. He stormed at the village superstitions, mocked the painted shrines, and even tore off the finger of one of the wooden gods. The village was horrified and, as a result of his "sacrilege," he was banished and sent to Hong Kong. A few months later he entered Queen's College, applied himself to the Bible, and spoke so ardently about Christianity that he converted two younger students.

He was now eighteen, time to prove his maturity and assert himself as a husband. As was the custom, his family arranged a marriage, and a farmer's daughter from a neighboring village was selected. The boy's iconoclastic insolence was forgiven; there was a wedding ceremony and, after it, the bridegroom returned to Hong

Kong and the bride took up her duties in her mother-in-law's household.

At nineteen the youthful zealot toyed with the idea of being a missionary. But he was already devoted to another cause. Revolted at the barbarism of the slave system which permitted families to sell their sons into bondage and their daughters into prostitution, he identified himself with the shackled men and women. He was equally outraged at the corruption and weakness of his country's rulers who were either unable or unwilling to resist foreign aggressors. He studied means of reform, encouraged a group of striking shipyard workers, and looked hopefully forward to the overthrow of the imperialists. Meanwhile, thinking of a direct way of helping his people, he determined to study modern medicine. He became an assistant at the Pok Tsai Hospital in Canton and in 1887, when Dr. James Cantlie opened a new hospital in Hong Kong, Sun Yat-sen was the first pupil to enroll. Five years later he was among the first to graduate. During these years he engaged in secret activities until he became as proficient in propaganda as in surgery. He was twenty-nine when he announced the maxim, a quotation from Confucius, which was to be his motto through life: "The Earth, the Universe, belongs to Everyone." He organized a hard-core group known as the "Dare-to-Dies," and planned his first revolutionary plot. It was discovered; his associates were arrested and executed; he was the only one to escape.

Sun Yat-sen was already acquainted with Charlie (Yao-ju) Soong, American-educated, Methodist-trained industrialist, whose second daughter, Chingling, was to become Sun Yat-sen's second wife. Soong's other daughters were to marry similarly famous men. The eldest, Eling, was to be the wife of H. H. Kung, the banker who has been called the Chinese Morgan; the youngest, Mayling, was to be the active partner as well as the wife of the Generalissimo, Chiang Kai-shek. Soong was the same age as Sun; he, too, in youth had given up the idea of being a missionary in order to put progressive political ideas into action. He had become Sun Yat-sen's secretary, assistant, and ally. He had organized a publishing firm, ostensibly for the printing of religious literature, but which soon had begun to turn out startling and provocative documents. "No other printer dared take the job," wrote Emily Hahn in *The Soong Sisters*. "The Imperial Court was watchful and its methods bloodthirsty. Dr. Sun therefore depended upon his friend and co-worker, who cheerfully risked his life and the welfare of his family for this new dream which had taken the place of the old. Soong published Bibles and tracts and pamphlets preaching peace on earth and revolution. He gave his Bibles away in the street and then went home to discuss new plans of overthrowing the government."

After the failure of his revolutionary coup, Sun Yat-sen was forced out of China. During the first of his many fugitive periods abroad, he traveled to Hawaii, the United States, and England, raising funds to carry on his campaign against the imperialists. The government put a price of fifty thousand dollars on his head, but he managed to escape capture by the narrowest margin. In London he was kidnaped and imprisoned in the Chinese Legation. Before being sent back to China for execution, he succeeded in smuggling out a note to his old friend and medical colleague, Sir James Cantlie, who made such a stir that the British government effected his release. The episode made the Chinese doctor known throughout the world; his name became synonymous with determination and fearlessness. "No gun ever manufactured works fast enough to get Sun," said one of his followers, who amplified the metaphor by adding, "his lightning-like adaptation to circumstance is quicker than the explosion of a shell." For a while he took refuge in Japan. The price for apprehending him was increased. Undeterred, Sun kept in touch with military men as well as underground workers; with the secret aid of General Hwang he founded a Patriots' Association. In 1910 he was in the South Sea Islands, a hunted man, a failure as a prophet, a lost hope as a leader. He did not despair; the communications were delayed, the messages were often intercepted, but the crusade went on.

Sun Yat-sen was in America when the word of revolution became a deed. It began in September, 1911, with a bomb explosion in Hankow, spread through a dozen districts, and overwhelmed the government troops. Although Chiang Kai-shek, who had come under Sun's influence in Japan, was just out of military school, he was appointed Chief of Staff in Hanchow. The news reached Sun in Colorado. He started east; learned, from a St. Louis newspaper, that he had been appointed the first president of the new republic; and went on to London. He reached China early in January, 1912, and took the oath as provisional president of the national convention at Nanking.

No one was more aroused than the three Soong sisters, who were to bring back to China the libertarian ideals with which they had been infected at Wesleyan College in Macon, Georgia. When Chingling heard the details of the revolution she was so stirred that she made the college paper a sounding board for her excitement. Her article, in *The Wesleyan*, April, 1912, was headed "The Greatest Event of the Twentieth Century." As quoted by Emily Hahn, it began: "One of the greatest events of the twentieth century, the greatest event since Waterloo, in the opinion of many well-known educators and politicians, is the Chinese Revolution. It means the emancipation of four hundred million souls from the thralldom of an absolute monarchy, which has been in existence over four thousand years, and under whose rule 'life, liberty, and the pursuit of happiness' have been denied. It also signifies the downfall of a dynasty whose cruel extortions and selfishness have reduced the once prosperous nation to a poverty-stricken country. The overthrowing of the Manchu government means the destruction and expulsion of a court where the most barbaric customs and degrading morals were in existence . . . Napoleon Bonaparte said, 'When China moves, she will move the world.' The realization of that statement does not seem far off. A race amounting to one-quarter of the world's population, inhabiting the largest empire of the globe, cannot help but be influential in the uplifting of mankind."

Although Chingling's enthusiasm was justified, it was premature. On February 12, 1912, an imperial edict announced the abdication of the Emperor and the establishment of the democracy, whereupon the man who was to become known as the Father of the Chinese Republic resigned as its first president. As soon as he had formed his Cabinet, Sun had misgivings about his ability to fill the office of chief magistrate. Troubling matters of state would have to be settled, and he had no training as an administrator; defections and dissatisfactions would have to be dealt with, and he lacked over-all authority. The new republic needed a president who was already known by the masses, one who could unite the whole country. Sun thought he knew the man. As his successor he selected Yuan Shih-K'ai, a liberal statesman who had persuaded the Ch'ing government to grant several reforms. In his speech of resignation Sun declared: "North and South are brought together by the abdication of the Emperor. Yuan promises to support the republic. He is a man experienced in affairs of state, and a loyal supporter of that democracy for which we have labored so long."

It was soon apparent that Sun was mistaken. Yuan was not a democrat but a dictator. Sun became Director General of Transport and Trade, but as the founder of the Kuomintang (People's Party), he devoted himself chiefly to the preparation and spread of propaganda. Yuan took advantage of his position and played politics with a high and heavy hand. Many commentators believe that Yuan planned to usurp power long before he joined the revolutionists. In *Sun Yat-sen and the Chinese Republic* Paul Linebarger calls him a Chinese Judas, an opportunistic traitor, a murderer, a tyrannical monster opposing the advance of the people. "It is accepted as a matter of Chinese history that Sun was tricked out of the presidency by Yuan, who made Sun believe that he, Sun, could do a greater work in improving the economic condition of China as its railroad builder and director rather than by giving up his whole day's work to listening to the supplications of office-seekers and franchise-grabbers . . . Yuan the Red was to make the blood of Chinese patriots run redder than red." Other and more impartial historians of the period are disinclined to believe that Yuan worked to undermine Sun's prestige. They maintain that Sun's subsequent troubles were inherent not only in the differences between the two men but in the situation itself.

The troubles came fast. Within a year the break with Yuan was complete. North and South were divided; Sun was forced into open conflict with the man he had appointed president. By this time Yuan was in command of a large and disciplined army, and after a brutal battle at Nanking, Sun was once more an exile. He was in Japan in December, 1915, when Yuan declared himself Emperor. Provinces revolted and many of his supporters deserted him. A reign of terror followed. Bands of marauders swept through the country, pillaging, looting, and burning. Six months later, at the height of the savagery, Yuan died. Sun came home to continue the interrupted formation of his constitutional government, but the conditions were unfavorable. The country was split by many factions. New gangs of armed ruffians sprang up and, before they could be seized, disappeared. Every little village politician was intent upon being a national leader. The country rioted in lawlessness; there were no authorities to whom to appeal.

There had been a brief respite of romance, but even this was attended by troubles. Ever since she had been a child, Chingling Soong had admired Sun Yat-sen, whom she and her sisters had regarded as a busy but gracious uncle. When, as a young co-ed in Georgia, she had written about the victorious revolution, she had idolized the revolutionary. Now she was in love with him. She was twenty; he was close to fifty. Her family was dismayed. It was not the difference in ages to which they objected, but to the fact that Sun was already married and that, since both he and Chingling were Christian, such a marriage would be bigamous. Besides, even if, according to Chinese custom, Sun were to take a second wife, such an arrangement was possible only when it was properly approved, or, better still, proposed by the heads of both families involved. But Chingling had not been an American schoolgirl for nothing. She begged, coaxed, threatened and, when all her pleadings and protestations were unavailing, she ran away and married her hero.

In 1920 Sun took up his work in Canton. Conditions in the South were propitious. The warlord Chen Chiung-ming had defeated the hated Kwangsi faction, and since he was friendly to the fighting doctor, had made it possible for Sun to re-establish himself. Once more Sun was hailed as President, even though his power did not extend beyond Southern China. A little later he urged Chen to extend the sphere of their influence northward, to bring idealism as well as strength into the conflict before civil wars wrecked the country. Chen demurred and finally refused to move. Hurt and resentful, Sun organized his own army and led his troops northward. He was, however, unable to finance a long campaign and, upon his return, dismissed Chen from office. Chen, not unnaturally, was aggrieved; he turned against Sun and started a counter-movement. Chen's troops got out of hand, attacked Sun's headquarters, and forced Sun to flee, while Chingling escaped disguised as an old countrywoman.

Warring cliques were ruining the country. Sun tried desperately to reunite them. He had watched the Russian revolution with sympathy and displayed a great interest in the development of the Soviets. He did not, however, believe the Russian system could be introduced into China because, he said, "there do not exist the conditions for the successful establishment of either Communism or Sovietism." Nevertheless, he agreed that Chiang Kai-shek should receive aid and instruction from Russia's military advisers, and the Kuomintang was reorganized along Communist lines. As matters grew worse, Sun could not refrain from violence and mass executions in order to consolidate his position. He was sustained by the workers and students, but he lost the support of the politicians, landowners, and other conservatives.

More disturbances troubled the divided nation. War broke out in the north as well as in Peking and the valley of the Yangtze. Accompanied by Chiang Kai-shek, Sun threw himself into the conflict. Fresh alignments were formed and broken; new alliances resulted in new betrayals. At the height of the crisis Sun was invited to join others, including his enemies, in a call for a people's conference. He was extremely dubious about the sincerity of the invitation, but he could not refuse. He was a sick man when he set out for Peking.

He had been suffering from influenza and what had been diagnosed as some sort of liver ailment. In January, 1925, after having reached Peking, he was afflicted with a raging fever and a pulse of 120. Cancer was suspected. By the end of the month, the pulsebeat quickened to such an extent that it was apparent his heart could not stand the strain much longer. A last-minute operation was decided upon and it was discovered that the cancer was far advanced. Ultraviolet rays were applied and sedatives were administered to dull the pain, but there was no hope. Scarcely breathing but still whispering disjointed words about freedom and unity, he was moved to the house of Doctor Wellington Koo, and there he died, March 12, 1925.

The libertarian movement he had directed did not end with Sun Yat-sen's death. By 1946, after years of continued civil war, the fermenting force had shaped a National Government headed by Chiang Kai-shek. The regime did not stay in power for long. "The prestige of the National Government rapidly fell," reported Kenneth Scott Latourette in *A History of Modern China.* "Internal dissensions, corruption, and failure to bring peace and the longed-for reconstruction led many to the conclusion that any regime would be better." In 1949 the National Government suffered a military collapse, and in October of the same year a communist People's Republic of China was proclaimed with Mao Tse-tung as Chairman. A year later, Chiang Kai-shek and his army retained only a few islands off the coast and made their headquarters on Formosa. With United States aid they had dedicated themselves to recapturing the mainland and eventually destroying Chinese communism. It is impossible to predict the ultimate outcome with any certainty. It is certain, however, that whatever the end may be, it had its beginnings in the dream of Sun Yat-sen.

Wilbur Wright

[1867-1912]

and

Orville Wright

[1871-1948]

"Human flight is not only impossible but illogical."

THEY DID what everyone knew could not be done. "Human flight is not only impossible but illogical," said the distinguished astronomer, Professor Simon Newcomb, who assured his readers that a new metal or a new force in nature would have to be discovered before man could fly. What is more, asserted Newcomb, even if by some miracle a man should invent a power-machine that could get off the ground, it would inevitably crash and kill its pilot. "Once he slackens his speed, down he begins to fall. Once he stops, he falls a dead mass." Professor Newcomb published his conclusions in 1903, at the very moment when the Wrights, at Kitty Hawk, were about to demonstrate the "illogical" mechanism that would, within a quarter of a century, revolutionize old concepts of geography, shrink distances, and change man's dreams of flying from wild fantasies to the shortest, swiftest, and most spectacular means of transportation.

Five hundred years before the first take-off of the first airplane, Leonardo da Vinci had designed a tentative flying machine, and men had made ascents in balloons for more than a hundred years before the birth of the Wright brothers. Other experimenters had gone up in uncontrollable craft that were lighter than air, but the Wrights were the first to fly a heavier-than-air machine in sustained and mechanically controlled flight.

There was nothing spectacular about the men who, according to the monument erected at Kitty Hawk in 1932, conquered the air "by dauntless resolution and unconquerable faith." Until they became famous, they were, to most people, uninteresting and uncommunicative middle class citizens, practical businessmen whose incongruous hobby was aeronautics. Their father, Milton Wright, had been born in a log cabin in Indiana, and the pioneer background was always apparent, even after he became a Bishop of the United Brethren in Christ. There were five children: two older brothers, Reuchlin and Lorin, and a sister, Katherine. Wilbur was born April 16, 1867, on a small farm near the town of Millville, Indiana; Orville, the youngest, was born August 19, 1871, in Dayton, Ohio, which was to become the family home. It was within the circle of the family that the brothers formed the union which was as lasting as it was unassailable. Their classroom work was fitful. Wilbur left school when he was fourteen; Orville tried high school but did not stay long enough to get a diploma. They did not even think of a college career; in common with Edison and Ford, they had little education and no scholarly training. They learned by doing.

Although their father was a minister, he did not discourage the boys' peculiar proclivities for earning money. Orville was only six when he and another boy collected old bones and sold them to a fertilizer factory; at eleven he increased his spending money by making kites for his playmates, picking up scrap metal for a junk dealer, and folding papers for a church publication. Wilbur, four years older, led Orville in inventiveness; their first joint product was a wooden lathe with marbles for ball bearings. At twelve Orville became interested in printing, and Wilbur helped him build a press. Before he was eighteen Orville determined to be a publisher and issued the *West Side News,* which announced that it was "published in the interests of the people and business institutions of the West Side. Whatever tends to their advancement, moral, mental, and financial, will receive our closest attention." One of the contributors was a young Negro, an elevator boy, Paul Laurence Dunbar, who was to achieve fame with his *Lyrics of Lowly Life.* During the next few years the brothers published small weeklies, *The Midget, The Evening Item, Snap-Shots,* and did the printing for *The Tattler,* a paper edited by Dunbar for Negro readers. It was a partnership which grew closer with time and experience. The brothers knew each other so well and answered each other's demands so instinctively that they needed no one else. They never thought of marriage; there was never even a transitory romance in their lives. They completed each other; together they performed more than double the achievements that either could have accomplished alone.

Mechanics, particularly mobile machines, fascinated them even in childhood. Their first "real" toy was a small gyroscope, a wheel mounted in a ring that, when spun rapidly, kept its balance on a knife-blade or the rim of a cup. Another toy made an indelible impression on the youngsters. This was a miniature helicopter, a little flying machine made of bamboo and paper, with wound-up rubber bands for motive power. Before they were in the teens, Wilbur and Orville were making improvements on it. Bicycles were their next mobile interest, toys from which they earned a living. Wilbur was twenty-five and Orville twenty-one when they started to rent and sell bicycles. Then they began to manufacture them, assembling the machines in a room above their shop. But, although they were turning a pastime into a profitable business, the memory of the air-climbing helicopter kept plaguing them. By the time Orville was in his mid-twenties, he and Wilbur were collecting a small library of items about flying. Their hero was the German expert, Otto Lilienthal, who had not only studied but practiced gliding, taking off from the side of a hill and maintaining himself in brief but successful hops. When Lilienthal was killed in one of his glider flights, the Wrights were distressed but not discouraged. They pored over his findings, especially *The Problem of Flying and Practical Experiments in Soaring*. They wrote to Samuel Pierpont Langley, secretary of the Smithsonian Institution, and read his *Experiments in Aerodynamics*. Following Langley's lead, they examined the *Aeronautical Journal* of 1895, 1896, and 1897, Mouillard's *Empire of the Air,* and the highly suggestive *Progress in Flying Machines* by Octave Chanute, who became their valued friend and constant stimulator, whose influence is appreciatively detailed in Elsbeth E. Freudenthal's *Flight Into History*.

They decided to build their own glider, a biplane which departed radically from those built previously. Studying the erratic behavior of other planes, they fitted a stabilizer to the front of their construction, a small auxiliary plane or elevator, which could be controlled by the pilot. Tilted during flight, it would make the machine rise higher; depressed it would reverse the ascending movement. Lateral balance was a greater problem. Taking a cue from the gulls, they studied the balancing power of wings that were curved or "warped" instead of flat. The Wrights' flexible warping of the wings of a glider was a revolutionary change, and it was on this that their later patents were based. An operator could vary the movable sections at the ends of the wings—now known as ailerons—and, once launched, keep the machine in the air. The bicycle business suffered while their Dayton workshop was cluttered with wooden struts, a dozen types of tubing, sprockets, propeller shafts, and hitherto unknown odds and ends. By August, 1900, the new type of glider was built. It weighed fifty pounds, looked like a chicken coop attached to a kite, and cost fifteen dollars. Upon advice from the Weather Bureau at Washington, the Wrights decided that a sandy strip of North Carolina beach was the most promising for their experiment—open country and equable winds—and it was to Kitty Hawk that they took their glider.

The first results were not too satisfactory, but the kite builders learned several things. They learned that they could control their gliding flights, and that actual flying was not far off. As soon as the brothers returned to Dayton, they built a larger machine— larger than anyone had ever tried to fly—tested it at Kitty Hawk and, although no flight had more than a few seconds duration, broke all existing records for distance in gliding. Now they set to work with a new access of energy. Back in Dayton they constructed wind tunnels; built more than two hundred wing models; and, though completely self-taught, made complicated tabulations and computed countless intricate mathematical formulas. "We saw," they wrote later, "that the calculations upon which flying machines had been based were unreliable, and that all were simply groping in the dark. Having set out with absolute faith in the existing scientific data, we were driven to doubt one thing after another till finally, after two years of experiment, we cast it all aside and decided to rely entirely upon our own investigations. Truth and error were everywhere so intimately mixed as to be undistinguishable . . . We had taken up aeronautics as a sport. We reluctantly entered upon the scientific side of it, and we soon found the work so endlessly fascinating that we were drawn into it deeper and deeper."

In the fall of 1902, the Wrights brought their improved glider to Kitty Hawk for their third stay. The wing span was now thirty-two feet; the wing-warping mechanism was improved; a tail had been added. Ignoring the old "established" tables of air pressure, and proceeding according to their own checked and rechecked calculations, they made over one thousand gliding flights, some of them more than six hundred feet, in two months. The important part, however, as Wilbur testified later, was that, for the first time in history, "lateral balance had been achieved by adjusting wing tips to respectively different angles of incidence on the right and left sides. It was also the first time that a vertical vane had been used in combination with wing tips, adjustable to respectively different angles of incidence, in balancing and steering an aeroplane."

They were now ready for the next step: the first power flight. Wilbur was thirty-six, Orville thirty-two. They were lean, wiry men; both had steel-blue eyes and a hawklike look. Wilbur was the taller; he was an inch-and-a-half short of six feet. Orville was the heavier but, although he weighed five pounds more than Wilbur, he barely tipped the scales at 145 pounds. Some people found that Orville's features—the long face, pursed mouth, and short mustache—reminded them of Edgar Allan Poe's; but Orville was cheerful, socially charming, and always pleasantly if not effusively amiable. Wilbur was the more reserved; "reclusive," "solitary," "sphinxlike" were among the adjectives used to describe him. "He throws out thirty words like an engine," wrote Heinrich Adams in *Flug.* "Then he keeps silent, as though he had been turned off mechanically." Wilbur was not taciturn but laconic. Once when called upon to make a speech, he got up reluctantly and said, "I know of only one bird that talks—the parrot. And it is not a good flyer." After the Wright Company became a great financial enterprise and Wilbur was reproached for being cavalier about his mail, he murmured, "Maybe those letters should be opened. But if you open a letter, there's always the danger that you may decide to answer it. And if you do that, you are apt to find yourself involved in a long correspondence." In *The Life and Work of Wilbur Wright,* Griffith Brewer portrays Wilbur as an ascetic, and quotes him as saying that the most enjoyment in life consisted of relief from discomfort. "To try to be always comfortable and happy was a mistake, for, if one succeeded, life became unbearably monotonous." The asceticism was part of the Wright nature. Neither Wilbur nor Orville drank or smoked; they strictly observed the Fourth Commandment about keeping the Sabbath holy. They were too modest and too busy to have their pictures taken; their dislike of publicity was almost an obsession. They dressed like the conventional businessmen they were; it was a queer sight to see Orville get in a glider in street clothes, disdaining helmet, goggles, and gauntlets, or watch Wilbur piloting a plane in an ordinary gray suit and a high starched collar. Wilbur gave the architect, Cass Gilbert, the impression of "a provincial boy who had an underlying sense of humor and perfect confidence in himself, but with a slightly provincial cynicism as to how seriously the other man might regard him."

The cynicism was purely protective. Both brothers had need of it when the scoffers mocked them for the thousandth time with the taunt that "if God meant men to fly, he would have given them wings." The gasoline engine had been thoroughly developed, and the Wright brothers decided that it was the most suitable engine for their purpose. But the companies were too busy to make a motor to their specifications and they had to build their own. It was a strange thing that the Wrights put together in the summer of 1903. Fred C. Kelly describes it graphically in his biography, *The Wright Brothers:* "The wings of this power machine had a total span of a few inches more than forty feet; the upper and lower wing surfaces were six feet apart. To reduce the danger of the engine ever falling on the pilot, it was placed on the lower wing a little to right of center. The pilot would ride lying flat, as on the glider, but to left of center, to balance the weight. To guard against the machine rolling over in landing, sledlike runners extended far out in front of the main surfaces. The tail of the machine had twin movable vanes instead of a single vane as in the 1902 glider."

In November, 1903, the new machine was tested at Kitty Hawk. Defects were discovered and rectified; parts were discarded and others substituted. On December 14, Wilbur took his position as pilot. He kept the machine in the air only three and a half seconds, but he had been able to get it off the ground and had demonstrated that it *could* fly. It took two days to repair the broken parts, and when it was Orville's turn the outlook was discouraging. The morning was raw and cold; a freezing northeaster turned the puddles into ice; the wind blew twenty-seven miles an hour; the Wrights wore no overcoats which might hamper freedom of movement. It was a queer contraption that slid down the track on December 17, 1903. The engine sputtered, the rudder quivered, but the machine rose. The flight lasted only twelve seconds, but, according to Orville's own account, it was the first time that a machine carrying a man "had raised itself by its own power into the air in full flight, had sailed forward without reduction of speed, and had finally landed at a point as high as that from which it started." On the fourth flight of this memorable day Wilbur manipulated the controls with the ease of a veteran and kept the machine flying steadily for fifty-nine miraculous seconds. The world was oblivious of the event—the press ignored it—but something of extraordinary significance had occurred: a weak and wingless biped had lifted himself above the law of gravitation. Man had flown.

There followed a series of increasingly powerful flights, radical alterations, rapid improvements. Since Kitty Hawk was too far from home, the Wrights confined their activities to a field locally known as the Huffman Prairie, near Dayton. It was not until their fifty-first flight that the machine surpassed the achievements at Kitty Hawk and stayed aloft for more than one minute. Then, in 1904, they managed to make a couple of five-minute flights. A year later they were flying eleven miles at a time; they increased it to fifteen, then twenty. On October 5, there was a flight of twenty-four miles which lasted over a half-hour. But, as Fred Kelly points out in his chapter "It Still Wasn't 'News,'" the newspapers were skeptical. The daily journals were not only indifferent but scornful. The *Scientific American* referred to the "alleged" flights; the fact that they had been ignored seemed to prove that they had not happened When the *New York Herald* correspondent, Byron Newton, submitted an eye-witness account of the Wrights' exploits to a magazine, his article was brusquely rejected. "While your manuscript has been read with much interest," wrote the editor, "it does not seem to qualify either as fact or fiction." The United States Army was uninterested and remained unconcerned.

Europe had gone "air crazy" and in 1908 Wilbur went to France where he broke all records by rising to a height of 360 feet, circling high in the air for one hour and fifty-four minutes. Meanwhile Orville was breaking records in America, winning prizes, and beginning to overcome the apathy of the War Department.

After 1910 the erstwhile bicycle makers became manufacturers of airplanes. Although they sometimes flew, they turned their attention to building rather than to flying. Suddenly they found themselves beset with imitators, infringements on their patents, conflicting claims, and long-drawn-out law suits. Eventually they won, but not before Orville lost his partner. Worried about the patent litigation and weakened by overwork, Wilbur succumbed to typhoid fever and died May 30, 1912. He was just starting his forty-sixth year.

For a while Orville tried to carry on the business, but he found he could not run it alone. Three years after Wilbur's death, he sold the company and all the patents. He never quite abandoned his researches—he was consultant for several aircraft factories—but his withdrawal from the industry was a thinly veiled retirement. He rarely appeared in public; he pleaded poor health as an excuse for not answering letters. Although he refused to be drawn into arguments about his contemporaries, he entered into a long controversy with the Smithsonian Institution, which he believed had stressed the importance of Langley's work at the expense of the Wrights'. In his fifties he seemed prematurely old, yet he survived Wilbur by thirty-six years. In his seventy-seventh year he contracted a series of severe colds; a heart attack was followed by congestion of the lungs, and he died January 30, 1948.

A month after his death a jet fighter plane, the Navy's FJI, set a new speed record, flying the 950 miles from Seattle to Los Angeles in one hour and fifty-eight minutes. The original Wright Brothers airplane which had hovered for twelve seconds at Kitty Hawk was still in existence, enshrined in the South Kensington Museum. It has not been proven that it vibrated slightly at the news, nor that Professor Newcomb turned over in his grave.

Marie Curie

[1867-1934]

"Pierre's first gift was a copy of his latest pamphlet, 'On Symmetry in Physical Phenomena: Symmetry of an Electric Field and of a Magnetic Field.'"

THE DISCOVERY of a new element which was to become a powerful weapon against disease was accomplished by a thirty-five-year-old woman working with her husband in an abandoned shack. She was born Marya (nicknamed "Manya") Sklodovska in Warsaw, Poland, November 7, 1867. Her father was a scholar who taught physics in the Warsaw high school; her mother was a musician who had been principal of a girls' academy. There were four other children: Sophie or "Zosia," the eldest; Joseph or "Jozio," the only boy; Bronislava or "Bronya"; Helen or "Hela." Marya was the youngest. All the girls had delicately molded features, luminous skin, and penetrating steel-gray eyes that set their blonde beauty apart from mere prettiness.

Marya's education progressed in spite of two handicaps: the restraints put on her precocity and the tyrannies which every Pole had to endure under a "holy" Russian domination. Polish history was distorted; the Polish "accent" was ridiculed; all studies were conducted in Russian, the language of the conqueror. Marya's father, judged insufficiently subservient, was punished by a demotion in tutorial rank and a reduction in salary. As a consequence, the Sklodovskis had to take in boarders—at one time there were ten roomers in an already crowded household, young people who had to be instructed, disciplined, and cared for as well as lodged and fed in a house that was no longer a home but a barracks. Zosia and Bronya contracted typhus from one of the boarders, and Zosia, barely sixteen, succumbed to the virulent fever. Two years later Marya's mother, who had concealed a long struggle against poverty and illness, died of tuberculosis. It was a saddened eleven-year-old child that faced the world with a bewilderment in which there was an unacknowledged but nagging resentment.

During the first years of her adolescence Marya was outwardly a model pupil and secretly a little rebel. She won awards, medals, and "prizes" of Russian books, but on the way to school she never failed to spit on the monuments erected by the Russian authorities to the traitors of her country, "the Poles faithful to their Sovereign." Free of school, recovering from her losses, she blossomed into a young lady who enjoyed her passing pleasures. With her companions, she hunted for wild strawberries, swam, fished by torchlight, played battledore and shuttlecock, climbed the Carpathians, and danced her way through the wild "kulig," a combination of sleigh ride, carnival, and fancy dress ball. "I have no schedule," she wrote to one of her friends. "I get up sometimes at ten o'clock, sometimes at four or five (morning, not evening!), I read no serious books, only harmless and absurd little novels . . . Thus, in spite of the diploma conferring on me the dignity and maturity of a person who has finished her studies, I feel incredibly stupid. Sometimes I laugh all by myself, and I contemplate my state of total stupidity with genuine satisfaction."

Back in Warsaw, Marya joined a group of "positivists," ardent seekers who followed the underground movements of the day, read proscribed pamphlets, and discussed the possibilities of reform. The secret sessions of the "Floating University" were idealistic and probably naïve, but the girl of seventeen never forgot them. Forty years later, she wrote: "The means of action were poor and the results obtained could not be considerable, yet I persist in believing that the ideas that guided us then are the only ones which can lead to true social progress. We cannot hope to build a better world without improving the individual. Toward this end, each of us must work toward his own highest development, accepting at the same time his share of responsibility in the general life of humanity."

As he grew older, M. Sklodovski could not continue to take care of the student-boarders, and his income shrank to almost nothing. The family moved to smaller quarters and it was necessary for the children to find ways of supporting themselves. At eighteen, Marya became a governess. Part of her small salary she sent to her twenty-one-year-old sister Bronya, who had gone to Paris to study medicine, and whom some day she hoped to join in the land of liberty, equality, and fraternity. She barely survived her first position in which the cultured and protectively reared young girl had to endure a family of boors demoralized by wealth. "I should not like my worst enemy to live in such a hell," she wrote to one of her cousins on December 10, 1885. "It is one of those rich houses where they

speak French when there is company—a chimney-sweeper's French
—where they don't pay their bills for six months, and where they
fling money out of the window, even though they economize nig-
gardly on oil for lamps. They have five servants. They pose as liberals and, in reality, are sunk in the darkest stupidity."

A few weeks later she had a situation which presented other problems. She was employed by an agriculturist with a comparatively
small estate and a large family. There was a pleasure garden with
a croquet ground; the lessons were easy; the eighteen-year-old
daughter became her boon companion; there was time enough for
her to pursue her studies in physics and mathematics. She was even
allowed to discuss "the labor question" and, in line with her "pos-
itivist" philosophy, to teach a group of illiterate young peasants.
But Marya made a mistake that caused much wretchedness: she fell
in love with Casimir, the eldest and favorite son of her employer.
His mother and father were fond of Marya, but they could not
countenance a serious breach in the social pattern; marriage to a
governess was out of the question. Casimir went back to the university and Marya stayed on. She would have liked to give notice,
but she could not afford the luxury of hurt pride. She was still
sending part of her salary to Bronya and saving the rest for the
time she could go to Paris, live with Bronya, and study at the Sorbonne. Although she finally took another position, she remained a
governess for another five years; she was twenty-four before she persuaded herself to leave her father and Hela, "the minor child of
the family," get into a fourth-class railway carriage, and set out for
France.

Bronya had married a Polish revolutionary and fellow-student
named Dluski, and Marie—she had Gallicized her name when she
registered as a student in the Faculty of Science—went to live
with them. Dluski began treating his first patients; Bronya acted as
consultant on women's diseases; and Marie worked over her equations and solutions. It was a happily busy circle, but it had to be
broken. Bronya was to have a baby, and Marie found that the one-
hour trip to the university was too long and too expensive—for the
price of two omnibus fares she could buy her lunches. In March,
1892, she moved to a flat in the Latin Quarter. The room was tiny,
cold and bare as a monk's cell, but it was only a fifteen-minute
walk from the chemistry laboratory, and Marie had no time to
realize that it was as shabby as it was uncomfortable. During the
next two years she moved from one dingy lodging to another, from

a sloping attic six stories high to a garret that was always dark except for an underwater glimmer that came through a skylight in the roof. She struggled on a few francs a day, contributed by the Dluskis, lived on tea and bread, and starved herself to such an extent that she fainted in one of her classes. Summoned, Dr. Dluski made her confess that all she had eaten in twenty-four hours was a bunch of radishes and a few cherries. Her brother-in-law took her to the flat, where Bronya fed and cared for her, but after a few days she insisted on returning to her attic study.

Her head was full of the forthcoming examinations. She had little time for anything except chemicals and calculus; although her beauty continually attracted admirers, she had no time for men. She had once been in love with a man—long ago, it seemed to her—now she was in love only with her studies. Working with a fixed purpose and unrelenting intensity, she grew thin and was on the point of breaking. But her will strengthened her body as well as her spirit and triumphed over every setback. At twenty-six she passed first in the Master's examination in physics; a few months later she was second in the Master's examination in mathematics. Her persistence was further rewarded with a scholarship—the six hundred rubles attached to it seemed a fortune—but she continued to live as frugally as ever. "She was proud of her poverty," wrote one of her daughters, Eve Curie, in the vivid and moving biography, *Madame Curie*, "proud of living alone and independent in a foreign city. Working in the evening beneath the lamp in her poor room she felt that her destiny, still insignificant, mysteriously related itself to the high existences she most admired, and that she became the humble unknown companion of those great scientists of the past, who were, like her, shut into their ill-lighted cells, like her, detached from their time, and, like her, spurred their minds to pass beyond the sum of acquired knowledge . . . These four heroic years were not the happiest of Marie Curie's life but the most perfect in her eyes, the nearest to those summits of the human mission toward which her gaze had been trained." It was when she was most engrossed in her mission and in as unromantic a mood as possible that she met Pierre Curie.

Learning that Marie needed a workroom with larger equipment than the one available to her, a mutual acquaintance brought the young Polish student and the mature French teacher together. Marie left a record of her first impression of the man: "When I came in, Pierre Curie was standing in the window recess near a door leading to the balcony. He seemed very young to me, although he was then aged thirty-five. I was struck by the expression of his clear gaze and by a slight appearance of carelessness in his lofty stature. His rather slow, reflective words, his simplicity, and his smile, at once grave and young, inspired confidence. A conversation began between us and became friendly; its object was some questions of science upon which I was happy to ask his opinion."

Pierre Curie was born May 15, 1859, in Paris. The Curies were Protestant Alsatians, progressive scholars occupied with science. The father had been a physician, author of books on tuberculosis, and a research worker in the Museum of Natural History in Paris. A brother, Jacques, was also a researcher and laboratory worker. Doctor Curie had been particularly concerned about Pierre, whose methods of learning were decidedly unorthodox. Instead of sending Pierre to school, the father taught him and supervised his schooling until the boy was sixteen, at which age Pierre received his Bachelor of Science degree. At eighteen he obtained a Master's degree in physics. Before he was twenty-four, he and his brother had invented an apparatus capable of exactly measuring the smallest quantity of electricity. In his late twenties and early thirties Pierre Curie specialized in work on crystalline physics, invented an extra-sensitive scientific scale, and in his researches on magnetism, discovered a fundamental law, now known as "Curie's law."

He was something of a misogynist when he met Marie, but he was fascinated by the Polish girl who, instead of flirting with him, discussed quartz and crystals. A long courtship was conducted in strictly scientific style. His first gift was a copy of his latest pamphlet, "On Symmetry in Physical Phenomena: Symmetry of an Electric Field and of a Magnetic Field." Marie weighed the probabilities involved in the situation, and hesitated. Ten months later the two were married. Since both were freethinkers, it was a civil ceremony. There were no rings; and when Dluski's mother offered to supply the traditional white wedding dress, Marie wrote, "If you are going to be kind enough to give me one, let it be practical and dark, so I can wear it afterwards to go to the laboratory." Their honeymoon was spent roaming the woods beyond Paris, sometimes on foot, sometimes on the bicycles which, even after they became famous, they retained as their favorite form of transportation. In 1895 they settled down in a little flat and Marie, who never before had prepared a meal, diligently learned to cook like an expert Frenchwoman. Housekeeping became merely another experiment, and the kitchen was no problem as soon as she decided to treat it like a laboratory. Pierre and Marie rarely went to the theater or visited friends for a social evening. They needed no diversions, for they never had enough of each other. Their mutual joy was increased by two daughters: Irène, born during the second year of their marriage, and Eve, born seven years later.

In 1895, the year that the Curies were married, Wilhelm Roentgen discovered the mysterious X-rays. At the same time Henri Becquerel found that uranium salts emitted other unknown rays without exposure to light. Happening to leave certain compounds next to a photographic plate in a darkroom, Becquerel was astonished to find a distinct impression on the plates, although they had been wrapped in thick black paper. Something unforeseen had affected the plates, penetrating through the solid protection. The "Becquerel rays," which pierced objects opaque to light, excited the Curies to such an extent that Pierre dropped his other researches to collaborate with Marie on what was now her single, all-compelling project: to track down, study, and if possible isolate the substance which had the extraordinary power of penetration. The handicaps were tremendous; the Curies were limited in means, material, and equipment. Their laboratory was a crude wooden shed, a storeroom for which the School of Physics had no further use. The room was always damp, steaming in summer, a little above freezing point—about forty-two degrees Fahrenheit—in winter. The Curies began by examining all known pure chemicals as well as chemical compounds, and found that uranium was not the only element which had the power of emitting rays. There was thorium. And there were others. The Curies could think of nothing but this elusive radiance; the secret of radioactivity so tormented Marie that she often weakened under the strain. But she was always eager for the new experiment, the next step.

The next step was a large one. Marie discovered that certain compounds were many times more powerful than could have been estimated from the amount of uranium and thorium contained in them. The results were checked and rechecked until the conclusion was inevitable: the intensity of radiation indicated a completely new element—an element of unbelievable strength. The intensity was greatest in pitchblende, an ore of uranium, and although the Curies realized that the active substance was present in small quantities, perhaps one per cent, they could not have foreseen that the element in the ore was so minute: less than a millionth part. Obtaining sufficient pitchblende was an almost insuperable problem. The ore was expensive, and the Curies could not hope to purchase the tons of it that were required for their purpose. They figured that after uranium had been extracted from pitchblende, the residue would contain traces of what they were seeking. Since the residue had practically no market value, the Curies arranged to buy the metallic leftovers from the ore extractors at little more than transportation costs. It was more than a year before the Curies could announce the first of their significant discoveries: the existence of a new element which they called "polonium, from the name of the original country of one of us," Polonia being the ancient form of Poland. It was an auspicious beginning.

Marie's tasks were those of a day laborer. She filled the shed with great jars of liquids and precipitates, treated the tons of pitchblende residue pound by pound, mixed the boiling matter in a smelter. But she did not stop being an ideal wife and mother. She made gooseberry jellies, prepared appetizing meals, and began to educate her first child. The laboratory almost killed her. The place was so cold that heat from a small stove could not be felt five feet away; the roof leaked; there was no chimney to carry off the semi-poisonous fumes. "And yet," Marie wrote at a later date, "it was in this miserable old shed that the best and happiest years of our life were spent entirely consecrated to work. I sometimes passed the whole day stirring a mass in ebullition, with an iron rod nearly as big as myself. In the evening I was broken with fatigue."

Somehow, the Curies managed not only to survive but to surmount every obstacle. Six months after their discovery of polonium, they published a paper announcing another hitherto unknown element they had found. "Various reasons lead us to believe that the new radioactive substance contains a new element to which we propose to give the name: radium." However, forty-five months were to pass until, in 1902, Marie Curie produced a decigram of pure radium. The power of its radioactivity was greater than that of uranium by a factor of one and one half million.

Between 1899 and 1904 the Curies published more than thirty scientific papers. They were on such subjects as the chemical effects of radium rays, on radioactive bodies, on the heat spontaneously disengaged by radium salts, on the possibility of radioactive transformation of atoms. They discovered that, although radium could cause dangerous and sometimes fatal burns, it was highly efficient in dealing with certain diseases. It destroyed infected cells, stopped harmful growths, and even arrested some forms of cancer. In 1902 the Academy of Science gave the Curies 20,000 francs "for the extraction of radioactive matter." The University of Paris accorded Marie the title of Doctor of Physical Science, "très honorable." In 1903 the Nobel Prize in Physics was divided between Henri Becquerel and the Curies for their pioneering discoveries in radioactivity.

The impoverished strugglers had uncovered an inexhaustible Golconda—a single gram of radium was worth $150,000—but the Curies refused to take advantage of their unique situation. Instead of regarding themselves as proprietors, central figures in a hugely profitable industry, they decided that such an attitude would be "contrary to the scientific spirit," that radium, with its healing power, belonged to no person but to the world. "We took out no patent," wrote Marie, "and we have published the results of our research without reserve." The Nobel Prize money permitted Pierre to give up the drudgery of teaching. Abetted by Marie, he refused publicity and specious "honors" with the same firmness he had declined them in the past. When it was proposed that he accept the coveted decoration of the Legion of Honor, he wrote: "Please be so kind as to thank the Minister and to inform him that I do not feel the slightest need of being decorated, but that I am in the greatest need of a laboratory." Visitors, journalists, and photographers invaded the premises of the couple who, a year before, were unknown to the general public. Their mailbox was crammed with requests for endorsements, invitations to important functions, offers for a lecture tour of the United States, laudatory sonnets, communications from helpful otherworldly "spirits"—"yesterday," Marie wrote to her brother, "an American wrote to ask if I would allow him to baptize a race horse with my name." After unaccountable delays, Pierre was finally taken into the Academy of Science "without," he wrote, "having desired to be there and without the Academy's desire to have me." He was made full professor at the Sorbonne and urged to devote himself to research. A wealthy woman proposed to build a modern laboratory for the Curies. But Pierre was not to enjoy the promise of the future for long. On April 19, 1906, a little more than two years after receiving the Nobel award, he went to call on his publisher. It was a rainy day; the streets were crowded and slippery. Attempting to cross the street, he failed to see an oncoming dray. The horses reared; Pierre tried to hang onto one of them, but was knocked down. For a moment he seemed safe. He escaped the horses' hooves but the wheels crushed his skull, and the precious brain was strewn among the muddy cobbles.

When the dead man was brought home, Marie could not be separated from the body. Her grief was unconcealed, her mourning unabashed. The diary from which her younger daughter, Eve, has quoted deeply moving paragraphs, is pathetically eloquent. "Pierre, my Pierre," she wrote after the funeral, "you are there, calm as a poor wounded man resting in sleep, with his head bandaged. Your face is sweet and serene; it is still you, lost in a dream . . . I kissed your eyelids which you used to close so that I could kiss them, offering me your head with a familiar movement . . . We were made to live together, and our union had to be . . . Your coffin was closed and I could see you no more . . . Then the dreadful procession of people . . . They filled the grave and put sheaves of flowers on it. Everything is over. Pierre is sleeping his last sleep; it is the end of everything, everything, everything."

A woman in her fortieth year, whose ash-blonde hair was graying, whose beauty had acquired a stern serenity, Marie was alone now. At first she felt it impossible to go on with her work. ("In the street I walk as if hypnotized, without attending to anything . . . I do not desire suicide. But among all these vehicles, is there not one to make me share the fate of my beloved?") Then she remembered it was his work also, and she went back to the laboratory. Offered the post of successor to Pierre, she accepted. She did not know whether this was good or bad but, as she confided to him in her diary, "I would like at least to make an effort to continue your work. Sometimes it seems to me that this is how it will be easiest for me to live; at other times it seems that I am mad to attempt it." During the day she filled her head with tables of radioactive constants and classifications of the radio-elements, but at night, at her secrétaire, she emptied her heart. "My Pierre, I think of you without end . . . Yesterday, at the cemetery, I did not succeed in understanding the words 'Pierre Curie' engraved on the stone. The beauty of the countryside hurts me, and I put my veil down so as to see everything through my crepe." "My little Pierre, I want to tell you that the laburnum is in flower, the wisteria, the hawthorn and the iris are beginning—you would have loved all that . . . I want to tell you that I no longer love the sun or the flowers. The sight of them makes me suffer. I feel better on dark days like the day of your death; and if I have not learned to hate fine weather, it is because our children have need of it."

It was the children to whom she turned whenever she was free of the laboratory; she rented a house for the two girls and her father-in-law who had no one else to care for him. Her success as a teacher was unqualified; her pupils grew in number and devotion. Andrew Carnegie endowed a series of annual scholarships. The Nobel Prize was given to her again in 1911 for the work done since her collaborator's death. It was the first time that anyone had twice received the award, but Marie insisted on regarding it as "an homage to Pierre Curie." The Sorbonne and the Pasteur Institute founded a double laboratory for her own explorations and for biological research. When the "Institute of Radium: Pavilion Curie" was dedicated in 1914, Marie uttered the plea of Pasteur: "Take an interest, I urge upon you, in these holy dwellings to which the expressive name of laboratories is given . . . They are the temples of the future. It is there that humanity grows bigger, strengthens and betters itself."

Marie never stopped working in the "holy dwelling" to serve humanity. She left it only when she felt she could serve it more effectively. When the First World War swept over Europe, she brought the healing power of radium to the front lines. She started by converting a Renault passenger automobile into a "radiological car," but before the war was over, she had organized twenty mobile units and installed radiological equipment in more than two hundred hospital rooms. After the war she visited America, where women had subscribed enough money to purchase a gram of radium, a gift which was presented to her by President Harding at the White House. Her acceptance stipulated that the radium was not to be her property but "must belong to science." She was feted in Carnegie Hall and in the colleges, accompanied by her daughters Eve, who was to become a brilliant writer, and Irène, the scientist, who, with her husband, Frédéric Joliot, was to receive the Nobel Prize in 1935 for the synthetic production of radioactive elements.

Marie Curie did not live to enjoy her children's glory. Back in her Paris laboratory she busied herself with new calculations, but she was working against time. At fifty-eight she journeyed to her native Poland to lay the cornerstone of the Radium Institute of Warsaw. At sixty-two she paid her second visit to America and received another gram of the precious element. At sixty-five she was still working twelve to fourteen hours a day, but she was laboring against an increasing physical handicap, the threat of blindness. She kept her fears to herself, but finally she wrote to her sister Bronya: "My eyes have grown much weaker, and probably very little can be done about them. As for my ears, an almost continuous humming, sometimes very intense, persecutes me." She suspected that radium might have something to do with her ailment, but she could not be sure. There were four operations for double cataract; Eve spoon-fed her blind mother until she could see again. Marie, now an enfeebled but determined old lady, was working on the preparation of actinium X when she felt great pain in another part of her body. X-ray photographs revealed a stone in her gall bladder, but she refused to submit to an operation which would interfere with her work. In May, 1934, a sudden fever compelled her to leave the laboratory. She never returned to it. Suffering from bronchitis and (although the doctors were slow to acknowledge it) from exhaustion, she held on for a while, sank, rallied, and died of pernicious anemia at the sanatorium in Saint-Cellemoz, July 4, 1934. She was sixty-six years and eight months old, a simple unselfish worker, the greatest woman scientist in history and one of mankind's humblest benefactors.

Frank Lloyd Wright

[1 8 6 9 -   ]

*"I intend to be the greatest architect that
ever lived."*

E ARLY IN LIFE," wrote Frank Lloyd Wright, "I had to choose between honest arrogance and hypocritical humility. I chose
honest arrogance, and have seen no reason to change." At the
very beginning of his career he announced his determination to be
not only the best architect who had hitherto been born but better
than any who might appear. "I intend," he said flatly, "to be the
greatest architect that ever lived." Before he was seventy his admirers were convinced and most of his detractors were willing to
concede that his arrogance was honest and not entirely unjustified.
At eighty he was universally considered the most original architect
that the New World had produced and, as Lewis Mumford wrote,
"one of the most creative architectural geniuses of all time . . . the
Fujiyama of American architecture, at once a lofty mountain and a
national shrine."

Frank Lloyd Wright was born June 8, 1869, in Richland Center,
Wisconsin. His mother was Anna Lloyd-Jones, daughter of a Welsh
hatter and Unitarian preacher who had migrated to Wisconsin.
His father was William Russell Cary Wright, whose stock was English, who came from Hartford, Connecticut, and who had tried half
a dozen ways of making a living. William Wright had studied medicine, then law, then abandoned both. He became simultaneously a
musician and minister. At the time he met Anna he was traveling
through Wisconsin teaching singing; after his marriage to her he became a preacher. Frank was the first child—there were two younger
sisters, Jennie and Maginel—and, when the boy was three, the father was called to a Boston church. Before long they were back in
Wisconsin where William Wright attempted to run a conservatory
of music in Madison. Maladjusted, withdrawn and unhappy, the father was a failure in everything, including marriage, and the mother
turned more and more to her firstborn. "The lad was his mother's
adoration," wrote the architect in the third person style which he
affected in his *Autobiography*. "She lived much in him"—which did

379

not help the strained relations between husband and wife. Finally
Anna and her husband agreed upon a separation; he disappeared
and the family never saw him again. Anna had no difficulty obtaining a divorce.

Anna Wright was always fascinated by buildings. Before he was
born, she had decided that her first child was to be a son and
that he would become an architect. Although she was "poverty
pinched," she made every sacrifice to have him well educated, but
he was not an indulged or self-indulgent youth. At fourteen he
earned money on his uncle's farm, and when he went to college, he
worked afternoons in an architect's office to pay for his schooling.
Since the University of Wisconsin did not have a School of Architecture, he enrolled for a civil engineering course. He did not regret the choice or the necessity. "Fortunately," he comments in the
Autobiography, "by the limitation he was spared the curse of
the 'architectural' education of that day as sentimentalized in the
United States with its false direction in culture and wrong emphasis
on sentiment."

He continued working his way through the university but, before
graduation, he became impatient with what he felt was time
wasted. He was anxious to ease the financial situation at home and
eager to be on his own; in spite of his mother's misgivings, he left
Madison and went to Chicago. He applied to one architectural firm
after another until he was taken on as a "tracer" at eight dollars a
week. He borrowed ten dollars (which he sent to his mother) to be
paid back at two dollars a week. "Here," he said at seventy-four,
"started a characteristic process continuing to this day."

After a very short time, he applied for a raise and was refused;
he quit the job, immediately got another for much more money, and
was told to go ahead and design. At first overjoyed, he quickly
realized that he was not yet ready for either the work or the salary;
he thereupon resigned, asked his previous employer to give him
back his job, and got it. Soon, however, he was earning enough to
bring his mother and sisters to Chicago, and the family settled in
the nearby suburb of Oak Park.

Before he was twenty Wright obtained a position as draftsman-
designer with the firm of Adler and Sullivan. Louis Sullivan was the
most advanced architect in Chicago, perhaps in the whole country,
at the time. Sullivan was a difficult man to work for but Wright
was devoted to him, dedicated himself to Sullivan's slogan, "Form
follows Function," and always referred to him as "Lieber Meister."

It was a time of ardor. Wright had fallen in love with a beautiful girl, Catherine Tobin. When they were married Wright was not twenty-one, Catherine barely eighteen. Sullivan loaned him enough money to build a small house, and Wright, insured by a five-year contract, agreed to pay the indebtedness back month by month. With a sententious flourish that characterized his literary style, he carved a phrase over the fireplace: "Truth is Life." "Soon after," he added, "it occurred to me that Life is Truth."

Children also occurred to him soon after. There were six in all: Lloyd, John, Catherine, Frances, David, and Robert Llewellyn. Although Wright claims he disliked fatherhood per se, he seems to have been an exciting if not an exemplary father. Each child was taught a different musical instrument, and since the mother played the piano, there was no lack of impromptu concerts with Wright as creative listener. In *My Father Who Is on Earth,* an obviously worshipful memoir, his son John described the man: "Brown eyes full of love and mischief; a thick pompadour of dark, wavy hair . . . He looked like Beethoven . . . The unrestrained character and the peculiarities of his genius caused him to have little in common with his neighbors . . . It was Dad's desire that his children should grow up with a recognition for what is good in the art of the house. He believed that an instinct for the beautiful would be firmly established by a room whose simple beauty and strength are daily factors." Long before he formulated his philosophy, Wright knew that the architect built "for the life lived in the building."

By 1893, while his contract with Sullivan still had some time to run, Wright was augmenting his income by taking a few private commissions on his own time. When Sullivan learned of this, he was understandably aggrieved and Wright, irascible because he was wrong, defiantly threw up his job. Although he realized his error, he could not get himself to acknowledge it, and it was twelve years before he resumed his intimacy with "Lieber Meister." He was not quite twenty-five when he started private practice in Chicago. A success from the start, he was never without commissions. The houses he designed were so personal and distinctive that patrons regarded them with the affection usually reserved for living things. He did not have clients but converts, devotees who hailed every departure with championing hallelujahs. Nevertheless, his carelessness with money kept him in a state of near-insolvency. It was his method, as well as his wife's, to draw checks until they came back stamped "Not Sufficient Funds." Then they knew they had no more money in the bank. "God give me the luxuries of life," he said with undisturbed equanimity, "and I will willingly do without the necessities."

Successful though he was, public recognition of his work came slowly in his own country. With remarkably few exceptions, his fellow architects belittled his innovations, mocked his theories as spectacular nonsense, brushed aside his designs as "impractical," and, worse, ignored the solidity of his accomplishments. Yet, before he was forty, his work had been extolled in Europe and an illustrated record of his achievements had been issued by a publishing firm in Germany. His departures from contemporary fashion were to undergo many developments, but his concept of Organic Architecture had already taken shape. He began by eliminating irrelevant ornaments, discarding approximations of elaborate foreign elements, avoiding sacrosanct but obsolete precedents. A stubborn noncompromiser, he maintained that "Principle is the only safe precedent." The first house Wright designed on his own was small but revolutionary. At the time (1893) all homes were equipped with high basements, attics with jutting dormers, boxlike structures consisting of boxes within boxes. Rooms were sealed off, connected with other rooms by doors in partitions and dark halls. First of all, Wright dispensed with the ugly hole of the basement. The attic was abandoned. "Step by step," explained Edgar Kaufmann, Jr., in his commentary on Wright's later work, "all closed spaces overhead were added to the rooms, were used to live in. The substantial fireplace emerged. The sense of interior space as the reality of the building was born—the essence of Organic Architecture . . . The kitchen became an attractive feature . . . incorporated with dining area and living room: the 'open plan.' Furniture began to be built in. Floor spaces everywhere became living spaces, expanded by terraces and balconies. A sense of broad shelter was emphasized overhead as the outside and inside began to mingle." Other technical innovations followed, features which are now accepted as familiar but were radical departures in his day: the floor-to-ceiling picture window; the concrete floor slab without basement but with gravity, or floor, heat; low pitched roofs with wide overhang; and other means of achieving a sense of spaciousness.

Out of Wright's conception of the organic house came an appreciation of the relation between design and material, as well as his most dramatic pioneering triumph: freedom of form. Rebelling against the time-sanctified cube or parallelepiped, his abhorred "box," Wright did not devote himself to merely one other form but rather to an ever-enlarging variety of forms, while most of his contemporaries contented themselves with variations on the traditional structures. Even such a fantastic building as New York's seemingly suspended glass-walled Lever House is, as Wright scoffs, merely an upended "box on sticks," a sorry contrast to his daring free-form skyscraper in Bartlesville, Oklahoma. Every new site and situation called forth a whole new set of shapes and details—Wright was never a slave to patterns, including his own.

Part of Wright's boldness lies in his feeling for the materials he employs. He does not conceal the rough power of stone; he would consider it a sacrilege to hide the wavelike contours of good grained wood. The Larkin Building, put up in Buffalo in 1904, was one of his first great protests in brick and mortar against excess decoration and senseless elaboration. Significance was demanded and achieved by respecting the very nature of the materials, from the then-startling glass doors and metal furniture to the lighting system especially designed in steel.

Unable to share his seemingly intuitive knowledge of the capabilities of his materials, the authorities continually made trouble for Wright. The building codes, failing to allow for his combination of imagination and practicality, almost invariably opposed his projects. Time and again he had to prove that his structures would stand up; time and again his calculations were right and the "experts" wrong. In 1936, when Wright planned the Administration Building for the Johnson Wax Company in Racine, Wisconsin, the tapering mushroom supports he designed were labeled unsafe by the building overseers. The architect thereupon constructed one of the slender columns and piled more than the required weight upon it to demonstrate that it was not only safe but unprecedentedly strong.

Each drawing Wright made was not only a new attempt to solve the old problem of space and shelter, but a new statement of purpose and a declaration of human progress. He used many different ways to "break open the box" and free the occupant from its constraint. The use of the cantilever gave him his greatest opportunity to destroy the stereotyped, inhibiting shape. "You could put the load under the center of the beam or you could reduce the span between the corners by moving the supports inward and leaving the corner open. Now the walls could be merely screens and the corners could be knocked out—man could look out of the corner where he had never looked before. What could happen horizontally could also happen to the vertical corner. Walls could be screens independent of each other; the open plan appeared naturally; the relationship of inhabitants to the outside became more intimate; landscape and building became harmonious and, instead of a separate thing set up without regard to the site, the building, site, and landscape became inevitably one." Wright was justified in boasting that the life of the individual was broadened and enriched by the new concept of architecture, by light and the sense of liberty attained through freedom of space.

Wright was about forty when his marital troubles began. "Domesticity bore down heavily," he records vaguely, and he asked Catherine for a divorce. She replied that if he repeated the request a year from then, she would agree. At the end of the year he was still insistent, but Catherine had changed her mind. Wright was outraged—"only to the degree that marriage is mutual is it decent." Without further argument, he left home and the United States and went to Italy. His autobiography discloses that he did not go alone. He was accompanied by Mrs. Mamah Bouton Borthwick Cheney and, pursued by "newspaper publicity and relentless persecution," remained in exile for about two years. In 1911 he returned to Wisconsin. He went to Spring Green, where he had some property, and there he began to build Taliesin (the name of a Welsh poet, which also means "Shining Brow"), "to get my back against the wall and to fight for what I saw I had to fight." Mrs. Cheney became not only his companion but his collaborator; together they translated Ellen Key's *Love and Ethics*. She and her two children were living at Taliesin when Wright was called to Chicago to create the Midway Gardens, an early correlation of architecture, sculpture, painting, and music. While he was away from home, supervising the construction, there occurred a tragedy of unbelievable proportions. A fanatical Negro butler insanely believed he was an instrument of God; one night in August, 1914, he threw lighted torches into a room which he had already soaked with kerosene. He waited outside, and as the occupants fled to escape the fire, struck them down with an axe. He killed seven people, including Mrs. Cheney and the two children. This unspeakable disaster was hailed by many as a just "retribution" and moralists all over the country were gratified. The censure had one salutary result: it roused Wright from his abysmal grief. Outraged at the attacks, Wright rebuilt Taliesin.

Shortly after, Wright was selected by the Japanese government to erect an Imperial Hotel, which was to serve as a social clearinghouse as well as a monument of the empire. Wright went to Japan, spent years studying earthquake conditions, and designed a building which would resist the shock of earthquakes. Instead of being "fixed" on treacherous rocks, it figuratively floated. Wright realized that, instead of rigidity, flexibility and resiliency must be the answer to the ever-recurring nightmare threat; he designed a building that could "flex and return to normal." In 1924, several years after the Imperial Hotel had been built, one of the worst quakes in the history of Japan leveled Tokyo, but the Imperial Hotel was not affected. It rocked in the upheaval but, to quote from Alexander Woollcott's "Profile" of Wright in *The New Yorker,* "as the temblor passed, settled quietly back into position with no crack or dislocation." Until it was destroyed by bombing during the Second World War, the Imperial was a place of refuge during earthquakes—"all the town," wrote Woollcott, "tried to crowd into the terraced courtyards, seeking the protection of a god that can laugh at an earthquake."

Before Wright left for Japan he had met a woman, Miriam Noel, who had written sympathetically to him after the Taliesin tragedy. She was a Christian Scientist, a sculptress, and something of an eccentric—she sported a monocle—with grown children. They met, entered upon a "voluntary, open intimacy," and he took her with him to Japan. During Wright's four years' stay in the Orient, Catherine finally consented to a divorce, and he married Miriam. Unfortunately, the marriage was ill-starred from the beginning. Miriam had long periods of psychological disturbance and, by the time Wright was ready to leave Japan, he was also ready to leave Miriam. He returned to America to face another misfortune. The rebuilt Taliesin burned down. He built it up again.

Wright was beginning to dream in terms of cities rather than individual buildings. He recognized the fact that modern man lived in a mechanized world and that it was an expression of neurotic nostalgia to pretend otherwise by putting up replicas of a "dear, dead past." On the other hand, he scorned the inorganic, mechanistic functionalism of the so-called "International Style" publicized by Walter Gropius and his pupils. "The machine should build the building," said Wright, "but it is not necessary to build as though the building, too, were a machine." The architect was not yet ready to present to the world his model for Broadacre City, a development based upon his theory of decentralization; but he was devoting more and more thought to the freedom that could be secured by "going forward to more intelligent use of man's heritage: the ground." In the ideal community everyone could enjoy his birthright, with an acre of land for each person.

Before he got around to answering the moot question of congested centralization, Wright was again emotionally involved. He met Olga (Ogilvanna) Lazovich and was irrevocably committed to her. She was dark and handsome, unusually intelligent, a person of culture and breeding, a divorced woman with a daughter, Svetanna. When Miriam, who had returned to America, learned that they were living together, she sued Wright, using every possible private and public means of harassment. It was another field day for the newspapers, especially after Miriam located Ogilvanna's former husband and persuaded him to press charges of kidnaping and to brand Wright as a criminal by invoking the Mann Act. While the scandal sheets splashed stories of the lawless architect and his "Montenegran dancer" across their syndicated columns, Wright and Olga were arrested and jailed. The violent controversy finally subsided, the entanglements were straightened out, and on August 25, 1928, Wright was legally married to Olga, by whom he had a daughter, Iovanna.

Wright remained the great uncompromiser. He continued to startle the world with his inexhaustible flair for experiment, his unqualified vitality and prodigal variety. Each architectural unit differed in form, but not in principle, from its predecessor: the Edgar J. Kaufmann house, "Fallingwater," at Bear Run, Pennsylvania, the first house in Wright's experience to be built of reinforced concrete, where the building, growing from its site, seemed to be part of both the rock-ledge and the stream; Taliesin West, built near the Arizona desert where a complete change in terrain caused a complete change in form; the Heliolab, the Johnson Laboratory Tower at Racine, where the mushroom-type floor slabs are cantilevered out around a central core and the walls, which bear no load, are a transparency of glass tubing; the extraordinary Morris gift shop in San Francisco with a windowless façade, a subtly insinuating arch, and a plastic bubble skytop; Florida Southern College at Lakeland, the gayest, airiest, and most unconventional campus in America; the projected new Guggenheim Museum on New York's Fifth Avenue, which, instead of being a cellular composite of separate compartments, is one great rounded space where, by means of a spiral-like ramp, the exhibits are on one continuous floor.

Wright's program was buoyantly announced, emphasized, and reiterated in his published volumes which, in a sometimes irritating hortatory-mystical manner, stressed the kinship of the structure and the site—a house should grace its surroundings rather than disgrace them. As a protest against the habit of importing foreign woods and marbles, Wright proclaimed the beauty and dignity of local materials. His conviction that "organic buildings are always of the land," was amplified to read "and *from* the land." Much of his later work was aided and abetted by the Taliesin Fellowships, a group of fifty-odd disciples, who not only did Wright's drafting but all the repairing around the place, the farming, the supplementary handcrafts, and considered it the greatest privilege to be selected to do the work.

Wright was nearing seventy when the honors began to pour in. He was awarded the Gold Medal of the Royal Institute of British Architects in 1941 and, after a cautious waiting period of eight years, the American Institute of Architects followed suit with their Gold Medal. He was already an honorary member of academies in fifteen different countries. In 1953 the Gold Medal of the National Institute of Arts and Letters was presented to him with this tribute: "You have created an architecture in which you have been thoughtfully aware of the powerful forces implicated in the new inventions and, though philosophically concerned with the machine, you have never held that it should heedlessly produce more machines or more machine-like objects. On the contrary, you have felt that it should be used to make a world in which function may be controlled so as to emancipate enslaving forms and to increase the possibilities for new-founded cities whose broad acres will furnish that beauty of life for which man has ever sought."

In reply Wright murmured that this and other late honors were beginning to infect him with the disease of humility. The contagion was not serious. The taint of humility did not deter the octogenarian from assuring a body of students that, if they stuck to their studies and carefully followed the textbooks, they would have careers of competent and profitable mediocrity. Nor was the old cantankerousness missing when, shaking his white mane, he told another group attending a symposium that they were wasting their time in today's schools. "We have no culture," he said on another occasion, "we have only a civilization. We have power, the consequence of excess. But excess is artificial; it should not be confused with exuberance. Exuberance," said the eighty-four-year-old *enfant terrible,* with a nod at William Blake, "is beauty." He was entitled to the epigram. He could point, with confident loftiness, to some six hundred and fifty highly individualized structures—proofs of a tireless exuberance, fresh and organic in every living line.

Mohandas Karamchand Gandhi

[1 8 6 9 - 1 9 4 8]

*"He had the might of a dictator and the
mind of a democrat."*

NTIL THE EARLY YEARS of the twentieth century India, to the
average Occidental, was as far removed in concern as it was
remote in distance. By 1940, however, it had violently in-
truded itself and its incalculable possibilities upon the attention of
the entire world. This was due almost wholly to one man, Mohandas Karamchand Gandhi, an undersized, unpretentious, and
deeply religious Hindu, sometimes described as a saint attempting
to be a politician, although Gandhi insisted the truth was the other
way around.

He was born October 2, 1869, in Porbandar, a small seashore
town in the province of Bombay on the western coast of India, on a
peninsula where the people speak Gujarati. Although his grandfather had once been prime minister of Porbandar and his father had
served in a similar capacity in two smaller states, their tasks were
more managerial than diplomatic, and both men were overseers
rather than statesmen. According to Hindu tradition, people were
divided into four castes. The Brahmins, wise men, and priests were
ranked highest. Then came the aristocrats, leaders, and warriors.
The merchants, traders, and shopkeepers were third, while the
workers were the fourth and lowest class. The Gandhis belonged to
the third class—the name Gandhi originally meant grocer—but they
lived in comfort that was close to luxury. There were no Western
influences in the home, but there were many books, musical instruments, ornaments of ivory and gold. Mohandas, who was the fourth
child of his father's fourth wife, had a nurse of his own. His childhood was uneventfully secure and serene. He succumbed to normal
boyhood temptations: he smoked surreptitiously, ate a little meat—
forbidden by his sect—and stole a few coins from his brother. When
his fifteen-year-old conscience made him confess his misdeeds to his
father he braced himself for the expected punishment, and when
his father, weeping, forgave him without a blow or even exacting a
penalty, Mohandas was overcome. Indian lore accepted the com-

bination of understanding, love, and truth as the highest good, but this was his first concrete experience of the application of those abstract virtues. He never forgot it.

In accordance with the country's custom, Gandhi was married at thirteen. His bride, Kasturbai, daughter of a Porbandar merchant, was his own age—he had been betrothed to her for years. Such child-marriages were possible because of the traditional economic arrangement: the adolescent couples lived in the home of the groom's family. Gandhi's marriage made him lose a year's schooling. He hoped to teach what he knew to Kasturbai who was illiterate when he married her, but she never learned to read or write anything except the simplest Gujarati. Nevertheless, he adored and desired her constantly. His youthful passion was both a torture as well as a delight; years later he tormented himself with the fact that when his father died, instead of being at his side, Gandhi was in bed with Kasturbai. When his first child died soon after birth, the parents being barely fifteen, Gandhi blamed this, too, on his uncontrolled desire.

At nineteen, after his father's death, Gandhi was sent to England to study law. Gandhi would have preferred to study medicine, but the family felt that a law degree would insure a position in the field of management and diplomacy. Leaving his wife and a second child (a boy named Harilal), Gandhi arrived in London in 1888. A photograph taken at twenty is anything but flattering. The abundant black hair is slicked down and parted on one side of the head; the eyes are dark and so deep-set that one of his biographers says they mirrored puzzlement, fright, and yearning. The other features were unattractively prominent: abnormally large projecting ears, a long beaklike nose, and a sensitively sensual mouth distorted by a too-full and almost pendulous underlip. During his first stay in England Gandhi's foreign appearance was accentuated by his meticulous adoption of Western haberdashery, including starched white collars, striped vest, formal morning coat, patent leather shoes with spats, high silk top hat, gloves, and cane. In contrast to this raiment, he lived simply; he walked miles daily to save carfare; he made a few friends but was inarticulate in a gathering of any size. He studied Latin, French, and physics as well as law; his extra-curricular activities included the reading of English and American literature as well as a comparison of Western and Eastern religions. Oddly enough, it was in England that he first read, in an English translation, the great Indian allegorical epic, the *Bhagavad-Gita,* from which he derived his central philosophy and way of life.

In 1891, having passed his bar examinations, Gandhi returned to an India in which he seemed inept as a lawyer and insecure as a layman. The atmosphere of the corrupt provincial states, with their intrigues, deceptions, and fawning hypocrisies, dismayed him. When a business firm proposed that he go to South Africa to take care of their legal matters there, he gladly accepted. It was to be a brief stay, but Gandhi practiced there twenty years. When, at twenty-four, he arrived in South Africa he found rampant discrimination against Indians, who were treated as inferiors. The British imposed humiliating restrictions similar to the American "Jim Crow" laws, and Gandhi resolved to ignore them. When told by a magistrate to take off his turban in court, he refused and was sneeringly called a "coolie" barrister. Traveling first-class, he was told to go into the third-class cars, even though he had a first-class ticket; when he objected, he was thrown out and beaten. It was obvious to Gandhi that ignoring the situation was not enough. He saw that, although no one had dared question the status quo, there would have to be protests and, to implement the challenge, action. Accordingly, he started to organize the South African Indians in an effort to better their conditions. As a beginning he made them realize that, in order to get their claims respected, they had to be self-improving, worthy of respect. Gandhi's power was singular. Although he was only twenty-five, he moved men by the directness of his vision and the purity of his purpose. He united the recognition of a need with the necessity of doing something about it; his fearlessness in the face of injustice roused others to do what they never would have done on their own.

During his two decades in South Africa, Gandhi's development was greatly influenced by the work of three Western authors: a Russian novelist, Tolstoy; an English critic, Ruskin; and an American essayist, Thoreau. Tolstoy's *The Kingdom of God Is Within You* showed him how to apply a program of nonresistance in terms of social practice. Thoreau taught him the right, even the virtue, of civil disobedience. But it was Ruskin who affected him most. Ruskin's *Unto This Last* filled him with a sense of the dignity of labor. Originally the Hindu traditions had reflected the equal integrity of men, regardless of their activities; but the caste system had degenerated and, after many centuries, had debased physical labor to inferior status. Those who did the most disagreeable physical chores were the "untouchables," consigned to the lowest depths of permanent discrimination. Inspired by Ruskin, Gandhi aimed to change all this and, in so doing, changed not only himself but an entire system of thought. It may have been unusual for Gandhi to want to live a godly life, although Indian religious training might have led to this. But his conviction that labor must be restored to dignity was radical, and his conclusion that the only good economy is that which conduces to the good of all was revolutionary.

Gandhi's first efforts were in the nature of appeals. He wrote letters to newspapers and officials, prepared circulars, drafted pamphlets. He addressed meetings and found that fervor made him eloquent. When he realized that his work in Africa would take a long time he went back to India for his family, which now included a second son, Manilal. By the time he returned, his propaganda had proved so successful that he was considered "undesirable" and the ship he was on was not permitted to dock. Finally, after twenty-three days of waiting, the passengers—Indian laborers whom he had recruited—were allowed to land, but Gandhi himself was warned not to disembark except under cover of darkness. Scorning subterfuge, Gandhi came ashore openly in full daylight, was attacked by an organized mob, kicked, stoned, and badly bruised. Only the belated protection of the police saved him from being lynched; but Gandhi refused to register a formal complaint. Instead of prosecuting the attackers, he forgave them. The refusal to be, in any sense, a persecutor did not lessen the power of his appeal.

Gandhi was thirty when the Boer War broke out. Although his sympathies were with the Boers, he felt that, since he was a British citizen, he had an ethical obligation to volunteer on the English side. This seeming contradiction of his ideas of nonviolence and pacifism was typical of Gandhi's sometimes paradoxical positions. His attitudes were not always popular, his followers did not always understand them, but they were logical. They were, to Gandhi, the natural consequence of a truth and, therefore, consistent and inescapable. It was with such a logic that he was to participate in the First World War and, although he could not be persuaded to do actual fighting, he organized and worked in the ambulance corps. After the Boer War he tried to settle down in his native land, but he was called back to Africa, where his popularity as a leader was matched by his success as a lawyer. Wealth did not make him less aware of inequalities. On the contrary, he took an increasingly active part in the social struggle, even to the extent of applying his principles to the casual details of everyday living. Unpleasant details were not relegated to menials and "untouchables" but, to put principle into practice, were performed jointly by the servants and the family. This included Gandhi himself; he was not above emptying the chamber-pots.

As his income grew, Gandhi put aside much of it for social progress; he set up a trust fund for aid to Indians in South Africa. He changed his life on the basis of his adaptation of Ruskin's thinking: "that the life of labor—the life of the tiller of the soil and the handicraftsman—is the life worth living." To Gandhi nothing had meaning unless it was translated into a mutual enterprise: the art and work and love which brought about the full realization of life. On the farm which Gandhi bought, his disciples and their families were co-workers as well as students; the aim was to be as self-sufficient as possible. All labor was shared; the flour was ground by hand. It was on the farm that Gandhi extended his disciplines of self-control. He denied himself rich food and all seasonings, limiting himself to the simplest vegetarian diet, trying to determine how few nuts and grapes were enough for active existence. He put a check upon his overabundant virility. In his thirty-seventh year, by which time he had four sons, he curbed all sexual desire. He remained continent until the end of his life. He believed that cutting off all sensual appetites would have two results: the energy saved or sublimated would give him added power to lead the good life and do good things; the self-control developed would bring him nearer to the source of all Good which is God.

Meanwhile, Gandhi had become an editor, a role which he maintained until his death. He used journalism partly as a medium for reforms, and partly as a sounding board, balancing the extremes of experiment with a recognition of errors. At thirty-eight he called a mass meeting in Johannesburg to protest the pending legislation to make all Indians register and be fingerprinted. Gandhi persuaded everyone to make a solemn vow collectively and individually not to obey the ordinance if it became a law, even though disobedience meant jail, beating, or death. This type of opposition, which Gandhi was to teach the people of India to use time after time, was called *Satyagraha,* literally "the force of truth" or "truth-love." The government paid no attention to the opposition. The act was adopted; Gandhi refused to obey it and was sentenced to a term in prison. He told Louis Fischer, author of the brilliantly illuminating *The Life of Mahatma Gandhi,* "Jail is jail for thieves and bandits. For me it was a palace. I was the originator of jail-going even before I read Thoreau."

It was in jail that Gandhi did his most concentrated reading and much of his meditating. According to Fischer, he spent 249 days in South African prisons and 2,089 days in Indian jails. Gandhi argued that if everyone resisted unjust discriminatory laws, a government would find it impossible to jail the entire population—a philosophic proposition which, later, was fulfilled in fact. At this juncture, the South African leader, General Smuts, offered to repeal the act if the Indians would register voluntarily. Although he was severely criticized, Gandhi accepted the compromise. Like many of his followers, he was doubtful of Smuts, but he insisted that, since love and truth and trust were interrelated, any negotiation implied a basis of trust. If you are deceived you can start over; but if you do not trust, you can never advance. Following this line of reasoning, Gandhi was the first to register, even though many of his adherents felt he had betrayed them. As a result, he was vilified, beaten, and almost killed.

General Smuts broke his promise; the objectionable act was not repealed. Had Gandhi been a visionary, he would have been ruined. But he was not an idealistic dreamer; he was a practical politician. He recognized the exigencies of a situation and gave in to them, knowing that once a thing is set in motion, it was no longer the thing itself which could be counted upon, but the effects it had on everything else. These effects he understood—and having been trained not to be impatient of time, he could wait to utilize them. Therefore Gandhi's mistake did not destroy him. He declared that it proved the power of *Satyagraha* to uncover concealed schemes, reveal the truth, give the opponent another chance to discard base motives, and make the victims see more clearly. The Indian contingent was now unanimous, and Gandhi headed a group more solidly united than ever. Discarding European dress, and adopting a white smock, loincloth, and sandals, he led thousands of men, women, and children in a prolonged protest march. The miners struck in sympathy. When the white railroad employees joined the strike, the government knew it was losing, Smuts sought new negotiations, and the resultant Indian Relief gave Gandhi the victory he had fought for so long and, in spite of seeming derelictions, so steadfastly.

At forty-six Gandhi returned to India with one aim: to free it from British domination. It seemed an impossible goal. India was not only vast in area, but divided into many tribes, tongues, sects and religions, chiefly the opposed Hindu and Mohammedan. He began agitating for Indian home rule in the same way he had operated in South Africa. His first appeal to his countrymen was to their dignity. He reminded them they were Indians, inheritors of a pure faith and a magnificent culture. He hoped to see that culture restored and reanimated. He spoke up for a respect for all classes and castes. He did not want to see India liberated from foreign despotism only to live under the yoke of a native tyranny. He wanted the illiterate myriads, the undernourished and underprivileged, liberated from their own self-imposed chains, so that as they struggled toward freedom they would advance toward enlightenment. As the leader of the Indian National Congress, he campaigned fiercely for cleanliness in an effort to raise the standard of living and, as a consequence, lower the mortality rate. He attacked unflaggingly the institution of untouchability and brought an "untouchable" girl into his home—an act as shocking to a tradition-bound Indian as a white man's adoption of a Negro child would be to the average Southerner. In protest against what he considered injurious industrialization and in an effort to revive village crafts, he advocated the use of homespun and urged everyone to spin.

The nationalist organization grew wider and spread deeper, but it took a particular situation to set it in motion. Gandhi visited Champaran, a district where Indian sharecroppers were being robbed by English plantation owners. The alarmed British officials attempted to restrain any activity by Gandhi and served him with a summons. In court Gandhi pleaded guilty to the charge of disobeying an order to leave the district. The peasantry was alerted to action, and Gandhi's civil disobedience program forced a settlement. The outcome was more than an episode; it was a turning point. It proved, for one thing, that even an imperial power could not bully a citizen in his own country. But Champaran was most significant because, wrote Louis Fischer, "it did not begin as an act of defiance. It grew out of an attempt to alleviate the distress of large numbers of poor peasants. This was the typical Gandhi pattern: his politics were intertwined with the practical, day-to-day problems of the millions. His was not a loyalty to abstractions; it was a loyalty to living, human beings. In everything Gandhi did, he tried to mold a new free Indian who could stand on his own feet and thus make India free . . . He was," Fischer concluded, "a natural fighter and a born peacemaker . . . He had the might of a dictator and the mind of a democrat." He distrusted the machine age not because he objected to the machine—"the human today is a most delicate piece of machinery," said Gandhi—but to the fact that "machinery helps a few to ride on the backs of the many." He believed in Marx's theory of labor's surplus value and the workers' inevitable conflict with capitalism, but he did not encourage the overthrow of capitalism by force, and his opposition to violence made him hostile to the communist state and all forms of totalitarianism. He campaigned unceasingly for spiritual as well as physical freedom. He wrote vivid polemics, stirred meetings, impelled without inciting action, and fasted vigorously. He did not fast for publicity or in an effort to frighten his opponents, as his detractors charged; he fasted because it was the most striking way of calling his own people's attention to the essential needs of an issue, of reassuring them that someone was willing to suffer and die for the principles involved.

A burning inspiration to his countrymen, he was a cold taskmaster to his family. He imposed his self-severity upon his sons who could not live up to his demands—the oldest, Harilal, became a drunkard, a wastrel, and a convert to Mohammedanism. Although Gandhi tried to shrug off greatness, he came to be loved as his country's Mahatma, "Great Soul," a title conferred only on a saint. The faith he inspired was not a blind belief but an appreciative awareness of his aims. "He had," said Gopal Gokhale, the Indian sage, "the marvelous spiritual power to turn ordinary men around him into heroes and martyrs." He applied the homilies of the Sermon on the Mount, especially the injunction to return good for evil, to every situation. Others had preached passive resistance, but Gandhi's practice of nonviolent civil disobedience was one of the most daring—and one of the most successful—experiments in the history of government.

Although Gandhi refused to let his followers take up arms, he had other weapons. One of these was the *hartal,* a general strike, during which all shops closed, while the workers stayed at home, fasting and praying. Gandhi used it to touch off a campaign against a restrictive act passed by the British in 1919. Its success was scarcely noticed, but it was epochal; it marked the beginning of the end, twenty-eight years later, of British rule.

The years between 1919 and 1947 were packed with political-spiritual activities. Gandhi grew frailer, a wisp of a man, his dark eyes exaggerated by huge, round, steel-rimmed spectacles; by the time he turned sixty he was toothless, bald, wrinkled, almost ugly. Only the hands stayed young, beautiful and eloquent, matching his ageless spirit. Beloved and more influential than ever, he traveled up and down India, speaking to audiences of hundreds of thousands. Sometimes, when he was too exhausted to speak, he would sit cross-legged on the platform in silence; the audience would remain transfixed, and there would be established a communication more potent and subtle than speech. There were many setbacks, compromises, reversals. When a *hartal* was followed by violence, Gandhi would call off the strike on the grounds that the people were not sufficiently trained in the technique of civil disobedience. After the British massacred Indians at Amritsar, Gandhi, as President of the All-India Home Rule League, advocated stricter noncooperation, was arrested, was sent to prison, fasted, and continued to call for sedition. This was a pattern which he followed for more than a decade. At sixty-one he walked twenty-four days, leading a great contingent on foot to the seashore. There he picked up salt in a dramatic defiance of the British salt tax, and his arrest made not only Asia but the Western world aware of England's cruelty to India. As a result, Great Britain took the renewed negotiations more seriously. Gandhi went to London for a conference and, while there, had tea with King George V and Queen Mary at Buckingham Palace. He appeared in nothing more than his habitual loincloth, sandals, and a light shawl. When asked whether he considered his raiment sufficient for a royal audience, he answered, "The King wore enough clothes for both of us."

Until the end, the imperialists held on with typical British doggedness. But Gandhi was equally dogged and even more determined. Again and again Gandhi initiated new civil disobedience programs, was imprisoned, went on epic fasts, drew up a pact between Hindus and Moslems that smashed tradition by declaring that no one should be considered "untouchable" by virtue of his birth. It became more and more difficult for Great Britain to dominate the situation. The end was foreseen by 1942 when Sir Stafford Cripps offered to give India full-fledged Dominion status. But Gandhi insisted that India must be nothing less than an independent democracy, not a divided satellite, and at seventy-three, he refused to give in to expediency. His problem now was staggering: how to achieve unity in his own country. He spent all his time in an effort to end the enmity between the two largest factions, the Moslems (Mohammedans), who occupied most of Pakistan, and the Hindus. In his mid-seventies he worked desperately but untiringly, and at considerable risk, going among the people, setting endless examples, spending nights, wherever possible, in some Moslem peasant's hut, talking, explaining, seeking to replace jealousy and resentment with love, to supplant prejudice with understanding and cooperation.

He was not successful. The difference between the two sects grew into violent clashes; blood was spilled; the antagonisms seemed irreconcilable. Compromise had always been an integral part of Gandhi's plan and so, reluctantly but resignedly, he bowed to the majority. His last long fast—an ordeal which almost killed him—brought amity between the factions in Delhi; he still hoped to repair the damage done by those who were determined to separate India and Pakistan. Again he failed. There was not enough time for him to complete his work for unity. On Sunday, January 25, 1948, shortly after his fast, he attended a prayer meeting. There were even larger crowds than usual. In the front row was an Indian, Nathuram Godse. When Gandhi rose to give the blessing, Godse, a fanatic Hindu who felt that Gandhi had taken the Moslems' part, fired a pistol three times. Gandhi was hit by all three bullets. Mortally wounded, he cried "Rama," the Indian word for God, and died almost instantly. He was spared the ironical knowledge that, like many another martyr, he had been struck down by one of those he had dedicated himself to save.

Edwin Arlington Robinson

[1 8 6 9 - 1 9 3 5]

"The world frightens me."

AN UNNATURALLY LACONIC and abnormally reticent poet—so shy that he had to drink himself into even an ordinary conversation—Edwin Arlington Robinson challenged contemporary values and questioned the current price of success more caustically than any poet of his day. Even in youth Robinson discovered that he would have to live in a hard world with a harsh set of imperatives. He was born December 22, 1869, in the village of Head Tide, Maine; but before he was a year old, his family moved to nearby Gardiner, a manufacturing town of some four thousand people. It was in Gardiner (the "Tilbury Town" of his poems) that he lived until he was twenty-seven and it was here that he was least lonely and most nearly at home. His father was a former ship's carpenter who had acquired a general store and, during Robinson's youth, was a well-to-do landowner, stockholder, councilman, and bank director. There were two older brothers, Dean, who was schooled to become a doctor, and Herman, who was expected to be a businessman. Edwin, the youngest, was also the quietest. He retreated into hours of abstraction and, fearing a hostile world, refused to compete. Even as a child, he knew he was "never going to be able to elbow [his] way to the Trough of Life." He read poetry at five; at eleven he began to write it. Before the boy was out of his teens, his father's health began to fail and he seemed to die daily. The gifted Dean had given up a country practice, and as a result of dosing himself with morphine for neuralgia, had become a drug addict. Shortly after attaining his majority, Robinson seems to have had premonitions of his later unhappily speculative, lonely life, his self-identification with failure, and a preoccupation with his fellows in frustration. "The truth is I have lived in Gardiner for nearly twenty-two years and, metaphorically speaking, have hardly been out of the yard . . . Solitude tends to magnify one's ideas of individuality; it sharpens his sympathy with failure . . . It renders a man suspicious of the whole natural plan and leads him to wonder whether the invisible powers are a fortuitous issue of unguided cosmos, or the cosmos itself."

In the fall of 1891 Robinson entered Harvard. Determined to be an author, he submitted to the *Harvard Monthly* a dozen poems, including several verses now enshrined in the anthologies, but they were all rejected. After two years, Robinson had to give up college. Mills were shutting down, banks were closing, established firms were bankrupt; four million men were out of work when Coxey's unemployed "army" marched on Washington. The Robinson fortunes had shrunk disastrously. The father had died. Dean was a tragic ruin, suffering from hallucinations. Herman, the bewildered businessman, had invested unwisely and was trying to comfort himself with drink and futile dreams. Edwin, realizing that he would have to support himself, but also realizing that he was perfectly helpless "in what the world calls business," tried his unsure hand at short stories in the manner of François Coppée's *contes,* stories about "the humble, the forgotten, the unknown." But sonnets and villanelles interfered and, though he tried to write plays later in life, he had no talent for anything except poetry.

A mastoid infection, incurred when a boy, had destroyed some of the small bones in the ear, and Robinson became fearful about losing his hearing; he was also worried about his weak eyes. His apprehensions were aggravated by his feeling of dependence. "You cannot conceive," he wrote to a friend, "how cutting it is for a man of twenty-four to depend on his mother for every cent he has and every mouthful he swallows." "The world frightens me," he confessed. His prose sketches came back with a curt comment; a poem now famous ("The House on the Hill") was accepted without payment by an inconspicuous quarterly; another poem was printed in a magazine which reimbursed him with a year's subscription. His first "commercial" publication occurred in 1895 when *Lippincott's Magazine* published a sonnet about Poe. The fee was seven dollars and Robinson was twenty-six years old.

In 1896 Robinson put together a manuscript of one hundred pages, entitled it *The Torrent and the Night Before,* and sent it out hopefully. It was twice rejected. Finally an uncle by marriage, who was connected with the Riverside Press, arranged to have three hundred and twelve paper-bound copies printed (privately) for fifty-two dollars. The book carried a quaint and somewhat self-conscious dedication: "To any man, woman, or critic who will cut the edges of it—I have done the top." The response was not great, but the few reviews were pleasant enough to encourage the author to try for a wider audience. Richard G. Badger, a "vanity publisher," offered to bring out a new edition for a "modest fee." A few poems were dropped, some new ones added, a Harvard friend advanced the money, and *The Children of the Night,* containing some of Robinson's most vividly drawn portraits, was published in 1897.

Suddenly Robinson could not stand Gardiner. He could not sleep. He could not work. He could not even endure the atmosphere. At twenty-seven, he said to his brother Herman's wife, "I don't expect to live to be forty; whatever I do has got to be done soon." Collecting a few hundred dollars from his share of his father's estate, he went to New York. At this time a contemporary described him as "a slender figure, erect, distinguished, breeding and race in every line." If the breeding and race were not apparent to everyone, the sharp-boned, quizzical scholar's face called for attention. The high forehead was already faintly lined; the mouth was small and set; the prim spectacles could not conceal the brown eyes quietly burning with tension and curiosity. A new long poem, modeled on a garrulous but splendid derelict who had become one of Robinson's New York cronies, *Captain Craig,* was rejected by Scribner's. Robinson sent the manuscript to Small, Maynard, where it languished, was accepted for publication, was mislaid, lost, and finally discovered in a Boston brothel where a member of the editorial staff had left it. By that time the firm, under new management, had decided against publishing *Captain Craig,* and it was not until two friends subsidized the book that Robinson's third volume appeared. Robinson was thirty-three and, so far, the only money he had earned from poetry was the seven dollars for the sonnet to Poe. The magazines, devoted to sweetly trilling, soothing little lyrics, refused to consider his acidly etched stanzas. He moved from one New York flat and rooming house to another, each one meaner and dingier than the last. He frequented saloons and, drinking to give himself momentary confidence, lived on the free lunch that went with the whiskey. He refused invitations to dine with his more affluent friends because his suit was too seedy. In desperation he took a job at twenty cents an hour for a ten-hour day. The job was in the New York subway, then being built, checking the loads of material, working underground, living, he said, in his own hell.

Nine months later the section of the subway was completed and Robinson, out of work, again faced a winter of terrible privation. An accident that was almost a miracle rescued him. One of President

Theodore Roosevelt's young sons had discovered Robinson's *The Children of the Night* and had sent it to his father. Roosevelt, a fighting politician and a president who, nevertheless, had a genuine feeling for literature, was not only impressed but moved. He sent for the poet, and after considering making him an immigration inspector at Montreal or in Mexico, decided that America needed her poets at home and in June, 1905, made Robinson a special agent in the New York Custom House at what was then a lordly salary of two thousand dollars a year. "I want you to understand," Roosevelt told him, "that I expect you to think poetry first and Customs second." Robinson was elated; there was time now for the poems he had been unable to write. He could live in something better than squalor; he could even, as he informed a friend, "own two pairs of shoes at the same time." Roosevelt had found not only a living for Robinson but, by virtue of an appreciative article in *The Outlook*, an audience for him.

Four years later, when the poet was forty and Roosevelt was no longer in the White House, Robinson lost his post. Another volume, *The Town Down the River*, appeared and received cautious reviews; even the praise was qualified by misgivings about the poet's "crudities," "obscurities," and "perversities." Lonely and isolated, Robinson began drinking again, this time more heavily. He borrowed money from his circle of bohemian friends. Again he was rescued, this time by Hermann Hagedorn, who became his first biographer and who brought him to the MacDowell Colony, a haven for creative artists. Here, deferred to and, as he grew older, idolized, he spent his summers, dividing his winters between New York and Boston. The poetry began to flow steadily now, and the poems flowered into books: *The Man Against the Sky*, with a title poem which many considered his most important single utterance; *The Three Taverns*; three book-length narrative poems, curiously modernized Arthurian legends (*Merlin, Launcelot, Tristram*); *Avon's Harvest; Roman Bartholow*. In 1921, Robinson's *Collected Poems* won the Pulitzer Prize. Twice again Robinson was given the coveted award: in 1924 for *The Man Who Died Twice*, and in 1927 for *Tristram*, which was also distributed as a Literary Guild book choice to the several hundred thousand club members, one of the rare times that a Book Club has distributed a volume of poetry. After a short interval of comparative affluence the worries returned, and Robinson drove himself to attempted successors of *Tristram: Dionysus in Doubt, Cavender's House, The Glory of the Nightin-*

gales, Matthias at the Door, Talifer. When Robinson was sixty, his work became prolix and labored. Writing for an income, frightened of the past and fearing for the future, he accelerated his output and determined to publish an annual volume. Each year for seven years, until the very month of his death, he planned and issued a narrative poem in which maladjustment as well as physical fatigue was increasingly apparent. Some of the books, such as *Amaranth,* are extended nightmares; others, like *Nicodemus,* are full of echoing murmurs, garrulous ghosts mocking Robinson's taciturn past. Some seem to be allegories, but it is hard to tell whether Robinson is sympathizing with his lost shadows or satirizing them. He gave his characters memorable names but, as Malcolm Cowley observed, "he sometimes forgot to give them faces."

In his later years, he grew more tolerant of "company," but he never lost his distrust of most men and almost all women. He never married; he was never in love. When the irresistible dancer Isadora Duncan tried to seduce him, he could not let himself yield to her bacchante blandishments. At sixty he was lonelier than ever; he rarely left his rooms; his last winters were full of suffering. At sixty-six he weakened alarmingly, chiefly because of a growth in the pancreas. At the New York Hospital, where he was brought in a pitiable condition, it was found that a successful operation would be impossible, and he died there, April 6, 1935.

Upon his death there ensued the inevitable belated tributes. Robinson was especially praised for his single-mindedness, undiverted concentration, and "the dignity with which he wore his fame." It was also pointed out that Robinson's grim and pessimistic attitude kept him from the large audience he had temporarily found with *Tristram.* But Robinson had always winced at the charge of pessimism. "The world," he said, "is not a 'prison-house' but a kind of spiritual kindergarten where millions of bewildered infants are trying to spell 'God' with the wrong blocks." His theme was not hopelessness but loneliness; his heart went out to all the dream-lost drinkers and illusion-led failures with whom he could identify himself. He created an entire gallery of strange but recognizably American figures: Richard Cory, who "glittered when he walked" and fluttered pulses but who, one calm summer night, "went home and put a bullet through his head"; Miniver Cheevy, born too late, in love with the past, sighing "for what was not," who coughed "and called it fate, and kept on drinking"; Bewick Finzer, the wreck of wealth, coming for his pittance, "familiar as an old mistake, and futile as regret"; Fernando Nash, the tortured soul "who lost his crown before he had it"; Mr. Flood, the battered but ingratiating old ruin, lifting his jug on a moonlit road above the town

> Where strangers would have shut the many doors
> That many friends had opened long ago.

Robinson's characters are lit with a New England shrewdness, a blend of sympathy and irony, but the wry humor does not detract from the real love. It is with tenderness as well as sadness that Robinson protests against "our shopman's test of age and worth"; but he can cry out angrily against the corruption which comes with prosperity and man's cruelty to his fellow men:

> Tell me, O Lord—tell me, O Lord, how long
> Are we to keep Christ writhing on the Cross!

Robinson was no innovator; he never attempted to create new techniques or widen the gamut of traditional verse. He was essentially a revitalizer of old forms. He sharpened the outlines of the sonnet. He put strength and substance into attenuated French forms like the archaic ballade and villanelle; he used light verse with almost incongruous seriousness and turned the patterns employed so mincingly by Praed and so pertly by Dobson into brusque narratives and tragic little dramas. He gave the terse portrait poem a keener line than it had ever attained in America. If Robinson lacks luxuriance, if his conversations are a little too brilliant and the language a little too literary, his tone is precise and his taste is fastidious. His compressed epigrammatic phrasing freshened the traditional measures he loved and ennobled. His placidity was born of pain, and his tart idiom was the result of galling struggle. Opposed to the accepted standards of his time, he repudiated crass materialism as a justification of existence. Turning away from the complacent platitudes of his contemporaries, Robinson made a fanfare of failure and, as a spokesman for the downtrodden, the despised and the rejected, wrung a bitter triumph from defeat.

Henri Matisse

[1869-1954]

"He does more harm than alcohol."

THE BIOGRAPHY of Henri Emile Benoît Matisse consists of little more than a catalog of paintings. His art was his life; it may be said that he lived only on canvas. He was born December 31, 1869, in Le Cateau, a little town in Picardy, in the northern border country where France joins Flanders. His father was a grain merchant and hoped that his son, the older of two boys, would become a lawyer. Henri obediently prepared himself for the law, but his studies were interrupted by a severe illness. While convalescing he began to sketch the objects about him; he discovered a little manual, *How to Paint,* and in spite of parental objections, abandoned thoughts of a legal practice and determined to live by art alone. He took lessons in commercial design—a course given to makers of embroidery, of which there are reminders in Matisse's interiors—but he was twenty-three before he studied art systematically. At twenty-nine he married Amélie Payare of Toulouse, who bore him two sons, Jean and Pierre, and a daughter, Marguerite.

Matisse did not begin as a radical who scorned the academic tradition. His first teacher was the popular Bouguereau whose omnipresent nymphs seemed to be made of sponge cake and pink sugar. An instinctive distaste for the prettified third-rate sent Matisse to the studio of Gustave Moreau who, though not a great painter, was a stimulating influence, a teacher who urged Rouault, Dufy, and others besides Matisse to throw off their borrowed styles and discover their own idioms. Matisse was slow to declare his independence. He earned a little money by making copies of the Old Masters in the Louvre, chiefly for small provincial museums. In spite of his later reputation as an anarch, he never really repudiated tradition. He appreciated the skills of his predecessors and incorporated into his own experiments the lessons he had learned from the academicians. "I have always maintained one foot in the Louvre," he said, "so that, even when going forth adventuring, I always have an anchor in the native land."

That anchor was temporarily cast off when Matisse joined the

Impressionists and then went beyond them. In 1897, when he was almost thirty, he justified Moreau's prediction that Matisse would some day "simplify" painting. The prophecy was not wholly fulfilled by the rather elaborate "La Desserte," but the painting was sufficiently original to outrage the members of the *Salon de la Société Nationale*. Gertrude Stein has described the event unforgettably: "Matisse spent the winter painting a very large picture of a woman setting a table, and on the table was a magnificent dish of fruit. It had strained the resources of the Matisse family to buy this fruit. Fruit was horribly dear in Paris in those days, even ordinary fruit; imagine how much dearer was this very extraordinary fruit, for it had to be kept until the picture was completed, and the picture was going to take a long time. In order to keep it as long as possible they kept the room as cold as possible, and that under the roof and in a Paris winter was not difficult. Matisse painted in an overcoat and gloves, and he painted at it all winter. It was finished at last and sent to the salon, and there it was refused . . . These were very dark days and he was very despairful." Unable to sell his new paintings, he tried to earn a living as a sculptor, while his wife made and sold hats.

In 1904 the fabulously perceptive dealer, Ambroise Vollard, discoverer of Cézanne, gave Matisse his first one-man show. It was not a financial success—Vollard managed to sell only one canvas which netted Matisse barely one hundred francs—but it was evident that a new talent, with an expressiveness so candid as to seem bizarre, had arrived. Fascinated by a series of Japanese prints he had discovered in Paris, Matisse began to imitate their absence of perspectives and shadows. In 1905, when he was thirty-six, Matisse took another step into strange territory. He aligned himself with the young radicals who, after their showing in the *Salon d'Automne*, were dubbed "Fauves" or "Wild Beasts" and who accepted "Fauvism" as a half-proud, half-protesting characterization.

It was an age of isms. Fauvism had been preceded by Impressionism, Post-Impressionism, Divisionism, and Pointillism. It was followed by Expressionism, chiefly in Germany; Futurism in Italy; Vorticism in England; Surrealism and Abstractionism all over the world. The "Wild Beasts" took liberties with their objects; they painted ideas rather than things; they changed shapes arbitrarily to express a mood; they rendered their feelings in more violent colors than had ever been put together on canvas. They were howled down as "madmen," "degenerates," "criminals," "senseless betrayers

of Nature"; they were charged with a deliberate conspiracy to outrage the decencies and insult the public. Matisse's arbitrary arrangements and "simplified" color schemes made the critics particularly furious. They held that he was an anarchist dedicated to
destroy all tradition. "He is a poison," "he does more harm than
alcohol," "his is an extension of insanity" were a few of the phrases
with which his innovations were greeted. Summarizing the ingenu-
ous quality of the man who "began by being notorious and, considerably later, achieved fame," the American critic, Henry McBride,
wrote: "Almost at the beginning of his career Matisse looked about
him for encouragement in his desire for spontaneity of expression
and found it only in the drawings of children. Not being a child
himself, he felt it necessary to throw overboard a lot of stiffening
mannerisms that had been taught in the schools, and he suddenly
began painting with the carefree abandonment to the sheer pleasure of painting that all children show in their beginnings . . . All
the great Matisse pictures hide completely the traces of preparation
and seem improvisations."

It was Gertrude Stein and her brother Leo who saved Matisse
from poverty. They bought his paintings in quantity, propagan-
dized for them, encouraged Americans to collect them, and created
a vogue for his flat but sumptuous compositions. Emboldened by
the unexpected response, Matisse opened an atelier for painters. It
is significant that, at the height of his most experimental period, he
said to one of his students: "You must not think you are committing
suicide by adhering to nature and trying to picture it with exactness. In the beginning you must subject yourself to the influence of
nature. After that you can motivate nature and perhaps make it
more beautiful. But you must be able to walk firmly on the ground
before you start walking on a tight-rope."

In his forties Matisse looked like the proverbial intellectual: high
forehead, thinning hair, quizzical mouth, keen eyes framed in a
pair of large spectacles. The trim beard streaked with gray gave
him the appearance of a minor official, a professor of mathematics
or, when he was in an affable frame of mind, a country doctor relaxing between diagnoses. In later life the beard almost vanished; the
eyes grew dimmer; the mouth thinned. But the eager speculative
look never left the artist even in his eighties. Travel delighted and
inspired him. Before he took up permanent quarters in Nice in
1917, he wintered in Morocco, and his North African sojourns are
reflected not only in a tireless succession of odalisques but in lush

variations of rich textiles, gaudy wallpapers, luminous fruits and flowers, all of them done with joyful ease, registering a tone that is nothing less than a continuing vibrato. In 1930 Matisse journeyed to Tahiti to inspect the setting which had entranced Gauguin. He also made trips to the United States, during one of which he acted as a judge in the Carnegie Exhibition.

It was not, however, until he was past sixty that Matisse was hailed as a great French classic and ranked with Cézanne, the one contemporary whom Matisse had worshiped as a young man. Yet no two painters of a period could be more dissimilar. Although Matisse never tired of painting women, he painted them without passion, even without individuality. Cézanne made his landscapes as personal as his figures; Matisse made his people even more impersonal than the landscape. Unlike Cézanne, Matisse was interested in the human body not because it represented a man or a woman, but because it offered endless opportunities for rich rhythms and multiple designs. Although Matisse placed his odalisques against brilliant backgrounds, the houris themselves are without fleshly appeal; his nudes are the most sexless of the century. "The chief aim of color," Matisse wrote in "A Painter's Notes" in *La Grande Revue* (1908), "should be to serve expression as well as possible . . . A work of art must carry in itself its complete significance and impose it upon the beholder even before he can identify the subject matter . . . What I dream of is an art of balance, of purity and serenity devoid of troubling or depressing subject matter, an art which might be for every mental worker (be he businessman or writer) like an appeasing influence, like a mental soother, something like a good armchair in which to rest from physical fatigue." While one may suspect that when he wrote this, Matisse had at least the tip of a tongue in his cheek, the expressed dream of unemotional balance is not unlike the silent credo of his paintings.

Color is the crux of Matisse's work. It is not merely the unifying agent but often, by curious repetitive devices, the pattern itself. Matisse deepened "significant form" by dispensing with perspective, spurning realism, and concentrating upon the design. He used black outlines whenever he wanted to accentuate a form; he reveled in such unorthodox combinations as orange and pink, scarlet and purple. Like the Impressionists, Matisse discarded the usual soft gradations of shading and, by abrupt contrasts of color, achieved not only a directness of design but an intensity which struck the observer with an almost physical impact. He was so intent upon design per se that he would begin a detail boldly—a hand, a foot, a flower—only to let it remain unfinished, a kind of calligraphy, meandering but meaningful.

At eighty Matisse designed and decorated an entire chapel (the *Chapelle du Rosaire des Dominicaines*)—doors, stained glass windows, stations of the cross, choir stalls, candlesticks, crucifix, tile, even the priests' chasubles—in the town of Vence, not far from his home in Nice. At eighty-three, crippled by an intestinal operation and confined to bed, he was still at work. By this time many considered him the greatest of living painters. Only the Philistines objected to his brusque transformations and distortions which at first shock but finally charm the eye. Only an occasional critic protested that his arabesques were mannered, that he escaped reality and fled from thinking by devoting himself to untroubling diagrams of devitalized women and such soothing motifs as a piece of embroidery, an interlacing of leaves, the trailing course of a tendril.

Matisse remained undisturbed by his belittlers. In an article written in his eighty-fifth year he asserted that the artist is a man who "succeeds in arranging, for their appointed end, a complex of activities of which the work of art is the outcome." Undistorted vision is one of the most important elements of what Matisse considered the "complex of activities." He went on to say that the average observer sees everything more or less distorted by acquired habits, prejudices, points of view. "The artist," he maintained, "must look at life without prejudices, as he did when he was a child. If he loses that faculty he cannot express himself in an original, that is, a personal way." He maintained that faculty until he died of a heart attack, November 3, 1954.

Even his least sympathetic critics agreed that, although Matisse chose his colors with almost perverse boldness, he used them with precision. In all the contradictions of flat color there are no clashes. Nothing is harsh or strained; everything is so straightforward as to deceive the casual eye, and what seems flat at first glance becomes suggestive, then persuasive, and finally inevitable. What Matisse has to say is said with great directness, a forthright set of conventional statements—most of them as commonplace and frankly bourgeois as the man himself. But the manner is anything but conventional, and if the subject matter is seldom challenging, Matisse makes the observer forget the subject by expressing the obvious in terms of the extraordinary.

Nikolai Lenin

[1870-1924]

"From Spark to Flame."

THE MAN known as Nikolai Lenin was christened Vladimir Ilich Ulianov. He was born in the little Russian city of Simbirsk in 1870. There is some confusion (chiefly due to the differences in the old and new Russian calendars) about the exact date of his birth, but most authorities agree on April 9. His father was Ilya Nicolaevitch Ulianov, a schoolmaster and an organizer of rural schools who had been promoted to superintendent of schools in the district of which Simbirsk was the seat. His mother, Maria Alexandrovna, daughter of a doctor, was brought up in comfort and trained in culture. She had an income from property which, with the inspector's salary, enabled the Ulianovs to live somewhat better than the families of the average bureaucrat. There were six children, of whom Vladimir was the third. The oldest child was Anna, the next was Alexander; the three youngest were Olga, Manyasha, and Dmitri.

The Ulianovs differed little from their neighbors. The growing boys and girls were as intelligent as one might have expected from the union of a teacher and a doctor's daughter, but they were not spectacularly intellectual. An academic and even a dull future might have been predicted for them when their security was suddenly threatened. Vladimir was sixteen when his father died, and although his mother's small income kept the family from actual need, the household was violently disturbed. A second tragedy, which occurred a year later, was more far-reaching in its final effects. Alexander, who had been studying science at St. Petersburg University, had become involved in a small group of student revolutionaries, common in Russia during the last half of the nineteenth century. They had plotted against the life of Tsar Alexander III, had been apprehended, and had been hanged. The name by which Alexander was known to his group had been "Lenin," and it was this *nom de guerre* which his younger brother later adopted as his own.

The double blow of death and shame broke the mother's health.

The Ulianovs were no longer socially acceptable, but Vladimir stuck to his studies so grimly that he received a gold medal upon his graduation from high school. Partly to escape the lingering opprobrium and partly to permit Vladimir to enter the university, the family moved to Kazan. There he began to study law but, within a few months, was expelled for participating in radical student activities. Denounced with thirty-eight others for sedition, he was banished to a village where, with his enormous capacity for application, he continued studying law under his own tutelage. At twenty-one he passed the examinations at St. Petersburg University and, a year later, started to practice law in Samara.

Although he was qualified to be a successful attorney, his career was not to be that of lawyer but revolutionist. He had already discovered the writings of Karl Marx; during the next few years he studied the Marxian philosophy as intensively as he had studied law, moved to St. Petersburg, and began his work as a revolutionary. With his stiff white collar surmounting a neat suit, his carefully brushed hair and trimmed Vandyke beard, he looked like an accountant, an inconspicuous merchant, a minor musician, an instructor in physics—anything but a disturber of the social order. He kept his real name for legal purposes and as a respectable front. For his propaganda work as teacher and speaker with the socialist groups in the rapidly industrializing centers he used the "underground" name of Nikolai Lenin.

Conditions in Russia had always been deplorable for large parts of the population. They were now becoming unspeakable. The Tsar's private family, as well as his "official family" of nobles, lived in reckless luxury. The wealthy farmers who owned huge tracts of land were a particularly prosperous part of the idle rich. Factories were expanding and their owners were making fortunes. On the other hand, the standard of living for the factory workers as well as the peasants was desperately low. The Tsar was known as the "Little Father," but his role was paternal only in the most repressive sense; he felt that his people were nothing more than children and punished them whenever they incurred his least displeasure. When, during the famine of 1891, many peasants died of starvation, Lenin saw that the peasantry was as much a part of the oppressed masses as the exploited workers in industry; it was his idea that the socialist state could not succeed until the peasants became the active allies of the proletariat.

At twenty-five, he was already a leading revolutionist. After a trip abroad to meet the agitator George Plekhanov, known as "the Father of Russian Socialism," he organized the Union for the Liberation of the Working Class and began the printing of its newspaper. Within a few months he was arrested, spent all of his twenty-seventh year in prison awaiting trial, studying, writing, and directing outside activities by means of a smuggled code. One of his group, Nadezhda Konstantinovna Krupskaya, was an educated middle class Russian. To facilitate the handling of secret communications, she claimed that she was Lenin's fiancée, and was allowed to visit him in prison. In February, 1897, Lenin was brought to trial and condemned to three years exile in Siberia. The sentence of three years, considered light, was because his crime was one of intention rather than committal. Some months later Nadezhda was also arrested and sentenced to exile. In the hope that she could continue her Marxist studies and activities, she again asserted that she was Lenin's fiancée, and requested the court to send her to him. The judge said that the number of exiles in Yenisei Province could not be increased with safety, but if she and Lenin were married, he would be willing to count the two as one. Lenin was twenty-eight when he married Nadezhda; her mother accompanied her into exile, and until her death, kept house for her daughter and son-in-law wherever they went. Although theirs was scarcely a love match, and although they were married by the necessity of a court order, Lenin and his wife became completely devoted to each other. She was not merely his unquestioning follower, but his always dependable partner.

Nearing thirty, Lenin finished a piece of writing started in prison: *The Development of Capitalism in Russia,* an important economic landmark. A few months later Lenin's term of exile expired, but as soon as he returned to St. Petersburg he was arrested. When he was freed, he hurried to Switzerland where, with the much older Plekhanov's endorsement, Lenin undertook the publication of a magazine called *Iskra.* It was printed in Munich; its motto was "From Spark to Flame"; and its aim was to form a centralized underground revolutionary party which would act as a spearhead against oppressive Tsarism. Realizing that the peasants' hunger for land was as important as the factory workers' need of security, Lenin planned a hegemony of the laboring class within a democratic movement. *Iskra* was smuggled into Russia, copy by copy. Working secretly and living underground became not only an elaborate technique but, to the exiled revolutionaries, a normal way of life.

During the next seventeen years, Lenin's life was a record of arrests and escapes, long concealments and sudden emergences. He lived almost all the time out of his homeland, moving from one country to another. He and his wife somehow managed to exist on the pittance he allowed himself as editor—a salary fixed at the rate paid to the cheapest worker, the least skilled printer. His clothes were always outworn, his rooms wretched, and the food inadequate. But his writings were making converts and his name was becoming known all over Russia. His pamphlets were simply written; Lenin had the genius to translate abstract ideas and complicated theories into the vocabulary of the common man. He drove home a few insistent facts: No man has a right to live by exploiting the work of another man. The worker has a claim to the results of his work. The workers were reminded of Marx's epigram that they had nothing to lose but their chains and that once they were united, their chains would drop off.

In 1902 while he was publishing *Iskra* in London, he was joined by another young revolutionary just escaped from Siberia, Leon Trotsky. Trotsky, a brilliant and dynamic speaker, became one of Lenin's most fervent supporters. A year later a difference of opinion developed into what was to become a historic split in the Russian Social-Democratic Party. Lenin wanted only active revolutionaries in the party. Trotsky believed in admitting nonactive sympathizers. Lenin won the greater amount of votes, and his group became known as *Bolsheviki,* which means the majority. The opposition, or minority members, were called *Mensheviki.*

Lenin was thirty-five when mounting unrest made Russia seem ripe for revolution. On January 9, 1905, a group of workers, led by a priest, made a pilgrimage to the Winter Palace, where the royal family was living. It was to be a quiet demonstration to show the Tsar, whom they devoutly regarded as their "Little Father," how undernourished they were and how impossible it was for them to live on the prevailing wage-scale. As they approached the Palace they were fired upon without warning by Cossack guards. Two hundred of them were killed. The news spread rapidly and helped to destroy the traditional reverence which the Russian people had for their ruler. The dependence on the "Little Father" was still further damaged when, during the same year, the military forces suffered defeat in the futile Russo-Japanese war. Strikes and uprisings led Lenin to feel that this was the right time for the masses to make themselves felt and he returned to Russia. For two years he traveled about the country, haranguing, inciting, and organizing guerrilla bands; but the Tsar placated the people by giving an elected body, the Duma, a small voice in the government. He also permitted workers to elect committees (Soviets) to petition the employers. Wages were slightly increased and hours shortened. By the end of 1907 the revolutionary fervor had waned, the trouble-makers were again in trouble, but Lenin managed to make his way through Finland to Sweden.

Living on a minute salary as chairman of the Bolshevik Party, Lenin was financially worse off than ever. He was in difficulties on all fronts: hounded by Imperial Russia, trying to resist pressure from the Mensheviks on one hand, and from the anarchists and terrorists on the other. He had lost Trotsky as his ally but he had gained two new friends: the celebrated writer, Maxim Gorky, and the tough-minded young extremist known as Joseph Stalin. Lenin was living in Paris when he wrote *Materialism and Empirio-Criticism,* a book which his appraisers have regarded with widely differing conclusions. In *A History of Modern Philosophy,* Frederick Mayer considers the book an attack against mysticism, "a most significant contribution to dialectical materialism . . . which does not regard nature as inert and, hence, is not undermined by the discoveries of quantum physics, which reduces matter to forms of energy. Lenin thus made it clear that dialectical materialism should not be identified with eighteenth-century views of matter, which were impregnated with incorrect scientific concepts, and is not primarily concerned with the essence of the material world . . . It is not the contemplation of the objective world which counts; rather it is the control through which we channel the powers of nature and make them useful to mankind." On the other hand, in his biography of Lenin, Valeriu Marcu calls the book "a cauldron of invective and constructive thought—a book in which profundity alternates with mere abuse . . . If anyone else had written it, no one would remember it."

The Lenins moved from Paris to Cracow, Poland, nearer home and their followers. Nadezhda broke down while helping Lenin with a series of complicated statistics, and underwent a serious operation. However, she not only recovered but resumed her difficult and unremitting work. Although the doctors warned that her heart had been damaged and that continued activity would kill her, she survived her husband by fifteen years. In August, 1914, the Lenins were in Galicia, a part of Austria, when Austria declared war against Russia. Lenin was arrested, but when it was proved that he was scarcely a spy for the Russian government, he was released. He moved to Switzerland.

The First World War was a blow to international socialism. According to Marxism, such a war would solidify the workers' struggle in each capitalist country. The workers would unite to oppose participation in the conflict and move toward revolutionary civil war. Nothing of the sort happened. The German socialists supported their country's military aims; Plekhanov broke completely with Lenin and urged that the Russian socialists help the Russian war effort. Lenin was one of the few who stood firm. He called upon the proletariat of each belligerent nation to oppose the triumph of nationalism and work for the ultimate victory of socialism. The only group that stood with Lenin was the Bolsheviks and, as a consequence, the five Bolshevik members of the Duma were exiled.

Realizing that international revolution was out of the question, Lenin summoned all his energies to prepare the Russian proletariat for the role they were to play in their own country. He was helped by the debased conditions within Russia. The country was unable to maintain its army properly; the soldiers were ill-clothed and half-fed. Profiteers made incalculable fortunes while working conditions were forced back to the lowest pre-reform levels. Hysteria ruled. It was even rumored that Tsar Nicholas was trying to arrange for a separate peace with Germany. This alarmed the court aristocrats who were not only making money because of the war, but who felt safer with the army on the battlefields rather than with restless and possibly rebellious troops at home. Their dissatisfaction resulted in the murder by three nobles on December 16, 1916, of the ex-monk Rasputin, the recognized "power behind the throne."

The demoralization was now complete. The rapidly unfolding drama of revolution was building to a climax. On February 23, 1917, women workers in the St. Petersburg mills went on strike. Men workers poured into the streets to join them. Most industry and all traffic stopped. The police charged the crowds and fighting began to rage. The army was called out. But the army garrison and the Cossack troops began to fight on the side of the people against the police. At the end of the fifth day, the people had triumphed and a full scale rebellion had ended.

The long-anticipated revolution had occurred, but there was no organization to guide it. When the workers and soldiers elected a group of representatives as their Soviet, the Duma stepped in and offered to work with them. When, however, a provisional government was set up, no member of the Soviet was included. One of the ministers, Kerensky, became president, forced the Tsar's abdication, and pledged his government to continue the war on the side of the Allies.

Communications were so bad that Lenin did not even hear about the revolution until a month after it had happened. He determined to return to Russia, but no one of the allied nations, including his own country, wanted Lenin back home. He was finally able to get through the enemy territory of Germany only because the Germans knew that he was opposed to Russia's continuing the conflict. As soon as he arrived at St. Petersburg, he attacked the provisional government because of its compromises, and kept calling for Russia's withdrawal from the war. The people echoed his protests. There were demonstrations and fresh uprisings. In reprisal, the Kerensky government charged that Lenin was collaborating with Germany, and Lenin again went into hiding and waited for a final recall. A revolt on the part of General Kornilov, who hoped to form a military dictatorship, weakened Kerensky's control and increased the strength of the Bolsheviks. When the Bolsheviks seized a palace in St. Petersburg and set up headquarters there, Lenin returned, estimated the forces involved, and decided to strike at once. The event known as the October Revolution occurred October 25, 1917, by the Julian calendar reckoning. By our calendar it began on November 7. The date marked the first convening of the Congress of Soviets from all over Russia, and it was in their name that Lenin seized power. The Central Committee of the Bolshevik Party, of which Stalin was a member, was the organizing unit. Trotsky, who had broken with the Mensheviks and had joined Lenin, was directing the military offensive. There was some street fighting, but "the ten days that shook the world" were accompanied by less bloodshed than any previous revolution of such proportions.

Lenin's victory did not change either the man or his habits. He continued to live in surroundings that were not only plain but austere. Marcu quotes one who visited him after he had been a dictator for three years: "I saw more than one workman's home which was more richly furnished . . . I found Lenin's wife and sister at supper—as modest a meal as that of any average Soviet official at the time. It consisted of tea, black bread, butter, and cheese." Lenin was not an impressive-looking man. He was below middle height; his features were plebian and strongly Slavonic. Only his massive forehead gave him a look of power. In her biography of Lenin, Nina Brown Baker describes him on his return to Russia in 1917 as "a bald little man in a shabby coat, somewhat paunchy, with a reddish beard. He was forty-seven years old, and looked older. He could scarcely have seemed more commonplace until he smiled. Everyone who knew Lenin spoke of the way his smile transformed his homely features."

Lenin proceeded to the construction of the socialist state by dividing the land among the peasants. At the same time all industries, financial institutions, national resources and utilities ceased to be privately owned. The name of the Bolshevik Party was officially changed to the Communist Party, and the Marxist doctrine was incorporated in two slogans: "Production for use, not for profit." "If a man will not work, he shall not eat." On January 7, 1918, Lenin abolished the constituent assembly and established the dictatorship of the proletariat—a step toward the theoretical though by no means actual abolition of class divisions. On March 15, 1918, Russia entered negotiations with Germany, came to terms at Brest-Litovsk, and withdrew from the war.

A treaty had been signed, but there was no peace. There was internal as well as external opposition. The *kulaks,* owners of large farmlands, resisted the proletarian dictatorship, and there ensued a period of relentless bloodshed and ruthless extermination. The *Cheka,* the secret police set up by the Soviets, discovered a plot to do away with the top officials. The conspirators were caught and executed after a secret trial—the first of a long series of such procedures—and there began what became known as the Red Terror. External opposition came from the Allies, whose cause Russia had deserted, and who supported various moves to overthrow the new regime. Czechoslovakian troops seized Russian land and promised to restore the throne to the Tsar. Faced with this rather remote threat, the Soviet of the country place where the royal family were interned acted without investigation or compunction. The Tsar, the Tsarina, and their five children were brutally murdered. Civil war broke out. The Red Guards were challenged by the White Guards, formed mainly of military school cadets, young members of the upper middle classes. For a while it seemed that the counter-revolutionists might be successful, but in 1921 they were decisively defeated by the conscripted Red Army.

It was not until 1921 that Lenin could begin to build the economic and social structure of which he had dreamed. Inaugurating the New Economic Policy, he found it necessary to allow for private industry in the distribution of goods. At a time when his backward country was still dependent on manpower, he drafted a plan for a vast electrification of Russia, stating that "Socialism is a Soviet government—electrified." He stressed the need for permitting national groups free development within the country and applied principles of national self-determination to colonial peoples. The Russian Orthodox Church ceased to be the state religion. Marriage and divorce, formerly under the tax-supported Church, became the province of the government.

In 1922, when reconstruction was recognizably under way, Lenin was unmistakably exhausted. Sclerosis of the cerebral arteries caused a slight apoplectic stroke. A few months later a second stroke partially paralyzed him. Brief periods of improvement were followed by increasingly alarming relapses, and on January 21, 1924, in the model town named after his friend Gorky, he died. He had transferred the nation's capital to Moscow, and it was there they buried him, in a tomb by the wall of the Kremlin.

Like Gandhi, Lenin was driven by an unwavering singleness of purpose. Unlike Gandhi, however, Lenin was in love with an idea rather than with the people who were to benefit from that idea. Gandhi was a compassionate and saintly spirit, irrevocably attached to the least of human beings; Lenin was a coldly scientific calculator who could not be bound by personal attachments. Even when his program was at the point of failure, Gandhi found it impossible to sacrifice a single individual; in order to carry out *his* program, Lenin was willing to liquidate anyone. "Lenin's conception of a ravaging and ravaged world," wrote Robert Heilbroner in *The Worldly Philosophers,* "internally corrupt and externally predatory, is still the official Soviet explanation of the world in which we live. Its validity was again affirmed by Stalin in 1952." Marx had theorized that the state would ultimately "wither away," but Lenin, the theorist whom conditions had changed into the man of action, knew that the end would come only after a series of long and lethal blows. His writings have been variously interpreted; his influence is part of an acrimonious and endless controversy. Unlike other dictators, he was not a power-hungry fanatic or a possessed paranoiac. Opposed to one-man rule, he seized power not to enlarge his stature or aggrandize himself, but to make people take power in their own hands. "The word must be," he said, "power to the Soviets; land to the peasants; bread to the hungry; and peace to the peoples."

Georges Rouault

[1 8 7 1 -   ]

*"The brutal and the breath-taking, the
vulgar and the pitiful."*

THE MOST deeply religious artist of our time was, with the exception of Van Gogh, the most violent painter of the last hundred years. Although in the tradition of the great experimentalists, the canvases of Georges Rouault were a galvanic contrast to such Impressionists as Cézanne and Renoir. Where Cézanne limited himself to a generally light palette, abjuring the bitumens and heavy ochres, Rouault piled on his colors in layers of bold reds, chromes and browns, intensifying them with broad black outlines. Where Renoir bathed his subjects in a warm and limpid loveliness, Rouault exposed them fiercely with every extremity of emphasis from turbulent horror to agonized mysticism.

It has been maintained that the sense of tension in Rouault's paintings may have stemmed from the circumstances of his birth —he was born May 27, 1871, in Paris while that city was being bombarded by the enemies of the Commune, and it is said that his mother was driven to a cellar during her labor pains. "A less romantic but perhaps more pertinent fact," wrote James Thrall Soby in *Georges Rouault: Paintings and Prints,* "is that he grew up under the affectionate eye of a grandfather who admired Callot, Rembrandt, Courbet, Manet, and owned lithographs by Daumier . . . This grandfather desperately wanted Rouault to become an artist." Roualt's parents were hard pressed—his father was a woodfinisher in a piano factory—and at fourteen he was apprenticed to a maker of stained glass. "My work," wrote Rouault, "consisted in supervising the firing, and sorting the little pieces of glass that fell out of the windows they brought us to repair. The latter task inspired me with an enduring passion for old stained glass."

While employed as apprentice, still in his teens, Rouault attended evening classes at the *Ecole Nationale des Arts Décoratifs;* at twenty he enrolled in the *Ecole des Beaux-Arts.* Here he came under the influence of Gustave Moreau, a second-rate romantic artist. But Moreau was an unusually tolerant teacher who never forced

his sentiments or his style on his young students and encouraged
them to seek anything but superficial values. "Art is a furious
tracking down of the inner feelings solely by means of plastic expression," Moreau insisted, and Rouault was quick to respond to the
"furious tracking down" and give tumultuous play to "the inner
feelings." Rouault became Moreau's favorite pupil; the relations between the two men remained close; and when the teacher died in
1898 Rouault was appointed director of the Moreau Museum.

During his early years as a student, however, Rouault schooled
himself in the classics. Those who still complain about Rouault's
"anatomical defects" and his "inability to draw" should examine the
carefully modeled studio pieces produced in his twenties, the
graphic self-portrait done at twenty-five, the Rembrandt-like
"Quarry" painted at twenty-six.

At thirty Rouault already looked like an ascetic. The beard which,
in the mid-twenties, had been softly curled, was hard clipped; the
once amiable eyes were coldly questioning; the mouth was no
longer mild but grimly set. He was obviously unhappy, and his de-
jection expressed itself in a series of depressing landscapes, dull
blue in tone and heavy in spirit. It was about this time (in 1903)
that Rouault met Léon Bloy, the dedicated and impassioned Catholic writer. Bloy's combination of spiritual yearning and despair fascinated Rouault. Rouault also was repelled by the modern world and,
like Bloy, longed, "at a time when everything seemed lost, to
thrust at God the outcry of dereliction and anxiety for the orphaned multitude which the Father in his celestial heights seems
to be abandoning and which no longer has the strength even to die
bravely." He began to spread upon canvas a gospel of terror and
disaster. Determined to portray the hideousness of evil, he devoted
himself to studies of ugly prostitutes, loathsome sensualists, male
as well as female, hideous nude odalisques and repulsive sirens,
cheap charlatans, tired and tragic clowns. Confronted with the
visualization of his own logic, Bloy was shocked. He had hoped that
his friend and disciple would become a modern Fra Angelico, translating the soulfulness of the men of the Renaissance into terms of
the contemporary world. Instead this artist, wrote Bloy, "whom
one would have believed capable of painting seraphim, seems to
think of nothing but atrocities and vengeful caricatures."

But, though Rouault and Bloy remained friends until the author's
death in 1917, the painter never altered the fixity of his vision. The
"atrocities" seemed even more atrocious when they were first ex-

hibited in the *Salon d'Automne,* of which Rouault was one of the founders and which was subsequently dubbed the "Salon des Fauves." The "Fauves" or Wild Beasts included Matisse, Derain, and Friesz, as well as Rouault, and the public, faced with radical innovations, reacted in the customary manner: the work was regarded as obscure, obscene, insincere, insane, and generally incomprehensible. Rouault was, perhaps, the most scorned, especially for the double darkness of his tone and mood. The condemnation grew more severe when, a few years later, he exhibited at the *Salon des Indépendants.* Bloy wrote to him: "I have only two words to say to you, after which you will no longer be for me anything more than a lost friend. First, you are exclusively interested in the ugly; you have a vertigo of hideousness. Secondly, if you were a man of prayer, an obedient soul, you could not paint these horrible canvases." No one saw that Rouault's "degrading" canvases were a deep complaint, a protest to man and a "thrust at God" against human degradation and the defeat of the spirit. No one understood that his tortured nightmare faces were not drawn with cynicism or loathing but with an "inner necessity" of pity, a compassion for all the wretchedness of the modern world.

In his late thirties Rouault seemed poised for a great leap. His style alternated between a harsh satire, as shown in a series of bitter revelations of judges as miscarriers of justice, and a casual tenderness, evidenced in pictures of ordinary people, peasants, bathers, everyday women and children. The color deepened; the planes were accentuated by heavy black contours. The "stained glass method," a reminder of Rouault's original trade, manifested itself with power and persuasiveness.

That method became Rouault's identifying style. It marked the world-weary clowns painted in his mid-forties, the magnificent self-portrait painted at fifty-eight, the pictures of Christ, the crucifixions, and other religious compositions of his sixties. He did not confine himself to canvas. He made more than sixty large prints— there were to be a hundred—for André Suarès' *Miserere et Guerre;* a portfolio of lithographs, personal portraits and circus figures, for the publisher E. Frapier; illustrations for a book of his own poems, *Paysages Légendaires;* more than one hundred wood-engravings, as well as twenty-two etchings, for *Les Réincarnations du Père Ubu* by the art dealer, Ambroise Vollard; designs for wood tapestries; settings for a ballet, *Le Fils Prodigue (The Prodigal Son)* with music by Prokofiev. Age did not soften his style. The

"Biblical Landscape" and "The Infant Christ Among the Doctors" painted at seventy-five are among Rouault's outstanding accomplishments; they even show a gain in reverential feeling without the loss of his characteristically somber intensity.

More fortunate than most painters, Rouault lived to see the power of his fierce and almost fanatic unloveliness acknowledged by critics and collectors all over the world. His extraordinary concentration was pithily summarized in 1947 by James Thrall Soby: "A devout Catholic and devotional painter in a period when artists more often have run the gamut of anti-religious feeling from indifference to irreverence; a painter of sin and redemption in the face of prevailing estheticism and counter-estheticism; an artist with a limited vision of unlimited ferocity in contrast to many other leading painters who have scanned and pivoted but seldom stared fixedly for long."

If Rouault is to be compared to any other contemporary artist, it must be to a poet rather than to a painter. In his harsh juxtaposition of the brutal and the breath-taking, of the vulgar and the pitiful, Rouault is kin to the T.S. Eliot of "The Waste Land" and the Sweeney poems; in his apocalyptic and darkly devotional creations he suggests the later Eliot who wrote "Ash-Wednesday," "Journey of the Magi," and "Four Quartets." Like Eliot, Rouault progressed from driving desperation to desperate belief. Nothing is placidly resolved; sin and expiation play a continual counterpart; all—clowns and Christs, places no less than people—are burdened with a terrible sense of suffering. But for Rouault, as for Eliot, the brutality compels our pity, and in the suffering is our salvation.

Marcel Proust

[1 8 7 1 - 1 9 2 2]

*"Little boy lost . . . torn between integrity
and expediency."*

A FRAIL ECCENTRIC, riddled with suffocating allergies, Marcel
Proust kept himself alive by drugs and will power to finish
what is perhaps the longest narrative in existence and certainly one of the greatest novels of the twentieth century. Except
for a few youthful essays, *A la Recherche du Temps Perdu* (usually translated as *Remembrance of Things Past* but literally
In Search of Time Lost) is his one book or, rather, it is a single
interlocked volume of sixteen books, part fiction, part autobiography, and a portrait-panorama of an entire society.

Proust was born July 10, 1871, in Auteuil, then a fashionable
rural suburb of Paris. The family was comfortably well-to-do, in
the upper brackets of the middle class. His father, Dr. Adrien
Proust, was not only a practicing physician but a professor at the
Paris School of Medicine and head of the French medical health
service. His mother was Jeanne Weil, a beautiful and cultured Alsatian Jewess, who adored and spoiled her worshiping and completely dependent child. There were two sons. Robert, the younger,
derived his robust health, profession, and plain common sense from
his father; Marcel, two years older, inherited the nerves and hyper-
sensitivity of his mother. At nine Marcel suffered a choking spell;
the attack was diagnosed as asthma and subsequent events aggravated the illness. Asthma is often associated with psychological
disturbances, perhaps even resulting from them; Proust became a
chronic asthmatic, a semi-invalid who remained—or determined to
remain—a sick man until he died. He clung passionately to his
mother; one of the most poignant moments in *Swann's Way,* the
first installment of *Remembrance of Things Past,* is the fierce depression of the author as a little boy whose mother has forgotten to
give him the customary goodnight kiss and who, lying awake,
plans to send a surreptitious note to be slipped in her hand during
dinner. The "Overture" pictures him lying disconsolately "in the
shroud of my nightshirt," in a torture of resentment and remem-

brance. "So much did I love that goodnight that I reached the stage of hoping that it would come as late as possible, so as to prolong the time of respite during which Mamma would not yet have appeared. Sometimes when, after kissing me, she opened the door to go, I longed to call her back, to say to her 'Kiss me just once more.' But I knew that then she would look displeased, for the concession which she made to my wretchedness and agitation always annoyed my father, who thought such ceremonies absurd . . . And to see her look displeased destroyed all the sense of tranquillity she had brought me a moment before, when she bent her loving face down over my bed, and held it out to me like a Host, for an act of Communion in which my lips might drink deeply the sense of her real presence, and with it the power to sleep."

There was little difference between the "I" of the autobiographical novel and the "Marcel" of actual life. When he was adult, Proust often addressed his mother in the same injured and agonized tone of the hurt little boy. "The truth is," he wrote in one of the letters to his mother, after she had reproved him for leading a life which was not only frivolous but dangerous, "as soon as I feel better, my kind of life, which helps to make me better, exasperates you . . . This is not the first time. I caught cold the other evening—if it turns to asthma, which will most likely happen, I am sure that you will be nice to me again. But it is sad not to have affection and good health at the same time." The note of grievance often mingles with a confusion of subdued hysteria and self-pity.

Regarded by his father as a weakling who had disappointed him and a prodigy whom he could not understand, Marcel was brought up and educated almost entirely by his mother. She tried to strengthen his morale by prodding him to work—he was lazy about lessons—but whenever she scolded him, Marcel would have another prolonged coughing spell, and his mother would be compelled to relinquish the role of preceptor for that of nurse. He retreated to the library, where he translated life into literature; it was said that he absorbed books and read people. He looked forward with special eagerness to the periods when the family summered in his father's native Illiers, which became the Combray of Proust's half-fictional world, and the coastal town of Cabourg, which was metamorphosed into Balbec. Meanwhile, he underwent an irregular schooling. He attended the Lycée Condorcet, where he discovered the social philosophy of Saint-Simon and dreamed of becoming the critic-chronicler of the society of his own times. His father urged him to train for a career as diplomat; but after he had served a token term in the conscript army, Proust evaded the issue by registering simultaneously in three institutions: the School of Political Science, the Law School, and the Sorbonne. At the Sorbonne he was greatly influenced by Henri Bergson's emphasis on the imagination and intuition, and when Bergson married Proust's cousin, Mlle. Neuberger, the novelist was proud to be best man.

At twenty-one Proust was a debonair and popular young man-about-town. Like his mother, he was olive-skinned with shining black hair and heavy-lidded dark eyes, "meltingly expressive." "A continual smile, amused and inviting," writes Léon Pierre-Quint, "hesitated and then fixed itself motionless on his lips . . . He gave one the impression of an overgrown child, indolent and over-observant." Delicately built, his shy and effeminate manners made him a favorite with the somewhat older ladies who alternately teased and mothered him. His immediate circle revolved about the arts, but he determined to enter the exclusive aristocratic world as well. He made his social debut in the salon of Madame Geneviève Strauss who, before the premature death of Bizet, had been the composer's wife, and she introduced him to other cultural arbiters. Among those who attracted him particularly was Madame Arman de Caillavet, the beloved friend, traveling companion, and provocative inspirer of Anatole France. Her daughter-in-law, Jeanne Maurice Pouquet, whose first husband was Gaston de Caillavet, sympathetically but adroitly pictured Proust as a young dilettante in her *Anatole France and His Muse:* "The frequenters of Mme. Arman de Caillavet's salon saw Marcel very often on Sundays, his head thrown back and hanging on his shoulder, sitting, almost lying, in one of the deep lounges . . . He always used to sink into a heap, as if overcome by a perpetual lassitude, which the future proved, alas, not to be a mere pose. Although his face was serious and his great brown eyes were melancholy, his very white teeth lit up his pale countenance, and his laughter broke forth on the slightest pretext. He was handsome, charming, and nice. This last epithet, which he used so often himself, best describes his character, his ways, his manner, his greeting, his willingness, and his friendship. Everything in him was nice. How good, how sensitive he was! How grateful for the slightest service, the tiniest attention! And how frightfully and unreasonably sad he would become if he were hurt, or if he even thought he had reason to feel hurt!" He liked to associate with young girls as well as boys —forbidden to play anything as strenuous as tennis, he delighted to plan their picnics—but no girl ever took his attentions seriously and his male comrades merely flattered him when they pretended to be jealous.

If, due to his fixed affection for his mother, his emotional life was ambivalent, there was no uncertainty about the life of the intellect. He knew he would be a writer even before he began to write. In his early twenties he became a member of a group which, cultivated in Madame Strauss's salon, flowered into a little magazine, *Le Banquet*. It had some of the preciousness and a few of the pretensions of England's *The Yellow Book;* Proust contributed a few pieces in the affected style of the period. He also contributed journalistic items, social notes and gossip, to *Le Figaro*. The pieces had little literary distinction but they were outlets for his love of little scandals, his delight in high-toned if malicious badinage, and his first experiments in juxtaposing the haut monde and the demi-monde.

He was twenty-five when he published his first volume, *Les Plaisirs et les Jours,* a collection of fragile essays, poems, reveries, and impressionistic sketches. To his contemporaries the most important part of the book was the preface, which Madame Caillavet had prevailed upon Anatole France to write; in it France referred to the youthful Proust as "a guileless Petronius." However, to a student of Proust today the most revealing thing in the volume is the dedication: "To my friend, Willie Heath, who died in Paris, October 3rd, 1893." Proust was twenty-two at the time of the young Scot's death, but his grief was still great when, three years later, he described the companion whom he used to meet in the Bois: "In the mornings we used to meet; you, having seen me coming, waiting for me under the trees—standing there, resting, like one of those young lords Van Dyck liked to paint. You seemed to share their pensive elegance . . . But if the gracefulness of your pride belonged to the art of Van Dyck, you owed even more to Vinci, through the mysterious intensity of your spiritual life. Often, your finger uplifted, your eyes impenetrable and smiling in the face of some enigma you would not reveal, you appeared to me like the young John the Baptist by Leonardo. At that time we had a dream, almost a plan, of living more and more closely with one another, surrounded by understanding and magnanimous men and women, sheltered by them from the vulgar barbs of wickedness and stupidity . . . Too feeble to desire the good, too respectable to enjoy evil fully, knowing only suffering, I have been able to speak of them with enough pity to purify these little sketches."

Of equal significance is a passage in which Proust compared himself to Noah in the ark, and, by a surprising association of ideas, saw a relation between his dead friend and his mother, the dove who, when he was ill and the world was dark, returned to reassure him. But when he was well, his mother failed to beat her wings and hover over him. "One has to start to live again, to turn outwards from oneself, to hear harder words than those of my mother—even worse, hers, always so sweet until then, when they became stamped with the severity of life which she had to teach me . . . 'Grace' of illness—the gentle faithfulness of a mother and of a friend which so often seemed like the very face of our own sorrow, or like the protection which our weakness demanded, but which ceased on the threshold of convalescence—I suffered so often when I felt you so far from me, all you exiled descendants of the dove of the ark."

Before he was thirty Proust showed self-destructive tendencies. Almost defeated by a hopeless dichotomy, he was torn between integrity and expediency. On the one hand he desired to speak and write frankly; on the other, he was aware of the need for concealment. The struggle between what he wanted to disclose freely and what he had to hide from the public, his parents, and even himself, made the daily adjustments increasingly hazardous. There were times when it was literally difficult for him to breathe. With the death of his father in 1903 and that of his mother two years later he grew more hypochondriacal and unhappy. His mother's death was a blow from which, as a person, he never recovered. "When she died," wrote Charlotte Haldane in her study, *Marcel Proust,* "he was orphaned at the age of thirty-four, an age at which a normal adult has long outgrown the terrifying loneliness of knowing himself to be an orphan. At the onset of full maturity Marcel's reaction to the loss of his mother was no different from what it might have been had she died during his childhood or adolescence. He was, and remained until the end of his days, a little boy lost." He never forgot or forgave her; she was the dove, the consoling, hopeful messenger, who had left him hopelessly alone. Her death made any possible relation to any other woman impossible; yet although he shrank from acknowledging it, the loss was his liberation. Fastening the overgrown boy to her image forever, she freed the writer.

Proust was now ready to start his major work. He had insinu-
ated himself into the graces of high society. His charm and affability, abetted by a reputation as the author of pleasant trifles,
brought him to the attention of Count Robert de Montesquiou, the
degenerate fashion-plate of the day, to whom he humbled himself,
and Princesse Mathilde, Napoleon III's sister, at whose feet he literally knelt and whose toes he kissed. He did not stop at servility if
it served his purpose. Inordinately ambitious and extraordinarily
curious, Proust observed everything and forgot nothing. The memories of a desolate child grew into a saga of universal decay and
disintegration. The aimless hours and the magnificent moments, the
slyly malicious rumors and the frankly sordid liaisons, the innocently virtuous and the cynically vicious, were impartially joined.
Imperceptibly they changed proportions, transformed into a vast
study of the breaking down of barriers between the classes, the
slow interpenetration of the vigorous bourgeoisie and the decadent
aristocracy. With the merest show of disguise, Proust put all the
people he knew into *Remembrance of Things Past*. The infamous
Count Robert de Montesquiou was the model for the sinister Baron
Palamède de Charlus—both were absurdly boastful of their lineage,
frankly perverted, and careless about their indiscriminate homosexuality. Charles Haas, the banker-friend of the family, became
the mysterious, much-enduring, and admirable Charles Swann.
Proust's housekeeper, Céleste Albaret, was the prototype for the
knowing peasant-servant, Françoise. Proust denied that these, as
well as his other characters, were taken from life and maintained
that they were all composites; but there is little doubt that the portraits were drawn, retouched, possibly distorted, from live figures.
Praised for the exactness of his minute details, Proust refused to
accept the compliment. "Even those who were favorably impressed," he wrote, "congratulated me on the 'microscopic' thoroughness with which I had discovered them [the details] when, on
the contrary, I had used a telescope to reveal things that only appeared to be so very small, because they were at a great distance
and were, in fact, each a world."

There is only one character which is never convincing. The
girl Albertine, with whom the narrator is agonizingly in love,
eludes the reader for the same reason that she eluded her author.
Intended to be an enigma, she is merely a synthetic substitute. Albertine is portrayed as a shadowy Lesbian, accepting her lover's
gifts, his protection, and his home. but betraying him, chafing at

his possessiveness and cheating him at every opportunity. If one imagines the original Albertine a male homosexual instead of a Lesbian, Proust's failure becomes comprehensible if not clear. "The legend is by now pretty well established," writes Charlotte Haldane, "that she was, in fact, a boy, or a young man, with whom the narrator may have had an emotional relationship." Since most of Proust's characters were composite portraits, it is possible that there was more than one "Albert." But when we remember that the fictitious Albertine was killed in a riding accident, an essay Proust wrote in 1919 has more than a little relevance. Part of the essay refers to Agostinelli, Proust's chauffeur (later his secretary) and contains this footnote: "I did not foresee that seven or eight years later this young man would ask to be allowed to type one of my books, would learn to fly under the name of 'Marcel Swann,' in which his friendship chose to combine my Christian name with the name of one of my characters, and that, at the age of twenty-six, he would be killed in an airplane crash."

Remembrance of Things Past has been characterized as a novel that was written to explain why it was written. In a sense this is true, for Proust was preoccupied with what was to be both a personal confession and a social criticism. The critic had to justify the obsequious climber; the snob had to be transcended by the satirist. Proust began his mammoth novel a year after his mother's death, when he was thirty-five, worked at it until the day of his death, seventeen years later. It took him almost seven years to finish the first fifteen hundred pages. No magazine would serialize it; no publisher would consider printing it. Finally, Proust paid a small and almost unknown publisher to issue the first part, and *Du Côté de Chez Swann (Swann's Way)* appeared in 1913. It was scarcely noticed by the reviewers. Five years were spent on the next installment, *A l'Ombre des Jeunes Filles en Fleurs (Within a Budding Grove)*, which, unlike the first and finer section, aroused the readers, captivated the critics, and won its author the Goncourt Prize. In the four remaining years of his life Proust finished *Le Côté de Guermantes (The Guermantes Way)*, *Sodome et Gomorrhe (Cities of the Plain)*, *La Prisonnière (The Captive)*, *Albertine Disparue (The Sweet Cheat Gone)* and *Le Temps Retrouvé (The Past Recaptured)*—the last three, comprising two volumes each, appearing posthumously.

Remembrance of Things Past includes many characters and multiple conflicts building two broad themes. The first is the rise and fall of a society, an end-of-the-century loosening of inflexible codes, and the dissolving of social strata. This theme is emphasized by the intermixture of the Guermantes (the aristocracy), the Swanns (the comfortable and intellectual middle class), and the Verdurins (the persistent and powerful new-rich). The second and more symbolic theme is man's struggle against Time—hence the general title: *In Search of Time Lost.* Wordsworth declared that poetry was emotion remembered in tranquillity. Proust found that not only poetry but reality was an experience relived in the memory; reality was not so much the event as the reanimating flow between the past and the present. The last few pages of *The Past Recaptured* (or, as it is sometimes called, *Time Regained*) furnish the key: "It was the idea of incorporated time, of the years, past, but not separated from ourselves, that I wanted to bring out strongly in my book." Proust believed that men loom considerably larger in Time than they do in Space; their present is unalterably shaped by the past. His characters do not "grow" in the ordinary sense of the verb; they develop and unfold, conditioned not so much by varying circumstances as by predetermined reflexes, previous patterns of associations. The most vivid insights in Proust's work do not rise from wisdom or applied intelligence, but from chance sensations and their buried associations—a "madeleine," a little cake dipped in a cup of tea; the sight of a church steeple; the look of three old trees; the accidental tinkling of a spoon against a plate; the blow of a hammer testing the wheels of a railway train. Proust's subconscious memory was the means by which he triumphed over the obliterating power of Time. Examining himself, Proust finally realized why, no longer troubled by his self-contradictions, he was "indifferent to the vicissitudes of the future." As he wrote in *Time Regained:* ". . . the being within me sensed what it had in common in former days and now, sensed its extra-temporal character, a being which only appeared, when through the medium of the identity of past and present, it found itself in the only setting in which it could exist and enjoy the essence of things, that is, outside Time."

Proust has been compared to Fabre because he analyzed human society as Fabre studied insect societies; to Bergson because of his preoccupation with Time; and to Joyce because of his explorations of the subconscious. But, unlike Fabre, Proust was not only an annotating observer but an analytical commentator. Unlike Bergson,

Proust regarded Time as a destructive rather than a creative force. Unlike Joyce, who is subjective, Proust is objective; in contrast to Joyce's technique, Proust's associations are not "free" but tightly linked in a long chain of memories. *Remembrance of Things Past* is, first and last, a uniquely expanding autobiography which is a masterpiece of sensibility.

During the writing of his major work, Proust immured himself in neurasthenic seclusion. Street noises, pollen, dust, even the light of day affected his nerves so disastrously that he spent most of his hours in a room lined with sound-proof cork battens and with shutters closed against the sun. Windows were never opened; steam heat was never permitted; when women occasionally visited him, his servant saw to it that they had neither flowers nor perfume. He slept fully clothed in winter; even in warm weather he wore sweaters and mufflers in bed, as well as stockings, nightcap, and gloves. The room was always thick with the smoke of fumigation. When Proust moved from the family home, he "emigrated" to a flat on the fourth floor of an old house. The place was dark, but darkness suited his recessive nature. It looked, said his most scrupulous biographer, Léon Pierre-Quint, "like a servant's room . . . He hoped soon to move; he said he was merely camping there. But he was never to leave this strange and hostile abode. He never managed even to get his books out of storage. In the salon, the chairs were covered with dust-cloths. A chandelier stood in the middle of the floor. He remained in bed for longer and longer periods; the bed was never made. Medicine bottles and empty jars were everywhere, mixed up with masses of manuscript. Old newspapers littered the floor. Amongst all this appalling disorder were the twenty large notebooks, piled on a table, which contained the last installments of his work."

Once in a while Proust ventured out at night, for the night air seemed to affect him less harmfully, but after a few brief dissipations, he scurried back to his dismal room with relief. Living on a diet of anodynes and false stimulants, his condition grew rapidly worse. He had to take narcotics in order to rest, and after veronal had put him to sleep for three days, caffein and adrenalin were required to keep him awake. At fifty-one, he contracted pneumonia, but he would not summon a doctor. His brother, Dr. Robert Proust, had to force his way in to attend him. Proust refused to talk to him and brushed aside the medicaments, moaning that he had work to do. His last hour was devoted to proofreading. He particularly wanted to make some changes in his description of the dying writer, Bergotte, because, he said, "I have several retouchings to make, now that I find myself in the same predicament." As he gave the episode its last fatal touch, the amending pencil fell from his hands and he died, November 18, 1922.

Theodore Dreiser

[1 8 7 1 - 1 9 4 5]

*"He had no talent, but a great deal of
genius."*

O NE OF the most censored and suppressed of American novelists, Theodore Dreiser was decried and defended with almost hysterical zeal. Two eminent firms refused to bring
out his books after they had contracted to publish them; other publishers were prevailed upon to reject his manuscripts without reading them. A writer who seems merely dogged and somewhat dull to
readers of today's high-pitched and swift-paced fiction, Dreiser was
treated as though he were a disgraceful exhibitionist, an insidiously
evil influence, whose banned books were surreptitiously read as
pieces of subversive pornography. He began as a doubting, defenseless boy and, until the end of his life, remained confused by "the
brittle cruelty of life." His very confusions fumbled their way into
a series of books which, ungainly and frequently malformed, transfixed an epoch and made a literature of insecurity.

Christened Theodore Herman Albert Dreiser, he was born August 27, 1871, in Terre Haute, Indiana, in what was supposed to
be a haunted house. Since he was alarmingly small and sickly, his
superstitious mother summoned a neighboring crone, purported
to have the powers of a witch, to save her son. The conjuration had
to be done by stealth, for his father, who had fled Germany in his
twenties to avoid conscription, was a strict Catholic. John Paul
Dreiser was a failure. Once a fairly prosperous manager of a mill,
he was reduced to the status of a day laborer who had trouble finding odd jobs, while his Mennonite wife ran a boarding house and
took in washing. The children—Theodore was the twelfth of thirteen—lived on fried potatoes and cornmeal mush; they learned to
steal coal from the railroads; they were usually without shoes. Delivering bundles of laundry which he could scarcely carry was only
one of Theodore's childhood chores and, long before he was aware
of bitterness, he could not help but contrast his family's grinding
poverty with the comforts all about him. The contrasts were accentuated by his older brothers, Paul and Rome, who were drifting

about the country and whose occasional visits were marked with swaggering stories of a gay and irresponsible world, a world to which his sisters were only too eager to succumb. The father thundered, railed against his daughters and reproached his wife; but Theodore's mother, whom he remembered as "thoughtful, solicitous, wise, and above all, tender and helpful," defended the children, the more so since the father did nothing to protect them.

It was his father who, in a desperate effort to save young Theodore from sinful pleasures, sent him to a parochial school. The religious training to which the boy was subjected was not a success. He feared the black-clothed priests, shrank from the grim classrooms, and dreaded the ritual. When the family moved from Terre Haute to other towns in Indiana, he reluctantly continued to attend Catholic schools until the family went to Chicago. There was no time for childhood play. Before he was seventeen, he worked as a dishwasher in a dingy restaurant, stove cleaner, car-checker in the train yards, clerk in a hardware store. At eighteen he was earning five dollars a week when a former teacher made it possible for him to spend a year at Indiana University. He was nineteen when his mother died. Because she had been unable to go to church and take communion, the priest withheld his blessing. Although she finally was buried in consecrated ground, Theodore felt fresh resentment against the Church and, eventually, turned away from it entirely. There were other jobs—canvasser for a real estate agent, wagon-driver for a laundry—before he found himself in a newspaper office. As a twenty-year-old reporter he discovered the extremes of misery and apathy, and learned that neither was "news." He moved on to St. Louis where, during a popularity contest for schoolteachers conducted by his paper, he met Sara (Sallie) White, fell in love and, five years later, married her. Before his marriage, he had read indiscriminately—Dickens and Du Maurier, Hawthorne and Balzac—and had moved from St. Louis to Toledo, Cleveland, Pittsburgh, and New York.

Paul, the oldest brother, and two of his sisters were living in New York when Theodore, now twenty-three, arrived there. One ("Carrie") had been seduced and supported by an architect, but she had given him up for a restaurant manager with whom she had run away. The man was married and had stolen some fifteen thousand dollars (most of which he returned to escape prosecution), but she worked for him and helped him. Meanwhile, she took care of another sister who was pregnant with the child of a wealthy lover too well-connected to marry her. "Carrie" seemed such a heroine to her young brother that, later, he made her the central figure of his first novel. Refusing to add to her burdens and wanting to be independent of Paul, he took a room in a flop-house, got an assignment on the *New York World,* was dismissed, and almost starved. It was Paul who rescued him. Paul Dresser, as he called himself, was a celebrated actor, entertainer, author and composer of some of the most popular songs of the day, barber-shop melodies and sentimental thrillers, such as "Just Tell Them That You Saw Me," "The Letter That Never Came," "The Blue and the Gray," "My Gal Sal," and the rollicking hit, "The Bowery." Paul was a sensuous, Falstaffian fellow, weighing three hundred pounds, in his late thirties, fifteen years older than Theodore. In "My Brother Paul," written after Paul died of pernicious anemia in 1906, Theodore recalled, almost tearfully, the ebullience mixed with gentleness, the tolerance and tenderness which were the big playboy's outstanding qualities. For a while, he and Paul worked together; Theodore supplied the first verse and chorus of what was to become Dresser's greatest hit, "On the Banks of the Wabash," and Paul got him a position with his publishing firm. The firm put out a magazine of songs and stories, printed his name on the masthead as "Editor and Arranger," and allowed him to editorialize on corrupt metropolitan politics, anthropology, the European situation, the future of women, alcoholism, and possible inhabitants of Mars.

Two years later he decided that, although he had a steady income, his scope was too limited. He found work elsewhere, and by the end of 1928 his free-lance abilities enabled him to get married. During the next few years he was a thoroughly successful hackwriter. He depicted the viciousness of New York's slums, the sweatshops, and the squalor of the jobless; but he defended the corporations against the charge of "soullessness," because "no corporation is soulless which helps all others in helping itself." He buried his deep-seated sympathies and instinctive identification with the poor in banalities and the rhetoric of the advertiser's jargon. He was twenty-eight when, in a spasm of revulsion, he threw overboard the glib enthusiasms and false optimisms, and wrote *Sister Carrie.*

Sister Carrie, Dreiser's first novel, is perhaps his most popular. Its popularity may be due to its subject matter. Seduction and adultery, spiced with sadness, robbery, and general amorality are standard ingredients of the perennial best-seller. But Dreiser had built *Sister Carrie* around the story of his complacently ruined sister, and unprettified realism gave the tale a simplicity and candor utterly unlike the smirking sexuality of its genre. It was the candor of *Sister Carrie* which, with its incongruous dignity, outraged the sensibilities of the genteel. The proprieties were only partly observed; for, although the man, Hurstwood, completes the proverb about the wages of sin by committing suicide in a Bowery lodging-house, Carrie not only survives but fulfills her destiny as a woman. Harper and Brothers, to whom the manuscript was submitted, immediately rejected it. Dreiser tried a younger firm of publishers, Doubleday, Page and Company, and Frank Norris, author of the realistic *McTeague*, editorial reader at Doubleday, advised publication. After the book was set up, Doubleday's wife read the proofs and was so shocked by its frankness that, although the publishers were legally bound to issue the volume, they refused to advertise it, kept most of the small edition at the printer's, and virtually suppressed it. A few reviewers commented favorably on the author's power of characterization, but most of the reviews were cautious and noncommittal. Only a few hundred copies were sold and Dreiser was convinced that he was as much a failure as his father.

At thirty he was too disappointed to attempt anything more than occasional sketches. Worse, he was hopelessly destitute. He sent his wife back to her family in Missouri, moved from cheap dwellings in New York to Virginia to Pennsylvania and back to New York. He developed hypochondria and felt that he was losing sensation in his fingers; he could not sleep, imagined that he was being spied upon, and thought of himself as a split personality. He moved, wrote Robert H. Elias in *Theodore Dreiser: Apostle of Nature,* "into a cell-like room that cost only a dollar and a quarter a week, and restricted himself first to two meals a day, then to one, then to a bottle of milk and a loaf of bread, supplemented by an apple and perhaps some vegetable he could pick up in the streets of the public market and heat on the oil stove that warmed his room." He sank so low that he appealed for help to a charitable organization and was refused. He was suicidal, in the midst of a mental and physical breakdown, when Paul, with whom he had quarreled, met him by chance and saved him again. Paul insisted on his accepting money—"Why, Thee, I owe you half of 'On the Banks,' and you know it! You can't go on living like this!"—supplied him with clothes and took him to Muldoon's famous health resort in Westchester.

Restored in spirits, his nerves repaired, Dreiser worked for the New York Central, mostly out of doors, for six months and felt sufficiently rehabilitated to try editing again. In 1905, he was hired as fiction editor of Street and Smith, purveyors of trashy romances and the kind of fiction later to be known as "pulp" stories. "One of his jobs," wrote H. L. Mencken in his chapter on Dreiser in *A Book of Prefaces,* "was to reduce a whole series of dime-novels, each 60,000 words in length, to 30,000 words apiece. He accomplished it by cutting each one into halves, and writing a new ending for the first half and a new beginning for the second, with new titles for both. This doubling of their property aroused the admiration of his employers; they promised him an assured and easy future in the dime-novel business." This was more—and less—than Dreiser bargained for, and within a year he became managing editor of the *Broadway Magazine* and, in another year, was appointed director of the Butterick "trio": the *Delineator,* the *Designer,* and *New Idea Woman's Magazine.* His was not merely a middle-of-the-road policy but one plainly to the right of it. "We cannot admit stories which deal with immoral relations," he announced, "or which are disgusting in their realism and fidelity to life." Such sentences must have been hard for Dreiser to write, the more so since *Sister Carrie* had been reissued by a new publisher, who had bought the original plates and who advertised the book as "a curtain raised on a generally unwritten phase of life," full of "sensational revelations—the realism of Zola without the faults!" Having acquired control of the *Bohemian,* Dreiser planned to print the kind of sharp and satirical pieces which never could appear in Butterick's mild-mannered ladies' journals, but a few months of this was all he could manage. Five years of contriving worthless feature stories, feeble controversies, and false sensations was depressing and degrading. He was not yet forty and another breakdown was threatening. To save himself from it, he gave himself over to his second novel, *Jennie Gerhardt.*

As in his first novel, Dreiser presented the portrait of a woman seduced by one man and the mistress of another. Like Carrie, Jennie is amoral. ("Did anything matter except goodness—goodness of heart?" she inquires.) But she is portrayed with more skill; the delineation is subtler, the drama more direct. Both books, in spite of their spectacular elements and sensual appeal, are tragic; but, as Mencken remarked, "the tragedy of Carrie and Jennie is not that they are degraded but that they are lifted up, not that they go to

the gutter but that they escape the gutter and glimpse the stars."
The writing of *Jennie Gerhardt* was a catharsis, a purging of
Dreiser's self-destructive doubts; in a release of energy he completed six books within the next six years. He made his first trip
abroad and, in *A Traveler at Forty,* recorded his impressions of
England, Germany, and Italy with naïve honesty. For the most
part he abandoned his native style for an assumed stylishness, but
the Dreiserian attitude is maintained; it is revealed flatly and incontrovertibly in the much-quoted statement: "For myself I accept
now no creeds. I do not know what truth is, what beauty is, what
love is, and what hope is. I do not believe any one absolutely, and
I do not doubt any one absolutely. I think people are both evil and
well-intentioned." Thus Dreiser rejects the stereotypes of judgment,
the blacks and whites of lazy thinking, and accepts (for everyone)
the continual shifts, contrasts, and contradictions of men and
morals.

Before Dreiser published his travel book, he was engrossed with
a study of an artist in conflict with convention (*The 'Genius'*) and
a full-length portrait founded on the career of the capitalist,
Charles T. Yerkes, who had amassed a great fortune, had gone to
prison for embezzlement, had made another fortune after being
released, and had accumulated mistresses, Old Masters, and law-
suits with equal enterprise. Yerkes was the model for Cowperwood,
the leading figure in Dreiser's "trilogy of desire," a tremendously
well-documented saga of a ruthless industrialist's rise and fall. In
the three volumes—*The Financier,* 1912, *The Titan,* 1914, and
The Stoic, posthumously published in 1947—Cowperwood is
shown as the strong man who is also the shrewd manipulator, spec-
ulating with other people's money, forcing his way to power. "So
far as he could see," says his creator, "force governed this world—
hard, cold force and quickness of brain. If one had force, plenty of
it, quickness of wit and subtlety, there was no need of anything
else." Critics agree that the final volume in the series, *The Stoic,* is
a dispiriting affair in which Cowperwood sinks, as his last mistress,
using him as he has used so many others, rejects the very values
which elevated him. But there is divided opinion whether *The
Financier* or *The Titan* is the more intensive and analytical work:
exposures of the spirit of profit in an acquisitive society. "Money
was the medium of these novels," writes Maxwell Geismar in his
chapter, "Theodore Dreiser: The Double Soul," in *Rebels and
Ancestors.* "The epoch of social transition in the United States

during the last half of the nineteenth century marked the change from a relatively simple economic order based on productive work and more or less durable values to the consolidation of industrial empire under the dominance of finance capitalism. In Dreiser's work this epoch became a completely self-contained and remorselessly logical universe in itself, whose only goal was power, whose primary emotions were greed and cunning, whose main activity was to manipulate and exploit."

If the zealous guardians of morality withheld their indignation about the first two volumns of the trilogy, they could not contain themselves when Dreiser published *The 'Genius.'* The central figure, Eugene Witla, unlike Cowperwood, is the victim of his wavering emotions. Although the story deals with physical love, it reveals passion as a destructive force and is, therefore, almost a moral preachment. Nevertheless, the puritans were aroused. Stuart P. Sherman, the most influential critic of the day, pointed out the difference between a truly realistic novel and Dreiser's "naturalistic" novel—the first being "a representation based upon a theory of human conduct," while the second was "a representation based upon a theory of animal behavior." Ministers began denouncing the book from their pulpits; the Western Society for the Prevention of Vice charged it was a fearful exhibit of "obscenity and blasphemy"; the New York Society for the Suppression of Vice saw to it that the book was suppressed. Bookstores refused to stock *The 'Genius';* many libraries not only took the volume off their shelves but barred all of Dreiser's other works.

As might have been expected, Dreiser's chief reaction was anger. As though to emphasize his disgust, he published a four-act play, *The Hand of the Potter,* an unbelievably bad pathological drama, which grieved his friends and caused fresh attacks. Dreiser's second reaction was a retreat into mysticism. He brought out *Plays of the Natural and Supernatural,* in which vague spirits, wraiths, and unseen voices dominate the scene and a monstrosity of a child tries to capture an imaginary blue sphere. Dreiser's admirers were puzzled that he should care to preserve these lugubrious fables written in terms of high school melodrama, but Dreiser was exploring his "other side." He toyed with theosophy, attended sessions at which messages were received from a ouija board, and praised the crackbrained pseudo-scientific theories of Charles Fort.

After the publication of a volume of short stories and before offering his next major work, Dreiser got together a collection of his random writings and issued them under the title *Hey Rub-a-Dub-Dub,* nominally a book of essays. All the old Dreiserian themes are here, but they are reduced to the level of an adolescent's musings on Life and Death. That Nature is cruel is scarcely a remarkable finding, but Dreiser drives home the fact as though he had stumbled upon the secret of some mysterious rite. Although there are passages of unquestionable truth and penetration—"Democracy must do at least as well as Autocracy or it ought to shut up shop"—the writing is sadly jejune, an embarrassing parade of platitudes, the product of a fifty-year-old sophomore. The title may have been meant to suggest that Dreiser considered existence irrational as a child's nonsense nursery rhyme, but he could not resist adding a portentous subtitle: "A Book of the Mystery and Wonder of Life."

Dreiser had been separated from his wife since 1909, but she refused to give him a divorce. After she died in 1942, he married a distant cousin, Helen Parks Richardson, who had been his companion for more than twenty years.

An American Tragedy, published when Dreiser was in his mid-fifties, was the major work of his later period. Dreiser took the newspaper reports of an actual crime, and gave a not unusual murder the significance of a social parable: a crime brought about by the very society which self-righteously repudiated not only the act but the motive. Again money and social acceptance were Dreiser's leading themes. But this time his hero-victim was a weakling, caught between the low background which he scorned and the dangerous heights which he sacrificed everything to reach—a case history that was a nightmare version of a Horatio Alger story in reverse. Although the book was a long, slow-moving narrative in two volumes, it was an immediate success. The censors managed to have it banned in Boston and other cities at the very moment it was being hailed as "the greatest American novel of our generation." It was dramatized and played to enthusiastic audiences; the motion picture rights were bought for ninety thousand dollars. Dreiser was encouraged to bring out a new selection of his short stories, a collection of his free-verse poems, and prepare the second volume of his autobiography. He made another trip to Europe and wrote the controversial *Dreiser Looks at Russia.*

As he grew old, Dreiser allowed himself to utter predictions, deliver oracular judgments, and offer political advice. He was wrong most of the time. He championed the Spanish Loyalists but

equivocated about Hitler and argued that Nazi Germany was
merely seeking security for its people; he was alternately for and
against Roosevelt; he conceived of a union between Oriental intuition and Marxian economics. Essentially he was torn between
his old belief that mankind was helpless and a new hope that,
somehow, it could be helped; by the conviction that the unhappy
fate of humanity was predetermined but that, nevertheless, mankind must learn to choose its destiny. Sick and confused, he turned
to the dream of brotherhood as an expression of his abiding social
sympathies. Refusing to be termed a communist, he called himself
an "equitist," but he believed that communism might promote the
cause of justice and equity and, at seventy-four, joined the Communist Party. Many considered this a foolish gesture, but it was
religious conviction that made him seek a fusion of Marx and
Saint Matthew. He worked on *The Bulwark,* an unrecognizably
idealized portrait of his father, a book which, announced in 1916,
had taken him almost thirty years to complete. His hypochondria
had developed into genuine illnesses; his steel-gray eyes had lost
their fire; his heavy body sagged. A severe kidney attack came suddenly and he died December 28, 1945.

Dreiser can scarcely be considered a writer's writer. His style, as
even his most ardent defenders concede, is graceless. It is full of
wornout stereotypes, overloaded with sententious phrases, and
clogged with muddy trivialities. "Laborious," "clumsy," "inept,"
"exasperating," are a few of the adjectives which Mencken, his
doughtiest defender, uses to describe Dreiser's "molelike diligence
—an endless piling up of minutiae, an unshakable determination
to tell it all." To other critics Dreiser seems a lumbering elephant
slowly shouldering his way through a particularly dense jungle,
crushing the undergrowth, trampling down trees, but making a
new path.

As a thinker Dreiser was a problem to himself. His mind was a
ragbag of schoolboy philosophies. He believed in fatalism and free
will, in man's natural depravity and man's native goodness. He
wanted to remain a spectator and, at the same time, reform the
world; unable to do both, he wavered between dreams and disillusion. In *A Hoosier Holiday,* a mixture of nostalgia and cynicism,
he confessed sadly that nature was full of nameless brutalities but
that, on the other hand, "the high councils of nature" must have
considered cruelty necessary. He spoke up for the underdogs, the
"dear, crude, asinine, illusioned Americans," but he despised

"dogma-bound" communities. Aware of his inability to think his way out of the blind alleys into which his intelligence had led him, he cried out, "Oh, to escape this endless cogitation!"

When Dreiser dropped his muddled attempts at philosophizing and turned to the novelist's problems, the struggle took on major importance. The callow thinker, "confused and dismayed" before "inscrutable forces," disappeared as the mature craftsman recaptured a degenerate and dying society and restored it to frenzied life. Unable to reconcile the swiftly crowding and contradictory phenomena of the turn of the century—the booming progress of American industrialism and the threat of William Jennings Bryan's "socialistic" populism, the triumphs of power-driven farm machinery and the decline of the farmer, the timid attempts at social reform and the violent denial of women's rights—and abandoning attempts to solve "the ultimate meaning of existence," he created timeless characters and projected a shoddy society with unforgettable power. He added something rough-hewn and ungainly but massive to literature. It was said that he had no talent but a great deal of genius. The lack of talent made him vulnerable; but although many of his successors wrote with far more finesse than Dreiser ever achieved, it was his desperate earnestness and lifelong war with timidity and prudery that won them the prerogative to write honestly and without fear.

Stephen Crane

[1 8 7 1 - 1 9 0 0]

". . . all inside—he had no surface."

The *Red Badge of Courage,* an immortal depiction of an army at war, was written by a twenty-three-year-old youth who had never seen a battlefield. The *Atlantic Monthly* pronounced it great enough "to set a new fashion in literature," and H. G. Wells, speaking of its spreading influence, hailed it as "the first expression of the opening mind of a new period . . . a record of intensity beyond all precedent." The intensity was its author's undoing. He spent himself in a fury of creative energy and was dead before he was thirty.

The fourteenth and youngest child of Jonathan Townley Crane and Mary Helen (Peck) Crane, Stephen Crane was born in Newark, New Jersey, November 1, 1871. His father, who died when the boy was nine, was an uninspired but devout Methodist minister; his mother, equally pious but more enterprising, took care of the children by writing pieces for religious publications. Stephen inherited his mother's talent. In his early teens, when the family lived in Asbury Park, he gathered social gossip and other "news items" about the summer visitors; when he became a student at Syracuse University, after a year at Lafayette College, he paid most of his expenses by acting as college reporter for the *New York Tribune.* He was a careless yet satisfactory student; he skimmed over the textbooks, but the facts imprinted themselves on his retentive mind. Tall and thin, with bright blue eyes, he looked the athlete which he was, the popular captain of the baseball team.

His mother died when he was eighteen and although, considering the size of the family, he was by no means alone, he decided to go his own way. Joining a group of other young writers and artists, he found lodgings on New York's lower East Side and, for five years, turned out random sketches, sold a few bits of journalism, and kept himself from starvation. At twenty-one he completed a novel, but no publisher would consider issuing it. *Maggie: A Girl of the Streets* was a strange book to have been written by the son of two pietistic parents. It concerned a prostitute, a broken flower that had "blossomed in a mud puddle"; it detailed the raw violence of the slums; it employed a language that was loose and often vindictive. An obscure publisher finally consented to publish the work on two conditions: Crane would have to put up the money for the publication, and the name of the publisher would not appear anywhere in connection with it. Crane borrowed the money from one of his brothers and, afraid that knowledge of its authorship might destroy his reputation as a journalist, signed it with a pseudonym, "Johnston Smith." A hundred copies were disposed of, and Crane kept himself warm for a few days by burning the rest, like Rodolfo in *La Bohème,* in the fireplace. The first unreservedly realistic American novel, anticipating Dreiser's *Sister Carrie* by seven years, it was noticed by a few reviewers, but there was no critical stir. Other writers felt its impact. Hamlin Garland praised the book, and William Dean Howells said that the integrity and purpose was "as present in the working out of this poor girl's squalid romance as in any classic fable."

The newspapers were receptive to his articles and he worked with more deliberation on his next book. This was *The Red Badge of Courage,* published in 1895, when Crane was not yet twenty-four. The background is the Civil War, but it could be any war fought in the pre-atomic age by bewildered soldiers. The men are all sorts, cowardly, swaggering, foolhardy, covering their fears with poor jokes and pitiful boasts. The story is told in flashes, one fitfully succeeding the other; the men are anonymous. The small heroisms and the great horrors of warfare are seen from these men's point of view; the common soldiers, who were farmers and blacksmiths and clerks and mule-drivers, know nothing about the plan of battle or even about the reasons why the war is being fought. Crane's "search in esthetic was governed by terror," writes Thomas Beer, Crane's first biographer, and the novelist Joseph Hergesheimer adds, "Thereafter all novels about war must be different; the old pretentious attack was forever obliterated." The hero's realization of his cowardice and the explication of his sense of guilt are presented without heroics, but they are no less terrible for seeming casual. The conflict is revealed on many levels. Beauty struggles beneath the bloodshed, and the poet makes himself felt in the description of a dying soldier walking painfully, "as if he were taking care not to arouse the passion of his wounds"; in the symbol of an awe-striking sacrament, "the red sun was pasted in the sky like a wafer"; the lyrical picture of the battlefield just before dawn: "In the gloom before the break of day their uniforms glowed with a deep purple hue. From across the river the red eyes were still peering. In the eastern sky there was a yellow patch like a rug laid for the feet of the coming sun; and against it, black and patternlike, loomed the gigantic figure of the colonel on a gigantic horse."

Although *The Red Badge of Courage* was much praised, it was not a greatly profitable venture; it brought Crane less than a hundred dollars. It made him, however, a celebrity, and he was given a travel assignment which took him to Mexico. When Greece and Turkey went to war in 1896, the editor of the *New York Journal* decided that, on the basis of his book about war, Crane would be the ideal war correspondent and sent him to cover the Greco-Turkish conflict. Crane went gladly. He had been involved in several scandals. One of the girls in whom he was interested had been arrested as a street-walker while in his company; when Crane came to her defense, the police claimed that they had found narcotics in his room. Another girl blackmailed him and sued for support; a third sued to get back money which, she said, he had borrowed from her. Crane was barely twenty-six, but dark legends were already gathering about him.

On his return from Greece, he was ordered south. Cuba was in a state of insurrection, and although the Spanish-American War would not occur for another two years, America's sympathies were roused by the islanders' battle-cry, *Cuba Libre*. Hearst's newspapers were doing everything possible to bring about an active state of war. There was much illegal gun-running, and Crane was sent to report the filibustering expeditions. The ship that carried him was wrecked; before the passengers were rescued, Crane and three other men were tossed about in an open boat for several days. A year later this episode was turned into what William Dean Howells called "the finest short story in English," the title story of *The Open Boat and Other Tales of Adventure*. To accentuate the tension, Crane understated every phase of the blow, from the ominously calm opening, "None of them knew the color of the sky," to the last quiet line. The shock and exposure of the near-tragedy undermined his health. He developed a continual cough; his lungs were affected; his athletic frame shrunk. He was twenty-seven when he went to England with Cora Howarth Stewart.

Cora Stewart had run a brothel in Florida, where Crane met her. A New Englander by birth, she had married an English captain who was heir to a title; she had been several men's mistress. A handsome, full-blooded, and adventurous blonde, several years older than Crane, she fell completely in love with him. Although she had never received a divorce from Captain Stewart, she married Crane in London, and devoted herself to taking care of him. When the doctor advised sunnier skies and a warmer country, she went with him to Greece and tried to nurse him back to health. Thinking himself better, he returned to England, where he and Cora established themselves in Surrey. He met Joseph Conrad, who, when gossip spread through the village, became his stout defender, and Crane seemed at ease among the other literati. But the gossip grew worse. Strangely enough, it did not attack Cora but centered about Crane. He had written familiarly and in detail about prostitutes; therefore, it was argued, he was a libertine, a lecher, possibly a procurer. His complexion grew sallow and his eyes feverish; a straggling mustache gave him the look of a sick poet—his last photographs bear a startling resemblance to Rilke—and, since he had sudden spells of tiredness, people remembered the story of narcotics being discovered in his room and he was said to be a drug-addict. When the Spanish-American War broke out, he was happy to return to America and accept an offer to send despatches from Cuba.

It was, however, too late. There was now no question about the tuberculosis, and in an effort to keep up his spirits, Cora arranged to take over a house in Brede, Sussex, and there Crane fought desperately against time. He wrote panoramic descriptions of the world's great battles (which were posthumously published) for *Lippincott's Magazine,* added to the boys' juvenile tales, *Whilomville Stories,* which were appearing in *Harper's Monthly,* and began a similar series for girls. But he was far gone. Hemorrhages stopped all work, and he was taken to a sanatorium in the Black Forest, Germany, where, at the age of twenty-nine years and seven months, he died, June 5, 1900. His body was taken back to the United States and buried in Elizabeth, New Jersey.

Besides his prose, Crane wrote a small but important body of poetry. His second book, published in the same year as *The Red Badge of Courage,* was a book of poems, *The Black Riders and Other Lines.* Another book of poems, *War Is Kind,* appeared two years before he died. At first glance both volumes seem to be a willful juxtaposition of blasphemy and sentimentality. Although the sentiments are cryptic, they intensify without softening the severity with which Crane communicated his misgivings. Again and

again the poems express Crane's anxious desire to flee this threat-
filled world and his realization that, outside of death, escape is
impossible. The tone is usually bitter; the key is often as mordant
as:

> In the desert
> I saw a creature, naked, bestial,
> Who, squatting upon the ground,
> Held his heart in his hands,
> And ate of it.
> I said, "Is it good, friend?"
> "It is bitter—bitter," he answered;
> "But I like it
> Because it is bitter,
> And because it is my heart." [1]

The above is from the early book, *The Black Riders*. The attitude is not perceptibly altered in the following, from the later *War
Is Kind:*

> "Have you ever made a just man?"
> "Oh, I have made three," answered God,
> "But two of them are dead,
> And the third—
> Listen! listen!
> And you will hear the thud of his defeat." [2]

Not all the poems are as clenched as this. Some are bright extensions of protest; some are the murmurs of a discouraged spirit;
some are the cries of angry frustration. But there is nothing negligible in the least of them. Acidulous and brilliant, misunderstood in
Crane's own time, they have not been sufficiently appreciated in
ours. Only a few of those who practice Crane's elliptical concisions
have analyzed his experiments in free verse or have properly measured his efforts to find new cadences in unrhymed lines and new
rhythms in sharply edged parables.

Writing a kind of poetry that must have tasted acrid on the
sweets-craving palates of the nineties, he was twenty years ahead
of the Imagists, that school of poets which, using the language of
common speech, presented images cleaned of excessive ornamenta-
tion to concentrate on a poetry which is "hard and clear, never
blurred or indefinite." It was not until a quarter of a century after

---

[1] Copyright 1922 by William H. Crane. Copyright 1925, 1926, 1930 by Alfred A.
Knopf, Inc.
[2] Copyright 1922 by William H. Crane. Copyright 1925, 1926, 1930 by Alfred A.
Knopf, Inc.

Crane's death that a publisher was willing to risk a *Complete Works of Stephen Crane;* another five years passed before a *Collected Poems* appeared.

Crane, said Conrad, was a writer who not only got under the skin but was "all inside—he had no surface." In a review of a Stephen Crane *Omnibus* published in 1952, Alfred Kazin made the same point but put it somewhat differently: "He is the one American prose writer between Thoreau and Hemingway whose sensitiveness to physical sensation is so acute that he makes you feel, as only Hemingway and Faulkner now do, that he has earned his own style every inch of the way. The ordeal of the American land is in his prose; his sentences have the thunderclap of a man hitting the earth."

Riddled by illness that ate away his strength and betrayed by experiences which seared his soul, Crane was a naturalistic writer without stopping to think about naturalism. He made an image of a new and clear-cut world. The actual world in which he lived was not only too much with him but too much for him.

Bertrand Russell

[1 8 7 2 -   ]

"The wish to discover whether we possess anything that can be called knowledge."

A PHILOSOPHICAL MATHEMATICIAN (or mathematical philosopher) and a reappraising historian, Bertrand Russell persisted in an attitude which was skeptical, unpopularly corrective, and doggedly constructive. Opposed to the quick acceptances and glib affirmations of routine thinking, he was not without his own contradictions. A conflicting spirit in a confused world, he was unable to shape his life and works into a consistent pattern. The father of four children and an authority on child training, he founded a progressive school which turned out to be a flat failure. An apparently unromantic theorist who wrote scientifically about the perfect marriage, he was a peripatetic husband, divorced three times, who married his fourth wife when he was over eighty.

He was a controversial figure practically from birth. When he was three, the British Crown took him under protection as its ward after his father had announced that his son would be raised as an agnostic. Born May 18, 1872, at Trelleck, in Monmouthshire, England, a few miles from picturesque Tintern, he was christened Bertrand Arthur William Russell. His grandfather was a Prime Minister, the first Earl Russell; Bertrand Russell became the third Earl when he was fifty-nine. It was from this grandfather, who, in 1832, introduced a revolutionary Reform Bill, that the youth inherited a liberalism which was to last a lifetime. As a child, he attended the Episcopalian and Presbyterian churches on alternate Sundays, with the result that he was a non-church-going disciple of Darwin at eleven. At the same age he announced his first revolt: he was willing to accept the Definitions of Euclid, but he balked at the Axioms as not being "self-evident."

Until he was eighteen, Russell was educated at home by German governesses and English tutors, whom he embarrassed by a precocious grasp of mathematics. At eighteen he went to Cambridge and, after graduating, lived in Paris, where he was attached to the British Embassy, and in Berlin, where he studied economics. At twenty-two he met and married Alys Whitall Pearsall Smith, sister of the Philadelphia Quaker essayist, Logan Pearsall Smith, and settled in Sussex. There he devoted himself to an examination of his two favorite studies, arithmetic and philosophy, with excursions into the fields of feminism and socialism. He and his wife became members of the Fabian Society, sparred verbally with George Bernard Shaw, and delighted in their fellow Fabians, especially Sidney and Beatrice Webb. At this period, when Russell was twenty-nine, he wore a dangling black mustache that made him look like an intellectual young walrus, but his eyes were the eyes of a disillusioned leprechaun. In her posthumous memoirs, Beatrice Webb left this portrait of him: "Bertrand is a slight, dark-haired man, with prominent forehead, bright eyes, strong features except for a retreating chin, nervous hands, and alert quick movements. In manner and dress and outward bearing he is most carefully trimmed, conventionally correct and punctiliously polite. In speech, he has an almost affectedly clear enunciation of words and preciseness of expression. In morals, he is a puritan; in personal habits, almost an ascetic, except that he lives for efficiency and, therefore, expects to be kept in the best physical condition. But intellectually, he is audacious—an iconoclast detesting religious and social conventions, suspecting sentiment, believing only in the 'order of thought' and the 'order of things' in logic and science."

The picture of the puritan was to be altered rudely in the next few years. Russell was, as Beatrice Webb concluded, "intolerant of blemishes and faults in himself and others . . . he loathed lapses from men's own standards." He was impatient with any lack of perfection, whether the lack was in his wife or the world. He had started out with the conviction that science was the source of all human progress. "Youthful ambition," he wrote in the introduction to his *Selected Papers*, "made me wish to be a benefactor of mankind. I hoped to pass from mathematics to science, and lived a solitary life amid daydreams such as may have inspired Galileo or Descartes in adolescence. But it turned out that, while not without aptitude in pure mathematics, I was completely destitute of concrete kinds of skill which are necessary in science. Science was therefore closed to me as a career. At the same time, I found myself increasingly attracted to philosophy, not, as is often the case, by the hope of ethical or theological comfort, but by the wish to discover whether we possess anything that can be called knowledge."

It was the pursuit of knowledge that made Russell first the challenging inquirer, then the storm center, the enemy of the state, the branded "immoralist," and finally the authentic but never dogmatic seer. His first book, published at twenty-four, was a study of German social democracy and was followed by essays on geometry, the philosophy of Leibnitz, and a thesis which held that mathematics and logic are identical. He was thirty-eight when, with A. N. Whitehead, he completed the manuscript of *Principia Mathematica,* "which contained all that I could hope to contribute toward the solution of the problem which had begun to trouble me more than twenty years earlier. The main question (whether we possess anything that can be called knowledge) remained, of course, unanswered; but incidentally we had been led to the invention of a new method in philosophy and a new branch of mathematics."

The method may not have been altogether new, but it served to expose the limitations of the logical-analytic approach to the ascertainment of truth. Knowledge is mainly empirical, the result of observation, examination, and analysis. But logic and mathematics go further, Russell demonstrated: they investigate empirical knowledge and explore the implications that lie in and beyond established facts. "It appears from our analysis of knowledge that, unless it is much more restricted than we suppose, we shall have to admit principles of nondemonstrative inference which may be difficult to reconcile with pure empiricism." It was this negative note, the "methodological doubt," that Russell extended not only to philosophical speculation but to the very language used by philosophers. We can only assume, he warns us. We cannot be positive about anything until we have "proved" every phrase as well as every "fact"— and, in the meanwhile, we should suspect, or at least cautiously examine, everything we think we "know."

Russell was forty-one when the third and last volume of *Principia Mathematica* was published. He visited the United States, delivered the Lowell lectures at Harvard, and returned to England on the verge of the First World War. His innate pacifism was strengthened and his faith in the intellect was shocked at the readiness with which the liberals supported "the war to end war." Undeviatingly opposed to conscription, he fought against the slogans which justified the horrors of warfare. "Intellectual integrity made it quite impossible for me to accept the war myths of any of the belligerent nations," he wrote a quarter of a century later. "Indeed, those intellectuals who accepted them were abdicating their functions for the joy of feeling themselves at one with the herd. If the intellectual has any function in society, it is to preserve a cool and unbiased judgment in the face of all solicitations to passion. I found," he added ironically, "that most intellectuals have no belief in the intellect, except in quiet times."

Russell soon took an active part in the defense of conscientious objectors, was fined, and as the result of a pamphlet he had written, lost his lectureship at Trinity College. A little later one of his articles was found to be not only subversive but harmful to the cause of the Allies, and Russell was sent to prison for six months. The confinement was not wasted; during the imprisonment he finished a so-called textbook, *Introduction to Mathematical Philosophy.* "Every page he wrote," said H. W. Leggett in *Bertrand Russell, O.M.,* "had to be read by the Governor of the prison before it went to the publisher, and that individual is reputed to have given himself some bad headaches over the manuscript, of which he scarcely understood a word." By this time, Russell had ceased to be a retired academician of whom no one had heard; he was now a public person, looked upon either as a notable martyr or a notorious traitor. He briefly considered emigrating to America with D. H. Lawrence and founding a pacifist-utopian colony there, but he decided that his mission was to remain in England, at least until the war was over.

After the war he traveled through Russia, which he distrusted and feared—"I realized how profound is the disease in our western mentality which the Bolsheviks are attempting to force upon an essentially Asiatic mentality"—and China, which he admired almost without reservations. Nearing fifty, after twenty-seven years of marriage, he was divorced, and thereupon married Dora Winifred Black, who became his collaborator on *Prospects of Industrial Civilization.* She was also, with Russell, co-founder of the Beacon Hill School for youngsters of both sexes between the ages of four and ten. It was an aggressively modern school, so progressive as to seem anti-British. There were no rules, no religious instruction, no cricket, no football, no physical punishments. The children were permitted to read what they liked and, within limits, do what they wanted to do; they bathed together unclothed, and all questions were answered with complete honesty. This horrified the average person and even the somewhat-better-than-average-parent, but few of the remonstrators considered the positive principles on which the school was run. Russell stressed four characteristics which were the basis of character. He listed them in *Education and the Good Life;* (1) Vitality: Fearless self-discipline. "No one should learn

how to obey, and no one should attempt to command . . . Our
purposes should be our own, not the result of external authority,
and our purposes should never be forcibly imposed upon others."
(2) Courage: self-respect and self-reliance. Any child "will have to
fight against contrary habits and will consequently be met by resentful indignation." (3) Sensitivity: The right education produces
sensitivity to abstract causes and ideas rather than to personal and
quickly roused emotional stimuli. (4) Intelligence: Curiosity is the
key to exploration, discovery, receptivity to knowledge. It is a creative impulse which, unfortunately, "grows weaker with advancing
years" until "with the death of curiosity we may reckon that active
intelligence, also, has died." In spite of Russell's principles, or possibly because of them, his venture was regarded with suspicion and
the school failed.

At about the same time Russell's second marriage also failed. The
divorce from his first wife had received little notice. The divorce
from Dora Russell, however, was more spectacular, largely because
of a book Russell had published, *Marriage and Morals*. In this work
Russell contended that the rigidity of the divorce laws had made
marriage not so much a noble institution as a penal institution;
that, since men and women do not have sexual relations for the sole
purpose of having children, education in birth control is necessary;
and that pre-marital sexual relations are advisable. Moreover, Russell defended extra-marital intercourse; "I think," he maintained,
"that, where a marriage is fruitful and both partners to it are reasonable and decent, the expectations ought to be that it will be lifelong, but not that it will exclude other sex relations." Reasonable
and decent the Russells undoubtedly were; moreover, since there
were two children, the marriage should, by Russell's standards, have
been lifelong. But both partners were unable to take the other's
extra-marital affairs (they refused to call them infidelities) either
casually or philosophically, and in 1932 they were legally separated. Two years later they were divorced; after two more years,
when Russell was sixty-four, he married his assistant in research,
Helen Patricia Spence. At sixty-five he became the father of a son.

In his early and middle sixties he produced a rich variety of volumes with particular meaning for our time. Perhaps the most important is *Freedom and Organization,* a survey of the century from
1814 to 1914, a history which, by the use of a forceful narrative
style, Russell made as exciting as a work of scientific fiction. It is a
revaluating and clear-headed, if sometimes cantankerous, résumé

of one hundred years, in which Russell dissects such notables as the dictatorial Metternich; the leonine Bismarck, whom he admires; the coldly logical Malthus, whom he appreciates; and the revolutionary Marx, whom he assails. Russell found Marx dubious as a philosopher and dangerous as an economist. As a mathematician he ridiculed Marx's controversial theory of surplus value; he challenged Marx's contention that power is in the hands of the unscrupulous rich, and concluded that the doctrine of class war had ruined liberal thought by intimidating the fearful and frightening the conservatives into reaction. But he was not sanguine about capitalism and he doubted that industrial democracy was the answer. "The nineteenth century was brought to a disastrous end by a conflict between industrial technique and political theory . . . Plutocracy, the actual form of government in western countries, was unacknowledged and, as far as possible, concealed from the public eye."

In Praise of Idleness, published a year after *Freedom and Organization,* is a startling contrast in style as well as in subject. Bantering in tone, it is packed with surprises and spiced with epigrams as witty as: "Science, while it diminishes our cosmic pretensions, enormously increases our terrestrial comfort. That is why, in spite of the horror of the theologians, science has on the whole been tolerated." "Work is of two kinds: first, altering the position of matter at or near the earth's surface relatively to other matter; second, telling other people to do so."

At sixty-six Russell revisited the United States and gave lecture courses at the University of Chicago, the University of California at Los Angeles, and at Harvard, where he delivered the William James lectures. When, in 1940, he was given a chair as Professor of Philosophy at the College of the City of New York, there were loud cries of protest. Worried parents who had heard of *Marriage and Morals* without bothering to read it charged that Russell was trying to pervert their children with his distorted views on sex, his advocacy of free love, and his "general immorality." When Russell was assailed with such epithets as "salacious," "lecherous," "libidinous," "atheistic," and "subversive," he recalled that the same accusations were leveled against Socrates. Despite the fact that the president of the college testified that Russell taught nothing but logic and mathematics, a suit was brought to have the appointment annulled on the ground that Russell was a "pernicious influence." John Mc-Geehan, a Justice of the Supreme Court of New York, revoked the appointment, and declared it was "an attempt to establish a Chair of Indecency." Russell thereupon accepted an invitation to lecture on philosophy at the Barnes Foundation near Philadelphia, bought a house in Merion, Pennsylvania, for himself and his children, quarreled with Barnes and, after two years, returned to England.

During the Second World War Russell ceased to be a conscientious objector. He did not "renounce" pacifism, but he held that the democracies had to be supported in the world struggle against fascism. At seventy he was as anti-mystical, ironic, and recalcitrant as ever; he described himself as "a happy pessimist." At seventy-six he published another examination of the intelligence which, with characteristic imperturbability, he entitled *Human Knowledge: Its Scope and Limits.* He began a series of broadcasts which raised the standard of radio and won a public to a new level of literacy. At seventy-seven he was a passenger on a Norwegian flying-boat which crashed. Twenty people were drowned, but Russell, fully clothed, managed to swim in the icy sea until he was rescued. A few days later he delivered a scheduled lecture. At seventy-eight he received the Nobel Prize for Literature as a great writer who was also a great humanist.

His eightieth birthday was the occasion for international tributes. The magazine *Life* recalled that when Russell was awarded the Nobel Prize, he denied that he had contributed anything important to literature, and *Life* added: "A great mind is still annoying and adorning our age." When he gave a filmed interview, it was apparent that his mind was as quick as ever to detect prejudice, pretension, and fraud. He seemed younger than he looked at sixty. The mustache had disappeared long ago; the features were sharper, the lips firmer, the eyes livelier.

A month after his eightieth birthday the champion of trial marriages decided that he had had enough of the marital state and was divorced for desertion. However, a few months later, he married for the fourth time. His bride was Edith Finch, a former teacher at Bryn Mawr College. The amazing vitality of the man was proved by the books which he wrote after eighty, works which exposed the dangers of dogmatism more keenly than ever. Between 1950 and 1952 Russell published *Unpopular Essays, New Hopes for a Changing World,* and *The Impact of Science on Society.* In 1953, Russell entered a new field. The author of some sixty-five books and pamphlets turned to the writing of short stories published under the title, *Satan in the Suburbs,* and, in 1954, celebrated his eighty-second birthday by bringing out his second work of fiction, *Nightmares of Eminent Persons.*

In everything he wrote, Russell had what Irwin Edman called "the rare gift of exposition which turns popularization into an art." The touch is light and always lucid; the manner is elegant without being artificial or finicky. The mood is alternately rebellious and sober, but the sobriety is accompanied by many reservations and even the recklessness seems measured. Russell continually spoke up for "the free mind which is the glory and torment of the western world . . . In spite of death, Man is yet free, during his brief years, to examine, to criticize, to know, and in imagination to create. To him alone, in the world with which he is acquainted, this freedom belongs; and in this lies his superiority to the resistless forces that control his outward life."

In an obituary which Russell planned for publication in the *London Times* on June 1, 1962, "on the occasion of my lamented but belated death," he concluded: "His life, for all its waywardness, had a certain anachronistic consistency, reminiscent of the aristocratic rebels of the early nineteenth century. His principles were curious, but, such as they were, they governed his actions. . . . He appeared, in extreme old age, full of enjoyment, no doubt owing in large measure, to his invariable health; for, politically, during his last years, he was as isolated as Milton after the Restoration. He was the last survivor of a dead epoch."

Gertrude Stein

[1 8 7 4 - 1 9 4 6]

"Simplify! Simplify!"

THE BATTLE that raged about Gertrude Stein was fought along bitterly contested and closely drawn lines. There was no middle ground. Her detractors ridiculed her as a literary fraud, a "medium" who employed automatic writing to mock the critics and hoax the readers, a rich and garrulous dilettante who, pretending to set the fashion, merely followed the latest fad, "a clinical case of megalomania." A small but fervent circle regarded her not as a writer but a religion, the century's most radical innovator, a scientific student of literature who, in a series of strange but convincing demonstrations, had brought about a one-woman Revolution of the Word. To the great majority of uninstructed readers she was merely a controversial "name." A few sampled her work, found it incomprehensibly puzzling, and concluded that she was, as her critics charged, "the high priestess of the cult of unintelligibility."

She was born February 3, 1874, in Allegheny, Pennsylvania, the daughter of Daniel and Amelia Keyser Stein. The family was affluent—her father was vice-president of a prosperous street railway—and fond of travel. Her older brother, Leo, and she spent their early years in Vienna and Paris and their childhood in California. Even as a very young girl she was a devoted and avidly indiscriminate reader; she devoured books, she said, "going through whole libraries, reading anything, everything." Years later she remembered poring over Smollett, Scott, Shakespeare, Bunyan, Fielding, Wordsworth, and the *Congressional Record* with equal absorption. At nineteen she studied at Radcliffe, where she specialized in psychology and became a favorite pupil of William James. The night before her final examination she went to the opera and a late party afterwards. "Dear Professor James," she wrote at the head of her paper, "I am so sorry, but I do not feel a bit like an examination paper on philosophy today." "Dear Miss Stein," James wrote in reply, "I understand perfectly. I often feel like that myself"—and gave her the highest mark in the course.

It was at Radcliffe that she made some experiments in automatic reading and writing. Together with a graduate student, Leon Solomon, she proceeded on the theory that a creative action can be performed without conscious attention, and the results of the collaboration were published in 1896 in the *Psychological Review* under the title, "Normal Motor Automatism." It was Gertrude Stein's first printed piece of writing and much was made of it after she became famous. "The words and phrases fitted together all right, but there was not much connected thought," she said in a later estimate. "For example: 'When he could not be the longest and thus to be, and thus to be, the strongest.' " Thirty-eight years after the Radcliffe experiments Professor B. F. Skinner discovered the paper. In "Has Gertrude Stein a Secret?" he concluded that all Gertrude Stein's subsequent writing was more or less of a piece with the article published in the *Psychological Review* and that "the work of Gertrude Stein in the *Tender Buttons* manner is written automatically and unconsciously in some such way as that described." Miss Stein differed. In one of her autobiographical passages she maintained that (a) the experiment was not successful and (b) that it did not produce verifiable automatic responses. "I did not think it was automatic," she wrote with her characteristic disdain of punctuation. "I do not think so now, do not think any university student is likely certainly not under observation to be able to do genuinely automatic writing . . . No; writing should be very exact and one must realize what there is inside in one and then in some way it comes into words and the more exactly the words fit the emotion and more beautiful the words that is what does happen and anybody who knows anything knows that thing." Nevertheless, the experiments on the distraction of attention seem to have developed her word sense and stimulated further linguistic experimentation.

In this she was encouraged by her mentor, William James. She was already aware of the nuances of words and ideas which James had suggested in his *Psychology*, particularly in a chapter entitled "The Stream of Consciousness," a term which heralded an entirely new literature. "When we take a general view of the wonderful stream of our consciousness," wrote James, "what strikes us first is the different pace of its parts. Like a bird's life, it seems to be an alternation of flights and perchings. The rhythm of language expresses this, where every thought is expressed in a sentence, and every sentence is closed by a period. The resting places are usually occupied by sensorial imaginations of some sort . . ." Gertrude Stein was fascinated by the double image of consciousness as a flowing stream and a flight of birds, a constant activity with alternations of "flying" and "perching." She was also excited by "The Sense of Time," in which James traced the fluidity of time as well as consciousness and showed that, at the very moment of considering the present, "it has melted in our grasp . . . gone in the instant of becoming." This thought became one of the cardinal points of her later theorizing. With increasing determination she sought to give her work a feeling of uninterrupted time, a Jamesian sense of the overflowing moment and the "continuous" present.

At twenty-three she entered Johns Hopkins University, where she studied medicine for four years but, although her work was excellent, she left without taking a degree. She was interested only in study, not in high marks. Her education took a new turn in London, where she devoted a year to Elizabethan prose. Paris was the center of intellectual ferment at the beginning of the twentieth century and in 1903, with Alice B. Toklas, a San Francisco friend who became her lifelong companion, she settled in the French capital. Except for a visit thirty years later, she never went back to America. For a while she lived with her brother Leo, art connoisseur and author of *The A B C of Aesthetics,* but their differences in taste and temperament led to continual quarrels. Leo collected the works of the new and little-known painters, but Gertrude often claimed that she had discovered them. Moreover, Leo was not impressed by the manner in which his sister was planning to write. He was tolerant about her first departures from the norm of English composition, but he grew more and more irritated by her fondness for prolonged repetition. "When Jesus said 'Verily, verily,'" he wrote to Hutchins Hapgood, "the second 'verily' added much to the expression. But if he had said 'Verily, verily, verily, verily, verily, verily, verily,' it wouldn't have been so good." Besides their other differences, Leo resented Gertrude's masculine manner, emphasized in her clothes as well as her speech, and her compulsion to dominate. She was four-square in conversation and appearance, thickset and short. Her hair was closely cropped; her eyes were black and sharp. The portrait painted by Picasso caught her in a half-meditative, half-argumentative mood, bending forward, about to trap an unwary opponent. But her features were stronger than those Picasso gave her. Her face was a forceful contradiction; she had the look of an aggressive Buddha or a Roman senator wrapped in tweeds. Overshadowed by his domineering sister, and finding himself out of place in a household run by two women, Leo left. He

felt released, he said, from a complicated family relationship, "a prolonged disease, a kind of mild insanity."

The house in the Rue de Fleurus became a center for advance
guard writers and artists. As a patron of the arts, Gertrude Stein
made friends with Picasso, Matisse, and Braque before they
achieved fame; she bought their canvases and hung them proudly
on her walls. As hostess of an elegant salon she attracted young authors, charmed them with her forthrightness and, although she was
just beginning to write, influenced them by her salient honesty.
F. Scott Fitzgerald, Sherwood Anderson, and Ernest Hemingway
(another with whom she quarreled) were among those who benefited from her advice to "Simplify! Simplify!"

Her own use of the art of simplification was evident but not too
insistent in her first book, *Three Lives*. Published when she was
thirty-five, *Three Lives* was not, as might have been expected, concerned with the careers of artists and writers, but with the simple,
tender, and tragic lives of two German servants and a Negro prostitute. "The Good Anna" is a cousin to the innocent woman in Flaubert's "A Simple Heart"; "The Gentle Lena," a milder version of
Anna, is described by the title; but "Melanctha" is a work of
greater dimensions. It was, said Carl Van Vechten, "perhaps the
first American story in which the Negro is regarded as a human being and not as an object for condescending compassion or derision." "In a style which appears to owe nothing to that of any other
novelist," wrote Edmund Wilson in *Axel's Castle*, "she seems to
have caught the very rhythms and accents of the mind of her heroines. We find ourselves sharing the lives of the Good Anna and the
Gentle Lena so intimately that we forget about their position and
see the world limited to their range, just as in Melanctha's case
. . . we become so immersed in Melanctha's world that we quite
forget its inhabitants are black." The reviews of *Three Lives* were
few and noncommittal. The *Nation* found the form eccentric and
difficult, but granted that the book had vitality and that "whoever
can adjust himself to the repetitions, false starts, and general circularity of manner will find himself very near real people."

In the next volume (which, in common with all her work until
The Autobiography of Alice B. Toklas, was paid for by the author) Gertrude Stein increased her mannerisms and purposely emphasized the "general circularity." *The Making of Americans* is a
disjointed union of unrelated units through which the novelist hopes
to project the history of "the old people in a new world, the

new people made out of the old." Nothing happens: there is no
plot; the narration is static. The book purports to be, more than
the story of a single family, "the history of everyone who ever was
or is or will be living." Life, according to Gertrude Stein, was a
monotonous round of ordinary events. She made this plain by
amassing all the banalities, platitudes, and trivialities of existence
and recounting them with unwearying, unchanging regularity.
"She presents her material," wrote Rosalind S. Miller in *Gertrude
Stein: Form and Sensibility,* "in a redundant fashion by repeating
words and situations in a seemingly endless way . . . and this repetition represents the monotonous flow of time." In *Gertrude Stein:
A Biography of Her Work,* Donald Sutherland points out the
"fairly adventitious situation or quality" to the separate interior existences of the men and women in *The Making of Americans:* "The
quality of being a son or an uncle does not depend at all on the
specific parents or nephews who objectively create the position.
The individual people in the book go on and on as themselves . . .
As living beings, as verbs, they are intransitive, and they tend to be
present participles: 'Many having resisting being have it in them all
their living when they are beginning and then on to their ending
have it to have suspicion always naturally in them and this is a natural thing for them to have in them because they have resisting being have it in them to be knowing that always someone is doing the
attacking.' " The commentator is not disturbed that Gertrude Stein,
having abjured punctuation and having fallen in love with the par-
ticiple, has made her meaning all but impenetrable to the reader.
On the contrary, Sutherland finds that "the work itself, the sequence of statement and ideas, makes the stream of thought perfectly objective and available to anyone who can read English . . .
The basis of communication is intellectual, not emotional, and is
very simple . . . The subjectivity of Gertrude Stein in this work is
very nearly anonymous . . . the stream of thought is scarcely qualified by biographical feeling, as it is in Proust, for example. This
anonymity or 'commonplaceness' or impersonality of mind is, of
course, in her case an intellectual thing, even a scientific discipline;
but it is parallel to and very like the mentality of the saints whose
biographies are lost in their absorption in the present general miracle and the state of grace." Idolatry can go no further.

Gertrude Stein's next book, published when she was forty-one,
was a still wilder venture in dislocation and disorganization. Picasso
and Braque were experimenting in reducing objects to abstrac-

tions in terms of paint; Gertrude Stein attempted to do the same
thing in terms of syllables. *Tender Buttons*, subtitled "Objects Food
Rooms," is a series of "still life" arrangements written as a cubist
might paint them. She chose such objects as a chair, a piano, an
orange, a box, a flower, a postage stamp, eggs, an umbrella, rhu-
barb, a seltzer bottle; she tried to shock the reader into seeing each
subject as a new and vivid thing, something that he might have casually encountered but had never actually *seen* or *realized.* Just as
the painters rearranged forms and disconnected the object from its
superficial aspect to reveal its essence, so she recomposed sentences,
destroyed syntax, and flung the conventions out of the window. Although she had depicted real people in *Three Lives* and *The Making of Americans,* the human element no longer interested her. She
was excited by words, by the correlation of sight, sound, and sense
evoked by the words themselves. All the associations of the word—
its possibilities as a rhyme, as a pun, as an ambiguous association—
captivated her to the exclusion of everything else. She avoided events
and actions because "nowadays everybody all day long knows what
is happening and so what is happening is not really interesting . . .
I began to wonder at about this time just what one saw when one
looked at anything really looked at anything. Did one see sound,
and what was the relation between color and sound, did it make
itself by description by a word that meant it or did it make itself
by a word in itself . . ."

This seems to be the key to such pieces from *Tender Buttons* as
the following:

A CUTLET

A blind agitation is manly and uttermost.

CHICKEN

Alas a dirty word, alas a dirty third alas a dirty third, alas
a dirty bird.

MILK

Climb up in sight climb in the whole utter needles and
guess a whole guess is hanging. Hanging hanging.

A METHOD OF A CLOAK

A single climb to a line, a straight exchange of a cane, a
desperate adventure and courage and a clock, all this which
is a system, which has feeling, which has a resignation and
success, all makes an attractive black silver.

Although these excerpts are not written in a foreign language, they demand interpretation. Unfortunately, no two interpreters seem to agree on the meaning of the cryptically arranged phrases. Donald Sutherland disposes of the last tender button with airy ingenuity:

> "What is being described here is of course not what everyone knows about cloaks or expects of them generally but what was actually experienced in looking directly at one once, the style of the lines and folds felt as a distinct impression—their dash and regularity at once. In this poem at least one can reconstruct closely enough what the original experience was like. The 'clock' may be a metaphor for regularity of interval in the folds, but otherwise the ordinary meaning of each word is enough to re-create the experience about as sharply as any experience of the kind can be re-created in words."

Rosalind Miller is more tentative about the same subject. She believes that two different associations are being brought to mind, although one is related to the other. She proceeds cautiously:

> "There is a cloak and a clock image, which in turn may mean two things: a play on words or a situation involving a cloak and a clock. 'A single climb to a line, a straight exchange to a cane,' may imply the hand of the clock climbing or moving up to the next line which marks off the minutes on the face of the clock. The last part of the line might mean that the large hand, directly across from the small hand, forms a straight line or resembles a cane; but the cloak image implies a person who may be glancing at the clock and then, noticing the lateness of the hour, picks up his cane to leave. With the addition of 'a desperate adventure and courage and a clock,' the picture begins to broaden: the clock shows the arrival of a certain hour which means that the persons must leave for an adventure involving courage. Then 'all this which is a system which has feeling, which has resignation and success' adds some tension and a philosophy of life. The clock may be a symbol for time or life; life involves a feeling which is composed of many moods and experiences—in this case 'resignation and success.' But all of these things together 'make an attractive black silver.' In this case the 'black silver' may refer to the cloak—a black cloak lined in white satin which gives the appearance of silver. Here the mention of the cloak substantiates the idea of adventure. Or the 'black silver' may mean the clock—i.e., the black hands on a silver face. If this last idea is accepted then the line may be interpreted

to mean that life is conducted and based on the movement
of the hands of the clock around the face."

Thus "Toasted Susie is my ice cream"—a phrase which was ban-
died about to everyone's delight—could mean that Susie is a delec-
table little dish or that Susie might be sunburnt and, quite literally,
the toast of the town. "A rose is a rose is a rose"—another much-
quoted Steinism—could indicate that fancy descriptions of roses
have been overdone, and the plain repetition (an emphasis on the
pure essence of rose) could be considered a triumph of flat and
complete finality. In any case, Gertrude Stein took criticism with
calm but not untroubled seriousness. She believed that her disinte-
grations were reflecting the disintegrated spirit of the age, and that
she was prolonging a sense of the present by her restatements, repetitions, and reorganizations. By "groping for a continuous present and
using everything again and again" she endeavored to picture the
period in which she lived. "It is a time when everything cracks,"
she wrote, speaking of Picasso, "where everything is destroyed, everything isolates itself, it is a more splendid thing than a period
where everything follows itself."

Tender Buttons was followed by a series of portraits of persons
done in the same manner as her depiction of household objects, as
abstruse in idiom as an abstractionist's design; by *Geography and
Plays,* a more than ordinarily misleading title; by a quasi-novel,
Lucy Church Amiably; and by *Useful Knowledge,* another ironic
misnomer. Act Three of "What Happened" is typical of Gertrude
Stein's "dramatic" style. It begins: "A cut, a cut is not a slice, what
is the occasion for representing a cut and a slice. What is the occasion for all that. A cut is a slice, a cut is the same slice . . ."

Nearing fifty, Gertrude Stein suddenly discarded all her tricks of
transposition and distortion to write what became her most popular
work. Using her friend as a subterfuge to tell the story of her own
life, she wrote *The Autobiography of Alice B. Toklas,* a lucid,
chatty, and altogether ingratiating book of reminiscences. Combining anecdotes, portraits of celebrities, philosophical asides, and explanations of her idiom, she scarcely concealed her opinion that she
was a genius and that she had helped shape her epoch. Her right to
speak for her generation was, however, disputed by some of the
very people she claimed to have influenced. In "Testimony Against
Gertrude Stein," Matisse and others protested that her "hollow, tinsel bohemianism and egocentric deformations" had misrepresented
the ideas of the period "without taste and without relation to real-

ity." Most readers, however, were so happy to find a work of Gertrude Stein which was intelligible that the book was even more discussed than her more characteristic obscurities.

On the strength of the success of the *Autobiography,* she returned to the United States for a lecture tour and to witness the production of her *Four Saints in Three Acts,* set to music by Virgil Thomson, an "opera" which is a triumph over its half-mystical, half-whimsical but wholly motionless (as well as emotionless) libretto. One of the leading passages, "Pigeons in the grass alas" became a password among the intelligentsia. "You are so easy to understand when you speak," a clubwoman said during the question period of a lecture. "Why don't you write the way you talk?" "Why should I?" replied Miss Stein. "Do you think that Shakespeare talked in blank verse?"

During the First World War Gertrude Stein drove a Ford to the front lines and distributed food and other gifts to the wounded and hospitalized. The GI's enjoyed the woman—they appreciated the open-handedness, the flashing retorts, the ringing laugh—although they did not appreciate the writer enough to interest themselves in her work. When the Nazi Armies occupied Paris in the Second World War, she walked more than seven miles every other day to procure food. "Hers is a powerful personality," wrote Francis Hackett. "It took the American Army to liberate her." *Wars I Have Seen* pictures not only the fall of France but the occupation and liberation. *Brewsie and Willie* is full of pictures of soldiers who are not like soldiers but what Gertrude Stein thought soldiers were like. It was her last book, written when she was seventy. The following year her amazing energy vanished and her frame shrank visibly. She was planning to return to the United States when it was discovered that she was suffering from cancer, and she was sent to the American hospital in Neuilly-sur-Seine. She was there only a week when, as concerned as ever about her work, the seemingly endless vitality gave out and she died July 26, 1946. "What *is* the answer?" she asked, just before her death. "Well then," she laughed, as there was no reply, "what is the question?" Her last breath was the query of a lifetime.

After her death critical opinion was more sharply split than before. There were the scoffers, those who referred to her "logorrhea, a running of the vowels," and those who, irritated by her "syllabic babbling," agreed with Van Wyck Brooks that "the infantile became fixed in herself because her imagination was unpeopled." Her more tolerant critics conceded that she undoubtedly had talents but that she never developed them, that she was a brilliant beginner but never grew up, that she could help everyone except herself. Even her admirers had to apologize for the fact that her countless accretions so seldom embodied an important event or even an episode, that she made so little appeal to recognizable emotions, and that with the exception of the early work, everything was intellectually contrived, cold, inhuman. Only a fanatic votary could be pleased by her coy, third person self-adulation, the interpolations which were not so much irrational as irrelevant, the childish jingles, sentimental rhymes, bits of old doggerel ("When this you see remember me") interpolated in what seem to be serious speculations, to say nothing of such lapses as the self-conscious "tribute" to her dog: "Listening to the rhythm of his water drinking made her recognize the difference between sentences and paragraphs, that paragraphs are emotional and that sentences are not."

Lately there has been a reappraisal, largely in her favor. It has been maintained that Gertrude Stein did not play with words in a haphazard and willful way but, as a grownup child, with the building blocks of language. Language, it was argued, tends to grow stale. Cluttered with literary accumulations, colloquial platitudes, and age-long associations, words lose their pristine freshness. Because of our stereotyped responses to stereotyped phrases, a continual revitalizing of language is necessary. This, Gertrude Stein believed, was her function. She reacted to overelaboration by oversimplification; against what she considered an effete literature she pitted a primitive, even a barbaric, youthfulness. She juxtaposed the nonsensical, the clinical, and the spectacular to attain her objective. ("You say you do not like me to repeat but why not if it makes you listen.") She was always trying "a new thing in a new way," even though her departures, which suggested constant change, were constantly the same only more so. She did not mind goading and worrying the reader as long as she worried him into wakefulness. As a communication her work was a failure. But as a language experiment it was a successful influence on those who applied her detached and simplified "exactitudes" to the human problems of the "continuous present."

Robert Frost

[1874 -   ]

"His poems are people talking."

THE MOST AUTHENTIC INTERPRETER of New England, Robert Frost, was born in San Francisco, March 26, 1874. The native tone as well as the terrain is immediately apparent in the titles of his books—*North of Boston, Mountain Interval, A Further Range, New Hampshire, Steeple Bush*—and the poet's birth in the Far West was something of a geographical accident. Both his parents had been country schoolteachers born in the East, where his forefathers had lived for eight generations. His mother came from a Scottish seafaring family of Orkney origin; his father's people had migrated from England. His father, William Prescott Frost, was a natural nonconformist. He gave up teaching, revolted from Republican New England and moved to California, where he became an editor on the *San Francisco Bulletin,* a hotly Democratic paper. As a "copperhead" his sympathies were wholly with the South and, although the Civil War had been concluded a decade before his son was born, he christened the boy Robert Lee Frost. William Frost threw himself into local politics, but his health could not stand the strain. He died of tuberculosis in his early thirties, and his widow took her son and daughter back to Lawrence, Massachusetts, to live with Grandfather Frost. Robert was then ten years old.

His mother resumed teaching, and in between chores and various odd jobs, Robert went to school—there had been no formal schooling in California. Although he managed to get himself in (and out) of college, he said "My year and a half of the ungraded district school and four years in Lawrence High School were the heart of my education." In his twelfth year, he had begun to pick up small change as a hired hand on a farm and as a pieceworker in a shoeshop. At sixteen he pushed a bobbin wagon in a Lawrence textile mill. At eighteen he tended the dynamos and trimmed the carbon-pencil lamps over the spinning machines.

He had entered Dartmouth when he was seventeen, but quit suddenly after three months. He was restless, sure of only one thing:

he could not be trained by textbooks. He took his mother's place teaching for a term, tried farming after a fashion, set out to promote a Shakespearean reader, and gave up his attempt to be an impresario after the reading failed to impress the audience. At nineteen he tried his hand at journalism. He began as a reporter on the *Lawrence Sentinel,* transferred to the *American,* and gravitated to the editorial page as an irregular columnist. He wrote random paragraphs, little pieces on pastoral subjects which turned up later in his poetry. At twenty-one he married his high school sweetheart and co-valedictorian, Elinor White, an unusually pretty girl, and, determined to complete his formal education, entered Harvard. He wanted to study under William James, but he was not eligible for courses with the great philosopher. He wrestled manfully with the curriculum for two years, decided it was not worth the effort, and left.

For the next five years, Frost farmed. Then he began part-time teaching at Pinkerton Academy in Derry, New Hampshire, to support his growing family. (Robert and Elinor Frost, who died in 1938, had six children, only two of whom were living in 1955.) At twenty-seven he taught psychology at New Hampshire State Normal School at Plymouth, varying his studies with readings from the plays of two Irish dramatists, J. M. Synge and George Bernard Shaw. It seemed that teaching was to be his career.

Meanwhile, he had been "indulging" in poetry. He wrote his first poem when he was not quite fifteen; it sprang straight out of a book which fascinated him, Prescott's *Conquest of Mexico,* and grew into a long ballad which was published in the Lawrence High School *Bulletin.* He was nineteen when his first "professional" poem was published in *The Independent,* for which he was paid fifteen dollars. If he had any hope that he could live by poetry alone, he was disappointed although not disillusioned. He was right to keep his illusions; later recognition proved that poetry could support him. During the next fourteen years, *The Independent* printed six more of his poems; none of the other magazines showed any interest in a kind of poetry that departed from the stereotypes of sentiment and showed the countryside in its quiet, sometimes drab, but always true colors. It was twenty years after the appearance of "My Butterfly" that his first book was printed—in England. He had gone to England for various reasons. Beaten as a farmer, he had sold his acres—he was tired of wresting a living from stubborn soil by "cultivating rock"; teaching had been so successful that he feared he might be committed to it; he wanted to find out "whether I had it in me to think and write." The Frosts settled temporarily in rural Buckinghamshire, since Mrs. Frost expressed a wish "to live under thatch." Frost tried farming again and found that two of his neighbors were poets. He met other writers, notably Rupert Brooke and Edward Thomas, who was so deeply influenced by Frost that he dedicated his first volume to the American poet.

One evening in 1913 Frost was shuffling through the poems he had written, most of which had not been printed. In his hands was the work of twenty years. He had always admired the poetry of W. E. Henley and he suddenly decided to send the manuscript to Henley's publisher. Although he was totally unknown, the little book was immediately accepted. Taking a phrase from Longfellow's "My Lost Youth," it was entitled *A Boy's Will*. When the book appeared, Frost was thirty-eight years old.

The reviewers liked Frost's unaffected lyrics, his simple vocabulary, and sharp observation; they commented on his way of turning usually forgotten thoughts into unforgettable phrases. But it was Frost's second volume, which appeared a year later, that made him famous. Critics on both sides of the Atlantic regarded *North of Boston* as a set of modern idylls which were both simple and psychological. They praised his powerful use of plain language, his lack of the traditional "poetic diction" and, most of all, the rendering of native subject matter in a heightened tone which, nevertheless, carried the accent of casual speech. Mark Van Doren maintained that Frost's singularity consisted in the conversational tone he built into his verse and which, somehow, attained eloquence. "Whether in dialog or in lyric, his poems are people talking . . . The man who talks under the name of Robert Frost knows how to say a great deal in a short space, just as the many men and women to whom he has listened in New England and elsewhere have known how to express in the few words they use more truth than volumes of ordinary rhetoric can express."

North of Boston is subtitled "A Book of People." It is also a book of backgrounds as living and powerful as the people they overshadow. Frost dramatizes a stone wall, an empty cottage, a grindstone, a forgotten woodpile left

> To warm the frozen swamp as best it could
> With the slow, smokeless burning of decay.

He also creates a series of grim dramas—many of them virtually one-act plays—out of the isolated lives, the poignant hardships and acrid humors which are found in a region caught between a decaying agrarianism and an encroaching industrialism. Like his fellow New Englander, the poet Edwin Arlington Robinson, Frost sees the evil of self-love and ambition that lurks everywhere, but unlike Robinson, he believes in the healing sanities of woods and weeds and all that emanates from the soil. With Robinson also he shares a laconic but understanding love for the people who, old, discarded, or merely neglected, are too poor and too proud to be successful.

It is the people who dominate *North of Boston*. "Home Burial" blends the strange and the familiar with unusual effect. The talk is the talk of everyday, but the situation is extraordinary—common in words, uncommon in experience. Even the stains of mud on the man's shoes take on a significance that is horrifying because it is so matter-of-fact. The "Witch of Coös" is a ghost story in which the homeliness is part of its surprise; the buried bones of a murdered man mount the cellar steps to a narration which casually mixes prattle with terror. "The Code" is another example of extremes: a comedy and near-tragedy in which a farcical episode uncovers a basically grim conviction. "The Fear" is muted melodrama, a superb achievement in tension and anti-climax. "The Housekeeper" is an instance of pure talk not only in poetry, but talk *as* poetry. It is a domestic drama in which four ordinary people are involved, although the central figure—the extraordinary one—does not disclose her mind and, although she is fully realized, does not even appear. "A Hundred Collars," "The Mountain," and "A Servant to Servants," say all there is to say about isolation and the precarious balance between pathos and half-pitying humor. "Mending Wall" is a whimsical one-man debate, a rustic monolog in which bantering speculations are enclosed between two opposed adages: "Something there is that doesn't love a wall" and "Good fences make good neighbors." "The Death of the Hired Man," one of the most touching poems in modern literature is told in undertones, a poem which is not so much heard as overheard.

In early 1915 Frost returned to the United States to find himself a celebrity. Much to his surprise the man who had left his country an unknown writer came back to be hailed a leader of "the new era in American poetry." Critics fought over him; movements claimed him. Ezra Pound, who had befriended and patronized him in London, had failed to make him an Imagist. Later appraisers were no more successful in their efforts to dispose of him as a Classicist, a Humanist, a Realist, or a Ruralist. "If I must be classified," he wrote in a letter, "I might be called a Synecdochist, for I prefer the synecdoche in poetry—that figure of speech in which we use a part for the whole."

That playful statement is a key to Frost's method. Without telling too much he suggests all. With a genius for suggestion Frost takes the amorphous speech of everyday and gives it a shape. Prodded into taking a stand on realism, he wrote: "There are two types of realists—the one who offers a good deal of dirt with his potato to show that it is a real potato, and the one who is satisfied with the potato brushed clean. I'm inclined to be the second kind. To me the thing that art does for life is to clean it, to strip it to form." This is typical. He luxuriates in serious banter and flourishes in the play of ambiguities. In another letter he enlarged on the power of words and the magic by which they turned a craft into witchcraft. "Sometimes I have my doubts of words altogether, and I ask myself what is the place of them. They are worse than nothing unless they do something, unless they amount to deeds as in ultimatums and war-cries. They must be flat and final like the show-down in poker from which there is no appeal. My definition of literature would be just this: words that have become deeds." Frost's letters, still to be published, supplement his life and work in the same way that Keats's letters round out his poetry.

The breadth and quality of Frost's thought were part of his landscape—and the landscape showed in his face. Carved out of native granite, the features were sharp and the effect would have been cold had it not been for the pale blue and quizzical eyes, the lightly mocking smile, and the sensual bee-stung underlip. His was a stubborn scholar's face, masking the irrepressible poet's. Later, in a preface to his *Collected Poems* he made the distinction: "Scholars and artists thrown together are often annoyed at the puzzle of where they differ. Both work from knowledge; but I suspect they differ most importantly in the way their knowledge is come by. Scholars get theirs with conscientious thoroughness along projected lines of logic; poets theirs cavalierly and as it happens in and out of books. They stick to nothing deliberately, but let what will stick to them like burrs when they walk in the fields."

Immediately after his return to America, Frost did a characteristic thing: he bought a farm. Buying farms continued to be his favorite weakness. The first one he occupied was on a climbing hill outside of Franconia, New Hampshire, and this was followed by others in South Shaftsbury, Concord Corners, and Ripton, Vermont. Since he could not earn a living by farming, he turned to lecturing and let culture support agriculture. A spontaneous and brilliant talker, he enchanted audiences by "saying" the poems which found their way into countless anthologies and textbooks. He also went back to college, not as a scholar or even as a teacher, but as a "poet in residence," a campus influence, "a sort of poetic radiator." From his fortieth year on, he spent much of his time at various institutions of learning: his special stays were at Dartmouth, Michigan, and principally, Amherst, to which he came to "belong."

The volumes which followed *North of Boston* marked a continual increase in the ability to make poetry talk as well as sing. There was occasional raillery, but the mood was reflective, seasoned in experience, fresh in emotion. Frost triumphed in the subdued, even flat, tone and the slight ironic twist. Sometimes the poems conversed; sometimes they made their own tunes; mostly they talked and sang together. *Mountain Interval,* which was published in 1916, sustained the strength of the preceding narratives with their sinewy speech and suggestive understatements. Such blank verse monologs as "An Old Man's Winter Night" and "Birches" are particularly flexible, especially when set off by a new strain of intimate and intensified lyrics. "Fire and Ice," for example, is a masterpiece of condensation, a somber fancy wrapped in an epigram.

> Some say the world will end in fire,
> Some say in ice.
> From what I've tasted of desire
> I hold with those who favor fire.
> But if it had to perish twice,
> I think I know enough of hate
> To say that for destruction ice
> Is also great
> And would suffice.[1]

Honors descended thickly upon Frost in his middle years. He received the Gold Medal from the National Institute of Arts and Letters, citations from forums, schools and book clubs, and honorary degrees from more than a dozen colleges and universities. He won the Pulitzer Prize four times—for *New Hampshire* in 1924, for *Collected Poems* in 1931, for *A Further Range* in 1937, for *A Witness Tree* in 1943—Frost having been the only poet ever to win that quadruple distinction. The honors and rewards did not affect the man or his work. There seemed to be something prophetic about the last lines of the first poem in his very first book:

> They would not find me changed from him they knew—
> Only more sure of all I thought was true.

Although the chorus of praise was loud, there were a few discordant notes. His detractors felt that he had sacrificed his early effortlessness to "play with the role of a self-conscious homespun philosopher." Some of his admirers regretted that he avoided most of the problems of the day or, when he touched upon them, spoke as an arch conservative. Lines like the following, from "A Considerable Speck," were quoted as an expression of his resentment against all social welfare efforts:

> I have none of the tenderer-than-thou
> Collectivistic regimenting love
> With which the modern world is being swept . . .

"I never dared be radical when young/ For fear it would make me conservative when old" was one of the teasing jibes which were deplored. "His own native shrewdness began to get the upper hand; and, although his lyrical gift remained very nearly untouched, he began to shift his sympathy, with almost imperceptible slowness, away from wildness and unpredictability, toward the weather-safe side of existence," wrote Louise Bogan in *Achievement in American Poetry*. "He advocated none but the simplest virtues and expressed the most graspable ideas . . . Frost's final role—that of the inspired purveyor of timeless and granitic wisdom—has proved acceptable to all concerned, including the poet himself . . . He has come to hold so tightly to his 'views' that they at last have very nearly wiped out his vision." The complaint was echoed in *Poetry and the Age* by Randall Jarrell: "This poet is now, most of the time, an elder statesman, full of complacent wisdom and cast-iron whimsy . . . Sometimes it is this public figure, this official role, that writes the poems, and not the poet himself; and then one gets a self-made man's political editorials, full of cracker-box philosophizing, almanac joke-cracking . . . one gets the public figure's relishing consciousness of himself, an astonishing constriction of imagination and sympathy; one gets sentimentality and whimsicality, an arch complacency, a complacent archness, and one gets Homely Wisdom till the cows come home." Yet Jarrell is almost unreserved in his tribute to the "other" Frost, whose work is the most certain to endure. "No other living poet," says Jarrell, "has written so well about the actions of ordinary men . . . the many, many poems in which there are real people with their real speech and real thoughts and real emotions—all this, in conjunction with so much subtlety and exactness, such classical understatement and restraint, makes the reader feel that he is not in a book but in a world, and a world that has in common with his own some of the things that are most important in both . . . The grimness and awfulness and untouchable sadness of things, both in the world and in the self, have justice done to them in the poems, but no more justice than is done to the tenderness and love and delight."

Poets are said to lose the singing impulse as they grow older. The reverse is true of Frost; the work of his fifties and sixties is distinguished by its lyrical vitality. "Happiness Makes Up in Height for What It Lacks in Length," "Choose Something Like a Star," "Closed for Good," "The Gift Outright," one of the least flaunting but most persuasive patriotic poems ever written, "Directive," "Come In," and a dozen others are seemingly casual but full of so many nuances that they unfold level after level of meaning with each rereading. "Come In" is quoted not because it is the best of those mentioned, but because it is one of the shortest and most recent:

> As I came to the edge of the woods,
> Thrush music—hark!
> Now if it was dusk outside,
> Inside it was dark.
>
> Too dark in the woods for a bird
> By sleight of wing
> To better its perch for the night,
> Though it still could sing.
>
> The last of the light of the sun
> That had died in the west
> Still lived for one song more
> In a thrush's breast.
>
> Far in the pillared dark
> Thrush music went—
> Almost like a call to come in
> To the dark and lament.

> But no, I was out for stars:
> I would not come in.
> I meant not even if asked,
> And I hadn't been.[1]

On his eightieth birthday there appeared *Aforesaid,* a book of Frost's favorite poems selected by the poet himself. It is significant that only a few of the dark monologs were included. Frost had not repudiated the harsher note ("Provide, Provide" and "The Lovely Shall Be Choosers" were there) but the emphasis was on the unexpected phrase, the shift of thought on which the poem turned. "A poem is never a put-up job, so to speak," wrote Frost in an epistolary aside. "It begins as a lump in the throat, a sense of wrong, a homesickness, a lovesickness. It is never a thought to begin with. It is at its best when it is a tantalizing vagueness . . . It finds its thought or *makes* its thought. I suppose it finds it lying around with others not so much to its purpose in a more or less full mind. (That's why it oftener comes to nothing in youth before experience has filled the mind with thoughts. It may be a big emotion then, and yet find nothing it can embody it in.) It finds the thought and the thought finds the words."

In an introduction to E. A. Robinson's posthumous *King Jasper,* Frost said that the style was not only the man but that style was the way the man takes himself. "If," he maintained, "it is with outer seriousness, it must be with inner humor. If it is with outer humor, it must be with inner seriousness." The sentences, primarily a tribute to Robinson, are an almost perfect description of Frost's manner. His style, so characteristically quirky, so colloquial and so elevated, has its own way of uniting opposites. It combines observed fact with suddenly soaring fantasy. Or, rather, it is not a combination but an alternation, an intellectual prestidigitation, in which fact becomes fantasy and the fancy is more convincing than the fact. The inner seriousness and the outer humor continually shift their centers of gravity—and levity—and it becomes plain to all that Frost's banter is as full of serious implications as his somber speculations, that his playfulness is even more profound than his profundity.

Frost always preferred to let the poem speak for itself, even (or especially) when it is capable of more than one interpretation. Abhorring pretentious scholarship, as practiced, for example, by the

---

[1] From *Complete Poems of Robert Frost.* Copyright, 1930, 1949, by Henry Holt and Company, Inc. Copyright, 1942, by Robert Frost. By permission of the publishers.

gloomy grammarians of the New Criticism, he rarely explains. In a preface to his *Collected Poems,* however, he clearly indicated his fondness for the unpredictable play of thought, the element of surprise which is the life of poetry. "A poem," he wrote, "begins in delight and ends in wisdom. It has an outcome that, though unforeseen, was predestined from the first image of the mood . . . No surprise for the writer, no surprise for the reader. For me the initial delight is in the surprise of remembering something I didn't know I knew."

It is not hard to discover the reason for Frost's popularity. Readers who know nothing of his pioneering poetic vocabulary and are unconscious of the finesse with which it is employed, are grateful to him. They have been charmed and, at the same time, challenged. They are happy because they have learned something new while they were experiencing something old—the initial delight of "remembering something" they didn't know they knew. Never has poetry accomplished a more complete act of sharing.

Guglielmo Marconi

[1 8 7 4 - 1 9 3 7]

"There are no limits in science."

THERE IS a legend that when Guglielmo Marconi was born in Bologna, Italy, April 25, 1874, a neighbor rudely called attention to the infant's abnormally large ears. Whereupon his mother roused herself to retort, "That is so he can listen to things other people cannot hear." The child's hearing, sensitized to music by his Irish mother, seemed unusually acute, and as the boy was unusually shy, his father, a wealthy Italian businessman, decided not to subject him to routine schooling. Until he went to such centers of learning as Florence and Leghorn, Guglielmo was educated privately by tutors and by the books he found in his father's library. It was, in the main, a scientific library, and the boy pored over tomes about the physical sciences almost as soon as he could read. Electricity fascinated him, and by the time he was twelve, he was connecting wires and playing with batteries in the attic which his father let him use as a laboratory. He thought a lot about the chemistry of the air; at thirteen he tried to extract nitrate from the atmosphere.

He was fourteen when Heinrich Rudolph Hertz published the results of his experiments with air-waves. The theory that there were "waves" in the air was not new. In 1864 the mathematician James Clerk Maxwell had not only demonstrated the electromagnetic theory of light and the existence of electric waves, but had suggested their length as well as their velocity. Since his theory could not be proved, it remained a theory, considered impractical by everyone except Hertz and one or two other experimenters. Young Marconi was wildly excited when he read that Hertz had been able to send electrical waves across a room, inducing a visible spark twenty feet from his electric oscillator, without any connecting wires. He immediately began to speculate on the fantastic powers latent in wireless transmission. Could messages, music, or the speech of men and women be projected, and perhaps preserved, by using the air itself as a medium? If an impulse could be thrown a few feet without wires, why not a few miles? Why not across the world? There flashed upon him the idea, "I might almost say the intuition," he wrote later, "that these waves might, in a not too distant future, furnish mankind with a new and powerful means of communication."

At sixteen Marconi knew his life's purpose. Shortly afterwards he studied under Augusto Righi, a professor of physics who was experimenting in electromagnetism at the University of Bologna. Other eminent scientists were endeavoring to put the Hertzian waves to work, but young Marconi was not abashed. He rigged up an apparatus of combined parts, using an induction coil, a Morse signaling key, and a transmitter with a multiple discharger or spark "gap," the latter having been used by Righi. He "borrowed" another device from Edouard Branly, a Parisian physicist. Branly had used a glass tube filled with metal filings which cohered when an electric discharge was applied and which afterwards fell apart when subjected to a mechanical shock. Marconi took the principle and improved the construction. He packed a thermometer-thin glass tube with nickel dust and sent a current through the particles which cohered and thereupon acted as a conductor. When tapped with a light blow—the "hammer" was the small tongue of an electric doorbell—the filings fell apart and "decohered." Marconi tried other metals—iron, copper, zinc, brass—and decided that a nickel-silver composite was the most sensitive. He increased the responses and refined the instruments. He discarded the two rods of the Hertzian oscillator and connected one terminal of the spark discharger to a metal conductor on top of a pole. The other terminal was attached to a metal plate sunk in the earth. By this step, wrote Orrin Dunlap in his biography of the inventor, "wireless went out of the laboratory and into the air. There now seemed no limit to what the embryonic sparks might not do and where they might not go."

Although he had to overcome many failures, Marconi already had a few minor triumphs. He could press a key on the third floor of the villa and ring a bell in the basement. On a machine upstairs he could tap out three dots—the Morse letter *s*—and his father would hear the signal on the receiver which Guglielmo and his older brother set out on the lawn. His next test was to put more sending power into the waves, to concentrate them into beams and give them greater drive. Soon the sparks snapped with increased force; the reception became clearer and sharper. Marconi was twenty-one when he sent a message from his father's country house at Pontecchio near Bologna, and transmitted it a distance of one mile. The next year he increased the power of his primitive apparatus and established communication at double the distance.

Influential friends tried to interest the Italian government in Marconi's potentialities, but the authorities were not impressed by what seemed nothing more than a useless exhibit of precocity. Aided by his father, and encouraged by the experiments of Sir Oliver Lodge, Marconi set out for England. He was twenty-two years and six weeks old when he conducted a series of astonishing demonstrations there and took out the first patent ever issued for wireless telegraphy. A message was flashed ten miles across the Bristol Channel, whereupon Italy invited Marconi to return to his native land. He set up a station on the Italian Riviera, at Spezia, and contacted warships twelve miles out at sea. By the time his Wireless Telegraph and Signal Company had been formed, Marconi had gone back to England, where messages were exchanged across the English Channel.

Scientists were now certain that a youth had achieved a major development in scientific progress. The public, however, was not convinced until 1898, after the first wireless apparatus was installed on a lightship. A few months later the lightship was run down by a steamer. Wireless calls for help were flashed to a lighthouse, lifeboats were sent out, and the crew was dramatically rescued. The distances of transmission increased rapidly; during naval maneuvers wireless messages were conveyed seventy-four miles.

Although the newspapers called wireless one of the wonders of the modern world, Marconi felt he had only made a beginning. If wireless could span the Channel, he maintained it could cross the Atlantic. Professors, chained to the textbooks of the past, argued it was impossible. Electromagnetic impulses, they contended, traveled in straight lines. Instead of answering the skeptics Marconi proved that the Hertzian waves follow the curvature of the earth as streams and rivers do.

Already famous, he remained serious and reticent, devoted to the details of his work. Asked to explain wireless to the incredulous layman, "the boy wizard" offered a simple comparison by way of illustration. "Everyone knows how sound is transmitted by vibrations and air," he said. "For instance, if you fire a cannon, the concussion produced by the explosion of the powder causes the air to vibrate, and so far as these vibrations extend just so far is sound audible. Well, my vertical wire carries the electric vibrations up into the air and produces certain vibrations in the atmosphere. These vibrations extend in every direction and continue until they reach a receiving instrument. Thus a message can be transmitted through the air for as great a distance as you can cause vibration to proceed."

In the fall of 1899 Marconi sailed to the United States. James Gordon Bennett, owner of the *New York Herald,* had arranged to have him report the America Cup yacht races by means of wireless. He was excited by his visit to New York and, although "not frightened that your big steel buildings will stop wireless," was nonplused by the interviewers who followed him everywhere. One of the reporters described him as "no bigger than a Frenchman and no older than a quarter century. He is a mere boy, with a boy's happy enthusiasm and a man's view of his life-work. His manner is a little nervous and his eyes a bit dreamy. He acts with the modesty of a man who merely shrugs his shoulders when accused of discovering a new continent."

It was literally a new continent in every way for Marconi. His chief reason for coming to America was to accomplish "the big thing"—to establish wireless communication between the New World and the Old. (Before he died he was to cross the Atlantic eighty-nine times.) In October, 1900, he supervised the building of a great transmitter, a hundred times more powerful than any he had constructed. It was put up at Poldhu, in Cornwall, at the furthest southwest reach of England. In January, 1901, he tested the power of the beams. Six months later a cyclonic storm tore down the huge masts he had erected, and all of them had to be rebuilt. Similar towers put up on the receiving end on Cape Cod, Massachusetts, were blown down later, and the American site was shifted to St. John's, Newfoundland. There were innumerable difficulties. The weather was continually bad; trial balloons were ripped away; Marconi could not get a structure up to the required height. As a last resort he raised his Newfoundland aerial to four hundred feet by using kites to hold up the antennae.

Finally, on December 12, 1901, Marconi sat in a tower at St. John's and waited for the signal from Cornwall. It came, faintly at first and then stronger—the Morse code for the letter *s*—and the world learned that an ocean had been bridged by an insubstantial miracle. The young inventor was hailed as "the hero of the hour," "the epoch-making Marconi," "master of space," whose name "will stand through the ages among the very first of the world's great inventors." "When Signor Marconi succeeded in sending the letter *s* from Cornwall to Newfoundland," wrote the scientist-author Sir

Oliver Lodge, "it constituted an epoch in human history . . . One feels like a boy who has been strumming on the silent keyboard of a deserted organ, into which an unseen power begins to blow the vivifying breath. Astonished, he now finds that the touch of a finger elicits a responsive note; and he hesitates, half delighted, half frightened, lest he should be deafened by the chords which he can now summon almost at his will."

Marconi was too preoccupied to think of marriage until he was past thirty, and his first matrimonial venture ended unsuccessfully. The marriage started under the best auspices—his wife was the Honorable Beatrice O'Brien, the Irish daughter of Lord Inchiquin —and although it lasted nineteen years and resulted in three children, it was terminated in 1924. Three years later, when Marconi was fifty-three, he married another titled beauty, Countess Maria Cristina Bezzi-Scali, whose family belonged to the old Papal aristocracy. The second union was regally celebrated; a Prince officiated at the civil wedding ceremony and a Cardinal performed the religious rites. Marconi learned to live luxuriously. He spent more time on his yacht, on which he installed a small laboratory, and was treated more as a noble than a scientist. He again became a father; his daughter received the appropriately symbolic name of Elettra.

Marconi persistently broadened the scope of his pioneering work. In 1902, he had patented the magnetic detector and had followed it with another astounding invention, the horizontal directional aerial. He had studied the properties of ultra-short waves—fifteen meters wavelength in comparison with the two thousand of his early experiments—but had put aside these researches to concentrate on the problem of lengthening the waves up to about twelve thousand meters, waves which seemed to diminish in strength during daylight. As he grew older, he returned to his early studies and discovered the power of short waves which could be concentrated, focused, and beamed in any direction. He proved that short waves could be aimed at any part of the world and carry messages without distortion or "fading" either during the day or at night.

Another tremendous advance had been made in man's need for communication. Others, such as John Ambrose Fleming and Lee De Forest, were to apply the results of Marconi's genius to other mediums, presenting entertainment as well as communicating ideas. Fleming's thermionic valve led to De Forest's vacuum tube and, thus, to radio and talking pictures.

In 1909 Marconi was doubly honored. He was made a member

of the Italian Senate and was awarded the Nobel Prize for physics. In 1919 he was chosen to sign the peace treaties with Austria and Bulgaria, and he was plenipotentiary delegate to the Paris Peace Conference. In 1929 he was created a Marchese. He was planning further extensions of the wireless—possibly a beam to outer space with the moon as target, or a message to Mars—when he collapsed from overwork. He did not know what was wrong; the dynamic genius merely said he was "very, very tired." He sank so rapidly that, although oxygen was administered, he could not rally. He died July 20, 1937.

To the day of his death Marconi was modest about his achievements; he was always uncomfortable when praised for having "annihilated space." He regarded radio not as "the miracle with world-girdling wings," but as a symbol of progress. "There are no limits in science," he said. "Each advance merely widens the sphere of exploration." He was sufficiently gratified that his fifty preoccupied years had somewhat widened that sphere.

Winston Churchill

[1874-   ]

" 'I am finished,' he wrote in 1915."

ON HIS SEVENTY-NINTH BIRTHDAY, the Prime Minister of England, Winston Leonard Spencer Churchill, published the concluding volume of his six-volume memoirs, *The Second World War.* He had already written more than thirty other books, none of which could be accused of being light or laconic. Four monumental tomes had been devoted to an account of his illustrious ancestor, *Marlborough: His Life and Times;* a biography of his father, Lord Randolph Churchill, had run two volumes; his war speeches had been edited and compressed into six volumes; he had even ventured into fiction with the long, lurid, but prophetic *Savrola, a Tale of the Revolution in Laurania.* Authorship, however, was only one of the many occupations of the soldier, journalist, historian, politician, orator, and statesman who had served under five sovereigns—a man whose career was framed in superlatives, the most bitterly hated member of the House of Commons, the most fanatically loved leader, and incontrovertibly one of the most protean figures of the century.

He was born November 30, 1874, at Blenheim Palace, the third son of Lord Randolph Churchill, and a direct descendant of the mighty Marlborough, to whom Queen Anne had given the crown property of Woodstock, and for whom the famous architect, Sir John Vanbrugh, had built the magnificent edifice at Blenheim. His mother was an American, Jennie Jerome, a New Yorker possessed of great beauty and even greater fortune. It was probably his premature birth, as well as his eagerness to succeed which, as he grew up, led his contemporaries to call him "Young Man in a Hurry" and, later, "Pushful, the Younger." He was belligerent from the beginning. He rebelled against authority; wore out his nurses, and laughed at his tutors. He was, wrote Robert Lewis Taylor in *Winston Churchill: An Informal Study of Greatness,* "mule-headed to a degree. His appearance left no doubt of the smoldering fires within: he was small, red-haired, peppered with freckles, had a slightly pug nose and a mouth that signaled competition as plainly as a signpost.

His eyes were blue and gazed out with unflinching calm, and a touch of impatience, on children and grownups alike." Churchill maintained the appearance of a truculent child all through his life. Even at eighty, when he was quite bald, his face was bland, round and pink. When an admiring mother informed him that her newborn child resembled him, Churchill replied, "Of course. All babies look like me."

Before the boy was two years old, his grandfather was given the position of Viceroy of Ireland, and Winston spent the next few years in Dublin, resisting discipline, making up his own games, and playing with toy soldiers. He never ceased playing with them, and it is said that his father, watching him deploy his more than a thousand tin troops, knew that his son was destined to be a commander.

Formal education was a torture for young Winston. At seven he was sent to a school near Ascot which prepared for Eton. There he chiefly learned to hate Latin. He was often caned, but the floggings could not beat him into surrender. When he kicked the headmaster's straw hat to pieces, he became the school's idol. Hoping to improve his manners, as well as his health, which had suffered during the two years at Ascot, his family removed him to the Brighton seashore, where he went to a school conducted by two elderly ladies. Here he had more liberty. He was allowed to swim, ride, and read his favorite fiction, *King Solomon's Mines* and *Treasure Island;* but he was happiest when engaged in some form of mischief. One of his teachers, Vera Moore, threatened to resign if he kicked her shins once more. "He was," said Miss Moore, "the naughtiest boy in the class. In fact I used to think he was the naughtiest small boy in the world." He delighted in impertinences. Once when the youngsters were called upon to announce the number of demerits they had received during the day Winston proudly shouted "Nine!"

This seemed high even for the most undisciplined boy of the class, and the teacher repeated "Nine?"

"I said 'Nein.' " replied Winston. "I was talking German."

After three years of Brighton, Winston was sent to Harrow, which, because of its healthier location, the family had chosen instead of Eton. Here things went even worse. Winston was given a Latin entrance examination to fill out, and when he handed it back, it was blank except for the numeral one enclosed in brackets, some smudges, a large blot, and his signature. He was the lowest boy in the lowest form, self-assertive and, in consequence, generally unpopular. Far from stupid—he was, on the contrary, extremely literate and loquacious—he would not apply himself to anything in which he was not definitely concerned. "Where my reason, imagination, or interest was not engaged I could not or would not learn," he recalled in *My Early Life*. He resisted the classical education which his schoolmasters tried to force upon him, but he was compelled to sweat through Caesar, Ovid, and Virgil. He found some compensation in English Composition and began to respond to the cadences of the great English stylists. "I got into my bones the essential structure of the ordinary British sentence, which is a noble thing. And when, in after years, my schoolfellows, who had won prizes and distinction for writing such beautiful Latin poetry and pithy Greek epigrams, had to come down again to common English to earn their living or make their way, I did not feel myself at any disadvantage."

Churchill disliked sports almost as much as he despised the classics. He refused to cheer at, much less participate in, the football and cricket matches; the only form of athletics in which he distinguished himself was the Fencing Competition which he won when he was seventeen. The next year his father, troubled by his son's scholastic incapacities and his penchant for dangerous escapades—the boy had almost killed himself trying to blow up a "haunted house" with a gunpowder-filled ginger-beer bottle—remembered the toy soldiers and concluded that the best place for his backward boy was a military school. The seventeen-year-old Winston was delighted at the prospect of going to Sandhurst, but he had difficulty being admitted. He failed twice to pass the entrance examinations and, only after cramming with a specialist, was he able to get through the third test. His marks were so low that, instead of being qualified to join the crack regiment on which his father has set his heart, he was assigned to the disdained cavalry. The cavalry catered to young men from wealthy families, the horsy set whose intellectual standards were not nearly so high as their financial status. Churchill was not cast down. He said he preferred riding to walking.

Sandhurst changed Churchill. It did not eradicate his truculence or curb his artfulness, but it trimmed, tightened, and shaped him. He no longer delighted in taking exception to everything; he had found a purpose. He applied himself to the study of warfare; he gave himself wholeheartedly to lessons in map-making, fortifications, tactics, administration, and military law. He also grew aware of public affairs. His father's sister had married Lord Tweedmouth,

Gladstone's righthand man, and the youth listened to the Liberals expound their views on Home Rule at the dinner table or wrangle with the Conservatives in the House of Commons. He found himself in politics at the age of nineteen. During his last school term he made his first speech at a London meeting—a vehement protest against a Mrs. Ormiston Chant and her prohibition movement whose placards, as a result of Churchill's eloquence, were torn down and whose teetotalism was badly jarred. The occasion more than the "cause" excited Churchill; he had discovered his unknown forensic powers. A speech defect made it impossible for him to pronounce the letter *s* with any accuracy; but, in spite of the impediment, Churchill lisped his way through "I must say" and "I rejoice to see" to become one of the greatest orators of the period.

At twenty, a poised, self-possessed, copper-haired and smiling young man, he received the reward of his studies at Sandhurst: the Queen's Commission. His father had not lived long enough to witness the event. The estate was just large enough to settle the debts; the young cavalry officer could not support himself, to say nothing of a horse. Fortunately his mother still had ample means, and Winston was given an allowance of five hundred pounds per annum. It was not nearly as much as his brother officers had at their disposal, but the expenses were light; there were five months' leave every year; and the social distinction was gratifying.

For a while, Churchill was content to play the young blade-about-town, but he was too ardent to remain idle, too active to rust in peace. He looked around for something which might spell trouble, preferably a war. He found it in Cuba. It was a shabby little conflict, a second-rate war at the best, a disorderly series of guerrilla raids and reprisals, but it was something. Taking advantage of his leave, Churchill got an assignment as war correspondent for the *Daily Graphic,* sailed for Cuba with a fellow-Hussar, and the two were received by the Spanish authorities as though they were emissaries from the British government. The couple were liberally supplied with rum and cigars, which Churchill consumed in vast quantities, were furnished with horses, given an escort, and received the traditional baptism of fire. It was enough. After a few weeks of mosquito-infested, malaria-riddled jungle skirmishes, Churchill and his friend returned to England to learn that their company had been ordered to prepare for service in India.

Churchill was twenty-two when his regiment arrived in Bangalore. His duties there were far from onerous. He moved into a rose-covered bungalow, which he shared with three other officers, drilled most of the morning and slept all afternoon until five o'clock when polo, the really serious business of the day, began. Churchill enjoyed the frenzied chukkers, but he relished the enforced siestas less than his colleagues. His overactive mind could not rest during the three and four hours around noon when everyone was dozing, and he sent to England for books. Formerly he had been content with tales of adventure; now he found himself engrossed in Plato's *Republic,* Macaulay's *History of England,* and Gibbon's *Decline and Fall of the Roman Empire.* Although he read them for diversion, the muscular vigor and sonorous style of the majestic works penetrated his consciousness; echoes of Macaulay and Gibbon reverberate through the books he wrote and the ringing speeches he made.

A year later fighting broke out along the northwest frontier of India. Churchill, wangling a job as war correspondent, persuaded his colonel to let him join the force that had been sent to suppress the Pathan uprising. For his part in the punitive expedition, Churchill was mentioned in dispatches as having "made himself useful at a critical moment"; his articles, as well as his courage, were praised; his first book, *The Story of the Malakand Field Force,* an expansion of his battle pieces, was published when he was a few months more than twenty-three. The book was a financial success—the royalties amounted to more than two years' pay of a second lieutenant—and, encouraged by its reception, he started a novel, *Savrola,* a cross between a gaudy Zenda-like dream of escape fiction and a critique of revolution. Churchill was, however, more a soldier than a writer, and when he heard that the Anglo-Egyptian Army was about to launch an offensive to rid the Sudan of the Dervishes, he resolved to be a part of the campaign. He had some trouble convincing his superiors that he was needed—the Commander-in-Chief, Sir Herbert Kitchener, obviously did not want him—but his mother pulled the necessary diplomatic strings and Churchill, once more reinforced by an assignment as correspondent, was attached to the 21st Lancers as a supernumerary lieutenant.

The war in the Sudan increased Churchill's dual prestige as fighter and author. The Lancers played a leading part in the battle of Omdurman—their cavalry charge, a reminder of Balaclava's archaic Light Brigade, was one of the last of its kind—and Churchill's account of the conflict, *The River War,* was not only esteemed by

the critics but so relished by readers that a second edition of the
expensive book was issued within a few months of the first. At
twenty-four, upon his return to England, the soldier-journalist made
a second foray into politics. He fought a by-election in Oldham as a
Conservative whose policies were vague and whose principles were
dubious. He accepted the Tory platform of the vested interests and
the status quo; he espoused a Tithes Bill but, when it appeared to
be an unpopular measure, discarded it. When Arthur Balfour,
leader of the House of Commons, learned of the defection, he said
unhappily, "I thought he was a young man of promise, but it appears he is only a young man of promises." Badly beaten at the
polls, Churchill licked his political wounds, and went back to sol-
diering. Six months later, the defeated candidate was a famous
hero.

South Africa was the scene of his exploits. The Boers, descendants of farmers of the Transvaal and Orange Free State, resented
the invasion of English fortune-seekers who were crowding the region, attracted by the gold and diamond mines, and hopeful of
uniting the independent republics under British rule. When England placed troops on the Transvaal border, President Paul Kruger
sent an ultimatum, and London promptly declared war. The South
African War, hailed by the Tory imperialists, was assailed by the
Radicals and most of the Liberals. An unpopular and humiliating
struggle, it took almost three years for the greatly superior English
forces to gain a doubtful decision through shockingly ruthless methods—120,000 Boer women and children had been packed into a
concentration camp and 20,000 of them had died of brutalities.
But although England suffered a serious loss in prestige, Churchill
achieved national prominence. He went to South Africa as war correspondent of the *Morning Post,* got himself on an antiquated armored train, took charge of operations when it was derailed, was
trapped and taken prisoner. Two weeks later he escaped. He was
hunted and a price was set on his head—he resented the fact that
his value was assessed at only twenty-five pounds. Handbills described him unfeelingly: "Englishman, 25 years old, about five feet
eight inches tall, indifferent build, walks with a forward stoop, pale
appearance, red-brownish hair, small and hardly noticeable mustache, talks through his nose and cannot pronounce the letter *s* properly." He could not speak the language of the country, but he
managed to evade his pursuers, found shelter with an expatriated
Englishman, hid himself in a freight car under bales of wool, and

reached the British colony. His exploits were widely heralded, but the military authorities scorned his reports on the high morale of the enemy and the superiority of the individual Boer soldier. A group of officers wired him: "Best friends here hope you will not continue making further ass of yourself." In spite of the admonitions of his elders, Churchill was unabashed. His was a headline triumph, and he was bound to relish it. He tried to seem modest, but it is not easy to be self-effacing when one is a national idol in his mid-twenties.

On the strength of the acclaim, Churchill returned to Oldham and once again stood for public office. This time, thanks to patriotic fervor, he had no trouble winning. Before he entered Parliament he made a lecture tour of England, which netted him almost five thousand pounds, and supplemented this by touring America, where he amassed another ten thousand pounds. In the United States he was billed as "the hero of five wars, the author of six books, and the future Prime Minister of England." Mark Twain introduced him to a New York audience as "the definitely perfect man—son of an English father and an American mother." By the time he returned, the proceeds of his books and lectures totaled an equivalent of one hundred thousand dollars. Churchill's star was not only in the ascendancy but had risen to a considerable height when, at twenty-six, he took his seat in the House of Commons.

As a speaker Churchill held audiences by his way with words, his elocutionary surprises, his vivid turns of phrase which, carefully rehearsed, had the ring of brilliant spontaneity. As a thinker, he did nothing to disturb the minds of his listeners. He developed a manner of stating stereotyped ideas so that they seemed daring; even the most critical of his hearers were so taken with the challenging manner that they failed to realize how conventional the matter was. In *Winston Churchill: The Era and the Man,* Virginia Cowles explains the paradox which prompted Churchill to proffer unoriginal ideas with striking originality. "He was a man of action rather than thought. He did not feel compelled to examine accepted principles and value them for himself . . . Far from anticipating the new forces of the century, his energies were bent on turning the clock back to the generation before, when Victorian conceptions were in the full bloom of maturity. He preached all the fading doctrines of a fading age: he stood for isolation from Europe and for a small army; for Imperialism; strict economy; Free Trade; no increase in the income tax. These were the ideas of the past, and as the new century progressed every one of them was to perish."

"I adopted quite early in life a system of believing what I wanted to believe," Churchill said candidly. He acknowledged that he took his politics unquestioningly from his father, the highly conservative Lord Randolph who seemed to have possessed the keys to popular oratory and political action. Young Churchill also fancied that he carried on the tradition of his swashbuckling ancestor, the soldier-politician, John Churchill, first Duke of Marlborough, who was, according to Churchill's biography, not only a great commander but virtually Master of England. He developed a wit that was so flexible he could use it either as a stiletto or a bludgeon. "Mr. Chamberlain loves the workingman," he purred on one occasion. "He loves to see him work." "Mr. MacDonald," he remarked sardonically, "is the greatest living master of falling without hurting himself." Before long it was rumored that Churchill seemed to love dissidence for its own sake. His enemies declared that he considered himself too big for the party; his friends countered by saying that party came second and personality first. Suddenly he began to attack the Tories, to advocate a soft peace with the Boers, a strong defensive Navy, and complete opposition to continental wars. As a logical consequence, and to the discomfiture of his fellow-Conservatives, he moved over to the Liberal side of the House. Three years later the Liberal Party overthrew their adversaries in the General Election of 1906, and Churchill was given the post of Under-Secretary for the Colonies.

While the Liberals were battling their Conservative opponents, the championless Suffragettes, shouting "Votes for Women," were busily breaking windows and attacking Churchill. Two years later their demonstrations were so successful that they caused him to lose an election. He ran in another county, a Liberal stronghold, and was returned to office. Reappointed to the Cabinet, this time as President of the Board of Trade, Churchill felt secure enough to get married; his wedding with the beautiful Clementine Hozier, which took place in the fall of 1908 in St. Margaret's Church (significantly next to Westminster Abbey) was almost a royal event. Churchill's ascent was spectacularly apparent when, at thirty-six, he was appointed Home Secretary and, a year later, First Lord of the Admiralty. His role was difficult and often dangerous; he was the accepted target, blamed for every minor disturbance and major calamity. At home, England was riddled by bitter and often bloody strikes; abroad a series of crises, largely caused by the struggle for overseas markets following upon colonial expansion, threatened a tense and fearful world. The flimsy façade of leagues and alliances failed to hide a savage armaments race which involved all Europe. By 1914 Anglo-German relations had grown steadily worse, and only a provocative incident was needed to set off a general conflict. On June 28, 1914, an Austrian archduke was assassinated by a member of a Serbian terrorist society. Germany backed up Austria; Russia stood behind Serbia; France deliberated and hesitated but mobilized; German troops, aiming at Paris, invaded Belgium; England declared itself in a state of hostilities with Germany, and the First World War began.

At the beginning of World War I, Churchill was one of the most powerful figures in the British Empire. Dynamic, persuasive and, when the occasion demanded, truculent, he altered the conduct of land fighting, inspired the invention of new weapons, and changed old concepts of warfare. He stressed the importance of aviation when heavier-than-air flying machines were still dubious experiments and German gas-filled Zeppelins controlled the skies. He revolutionized the employment of infantry and made trench warfare practically obsolete by the emergence of "an armored car," a land battleship which became the tank. Nevertheless, Churchill remained in power less than a year. Those who scoffed at the tank—orders for all except one were canceled—resented his authority as well as his self-assurance; his inability to consider the views of others made more and more enemies as the war dragged on. The disasters at Antwerp and the Dardanelles were blamed on him, and ten months after the outbreak of the war he was no longer First Lord of the Admiralty. In another five months he was dismissed from the Cabinet.

"I am finished," Churchill told a friend. "I am banished from the scene of action." He was still a member of the House of Commons, and as part of the "patriotic Opposition" he pursued a course of pugnacity, attacking complacence and the blind policy of "muddling through." He had time for his hobby, painting, and his family; there were, by 1916, three children: Diana, Randolph, and Sarah. (A third daughter, Mary, was born six years later.) Gradually he was restored to a position of power. As governments fell and new ones were formed, Churchill re-entered the Cabinet. In spite of a bombardment of protests Lloyd George made him Minister of Munitions. After the Armistice, he was appointed Minister of War, with the Air Ministry under his aegis. He was transferred to the Colonial Office, after which he deserted the weakened Liberal Party, attacked the Laborites, flirted for a while with the idea of a coalition, and finally threw in his lot with the Tories. In 1924 the Conservatives again came into power and Stanley Baldwin appointed Churchill Chancellor of the Exchequer.

Churchill's opponents did not fail to point out his waverings and inconsistencies. "The only side he sticks to," said one of them, "is his own side." When he was denounced for abandoning Free Trade, he replied nonchalantly, "There is nothing wrong in change, if it is in the right direction . . . To improve is to change," he went on, placidly adding, "To be perfect is to have changed often." Lord Oxford called him "a genius without judgment." True to his nature, he went to extremes. He grew more conservative than the Conservatives; he out-toried the Tories. In 1929 the Labor Party, supported by the Liberals, achieved a sweeping victory, and Baldwin was allowed to form another government on condition that Churchill was no longer included in the Cabinet. He was fifty-five when he stepped down from his eminence; ten years passed before he again held office.

During the so-called idle decade, his "lotus years," Churchill retreated to his country manor at Chartwell, and devoted himself to the ever-accumulating reminiscences which were to emerge as one of the most important political-historical documents of the period. The four volumes of *The World Crisis* displayed its author as one of the greatest talkers of his time, master of a style that was already classified as "pure Churchillian" and a reader appeal that brought him the reward of about one hundred thousand dollars. This sum was further amplified by his immense biography of Marlborough, by sporadic lectures, and by a series of magazine articles. He developed another hobby, masonry, and when the Bricklayers' Union objected, he applied for membership in the union and proved that he could build a brick wall and tile a roof with the best of them. He was, however, not allowed to retire from public life; although he was no longer in the Cabinet, his constituents returned him to Parliament.

When Hitler made his first pronouncements concerning Germany's right to rearm, Churchill had no national prejudice against the man. "I knew little of his doctrine or record and nothing of his character," he wrote in *The Gathering Storm*. "I admire men who stand up

for their country in defeat, even though I am on the other side."
Subsequently Churchill read *Mein Kampf,* foresaw the pattern of
the world conquest, and envisioned the shape of the war to come.
Seven years before the German Armies overwhelmed the Low
Countries, he warned the House of Commons that the Germans
were not, as Hitler protested, merely asking equal status. "All these
bands of sturdy Teutonic youths marching through the streets and
roads of Germany, with the light of desire in their eyes, are not
looking for status. They are looking for weapons." He argued, he
coaxed, he thundered, he pointed out that Germany was building
an unprecedented submarine navy and a fearsome, fully mechanized army founded on the very tanks which his detractors had belittled. He became a one-man forum against the Nazis, and he became a nuisance. The opposition nodded in somnolent assent, and
waved the alarmist away. In 1934 Churchill informed Parliament
that the Hitler strategy called for a great armada of planes and predicted that London would be ruinously bombed from the air. But
the Prime Minister, Stanley Baldwin, was busy preventing King
Edward from marrying an American, a commoner; Neville Chamberlain was placating Hitler; and England, putting a dagger in the
back of the League of Nations, bowed to Italy's conscienceless dismemberment of Abyssinia. Although Churchill harangued, England
did nothing while Germany occupied the Rhineland and exercised
a free hand in Eastern Europe. Baldwin who had rebuked Churchill with "there will be no great armaments in *this* country," refused
to worry; Chamberlain capitulated shamefully to Hitler at Munich
("to preserve peace in our time") and, less than a year later, Germany invaded Poland and initiated the Second World War.

Churchill the Warmonger was now hailed as Churchill the
Prophet. Chamberlain, who had succeeded Baldwin as Prime Minister, had little trouble persuading the inexhaustible and indomitable veteran of sixty-five to take over the Navy, and the Admiralty
flashed a welcome message to every unit of the Fleet: "Winston is
back!" Churchill was England's symbol; the face of the British lion
assumed the pugnacious features of the restored First Lord of the
Admiralty. A few months after the outbreak of World War II
Chamberlain was compelled to step down and the King asked
Churchill to form a coalition government. On May 10, 1940, Churchill made his first speech as Prime Minister. "I have nothing to offer," he told the British people, "but blood and toil, tears and
sweat."

Churchill, the rhetorician, was aware of the powerful understatement. He offered more than fanatical devotion and unsurpassed leadership. He made plans to invade the German coast and, for that purpose, devised new types of amphibian tanks, armored fighting vehicles, experimental landing craft. Long before D-Day, when the Allies landed in France and an artificial harbor was constructed for that event, Churchill suggested the construction of "a number of flat-bottomed barges or caissons, made not of steel but of concrete . . . They would float when empty of water, and thus could be towed across to the site of an artificial island. On arrival at the buoys marking the island, the sea-cocks would be opened and they would gradually sink to the bottom . . . By this means a torpedo-proof as well as weather-proof harbor would be created in the open sea, with regular pens for destroyers and submarines, and alighting-platforms for aeroplanes." He also offered such intangibles as courage, inspiriting and invincible faith. After King Leopold of Belgium unaccountably surrendered to the Germans, forcing the nightmare evacuation of Dunkirk, when France fell, with Russia already aligned with the Nazis, Churchill faced his Cabinet. "Gentlemen," he announced grimly, "we are alone. For myself," he added, "I find it extremely exhilarating." When Germany seemed about to launch the long-threatened invasion of Britain, he exhorted his fellow-countrymen: "We shall defend our island, whatever the cost may be. We shall fight on the beaches. We shall fight on the landing grounds. We shall fight on the fields and in the streets. We shall fight in the hills. We shall never surrender." He strengthened a nation's resolve with: "Let us brace ourselves to our duties, and so bear ourselves that, if the British Empire and Commonwealth last for a thousand years, men will say: 'This was their finest hour.'"

It was Churchill's stubborn refusal to acknowledge the apparent triumph of the Nazi Armies that kept a battered England fighting and gave Russia and the United States time to organize their vast resources in supplies and manpower; it was Churchill who welded the "grand Alliance" which brought the United States pounding from the West and the U. S. S. R. hammering from the East. His friendship with Roosevelt was solidified during the rendezvous at Newfoundland in 1941 when the Atlantic Charter—the document setting up ideal peace terms—was signed. During the war the two men met a dozen times and Churchill was a favorite guest, almost a member of the family, at the White House. Eleanor Roosevelt recalls that both men were nostalgic for the world that existed before the war and that, although Churchill knew it could never be the same again, he said that "all he wanted to do was to stay in office until he had seen the men come home from the war and until they had places in which to live." Churchill's camaraderie with Stalin was personal rather than political. Both leaders were reckless, aggressive, great fighters as well as great eaters and drinkers. Churchill regarded the rise of Communism with horror. "Was there ever a more awful spectacle in the whole history of the World than is unfolded by the agony of Russia?" he said in January, 1921. "It is now reduced to famine of the most terrible kind—not because there is no food—there is plenty of food—but because the theories of Lenin and Trotsky have fatally and, it may be, finally, ruptured the means of intercourse between man and man, between workman and peasant, between town and country . . . because they have driven man from the civilization of the twentieth century into a condition of barbarism worse than the Stone Age, and have left him the most pitiable spectacle in human experience, devoured by vermin, racked by pestilence, and deprived of hope." But twenty years later the twists of fortune and the ways of war prompted Churchill to refer to the Russians as "glorious warriors" and "mighty heroes" as the armies under Stalin kept Hitler's hordes engaged before Moscow and at Stalingrad, and prevented them from returning westward to invade England. "No one has been a more consistent opponent of Communism than I have been for the last twenty-five years," he announced in a challenging broadcast the day after Germany attacked Russia. "I will unsay no word that I have spoken about it. But all this fades away before the spectacle which is now unfolding. I see the Russian soldiers standing on the threshold of their native land, guarding the fields which their fathers have tilled from time immemorial . . . Can you doubt what our policy will be? We are resolved to destroy Hitler and every vestige of the Nazi regime . . . We will never parley, we will never negotiate with Hitler or any of his gang. We shall fight him by land, we shall fight him by sea, we shall fight him in the air, until, with God's help, we have rid the earth of his shadow and liberated its peoples from his yoke. Any man or state who fights on against Nazidom will have our aid."

After the war Churchill maintained an ambiguous attitude toward the U. S. S. R. Knowing that Russia would dominate the Continent and, perhaps, Asia, he called for a federation of English-speaking nations. At the same time, he was opposed to any warlike gestures in the direction of Russia. His voice never lacked authority even when he was intermittently in and out of power. Two months after the victory of the Allies, there was a General Election and the men and women whom Churchill had saved from despotism exercised their freedom to vote their hero out of office. Various reasons were given for the overthrow of a great leader at the peak of his fame. He was, it was said, by nature a Tory, out of sympathy with the problems of the poor and underprivileged; he was too old as well as too rigid to guide his country through the inevitable reconstruction period; he had made the mistake of holding on to power after he had done his job of concluding the hostilities. His enemies charged that, although he was needed (a militant and necessary evil) during the war, he had always been an irresponsible peacetime leader. All these arguments may have contributed to his rejection, but the main reason was the overwhelming wish to forget everything connected with the war and the unreasoning but deep-rooted desire for change. Not being superhuman, Churchill was hurt and resentful; he became an embittered leader of the Opposition. "At the outset of this mighty battle," he wrote in his history of the Second World War, "I acquired the chief power in the State, which henceforth I wielded in ever-growing measure for five years and three months of world war, at the end of which, all our enemies having surrendered unconditionally or being about to do so, I was immediately dismissed by the British electorate from all further conduct of their affairs."

It was some time before Churchill recovered from a sense of shocked frustration. Gradually his natural ebullience and volatility reasserted themselves, and he flew into action with as much zest as when he was cutting down Pathans or hurling deadly diatribes at the Laborites. He toured England and America, speaking with the old vibrancy and adding new phrases to the language, such as, when referring to Russia's secret preparations, he said "an iron curtain has descended across the Continent." He plunged into his richly documented account of World War II and, with the help of a large array of statisticians, scientists, military experts, scholars, and other researchers, a specially built recording machine, and a staff of six secretaries working day and night in eight-hour relays, he produced six volumes, for which the American serial rights alone brought him close to two million dollars. The separate titles are *The Gathering Storm, Their Finest Hour, The Grand Alliance, The Hinge of Fate, Closing the Ring,* and *Triumph and Tragedy.* To the last he appended a mournful subtitle: "How the Great

Democracies Triumphed, and So Were Able to Resume the Follies Which Had So Nearly Cost Them Their Life." The problems of understanding and living with Soviet Russia, the once "great and gallant ally," as well as a settlement to end the "cold war," were left unsolved.

During the six years spent in writing the memoirs, Churchill was preparing to change the tragedy of his humiliating defeat to a heroic drama with a triumphant ending. In 1951 another General Election gave him the climax he was seeking, and he was once more Prime Minister. He was proud to serve, he said, "not because of love for power and office. I have had an ample feast of both . . . It is because I have the feeling that I may through things that happened have an influence on what I care about above all else—the building of a sure and stable peace."

Churchill's seventy-ninth birthday was celebrated by world acclaim, synthesized by a memorial volume, *Churchill By His Contemporaries,* a series of affectionate homages to the dazzling and uneven career of the war correspondent, novelist, artist, humorist, orator, soldier, parliamentarian, political opponent, and, as summarized by Bernard Shaw, "Churchill, the Man of Talent." Shaw was gracious (or defensive) enough not to recall the interchange of thrusts when he sent Churchill two tickets for the opening of one of his plays with a note: "Come to the first night and bring a friend —if you have a friend." To which Churchill acidly replied: "Too busy to come to the opening, but will be there the second night—if there is a second night."

Churchill's pronouncements were usually sharpened with flickering wit. *A Churchill Reader* is practically built around such epigrams as: "A fanatic is one who can't change his mind and won't change the subject." . . . "Personally I am always ready to learn, although I do not always like being taught." . . . "Any clever person can make plans for winning a war if he has no responsibility for carrying them out." . . . "It is better to have a world united than a world divided; but it is also better to have a world divided than a world destroyed."

Toward the middle of his seventy-ninth year, the most colorful and controversial of statesmen had been made a Knight of the Most Noble Order of the Garter by Elizabeth the Second. A few months later Sir Winston Churchill received a greater tribute: he was awarded the Nobel Prize in literature not only for his writings but for his wartime speeches against "a monstrous tyranny never surpassed in the dark, lamentable catalog of human crimes." The Swedish Academy, which conferred the honor, stated that he had been chosen "for his mastery of historical and biographical description, as well as the brilliant art of oration with which he has defended human values."

The award was fitting not only for oratory and history. It was also a recognition of the embattled personality who had inscribed his most ambitious books with a revealing "moral of the work." The words were restrained, succinct and noble—"In War: Resolution. In Defeat: Defiance. In Victory: Magnanimity. In Peace: Goodwill." It was a motto worthy of being borne on the proudest shield and the loftiest banner.

Albert Schweitzer

[1 8 7 5 -   ]

"Reverence for life."

I AM IN COMPLETE DISAGREEMENT with the spirit of the age because it is filled with disdain of thinking. This attitude can be explained to some extent by the fact that thought itself has never yet reached the goal which it must set before itself . . . The only possible way out of chaos is for us to come once more under the control of the ideals of true civilization." These words were not written by an immured philosopher, protecting his privacy with a barrier of abstractions, but by an active preacher, a creative musician and practical organ-builder who abandoned civilization, as well as a successful career, to spend his life among uncivilized creatures at the edge of the primeval jungle.

Albert Schweitzer, one of the saintliest figures of modern times, was born January 14, 1875, at Kaysersberg, in German Alsace. His ancestors on both sides were ministers and musicians. His paternal grandfather was an Alsatian organist and schoolmaster, whose three brothers held similar posts. His maternal grandfather was a pastor, and his father was the leader of an evangelical congregation. Albert was the second of five children, there being, besides himself, three sisters and a brother. At five he began picking out melodies on the piano with one finger; at seven he played hymn-tunes on the parlor-organ and made up his own harmonies. He was barely nine when he substituted for the organist at a church service in Grünsbach, where the family had been brought shortly after his birth. He was educated at various Alsatian schools, paid particular attention to natural science, took occasional lessons from Charles Marie Widor, the great French organist, and, at eighteen, entered Strasbourg University. There he devoted himself to theology and music; during his student years he was filled with an inextinguishable and undivided veneration for Bach and Jesus. At twenty-two he went to Paris to study philosophy at the Sorbonne and organ-playing with Widor, developing in both a "plastic" style which he never could acquire in Germany.

At twenty-four Schweitzer took his degree in philosophy and obtained a position as preacher at the Church of St. Nicholas in Strasbourg. He was also accepted as a university lecturer on theological subjects. His understanding of the origin and early Christian development of the Last Supper and Baptism led to a probing reappraisal, *The Quest of the Historical Jesus,* the first edition of which appeared in 1906. At about the same time Schweitzer's monumental book on Bach appeared. Differing with those who ranked the great eighteenth-century master of polyphony as a severe classicist, Schweitzer presented a Bach who was not only a poet but a tone painter. "His music is poetic and pictorial because its themes are born of poetic and pictorial ideas. Out of these themes the composition unfolds itself, a finished structure in terms of tone . . . Its essence displays itself as Gothic architecture transformed into sound." As a corollary to his work on Bach, as well as his own performances, Schweitzer also published *The Art of Organ Building and Organ Playing in Germany and France.* He became an authority on the reconstruction of old models and the building of new ones. Designs were sent to him for approval or revision; he made many trips to help the restoration of ancient instruments. An acknowledged authority at twenty-nine, he seemed to have a lifetime of security ahead of him.

At thirty, Schweitzer made a dramatic decision. He determined to become a medical student in order to go to Equatorial Africa as a doctor. His friends were astounded. One of them tried to conceal his sense of shock with a flippancy: "In Europe you saved old organs; in Africa you want to save old Negroes." Schweitzer had conceived of his plan years before. Even as a student it had struck him as unfair that he should be allowed to lead a carefree life in the midst of suffering. One morning when he was in his twenty-second year he came to a definite resolution: "I would consider myself justified in living for art and science until I was thirty in order to devote myself from that time on to the direct service of humanity. Many a time I had tried to settle what meaning lay hidden for me in the saying of Jesus, 'Whosoever would save his life shall lose it, and whosoever shall lose his life for My sake shall save it.' The answer was found. In addition to the outward, I now had inward happiness."

Schweitzer did not plan to leave Europe. For a while he thought of looking after abandoned children and educating them; but the organizations which had charge of destitute and neglected children would not cooperate with him. He then considered devoting himself to tramps and discharged prisoners; but this, too, turned out to be impractical. A magazine put out by a Paris missionary society carried an article on the need for doctors in Gabon, the northern province of the Congo Colony. When Schweitzer finished the article, he knew that his search was over. He was not too surprised to find that all his relatives and friends joined in remonstrations, for he realized that, although men believed in the sayings of Jesus, only a few were willing to act upon them. "I felt as a real kindness the action of persons who made no attempt to dig their fists into my heart, but regarded me merely as a precocious young man, not quite right in his head, and treated me correspondingly with affectionate mockery."

His associates were surprised to hear that Schweitzer had chosen Africa, and still more startled to learn that Schweitzer wanted to go not as a missionary but as a doctor. His reply to them was simple and characteristic of the man: "I wanted to be a doctor that I might be able to work without having to talk. For years I had been giving myself out in words, and it was with joy that I had followed the calling of theological teacher and of preacher. In this new form of activity, however, I would not merely be talking about the religion of love, but would be putting it into actual practice."

For the next seven years Schweitzer applied himself to the study of medicine. He also engaged in further explorations of the historicity of Jesus and, with Widor's collaboration, prepared the first five volumes of a radically new edition of Bach's organ music. He was thirty-seven when he finished his researches in tropical diseases, completed his internship at the hospital and, with his newly married wife—Helene Bresslau, daughter of a historian—set out for the little African settlement of Lambaréné. The conditions there were disheartening. The buildings in which he expected to conduct his medical practice had not been built; his consulting room was an old, filth-encrusted chicken house close to his living quarters; the heat was unbelievable. For a while he was unable to find natives who would serve as orderlies and interpreters. But word spread that a doctor had come to Lambaréné, and soon the sick came on foot and in canoes from distances up to two hundred miles. He treated not only malaria, sleeping sickness, dysentery, and leprosy (the chief diseases of the region), but operated on cases of hernia, ulcers, and elephantiasis. Although he had put aside his gifts as doctor of divinity, the missionaries persuaded him to preach and, with the aid of an interpreter, he found it a fresh and uplifting experience.

"It was," he said, "a glorious thing to preach the sayings of Jesus and Paul to people to whom they were altogether new." In his "spare time" Schweitzer worked on the last three volumes of the Bach organ music and kept up his organ technique by playing on a specially equipped piano.

Schweitzer and his wife, who had become his nurse as well as his amanuensis, had been in Africa less than a year when the First World War broke out, and as Germans in a French possession, they were held as enemy aliens. "That white people were making prisoners of other whites and putting them under the authority of black soldiers was something incomprehensible to the natives," Schweitzer wrote in *Out of My Life and Thought*. Faced with the problem of a civilized world at war with itself, he set to work. Two days after his internment, he began his *Philosophy of Civilization*. Sixteen months later, Schweitzer was permitted to visit the ailing wife of a missionary who lived more than a hundred miles upstream. "Lost in thought," he recalls, "I sat on the deck of the barge, struggling to find the elementary and universal conception of the ethical which I had not discovered in any philosophy. I filled sheet after sheet with disconnected sentences, merely to keep myself concentrated on the problem. Late on the third day, at the very moment when, at sunset, we were making our way through a herd of hippopotami, there flashed upon my mind, unforeseen and unsought, the phrase Reverence for Life. The iron door had yielded: the path in the thicket had become visible. I had found my way to the idea in which affirmation of the world and ethics are contained side by side. Now I knew that the ethical acceptance of the world and of life, together with the ideals of civilization contained in this concept, has a foundation in thought."

Reverence for life sustained Schweitzer through one hardship after another. It preserved him when he was shipped back to Europe and placed in the internment camps of Garaison and Saint-Rémy, where he was put in a building which had been a hospital for the insane and had housed Van Gogh. When the Armistice came, he seemed somehow to have stored up physical as well as spiritual strength. He was more determined than ever to go where he was needed. He gave organ recitals and delivered lectures to raise funds for continuing his work at Lambaréné. Concertizing and lecturing took him to Switzerland, Sweden, Denmark, and England, but in 1924 he was back in Africa.

This became the pattern of Schweitzer's life. Whenever his hospital needed drugs or medical supplies he would undertake a lecture tour, interspersed with performances on the great organs of Europe. In 1949, he visited the United States for the first time in order to address the Goethe centennial at Aspen, Colorado. In 1950, the National Arts Foundation conducted a poll among the artists, musicians, and authors of eighteen countries, and Schweitzer was proclaimed "The Man of the Century." Being human, he was pleased. But he was much happier because of his discovery of a perpetual spring and prouder of the seven hundred and fifty huge concrete blocks which he had made to line it. He was equally delighted when his young daughter, sharing his love for everything that lives, played with the six chimpanzees and five antelopes that made themselves at home in the hospital yard. A member of the Albert Schweitzer Fellowship, which had been founded when Schweitzer was sixty-five years old, described a typical scene in Lambaréné: "At seven-thirty the bell rang for breakfast, and we came out into the strange world which darkness had covered, as we came into it the night before. And what a world! Under the house and around it, is a veritable menagerie: chickens, geese, turkeys, cats, dogs, goats, antelopes, birds, etc. A pelican is a faithful devotee and it comes back daily to mingle with the congregation of birds and beasts which have gathered around Dr. Schweitzer . . . He is truly another St. Francis of Assisi . . . Nights, as he writes on his philosophy, a yellow and white cat which he saved as a kitten, curls up around his lamp."

Nearing eighty Schweitzer's hair was white and thick as ever; his brilliant blue eyes still looked at a world with tolerance and, in spite of its daily injustices, with trust. He was by no means convinced that it was the best of all possible worlds; he was even willing to be considered a self-divided idealist: a pessimist by what he had seen of humanity and an optimist by what he hoped it might someday become. "In my judgment of the situation in which mankind finds itself at present, I am pessimistic. I cannot make myself believe that the situation is not as bad as it seems to be; I am inwardly conscious that we are on the road which, if we continue to tread it, will bring us into the 'Middle Ages' of a new kind . . . And yet I am optimistic . . . If men can be found who revolt against the spirit of thoughtlessness, and who are strong enough to let the ideals of ethical progress radiate from them as a force, there will start an activity of the spirit which will be great enough to rouse a new mental and spiritual disposition in mankind . . . To everyone, in whatever state of life he finds himself, the ethics of reverence for life do this: They force him without cessation to be concerned with all the other human destinies which are going through their life-course around him, and to give himself, as man, to the man who needs a fellow-man. They will not allow the scholar to live only for his learning, even if his learning makes him very useful, nor the artist only for his art, even if by means of it he gives something to many. They do not allow the busy man to think that with his professional activities he has fulfilled every demand upon him. They demand from all that they devote a portion of this life to their fellows."

Such a demand was the heart of Schweitzer's "reverence for life." But it implied something beyond reverence. It asked for a life which was actively, not passively, Christian; a life in which getting and spending, contrary to the spirit of the times, came second and sharing came first.

In October, 1953, Schweitzer was awarded the Nobel Peace Prize, a tribute to the devoted individual who had been called "the twentieth century's matchless human being." Although he was deeply touched, he did not go to Sweden to accept the honor; he was too occupied with the unknown, unnumbered human beings who were dependent upon him in Africa.

Thomas Mann

[1 8 7 5 -   ]

"Artist with a bad conscience."

I
T IS GENERALLY AGREED that the twentieth-century autobiographical novel attained new dimensions in the works of a Frenchman,
Marcel Proust; an Irishman, James Joyce; an American, Thomas
Wolfe; and a German, Thomas Mann. Until Mann began his later
epical narratives, he was as disturbed as any of the other self-tortured writers. He was, like them, concerned with the artist's sense of
"separateness" from his fellows and the cost of his enforced isolation,
the more so since Mann had been brought up in the world of the
prosperous middle class.

He was born in an old Hanseatic town, the free city of Lübeck,
on June 6, 1875, and was christened Paul Thomas Mann—his first
writings, contributions to a students' magazine, were signed "Paul
Thomas." The Manns had been important people for generations.
His paternal grandfather was an outspoken liberal who had been
Consul to the Netherlands. His father was a wealthy grain merchant
who had been a Senator and twice Mayor of Lübeck; conservative but not conventional, he had married the Portuguese-Creole-
German daughter of a South American planter. Their first child
was Heinrich who, like his grandfather, became a noted liberal and,
like his brother, a novelist. Thomas, the second son in a family of
five children, admired his father's dignity and fastidiousness, but
he adored (as he recounts in the short autobiographical novel,
Tonio Kröger) "his beautiful black-haired mother, who played the
piano and mandolin so wonderfully . . . and who was so absolutely different from the other ladies in the town."

School was something which had to be endured, "a stagnating,
unsatisfying time," remembered chiefly because it was rigidly Prus-
sianized and roused "a sort of literary opposition to its spirit, its discipline, and its methods of training." Young Thomas derived more
instruction, as well as pleasure, from his brother's toy theater and
the books he read at home—the little tales of Hans Christian Andersen and the great legends of Homer. When he was fifteen his
father died and the family firm, whose fortunes had been steadily

declining, went into bankruptcy. The great house was put on the market; most of the antique furnishings were sold; and his mother moved herself and the younger children to the south, to the warmer and more exciting city of Munich. Thomas remained in Lübeck, with his brother Heinrich, to finish his schooling. He wrote romantic verses in imitation of Goethe, Schiller, and Heine, submitted them to a little magazine, not inappropriately named *Spring Storm,* and thrilled to see himself in the permanent glory of print. At nineteen he rejoined the family in Munich, a serious, somewhat self-important, dark-gray-eyed youth with a fixed purpose: to be a writer. He found work in an insurance office, "with the word temporary in my heart," kept the accounts, composed fiction by stealth, and had his first short story accepted, published, and praised. Within a year, Mann struggled free of the hated clerical routine, "surrounded by snuff-taking clerks," and, since there were sufficient funds from his father's estate to permit another year of education, he studied philosophy and literature at the university. His mother gave him twelve more months of freedom, which he spent in Italy. Heinrich was already there, at work on a long book, and Thomas began to produce short stories, a collection of which, *Der Kleine Herr Friedemann* (*Little Mister Friedemann*), appeared in Mann's twenty-third year.

Meanwhile, encouraged by Heinrich, Thomas had been engaged on a work of intimidating size, and when he returned to Germany in 1898, he brought back the manuscript of *Buddenbrooks.* His publisher begged him to cut it in half but, although Mann was only twenty-three, he insisted that the multiple saga of his forebears, his family, and the society which they represented could not be told in less space. In spite of the publisher's misgivings, *Buddenbrooks* was published in two volumes at the end of 1900 and was a startling success; a one-volume edition was brought out within a year and Mann was hailed as a dazzling portent. The book was translated into every living language. It became a contemporary classic; it appeared, next to the Bible, on every living-room table in Germany; by 1935 the German edition had sold over one million copies. When Mann was awarded the Nobel Prize in 1929, the citation specifically read: "Principally for his great novel, *Buddenbrooks.*"

The story of *Buddenbrooks* is indicated by its subtitle: "The Decline of a Family." In a narrative of three generations set in the middle of the nineteenth century, Mann imaginatively traces the rise

and fall of his own people, the steady loss of money and the increasing gain in culture. The treatment is naturalistic but the
underlying theme is metaphysical. Mann had fed on Schopenhauer
and Nietzsche, whose barbaric philosophy he loathed but whose
style intoxicated him; he employed the realistic method to ask a
spiritual question, Nietzsche's "has existence a significance?" Mann,
like his alter ego, Tonio Kröger, stood between two worlds, the
world of the ordinary citizen and the world of the maladjusted artist
—"I am at home in neither, and I suffer in consequence . . . My
father, you know," Mann summarized near the end of *Tonio
Kröger,* "had the temperament of the north: solid, reflective, puri-
tanically correct, with a tendency to melancholia. My mother, of
indeterminate foreign blood, was beautiful, sensuous, naïve, passionate, careless and, I think, irregular by instinct. The mixture was no
doubt extraordinary and bore with it extraordinary dangers. The
issue of it: a *bourgeois* who strayed off into art, a bohemian who
feels nostalgic yearnings for respectability, an artist with a bad conscience. For surely it is my bourgeois conscience makes me see in
the artist life, in all irregularity and all genius, something profoundly suspect, profoundly disreputable; that fills me with this
lovelorn *faiblesse* for the simple and good, the comfortably normal,
the average unendowed respectable human being."

At thirty Mann married Katia Pringsheim, daughter of a celebrated mathematician and art collector. For the next twenty-eight
years he lived happily, creatively, and in unostentatious luxury.
Besides his sumptuous home in Munich, he had a cottage on the
Isar and another summer residence on the dunes of Nidden in Me-
melland. Six children were born—three girls and three boys. One of
his sons, Klaus, became a writer; one of his daughters, Erika, became an actress and married W. H. Auden. Shortly after Mann's
marriage, he wrote *Königliche Hoheit (Royal Highness)*, another
variation of the aristocratic hero as artist beset by the vexed problem of belonging to two societies; but the tone is lighter than in the
preceding books and justifies its claim to being "a comedy in the
form of a novel." The First World War was threatening, and fifteen
years were to pass before the publication of what has been considered Mann's major work.

Death in Venice, one of the most famous novellas of the period,
was the product of Mann's middle thirties. The story centers about
an exhausted, aristocratic, and deracinated esthete, Gustave von
Aschenbach, and his compulsive attachment to a young Polish boy,

who is, to him, the embodiment of all that is beautiful and unattainable. No words are exchanged between the two; but although the town is in the throes of a plague, Aschenbach is willing to remain and die of the affliction rather than lose sight of the youth who has become (he tells himself) "beauty's very essence; form as divine thought, the single and pure perfection which resides in the mind." There is no plot; there is practically no action. But in the abnormal adoration for what is rare and exquisite, Mann creates an atmosphere of tension which is close to terror, an evocation of a beauty which is both inspiring and sinister. *Death in Venice* plays new and macabre variations on Mann's favorite themes: the perils and perversities of art, the danger of preoccupation with the unfamiliar, and the loneliness of the isolated soul. "The careful reader will note," wrote Joseph Warner Angell in *The Thomas Mann Reader*, "that Aschenbach is absolutely alone throughout the story, except as he speaks to those who can inform or serve him. His absorption with the idea, his yielding to the *image* of Tadzio's beauty separates Aschenbach from his art, which is communication, and from his morality, which is loyalty, and he plunges into the abyss of solitude."

During the First World War Mann wrote practically no fiction. His "war service with the weapon of thought" was represented by his *Reflections of an Unpolitical Man*. His convictions, he said, were moral and metaphysical, not political and social; but his tastes as well as his traditions were proudly Germanic, chauvinistic, and even belligerent. A few years later, Mann was no longer so positive of the values of conservatism; the urgent issues of the day crowded in upon him. He examined his conscience as well as the position in which he had placed himself. He saw that he had been wrong, that he could no longer ally himself with a culture which was not only anti-political but anti-progressive.

It was in this self-examining frame of mind that he wrote *The Magic Mountain*. Critics who had acclaimed *Buddenbrooks* as the first purely German novel of the period, characterized *The Magic Mountain* as the first purely European novel. It was Mann's second masterpiece. The idea for it had come to Mann in 1912 during a three weeks' visit to a sanatorium where his wife was being treated for a lung ailment. He first thought of the book as a comedy, a "droll conflict between macabre adventure and bourgeois sense of duty." But "the fascination of death, the triumph of extreme disorder over a life founded upon order and consecrated to it" grew into a huge parable of a sick civilization. *The Magic Mountain* is written on at least two levels, the realistic and the symbolic. On the naturalistic level, it concerns an innocent and open-minded middle-class youth, Hans Castorp, who visits his cousin in a Swiss sanatorium for the tubercular. He plans to stay three weeks but he remains seven years. Here he undergoes many adventures of the flesh and spirit and discovers a new world in microcosm. He is deeply influenced by individuals of all nationalities: a German doctor, a Russian woman, with whom he falls in love, a Dutch planter, and a Slavic psychologist, among others. He hears long and involved arguments, declines into an almost deathlike apathy, and suddenly finds himself rescued from inactivity, the retreat from life which is the enchantment and curse of solitude, the baleful "magic" of the mountain. On the symbolic level, the book is a critical fable, a probing of nationalism and liberalism, a juxtaposition of comedy and tragedy in which all the characters tend to become allegorical figures: "A man lives not only his personal life as an individual, but also consciously or unconsciously, the life of his epoch and his contemporaries."

The atmosphere of *The Magic Mountain* is, in the literal as well as the metaphorical sense, rarefied. It suffers from its high altitude and a kind of attenuation which too often makes the speeches sound like a bloodless set of essays. Mann cannot restrain his erudition nor his fondness for displaying it. Nevertheless, the range of his interests, the vigor of his intellect, and the subtlety of his characterizations make *The Magic Mountain* a unique work of the imagination: a panoramic novel which is also a study of the twentieth-century world and the decay which has infected it.

The realization of the extent of that decay did not occur to Mann at first, not even when Hitler made his cynical attacks upon democracy. His brother Heinrich as well as his older children urged him to protest the excesses of the encroaching totalitarianism; but Mann, the "unpolitical man," temporized. He could not bring himself to speak out against a Germany which, although changing radically, still seemed to represent the conservative culture of which he felt himself an integral part. The full implications of Nazism struck him only when the Reichstag fire revealed the criminal ruthlessness of National Socialism. Alarmed and aware now, he warned his compatriots against the terror of "romantic barbarism." At that time he was in Switzerland, at work on his Joseph tetralogy. He never returned to his native land. In 1933, after he had settled in

Zürich, his property was confiscated, his books were burned and, three years later, he was deprived of his German citizenship. In 1938 he took up residence in the United States, where he lectured at Princeton University. After building a home in California, in 1944 he took the oath of allegiance as an American citizen. He gave his support to causes engaged in anti-Fascist activities, and in *The Coming of Democracy* excoriated "that habit of thought which regards life and intellect, art and politics as totally separate worlds." Even when he was most prophetic in his appraisal of the future course of civilization, he did not dogmatize. "If I was in error at the age of forty," he said, "I do not imagine that I possess the Truth today. Truth can never be a possession, only an eternal aspiration. May it be said of each one of us that he spent his life honestly and restlessly striving for the true and the good."

In America Mann finished the four volumes which he had begun in Germany, pursued in Palestine, and continued in Switzerland. When he was fifty a Munich artist had shown him a portfolio of drawings he had made to illustrate the legend of Joseph and asked Mann to supply a prefatory note. "Full of meditation, of tentative, groping speculation and the forecast of a new thing," as Mann recalled in *A Sketch of My Life,* he reread the Biblical story and remembered Goethe's comment: "This simple story is utterly charming, but it is too short; one is tempted to fill in the omitted details." Goethe's sentence, said Mann, furnished "the readiest and most plausible explanation for my venture." He was fascinated with the idea of leaving the sphere of the bourgeois present and reanimating a mythical set of situations which would "pierce deep, deep into the human," exploring man's "origin, his essence, his goal."

The Joseph books took Mann sixteen intensive years to complete. The first volume, *Joseph and His Brothers* (published in England as *The Tales of Jacob,* after the original German, *Die Geschichten Jaakobs*) appeared, after six years' work, in 1934. It was followed a year later by *Young Joseph. Joseph in Egypt* was published in 1938, and *Joseph the Provider,* the happiest of the volumes, composed entirely in America, in 1944. Although Mann preserved the line of the Biblical tale and embellished it with an imposing array of authentic archaeological details, the perspective is altered; the time and place are brought into focus through the mind of a modern analyst. Like Hans Castorp, Joseph enters a strange and unhealthy environment as an innocent and impressionable youth. Once again Mann's mixture of realism and symbolism propels the story, and the events revolve about the author's almost obsessive theme: the artist and his struggle with society. Joseph, the dreamer and interpreter of dreams, is betrayed by his brothers because of his beauty, maligned and imprisoned because of his virtue, and finally freed and elevated because of his faith. Although he is rewarded with a triumphant finale, instead of the tragic death reserved for most mythical heroes, Joseph is the artist-martyr, the redeemer as well as the provider, who, through his vicarious sufferings, saves his people.

During the ten years while the four volumes of *Joseph and His Brothers* were appearing, Mann issued all of his fiction prior to 1940, except the long novels, under the title *Stories of Three Decades*. In this period he also published a notable book of essays, *Freud, Goethe, Wagner;* several political documents; *The Beloved Returns,* a novel about the aged Goethe (more accurately described by its German title, *Lotte in Weimar*) in which Mann uses the stream-of-consciousness technique to transcribe Goethe's morning meditations; *The Transposed Heads,* a fantasy on a Hindu theme; *The Tables of the Law,* a variation on the subject of Moses and the Decalog, a short novel which seems a kind of postlude to the Joseph saga; and *Essays of Three Decades*.

At seventy-three Mann again paid his respects to Goethe with *Doctor Faustus* and, at the same time, reverted to his favorite topic: the embattled and ambitious artist. In this version of the Faust legend, the hero is a composer and he sells his soul to the devil, not for youth or power, but for fame. This allows Mann, through the device of letting the hero's rather pedantic friend tell the story, to create a complicated counterpoint of double meanings, social criticism, political allegories and, in his description of the huge cantata, "The Lamentation of Doctor Faustus," to compose a gigantic musical composition (in words) in which "the dark tone-poem permits no consolation, appeasement, transfiguration," nothing but a "hope beyond hopelessness, the transcendence of despair."

In his eightieth year Mann embarrassed his admirers by publishing *The Black Swan,* a grisly, gynecological tale about a middle-aged woman who, during her menopause, falls sickeningly in love with a youth only a few years older than her young son, dreams continually of consummating her desire, and discovers she has cancer. The tortured plot is underscored by being written in a language which is turgid to the point of parody.

Mann's faults are woven into the fibers of his style. He treats his subjects with a heavy Wagnerian orchestration, or, to employ the jargon of another art, with a thick impasto of color upon color. He has no talent for concision—even his short stories are stretched far beyond their material—and his long-windedness, swollen by a passion for repetition, rarely permits a flash of sudden insight. Mann's symbols are not only burdensomely detailed but doubly underlined; the pace is slow; there is commentary within commentary. Each work is a massive example of Teutonic *Tüchtigkeit,* the so-highly-esteemed but overloaded "thoroughness." Yet, if Mann's results are produced by careful assembly, the method is not to be undervalued, for the slow accretion builds into something monumental. The approach, the pontifical manner, may be German; but the application, the creative and unquestionably lasting effect, is universal.

The universality was immediately acknowledged upon Mann's death at the age of eighty. Drawn by the pull of Europe and the hope of helping to reunite a divided Germany, Mann had gone to Switzerland in 1952. He was suddenly taken ill in Zurich and died there of a blood clot on August 12, 1955. West and East Germany outvied each other to acclaim the author as "a herald of the best traditions of humanism."

By an unhappy irony, Mann's gayest novel appeared a month after his death. For more than thirty years Mann had been teased by an idea and a character that had come to birth as a fragment of a novel in 1921. When *Confessions of Felix Krull, Confidence Man* was posthumously published in 1955, it was hailed not only as an entertaining comedic work but as the great picaresque novel of the age. Part parody and part sardonic wisdom, *Felix Krull* is not only the story of an artist-actor-adventurer but a critical portrait of his times. While the world was praising the seriousness of his efforts to bring new reality to the present, Mann was presenting from his grave the merriest of his books out of the tribulations of the past.

Rainer Maria Rilke

[1 8 7 5 - 1 9 2 6]

" 'The Santa Claus of loneliness.' "

RAINER MARIA RILKE, probably the greatest German poet since Goethe and Heine, was not a German and lived in Germany only a few of his fifty-one years. He was born December 4, 1875, in Prague, of old Bohemian ancestry. His childhood was strange and unhappy. The recessiveness which characterized the grown man stemmed from his earliest years. His mother, who had lost an infant daughter, brought him up as a girl—he was actually christened Renée—and, until he was six, he was dressed in girl's clothing, wore curls, and was given dolls and a toy kitchen for his playthings. He helped with the housework, was taught the importance of dusting furniture, and was made to take pride in his "uniform": a big apron and little chamois gloves.

"My life had no real foundation," he wrote at forty to Magda von Hattingberg. He developed a secret life and, even as a child, found recesses within himself "where things might be stored that no one could find . . . When I come to think of it, I yearned for a reality before which the monstrous everyday tedium surrounding me would be revealed as puny, perplexed, humbled, outdistanced, indeed, actually denying its own existence. Sometimes I looked to my family for such a reality, dreaming that the family might turn out to occupy a position of inconceivable high privilege heretofore denied it." But the boy had to give up the fantasy of escape when his father sent him to military school. He was ten years old, already trying to resist the pressure of the confining everyday world and beginning to be a solitary self, when he turned hopefully to a protective uncle. It was another wish-fulfillment which made him picture this uncle as one who had intimate connections with some great lord "or even the Emperor himself [who] would exert a rescuing interest in my situation. At other times, it seemed to me that such intervention could be expected only of God—and then I felt on a footing of trust with Him, in which I was by no means reticent with proposals for the doom of the military school." But the military schools were inescapable realities. Rilke suffered through two of them until he was fifteen. "Five years—such was the length of my military education—what years they were! No one has ever stayed so long under water! . . . I was subjected to unmerited brutalities—suffered blows without ever returning them . . . I sat up in bed, folded my hands, and prayed for death." The brutal experiences, especially at the first school, St. Pölten in Moravia, left a trauma which lasted a lifetime.

Rilke's sense of insecurity was aggravated when his parents separated. His affections were transferred to his father's eldest brother, Jaroslav, who engaged private tutors for the boy, and when the beloved uncle died, the seventeen-year-old Rainer was driven to the verge of suicide. A year at a business school had come to nothing; he was twenty before he passed his examinations for the University of Prague. He took courses in literature, metaphysics, and the history of philosophy, turned to law as a possible profession, but after a single semester, fled to Munich to study art. A few months later he abandoned all classwork for travel—financed by a small inherited income—and embarked on a series of wanderings, sudden friendships, rhapsodic but unsatisfactory and usually short-lived romances.

In 1897, after an aborted engagement with Valery ("Vally") David-Rhonfeld, who not only inspired his first book but paid the cost of its publication, Rilke met Lou Salomé. An enigmatic woman who, at twenty, had fascinated and deeply disturbed Nietzsche, Lou Salomé was now thirty-five and married; Rilke was not yet twenty-three. As soon as they met she "took him into her arms and gently rocked his soul." They became lovers at once, and although they separated soon after and Rilke married a few years later, the bond was never broken. Lou Salomé remained his intimate confidante, his most cherished correspondent and, with the blurring of time, became transformed into his ideal woman.

Meanwhile, Rilke had learned to transmute the routines of regimentation into images of escape. His first book, the Heinesque *Leben und Lieder* (*Life and Lyrics*), had been published when he was nineteen; the somewhat more original *Traumgekrönt* (*Dream-Crowned*) appeared three years later. With *Advent, Geschichten vom Lieben Gott* (*Stories About God*) and *Das Buch der Bilder* (*The Book of Pictures*) there emerged Rilke's main concern: the question of reality; of what, in a bewildering and almost unbelievable world, is sufficiently real to hold man's faith.

Between his twenty-second and twenty-fifth years, Rilke made successive changes of place in what was to become a lifetime pattern. He moved to Munich, Berlin, Italy, and Russia, which he characterized as "the home of my instinct," met Tolstoy and learned Russian. Returning from his second journey to Russia he went to the village of Worpswede, an art colony, where he met Clara Westhoff, a sculptress, one of Rodin's pupils. The following year he married her and she bore him a daughter, Ruth. But Rilke was too fitful to settle down. He lived in Paris for a while, met Rodin, spent the spring in Viareggio on the Italian Riviera, lived ten months in Rome, six months in Denmark and Sweden, and returned to Paris where, at thirty, he became Rodin's secretary. Incompatible with the man but greatly influenced by his sculpture, Rilke envisioned a poetry which would not be *about* "things" but would *be* them, a poetry which would make his objects stand by themselves, filling space with their solidity. The so-called *Dinggedichte* (*Poems of Things*) have been variously characterized as "anthropomorphic" and "cosmomorphic." Hans Egon Holthusen, in *Rainer Maria Rilke,* writes: "Under the emblem of humility, of selfless devotion to 'die Dinge,' the world is conquered by the all-in-one of feeling. Magical and, at the same time, intelligible, the activity of feeling leaves its subjective confine and informs the object or a whole cosmos of objects." W. H. Auden, recalling the power of the things which, out of his isolation, Rilke gave the world, referred to:

> . . . Rilke, whom "die Dinge" bless,
> The Santa Claus of loneliness.

Lonely he was, and remained lonely by choice. Needing to be alone most of the time, he was ambivalent wherever he went; in Paris, as elsewhere, he felt himself both attached and exiled. He was, wrote C. F. MacIntyre in an introduction to a translation of fifty selected poems, "a man who spent his days in museums, galleries, studios, libraries, public parks and gardens; a wanderer of the streets by night, often even of the more sinister boulevards, a brooder on the many bridges over the Seine." Rilke not only understood loneliness, he appreciated it to the fullest; he made a credo out of it. Replying to a young poet who complained of being unhappy alone, Rilke assured him: "What's needed is just this: Loneliness, vast inner loneliness. To walk in one's self and to meet no one for hours on end—that is what one must be able to attain. To be lonely in the way one was lonely as a child, when the grownups moved about involved in things that appeared important and big because the Big Ones looked so busy, and because one understood nothing of what they were doing. And if, one day, one comes to perceive that their occupations are miserable, their professions moribund and no longer related to life, why not go on regarding them, like a child, as something alien, looking out from the depths of one's own world, from the very expanse of one's own loneliness, which is, itself, work and rank and profession." Only rarely did Rilke establish normal relations with his fellow-men and enjoy the give-and-take of social intercourse; he was still a young man when he concluded that human influences were "disastrous" and life itself hostile.

Loneliness and restlessness, intense introspection and a Proustian gift of total recall, went into the poetry. "To write one line," confessed Rilke in *Die Aufzeichnungen des Malte Laurids Brigge (The Notebooks of Malte Laurids Brigge,* published in the United States as *The Journal of My Other Self)* "a man should see many cities, people, and things. He must learn to know animals and the way of birds in the air, and how little flowers open in the morning. He must be able to think back to unknown places—to partings long foreseen, to days of childhood . . . and to parents . . . to days at sea . . . to nights of travel . . . One must have sat by the dead in a room with open windows . . . But it is not enough to have memories. One must be able to forget them and have vast patience until they come again . . . And when they become blood within us, and glances and gestures . . . then it can happen that, in a rare hour, the first word of a verse may arise and come forth."

The wanderings and the poems continued: Belgium, Capri, Munich, Biskra, Carthage, Naples, Tunis, a month in Algiers, three months in Egypt. *Das Stundenbuch (The Book of Hours), Die Frühen Gedichte* (Early Poems), *Das Marienleben (The Life of the Virgin Mary),* translations of Elizabeth Barrett Browning's *Sonnets from the Portuguese, Neue Gedichte (New Poems* in two volumes). After completing the last of the new poems Rilke was overcome with a feeling which he could not analyze. He was apprehensive and despondent, but tense, aware that some change was impending. He had achieved "the work of sight," now he wanted to see and think with the heart. All he had done with "outer forms" was only a preparation for an expression, the "inward" sense. As J. B. Leishman wrote in the preface to *Duino Elegies,* he was ready for "the fashioning forth of some ultimate vision of human life and destiny and of the true relationship between the looker and that world on which he had looked so intensely and so long." Rilke was thirty-five when he felt the change coming. Although he could not guess what shape it would assume, he waited and suffered. Separated from his wife, he became physically ill and mentally depressed; he feared that he had lost his creative power; he looked like a frustrated and desperate ascetic.

Fortunately, he had become acquainted with the Princess Marie von Thurn und Taxis-Hohenlohe; he had stayed as her guest in the castle of Duino, near Trieste. A year and a half later he revisited Duino and, for several months, remained alone in the castle. One day he had one of his mystical experiences. "Something strange encountered him," as he related in the third person. "Walking up and down with a book, as was his custom, he had happened to recline in the fork of a shrublike tree and felt himself so agreeably supported and so amply reposed that he remained as he was, without reading, completely received into nature, in an almost unconscious contemplation. Little by little his attention awoke to a feeling he had never known: it was as though almost imperceptible vibrations were passing into him from the interior of the tree . . . It seemed to him that he had never been filled with more gentle motions; his body was being somehow treated like a soul, and put in a state to receive a degree of influence which, given the normal apparentness of one's physical conditions, really could not have been felt at all." It was as if he "had got to the other side of Nature." During this period at Duino he heard a voice calling to him: "Who, if I cried, would hear me among the angelic orders?", and thereupon wrote down the words which form the opening sentence of the *Duineser Elegien* (*Duino Elegies*), which took him ten years to complete. "Everywhere," he wrote at a later time, "appearance and vision came, as it were, together in the object; in every one of them a whole inner world was exhibited—as though an angel, in whom space was included, were blind and looking into himself. This world, regarded no longer from the human point of view, but as it is *within* the angel, is perhaps my real task." Blake screamed because he saw God put his forehead against the window, and he beheld "a tree filled with angels, bright angelic wings bespangling every bough with stars"; Rilke looked through the branches of a tree at night and saw the universe face to face.

The Angel who makes his appearance in the *Elegies* is not the traditional Christian angel. Certain Rilke commentators have called the Angel "God's pseudonym"; Rilke himself says that the Angel "is the creature in whom the transformation of the visible into the invisible appears complete"—a spirit as far beyond all the dreams and achievements of man as God is beyond the angel. Rilke devoted himself to the world "within the Angel," to the "other side of Nature," a sense of "inwardness" in which all things as well as thoughts are interrelated. Instead of the "here and now" Rilke directs himself to the "there and forever" in an ecstasy of pure feeling. The main theme of the *Elegies* is lamentation balanced by acceptance and fulfillment—a giving up of intellectual consciousness for the innocence of children and animals, for a sense of continuity, an "otherness" which is identified with the timeless wonder of Being and Becoming. Rilke hopes for a triumph of creative vision over sterile reality. He satirizes the vulgar modern society, the smugness of the average church-goer and emptiness of "ready-made" religion "as clean and closed and disappointing as a post-office on Sunday." Far from making a grim religion of resignation, Rilke heralds surrender as a preparation for spiritual struggle and regeneration. Death is not a defeat but a transmutation.

The lamentation of the *Elegies* is answered by the jubilation of *Die Sonnete an Orpheus* (*Sonnets to Orpheus*), written in Rilke's forties. A burst of joy after grief, it is a paean of affirmations as surprising as it is overwhelming. Nevertheless, Rilke was lonelier and more restless than ever. Once more he made the round of cities, and once more he complained that people were always his undoing. "Must I not then keep myself well-stoppered," he wrote to his dear "Benvenuta" (Magda von Hattingberg), "as the merchants do their attar of roses? . . . Why should I not say that I prefer to be alone? In the same breath with which I implore God to *let* me love you, I beg him, I implore him to strengthen my will for militant solitude, for such is the destiny of every fiber of my being."

In nothing was Rilke more ambivalent than in his relations to women. He considered the highest type of passion that which was unfulfilled, even unrequited. Love that expects no return, barely recognition, is what he asked from his admirers. "I really believe I sometimes get so far as to express the whole impulse of my heart . . . in gently laying my hand on a shoulder." Rilke's ideal great lovers were wholly feminine, undemanding, understanding—"everything performed, endured, accomplished" as contrasted with "man's absolute inefficiency in love."

In his mid-forties he was established in the Swiss Château de Muzot, near Sierre. There were occasional trips to Paris and Italy, but he seemed settled in Switzerland. He went into a nursing home for two months in 1923; before he was fifty, it was apparent that he was afflicted with leukemia. A rose, Rilke's favorite symbol, hastened his death. Cutting a bouquet of flowers for Nimet Eloui Bey, an Egyptian admirer, Rilke pricked himself on a thorn and blood poisoning set in. The infection complicated the leukemia which had weakened him, and he died December 29, 1926. He was buried at Raron, Valois, Switzerland.

Until recently Rilke's admirers were a fervent few. His distinction threatened to be that of "a poet's poet" even in Germany; no lines of his are to be found in Vesper's popular two-volume compilation, *Die Ernte Seit Goethe* (*The Harvest Since Goethe*), although Rilke was forty-eight when the anthology appeared. Slowly the rare essence of the poet revealed itself, persuading awakened readers to explore Rilke's world beyond consciousness, following the wavering line between sensuousness and hyper-sensibility. Although most critics concede Rilke's permanence, there is disagreement concerning his different styles. Like Yeats, Rilke turned from the fluent and traditionally formed lyrics of his first manner to an expression of such variety and depth that even some of his translators found it cloudy and obfuscating. "After he had finished the last of these books [*Neue Gedichte*, published when Rilke was thirty-three], a great artist began to grow dim," wrote C. F. MacIntyre. On the other hand, the poet Louise Bogan considers that Rilke's *Duino Elegies* not only "mark the summit of his career" but stand "as the most profound poetic work of the twentieth century . . . In the *Elegies* the ills of our time are traced back to their source, to the spiritual infection of a world without values."

Rilke's thirty books of poetry, stories, memoirs, and translations, as well as several posthumously issued volumes, present innumerable difficulties. Even a trained German reader will be troubled by the rapidly colliding images, the bizarre figures of speech, the double meanings and countless word-plays with which Rilke fashioned a new language. In an idiom which is both subtle and extraordinarily intense, Rilke multiplied visual and emotional references to achieve a fusion of outer and inner experience, bringing "appearance and vision" together in the object represented. J. B. Leishman, one of Rilke's most sensitive translators, makes an illuminating comparison when he writes: "Rilke often finds himself confronted with the limitations of language: sometimes the particular shade of meaning, the particular tone of feeling he wants a word to bear is not naturally and immediately determined by its particular position; it will only, as Hopkins would say, 'explode' when the reader comes to it with recollections of it in other contexts, even, perhaps, in other works."

The reference to Hopkins is not only appropriate but pointed. Like Hopkins, Rilke suffered from an excess of ecstasy; a breathless rapture led him to evoke indescribable emotions in an effort to express the inexpressible. The poet Stephen Spender, another of Rilke's translators, calls attention to Rilke's "exaggerations of a style of thinking" that often results in "a facility of attaining the timeless, the nameless, the infinite, etc., which gives the reader the feeling that the poet's very highmindedness can betray him into a kind of spiritual opportunism." It is also true that Rilke's esoteric symbols and private associations make it hard for the reader to find his way among the ambiguities. But even when the communication is clouded, it comes through, and the orphic utterances rise to a height of magic. Attempting to say more than the mind can shape and the tongue can utter, the idiom is sometimes clogged, sometimes turbulent, but it has the strange effect of exact description in the midst of incantation. There is magnificence in Rilke's double vision which tries to break through the barrier of the senses; and even for those who comprehend it only in glimpses, there is nobility in the poetry which continually strives to unite thought and action, desire and fulfillment, in a sustained flash of revelation.

Isadora Duncan

[1878-1927]

"Born under a dancing star."

BEGINNING in Europe and spreading through the world, a one-woman revolution in the dance was accomplished by a reckless but resolute young American, Isadora Duncan. She was born May 27, 1878, in San Francisco by the sea. Her first idea of movement, she wrote in her embarrassingly self-conscious autobiography, *My Life*, "came from the rhythm of the waves. I was born under the star of Aphrodite, who was also born on the sea." From the beginning she had a penchant for identifying herself with nothing less than elemental significances.

Her father, of Scottish descent, was a plausible opportunist who made and lost four fortunes. Her mother was a devout Irish Catholic until her husband left her for another woman, after which she became an equally devout atheist, a disciple of Robert Ingersoll. There were four children—two boys and two girls—and she raised them all to be rebels. A frustrated musician, she gave piano lessons, recited sentimental verse, and taught her brood the best second-rate literature. The Duncans lived from hand to mouth and from lodging to lodging, but Isadora remembered her childhood as an exciting, untrammeled state, a state which became the pattern of her later nomadic existence.

The urge to teach was as great—and as early—as the urge to dance. At the age of six she collected half a dozen neighborhood babies and, since most of them were too young to walk, seated them on the floor and showed them how to wave their arms and sway from the hips. This was, she said, her School of the Dance. All her life Isadora was to try to bring into reality this dream of a School, a dream that she kept pursuing from continent to continent. At eight she earned a few pennies by teaching dance steps to little girls, and at ten she informed her mother that now she knew how to make money and school could not teach her anything she wanted to know. Hoping to make her daughter an accomplished danseuse, Mrs. Duncan took Isadora to a local ballet teacher, but the girl refused to stand on her toes, saying it was "ugly and against nature." After the third lesson she left the class and never recovered from her revulsion against the ballet. Much of what she later achieved was done as a continual protest against the ballet schools with their "inane coquetry" and "the stiff and commonplace gymnastics which they called dancing." With the exception of social dancing and musical comedy routines, there was nothing besides the ballet which could be called Dance when Isadora began "interpreting" the music of the masters.

When she was seventeen her mother took her to Chicago, hoping to find a producer for Isadora's interpretations of Mendelssohn's "Spring Song" and other favorite melodies of the period. No manager was interested. Isadora's mother pawned what few possessions they had, and for a week they lived on tomatoes. Finally the manager of the Masonic Temple Roof Garden agreed that Isadora could perform her "Spring Song" if she followed it with something that had "frills and kicks." It was her first engagement, but after a successful week, she refused to extend it. In Chicago Isadora fell in love with a Polish painter and, although it was discovered that he had a wife abroad, Isadora cherished "the insane passion with which I had inspired Miroski." Because of her mother's unhappiness, Isadora had rejected the idea of marriage. "All my childhood seemed to be under the black shadow of my mysterious father, and the terrible word divorce was imprinted upon the sensitive plate of my mind . . . I decided (at twelve) that I would live to fight against marriage and for the emancipation of women and the right for every woman to have a child or children as it pleased her." Her mother hurried her off to New York.

Before they left Chicago, the Duncans had met Augustin Daly, the famous theatrical producer and, obtaining an interview, Isadora made a speech. "I have a great idea to put before you, Mr. Daly," said Isadora with consummate conviction. "I have discovered the dance. I have discovered the art which has been lost for two thousand years. I bring you the idea that is going to revolutionize our entire epoch. Where have I discovered it? By the Pacific Ocean, by the waving pine-forests of Sierra Nevada . . . I am the spiritual daughter of Walt Whitman. For the children of America I will create a new dance that will truly express America . . ." Unable to stem the overflowing tide of youthful oratory and self-assurance, Daly muttered that there might be a part in a pantomime he was putting on, and a few weeks later Isadora was rehearsing on Twenty-ninth Street and Broadway. When the pantomime failed,

Daly put on *A Midsummer Night's Dream.* Ada Rehan was Titania and Isadora, as one of the fairies, was allowed to dance the Mendelssohn Scherzo in the wood scene. She disliked the tinsel wings; she left the company when she had to sing as well as dance in the chorus of an English musical comedy, *The Geisha.*

On the strength of the few dollars saved from her daughter's salary, Isadora's mother rented a small one-room studio in Carnegie Hall and summoned the rest of the family east. Mrs. Duncan found a few piano pupils; Augustin determined to be an actor and joined a touring company; Raymond got a part-time job on a newspaper; and Elizabeth relieved Isadora of most of the teaching. Since the income was not quite enough to pay the rent, they hired out the studio by the hour to elocution and music teachers; which meant that, when the place was occupied by their tenants, the Duncans had to walk briskly in Central Park to keep warm. Isadora enlarged her repertoire; she evolved dances to the sugary strains of Ethelbert Nevin's popular "Narcissus" and his "Ophelia." Later Nevin himself arranged several recitals for her in small concert halls and Isadora was also seen in New York drawing rooms. But the Duncans' expenses continued to be greater than their income. With gypsy-like nonchalance they had left Carnegie Hall for two large and expensive rooms at the Windsor Hotel from which they were about to be evicted. "The only thing that can save us," said Isadora cheerfully, "is for the hotel to burn down." At this period of her life the fates were on Isadora's side. The next day the Windsor burned to the ground, and the Duncans moved again. They boarded a cattle boat for England.

At twenty Isadora was attractively fresh but not unusual looking. In spite of the later idealizations by artists and the soft-focus flattery of such photographers as Arnold Genthe, she was not beautiful. The nose was a little too pert; the cheeks were a little too full; even in youth there was the beginning of a double chin. But the mouth was delicately molded, serious and sensuous, the eyes were challenging, and the whole expression was that of vibrant expectancy. In repose she differed little from thousands of American girls; it was only when she moved that Isadora took on beauty and showed that she had been born under a dancing star.

In London the Duncans spent most of the time at the British Museum. An English translation of Winckelmann's *Journey to Athens* stimulated their interest in Hellenic culture. There were a few garden parties and drawing room entertainments at which Isadora continued to interpret Mendelssohn and Nevin, accompanied by her mother, while Elizabeth read some poems of Theocritus, and Raymond delivered a talk on the subject of dancing "and its effect on the psychology of future humanity." As a result the Duncans accumulated quite a lot of kudos but no cash. They lived, somehow, on watered soup and penny buns. Isadora met many celebrities, the Prince of Wales and Ellen Terry, and joined Frank Benson's Shakespeare Company. Since she never got any further than playing the first fairy in *Midsummer Night's Dream,* another move was indicated. The next stop was Paris.

In Paris at twenty-two, Isadora became a different being. She haunted the Louvre, studied the Greek vases and bas reliefs, and tried to fit them to a music which "seemed to be in harmony with the rhythms of the feet, the Dionysiac set of the head, and the tossing of the thyrsus." Raymond painted Greek columns around the wall of their studio; the Duncans discarded shoes in favor of sandals; Isadora shed her little lace dress and slippers, and danced in bare feet and a light tunic—a costume as sensational then as nudity would be today. Influenced by the Greek paintings and sculptures, she was also stirred by the bronzes of Rodin and the tragic dancing of the Japanese Sada Yacco. She declared that she was seeking the source of the dance "which might be the divine expression of the human spirit through the medium of the body's movement . . . The ballet school taught the pupils that the central spring of all movement was found in the center of the back at the base of the spine. From this axis, says the ballet master, arms, legs and trunk move freely, giving the result of an articulated puppet." Isadora "discovered" that the central spring, "the crater of motor power," was in the solar plexus. "What she was primarily concerned with," wrote John Martin almost half a century later, "can only be called basic dance—not a trade or a profession or even an art to begin with, but a biological function. She was not seeking to invent or devise anything, but only to discover the roots of that impulse toward movement as a response to every experience, which she felt in herself and which she was convinced was a universal endowment. Without benefit of formal psychology, she knew as no other dancer on record had known, that spontaneous movement of the body is the first reaction of all men to sensory or emotional stimuli."

There were many doubts as to the validity of Isadora's theories, but there was never any question about their realization in the flesh. She expressed primary emotions, the leap of love or the lamentation of despair, and began to affect larger and larger audiences with her own joy and grief. Composers and playwrights thronged to her; artists vied with each other not only to capture her exquisite movements but to praise the revival of the ancient terpsichorean art. Rodin himself wrote that Isadora had "attained sculpture and emotion effortlessly . . . She has properly unified Life and the Dance."

In her effort to express life not only in the dance but fully in herself, Isadora planned to relinquish her virginity as simply as she had discarded her slippers. It was not so easy. One night she sent her mother and Raymond to the Opera, clandestinely bought a bottle of champagne, "donned a transparent tunic, wreathed my hair with roses, and thus awaited André, feeling just like Thaïs." The young man was startled. He fidgeted, perspired, and departed almost as soon as he entered, leaving Isadora to weep over the ineffectual roses and champagne. She induced another young man to take her to a hotel room, but he fell on his knees beside the bed, overcome by her purity. This became the pattern of Isadora's amatory life. She was always importunate, always overaggressive in affairs of the heart and, although she had many lovers, she frightened more men than she seduced. The perfect example of the artist as narcissistic adventurer, she borrowed unscrupulously, lived thoughtlessly, and loved irresponsibly. She boasted that her life called for "the pen of Cervantes—or Casanova."

The Duncans moved eastward, to Berlin, Vienna, Budapest. Mendelssohn was exchanged for the more restrained classicism of Gluck. Isadora designed her stage to emphasize the contrast of severity and sensuousness. Purged of all settings and specious decorations, the stage was bare. Long curtains—pale blue, soft green, or neutral gray—disappeared in the upper darkness and fell in folds at the back and sides. The imagination was given full play as a rose-colored spotlight focused on a single figure clad only in a wisp of diaphanous stuff. Her hair was lightly coiled, parted in the middle, suggesting an innocent votary until, loosened, it belonged to a love-drunk dryad or a maddened fury. The dances began. She was a child playing ball and knuckle-bones on the seashore of Chalkis; she was one of the sad companions of Orpheus; she was a Happy Spirit rejoicing in the Elysian Fields . . . The end always came too soon. It was more than a success; it was a revelation.

It was in Budapest that Isadora improvised a new dance which caused a delirium of enthusiasm, "The Blue Danube" of Strauss, and found her first lover. ("He was tall, of magnificent proportions, a head covered with luxuriant curls, black, with purple lights in them . . . a young Hungarian of godlike features and stature, who was to transform the chaste nymph that I was into a wild bacchante.") Isadora's taste was almost as bad as her prose style. In a chapter devoted to her in *Twelve Against the Gods,* William Bolitho wrote: "The affairs themselves seem of impenetrable banality, except for the generosity which she put in them, which is very likely as rare as its confession. The men who figure, robed in girlish adjectives, are almost embarrassingly awkward." Nevertheless, Isadora was enraptured with her Romeo, a stock company actor whose mood changed with every role. She was in despair when the run of *Romeo and Juliet* was over and he had to play the part of Mark Antony. His passion cooled; he delivered orations when Isadora asked for kisses; he told her that a man must consider his career. Let down by love, Isadora remembered her art. She returned to Germany, to the expensive spas where, with a kind of malicious irony, she put on a short red tunic and danced the Dance of the Revolution. She went on to Munich, where the students unharnessed the horses from her carriage and drew her through the streets. She appeared at the Berlin Opera House, and the audiences demanded encore after encore.

At twenty-six Isadora paid her first visit to Greece. Raymond insisted that their voyage should follow that of Ulysses and, although they suffered from the primitive violence of the trip, they felt that their arrival on Greek soil was a kind of homecoming. After viewing the Parthenon, they decided to build a temple. A cornerstone was laid, a priest officiated, and a black cock was offered as a sacrifice. The Duncans determined to stay in Greece forever. They planned to greet the rising sun each day with songs and dances, "after which we were to refresh ourselves with a modest bowl of goat's milk. The mornings were to be devoted to teaching the inhabitants to dance and sing, to celebrate the Greek gods and give up their terrible modern costumes. The afternoons were to be spent in meditation, and the evenings given over to pagan ceremonies with appropriate music." Alas, the program so raptly conceived remained unrealized. The Duncans discovered there was no water to be had for miles, the artesian well-drillers failed to find a vein, and the structure was left uncompleted. However, Isadora salvaged something from the trip. She found and trained a group of Greek boys to chant the choruses from *The Suppliants* of Aeschylus and brought them to Vienna.

The Viennese were unappreciative. They preferred their Strauss to her Aeschylus and were appeased only when Isadora gave them "The Blue Danube." As the tour progressed, the Greek boys presented a further problem. By the time they reached Berlin their habits as well as their voices began to change; they lost their pitch and their primal innocence, and had to be packed off to Athens. Isadora continued her passionate pilgrimage. At Bayreuth she danced a new version of the Tannhäuser Bacchanale and fell fiercely in love with a German author, Heinrich Thode, whose response was ecstatic but strictly spiritual. ("My soul was like a battlefield where Apollo, Dionysus, Christ, Nietzsche, and Richard Wagner disputed the ground.") In St. Petersburg she clothed herself in cobweb tissue to express the delicate nuances of Chopin and made love to Stanislavsky, who gently repelled her. ("Something within me revolted at always playing the role of Egeria.") In Berlin she fulfilled one of her dreams and, with her sister, Elizabeth, opened the Isadora Duncan School for talented children who were to become disciples and would, in turn, teach the true art of the dance to thousands of less favored children. Some of the patrons demurred when Isadora appeared in public in the filmy costume she wore on the stage. Her bare legs shocked her sponsors, but Isadora convinced them that a stockinged foot was no more virtuous than a naked one. A year later a more intimate scandal rocked and almost ruined the school.

Isadora was twenty-seven when she saw Gordon Craig, an artist and scenic designer. He was the son of the famous actress, Ellen Terry. Their mutual infatuation was consummated a few hours after they met. ("His white, lithe, gleaming body emerged from the chrysalis of clothes and shone upon my dazzled eyes . . . So must Endymion, when first discovered by the glistening eyes of Diana, so must Hyacinthus, Narcissus, and the bright, brave Perseus have looked.") Isadora felt that they were not two persons, but two halves of the same soul. For two weeks she remained locked in Craig's studio; since there was no couch, they slept on the floor. Craig was not an ordinary human being; when he walked down the street Isadora had a vision of a High Priest promenading in buried Thebes. The period of adoration did not last long. Soon they found fault with each other's routines, quarreled, fought over the relative importance of their careers, and tried to shout each other down until Craig stormed out and slammed the door. At last Isadora went to Holland to recover and to have her baby. She called it Deirdre, in memory of the tragic Irish queen.

Unable to live with Craig and incapable of living without love, Isadora fretted for almost a year. Remembering "the wisdom of the homeopaths," she looked for a remedy, a small dose of the sickness from which she was suffering, and found it in a debonair young Dutchman whose lifework was the collecting of eighteenth-century snuff-boxes. She ran off to Russia with him and his eighteen trunks —"better the pleasure which lasts for a moment than the sorrow which endures forever"—and composed the lightest of her dances, Schubert's "Moment Musical." A year later she was in New York, meeting the intelligentsia and dancing Gluck's "Iphigenia." Her performances caused a sharp split in opinion. The usual outcries of "indecency," "desecration of art," and "vulgar exposure" were emitted by the Philistines—because she danced in bare feet her performance was banned in Boston—but even so sympathetic a critic as Carl Van Vechten found that one of the Gluck dances was "more or less a sacrilege" and her Beethoven was "a perverted use of the *Seventh Symphony*." What the critics refrained from saying was that Isadora had fallen into the deplorable habit of destroying the very mood which she had evoked by interlarding her dances with long speeches full of sententiousness and self-adulation. She called herself a "cerebral," and none of her friends had the courage to correct her.

Back again in France, thirty-two, and again impoverished, she met the millionaire, Paris Singer. She promptly christened him Lohengrin because he was tall, blond, and bearded, and because he was the knight who had come to rescue her. His yacht carried them over the Mediterranean, up the Italian Riviera, down the Nile, off to Brittany. There were fabulous parties, carnivals in Nice, fêtes in Paris, banquet festivals in Versailles, where the entire Colonne orchestra played as the guests progressed from caviar to teacakes. The rebel in Isadora had a hard time adjusting to these extravagances—she was often unpleasantly aware of the stokers in the engine room and wondered whether Lohengrin knew "what sort of red-hot revolutionary he had taken aboard"—but she got used to the fine wines, furs, perfumes, and the gowns of Paul Poiret, "who could dress a woman in such a way as also to create a work of art." In 1911 she and Lohengrin sailed for New York, occupying the largest suite on the finest boat. But after a triumphal beginning, the tour had to be abandoned when Isadora's pregnancy became too obvious. She returned to France, where her son Patrick was born on the shores of the Mediterranean.

Lohengrin offered to marry Isadora, but she was too restless and too creative to spend the rest of her life imitating the idle. As with Craig, there were angry scenes, recriminations, loud harangues about his place and her mission. In common with her other unions, this one was severed by Isadora's capricious wrong-headedness and her stubborn volubility; she who could dance her way into men's hearts talked her way out of them. She was not, as she thought of herself, an independent individualist. She shunned marriage because she refused to be dependent on any man; but she was always looking to be supported by chance acquaintances, by patrons, by wealthy women and masculine spendthrifts, by the very society which she scorned but which, like the born bohemian, she felt owed her a living.

Tragedy overtook Isadora in her thirty-fifth year. Temporarily reunited with Lohengrin, she sent the two children and their nurse for a ride. The automobile got out of control, the brakes would not hold, and the car plunged into the Seine. Isadora, deluding herself that her lover had come back to take care of her, woke from her daydream when Lohengrin staggered in, crying, "The children—the children are dead."

The death of the children changed Isadora terribly. Life went on for her, but it was another woman who lived it, a coarser woman suffering less from sorrow than from a self-destructive recklessness. She grew heavier in body, slower in response, a victim of sporadic impulses. Living on sensations, she took on lovers indiscriminately: an accompanist whom at first she found repulsive but who made her "whole being go up in flames"; a young Italian sculptor who was about to be married; a doctor who concluded that her soul was sick and the only thing that could cure her was love and still more love; a pretty homosexual whom she enticed from his bevy of boy friends; a South American tango dancer; a pianist who became her flaming Archangel but who deserted her for one of her young pupils; nameless artists, poets, musicians—"I had discovered that love might be a pastime as well as a tragedy, and I gave myself to it with pagan innocence."

With the coming of the First World War, Isadora the dancer came fitfully to life, but she had to fight new terrors and suffer unforeseen blows. Her ideal school was turned into a hospital—"a charnel house of bloody wounds and death"—and finally into a factory for the production of poison gas. A baby, who she hoped might take the place of the dead children, died a few hours after it was born. Nevertheless, the dream of an Academy persisted, and in 1921, at the invitation of the Soviet government, she went to Russia to establish a school of dancing in Moscow.

A year later she threw her principles away and married Serge Essenin. Isadora was forty-four; Essenin was twenty-seven, a good-looking, dissolute, cruel and half-crazy Russian poet. She could manage only a few disjointed phrases of his language; he knew no English and refused to learn it. He drank stupidly, humiliated Isadora by making fun of her dancing, and when she mildly remonstrated, threatened to shoot her. She took him to America where she was acclaimed with superlatives and where, after having been detained at Ellis Island, he was put on show. A double portrait taken in New York shows a big blond boy and a possessive Isadora looking not so much like a wife as a triumphant mother proud of her sulky but fascinating son. Back in Europe, Essenin resumed his favorite sport of wrecking furniture and smashing windows. Several times the authorities arrested him, but Isadora interceded, pleading that he suffered from epilepsy. After wrecking a particularly elegant hotel suite he was placed in an insane asylum, and again Isadora obtained his freedom when she promised to control him. At last he slashed his wrists, wrote a poem, signed it with his blood, and hanged himself. Isadora went into a paroxysm of mourning. She did not survive him long.

In July, 1927, in Paris, in the forty-ninth year of her life, she gave what her admirers considered her greatest concert. People remarked that she had never flourished her scarf with a greater joy of life. It was the scarf that killed her. Two months later, on September 14, she went for an automobile ride, wearing the scarf which she waved so often as a symbol of freedom. As the car started, the fringes caught in the spokes of the wheel, the scarf suddenly tightened, strangled her, and broke her neck.

The obituaries gave little indication of the confusing mixture of her "divine" purpose and her disastrous entanglements, her shoddy gestures and her sheer genius. Her mission was the communication of wonder; she fulfilled it eloquently when she danced her message, foolishly when she explained it. She never learned to separate beauty from banality, pretentious nonsense from pure divination. But her art was more than a vogue; it was a purging force. It cleared the stage of a clutter of false conventions and, freeing the body of corseted and petticoated absurdities, liberated its movements. Isadora Duncan brought about a revolution not only in the dance but in the modern mind, healthier for her pioneering art. Actress as well as artist, she essayed many roles and overplayed them all—the delayed adolescent, the disillusioned femme fatale, the discursive Chorus, the Tragic Queen. Hers was a protean melodrama, and she cast herself in the full glare of the limelight where, wrote Bolitho in 1929, she attained "a greater fame and influence than any other American woman ever achieved."

Albert Einstein

[1879-1955]

*"I cannot believe that God plays dice with
the cosmos."*

AT THE AGE of twenty-six Albert Einstein published his theory
of relativity. Soon thereafter it was said that only twelve men
were intelligent enough to understand its implications. Forty
years later, when the U. S. Army Air Force dropped the atomic
bomb on Hiroshima, August 6, 1945, eighty thousand people died
as the result of an application of his abstruse reasoning. By this time
it was agreed that the young lecturer's theories had caused the
greatest revolution in science since Galileo.

He was born March 14, 1879, at Ulm, a small Württemberg city
in Bavarian Germany. The Einstein family was well-to-do; the father,
an engineer, owned the town's electro-technical works, but business
made it imperative for the Einsteins to move to Milan, Italy, in
1894. Most of Albert's youth, however, was spent in Munich, where
he received his early education. Unlike most of his fellow students,
the boy was not interested in the military shows and glories of the
New Germany; he turned away from the prevailing belligerence to
the serenity of Beethoven and Mozart and the books of the philosophers. At fifteen he had mastered the works of Euclid, Newton, and
Spinoza, and had earned the nickname of "Old Father Bore." At
seventeen he studied at the Zürich Polytechnical School in Switzerland, and although his father urged him to learn a trade, such as
electrical engineering, young Einstein determined to explore the
world of science, a world of order in sharp contrast to the chaotic
and bitterly competitive world of business. He heartened himself
with Emerson's line: "If a man plant himself indomitably on his instincts, the world will come round to him." He decided to specialize
in mathematics and physics. Attending the University of Zürich, he
taught in that city's high school and, a little later, in a school at
Schaffhausen. At twenty-two he became a Swiss citizen, married a
former fellow-student, Mileva Marec, a mathematician in her own
right, and worked in the patent office at Berne. He was a pleasant
and conventionally good-looking young man with a carefully

trimmed black mustache and neatly brushed dark hair. Only the eyes dispelled an impression of the commonplace; the eyes were both brooding and brisk, restless with energy and intense in quick perception.

In 1905 the *Annalen der Physik* published a thirty-page paper by Einstein, "On the Electrodynamics of Moving Bodies," a modestly entitled and seemingly academic document which was destined to alter our whole conception of the properties of matter as well as the structure of the universe. Its revolutionary import was not grasped at first, but it became apparent by 1920, when a translation of Einstein's *Relativity, The Special and General Theory* challenged physicists and mathematicians throughout the world.

Newton's followers were convinced that motion and rest were absolute and measurable; Einstein demonstrated that motion and rest are relative: measured differently by different observers. From this starting point, he proceeded to demolish the more sacred absolutism of length, mass, and time—the three fundamental measures on which all other quantities depend.

Such a drastic revision of concept was not completely unheralded. Herbert Spencer had already posed the problem of the sailor walking west on a ship sailing east at the same speed. Does the man move or not? To anyone on the vessel he is incontrovertibly in motion, but an observer on shore would conclude he was making no progress. This sort of discussion of relative motion was well known before Einstein's time, but suffered the failure that it could not be applied to the motion of light. Since it could not, the necessity remained of assuming somewhere in the universe a reference point which was absolutely at rest.

To this conceptual difficulty were added a number of more substantial cracks in the smooth edifice of Newtonian science: astronomers had computed that even with all possible influences accounted for, the planet Mercury deviated slightly but steadily from the path that Newton's laws of gravity predicted; Michelson and Morley had, in 1887, failed to detect the expected differences in the earth's motion (as it circled the sun) with respect to the "reference point at rest"; the Curies had shown that radium continuously emitted energy with no visible source; and Kaufmann found, in 1901, that rapidly moving electrons were inexplicably heavier than stationary ones.

It is to Einstein's profound credit that these and other flaws seemed to him not causes for many small adjustments in scientific thought, but rather evidence of an underlying new law of nature. He assumed that the anomalous experiments were right, and built on that assumption.

In the symbols of mathematics, Einstein reasoned that any observer had an equal right to consider himself "at rest." If the speed of light appeared the same—approximately 186,000 miles per second—to all observers, it required a shrinkage of dimensions along the direction of motion. Such a shrinkage—the Lorentz-Fitzgerald contraction—had been postulated in 1895 as a mathematical artificiality; Einstein proved it to be a physical reality. For example, a round ball moving at 161,000 miles per second past an observer would appear flattened from front to rear to half of its normal thickness; at the speed of light it would appear as a flat disc with no thickness at all. The important consequence of this is that nothing can move faster than the speed of light.

The same analysis showed that events which seemed simultaneous to one observer might not seem simultaneous to another. Specifically, a clock appears to run slow when there is relative motion between it and an observer.

Though length and time were now both changeable, Einstein found that a combination of the two—a "space-time interval" which includes distance and duration—was constant to all observers. The invariance of this interval is a basic justification of order in the universe, replacing the separate problems of space or time alone.

With no further assumptions, the contraction of rapidly moving lengths and the slowing down of rapidly moving clocks are sufficient to show quite simply that rapidly moving masses appear heavier than their "rest mass." This mass increase vindicated Kaufman's experiments and led to the now famous interrelationship between mass and energy.

In Newtonian physics, if a moving object is pushed, the push speeds it up and the energy of propulsion becomes kinetic energy of the object's motion. Repeated pushes will give increased speed, without any limit. Einstein had shown that nothing could exceed the speed of light and that masses increased at high speeds. This meant that, near the speed of light, a push contributes only partly to increased speed, with the remainder going to increase the object's mass. The mass increase could be directly related to the energy of the push, to give the simple but overwhelming equation $E = mc^2$.

Here Einstein showed his genius by asserting that not only the relativistic mass increase had its equivalent energy, but that *all* matter was concentrated energy. The equation signified that the latent energy (E) in any object is equal to its mass (m) multiplied by the square of the enormous speed of light (c^2). "But," said Einstein, "if every gram of material contains this tremendous energy, why did it go so long unnoticed? The answer is simple enough: so long as none of the energy is given off externally, it cannot be observed . . . For a mass increase to be measurable, the change of energy per mass unit must be enormously large. We know of only one sphere in which such amounts of energy per mass unit are released: namely, radioactive distintegration."

Thus were the Curies' results explained, and the way opened to search for the conversion of greater masses: a search which led to the tremendous energies of the atomic bomb. Einstein denied that he was "the father of the release of atomic energy." "My part in it," he wrote in *Atomic War or Peace,* "was quite indirect. I did not, in fact, foresee that it would be released in my time. I believed only that it was theoretically possible. It became practical through the accidental discovery of chain reaction, and this was not something I could have predicted." Nevertheless, in 1939, after American physicists had failed to persuade the Army and Navy of the importance of the Atomic Project, it was Einstein's letter to Roosevelt describing the incredible potency of atomic energy that made the United States build the bomb before the enemy constructed it.

Far-reaching as these results were, they were all outgrowths of the early Special Relativity theory. The General Relativity, which was published in 1915, caused even wider revision of the concepts of our universe. Drawing from the most recent advances in mathematics, and adding to them his own original techniques, Einstein formulated the Principle of Equivalence. This principle asserts that there is no basic difference between the forces of gravity and of acceleration. But the "force" of acceleration is not a force—when we feel it in a car that suddenly starts, stops, or turns, we are only feeling a changing state of motion. Einstein found that gravity could also be so considered if the properties of space changed near large masses. This change—thought of by some as a "bending" or curvature in a fourth dimension—led to effects predominantly agreeing with Newton's "force" of gravity. However, an additional term in the equation gave slight differences in the immediate neighborhood of such large masses as the sun. These differences proved to account exactly for the unexplained deviations of Mercury, the planet closest to the sun.

Furthermore, if gravity was a property of space itself, rather than a force, then light was subject to gravity, and wherever a light-ray entered a gravitational field it would be deviated or "bent." This was too much for all but the most visionary physicists; but Einstein insisted that his theory could be proved by factual evidence. He suggested a test which would chart the path of starlight in the gravitational field of the sun. The stars normally being visible only at night, the only time when the stars and the sun can be seen together is during an eclipse. Einstein therefore proposed, as related by Lincoln Barnett in *The Universe and Dr. Einstein,* "that photographs be taken of the stars immediately bordering the darkened face of the sun during an eclipse and compared with photographs of those same stars made at another time. According to his theory the light from the stars surrounding the sun should be bent inward, toward the sun, in traversing the sun's gravitational field; hence the *images* of those stars should appear to observers on earth to be shifted outward from their usual positions in the sky. Einstein calculated the degree of deflection that should be observed and predicted that for the stars closest to the sun the deviation would be about 1.75 seconds of an arc. Since he staked his whole General Theory of Relativity on this test, men of science throughout the world anxiously awaited the findings of expeditions which journeyed to equatorial regions to photograph the eclipse of May 29, 1919. When their pictures were developed and examined, the deflection of the starlight in the gravitational field of the sun was found to average 1.64 seconds—a figure as close to perfect agreement with Einstein's prediction as the accuracy of instruments allowed."

Einstein referred to the international reception of this triumph with dry humor. It is merely, he wrote, another proof of relativity. "Today in Germany I am hailed as a German man of science and in England I am pleasantly represented as a foreign Jew. But if ever my theories are repudiated, the Germans will condemn me as a foreign Jew and the English will dismiss me as a German."

At this time Einstein, who had been professor of theoretical physics at the German University in Prague, was a member of the Prussian Academy and had moved to Berlin. His first marriage, of which two children had been born, had ended in divorce, and in 1917 he had married his first cousin, Elsa Einstein, who was his beloved companion until her death in 1936. At forty he became a world traveler and visited England, France, the United States, China, Japan, and Palestine.

Although not politically minded, Einstein never hesitated to take sides whenever confronted with violence. A lover of peace and a champion of the poor—he gave his Nobel Prize money to charity— he dared to fight aggression in a nation that was becoming a synonym for aggressive intolerance. The Nazis harried him and when Hitler came into power, Einstein was branded a public enemy. Forced out of the Academy in 1933, he forsook Germany and came to America, where he was given a lifetime professorship at the Institute for Advanced Study in Princeton, New Jersey. He became an American citizen in 1940. His devotion to the freedom-loving spirit of man had been declared in a series of papers and pamphlets, convictions and beliefs collected in two volumes of general writings, *The World As I See It* and *Out Of My Later Life*. Typical of his hatred of brutality is the noble indignation of his paragraphs on "Moral Decay." "Today," wrote Einstein in 1937, "we must recognize with horror that the pillars of civilized human existence have lost their firmness. Nations that once ranked high bow down before tyrants who openly assert: 'Right is that which serves us!' The quest for truth for its own sake is not to be tolerated. Arbitrary rule, oppression, persecution of individuals, faiths and communities are openly practiced in those countries and accepted as justifiable or inevitable . . . One misses the elementary reaction against injustice—that reaction which in the long run represents man's only protection against a relapse into barbarism . . . Let us refuse to accept fatal compromise. Let us not shun the fight when it is unavoidable to preserve right and the dignity of man." It was this reaction which turned the congenital pacifist into the dedicated warrior for humanity.

Though his Special and General Relativity had wrought more of a revolution in science than the works of any other man, Einstein continued seeking more accurate descriptions of the universe. In 1921 his modifications of the prevailing theories of radiant energy —in particular his extension of Planck's quantum principle that radiant energy is emitted in a broken stream of particles or "quanta" —won him the Nobel Prize. The results of his investigations from 1906 to 1920 included the equation known as Einstein's Photoelectric Law, which changed the course of physics and spectroscopy, and made possible the more dubious benefits of television.

In 1950, Einstein published an appendix to the third edition of the volume, *The Meaning of Relativity*, which first appeared in 1922. The appendix was the culmination of a thirty-five-year search for a simple unifying principle (the Unified Field Theory) underlying all manifestations and forms of creation. Modern science had become the scientists' race for simplifications. Conglomerate matter had been reduced to ninety-two elements; these elements had been divided into minute particles; the natural forces of nature, with their widely differing manifestations, had been "simplified" into a few types of force fields, while light, heat, and other forms of radiation had been classed as electromagnetic waves differing in length and frequency. Einstein's early work reduced these still further. The astronomers had proved Einstein's theory that space and time were joined in a flowing continuum, using his General Theory to advance the concepts of the curved universe and to explain the creation of stars, planets, and galaxies. The explosion of the atom bomb—an explosion which converted a tiny bit of matter into the blasting power of 20,000 tons of TNT—proved that matter was merely unreleased energy, and that matter and energy were two different manifestations of a single cosmic entity.

But Einstein was not satisfied; he was after the unattainable simplicity: a proof that the whole physical universe is one continuity, a rising and falling and never-ending stream. Most of his fellow-physicists held that the universe is discontinuous, composed of infinite and infinitesimal particles and atoms (or quanta) of energy. The quantum physicists held that, since everything was both "particles" and "waves," the universe was dual; one of its chief tenets was the ultimate unpredictability of things, with chief emphasis on probability. This, known as the Uncertainty Principle, compelled the conclusion (with which practically all physicists agreed) that neither causality nor determinism can be found in nature. Einstein, as William L. Laurence summarized the Unified Field Theory in *The New York Times*, "alone has stood against all these concepts of the quantum theory. Admitting that it has had brilliant successes in explaining many of the mysteries of the atom and the phenomenon of radiation, he maintains that the theory of discontinuity and uncertainty, of the duality of particle and wave, and of a universe not governed by cause and effect, is an incomplete theory, and that eventually laws will be found showing a continuous, non-dualistic universe, governed by immutable laws, in which individual events are predictable." Long before this Einstein had declared his faith in a completely logical universe; "I cannot believe," he said, "that God plays dice with the cosmos."

"The field concept," Einstein explained when he issued an addendum to the startling appendix in his seventy-fifth year, "seems inevitable, since it would be impossible to formulate general relativity without it . . . However, it has before it the gigantic task of deriving the atomic character of energy." The symbols which he used to postulate the perfect universe were so forbidding that even master mathematicians will require years of labor to extract the factors applicable to experimental justification. Until then, the electronic "brains" are helpless because the mathematicians do not know how to "translate" the equations for the machines. Until Einstein's field concepts can be tested in terms of concrete reality, it will not be certain that Einstein has come to the end of the search, or whether an end can ever be indicated.

Nearing seventy-five, Einstein was honored all over the world. His presence at a dinner helped raise several million dollars to build the Albert Einstein College of Medicine projected by Yeshiva University. The man who had changed practically every concept of space, time, and energy was growing old, but he refused to grow venerable. Although he resembled the traditional bespectacled, bewildered, felt-slippered, absent-minded professor, he looked much more like a slightly raffish but somehow leonine saint with a disordered halo of wild white hair. His son, Hans Albert Einstein, gave a few insights into his private life: "With the exception of mathematical puzzles, he has little interest in games—he does not even care for chess. He has never, to my knowledge, attended a horse race, a baseball or a football game. But he loves boating and he's an experienced yachtsman. His favorite sport is, of course, walking. But he hates to climb. Even the sight of mountains depresses him—they bear down on him, he says. He smokes pipes—usually short ones. He reads widely. What interests him, besides science, is history, biography, essays. He is fond of fine pictures, but he does not collect them . . . Father doesn't go in for religious ritual, but in the interest of charity I have seen him, wearing the traditional skullcap, play his violin in a synagogue."

Never a dogmatist, Einstein never belittled the power of religion. A philosopher as well as a physicist, he believed that the mystic transcended the materialist, and that it was impossible to draw the line between the physical and the metaphysical. "The most beautiful thing we can experience is the mysterious," he declared. "It is the source of all true art and science. He to whom this emotion is a stranger, who can no longer pause to wonder and stand rapt in awe, is as good as dead; his mind and eyes are closed. The insight into the mystery of life, coupled though it be with fear, has also given rise to religion. To know that what is impenetrable to us really exists, manifesting itself as the highest wisdom and the most radiant beauty which our dull faculties can comprehend only in their most primitive forms—this knowledge, this feeling, is at the center of true religiousness. In this sense, I belong in the ranks of devoutly religious men."

Einstein spoke not only as the man of faith but as the man of science, for he contended that "the cosmic religious experience is the strongest and noblest mainspring of scientific research." Inspired by the great thinkers who had defined the universe, Einstein especially praised Spinoza and his "geometric form of argumentation." It was in the Dutch philosopher that he found something which led him to discover the equivalence of matter and energy. "In Spinoza," said Einstein, "one finds the majestic concept that thinking (the soul) and extension (the naturalistically conceived world) are only different forms of appearance of the same 'substance.' " To the question whether, as a scientist, he could ever hope to quiet man's fears and give him the assurance of a unified universe based only on a few mathematical formulas, Einstein replied that he was like a paleontologist who had only two bones with which to reconstruct a mysterious prehistoric animal. "Meanwhile," he said, "the only proper attitude is patience—patience and resignation supported by good humor and a certain indifference to the importance of one's continued existence . . . We scientists will not change the hearts of other men by mechanisms, but by changing our own hearts and speaking bravely. We must be generous in giving to the world the knowledge we have of the forces of nature, after establishing safeguards against abuse. We must realize we cannot simultaneously plan for war and peace . . . When we are clear in heart and mind—then only shall we find courage to surmount the fear which haunts the world."

After a sudden brief illness, Einstein died at the age of seventy-six. Apparently he had been suffering from hardening of the arteries, which caused an arterial rupture, and death occurred on April 18, 1955.

Joseph Stalin

[1 8 7 9 - 1 9 5 3]

"Genghis Khan with a telephone."

IS WORSHIPERS extolled him as "Our Father" and "The Sun of our Lives"; cities were named after him, his photograph replaced the icons; he was idolized as a god, omniscient, omnipotent, and infallible. His enemies regarded him as an evil genius, an unscrupulous, inhuman, and merciless Machiavelli, who never hesitated to repudiate his promises and betray his supporters. To most of the world, the man who controlled the destinies of more than 800,000,000 people and exercised more power than any other figure in history was, in Churchill's phrase, "a mystery wrapped in an enigma."

He was born in the little Georgian village of Gori, December 21, 1879; his name was Joseph Vissarionovich Djugashvili. His ancestry was mixed with a wild Oriental strain. His father was an illiterate shoemaker who, in his frequent drunken fits, sullenly beat the boy. His mother was a laundress, a devout church-goer, who hoped that her son, whom she called "Zozo," would be a priest. She worked overtime to send him to a local church school before he was nine. When he was fifteen, she managed to obtain a scholarship for him in the Tiflis Theological Seminary, where he remained until he was nineteen. There is a persistent legend that when young Joseph sang in the choir his voice quivered with emotion, but the records reveal nothing so devotional. On the contrary, they show that Joseph spent much of his time with a rough crowd as "king of the streets" and that what books he read were forbidden documents smuggled in from the outside. One entry in the school's register of discipline reads: "Djugashvili was discovered reading *Literary Evolution of the Nations* on the chapel stairs. This is the thirteenth time he has been discovered reading such books." While in the Seminary, he became a member of a secret society, part of the socialist movement. After he challenged authoritarian dogmas he was expelled for heresy.

Cut off from his family, he supported himself by working at night in the Tiflis Observatory; during the day he discoursed on the

Marxian doctrine to railway and transportation workers, whom he helped to organize. Before he was twenty-one he took part in a demonstration which was put down by the Cossacks. He had to go into hiding. At this time he called himself "Koba," the name of a mythological Georgian hero.

At twenty-two he was elected a committee member of the Social Democratic Labor party; he went to Batum, led a strike of oil workers, and was arrested. Concealed copies of Lenin's *Iskra* (*The Spark*) found their way into the prison and he continued to study Marx and Lenin's application of Marxism. When he learned of the party split between the aggressive Bolsheviks and the moderate Mensheviks, he determined to ally himself with Lenin and the other extremists.

During the next twelve years he was sentenced six times to Siberia. Each time he escaped, worked his way back, and continued his activities. On one occasion he led a group of revolutionists who held up two carriages containing government funds and "expropriated" 340,000 rubles for the Bolshevik party. In his late twenties he assumed the name of Stalin ("Steel") and became famous for his physical toughness as well as his ideological tenacity. At thirty, a political prisoner under the Tsarist regime, he was compelled to lead his fellow prisoners and march in single file between two lines of soldiers and take the blows from their rifle butts. Refusing to "run" the gantlet, the man of steel walked slowly and defiantly down the line, beaten and bleeding, with his head high. It was this nerveless self-discipline he demanded from his followers; he was ruthless when he did not get it.

During an interval between one prison and another, he helped found *Pravda,* which became the official organ of the Bolshevik party. In 1912 he was betrayed by Malinovsky, a supposed comrade who was actually a government spy, and once more was sent to Siberia. This time, cut off from all communications, it seemed that any effort was futile and that his work was at an end. The news of the First World War roused the hope that the Russian autocracy could not last much longer, but it was not until after the revolution of 1917, when the Provisional Government took over, that he was released along with other political prisoners. Stalin was forty when he came to Petrograd and joined Lenin, who had made his way across Germany, and Trotsky, who had come from America. Trotsky was Lenin's favorite. He overshadowed all his colleagues by virtue of his learning, his brilliant writing, and his dramatic power of speech. Stalin was sent to the front, where, having studied Clausewitz, he followed the Prussian general's tactics and succeeded in putting down the counter-revolutionaries.

Stalin and Trotsky were at loggerheads when Lenin suffered his first stroke in 1922. Two years later, when Lenin died, the feud between the two men had developed into deadly hatred. Lenin, who recognized Stalin's determination but distrusted his purpose, had written in his will: "Comrade Stalin, having become a general secretary of the Party, has concentrated tremendous power in his hands, but I am not sure he knows how to use that power properly . . . Stalin is too rough, and this fault becomes insupportable in the office of a general secretary. Therefore, I propose that the comrades find a way to remove Stalin from that position and appoint another man more patient, more loyal, less capricious . . . On the other hand, Comrade Trotsky is distinguished not only by his exceptional abilities—he is the most able man on the committee—but also by his too far-reaching self-confidence and a disposition to be too much attracted by the purely administrative side of affairs."

After Lenin's death, there was a short triumvirate. It included Stalin, Zinoviev, and Kamenev, but Trotsky was not a part of it. In the next few years, Stalin played one group against another and undermined Trotsky's persuasiveness. Stalin was not only a shrewd politician but an implacable leader whom no one dared oppose. He declared that Trotsky was a visionary who had dreamed of world-wide revolution at a time when international revolution was impossible, whereas all revolutionary efforts should consist of "building socialism in a single state," that state being Russia. Trotsky maintained that Stalin had taken possession of power, not with the aid of personal qualities, but with the aid of an impersonal machine. "Stalin did not create the machine, but took possession of it . . . Stalin," wrote Trotsky in his uncompleted *Stalin: An Appraisal of the Man and His Influence,* "is a past master of the art of tying a man to him not by winning his admiration, but by forcing him into complicity in heinous and unforgivable crimes." Stalin was fifty when he had Trotsky driven from the country he had done so much to liberate. Twelve years later Trotsky was murdered in Mexico.

A reign of terror began in the 1930's. Countless thousands—members of the Red Army General Staff, small landowners, and mere critics of Stalin's methods—were killed, while many times their number were imprisoned. Most of those who had been closest to Lenin were relentlessly liquidated. Sergei Kirov, Zinoviev's successor, was assassinated in 1934. A few months later there began the so-called "purge trials" which did not end until 1937. Men who had devoted themselves to Lenin and his principles—party organizers, soldiers of the revolution, small propagandists as well as high officials—were accused of being agents of the corrupt bourgeoisie, of conspiring with Nazi Germany, of planning to restore capitalism. They were even accused of being criminals retroactively, of plotting treason at a time when they were risking not only their own lives but those of their families in the revolutionary struggle. Leading generals were executed, and a little later, those who had condemned them were also executed. Hundreds of thousands of government functionaries and party members, charged with being Trotskyites, saboteurs, "fascist wreckers," were cold-bloodedly killed or sent into exile. The trials were secret; there were inexplicable and implausible "confessions." Trotsky was tried in absentia and violently condemned. As *The New York Times* wrote, "From the indictments and the 'confessions' of the accused, it appeared that the Bolshevik revolution was carried out, and the Soviet regime established, by traitors with the aid of traitors." The word "brotherhood" became a mockery, and the dream of a classless society turned into a nightmare as, after seven major purges, all classes were subjected to fear, terror, and cruelty.

In spite of the violence with which Stalin was identified, his appearance was far from bloodthirsty. He was a mild-looking little man with a round face, a shock of wiry hair, and the mustache of an amiable walrus. He was short—five feet six—but he weighed close to a hundred and ninety pounds. He was built, said Harry Hopkins, "like a football coach's dream of a tackle, with hands as huge and as hard as his mind." General Walter Bedell Smith, former Ambassador to the Soviet Union, pictured him as one who was "not by any means the unattractive personality which some writers have depicted. Indeed, he has genuine charm when he chooses to exercise it. While not tall, he gives the impression of great strength. . . . The most attractive feature of Stalin's face is his fine dark eyes, which light up when he is interested." He rarely dressed formally even at formal affairs; instead he usually wore a common soldier's uniform. He smoked a cheap pipe; chess was his favorite diversion. Visitors to the Kremlin recalled that he was a proud and affectionate father who brought up his children in the simplest surroundings. Churchill described his apartment as anything but ostentatious: a bedroom, a dining room, a workroom, and a bath.

Stalin's domestic life was a guarded but fairly public secret. His first wife, Ekaterina Svanidze, bore him a son, Jacob, of whom nothing is known after he became a German war prisoner during the Second World War. She died, after a lingering illness, in 1907, and in 1919 Stalin married Nadya Alliluyeva, the seventeen-year-old daughter of an old revolutionary companion. There were two children by this marriage, a son, Vassily, who became a lieutenant-general in the Soviet Air Force, and a beautiful red-haired daughter, Svetlana. Nadya died mysteriously in 1932; it was said that she committed suicide. Little is known of his third wife except that her name was Kaganovich.

Even his most embittered opponents admitted that Stalin "did some good." As a matter of record, not since the time of Peter the Great had a country been so transformed. Inspired by a rehabilitation scheme of Trotsky's, Stalin presented the first of his Five-Year Plans, which brought about colossal social and economic upheavals and changed Russia from a half-barbaric nation to a modern state. Following Lenin's lead about the need for electricity, Stalin assembled the reports of a thousand experts, put the technicians to work, and industrialized a backward land with a gigantic Electrification Plan. Irrigation brought life to exhausted soil; tractors supplanted the ox; one acre with modern machinery produced more than a dozen acres operated by previous primitive methods. Those landowners, farmers, and peasants who objected to collective farming were punished by having their land confiscated, by being starved by famine, and pitilessly exterminated. Profound changes took place in education. Illiteracy, which under the Tsars had been reckoned at 79 per cent, fell to 10 per cent. Enthusiasm for the benefits of technology brought about a passion for science. In 1916 there were only about 200 laboratories in Russia; twenty years later there were more than 2,000. At the same time, knowing that revolutionary progress would not ensure peace, Stalin prepared for war.

By this time he was the complete dictator. Stern, savage, semi-Oriental, he was, said someone, "Genghis Khan with a telephone." He saw a Second World War looming, but hoped to keep Russia out of it. When the Nazis threatened, he played for time, had his diplomats negotiate with Hitler, and finally signed a mutual non-aggression pact. When Hitler violated the treaty and swiftly invaded the U.S.S.R. it seemed that nothing could stop the German advance. Town after town fell; the very heart of the country was threatened when the attackers ringed Moscow. It was then that Stalin emerged as a superb strategist and an unyielding force. The government had fled to safety in Kuibyshev, but Stalin remained in the Kremlin with some of his staff. He had previously ordered a "scorched earth" policy; now, before the Germans could dig in for the winter, he ordered a counter-offensive and drove the Nazis into a retreat almost as disastrous as Napoleon's. Two years later Hitler called up fresh troops and the Wehrmacht's crack divisions circled Stalingrad. Stalin steeled the beleaguered garrison with "Not a step back." And there, in one of the greatest reversals in history, the Russians held fast, counter-attacked, and decimated an enemy army of 300,000 men, thus making possible a final Allied victory.

Conferences with the "Big Three" at Teheran, Yalta, and Potsdam, reinforced by lend-lease supplies from the United States, seemed to promise future cooperation between Russia and the democracies. But after the end of the global conflict, mutual distrust developed; good feeling diminished and suspicion deepened when Russia pulled down what Churchill called an "iron curtain," and made rapprochement with the western powers increasingly difficult. The Soviet Union joined the United Nations, but at Yalta, Stalin had insisted on an absolute veto power; subsequently he used that power in a way that often paralyzed the United Nations, prevented them from resisting aggression, and obstructed cooperative action on any world problem.

All authority was now vested in Stalin. At the beginning of government by the Soviets there had been four congressional meetings each year. In the fourteen years between 1925 and 1939 there were just four meetings; after 1939 there were none. To safeguard his gains, Stalin embarked on a huge campaign of consolidation. It has been argued that his object was not so much the spread of communism as the traditional imperial policy of attaining security and, eventually, world leadership for Russia. In any case, after Carpatho-Ukraine was ceded to Russia, Poland, Hungary, Yugoslavia, Bulgaria, and Czechoslovakia came under his control. When noncommunist parties in these countries seemed to possess any strength, they were reduced to impotence. Sometimes violence was necessary, as in Czechoslovakia, to keep the "satellite" states in line. In 1948 Marshall Tito broke with Stalin and, although still insisting that Yugoslavia was Communist, refused to take orders from the Kremlin. To forestall any further "deviations" or defections, Stalin saw to it that most of the subordinate communist states repudiated their leaders. Among the hitherto important and patriotic top Communists purged were Anna Pauker in Rumania, Slansky in Czechoslovakia, Gomulka in Poland, Rajk in Hungary, and Kostov in Bulgaria.

As the uneasy peace degenerated into the "cold war" Stalin grew more remote and recalcitrant. He refused to participate in the Marshall Plan, although his country needed economic aid, and surprised his antagonists by building up a vast network of factories which brought heavy industry to an unprecedented height. In spite of the devastations caused by war, consumer goods and agricultural production soared far beyond pre-war levels, while at the same time, Russia produced marvelous aircraft, submarines, jet fighter planes, guided missiles, atomic and hydrogen bombs. The western powers argued, objected, and sent protesting notes. But Stalin was impervious to western diplomacy. "If any foreign minister begins to defend to the death a 'peace conference,' " he wrote, revealing a flair for irony as well as a congenital cynicism, "you can be sure that his government has already placed its order for new battleships and airplanes. A diplomat's word must have no relation to action. Good words are a mask for the concealment of bad deeds. 'Sincere diplomacy' is no more possible than 'dry water' or 'iron wood.' "

While Stalin was still alive, dozens of commentators strove to explain his power in terms of a peculiar fusion of savage contempt and stony confidence, of a disdain which was matched by his daring. In *How Russia Is Ruled* Merle Fainsod maintained that Stalin's position was achieved by the mutual control and rivalry of the Party, the secret police, the state administration, the army, and industrial management. These groups, however, were not puppet organizations but "power structures in their own right," the techniques of control being those of indoctrination, prestige incentives, punitive measures, repressions and rewards, "with periodic concessions and breathing spaces." In *From Lenin to Malenkov* Hugh Seton-Watson reminded readers that, contrary to Marxist dogma, the backward countries, not the highly developed nationalities, permitted communism to take power, and concluded that Stalin's workers' state was "a combination of the economic exploitation of early capitalism with the political terror of modern totalitarianism." In *Russian Assignment* Leslie C. Stevens asserted that, in spite of "the blight of total statism," there was a clear distinction between the Russian people and Stalin's regime, and that "the problems created in a decent people by the forced maintenance of power will somehow in the end destroy that power."

"Power corrupts," said Lord Acton, "and absolute power corrupts absolutely." Stalin had achieved absolute power. Unlike Lenin, who encouraged free discussion and individual differences, Stalin permitted no shades of opinion. Any difference was condemned as a defection, and the unlucky perpetrator was forced to make public recantation of his sins. Art, music, and literature had to conform to Stalin's prejudices; writers, artists, and even musicians were rated according to their ability to conform. Stalin repeated that the state was not meant to be of service to the individual but that, on the contrary, man was meant to serve the state.

Approaching seventy, Stalin entered a period of deification. Every museum, every home, every room in every public building displayed his portrait. His statue was omnipresent; his bust eyed the travelers in every railroad station and stared at the students in every school. The ubiquitous likenesses implied that Stalin was everywhere, watched everyone, and knew everything. He was the glorified, supreme leader, undisputed master of one-third of the world's people when, in early 1953, he suffered a stroke. It was kept secret, and "corrected by extraordinary curative measures." A second attack caused a brain hemorrhage and a collapse. This time the extraordinary measures failed to effect a cure. Four days later, due to "a growing circulatory and respiratory insufficiency," Stalin died, March 5, 1953. He was not quite seventy-four and he had been in power twenty-nine years.

Lytton Strachey

[1 8 8 0 - 1 9 3 2]

*"Clean brevity; dispassionate truth; free
spirit of inquiry."*

To his early confreres, Lytton Strachey seemed scarcely the
person who would revolutionize the writing of historical biography. A shy man who lived with his mother until she died,
he was grotesquely tall and abnormally thin. His unnaturally pale
skin, flaming red beard, and staring eyes made him still more startling. He looked as if he had been drawn for one of Edward Lear's
absurd limericks. His posture was that of an elongated crane, but
his persistence was a gadfly's. When he was with his cronies, the
half-dozen writers who formed London's "Bloomsbury Group," he
always sat quietly, hardly speaking, but owlishly alert; "hunched
in a corner," reported Vincent Sheean, "all beard and spectacles,
not even appearing to listen, but waiting the opportunity to
pounce." He liked domesticity, but he never married.

Born in London, March 1, 1880, (Giles) Lytton Strachey came
of an exceptional family. He was the son of General Sir Richard
Strachey, an Indian administrator, and Lady Jane Strachey, a distinguished essayist; the editor of the *Spectator,* St. Loe Strachey,
and the political economist, John Strachey, were his cousins. Educated at Trinity College, Cambridge, he made a reputation while
an undergraduate with a prize-winning poem. The judges who
gave the award for his academic and traditional set of verses could
never have suspected that Strachey would become one of the period's most famous tradition-smashers. As soon as he was graduated,
Strachey forgot his gentle stanzas and devoted himself to a stabbing
prose. He wrote with deliberation—he was thirty-two before his
first volume appeared—and it was not until he was forty that a
collection of his essays, innocuously entitled *Eminent Victorians,*
caused a critical furor. These were strange biographical studies,
caustic and probing, sly and savage; they bewildered the cautious
scholiasts and delighted the young rebels. Here was a historian who
dared to make an art of biography—"that ill-digested mass of ma-

terial, slipshod style, tedious panegyric"—and turn the exposé from a sensation into a school. Strachey followed these brief indictments of a snobbish, scheming society with works of greater scope and larger dimensions: *Queen Victoria, Pope, Elizabeth and Essex*. He applied the then-revolutionary psychoanalytical method to figures which previously had resisted analysis of any kind. With uninhibited candor, fierce curiosity, and a touch of malicious glee, Strachey tore veil after veil from sacrosanct shrines. It was not with rude iconoclasm, however, but with a surgeon's detachment and a scholar's precision that he cut through the rigid pietism, the swaddled sentiment, and the prudish reticences. Seeking unsuspected truths rather than glibly restated conclusions, Strachey's aim was speculative rather than predetermined, esthetic not ethical.

Strachey insisted that biography should be at least as interesting and even as exciting as fiction, and the results were spectacular. His slogans—"clean brevity," "dispassionate truth," "free spirit of inquiry"—became the manifesto of a new school. Using words with poetic finesse, he swiftly flashed a personality onto the page. The verses which Pope aimed at his enemies are "spoonfuls of boiling oil, ladled out by a fiendish monkey at an upstairs window"; on the other hand, Molière's comedies make "light and frivolous things as ernal as the severest and weightiest works of men."

Several things were charged against Strachey. It was said that he wrote (or rewrote) history like a novelist, that he used facts only to negate them with fanciful conclusions, that his forte was a kind of feline praise which was worse than a forthright attack, that he dipped his pen in vitriol to write letters about the defenseless dead. But Strachey's best work was neither invidious nor destructive. He recognized gold wherever he found it, and he made the true metal of his effigies shine through the gilt and tarnish. It was also said that Strachey cultivated a style for style's sake, that he saw life in terms of literature and, although he prided himself upon his restraint, he distorted details and turned character into caricature. However, in the very act of examining his subjects, Strachey often fell in love with them. He began work on his portrait of Queen Victoria in a spirit of dry ridicule but, wrote Frank Swinnerton, "as the months passed . . . he found laughter fade before a growing respect, admiration, affection. He found her a queen after all." A laudatory lecture by Max Beerbohm, published in 1944, praised Strachey's narrative power, his penetrating irony, his dramatic and, at times, melodramatic effectiveness. Although uncritical, the essay reminds us, wrote Louis Kronenberger, "as we need to be reminded, of the sheer pleasure that Strachey provides."

It is a question whether Strachey's brilliance will survive his mannerisms. Many readers prefer him in such shorter works as *Portraits and Miniatures* and *Books and Characters*—"Lady Hester Stanhope," that splendid *tour de force,* is a favorite choice—but there is no question that, before Strachy died in 1932, his influence was international. With his power of revaluation, incisive skepticism, and challenging imagination, he not only changed the biographer's approach, but also made the reader look for the living men and women too often buried in the stolidly official biographies.

Oswald Spengler

[1 8 8 0 - 1 9 3 6]

"Without reason, without hope."

BEFORE Friedrich Nietzsche went completely mad he had completed various prophetic books which, for all their pessimism, were illuminated by wild insights and flashes of clairvoyant vision. The writing was alarming if ambiguous, but Nietzsche would have been aghast to see his cryptic utterances applied literally in the political terrorism of Hitler and the philosophical hopelessness of Spengler's despairing *The Decline of the West*. Nevertheless, the nineteenth-century rhapsodic prophet of doom not only prepared the way for his twentieth-century disciples, but was surpassed by the dictator's murderous hymns of hate and the scholar's calm but horrifying chant of disaster.

Oswald Spengler was born May 29, 1880, at Blankenburg, a small town in the idyllic Harz mountains of Central Germany. His lineage consisted of two strikingly different strains. His mother's people boasted of their theatrical blood: his aunt was a professional dancer and his maternal grandfather had been a balletmaster. His father's forebears, who had come from South Germany about three hundred years before, had been engineers and mining technicians, and Spengler's father followed their profession until the mines failed to show a profit and the family moved to Halle. There were three younger sisters; Oswald was the only son. At Halle the boy attended high school and the local university; later the universities of Munich and Berlin. Although he was granted a Ph.D. from the latter institution for a thesis on the ancient Greek philosopher, Heraclitus, his main interests, as might have been expected in a child of the engineering Spenglers, were mathematical and scientific.

At twenty-three he began teaching not only mathematics, but geography and history, first in Saarbrücken, then in Düsseldorf and Hamburg. At thirty he received a sabbatical leave of absence and, after a year, decided he had still not learned enough. Without a qualm he renounced teaching. The climate of Berlin had been too severe and he moved to Munich, a city which he found more salubrious in every respect. He had inherited a small income, which was slightly increased by the reviews he wrote, but the First World War wrecked his finances. He had to live in an unheated room in the meanest part of Munich, eating occasionally in workmen's shelters, and living chiefly on tea. He was always cold, insufficiently clothed, writing by candlelight, unable to buy the books he needed for reference or even coal to warm his garret. In his early thirties his face was already worn. The mouth was grim; the cheek bones stonily pronounced; the eyes hard; the head bullet-shaped and aggressively bald. Although his ancestry was anything but North German, everyone considered him the pure Prussian type.

At thirty-eight Spengler, unsocial and almost totally unknown, published a volume which was not only to affect Prussianism but was to cause reverberations throughout the world. *The Decline of the West* appeared in 1918, toward the end of Germany's bid for power in the First World War and, translated into a dozen languages, disturbed historians and scholars in America and Japan as well as in all the European countries. In it Spengler predicted the downfall of a civilization whose promise had not been fulfilled and the rise of a force which was to be both annihilating and reanimating. Fascism and National Socialism offered to complete the process of destruction and set out to prove that, far from being an age of progress, our civilization was decadent. Spengler saw no future for the victors; he prophesied that the white conquerors would be superseded by another race, probably Mongolian and Asiatic. A second and more sharply defined version of *The Decline of the West* was published in 1923, and stressed Spengler's conclusion, by way of Nietzsche, that civilization as we know it is merely mankind growing old and that it is about to end. Western man, having become civilized, is effete, infirm and defenseless, and, therefore, must die.

Drawing a parallel between the modern and the ancient world, Spengler maintained that his work represented a new philosophy: *"the* philosophy of the future, so far as the metaphysically-exhausted soil of the West can bear such." Every culture, said Spengler, went through four distinct seasons: spring, summer, autumn, and winter. In the West, culture's spring was represented by the Middle Ages, a period of crusading vigor, the age of the great cathedrals, the free-flowering arts, the creative aristocracies. The Renaissance was culture's summer, with the towering geniuses of

Leonardo da Vinci, Galileo, Shakespeare, and literate man's liberation from ignorance and supernaturalism. Autumn came with the
Reformation; aristocratic culture degenerated into middle-class
conventions, an existence in which a specious intellectuality replaced deep instincts, and a dependence upon reason proved to be
a feeble substitute for faith. The nineteenth century was our winter
of discontent and doom. Civilization completed and killed itself
with the growth of the modern city, the power of money, and the
dominance of the masses.

The city, charged Spengler, exhibits all the symptoms which has
brought the Western world to its inevitable end. It destroys the
true value of things, since all its values are appraised in terms of
money. Its cultural aspects, as well as its social customs, are opposed
to the less sophisticated who live in small towns and hinterlands,
and present "an uncomprehending hostility" to the "keen and cold
intelligence" which confounds them. Moreover, the city is the out-
growth of imperialism, the dead-end of civilization. Cultured man
applied his energies inward; civilized man directs his energies outward, a seemingly vital but actually self-defeating expansion. "The
expansive tendency is a doom, something daemonic and immense
which grips, forces into service, and uses up the late mankind of the
world-city stage, willy-nilly, aware, or unaware." Our future is win-
try, bleak and inexorable; "we have no right to expect anything
good in the face of facts. . . . Only dreamers believe there is a
way out. Optimism is cowardice. We are born into this time and
must bravely follow the path to the destined end. There is no other
way. Our one duty is to hold on to the last position, without reason, without hope."

As for the arts, we are shamed by the Orient; Western culture
has gone down with Western civilization. We have, said Spengler,
ruined classicism with soulless sentimentalities and destroyed pure
form with multiple but meaningless decorations. "What do we
possess today? A faked music, filled with the artificial noisiness of
massed instruments; a faked painting, full of exotic and absurd
effects, which, every ten years or so, concocts some new 'style' which
is, in fact, no style at all." We have, in essence, a succession of
imitations and distortions, splintered mirrors, reflections of reflections.

Spengler regarded the future with a resigned and almost gleeful
pessimism. He awaited Nietzsche's "eternal recurrence" with mingled fear and satisfaction. We have come full circle, he chortled; a

new cycle is about to begin with the debacle of an outworn civilization and the return of a healthy and invigorating barbarism. A new elite, young and ruthless, will take over and rule mankind. As H. Stuart Hughes wrote in *Oswald Spengler: A Cultural Estimate,* "In view of his cyclical theory of human development and his scepticism about man's ethical potentialities, Spengler dismissed as an illusion the idea of progress in history. Democracy he considered a pious sham. World peace he regarded as both unattainable and undesirable. The twentieth century, he predicted, far from being the century of peace, progress, and democracy that his contemporaries imagined, would prove to be an era of tyranny, imperialism, and virtually constant warfare."

Spengler's fatalism was accepted by a ruined as well as a resurgent Germany. The defeated Germans were comforted by being assured that their defeat was part of a universal downfall, and the emerging Nazis were heartened by his prophecy of a new and Aryan elite unprecedented in its destructive savagery. For a while Spengler was one of the gods of the Nazi hegemony, but his distrust of regimentation and his own particular kind of arrogance kept him from participating in National Socialism. Although he was not molested, his activities were limited, and remaining quiet in a wildly psychotic Germany, he lived the rest of his life in shadowed solitude. In his fifty-sixth year he suddenly collapsed. He had been suffering from headaches for some years, but he was seemingly in good health when he was struck down by a fatal heart attack on May 8, 1936.

Others had anticipated Spengler's forebodings and had made similar prognoses of a dying civilization. The Italian historian, Giambattista Vico, had charted the lives of nations and had indicated a series of *ricorsi,* or historical returns, passing through various civilizing phases from one barbarism to another. In the 1890's the American Henry Adams felt that the democratic experiment was nearing its finale of failure—"allowing for our rapid movement we ought still to have more than two hundred years of futile and stupid stagnation"—while his brother, Brooks Adams, was even more convinced of the breakup of Western civilization. Our misdirected surplus energies, he thought, are bringing about such an accumulation of tensions that all the structures of modern man will crack and shatter. "At length a point must be reached when pressure can go no further," wrote Brooks Adams in *The Law of Civilization and Decay,"* and then one of two results may follow: A stationary period may supervene, which may last until ended by war, by exhaustion, or by both combined. . . . Or disintegration may set in, the civilized population may perish, and a reversion may take place to a primitive form of organism."

No one, however, was so implacable and appalling as Spengler in his insistence that democracy is a synonym for dissolution, that peace is a mere passing away into death, that, since philosophers no longer have any real understanding of life, philosophy is futile, and that there is no progress except a progress toward decay. He had followed *The Decline of the West* with *The Hour of Decision* and other essays as well as political writings, some of which were posthumously published; but nothing he wrote subsequently had either the impact or the imagination of the work which he completed in his mid-thirties. Startling his readers, he also stimulated them when, comparing our civilization with the long span of Chinese, Egyptian, Indian, Greek, and other cultures, he characterized the spirit of Europe and America as "Faustian," a spirit which, although aging and wasted, not only hoped to comprehend but to achieve everything, including the impossible. Closing the first part of his major opus with a flourish of fatalism, Spengler concluded: "For us whom a destiny has placed in this culture and at this moment of development—the moment when money is celebrating its last victories and the Caesarism which is to succeed approaches with a firm step—our direction, willed and at the same time obligatory, is set for us within narrow limits. . . . We have not the freedom to choose, to reach to this or to that, but only the freedom to do what is necessary—or do nothing. And a task that historic necessity has set will be accomplished with the individual or against him."

Many historians disagreed with Spengler's theory of "the determinism of inevitable decline" and the repudiation of the enlightenment and the liberties attained after centuries of struggle. Few, however, disagreed that its influence was powerful and widespread. "Spengler had almost everything to qualify him as the first of the post-war prophets," wrote Quincy Howe in *The World Between Two Wars*. "He had the faculty of making his readers feel that in understanding him they had thereby joined the elect. They could not all become Caesars, but at any rate they would know what to expect and how to adjust themselves to the inevitable. The emergence of Wilson and Lenin appeared to confirm Spengler's prediction about the role great men would play in the twentieth century. His emphasis on practical results appealed to a generation weaned on the pragmatic philosophy of William James. His worship of 'technics' suited the scientific temper of the times. But above all Spengler offered a fatalistic formula to replace Western man's lost religious faith. And as his fame spread from defeated Germany to shell-shocked Europe and from shell-shocked Europe to the bewildered United States, it became more and more apparent that nobody had won the war and that everybody had lost it."

Spengler's work has been attacked as a typically German pretense of omniscience, as a book which "reeks with unpardonable exaggerations delivered in a tone of dogmatic certainty," as a series of brilliant but misleading metaphors, as an extended rationalization of personal prejudices. His detractors may be right and Spengler may be wrong in his despondent augury. But, picturing the rise of a new barbarism, he forces us to reappraise the quality of our culture and the permanence of our civilization. His method may be unscientific and his metaphysics suspect, but his major premises —together with such omens as the rising tide of color and the inescapable clash between East and West—are more timely now than when they were pronounced in the early years of the twentieth century. Spengler speaks with particular significance to a society weakened by wars and sickened by depressions. What with seething unrest in Asia and Africa, worldwide national uprisings and international war-psychoses, the manifestation of Communist Russia as a commanding power, the armaments race growing more frantic with the stockpiling of atom and hydrogen bombs and other weapons of almost total destructiveness, *The Decline of the West* remains a fearful and continuing portent.

Alexander Fleming

[1881-1955]

"A triumph of accident."

As opposed to the revolutionary discoveries in atomic power the revolution in medical science was universally approved. Where the eruptive force of nuclear weapons threatened to shorten man's life, if not to destroy it altogether, the so-called wonder drugs promised to extend his existence beyond the prophet's fondest life expectancy. The problem of destroying sick and harmful cells without damaging healthy ones has by no means been solved, but contemporary triumphs with the almost miraculous antibiotics, sulfa drugs, and hormones suggest a future free of today's mysterious and malignant diseases.

The discovery of penicillin, the greatest disclosure in the practice of medicine since Pasteur, was due to a Scottish bacteriologist, Alexander Fleming, who was born at Lochfield, Darvel, in Ayrshire, August 6, 1881. He was the youngest of eight children and his father, a farmer, hoped that the last child of his second wife would continue to cultivate the family acres. Young Alexander hoped so, too. He enjoyed the life of the land, cut peat, fished for trout, snared rabbits, and roamed the countryside with the sheep. "Living as we did at the end of the road, and up on the edge of the moor," he recalled, "we considered ourselves a bit better than the boys in the town; they did not know how to climb and they did not know where to find peewits' eggs. . . . I might have stayed on the land and become a farmer—not at Lochfield, for my brother Hugh was there—but on some other farm in the neighborhood. I might have been a very good farmer, who knows, and I might have had the finest Ayrshire herd in the country."

At fourteen, his background was suddenly altered when he was sent to London to join one of his older brothers. He had attended Kilmarnock Academy, where Robert Burns and Robert Louis Stevenson had their schooling and, though England became his country and London his center, he never lost his Scottish accent. After studying at the Polytechnic he enlisted in the Scottish Volunteers, became a crack shot and an expert swimmer. It was his swimming which radically changed his career. His brother Thomas was a general practitioner in the Marylebone Road; two other brothers, John and Robert, were studying optometry. "My brother Thomas pushed me into medicine," he said, "and I had to choose a medical school. There are twelve such schools in London. I did not know any of them, but I had played water-polo against St. Mary's—so to St. Mary's I went."

At St. Mary's, Fleming studied under the eminent bacteriologist, Almoth Wright. He learned to observe closely, to develop a formidable memory and to work economically. The last came easily to the man who described himself as "just a canny Scot who cannot bear to throw away anything—not even a contaminated Petri dish." He participated in every sport and took practically every prize and scholarship offered in Physiology, Hygiene, Medicine, Pathology, Pharmacology, and related subjects. After his apprenticeship he worked in the laboratory and, by the time he was twenty-eight, had won honor after honor for his researches and diagnostic discoveries.

The First World War took Fleming out of England. In 1914, shortly after his thirty-third birthday, joining Wright, he went to Boulogne as an officer in the Royal Army Medical Corps and established himself in the city's Casino. It was dangerously overcrowded with badly wounded, pain-protesting soldiers, many of them suffering from gangrene. The improvised laboratories, according to Fleming, "consisted of two subterranean bathrooms which were periodically flooded with sewage." Fleming was shocked not only by the hell of battle but by the staggeringly unnecessary casualties. He saw men die of wounds that should have healed; he saw powerful antiseptics fail to halt the bacteria they were supposed to attack. Although he was frequently cited in dispatches, he was disheartened. He felt that he had not fulfilled the function of a man dedicated to healing.

Fleming was thirty-seven, bearing the rank of captain, when the war ended and he was demobilized. Returning to London, he determined to devote himself to immunology, hoping to find something which would be an effective bacteria killer without hurting healthy tissue. Experience as well as experiments had convinced him that the most important antibacterial agents in the body were the cells themselves. It was "natural immunity" that he sought. . . . "I could never forget the importance of the body's natural defences."

He published significant papers on experimental pathology; one of the most important was "Observations on a Remarkable Bacteriolytic Substance (Lysozyme) Found in Secretions and Tissues"— lysozyme, a precursor of penicillin, being "a bacteriolytic ferment which acts on certain bacteria and causes their rapid dissolution." The year before his discovery of lysozyme Fleming had married Sarah Marion McElroy, whose twin sister was the wife of his brother John.

He was a soft-spoken, gray-haired, finically neat scientist of forty-seven, puzzling over various compounds when on a summer day in 1928 he noticed a strange phenomenon in his laboratory. One of the Petri dishes, a shallow glass plate, held a culture of staphylococcus germs, and a mold had gathered on part of it. It was not too unusual a manifestation, but this one was caused by a particular and history-making speck of dust. Legend has it that the activating spore of mold had floated in from a beer barrel in a nearby saloon. What startled Fleming, however, reminding him of the action of lysozyme, was that the area surrounding the mold was clear of the staphylococci; some unknown agent within the mold had killed what had been living germs. Closer examination with the microscope revealed the mold in action; Fleming could actually see the bacteria shrinking. "Nothing is more certain," he wrote afterward, "than that, when I saw the bacteria fading away, I had no suspicion that I had got a clue to the most powerful therapeutic substance yet used to defeat bacterial infections in the human body."

He called the substance penicillin, since it came from the mold botanically known as *Penicillium,* or "little brush," because of the brushlike ends of the infinitesimal fibers. Since it was the common mold that gathers on cheese and stale bread, it was easy enough to produce. Obtaining a pure culture, Fleming "grew" it on bread, cheese, and fruit, but soon discovered that it flourished best in meat juices. Experiments proved its potency. Following Pasteur's classic method, mice were infected not only with large doses of staphylococci but with streptococci and pneumococci; they were then inoculated with the liquid. The germs disappeared, and the mice showed no sign of deleterious effects. Further tests showed that the liquid form of the mold prevented growth of various cocci even in dilutions up to 1 in 800. When he published his findings in the June, 1929, issue of the *British Journal of Experimental Pathology,* Fleming announced, in what has been called one of the most remarkable understatements of the times: "Penicillin may be an efficient antiseptic for injection into areas infested with penicillin-sensitive microbes."

The mold from which penicillin is derived was not merely, as Fleming modestly said, "a triumph of accident" but a combination of endless research, unrelaxing observation, and definitely favorable circumstances. The discovery arose, said Fleming in his Nobel Prize lecture, "simply from a fortunate occurrence which happened when I was working on a purely academic bacteriological problem which had nothing to do with bacteriological antagonism, or molds, or antiseptics, or antibiotics. In my first publication I might have claimed that I came to the conclusion, as a result of serious study of the literature and deep thought, that valuable antibacterial substances were made by molds, and that I set out to investigate the problem. That would have been untrue, but I preferred to tell the truth: that penicillin started as a chance observation. My only merit is that I did not neglect the observation, and that I pursued the subject as a bacteriologist."

In common with almost all epochal discoveries, penicillin was neglected for years. "This business of fussing with fungi," wrote Donald G. Cooley in *The Science Book of Wonder Drugs,* "making herb extracts and so on was scarcely respectable in leading scientific circles. It was all a bit too witch-doctorish, savoring of superstition and folk-lore, like the belief of some ignorant people that a poultice of molded bread made a wound heal more cleanly. The nature of pharmaceutical research was overwhelmingly along lines of laboratory synthesis of organic molecules, and the impact of sulfas gave tremendous impetus to such directions." Fleming kept "cultivating his molds" but he did little about them. For ten years the power of penicillin remained in suspension.

Fleming's paper, however, had made a great impression upon a few of his more progressive colleagues. Two Oxford University specialists, Dr. Howard W. Florey and his German associate, Dr. Ernst Boris Chain, spent month after month attempting to extract the essential substance from Fleming's mold. At last they obtained a concentration—about a teaspoonful of yellow-brown powder—of the powerful bacteria killer, the first salt of penicillin, and tested it on various bacteria, then on mice. On February 12, 1941, the first dose of isolated penicillin was injected into a human being. The patient, a London policeman badly infected with staphylococci, was critically ill; his face was a mass of abscesses and he was wasting away with a fever of 105 degrees. He had failed to respond to any drug, including the violent sulfanilamide. After a single injection of penicillin his temperature immediately dropped, but there was not enough to combat the damages which already had been done and the patient died. A small amount of the precious substance had been extracted from his urine and, after months of further concentration, another patient—a boy, fifteen, dangerously infected with streptococci—was treated and, overnight, was rescued from death. A few months later Fleming himself injected the drug into the spinal canal of a dying friend and, within a week, the man completely recovered.

Penicillin suddenly became the world's most needed drug. The Second World War had begun, and England, crippled by bombings and requiring every available foot of factory space for arms, could not hope to produce the drug in sufficient quantities. Dr. Florey flew to the United States, arranged for mass production, and whereas in 1942 there was barely enough penicillin to treat a hundred patients, within a year countless thousands of lives were saved by the most potent and, at the same time, the least toxic of all antibiotics. In 1943 Fleming was made Fellow of the Royal Society. The following year he was knighted and, in 1945 together with Florey and Chain, was awarded the Nobel Prize.

Other molds, chiefly derived from various soils, were developed. Dr. Selman A. Waksman of Rutgers University produced a germ-annihilating microorganism from New Jersey earth and called it streptomycin. Another microbiologist, Paul Burkholder of Yale, extracted chloromycetin from a sample of Venezuela dirt; it stopped an epidemic of typhus in South America. At the age of seventy-five Benjamin Duggar, a retired professor of botany who had specialized in the study of mushrooms, incubated a yellow mold out of Missouri mud and—because of its aureate or golden color—named it aureomycin. A commercial chemical firm in Brooklyn literally unearthed terramycin from some decayed Indiana soil. By this time there was no doubt that a new period in medicine had arrived—an era of chemotherapy which derived its power from the combative strength of a few soil-inhabiting microorganisms.

Continual refinements were made to check the sometimes excessive power of the antibiotics and the allergies with which some patients reacted. Thanks to Fleming, however, the world of medicine had undergone a complete change. Mastoid operations, feared by every parent of growing children, disappeared; the dread middle-ear infection could be cured by an antibiotic in a few hours. Within a decade the number of patients operated for mastoiditis fell in a Boston children's hospital from more than three hundred a year to five. Appendicitis, and the once almost fatal peritonitis, as well as meningitis, tularemia, and puerperal fever no longer terrify. The world owes much of this to Fleming who, feeling that younger men should carry on his work, retired at the age of sixty-seven. Combining his passion for bacteriology and his favorite hobby, painting, he ornamented his walls with brilliant enlargements of germ cultures, abstractions reminiscent of modern stained glass executed with the skill and devotion which had gone into his dedicated work. His seventieth birthday found him resigned to retirement but reluctant to forgo further researches in microbiology. "I have still got a few useful years before me," he said. "The happy man keeps on working."

Fleming was in his seventy-fourth year when he was struck down by a heart attack. Death occurred March 11, 1955, in his London home, a few blocks from the laboratory where a sealed container preserves Fleming's original mold, the "ancestor" from which most of the world's penicillin is descended.

Pablo Picasso

[1881 -]

"Painting is not done to decorate apart-
ments . . . It is an instrument of war
against brutality and darkness."

WHEN, after a period of imitation, an artist finds his own idiom he is usually glad to stick to it, even to capitalize on it. The layman can immediately recognize, let us say, "a typical Renoir" or "a typical Rouault." But "a typical Picasso" is not the product of a carefully cultivated method; it can be a picture in any of half a dozen totally different styles. Picasso has gone through so many radical changes—a superb artist in all of them—that he has discarded one manner after another. He has not "evolved"; he has simply never been satisfied to see (and paint) things, places, and people in any one set style. Unquestionably the most variable and volatile artist of our times, perhaps of all time, Picasso is the intellectual creator at the top pitch of experiment.

He was born October 5, 1881, at Málaga, Spain, and was christened Pablo Nepomuceno Crispiniano de la Santissima Trinidad Ruiz y Picasso. The boy's companions shortened the imposing set of titles to Pablo Ruiz. His father, José Ruiz Blasco, of Basque descent, was an art teacher, and when the youth exhibited his first paintings he used both his mother's and his father's names and signed them P. Ruiz Picasso. It was not until he was twenty that he dropped his father's name, as being too common, and adopted that of his mother, as being more unusual as well as more euphonious.

Picasso, it is said, was born with a pencil in his hand. He was not only a precocious draftsman but a decided artist before he entered his teens. At fourteen he drew portraits that are preserved today as examples of expressive realism and depth of modeling. After the family moved to Barcelona, where his father became professor, Pablo, then not quite fifteen, was admitted to the School of Fine Arts. The time allowed for the difficult entrance tests was a month; Pablo passed them in a day. At sixteen he exhibited at the Fine Arts Exhibition in Madrid and won an award. A few months later he had his own studio. Besides his easel, he possessed only a bed and a chair, so he painted ornate and luxurious furniture on the walls. He wandered about the streets, the docks, the cabarets, and drew everything he saw: idlers, nuns, prostitutes, dock-workers, dogs, fashionable women, whom he delighted to caricature, weary old men and lusty cab-drivers.

At nineteen he paid his first visit to Paris, and it was already obvious that he would be a success. Within a month he sold three canvases. He returned to Madrid, where he started a magazine entitled *Young Art* and had a showing of his pastels, but soon went back to Paris. He was strongly influenced by the acrid Bohemian studies of Toulouse-Lautrec, the bold brushwork of Van Gogh, and the flat color masses of Gauguin. Consequently he ceased to paint in soft tones and blurred outlines and adopted a more discriminatory palette. Having learned from many sources and having schooled himself in various styles, he was ready for his first wholly original work. He was twenty when he began painting the remarkable series of poor, unhappy men and women with emaciated bodies, bony hands and long thin fingers, pathetic mothers and children, beggars, wretched acrobats, cripples, hungry couples, outcasts. The canvases were drenched in blue—the color of melancholy—sad ceruleans and muffled azures—and the pictures were not so much portraits of forlorn people as symbols, metaphors of the misery of their world. Recalling his sympathy as well as his distress, in *Picasso and His Friends,* Fernande Olivier inquires whether his work was "cerebral, as I have understood it since, or did it record a profound and desperate love of humanity, as I thought then?" At twenty-three he was, she remembers, "small, dark, thickset, unquiet and disquieting, with somber eyes, deepset, piercing, strange, almost without motion. Awkward gestures, womanish hands, carelessly dressed. A heavy shock of hair, black and glossy, cut across an intelligent and stubborn brow. He seemed half-Bohemian, half-workman." He painted at night, frequented the dives, sported a Browning automatic, attended prize fights, and fell in love with the circus.

It was his passion for the circus, not only for the performers in the ring but for the circus-folk backstage, that gave his art a new and happier turn. There still is a look of distraction if not distress about Picasso's jugglers, harlequins, merrymen, and mountebanks —his clowns are conspicuously sad—but the color is no longer cold. The preceding so-called Blue Period (which Picasso now considered overemotional) gives way to the Rose, or Pink, Period in which a lack of physical gayety is compensated by delicate reddish tans and warm terra cottas. A trip to Holland may have determined him to discontinue the attenuated forms and gaunt features of the Blue Period, for his portraits take on a rounded sweetness and firm flesh, as well as an ageless nobility—an amazing performance for a youth not yet twenty-five. It is a world of half-lights, like Rilke's, beyond everyday reality; but the people who live in it are both severe and serene. "In their very expressionlessness," wrote Maurice Raynal, "we discern Picasso's single-minded concern for style. Constantly refining the saliencies of form, polishing the disciplined framework of his line, he makes his way towards a new classicism. This he carries to an incredible degree of perfection. It is no exaggeration to say that several compositions of the Rose Period stand comparison with the noblest masterpieces of painting."

At twenty-five Picasso was already an established painter. He was collected and panegyrized by Gertrude Stein; the Russian dealer, Sergei Shchukine, bought more than fifty large canvases. Gertrude Stein says she gave Picasso eighty sittings for the portrait which he painted of her; but, just before he completed the work, he was dissatisfied with the result and wiped out the face. It was many months later, when he returned from a trip, that Picasso painted in the features—this time without using his model. He was beginning to draw less from the image and more upon his imagination.

The paintings of his Parisian friends, and particularly the group of "wild beasts" led by Matisse and including Rouault, Vlaminck, and Derain, made Picasso think of the possibility of painting as an autonomous art. He was not yet ready to discard representation, but he was beginning to envision an art which was primarily and, perhaps, purely pictorial—a further application of the much-condemned "art for art's sake," which would not be against nature but *unlike* nature, an art which would not merely distort but invent. His colleagues had discovered the masks and wood sculptures of the African Negroes, and Picasso was fascinated by the sharp angles, abrupt planes, and dramatically distorted combination of naïveté and ferocity. They evoked an "esthetic shock" which challenged the canons of conventional art, mocked perspective, and suggested a new dimension for painting. The new dimension was to be cubism; but as yet, Picasso was only exploring the possibilities of geometrical forms. "The idols of the primitive tribes of Africa had a real value for Picasso," writes Christian Zervos, "only insofar as they helped him modify his esthetic experience and attempt a new picture of the world where natural experience and the supernatural overlap to form a unique reality."

That "unique reality" is startlingly revealed in "Les Demoiselles d'Avignon," which Picasso painted at twenty-six and which burst upon the art world with a new and highly controversial esthetic. Zervos says that this "about-face of all esthetic values marked the beginning of a period which revolutionized painting and enriched all art." " 'Les Demoiselles d'Avignon,' " writes Alfred H. Barr, Jr. in his comprehensive and scrupulously annotated *Picasso: Fifty Years of His Art,* "may be called the first cubist picture, for the breaking up of natural forms, whether figures, still life or drapery, into a semi-abstract all-over design of tilting, shifting planes compressed into a shallow space is already cubism. . . . 'Les Demoiselles' is a transitional picture, a laboratory or, better, a battlefield of trial and experiment; but it is also a work of formidable, dynamic power unsurpassed in European art of its time."

With his friend and fellow-painter, Georges Braque, Picasso made continually bolder ventures into the potentialities of cubism. Cézanne had hinted that landscapes and common objects seemed composed of cones, cylinders, and spheres; Picasso and Braque enlarged the suggestion to include the cube. It was not long before they confined their compositions to prisms, triangles, and other sharp-angled forms in order to achieve a simulation of solid geometry. Seurat had called painting "the art of hollowing a surface"; Picasso proceeded to make a contrary art, building up the surface by filling it with masses of pure volume. He analyzed what he saw and rebuilt it with the eye of the imagination rather than with the imperfect and idiosyncratic physical eye. Picasso taught himself to behold an object, according to Maurice Raynal, "from several sides at once, just as the inner eye conceived it, and in the artist's imagination it corresponded not to a mere visual scheme of things, but to a statement, as it were, in which the subject was summed up and contained, once for all. It was no longer in the nature of a picture to set up as a representation, with overtones of anecdote and association; it had to become a statement by itself, a self-sufficient *datum.*"

In an ascetic effort to establish the principle of the *structure* of things rather than the principle of the *aspect* of things, Picasso declared his preoccupation with form not only by modifying the shapes of his subjects, but by forsaking his formerly vibrant colors and restraining himself to dry tones that have no distracting charm: cold grays, unalluring browns, beiges, and dull sepias. Picasso went to the very limits of severity in his desire to wrest the essence from his objects and rescue the "pure design" from the clutter of accumulated and nonessential details. In the intricately angular modulations, however, and the irregular plastic planes, Picasso dissected anatomy so scientifically that, although the operation was a brilliant success, the subject often failed to survive. Masked by shifting horizontals and verticals, the subject almost ceased to exist; it became a suggestion, a vague indication, a theme lost in a complexity of variations, an "ideogram." The true Picassophile divides this period into proto-cubism, analytical cubism, hermetic cubism, synthetic cubism, rococo cubism—there is even a completely contradictory but solemnly announced "curvilinear" cubism.

Although Picasso rarely explained his progress, he was willing to defend his addiction to cubism. In a statement to Marius de Zayas, published in *The Arts*, May, 1923, Picasso maintained that "cubism is no different than any other school of painting. The same principles and the same elements are common to all. The fact that for a long time cubism has not been understood and that, even today, there are people who cannot see anything in it, means nothing. I do not read English—an English book is a blank book to me. This does not mean that I blame anybody but myself if I cannot understand what I know nothing about . . . Mathematics, chemistry, psychoanalysis, music, and whatnot, have been related to cubism. All this has been mere literature, not to say nonsense, which has brought bad results, blinding people with theories. Cubism has kept itself within the limits and limitations of painting, never pretending to go beyond it. Our subjects may be different, as we have introduced into painting objects and forms that were formerly ignored. We have kept our eyes open to our surroundings, and also our brains." Picasso not only kept his eyes open but continued to keep his critics in such a state of excited controversy that he was a legend before he was out of his twenties. He was only thirty when eighty-four of his works were exhibited in his first one-man show in America, in April, 1911.

Picasso did not stop with cubism after he had seemingly exhausted it. He went on to further and even more drastic experiments. For a while, he played with collages, superimposing paper and other things on his surfaces, and painting over or around them.

As if to show that beauty could be evoked by the most common-place materials, he pasted on newsprint, pieces of string, scraps of paper, bits of linoleum, cloth, sand, glass, simulated wood, a torn page of sheet music, and added charcoal, ink, or oil. The technique of collage, a kind of simplified mosaic, placed the emphasis on texture and, blending the realism of ordinary stuff with extraordinary unreality, achieved a kind of painter's paradox: a bizarre and florid austerity.

At thirty-four, having abandoned realism for about ten years, Picasso made another turnabout and drew graphic and carefully naturalistic portraits of his friends and associates. This so-called "Classic Period" was extended after he went to Rome, where he designed the curtain, scenery, and costumes for the ballet, "Parade," produced by Sergei Diaghilev with music by Erik Satie. He met Stravinsky, drew the memorable portrait of the composer, and sketched the cover for his "Ragtime." He enjoyed being with the members of the Russian Ballet—"we rehearsed in a Roman cellar; we walked in the moonlight; we visited Naples and Pompeii"—and married one of the troupe, a young dancer, Olga Koklova. She bore him a son, Paul, whom Picasso immortalized in two particularly winning portraits: one, painted when the boy was three, as a wistful harlequin; the other, when he was four, as a pert and slightly impudent Pierrot. Throughout his thirties Picasso displayed his virtuosity, as well as his refusal to be bound to any style, by making abstractions, cubist patterns, decorative landscapes, and delicate line drawings which have been compared to Ingres' slim elegancies.

Picasso's "Neo-Classical" period began in his late thirties. Making his home in the semi-tropical French Riviera, he turned out flower pieces, baroque arrangements of fruit, bodies as lush and alluringly rounded as though he had never seen a cube. When he entered his forties, the figures attained heroic proportions as the aftermath of the First World War threw him back to his old concern with humanity. Some of them, like the much-reproduced "Woman in White," are tender, softly palpable, but most of them seem hewn out of antique rock. They are classical not only in their solidity but in the sense that they emphasize form rather than content, dignified tradition rather than romantic experimentation. "Monumental," "impassive," "immovable" are a few of the adjectives with which the critics described the heavy-limbed, sculptural paintings.

During the next twelve years Picasso went through various metamorphoses. He made "constructions" of wire, wrought-iron, and wood; he wrote surrealist poetry; he turned sculptor and created gigantic heads, animals, and curious deformations; he drew projects for monuments. He let his fantasy loose in a flood of abstractions, some of which are violent and revolting, symptomatic of some deep disturbance, but many of which, filled with graceful arabesques, take pleasure in sheer design. It is as if Picasso were calling attention to the beauty of the fluent line, an art in which there is no meaning beyond the pattern or, rather, in which the pattern *is* the "meaning" and the form is absolute.

The Spanish Civil War, which began when Picasso was in his mid-fifties, found him in Spain on the side of the embattled Loyalists. He had been a noncombatant foreigner, a Spaniard living in France, during the First World War; but now, although he had held himself aloof from politics, he became an active partisan of the republican government, aligned against the tyranny of the Franco-led rebels and their military insurrection. An ardent propagandist, he became director of the Prado and was instrumental in saving the museum's treasures from destruction. "Painting is not done to decorate apartments," he declared. "It is an instrument of war for attack and defense against the enemy . . . against brutality and darkness." When the Nazi airplanes, joining the Spanish Fascists, bombed and wiped out the peaceful Basque town of Guernica, Picasso began what many believe to be his most expressive if not his most significant work. On a mammoth canvas, three hundred feet square, Picasso uttered his protest against the cruelty and barbarism of all war, and against this war in particular. "The Spanish struggle is the fight of reaction against the people, against freedom," he stated, while at work on the painting. "My whole life as an artist has been nothing more than a continuous struggle against reaction and the death of art . . . I clearly express my abhorrence of the military caste which has sunk Spain in an ocean of pain and death."

Picasso's outrage is implicit in the terror-evoking images of "Guernica," but its symbols—monsters, broken human bodies, distorted bulls, screaming horses, painted in gray, black, and white—are, though horrible, far from "clearly expressed." Alfred H. Barr devotes several pages of his book on Picasso to an examination of the huge painting which was exhibited in the Paris World's Fair of 1937. He quotes Vernon Clark who, in *Science and Society,* wrote that "Guernica" was "the culmination *ad absurdum* of all the trends, artistic and psychological, that the artist has developed in the past," and, in *Babel's Tower,* Francis Henry Taylor, director of

New York's Metropolitan Museum of Art, sneered at what he considered a "banality of overstatement." On the other hand, the English poet and essayist, Herbert Read, hailed "Guernica" as "a monument to disillusion, to despair, to destruction . . . His symbols *are* banal, like the symbols of Homer, Dante, Cervantes. For it is only when the widest commonplace is infused with the intensest passion that a great work of art, transcending all schools and categories, is being born; and, being born, lives immortally." Granting that Picasso spoke of a world catastrophe "in a language not immediately intelligible to the ordinary man," Barr concludes that "if this work does not entirely explain itself, it can be defended very easily. Let those who find the 'Guernica' inadequate point to a greater painting produced during the past terrible decade or, for that matter, during our century."

From 1937 on, many of Picasso's canvases are distressed, usually disquieting and often disruptive. We are confronted with diabolical effigies and shocking deformations, as though the artist could not stop registering his disgust of people torturing each other in a world bent on its own destruction. More and more he turns away from surface appearance and, in a body of work which is "not immediately intelligible to the ordinary man," perfects an enigmatic but powerful art. His portraits are no longer likenesses; they are emblematic, frightening, as though Picasso were trying to paint the inside of the face, the mind behind the mask. The features are often redistributed; profile and full face appear together; a nose takes the place of an ear. But the "simultaneity" of two different aspects has a distinct purpose. Picasso hopes to give a feeling of the live and active person, not a static replica; he presents a face with all its complexity of planes in motion, moving not only in space but time. "If many of his canvases seem strange and undecipherable," wrote André Leclerc, "it is because our vision, accustomed to encounter only one aspect of things, finds it difficult to encompass several aspects at the same time." It is as though Picasso were aware of Blake's "Auguries of Innocence," with its gnomic wisdom:

> We are led to believe a lie
> When we see *with,* not *through,* the eye.

Besides his "double-faced" heads, Picasso made further explorations into the depths of abstraction, wrote an ironic nightmare play, and was planning still more daring projects when the Second World War began.

Picasso was in Paris when the German army of occupation captured the city. Although he knew that his art was considered "degenerate" by the Nazis and that he was in constant danger, he could not be persuaded to escape. He remained in Paris during the entire occupation and refused offers to collaborate with the enemy; on the contrary, he took pleasure in distributing reproductions of "Guernica." After the liberation, he became the father of two children, Claude and Paloma, by a woman forty-two years his junior, and moved to Vallauris, near Antibes, on the French Riviera. Again his art underwent a change. The painting shows a new enthusiasm, a feeling of relief, even of light-heartedness. Always inventive, he tried new techniques in lithography, found a new-old medium, ceramics, and worked with clay as creatively as with pigments. He delighted in mixing, kneading, and firing the material, playing with modern adaptations of archaic plates, pitchers, and pots of multiform shapes, goatlike jugs, woman-formed vases, teapots modeled after birds with beaks for spouts.

In his seventies, Picasso was still the constant innovator and complete iconoclast. A "Mediterranean Landscape," painted in 1952, is bolder in color and composition than any similar work by his "school"; "Massacre in Korea" is relentless in its contemporary ghastliness. A one-man show of his work in Rome (May, 1953) included fifty Picassos never seen before, and the exhibit filled fourteen rooms of the Museum of Modern Art.

Critics have never stopped disputing whether Picasso's many-sided and opposed manners are the result of logical growth, arbitrary willfulness, or a compulsion to discard every new departure for one still newer. His admirers consider it praiseworthy that, as soon as he mastered one style, Picasso was impatient to try another. His opponents point to these very changes of direction as a proof of a lack of serious purpose; they claim that Picasso has been so preoccupied with method that his work has lost meaning. "He has stubbornly resisted his experiences," wrote Thomas Craven in *Modern Art*. "He has no interest in life; he is interested only in art —in the mechanical formation of pictures. He has used his nimble intelligence to complete the withdrawal of art into the inorganic world . . . His art is perfect because it offers nothing; pure because it is purged of human content; classic because it is dead."

Although Picasso never replied to such sweeping denunciations, he showed (implicitly in "Guernica" and other paintings, explicitly in his few writings) that artists who live with spiritual values cannot remain indifferent to the conflicts about them, struggles "in which the highest values of humanity and civilization are at stake." Picasso assumes that form itself, no matter how arbitrary—he does not believe there is such a thing as "abstract" art—has a deep function and that art is the balancing and harmonizing of man's emotions. "If the subjects I have wanted to express have suggested different ways of expression I have never hesitated to adopt them," he wrote. "Whenever I had something to say I have said it in the manner I have felt it should be said. Different motives inevitably require different methods of expression. This does not imply either evolution or progress, but an adaptation of the idea which one wants to express and the means to express that idea." Praising one of his pictures as "the result of sudden vision, rather than of calculated manipulation of form," James Thrall Soby spoke of Picasso's "acuteness of discovery. And finally," he concluded, "he was and remains one of the most extraordinary creators of imagery . . . in the long history of art."

Franklin Delano Roosevelt

[1882-1945]

*"There is nothing I love so much as a
good fight."*

THE ONLY MAN ever to be elected four times to the Presidency of the United States, Franklin Delano Roosevelt, was both worshiped and despised, glorified as a dedicated crusader and vilified as a destructive tyrant. A cripple, living at a time of the severest depression and the worst war in history, Roosevelt taught the world that "the only thing we have to fear is fear itself."

He was born January 30, 1882, the only son of James Roosevelt II and his second wife, Sara Delano, at Hyde Park, New York. On both sides the family was deeply rooted in American soil. The Roosevelts had a double line in the New World. The senior line, which produced Theodore Roosevelt, was mainly of Dutch origin; the first Roosevelt arrived in New Amsterdam in 1644. The junior line, from which Franklin Delano was descended, was a mixture of Dutch, English, French, German, and a strain of Swedish. His mother's family traced their ancestry back to Philippe De la Noy (anglicized into Delano), a Flemish seafarer who was born in Leyden of French parents and settled near New Bedford, Massachusetts, in 1624. It was undoubtedly from the Delanos that the thirty-second President inherited his passion for ships and anything which had to do with the sea.

The Roosevelts were not merely a family but a dynasty. Chiefly, they were businessmen. Isaac Roosevelt (who, like many early Americans, was given a patriarchally Hebraic name) was Franklin's great-great-grandfather, a wealthy banker, merchant, senator, and soldier in the Revolutionary War. His grandson, the first James Roosevelt, retired to the country and purchased the expansive, rolling estate of Hyde Park in Dutchess County, along the Hudson River. The Delanos were equally affluent. Franklin's mother was a beautiful, dominating, and class-conscious woman whose sense of *noblesse oblige* gave her tremendous confidence, a power of self-assurance which she transmitted to her only child. The boy was reared in unostentatious luxury; sailing was his favorite occupation, and he loved to navigate his boat in the tricky waters of Passamaquoddy Bay between Canada and Maine. Before he was fifteen he had been taken to Europe ten times, had learned German in a folkschool in Nauheim, and had already achieved an adolescent cosmopolitism. It was inevitable that, at fourteen, he should be sent to upper-class Groton to prepare for college.

At Groton young Roosevelt did not distinguish himself either as a student or a mixer. None of his courses seemed to interest him. He played tennis and read sea stories; but he missed his mother, to whom he wrote devotedly and regularly three times a week. At sixteen, however, he became suddenly concerned with controversial subjects, and in debates his attitude was always that of a liberal. He spoke in favor of Philippine independence and against restrictions in immigration. At seventeen he was already a dissident. Differing from his fellow Grotonians, the young nonconformer held strange views for the patrician son of a country gentleman. "He became," said John Gunther in *Roosevelt in Retrospect,* "conscious of Jews (though there were certainly none in the school of that day), and he went to a lecture by a Negro on the lack of Negro education in the South. He became intensely interested in the struggle of the Boers against the British in South Africa; he took the Boer side wholeheartedly, and even raised money for their cause."

His passion for the sea was so great that he schemed to run away from Groton and enlist in the Navy—a plan prevented by an attack of measles—and he comforted himself with the thought of entering the Naval Academy at Annapolis upon graduating from Groton. His father, however, had determined he should attend Harvard, the Alma Mater of the Roosevelts, including Franklin's cousin, the famous Theodore, and so he entered the university in the fall of 1900. A restless eighteen, he tried out for football, but did not try hard enough to make the team; pulled a freshman oar because he was built for rowing and because it was expected of him; then gave up athletics for journalism. A scoop got him an important position on the *Crimson,* the college newspaper, of which he became managing editor and president.

The most colorful as well as the most important part of his four years at Harvard was the courtship of Anna Eleanor Roosevelt, his fifth cousin once removed, whom he had known since childhood. The young lovers were engaged during his senior year, but the opposition of Roosevelt's mother was so persistent that the marriage was delayed until 1905, when the groom was past twenty-three and his bride twenty-one. President Theodore Roosevelt came up from Washington to give away his favorite niece, an orphan, who was also his godchild.

At the time of the wedding, Roosevelt was attending Columbia Law School. Two years later, planning to specialize in admiralty law, he was admitted to the bar. In the meantime his father had died, and he took over the duties of host at Hyde Park, where his first two children were born. His position as country squire brought him into local politics and, because a corrupt Tammany Hall under unusually bitter fire needed a respectable front, he was nominated for the State Senate. Roosevelt's name was more than respectable; it was popular. Moreover, it was hoped that some of the magic of Theodore's reputation might rub off on Franklin. No one expected much, for the junior Roosevelt was a Democrat running in uncompromisingly Republican territory—only one Democrat had been elected State Senator since the Civil War. Roosevelt accepted the challenge without fear. He was already a vivid personality: tall and thin with bright blue eyes and fair hair; the lean features were sharply cut, the nose strong, the jaw slightly jutting. The *New York Herald* declared that, if he were not already wealthy, "his handsome face and his form of supple strength could win him a fortune on the stage." Scorning predictions and unfavorable precedents, Roosevelt determined to win—he said "there is nothing I love so much as a good fight." He put the enemy on the defensive with a hard-hitting campaign, storming, cajoling, threatening the opposition in towns and villages where he had always taken his hold for granted, covering the back roads in an old Maxwell, the first time any candidate had campaigned by automobile in New York State. To everyone's surprise except his, he won. He left his law firm and went to Albany.

As a State Senator Roosevelt maintained a liberal attitude in a tightly conservative legislature; he favored progressive measures, including the then-controversial question of woman suffrage. It was only natural that he should support a progressive like Woodrow Wilson and, at the Democratic convention in 1912, he was partly responsible for Wilson's nomination. When Wilson became President, Roosevelt, at thirty-one, was appointed Assistant Secretary of the Navy, a post which was the fulfillment of a dream. The First World War gave him full play to exercise his knowledge of ships, naval relations, and men. He went, via destroyer, on a secret mission to examine naval installations; his advocacy of submarine chasers helped defeat the dreaded German undersea craft. The Armistice of 1919 came just as he was about to engage in more active service as lieutenant commander.

Roosevelt was thirty-eight when the Democratic convention met in San Francisco in an atmosphere of profound depression. The war had been won, but the peace had been lost. Wilson's plan for international understanding, the League of Nations, had been rejected by the Senate; having suffered a stroke, Wilson himself was dying. James M. Cox of Ohio was chosen as a compromise candidate and Roosevelt received the nomination for Vice President. Although the pair campaigned desperately—Roosevelt made more than eight hundred speeches—they were disastrously beaten by the Harding and Coolidge ticket of Republican reaction, with its appeal for "return to normalcy."

Less than a year after returning to private practice, Roosevelt was struck down by an almost fatal catastrophe. In August, 1921, while the family was spending a vacation at their New Brunswick retreat on Campobello Island, Roosevelt ended a day of extreme exertion with a swim in the icy waters of the bay. A chill developed, then fever, then partial paralysis. After several false diagnoses, it was agreed that he was a victim of poliomyelitis. He was terribly crippled—he lost the use of his legs and never could walk a step without heavy braces and crutches. Except by a complicated and exhausting effort, he could not get up from a chair unassisted; he could not even stand without a cane or some person's support. It was taken for granted that his public life was finished; his mother urged him to resign himself to a life of invalidism and retire to the consolations of Hyde Park. But Roosevelt would not accept defeat. A year after the blow, he began to overcome the exhausting handicaps and resume his work. He discovered a bathing pool in an obscure resort, Warm Springs, Georgia, which was full of mineral salts and of a high specific gravity. It checked the damage of his disease and restored some sensation to his limbs; he felt a tingling in his toes for the first time in almost three years. After that, Roosevelt visited the place twice a year, spent a great deal of money (about a quarter of a million dollars) to improve it, and, having bought the property, incorporated it into a nonprofit clinic for the treatment of poliomyelitis. By the time he was forty-two he was able to attend the Democratic convention in New York on crutches; four years later he electrified the convention in Houston, Texas, when, discarding his crutches, he appeared, held up by steel braces which supported him from foot to hip.

It was in 1928, after Alfred Smith had been chosen the Democratic standard-bearer for President, that Roosevelt was nominated for Governor of New York with Herbert Lehman, a forward-looking banker, as running mate. The contest was close; Smith was defeated for President, but Roosevelt won the Governorship. Four years in the gubernatorial seat made him a logical candidate for the Presidency in 1932. While he was still Governor and the country seemed helpless in the grip of an intolerable depression, he spoke prophetically of "the forgotten man." Recalling preceding crises, he said: "These unhappy times call for the building of plans that rest upon the forgotten, the unorganized but the indispensable units of economic power, for plans that build from the bottom up and not from the top down, that put their faith once more in the forgotten men at the bottom of the economic pyramid." This was the keynote of the speeches he made when, at fifty, he campaigned for the Presidency in 1932. He pledged himself to "a new deal" for the American people. "Every man has a right to live, and this means he also has the right to make a decent and even comfortable living," he contended. "Our industrial and agricultural mechanism can produce enough and to spare. Our government, formal and informal, political and economic, owes to everyone an avenue to possess himself of a portion of that plenty sufficient for his needs, through his own work." He spoke proudly of the country's limitless resources, then pointed indignantly to the fifteen million unemployed, starving in the streets, huddled in the breadlines, living in disgraceful "Hoovervilles," cardboard shacks and miserable huts made of discarded orange crates. "The country needs and, unless I mistake its temper, the country demands bold, persistent experimentation. It is common sense to take a method and try it. If it fails, admit it frankly and try another. But, above all, try something. The millions who are in want will not stand by silently forever while the things to satisfy their needs are within easy reach . . . We need enthusiasm, imagination, and the ability to face facts, even unpleasant ones, bravely. We need to correct, by drastic means, if necessary, the faults in our economic system from which we now suffer. We need the courage of the young."

The daring of such appeals at such a moment, the combination of Roosevelt's magnetic personality and the country's distress, proved that Roosevelt had not only a correct appraisal of the situation—he saved the country from bloody strikes and possibly a revolution—but a dramatic sense of timing. As a result he was elected by a huge majority. He was the first Democrat in eighty years to carry every state but six; he received 472 electoral votes to Hoover's 59.

The country was still in a state of panic, and Roosevelt's first task was to restore calm, if not confidence, to a nation riddled with apathy, doubt, and despair. "We need not shrink from honestly facing conditions," he said in his first inaugural address. "This great nation will endure as it has endured, will revive, and will prosper. The only thing we have to fear is fear itself—nameless, unreasoning, unjustified terror which paralyzes needed efforts to convert retreat into advance." As soon as he was elected he set in motion an elaborate machinery of reform. He imposed excess profit and dividend taxes, cut government salaries, reduced pensions, and got Congress to grant control of the banks, devalue the dollar, withdraw all the gold in the country and go off the gold standard.

This was only the beginning. Roosevelt called down to Washington a group of economists, scientists, writers, and teachers. Professional politicians jeered. Deriding the President's "naïve" notion that men who knew could also do, they scornfully referred to the group as "The Brain Trust." Roosevelt ignored the sneers. Within three months he and his "intellectuals" had organized and put into action a set of startling New Deal experiments: the Agricultural Adjustment Administration, the Civilian Conservation Corps, the Securities Act, the Farm Relief Act, the Tennessee Valley Authority, the Home Owners Loan Association, the Federal Relief Act, and, crowning them all, the National Industrial Recovery Act. Some of these were stop-gap legislation, emergency measures; some turned out to be failures. In 1933, however, they were imperative. The Securities Act curbed the runaway powers of Wall Street; the Civilian Conservation Corps found jobs for half a million jobless youths, setting them to reforestation and other constructive works; the Home Owners Loan Association made it easier to obtain small mortgages; the Tennessee Valley Authority stopped soil erosion, brought sanitation and electricity, flood control, and countless other benefits into a poverty-stricken part of the South; the National Industrial Recovery Act abolished child labor, controlled prices, prohibited unfair practices, raised wages, and tremendously improved working conditions by calling for collective bargaining, the right of labor to bargain with employers through representatives of their own choosing.

The resulting outcries were horrendous. The Republican newspapers (and the great majority of American journals were unswervingly Republican) boiled with vituperation. One columnist (Dorothy Thompson) attacked the New Deal as fascist; another (Frank Simonds) proved it was communist. Roosevelt stuck to his reforms, even though his enemies increased with every new law. "Tax the wealth" was a slogan which was not calculated to win friends among bankers and captains of industry. The masses, recognizing the humanitarianism of his program, were with him; it was obvious that he would be re-elected for a second term. In his acceptance of the nomination in 1936 he quoted the English judge who said "Necessitous men are not free men," and, training his guns at the "economic royalists," went on: "Better the occasional faults of a government that lives in a spirit of charity than the consistent omissions of a government frozen in the ice of its own indifference."

He instituted the Fireside Chat, a series of intimate talks via radio with a nation of listeners. Fifty million people at a time tuned in and hung on every word, held by the hypnotic vibrancy of the voice and the fabulous charm of the man. It was the astute politician, the actor conscious of his ability to manipulate his audience, as well as the protective "big brother," who began his public confidences with the sonorous salutation: "My friends . . ." His assured manner was justified; the people became not only his friends but his devotees.

It was a foregone conclusion that he would win again, but it was not foreseen that his second victory would be so much greater than his first. This time, running against Alfred M. Landon, former Governor of Kansas, Roosevelt achieved the most one-sided triumph in the history of Presidential elections. He won 523 of the 531 electoral votes, and lost only two states, the rock-ribbed Republican diehards, Maine and Vermont. His second inaugural address recognized that there was much to be done before the country could be restored to active health. "I see one-third of a nation ill-housed, ill-clad, ill-nourished," he announced. "I see millions lacking the means to buy the products of farm and factory, and by their poverty denying work and productiveness to many other millions." It was with a mixture of zealousness and wistfulness that he looked forward to the future: "I should like to have it said of my first administration that in it the forces of selfishness and lust for power met their match. I should like to have it said of my second administration that these forces have met their master." The opposition never forgave him such pronouncements; they lashed at the crusader with venomous hatred; they caricatured him as a machiavellian egotist and a mad anarchist. Roosevelt could not fail to be wounded. He was valiant but not invulnerable; he made mistakes in strategy as well as errors in judgment. He played into the hands of the enemy when, to overcome the obstructionists, he tried to "pack" the Supreme Court by asking Congress for power to increase the nine-man Court to fifteen. The plan was denounced even by leading Democrats, and it died without being put to vote. Considerably heartened by proof that he could be defeated, the Republicans began to organize a revolt. Congress, hitherto compliant, resisted Roosevelt's proposal for broader executive powers, especially his desire to create new Cabinet posts, including a Department of Public Welfare.

Meanwhile, the country was wrought up by two major concerns: the threat of war and the possibility that Roosevelt would break all precedents and seek a third term in 1940. The former dictated the latter. For a long time Roosevelt refused to commit himself on the hotly contested issue, but the spreading European war was involving a technically neutral America and, when the delegates in Chicago nominated him on the first ballot, he broke the national tradition set by George Washington at the beginning of the Republic. At fifty-eight he defended himself against the charge of dictatorship by saying that, at a time of international crisis, he had urged others to extend their service to the government and he was subject to the same demands and the same devotion. Preparedness for the coming war was his major problem. He had instituted military conscription —the first President to call for it during peace-time; he had exchanged fifty old American destroyers for a ninety-nine-year lease on British possessions in the Atlantic as naval bases for defense, and he had softened the restrictive features of the New Deal so that industry could turn out more guns, tanks, and other implements to make America the "arsenal of democracy." He had, moreover, drawn steadily closer to military cooperation with France and England. He ordered seizure of all German and Italian vessels in American ports, sent troops to Greenland, and, at a secret meeting with Winston Churchill, the English Prime Minister, drew up an Atlantic Charter designed to destroy Nazi tyranny and build a post-war world with universal freedom of the seas, self-determination of all peoples, abandonment of the use of force, the sharing of raw materials by all nations, including not only the victors but the vanquished.

The United States was forced into World War II on December 7, 1941, when the Japanese rulers began their fanatic and suicidal struggle for conquest by attacking Pearl Harbor. While the conflict raged on every sea and swept over every continent, Roosevelt stirred the world with his confident spirit. "The issue of this war is the basic issue between those who put their faith in the people and those who put their faith in dictators." He met again with Churchill, formulated a declaration for the United Nations, and made plans for an Anglo-American invasion of North Africa. He set up with Great Britain, wrote George Fielding Eliot, "the splendid agency of the combined chiefs of staff which resulted in the most successful combative warfare by a military alliance in all history." At Teheran he conferred for the first time with Stalin and Churchill, and determined upon the greatest step in the war: the smashing of Germany by an invasion of the west coast of Europe.

In 1944 Roosevelt once more broke all precedents by running for a fourth term as President. While not as spectacular as his earlier victories, the winning vote showed that the people had not lost faith in their leader. The Republicans assailed him with every vindictive epithet; the whispering campaign was loathsome. Nevertheless, their candidate, Thomas E. Dewey, received only 99 of the electoral votes to Roosevelt's 432. With all this overwhelming approval and other tokens of popular esteem, Roosevelt had thousands of acquaintances, millions of admirers, but only a few intimate friends. The strain was telling on him. He looked older than his sixty-two years. His hair had turned white; his features were gaunt, his expression was grim, his face was gray. He was a lonely and troubled man as he envisioned the end of a frightful war and the beginning of a frightening peace.

It was the difficult peace-to-come which brought him to Yalta for one more meeting with Churchill and Stalin. The Yalta conference has become a source of bitter disputes, an endless controversy; the defamers' cries of "appeasement," "betrayal," and "sellout" did not cease with Roosevelt's death or even soften with the 1952 defeat of the Democrats. The armies of the Soviet were occupying Poland; they were moving westward. Roosevelt had to bargain, and some of the bargaining was bad. He believed that a lasting peace was attainable, and he was wrong. Eager—perhaps too eager—for the war to end, he made concessions, but (although it is rarely mentioned) so did the Russians. "The tragedies that followed," wrote John Gunther, "did not derive so much from the conference itself as from the brusque alteration in Soviet policy later, and direct, callous Russian violation of what had been agreed upon." Perhaps Roosevelt should have foreseen this, but he was trying to achieve mutual understanding and goodwill, goaded by hope and trepidation.

A few weeks after his sixty-third birthday he outlined the consequences of Yalta to Congress. Tired and worn, he went to relax in Warm Springs toward the end of March. A fortnight later, while having his portrait painted, he complained of a sudden and particularly severe headache. Within three hours a cerebral hemorrhage caused a complete collapse. At 5:47 in the afternoon of April 12, 1945, the abrupt and incredible news was flashed that Franklin Delano Roosevelt was dead. The country was shocked almost into insensibility. The millions who, for thirteen years, had depended upon him, were suddenly without a guide. The day of his funeral men, women, and children wept unashamedly; all over the world heads of state and ordinary people met to console each other. He was survived by four sons, a daughter, and his wife, Anna Eleanor, who had become famous as a commentator, humanitarian, and glowing personality in her own right.

So much good and bad blood has been spilled in the name of Franklin D. Roosevelt that it is almost impossible to appraise him without emotion. His opponents were fond of saying that he "betrayed his class" by forcing legislation which hampered the beneficent growth of capitalism and limited free enterprise. The opposite may turn out to be true. History may show that, instead of betraying his class, he protected and even furthered its interests. There was a distinct split in the capitalist thought of his times. In order to recover from the depression of the Threadbare Thirties, a large part of Big Business was progressive to the extent of favoring government controls and government aids for its own preservation. Roosevelt's New Deal was the practical application of this progressivism. Roosevelt realized that the common man was not an allegorical figure, abstruse and vaguely idealistic, but, from the standpoint of the state, a consumer. Moreover, unless the common man could continue to function as a consumer, Roosevelt's class was doomed. The need was pressing and, in order to forestall one crisis after another, Roosevelt advocated the severe modifications and drastic changes which were to affect the future of capitalism not only in his own country but, by its very example, throughout the world.

Scorned loudly by his enemies as "That Cripple in the White House," he was quietly lauded by those who understood him as a citizen of the world, a world he tried to make more livable. He was, as Stephen Vincent Benét put it:

> A country squire from Hyde Park with a Harvard accent,
> Who never failed the people,
> And whom the people will not fail.

In spite of many resounding speeches, he was not a great writer; unhappy when disputed and unable to accept disagreement, he was not always a great man. But he achieved greatness. He radiated it everywhere. His summary of the Four Freedoms is a credo that cannot be forgotten. The First Freedom, he said, "is freedom of speech and expression—everywhere in the world. The second is freedom of every person to worship God in his own way—everywhere in the world. The third is freedom from want—everywhere in the world. The fourth is freedom from fear—which, translated into world terms, means a world-wide reduction of armaments to such a point that no nation will be in a position to commit an act of physical aggression against any neighbor—anywhere in the world.

"That is no vision of a distant millennium. It is a definite basis for a kind of world attainable in our own time and generation."

James Joyce

[1 8 8 2 - 1 9 4 1]

*"To achieve a multi-dimensional effect . . .
a multi-dimensional language."*

A TROUBLED LOVER of Ireland and a contemptuous hater of the Irish, whom he derided as "the most belated race in Europe," James Joyce lived in self-imposed exile most of his life, fighting an uneven battle against poverty, prejudice, failing health, and almost total blindness. In his youth he revolted against the narrow nationalism of the Irish Renascence—he ridiculed the Celtic Twilight as the "cultic twalette"—and turned against the chief figure of the movement by arrogantly telling William Butler Yeats, "We have met too late; you are too old to be influenced by me." Rejecting the misty symbolism and provincial myths of the Irish Revival, Joyce made a violently new language of symbols and, in a series of intricately related works, created a broad and often baffling mythology of the modern world.

Christened James Augustine Aloysius Joyce, he was born February 2, 1882, in a suburb of Dublin. His mother was a gifted musician whose affections were disturbingly divided between her husband and the Church. His father was a light-hearted, charming, and irresponsible fellow, from whom Joyce inherited his pugnacity and a fine tenor voice; enormously proud of his eldest son, he declared James was "the favorite of his sixteen or seventeen children." At six the boy was sent to a Jesuit school, Clongowes Wood College in Clane, where he remained three years. When he was nine, hearing his father extol the patriot Parnell, he wrote a precocious tribute which his father had printed and distributed in Dublin. At eleven he was sent to another Jesuit institution, Belvedere College, for four years. Here he received prizes for his essays, one of which was entitled "My Favorite Hero." It is significant that, even at fifteen, his hero was the wandering, storm-tossed Ulysses.

From his sixteenth to his twentieth year Joyce attended University College, was a pious student, and considered joining the Jesuit Order. Intensive reading in foreign literatures shifted his interests; before he was twenty he could not only read Latin but French and

Italian as easily as English. He studied Norwegian in order to read Ibsen in the original and, at eighteen, wrote an essay entitled "Ibsen's New Drama" which was published in the eminent *Fortnightly Review*. Joyce followed this with a letter to Ibsen, praising the Norwegian dramatist for his dogged devotion to truth and his "absolute indifference to public canons of art."

At twenty, after taking his bachelor's degree, Joyce felt he could no longer be a divided self, a "doblinganger," and left Dublin for Paris. Later he put his resolution in *A Portrait of the Artist as a Young Man:* "I will not serve that in which I no longer believe, whether it calls itself my home, my fatherland, or my church." He said much the same thing in a bitter diatribe, part of which runs:

> This lovely land that always sent
> Her writers and artists to banishment,
> And in a spirit of Irish fun
> Betrayed her own leaders, one by one.

All Joyce took with him to Paris was a letter of introduction, a couple of pounds, and a few poems. He hoped to study medicine at one of the colleges, but he abandoned the idea when he learned that he would have to pay the fee in advance. Unable to write anything marketable, he almost starved. Cocoa was his only food a great part of the time—in *Ulysses* cups of cocoa are not only a source of nourishment but a symbol of the sacrament—and he became ill. He had serious tooth trouble, and he could not afford dental treatment; the later damage to his eyes may have been due to neglect of his bad teeth. He thought of becoming a professional singer and dreamed of taking singing lessons; but this was out of the question since he could not pay a teacher. Six months later, he was called home. His mother was dying. She realized her condition; her pain was aggravated by her son's refusal to go to confession and become a devout follower of the Church.

Joyce's twenty-second year was crowded. He drank heavily for a while, and left home penniless, carrying his few possessions, including bedposts, from one dingy lodging to another. In the spring he got a position as a teacher at Clifton School in Dalkey, where he made further studies in foreign languages. He entered the tenor competition in the National Festival, hoping to achieve the success of the famous John McCormack, who had won the competition the preceding year. The audience was enthusiastic, the judges were impressed, and it seemed certain that he would win. But he refused to subject himself to the third requirement—a sight-reading test—on the grounds that it was wrong to expect a singer to do full justice to a musical composition without having studied it. Rather than compromise, he walked off the platform. His voice had created such an effect that an eminent coach offered to train him for the opera for a small percentage of his earnings, but he was not in a mood to discuss terms. At Dalkey, Joyce met Nora Barnacle and married her in October, 1904. He and his wife immediately left for Switzerland, where he failed to get a promised job, and went on to Trieste, where he became a teacher of languages in the Berlitz School.

For the next twenty-five years Joyce's history is a history of exile and suffering, of struggles for publication, of philistine hostility, of disappointments, delays, and desperations. A group of short stories was completed in his twenty-third year and accepted for publication. However, its naturalism was so offensive to the publisher that even after the book had been set up, he refused to issue it. Another publisher failed to fulfill his contract, but refused to sell the book back to Joyce, who was planning to publish it himself, broke up the type, and destroyed all the sheets. It was not until ten years later that *Dubliners* was published in London in 1914.

Joyce's first publication was a book of poems entitled *Chamber Music*—a later reference makes it plain that Joyce used the punning title in self-mockery. It appeared when Joyce was twenty-five, and it is the very antithesis of the writing with which Joyce became identified. Instead of being experimental, it is full of traditional echoes of seventeenth-century singers, the French symbolists, and the early lyrics of William Butler Yeats. Although the rest of his creative life was devoted to a search for new materials and original ways of expression, Joyce loved the music of the minor Elizabethans and, after his major prose departures, he returned to it in his mid-forties with the simple melodies of *Pomes Penyeach*.

Dubliners is a transitional work. Here Joyce acts as a suggestive reporter, revealing a conglomeration of unhappy episodes in the city of his birth. The first three stories seem to be fragments of his childhood; the others are grim and often merciless pictures which enraged his compatriots and which they vainly tried to repudiate. The portraiture ranges from the casual brutality of "Two Gallants" to the dry pathos of "Eveline" and the mixed coarseness and anguish of "Counterpart." "The Dead" is the most poignant as well as the most sensitive story; in it the hard realist begins to turn into the groping symbolist.

Isolated in Trieste, Joyce was faced with what he called "the delicate task of living" and supporting a wife and two children. He managed somehow "on a salary of eighty pounds a year for teaching the English language as quickly as possible with no delays for elegance." It was all of a decade before he finished *A Portrait of the Artist as a Young Man.* The book is not only a justification of its title but a frank autobiography of Joyce's first twenty years. He originally intended to call it *Stephen Hero,* and his choice of titles reveals Joyce's preoccupation with names and their magic associations. His central character remained Stephen, but the last name was discarded in favor of Dedalus, the heroic and fabulous artificer. The choice was particularly meaningful because Dedalus, who invented wings to lift man from the earth, symbolized the poet and his soaring imagination, as well as the basic idea of flight. But Dedalus (literally "cunning craftsman") was also the designer of the labyrinth, a symbol of the elaborately labyrinthine works which Joyce was beginning to construct. Joyce had chosen the name before he began the first of his three major works. George Russell, the agronomist who wrote poetry under the pseudonym "Æ," had started *The Irish Homestead* to promote modern agricultural methods and, incidentally, to publish the writers of the Celtic Movement. In 1903 he asked Joyce to contribute something simple ("rural? live-making? pathos?") for which the editor would pay a pound— "easily earned money if you can write fluently and don't mind playing to the common understanding . . . You can sign any name you like as a pseudonym." Joyce wrote three stories and signed them "Stephen Dedalus."

Portrait of the Artist as a Young Man is a double exposure: a nostalgic portrait of the Dublin which Joyce ambivalently loved and loathed, and a portrait of the young and rather precious writer, preoccupied with verbal associations and the incantatory power of words. Joyce-Dedalus is the aroused creator who, with a flourish of trumpets, goes forth "to encounter for the millionth time the reality of experience and to forge in the smithy of my soul the uncreated conscience of my race." The *Portrait* is a history of an education, a full-length study of an unusually perceptive adolescent groping toward maturity, and, at the same time, a candid case history of the esthete's coming-of-age. "The narrative of the *Portrait of the Artist,*" wrote Harry Levin in *James Joyce: A Critical Introduction,* "has scarcely emerged from the lyrical stage . . . The personality of the artist, prolonging and brooding upon itself, has not yet passed into the narration. The shift from the personal to the epic will come with *Ulysses,* and the center of emotional gravity will be equidistant from the artist himself and from others. And with *Finnegans Wake* the artist will have retired within or behind, above or beyond his handiwork." Meanwhile, the *Portrait* had difficulty getting itself published. It appeared as a serial in *The Egoist,* an advance guard magazine, but when it was issued as a book, sheets had to be imported from the United States as no publisher in England or Ireland would "for one moment entertain any idea of printing such a production."

Ulysses is a panoramic extension of Joyce's nostalgia. Like the epic from which it takes its name, it is a full-scale parallel of exile and wandering, of blundering search, distracting interludes, and ultimate resignation. The Homeric events, however, occur during an ordinary day (June 16, 1904) in Dublin, as experienced by Stephen Dedalus (Telemachus), Leopold Bloom (Ulysses) and his wife Molly (an unfaithful Penelope). There are also many minor characters, including Mrs. Bella Cohen who runs a brothel (Circe), Miss Douce and Miss Kennedy, barmaids (the Sirens), Mr. Deasy, schoolmaster (Nestor), the seventeen-year-old romantic exhibitionist, Gerty MacDowell (Nausicaa). But the narrative centers upon Bloom, who has lost a child, and is looking for a substitute son, and Dedalus, who has repudiated his family and his religion, and, disconnected with mankind, is seeking a father. "*Ulysses* takes the form of a quest," wrote William York Tindall in *James Joyce: His Way of Interpreting the Modern World,* "and the quester is almost everybody . . . Whether it have as its object tradition or what some call integration, the life-force or the five-year plan, the latest yogi from Los Angeles or Almighty God, the search is the same and so is its real object . . . Joyce symbolized the hunt for the father. With his own loss and need in mind, he made a suggestive image, perhaps the most adequate of all, for the central occupation of modern man."

Together Stephen Dedalus, the lonely self-conscious introvert, and Leopold Bloom, the genial extrovert, "the whole man," explore the gulfs between Homer's wine-dark sea and the side streets of Dublin. Sometimes the analogies with the Greek epic are fully developed, sometimes they are merely suggestive points of departure, but the symbols are patent to any student. The first three episodes concern Stephen Dedalus as thinker, teacher, and brooding wanderer. The first part, according to Stuart Gilbert's brilliant *James Joyce's*

Ulysses, a study almost as long as the work it analyzes, "serves as prelude to the narrative of Mr. Bloom's day, the main theme, and may be regarded as a 'bridgework' between *Portrait of the Artist as a Young Man* and *Ulysses* . . . He [Stephen] is still an intellectual exile, proudly aloof from the mediocrity of his contemporaries, and he still displays an ironic disdain for their shoddy enthusiasms, combined with a predilection for the 'abstruosities' inculcated by his Jesuit upbringing, the scholastic habit of dialectic and exact definition." Bloom enters in the fourth episode, which, with the scene in the bedroom, suggests Ulysses' dalliance with Calypso. Further analogies can be found as the book progresses: Bloom's fondness for soft music and scented soap: and the episode of the Lotus-Eaters; Bloom's appearance at a graveyard: and Ulysses' voyage to Hades; a visit to a newspaper office: and (with exceptional appropriateness) the Cave of the Winds; a tavern quarrel with a drunken, blindly furious Citizen: and the Cyclops' den. Finally, there is the unprecedented monolog in bed, that extraordinary tour de force, Molly Bloom's unbroken chain of thoughts, a single unpunctuated sentence of more than forty pages and some twenty-five thousand words, a vigorously earthy review of her life and a serene acceptance of it.

Long before *Ulysses* was printed in book form the heavy hand of the censor descended upon it. There were mutterings when it began publication as a serial in 1918 in *The Little Review.* When the Gerty MacDowell-Nausicaa episode appeared, the American Society for the Suppression of Vice got busy, the United States Post Office confiscated all copies on the charge of obscenity, the editors were fined and fingerprinted, and the serialization was stopped. An indignant admirer, Sylvia Beach, arranged to have the book privately printed in France, and Joyce was given the first copy, appropriately bound in the blue and white colors of Greece, on his fortieth birthday. The book became a collector's item; it was sold under the counter; it was reprinted in pirated editions for which Joyce, sharing D. H. Lawrence's similar ill fortune with *Lady Chatterley's Lover,* did not receive a penny. Five hundred smuggled copies were burned by the Post Office. It was not until fifteen years after its first serial installment that the book was cleared of the charge of pornography by the decision, since often quoted, of Judge John M. Woolsey, who ruled that, "whilst in many places, the effect on the reader undoubtedly is somewhat emetic, nowhere does it tend to be an aphrodisiac." Harry Levin calls attention to the fact that, in vindicating the book, Judge Woolsey described its effect "in terms of catharsis, the purge of the emotions through pity and terror that Aristotle attributes to tragedy."

For a long time the vindicators were in the minority, while the air was filled with invectives. "It is simply the foulest book that has ever found its way into print," said Alfred Noyes. Richard Aldington considered it "an invitation to chaos . . . the gravestone, the cromlech of naturalism." Joseph Collins' review in *The New York Times* was part adulation, part diatribe. On one hand he conceded that *Ulysses* was the most important contribution to twentieth-century fiction; on the other hand he dismissed Joyce as "the only individual that the writer has encountered outside of a madhouse who has let flow from his pen random thoughts just as they are produced." "I should very much regret your paying Mr. J. Joyce the compliment of an article in the *Revue des Deux-Mondes*," wrote Edmund Gosse, "the grand old man of English letters," to a member of the French Academy. "You could only expose the worthlessness and impudence of his writings . . . I have difficulty in describing to you in writing the character of Mr. Joyce's notoriety . . . It is partly political, partly a perfectly cynical appeal to sheer indecency . . . A literary charlatan of the extremest order . . . There are no English critics of weight or judgment who consider Mr. Joyce an author of any importance." Contrariwise, certain English critics (and creators) of decided weight and judgment differed sharply with such dismissals. Yeats called it "more indubitably a work of genius than any prose since the death of Synge." Speaking of the work as an epic, T. S. Eliot declared, "In using the myth, in manipulating a continuous parallel between contemporaneity and antiquity, Mr. Joyce is pursuing a method which others must pursue after him . . . It is simply a way of controlling, of ordering, of giving a shape and a significance to the immense panorama of futility and anarchy which is contemporary history . . . It is," concluded Eliot in a kind of special pleading, "a step toward making the modern world possible in art."

Between the experts' extremes of opinion the layman felt lost. In spite of the intricacies, the subject matter of *Ulysses* is not too forbidding—much of it can be read without any reference to the Homeric pattern. But the manner of telling presents so many difficulties that countless chapters, theses, pamphlets, and five entire books had to be written in explication. Nevertheless, *Ulysses* is not, as Collins intimated, a disorderly extravaganza which the author could not control. On the contrary, it has a severity of design, a disciplined logic, and a formalism so strict as to be classic. With its richly allusive word-plays, its cumulative evocations of music, mythology, philosophy, little-known books, strange characters, pagan lore, Catholic ritual, and arcane knowledge, *Ulysses* is unquestionably the most complex, the most confusing, and the most learned novel—if it is a novel—in all literature.

Joyce had taken seven years to complete *Ulysses;* when it was legally safe for Americans to read it he was fifty-two years old. He was going blind—before he died there were ten operations, all of which had to be performed without anaesthetics—and he was forced to write his manuscripts on thousands of large sheets of paper covered with huge letters. A tall, thin man, he was known wherever he went by his unusually courtly manners, his almost finicky elegance, and his amazing linguistic range. His exile was a series of unhappy dislocations—in a sense he never left Ireland, for his books are about no other place—and he was not permitted to rest anywhere with the feeling he might be at home. He was living in Trieste when the First World War drove him out of Austria into neutral Switzerland, where he made a home for himself in Zürich. After the Armistice he moved with his family to Paris, hoping for a prolonged spell of personal as well as universal peace. But illness, low finances, and family troubles continued to plague him. The income from his books was so small that he had to be helped by friends and anonymous well-wishers; much of the money he received went for the care of his daughter Lucia, who was in a sanatorium with a nervous affliction. Just when the prospect seemed brighter, he was again uprooted. In 1940 the Second World War sent the German armies swarming into France, and the Joyces were forced to move once more. Unable to get Lucia out of the country, they arrived in Switzerland with nothing besides their clothes, and only the help of contributions from America enabled them to return to Zürich.

Meanwhile, struggling against poverty, isolation, and rapidly failing eyesight, Joyce had finished his controversial *Finnegans Wake,* a monumental language experiment. In *Ulysses* the conflicting rushes of thought were channeled in smoothly flowing monologs; they were set off and relieved by the plain speech of the dialogs and the sharp lines of the narration. In *Finnegans Wake* there is no such division, nothing but a continuous, gathering, turbulent stream of ideas, an onrushing torrent of broken images, disjointed quotations, unrelated things, thoughts, and symbols in "the rivering waters of, hitherandthithering waters of. Night!" Night controls *Finnegans Wake* as day governs *Ulysses.* In order to liberate his narrative from the restrictions of time, Joyce composed *Finnegans Wake* as an accumulative dream. He endowed it with a dream's timelessness, its private language, and its irrational logic. Like *Ulysses,* this work is founded on myth, but it is an impersonal rather than a personal mythology which makes the central figure mankind itself. The protagonist is H. C. Earwicker: Here Comes Everybody: Haveth Childers Everywhere: Everyman. Attempting to embody the psychological, spiritual, and allegorical history of humanity in a single theme, Joyce wrote on several levels simultaneously. Here, intermingled, broken up, rearranged, and distorted are fragments from the philosophers, scientists, and historians: Sigmund Freud's *The Interpretation of Dreams,* and *The Psychopathology of Everyday Life;* James Frazer's studies of folklore and religion; Giambattista Vico's theory of cyclical patterns in the history of nations; Giordano Bruno's "coincidence of contraries," the conflict and reconciliation of opposites; Lucien Lévy-Bruhl's celebration of anthropological archetypes. To achieve a multi-dimensional effect, Joyce uses a multi-dimensional language. Snatches of popular songs are fractured by echoes of church liturgy; heroes of the past are assailed with today's headlines; the vocabulary is a welter of Shakespearean tags, perverted proverbs, slang, foreign idioms, philological monstrosities, dislocations, double talk, telescoped sounds, portmanteau words, parodies and puns . . . "the cross-correspondences from language to language," says L. A. G. Strong in *The Sacred River: An Approach to James Joyce,* "from experience to experience, the place-names, the incidents, the mistakes, the memories, everything in the life of everyman—everything, since man's thought first became recognizable, which has brought about that any one object or idea shall join hands with or recall another or be fused with it into a dream object or idea incomprehensible at first sight to the waking mind."

The pun seems to have been Joyce's favorite device. It was used lavishly in *Ulysses;* but in *Finnegans Wake* the humorist takes over and the pun runs riot, expanded into book-length. Joyce rollicks in such ambiguities as "Ibscenest nansence," "there's no plagues like Rome," "the water of the livvying goes the way of all fish," "poached eyes on ghost." A bass baritone becomes a "base barreltone"; a double reference to Freud and Lewis Carroll emerges as "We grisly old Sykos have done our unsmiling bit on 'alices, when they were yung and easily freudened"; Earwicker is a "handpicked" husband; the two washerwomen by the river Liffey burlesque the Tennysonian refrain by crying "Wring out the clothes! Wring in the dew!" It has been estimated that in *Finnegans Wake* alone there are some thousands of puns in a dozen languages—which makes Joyce the greatest punster since Shakespeare.

Although the scholar will be quick to recognize Joyce's mastery of language, his double and triple meanings illuminated by a contrapuntal prose, the average reader will be unable to make much headway in what must seem to him a crossword puzzle written in some indecipherable code. Joyce was the first to recognize this; he described *Finnegans Wake* lightly as a "prepronominal funferal . . . sentenced to be nuzzled over a full trillion times forever and a night till his noodle sink or swim by that ideal reader suffering from an ideal insomnia." Joyce was even willing to make merry with a bit of nonsense doggerel, mocking the music of the "Anna Livia Plurabelle" section:

> Buy a book in brown paper
> From Faber and Faber
> To hear Annie Liffie trip, tumble and caper.
> Sevensinns in her singthings,
> Plurabells on her prose,
> Sheashell ebb music wayriver she flows.

"It is not impossible," wrote Lewis Gannett in a review of Herbert Gorman's rewarding biography, "that Joyce himself may have regarded his *Finnegans Wake* as his greatest joke." Other critics suspected that the book might well be a gigantic hoax. They did not stop to consider that a sick man, to whom writing was an increasingly painful effort, would scarcely devote seventeen years of a serious life to playing a monstrous trick upon the public.

In his fifty-ninth year, Joyce's hardships increased. *Finnegans Wake* seemed a financial failure. Harassed by fears for the future and worried about what might happen to Lucia, he broke down. He developed a malignant duodenal ulcer, was operated upon, but after two blood transfusions, failed to recover, and died in Zürich, January 13, 1941.

"To assess Joyce's work fully," wrote L. A. G. Strong, "the critics must know as much as Joyce did." If this is a formidable demand upon the critics, it is an impossible one upon the readers. Without one of the many guides, an intelligent reader may enjoy considerable parts of *Ulysses;* but unless he is equipped with something like

Robinson and Campbell's *A Skeleton Key to Finnegans Wake,* he will give up the latter book after the first two or three pages. Yet, although Joyce's work bristles with difficulties, it is not wilfully obscure. It can be mastered, and, what is more, appreciated. Joyce is often ranked as a writer's writer, but he is much more than a virtuoso. His books added a new dimension to literature; in an era of lost security they represented a search for certainties. Technically, they explored limbos of language which no prose writer had ever envisioned; they gave formlessness a form. Speaking of Joyce's preoccupation with verbal structure, one of his critics remarked: "In the beginning there was the Word and the Word was Life; in the end there was only the word." That Joyce was both poet and pedant cannot be denied; but it is equally indisputable that he was an originator who was both outrageous and inspiring. He enlarged the Shakespearean soliloquy into an interior monolog of unexampled length, breadth, and richness. He was the first to employ the "stream of consciousness" as a running commentary, a tossing flood of free associations. He caught and preserved in a fluid amalgam— part speech, part sliding, suggestive syllables—the shapes of dissolving dreams. A genius who united the comic with the cosmic, a renegade Jesuit with the lustiness of a Rabelais and the savagery of a Swift, Joyce was an influence so great that imitators were inevitable and so unique that imitation was impossible.

Igor Stravinsky

[1 8 8 2 -   ]

"Beauty is the essence and glory of order."

WHEN *Le Sacre du Printemps* (*The Rite of Spring*) was presented to a Parisian public in 1913, the onlookers and listeners did not know whether to regard the work as a revolutionary ballet or a nihilistic attack on all musical traditions. Divided into violently rebellious objectors and even more hysterical devotees, the audience hissed its hate and screamed its approval in a mounting crescendo of whistles, groans, hoots, shouts, and catcalls. The uproar recalled the pandemonium which greeted the first performances (also in Paris) of Wagner's "revised" *Tannhäuser*. Except for the moments when the audience paused to catch its breath, the orchestra could not be heard, not even by the dancers on the stage. The American critic, Carl Van Vechten, remembered that a young man seated behind him stood up, and "the intense excitement under which he was laboring betrayed itself presently when he began to beat rhythmically on the top of my head with his fists. My own emotion was so great that I did not feel the blows for some time."

Yet emotion was the last thing that the composer, Igor Stravinsky, wanted to arouse. The purpose of music, according to Stravinsky, is "to create order between things and, above all, an order between man and time." Far from being an effort to communicate an emotion, or even a meaning, through his creations, Stravinsky's art is a coldly intellectual act; compositions consist of "the ordering of a given number of tones, according to certain intervals." Moreover, he resents the specious appeal to the senses, the romantic persuasion which Cocteau called "the blackmail of the heart." A rationalist, Stravinsky believes with Emerson (although with none of Emerson's transcendentalism) that "beauty is its own excuse for being," and sets about to achieve it in workmanlike fashion. "For me," he states simply, "composition is a daily function. Just as an organ which is not regularly used tends to deteriorate, so the creative ability of a composer becomes flaccid if he does not keep himself in daily training. Many people believe that one must wait to be inspired before one can create. I do not deny the existence of inspiration. It is a motivating force, necessary for every human activity, and by no means the exclusive property of the artist. Yet it only manifests itself when it is roused by exertion." Exertion, a constant exercise of the intellect, is the keynote of Stravinsky's continually varied music, his changeable but highly personal "thinking in sound."

Stravinsky was born in 1882, on St. Igor's day which, in the Russian calendar, occurs on June 5 and which, according to western calculations, is June 17. His father, Feodor Stravinsky, was a famous bass singer and music was a vital part of his third son's childhood in Oranienbaum, a suburb of St. Petersburg. Young Igor was "making pieces" at the piano before he was six, but he was not spectacularly precocious. The compositions which, at nineteen, he played for Rimsky-Korsakoff did not seem sufficiently "developed," and Stravinsky was twenty-four before the composer of *Scheherazade* consented to instruct him. Although Stravinsky progressed far beyond his teacher's piquant and elaborate Orientalism, he did not fail to appreciate his first stimulator. When Rimsky-Korsakoff's daughter married, Stravinsky wrote a symphonic poem entitled *Fireworks,* and when, four days after the nuptials, Rimsky-Korsakoff died, his pupil composed a *Chant Funèbre* to his master's memory.

Stravinsky was still studying, fashioning *Etudes* for the piano, when he met Sergei Diaghilev, who had already revolutionized the Russian ballet. Diaghilev was to produce more than seventy ballets; he was able to persuade such composers as Debussy, Falla, Prokofiev, Ravel, Auric, Poulenc, and Rimsky-Korsakoff to furnish the music; for the decor and costumes he won the cooperation of such painters as Picasso, Braque, Derain, Laurencin, and Rouault. Stravinsky was his enthusiastic collaborator from the start. He respected Diaghilev's aristocratic taste and patrician temper. "Born to command," Stravinsky wrote more than forty years after first meeting the impresario, "he knew how to make people obey him by sheer prestige and authority . . . He displayed characteristics of the enlightened despot, of the natural leader who knows how to drive the most unyielding elements." Following Diaghilev's guidance, Stravinsky gradually transformed himself from a provincial Russian to an international European.

It was in 1909 that Diaghilev commissioned Stravinsky to orchestrate two pieces by Chopin and to write *L'Oiseau de Feu* (*The Firebird*). It was with the latter work that Stravinsky made his tentative debut as musical innovator. *The Firebird* was founded on a Russian story, and Stravinsky was still responding to Russian influences when he planned his next work. This was to be an orchestral piece in which the piano would dispute with the orchestra in a half-playful and half-macabre manner. He had in mind a mechanical figure, "a puppet, suddenly endowed with life," Stravinsky wrote in his *Autobiography*, "exasperating the patience of the orchestra with diabolical cascades of arpeggios. The orchestra in turn retaliates with menacing trumpet blasts. The outcome is a terrific noise which reaches its climax and ends in the sorrowful and querulous collapse of the poor puppet . . . Soon afterwards Diaghilev came to visit me at Clarens, Switzerland, where I was staying . . . I played him the piece I had just composed and which, later, became the second scene of *Petrouchka*. He was so much pleased with it that he would not leave it alone and began persuading me to develop the theme of the puppet's sufferings and make it into a whole. ballet."

In *Petrouchka* Stravinsky begins to speak in his own idiom. For the most part, he depends on the accepted musical vocabulary— Russian folk-tunes, shimmering strings and woodwinds in the Wagnerian manner, a piano cadenza mocking the pyrotechnics of the conventional concerto—but an unmistakable originality breaks through. Different keys are curiously juxtaposed and even imposed upon each other to obtain an acrid polytonal effect; strange rhythms erupt and contradict each other; harmonic complexities express a spirit which is paradoxical: intellectual and, at the same time, primitive.

The next step toward freedom was more determined. Stravinsky was thirty-one when he completed the score of *Le Sacre du Printemps*. The subject was a prehistoric sacrificial feast which came to Stravinsky as a fleeting vision. "I saw in imagination a solemn pagan rite: sage elders, seated in a circle, watching a young girl dance herself to death. They were sacrificing her to propitiate the god of spring." Apart from the work as a theatrical spectacle—a stage peopled by bearlife troglodytes, frenzied women, hypnotized adolescents, and possessed virgins, with groups meeting, uniting, and splitting apart in a dance of natural forces—the *Sacre* is a masterpiece of controlled violence. It is, wrote Jean Cocteau, "a symphony impregnated with a wild pathos, with earth in the throes of birth, noises of farm and camp, little melodies that come to us out of the depths of the centuries, the panting of cattle, profound convulsions of nature . . ." Stravinsky's fresh and daring musical values brought the work to a tumultuous pitch. Everything seemed thrown into movement by centrifugal power. The rhythms were not only brusque but brutal; chords built on two opposed keys crashed starkly; pounding syncopations continually jolted the accents; the percussion, precise but asymmetrical, reached new heights of savagery. This music, wrote the critic, Emile Vuillermoz, "bends the men in rows, passes over the shoulders of the women like a hurricane over a wheat-field, throws them to the winds, burns the soles of their feet. Stravinsky's dancers are not merely electrified by these rhythmic disturbances, they are electrocuted." It is little wonder that the first performance of the *Sacre* struck its first hearers a succession of physical blows—something against which the audience felt it had to retaliate.

The effect of *Petrouchka* and the *Sacre* can scarcely be overestimated. The departures from the common grammar of music, the abrupt interpolations and the violent leaps of unrelated phrases inspired an entire generation of composers to find ways of expressing a new and sometimes exasperating music, the music of the modern world. It made demands upon those who were unacquainted with it—it was fitful, willfully overemphasized, relentlessly uncompromising—but unprejudiced listeners as well as all musical practitioners could not help but respond to the nervous energy, the liberating sweep of sound, the very power of its clashing dissonances.

Early in 1914, Stravinsky made a short voyage to Russia. It was his last visit to the country of his birth; he returned to Switzerland with ideas for more works with Russian backgrounds. Russian folk songs were the basis for three successive works: *Priboutki,* songs for a single voice and eight instruments; *Berceuses du Chat,* a vocal suite for a contralto and three clarinets; and *Renard,* a burlesque opera full of Russian folk melodies. Stravinsky was in Rome at the time of the Russian Revolution, and he immediately wrote a resounding orchestration of the *Volga Boatmen's Song,* which was played instead of the Russian hymn at the Diaghilev productions.

Meanwhile Stravinsky was engaged on another work which was definitely Russian in character. This was *Les Noces,* a wedding ceremony, using, said Stravinsky, "those ritualistic elements so abundantly provided by village customs which had been established for centuries in the celebration of Russian marriages. I took my inspiration from those customs, but reserved to myself the right to use them with absolute freedom." The freedom was obvious and, even for Stravinsky, startling. *Les Noces* is a kind of monster cantata, scored for an almost unbelievable combination: massed and solo voices, four pianos, and seventeen percussion instruments. There were no strings or woodwinds, no harmonic pleasantries or instrumental sonorities; choruses, piled on top of choruses, dwarfed the soloists—"the almost constant use of voices," wrote Arthur Berger in *Music For the Ballet,* "chanting in authentic folk accents, even shouting and at times screaming, is a guarantee against any intrusion not nakedly indigenous." *Les Noces* is perhaps one of the noisiest pieces of music ever composed, but it is a pulsing experience and a further rhythmical progress which, departing from the limitation of a regular meter, sets its own measures.

Stravinsky was still in Switzerland when he composed *L'Histoire du Soldat,* another Russian bit of folklore, the story of a shabby, deserting soldier who gets into the clutches of the devil. Adapting himself to the exigencies of wartime, Stravinsky scored the work with strict economy. There was a narrator, placed upon one side of the stage; a small orchestra consisting of only seven instruments (trumpet, trombone, clarinet, bassoon, violin, double bass, and percussion) was arranged in the other corner; and between them the play was acted out. *L'Histoire du Soldat* is a series of brief, thinly connected episodes, one of which was entitled "Ragtime." Stravinsky had his ear already tuned to the new music of America and, when he returned from the United States in 1916, he brought with him a fairly large collection of jazz. On November 11, 1918, the date of the Armistice, he composed a tribute to what, later, was to be his adopted country. He called it *Ragtime* too; although it was scored for only eleven instruments, it achieved a vigor and richness of sound which the composer has rarely surpassed.

None of Stravinsky's subsequent compositions caused anything like the excitement aroused by the early spectacular works; yet the influential circle of musical creators and creative listeners reiterated their belief in the importance of the abstract music which Stravinsky went on to write. Most of it was written in revolt against the pretentious tone poems and "program music" of the romantics, and much of it succeeded. There is a large contingent which holds that Stravinsky needs the stage, that it is, according to Minna Lederman, "the theater through which Stravinsky's music has most profoundly affected our time." But there is an equally positive group which contends that Stravinsky's nontheatrical compositions are his best, his most contemporaneously valuable, and probably his most viable.

At thirty-six, at the end of the First World War, Stravinsky exchanged his Swiss residence for a domicile in Paris where, sixteen years later, he assumed French nationality. It was here that a change occurred which, in its way, was as dramatic as Picasso's revolution. The musician's break was, however, the very opposite of the painter's. Picasso shifted from what seemed to be an established classical poise to an orgy of experimental distortions; Stravinsky turned from the wildest of harmonic and rhythmical excesses to an austere neo-classicism. He declared that music should be considered an exact science and, therefore, never should attempt to carry a message or mean anything other than itself. The work of Stravinsky's forties is increasingly "pure," aloof and abstract.

After forty, Stravinsky devoted himself more and more to classical forms. Disdaining for the time being the silken sensuality of the strings, he exploited the possibilities of the reeds and wind ensembles. He wrote an octet for wind instruments; a symphony, also for wind instruments, dedicated to Debussy; a concerto for piano and wind orchestra. Stravinsky disliked the combination of piano and violins; he believed that the timbre of the strings discolored and "consumed" the percussive sound of the piano; he favored the wind instruments because they were neglected and because "people have had enough of satiated sonorousness. They are desirous of something other than this overfeeding which distorts the true instrument and inflates it into something quite different from itself." Stravinsky's search for a purer sound and a sharper line brought him back to a reconsideration of the past. In *Pulcinella* he adapted a number of old melodies by Pergolesi, *Le Baiser de la Fée (The Fairy's Kiss)*. He also made free use of Tchaikovsky melodies, and when critics called his "borrowings" an outrage, Stravinsky replied "Rape may be justified by the birth of a child." Themes from other composers are easy to find in Stravinsky's pieces but, like T. S. Eliot's montages, they are absorbed by their context and transformed in the assimilation.

Traveling through Italy, Stravinsky found himself drawn to a past more remote than he had ever explored. As a result he asked his friend, Jean Cocteau, to translate a French text of *Oedipus Rex* into Latin. This suited Stravinsky's purpose perfectly for, since he knew little Latin, he was free to use the words as phonetic material, counterparts for the music, emphasizing the sounds and letting the sense take care of itself. This opera-oratorio was followed by another piece of lucent classicism, *Apollon Musagètes,* which had been commissioned by Elizabeth Sprague Coolidge after Stravinsky's first visit to America in 1925. In *Apollon Musagètes* Stravinsky restored the strings to their place as the dominating instruments of the orchestra and created a broadly melodic, subtly fluctuating line which recalls the dignity of Bach and Handel.

After Diaghilev's death in 1929, the composer turned almost entirely to nontheatrical compositions. Although Stravinsky continued to live in Europe, he looked to America for the future. In 1930 the Boston Symphony commissioned him to write a symphony in celebration of its fiftieth anniversary. Reluctant at first—"the symphony as we have inherited it from the nineteenth century seems foreign to us in language and thought"—he decided to combine human voices with the voices of the orchestra and, thereupon, composed the most impressive work of his neo-classical period. "According to my plan," he wrote in his *Autobiography,* "the symphony was to be a work with a substantial contrapuntal development, and for that I felt the need to enlarge the means at my disposal. I finally arrived at a choral and instrumental ensemble in which the two elements would be granted equal rank without predominance of one above the other . . . As to the words, I sought them among texts specifically created to be sung, and the first idea that came to mind was to have recourse to the Psalter." In the *Symphony of Psalms* Stravinsky once more made use of words as verbal sounds, this time from the Vulgate Latin. Entering his fifties Stravinsky was richly productive. Among the more important works are the *Duo Concertant* for violin and piano; a ballet, *Perséphone;* a concerto for two pianos; and a concerto for sixteen instruments.

At twenty-one Stravinsky had married his second cousin, Nadejda Soulima, who bore him three children: two sons, Theodore and Sviatoslav (nicknamed Soulima, after the family), and a daughter, Milene. After thirty-three years of marriage his wife died. Saddened by the loss and sickened with a decadent Europe, Stravinsky returned to the United States. At fifty-eight he married Vera Sudeikine at Bedford, Massachusetts, and made a home in his third fatherland, where he became an American citizen at sixty-three. At seventy he composed his first full-length opera, *The Rake's Progress,* inspired by the eighteenth-century engravings of William Hogarth and transmogrified into an aggressively twentieth-century fable by two poets, W. H. Auden and Chester Kallman. Once again Stravinsky dealt with a language that was not his own and, once more, he employed the syllables of the text as fragments of disparate sounds to be welded into sonant unity. Again the critics could not agree whether it was a representatively original work or a mélange prompted by other composers, chiefly Handel, Mozart, and Tchaikovsky, peppered with characteristic dissonances. Irving Kolodin, who disliked much of the music and most of the libretto, concluded, "It takes a great deal to discourage a master bent on expressing his immortal urge. Given access to some extraordinary springs of musical impulse, Stravinsky drenched the arid soil of the Auden-Kallman text with an amount of freshly felt, cunningly contrived music remarkable for any day, and, for our own, close to exceptional."

Stravinsky's Hittite profile, his high, slanting forehead, prominent nose and protuberant lower lip have been unforgettably drawn by Picasso and Cocteau. A dapper, birdlike little man—he measures exactly five feet four—he seems, even at seventy-one, to be built of springs that will never wear out. In an article in *Life,* Winthrop Sargeant, seeing a different image, remarked that "his aquiline nose and heavy horn-rimmed glasses give him the look of a deeply preoccupied grasshopper." The key-word is "preoccupied," the absorbed intellectual constantly in search of a subject.

There are those who maintain that Stravinsky's willingness to write "to order" has made him more a craftsman than a creator, that his contempt for feeling and his devotion to an anti-romantic musical system with mathematical precision have made him a victim of his own rationalism. On the other hand, his admirers insist that nowhere in music is there a greater vitality, a more astonishing wealth of detail, so phenomenal a contradiction of shocking experiment and placid accomplishment, and, finally, such an integration of furious rhythms and formal structures. Meanwhile, ignoring his critics, Stravinsky drives himself relentlessly to work. There are new chords to be tried, new combinations of instruments to be tested. He lives wholly in his music, shaping, cutting, and correcting it on a desk as severe as an architect's drafting table. Inspiration is only a prelude to labor; he knows, said the Dutch critic, Frank Onnen, "how to sublimate instinct to a regulating force." To Stravinsky a thing of beauty is not a joy until it conforms to discipline, bringing form out of chaos, fulfilling the stern definition of St. Thomas: "Beauty is the essence and glory of order."

Arthur Eddington

[1882-1944]

"Man's logic is his best instrument."

A BEGINNING and an end in numbers; in between, inspired scientific versatility. Thus the career of Arthur Stanley Eddington might be curtly summarized. Whether the end in numbers is a weakening of his earlier brilliance or whether it is the genius by which the future will mark him, has not yet been determined. In any case, the concept that is the Eddington Principle has provided a new approach to scientific thought.

Arthur Eddington was born December 28, 1882, in Kendal, fifty miles south of the Scottish border. His father, who owned and operated Kendal's Stramongate School, died two years after Eddington's birth. The widow took her son to Somerset, determined to give him the Quaker upbringing and proper education in which she and her husband had believed.

Facility and preoccupation with numbers came early. At the age of four, Eddington knew the multiplication table up to twenty-four. At six, the fascination of large numbers led him to an interest in astronomy. He was, even at that age, sufficiently well-equipped to study mathematics and, at ten, to use a three-inch telescope in exploring and learning the sky.

His mother, an advocate of superior education, entered him in the exclusive Brymelyn boarding school. Family finances were such that he could not be a boarding student, but she was justified in her belief that this institution could give him more in day classes alone than could full attendance at "common" schools. The boy's special interests were encouraged by his schoolmasters, so that he earned honors in the Cambridge Junior Local Examination at thirteen and a Somerset County Scholarship for 180 pounds two years later. These aided his precocious entrance, at fifteen, into Owens College in Manchester, where he won more scholarships.

In 1902 he entered Trinity College, Cambridge. Learning of the Tripos mathematics examinations, he competed for and won the first honor—"Senior Wrangler"—a full year earlier than any other contestant ever accomplished it.

His outstanding mathematical ability and liking for astronomy led him to become Chief Assistant at Greenwich Observatory where, within a year, he began a comprehensive study of the motions of stars. A year later, in 1907, his essay on stellar motions helped to indicate the shape and motion of the vast groups of stars that form our galaxy. He catalogued his researches in a 1910 publication: "The Systematic Motions of Stars," in which he compiled and analyzed the size, position, and motion of 6,188 stars.

At thirty-one Eddington was appointed Plumian Professor in astronomy; the following year he became a Fellow of the Royal Society and Director of the Cambridge Observatory. In this period he was engaged in a twelve-year study of latitude variations, leading to more accurate knowledge of the earth's motion, in further study of stellar movements, in the theoretical structure of stellar interiors, and in following attentively the then-unrecognized Einstein Theory.

Earlier scientists had treated conditions inside stars in a general manner, but Eddington combined thermodynamics with atomic physics to solve the specific problem of Cepheid variables, a large class of stars which exhibit periodic fluctuations of brightness from maximum to minimum and back. In some, the time to return to each maximum is a few hours; others have longer periods, up to over a year. The variations are not only changes in the star's temperature, but apparently also involve alternate blowing-up and shrinking of the whole star. It had been suspected that brighter stars pulsated more slowly; Eddington computed the conditions inside them and derived a rigorous relation between their weight and their frequency of pulsation.

A rough rule for relating weight and brightness was known from observation, but Eddington made the rule precise a few years later. Thus, from a Cepheid's period, its mass could be found; from its mass, its real brightness. If calculation showed that a faint long-period Cepheid should be extremely bright intrinsically, then it was clear that its faintness resulted from distance. The Cepheids might be compared to lighthouses, whose flashing signals tell their candle-power. From this and their apparent brightness their distances can be computed.

In many cases nebulae as big as our whole galaxy of stars exist far beyond the Milky Way; it is as if our sun were in the suburbs of one large town, with the stars around us the lights of the neighborhood. The nebulae outside of our galaxy are like the faintly seen lights of a faraway city, whose distance may be measurable only by the degree of faintness with which we perceive their lighthouses. Eddington's precise estimates of the Cepheid variables furnished a valuable and uniform yardstick for all astronomers.

The work on the inside of ordinary stars was less spectacular, but it applied the concept of radiation pressure to stellar interiors for the first time. Eddington assumed that this radiation pressure—an actual force or push of light when it is sufficiently intense—has the greatest influence on the star's structure. In "On the Radiative Equilibrium of Stars" Eddington's concepts not only derived the relation between mass and brightness of a star, but led eventually to an understanding of the different atomic reactions that provide the heat and light in different types of stars.

Eddington was Secretary to the Royal Astronomical Society from 1912 to 1917. In this post he received correspondence from Willem de Sitter, a Dutch mathematician. De Sitter knew of Eddington's interest in relativity, and sent him a copy of Einstein's General Theory and some explanatory papers. Since it was wartime, these remained for some time the only literature in England covering Einstein's latest work. Eddington was greatly impressed with its extensive use of numerical and geometric reasoning. He appreciated a work that used the fundamental properties of numbers and of space itself rather than the specialized properties of different materials. Though he protested that he should devote his time to his own work, he found himself spending more and more time explaining the General Theory of Relativity to his colleagues and, in simpler terms, to the public. He published a 91-page "Report on the Relativity Theory" in 1918, and in the next year went on an expedition to measure the bending of light beams in the sun's strong gravitational field, confirming Einstein's predictions. In 1920 he published *Space, Time, and Gravitation,* which augmented a clear exposition of Einstein's work with some of Eddington's own ramifications.

Space, Time, and Gravitation was the first of many popular works in which Eddington explained the methods and results of scientific investigation. In successive books (*Stars and Atoms, The Nature of the Physical World, The Expanding Universe, New Pathways in Science, The Philosophy of Physical Science*) he covered an ever-broadening scope and crystallized his own philosophy. He praised the continually speculative nature of science: "Our model of nature should not be like a building—a handsome structure for the populace to admire, until in the course of time someone takes away a corner-stone and the edifice comes toppling down. It should be like an engine, with movable parts." He was ready to accept the eventual repudiation of his own ideas: "The religious reader may well be content that I have not offered him a God revealed by the quantum theory, and therefore liable to be swept away in the next scientific revolution . . . If the scheme of philosophy which we now rear on the scientific advances of Einstein, Bohr, Rutherford, and others is doomed to fall in the next thirty years, it is not to be laid to their charge that we have gone astray. Like the systems of Euclid, of Ptolemy, of Newton, which have served their term, so the systems of Einstein and Heisenberg may give way to some fuller realization of the world." Thus, while Eddington refused to believe that contemporary ideas were fixed, he maintained a firm conviction that the principles of change and faith in science would persist. He returned to this view repeatedly in his philosophy to an extent that would appear to be religious rather than philosophical.

Eddington's popular exposition contained a wealth of conceptual pictures that translated the results of abstruse mathematics into comprehensible form. He compared gravitation to a dimple or "pucker" in the otherwise smooth fabric of space and time: bodies were "attracted" by gravity in the same way that a stone sliding over an icy pond may be "attracted" to a depression in the ice. His work on relativity suggested that the whole universe is curved in a fourth dimension so that it is closed on itself, rather than infinite. He compared this theory with the beliefs of a race of intelligent two-dimensional creatures living on the surface of a balloon. These flat creatures could have no knowledge of curves or of directions inside or outside of the balloon; its surface would be their whole universe. If one of them discovered that, heading away from his home in an apparently straight line, he eventually returned to it from the opposite direction, he would perforce postulate a kind of curvature alien to his way of thought, but one which three-dimensional humans could easily understand. Likewise, astrophysical calculations suggest that if a spaceship traveled (in an apparently straight line) for a great enough distance, it might eventually return from the opposite direction. This concept forces us to accept a curvature in a dimension we are incapable of visualizing. Furthermore, observations of distant nebulae seem to show them all moving away from us. Eddington pointed out that this is exactly analogous to the two-dimensional balloon inhabitant observing the recession of other inhabitants as the balloon was inflated. Eddington therefore felt that the fundamental viewpoint was not the apparent *recession* of nebulae, but the *expansion* of the whole four-dimensional curved universe.

This expansion was associated by Eddington with continually increasing entropy. (Entropy can be thought of as a randomness or disorder, or as a lack of availability of energy in the universe.) Eddington showed that the thermodynamic principle that entropy tends to increase is no more difficult to understand than the shuffling of a deck of cards. If a stacked deck is shuffled poorly once, some regularity will remain; with each successive shuffle the deck becomes less regular and more random until no order remains. From then on, further shuffling is extremely unlikely to restore the original order. Likewise, the energy available in the universe may be used up or lost in many ways, but can never be recreated.

By 1928 Eddington had summarized his work on stellar dynamics with *The Internal Constitution of the Stars.* This work, in addition to his previous high level of achievement, was instrumental in winning him knighthood at forty-eight. His time was spent in contributions to relativity theory, in lectures—both abstruse and popular—and in popular writing. His words were always chosen meticulously; he felt that a scientific exposition should have the completeness and harmony of a work of art. However, this need for careful accuracy kept him from joining in question-and-answer discussions. He was at a loss for words when first queried; he could only answer after prolonged, and often private, deliberation.

Once prepared, his lectures made no concession to gesture or oratory. He moved slowly and spoke gravely. His firm mouth and deep eyes—half hidden by a brush of brows and lashes—reinforced the immediate impression that this man's world was almost wholly one of thought. As a speaker, he was a paradox. His delivery was dull, but what he had to say was so pointed and provocative that the attentive listener could not help but be inspired. When not writing or teaching, he began to be more and more aware of spare time. For a while, he "wasted" it with bicycles and golf, with crossword puzzles and detective stories. He never considered "wasting" it with marriage. Then he began to work again. His speculative nature needed new exercise, and he found it in the type of geometrical reasoning that had so impressed him in Einstein's work.

This reasoning involved the most difficult types of calculus, but Eddington's principle was enunciated clearly in the *Relativity The-*

ory of Protons and Electrons in 1935. He stated that it should be possible to determine the numbers in physics—the "constants of nature"—by purely inductive reasoning. Universal truths should be ascertainable without measuring the speed of light or the weight of an atom. Certainly, something must be assumed at the beginning, but the assumptions were of a far simpler and more basic nature than hitherto believed possible.

For example, if one assumes initially that we live in a three-dimensional world, that time exists, and that electric charges can be positive, negative, or neutral, then one can construct a mathematical framework from these facts alone. This framework is tremendously complex (one formula can cover a dozen pages), but it can be manipulated so as to give measurable results. For example, Eddington's theory agreed with observation in concluding that the proton (which is the nucleus of the hydrogen atom) must be about 1,840 times as heavy as the electron which circles the outside of the hydrogen atom.

Eddington also gave the expected fractional deviation from the main laws of atomic physics (the "fine structure constant") as exactly $1/137$, at a time when experiments gave a different value. As later experiments have improved, their results are continually closer to Eddington's figure.

Eddington suggested a hypothetical atomic particle of weight between that of an electron and that of a proton. Subsequent research revealed the "meson" in cosmic rays and nuclear theory, with a mass exactly agreeing with his prediction.

Eddington even claimed the universe should contain 204×2^{256} particles. (Written out, this number is approximately equal to 16 followed by seventy-eight zeros.) All that astronomers can say is that their measurements of the mass of the universe is not inconsistent with that many particles. Yet even this conclusion, with its staggering and literally astronomical result, is different only in degree from calculating that honeycombs are best built with six sides, since both calculations are based on the properties of space and geometry. Scientists may well question whether such theorizing is sheer genius or merely advanced playing with numbers. Critics have pointed out many numerical coincidences among physical constants, coincidences fully as striking as Eddington's results.

After resisting cancer for two years, Eddington succumbed to the disease in 1944. He had explained and expanded many of his geometrical principles, but had left many more facets still to be investigated. Younger men will untangle the complexity of his work and apply it to new problems. The important thing is not whether Eddington's work is valid. Even if his methods or conclusions are wrong, the principle of obtaining results from logic alone is being used ever more widely. Geometrical reasoning is leading to greater knowledge not only of metal alloys but of nebulae and of living cells.

Eddington has left the knowledge, so easily lost sight of, that man's advance need not depend on instruments of science as long as man's logic is his best instrument.

Franz Kafka

[1 8 8 3 - 1 9 2 4]

"I have none of the qualities needed for a successful life."

THE INTERNATIONAL DISTRUST and universal insecurity which followed the Second World War were foreshadowed in the disturbing parables of a maladjusted but clairvoyant young Czech, Franz Kafka. Kafka was born July 3, 1883, in Prague. He was a lonely spirit from the beginning, a member of an oppressed and often suppressed race. The Czechs were a disdained minority within the Austrian Empire and, since Kafka was a Jew, he was one of a despised minority within the minority. His sense of isolation was increased by his inability to adapt himself to his environment. His mother, Julie Loewy, was an unusually sensitive woman characterized as "exotic and eccentric." The Loewys had been scholars and visionaries for generations, and, even as a young boy, Kafka felt himself in tune with them; but his father, Herman Kafka, a highly successful merchant who had established a large wholesale business in fancy goods, dominated the family. Franz's attitude to his father was painfully ambivalent. He was envious of and at the same time repelled by his father's powerful frame, his extraordinary physical strength, and his shrewd business judgment. A weak and spindly child, Franz worshiped him as a force and hated him as a tyrant.

He never recovered from this. When Kafka was thirty-six years old he wrote a book-length "Letter to My Father" which was a mélange of accusations, fantasies, and self-defensive protestations. The letter began, "Dear Father: You asked me once why I always say that I am afraid of you. At the time I did not know what to answer, partly because of the very fear which you strike in me." The letter then proceeds to pit Franz's weakness against his father's strength as well as the son's insecurity in contrast to his father's accomplishments. "Compare the two of us. Me, to put it briefly, a Loewy with certain Kafka-ish possibilities which, however, are not activated by the Kafka will to live, to succeed in business, to dominate and to conquer. You, on the other hand, are pure Kafka in strength, health, appetite, vocal power, speaking ability, self-approval, sophistication, perseverance, presence of mind, knowledge of people, and a certain magnanimity . . . From your armchair you ruled the world. Your opinion was always the right one; every other opinion was crazy, extravagant, *meshuggah,* abnormal. At that, your self-confidence was so great that you did not even need to be consistent; you could never be wrong . . . You could rant against the Czechs, then against the Germans, then against the Jews, and not merely for particular reasons but for no reason, so that finally no one was left but you. For me you had that mysterious quality which all tyrants have, whose privilege is based on personality, not on logic or intelligence." The letter is, in itself, a small autobiography. It discloses Kafka's timidity as a child and his self-distrust as a man; its details show how the father's self-assurance made the son question himself about every trifle until he was convinced of his own incapability. "You made me lose all possible self-confidence and exchange a boundless sense of guilt for it."

Kafka was already obsessed with a nerve-destroying fear and "a boundless sense of guilt" when he started school. He was the oldest child; two brothers died in infancy, and he felt himself isolated from three much younger sisters. Educated in German elementary and high schools, he went on to the Prague University, where his favorite studies were literature and languages. He joined a debating society and defended the work of the younger experimental writers. Before he was twenty-one he was made to realize that he could not remain a "Loewy dreamer" but would have to decide on a practical way of earning a living. Resisting pressure to enter his father's business, he determined to put his argumentative talent to use and turned from literature to law. He was twenty-three when he became Doctor of Law, but he never went into practice. Instead, he took a clerkship in a small insurance office and later procured a position in the workmen's compensation division of the Austrian government, a post which gave him some time for himself and the semi-autobiographical writings to which he turned as a release for his tensions.

Aware of a tendency to withdraw into solitude even in youth, he joined various groups in an effort to establish a rapport between himself and his fellows. Flattered by Dr. Rudolph Steiner, a mystical interpreter of Goethe, he flirted with anthroposophy and occultism. For a while he considered himself a Cabalist. Under the influence of such friends and fellow-writers as Max Brod and Franz

Werfel, he almost became a Zionist. But he was never at ease with more than two or three people, and he was unable to share or even understand group-thinking. After an hour of talk his nerves would give way, his lips would twitch, his extraordinary black eyes would burn, and he would be racked with headaches.

When Kafka was twenty-nine he became infatuated with a young Berlinese. His attachment was so intense that it alternately inspired and frightened him. Two years passed before he asked her to marry him and then, three months after they were engaged, Kafka broke off the engagement. He gave various excuses for the sudden, unhappy decision. He referred to his nervousness and general bad health—symptoms of tuberculosis had already manifested themselves—but his fear of marriage was much more psychical than physical. "The idea of a honeymoon fills me with dread," he wrote to Max Brod; his love was "buried to suffocation beneath fear and self-reproaches." His abrupt retreat from the responsibilities of married life recalls Kierkegaard's similar brusque renunciation; like Kierkegaard, Kafka also blamed his complicated and unresolved relationship with his father. He said it explicitly in one part of the unashamedly self-revealing "Letter to My Father": "The most important obstacle to marriage is the already ineradicable conviction that, in order to preserve and especially to guide a family, all the qualities I see in you are necessary—and I mean *all* of them, the good and the bad, just the way they are organically united in you: strength, coupled with a tendency to ridicule the other fellow, health and a certain recklessness, speaking ability combined with aloofness, self-confidence and dissatisfaction with everyone else, sophistication and tyranny, knowledge of people and a distrust of most of them." Kafka tried to repair the damage and, at thirty-four, became engaged to the girl a second time, but the idea of consummation remained as great an obstacle as ever and the affair terminated in a breakdown. By this time Kafka was seriously ill and desperately alone.

He had already issued a collection of essays and some short stories, one of which, "The Stoker," was awarded a prize and became the first chapter of his fantasy, *America*. But none of his major works was ever finished and, except to a small circle, Kafka remained unknown until years after his death, when his three uncompleted novels were posthumously published and translated. His health worsened during the First World War. He was never without funds, but the coal shortage affected him badly. He began to spit blood. When the trouble was diagnosed as "pulmonary catarrh," he was persuaded to stay with his youngest sister who was in charge of an estate at Zurau, near Saaz. For a while, he seemed to be recovering and he worked frantically on *The Trial* and *The Castle*. But the coughing spells grew more protracted, and Kafka spent most of his few remaining years in various sanatoriums.

In his fortieth year he fell in love with Dora Dymant, an eighteen-year-old Polish Jewess, and together they went to Prague. But the romance was doomed; his illness was reaching a critical stage. Realizing the gravity of his condition, his parents insisted that he should be hospitalized and he was taken to the Wiener Wald Sanatorium for consumptives. He had been driven there in an open car and, caught in a sudden storm, arrived wet to the skin, shivering, and almost inarticulate. The place was overcrowded; Kafka was put in a ward-bed next to a man dying in agony. Finally, he was moved to a private room in the Kierling Sanatorium at Klosterneuberg, near Vienna, and there he died, June 3, 1924, exactly one month before his forty-first birthday. His body, taken back to his native city, was buried in the Jewish cemetery in Prag-Strasschnitz. The entire family was marked for extermination. No male survived; his three sisters died in the concentration camp at Auschwitz.

Kafka's books form a saga of frustration, a nightmare search for lost security. This effort to reach a strong haven, a firm but friendly authority, becomes the more distracted as Kafka realizes it cannot be found. The dichotomy is the center of *The Trial,* in which the hero, a commonplace and inconspicuous bank assessor, is arrested, although he has never committed a crime or broken a law. He never sees his accusers; he does not even know the charges against him. Reluctantly he hires a lawyer, an act which makes him conscious of a sense of guilt, the more so when his attorney, a shabby frightened fellow, tells him that mysterious documents may be produced and that the trial may go on forever. "Lie low; never draw attention to yourself," the lawyer advises. "Accept the prevailing conditions." Referred to one authority after another, the harried man is never admitted to the presence of the judges. Nothing specific is said, but it is obvious to him that his guilt is everywhere assumed, and although he realizes that the trial is "only a trial if I recognize it as such," he also realizes that "there is a great organization at work" which includes the very society to which he belongs. Since the law is unable to help him, he turns frantically to religion, but he discovers that the priest also is part of the secret Court. The vague but ever-threatening atmosphere suddenly clears in a scene of violent action; two frock-coated agents of the hidden organization apprehend him and he is stabbed to death. (Three decades after it was written, *The Trial* was made into a drama by André Gide and Jean-Louis Barrault and into an opera by Gottfried von Einem.)

The theme of frustration is extended in *The Castle*. In this novel the hero has been offered work as a land surveyor by the authorities of a great and enigmatic castle, on a hill "veiled in mist and darkness, lying in an illusory emptiness." But when he appears for an interview, he is refused admission. He tries various means of entrance, but although he is never explicitly repudiated, his position is never recognized and he turns from one source to another in an effort to achieve status. First he attaches himself to the family of Amalia, whose brother acts as a messenger from the castle; but he learns that she repelled the advances of Klamm, an important castle official, and her family has been ostracised. He then seeks the help of a barmaid, Frieda (Peace), who has been glad to be Klamm's mistress. He is permitted a clandestine glimpse of the powerful official and is allowed to remain in the village, but he knows that he will never receive the desired interview and that he will never gain entrance to the sought-for haven.

The omnipresent but unknown enemy is hidden in the satirical banter of *America*. Here the feeling of anxiety is transmuted into a dream of escape, a half-farcical, half-pathetic adventure in a curious Never-Never-Land which Kafka imagined America might be.

The central characters in the novels, which Max Brod, Kafka's closest friend and literary executor, called "a trilogy of loneliness," are self-acknowledged psychographs of the author. Kafka makes this plain not only by their mutually desperate search to establish themselves but by the fact that all of them bear the first letter of his surname. The hero of *America* is "Karl Rossman"; the trapped protagonist in *The Trial* is "Joseph K"; the pitiful outsider in *The Castle* is saved from anonymity only by the initial "K." All these seekers are involved in a series of painful mishaps, misunderstandings, and heartbreaking unfulfillments. "Not since the Book of Job," wrote Brod, "has man's spirit left any record comparable in bitterness with Kafka's *The Trial* or *The Castle:* justice presented under the image of a machine planned with an inhuman refinement of cruelty." Yet there is no resentment, scarcely a reaction, not even in *The Castle* where the hero-victim vainly tries to get the attention of the authority who, like Kafka's father, is part tyrant and part God. There is, instead, a resigned acceptance, an acknowledgment of inadequacy and a recognition of guilt. The nagging question persists: Of what is Kafka guilty? On the conscious level, he does not know and he never learns. But it is apparent that he considers himself guilty of a crime which, in Kafka's unconscious, is a sin against the Kafkas—the sin of being a failure.

Interpreters of Kafka have taken two different viewpoints regarding his monstrous fables—fables whose morals are discomfiting when they are obscure, and nihilistic when they are clear. One school regards his work as a tragic expression of life which depicts the world as a hopeless wasteland, a barren homelessness where there is not even a hiding place. Kafka himself said he reflected the negative elements of his age. "I have none of the qualities needed for a successful life; all I have is my share of human weaknesses," he wrote in one of his notebooks. "I have absorbed all that is negative in my own time . . . No share of the positive values of the age has been passed on to me. I was not, like Kierkegaard, led into life by the now heavily sinking hand of Christianity, nor have I, like the Zionists, caught the last fringe of the flying prayer shawl of the Jews. I am either an end or a beginning."

Kafka's sense of isolation, the feeling of being lost in a world of bureaucracy and mechanized industrialism, has been well expressed by Harry Slochower in *Franz Kafka—Pre-Fascist Exile:* "Kafka saw the cosmos as a whole held down by close-knit stages, impenetrable and irremovable, and lost in an infinite regression. Within this labyrinth, the air hangs dull and heavy, stifling every daring effort. Everywhere, the little man is threatened by dark forces as in a nightmare. The feeling of oppression never leaves one, and is intensified by the very fact that the dreaded blow is *not* struck, but continues to hover about . . . The result of not being at home either with the innocent or the fully conscious was metaphysical fear and loneliness. Kafka's work depicts this lonesomeness of the individual in a world where hierarchial impediments are intertwined with the nature of existence. It is a basic indictment of Being, as involving the torturous compulsions and crucifixions of man's daily, bagatelle demands, a commentary on man's anxiety in the presence of an anonymous, ubiquitous enemy."

Another school considers Kafka's evocations of veiled menace, postponed crises, and pathetic exclusions as deeply religious allegories. Both *The Trial* and *The Castle* have been interpreted as allegorical presentations of the gap between human codes and heaven's justice, between man's pretensions of wisdom and his inability to reach or even comprehend God. Man's entanglement in ritual, red tape, legal procedure, and conflicting systems of thought is symptomatic of the misapprehensions which intervene between him and his understanding of God's nature. According to the English critic, Edwin Muir, Kafka's best translator, the chief clue to Kafka is Kierkegaard's dogma of the incommensurability of the divine and human law. "Man is incapable of apprehending the divine law, and it is quite possible for that law to appear immoral in his eyes . . . Yet it is man's duty to direct his life in accordance with the law whose workings he cannot understand."

Kafka's admirers outdo themselves in superlatives. They claim that his combination of a simple, lucid style and staggering subject matter gives his work an unexampled force and finality. Muir said that "there is no other writer of his age—and it was the age of Rilke and Proust—whose work carries so continuously the mark of greatness," and Waldo Frank concluded flatly: "When the history of the novel of the past one hundred years is written, Kafka will be accepted as the equal of Dostoevsky." Reservations were made concerning the method—many readers were repelled by such a story as "Metamorphosis" which depicted man as a cockroach—but no one questioned either Kafka's intensity or his integrity.

In Kafka we find humanity isolated, unloved and unprotected, divested of all supports. Examining his own repressions and frustrations, Kafka magnified them into an analogue of modern man, defeated and impotent when faced with demands he cannot understand and, therefore, cannot expect to fulfill. The world to Kafka was a place where the "causes" were baffling for being incomprehensible, and daily existence terrifying for being increasingly irrational. For him there was a dignity, even a subdued heroism, in a life which was a perilous journey toward a constantly receding goal—a travail that must be undergone with a minimum of hope but a maximum of determination.

Sinclair Lewis

[1885-1951]

"He lodged a piece of the continent in the world's imagination."

IT IS A QUAINT PARADOX that Sinclair Lewis, the first American to win the Nobel Prize for literature, received the award for books which laid bare the cheap quality of local thinking, the shabby level of native social standards, and the hypocritical camaraderie of American business life. Born February 7, 1885, in Sauk Center, Minnesota, Lewis depicted his birthplace as "Gopher Prairie," the typical small town of the Middle West, anti-cultural, thickly home-spun, and esthetically depressing. His father was a country doctor, idolized by his son and idealized by him in his novels, but his affection did not extend to a fondness for his semi-bucolic, semi-urban backgrounds. Even as a boy, Lewis was fascinated by the sophisticated East and, after attending the local schools, went to Yale, where he became editor of the literary magazine and was graduated in 1908. He was a lanky, rawboned youth; the tight fore-head of a bulging brow was thatched with sandy red hair; his freckled face was already pocked with a severe acne which grew worse with age. As an undergraduate, he wrote incessantly in a key of lush romanticism, purpling his prose and poetry—his first efforts were all in verse—with passages of swooning rhetoric. "It may be interesting to note," he declared in a backward glance at forty-five, "that one who was later to try to present ordinary pave-ments trod by real boots should have written nearly always of Guin-evere and Lancelot, of weary bitterns among sad Irish reeds, of story-book castles with troubadours vastly indulging in wine, a com-modity of which the author was singularly ignorant." Later, he re-membered ironically, "in regions where castles and the memory of troubadours really did exist—in Kent and Cornwall, Fontainebleau and London and Rome—he sat writing of Minnesota prairie vil-lages."

A dissident collegian, he espoused lost causes and socialism; when Upton Sinclair's cooperative colony at Englewood, New Jersey, needed helpers, Lewis volunteered to work as janitor and laundryman. When the unhappily named Helicon Hall burned down, Lewis was a disillusioned but still stubborn radical. He drifted down to Panama, where he failed to get a job on the great canal that was being dug, and reached California, where he lived for a year and a half on borrowed money and wrote short stories which were returned almost as fast as they were sent out. Gradually he found his way back East. He was a reporter in Iowa; a junior assistant on a Washington, D. C., magazine for the deaf; a sub-editor at twenty-five in a New York publishing house at fifteen dollars a week. "This was my authentic value on the labor market," Lewis remarked wryly in the autobiographical note he prepared for the Nobel Foundation in 1930, "and I have always uncomfortably suspected that it would never have been much higher had I not, accidentally, possessed the gift of writing books which so acutely annoyed American smugness that some thousands of my fellow-citizens felt they must read these scandalous documents, whether they liked them or not." For the next five years he earned a living as office boy with one publisher and manuscript reader with another; as assistant editor of *Adventure*; as editor of a newspaper syndicate; as advertising writer, cataloguer, and book-reviewer; as author of *Hike and the Aeroplane*, his first book, a boy's story, written at twenty-seven under the pseudonym of "Tom Graham."

At twenty-nine he married Grace Hegger, from whom he was divorced eleven years later. In 1928 he married the journalist and columnist, Dorothy Thompson, a marriage which lasted fourteen years; when it was dissolved, the custody of their son, Michael, was given to Miss Thompson. A son by his first marriage was killed in the Second World War; he had been named Wells because of Lewis' admiration for the English novelist and polemicist, H. G. Wells— "his casual humanness, more even than his indignation at cruelty or his sense of order, which is science, made H. G. so great ... a discoverer of importance in the pettiest and drabbest 'character.'"

Wells's influence, diluted but definite, is apparent in Lewis' early novels: *Our Mr. Wrenn*, written at twenty-nine, the story of a New York clerk who frees himself from Philistine respectability; *The Trail of the Hawk*, published the year following, in which the son of a midwestern carpenter is emancipated from provincial conventions, becomes a wanderer, and finally discovers the new and miraculous world of aviation; *The Job*, in which the freedom-loving protagonist is a woman struggling with a business career; *The Innocents*, a middle-age adventure and middle-class love story; *Free*

Air, which, centering about an eastern society girl and a midwestern mechanic, breezily presents the conflict between conformity and independence.

All of these were written before Lewis had reached his midthirties, and in all of them except *The Innocents* the author manipulated the plots to project a collision between the elements of convention and revolt, between the rigid upholders of dogma and the questioning nonconformer, the established high priests of the status quo and the essential iconoclast. But the struggle was only faintly indicated; it was glossed over with contrived situations and specious solutions—easy-reading compromises which the later Lewis dismissed as purely manufactured products, "dead before the ink was dry."

Turning thirty-five Lewis suddenly abandoned slick fiction in favor of uncompromising honesty and unflinching realism. Formerly he wrote to please; now he wrote to tell the truth, no matter how much displeasure he might cause or whether he would be read at all. The result was a novel, *Main Street,* and it was not merely a publishing event but an explosion which shook the nation and shocked a great part of it. The earlier novels had done only moderately well, but, thanks to Lewis' violation of village taboos, *Main Street* became a controversy which sold a million copies, was translated into all the European and several Asiatic languages, and shot its author into international prominence. It was a championing, even a naïve glorification, of the rebellious spirit and an attack on the narrow mentality which governs small towns wherever "the dollar sign has chased the crucifix off the map." It was also his first novel, Lewis observed, "to rouse the embattled peasantry . . . One of the most treasured American myths had been that all American villages were peculiarly noble and happy, and here an American attacked that myth. Hundreds of thousands read the book with the same masochistic pleasure that one has in sucking an aching tooth."

In between the early and later novels Lewis supported himself by the making and marketing of short stories. He wrote and published almost two hundred before he was persuaded to choose the best of them for a volume of *Selected Short Stories.* This was in 1935, when Lewis was fifty, and the choice was not easy, for he had no respect for his potboilers. "To the stories published since 1930 the author feels some relationship, but he reads the others with a skeptical eye. They are so optimistic, so laudatory. They are so certain that large, bulky Americans are going to do something and do it quickly and help the whole world by doing it . . . I think," he ended his deprecating introduction, "a couple of these stories are fairly good." Meanwhile Lewis' head was full of novels, penetrating and provocative. *Babbitt,* published two years after *Main Street,* made almost as much stir as its tendentious and goading predecessor. Lewis thought of it as "the story of the Tired Business Man, the Man in the Pullman smoker, our American ruler." He originally intended to call it *Pumphrey,* then *Burgess,* then *Jefferson Fitch,* and finally decided on *Babbitt* because "it sounds commonplace and yet will be remembered." This tale of the average bumptious businessman was so indigenous that when it was published in England it carried an explanatory introduction by Hugh Walpole and a glossary of some 125 American expressions. Placed in Zenith, which closely resembles Minneapolis, *Babbitt* did for—or against—the large city what *Main Street* did for the small town. Zenith is Gopher Prairie grown up in size but not in grace or goodness. Here again are the little cheats and big hypocrisies, the gimcrack values and charlatan virtues, money as a gauge of success and merchandise as a measure of the Good Life. "The standard advertised wares—toothpastes, socks, tires, cameras, instantaneous hot water-heaters—were his symbols and proofs of excellence; at first the signs, then the substitutes for joy and passion and wisdom."

A realist who was, at the same time, a satirist and baffled visionary, Lewis continued to assail the complacency of material progress. In *Arrowsmith,* sometimes considered the most restrained and most completely realized of his books, he waged a furious and losing battle to protect the doctor-scientist from commercial adultery. In *Elmer Gantry* he struck out at the unctuous, canting high-class preachers as well as the quacks, false prophets, and howling revivalists who were making religion a hideously profitable trade. *The Man Who Knew Coolidge* is a large-scale cartoon, an exposure of the stupidity of the arrogant and self-righteous know-nothings who run business, shape opinion, and determine the mores of the community. Its central figure, Lowell Schmaltz, is undoubtedly a fraud but he is also unquestionably the Voice of Authority. *Dodsworth,* which embodies a more complex figure than Lewis' other merchants, pits the protagonist against personal as well as economic pressures and points the triumph of Big Business over the engulfed individual. "He had no longer the dignity of the craftsman. He made nothing; he meant nothing; he was no longer Samuel Dodsworth, but merely part of a crowd vigorously pushing one another toward nowhere." *Work of Art* seemed to come to the grim conclusion that, in America, the artist was the man who could not only make a success but an art out of running a hotel.

Once his idiom was established, Lewis had to run the gauntlet of critical disapproval. The charge most commonly brought against him was his lack of nuances—"I hate to take my foot off the loud pedal," he once said—and his black-and-white exaggerations. His detractors objected that he was a better hand at caricature than at character, but Lewis built his books with beautiful solidity and enriched them with the most delicately revealing inflections of ordinary speech. Never a mere photographer, his portraits show subtleties of light and shading; he was a skeptical reporter who hoped to be not only a craftsman but a constructive reformer. When the Pulitzer Prize was awarded to *Arrowsmith* in 1926, Lewis refused to accept the honor and aroused a storm of comment, mostly adverse. His passion for literary freedom made him conclude that all prizes, like all titles, were dangerous. "Seekers for prizes tend to labor not for inherent excellence but for alien awards: they tend to write this, or timorously to avoid writing that, in order to tickle the prejudices of a haphazard committee." Four years later, he almost apologized for accepting the Nobel Prize, especially since Theodore Dreiser, Willa Cather, James Branch Cabell, and other writers whom he named as prizeworthy had, unlike him, refrained from scoffing at American institutions.

Lewis went on to further diagnoses and dissections. After he reached fifty, he alternated between trivial and tremendous themes, but he atoned for every weakly conceived work with a powerful one. The trivial *Ann Vickers* was followed by the horrifying *It Can't Happen Here,* a frightening forecast of a possible fascist dictatorship in America. The innocuous *Bethel Merriday,* a theatrical fairy tale of the theater, was succeeded by *Gideon Planish,* another attack on smug custom and the double standards of morality and money. The hollow domestic drama of *Cass Timberlane* is offset by the squarely faced racial problems of *Kingsblood Royal.* Throughout all of them Lewis slyly travestied or roughly hammered away at the division between a moral assumption and its practical application— the pretended scorn of money (expressed in such favorite clichés as "filthy lucre" and "root of all evil") and the measurement of a man's ability, his very respectability, in terms of his financial standing.

Strangely enough, after Lewis was finally accepted as a reformer, he grew increasingly conservative. He had often talked of writing a "labor novel," but he mistrusted the unions and could never really understand the worker. He liked young people around him, but inveighed against the radicalism of American youth; *The Prodigal Parents*, the poorest of his twenty-two novels, is an attack on the younger generation in which the former Babbitt-scorner becomes the defender of Babbittry. He became uncertain of his position, unsure of his "place." After his second divorce, Lewis left the Vermont country home he had shared with Dorothy Thompson and tried to re-establish himself in a New York penthouse, in a vast mansion in Duluth, Minnesota, on a sumptuous estate near Williamstown, Massachusetts. But fits of contentious garrulousness and sudden truculence, usually the aftermath of drinking, had alienated many of his friends, and he was lonely in the midst of his rich possessions. Worse, he was ill. Forced to give up alcohol, he consumed great quantities of candy until sweets, too, were forbidden. Yet he never stopped reading, researching, and writing. At sixty-four he published his first historical novel, *The God-Seeker*, which was a dogged but unrewarding effort. Sick, but still determined to work on a new book (the posthumous *World So Wide*) he went to Italy, where he rallied, collapsed after an attack of pneumonia and died, far from everything that was familiar, in Rome, January 10, 1951.

A mingled stream of idealism and irony runs through all of Lewis' work: a hope for the countless Main Streets and a hatred for all the frauds that fatten on the provinces. The work is also marked by inconsistencies, chiefly because, although Lewis was sure enough about his direction, he was never positive about the goal. It is not only that the older Lewis rebukes and contradicts the young Lewis, but that the mature author is sometimes suspicious of his own objectives. The reader is often left to grope among uncertainties, for Lewis seems to be a Utopian who makes fun of Utopias, an anti-sentimentalist who wallows in orgies of folksy sentiment, a mocker of Rotary Clubs who, confronted with radicalism in action, changes from a rebel to a Rotarian. Lewis is a curious anomaly: a true believer who has lost his faith, a man of good will who hopes somehow to unite a profitable socialism and a profitless capitalism. It is true that he brandishes the torch of Art and Poetry in the faces of the Philistines, but his artists are futile dreamers and his poets are dedicated to the commercial cliché. This ambivalence is the key to the confusion of Lewis' program and his principles, the announcement of a fighting purpose and the failure to carry it out. The central figure of the Lewis saga is Babbitt, a symbol who bears various names; he is the standardized citizen, the prefabricated bourgeois, the assembled, watertight, weatherproofed middle class man. But it is doubtful that Lewis loathes him more than he loves him, for Babbitt and his creator are self-torturing but self-preserving Siamese twins, one divided but inseparable flesh.

First and last, however, Lewis is one of the century's sharpest delineators of manners and perhaps the most accurate recorder of his country's speech. He has, wrote the English novelist, E. M. Forster, "lodged a piece of a continent in the world's imagination." Uniquely combining shrewd wit and broad humor, he endowed absurd and even repulsive figures with a compelling plausibility. Even when he was most sardonic—in the full-length images of the viciously unprincipled revivalist, Elmer Gantry; the platitude-worshiping poet, T. Cholmondeley ("Chum") Frink; the endlessly discursive bore, Lowell Schmaltz; the fascist terror, Buzz Windrip—he drew his characters in clean and searing lines. His novels are essentially a gallery of portraits as native and representative of his country as Pickwick, Don Quixote, Siegfried, Raskolnikov, and Cyrano are of theirs. "Until George F. Babbitt was born in Sinclair Lewis' pages," wrote Lewis Gannett in an obituary note, "not another character in American fiction, with the possible exception of Tom Sawyer, had made himself a recognized citizen of the international world." Whether drawn with brooding fondness or blistering contempt or with a troubled mingling of both emotions, the portraits are as precise, as discerning, and as brilliantly accomplished as the swift savageries of Rowlandson and the crowded commentaries of Hogarth. They are, to confine the comparison to Lewis' own genre, the kind of books Dickens might have written and the kind of people he might have delineated had Dickens acquired an impressionistic point of view, a twentieth-century staccato style, and a ringing American accent.

Ring Lardner

[1 8 8 5 - 1 9 3 3]

"He had the habit of catching human beings
when they think no one is looking at them."

RING LARDNER is a textbook case of a writer who began as a sportive humorist and ended as an unsocial satirist. His early stories achieved new dimensions in the idiom of popular entertainment; his later work was considered cruel, tortured, despairing, and self-despising. The critic-journalist William Bolitho rated him as "the greatest and sincerest pessimist America has produced."

He was born March 6, 1885, in Niles, Michigan, and was christened Ringgold Wilmer Lardner. When he grew up he changed his name to Ring W. Lardner, and then discarded the middle initial fearing, he said, that people might say it stood for Worm. After he had graduated from high school he thought of going to the University of Michigan so that he might "take football and dentistry." But Michigan was too much like home and, since Illinois seemed to hold the promise of something fresh and foreign, he went to Chicago's Armour Institute. There, at eighteen, he studied mechanical engineering, but he did not stay long. At the end of the first semester he "passed in rhetoric and out of Armour." He turned to railroading and worked for a while as local freight agent, but he was discharged when he sent a large shipment of cream cheese to the wrong place. He was boy-of-all-work in a gas office where he earned six dollars a week. When Ring was not quite twenty, his brother was offered a place on the South Bend, Indiana *Times,* and when he could not accept the position, Ring snatched it. For two years he was a catch-as-catch-can reporter, covering the law courts, police stations, ball games, reviewing the current films, and writing blurbs for any entertainment that might come to town.

At twenty-two, he was a professional journalist with a growing reputation. His sports stories began to be quoted and his column, "In the Wake of the News," which began in the *Chicago Tribune* in 1913, was cited as a model. He was still in his twenties when his wry but rollicking stories about Jack Keefe, a fictional Chicago pitcher, were featured in *The Saturday Evening Post* and attained an even greater popularity when they were published in a volume entitled *You Know Me, Al*. While readers laughed uproariously at the misadventures of Lardner's doltish hero, critics were becoming aware of a new language with which Lardner was enlivening native fiction. Henry L. Mencken was among the first to praise the skill and subtlety with which the humorist anatomized his characters: "I doubt that anyone who is not familiar with professional ball players intimately and at first-hand will ever comprehend the full merit of the amazing sketches in *You Know Me, Al;* I doubt that anyone who has not given close and deliberate attention to the American vulgate will ever realize how magnificently Lardner handles it."

In 1911, while Lardner was still a reporter in his mid-twenties, he married Ellis Abbott. He was a handsome, large-boned, heavyset six-footer weighing two hundred pounds. He delighted in fatherhood, proud to be the progenitor of four gifted sons. John, the oldest, followed his father's early proclivities and became a noted sports-writer, columnist, and author of many non-fiction pieces. James joined the Abraham Lincoln Brigade during the Spanish Civil War, fought on the Loyalist side, and was lost in the battle of the Ebro. Ring, Jr., usually called Bill, also became a writer. David, the youngest, died heroically when, a war correspondent in the Second World War, he was killed in action at Aachen.

Lardner astonished his colleagues as well as the critics. The journalist turned sports-writing—until that time a routine job of reporting—into something which was broadly comic and, at the same time, unexpectedly caustic. The style, attempted by countless imitators, was found to be inimitable. The speech perfected a composite of ordinary American and extraordinary English—it was inevitable that it was sometimes referred to as "Ringlish." *Gullible's Travels* and *Treat 'Em Rough* continued in the vein of knockabout humor which characterized his first volume.

By the time he had reached his late thirties, Lardner the humorist had been supplanted by Lardner the satirist. *How to Write Short Stories* and *The Love Nest* are full of ludicrous incidents and bizarre situations, but the people in them are no longer confined to a limited area and a single level of entertainment. The locale of "Alibi Ike" is still the baseball diamond and the plot is still absurd, but the alternately pretentious and apologetic outfielder, Frank Farrell, is not a clown but a living person as sharply drawn as a character in Dickens. On one level "Haircut" is a garrulous barber's irritating monolog; on another level it is an unforgettably savage etching of a small-town practical joker. "A Day with Conrad Green" rips the glamour from the world of the theater and, tracing a few hours in the day of a blatantly successful manager, not only reveals the shoddiness of "show business" but paints a portrait of loathsome dishonor. "The Love Nest" is another triumph of indirect narration; seen through the eyes of a reporter sent to interview a pompous film magnate, the reader is teased, shocked, and finally shaken by a picture of domestic horror and degradation. "Zone of Quiet" starts off as a comic cartoon of a trained nurse and grows into the apparition of a terrifying person. "Mr. and Mrs. Fixit," a small saga of follies, is an equally incongruous mixture of buffoonery and dreadfulness. "The Maysville Minstrel" begins as a coolly realistic report, drops into burlesque, and ends not only in bitterness but something close to heartbreak. "Some Like Them Cold," which was amplified into a popular play, *June Moon*, is a parade of illiteracies which turns the opening light gayety into a grotesque aftermath. "Champion" is unadulterated cruelty, the condensed history of a vicious pugilist who beats and badgers his way to fame, and whose false legend of goodness and gallantry is preserved by the newspapers for an idol-worshiping public.

When ten of the stories were collected in 1924 Lardner acted as though he, hitherto a comic sports writer, were guilty of effrontery and would be upbraided for taking his subjects seriously. Thereupon he belittled himself. He began the volume with a burlesque preface —the ten short stories being appended as "samples" of How to Write. The so-called instructions were purportedly written by a bumptious illiterate, and each story was introduced with a nonsensically misleading and wholly derisive sentence or two. The seemingly hilarious but actually heartless tale, "A Frame-Up," was characterized as: "A stirring romance of the Hundred Years' War, detailing the adventures in France and Castile of a pair of well-bred weasels. The story is an example of what can be done with a stub pen." The savagery of "Champion" became all the more shocking since it followed the author's falsely mocking summary: "An example of the mystery story. The mystery is how it got published."

Although most of the creatures in these stories are boors, odious fools, middle-aged adolescents, fakes hiding behind false fronts, cheapjacks, and worse, Lardner rarely makes fun of them. With the exception of his showing-up of Midge Kelly in "Champion," he lets them exhibit their own inanities and pretensions. Once in a while the disgust breaks through. More often there is a wry tenderness for the thoughtless and the slow-witted, like the old couple in "The Golden Honeymoon," whose lives are, from the observer's point of view, meaningless and whose days are empty of everything that matters.

When the tales were brought together in *How to Write Short Stories* and *Round Up* most of the critics went to the extreme of analysis. They examined Lardner as a disillusioned misanthrope, a hater of the products of his age. "An authentic commentator on American capitalism in its frantic flowering," wrote Maxwell Geismar in *Writers in Crisis*, "Lardner became the mordant chronicler of a moribund social order." What the critics minimized and often forgot was the irreducible comic element, the sheer fun which made even the most clinical exposures laugh-provoking. Lardner's sense of playfulness manifests itself not only in his deadpan descriptions and his astonishingly accurate dialogs, but his incidental puns: "the connubial yokel," "the highpolloi," "marred (instead of married) life," nerve-twitched women who shake like "an aspirin leaf." In his nonsense plays the irrepressible comedian achieves heights of the ridiculous attained only by Edward Lear and Lewis Carroll. He anticipates the wild incongruities of surrealism in *Cora, or Fun at a Spa, Clemo Uti, the Water Lilies, I Gaspiri, the Upholsterers,* and *Taxidea Americana,* with such stage directions as: "A public street in a bathroom." "Three outsiders named Klein go across the stage three times." "The curtain is lowered for seven days to denote the lapse of a week." "Cora enters. She looks as if she had once gone on an excursion to the Delaware Water Gap."

Lardner was disturbed by the embrace of the intellectuals. Afraid that he could not live up to the claims they had made for him, he ridiculed himself in a blandly spurious autobiography, *The Story of a Wonderman,* and invented a fatuous, cliché-ridden secretary-biographer to add an obituary and make fun of his work. ("The Master is gone, and who will succeed him? Perhaps some writer still unborn. Perhaps one who will never be born. That is what I hope.") Misled by his self-deprecations, his critics continued to detect pathological symptoms in the least of his skits. Geismar, for example, found the inimitable sharpness and misapprehension of childhood and "the stammering baseless bliss—the apotheosis of Lardnerian love" in "The Young Immigrunts," which Lardner wrote as a casual parody of "The Young Visiters," the diary of a precocious child. Lardner covered his fear with a self-mockery which sometimes turned into masochism. But it was not, as has sometimes been implied, a self-destroying self-concern. If he was often bitter about the society in which he moved, he was careless about himself. He covered his sensitivity with a cloak of sarcasm, a protective contempt for the loud hucksters, the smug suburbanites as well as the braggarts of the Big Town, the self-servers, worshipers of the genie of the jackpot. Too conceited to understand anything beyond their limited concerns and too arrogant to show sympathy for their own kind, the people Lardner pilloried are unaware of being scorned. It is they who are the scorners, mockers of emotion, free of love and contemptuous of loyalty.

The first sign that Lardner was not tough and hardy, as his great frame seemed to suggest, came in 1926. A persistent cough and general weariness made him submit to an examination. The illness was diagnosed as tuberculosis and, although it was a light case, he became depressed. The depression lasted longer than the condition warranted. He could not understand it. He was even affected by a strange sense of guilt, a feeling that something had happened which, somehow, he should have prevented. By this time he was a famous writer, but he was skeptical about fame. A darkness had begun to grow in him and, as the naturally modest man became doubtful about people, he became more and more reticent about himself. "There are times in reading Lardner," wrote Gilbert Seldes in an introduction to *The Portable Ring Lardner,* "when you feel his total sympathy with Swift's terrible verdict on humanity—that we are the most odious little race of vermin that ever inhabited the planet; you feel his sympathy with the half-hidden sardonic side of Mark Twain's temperament. He takes less pleasure in the accidents of human behavior than Twain did and is not so thoughtful as Swift; but, like both of these, Lardner has the habit of catching human beings when they think no one is looking at them . . . He wrote a language which corresponded to the way his people thought and he used the words he heard them speak, spelling them as the speakers imagined they should be spelled . . . If he disliked humanity as a whole and had little hope for it, he was, like many misanthropes, possessed of an exceptional power to make himself loved."

The sense of fascinated liking, even of love, which readers brought to the reading of Lardner, did not stop when he had to give up writing fiction and, confined to his home—which he alternately called "No Visitors" and "Out to Lunch, New York"—limited himself to occasional columns. His popularity never waned, but he no longer enjoyed it. In his mid-forties he had a breakdown and was hospitalized for almost two years. There was a radio in his room, and, partly to amuse himself and partly to exercise his talent for satire, he turned out some of the best reviews of broadcasting ever published. But he could not overcome an ever-increasing depression and feeling of defeat. He was too tired to care. His heart gave out and he died at his home in East Hampton, Long Island, September 25, 1933.

D. H. Lawrence

[1885-1930]

"He was sure that instinct was superior to intelligence."

MODERN LITERATURE presents no more remarkable picture of a maladjusted, self-tortured genius in a world of stretched nerves and almost unbearable tensions than the life and works of David Herbert Lawrence. "Ours is essentially a tragic age," is the way Lawrence introduced *Lady Chatterley's Lover,* "so we refuse to take it tragically. The cataclysm has happened, we are among the ruins, we start to build up new little habitats, to have new little hopes. It is rather hard work: there is no smooth road into the future: but we go round, or scramble over the obstacles. We've got to live, no matter how many skies have fallen."

Lawrence was born September 11, 1885, in the colliery town of Eastwood, a grimy hamlet on the border between Derbyshire and Nottinghamshire. There were five children (three sons and two daughters), of whom David Herbert was the next-to-youngest, in the drab brick house tilted on the mean little street sliding downhill. His father, an illiterate day-laborer, worked all his life in the coal mines and could scarcely write his name. His mother, a former schoolteacher, was genteel, intolerant, and dominating. Lawrence remembered his father, distorted by images inherited from his mother, as a drunken brute, but his mother was unquestionably held by her husband's unquenchable high spirits; she had, in fact, been won by "his graceful dancing, his musical voice, his gallant manner, and his overflowing humor." Lawrence was always frail; he never fully recovered from an early attack of pneumonia. As a boy he developed a nervous, hacking cough that never left him. He was a shy, unimpressive student who, nevertheless, won a scholarship to the Nottingham High School and, at sixteen, fell in love with a neighbor, Jessie Chambers. It was a romantically literary love, later fictionalized and heightened in *Sons and Lovers.* Devoted to his mother, the boy had grown up to think of love as a spiritual thing not to be debased by physical demands. It was as a reader and embryonic writer that he shared his discoveries with Jessie.

By the time he was seventeen, Lawrence was a pupil-teacher in the town of his birth. For four years he served his apprenticeship in a "savage teaching of collier lads." Meanwhile he continued to study, chiefly reading, botany, and French. The last subject was taught by Professor Ernest Weekley, with whom Lawrence was to become singularly involved a few years later. At twenty-three he began teaching an upper class in the Davidson Road School at Croydon, South London. Here Lawrence did not show as much aptitude for the teaching of literature as for his delicate drawings of flowers. To disguise his boyishness, he grew a small sandy mustache; but his delicacy was obvious in the smooth, hairless cheeks, the weak chin, and the thin sensitive hands, as well as the soft voice which sometimes rose into unexpected shrillness.

Lawrence was still in his teens when he determined to sublimate his inner conflicts by writing about them. He began with poems, flower pieces—"any young lady might have written them and been pleased with them, as I was pleased with them. It was after that, when I was twenty, that my real demon would now and then get hold of me and shake real poems out of me, making me uneasy." His first novel, however, started at twenty, suggests the cycle of fulfillment-frustration which became Lawrence's chief preoccupation. Completed after four years of spasmodic efforts, *The White Peacock* is Lawrence's earliest piece of self-exposure. Set against his native background, full of thick poeticisms and pathetic fallacies, it smoulders with anguish, a significant prelude to all the subsequent works of muffled passion and final defeat.

He was twenty-five, struggling between teaching and writing, when his mother died. Instead of being freed by her death, his deeply cored love for his mother was more centered than ever. "The world began to dissolve around me . . . passing away substanceless —till I almost dissolved away myself . . . Everything collapsed, save the mystery of death and the haunting of death in life." During the next two years the need of being loved drew him to various girls—he became engaged to one of them—but his attachment to his mother was so strong, stronger even than when she was alive, that he could not attach himself to any other woman. His physical ills were aggravated by psychosomatic symptoms; he suspected that his cough was an indication of consumption. He gave up teaching with a mixture of fear and relief, a state of mind which persisted for a long time, as implied in his poems and stated explicitly in a letter: "I still dream I must teach—and that's the worst dream I ever have. How I loathed and raged with hate against it, and never knew!"

Lawrence was twenty-seven when he met Frieda von Richthofen Weekley. She was thirty-one, daughter of a German baron, the wife of Lawrence's one-time professor, and the mother of three young children. Lawrence immediately transferred his seemingly fixed filial devotion to the woman who had the authority of mature motherhood fused with the physical allure of an ardent girl. His liberation was immediate; he and Frieda left England and went to Germany, Austria, and Italy, where they lived during more than a year of trouble before she obtained a divorce and they were able to marry. The experience is compacted in his third volume of poetry (the first two were appropriately entitled *Love Poems* and *Amores*), the candidly autobiographical *Look! We Have Come Through!* "Of this volume," Lawrence wrote, "the first few poems belong to England and the end of the death-experience." But the body of the book starts the new cycle which was Lawrence's new life. "After much struggle and loss in love" Lawrence made it plain in his preface that the protagonist throws in his lot with a woman who is already married. "Together they go into another country, she perforce leaving her children behind. The conflict of love and hate goes on between the man and the woman, and between these two and the world around them, till it reaches some sort of conclusion, and they transcend into some condition of blessedness." The last phrases tremble on a note of pathos, for the reader already knows that the search for peace through love will go on desperately, and that the title, *Look! We Have Come Through!*, is the expression of a forlorn wish rather than the triumphant fact it pretends to be.

At twenty-eight, while living above the Italian Lake Garda, Lawrence finished his third novel and his most revealing piece of painful autobiography, *Sons and Lovers*. It is the story of the young Lawrence's crippling relations with his mother and his frustrated romance with Jessie Chambers, "Miriam" in the book. He summarized it in a letter to his publisher: "A woman of character and refinement goes into the lower class, and has no satisfaction in her own life. She has had a passion for her husband, so the children are born of passion . . . But as her sons grow up, she selects them as lovers—they are *urged* into life by their reciprocal love of their mother. When they come to manhood, they can't love because their mother is the strongest power in their lives, and holds them . . . The younger son gets a woman who fights for his soul—fights his mother.

The battle goes on between the mother and the girl, with the son as object. The mother gradually proves the stronger because of the tie of blood. The son decides to leave his soul in his mother's hands and, like his elder brother, go for passion. But almost unconsciously, the mother realizes what is the matter and begins to die. The son casts off his mistress, attends to his mother dying. He is left in the end naked of everything, with the drift towards death." Many of the reviewers misread the purport of the book—one of them spoke of "the beautiful bond uniting the two chief characters" and *The New York Times* captioned its review "Restless Son and Heroic Mother" —but most of the critics realized that a new force, linking Sophocles and Freud, had catalyzed the violent conflicts of its nature into an extraordinary work of art.

At twenty-nine Lawrence published his first collection of short stories, *The Prussian Officer*. *The Rainbow,* Lawrence's fourth novel, a driving work agitated by a wildly disturbing beauty and a physical sense of hurt, was issued in 1915. By this time Lawrence had formulated his credo about an elemental, super-rational life. He was sure that instinct was superior to intelligence, and that the subconscious generated the only light to save the sick spirit of man from "heavy, sealing darkness," immovable and impenetrable. "My great religion is a belief in the blood, the flesh, as being wiser than the intellect. We can go wrong in our minds. But what our blood feels and believes and says, is always true." Lawrence's instincts may have been superior to his intelligence, but his beliefs led him from personal troubles to public disasters. *The Rainbow* was merely the first of his works to run afoul of the law. This novel of tormented love and unsatisfying passion was attacked by England's three leading critics and, because of a frankly sexual episode and a hint of Lesbianism, was suppressed. The publisher cravenly pleaded that he had not read the manuscript, that he was horrified to discover its indecencies, and the first edition was withdrawn. Readers, however, were not slow to discover the massive imagery and hypnotic power of the work, its subtly changing repetitions and symbol-crowded rhapsodies building cadence upon cadence. Even its detractors conceded that, although *The Rainbow* was distressingly febrile, it was flushed with a moving, animal vitality.

The First World War was a source of fresh trouble for Lawrence. Since everything he wrote was concerned with the possibility of a larger life for man, Lawrence was distressed by "organized mass murders," disgusted with humanity's drive toward death. He and

Frieda retreated to what seemed a haven, the little Cornwall town of Zennor on the south coast of England. There he dreamed of founding a community of kindred souls, a post-war Utopia on some ideal island, a realization of Coleridge and Southey's never-built, ivory-towered Pantisocracy. It was at this time that Lawrence covered his chin with a beard, a scraggly reddish fringe that accentuated his flimsy build and faunlike features. One of his friends jestingly spoke of it as Lawrence's "red badge of courage," symbolizing an effort to look and act like other men. But there were no friends in Cornwall. Although he tried to be sociable, the townspeople mistrusted the queer artist who did the cooking and scrubbed the floor of his little shack; they grew increasingly suspicious of the outsider with his unhappy air and unconventional ways. It was wartime. Germany was the enemy, and Lawrence had a German wife, whose brother, Manfred von Richthofen, was a famous German flyer. It was more than likely, thought the people of Cornwall, that the Lawrences might be spies. The likelihood grew into a conviction. Their lights were interpreted as signals, the cottage was searched, and the Lawrences were driven out. They went back to London, Frieda sadly, Lawrence furiously.

During the next two years they were driven from one domicile to another—London, Berkshire, Derbyshire, the Midland hills—until the war was over, and in the autumn of 1919, the Lawrences left England for the Continent. In spite of Lawrence's productivity, they were poorer than ever. Publishers looked on Lawrence as a bad risk. He continued to write with nothing more encouraging than his own frenzied energy and almost fanatic will. At thirty-five he published *Women in Love,* which he called "something of a sequel to *The Rainbow."* In it the Lawrencean hero announces the author's ideal of a super-sexual love, a state of pure being, "the individual soul taking precedence over love and desire for union, stronger than any pangs of emotion," an acceptance of "the obligation of permanent connection with others, but which never forfeits its proud individual singleness, even while it loves and yields."

The quest for "singleness" drove Lawrence through six years of wandering. Searching for a security that would be a reaffirmation and final establishment of self, he left England in 1919 and returned to it only for brief visits. He literally ran away. Sometimes he realized that he was trying to run away from himself. "I wish," he wrote to a friend "I were going to Thibet—or Kamschatka—or Tahiti—to the ultima, ultima, ultima Thule. I feel sometimes I should go mad, because there is nowhere to go, no 'new world.' " Wherever he was, Lawrence wanted to be somewhere else, and soon after he arrived at the new goal he would write, "This place is no good." Then he would be off again in quest of the dark magic and the fading illusion. Instead of ultima Thule, he went to Baden-Baden, the Abruzzi hills, Capri, Taormina, Sardinia, Austria, then halfway around the world to Ceylon, Australia, Tahiti, and America. In 1920 at the invitation of Mabel Dodge Luhan, he came to Taos, New Mexico, where, with trips to Old Mexico, he remained for three turbulent years. In 1924 he tried Europe again but, within a few months, he came back to the New World. In February, 1925, in Mexico City, he suffered a violent attack of what he was forced to recognize as tuberculosis. Although he was not yet forty, he knew he had not much longer to live.

It was in the southwest of the United States and in Mexico that Lawrence conceived of himself as prophet and leader. Once again he dreamed of a phalanstery of creative thinkers, artists, workers. He had a vision of the Indian as the hope of survival in "a world of corruption and cold dissolution." Here was Rousseau's noble savage whose "blood-stream consciousness" placidly but firmly resisted the degenerating mechanical toys and tricks of twentieth-century civilization. Some of Lawrence's consequent celebrations of primitive power are raptly mystical; some, like his yearning for "the lost magic" and "the dark Gods," are silly to the point of being nonsensical. It was at this period, however, that Lawrence, in spite of impending doom, wrote some of his most revealing works. *The Plumed Serpent* and *Mornings in Mexico* are full of Lawrence's ecstatic response to nature, his sudden if short-lived joy in each new place, and his rare gift of intimacy with every object as well as every person he encountered. The books also reveal Lawrence's more vulnerable side: his exaggerated sun-worship, his grotesque "blood-knowledge," and his messianic delusions. Worse, his absurd assumptions of leadership were linked with an anti-democratic hunger for power and a yearning for an aristocracy of the elite, idiosyncrasies which proved him to be as naïve as "proto-fascist."

Strangely enough, as Lawrence's philosophy grew irritatingly inconsistent, the quality of his writing grew clearer and more penetrating. The work of his last eight years vibrates with superabundance. An inexhaustible improviser, Lawrence took any thing he observed—an Indian or an insect, a sunset or a cow—and it became an active symbol, filled with his vital responsiveness. "He had," wrote the English novelist, David Garnett, "the power of imparting the deeper, unexpressed feelings about ordinary things . . . a genius for seizing the fleeting, most essential, momentary emotions which are charged with intense significance, but which fade as they are felt." This sensorial penetration was a source of continual annoyance to Lawrence's squeamish critics but a revelation to all creative writers. "Lawrence attempted very difficult things with writing," declared Anaïs Nin in *D. H. Lawrence: An Unprofessional Study.* "He would give it the nuances of paint: thus his efforts to convey shades of color with words that had never been used for color. He would give it the rhythm of movement, of dancing: thus his wayward, formless, floating, word-shattering descriptions. He would give it musicality, cadence: thus words sometimes used less for their sense than for their sound. It was a daring thing to do. Sometimes he failed. But it was certainly the crevice in the wall, and it opened a new world to us."

All this was achieved because, in a tottering world, Lawrence had one mainstay: the stabilizing support of Frieda. Nothing, not even Frieda, could give him peace—their quarrels, though soon healed, were epical; they included physical violence and bitter recriminations. There were times when Frieda expressed a longing for her children and Lawrence raged with resentment, the more so since she had no children by him. But Frieda, understanding his ungovernable fury, made him her child and encouraged the artist while she comforted the man. They were exact opposites in social class, training, and temperament; but, by a freak of circumstance or a genius for adaptation, the daughter of the aristocrat had become the assured earth-mother, solid and simple. He struggled against his dependence on her and, in exasperation, inveighed against all women. Yet it was to women, not men, that he turned for literary stimulation and even for collaboration. Several episodes in *Sons and Lovers* were originally written by Jessie Chambers, Lawrence's youthful sweetheart and the defeated heroine of the book; parts of *The Trespasser,* Lawrence's second novel, were adapted from a manuscript by Helen Corke, a fellow-teacher to whom Lawrence was drawn in his mid-twenties; his Australian narrative, *The Boy in the Bush,* is a rewriting of M. L. Skinner's *The House of Ellis;* he urged Catherine Carswell (according to her appreciation in *The Savage Pilgrimage*) to furnish him with the background for a projected Scottish novel; he offered to work with Mabel Dodge Luhan on an extended story of her life. Other women claimed and tried to possess him, but Frieda was his answering need.

In September, 1925, two weeks after his fortieth birthday, Lawrence left America, hoping to return. It was a forlorn hope. Still searching for sun and health Lawrence again went from place to place—a town near Genoa, a suburb of Florence, a spot in Switzerland, Austria, Germany, the Balearic Islands and, finally, France. This was Lawrence's last phase, but in it he wrote some of his most memorable prose and his noblest as well as his angriest verse. His preoccupation with physical desire and psychological inhibitions culminated in *Lady Chatterley's Lover,* an extension of the duel between the desperate demand of sex and the serenity of love. Nothing in contemporary literature roused a greater storm of protest. But, although there are passages of unrestrained animality, there is a deep undertone of tender pity—in fact, Lawrence first intended to call the book *Tenderness.* It was attacked, censored, prohibited (and, consequently, pirated by unscrupulous printers) as an obscene work; but Lawrence maintained that it was written in an effort to strike a balance between the coarse ugliness, the mental-spiritual sterility of the modern world, and the quickening phallic consciousness, "the source of all real beauty and all real gentleness . . . not the cerebral sex-consciousness, but something far deeper, the root of poetry, lived or sung." In *Lady Chatterley's Lover* the sexual act is disclosed not only as a completion but as a catharsis, an expunging of fear and shame, less of a gratification than a purification. This was scarcely the view held by the critical arbiters of the time. The book was damned as a piece of willful pornography and, since no reputable publisher would circulate it, Lawrence had to print it privately. "It is an appalling fact," wrote Rebecca West, "that man should speak of the functions on which depend the continued existence of his species and the tender life of the heart in words that cause shame and ugly laughter when they are spoken . . . Lawrence laid sex and those base words for it on the salver of his art and held them up before creation, and prayed that both might be transmuted to the highest that man could use."

The influence of *Lady Chatterley's Lover* was enormous. In *Pilgrim of the Apocalypse,* Horace Gregory said: "No novelist or poet living today finds it necessary to continue the half-century fight for sexual liberation in English writing. After *Lady Chatterley's Lover* all subsequent uses of the sex symbol are anticlimactic. It has been a long fight from the publication of Whitman's 'Song of Myself' through the Oscar Wilde trial, through twenty years of Freud to this last writing of a novel printed in Italy and Paris. The fight was won in 1928."

Lawrence had two more years left. In that time he wrote another novel, a metaphysical-religious inquiry (*Apocalypse*) which ends with a magnificat to the sun, several pamphlets (most of them prompted by the attacks on *Lady Chatterley's Lover*), more than a hundred poems, and half a dozen mordant short stories, including "The Rocking Horse Winner," the tale of a supernatural child in a money-mad family, a fable that turns into one of the world's great horror stories. There were frightening premonitions. His chest pained him; the tubercular attacks increased; there were bad hemorrhages. Although writing was a relief, it was also a strain. News from England made things harder to bear. A manuscript of his poems, *Pansies*, was seized at the order of the Home Secretary ("there was a rush of detectives to pick out the most lurid blossoms") and a show of his paintings was closed by the police. He kept on writing, trying to fulfill "his living wholeness and his living unison." Six months later the man who wanted to exult because "for man, as for flower and beast and bird, the supreme triumph is to be most vividly alive," was dead. The sun-worshiper had been too ill to appreciate the irony that he had left a villa named Beau Soleil for one named Ad Astra. It was there, in the old-world town of Vence, above the French Riviera, that he died March 1, 1930, midway in his forty-fifth year.

Lawrence's death was followed by a variety of posthumous volumes and a fair-sized library of biographies, memoirs, reminiscences, correspondences, estimates, and reappraisals, justifications by his supporters and self-justifications by his belittlers. It seemed that everyone who had come even briefly in contact with Lawrence wrote a book about him. There were, for example, Norman Douglas' slanderous "exposé," *D. H. Lawrence and Maurice Magnus*, and John Middleton Murry's vicious attack, *Son of Woman*. On the other hand, there were Catherine Carswell's fervently defensive *The Savage Pilgrimage* and Richard Aldington's balanced *D. H. Lawrence: Portrait of a Genius But . . .* Other memoirs of varying merit include Hugh Kingsmill's journalistic *The Life of D. H. Lawrence;* Mabel Dodge Luhan's *Lorenzo in Taos,* so inchoate that someone suggested it be renamed *Lorenzo in Chaos;* Jessie Chambers' early recollections, *D. H. Lawrence: A Personal Record;*

Frieda Lawrence's *Not I, But the Wind,* a direct, naturally prejudiced, but valuable account of Lawrence's life seen through wifely-maternal eyes; William York Tindall's mocking *D. H. Lawrence and Susan His Cow;* Knud Merrild's *A Poet and Two Painters,* an inconsequential remembrance of a winter in Taos; and Witter Bynner's misleading *Journey with Genius.* The two best interpretations are Horace Gregory's scholarly *Pilgrim of the Apocalypse* and Harry T. Moore's comprehensive *The Life and Works of D. H. Lawrence.*

While the final estimate of Lawrence is yet to be written and his place in literature is still uncertain, it is generally conceded that no one of his generation pursued the cry of sex so passionately and so painfully. Almost everything he touched was translated into the struggle, death, and resurrection of the crucified flesh. He wrote in an exaltation and terror of passion as though his throat "were choked in its own crimson." One homily was apparent in all his works: The world is sick with a soft-rotten culture; dominated by women, our arts, manners, and casual existence have become effeminized. Suffering from a "mind-perverted, will-perverted, ego-perverted love," the world will regain its happiness only when men regain their manhood, the wellspring of emotional sanity. In the short span of twenty years Lawrence wrote more than forty books in a desperate effort to illuminate his text. Physical frailty and what appear to be spells of psychic impotence made Lawrence over-emphasize virility: he exalted the historical hero, the strong man, the natural leader—the very things he could never become. Sometimes the work discloses a distinct sexual dichotomy or, rather, a union of both sexes. In *Lady Chatterley's Lover,* for example the writing is curiously hermaphroditic, as if the author could not decide whether to write from the standpoint of the oversensitized woman or the oversexed man. Lawrence's marriage to Frieda was another fact which he worried out in his fiction. He endowed his male commoners with ultimate power over the feminine aristocrats: Lady Chatterley gives up her home and title to live with a gamekeeper; in "St. Mawr" the wealthy Mrs. Carrington proposes marriage to her groom.

Lawrence's utterance is fitfully uneven; it ranges from the quietly reverberating to the embarrassingly shrill. But it is kept radiantly alive with an inner fire—"in Lawrence," said Elizabeth Bowen, "every bush burns." An intellectual whose emotions often led him down anti-intellectual dead-ends, Lawrence was, nevertheless, a reformer. "He came up," wrote Henry S. Canby, "when the bourgeois Victorian morality was losing its vigor, and he preached his gospel of virility just as the Methodists preached revivalism." With his insistence on sex as salvation, Lawrence held forth like a moralizing if inverted Puritan, an impassioned preacher whose eloquence was "the hot blood's blindfold art."

Ezra Pound

[1 8 8 5 -   ]

*"It is easy to belittle the eccentric theorist,
but the poet must not be deprecated."*

THE CASE of Ezra Loomis Pound is largely a case of mistaken identity. The mistake was his own and it was tragic; for Pound, unquestionably a poet, persuaded himself that he was also meant to be an expert in political propaganda. As a propagandist, he betrayed not only the artist but the man into garrulity, then scurrility and, finally, into treason against his country.

He was born October 30, 1885, in Hailey, Idaho. The family was of New England stock. Pound's mother was a distant relative of Henry Wadsworth Longfellow; his father, a government employee and something of a pioneer, put up the first plastered house in Hailey. The boy was taken to Pennsylvania in his infancy and was brought up in the East. A precocious reader, he entered the University of Pennsylvania at fifteen, began to study extra-curricular comparative literature and, at sixteen, enrolled as a special student "to avoid irrelevant subjects." At eighteen he transferred to Hamilton College in upstate New York, was graduated at twenty and, as a Fellow in Romance languages and literature, became "Instructor with professorial functions" at the University of Pennsylvania. Seemingly destined for an academic career, he took his Master's degree at twenty-one, went to Spain, France, and Italy, and spent a year on research for a thesis on the Spanish dramatist, Lope de Vega. Upon his return toward the end of 1907, he was invited to be on the faculty of Wabash College in Crawfordsville, Indiana, "the Athens of the West," Pound satirically recalled, "a town with literary traditions, Lew Wallace, author of *Ben Hur,* having died there." He was dismissed after four months, charged with "unconventionality," "bohemianism," and other more ambiguous misdemeanors, "all accusations," said Pound, "having been ultimately refuted save that of being 'the Latin Quarter type.'"

A born educator and a frustrated teacher, Pound struck out for Europe, determined not so much to learn as to teach his fellow Americans ("artists astray, lost in the villages, mistrusted, spoken-against") who had become expatriates. He landed in Gibraltar with eighty dollars and lived so thriftily that he was able to subsist for some time on the interest. He journeyed to Italy, where his first book, *A Lume Spente,* was published in Venice in 1908. It was a small book, a series of highly colored reflections of his reading, "a broken bundle of mirrors." A few months later Pound took up residence in London, joined the most advanced group of young writers, assumed leadership of its varied activities, and was appointed the unofficial literary executor of the Fenellosa collection of Chinese and Japanese poetry. In his twenty-fifth year he published two more small volumes of poetry: *Personae* and *Exultations.* Before he was twenty-seven the sum of his publications had reached five with *Canzoni* and *Ripostes.* At twenty-nine he married Dorothy Shakespear, by whom he had a son.

Pound's early poems are a curious amalgam of ancient French and modern English influences. The accents of the Provençal poets and medieval troubadours mingle with those of Browning, William Morris, Swinburne, Lionel Johnson, and lesser Pre-Raphaelites. Often the effect is not so much a combination as a contradiction, an alternating freshness and affectation. The rich archaisms of the ballades, the sestinas, and translations of other French forms are set off in bold relief by appearing next to the colloquial self-consciousness of:

> Come, my songs, let us speak of perfection—
> We shall get ourselves rather disliked . . .

and the naughty preciosity of:

> The gilded phaloi of the crocuses
> are thrusting at the spring air.

Pound was playing the young insurgent ("I mate with my free kind upon the crags"), scorning the bourgeois ("O generation of the thoroughly smug") and, although he had detested Walt Whitman, he was willing to make a pact, coming to the author of *Leaves of Grass* "as a grown child who has had a pig-headed father." "It was you that broke the new wood," he acknowledged. "Now is a time for carving." Within a few years Pound had carved a not altogether enviable place for himself. The first impression he made on the English was an unfavorable one. In his mid-twenties, he was, according to the painter-essayist-novelist, Wyndham Lewis, "an uncomfortably tense, nervously straining, jerky, reddish-brown young

American . . . He was a drop of oil in a glass of water. The trouble was, I believe, that he had no wish to *mix*. He just wanted to *impress*."

In this he succeeded. Pound's arrogance and his erudition became a legend. He lectured in a high and strident voice on new manifestations in the arts, helped to found *Blast,* the organ of the English Vorticists, and was made European correspondent for the magazine *Poetry,* which had just been organized in Chicago. He flaunted an aggressive red beard, and grew, said Lewis, "into a sort of prickly, aloof, rebel mandarin." He attracted disciples and repudiated them; his animadversions were harsh but never merely destructive. Among those who benefited from his criticism was T. S. Eliot who, at Pound's suggestion, cut *The Waste Land* to half its original length and dedicated the poem to Ezra Pound as *"il miglior fabbro"* (the better craftsman). In an introduction to Pound's *Selected Poems,* published in 1928, Eliot maintained that the diverse influences of the Provençal singers and the English poets of the nineties determined Pound's half-sparse, half-ornate utterance. "These influences were all good; for they combined to insist upon the importance of *verse as speech,* while from the more antiquarian studies Pound was learning the importance of *verse as song . . ."* Eliot believed that one of Pound's most indubitable claims to originality is his revivification of the past: "When he deals with antiquities, he extracts the essentially living; when he deals with contemporaries, he sometimes notes only the accidental." Nevertheless, Pound became increasingly concerned with his contemporaries, and the impact he made upon them was considerable. Eliot's debt to the slightly older poet was not only general but specific; Eliot's "Portrait of a Lady" and the intonation of "Prufrock" are anticipated in Pound's "Portrait d'une Femme" and "Villanelle: The Psychological Hour."

In 1914 Pound gathered a little band of poets who were protesting against the romantic excesses of contemporary poetry, wrote their manifesto, and gave the group a name. He called them Imagists, partly because they stressed the importance of the image itself, freed from its clutter of romanticism, and partly to adopt a discriminating term. The creed of the Imagists called for (1) the use of the language of common speech, but the employment of the exact word, not the merely decorative word; (2) the creation of rhythms based on cadence rather than on a strict metrical beat, new rhythms that expressed new moods—"we believe that the individuality of a poet may often be better expressed in free verse than in conventional forms"; (3) the production of poetry that is hard and clear, never blurred or indefinite. These tenets were the essentials of all good poetry, indeed of all good literature. Yet the statement of principles aroused a storm of argument and fury, particularly after the belligerent Amy Lowell adopted the credo and started a campaign for her own controversial purposes. Pound accused her of exploiting the group, violating its spirit and, misled by the very name, making the image so static that it became nothing more than the picture of a lifeless object. Scorning Miss Lowell's captured clan as "Amygists," Pound withdrew from the group, disavowed its anthologies, became English editor of *The Little Review*, sat out the First World War and, at the end of it, abjured London and moved to Paris.

In Paris Pound continued to irritate and stimulate his associates by his creative volatility and perverse bellicosity, as well as by a pretentious scholasticism which threatened to turn the poet into the pedant. At the same time, he developed a new and acrid style, conversational in manner, ironic in mood. *Hugh Selwyn Mauberley*, published when Pound was thirty-five, frankly faces the modern world with brilliant satire and adroit disdain. The poem is a chain of technical virtuosities, mellifluous passages jarred by purposeful roughness, a great flow of sensuous allusions interrupted and diverted by dissonant recollections. Eliot called it "a positive document of sensibility. It is compact of the experience of a certain man in a certain place at a certain time; and it is also the document of an epoch; it is genuine tragedy and comedy; and it is, in the best sense of Arnold's worn phrase, a 'criticism of life.'"

Nothing which Pound had previously attempted divided critical opinion so sharply as his *Cantos,* a series of broken but ambitious monologs. As they continued to appear over a quarter of a century, they were hailed by one school as the peak of his achievement, an almost inexhaustible epic, and by another school as the descent of an eccentric and wayward talent into an abyss of incoherence. There were to be a hundred "chapters" in Pound's major work. The first sixteen were printed in 1925; others appeared during the next twenty years; the ten *Pisan Cantos,* (so called because they were composed while Pound was imprisoned near Pisa in May, 1945) brought the count to eighty-four. Many readers who attempted to read the magnum opus decided that it was written in code and that there was no way of deciphering it. They were mistaken but not altogether wrong. Although the *Cantos* are not incomprehensible, they are anything but clear. To understand them the reader may have to plow through encyclopedias, foreign language dictionaries, cultural and political histories; he would also have to be aware of forgotten gossip about Pound's contemporaries and recognize the tenor of his rambling, disordered, and extremely private associations. At the best, the response to the *Cantos* is intellectual and painfully gradual, never emotional or immediate. "The student is recommended to read them about six times before their flavor can diffuse through the blood," writes an admiring poet, Richard Eberhart. As to Pound's scrambled idioms, his "polylinguality," or talking in tongues, "one becomes used to it," Eberhart says blandly and with no desire to sound humorous.

Only a scholar versed in multiple cultures could hope to follow the bizarre narratives and abrupt interjections, the sniggering asides and secret jokes, the parodies, imprecations, and ambiguous pronouns, the confusion of obscenities and occasional exaltations. Yet Pound always asserted that the scheme of the *Cantos* is severely formal; he said that he was writing a Human Comedy in many voices and dimensions. He began with a precise plan: the work was to be broadly fugal, with subject and counter-subject, using the repetitions of history as recurrent themes. But as the *Cantos* grew in number the author grew increasingly prolix. Pound assails democratic capitalism with a petulance that is close to hysteria; the outlines of the quasi-epic disappear in an agglomeration of Greek myths, Chinese ideograms, and preoccupation with usury, an obsession which eventually dominates and distorts the whole design. At the beginning Pound gave the reader to understand that the work had the architecture of Bach; as it progressed Pound liked to compare it to Dante. The Greek, Renaissance, and First World War passages represent the *Inferno;* the sinful history of money and banking forms the *Purgatorio;* the climactic finale (as yet unwritten) may reveal the *Paradiso.*

No poem of the period succeeded so completely in splitting the critics far apart from each other. "The *Cantos* form an unparalleled history of a world seen from the shores which are the home of our civilization," wrote Ford Madox Ford. "About the poems," demurred Edward Fitzgerald, "there hangs a dismal mist of unresolved confusion."

Pound's very contradictions, especially his gift for mixing plain speech and poetic diction, greatly influenced the style of his contemporaries. Even so eminent a poet as William Butler Yeats substituted Pound's colloquial manner for his own early lyrical incantations. Yet Yeats considered Pound "a sexless American professor, [who had] for all his violence, a single strained attitude instead of passion . . . a brilliant improvisator who had more style than form, a style continually interrupted, broken, twisted into nervous obsession, nightmare, stammering confusion."

The confusion bothered Pound's admirers, but they accepted his least speculations as though they were a new gospel. Pound gave them sufficient material for exegesis. Besides his poetry and an opera on Villon (*Le Testament*), Pound wrote and translated some fifteen volumes of prose, the most characteristic being *The Spirit of Romance, The A B C of Reading, Pavannes and Divisions* (expanded into *Make It New*), *Instigations, Polite Essays,* and *Social Credit: An Impact,* all of them rebelling against the traditional romantic response.

Pound abandoned France for Italy in 1924 and settled in Rapallo, a sunny corner of the Italian Riviera. He left it in 1939 for a short visit to the United States and succeeded in arousing bitter controversies by his praise of fascism and his favorable comparison of Mussolini to Jefferson. His defenders were embarrassed; they pleaded that Pound's long separation from his country (and his natural audience) had given the expatriate a sense of isolation and excused his embittered and misapplied talent, his ill-timed blasts and irresponsible nose-thumbing, as well as his shallow application of Douglas' Social Credit System. But it was too late to help. Pound had never liked criticism; in his fifties he was beyond it.

After his return to Italy, his support of fascism became overt and active. In January, 1941, Pound started broadcasting propaganda by short wave from Rome. He attacked the United States and issued violent diatribes against the American system. He vilified Roosevelt, assailed democracy, spouted anti-Semitism—all of which he echoed in the later *Cantos*—gave aid and comfort twice a week to the enemy, and counseled fascist officials in opposition to his native land. The inspired *enfant terrible* had become the public traitor. In May, 1945, he was taken prisoner and indicted for treason. Brought to Washington, Pound escaped trial and the possible death penalty when four psychiatrists testified that he was of unsound mind. After a court hearing on February 14, 1946, Pound was committed to St. Elizabeth's Hospital as insane.

Three years later the sixty-three-year-old expatriate, still in an institution under suspended indictment for treason, was given the $1,000 Bollingen Prize for the *Pisan Cantos*. The award roused an angry controversy which blazed into fury when it was learned that the award had been made by the Fellows of the Library of Congress and was, therefore, assumed to have semi-official governmental approval. The Fellows, most of whom were American poets, disclaimed agreement with Pound's much-publicized views; they maintained that they were not concerned with Pound's politics but solely with his poetry. The dissension continued for months. It implicated not only a countryful of poets who took both sides of the old debate about "form" and "content," but, since the Bollingen Foundation had been founded by Andrew Mellon, it involved the giant Mellon industrial interests, and even Freud's erstwhile pupil, Dr. Carl Jung, because Bollingen was the name of Jung's Swiss retreat.

As a political economist Pound was bigoted, ineffectual, and absurd; as a person he was erratic and intermittently disbalanced. It is easy to belittle the eccentric theorist, but the poet's importance must not be deprecated. He was a champion of new writers as well as a pioneer of new forms. He fought complacency wherever he encountered it; he experimented in an idiom which he made his own and which he transmitted to many others who used it more flexibly if less forcefully than he did.

Many of Pound's critics asserted that his end was in his beginning, that his belligerent egocentricity contained the germs of his later madness. Even the least worshipful commentators remembered the early rebel with sadness. They recalled Pound's youthful appeal to the artists of his country (the "remnant enslaved, lovers of beauty, starved, thwarted with systems"), and his encouraging advice which ended proudly:

> I have weathered the storm,
> I have beaten out my exile.

In view of the circumstances, the boast was as tragic and pathetic as it was empty.

T. S. Eliot

[1 8 8 8 -   ]

*"The boredom, and the horror, and the
glory."*

IN HIS SIXTIES, a Nobel Prize winner, author of many formidable books and pamphlets, the most forbiddingly erudite essayist and the most uncompromisingly serious poet of his day turned to the writing of comedies. In itself this was surprising enough. Even more remarkable was the fact that, far from being esoteric and obscure, like much of his poetry, the plays were highly successful entertainments, popular "hits" on both sides of the Atlantic.

His full name is Thomas Stearns Eliot and he was born September 26, 1888, in St. Louis, Missouri, the youngest of six children. His father's family were Puritan New Englanders. His grandfather, who came from Boston, founded Washington University and the first Unitarian church in St. Louis; he was said to have been one of the instigators of the "underground railway" for runaway slaves before the Civil War. Eliot's mother was a civic leader, a reformer, and a poet who wrote a dramatic poem about Savonarola. Her gift was transmitted to her talented son, who was sent back to New England for his schooling. He attended Milton Academy and Harvard University, from which he received his A.B. in 1909, and his A.M. the year following. Going abroad, young Eliot studied at the Sorbonne and at Merton College, Oxford, and became a schoolmaster. His teaching career, which he disliked, lasted four years; a period as bank clerk lasted eight. Married at twenty-seven to Vivienne Haigh, a devotee of the ballet, he obtained a position with a London publishing firm, rose to full partnership, and in 1927 became a naturalized British subject. For those who sought explanation, he announced: "Here I am, making a living, enjoying my friends here; I don't like being a squatter; I might as well take the full responsibility." He also declared that he was "Anglo-Catholic in religion, royalist in politics, and classicist in literature."

He was a strange sort of classicist, especially since his early writings seemed the expression not only of a romantic nature but the work of a romantic experimenter. At nineteen Eliot was writing lyrics in the approved manner of the period, but before graduating from Harvard he discovered the French symbolists. In 1910, when Eliot was twenty-two, the Harvard *Advocate* printed his poem, "Humoresque," which bore a parenthetical "After J. Laforgue." Another, entitled "Spleen," carried overtones of Verlaine and Baudelaire, as well as distinct indications of the Eliot of "Prufrock." Its concluding lines are:

> And Life, a little bald and gray,
> Languid, fastidious, and bland
> Waits, hat and gloves in hand,
> Punctilious of tie and suit
> (Somewhat impatient of delay)
> On the doorstep of the Absolute.

Many years later, Eliot acknowledged the influence. Referring to Arthur Symons' *Symbolist Movement in Literature,* Eliot wrote, "But for having read his book, I should not, in the year 1908, have heard of Laforgue and Rimbaud; I should probably not have begun to read Verlaine; and, but for reading Verlaine, I should not have heard of Corbière. So the Symons book is one of those which have affected the course of my life." However, even as an undergraduate poet, Eliot did not merely repeat what he had learned from his models. To the subjective emotions of the French symbolists Eliot added an awareness of the disturbed states which provoked them and supplied psychological analyses to the expression of feelings. In a manner which became increasingly elliptical, he voiced the creeping disillusion of his time, reflected in one of his favorite quotations from Dryden's "The Secular Masque":

> All, all of a piece throughout:
> Thy chase had a beast in view;
> Thy wars brought nothing about;
> Thy lovers were all untrue.
> 'Tis well an old age is out,
> And time to begin a new.

Eliot was still struggling with a style that was half scholarly, half colloquial, when, at twenty-three, he began his first important poem, "The Love Song of J. Alfred Prufrock." The symbolists had indicated a method "of transmuting ideas into sensations, of transforming an observation into a state of mind"; Baudelaire had furnished him with a key for a whole new stock of images. "It is not merely in the use of imagery of common life," Eliot wrote years later, "not merely in the use of imagery of the sordid life of a great metropolis, but in the elevation of such imagery to the *first intensity* —presenting it as it is, and yet making it represent something much more than itself—that Baudelaire created a mode of release and expression for other men."

"Prufrock" was Eliot's first full employment of the "use of imagery of the sordid life of a great metropolis" to represent something "more than itself." Eliot prefaced the poem with a quotation from Dante but, unless the reader knew *The Divine Comedy* or could read Italian, he could scarcely realize that Eliot was giving him the key by suggesting that his Prufrock echoes Dante's Guido da Montefeltro, who said: "If I thought my story [my answer to you] would get back to the world, then this flame would shake no more. But since, if what I hear is true, that none did ever return alive from these depths, I answer you without fear of misrepresentation." Prufrock is not in hell. But he, too, is in the depths of indecision and disillusion which create a hell of the modern world, and his story presents an allusive picture of decadence against the background of a sterile society. Concentrating on moments of intensity, omitting all but the most powerful images, Eliot portrays a tired world through the words of a tired, inadequate, yet self-sufficient, ultrafastidious dilettante. The title sets the mood with its contrast between the alluring "Love Song" and the business-like signature of "J. Alfred Prufrock." The discord suggested by the incongruous title is furthered by the opening stanza. It begins promisingly:

> Let us go then, you and I,
> When the evening is spread out against the sky . . .

which is followed by a sudden shock, a simile which is a revulsion, a reminder of a sick world's desperate condition: "Like a patient etherised upon a table."

The poem proceeds to emphasize its inherent ironies. Bizarre but logical images carry the reader into the sordid world of "half-deserted streets, the muttering retreats of restless nights in one-night cheap hotels, and sawdust restaurants with oyster-shells"—

> Streets that follow like a tedious argument
> Of insidious intent
> To lead you to an overwhelming question . . .

The question remains unanswered as the speaker threads his way through "the yellow fog that rubs its back upon the window-panes" and finds himself in a room where "women come and go, talking of Michelangelo." There he loses himself among trivialities and intensities; he is aware of great emotions and the failure to measure up to them. An inhibited, prematurely old young man, a spectator of life but not a participant—"I have measured out my life with coffee spoons"—Prufrock is conscious of passion everywhere about him, but he cannot rouse himself to respond to it.

> Do I dare
> Disturb the universe? . . .
> And should I then presume?
> And how should I begin?

Prufrock can live only in terms of evasion. He escapes the invitation of love, which is a challenge to live, by summoning the dead past. Retreating from any overt act and the fearful likelihood of his inability to perform it, Prufrock wishes he were something less than human.

> I should have been a pair of ragged claws
> Scuttling across the floors of silent seas.

The mockery of the title becomes clear for, as F. O. Matthiessen pointed out, "Prufrock can give utterance in soliloquy to his debate with himself only because he knows no one will overhear him. The point of calling this a 'Love Song' lies in the irony that it will never be sung." The full significance of the epigraph from the *Inferno* is now revealed, for the inscription clinches the closed circle of Prufrock's isolation as each verse discloses the defeat of the irresolute man, safe only in his dream-life, too priggish for pathos, too sunk in the depths ever to "return alive" to this world.

Most of the early poems collected in *Prufrock and Other Observations* are in the vein of the title poem. The tone is satirical, the technique complex. Traditionally elevated rhetoric is not so much contrasted as combined with an utterance that is purposely flat. Everything is in conflict: the verse reflects a world where the noble degenerates into the tawdry, the beautiful is mixed with the banal, and appearance is confused with reality. "Our civilization comprehends great variety and complexity," wrote Eliot in an essay on the metaphysical poets, "and this variety and complexity, playing upon a refined sensibility, must produce various and complex results. The poet must become more and more comprehensive, more allusive, more indirect, in order to force, to dislocate, if necessary, language into his meaning." Although these sentences were not meant as a

reply to his critics, they serve as a partial answer to those who contended that Eliot was willfully obscure and delighted in obfuscation.
Eliot anticipated the charge that, like Baudelaire, he was fascinated by the ugly and repulsive in nature rather than by the comforting elements of existence. In *The Sacred Wood* he wrote: "The
contemplation of the horrid or sordid or disgusting, by the artist, is
the necessary and negative aspect of the impulse toward the pursuit of beauty." He amplified this statement in "The Use of Poetry":
"The essential advantage for a poet is not to have a beautiful world
with which to deal; it is to be able to see beneath both beauty and
ugliness: to see the boredom, and the horror, and the glory."

The exploration of "the boredom, and the horror, and the glory,"
the union of the mellifluous and the discordant, is extended in *The
Waste Land*, published when Eliot was thirty-four. The poems written between "Prufrock" and *The Waste Land* mingled the irony of
the symbolists with the wit of the seventeenth-century metaphysical poets. The satirical attitude may have been assumed, but the
mood was genuine and sincere. Avoiding personal emotion, self-
mocking, and seemingly detached, Eliot underlined the flippancies
and obliquities with a mordant incisiveness, a cold disdain. In *The
Waste Land* Eliot went further. He mixed "memory and desire" in
an idiom altogether new to English poetry. The verse was a curious
amalgam: colloquial speech joined to and jarred by recondite references, blending, with subtle associations, the horrifying and the
ridiculous.

The Waste Land bristles with difficulties and, as a consequence,
has had many differing interpretations. One school of commentators
sees the poem as a mosaic of quotations skillfully arranged to form a
minor epic. Another school of critics considers it a prolonged regeneration myth. A third contends that it is an expression of faith in
Christianity. A fourth (the most popular) holds that it is a picture
of the social decay of a barren world, corrupt in manners, desolate
in outlook, and bankrupt in moral values. *The Waste Land* did in
poetry what Hemingway's *The Sun Also Rises* did in prose: it became the manifesto of a "lost generation." The intellectual young
men and the precocious adolescents hailed it as their Bible. Speaking for his fellows, the English poet, Louis MacNeice, declared:
"*The Waste Land* was the poem which most altered our conception of poetry and, I think one can add, of life . . . It is possible
that at the age of eighteen we knew, however unconsciously, more
about waste lands than most earlier generations did—or than any

adolescent ought to know . . . What is certain is this: to have painted the Waste Land so precisely, that those who had never to their conscious knowledge been there could so fully recognize it at first sight and at every subsequent meeting could find it still as real or more so, was the feat of a great poet."

Although the critics differed widely in their interpretation of *The Waste Land,* most of them agreed that Eliot's leading theme here, as elsewhere, was disgust with the contemporary world and despair of man. The atmosphere was both miasmic and chokingly arid. The erotic element had disturbed him from the beginning—two of his early poems, written in French ("Dans le Restaurant" and "Lune de Miel") offended average readers with their contemptuous and repulsive attitude to the power of sex. In *The Waste Land* and in subsequent works, Eliot made sex loathsome and, distressed by its demand, turned away from it in almost unnatural revulsion. He uncovered death-in-life everywhere. He explored a vast region of drouth and charted the detritus of civilization: vacant lots cluttered with old newspapers and rusted machinery, musty parlors and filthy side-streets, rats' alleys "where the dead men lost their bones," suspicious boarding-houses, and rivers that sweat oil and tar where once a queen glided by on a gilded shell. In order to depict a fractured time composed of splintered cultures, Eliot broke the continuity of his verse into jagged segments and interrupted the flow of every idea with another fragment of literature. Many readers complained that his poems were puzzling montages, compendiums of quotations without quotation marks, and it is true that Eliot embellished his lines with excerpts, phrases, and "broken images" from a most remarkable variety of sources: *The Aeneid,* Henry James, a sonnet by Meredith, a biography of Edward Fitzgerald, Edmund Spenser, Sherlock Holmes—Eliot was a great admirer of Conan Doyle's detective—Cavalcanti, Dante, Shakespeare and the lesser Elizabethan dramatists, Jessie Weston's *From Ritual to Romance,* Wagner's music dramas, Frazer's *The Golden Bough,* Ecclesiastes, the twisted echo of a sentimental ballad by Theodore Dreiser's brother, a nursery rhyme . . . to name only a few. Nevertheless, Eliot's borrowings amplify the suggestiveness of the passages in which they are incorporated. "Eliot," wrote Edmund Wilson, "manages to be more effective precisely where he might be expected to be least original—he succeeds in conveying his meanings, in communicating his emotions, in spite of all his learning or mysterious allusions, and whether we understand them or not . . . He has been able to lend even to the rhythms, to the words themselves, of his great predecessors a new music and a new meaning." Eliot himself contended that one of the surest tests of a poet's sensibility is "the way in which a poet borrows. Immature poets imitate; mature poets steal; bad poets deface what they take, and good poets make it into something better or, at least, something different."

"The Hollow Men," which emphasizes the barrenness of *The Waste Land* in a still more cruel state of desolation, characterizes the end of a period. In one of the most hopeless poems ever written, Eliot rivets our gaze upon an exhausted world—"shape without form, shade without colour, paralysed force, gesture without motion." Men, figures stuffed with straw, gather on stony soil in a valley of dying stars. They are empty, without vision; they lean together without thought; their dry voices whisper meaninglessly. The poet proceeds on various levels of ambiguity, through a land of stone images and death's dream kingdom. Here man cannot even die decently. He approaches his shabby end by way of a nursery rhyme ("Here we go round the prickly pear") and concludes it with another jingle. A child's game turns into an ironic litany of complete frustration:

> This is the way the world ends
> This is the way the world ends
> This is the way the world ends
> Not with a bang but a whimper.

After "The Hollow Men" Eliot's poetry deepened in tone and grew more extensive in breadth. "Journey of the Magi," "A Song for Simeon," and "Ash-Wednesday" trace the progress of the intellectual soul in new guise as well as new subject matter. "Ash-Wednesday," the most imposing poem of Eliot's late thirties, at first seems a composite of devotional verse, a pastiche of *The Book of Common Prayer,* ecclesiastical ritual, and Latin liturgy. Helen Gardner, one of Eliot's most ardent admirers, doubts whether the assembled phrases "fulfilled their proper function except for a small minority of readers. I think they were felt as an irritant by the majority, to whom they brought no real association of prayer and worship, but merely the suggestion of conventional religious phraseology." On the other hand, there were those who rated "Ash-Wednesday" as a truly great poem, beginning in desperation, rising in hope, and ending in a resigned peace. Replying to those who believed that Eliot's religiosity had limited his vision as well as his poetry, Edwin Muir wrote, "A church is the only kind of institution in which the individual can hold communion not only with the living, but with the dead as well; and so membership of a church was perfectly consonant with Eliot's view of life and his development as a poet. 'Ash-Wednesday' is one of the most moving poems he has written, and perhaps the most perfect."

There continued to be, however, many dissidents. Eliot's followers recognized his remarkable half-narrative, half-lyrical gift; but most readers were perplexed by imagery that rose from hidden associations, rather than a logical sequence of ideas, and which derived from a complex of unfamiliar literatures, remote philosophies, and oddments of learning in half a dozen languages. It was apparent that this was poetry for the few, but for those few it was poetry that excited their minds and stirred their imaginations.

Eliot continued to undergo a set of unexpected changes. He emerged as a playwright, composed provocative essays, turned out book reviews, and wrote *Old Possum's Book of Practical Cats,* a book which will be enjoyed by every cat lover and every fancier of light verse. *The Rock* is an eloquent pageant play. *Murder in the Cathedral,* a consideration of the essence of martyrdom, abandons private references and literary references for straightforward action, simple unity, and a language that is not only lucid but impassioned. Eliot refused to conform to any single pattern.

As in his verse, so in his looks. He resembled the conventional picture of a banker, rather than the typical notion of a poet. Six feet tall, he carried himself with a haggard, hawklike elegance, although he began to stoop a little and his ascetic face grew gaunt as he approached sixty. His beautifully modulated voice recorded many of his poems with a grave and appropriately sepulchral inflection. In a *Life* profile T. S. Matthews described him as "a shy man who has built up a shy man's defense against the crude clangors of the outside world. When he is listening or talking, his face is benign and quizzical, rather like a kindly but sharp-minded old spinster who could obviously say a good deal more than she does—if she knew you better, or were not so polite." Eliot has also drawn his own portrait, which is only partly a caricature in the manner of Edward Lear:

> How unpleasant to meet Mr. Eliot!
> With his features of clerical cut,
> And his brow so grim
> And his mouth so prim

And his conversation, so nicely
Restricted to What Precisely
And If and Perhaps and But . . .

Eliot was past fifty when he wrote in this frisky style; most of his devotees, not suspecting the comic spirit which was to surprise the world ten years later, dismissed such trifles as excusable but scarcely praiseworthy diversions. They preferred to think of Eliot only as the serious analyst of man's agonies and as an unsurpassed character creator. Although they were not justified in dismissing Eliot's other talents, they were right in regarding him as one who had the power of dramatizing drifting, lone, and largely neurotic individuals and making them symbols of sensibility. His unforgettable *personae* include the precious, indecisive, and impotent Prufrock as well as his opposite, the vulgar, extrovert Sweeney; the faunlike Mr. Apollinax, whose laughter "tinkled among the teacups"; a dirty, lecherous waiter; an infatuated American commercial traveler, "Chicago Semite Viennese"; an old man in a decayed and drafty house; a house agent's clerk "on whom assurance sits as a silk hat on a Bradford millionaire"; a lady tortured with nerves and boredom; a tired typist undergoing an automatic, loveless seduction . . . The Eliot method of manipulating character had not yet reached its unfolding in the theater, but it was approaching the stage. Before Eliot could create his light comedies, he was to compose his most profound poetry.

The first of the *Four Quartets* had appeared when Eliot was nearing fifty; with "Little Gidding," the last of the Quartets, he completed what many have considered the greatest philosophic poem of the twentieth century. It was said that it attempted to go "beyond" poetry in the way that Beethoven, in his last quartets, tried to go "beyond" music. In *Four Quartets* Eliot explored the meaning of time and timelessness, as well as the sense of the present and the sense of poetry. The allusions are remote but not nearly as complex as those in *The Waste Land,* and the skilfully interwoven repetitions furnish a music only tentatively sounded in Eliot's preceding work. There are designs within designs, and the patterns are intricately related in a kind of four-part harmony: the mixed symbols of the four seasons and the four elements, the dexterous alternation of slow-paced unrhymed monologs and rapidly rhyming lyrics. In a series of contrasts between the center of existence, "the still point" and "the turning world" of daily life, Eliot probes into, as he said in "Tradition and the Individual Talent," the historical sense which "involves a perception, not only of the pastness of the past, but of its presence." Only in this realm can the soul find itself: love is still and timeless, perfect in Being, as distinguished from desire, which is temporal, restless, and uncompleted in the state of Becoming. The refrain of time present and time past is accompanied by meditations on the difficulty of communication As craftsman Eliot complains of the twenty years, largely wasted, between two wars—

> Trying to learn to use words, and every attempt
> Is a wholly new start, and a different kind of failure
> Because one has only learnt to get the better of words
> For the thing one no longer has to say, or the way in which
> One is no longer disposed to say it. And so each venture
> Is a new beginning, a raid on the inarticulate,
> With shabby equipment always deteriorating
> In the general mess of imprecision of feeling,
> Undisciplined squads of emotion.

In 1947, after spending the last seven years of her life in a nursing home, Eliot's wife died. The following year Eliot received two great honors: The British Order of Merit and the Nobel Prize for "work as a trail-blazing pioneer of modern poetry." Eliot might well have retired into a dignified twilight of life but, at sixty-two, he startled everyone by claiming attention as a writer of comedies. He was still a classicist—he had summoned the Greek spirit by introducing the Eumenides in *The Family Reunion*—now he went back to the *Alcestis* of Euripides for *The Cocktail Party*.

A great success in the United States as well as England, *The Cocktail Party* fused the gifts of the wit and the poet, the satirist and the former agnostic turned God-seeker. Centering about the lives of a few members of a frivolous society, Eliot bewildered his audiences by unaccountably changing three comic figures of the first act into a holy trinity, and ending the plot with a twist which the listeners found either saintly or sadistic. *The Confidential Clerk,* which was produced three years later, also owed something to Greek drama—the central situation occurs in *Ion*—but Eliot transformed it into an intellectual farce, part Euripides and part Gilbert and Sullivan, complete with the mixed-up babies, mistaken identities, and the old nurse who, at the fall of the curtain, straightens out everything. Beneath the wry humor of the situation and the nimbleness of the repartee, Eliot employs a flexible blank verse to inquire into the relation between father and son (and, by inference, between God and man), brilliant speculations about love, loneliness, and (Eliot's recurring theme) the nature of reality. He also touches upon a salient disease of our age: the insistence on "importance," not only on accomplishment but on "bigness." The drive to be successful forces the characters to become what they never wanted to be. The powerful financier had dreamed of being a potter and the confidential clerk is a disappointed organist; both have to learn that "if you haven't the strength to impose your own terms upon life, you must accept the terms it offers you."

At sixty-five Eliot was the most discussed poet and critic of the period. A dozen full-length books analyzed his prose and verse; a bibliography listed 285 critical studies about him, including theses and magazine articles. Malcolm Cowley remarked that Eliot's "rather slender production [of poems] sometimes seems to be buried under an accumulated mass of glosses and explications." Not all the estimates were favorable; on the contrary, Eliot was the center of many controversies. He was attacked with equal violence for his political conservatism and his literary avant-gardism. The tendentiously savage *The T. S. Eliot Myth* by Rossell Hope Robbins indicted Eliot for being anti-humanist as well as anti-democratic; an apologist for fascism who is quasi-racist and definitely anti-semitic; an opponent of universal suffrage who contends that higher education should be limited to a favored few; a believer in the damnation of unbaptized infants; a maladjusted spirit who fears progress, hates the world, and loathes the regenerative process which populates it; a poet bored by "birth and copulation and death"—in short, a man who is, at the best, condescending in social problems, orthodox in religion, and reactionary in politics. "One of the most astonishing things about Eliot," wrote Stephen Spender in *The Destructive Element,* "is that a poet . . . should seem so blinded to the existence of people outside himself." Spender's further criticism of Eliot's blend of aggressive Catholicism and Old Testament "intense nationalism and self-sufficiency" was amplified by Horace Gregory: "It is toward this danger that Eliot has been moving, a danger which may at last obscure the values of his poetry and leave him, at the end of a career, an isolated symbol of post-war sensibility."

The sensibility was never questioned. Eliot's method made it difficult to comprehend his work without considerable study; but the extraordinary compression, the loosely logical but interknit connection of ideas and effects, "the alliance of levity and seriousness," the very obliquity of his language rewarded the studious reader with

rich suggestiveness. It brought back the power of the poetic line
to the theater and, with its fusion of the ordinary and the exalted,
renovated the entire structure of verse. No poet of his day exposed
a whole civilization in a picture more trenchant and excoriating
than:

> And the wind shall say: "Here were decent godless people;
> Their only monument the asphalt road
> And a thousand lost golf balls."

"Poetry," wrote Eliot, "may make us see the world afresh, or some
new part of it. It may make us from time to time a little more
aware of the deeper, unnamed feelings to which we rarely penetrate." Eliot's fluctuating forms made not only his technique but his
thought more mobile; it permitted the reader to see a new or unsuspected part of the world with a greater awareness than he had
hitherto possessed. There is something to be said for those who have
found Eliot lacking in warmth, limited in sympathy, and restricted
in emotional range, but there can be no question about his importance as a "maker." Eliot's early concern with individual consciousness and his later preoccupation with man's conscience, his very
mystifications, concentrated in fresh audio-visual images, challenged
writers, as well as patient readers, and put them in his debt. His
unique blend of borrowings and vividly original figures, his private
anxieties and even more private visions, his nervous rhythms and
tangential style may have made him the exegetic scholars' pet, the
fashionable idol (as well as the victim) of cliques and coteries. But
the total effect of his work unquestionably raised the pitch, enlarged the vocabulary, and changed the direction of contemporary
poetry.

For permission to reprint quotations from *Collected Poems* 1909-1935 by T. S.
Eliot, copyright, 1936, and from *Selected Essays* 1917-1932 by T. S. Eliot, copyright,
1932, the author is indebted to Harcourt, Brace and Company, Inc., and Faber &
Faber Ltd.

Eugene O'Neill

[1 8 8 8 - 1 9 5 3]

"The world drives men to assume characters
which are not their own."

ON DECEMBER 3, 1953, America's greatest dramatist, the playwright who had been awarded the Nobel Prize and had
won the Pulitzer Prize three times, was buried in a bare
casket. Only three mourners were present: his wife, his doctor, and
a nurse. It was the dead man's wish that there should be no ceremony of any sort. There were no prayers at the side of the grave.
No hymns were sung and not a word was said as the body of Eugene O'Neill was lowered into the earth.

Eugene Gladstone O'Neill was born October 16, 1888, in a third
floor backroom of a family hotel in New York City. He was the
second son of James O'Neill, a matinee idol, the perennial star of
The Count of Monte Cristo, and Ella Quinlan O'Neill. During his
first seven years the boy traveled up and down the country with his
father's touring troupe. It was not until his eighth birthday, when
he was put in a Roman Catholic boarding school, that he had any
regular education. At thirteen he was a student at Betts Academy
in Stamford, Connecticut; unvisited by his family for long periods,
even his vacations were spent alone. At eighteen he entered Princeton. He was there less than a year. In a spasm of combined resentment and high spirits he hurled a beer bottle through a schoolmaster's window and was expelled from the university. The tossed
bottle ended his formal education.

At nineteen O'Neill began a long series of erratic wanderings. He
left his job in a New York mail-order firm to prospect for gold in
Honduras, explored the jungles, contracted a tropical fever, and
shipped back home. Back in America he married Kathleen Jenkins,
by whom he had a son, Eugene, Jr., and was given the position of
assistant stage manager of his father's company; but he could not
adjust himself to either domesticity or the routine of the theater.
He shipped as an ordinary seaman on a freighter and landed in
Buenos Aires. He remained a sailor, traveling from South America
to Africa and back, for a year, and finally worked his way to New

York, where he went on a prolonged carouse. The spree ended in New Orleans, where his father was playing. Here he became an actor, but he remained in that role only four months, went north and took a job as reporter on the *New London Telegraph*. His work as a newspaperman lasted another four months. He disliked news-gathering and claimed that confinement was ruining his health. A physical examination showed that he had a light case of tuberculo-sis, and he was sent to a sanatorium in Connecticut.

It was during the five months spent at Wallingford, Connecticut, that the disorganized fragments of O'Neill's early life came into focus. His mind began, as he said, "to establish itself, to digest and evaluate the impressions of many past years in which one experi-ence had crowded on another with never a second for reflection." He also began reading, chiefly plays. It was Strindberg, he said, who "first gave me the vision of what modern drama could be, and inspired me with the urge to write for the theater." O'Neill's condi-tion had improved and, as soon as he was discharged, he got to work; he wrote eleven one-act plays, most of which reflected the grim influence of the Swedish dramatist, and two long ones. It did not require much rereading for him to realize that most of what he had written was not only unplayable but unpublishable. He tore up all the plays except six of the least lurid one-acters, and these his father had printed for him in a volume entitled *Thirst and Other Plays*. He was twenty-six; gratified that his wayward son had found a way to channelize his restless energy, his father paid for a year's tuition in George Pierce Baker's drama workshop at Harvard.

At twenty-eight, with a satchel full of scripts, he went to Prov-incetown and saw his first play produced. It was *Bound East for Cardiff* and was put on by a stock company which had just been organized in a barn on one of the wharves. The venture was so suc-cessful that the Wharf Theater transferred its activities to New York's Greenwich Village and became famous as the Provincetown Players. In the three years between 1917 and 1920, this group staged ten of O'Neill's one-act plays (most of them about the sea); three of them—*Ile, The Moon of the Caribbees,* and *The Long Voy-age Home*—were printed in *The Smart Set*. His first full-length play, *Beyond the Horizon*, produced in 1920, ran for more than a hundred performances and was awarded the Pulitzer Prize.

Crude though the early plays undoubtedly are, they are not pat-terned on tailor-made entertainments, competently contrived. They are not pretty or comforting; they thrash about in darkness to find a wild beauty in things that are violent and ugly. They are sometimes tawdry, sometimes terrible, but they are never trivial. O'Neill did not shrink from the contemplation of the world's pain and prevailing evil. His heroes are doomed—one commentator speaks of O'Neill's "haunted heroes"—not by the gods but by the lack of them, and no less tragic for being helpless. Tragedy stares bleakly out of *Anna Christie,* which won the Pulitzer Prize in 1922, and *Strange Interlude,* which, in 1928, brought O'Neill the national honor for the third time. Two years later, when another American, Sinclair Lewis, accepted the Nobel Prize with a half-modest, half-sarcastic speech, Lewis startled his hearers by saying: "Had you chosen Eugene O'Neill, who had done nothing much in American drama save to transform it utterly in ten or twelve years, from a false world of neat and competent trickery to a world of splendor and fear and greatness, you would have been reminded that he has done something far worse than scoffing—he has seen life as not to be neatly arranged in the study of a scholar but as a terrifying, magnificent, and often quite horrible thing, akin to the tornado, the earthquake, the devastating fire."

It was to "the devastating fire" that O'Neill devoted himself. He broke every law of dramaturgy to project his passionate intensity across the footlights. *The Emperor Jones* violated the rule against long speeches by being practically a monolog and broke the edict about changing an established mood by shifting the line of the play from modern realism to primitive fantasy. *The Hairy Ape* turned fantasy into expressionistic symbolism. *The Great God Brown,* a showing-up of the split life of a seemingly happy businessman, emphasized the double meaning of the action and revealed the hidden symbols of failure by the use of masks. "The basic idea of the play," wrote Frederick C. Packard, Jr., "is that the world drives men to assume characters which are not their own, and they wear masks to hide their true selves—false faces molded in the likeness of the persons they have become." The tension of *Lazarus Laughed* was increased by the sound of choral chants. *Strange Interlude* revived the "aside," and gave validity as well as unsuspected strength to the expression of inner thoughts, a powerful exposure of the mind which had been discarded as a wornout theatrical device. *Mourning Becomes Electra* stretched the resources of the theater to the uttermost. Dispensing with "the classic unities" and the traditions of "theater time," it ran five hours (requiring a dinner intermission) and brought, wrote Brooks Atkinson in his review in *The New York*

Times (November 1, 1931), "the cold splendors of Greek tragedy off the sky-blue limbo of Olympus down to the gusty forum of contemporary life . . . It rose out of our moribund drama like a lily from the black slime of the swamp." John Mason Brown called it "an achievement which restores the theater to its highest state," and, in his introduction to *Nine Plays by Eugene O'Neill,* Joseph Wood Krutch remarked: "Once more we have a great play which . . . means the same thing that *Oedipus* and *Hamlet* and *Macbeth* mean—namely, that human beings are great and terrible creatures when they are in the grip of great passions, and that the spectacle of them is not only absorbing but also and at once horrible and cleansing."

The character of O'Neill's life changed almost as rapidly as the form of his plays. Working in many moods, he tried many places, but he did not find it possible to live in any one spot for any length of time. He tried New England, then Bermuda, then France, the Sea Islands off the coast of Georgia, Tao House across the bay from San Francisco, New York, Cape Cod. His first marriage had lasted less than three years. In his thirtieth year he married Agnes Boulton, by whom he had two children, a son, Shane, and a daughter, Oona, and from whom he was divorced in 1929. At forty-two he married Carlotta Monterey, a beautiful actress, and began planning *A Tale of Possessors Self-Dispossessed,* a cycle of nine related plays which were to form a saga of the rise and fall of an American family from 1775 to 1932. He had, to all appearances, completely recovered his health. He was bronzed by the sun; his hair, though graying, was still thick; his bulging brow, mobile mouth, and dramatic cheekbones were intensified by brooding eyes that would suddenly blaze with questions.

At forty-five O'Neill surprised his admirers with *Ah, Wilderness!* which, since it was a sentimental comedy of adolescence, was a popular success. Approved by audiences which had hitherto been repelled by O'Neill's dramatization of "the sickness of today: the materialistic myth of success," *Ah, Wilderness!* ran for almost three hundred performances. It made up for many reverses, denunciations, and difficulties. It had been hard to get the controversial *All God's Chillun Got Wings* on the stage because the authorities feared it might lead to race riots. *Desire Under the Elms* was so violently attacked for its "undisguised immorality" that the New York theater which presented it was almost compelled to close. The play was not permitted to be shown in Boston, and, after a few performances in Los Angeles, the police arrested everyone in the cast for taking part in an indecent entertainment.

The award of the Nobel Prize in 1936 came as a rebuke to the Philistines and an unexpected tribute to the playwright. Remembering the statement made six years before by Sinclair Lewis, O'Neill was equally deprecating. "This highest of distinctions," he wrote, "is all the more gratifying because I feel so deeply that it is not only my work which is being honored but the work of all my colleagues in America—that the Nobel Prize is a symbol of the coming of age of the American theater. For my plays are, through luck of time and circumstance, merely the most widely known examples of the work done by American playwrights since the World War . . ." O'Neill was understating the case. His works were not only more often performed than any contemporary dramatist except Shaw but, with the exception of Shaw and Shakespeare, he was the most widely read playwright who had written in the English language.

Suddenly O'Neill lost his "luck of time" and his power. He declined physically and creatively; the very height of his achievement made the descent seem all the more precipitous. *Days Without End* floundered, and there was an interval of twelve years before *The Iceman Cometh,* an enigmatic failure, brought O'Neill back to the theater in 1946. *A Moon for the Misbegotten* closed during its out-of-town tryout. The playwright who had made a million dollars was a sick, unhappy man at fifty. His family life went to pieces. He had never forgiven his daughter, Oona, for marrying the comedian, Charlie Chaplin. His younger son, Shane, had been in a federal clinic for addiction to narcotics. His older son, a teacher who was also a brilliant Greek scholar, had committed suicide in 1950. O'Neill's physique shrank to skeletal gauntness; his eyes became black hollows; the skin of his face seemed too tightly stretched over thin bone. At fifty-six a muscular ailment made writing difficult; a little later he could not hold his pen. Hospitalization was no help. There was a general slowing-up of all faculties and a convulsive twitching of the hands. The palsy and growing rigidity indicated Parkinson's disease; a diagnosis showed a "pre-senile arterial sclerotic condition." He tried to dictate, but he had always composed in microscopic longhand and found that he could not create in any other way. He destroyed much of what he had written on the cycle started twenty years before, and left the autobiographical *Long Day's Journey Into Night* with the stipulation that it must not be produced until twenty-five years after his death. He had been a prisoner of his disease for more than ten years when, completely incapacitated, he contracted bronchial pneumonia and died at sixty-five, November 27, 1953.

In a not too laudatory obituary, *Time* conceded that "before O'Neill, the United States had theater; after O'Neill it had drama . . . Greek tragedy is tragedy of Destiny: man's fate is in his stars. Shakespearean tragedy is tragedy of character: man's fate is in his will. Through suffering and death, Greek and Shakespearean tragic heroes appeased the gods and found redemption. O'Neill's audiences were almost as suspicious of God, Will, and Destiny as of a flat earth. Bowing to his time, O'Neill wrote the tragedy of Personal Psychology: man's fate is in his genes and hormones." It was as a victim of circumstance that the hero of *The Great God Brown* declared: "Man is born broken. He lives by mending. The grace of God is glue." In *Mourning Becomes Electra* O'Neill twisted the climax of the Greek legend by withholding the traditional catharsis and making the leading character cry out: "There's no one left to punish me. I've got to punish myself!"

When O'Neill failed, he failed abysmally; but his failures were due to an excess of purpose, never to an impoverishment of the imagination. If he sometimes toppled from the peaks, it was because he refused to admit that they were inaccessible and because, in any case, he preferred to die on the lonely heights rather than live on much-traveled highroads. He was primarily concerned with "the death of the old God and the failure of science and materialism to give any satisfying new one for the surviving primitive religious instinct to find a meaning for life in, and to comfort its fears of death with." His many-peopled dramas transmitted the ecstasies and tensions and terrors of human beings because, as John Mason Brown wrote in his final estimate, "his characters were not merely in conflict with one another. They were at war with the agents controlling their destiny, and these agents were not indifferent to them. This link between mortals and forces shaping their lives was the mighty concern which gave a kind of majesty to the feeblest of his plays."

It is too early to determine O'Neill's final status as dramatist. It is obvious that he was a provocative innovator, a breaker of established forms and a builder of new ones. It is less certain that his plays have the viability which will assure permanence in the living theater. At present, only a few of his many plays—chiefly the shorter ones—are performed by scattered repertory companies. None of his major works is to be found, as are Shaw's and Shakespeare's, in production somewhere all the time. The quality of O'Neill's writing, the persuasion of his plots, and the credibility of his characters are still debatable, but the importance of his influence is unquestionable.

Charles Chaplin

[1 8 8 9 -   ]

"Pan, too, had been much assailed . . ."

HE OFFENDED the moral susceptibilities of a great number of people. He was considered so politically "controversial" that he was expelled from the country in which he lived. But he was the only actor ever to achieve anything like universality, and critical opinion about the uproariously funny and pitifully sad little tramp was expressed only in superlatives. One of his biographers, Theodore Huff, wrote that "he made more people laugh than any other man who ever lived. Beyond this, he is a symbol of the age, the twentieth-century Everyman. In Gilbert Seldes' apt phrase, Chaplin was 'destined by his genius to be the one universal man of modern times.' " A more detached commentator, Max Eastman, said, "in the History of Great Fame, no chapter will be more astounding that that in which this little modest actor of one role . . . became in three short years known and loved by more men, and more races and classes of men, than anyone, even the great religious leaders, ever had been before."

He was born in London, April 16, 1889, and was christened Charles Spencer Chaplin. The date and place are definite, but there is no record of such a birth under such a name—which may mean that the "Chaplin" was an assumed rather than the actual name. His father, a music hall baritone, also known as Charles Chaplin, was the son of French Jews who had become Anglicized. His mother, Hannah, whose maiden name is not known, and is supposed to have been part Irish, part Spanish—Chaplin always refused to clarify the facts—was a singer and dancer. She had three sons by a previous marriage, and one of these, Sidney, born four years before Charlie, took the name of his stepfather.

The Chaplins were usually in financial difficulties. The father drank to excess; the mother, a woman of singular penetration, worried herself into a decline. The two children were brought up backstage; Charlie was taught to sing before he could talk and to dance as soon as he could walk. When he was five he made his first stage appearance as a replacement for his mother, who had been taken suddenly ill. He was so carried away with the small sensation he created that he had to be dragged off the stage. A year or so after, his parents separated and, a little later, his father died of alcoholism. Worry and unhappiness ruined his mother's stage career. The situation was so desperate that both boys had to be placed in a charity home. When his mother was well enough, she took the children back and supported them by sewing. By the time Charlie was seven, he was helping the family by appearing with a children's music hall act. At the end of the engagement he was afforded two years of schooling at Hern Boys College, the only formal education he ever had.

Sidney had gone to sea and Charlie was at school when his mother suffered a mental breakdown and was taken away to an institution. Completely alone, Charlie lived on the streets. He picked up a few pennies by running errands and doing other odd jobs. Even when the waif became a millionaire he worried about money; the fear of poverty, never dispelled by the luxuries of Hollywood, was stamped on him in the side-streets of London.

Sidney returned from his voyage with a little capital, located his half-brother and decided to pool their combined talents. Acting as agent, he got the ten-year-old boy an engagement at the London Hippodrome and, within a few years, Charlie became one of the most popular child actors in England. He and Sidney transferred their mother from the institution to a convalescent home, but her condition still did not improve sufficiently for her to rejoin her children; she did not even recognize them.

As a gawky adolescent whose voice was changing, Charlie found that he could not remain a child actor in the legitimate theater and was forced back into vaudeville, where he rediscovered the gift for comic pantomime. Sidney, too, had gone into vaudeville with a famous pantomime group known as the Fred Karno Company, and he got Charlie a job with the troupe.

Charlie was not quite twenty when he came to the United States as a top comedian—a clown who had a drunken dude specialty— with a Karno touring group. He was twenty-four, making $50 a week in the vaudeville routine, when he was offered a movie contract with Keystone Films at $150 a week. In November, 1913, Charlie completed his contract with the Karno outfit and left for California.

The rapidly developing film industry was undergoing a major change. The early success of the cinema and the competition of European producers were influencing the American studios to decrease the output of their early stock products, the short films, and concentrate on feature-length pictures. Cecil B. De Mille, Sam Goldwyn, and Jesse Lasky were working on an adaptation of the stage play, the "Squaw Woman"; D. W. Griffith was planning the huge, semi-documentary drama, "The Birth of a Nation." For the time being, the comedy field was unaffected; it continued to turn out one- and two-reel items at the rate of one a week. During his own days as a comedian, Mack Sennett, head of Keystone, had learned movie techniques from Griffith. He turned out madly paced pieces of non-sense, with sequences and gags usually made up on the scene, almost always culminating in a wildly uproarious chase. Sennett was dubious about Keystone's new comedian—Chaplin's tempo had always been deliberate and he resisted all efforts to speed him up—but the very first reviews convinced Sennett that Chaplin was an original and indisputable laugh-getter.

The shabby apparel with which Chaplin was to become identified was an accident. Sennett had ordered Chaplin to report on location, wearing something funny. In a hurry Chaplin picked up whatever he could find: baggy pants which were the property of a famous fat comedian; oversized shoes, belonging to another comic star; a rusty derby, too small for his head; a coat too tight even for his slender frame; an incongruously dapper bamboo cane, and a tiny "tooth brush" mustache. The costume, wrote Theodore Huff in his analytical biography, *Charlie Chaplin,* "personifies shabby gentility—the fallen aristocrat at grips with poverty. The cane is a symbol of attempted dignity, the pert mustache a sign of vanity." The appealing and often pathetic figure was still to emerge. During the first year in which he appeared in thirty-five films, he was a good-for-nothing and completely unsympathetic character, but his comic effects were so hilarious that, only thirteen weeks after making the change from vaudeville to the "flickers," he was allowed to write and direct all his films. His contract with Keystone ran for twelve months. When the year was up, Sennett offered to raise Chaplin's salary from $150 to $400 a week; but a rival concern, the Essanay Company, lured the comedian away with a weekly stipend of $1,250—almost ten times what he was making. By the end of the year with Essanay, Charlie's value had increased ten-fold again. This time the Mutual Company outbid all the others with a history-making offer of $10,000 a week and a bonus of $150,000. It was, however, with difficulty that Chaplin was persuaded to leave his small hotel room in an unfashionable section of Los Angeles and move to suitable quarters.

During his year with Essanay, according to Huff, "the immortal and world-famous character of the tramp—the tragi-comic vagabond so perfectly symbolizing the universal underdog—came into being . . . possibly the most significant artistic archetype of this century." The little shuffling tramp achieved lasting life in twelve pictures made for Mutual. They reveal not only Chaplin's sensitive handling of situation and story, but the subtly changing nuances of his inimitable pantomime. The pictures made the war-torn world of 1916 and 1917 a little happier and Charlie more beloved. Millions enjoyed "The Floorwalker," "The Count," "The Immigrant," "Easy Street," and the others which have become classics and, even though the prints are inferior, are still shown in Chaplin Festivals.

While Chaplin was adored, he was also attacked. His detractors pointed out that, although he made his money in the United States, he refused to become a citizen or enlist. The feeling that he was a "slacker" was particularly strong in England because he still retained British citizenship. The publicized fact that he could not pass the Army's physical requirement and his two-month bond-selling entertainment tour failed to quiet his critics.

It was at this time that Chaplin signed a million dollar contract with First National, plus a bonus of $15,000. He became his own producer, had his own studio, and shared in the profits. To this period belong some of his celebrated pictures, such as "Shoulder Arms" and "The Kid," in which Jackie Coogan, a find of Chaplin's, created a sensation as a child actor.

Until he was nearly thirty Chaplin's life had been quiet, scandal-free, and without any serious involvement. He had made his leading lady, Edna Purviance, nationally known and many hoped he would make her his wife. He was, however, still a bachelor—handsome, rich, and famous—when he became infatuated with a sixteen-year-old movie ingenue, Mildred Harris. On October 23, 1918, they were suddenly married. A baby born the following summer lived only three days. It was not long before Chaplin separated from his child-bride and, after a prolonged series of charges and counter-charges and a great deal of wrangling about money, a divorce was obtained. He was to grow more and more emotionally unstable, intensely complicated and blithely egocentric. Living compulsively, he behaved as though his gifts entitled him to special privileges. For years, his audiences did nothing to disillusion him. In 1921 he visited Europe—partly to escape the newspaper gossip and partly to restore his depleted creativity—and was acclaimed by crowds as though he were a returning hero.

Chaplin's temperament, as well as a sporadic streak of irresponsibility, made his personal life extremely difficult. Until he was well in his fifties his amatory and marital record was anything but pleasant. In 1924 he was frequently seen with Lolita McMurry, who used the name of Lita Grey, and who was, like his previous wife, sixteen years old. Again there was a hurried marriage, a marriage clearly unsuitable and unfortunate even before it took place in November, 1924. In June, 1925, Chaplin became the father of Charles Spencer, Jr.; the following year a second son, Sydney Earle, was born. In 1927 the papers were again filled with the domestic troubles of the Chaplins. There were angry denunciations on both sides; Lita charged flagrant infidelities and hinted at unmentionable immoralities; he retorted that he had been forced into marriage and that his wife's family had conspired to extort a vast sum of money from him. Lita's unsavory forty-two-page complaint was offered for sale and bought by thousands and, although Chaplin pleaded that an artist's private life should be considered apart from his work, women's clubs expressed their outrage and a section of the public was so agitated that several of Chaplin's films were banned. Chaplin could not stand the strain. He suffered a breakdown and settled the case for a cash settlement to her of $600,000 plus a $200,000 trust fund for the two boys, and attorney's fees which brought the total close to a million dollars. Lita made the best of a good bargain and married twice after the divorce.

Chaplin had learned something of the ways of the world, but not enough. For a considerable interval his name was connected with one woman after another. It was reported that he was engaged to the exotic Polish actress, Pola Negri, seriously attached to the ambitious Claire Windsor (originally Olga Cronk of Kansas), and deep in a romance with the sculptress Clare Sheridan. After he met Paulette Goddard, their relationship seemed to content him. For about eight years he kept the curious in a state of mystification; he refused to divulge where and when he had married Paulette, if he had married her at all, and his refusal was seized upon with malicious glee by the gossips, since he and Paulette were living together openly. It was only in 1942, two years after they had separated and a divorce had been quietly obtained, that a marriage was disclosed to have taken place at Canton, China, in 1936.

In 1943 Chaplin was once more the defendant in a spectacular court case. Joan Barry, a young, stage-struck waitress, brought a paternity suit against him. In the course of the action it was revealed that he had given her a contract, had sent her to the renowned German director, Max Reinhardt, and within a year had tired of her and her importunities. She got into his house, made scenes, threatened to kill him and commit suicide, and was arrested for vagrancy. When her baby was born, blood tests proved that the man she accused was not the father but, probably because of his acknowledged relations with her, the court compelled Chaplin to assume financial responsibility for the child.

In the midst of the Barry case, the public was further startled by the news of a fourth Chaplin marriage. To make matters more sensational, his new bride was again extremely youthful: the much-publicized, glamorous eighteen-year-old Oona O'Neill, daughter of the playwright, Eugene O'Neill, who thereupon disowned her. The marriage, which occurred on June 16, 1943, when Chaplin was fifty-four, apparently brought him a real companion as well as a satisfying romance. There were no further scandals, and the immoralist, whom the columnist Westbrook Pegler denounced as an "alien, guilty of a degree of moral turpitude which disqualifies him for citizenship," turned into a contented family man. In 1953 he and his present wife became parents for the fifth time when a boy was born in Europe.

Chaplin, however, had been making enemies not only because of his wayward emotional impulses but because of his political tendencies. His early work had received total popular acceptance. There was always a trace of social feeling in his portrayals of the rejected little fellow—the actor who played the tramp could not forget the nights when, as a child, he had huddled in doorways and slept on the London embankment. But after 1922 his sympathy with underdogs and the underprivileged began to deepen into something like social documents. His first departure was the production of "Woman of Paris," the serious study of a demimondaine, a picture in which he did not appear at all. He directed himself in "The Gold Rush," which many consider a masterpiece of excruciating farce and heart-rending pathos. The "text" of "The Gold Rush" is man's greed, and the sermon is all the more effective because it is preached by a clown, a fantastic misfit who lets the theme outline itself in a hysterical mixture of absurdity, satire, and suspense. In "City Lights" Chaplin upset all calculations. He presented a silent picture three years after talking pictures had made all silent films obsolete—and showed a profit of five million dollars. In this picture he broke another precedent by daring to add tragedy to slapstick. The plot of "City Lights" concerns a blind girl befriended and beloved by a tramp who blunders into a friendship with a drunken, manic-depressive millionaire, gets money from him for an operation which will restore the girl's sight and, when she is able to see, loses her. The ending is equivocal but inevitable; the poignance, never permitted to become maudlin, is enhanced by the shriekingly comic scenes which precede it.

Chaplin was now a multiple creator: scenarist and director as well as performer. He also appeared as a composer. "City Lights" and the subsequent films were furnished with music which he wrote and which was woven into the substance of the pictures. Although the serious element did not always predominate, it made his later pictures more critical of custom and, therefore, controversial. "Modern Times," again silent except for music and a few sound effects, was going to be called "The Masses," and the preposterous episodes do not conceal the fact that it is scarcely what the moviegoer expected; it is a crazy satire on the modern industrial world and, in particular, on mass production. "The Great Dictator," in which Chaplin took advantage of his makeup to portray the real Hitler, used ridicule as ammunition. Playing the part of a bashful Jewish barber, Chaplin spoke for the first time in any of his productions. Some said he spoke too much. The concluding monolog was much criticized—the comedian was reminded that he was a clown and should play with props, not with ideas—but Chaplin contended that he could not help being "a human being who wants to see this country a real democracy, free from the infernal regimentation which is crawling over the rest of the world."

During the next years Chaplin aired his political opinions and created almost as much stir and as many antagonisms because of his principles as he had because of his sexual entanglements. He called "prematurely" for the defeat of fascism and the establishment of a second front in 1942; he supported Henry Wallace in what was considered a dangerously leftist position; he advocated an understanding with Russia. When he was accused of being a Communist or a "fellow traveler," he answered, "I am not a Communist; I am a peacemonger." When he was upbraided for not becoming a citizen of the country in which he had made a fortune and had been living for two decades, he retorted, "I am an inter-

nationalist, not a nationalist. That is why I do not take out citizenship anywhere."

That he did not attempt to conciliate his assailants was obvious
when he produced "Monsieur Verdoux." In the bitterest of all his
pictures, Chaplin forsook the little tramp and appeared as a clever
and conniving bank clerk who had decided that in order to live
comfortably he must make himself wealthy. He needs money "to
support home and family" and gets it by marrying well-to-do
women and murdering them. (Chaplin discarded the original punning title, "Lady Killer.") Chaplin presented "Monsieur Verdoux"
as a wicked parable of Big Business. The central figure expressed,
said Chaplin, "the feeling of the times we live in. Out of catastrophe
come people like him. He typifies the psychological disease of depression." The method, murder, is morbid; the treatment is incongruously but, granting its premise, logically comic. James Agee
called the picture "a landmark not only in Chaplin's long career but
in the progress of the American screen." Most of the critics disagreed. They found it too somber, too symbolic, and, too often, in
reprehensibly bad taste. "Monsieur Verdoux" was picketed by the
Catholic War Veterans; many motion picture houses refused to
show it. Although it received many awards in Europe, it was
a financial catastrophe, his first failure. It was believed that Chaplin was finished.

Instead of retiring, the man whom George Bernard Shaw called
"the only genius developed by the motion pictures" came back
with fresh energy. He emerged in an entirely new role. At sixty-
three he produced "Limelight," for which, in addition to his usual
directing, writing, and scoring, he devised a ballet. In a semi-autobiographical role, he cast himself as a broken-down but once famous
music hall comic who has lost his self-confidence as well as his audiences. "It is in every sense a summing up," wrote Arthur Knight in
The Saturday Review, "an epitomizing of the comedian's fundamental philosophies and attitudes about life, about love, about audiences, about comedy . . . An overwhelming emotional experience, it is concerned far less with the play of emotions than with
the play of ideas." "It is a kind of cinematic poem about humanity,"
said Otis L. Guernsey in the *New York Herald Tribune,* "and if it
does not scan mathematically, it touches the heart with dramatic
images of longing." Other critics did not subscribe to such enthusiastic summaries. Chaplin was accused of verbosity, of egocentrism,
of old-fashioned techniques as well as old-fashioned sentiment. But

only a few gainsaid his ability to portray a man—or mankind—hounded by his frailties and harried by time, but who refuses to accept defeat.

"Limelight" exposed what had been growing increasingly apparent: the difference between the Charlie everyone loved and the Chaplin of whom people were suspicious. Chaplin had previously raised questions about the individual threatened in a regimented society, but now he was advertising himself as a serious thinker and, worse, people were beginning to listen. The funnyman, said his adversaries, was suffering from delusions of intelligence. At about the time "Limelight" opened, Chaplin took himself and his family abroad for a trip. While he was on shipboard, the Attorney General of the United States issued the statement that the comedian would not be permitted to re-enter this country without a hearing which would investigate his political and moral history. The action aroused an international storm of comment. On April 17, 1953, Chaplin announced from Switzerland that he had reluctantly decided to give up residence in the United States because of the campaign of official vilification against him. Reporting this over the airwaves, the news analyst Elmer Davis commented: "We need no longer fear the overthrow of the country by an actor who lived here forty years without accomplishing it. When all else about Attorney General McGranery is forgotten, he will be remembered as the man who kept out of America one of the greatest artists of our day."

Whatever the verdict of history may be, Chaplin will occupy a unique place in its pages. He will go down as a daring originator in a new medium, a political cause célèbre, and the object of more love and hate than has been expended upon any except such figures as Churchill, Roosevelt, and Hitler. In *The Great God Pan* Robert Payne traces Chaplin's descent from the goat-footed demi-god through Deburau, Grimaldi, and the great clowns of the past to his position as the greatest jester of his day, "half god, half man, and always vagabond, brother to St. Francis and the moon." Pan, too, had been much assailed—he was anathema not only to the Puritans —but, like his mythical progenitor, Chaplin will undoubtedly achieve a balanced and not unfavorable reckoning. When his personal maladjustments are forgotten, there will remain his image on the screen, the moving shadow, a living presence, whimsical, willful, and richly communicative, telling unknown, even unborn, multitudes about the love and hopes of hard-pressed humanity.

Adolf Hitler

[1889-1945]

"The gutter had come to power."

ADOLF HITLER was an unschooled Austrian, a derelict of the Vienna slums, who, for a few cataclysmic years, lifted a shattered Germany into a ruthless world power and plunged a sick Europe into almost irremediable chaos. He was born April 20, 1889, in the little town of Braunau, on the frontier between Austria and Bavaria. His father, Alois, was the illegitimate son of a peasant girl, Maria Schicklgruber, and he bore her name until, at thirty, it was legitimized as Hitler. The Hitler family (also known as Hiedler and Hüttler) intermarried to the point of incest and were wanderers and vagrants; but the Pölzls, Hitler's maternal ancestors, founded a stable line of farm laborers. Hitler's father, a petty official, married three times. His first wife was fourteen years his senior; the marriage was childless and, after sixteen years, was dissolved. His second wife was a hotel cook, mother of a son born out of wedlock. She died of tuberculosis a year later, and six months after her death he married his third wife, a second cousin, who was twenty-three years younger than himself. By this marriage there were five children, three of whom died at an early age. Adolf was the third child of the third marriage. The only kindred with whom he kept up any sort of relation was Angela Raubal, his half-sister— the daughter of his father's second marriage—and her daughter Geli, with whom Hitler was to fall tragically in love.

At six when he entered the village school, Adolf Hitler was much like other Austrian country boys except that he was unusually resentful of his father who, nearing sixty, was more like a petulant grandfather than an understanding parent. His education was conventional, but when he was eleven he challenged authority by declaring he would not study to become a civil servant because he had decided to be a painter. At first his father thought he meant a house-painter and expressed his disappointment, but when he realized that Adolf meant to become an artist, he raged violently. He raged in vain.

This was Hitler's first triumph, and he took advantage of it. When he entered a secondary school at Linz he refused to study and was so recalcitrant a pupil that he was not given the customary certificate. "I studied only what gave me pleasure" he wrote later in his autobiography, *Mein Kampf (My Struggle)*. "Anything that did not interest me, I completely sabotaged." In 1903 his father died, and two years later Hitler, at sixteen, left school for good. The final report shows that his grades were barely adequate; though his free-hand drawing was "laudable," his writing was "displeasing" and his knowledge of German "unsatisfactory."

Free of parental and scholastic discipline, Hitler loafed around the suburban home in Urfahr, a suburb of Linz, and avoided work of any kind. Uncertain of himself and suspicious of others, he declined to form a friendship or enter into any association which might make him submit himself to another's judgment. He attended a private art school in Munich for a few months, and, at eighteen, with his mother's support, prepared to attend the Academy of Fine Arts in Vienna. Although he submitted several "classic" heads, to his intense chagrin he was not accepted. A year later he tried again, but the rejection was still more crushing; he was not even permitted to take the test. He consoled himself that, like all great artists, he was a misunderstood genius. When his mother died he was not yet twenty; he did not know what to do, but he knew where to go. "With my clothes and linen packed in a valise and with an indomitable resolve in my heart, I left for Vienna. I hoped to forestall fate . . . I was determined to become 'something'—but definitely not a civil servant."

In Vienna he scraped along, keeping himself going with one menial job or another. Later he liked to boast that he earned his daily bread as a painter, but he was unable to draw the human figure or create a single original composition. He copied landscapes and buildings, painted postcard views of Vienna, which he peddled through a chance acquaintance, a tramp from Bohemia, until he quarreled with his partner over a division of proceeds. He picked up occasional pennies shoveling snow, carrying suitcases at a railroad station, beating carpets, and even begging from drunken men. He slept in alleys, on park benches and, when he could afford it, in a rooming house for men who were down and out. He stood in line for a cup of free soup; sometimes he was lucky enough to get a piece of horse sausage with a crust of bread. He was an unattractive figure. His face was soft and round; his complexion was pasty; an untidy hair lock slanted across his forehead. His hair was long and when, at twenty-one, he grew a beard, he was, said one of his room-mates, "an apparition such as rarely occurs among Christians."

It might be supposed that his condition, as well as his associates, would make him sympathetic toward the impoverished masses. On the contrary, he scorned them. "The workers," he said, "are filthy and self-indulgent. They know nothing but their belly, booze, and women." "Everybody who properly estimates the intelligence of the masses," he wrote in *Mein Kampf*, "can see that it is not developed enough to enable them to form general judgments on their own account." He refused to join a trade union and hated the working-class movement; he saw the workers as "an ever-increasing and menacing army of people" which could be manipulated if the method was sufficiently brutal. "Whatever goal man has reached, he has reached by his originality plus his brutality."

It was brutality rather than originality which counted with Hitler. A general distrust was channeled into an unreasoning and unlimited hatred for laborers, liberals, Social Democrats, and, most of all, Jews. Hitler's anti-Semitism was a lurid composite of nightmare fantasies, but it was so deeply embedded in his consciousness that it became a driving fury. He seriously pictured the average Jewish youngster as a sleek, black-haired seducer lying in wait, "for hours on end, satanically glaring and spying on some unsuspicious girl . . . adulterating her blood and removing her from the bosom of her own people . . . The Jews," he went on to say in *Mein Kampf*, "were responsible for bringing Negroes into the Rhineland with the ultimate idea of bastardizing the white race." Contemptuous of those with whom he had to associate, Hitler felt himself a member of the superior race, and he therefore hated all who preached equality. He read enough Marx to reach the conclusion that, since Marx was born a Jew, all Jews were Communists; so to his anti-Semitism he added a lifelong loathing for humanists, internationalists, reformers, intellectuals—all those who question the "aristocratic principle of Nature's inequalities." The Jews, backed up by the intellectuals, denied the supremacy of certain races and thus attempted to shake "the very foundations of human existence."

In Alan Bullock's carefully annotated and analytical *Hitler: A Study in Tyranny*, the author shrewdly comments: "In all the pages which Hitler devotes to the Jews in *Mein Kampf* he does not bring forward a single fact to support his wild assertions . . . To read these pages is to enter the world of the insane, a world peopled by hideous and distorted shadows. The Jew is no longer a human being; he has become a mythical figure, the incarnation of evil, into which Hitler projects all that he hates and fears—and desires. Like all obsessions, the Jew is not a partial but a total explanation. The Jew is everywhere, responsible for everything—the Modernism in art and music Hitler disliked; pornography and prostitution; the anti-national criticism of the Press; the exploitation of the masses by Capitalism, and its reverse, the exploitation of the masses by Socialism; not least for his own failure to get on." Hitler boasted that his discovery of the "Jewish World Conspiracy"—the misapplication of a transparent satire originally directed against Napoleon III— transformed him from a homeless Austrian into a passionate Pan-German, from "a weakly world-citizen into a fanatic, fighting anti-Semite."

The Nationalist idea and the idea of leadership were taking form in Hitler's mind before he was twenty-four. He watched a parade of Viennese workmen at a mass demonstration and felt that "the psyche of the masses is accessible only to what is strong and un-compromising . . . The masses prefer the ruler to the suppliant . . They feel little shame in being terrorized intellectually and are scarcely conscious of the fact that their freedom as human be-ings is abused . . . The art of leadership consists of consolidating the attention of the people against a single adversary and taking care that nothing will split up this attention . . . The leader of genius must have the ability to make different opponents *appear* as if they belonged to one category." Tell big lies, he insisted. Do not qualify or concede a point, no matter how wrong you may be. Do not hesitate or stop for reservations. "The masses are always more easily corrupted in the deeper strata of their emotional natures than consciously, and thus fall victims to the big lie rather than the small lie, since they themselves often tell small lies but would be ashamed to resort to large-scale falsehoods." Vehemence persuades the masses—the louder the statement the more plausible it seems— and passion convinces them. "The masses always respond to com-pelling force . . . Since they have only a poor acquaintance with abstract ideas their reactions lie more in the domain of the feel-ings, where the roots of their positive as well as their negative atti-tudes are implanted. The driving force which has brought about the most tremendous revolutions has never been a body of scientific teaching, but always a devotion which has inspired them, and often a kind of hysteria which urged them into action . . . Whoever wishes to win over the masses must know this key . . . It is not

objectivity, but a determined will, backed up by power where necessary." The greatest demagog in history, Hitler fused the cool cynicism of Machiavelli with the agitating oratory of a mob spellbinder,
plus a compulsive ruthlessness that was all his own.

At twenty-four, a failure with a fanatic longing for power, Hitler
left Vienna. Twenty-four years more were to pass before he returned to the city, entering it as a conqueror. He went to Munich in
the spring of 1913. It has never been established how he supported
himself. He painted and sold a few chromos, but he spent most of
his time shouting on street-corners in his high-pitched, hysterical,
somehow hypnotic voice. He harangued in taverns and extended
his megalomania into an awakening Nordic supremacy, a glorification of the Teutonic mythology, and the rearming of Germany. In
August, 1914, his dream began to be translated into active reality.
The First World War broke out, and Hitler enlisted in the Bavarian
Army.

Hitler's career as a soldier was undistinguished, but he found
his place. He was at home in a world at war. Although he was only
a corporal when the war ended, and his chief duty was the carrying
of dispatches, he was awarded the Iron Cross. The defeat of Germany increased his scorn of those in power. He regarded the men
who signed the peace treaty as traitors; the thought of a German
democratic republic was intolerable to him. He had entered the war
with a contempt for the masses. He left it, wrote Konrad Heiden
in *Der Fuehrer,* "with an equal contempt for the leaders. He felt
that these leaders trembled before what he called the rabble; in
later years he was still scornful of the timidity of this upper class
who handled with kid gloves those they should have trodden under
their feet. That they did not slaughter ten or twelve thousand
socialist agitators by poison gas seemed to him their greatest blunder." He had already taken part in anti-democratic demonstrations; now he determined to use propaganda for his own purposes.
He joined the so-called German National Socialist Workers' Party
(abbreviated as Nazis) whose symbol was the swastika, or crooked
cross. He recruited squads of rowdies and thugs to break up meetings and terrorize opponents. He told an audience that his movement would ruthlessly prevent all gatherings and all lectures that
might "distract" the minds of listeners. He proved that his strong-
arm organization could ride roughshod over the other parties and
earn the fear, if not the respect, of his enemies. "The reputation of
our hall-guard squads stamped us as a political fighting force and

not as a debating society." Adopting the fascist salute, which Mussolini had popularized as a symbol of renascent Roman imperialism, Hitler decided to follow Mussolini's lead and incite the people, lashing them into a frenzy. "We will preach struggle, the inexorable struggle against this parliamentary brood, this whole system which will not cease before either Germany has been totally ruined or else one day a man with an iron skull appears. His boots may be dirty, but he will have a clean conscience and a steel fist; he will put an end to speeches and show the nation some action."

Conditions in Germany quickened the growth of extremist parties. A rapidly accumulating depression caused the worst inflation the country had ever experienced. The mark, which was four to the dollar in 1918, dropped to seventy-five by 1921, to four hundred in 1922, and continued to fall every month thereafter. By the middle of 1923 the mark could be reckoned only in astronomical figures: it stood at 150,000 to the dollar in July, a million in August, and on the first of November a dollar could buy one hundred and thirty thousand million marks. The Nazis benefited hugely from the collapse of the currency, food shortages, unemployment, and the general bankruptcy. Thriving on panic, they offered themselves as the only party with sufficient power to rescue the nation from insolvency, from internal disorders and external demands. They called for outright repudiation of the hated Versailles Treaty and the restoration of a strong Germany, appeals which found widening popular response. Hitler knew how to simplify complicated grievances and resentments; what was more, he knew exactly how to play upon the people's frustrations and turn them into wish-fulfillments, dreams of glory. Thus, irrespective of a brutal secret police, he could count on the support of the misled masses. When the moment seemed ripe for revolution, Hitler persuaded the party to provoke civil war; in November, 1923, the Nazis attempted to take over the Bavarian State government. Partly because it was insufficiently organized, partly because it was premature, the *putsch,* or armed uprising, did not succeed, and Hitler was arrested. He had failed again, but this time he had failed on a large scale.

He was now thirty-five, one of the most talked-of men in Germany. His trial was a political triumph and the nine months' imprisonment made him a martyr. In prison he wrote most of *Mein Kampf,* which became the Nazis' Bible, kept in constant touch with his henchmen, and reorganized the party so that it was tighter and tougher than ever. After he was pardoned, Hitler went to work to solidify his position. For five years he attacked and cajoled, intrigued and intimidated, got rid of lukewarm supporters and all those who might some day stand in his way. He won the support of important industrialists, who were impressed by his anti-labor program, and generals, who thought they could use him to strengthen an enfeebled army. He fused the national discontent with his own unscrupulous opportunism and again set out to capture the government.

This time he knew better than to attempt armed revolt; at forty he had learned that power can be attained more effectively and the State captured more easily by means that looked legal. He set about to win the electorate by a vast campaign of frenzied oratory and brazen trickery. He promised homes to the homeless, employment to the jobless; most of all, he appealed to the downtrodden to rise and declare their superiority with him. The Nazi vote justified his strategy—his opponents on the right and left stubbornly refused to unite against him—and his legalized conspiracy against the State was conclusive. At forty-four, the incompetent painter of postcards, the Viennese guttersnipe, forced the President of the Republic, the aging war hero, Marshal Hindenburg, to appoint him Chancellor. From that day, January 30, 1933, Hitler was, in word and dreadful deed, the overlord of Germany who threatened to rule all Europe and, then, "tomorrow the whole world."

Hitler's progress from Chancellor to Dictator was swift. He gave his associates, chiefly Goering and Goebbels, power to smash the opposition at any cost. Goering was Hitler's most brazen mouthpiece, contact man, and director of the Party's worst intrigues; Goebbels, as head of the so-called Ministry of Public Enlightenment, was chief of propaganda. Hitler's underlings set fire to the Reichstag building and accused the Communists of having committed the crime. This was a pretext for the suspension of all guarantees of private property, personal liberty, the right of free expression, freedom of the press, and privacy of postal communications. "My measures," announced Goering, "will not be crippled by judicial thinking. I do not have to worry about Justice; my mission is to destroy and exterminate." Using an emergency edict as a Law for Removing the Distress of People and Reich, Hitler set aside the Constitution. As Alan Bullock said, "The street gangs had seized control of the resources of a great modern State; the gutter had come to power." On July 14, 1933, a law was enacted which officially constituted the Nazis the only political party in Germany.

After many acts of terrorism, of private murders, party purges and blood-baths, Hitler became the Fuehrer, the leader who was the complete Dictator. As Head of State he took over the army, and compelled the soldiers to take a "holy oath" of allegiance which called for unconditional obedience to Hitler himself. The man who had overcome his country now determined to conquer a continent.

As a first step, Hitler bolted the League of Nations and, although there was much grumbling, less than a month later Great Britain conciliated Germany with new arms concessions. Hitler took full advantage of the international situation. He had a genius for detecting the weaknesses of his enemies and exploiting their differences. He had risen to prominence by capitalizing on the disunity in his own country. Now he made a bid for world power by utilizing the dissensions of the nations allied against him. He played England against France, France against Poland, and Russia against the Western powers; he saw to it that the Disarmament Conference at Geneva ended in failure. He reinstated universal military service in Germany, and increased the devotion of his hand-picked elite by giving them the jobs of Jews whom he drove out of business, education, journalism, and the theater. Having determined what should be permitted and what should be purged, he began by destroying communications—the bulwark against chaos—and burning "subversive" books. At first the Nazis burned books which showed communist sympathies. Then the bonfires grew larger and the books thrown on the piles were those by Jews—Freud, Heine, and "Aryanized" writers suspected of having had a Jewish grandmother. The bookburners did not stop until they had put to the torch the writings of Social Democrats, war veterans tired of war, dissident scientists, and all nonconformists who had dared to be critical of the excesses of power politics.

In 1936 Europe seethed with crises. Fascist Italy defied the League and won a cheap victory by bombing defenseless Ethiopia out of existence. The high-minded League reproved Mussolini but deserted his victim. Civil war raged in Spain, with Italy and Germany on the side of the rebel, General Franco, and Russia on the side of the Loyalists, while Great Britain and America stood aloof. Combining daring with a fine sense of timing, Hitler took his first international gamble and moved troops into the Rhineland. He notified the other powers that Germany no longer considered herself bound by previous treaties. The other parties complained to the League but, as before, nothing was done. In January, 1937, France and Great Britain proposed the withdrawal of all foreign "volunteers" fighting in Spain. Italy and Germany instantly rejected the proposal; moreover, Hitler decided to extend more aid to the Spanish Fascists. He went further: he repudiated the Treaty of Versailles, shrugged off Germany's guilt, and demanded the return of her lost colonies.

Hitler threatened his adversaries with a combination of bluff, showmanship, and totalitarian aggressiveness. 1938 was a year in which he wrecked what remained of the uneasy peace. He embarked on a campaign of "liberation," seeing himself as the Nietzschean superman, "clad in the armor of hardness, free of the meekness and degeneracy of Christianity." He had already announced himself as the instrument of Destiny. "Providence has chosen me to be the greatest liberator of mankind. I free man from the fetters of a filthy and humiliating self-torture—the chimera called conscience—and from the requirements of freedom and personal independence, which only very few are able to endure." The first country which he freed from the burden of free will was Germany. Austria was next. Massing troops on the Bavarian frontier, he forced the resignation of the Austrian Chancellor, Kurt von Schuschnigg, and on March 12, entered Vienna, where he was cheered by carefully rehearsed mobs. He waited only a few months before making new demands. In September he became the militant champion of the "mistreated" Germans in Czechoslovakia. After a humiliating parley, Great Britain and France urged the Czechs to surrender the Sudetenland. On the thirtieth of September Hitler played another trump card, intimidated the allies, and triumphed at Munich when France and Great Britain agreed to the dismemberment of Czechoslovakia, the country they had promised to protect. Prime Minister Chamberlain returned to London, smugly assuring England that at Munich he had achieved "peace in our time."

At fifty Hitler seemed invulnerable. Except for the penetrating and almost hypnotic eyes, there was nothing remarkable about his appearance. His face was a contradiction of the bland and the bizarre. He looked like a badly madeup malevolent clown; the commonplace brow, the thin mouth, and the absurd little mustache reminded one of Charlie Chaplin, if Chaplin's pathetically comic expression could have been distorted by hate. He was a monster who had no bad habits; he did not smoke, drink, or eat meat. He was without love and, for many years, without a love affair of any kind. He was possessively devoted to his young niece, Geli, who was shot to death in his apartment when she was in her early twenties. Although no motive for the act was ever given, the verdict was suicide and, some time later, Hitler consoled himself with Eva Braun, with whom he made a domestic "arrangement." He disliked conversation and could not brook the slightest difference of opinion; he refused to listen to anyone or anything except to Wagner's "Nordic" music dramas and military bands, "the music of victory."

Victories came one after another in his fifties. The year 1939 had barely started when Hitler came out for complete and undisguised force—"force is the first law . . . force alone creates right." He ordered Slovakia to break from its parent government, fomented a small revolution which dismembered the remnants of Czechoslovakia, and entered Memel, which he annexed to the Reich. In April Hitler scrapped the War Renunciation Treaty with Poland and the Naval Limitations Pact with England. He rebuffed Roosevelt's plea for peace and demanded Danzig. In May Germany and Italy signed a military pact, and in August Hitler talked Russia into a pact of mutual non-aggression. This protected Germany from the two-front war which Hitler dreaded, and which he now thought would never take place. Seemingly safe from a threat from the East, Hitler invaded Poland on September 1, annexed Danzig, and wantonly bombed Warsaw and other open cities. Two days later, Great Britain and France entered the conflict and the Second World War began.

Hitler's star was balefully ascendant in 1940. His armies swept over Poland and, for a short time, he paused; it seemed he would maneuver for a negotiated peace with the western allies. But the *Sitzkrieg,* or "Sit-Down War," suddenly changed to the *Blitzkrieg,* the lightning blow. The Nazis stormed through the Netherlands, Belgium, and Luxembourg. Holland and Belgium surrendered in May, and the British army was trapped. Although most of the British forces were rescued from the beach at Dunkirk, all tanks and matériel were lost. On June 13 the Nazis marched into Paris; three days later Marshal Pétain assumed the Premiership of France and asked Hitler for peace terms. In July Germany launched mass air attacks against England, bombing and ruining such nonmilitary objectives as the cathedral town of Coventry. Eager to be in on the kill, Italy declared war on beaten France—Roosevelt called it "a stab in the back"—while Rumania and Hungary joined the Nazis. By the end of the year, the swastika flew over most of Europe, including Norway and Denmark.

1941 marked another triumphal progress for Hitler. He marched on Greece, which England tried to save with too little and too late, and Yugoslavia, which signed with the invader. Thinking that there would be no further resistance in the West, Hitler ceased to worry about a war on two fronts, and, in a surprise move, turned on his Eastern ally. In the first few weeks of the attack on Russia the Nazis broke the Stalin Line, and spread out toward Kiev, Moscow, and Leningrad. Experts predicted that the Russian Army would be decimated within three weeks and that Russia would capitulate within six. The Nazis continued their drive deep into Russia, took Kiev, Orel, and encircled Leningrad. Hitler thereupon declared that Russia was defeated, doomed, and would never rise again.

When Japan bombed Pearl Harbor, forcing America into the all-out struggle, Hitler, contemptuous of the "decadent democracies," declared war on the United States. That Hitler was determined upon a campaign of systematic extermination was evident not only from his scorn of "inferior races" and "do-nothing democrats" but from the magnitude and unspeakable horrors of his concentration camps. What disease, starvation, and torture failed to accomplish was achieved by injections, burnings, and gas chambers. According to the minutes of the Nuremberg Trials, at the outbreak of the war there were nine and a half million European Jews; at the end of the war less than three million were left alive.

Such measures appealed to Hitler as a sadist who was also an inhuman strategist. "Brutality is respected," he shrieked. "The plain man in the street respects nothing but brute strength and ruthlessness. The people need fear. They want someone to frighten them and make them shudderingly submissive . . . They need something that will give them a thrill of horror . . . Terror is the most effective political instrument. I shall not permit myself to be robbed of it simply because a lot of stupid mollycoddles choose to be offended by it." In *The Voice of Destruction* Hermann Rauschning reports Hitler scolding his advisors, stamping his feet, banging his fists on tables, like a spoilt child or an hysterical woman, screaming: "The most horrible warfare is the kindest. The important thing is the sudden shock of an overwhelming fear of death. These so-called atrocities spare me a hundred thousand individual actions against disobedience and discontent. People will think twice before opposing us when they hear what to expect in the camps."

In spite of terrible losses, undeterred by the classic tragedy of

Napoleon, Hitler hurled his men into the engulfing depths of Russia, only to be halted at Stalingrad, where more than one million soldiers stood bloodily engaged. Italian losses had to be made good, too, and Hitler sent the dashing Rommel to Africa. But, after initial successes, Rommel was stopped; the French scuttled their fleet to save it from Nazi seizure; and, in the largest operation in history, America and England landed a huge army in North Africa. The Americans used Sicily as a jumping-off place and swarmed into southern Italy. The tide began to turn against the invincible Fuehrer. In 1943 America plunged spearheads deeper into the soft underbelly of Fortress Europe, and the Red Army drove Hitler's battered soldiers back. Mussolini's regime collapsed, and Italy surrendered unconditionally. When the Nazis seized Rome, Italy turned on her late ally. U. S. Army planes started a round-the-clock bombardment of German industrial centers. In one night Bremen was rocked by five hundred planes; Berlin was attacked more than a hundred times; Hamburg was reduced to a rubble heap.

By 1944 Hitler's generals knew they were beaten, but Hitler was far more concerned about his prestige than about his countrymen. He shouted that peace was impossible and hysterically commanded that every soldier must die rather than retreat. The Russians turned defense into an offensive on all fronts; they retook Odessa, Sevastopol, Minsk, surged over Rumania, and compelled Hungary to plead for an armistice. On June 6 (D-Day) American, British, and Canadian forces landed on the French beaches; two months later other detachments occupied parts of southern France. In September the Americans entered Germany. By February, 1945, they were driving eastward toward Berlin while the Russians were approaching it from the east.

An attempt had been made on Hitler's life by a group of his generals, but Hitler, though wounded, had miraculously escaped death. He refused to concede defeat. Except to issue heartless orders that condemned thousands to die, he withdrew from all activity. He would not visit the bombed cities, and refused either to negotiate for peace or lead his broken army in a last desperate stand. He buried himself in a bomb-proof shelter, surrounded by a few sycophants and his mistress. When, at the end of April, 1945, the Russian flag was raised over the Reichstag and Russian shells exploded over his seemingly secure bunker, Hitler knew the end had come. He prepared a will, which is a masterpiece of vanity and self-deception. Instead of expressing remorse or even sorrow for the colossal calamities he had caused, he still saw himself as the inspired rescuer, the liberator, "actuated solely by love and loyalty." He declared that the six years of war, "in spite of all setbacks, will go down in history as the most glorious and valiant demonstration of a nation's life-purpose." Then, while his driven soldiers were still fighting to defend him, he chose a coward's death and shot himself. His mistress, whom he had married a few hours before, swallowed poison. His incineration in a ring of flaming gasoline was a poor Wagnerian finale, a shabby Dusk of the Gods. The date was April 30, 1945.

The revulsion was swift. The avenging savior, the assuaging hero of the hopeless, shrank to the proportions of a ranting actor in some monstrous melodrama. The cruelties he accomplished and the evils he perpetrated seem as unbelievable today as the terrors of a passing nightmare. But the undissipated forces of hate, bigotry, and brutality which he unloosed have left their hideous mark upon the world.

F. Scott Fitzgerald

[1 8 9 6 - 1 9 4 0]

"I wish I were twenty-two again."

LITERARY HISTORIANS who give every decade the status of an Era have failed, so far, to find the chief representative of the present Age of Anxiety. They seem agreed, however, that the spokesman of the 1920's, the Age of Confusion, was the self-confused and self-doomed voice of his generation, F. Scott Fitzgerald. He was born September 4, 1896, in St. Paul, Minnesota, and was proudly christened Francis Scott Key Fitzgerald in honor of a distant cousin on his mother's side. The family got along in genteel but embarrassing poverty; his father was a defeated mediocrity who lost his job when Scott was ten. Thirty years later, when Fitzgerald was convinced of his own defeat, he remembered that he felt a premonition of disaster even before his father told the news. "That morning he had gone out a comparatively young man, a man full of strength, full of confidence. He came home a broken man. He had lost his essential drive, his immaculateness of purpose. He was a failure the rest of his days." Defeat and disaster (with their compensating images of wealth and arrogance) were twin themes which Fitzgerald elaborated with bitter variations all his life. He was, as he told the author John O'Hara in his late thirties, "half black Irish and half old American stock with the usual exaggerated ancestral pretensions . . . Being born in an atmosphere of crack, wisecrack and countercrack, I developed a two cylinder inferiority complex . . . I spent my youth in alternately crawling in front of kitchen maids and insulting the great."

Poor though the Fitzgeralds were, Scott was his mother's pampered son. An aunt made it possible for him to attend Newman, a fashionable Catholic boarding school in New Jersey, where Fitzgerald made himself unpopular. He was too good looking—his small frame, fine features, fair skin, bright blond hair and brilliant green eyes gave him an almost feminine prettiness. He refused to play football; a born debater, he argued with everyone. Part of this was a natural resentment at finding himself "a poor boy in a rich boy's

691

school." Things did not go much better for him when he entered Princeton at seventeen. He associated himself with the undergraduate literati, chiefly with John Peale Bishop, who remained a lifelong intimate, and Edmund Wilson, Jr., who became his "literary conscience" as well as his literary executor. He did not want to repeat the errors of Newman, so he tried out for football; but he was barely five foot seven and his meager one hundred and thirty-five pounds precluded his making the freshman squad. Turning to his creative talents, he went in for dramatics. He wrote an operetta for the Triangle Club and, although he was never in the performance —his grades became so poor that extra-curricular activities were prohibited—his photographs in costume were circulated by the publicity department as "The Most Beautiful Show Girl in Princeton's New Musical Play."

During a holiday homecoming he fell in love for the first time. He was nineteen. The girl was Ginevra King, sophisticated in her teens, delicately reared, rich and aloof. Arthur Mizener, Fitzgerald's best biographer, characterized her as "the beautiful, magnetic girl who was always effortlessly at ease and surely seemed like this to Fitzgerald, with his imagination, his genteel poverty, and his uncertainty . . . Though she conquered everywhere quite deliberately, she remained essentially untouched, free. This was the girl he was to make the ideal girl of his generation, the wise, even hard-boiled, virgin . . . To the end of his days the thought of Ginevra could bring tears to his eyes, and when, twenty years after they had parted, he saw her again in Hollywood, he very nearly fell in love all over again with that imagined figure." The romance was never consummated; neither did the eminent Princetonian that Fitzgerald dreamed of becoming ever emerge. He lost a year because of continued bad grades and, although he got as far as his senior year, he never graduated and he never became a campus favorite. He failed to get elected to the presidency of the Triangle Club, and he had to face the grim fact that Ginevra would never marry him. He took it hard. "Taking things hard," he confided much later to his Notebooks, "that's the stamp that goes into my books so that people can read it blind like Braille."

The First World War did not stir Fitzgerald to enthusiastic paeans of patriotism—"this insolent war is beginning to irritate me," he wrote Wilson, "but the maudlin sentimentality of most people is still the spear in my side." Nevertheless, he applied for a commission. It came when he was a month past twenty-one, and he went to war, he wrote his mother, "coldbloodedly and purely for social reasons." He was never sent overseas. Instead he spent his time at several camps, and at Fort Leavenworth, where he was admittedly "the world's worst second lieutenant," he completed a novel, *The Romantic Egoist*. Shortly after the manuscript was politely rejected, he learned that Ginevra was going to be married. At about the same time, at a camp dance, he met Zelda Sayre, a vividly attractive and self-assured eighteen-year-old Southern girl, literally the belle of the ball. The two fell immediately in love and made romantically vague plans for the future. In February, 1919, Fitzgerald received his honorable discharge from the Army.

A private citizen again, Fitzgerald determined to make a career as a journalist and marry Zelda as soon as she could come to New York. After seven newspapers turned him down—"I failed," he said, "to impress the office boys"—he got a position writing copy for an advertising firm at ninety dollars a month. Nights he devoted to short stories, and they returned as promptly as he sent them out. Before H. L. Mencken and George Jean Nathan bought his "Babes in the Woods" for the *Smart Set* for thirty dollars, he had collected one hundred and twenty-two unsigned printed rejection slips. His letters to Zelda grew more worried as hers grew more fretful. Fearful of losing her, Fitzgerald spent what little money he had on a trip to Zelda's home in Montgomery, Alabama. But he was unable to get her consent to an early wedding, or any marriage at all, so he came shabbily back to New York—boldly boarding a Pullman but sneaking through to a daycoach—gave up his job, flung himself into a drunken spree which lasted three weeks, and returned to his home in St. Paul. There he set to work on the novel which he had discarded but never abandoned. He took all the best passages from *The Romantic Egoist,* rewrote the episodes but threw away so little that when the book appeared a friend spoke of it as "The Collected Works of F. Scott Fitzgerald." He was just twenty-three when he sent the manuscript, now titled *This Side of Paradise,* to Scribner's. Within two weeks the editor, Maxwell Perkins, accepted it enthusiastically and congratulated the author on its abounding energy and life. Fitzgerald felt that the tide was turning for him; but Zelda was not yet convinced. Perkins promised a substantial sale for the novel upon publication in early spring and, buoyed by the prospect, Fitzgerald refurbished his old stories and created new ones— he wrote nine in the last three months of 1919. All of them began to sell, and at gratifyingly increased rates. *The Saturday Evening Post* paid him $1000 for two stories which, less than a year before, had been rejected by a dozen different magazines.

The success of *This Side of Paradise* (semi-autobiographical, including college petting parties, the advertising agency, the broken romance, and the three-week drinking bout) was spectacular; it surpassed all Fitzgerald's expectations. The reviews were mixed—critics had no trouble pointing out the stylistic affectations, literary borrowings, and downright errors in language—but no one challenged the quick felicities and almost compulsive vitality. Edmund Wilson admitted that the book "commits almost every sin that a novel can possibly commit, except" he added, "the unpardonable sin: it does not fail to live." A hectic rather than a happy gayety vibrated through its pages and gave it the distinction of being both the most romantic and the most disillusioned American novel of college life. Within a few months it became the undergraduate's Bible and its author was the acknowledged leader of the Torrid Twenties, laureate of The Jazz Age and its excessive accent on youth. It was a golden boom-time of stock market speculation and political corruption, the heyday of illicit orgies as the unpopular prohibition laws were lightly violated by well-established organizers and purveyors of bootleg liquor. Fitzgerald was its shining symbol, the Golden Boy with a dazzling future. Zelda was now persuaded to come on to New York and on April 3, 1920, she and Scott were married.

Many years later he soliloquized on the frightening limitations of poverty and the even more terrifying power of wealth. The obsession with money never left him; it usually centered about Zelda. "The man with the jingle of money in his pocket who married the girl a year later would always cherish an abiding distrust, an animosity, toward the leisure class—not the conviction of a revolutionist but the smouldering hatred of a peasant. In the years since then I have never been able to stop wondering where my friends' money came from, nor to stop thinking that at one time a sort of *droit de seigneur* might have been exercised to give one of them my girl."

The young couple, soon to be the parents of an only daughter, Frances, immediately began living up to Fitzgerald's pictures of a dissipated and childishly dissolute period. They exaggerated the exaggerations of his heroes and heroines; they were "flaming youth" personified. Casting themselves as King and Queen of the Carnival, they flung themselves so ridiculously into the parts that they seemed to be purely fictional characters. They startled blasé New Yorkers by shouting scurrilities as they rode on the tops of taxis. They jumped into any available fountain, took off most of their clothes at a revue, and, a pair of Broadway bacchantes, danced the Charleston on dinner tables. They rang fire alarms and when the summoned firemen looked for the blaze, Zelda pointed to her breast and cried "Here!" It was so adolescently gay, so perfect a realization of a blithely irrational dream, that Fitzgerald echoed Alexander's grief after he had conquered the world. Riding down Fifth Avenue one day he felt the crying paradox of triumph and loss: "I bawled," he wrote, "because I had everything I wanted and knew I would never be so happy again."

Meanwhile, the parties had to be paid for and, although Fitzgerald was turning out highly profitable short stories in quantities, he was at twenty-four so deeply in debt that he offered his publisher his next ten books as security for a loan of $1600. Distressed by Zelda's extravagances and temperamentally incapable of budgeting his expenses, Fitzgerald lapsed into a cycle of drinking and driving himself to work, of writing and running away. The Fitzgeralds, like their fictive doubles, drifted from place to place, from one glittering riviera and one endless house party to another, "wherever people played polo and were rich together."

The first reflection of this period, a collection of short stories, *Flappers and Philosophers,* was nothing better than a gifted twenty-five-year-old author's hackwork; but his second novel, *The Beautiful and Damned,* was more searching if less successful than *This Side of Paradise*. It is a love story mutilated by the narcissism of the lovers, a satire spoiled by Fitzgerald's failure to detach himself from his characters, and a study in cynicism ruined by smartness. "Hitherto," wrote Wilson, "he had supposed that the thing to do was to discover a meaning in life; he now set bravely about it to contrive a shattering tragedy that should be, also, 100 per cent meaningless." Yet, concluded Wilson, "although the hero and the heroine are strange creatures without purpose or method, who give themselves up to wild debaucheries and do not, from beginning to end, perform a single serious act, you somehow get the impression that, in spite of their madness, they are the most rational people in the book. Wherever they touch the common life, the institutions of men are made to appear a contemptible farce of the futile and the absurd; the world of finance, the army, and finally the world of business are successively and casually exposed as completely without dignity or point."

Continuing to thumb his nose at dignity, Fitzgerald entertained lavishly on Long Island—in one year he spent thirty-six thousand dollars and was five thousand dollars in debt—wrote a play, *The Vegetable* which, when produced, was discovered to be a thin political satire and an instantaneous failure, and issued his second volume of short stories, *Tales of the Jazz Age,* which, besides slick potboilers, contains three of his most trenchant fables: "The Lees of Happiness," "May Day" and "The Diamond as Big as the Ritz." He was not yet twenty-seven. A few months later, the Fitzgeralds suddenly decided to exchange Long Island for Europe, to get away from "extravagances and clamor and from all the wild extremes among which we had dwelt for five hectic years." In France Zelda had a brief, abortive affair with a young French flyer and, although Scott's vanity was wounded and his inherently puritanic code outraged, he was tight-lipped about the matter. He even fancied that it had matured him. "I've been unhappy," he wrote to his publisher, "but my work hasn't suffered. I am grown at last." They went on to Rome, which Fitzgerald found so unpleasant that he quarreled with everyone and, as the result of a fight with a taxi-driver, was beaten and jailed. Capri seemed a haven, but it was January and they were wretched with grippe and colitis, so they went back to France, to "1000 parties and no work." The drinking was no longer sporadic but almost uninterrupted. "He was," wrote Arthur Mizener, "beginning to be drunk for periods of a week or ten days and to sober up in places like Brussels without any notion of how he had got there or where he had been." In five years he had earned a total of about $115,000, an annual average of $23,000, but he could not live within an income beyond the dream of most writers. "I can't reduce our scale of living," he wrote his publisher in all seriousness. "And I can't stand this financial insecurity." He still looked like a perennially handsome undergraduate and, like an adolescent desperate for attention, indulged in silly pranks, practical jokes which often backfired, and went to such excesses that many of his friends and a few of the hotels closed their doors to him. Trying to outdo her husband Zelda invented new excitements, including an attempted suicide, and Scott grew alternately more daring and depressed. "I wish I were twenty-two again," he wrote. "My work is the only thing that makes me happy—except to be a little tight—and for these two indulgences I pay a big price in mental and physical hangovers." In December, 1927, after being rootless expatriates for three years, the Fitzgeralds returned to America.

Meanwhile, Fitzgerald had published two books: *The Great Gatsby* and *All the Sad Young Men*. The second, which appeared early in 1926, is another chronicle of tinsel pleasures, although it contains "The Rich Boy" and "Winter Dreams," two of Fitzgerald's best short stories; but the first is undoubtedly his masterpiece. Fitzgerald still writes about self-gratifying escapists with their insistence on trivial excitements and basic insincerities, but the emphasis is no longer on casual kisses in countless speakeasies. His preoccupation with the spurious elite has given way to a troubled awareness of a sense of social complexities and a recognition of the role of the "outsider," the worker rather than the waster. Fitzgerald's central ambivalence shows through—a Byronic love of romance and the realist's scorn of the romantic; the poor boy's worship of wealth and the artist's scorn of money—but he begins to take sides. Jay Gatsby, formerly James Gatz, the upstart proletarian and gaudy racketeer, is revealed as a man of peculiar integrity vividly contrasted with the corruption of the aristocrats he envies, a human being worth more than " the rotten bunch" of the unscrupulous, untroubled rich. The critics almost unanimously commended the author's progress, although for different reasons. H. L. Mencken praised *The Great Gatsby* as an exposure of "the florid show of American life—the high carnival of those who have too much money to spend and too much time for the spending of it." T. S. Eliot hailed it as "the first step that American fiction has taken since Henry James."

After his return to the United States Fitzgerald again declared he would settle down in some quiet place and devote himself to the serious works he had in mind. But it was not long before the familiar pattern of restlessness and irresponsibility re-established itself, and it was almost ten years before the next novel got itself written. There was, first of all, a call from Hollywood which, with its promised pot of gold, he could not refuse. Once more there began the crazy round of parties and practical jokes. But Fitzgerald was no longer the precocious adolescent; he was thirty, and what used to be an amusing bacchanalian rout, became an embarrassing routine. A motion picture story featuring Constance Talmadge as a Jazz Age flapper was finally rejected and the Fizgeralds came back East where they bought an old mansion near Wilmington, Delaware, and literally put their house in order. Scott had begun a new novel abroad and expected to complete it in a few months. But the house was too big, Fitzgerald quarreled with Zelda, was rude to the neighbors, and the work bogged down. In less than a year they left the place, and the summer of 1928 saw them in Paris again. Zelda had determined on a career of her own and, although she had shown no more skill as a dancer than most young women, she determined without previous training—at the age of twenty-eight—to be a professional ballet dancer. Fitzgerald had made close to $30,000 the preceding year, but he was insolvent again. For the next two years he alternated between Europe and America, while Zelda practiced her *entrechats* and *jetés,* and he worked morosely at the stubbornly resisting material of his book. Unable to control his irritation with her as well as himself, he gave way to alternate fits of depression and belligerence; suffering made him insufferable. When it was apparent that she would never succeed as a dancer, Zelda began to go to pieces. In April, 1930, she collapsed. Fitzgerald brought her for psychiatric treatment to Switzerland, where the diagnosticians agreed she was schizophrenic. For the rest of his life Fitzgerald was to take care of a pathetic broken woman who, though sometimes well enough to be released from sanatoria and rest homes, never completely recovered and yet, by the paradox of her sickness, never had her intelligence destroyed. In 1932 he placed her in a hospital in Baltimore. Zelda spent her last years in an institution and died when a fire burned the place down.

In 1932, Scott was struggling to free himself from alcohol, but he now had more excuses for drinking. He fought with old friends and, in attacks of depressive negation, resigned himself to a friendless world. Speaking of Hemingway, he once said, "Ernest talks with the accent of success. I talk with the authority of failure." Somehow he managed to turn out nine short stories in two years, but he no longer could command high prices. Royalties on his books were practically nonexistent. When *Tender Is the Night* was published in 1934 it sold only a few thousand copies. The reviews were not only uncomplimentary but brutal; readers had tired of the depiction of a frivolous and sterile society and were turning to a future which would be more hopeful than Fitzgerald's past with "all Gods dead, all faith in man shaken." He exploited to the full, wrote C. Hartley Grattan, "the feverish beauty of a class in decay, the polished charm of a decadence that is not yet self-conscious." But Eliot had preceded him in charting the combined languors and horrors of *The Waste Land,* and the depressed readers of the Threadbare Thirties were looking toward comforting utopias rather than the arid earth which Fitzgerald still insisted on exploring. The story of a psychiatrist-husband and a psychoneurotic wife who ruin each other, it is, wrote Maxwell Geismar in *The Last of the Provincials,* "a novel of lost causes, or lost cures, as it represents Fitzgerald's most precipitous descent into the abyss, and fulfills the pattern of disaster which has been the core of his work." There are heart-breaking and mind-disturbing scenes in *Tender Is the Night,* but anxiety and exhaustion—Fitzgerald called it "emotional bankruptcy"—show through everywhere.

At thirty-eight he began a complete departure from anything he had ever attempted; it was to be a historical romance placed in the ninth century and called *The Count of Darkness.* Four instalments were written and published before he abandoned the work. At thirty-nine he made a selection of his uncollected short stories and grimly entitled it *Taps at Reveille.* With the exception of two stories ("Babylon Revisited" and "Crazy Sunday") there is a distinct deterioration in quality as well as impoverishment of feeling. The reviews ranged from the patronizing to the harsh. "It used to seem awful to Mr. Fitzgerald that youth should have to become manhood," wrote T. S. Matthews in *The New Republic.* "Now it seems even more awful that it can't."

Nearing forty Fitzgerald was convinced of rapidly approaching dissolution. He sensed breakdown even before he analyzed it in *The Crack-Up;* "an over-extension of the flank, a burning of the candle at both ends; a call upon physical resources that I did not command . . . a feeling that I was standing at twilight on a deserted range, with an empty rifle in my hands and the targets down. No problem set—simply a silence with only the sound of my own breathing . . . the disintegration of personality." For the first time since he had begun, several of his stories were returned. With masochistic fury he published a series of self-flagellating fragments of autobiography. For temporary security, if not for salvation, he turned once more to Hollywood.

Fitzgerald was a few months less than forty-one and forty thousand dollars in debt when he went to Los Angeles to repair his fortunes. Excited at having another chance of conquering a new world or, at least, a new medium, he remained sober for a while. But he could not escape the pattern of his past. He drank unsteadily and worked doggedly at adaptations of other men's creations, but his treatments roused no enthusiasm. He was especially wounded when the only script of which he was proud was rewritten by a Hollywood hack because Fitzgerald's dialog was not sufficiently "entertaining."

His reputation faded; the public was no longer aware of him. When Budd Schulberg, then a young script-writer, was told he was to collaborate with him, he exclaimed, "Scott Fitzgerald! I thought he was dead!" Fitzgerald's agent refused to advance money on stories that the exhausted author had not written and probably would never write. There seemed to be no more jobs for him in Hollywood; the drinking grew worse, and the abused body ached in protest. "I am tired of being old and sick," he complained—old at forty-three! At the same time he made hundreds of notes toward a novel in which the background was Hollywood the fabulous, the shopgirls' Eldorado and the false dream factory of America.

The first heart attack came in November, 1940. It frightened him into sobriety and renewed attention to the Hollywood novel, *The Last Tycoon,* which, though unfinished, revises and practically reverses Fitzgerald's early standard of values. He was resolved to make it his largest and most penetrating work; "I want to write scenes that are frightening and inimitable." A month later the heart struck again, this time fatally. When he died, December 21, 1940, he was three months more than forty-four years old.

Never were a man's life and work so intertwined as Fitzgerald's. It is hard to define where the writer ends and the legendary figure begins, impossible to separate the harassed creator from his unhappy characters. The man and his fictional figures share the dreams of immaturity, the anxieties of success and the agonies of failure, with equal intensity. In an *Esquire* piece entitled "Pasting It Together," written just before he went to Hollywood as literally a last resort, Fitzgerald cried out: "I only wanted absolute quiet to think out why I had developed a sad attitude toward sadness, a melancholy attitude toward melancholy, and a tragic attitude toward tragedy—why I had become identified with the objects of my horror and compassion."

At the time of his death all his volumes were out of print. Five years later, he was suddenly rediscovered. The Fitzgerald revival was heralded by the publication of *The Crack-Up,* edited by Edmund Wilson, a selection of intimate confessions, essays, notes, oddments, and a set of tender, irritating, and vividly revealing letters to his daughter. This was accompanied by *The Portable F. Scott Fitzgerald,* an omnibus gathering edited by Dorothy Parker. It was followed in 1950 by *F. Scott Fitzgerald: The Man and His Work,* a collection of appraisals and reappraisals edited by Alfred Kazin; Budd Schulberg's *The Disenchanted,* a lacerating novel manifestly based on Fitzgerald's last phase with flashbacks of his rise and fall; and Arthur Mizener's scrupulous and brilliant biography, *This Side of Paradise*. By 1953 it was no longer doubted that, in spite of his self-divisions, petty mischiefs and major maladjustments, Fitzgerald had written not, as some critics charged, with tongue in cheek but with his mind frantically on his bankbook. Although he died without accomplishing what might have been his best work, he delineated an enervated civilization in strokes that are incontestably clean and scenes that are unforgettable. The best of his books, like *The Great Gatsby*, will survive as documents of a personal crisis whose implications are universal. Unable to dominate the society he both idolized and despised, Fitzgerald was also unable, even unwilling, to destroy it. Although he finally scorned the worship of the bitch goddess, Success, he turned against it too late, and his tragedy was neither the tragedy of noble defeat nor of proud failure, but the casualty of irresolute and unresisting compromise.

William Faulkner

[1897-]

*"His work celebrates the dark grandeur of
destruction."*

L IKE T. S. Eliot, William Faulkner devoted himself, consciously
and unconsciously, to a world defeated by its excesses,
doomed by its sense of guilt, and destroyed by its pride and
pretensions, a decaying world waiting and even longing for death.
Like Eliot, he was awarded the Nobel Prize as the author of some
of the most powerful, if pessimistic, literature of his day. Unlike
Eliot, Faulkner remained close to the arid soil that had bred him;
he elected to cultivate his own Waste Land, the Southland, and
never thought of repudiating his cultural or political citizenship.

He was born September 25, 1897, the oldest of four brothers, in
New Albany, Mississippi. When he was only a few years old, his
father was shot in "an affair of honor," his grandfather became
involved in the shooting and, although no one was killed, his
mother decided to move the family to the nearby university town
of Oxford. There had been a history of shooting in the family.
William's great-grandfather, William Cuthbert Faulkner, had led a
wildly fictional life. He had run away from home at fourteen, enlisted as a private in the Mexican War, had come back a captain,
studied law, married his childhood sweetheart, raised a volunteer
regiment at the outbreak of the Civil War, and, at the end of the
war, built up a large legal practice. Famous at forty, he became a
legendary figure when, in partnership with a banker, he built a
railroad, turned into an author in his fifties with a best-seller, *The
White Rose of Memphis,* wrote *The Little Brick Church* as a reply
to *Uncle Tom's Cabin,* and was elected to the state legislature. His
multiple career ended when he quarreled with his partner, who,
after having been bought out, hated, waylaid, and killed him.
Known as The Colonel, he was William's boyhood idol; as Colonel
Sartoris he vivifies the pages of many Faulkner novels and short
stories.

The family had come down greatly since the days of The Colonel. William's father was a conductor on the family railroad at the

time of his son's birth, and the growing boy bemused himself with dreams of a colorful past as an escape from the commonplace present. He could not endure the classroom and never graduated from high school. His reading, which was undirected and uncorrelated, ran to extremes, from the pure romanticism of Keats to the turbid realism of Flaubert. He wrote poetry in his teens, but when the First World War threatened, he determined to be an aviator. He refused to become a U. S. Army flyer because he did not want to be bossed by "Yankees," and at twenty enlisted in the British Air Force. He was not, as legend has it, wounded in action in France; on the contrary, he was still in flight training when the war ended, and the only wound he received was the result of an Armistice Day celebration.

After returning to Oxford he supported himself by doing odd jobs of house painting, roof repairing, and carpentry. Meanwhile he stimulated his imagination with countless anecdotes and stories picked up from farmers and sharecroppers and Negroes and the local gossips. He gave himself one more try at formal education: attended the University of Mississippi at Oxford; but, failing in mathematics and English, he left without finishing the second year. Stark Young, a Mississippi author who had taught at the university, suggested that there might be something for Faulkner in New York, so he went north. He found nothing. He stayed with Young, washed dishes in a Greek restaurant for his food, and earned a few dollars a week by selling books in a department store—the nearest he came to a job in the publishing world. After six months of near-starvation, Faulkner learned that he could have a postmastership in his home town and returned to Oxford. Those who remember assert he was the world's worst postmaster. He never was on time; he was whimsical about sorting mail, keeping accounts, filing records; he opened and closed the office without regard to the convenience of the customers. When complaints reached the authorities, he resigned. He said he was glad that he would no longer "have to be at the beck and call of anyone who happens to have two cents."

He was twenty-seven when, after two years of farming, fishing, and hunting, the idea of being an expatriate appealed to him and he made up his mind to go to Europe. He got as far as New Orleans. There he met Sherwood Anderson, whose short stories he liked, associated for the first time with writers, and accepted the literati of New Orleans' French Quarter as a substitute for the Parisian bohemians of the Left Bank. He contributed to the group's advance guard magazine, *The Double Dealer,* as well as to the city's leading paper, and wrote two novels: *Mosquitoes,* a rather thin satire on society, and *Soldier's Pay,* a "hardboiled" report of a disfigured veteran's return, which *The New York Times* characterized as "an objective recital of irreconcilable factors of civilization meeting in an impasse of futility and irony . . . a novel without heroics or heroes." Neither novel was a success and, although Faulkner sold a few short stories, he had little hope of earning a living as a writer.

It was at this time that Faulkner began to create the large design into which practically all the subsequent work was to fit. With *Sartoris* and *The Sound and the Fury* he staked out, charted, and populated his own unique domain. He invented an imaginary county, "Yoknapatawpha," the original Indian name of the Yocona River, a region of once flourishing plantations and present desuetude, of mansions despoiled and estates ruined, of eroded cotton fields, rundown farms, and corrupted towns, of swamps and forests and the edge of what was still the wilderness in the poorest state of the Union. *The Sound and the Fury,* which is now generally considered Faulkner's greatest achievement, disturbed critics for several reasons. They were startled by its manner as much as its material, which was the depiction of a decadent, incestuous pseudo-aristocracy—the title reminded those who disliked the book of the rest of the Shakespearean quotation about life being a tale told by an idiot, signifying nothing. They were misled not only by the title but by Faulkner's method. *The Sound and the Fury* was the first of his books to break up the orderly routine of narration. Faulkner disrupted the usual sequence of events; he juggled the sections to show the violent disintegration of a family, sharpened characterization by the use of interior monologs in the Joycean "stream of consciousness," and made time seem as wayward as the mind of the idiot Benjy Compson, the symbol of ultimate ruin. Many found the manner purposely vague; it was remarked that Faulkner should be read backward, that his books could not really be read until they had been reread. At the same time, even the most puzzled critics acknowledged the virtuosity of his style, the plunging power of his writing, and the force of its impact. More than any of the preceding books, and more than most of the subsequent volumes, *The Sound and the Fury* dredged deep into the subconscious. Moreover, it presented a marvelous and unprecedented amalgam of innocence and depravity, of sick delusions, maturity's yearning for the security of early family affection, and childhood's memories lost in hopeless longings or, as in the case of Benjy, twisted into madness.

Although he was by no means popular, people were beginning to talk about Faulkner, to discuss his dark magic and the macabre beauty of his haunted borderlands. Faulkner never explained how the land came to be haunted. But death and degradation are implicit in everything he wrote; it is not too farfetched to say that his work celebrates the dark grandeur of destruction. The land and the landowners are accursed, he indicates, by having profited from slavery, by yielding to the money-ridden evils of reconstruction, and by coddling the remnants of an aristocracy which has lost courage and honor. A persistent rebel, unreconstructed and unassimilable, he was unsparing in the portrayal of its defeat. "This whole land, the whole South, is cursed," young McCaslin cries in "The Bear," one of the longest and most difficult of Faulkner's stories. "And all of us who derive from it, whom it ever suckled, white and black both, lie under the curse."

At thirty-two, in the same year in which *The Sound and the Fury* was published, Faulkner married Estelle Oldham Franklin, who had two children by a previous marriage. A child born to the pair failed to survive infancy, but a daughter, Jill, grew to be one of the very few things of which he was proud. Faulkner might well have been proud of his next novel, *As I Lay Dying,* composed while he was shoveling coal in the power plant of the university—he said he wrote most of it on the back of a wheelbarrow. The book is about the poor-white Bundrens, and particularly about the death of Addie Bundren, a hill-country woman, and her family's difficulties in getting her to the cemetery in Jefferson, while her flesh becomes putrescent, the vultures gather, a son goes mad, and her husband plans to get a new set of false teeth and marry a woman who had loaned him the shovels with which he digs his dead wife's grave. The subject may be repulsive, but Faulkner gives the sordid story such understanding, such penetrative force and raw poetry that it becomes a backwoods epic. Near the end, one of the characters expresses all human futility in what sounds like Faulkner's own credo: "How do our lives ravel into the no-wind, no-sound, the weary gestures wearily recapitulant, echoes of old compulsions with no-hand on no-strings; in sunset we fall into furious attitudes, dead gestures of dolls." Such an utterance furnishes a prose counterpoint to Eliot's "The Hollow Men," with its drab vista and sense of cosmic exhaustion:

> Shape without form, shade without color,
> Paralyzed force, gesture without motion . . .
> Remember us—if at all—not as lost
> Violent souls, but only
> As the hollow men,
> The stuffed men.

Nearing his mid-thirties, Faulkner determined to be a successful as well as a serious novelist; he wrote *Sanctuary*, "a cheap thing," he said, "deliberately conceived to make money." The plot is shocking to the point of being unbelievable; the scenes are unremittingly violent; the action, much of which takes place in a brothel, is brutally realistic. The chief characters are an impotent degenerate, who is also a killer, and a college girl who, after being grotesquely raped, becomes a nymphomaniac. In spite of its theme, there are passages which hold and shake the imagination, moments when the incredible suddenly becomes plausible and the nightmare turns into reality. A few commentators considered *Sanctuary* a transplanted myth about the blind Furies; others saw it as a symbol of the rape and degeneration of Faulkner's Southland. Most readers, however, did not pause to seek out allegorical implications; they read it for its orgies of sex and sensationalism. The censors stormed, and the public talked about it until it was a great commercial success. Hollywood rose to the bait, hired Faulkner to write a screen treatment (it appeared in a watered-down version as *The Story of Temple Drake*), and engaged him to work on other stories to be filmed. Whenever he wanted money he journeyed to Hollywood; he ceased to be concerned about the necessity of earning a living. As a script-writer he was almost as casual as he had been when a postmaster. It is said that he received permission to write one of his assignments at home instead of at the studio, and when the director was unable to reach him at the place he had rented, he learned that Faulkner had meant his request literally and had gone home to Mississippi.

In his desire to create a complete if imaginary world, Faulkner continued to amplify the Yoknapatawpha saga. He documented it in some of the wildest, catastrophic, and most agonized novels ever written in America. *Light in August*, one of Faulkner's most probing examinations of a rotting civilization, is a double narrative. It is the tale of a pregnant mountain girl searching on foot for the father of her unborn child, and it is also the polluted romance of a sex-driven old maid, who devotes herself to helping the Negroes, and the resentful but submissive young mulatto whom she destroys and who, in turn, destroys her. *Absalom! Absalom!* is a disrupted and unusually difficult melodrama of ruthless ambition, seduction, implied incest, and a doomed dynasty. Although the story is told tangentially by different characters, and the structure emerges in backward-reaching digressions, it reveals Faulkner's essential dichotomy: his feelings for human dignity and his peculiar aversion to the Negro and the Woman. *The Unvanquished* concerns another favorite Faulknerian theme: the family. In a series of short stories, originally written for widely circulated periodicals, Faulkner's swaggering great-grandfather is metamorphosed into a leading member of the Sartoris clan. In *The Wild Palms* two totally unrelated stories are printed in alternating chapters for no apparent reason except possibly to provoke the reader into greater awareness by confusion and contrast. The second story (published separately as "Old Man") seems to be subsidiary, but it is actually the more important half: the struggle of a convict who gives up freedom to get back into prison where he will not be troubled by women. *The Hamlet* is an ugly farce, the grimy Odyssey of a ravening family of insatiable invaders who victimize a community under the leadership of the cunning and unspeakable Flem Snopes— "Flem Snopes don't even tell himself what he's up to . . . not even if he was laying in bed with himself in the dark." *Requiem for a Nun* is the sorry aftermath of *Sanctuary*, embarrassing because of its pronounced exhibit of old prejudices and its implausible plot. *Intruder in the Dust* mingles bravery with brutality. The interrupting monologs of which Faulkner is fond and the quiet intensity of which he is master, unfold the tale of a Negro, wrongfully accused of murder, and the two boys, one white and one colored, who, with the assistance of an old spinster, save him from being lynched. Other narratives, such as the famous, much-anthologized horror story, "A Rose for Emily," "Ad Astra," and "That Evening Sun," extend the Yoknapatawpha series; a number of them were collected in *These Thirteen* and *Dr. Martino and Other Stories*.

They are all, as Malcolm Cowley wrote in his skillfully appraising introduction to *The Portable Faulkner,* "part of the same living pattern. It is this pattern, and not the printed volumes in which part of it is recorded, that is Faulkner's real achievement. Its existence helps to explain one feature of his work: that each novel, each long or short story, seems to reveal more than it states explicitly and to have a subject bigger than itself. All the separate works are like blocks of marble from the same quarry; they show the veins and faults of the mother rock." In *William Faulkner: A Critical Study,* Irving Howe considers the elaborate pattern from another but not too dissimilar point of view. "Despite the virtuosity that goes into most of Faulkner's books," says Howe, "their fundamental source is less the artificer's plan than the chronicler's vision . . . [Faulkner's work] results from submission to rather than control of his materials . . . as if the whole thing, no longer available to public experience, lived fresh and imperious in his mind . . . He has little need to construct, he needs only to call upon what is already waiting for him."

At fifty Faulkner was a national figure, an established writer who eschewed the company of writers and shunned literary gatherings. He did not scorn criticism, but he was noncommittal about the New Critics who made parables out of his novels and found universal myths in every local novelette. A small, wiry man with the tight mouth of a countryman and the quick eye of the gambler, Faulkner denied all preoccupations with art, esthetics, and the form for which he had been praised. "I'm just a farmer," he stated ingenuously, "who sometimes writes stories." It was as a farmer that he learned he had been given the greatest award a writer can receive: he was spreading lime on one of his fields in November, 1949, when his wife brought the news that he had won the Nobel Prize.

Faulkner's speech at the presentation ceremonies in Stockholm was a speech that surprised everyone not only because of its distinction but because of its dignity, modesty, and championship of the virtues Faulkner never seemed to practice. He spoke of "the old universal truths, lacking which any story is ephemeral and doomed . . . Until he (the writer) relearns these things, he will write as though he stood among and watched the end of man . . . I believe that man will not merely endure; he will prevail. He is immortal, not because he alone among creatures has an inexhaustible voice but because he has a soul, a spirit capable of compassion and sacrifice and endurance. The poet's, the writer's, duty is to write about these things. It is his privilege to help man endure by lifting his heart, by reminding him of the courage and honor and hope and pride and compassion and pity and sacrifice which have been the glory of his past."

The Stockholm speech was widely acclaimed; it sounded a note of affirmation and serenity which readers had never heard issuing from Faulkner's deep and gloom-darkened jungle of prose. In an estimate entitled "Faulkner: Sorcerer or Slave" Edith Hamilton commented: "In his speech Mr. Faulkner said that the writer's duty and privilege is to help men endure by lifting their hearts, not only by reminding them of what is good and great and enduring, but also by being a pillar of strength to them in their struggle toward it. In his books he reminds us only of the futility of all things human and the certain defeat of all men's struggles. When he accepted the prize in those words of singular nobility and profound truth, he was pronouncing the condemnation of the work which had won him the prize." At the same time, Miss Hamilton declared that Faulkner's special gift as a writer—"and it is a great gift—is that he can make anything live, no matter how ordinary and trivial . . . When he takes in hand what he deals with best— a flood, a fire, a storm—he can carry his reader away with him past all damning points of criticism . . . Wherein his special gift is most brilliantly shown is an experience which the reader feels as if it were his own, independent of the person in the book it is attached to, who was there only to give it a locality. There is no feeling necessarily of sympathy with the character or even of understanding him, but only of being oneself put through that suspense, that terror, that remorse."

The suspense and terror and, in a lesser degree, the remorse penetrate Faulkner's tightly knit chronicle of decay. Although the texture is tough, the quality of the material is uneven. Faulkner's naturalism has been compared to the "diabolism" of Baudelaire and the guilt-suffering drive of Dostoevsky, but there is no hint of the passion for redemption which agitates both the French poet and the Russian novelist. Far from craving the sustenance of religion, Faulkner thrives on revulsion. Sometimes the whole corpus of his work seems a revolt, as though the disillusioned Southerner were answering the artificial prettiness of his great-grandfather's *The White Rose of Memphis* with book after book of fearful and equally artificial ghastliness.

Almost four years after his Nobel Prize acceptance speech, Faulkner published *A Fable*, a departure from the Yoknapatawpha cycle.

He let it be known that he considered it his most ambitious work; even those who found his method of "delayed narration" hard to follow conceded its importance. In it Faulkner expressed the compassion, pity, and hope which he had said were the writer's duty to reveal. The book centers about a modern re-enactment of the Passion and the attempt by a Christlike army corporal to redeem the world. One critic praised the parallel; another compared the book to *War and Peace;* a third said that it contained some of the most powerful scenes Faulkner had ever conceived. But the majority found the book theologically murky, embodying a confused and sometimes self-contradictory sermon, a work which was formidable and baffling. For all his power, it was felt that, in making *A Fable* a set of symbols rather than a novel, Faulkner had overreached himself.

There are those who say that Faulkner is not primarily a novelist but a designer of skillfully interwoven short tales and that, to sustain his long narratives, he is forced to use all sorts of devices which pique the reader and make him fight his way through the resisting novels. They also point to his abnormal contempt for sex, his almost pathological condemnation of women and, except for family ties, his failure to acknowledge love. Critics have chided him for an overweening reliance on rhetoric and an inability to control the flood of words which, once spent, leaves him and the reader limp and gasping for breath—there is a single sentence in "The Bear" which runs on for more than two hundred lines. Others object that Faulkner is a strictly regional author, a victim of his prejudices, at home only in a topographically limited range and that, even here, his disclosures of the morbid, the twisted, and the horrible occur so often that they lose their force and evoke passing terror rather than essential tragedy.

At his best, however, Faulkner is not surpassed by any writer of the period. He combines the novel of direct action with the novel of analysis. To the horrors, grotesqueries, and spectral evils of Poe, Faulkner adds a Melville-like intensity of purpose; even his rapists, idiots, murderers, perverts, violating every concept of decent humanity, are hideously but recognizably human. The reader may be an unwilling observer of the Elizabethan deaths with which Faulkner strews his stage. He may shrink from the suicides, the fratricides, connivances and countless treacheries; he may even wish to persuade himself that these are fabricated terrors. But if he is fearful he is fascinated; and finally he is convinced that these violences, these outrages, are not only happening, but that in an atmosphere of defeat and a time of obsessive fear, they have to happen. Threatened with disaster and, at times, dementia, Faulkner's world is scarcely alluring; but it is unmistakably a world, and it is unquestionably his own.

George Gershwin

[1 8 9 8 - 1 9 3 7]

"He lived in a kind of fitful radiance."

BEFORE his tragically premature death at the age of thirty-eight, George Gershwin had not only changed the pattern of popular music in America but had quickened the pulse of music throughout the western world. Gershwin was born in Brooklyn, New York, September 26, 1898, the second son of Morris and Rose Bruskin Gershwin. "Most of our early boyhood," wrote his older brother Ira, "was spent on the lower East Side of Manhattan where my father engaged in various activities: restaurants, Russian and Turkish baths, bakeries, a cigar store and pool parlor on the 42nd Street side of what is now Grand Central Station, bookmaking at the Brighton Beach Race Track for three exciting but disastrous weeks. We were always moving. When my father sold a business and started another, we would inevitably move to the new neighborhood. George and I once counted over twenty-five different flats and apartments we remembered having lived in during those days. It was when we were living on Second Avenue that my mother added a piano to our home. George was about twelve at this time."

The piano was intended for Ira, but (as depicted with reasonable accuracy in a film-musical, *Rhapsody in Blue*) as soon as the piano was installed, George sat down and played a "piece" complete with left-hand harmonies. A few months later he was learning about Chopin and Debussy from Charles Hambitzer, who taught him the rudiments of piano technique, and playing Sousa marches at the morning assembly of the High School of Commerce. At fifteen he became a "professional" employed by a music publishing firm at fifteen dollars a week. He accompanied the "song pluggers," toured the vaudeville houses to report on acts, and tried to write popular tunes. Three years later he succeeded in getting a song published. At twenty-one he composed the entire score for a musical comedy (*La La Lucille*), and in the same year (1919) became a big name in Tin Pan Alley when the singer Al Jolson rocked the country with "Swanee."

"Swanee" was a prototype of the kind of song which was to

revolutionize the stereotyped and sentimentalized musical comedies of the time. It changed the lethargic imitations of old-fashioned Viennese operettas to swift-paced and exciting entertainments. "Swanee" was full of surprises; its nostalgia was spiced with humor; words and music went playfully, almost punningly, from suspension to cadence: "D-I-X-I-Even know my mammy's waiting." Most of all, it was American to the core of its syncopated heart.

After this the songs flowed easily and profitably; they cascaded over each other with a gusto and impudent gayety previously unheard in the theater. Gershwin put the country's fidgety feet and nervous high spirits into a dozen scores for Broadway musicals and countless individual songs, such as "I Got Rhythm," "Somebody Loves Me," "Maybe," "Liza," "Our Love Is Here to Stay."

Physically, Gershwin was challenging: a tall, slim personality. His face was dark and lean, his forehead high; the haughty and rather cold profile seemed copied from an ancient Assyrian carving. His smile was quick but half-sardonic, his manner was alternately defensive and defiant. He lived in a kind of fitful radiance, a man who did not exactly distrust people but, for the most part, did not need or understand them. He never married; his piano was wife, mistress, and private confidante. He was happiest at the instrument. There he would remain, indifferent to the fact that there might be other pianists in the room. "You see," explained Gershwin, "when I'm playing everyone is happy, and when anybody else is playing I'm miserable." Although he loved the music of the classical composers, and even liked a few tunes by his contemporaries, he gave no evidence of appreciation when he was at the piano. "An evening with Gershwin," remarked Oscar Levant, his friend and fellow-pianist, "is a Gershwin evening." Once, while improvising on one of his songs, Gershwin said, "I wonder if my music will be played a hundred years from now?" "It will be," replied Levant wryly, "if you are around." His hobby was painting, and to his canvases he brought something of the verve and wit of his music. One self-portrait is a full-length study of the pianist-painter; a long brush in his hand, he seems seriously at work—but he is clad in formal full dress, high hat, white tie, and tails.

A dramatically new career began for Gershwin in his mid-twenties. The band-leader Paul Whiteman had been making efforts to "elevate" dance music. He took the current down-at-heel jazz and "made an honest woman of her" by giving a concert entitled "An Experiment in Modern Music" in Aeolian Hall on Lincoln's Birth-

day, 1924. When Whiteman told the press in January that the
concert would include a new work by George Gershwin, no one
was more startled than Gershwin himself. "Some day, George, you
must write a concert piece for me," Whiteman had once said, and
George had assented with a vague "Some day I will." As soon as
Gershwin saw the announcement in the newspaper, he got to work.
Remembering a tricky theme he had jotted down in a notebook,
he thought of it as an opening. It was a long glissando for clarinet
(at that time considered practically unplayable) and it became
the tense, high-crying phrase which begins the "Rhapsody in Blue."
Gershwin completed the "Rhapsody" in three weeks. The impact
of the piece was tremendous and its success was instantaneous. It
galvanized the usually placid concert-goers and roused followers of
popular tunes to a sudden interest in serious music; its pace and
pungency, as well as its insinuating themes, appealed equally to
"lowbrows" and "highbrows." Everyone talked about it. It became
an American trademark; nothing ever composed in the United
States was so often and so universally performed.

Encouraged to extend himself, Gershwin increased his prodigious
output, alternating between light "commercial" pieces and music
in the larger forms. Whiteman's arranger, Ferde Grofe, had orches-
trated the "Rhapsody"; now Gershwin determined to do his own
orchestrations. He had little time for social diversions and, except
for tennis, none for sports. Instead, he buried himself in studies
with serious musicians, chiefly with Rubin Goldmark and Joseph
Schillinger. The erstwhile tunesmith of Tin Pan Alley was fascinated by Schillinger's mathematical concepts, by strange triads and
tetrads and unknown "pitch scales in relation to chord structures."
He filled pages with erudite notes on his lessons, curious graphs mysteriously headed "Rhythmic Groups Resulting from the Interference of Several Synchronized Periodicities" and "Groups with
the Fractioning Around the Axis of Symmetry."

A year after the "Rhapsody" was performed Gershwin appeared
as soloist in his "Concerto in F," a new work commissioned by
Walter Damrosch for the New York Symphony. Other symphonic
works followed in a sweep of productive vigor: "An American in
Paris"; "Second Rhapsody," which, with graphic appropriateness,
was originally entitled "Rhapsody in Rivets"; "Rhumba," later
called "Cuban Overture," a work which some critics considered
superior to Ravel's insistent "Bolero," but which is now conceded
to be an inferior production. All these vibrated with an unques-

tionably native rhythm and autochthonous strength. The "Rhapsody in Blue" was a mounting adventure in excitement full of the flamboyant youth and pulsing energy of the nation. The jazz-driven "Concerto" widened Gershwin's gamut; the English conductor-composer, Constant Lambert, wrote that it contained the "nerves, repressions, and complexities of the modern world." "An American in Paris" and "Second Rhapsody" were further liberations of the American idiom: the moaning, crooning "blues" set off by the happy bonhomie of walking tunes and percussive punctuation, the nostalgic *Weltschmerz* of escape pitted against the racketing skyscrapers, the sputtering neon-lit cities, the crazy syncopation of the crowded streets.

Meanwhile, abetted by the librettists George S. Kaufman and Morrie Ryskind, Gershwin put his stamp on another and hitherto unexplored field of American culture: musical satire. War, Politics, Big Business, and buncombe in high places were laughingly exposed in *Strike Up the Band, Of Thee I Sing,* (the first musical comedy to be awarded the Pulitzer Prize) and *Let 'Em Eat Cake,* all of them bristling with Ira's gleefully ironic lyrics. Written between 1930 and 1933, the trio established new dimensions in what had formerly been mere "amusements," and sounded a brash inventiveness in music for the theater.

In the fall of 1933 Gershwin began sketches for what was to be his major opus, *Porgy and Bess,* the first truly American music drama. Founded on a novel by DuBose Heyward, the "folk opera" took Gershwin two years to complete; nine months were spent on the orchestration. The longings and fears and rough joys of the story were lifted to crests of unabated vitality. No longer febrile, Gershwin's ingenuity manifested itself equally in the droll tunes, such as "A Woman is a Sometime Thing" and "It Ain't Necessarily So," the mock spirituals, and the fugal background of a crap-game, the contrapuntal play of swishing brooms, the beating of a carpet, the street-cries of crab-vendors, the murmur of men shuffling along to work, as Catfish Row stirred itself awake. The lullaby, "Summertime," and the concerted numbers revealed a maturity of conception and a greater breadth of feeling than the composer had ever attained. In his book, deprecatingly entitled *A Smattering of Ignorance,* Oscar Levant shrewdly pointed out that, despite Gershwin's half-dozen extended works, he never wrote a single score in a strict musical form. "He could never accustom himself to such restraints as sonatas, rondos, or any of the classic molds. The thematic fluency, the easygoing rhythmic freedom of the rhapsody or unrestricted fantasy was his natural genre."

Before he had reached his mid-thirties Gershwin had written nearly thirty musical comedies for stage and screen. In 1936 he and his brother were back in California. He was happily at work on his fourth film (*The Goldwyn Follies*) when the headaches began. At first his friends refused to take the attacks seriously; the pains were dismissed as "psychosomatic," "neurotic protests against Hollywood," "defense mechanisms." When his piano technique suddenly failed him and he collapsed at the studio, Gershwin was rushed to a doctor. Even then he would not believe anything serious was the matter. His condition was diagnosed as a nervous breakdown, but a second collapse made an X-ray imperative. An alarmingly developed growth on the brain was discovered, an emergency operation was performed, but the patient failed to survive. He died in Los Angeles, July 11, 1937. Gershwin was at the height of his creative activity, ready for fresh experiments, when the brain tumor killed him.

Two decades after his death, Gershwin's music was performed more often and was more widely acclaimed than ever. Critics still argued that the longer works were not sufficiently "developed," that the Rhapsody and Concerto consisted of a series of flaring improvisations, disparate if brilliant "epigrams" loosely strung together. But no one questioned Gershwin's genius for the unexpected, for turning what might have been an obvious statement into a sharp sensation and filling every phrase with fresh surprise, with delightful ingenuities and with—what is so rare in music—humor.

Record companies ransacked his old scores for forgotten numbers, and songs that had not been heard in thirty years not only were rediscovered but, with a new generation, attained a new popularity. It was now conceded that, besides creating a vivid musical vocabulary, Gershwin had performed a valuable and unprecedented function. He had broken down the barrier between popular and classical music or, as Irving Kolodin put it, between "formal" and "informal" music.

His ghost acted as international ambassador of good will when, in 1955, a touring company of *Porgy and Bess* captured all Europe and was rapturously hailed in Russia. Gershwin's place may not have been certified, but it was secure. He had pronounced the tone and the tempo of his age; he had given music a new racy speech and, for the first time in history, an American accent.

Ernest Hemingway

[1899-]

*"Half the young writers tried to imitate him
and half tried not to."*

ERNEST HEMINGWAY is the prime paradox of twentieth-century
literature. Spokesman for a "lost generation," he made a religion of irresponsibility; in love with disaster and obsessed
with death, he brought fresh life to American writing. He was
born July 21, 1899, at Oak Park, virtually a suburb of Chicago,
Illinois, and was christened Ernest Miller Hemingway. His father
was a doctor and sportsman, who, when his son was ten years old,
gave him a man-sized gun; his mother was an amateur musician
who hoped the boy would be a 'cellist.

His schooling was spasmodic and short. At fifteen he ran away
from home, returned to finish high school in 1917, and went to
Kansas City to work as a reporter. Before he was eighteen, he left
for France to join an ambulance unit, transferred to the Italian
infantry, was almost fatally wounded—more than two hundred
pieces of shrapnel remained in his legs the rest of his life—was
awarded the Croce de Guerra and the Medaglia d'Argento al
Valore Militare, returned home and married Hadley Richardson
in 1921. He tried journalism again—this time in Toronto—but,
like the warhorse in Job that "smelleth the battle afar off," Hemingway heard "the thunder of the captains and the shouting" in
Asia Minor, and found peace tedious if not intolerable. He went
to the Near East where, as a roving correspondent, he reported the
savageries of the Greco-Turkish war with the fascination of horror
—no reader can ever forget the picture of the retreating Greeks
breaking the forelegs of their mules and leaving them to drown in
shallow pools of water.

He was in his early twenties when he came to Paris and joined
a group of expatriates who had found writing and living in their
native United States exasperating as well as expensive. Gertrude
Stein, Ezra Pound, and Sherwood Anderson were the leaders of the
more determined experimental writers, and the young Hemingway
was drawn to all three, particularly to the first and last. Anderson

showed him the possibilities of a story without a plot and an idiom, clear and passionate, without rhetoric. Gertrude Stein advised him to leave out everything decorative or even descriptive and concentrate on a language in which every word is an act, a deed. "Remarks," she said, "are not literature." He had already learned many devices writing for newspapers. "You told what happened," he wrote many years later in *Death in the Afternoon,* "and, with one trick or another, you communicated the emotion aided by the element of timeliness which gives a certain emotion to any account. . . . But the real thing, the sequence of motion and fact which made the emotion and which would be as valid in a year or ten years or, with luck and if you stated it purely enough, always, was beyond me and I was working very hard to get it."

At this time Hemingway was a strange phenomenon, an athlete among the esthetes. Six feet tall, with a lion's head and a stallion's chest, he came into a room as if he were entering a prize ring. He was, in fact, a boxer who not only practiced but taught boxing; his favorite gesture was a feint to the jaw with, according to Ford Madox Ford, hands like prize hams. At twenty-four, determined to be an author instead of a journalist, he issued his first book. It was published in a small edition by an obscure press and its contents were made plain by the plain title: *Three Stories and Ten Poems.* A year later Hemingway got together a second book, *in our time*—the lower case title suggested either that the author was modest or that capital letters were too conventional. This was a set of epigraphs and post-war impressions which Hemingway liked well enough to incorporate in the volume. Using the old title but putting it in capitals, it was published in New York in 1924 as *In Our Time.* The book marked the emergence of an original, powerful, but immature writer unsure of his art and a little too sure of himself. *In Our Time* looks like a novel; it has chapter headings and an integrating set of characters. Actually it is a collection of short stories interlarded with the vignettes from the preceding book. But a kind of unity is established, for the italicized epigraphs act as commentaries upon the stories. At first glance the two kinds of writing seem to be contrasted. The vignettes belong to a world of violence, a world of war and other kinds of sudden death; the stories, manifestly autobiographical, belong to what seems a world at peace, chiefly reminiscences of the idyllic days when Nick (or Ernest) and his doctor-father went fishing and hunting together and the boy was fumbling through adolescence. But the stories show there is no real peace in the nostalgic world before the wars. Already at twenty-five Hemingway was fascinated by ferocity, not only by terrors and major tragedies, but by the heartlessness of nature and the casual cruelties of everyday. The theme of deception and random malevolence was continued in *The Torrents of Spring*, which was a tribute to and a parody of Sherwood Anderson, but a failure even as burlesque. In *The Sun Also Rises* Hemingway repudiated Anderson, along with Anderson's sexual-social mysticism, and became the idol of "the lost generation," a generation doubly lost after a war in which it could not believe and a peace in which it would not participate.

There were two reasons for Hemingway's sudden eminence: his attitude and his style. Both of these were based on resentment. Hemingway expressed the disillusion of thousands of young people, loss of faith, denial of standards, and bitterness at the frustration of all their hopes. This bitterness was masked in stoicism, but the generation was not sufficiently stoical to establish values of its own. Instead the men and women of a collapsed world—and especially the maladjusted and mutilated bohemians of *The Sun Also Rises* —turned to one sensation after another. Their twitched nerves made a fetish of violence; they "cried for madder music and for stronger wine," orgies of sex without love and, more despairingly, love without sex. Their heroes were bullfighters, hunters, athletes, primitive men whose simple strength seemed an antidote to the weakness of twentieth-century culture. Hemingway was their perfect protagonist. He shared his compatriots' hurts and cynicisms, their furies and frustrations, but he also surpassed them. He was not merely a writer but a fighter, a primitive, a glorifier of physical action. His writing and his being were of a piece. He found a new language, straightforward, simple—suspiciously too simple at times —stripped of all excess ornaments. The tone was dry and flat, but the implications were exciting; the dialogs were as artlessly plastic as conversation, but they were uncannily precise and almost unbearably intense. With this dual realization and rejection—the realization of a bankrupt society and the rejection not only of that society but its approved vocabulary—Hemingway created a vogue and founded a school. He caused a literary revolution whose social repercussions are still being felt. His manner was imitated not only by writers but by people who boasted they never read; his tight understatements started a fashion of hard-boiled fiction; his grim acceptance of accidental pain and irresponsible pleasure was echoed in volumes built on the strange combination of sick brutality and twisted sentimentality. At twenty-seven Hemingway had set the keynote for a new kind of literature. It was said that half the young writers tried to imitate him and the other half tried not to.

Living in Paris, going to the Tyrol for skiing and Spain for the bullfights, Hemingway was also writing some of the best short stories of the time. After his first marriage had ended in divorce in 1927, he married Pauline Pfeiffer, who bore him two sons; he returned to the United States, and published another collection of short stories, *Men Without Women*. Moving to Key West, Hemingway became an expert fisherman, overcompensated for spells of tiredness—his wounds still bothered him—by unremitting work and exhausting play, and, in 1928, finished *A Farewell to Arms,* generally considered his finest novel. *A Farewell to Arms* had been foreshadowed by two pages in *In Our Time.* But the scant plot of "A Very Short Story" is extended into a book-length dichotomy of degrading war and rewarding love, and the short story's sordid end becomes the novel's melancholy but ennobling tragedy. The hero's desertion after the hideous rout at Caporetto—an episode worthy of comparison with the retreat from Moscow in *War and Peace*—his disgust at the filth, lies, and chicanery necessary to keep the war going—"abstract words such as glory, honor, courage, were obscene beside the concrete names of villages, the numbers of roads, the names of villages"—and all the details of inhuman cruelty merge into a chorus of defeat against a counterpoint of doomed love. What some critic has called "the canon of death" assumes form; it becomes a fixed idea in practically all Hemingway's subsequent work. It is the central theme of his next book, *Death in the Afternoon,* a paean to bullfighting as an art, a special and highly stylized form of slaughter. In love with any kind of danger, Hemingway tried to become a bullfighter but, lacking grace as well as instinctive technique, he could not attain the status of an acknowledged matador. Nevertheless, although he remained a "novillero," he managed to add a few broken ribs to his other injuries. Besides chronicling the calculated skill of the bullring and the hysteria surrounding it, *Death in the Afternoon* is punctuated by asides about writing, which are alternately amusing, illuminating, and irritating; for good measure, there is a chorus of scorn for all "world-savers." The theme of destruction is sounded throughout the pages of *Winner Take Nothing* and *Green Hills of Africa,* in which the pleasures of bullfighting are exchanged for the thrills of big-game hunting. Death and dissolution are the joined themes of *To Have and Have Not.*

With *To Have and Have Not,* which takes place in and around Key West, the pattern of death assumed a somewhat different shape. Hemingway was now thirty-nine. The overthrow of the Spanish republic had sent repercussions throughout the world, and Hemingway was naturally anti-fascist. He was not ready to side whole-heartedly with the "world-savers," but his Harry Morgan, a cheated smuggler, represented as a heroic individual against a rotting society, becomes (unexpectedly and without logical motivation) a dying champion of solidarity. Morgan's half-literate mumbling became his author's motto: "No man alone now." The recognition of a pervasive social problem was a new thing for Hemingway, but the attempt to deal with it too tentatively and too late split *To Have and Have Not* into two parts of a broken book.

The death-wish and a faint hope of regeneration were mixed in *The Fifth Column,* a play that reads as easily as Hemingway's narratives. A luckless love—or a love affair—is once more pitted against the insanities of war, although in this struggle the hero is almost persuaded that the killings have a meaning. In 1938 the play introduced a volume entitled *The Fifth Column and the First Forty-Nine Stories.* The book contained some of the most famous writing of the period, stories strong enough to stand continual rereading in the anthologies and tough enough to withstand the squeamish softening of the Hollywood film-makers. Hemingway was still preoccupied with the feel and smell of death, but a greater tension and conviction were communicated by such stories as "The Snows of Kilimanjaro," "The Short Happy Life of Francis Macomber," "The Killers," "Fifty Grand," "The Undefeated"— all of them required reading in countless textbooks—and especially the less dramatic but more searching "Hills Like White Elephants" and "A Clean, Well-Lighted Place," two small but magnificent masterpieces.

At forty-two Hemingway published his largest and, in the opinion of many admirers, his most important work, a novel, *For Whom the Bell Tolls.* It was obvious that Hemingway had been looking for a theme that would reconcile his old concern with death and a new-found affirmation of life. He found it in Spain, in the struggle of the Loyalists against the Fascists. To point the moral, he introduced his account of what he believed to be a blow for human liberty and a sense of sharing, with part of one of John Donne's sermons: "No man is an *Iland,* intire of it selfe; every man is a peece of the *Continent,* a part of the *maine;* if a *Clod* bee washed away by the *Sea, Europe* is the lesse, as well as if a *Promontorie* were, as well as if a *Mannor* of thy friends or of thine owne were: any mans *death* diminishes *me,* because I am involved in *Mankinde;* And therefore never send to know for whom the *bell* tolls; It tolls for *thee."* Hemingway set out to amplify Donne's meditation that the loss of freedom anywhere means the loss of freedom everywhere. The central situation had been sketched in less than three pages in "Old Man at the Bridge," but Hemingway no longer looked at death dispassionately or clinically. Formerly his attitude had been the exact opposite of Keats's "Many a time I have been half in love with easeful death." Hemingway had been in love all the time with everything which made life dangerous, death desperate, and dying meaningless. Now he saw a purpose in both living and dying; he had found a "cause." His portrait of the Spanish War, wrote Alfred Kazin in *On Native Grounds,* "was less a study of the Spanish people than a study of epic courage and compassion. The idealism that had always been so frozen in inversion, so gnawing and self-mocking, had now become an unabashed lyricism that enveloped the love of Robert Jordan and Maria, the strength of Pilar, the courage and devotion of the guerillas, the richness and wit of Spanish speech, in a hymn of fellowship." For the first time Hemingway dealt in positives. He participated in a belief that was more than a hope for humanity. He had discovered brotherhood.

The feeling of fellowship and the joy of sacrifice withered with the defeat of the Loyalists. It vanished completely when, eight years later, Hemingway published *Across the River and Into the Trees.* The book which had been awaited with great expectations turned out to be a nightmare jumble of stereotypes with the American soldier-lover (now grown old and sick but not yet impotent) from *A Farewell to Arms* and the foreign doll-like Maria (now a garrulous juvenile delinquent) from *For Whom the Bell Tolls.* Worse still, the celebrated style degenerated into a rehash of repetitions; the narrative gift was lost in a welter of narcissistic snobberies; and the entire performance led the reader to conclude that Hemingway was parodying himself without humor just as he parodied Sherwood Anderson a quarter of a century before. Even the title was a prelude to dissolution, for it served as a "motto" uttered by a real

dying general (Stonewall Jackson) for a fictional general for whom
death was waiting.

The imminence of death is again the theme of *The Old Man and
the Sea,* published when Hemingway was fifty-four. A short novel,
it is another attempt to show man pitted against fate and, at the
same time, it establishes a sense of fearful kinship between the
forces of survival and the forces of destruction. The Old Man, a
shrunken Captain Ahab, fights a long and lonely duel with a huge
marlin, an ineffectual Moby Dick. The two are strangely paired.
The battle of equally matched strength and intelligence gives the
conflict a tragic dignity rarely attained by any of Hemingway's
contemporaries. "Now," soliloquizes the Old Man, "we are joined
together. And no one to help either one of us . . . Fish, I love
you and respect you very much. You are my brother . . . You
are killing me, fish. But you have a right to. Never have I seen a
greater, or more beautiful, or calmer or more noble thing than you,
brother. Come on and kill me. I do not care who kills who." The
tension does not end with the killing of the fish, for the Old Man's
disastrous return to port builds up a new set of suspenses. It seems
a small plot, a struggle between a fisherman and a fish, and yet
Hemingway communicates a greater excitement and creates a more
powerful symbolism than in all but his most extended works. Hemingway's admirers were not surprised when, in 1953, *The Old Man
and the Sea* won the Pulitzer Prize, but there were murmurs that
the award was some twenty years overdue. In the following year the
Nobel Prize was awarded to Hemingway for his "style-making
mastership," particularly as demonstrated in *The Old Man and the
Sea.* It was rumored that the authorities wanted to honor the writer
before he killed himself.

In January, 1954, a radio-flash announced his death. Hemingway
and his wife had gone to Africa on a safari, and the small plane in
which they had been flying had been sighted, wrecked, in the wild
upper Nile country. Newspapers carried comprehensive obituaries,
and there were editorials entitled "Danger was Hemingway's Forte"
and "Hemingway Braved Death With Joy." Millions who had
never read a Hemingway story were told that death was Hemingway's natural theme as a personal as well as an artistic philosophy,
that he always sought to come close to the ultimate sensation on the
edge of nonexistence. The morning editions were already on the
newsstands when it was learned that Hemingway was not only

alive but had escaped death twice. The landing gear of his plane was smashed, but the Hemingways had crawled from the damaged craft, had been picked up by a motor launch, and had boarded one of the search planes that had been sent out to look for them. When the rescue plane crashed and caught fire, Hemingway butted open the rear door, and he and his wife again escaped alive. Continuing his journey, Hemingway quipped "My luck—she is still running good," and added another characteristic episode to his history.

Everything Hemingway wrote provoked controversy, some of which found its way into *Ernest Hemingway: The Man and His Work,* edited by John K. M. McCaffery. But while the critics lashed each other, especially about the later books, the author lived quietly in Cuba with his fourth wife, Mary Welsh, a former war correspondent, whom he married in 1946. (After a divorce from his second wife in 1940, Hemingway had wed the writer, Martha Gellhorn, and had been divorced from her.) The critics, hot on the track of an elusive quarry, argued among themselves; they could not decide whether Hemingway's power proceeded from an extreme check on his emotions or from the extraordinary compactness of his prose. They tried to explain the magic by which he gave common idioms and familiar phrases a new significance. It remained for an English novelist, Ford Madox Ford, to describe it by indirection. "Hemingway's words," wrote Ford, "strike you, each one, as if they were pebbles fetched fresh from a brook. They live and shine, each in its place." It is an extraordinary sense of the living language that makes Hemingway pit words against each other, words that are casual and brutal, purposely colorless and plain, but, even when most commonplace, charged with excitement because of the author's skill in juxtaposition. Here the style is distinctly the man: hard, clean, close-clipped, persistently masculine; his very adjectives are appropriately, even aggressively, athletic and accurate.

The critics harried Hemingway and roused his spleen. He made petulant rejoinders; the sensitive author struck ridiculous poses and talked like an illiterate baseball player. This was one of Hemingway's more obvious failings. An intuitive as well as a disciplined intelligence, he made it a point to deride intellectuals with inexplicable rancor. He put weaklings and cowards into his books only to condemn them as hollow men without bothering to inquire what made them weak or cowardly or otherwise maimed. Another limitation was Hemingway's failure to create complete or even fairly credible women. Except for a few extremes, like the restless decadent, Lady Brett Ashley, and the earth-wise primitive, Pilar, it is impossible to believe in his heroines, the Marias, Catherines, Dorothys, and Renatas, except as complements to his virile and usually violent heroes. The women are either bright-eyed innocents or hard-drinking sophisticates, but they are all quietly submissive, a boy's dream of feminine response, quick and compliant figures. Nothing difficult—not even the give-and-take of ordinary human relations—is expected of them; there is no evidence of partnership. The real sharing that men require must be with other men, as Hemingway indicated in the title, *Men Without Women.* Chiefly the critics objected to the paucity of Hemingway's ideas and his unshakable symbol of death as the mystical union binding together the murderer and the murdered, bull and matador, man and marlin, in a kind of ritualistic love-death, an ecstasy of doom.

Yet, again and again, Hemingway insists that he is not concerned with death for death's sake; killing, he says "is the feeling of rebellion against death which comes from its administering." The reader is swept on by the swift progress of Hemingway's prose, the choked eloquence and dammed-up emotions, which, like rocks in a river, make the torrent flow more excitedly. Rarely has there been so sharp a focus on things seen and touched and cherished and lost; seldom has there been a greater intensification of passing time and its grim relentlessness. Never in American writing has there been so dramatic a conflict of bitterness and brilliance, incredible failures and unquestionable successes, physical ecstasy, intellectual exacerbation, shocking violence and lasting vitality.

Thomas Wolfe

[1900-1938]

". . . the fierce energy that will not be
beaten into form . . ."

THOMAS WOLFE was the epitome of gigantic need and illimitable excess, a symbol of the "enormous space and energy of American life," its rawness and richness, its frenetic successes and stupendous failures. The man who might have stood for the portrait of the magnified American hero—a shaggy black-haired, burning-eyed, six-foot-six Paul Bunyan, a craftsman who built everything on a monstrous scale—was vulnerable to the least murmur of criticism, tormented by the passing of time, and fearful of loneliness and the sense of being lost. Nothing ever conceived in America, except by Whitman, vibrated with so exuberant and desperate a craving for life—*all* of life, experienced simultaneously and on every level—as the four novels of the writer who died before he had lived thirty-eight years.

He was born October 3, 1900, in Asheville, North Carolina, and was christened Thomas Clayton Wolfe. His father was a stonecutter who had a great respect for literature and loved to read poetry aloud. Wolfe's childhood was full of the oratorical rhythms of Shakespeare's soliloquies and Gray's "Elegy," but it was also full of misery. His mother became a boarding-house keeper, and as Tom was the seventh child, youngest by six years, the meanest of chores fell to him. As he grew up, he earned a few pennies by peddling papers in the back streets, running errands, going into the Negro quarters to fetch a reluctant servant, and drumming up trade for the boarding establishment. By the time Tom was fifteen the family managed to send him to the University of North Carolina, where he became editor of the college newspaper as well as the college magazine. He intended to be either a lawyer or a journalist and, although he wrote several one-act plays during his last two college years, it never occurred to him that he might become a professional author. One of the plays ("The Return of Buck Gavin: The Tragedy of a Mountain Outlaw"), which he wrote at seventeen, was not only produced at the college, with the author as leading man, but published in *Carolina Folk Plays*. At eighteen he was employed on the docks at Newport News, Virginia, not, according to later legends, as a working colossus, but as a checker. Ideas for poems and plays kept nagging his mind and, after graduating from the university in 1920, he went to Harvard, where he became a member of Professor George Pierce Baker's famous "47 Workshop," which Eugene O'Neill had attended a few years earlier.

Writing came easily—often too easily—to Wolfe. Words flowed from him freely, inexhaustibly, furiously, as though they had been held back too long, sudden freshets released and rushing uncontrollably out of orderly channels. At twenty the river which was to carry him in full flood was taking an uncertain course, but it was already beginning to rise. New plays were written, were praised, but were always rejected. Everyone was impressed with Wolfe's dramas, but no one wanted to produce them. "I am acquiring patience," he wrote after one of his manuscripts had been held for several months and "regretfully" returned. "And I am quite willing to wait for the unveiling exercises. All that really matters right now is the knowledge that I am twenty-three, and a golden May is here. The feeling of immortality in youth is upon me. I am young and I can never die. Don't tell me that I can. Wait until I am thirty. Then I'll believe you."

Unable to wait for "the unveiling exercises," Wolfe took his M.A. at Harvard and, in his twenty-fourth year, received an appointment as instructor in the Washington Square College of New York University. He was anything but a dedicated teacher; he looked on his appointment as a job and was determined to be a playwright. He wrote frankly to Homer Watt, chairman of the English Department: "It is only fair to tell you that my interests are centered in the drama, and that some day I hope to write successfully for the theater and to do nothing but that." Wolfe did not care for his surroundings or his associates; he lampooned them sardonically in a section entitled "School for Utility Cultures" in *Of Time and the River*. Although he spent six years as a teacher in New York, he spent most of them in retreat from the classroom.

He had already begun to think of a kind of novel when he went abroad for a year. Forced to resume teaching, he returned, ran away again, and, in the fall of 1926, found himself in London. Alone, and in a foreign country, he began his book. Back in New York, after two and a half years more of teaching all day and writing all night, he finished it. "The book took hold of me and possessed me," he wrote in his revealing quasi-diary, *The Story of a Novel.* "In a way, I think it shaped itself. Like every young man, I was strongly under the influence of writers I admired. One of the chief writers at that time was Mr. James Joyce with his book *Ulysses.* The book that I was writing was much influenced, I believe, by his own book, and yet the powerful energy and fire of my own youth played over and, I think, possessed it all. Like Mr. Joyce, I wrote about things that I had known, the immediate life and experience that had been familiar to me in my childhood. Unlike Mr. Joyce, I had no literary experience. I had never had anything published before. My feeling towards writers, publishers, books, that whole fabulous far-away world, was almost as romantically unreal as when I was a child. And yet my book, the characters with which I had peopled it, the color and the weather of the universe which I had created, had possessed me, and so I wrote and wrote with that bright flame with which a young man writes who never has been published, and who yet is sure all will be good and must go well."

It was an incredibly big book. It contained some 350,000 words and was to be called *O Lost!* During the writing Wolfe had been sustained by the stage designer Aline Bernstein and, during the difficult process of trying to shape the material for publication, by the editor of Scribner's, Maxwell Perkins—two close friends whom he extolled, wounded, loved, and needed, and from whom, to save his half-arrogant, half-guilty pride, he eventually severed himself. The work, finally called *Look Homeward, Angel,* was published a few days after his twenty-ninth birthday. Wolfe had worried that he had exposed himself—"the awful, utter nakedness of print, that thing which is for all of us so namelessly akin to shame came closer day by day"—and he was relieved when most of the critics hailed the book with surprised superlatives. He was, however, unprepared for the howls of outrage which arose from his home town. He was irrevocably hurt when he heard that the book had been denounced from the pulpits and reviled on street corners. "I received anonymous letters full of vilification and abuse . . . One venerable lady, whom I had known all my life, wrote me that although she had never believed in lynch law, she would do nothing to prevent a mob from dragging my 'big overgroan karkus' across the public square." Although Wolfe suggested that his book was a work of fiction, that he "meditated no man's portrait," there is no question but that *Look Homeward, Angel* is, in common with all of Wolfe's novels, almost literally autobiographical. "We are," he acknowledged, "the sum of all the moments of our lives—all that is ours is in them: we cannot escape or conceal it. If the writer has used the clay of life to make his book, he has only used what all men must, what none can keep from using . . . Dr. Johnson remarked that a man would turn over half a library to make a single book: in the same way a novelist may turn over half the people in a town to make a single figure in his novel."

Success disturbed Wolfe more than it delighted him. He worried about what the critics would expect of him, and began to worry about his next book, and the one which was to follow the second novel, and the one after that, and then the next . . . Six months after publication, his book went so well that he was able to resign from the faculty of New York University and, assisted by an award of a Guggenheim Fellowship, go abroad again. In Paris he felt a great wave of homesickness and, in "the almost intolerable effort of memory and desire," recreated and enlarged the entire progress of his life. The past came back to him "loaded with electricity, pregnant, crested, with a kind of hurricane violence." He says that the second book was not really written; it wrote him. It was to be called *The October Fair,* but the onrushing memories bore him along on a "torrential and ungovernable flood," and he decided on the inevitable title *Of Time and the River.* At first there was neither shape nor structure. It seemed unlikely to him that a novel could ever result. Wolfe was right. It turned into an uplifted and endless rhapsody. "I wrote about night and darkness in America, and the faces of the sleepers in ten thousand little towns; and of the tides of sleep and how the rivers flowed forever in the darkness. I wrote about the hissing glut of tides upon ten thousand miles of coast; of how the moonlight blazed down on the wilderness and filled the cat's cold eye with blazing yellow. I wrote about death and sleep, and of that enfabled rock of life we call the city. I wrote about October; of great trains that thundered through the night; of ships and stations in the morning; of men in harbors and the traffic of the ships."

When Wolfe returned to America in 1931 he was still engaged in capturing not only the immensities but the vanishing minutiae of life—"all the flicks and darts and haunting lights that flash across the mind of man: a voice once heard; a face that vanished; the way the sunlight came and went; the rustling of a leaf upon a bough: a stone, a leaf, a door." In a basement flat in the Assyrian quarter of

South Brooklyn, Wolfe piled crowded page on page of the life story of his hero, Eugene Gant, filling huge packing cases with ledger after ledger. He could not bring the book to an end. Perkins would suggest the excision of an episode, and Wolfe would dutifully agree; but on the way back to Brooklyn he would think of a passage that seemed to be imperative and, by the time he had it on paper, it was double the length of the deleted segment.

With Perkins' aid, he cut again and again, only to find that his manuscript, something over a million words, was still twelve times the length of the average novel, and more than twice the size of Tolstoy's *War and Peace.* Wolfe intended to begin the novel with a description of a train-ride across Virginia at night, but what was meant to be an introductory chapter ran over 100,000 words—a book-length exposition—and it had to be sacrificed. "My spirit quivered at the bloody execution," wrote Wolfe. "My soul recoiled before the carnage of so many lovely things cut out upon which my heart was set. But it had to be done, and we did it . . . Chapters 50,000 words long were reduced to ten or fifteen thousand words; and, having faced this inevitable necessity, I finally acquired a kind of ruthlessness of my own, and once or twice did more cutting than my editor was willing to allow." Even when the book came to a kind of end, Wolfe was reluctant to surrender it. He wanted to cram into it detail upon detail, to reproduce in its entirety "the full flood and fabric of a scene in life itself." There was always something more, he felt, that needed desperately to be said, something to be added to the thousands of pages in the packing case. The book would probably never have been printed if Perkins had not taken advantage of a visit which Wolfe made in Chicago; editing the book during the author's absence, Perkins sent the manuscript to the printer. Wolfe protested that he needed six more months, but Perkins told him that he was no perfectionist like Flaubert who continually had to refine and polish, that his business was to get on with the books which were in him. Wolfe eventually completed his revisions on the proof pages. In March, 1935, after the author had worked on the continuation of his (or Eugene Gant's) story for almost six years, *Of Time and the River* appeared.

Afraid to face the reception—"I felt as if I had ruinously exposed myself as a pitiable fool who had no talent and who once and for all had completely vindicated the prophecies of the critics who had felt the first book was just a flash in the pan"—Wolfe left the country and arrived in Paris the day the book was published in the United States. For all his bulk and bravado, Wolfe was the most thin-skinned of artists. "My state is not bad," he wrote to the understanding teacher who was his first and, in many ways, his most lasting influence, "in spite of the fact that I am considered arrogant and proud—the proper coloration of one who was born without his proper allowance of hide." "He wrote to match his height, he roared to match it, he ate and drank to match it," wrote Pamela Hansford Johnson in the critical appraisal entitled *Hungry Gulliver.* "But among the Lilliputians of Altamont [Wolfe's fictional name for his native Asheville] he was a feeble Gulliver. Their miniature arrows had found their mark and sunk their poison." When he was assured that the second volume in the Gant series, like the first, was a success, Wolfe was not reassured. In the books which followed, he tried to evade the identifiable autobiographical elements of Eugene Gant by changing the man's name as well as his appearance.

Although the next two novels continue the saga of the writer's life—the four books are actually one book, one towering autobiography—Wolfe now calls his hero George Webber. Instead of the young giant with "the face of a demented angel," a phrase which applied to Gant, Webber is a squat fellow, "strong and heavy in the shoulders, arms absurdly long, big hands, legs thin, bowed out a little . . . a large head that hangs forward and projects almost too heavily for the short, thin neck." He has a simian look—the boys call him "Monk." But the disguise goes no further and is completely ineffectual. Except for the arbitrary distortions, Webber remains Gant and, with a somewhat toughened manner, Wolfe.

In *The Web and the Rock* and *You Can't Go Home Again,* both of which were published posthumously, the character of Gant-Webber-Wolfe changes only insofar as any man changes with age and experience. He is ambivalent, pitiful, perverse, sometimes even paranoiac, but always aware of his weaknesses; he analyzes his compulsive rages and ramping inconsistencies, balancing self-pity with self-mockery. Always he is something more than himself. He is (or meant to be) not only the ambivalent American artist but the symbol of America itself, intransigent and contradictory, looking to Europe for escape and inspiration and, at the same time, repudiating the past, denying any heritage but our own, crying, like Emerson and Whitman before him, "From the unique and single substance of this land and the life of ours, must we draw the power and energy of our own life, the articulation of our speech, the substance of our art."

Wolfe never had time to shape this substance nearer to his hungry heart's desire, to embody the "billion forms of America, the savage violence, and the dense complexity of all its swarming life." He was recovering from one of his gargantuan bouts of drinking when he became ill in July, 1938. He survived an attack of pneumonia but, during convalescence, succumbed when complications set in. He died, following an operation for acute cerebral infection, at Johns Hopkins Hospital in Baltimore on September 15, 1938, a fortnight before his thirty-eighth birthday. He was buried in Asheville, and a few words from *The Web and the Rock* were carved on his tombstone: "Death bent to touch his chosen son with mercy, love and pity, and put the seal of honor on him when he died."

Wolfe's faults are so obvious that it was all too easy for the critics to belabor them. The faults are part of his excess: the disorganized gusto, the fierce energy that will not be beaten into form, the confusion of philosophy and feeling, the contradiction between social consciousness and the failure to do anything about it. "Wolfe," wrote Bernard De Voto, "has mastered neither the psychic material out of which a novel is made nor the technique of writing fiction . . . One can only respect Wolfe for his determination to realize himself on the highest level and to be satisfied with nothing short of greatness. But, however useful genius may be in the writing of novels, it is not enough in itself." "His entire work is a forcing process," wrote the otherwise sympathetic appraiser, Pamela Hansford Johnson. "With every word he wrote he was trying to say more than any human being had ever said of the marvel of the earth and of man. He wanted to capture in words the experience of *nearly understanding* and, more preposterous and more wonderful, to be the first man in all the world to understand completely . . . Yet all Wolfe succeeded in producing was a history of violent endeavor." In an introduction to the English edition of *The Web and the Rock* J. B. Priestley, differing from most other critics, claims that this is not only the most varied and most massive but decidedly the best of Wolfe's books. Yet Priestley was compelled to add: "He [Wolfe] is apt to indulge himself, like a tipsy undergraduate at the end of a long evening, in long passages of a vague and bogus profundity, as if announcing, but at great length, that there is a 'something somewhere if we could only find it.' "

It is not enough to say that Wolfe is great in spite of his faults; the exaggerations, the wild monologs, the overextended raptures must be accepted as integrated and inseparable parts of the man. The pared concision, the brusque epigram was not for him. Wolfe luxuriated in length; he had to have great expanses to stretch himself. Forty thousand words are required to describe a daylong party in *You Can't Go Home Again;* in *Of Time and the River,* a single episode, the train journey previously mentioned, was finally condensed into some sixty pages of small print. One must also grant Wolfe's inability to distinguish between eloquence and verbosity, letting rhetoric slide into rant; his personal and general jealousies; his mixed envy and hatred of the well-to-do sophisticates, especially the Jews, the intellectuals, "the liberated princelings"; his incredible total recall which, superficially like Proust's, was without Proust's magic power of revelation. Properly balanced, the defects are minor blemishes when weighed against Wolfe's major accomplishments: the inexhaustible vitality—only in Rabelais and Joyce is there a swifter spate of words, a more joyful use of speech—the exuberant optimism; the enigmatic but noble summaries, the salutations to his native soil, a country compounded of "nameless fear and of soaring conviction, of brutal, empty, naked, bleak, corrosive ugliness, and of beauty so lovely and so overwhelming that the tongue is stopped by it, and the language for it has not yet been uttered." "I believe that we are lost here in America," he wrote in his Credo at the end of a half-bitter, half-exalted apostrophe to man, "but I believe we shall be found. And this belief, which mounts now to the catharsis of knowledge and conviction, is for me—and I think for all of us—not only our hope, but America's everlasting, living dream. I think the life which we have fashioned in America, and which has fashioned us—the forms we made, the cells that grew, the honeycomb that was created—was self-destructive in its nature, and must be destroyed . . . I think the true discovery of America is before us. I think the true fulfillment of our spirit, of our people, of our mighty and immortal land, is yet to come."

Wolfe tried too hard and stretched himself too far for perfection, but perfection was scarcely his aim. His furious desire to outreach time and space was bound to fail. But, as William Faulkner, Wolfe's fellow-Southerner and in many ways his opposite, contended, "Wolfe made the best failure because he had tried hardest to say the most . . . He was willing to throw away style, coherence, all the rules of preciseness, to try to put all the experience of the human heart on the head of a pin, as it were." Wolfe realized his intemperate appetite, his "almost insane hunger to devour the entire body of human experience," but he also knew that "having had this thing within me it was in no way possible for me to reason it out of me, no matter how cogently my reason worked against it . . . The only way I could get it out of me was to live it out of me."

"I'd rather be a poet than anything else in the world," he cried. "God! What I wouldn't give to be one!" Two posthumous volumes —*The Face of a Nation*, a collection of poetical passages from his writings, and *A Stone, A Leaf, A Door*, segments of his prose rearranged as verse—prove that Wolfe not only wrote prose-poetry but that Wolfe was a poet who happened to use the medium of prose. He mistakenly thought that he was not a poet because he put the emphasis on conventional form and refused to believe that his sprawling lines could attain the art he most admired. Nevertheless, the beat of ecstatic life, the rise and fall of tidal emotions, and the restless flow of the river of time are held in Wolfe's rhythmical, strongly cadenced lines. In no prose and only in a small body of verse has there been expressed a greater sense of urgency, of unhappy adolescence and its insatiable desires, of loving kindness and unexpected cruelty, the wanderings of the human spirit. Faintly concealed by its prose habit, the prefatory passage of *Look Homeward, Angel* emerges as naked poetry:

> Which of us has known his brother? Which of us has
> looked into his father's heart? Which of us has not
> remained forever prison-pent? Which of us is not
> forever a stranger and alone?
>
> O waste of loss, in the hot mazes, lost, among
> bright stars on this most weary, unbright cinder, lost!
> Remembering speechlessly we seek the great forgotten
> language, the lost lane-end into heaven, a stone,
> a leaf, an unfound door. Where? When?
>
> O lost, and by the wind grieved, ghost, come back again.

Equally eloquent, and equally full of poetic afflatus, is the end of *You Can't Go Home Again*. The book concludes with a long letter to Gant's editor, Foxhall Edwards (Wolfe's Maxwell Perkins), a rapt evocation which, with its premonition of Wolfe's early death, is not only a prophecy, Biblical in tone, but one of the most unquestionably moving, beautifully composed, and climactic poems of our time.

Something has spoken to me in the night, burning the
tapers of the waning year; something has spoken in the
night, and told me I shall die, I know not where. Saying:

"To lose the earth you know, for greater knowing; to lose
the life you have, for greater life; to leave the friends
you loved, for greater loving; to find a land more kind
than home, more large than earth—

"—Whereon the pillars of this earth are founded, towards
which the conscience of the world is tending—a wind is
rising, and the rivers flow."

Differing from Wolfe's diffuse style, such a passage is so perfectly
shaped, so classic in design, that its clear and almost formal rhythms
reveal the spirit free of the heavy flesh. They speak for the clairvoyant poet, beyond life, outliving death, completed and fulfilled.

André Malraux

[1 9 0 1 -　　　]

". . . the story of art is the story of man."

AT FIFTY-TWO a French novelist-politician who had veered from the revolutionary left to the reactionary right, visited the United States and announced that politics was threatening to destroy mankind and that only art could unite it. He amplified the theme in a monumental volume, *The Voices of Silence,* his "museum without walls," in which he maintained that all the absolutes except the absolute of art had vanished. As part of a new humanism, a spiritual reality, art, declared Malraux, "is the modern religion . . . Every masterpiece, implicitly or openly, tells of a human victory over the blind forces of destiny. The artist's voice owes its power to the fact that it arises from a pregnant solitude which conjures up the universe so as to impose on it a human accent; and whatever survives for us in the great arts of the past is the indefeasible inner voice of civilizations that have passed away. But this surviving yet not immortal voice soaring towards the gods has for its accompaniment the tireless orchestra of death . . . In our eyes the art of all civilizations has this in common: that it expresses a defense against fatality."

André Malraux's own "defense against fatality" took various forms and compelled him to lead several lives. He was born November 3, 1901, in Paris. His father was a well-to-do civil servant who believed in an unusually far-ranging education for his son. After excelling in classical studies at the Lycée Condorcet, André attended the Paris School of Oriental Languages, where he received a thorough understanding of Sanskrit and Chinese, as well as archaeology. At twenty he published a little book of prose poems and married Clara Goldschmidt, daughter of a German-Jewish financier. At twenty-three he joined his father in Indo-China, where he plunged into archaeological expeditions. He dug into ancient sites, explored temple ruins, and searched for buried Buddhist sculptures. A year of digging temporarily exhausted his interest in the past and he became involved with the present, in particular with the situation of colonial peoples. The Annamite revolt absorbed him and he joined the Annam League in its struggle for independence. Crossing the border into China, Malraux extended his political activities. He participated in the National Liberation Movement of 1925 and became associate Secretary-General of the Kuomintang founded by Sun Yat-sen. As one of a Committee of Twelve—Chiang Kai-shek was a fellow-member—he took part in the Canton insurrection and helped to accomplish the coalition of the Kuomintang and the Communist Party. His eloquence as well as his zeal was recognized, and he was given the position of Commissioner of Propaganda for the Kwantung and Kwangsi provinces. He was, at twenty-six, a confirmed revolutionist.

The things he saw and suffered in Indo-China, Shanghai, and Hong Kong burn through his first three novels. All three books are crowded with action and conflicting demands for power. The hero of *The Conquerors,* which appeared when Malraux was twenty-eight, is a Soviet agent in China, an organizer who directs propaganda during the general strike in Hong Kong in 1925. Trotsky called it "a romanticized chronicle of revolution," but Malraux insisted that the chief emphasis was on "the relation between individual and collective action rather than on collective action alone." *The Royal Way,* published a year later, has a background of archaeology in Cambodia, but its main purpose is to sound Malraux's theme of man's loneliness and, since man cannot defeat death, his determination to challenge it with all his reckless and destructive force.

The third novel, *Man's Fate,* made Malraux an international figure. It was hailed as a masterpiece, won the Goncourt Prize, and was translated into practically every living language. Like Hemingway, Malraux was preoccupied with death and violence but, differing from the American novelist, Malraux saw a stubborn and inescapable purpose propelling every action. The book dealt with another historical episode with which the writer was connected: the struggle between the communistic members of the People's Party, the Kuomintang, and the army of General Chiang Kai-shek. The intricate narrative of the crisis in Shanghai, two days in 1927, is a masterpiece of explosive writing. Philip Henderson declared that "outside of Dostoevsky and Gorky, there is perhaps no other book comparable to this in sheer naked intensity of its suffering." Geoffrey Stone said that it evoked "an atmosphere of impending doom . . . Malraux does not attempt to set off his communist and capitalist characters as neat foils against each other; they are, it is true, opposed, but opposed not so much because of qualities of their character as because they are placed in different systems whose movements pit them against each other." Malraux's people are, however, not merely the products of their environment, bitterly fighting their way to opposite goals, but sharers of a philosophy: an acceptance of cruelty and its barriers against communication, a determination to force the moment to its utmost, and a desperate affirmation of terror, loneliness, and sacrifice for some undefinable but greater future. Moreover, Malraux makes the reader believe that the passing hour is the hour of decision and that the destiny of the entire race is in the hands of a few embattled protagonists.

When Chiang Kai-shek broke with the Third International and held back the Communists in 1927, Malraux returned to Europe. He did not remain inactive. He became one of the leaders of the anti-fascist movement of the thirties; he dedicated himself to the cause of the underground workers in Europe and the masses everywhere. He dramatized the issue of fascism in *Days of Wrath*, which was received even more enthusiastically than *Man's Fate*. Kassner, its central figure, is a member of the German underground. Because he refuses to give up a paper containing the names of Communists, he is imprisoned in total darkness for nine days and is set free only when another Communist, calling himself Kassner, surrenders so that the real Kassner can resume his dangerous work. Malraux's passion for social betterment was not confined to the printed page. He spoke at mass meetings against all forms of nazism, excoriated Mussolini's black-shirt "adventurism," protested the brutal invasion of Abyssinia, and founded the International Association of Writers for the Defence of Culture.

In 1936 Malraux again found himself involved in revolutionary activities. When Franco set himself up as dictator of Spain, Malraux joined the Loyalists. He took a plane to Madrid, organized an air corps, and, although he was a relatively inexperienced aviator, flew sixty-five missions over fascist territory. He was twice wounded, was instrumental in halting the advance on Spain's capital, and toured France and the United States to plead for the Loyalists and raise money for their cause. His participation in the first phase of the Spanish civil war projects itself searingly but objectively through *Man's Hope*. He describes, wrote F. W. Dupee in *The Partisan Review*, "with precision and lyrical power the peculiar terrors of street fighting, the exaltation of the armed proletariat

. . . The real hero is the Republican Army." But Malraux does not commit himself incontrovertibly to one side, not even to the side he obviously favors. "Like most writers," continues Dupee, "he remains with a foot in both camps. The revolution is not static; it ebbs and flows . . . And the intelligentsia, slung between two classes, materially dependent on the bourgeoisie but facing spiritually towards the proletariat, vibrates to the rhythm of advances and retreats in the working class. Malraux's career reflects, more faithfully than that of most writers, the periodic crises of the European intellectuals."

Malraux continued to reflect those shifts and makeshifts. He favored Stalin and Trotsky alternately; he turned from paeans celebrating Marxist victories to epics of its defeat. At the outset of the Second World War he enlisted in a tank corps, was taken prisoner, escaped, and was active as a member of the underground Maquis. When the war came to an end, Malraux shocked most of his friends and all of his followers by aligning himself with the extreme rightist Government and becoming a supporter of the dictatorial Charles de Gaulle. When it was charged against him that the one-time revolutionist who declared he hated all wars had become a "warmonger," Malraux replied that it was the world and not himself that had changed.

No change was evident in the physical man. At fifty his green eyes still blazed, his hair was dark, and in repose his mouth was tighter than ever. The intensity of his spirit and the extent of his adventures kept him slender; a cold elegance was accentuated by a nervous tic which he acquired in China. His energy and loquacity were undiminished. Janet Flanner described him as "a phenomenal, peripatetic talker . . . As he walks, words and ideas rush from his brain and out of his mouth in extemporaneous creation, as though they were long quotations from books he has not yet written, and they flow at a rate that is almost the speed of thought, and sometimes faster than the ear can catch. His extravagant memory accompanies him as he paces back and forth, bringing reminiscences out into the air, along with history, art, and man's dangerous destiny—whatever he needs at the moment."

His life with Clara Goldschmidt had ended in divorce, and he had married Josette Clotis, a writer, who bore him two sons before she died in a railway accident. Two years later, in 1948, he married Marie-Madeleine Malraux, his half-brother's widow who had been left to him, said Janet Flanner, "as a desperate fraternal legacy in case he [Roland Malraux] never came back from wherever the Gestapo was taking him." Roland died in a concentration camp and Claude Malraux, another half-brother, was another of the casualties of the Resistance Movement. André was the only one of the three fighters to survive.

In 1953 Malraux published what many consider his most enduring if not his most exciting work: *The Voices of Silence*. Based upon an earlier exploration of the field, *The Psychology of Art*, Malraux presented a picture-history of man and his artistic expressiveness, from the neolithic scratchings on the caves of Dordogne to the modern world's incredible skyscrapers, from the functional Egyptian mummy-cases to the sometimes inscrutable canvases of Picasso. All art, Malraux implies, is a revolt, a protest against extinction, a rebellious act against death and man's tragic mortality. What the artist designs, paints, carves, erects, and, in one way or another, continually creates, is not so much a symbol as a concrete image planned to withstand the enmity of time. "How can we fail," cries Malraux at a pitch which is not only poetic but ecstatic, "to hear a voice calling across the ages, like the summons that sounded once across the foam of perilous seas, a call attuned in some elusive manner to that aura with which the genius of great artists has enhanced our knowledge and to the peal of silver bells which Michelangelo launches above the tombs of Florence—the same bells as those whose muffled chime rises from cities buried in the sea?" It is art that transfigures while it transfixes; it is art that molds, remakes, and preserves. For, maintains Malraux, the story of art is also the story of man.

Jean-Paul Sartre

[1905-]

". . . the hectic and impossible existence
that is known as the lot of man."

THE PHILOSOPHY of Søren Kierkegaard turned on a complex series of paradoxes, especially the paradox that the nearer man approaches God the nearer he comes to nothingness, yet this very nothingness is the fulfillment of his existence. A century after Kierkegaard's death, the problem of man as "existent" became the central concern of two opposed schools of modern philosophy. One school, believing that the great need of man is fundamental faith and religious orthodoxy, placed its emphasis on essence; the other, denying the presence of God, rejecting all gospels as well as the possibility of metaphysical knowledge, placed its emphasis on existence. The second school divided an array of critics into two antagonistic camps. Hailed as a new departure in philosophy and condemned as an outright denial of philosophy, Existentialism grew rapidly with every fresh controversy. Its basic cynicism was founded on hopelessness, but it grew immensely popular in the late 1940's due to the wave of disillusion following the Second World War. Its chief impetus came from the driving works of Jean-Paul Sartre.

Jean-Paul Sartre was born June 5, 1905, in Paris and, even in his childhood, was drawn to the study of philosophy. Educated at the Ecole Normale, he received his degree in his twenty-fifth year and taught philosophy in Le Havre, Laon, and Paris. In the early thirties he spent his spare time traveling, chiefly in Germany, Italy, Spain, Greece, and England, until on the eve of World War II, he was drafted into the Army. In 1939 he was stationed in Alsace as an artillery observer; a year later he was taken prisoner and kept in a German prison camp for nine months. Somehow he escaped to the unoccupied zone of France and, at thirty-five, resumed teaching. When the Nazi Army took over the government, Sartre remained in Paris, risking his life by becoming one of the most active members in the underground Resistance Movement.

It was at this time that Sartre began to formulate his own philosophy of paradox, a philosophy which maintained that external oppression is actually a liberating force; it frees the inner man to make his own daily, desperate decisions. He wrote in *The Republic of Silence:* "We were never more free than during the German occupation. We had lost all our rights, beginning with the right to talk. Every day we were insulted to our faces and had to take it in silence. Under one pretext or another, as workers, Jews, or political prisoners, we were deported en masse. Everywhere, on billboards, in the newspapers, on the screen, we encountered the revolting and insipid picture of ourselves that our oppressors wanted us to accept. And, because of all this, we were free. Because the Nazi venom seeped even into our thoughts, every accurate thought was a conquest. Because an all-powerful police tried to force us to hold our tongues, every word took on the value of a declaration of principles. Because we were hunted down, every one of our gestures had the weight of a solemn commitment." Sartre added a note of bitter stoicism: "The circumstances, atrocious as they often were, finally made it possible for us to live, without pretense or false shame, the hectic and impossible existence that is known as the lot of man."

Sartre learned that solidarity and solitude were not only essentials but hourly imperatives. "To those who were engaged in underground activities, the conditions of their struggle afforded a new kind of experience. They did not fight openly like soldiers. In all circumstances they were alone. They were hunted down in solitude, arrested in solitude. It was completely forlorn and unbefriended that they held out against torture, alone and naked in the presence of torturers, clean-shaven, well-fed, and well-clothed, who laughed at their cringing flesh, and to whom an untroubled conscience and a boundless sense of social strength gave every appearance of being in the right. Alone. Without a friendly hand or a word of encouragement. Yet, in the depth of their solitude, it was the others that they were protecting, all the others, all their comrades in the Resistance. Total responsibility in total solitude—is not this the very definition of our liberty? . . . There is no army in the world where there is such equality of risk for the private and the commander-in-chief. And this is why the Resistance was a true democracy: for the soldier as for the commander, the same danger, the same forsakenness, the same total responsibility, the same absolute liberty within discipline. Thus, in darkness and in blood, a Republic was established, the strongest of Republics. Each of its citizens knew that he owed himself to all and that he could count only on himself alone. Each of them, in complete isolation, fulfilled his responsibility and his role in history. Each of them, standing against the oppressors, undertook to be himself, freely and irrevocably. And by choosing for himself in liberty, he chose the liberty of all."

After the liberation of France, Sartre, the teacher and fighter, became the even more militant writer. Spurred by his own experiences and moved by the memory of all those forced to lead underground lives psychologically as well as physically, Sartre plunged into a study of the pathetic and absurd behavior of human beings. With pitiless clarity and a mixture of sympathy and cynicism he exposed the motives of man floundering in an apathetic world, a universe in which "nothing, absolutely nothing justifies his existence," and in which, pitted against an environment which is both hostile and purposeless, nothing but man's free will allows him to survive. Sartre expounded his feelings about man's precarious and almost hopeless situation in such novels as *The Age of Reason, The Reprieve, The Last Chance, Nausea*—books which represented a series of emotional crises in the lives of tormented people—and such plays as the propagandist *The Flies,* the violent *No Exit,* which takes place in hell, and the melodramatic *The Respectful Prostitute,* which delighted his admirers and alternately shocked and depressed the majority of theatergoers. At thirty-eight Sartre published his most important philosophical work, a treatise of some seven hundred pages, *Being and Non-Being.*

For Kierkegaard the ideal life was a constant search, an impassioned God-seeking. And, because of the infinite distance between the self and the God it loves, and hopes to find, the quest is a lifelong suffering and a final but, somehow, sustaining despair. Sartre opposed the whole concept of transcendence. "In the view of Sartre," according to Marjorie Grene in *Dreadful Freedom,* the best of the many books on Existentialism, "it is the very denial of God's existence, not the search for him, that makes the inner Odyssey of the self seeking the self philosophy's primary concern. The self that Existentialism seeks is each person's individual self, which he must forge for himself out of such senseless circumstances, such meaningless limitations, as are given him. This self-creation—the making of one's essence from mere existence—is demanded of each of us because, according to Existentialism, there is no *single* essence of hu-

manity to which we may logically turn as standard or model for
making ourselves thus or so. And there is no single concept of humanity, because there is no God."

Man, Sartre enounced, is personally and wholly responsible for
what he does, even for what he is. There are no values superior to
man or external to man. A man, therefore, may choose different
precedents for himself and not be subjected to prescribed standards
of thought or conduct. Regarded in this light, Existentialism is another version of Humanism or, in its emphasis on physiological and
psychological dissections of human nature, an inverted variation
upon it. As one of the expounders, Frederick Mayer, wrote: "It believes that man is the source and creator of all values, and that he
can realize his mission in life only by concentrating on his own
inner development."

Since each person is uniquely himself, unlike any other person,
no one should attempt to impose rules of conduct on anyone; individual choice is imperative and paramount. Yet no one can take
his liberty lightly; freedom is not a blessing but an almost insuffer-
able burden. Man, says Sartre with indubitable earnestness, is "condemned" to be free, for man is doomed to struggle in a world of
conflicting standards and counterfeit values. Recalling Kierkegaard's
picture of life as a continual state of dread, Sartre examines the
valuelessness of "values" and concludes that they are pretenses,
fraudulent comforts that cannot alleviate our insuppressible fears.
"There are," writes Sartre, "alarm clocks, signboards, tax returns,
policemen—so many barriers against dread. But as soon as I am
sent back to myself, I suddenly find myself to be the one who gives
its meaning to the alarm clock, who forbids himself, at the instance
of the signboard, to walk on a lawn, who lends its urgency to the
chief's order . . . I emerge alone and in dread in the face of the
unique and first project which constitutes my being; all the barriers
go down, annihilated by the consciousness of my liberty. I have not,
nor can I have, recourse to any value against the fact that it is I
who maintain values in being; nothing can assure me against myself. Cut off from the world and my essence by the nothing that I
am, I have to realize the meaning of the world and of my essence:
I decide it alone, unjustifiable, and without excuse."

It is part of the paradox of Existentialism that an unflinching
pessimist should turn out to be a moralist and that an uncompromising atheist should become a spiritual leader. But Sartre is the
voice of those who cry out against a world which has become in-

creasingly organized, against what Waldo Frank called "the collectivizing trend of society under machine production," against conformity of every kind. It is a protest which also expresses a need for redemption as well as the metaphysics of those whom someone characterized as "the emotionally unemployed."

A final estimate of Existentialism has not yet been achieved. On one hand, it has been damned as indecent, heretical, and viciously degenerate. It has been excoriated by such philosophers as Heidegger and Jaspers, who consider it the death of the philosophy of existence. Georges Gurvitch called it a "psychological isolation which nullifies itself" and stated that "Existentialism applies itself to the task of reducing existence to zero. This is the nausea of impotence." On the other hand, it has been eulogized as a revaluation of values, an effort to establish a heroic solitariness, a determination to stand equally against organized systems, sententious illusions, and collapsed conventions. Our repeated crises of anxiety, say the Existentialists, our dependence on principles which are worthless and standards which no longer exist, force us to fight against all dehumanization; only by such opposition can we hope to maintain individual identity which is the very essence of man's being. We speak, they say, for the countless men and women who believe they have been betrayed and who, having lost faith, feel themselves exiled even in communities, estranged and helplessly alone. "They insist," wrote Marjorie Grene, "on the essential optimism of their doctrine that 'man makes himself,' for there is always, until death, another chance. Granted, they would say, that, in their wide humanity, they explore the far corners of human life, the horrors and perversions uncharted by timorous captives of gentility. Granted, too, that, with honest ruthlessness, they expose the cant of a fraudulent, strictly bourgeois 'human dignity.' But just because of this very humaneness, this very honesty, they are decried as perverts and iconoclasts . . . and hence Existentialism, more even than the naturalism of Zola or Ibsen in their days, comes to mean the shocking, the sordid, or the obscene."

Only a few jaundiced bigots, however, failed to see the reasons for Existentialism and the serious problems it represented. Rooted in prejudice, they refused to acknowledge that its proponents were pitting a positive something—man's private and fearful freedom or a risky philosophic anarchy—against nothingness, a nihilism which infects the modern world. Only a few detached appraisers fairly measured the virtues and defects of a system which claims that "man is what he makes himself" and that there is no universal "spirit" of humanity but only the determining acts of men and women. One of the few calmly balanced and yet incisive analyses was written by Charles Frankel and published in *The Saturday Review* (September 3, 1953) under the title, "Seeing Things in Double Focus." "There is little doubt," Frankel concluded, "that we shall need very badly in the near future institutions which will act as deterrents against fanaticism and world idolatry, and which will stand out against the resurgent cult of the State and the growing pressures towards conformity . . . As an expression of the distracted modern spirit and as a form of shock treatment for the complacent, Existentialism has unquestionable merits. But terror produces its own form of inertia, and it is not an attractive antidote to complacency. And cosmic hypochondria is not a sound basis on which to build either a modern religion or a clear and candid mind." The Existentialists may dispute such a summary, but it takes more than the articulation of anguish to rid a world of agony.

W. H. Auden

[1 9 0 7 -   ]

*"People do not understand that it is possible
to believe in a thing and ridicule it at the
same time."*

BEFORE HE WAS THIRTY-FIVE, Wystan Hugh Auden was a disturbing phenomenon and an unquestioned influence on both sides
of the Atlantic. That his poetry marked a turning point as
well as a milestone was acknowledged when an entire volume devoted to the work of modern poets was entitled *Auden and After.*
The subtitle was equally significant: "The Liberation of Poetry:
1930-1941."

Auden was born February 21, 1907, in York, England. Son of a
retired medical officer, he was educated at Gresham's School, in
Holt, and at Christ Church College, Oxford. From his twenty-third
to his twenty-eighth year he taught school at Malvern, an experience echoed in the early "Ode: To My Pupils." The following year
he worked with a film unit. At thirty he received the King's Poetry
Medal, had an entire issue of an English magazine devoted to his
work, went to Spain and drove an ambulance for the Loyalists during the Spanish revolution. Two years later he married Erika
Mann, daughter of Thomas Mann, came to America, took out his
first papers, and, in 1946, became a citizen of the United States. By
this time, Auden was already the author of four books of poetry,
three plays, a collection of prose fiction, two books of travel, and
three anthologies.

Auden's early poetry is characterized by its startling ingenuity
and self-divided philosophy. The poet is merciless in his condemnation of "the old gang" which has made the world not only tragic
but tawdry, yet he cannot persuade himself to go over to the "other
side." He speaks for those who are bullied in war and exploited in
peace, but he is not one of them or even, except in a kind of abstract sympathy, whole-heartedly with them. Another obstacle
against complete participation is the closed-in feeling of the verse;
it is suspiciously tight and private. Auden was accused of writing
"for himself and a few friends" when he was actually trying to find

a way of externalizing and presenting to others what were inward-seeking thoughts and uncertain conclusions.

Social feeling breaks through clearly in *On This Island,* written when Auden was thirty, and *Another Time,* published three years later. The vocabulary becomes simpler, the utterance more direct. Auden juxtaposes staccato commonplace phrases and an elevated, even noble, diction to reconcile the vulgarities and occasional exaltations of everyday life; he uses the measures of light verse, the accents of popular songs, folk ballads and purposely crude rhymes, to contrast the latest findings of science with the oldest romantic dreams. Dignity and rowdiness dispute each other as Auden appears one moment as the fastidious scholar and the next as the man-of-the-people. The reader is often too bewildered by Auden's ambidexterity to appreciate the intensity. He might believe that the poet was essentially a wit after the caustic mockery of "Law, Say the Gardeners, is the Sun," with such a verse as:

> Law, says the judge as he looks down his nose,
> Speaking clearly and most severely,
> Law is as I've told you before,
> Law is as you know I suppose,
> Law is but let me explain it once more,
> Law is The Law.[1]

But, finding page after page of great tenderness and pure sensuousness, the reader might well conclude that only a naturally lyrical poet could have written such a love song as the one beginning:

> Lay your sleeping head, my love,
> Human on my faithless arm;
> Time and fevers burn away
> Individual beauty from
> Thoughtful children, and the grave
> Proves the child ephemeral:
> But in my arms till break of day
> Let the living creature lie,
> Mortal, guilty, but to me
> The entirely beautiful.[1]

Auden is perhaps the only modern poet who can completely express himself in the old-fashioned ballade or villanelle, or even that most artificial of French forms, the sestina—he employs the last to remarkable effect in the "Journal of an Airman" and in "Hearing of harvests rotting in the valleys." Stephen Spender, with whom

[1] From *Another Time* published by Random House, Inc., copyright 1940 by W. H. Auden.

Auden was closely associated in England, complained that Auden "sometimes overloaded his material," but Spender was quick to add that his work had "a vitality, an explosive violence, that leaves his contemporaries dazed." In his mid-thirties Auden published *The Double Man* and *For the Time Being* and made it apparent why he was considered the most provocative as well as the most unpredictable poet of his generation. In *The Double Man,* a single poem of some seventeen hundred lines, Auden speaks as the multiple man: the bravura performer and the finical craftsman, the jaunty iconoclast and the reserved classicist. The poem was hailed as a return to order, and the most experimental of contemporary poets was congratulated at having gone to school to Pope. *For the Time Being* consists of two long poems: "The Sea and the Mirror," which is an extraordinarily fresh if discursive commentary on Shakespeare's *The Tempest,* and the title poem, a Christmas cantata which, in its mixture of classic diction and colloquial speech, is a lively and even profound paradox. It was apparent, here and elsewhere, that Auden had accomplished a rare thing: he had broken down the barrier between light verse and oratory, between high spirits and high seriousness.

In common with Eliot, Auden had begun with poetry that was written out of revulsion, bitter in burlesque, desperate and morose in its sense of imminent catastrophe, "an immeasurable neurotic dread." As he matured, Auden synthesized not only the foreboding thought of his time but his own outrage against cruelty, a protest against cant and a suspicion of beauty without goodness. His despairing personal cry was vibrant with the voice of hurt humanity. As he neared forty, Auden's poetry grew in scope and compassion; it became, said Francis Scarfe, in *Auden and After,* "a clearinghouse for modern psychology and social doctrine. If Eliot is rooted to the past, Auden is topical to a fault, but he seems turned towards the future." His poetry embodies concepts from countless sources, but it is strong enough to carry suggestions, and sometimes essential ideas, from thinkers as diverse as Kierkegaard, Freud, Henry James, Matthew Arnold, Yeats, Rilke, Einstein, and Edward Lear, all of whom he has apostrophized, without being submerged by them.

Comparison to Eliot was inevitable for, although Auden had written no major work to be classed with *The Waste Land* or *Four Quartets,* he was recognized as the most influential poet after Eliot. It was observed there was a geographical as well as a poetic justice in the fact. Auden, born in England, had made his home in the United States, while Eliot, born in Missouri, had exchanged his American birthright for British citizenship. Again like Eliot, Auden had progressed from cynicism to mysticism, from a baffled distrust of civilization to a religious hope for it. He gave a name to an epoch in *The Age of Anxiety,* an anguished parable, which was awarded the Pulitzer Prize in 1948. *The Age of Anxiety* is a characteristic exhibit of Auden's virtuosity. Using the language of the 1940's, with its peculiar slang, it harks back to the time of the Anglo-Saxons and gets its strange effect from the tough, triply alliterative line of *Beowulf.* The result is so powerful a macabre morality play that the incongruity is unnoticed; Auden blends casual horror and a baleful *vers de société* (a patter which sometimes makes the speaker sound like the Freudian's Noel Coward) to construct a latter-day Purgatory. In this metropolitan "baroque eclogue," as Auden calls it, four people re-act the seven ages of man and seven stages of suffering in a New York bar. They progress from a morass of reminiscences through a desert of disillusion, with a lament for the lost leader—the lost "dad," the vanished God—to a final frustration which holds only a faint hope of other lives and other values. The opening of the second section is typical of the tone:

> Behold the infant, helpless in cradle, and
> Righteous still, yet already there is
> Dread in his dreams at the deed of which
> He knows nothing but knows he can do,
> The gulf before him with guilt beyond,
> Whatever that is, whatever why
> Forbids his bound; till that ban tempts him;
> He jumps and is judged; he joins mankind,
> The fallen families, freedom lost . . .[1]

By the time Auden had reached his mid-forties he was the author, collaborator, and editor of almost a score of volumes of poems, plays, and essays. Although he was conceded to be a protean writer, various voices were raised against his entertaining facility, his capriciousness, his mingling of solemn music and drawing room jazz. A victim of his own competence, he frequently became a target for a group of poets who reacted to the adulation of his followers with excessive fault-finding. "Looking back," wrote Kenneth Rexroth as the spokesman for some of the younger avant-

[1] From *The Age of Anxiety* published by Random House, Inc., copyright 1947 by W. H. Auden.

gardists in *New British Poets,* "it seems today that the Auden circle was more a merchandising co-operative than a literary school . . . His sympathy with Marxism, never too well grounded, has vanished and he has almost forgotten his special mythology, the Public Schoolboy, the garden party, the country house; and with Mr. Gerald Heard, sometimes science popularizer for the B.B.C., he has become the spokesman for a peculiarly American Hollywoodweary religiosity." On the other hand, Francis Scarfe, an almost equally severe though less malicious appraiser, found that Auden's liberating influence "broke down the new snobbery of intellectualism which was in danger of creating a minority-poetry . . . He was able to enlarge for younger writers the syntax, rhythm, and imagery of poetry. He also enlarged, quite definitely, the poetry-reading public."

This liberation was largely accomplished by Auden's very contradictoriness. Tall, with straw-yellow hair and light hazel eyes, he looked like an attenuated Puck, and it was his puckishness which worried his well-wishers. Some of them were inclined to agree with the critics who found him, for all his disturbing pictures of loneliness and malignity, lacking in seriousness. Auden did nothing to assuage their concern. On the contrary, he announced half-jestingly that not enough writers appreciate "the basic frivolity of art. People do not understand that it is possible to believe in a thing and ridicule it at the same time." This gave rise to a complaint that the statements in some of Auden's most earnest poems might not be a proof of belief "any more than a love poem is a proof that one is in love."

It is difficult to tell when Auden is deeply troubled and when he is merely exercising what Dudley Fitts called his "donnishly witty, flashing, attractively unkempt diction." His intellectual clowning and his natural compassion, his irresponsibility and his tenderness go hand in hand. There is nothing he cannot do with rhyme, half-rhyme, assonance, dissonance, and suspension. He is so superb a technician, so delighted with the play of a phrase, that it is almost impossible to draw the line between a fluency that falls into garrulousness and a loquacity that rises into eloquence. He perfected, moreover, a method of offsetting shallowness of feeling and triviality of subject by reviving the "occasional" poem which makes little demand in idea or form upon the reader but lures him with a celebration of the ordinary man and the everyday event.

In the later work, notably in a few of the poems in *Nones,* as well as some in *Another Time,* there is a human warmth and a humility only suggested in the dazzle of his early cerebrations. There is more observation and less abstraction, and far deeper feeling. Auden shows pity instead of contempt for those who are not certain that they like what they have but are sure that they want more of it. His images are, as before, often chill and ominous—someone has spoken of his "menacing mutter"—but his inventiveness is no longer exhibitionistic and his extraordinary erudition is not flaunted to display his rich resources but enlisted to intensify communication. A tribute to another poet ("In Memory of W. B. Yeats") never loses itself in rhetoric, but contrasts the one who sang "of human unsuccess in a rapture of distress" with the shabby state of the world:

> Intellectual disgrace
> Stares from every human face,
> And the seas of pity lie
> Locked and frozen in each eye.

Auden has moved from estrangement, the bravura of despair and "the cult of death," to a sense of sharing and a groping faith: The progress is from "Doom is dark and deeper than any sea-dingle" to "We must love one another or die." The most brilliant satirist and most spectacularly ambivalent poet of the period ends his poem on Yeats with this simple, definite, and significantly affirmative quatrain:

> In the deserts of the heart
> Let the healing fountain start;
> In the prison of his days
> Teach the free man how to praise.

Dylan Thomas

[1 9 1 4 - 1 9 5 3]

*". . . whirling images, wild metaphors, and
a high eldritch music . . ."*

A T TWENTY-ONE Dylan Marlais Thomas erupted upon the world
with a burning violence of emotion and an unmatched vehemence of diction. Without the usual tentative first offering
and seemingly without antecedents, he became the most exciting
poet of his time. In a tragically short life he published a few
small books of poems, a volume of stories and autobiographical
sketches, *Portrait of the Artist as a Young Dog,* and one play.
Through these he enriched English literature with whirling images,
wild metaphors, and a high eldritch music that added new sights,
sounds, and sensations to the living language.

Born October 27, 1914, in the Welsh seaport of Swansea, son of
an English teacher, he attended the town's Grammar School. He
was more attracted by the local folklore than by the classroom
curriculum, but otherwise he was undistinguished from his schoolmates. As a boy, he says he was "small, thin, indecisively active,
quick to get dirty, curly." His formal education was over when he
left the Grammar School. He earned a living as an actor, reporter,
reviewer, script-writer, and by various odd jobs. During the Second
World War, he served as an· anti-aircraft gunner; it is thought that
his experiences may have been sublimated in the sweep and explo-
siveness of Thomas' verse. At twenty-two he was married to Caitlin
Macnamara, by whom he had three children, two sons, Llewelyn
and Colm, and a daughter, Airon, and settled in the fishing village
of Laugharne, Carmarthenshire. His home, called The Boat House,
was once a ferry landing.

He began reading poems over the air for the British Broadcasting
Company in his mid-twenties. In 1950 he made his first visit to the
United States, returning two years later, and again in 1953. He
gave recitals in which he half-declaimed, half-sang the lines. No
one who heard him read poetry—his own or others—ever forgot the
rolling vigor of his voice, its melodic subtlety, and its almost hypnotic power of incantation. There was about him a Shelley-like con-

currence of passion and lyrical purity which was overwhelming. Even those who could not understand his poetry on the printed page, considered him the most persuasive reader of the day.

He made himself at home in America. "I don't believe in New York," he said, "but I love Third Avenue." He was especially fond of one seaman's bar—Dylan is Welsh for the sea—and friends spoke of it as his literary and social club.

At thirty-five, Thomas described himself as "old, small, dark, intelligent, and darting-doting-dotting eyed . . . balding and toothlessing." His slimness was gone, and he had grown corpulent, but he was heavy without being gross, slow without losing his grace. During his third visit to the United States he was to confer with Igor Stravinsky concerning plans for an opera. The beginnings of a plot had already been outlined and Thomas expected to elaborate it at the composer's home in California. His *Collected Poems* had just become a sensational success, and he was particularly happy as he celebrated his thirty-ninth birthday in New York. The festivities, however, ended in illness, followed by a sudden collapse. Thomas was taken to St. Vincent's Hospital, where it was discovered that he was suffering from encephalopathy, a virulent disease of the brain. He died on November 9, 1953, less than two weeks later.

Thomas was not quite twenty when his first volume *Eighteen Poems,* was written, but "the reeling excitement of a poetry-intoxicated schoolboy," said Kenneth Rexroth in *New British Poets,* "smote the Philistine as hard a blow with one small book as Swinburne had with *Poems and Ballads . . .* Thomas wrote like a savage chief on a scalp-taking expedition among the savages . . . In him the spiritual underworld of a suppressed civilization, the Celtic shadow cast by the Saxon torch, found voice and took flesh." When Thomas' three early books were combined in *The World I Breathe,* its author was hailed as the most spectacular of the Surrealists and the leader of the group of insurgent writers which called itself the Apocalypse. Recalling Joyce, Thomas luxuriated in the day-dream, bathed in the subconscious, strewed his pages with invented words and fused puns ("ship-racked gospel," "gallow grave," "minstrel angle," for "ministering angel") in an orgy of abandoned rhetoric. Acknowledging his indebtedness to Freud, he stated that "Poetry is the rhythmic, inevitably narrative, movement from an overclothed blindness to a naked vision . . . Poetry must drag further into the clear nakedness of light more even of the hidden causes than Freud could realize." Yet, as John Malcolm Brinnin pointed out in a review of *The Selected Writings of Dylan Thomas,* "in his free use of images from the unconscious, Thomas never follows the somewhat anarchic methods of surrealism, to which uncontrolled automatism is basic, but organizes his image-making faculty with consciously severe discipline . . . The method is one of metaphorical logic— successive 'explosions of meaning,' rather than a point-by-point distribution of thematic elements. Tensions of language and rhythm carry with them the excitement of perceptions immediately felt rather than studied and detailed."

In Country Sleep, published a year before Thomas' death, was a renewed justification of Thomas' claim that his poetry was "the record of my individual struggle from darkness toward some measure of light . . . To be stripped of darkness is to be clean, to strip of darkness is to make clean." The statement, as well as the book, was a refutation of the common assertion that Thomas was carefully obscure and purposely mad. It was also an answer to those who maintained that Thomas was Auden's deliberate opposite, that, in contrast to Auden's premeditated intellectuality, Thomas lost himself in merely boisterous emotionalism. On the contrary, Thomas continually sought with complete consciousness for the origin of his ego and identified himself with all the elemental powers of nature: "My world was christened in a stream of milk/And earth and sky were as one airy hill," "I dreamed my genesis in sweat of sleep," "I . . . suffer the first vision that set fire to the stars," and:

> The force that through the green fuse drives the flower
> Drives my green age; that blasts the roots of trees
> Is my destroyer.
> And I am dumb to tell the crooked rose
> My youth is bent by the same wintry fever.

"His syntax," wrote Elder Olson in *The Poetry of Dylan Thomas,* "is full of pitfalls for the unwary . . . He writes as if he were one of the Welsh enigmatic poets of the fourteenth century." Even to his admirers Thomas' originality was sometimes too extreme for comprehension, but the very critics who were confused by his fountain-like uprush of words did not question the power of his genius. There was no gainsaying the drive of his strange music, the strength of his lusty and often bawdy symbols, his ecstatic love of living and his loud joy in all its rich sensuality. "The closer I move to death, the louder the sun blooms," he cried with confident gladness. Only in Gerard Manley Hopkins is there such a constant and effusive sense of inventiveness, and nowhere in modern poetry is there so astonishing a mixture of gayety and grimness. Thomas is obsessed with the agonies of birth and the anxieties of death—remnants of an unorthodox training are heard in his curious reanimation of the Bible and his studies of Freud, a montage of mythology and psychopathology—but his natural exuberance cannot be suppressed.

Under Milk Wood was Thomas' last work. Originally commissioned by the British Broadcasting Company, tried out in the United States in May, 1953, with the poet himself reading two of the parts, it was expanded and completed just before his death. The poemplay is not a drama but a lyric pageant of people. The speech ranges from pure contemplation to limber, bawdy ballads. Nothing happens except in the minds of the characters who, during twenty-four reminiscent hours from dawn to dawn, the full circle of a spring day, are stirred to recall the casual and crucial moments of their lives. Humorous small talk mingles with terror, vague desires and rude carnalities overlap, drink and dreams make a rough chronicle which projects the spirit of a community, the coastal town in which Thomas lived and which, with an unearthly magic, he recreates and transfigures.

This is the beginning of *Under Milk Wood:*

> It is spring, moonless night in the small town, starless and
> bible-black, the cobble-streets silent and the hunched,
> courters'-and-rabbits' wood limping invisible down to
> the slowback, slow, black, crowblack, fishingboat-bobbing
> sea . . .

And this is its concluding "stage direction":

> The thin night darkens. A breeze from the creased water
> sighs the streets close under Milk waking Wood. The
> Wood, whose every treefoot's cloven in the black glad
> sight of the hunters or lovers, that is a God-built garden
> to Mary Ann Sailors, who knows there is Heaven on earth,
> and the chosen people of His kind fire in Llareggub's
> land, that is the fair-day farmhands' wantoning, ignorant
> chapel of bridesbeds, and to the Reverend Eli Jenkins,
> a green-leaved sermon on the innocence of men, the
> suddenly windshaken wood springs awake for the second
> dark time this one spring day.

There will always be complaints about Thomas' tempestuous virtuosity, his dazzling but precise choice of epithets, his seemingly feverish distortions which are actually the result of extraordinarily cool and careful reorganization. And there will, on the other hand, be a particular delight in the discovery of many lines which, in common with the best poetry, are untranslatable, poems that have an immediacy which is indefinable but unmistakable. His words were written, Thomas said, "for the love of man and in praise of God—and I'd be a damned fool if they weren't." The love of man and the praise of God overflow everywhere from the poems, notably those beginning "When all my five and country senses see," "Light breaks where no sun shines," "The hand that signed a paper felled a city," "And death shall have no dominion," "Through throats where many rivers meet, the curlews cry," as well as from the poignant evocation of "The Hunchback in the Park," the clear luxuriance of "In Memory of Ann Jones," and the simple carefree earthiness of "Fern Hill," with its blithe opening:

> Now as I was young and easy under the apple boughs
> About the lilting house and happy as the grass was green,
>   The night above the dingle starry,
>   Time let me hail and climb
>   Golden in the heydays of his eyes . . .

Instinctive rather than intellectual, Thomas' poetry is so genuinely impassioned, so deeply expressive—who can forget a phrase like "a grief ago"?—so buoyantly persuasive that, if it is forbidding at first glance, it is finally irresistible. If it is intemperate in pitch and indiscriminate in piling up word-pictures, it has the virtues of overabundance. For, as an earlier English poet, Laurence Binyon, wrote in a Blake-like couplet:

> . . . the spirit born to bless
> Lives but in its own excess.

The air Thomas breathed was taut with wonder. He rollicked through the world with savage innocence and took a child's delight in its rich and irresponsible tumult.

A Selected Bibliography

As THE HEADING indicates, this bibliography makes no pretension to being complete. With a few exceptions, it omits magazine articles, reviews, and books in foreign languages. It is, however, a list of the valuable and generally illuminating volumes to which, besides the works by the subjects themselves, the author had recourse during the progress of his book. The following titles are recommended not only as primary sources for greater detail but for stimulating and rewarding reading.

The arrangement of the names of the subjects is alphabetical. The arrangement of the book titles under each name is chronological.

SUSAN B. ANTHONY

Ida Husted Harper: *The Life and Work of Susan B. Anthony* (3 volumes). Bowen-Merrill Company, 1899-1908.
George Sherwood Eddy and Kirby Page: *Makers of Freedom*. George H. Doran Company, 1926.
Rheta Childe Dorr: *Susan B. Anthony: The Woman Who Changed the Mind of a Nation*. Frederick A. Stokes Company, 1928.
Constance Buel Burnett: *Five for Freedom*. Abelard Press, 1953.
Katharine Anthony: *Susan B. Anthony: Her Personal History*. Doubleday and Company, 1954.

W. H. AUDEN

Francis Scarfe: *Auden and After*. Routledge & Sons (London), 1942.
Richard Hoggart: *Auden: An Introductory Essay*. Yale University Press, 1952.

CHARLES BAUDELAIRE

Arthur Symons: *Charles Baudelaire: A Study*. Elkin Mathews (London), 1920.
François Porché: *Charles Baudelaire*. Horace Liveright, Inc., 1928.
Peter Quennel: *Baudelaire and the Symbolists*. Chatto & Windus (London), 1929.
Lewis Piaget Shanks: *Baudelaire: Flesh and Spirit*. Little, Brown & Company, 1930.
Enid Starkie: *Baudelaire*. G. P. Putnam's Sons, 1933.
Edward Morgan: *Flower of Evil: A Life of Baudelaire*. Sheed & Ward, 1943.
P. Mansell Jones: *Baudelaire*. Yale University Press, 1952.

HENRI BERGSON

Horace M. Kallen: *William James and Henri Bergson*. University of Chicago Press, 1914.

John Alexander Gunn: *Bergson and His Philosophy*. Methuen and Company (London), 1920.
Olive A. Wheeler: *Bergson and Education*. Longmans, Green & Company, Inc., 1922.
Jacques Chevalier: *Henri Bergson*. The Macmillan Company, 1928.

PAUL CEZANNE

Julius Meier-Graefe: *Cézanne*. Ernest Benn (London) 1927.
Gerstle Mack: *Paul Cézanne*. Alfred A. Knopf, Inc., 1935.
Ambroise Vollard: *Paul Cézanne: His Life and Art*. Crown Publishers, 1937.
Albert Coombs Barnes: *The Art of Cézanne*. Harcourt, Brace & Company, 1939.
John Rewald: *Paul Cézanne: A Biography*. Simon and Schuster, Inc., 1948.
Roger Eliot Fry: *Cézanne: A Study of His Development*. The Macmillan Company, 1950.

CHARLES CHAPLIN

Max Eastman: *Heroes I Have Known* ("Actor of One Role"). Simon and Schuster, Inc., 1942.
Theodore Huff: *Charlie Chaplin*. Henry Schuman, 1951.
Robert Payne: *The Great God Pan: Biography of the Tramp*. Hermitage House, 1952.
Peter Cotes and Thelma Niklaus: *The Little Fellow*. Philosophical Library, 1952.

ANTON CHEKHOV

Olga Knipper Chekhov: *A Few Words About Chekhov*. George H. Doran Company, 1924.
S. S. Koteliansky: *Anton Chekhov: Literary and Theatrical Reminiscences*. Routledge & Sons (London), 1927.
D. S. Mirsky: *A History of Russian Literature*. Alfred A. Knopf, Inc., 1947.
Lidiya Alekseyevna Avilova: *Chekhov in My Life: A Love Story*. J. Lehman (London), 1950.
Ronald Hingley: *Chekhov: A Biographical and Critical Study*. Allen & Unwin (London), 1950.
David Magarshack: *Chekhov: A Life*. Grove Press, 1953.

WINSTON CHURCHILL

Dwight D. Eisenhower: *Crusade in Europe*. Doubleday & Company, Inc., 1948.
Robert Lewis Taylor: *Winston Churchill: An Informal Study of Greatness*. Doubleday & Company, Inc., 1952.
Virginia Cowles: *Winston Churchill: The Era and the Man*. Harper & Brothers, 1953.
Charles Eade (editor): *Churchill by His Contemporaries*. Simon and Schuster, Inc., 1954.

STEPHEN CRANE

Thomas Beer: *Stephen Crane*. Alfred A. Knopf, Inc., 1926.
Matthew Josephson: *Portrait of the Artist as American*. Harcourt, Brace and Company, 1930.
John Berryman: *Stephen Crane*. William Sloane Associates, 1950.
Robert Wooster Stallman (editor): *Stephen Crane: An Omnibus*. Alfred A. Knopf, Inc., 1952.

MARIE CURIE

Marion Cunningham: *Madame Curie and the Story of Radium*. St. Catherine Press (London), 1917.
Eve Curie: *Madame Curie*. Doubleday & Company, Inc., 1938.
Irmengarde Eberle: *Radium Treasure and the Curies*. T. Y. Crowell Company, 1942.

CHARLES DARWIN

Charles H. Ward: *Charles Darwin: The Man and His Warfare*. John Murray, 1927.
Geoffrey H. Wells: *Charles Darwin: A Portrait*. Yale University Press, 1938.
Jacques Barzun: *Darwin, Marx, Wagner*. Little, Brown & Co., 1941.
Paul B. Sears: *Charles Darwin: The Naturalist as a Cultural Force*. Charles Scribner's Sons, 1950.

CLAUDE DEBUSSY

Romain Rolland: *Musicians of Today*. Henry Holt & Company, Inc., 1915.
Oscar Thompson: *Debussy: Man and Musician*. Dodd, Mead & Company, 1937.
Maurice Dumesnil: *Debussy, Master of Dreams*. Ives Washburn, 1940.
Piet Ketting: *Claude Achille Debussy*. Continental Book Company, 1947.
Edward Lockspeiser: *Debussy*. Pellegrini & Cudahy, 1949.

JOHN DEWEY

Sidney Hook: *John Dewey: An Intellectual Portrait*. The John Day Company, 1939.
Joseph Ratner: Introductory Essay (241 pp.) to *Intelligence in the Modern World* (*Selections from Dewey*). The Modern Library, 1939.
Various Contributors: *The Philosopher of the Common Man* (Essays in Celebration of Dewey's Eightieth Birthday). G. P. Putnam's Sons, 1940.
Sidney Hook (editor): *John Dewey, Philosopher of Science and Freedom*. The Dial Press, 1950.
Jerome Nathanson: *John Dewey: The Reconstruction of the Democratic Life*. Charles Scribner's Sons, 1951.

EMILY DICKINSON

Martha Dickinson Bianchi: *The Life and Letters of Emily Dickinson*. Houghton Mifflin Company, 1924.
Josephine Pollitt: *Emily Dickinson · The Human Background*. Harper & Brothers, 1930.

Genevieve Taggard: *The Life and Mind of Emily Dickinson*. Alfred A. Knopf, Inc., 1930.
Mabel Loomis Todd (editor). *Letters of Emily Dickinson*. Harper & Brothers, 1931.
George F. Whicher: *This Was a Poet: A Critical Biography of Emily Dickinson*. Charles Scribner's Sons, 1938.
Millicent Todd Bingham: *Ancestors' Brocades: The Literary Debut of Emily Dickinson*. Harper & Brothers, 1945.
Richard Chase: *Emily Dickinson*. William Sloane Associates, 1951.

FYODOR DOSTOEVSKY

Edward H. Carr: *Dostoevsky*. Houghton Mifflin Company, 1913.
Julius Meier-Graefe: *Dostoevsky: The Man and His Work*. Harcourt, Brace & Company, 1928.
Nikolas Berdyayev: *Dostoevsky: An Interpretation*. Sheed & Ward, 1934.
A. T. Yarmolinsky: *Dostoevsky*. Harcourt, Brace & Company, 1934.
Ernest J. Simmons: *Dostoevsky: The Making of a Novelist*. Oxford University Press, 1946.
René Fueloep-Miller: *Fyodor Dostoevsky: Insight, Faith, and Prophecy*. Charles Scribner's Sons, 1950.

THEODORE DREISER

H. L. Mencken: *A Book of Prefaces*. Alfred A. Knopf, Inc., 1917.
Theodore Dreiser: *A Book About Myself*. Boni & Liveright, 1922.
Theodore Dreiser: *A History of Myself: Dawn*. Boni & Liveright, 1931.
Robert H. Elias: *Theodore Dreiser: Apostle of Nature*. Alfred A. Knopf, Inc., 1948.
Helen Dreiser: *My Life with Dreiser*. World Publishing Company, 1951
Maxwell Geismar: *Rebels and Ancestors* ("Theodore Dreiser: The Double Soul"). Houghton Mifflin Company, 1953.

ISADORA DUNCAN

Isadora Duncan: *My Life*. Horace Liveright, Inc., 1927.
William Bolitho: *Twelve Against the Gods*. Simon and Schuster, Inc., 1929.
Max Eastman: *Heroes I Have Known*. Simon and Schuster, Inc., 1942.
Paul Magriel (editor): *Isadora Duncan*. Henry Holt & Company, Inc., 1947.

ARTHUR EDDINGTON

J. G. Crowther: *British Scientists of the Twentieth Century*. Routledge and Kegan Paul, Ltd. (London), 1940.

MARY BAKER EDDY

Mark Twain: *Christian Science*. Harper & Brothers, 1907.
Edwin Franden Dakin: *Mrs. Eddy*. Charles Scribner's Sons, 1929.
Hugh A. Studdert Kennedy: *Mrs. Eddy as I Knew Her*. Farallon Press, 1931.
Fernand E. d'Humy: *Mary Baker Eddy in a New Light*. Library Publishers, 1952.

THOMAS ALVA EDISON

George S. Bryan: *Edison: The Man and His Work*. Alfred A. Knopf, Inc., 1926.

Francis Trevelyan Miller: *Thomas A. Edison: Benefactor of Mankind*. John C. Winston Company, 1931.

H. Gordon Garbedian: *Thomas Alva Edison: Builder of Civilization*. Julian Messner, 1947.

Thomas A. Edison: *The Diary and Sundry Observations of Thomas Alva Edison*. Philosophical Library, 1948.

ALBERT EINSTEIN

Edwin E. Slosson: *Easy Lessons in Einstein*. Harcourt, Brace & Company, 1920.

Lincoln Barnett: *The Universe and Dr. Einstein*. Harper & Brothers, 1948; revised, 1950.

Albert Einstein: *Out of My Later Years*. Philosophical Library, 1950.

Philipp Frank: *Einstein: His Life and Times*. Alfred A. Knopf, Inc., 1953.

Antonina Vallentin: *The Drama of Albert Einstein*. Doubleday and Company, 1954.

T. S. ELIOT

F. O. Matthiessen: *The Achievement of T. S. Eliot*. Houghton Mifflin Company, 1935; revised and enlarged, Oxford University Press, 1949.

Stephen Spender: *The Destructive Element*. Jonathan Cape (London), 1935.

Raymond Preston: *"Four Quartets" Rehearsed: A Commentary*. Sheed & Ward, 1946.

Leonard Unger (editor): *T. S. Eliot: A Selected Critique*. Rinehart & Company, Inc., 1948.

Roy P. Basler: *Sex, Symbolism and Psychology in Literature*. Rutgers University Press, 1948.

Elizabeth Drew: *T. S. Eliot: The Design of His Poetry*. Charles Scribner's Sons, 1949.

B. Rajan (editor): *T. S. Eliot: A Study of His Writings by Several Hands*. Funk & Wagnalls Company, 1949.

Rossell Hope Robbins: *The T. S. Eliot Myth*. Henry Schuman, 1951.

Albert Mordell: *T. S. Eliot's Deficiencies as Social Critic*. Haldeman-Julius, 1951.

George Williamson: *A Reader's Guide to T. S. Eliot*. The Noonday Press, 1953.

WILLIAM FAULKNER

Harry Modean Campbell: *William Faulkner: A Critical Appraisal*. University of Oklahoma Press, 1951.

Malcolm Cowley (editor): Introduction and Notes to *The Portable Faulkner*. The Viking Press, 1951.

Frederick John Hoffman: *William Faulkner: Two Decades of Criticism*. Michigan State College Press, 1951.

Irving Howe: *William Faulkner: A Critical Study*. Random House, 1952.

Ward L. Miner: *The World of William Faulkner*. Duke University Press, 1952.
William Van O'Connor: *The Tangled Fire of William Faulkner*. University of Minnesota Press, 1954.
Robert Coughlan: *The Private World of William Faulkner*. Harper & Brothers, 1954.

F. SCOTT FITZGERALD

Paul Rosenfeld: *Men Seen: Twenty-four Modern Authors* ("Fitzgerald Before *The Great Gatsby*"). Paul Rosenfeld, 1925.
Malcolm Cowley: "Third Act and Epilogue." *The New Yorker* Magazine, 1945; revised, 1951.
Maxwell Geismar: *The Last of the Provincials* ("Orestes at the Ritz"). Houghton Mifflin Company, 1947.
Arthur Mizener: *The Far Side of Paradise: A Biography of F. Scott Fitzgerald*. Houghton Mifflin Company, 1950.
Lionel Trilling: *The Liberal Imagination*. The Viking Press, 1950.
Alfred Kazin (editor): *F. Scott Fitzgerald: The Man and His Work*. World Publishing Company, 1951.

GUSTAVE FLAUBERT

John Charles Tarver: *Gustave Flaubert: As Seen in His Works and Correspondence*. Constable and Company (London), 1895.
Emile Faguet: *Flaubert*. Houghton Mifflin Company, 1914.
Lewis Piaget Shanks: *Flaubert's Youth*. Johns Hopkins Press, 1927.
Francis Steegmuller: *Flaubert and Madame Bovary*. The Viking Press, 1939.
Henry James: *The Art of Fiction*. Oxford University Press, 1948.
Francis Steegmuller: *The Selected Letters of Flaubert*. Farrar, Straus & Young, Inc., 1954.

ALEXANDER FLEMING

L. J. Ludovici: *Fleming: Discoverer of Penicillin*. Dakers (London), 1954.

HENRY FORD

William C. Richards: *The Last Billionaire: Henry Ford*. Charles Scribner's Sons, 1950.
Harry Bennett: *We Never Called Him Henry*. Gold Medal Books, 1951.
Garet Garrett: *The Wild Wheel*. Pantheon Books, 1952.
Allan Nevins and Frank Ernest Hill: *Ford: The Times, the Man, the Company*. Charles Scribner's Sons, 1954.

SIGMUND FREUD

Fritz Wittels: *Freud and His Time*. Liveright Publication Corp., 1931.
A. A. Brill: *Introduction to the Basic Writings of Sigmund Freud*. Random House, 1938.
Hanns Sachs: *Freud: Master and Friend*. Harvard University Press, 1944.
Emil Ludwig: *Doctor Freud: An Analysis and A Warning*. Hellman, Williams & Company, 1947.

Patrick Mullahy: *Oedipus: Myth and Complex* ("The Theories of Sigmund Freud"). Hermitage Press, 1948.
Gregory Zilboorg: *Sigmund Freud: His Exploration of the Mind of Man.* Charles Scribner's Sons, 1951.
Ernest Jones: *The Life and Work of Sigmund Freud, Vol. I.* Basic Books, 1953.

ROBERT FROST

Gorham B. Munson: *Robert Frost: A Study in Sensibility and Good Sense.* George H. Doran Company, 1927
Sidney Cox: *Robert Frost: Original "Ordinary Man."* Henry Holt & Company, Inc., 1929.
Caroline Ford: *The Less Traveled Road: A Study of Robert Frost.* Harvard University Press, 1935.
Richard Thornton (editor): *Recognition of Robert Frost.* Henry Holt & Company, Inc., 1937.
Lawrance Thompson: *Fire and Ice: The Art and Thought of Robert Frost.* Henry Holt & Company, Inc., 1942.
Louis and Esther Mertins: *The Intervals of Robert Frost.* University of California Press, 1947.
Randall Jarrell: *Poetry and the Age.* Alfred A. Knopf, Inc., 1953.

MOHANDAS KARAMCHAND GANDHI

Romain Rolland: *Mahatma Gandhi.* The Century Company, 1924.
Robert Bernays: *Naked Fakir.* Henry Holt & Company, Inc., 1932.
Jethalal Shridharani: *War Without Violence.* Harcourt, Brace & Company, 1939.
Vincent Sheean: *Lead, Kindly Light.* Random House, 1949.
Louis Fischer: *The Life of Mahatma Gandhi.* Harper & Brothers, 1950.
George Edward Catlin: *In the Path of Gandhi.* H. Regnery Company, 1950.
Vera Brittain: *Search After Sunrise.* Macmillan & Company (London), 1951.
Reginald Reynolds: *A Quest for Gandhi.* Doubleday & Company, Inc., 1952.

GEORGE GERSHWIN

Merle Armitage (editor): *George Gershwin.* Longmans, Green & Company, Inc., 1938.

THOMAS HARDY

Lionel Johnson: *The Art of Thomas Hardy.* Dodd, Mead & Company, 1928.
Florence Emily Hardy: *The Early Life of Thomas Hardy.* The Macmillan Company, 1928.
Florence Emily Hardy: *The Later Years of Thomas Hardy.* The Macmillan Company, 1930.
Samuel C. Chew: *Thomas Hardy: Poet and Novelist.* Alfred A. Knopf, Inc., 1930.
Edmund Blunden: *Thomas Hardy.* Macmillan & Company (London), 1942.
Albert Joseph Guerard: *Thomas Hardy: The Novels and Stories.* Harvard University Press, 1949.

WILLIAM RANDOLPH HEARST

John K. Winkler: *W. R. Hearst: An American Phenomenon.* Simon and Schuster, Inc., 1928.
John Tebbel: *The Life and Good Times of William Randolph Hearst.* E. P. Dutton & Company, Inc., 1952.
Edmond D. Coblenz (editor): *William Randolph Hearst: A Portrait in His Own Words.* Simon and Schuster, Inc., 1952.

ERNEST HEMINGWAY

Gertrude Stein: *The Autobiography of Alice B. Toklas* ("Hemingway in Paris"). Random House, 1933.
Maxwell Geismar: *Writers in Crisis* ("Ernest Hemingway: You Could Always Come Back"). Houghton Mifflin Company, 1942.
Alfred Kazin: *On Native Grounds* ("Hemingway: Synopsis of a Career"). Harcourt, Brace & Company, 1942.
Edmund Wilson: *The Wound and the Bow* ("Hemingway: Gauge of Morale"). Oxford University Press, 1947.
Malcolm Cowley: "A Portrait of Mister Papa." *Life* Magazine, January 10, 1949.
John K. M. McCaffery (editor): *Ernest Hemingway: The Man and His Work.* World Publishing Company, 1950.
Carlos Baker: *Hemingway: The Writer as Artist.* Princeton University Press, 1953.
Charles A. Fenton: *The Apprenticeship of Ernest Hemingway.* Farrar, Straus, & Young, Inc., 1954.

ADOLF HITLER

Hermann Rauschning: *The Voice of Destruction.* G. P. Putnam's Sons, 1940.
Fritz Thyssen: *I Paid Hitler.* Hodder & Stoughton (London), 1941.
William Shirer: *A Berlin Diary.* Alfred A. Knopf, Inc., 1941.
Norman H. Baynes (editor): *The Speeches of Adolf Hitler* (2 volumes). Oxford University Press, 1942.
Konrad Heiden: *Der Fuehrer: Hitler's Rise to Power.* Houghton Mifflin Company, 1944.
Folke Bernadotte: *The Curtain Falls.* Alfred A. Knopf, Inc., 1945.
Alan Bullock: *Hitler: A Study in Tyranny.* Harper & Brothers, 1952.
H. R. Trevor-Roper (editor): *Hitler's Secret Conversations: 1941-1944.* Farrar, Straus & Young, Inc., 1953.

GERARD MANLEY HOPKINS

Humphry House (editor): *The Notebooks and Papers of Gerard Manley Hopkins.* Oxford University Press, 1937.
The Kenyon Critics: *Gerard Manley Hopkins.* New Directions, 1945.
Austin Warren: *Rage for Order: Essays in Criticism.* University of Chicago Press, 1948.
William Henry Gardner: *Gerard Manley Hopkins: A Study of Poetic Idiosyncrasy.* Yale University Press, 1948.

A. E. HOUSMAN

A. S. F. Gow: *A. E. Housman: A Sketch.* The Macmillan Company, 1936.
Laurence Housman: *My Brother, A. E. Housman.* Charles Scribner's Sons, 1938.
Percy Withers: *A Buried Life: Recollections of A. E. Housman.* Jonathan Cape (London), 1940.
Grant Richards: *Housman: 1897-1936.* Oxford University Press, 1941.

HENRIK IBSEN

George Bernard Shaw: *The Quintessence of Ibsenism.* Constable & Company (London), 1891.
H. B. Jaeger: *Henrik Ibsen: A Critical Biography.* McClurg & Company, 1901.
Archibald Henderson: *Henrik Ibsen* (2 volumes). Mitchell Kennerley, 1911.
Muriel Bradbrook: *Ibsen the Norwegian.* Chatto & Windus (London), 1946.
Janko Lavrin: *Ibsen: An Approach.* Methuen & Company (London), 1950.

HENRY JAMES

Rebecca West: *Henry James.* Nisbet and Company (London), 1916.
Joseph Warren Beach: *The Method of Henry James.* Yale University Press, 1918.
Van Wyck Brooks: *The Pilgrimage of Henry James.* E. P. Dutton & Company, Inc., 1925.
Stephen Spender: *The Destructive Element.* Houghton Mifflin Company, 1936.
Edmund Wilson: "The Ambiguity of Henry James" (in *The Triple Thinkers*). Harcourt, Brace & Company, 1938.
F. O. Matthiessen: *Henry James: The Major Phase.* Oxford University Press, 1944.
Elizabeth Stevenson: *The Crooked Corridor.* The Macmillan Company, 1949.
Michael Swan: *Henry James.* Longmans, Green & Company, Inc., 1950.
F. W. Dupee, *Henry James.* William Sloane Associates, 1951.
Leon Edel: *Henry James: The Untried Years.* J. D. Lippincott Company, 1953.

WILLIAM JAMES

Henry James: *Notes of a Son and Brother.* Charles Scribner's Sons, 1914.
William James: *The Letters of William James.* Little, Brown & Company, 1920.
Ralph Barton Perry: *The Thought and Character of William James* (2 volumes). Little, Brown & Company, 1935.
Houston Peterson (editor): *Great Teachers.* Rutgers University Press, 1946.
F. O. Matthiessen: *The James Family.* Alfred A. Knopf, Inc., 1947.
Lloyd Morris: *William James: The Message of a Modern Mind.* Charles Scribner's Sons, 1950.
Frederic Harold Young: *The Philosophy of Henry James, Sr.* Bookman Associates, 1951.

JAMES JOYCE

Stuart Gilbert: *James Joyce's "Ulysses."* Alfred A. Knopf, Inc., 1930; revised, 1952.
Frank Budgen: *James Joyce and the Making of "Ulysses."* Harrison Smith, 1934.
Herbert Gorman: *James Joyce.* Rinehart & Company, Inc., 1939; revised, 1948.
Harry Levin: *James Joyce: A Critical Introduction.* New Directions, 1941.
Joseph Campbell and Henry Morton Robinson: *A Skeleton Key to "Finnegans Wake."* Harcourt, Brace & Company, 1944.
W. Y. Tindall: *James Joyce: His Way of Interpreting the Modern World.* Charles Scribner's Sons, 1950.
L. A. G. Strong: *The Sacred River: An Approach to James Joyce.* Pellegrini & Cudahy, 1951.

FRANZ KAFKA

Angel Flores: *The Kafka Problem.* New Directions, 1946.
Harry Slochower and Others: *A Kafka Miscellany.* Twice a Year Press, 1946.
Max Brod: *Franz Kafka: A Biography.* Schocken Books, 1947.
Charles Neider: *The Frozen Sea: A Study of Franz Kafka.* Oxford University Press, 1948.
William Hubben: *Four Prophets of Our Destiny.* The Macmillan Company, 1952.
Willi Haas (editor): *Letters to Milena by Franz Kafka.* Farrar, Straus & Young, Inc., 1953.
Gustav Janouch: *Conversations with Kafka.* Frederick A. Prager, 1953.

SØREN KIERKEGAARD

Walter Lowrie: *A Short Life of Kierkegaard.* Princeton University Press, 1942.
Melville Chaning-Pearce: *Kierkegaard: A Study.* J. Clarke (London), 1948.
Marjorie Grene: *Dreadful Freedom: A Critique of Existentialism.* University of Chicago Press, 1948.
H. V. Martin: *Kierkegaard, The Melancholy Dane.* Philosophical Library, 1950.
William Hubben: *Four Prophets of Our Destiny.* The Macmillan Company, 1952.
Johannes Hohlenberg: *Søren Kierkegaard.* Pantheon Books, 1954.

RING LARDNER

Henry L. Mencken: *Prejudices: Fourth Series.* Alfred A. Knopf, Inc., 1926.
Maxwell Geismar: *Writers in Crisis.* Houghton Mifflin Company, 1942.
Gilbert Seldes: Introduction to *The Portable Ring Lardner.* The Viking Press, 1946.

D. H. LAWRENCE

John Middleton Murry: *Son of Woman: The Story of D. H. Lawrence.* Cape & Smith, 1931.
Mabel Dodge Luhan: *Lorenzo in Taos.* Alfred A. Knopf, Inc., 1932.

Horace Gregory: *Pilgrim of the Apocalypse.* The Viking Press, 1933.
Hugh Kingsmill: *The Life of D. H. Lawrence.* Dodge Publishing Company, 1938.
Knud Merrild: *A Poet and Two Painters.* The Viking Press, 1939.
William York Tindall: *D. H. Lawrence and Susan His Cow.* Columbia University Press, 1939.
Richard Aldington: *D. H. Lawrence: Portrait of a Genius, But . . .* Duell, Sloan & Pearce, Inc., 1950.
Witter Bynner: *Journey with Genius.* The John Day Company, 1951.
Harry T. Moore: *The Life and Works of D. H. Lawrence.* Twayne Publishers, 1951.
Harry T. Moore: *The Intelligent Heart* ("The Story of D. H. Lawrence"). Farrar, Straus & Young, Inc., 1954.

NIKOLAI LENIN

Valeriu Marcu: *Lenin.* The Macmillan Company, 1929.
Nina Baker Brown: *Lenin.* The Vanguard Press, 1945.
Frederick Mayer: *A History of Modern Philosophy.* The American Book Company, 1951.
Robert Heilbroner: *The Worldly Philosophers.* Simon and Schuster, Inc., 1953.
Hugh Seton-Watson: *From Lenin to Malenkov.* Frederick A. Prager, 1953.

SINCLAIR LEWIS

Maxwell Geismar: *The Last of the Provincials* ("Sinclair Lewis: The Cosmic Bourjoyce"). Houghton Mifflin Company, 1947.
Harrison Smith (editor): *From Main Street to Stockholm: Letters of Sinclair Lewis.* Harcourt, Brace & Company, 1952.
Harry E. Maule and Melville Cane (editors): *The Man from Main Street.* Random House, 1953.

ANDRÉ MALRAUX

Janet Flanner: *The Human Condition.* The New Yorker, November 6 and 13, 1954.

THOMAS MANN

James Cleugh: *Thomas Mann: A Study.* Martin Secker (London), 1933.
Joseph Gerard Brennan: *Thomas Mann's World.* Columbia University Press, 1942.
Charles Neider (editor): *The Stature of Thomas Mann: A Critical Anthology.* New Directions, 1947.
Joseph Warren Angell (editor): *The Thomas Mann Reader.* Alfred A. Knopf, Inc., 1950.

GUGLIELMO MARCONI

B. L. Jacot & D. M. B. Collier: *Marconi: Master of Space.* Hutchinson & Company (London), 1935.
Orrin Elmer Dunlap: *Marconi: The Man and His Wireless.* The Macmillan Company, 1937.
Douglas Coe: *Marconi: Pioneer of Radio.* J. Messner, 1943.

KARL MARX

William J. Blake: *Elements of Marxian Economic Theory.* The Cordon Company, 1939.

F. Mehring: *Karl Marx.* Covici Friede, 1940.

Edmund Wilson: *To the Finland Station.* Harcourt, Brace & Company, 1940.

Paul M. Sweezy: *The Theory of Capitalist Development.* Oxford University Press, 1942.

Jacques Barzun: *Darwin, Marx, Wagner.* Little, Brown & Company, 1949.

Robert L. Heilbroner: *The Worldly Philosophers.* Simon and Schuster, Inc., 1953.

HENRI MATISSE

Albert Coombs Barnes: *The Art of Henri Matisse.* Charles Scribner's Sons, 1933.

Aleksander Romm: *Matisse: A Social Critique.* Lear (New York), 1947.

Alfred Hamilton Barr: *Matisse: His Art and His Public.* Museum of Modern Art, 1951.

HERMAN MELVILLE

Raymond M. Weaver: *Herman Melville: Mariner and Mystic.* George H. Doran Company, 1921.

John Freeman: *Herman Melville.* The Macmillan Company, 1926.

Lewis Mumford: *Herman Melville.* Harcourt, Brace & Company, 1929.

Van Wyck Brooks: *The Times of Melville and Whitman.* E. P. Dutton & Company, Inc., 1947.

Richard Chase: *Herman Melville: A Critical Study.* The Macmillan Company, 1949.

Newton Arvin: *Herman Melville.* William Sloane Associates, 1950.

Jay Leyda (editor): *The Melville Log* (2 volumes). Harcourt, Brace & Company, 1951.

Lawrance R. Thompson: *Melville's Quarrel with God.* Princeton University Press, 1952.

FRIEDRICH WILHELM NIETZSCHE

Henry Louis Mencken: *The Philosophy of Friedrich Nietzsche.* Luce and Company (Boston), 1913.

Georg Brandes: *Friedrich Nietzsche.* The Macmillan Company, 1914.

Herbert Leslie Stewart: *Nietzsche and the Ideals of Modern Germany.* Longmans, Green & Company, Inc., 1915.

Willard Huntington Wright: *What Nietzsche Taught.* B. W. Huebsch, 1915.

Clarence Crane Brinton: *Nietzsche.* Harvard University Press, 1941.

Eric Russell Bentley: *A Century of Hero-Worship.* J. B. Lippincott Company, 1944.

William Hubben: *Four Prophets of Our Destiny.* The Macmillan Company, 1952.

EUGENE O'NEILL

Barrett H. Clark: *Eugene O'Neill: The Man and His Plays.* R. M. McBride & Company, 1929.

Joseph Wood Krutch: Introduction to *Nine Plays by Eugene O'Neill*. The Modern Library, 1932.
Sophus Keith Winther: *Eugene O'Neill: A Critical Study*. Random House, 1934.
Richard Dana Skinner: *Eugene O'Neill: A Poet's Quest*. Longmans, Green & Company, Inc., 1935.
Edwin A. Engel: *The Haunted Heroes of Eugene O'Neill*. Harvard University Press, 1953.

LOUIS PASTEUR

René Vallery-Radot: *The Life of Pasteur*. Doubleday & Company, Inc., 1912.
L. Descour: *Pasteur and His Work*. T. Fisher Unwin (London), 1922.
Samuel Jackson Holmes: *Louis Pasteur*. Harcourt, Brace & Company, 1924.
Piers Compton: *The Genius of Louis Pasteur*. A. Ouseley, Ltd. (London), 1932.

PABLO PICASSO

Willard Huntington Wright: *Modern Painting*. John Lane, 1915.
Clive Bell: *Matisse and Picasso*. Chatto & Windus (London), 1922.
Herbert Read: *Great Contemporaries*. Cassell & Company (London), 1935.
Albert Coombs Barnes: *The Art in Painting*. Harcourt, Brace & Company, 1937.
Alfred H. Barr, Jr.: *Picasso: Fifty Years of His Art*. Museum of Modern Art-Simon and Schuster, Inc., 1946.
Christian Zervos: *Picasso*. Fernand Hazan (Paris), 1951.
Maurice Raynal: *Picasso*. Albert Skira, 1953.

MAX PLANCK

Max Planck: *Where Is Science Going?* W. W. Norton, 1936.
Richtmyer and Kennard: *Introduction to Modern Physics*. McGraw-Hill Company, 1942.
Max Planck: *Scientific Autobiography and Other Papers*. Philosophical Library, 1949.

EZRA POUND

T. S. Eliot: Introduction to *Selected Poems by Ezra Pound*. Faber & Gwyer (London), 1928.
Edith Sitwell: *Aspects of Modern Poetry*. Duckworth (London), 1934.
D. D. Paige (editor): *The Letters of Ezra Pound*. Harcourt, Brace & Company, 1950.
Peter Russell (editor): *An Examination of Ezra Pound* (Essays by Edith Sitwell, Allen Tate, T. S. Eliot and others). New Directions, 1950.
Hugh Kenner: *The Poetry of Ezra Pound*. New Directions, 1951.

MARCEL PROUST

Léon Pierre-Quint: *Marcel Proust: His Life and Work*. Alfred A. Knopf, Inc., 1927.
Clive Bell: *Proust*. Leonard & Virginia Woolf (London), 1928.

Leon Derrick: *Introduction to Proust*. Paul, Trench, Trubner (London), 1940.
Harold March: *The Two Worlds of Marcel Proust*. University of Pennsylvania Press, 1948.
Frederick Charles Green: *The Mind of Proust*. Cambridge University Press, 1949.
André Maurois: *Proust: Portrait of a Genius*. Harper & Brothers, 1950.
Charlotte Haldane: *Marcel Proust*. A. Barker (London), 1951.
François Mauriac: *Proust's Way*. Philosophical Library, 1951.
Milton Hindus: *The Proustian Vision*. Columbia University Press, 1954.

AUGUSTE RENOIR

Ambroise Vollard: *Renoir: An Intimate Record*. Alfred A. Knopf, Inc., 1925.
Albert Coombs Barnes: *The Art of Renoir*. Minton, Balch & Company, 1935.
Rosamund Frost: *Pierre Auguste Renoir*. Hyperion Press, 1944.
Germain Bazin: Introduction to *Renoir*. A. Skira, 1947.
Walter Pach: Introduction to *Pierre Auguste Renoir*. H. N. Abrams, 1950.

RAINER MARIA RILKE

Frederico Olivero: *Rainer Maria Rilke: A Study in Poetry and Mysticism*. Heffer & Sons (Cambridge), 1931.
M. D. Herter Norton: *Letters to a Young Poet*. W. W. Norton & Company, 1936.
J. B. Leishman: Introduction, Commentary, and Appendices to *Duino Elegies*. W. W. Norton & Company, 1939.
Eliza Marian Butler: *Rainer Maria Rilke*. University Press (Cambridge), 1941.
F. Heerikhuizen: *Rainer Maria Rilke: His Life and Work*. Routledge & Kegan Paul, Ltd. (London), 1951.
Hans Egon Holthusen: *Rainer Maria Rilke: A Study of His Later Poetry*. Yale University Press, 1952.
Marcel Raval (editor): *Rainer Maria Rilke: His Last Friendship*. Philosophical Library, 1952.

EDWIN ARLINGTON ROBINSON

Hermann Hagedorn: *Edwin Arlington Robinson*. The Macmillan Company, 1938.
Emery Neff: *Edwin Arlington Robinson*. William Sloane Associates, 1948.
Ellsworth Barnard: *Edwin Arlington Robinson: A Critical Study*. The Macmillan Company, 1952.

AUGUSTE RODIN

Frederick Lawton: *The Life and Work of Auguste Rodin*. Charles Scribner's Sons, 1907.
Anne Leslie: *Rodin: Immortal Peasant*. Prentice-Hall, 1937.
Judith Cladel: *Rodin*. Harcourt, Brace & Company, 1937.

Victor Frisch and Joseph T. Shipley: *Auguste Rodin*. F. A. Stokes Company, 1939.
Rainer Maria Rilke: *Rodin*. Fine Editions Press, 1945.

FRANKLIN DELANO ROOSEVELT

Ernest Kidder Lindley: *The Roosevelt Revolution*. The Viking Press, 1933.
Marquis W. Childs: *They Hate Roosevelt!* Harper & Brothers, 1936.
John Thomas Flynn: *Country Squire in the White House*. Doubleday, Doran & Company, 1940.
Gerald White Johnson: *Roosevelt: Dictator or Democrat*. Harper & Brothers, 1941.
Donald Porter Geddes (editor): *F. D. Roosevelt: A Memorial*. Pocket Books, 1945.
Alden Hatch: *Franklin D. Roosevelt: An Informal Biography*. Henry Holt and Company, Inc., 1947.
Charles Austin Beard: *President Roosevelt and the Coming of the War*. Yale University Press, 1948.
James Aloysius Farley: *Jim Farley's Story: The Roosevelt Years*. Whittlesey House, 1948.
Robert Emmet Sherwood: *Roosevelt and Hopkins: An Informal History*. Harper & Brothers, 1948.
Eleanor Roosevelt: *This I Remember*. Harper & Brothers, 1949.
John Gunther: *Roosevelt in Retrospect*. Harper & Brothers, 1950.
James N. Rosenau (editor): *The Roosevelt Treasury*. Doubleday & Company, Inc., 1951.

GEORGES ROUAULT

Lionello Venturi: *Georges Rouault*. E. Weyhe, 1940.
James Thrall Soby: *Georges Rouault*. Museum of Modern Art, 1945.
Edward Alden Jewell: *Georges Rouault*. The Hyperion Press, 1945.
Wallace Fowlie: *Jacob's Night: The Religious Renascence in France*. Sheed & Ward, 1947.

BERTRAND RUSSELL

Harvey Wickham: *The Unrealists*. The Dial Press, 1930.
John Dewey (editor): *The Bertrand Russell Case*. The Viking Press, 1941.
H. W. Leggett: *Bertrand Russell: A Pictorial Biography*. The Philosophical Library, 1950.
Lester Dennon (editor): *The Wit and Wisdom of Bertrand Russell*. The Beacon Press, 1951.

JEAN-PAUL SARTRE

H. J. Blackham: *Six Existentialist Thinkers*. The Macmillan Company, 1951.
James Collins: *The Existentialists: A Critical Study*. Henry Regnery Company, 1952.
Kurt F. Reinhardt: *The Existentialist Revolt*. Bruce Publishing Company, 1952.
Iris Murdoch: *Sartre*. Yale University Press, 1953.

ALBERT SCHWEITZER

George Seaver: *Albert Schweitzer: The Man and His Mind.* Harper & Brothers, 1947.

Charles R. Joy (editor): *Albert Schweitzer: An Anthology.* Harper & Brothers, 1947.

John Middleton Murry: *The Challenge of Schweitzer.* Jason Press (London), 1948.

Hermann Hagedorn: *Prophet in the Wilderness.* The Macmillan Company, 1948.

Charles R. Joy (editor): *The Wit and Wisdom of Albert Schweitzer.* Beacon Press, 1949.

Joseph Gollomb: *Albert Schweitzer: Genius in the Jungle.* Peter Nevill (London), 1951.

GEORGE BERNARD SHAW

Archibald Henderson: *Bernard Shaw: Playboy and Prophet.* D. Appleton Company, 1932.

Eric Bentley: *Bernard Shaw.* New Directions, 1947.

Stephen Winsten: *The Quintessence of G.B.S.* Creative Age Press, 1949.

William Irvine: *The Universe of G.B.S.* Whittlesey House, 1949.

Maurice Colbourne: *The Real Bernard Shaw.* Philosophical Library, 1949.

Edmund Fuller: *George Bernard Shaw.* Charles Scribner's Sons, 1950.

A. C. Ward: *Bernard Shaw.* Longmans, Green & Company, Inc., 1951.

E. F. Rattray: *Bernard Shaw: a Chronicle.* Roy Publishers, 1951.

Louis Kronenberger (editor): *George Bernard Shaw: A Critical Survey.* World Publishing Company, 1953.

OSWALD SPENGLER

R. G. Collingwood: "Spengler and the Theory of Historical Cycles" in *Antiquity:* A Quarterly Review of Archaeology, September, 1927.

H. Stuart Hughes: *Oswald Spengler: A Critical Estimate.* Charles Scribner's Sons, 1952.

JOSEPH STALIN

John Allen (editor): *One Hundred Great Lives.* The Greystone Press, 1948.

Nikolaus Basseches: *Stalin.* E. P. Dutton & Company, Inc., 1952.

Gregory Klimov: *The Terror Machine.* Frederick A. Prager, 1952.

Alexander Orlov: *The Secret History of Stalin's Crimes.* Random House, 1952.

I. N. Steinberg: *In the Workshop of the Revolution.* Rinehart & Company, Inc., 1953.

Leslie C. Stevens: *Russian Assignment.* Little, Brown & Company, 1953.

Ernest J. Simmons (editor): *Through the Glass of Soviet Literature.* Columbia University Press, 1953.

Merle Fainsod: *How Russia Is Ruled.* Harvard University Press, 1953.

Hugh Seton-Watson: *From Lenin to Malenkov.* Frederick A. Prager, 1953.

GERTRUDE STEIN

Edmund Wilson: *Axel's Castle: A Study of the Imaginative Literature of 1870-1930.* Charles Scribner's Sons, 1931.

Rosalind S. Miller: *Gertrude Stein: Form and Intelligibility*. The Exposition Press, 1949.
Donald Sutherland: *Gertrude Stein: An Autobiography of Her Work*. Yale University Press, 1951.
Donald Gallup (editor): *The Flowers of Friendship: Letters Written to Gertrude Stein*. Alfred A. Knopf, Inc., 1953.

IGOR STRAVINSKY

Merle Armitage (editor): *Igor Stravinsky*. G. Schirmer, Inc., 1936.
Eric Walter White: *Stravinsky: A Critical Survey*. J. Lehmann (London), 1947.
Minna Lederman: *Stravinsky in the Theater*. Pellegrini & Cudahy, 1949.
Frank Onnen: *Stravinsky*. Continental Book Company, 1949.
Alexandre Tansman: *Stravinsky: The Man and His Music*. G. P. Putnam's Sons, 1949.

SUN YAT-SEN

Paul Linebarger: *Sun Yat-sen and the Chinese Republic*. The Century Company, 1925.
Henry Bond Restarick: *Sun Yat-sen: Liberator of China*. Yale University Press, 1931.
Lyon Sharman: *Sun Yat-sen: His Life and Meaning*. John Day Company, 1934.
Emily Hahn: *The Soong Sisters*. Doubleday, Doran & Company, 1941.
Stephen Chen and Robert Payne: *Sun Yat-sen: A Portrait*. John Day Company, 1946.
Kenneth Scott Latourette: *A History of Modern China*. Penguin Books, 1954.

DYLAN THOMAS

Henry Treece: *How I See Apocalypse*. L. Drummond (London), 1946.
Elder Olson: *The Poetry of Dylan Thomas*. University of Chicago Press, 1954.

LEO TOLSTOY

Ilya Tolstoy: *Reminiscences of Tolstoy*. D. Appleton-Century Company, 1914.
Edward A. Steiner: *Tolstoy: The Man and His Message*. Fleming H. Revell Company, 1914.
Ernest J. Simmons: *Leo Tolstoy*. Little, Brown & Company, 1946.
Janko Lavrin: *Tolstoy: An Approach*. The Macmillan Company, 1946.
W. Somerset Maugham: *Great Novelists and Their Novels*. J. C. Winston Company, 1948.
D. S. Mirsky: *A History of Russian Literature*. Alfred A. Knopf, Inc., 1949.
Alexandra Tolstoy: *Tolstoy: A Life of My Father*. Harper & Brothers, 1953.
Isaiah Berlin: *The Hedgehog and the Fox: An Essay on Tolstoy's View of History*. Simon and Schuster, Inc., 1953.

HENRI DE TOULOUSE-LAUTREC

Paul de Lapparent: *Toulouse-Lautrec.* Dodd, Mead & Company, 1928.
Arthur Symons: *From Toulouse-Lautrec to Rodin.* John Lane (London), 1929.
Gerstle Mack: *Toulouse-Lautrec.* Alfred A. Knopf, Inc., 1938.

MARK TWAIN

Albert Bigelow Paine: *Mark Twain: A Biography* (3 volumes). Harper & Brothers, 1912.
Van Wyck Brooks: *The Ordeal of Mark Twain.* E. P. Dutton & Company, Inc., 1920.
Clara Clemens: *My Father, Mark Twain.* Harper & Brothers, 1931.
Bernard De Voto: *Mark Twain's America.* Little, Brown & Company, 1932.
Edgar Lee Masters: *Mark Twain: A Portrait.* Charles Scribner's Sons, 1938.
Bernard De Voto: *Mark Twain at Work.* Harvard University Press, 1942.
Henry Seidel Canby: *Turn West, Turn East: Mark Twain and Henry James.* Houghton Mifflin Company, 1951.
Dixon Wecter: *Sam Clemens of Hannibal.* Houghton Mifflin Company, 1952.

VINCENT VAN GOGH

Julius Meier-Graefe: *Vincent: A Life of Vincent Van Gogh.* John Lehmann (London), 1922.
Vincent Van Gogh: *The Letters of Vincent Van Gogh to His Brother: 1872-1886.* Houghton Mifflin Company, 1927.
Vincent Van Gogh: *Further Letters of Vincent Van Gogh to His Brother: 1886-1890.* Houghton Mifflin Company, 1929.
Irving Stone (editor): *The Autobiography of Vincent Van Gogh (Founded on his Letters).* Houghton Mifflin Company, 1937.
Daniel Catton Rich and Theodore Rousseau, Jr.: *Van Gogh: Paintings and Drawings.* The Metropolitan Museum of Art and The Art Institute of Chicago, 1949.
Meyer Schapiro: *Van Gogh (The Library of Great Paintings).* Harry N. Abrams, 1950.
Robert Goldwater: *Van Gogh (The Pocket Library of Great Art).* Harry N. Abrams, 1953.

THORSTEIN VEBLEN

Stuart Chase: Foreword to *The Theory of the Leisure Class.* Modern Library, 1934.
Joseph Dorfman: *Thorstein Veblen and His America.* The Viking Press, 1947.
Max Lerner: Introduction to *The Portable Veblen.* The Viking Press, 1950.
Robert L. Heilbroner: *The Worldly Philosophers.* Simon and Schuster, Inc., 1953.
David Riesman: *Thorstein Veblen.* Charles Scribner's Sons, 1953.

PAUL VERLAINE

Harold Nicolson: *Paul Verlaine.* Constable and Company (London), 1921.
Henry Edward Berthon (editor): *Nine French Poets.* Macmillan & Company (London), 1930.
Marcel Coulon: *Poet Under Saturn: The Tragedy of Verlaine.* H. Toulmon (London), 1932.
Eric Bechhofer Roberts: *Paul Verlaine.* Jarrolds, Ltd. (London), 1937.
Joseph M. Bernstein (editor): *Baudelaire, Rimbaud, Verlaine.* Citadel Press (New York), 1947.

RICHARD WAGNER

Albert Lavignac: *The Music Dramas of Richard Wagner.* Dodd, Mead & Company, 1898.
George Bernard Shaw: *The Perfect Wagnerite.* Herbert Stone (Chicago), 1898.
Henry T. Finck: *Wagner and His Works* (2 volumes). Charles Scribner's Sons, 1901.
Ernest Newman: *Fact and Fiction About Wagner.* Alfred A. Knopf, Inc., 1931.
Ernest Newman: *The Life of Richard Wagner* (4 volumes). Alfred A. Knopf, Inc., 1933-1946.
Thomas Mann: *Freud, Goethe, Wagner.* Alfred A. Knopf, Inc., 1937.
Jacques Barzun: *Darwin, Marx, Wagner.* Little, Brown & Company, 1947.
Richard Wagner: *Letters: The Burrell Collection.* The Macmillan Company, 1950.
Leon Stein: *The Racial Thinking of Richard Wagner.* Philosophical Library, 1950.
Julius Kapp: *The Loves of Richard Wagner.* W. H. Allen (London), 1951.

H. G. WELLS

H. G. Wells: *Experiment in Autobiography.* The Macmillan Company, 1934.
Harold Williams: *Modern English Writers: H. G. Wells.* Sidgwick & Jackson, 1935.
Norman Nicholson: *The English Novelists Series: H. G. Wells.* Arthur Barker, Ltd., 1950.
Antonina Vallentin: *H. G. Wells: Prophet of Our Day.* John Day Company, 1950.

WALT WHITMAN

Bliss Perry: *Walt Whitman.* Houghton Mifflin Company, 1906.
Horace Traubel: *With Walt Whitman in Camden.* D. Appleton & Company, 1908.
Emory Holloway: *Walt Whitman: An Interpretation in Narrative.* Alfred A. Knopf, Inc., 1926.
John Bailey: *Walt Whitman.* The Macmillan Company, 1926.
Edgar Lee Masters: *Whitman.* Charles Scribner's Sons, 1937.
Newton Arvin: *Whitman.* The Macmillan Company, 1938.
F. O. Matthiessen: *American Renaissance.* Oxford University Press, 1941.

Hugh I'Anson Fausset: *Walt Whitman: Poet of Democracy*. Yale University Press, 1942.
Henry Seidel Canby: *Walt Whitman: An American*. Houghton Mifflin Company, 1943.
Van Wyck Brooks: *The Times of Melville and Whitman*. E. P. Dutton & Company, Inc., 1947.

THOMAS WOLFE

John S. Terry (editor): *Thomas Wolfe's Letters to His Mother*. Charles Scribner's Sons, 1945.
Maxwell Geismar (editor): Introduction and Notes to *The Portable Thomas Wolfe*. The Viking Press, 1946.
Pamela Hansford Johnson: *Hungry Gulliver*. Charles Scribner's Sons, 1948.
Herbert J. Muller: *Thomas Wolfe*. New Directions, 1948.
Thomas Clark Pollock and Oscar Cargill: *Thomas Wolfe at Washington Square*. New York University Press, 1953.
Richard Gaither Walser (editor): *The Enigma of Thomas Wolfe* (A Collection of Essays by Various Writers). Harvard University Press, 1953.

FRANK LLOYD WRIGHT

Frank Lloyd Wright: *An Autobiography*. Duell, Sloan & Pearce, Inc., 1943.
John Lloyd Wright: *My Father Who Is on Earth*. G. P. Putnam's, 1946.
W. M. Moser: *Frank Lloyd Wright: 60 Years of Living Architecture*. Wittenborn & Company, 1952.
Edgar Kaufmann, Jr. (editor): *Taliesin Drawings by Frank Lloyd Wright*. Wittenborn & Company, 1952.

THE WRIGHT BROTHERS

Wright Brothers: "Our Aeroplane Tests at Kitty Hawk." *Scientific American,* June 13, 1908.
Lester J. Maitland: *Knights of the Air*. Doubleday & Company, 1929.
Fred C. Kelly: *The Wright Brothers*. Harcourt, Brace & Company, 1943.
Elsbeth E. Freudenthal: *Flight Into History*. University of Oklahoma Press, 1949.
Mervin W. McFarland: *The Papers of Wilbur and Orville Wright* (2 volumes). McGraw-Hill Company, 1953.

WILLIAM BUTLER YEATS

William Butler Yeats: *Letters on Poetry*. Oxford University Press, 1940.
Louis MacNeice: *The Poetry of W. B. Yeats*. Oxford University Press, 1941.
Joseph Hone: *W. B. Yeats: 1865-1939*. The Macmillan Company, 1943.
Richard Ellmann: *Yeats: The Man and the Masks*. The Macmillan Company, 1948.
A. Norman Jeffares: *W. B. Yeats: Man and Poet*. Yale University Press, 1949.
James Hall and Martin Steinmann (editors): *The Permanence of Yeats* (*Selected Criticism*). The Macmillan Company, 1950.
T. R. Henn: *The Lonely Tower: Studies in the Poetry of W. B. Yeats*. Pellegrini & Cudahy, 1952.

EMILE ZOLA

Henry James: *Notes on Novelists*. Charles Scribner's Sons, 1914.
Matthew Josephson: *Emile Zola and His Time*. The Macaulay Company, 1928.
John Rewald: *Paul Cézanne: A Biography*. Simon and Schuster, Inc., 1948.
Angus Wilson: *Emile Zola; An Introductory Study of His Novels*. Secker & Warburg (London), 1952.
F. W. J. Hemmings: *Emile Zola*. Oxford University Press, 1953.

Index

A

"A la Promenade" (Verlaine), 199
A la Recherche du Temps Perdu (Proust), 424
A l'Ombre des Jeunes Filles en Fleurs (Proust), 430
A Lume Spente (Pound), 644
A Rebours (Huysmans), 202
Abbott, Ellis, 627
A B C of Aesthetics, The (Leo Stein), 460
A B C of Reading, The (Pound), 648
Abercrombie, Lascelles, 167
Abraham, Gerald, 15
Absalom! Absalom! (Faulkner), 707
Acharnians, The (Aristophanes), 261
Achievement in American Poetry (Bogan), 474
Across the River and Into the Trees (Hemingway), 722
Acton, John Dalberg-Acton, 1st Baron, 549
Acushnet (ship), 49
"Ad Astra" (Faulkner), 707
Adams, Brooks, 556
Adams, Heinrich, 364
Adams, Henry, 556
Addams, Jane, 189
Adler, Alfred, 242
Adler and Sullivan (architects), 380
Advent (Rilke), 515
Adventure (periodical), 620
Adventures of Huckleberry Finn, The; see Huckleberry Finn, The Adventures of
Adventures of Tom Sawyer, The; see Tom Sawyer, The Adventures of
Æ (pseudonym of George Russell), 338, 589
Aeneid, The (Virgil), 655
Aeronautical Journal, 362
Aeschylus, 528
Aforesaid (Frost), 476
Agassiz, Louis, 183
Age of Anxiety, The (Auden), 750
"Age of Bronze" (Rodin), 172
Age of Reason, The (Sartre), 742

Agee, James, 676
Agostinelli (Proust's secretary), 430
Ah, Wilderness! (O'Neill), 665
Albaret, Céleste, 429
Albert Edward, Prince of Wales (Edward VII), 525
Albert Einstein College of Medicine, 540
Albert Schweitzer Fellowship, 504
Albertine Disparue (Proust), 430
Alcestis (Euripides), 659
Aldington, Richard, 592, 640
Alexander III (Russia), 410
Alexander, Franz, 241
Alger, Horatio, 220
All God's Chillun Got Wings (O'Neill), 665
All the Sad Young Men (Fitzgerald), 697
"Allée, L'" (Verlaine), 199
Alliluyeva, Nadya, 546
Amaranth (Robinson), 403
Ambassadors, The (Henry James), 190, 194
America (Kafka), 614, 616
"American in Paris, An" (Gershwin), 714, 715
American Primer, An (Whitman), 44
"American Scholar, The" (Emerson), 44
American Society for the Suppression of Vice, 591
American Tobacco Company, 324
American Tragedy, An (Dreiser), 441
Amherst Academy, 133
Amherst College, 473
"Among Schoolchildren" (Yeats), 342
Amores (Lawrence), 634
Anatole France and His Muse (Pouquet), 426
Anatomy of Melancholy (Burton), 219
Ancelle (a notary), 68
Andersen, Hans Christian, 506
Anderson, Maxwell, 252
Anderson, Sherwood, 461, 703, 717-718, 719, 722
Androcles and the Lion (Shaw), 257
Angell, Joseph Warner, 509

Ann Veronica (Wells), 348
Ann Vickers (Lewis), 623
Anna Christie (O'Neill), 664
Anna Karenina (Tolstoy), 126-127
Annalen der Physik, 534
Annales de Mathématique, 281
Anne, Queen (England), 484
Another Time (Auden), 748, 752
Anthony, Daniel, 60, 61
Anthony, Lucy Read; *see* Read, Lucy
Anthony, Susan Brownell, 60-65
Antichrist, The (Nietzsche), 214
Antony and Cleopatra (Shakespeare), 255
Apel, Theodor, 15
Apocalypse (Lawrence), 640
Apollon Musagètes (Stravinsky), 603
Apple Cart, The (Shaw), 254, 258
Arch Street Presbyterian Church (Philadelphia), 135
Archer, William, 117, 248, 249, 250
Aristophanes, 261
Aristotle, 592
Arms and the Man (Shaw), 249, 251
Arnold, Benedict, 327
Arnold, Matthew, 749
Arosa, Achille Antoine, 303
Arrowsmith (Lewis), 622, 623
Art, L' (magazine), 71
"Art and Revolution" (Wagner), 18
Art of Organ Building and Organ Playing in Germany and France, The (Schweitzer), 501
"Art-Work of the Future, The" (Wagner), 18, 24
Arts, The (periodical), 569
Arvin, Newton, 53, 196
As I Lay Dying (Faulkner), 705
As You Like It (Shakespeare), 308
"Ash-Wednesday" (Eliot), 423, 656, 657
Assomoir, L' (Zola), 162
Atkinson, Brooks, 298, 664-665
Atlantic Charter, 495, 582
Atlantic Monthly, 191, 444
Atomic War or Peace (Einstein), 536
Attack Upon Christendom (Kierkegaard), 9
Attlee, Clement, 260
Aubert, Françoise-Emilie, 156; *see also* Zola, Françoise-Emilie
Auden, Wystan Hugh, 169, 204, 508, 516, 604, 747-753, 755
Auden and After (Scarfe), 747, 749
Aufzeichnungen des Malte Laurids Brigge, Die (Rilke), 517
"Auguries of Innocence" (Blake), 572
Augustine, St., 7
Aupick, General Jacques, 66, 67, 68
Aurevilly, Barbey d', 66, 67
Auric, Georges, 598
Auschwitz (concentration camp), 615

Autobiography (Freud), 243
Autobiography (Stravinsky), 599, 603
Autobiography (Frank Lloyd Wright), 379, 380, 384
Autobiography (Yeats), 337
Autobiography (Zweig), 243
Autobiography of Alice B. Toklas (Gertrude Stein), 461, 465, 466
"Ave Atque Vale" (Swinburne), 71
Avelova, Lidiya, 297
Avon's Harvest (Robinson), 402
Avril, Jane, 331
Axel's Castle (Wilson), 461

B

Babbitt (Lewis), 622
Babel's Tower (Taylor), 571
"Babes in the Woods" (Fitzgerald), 693
"Babylon Revisited" (Fitzgerald), 699
Bach, Johann Sebastian, 13, 500 f., 603, 647
Back to Methuselah (Shaw), 252, 258
Bacon, Roger, 345
Baille, Baptistin, 150, 156, 158, 159
Baiser de la Fée, Le (Stravinsky), 602
Baker, Abigail, 74
Baker, George Pierce, 663, 727
Baker, Mark, 74
Baker, Mary Ann Morse, 74; *see also* Eddy, Mary Baker
Baker, Nina Brown, 417
Baker, Samuel, 74
Bakunin, Mikhail Alexandrovich, 17
Baldwin, Stanley, 493, 494
Balfour, Arthur, 489
Balzac, Honoré de, 82, 83, 161, 174, 175, 191, 435
Banquet, Le (periodical), 427
Banville, Théodore de, 198, 200
Barbusse, Henri, 161
Bardac, Mme. Emma, 307
Bardac, Sigismond, 307
Bardach, Emilie, 119
Barnacle, Nora, 588
Barnes Foundation, 456
Barnett, Lincoln, 537
Barnum, Phineas Taylor, 36
Barr, Alfred H., Jr., 568, 571
Barrault, Jean-Louis, 616
Barrett, Edward Moulton, 133
Barrie, James M., 257
Barroom, The (Zola), 162
Barry, Joan, 674
Barth, Karl, 11
Bartlett, John, 75
Barye, Antoine Louis, 171
Barzun, Jacques, 5, 32
Basic Writings of Sigmund Freud, The (Brill), 239

Bassetto, Corno di (pseudonym of George Bernard Shaw), 249
Bastien-Lepage, Jules, 173
Bateau Ivre, Le (Rimbaud), 200
Battle-Pieces (Melville), 56
Baudelaire, Charles Pierre, 66-72, 99, 100, 173, 175, 198, 651, 652, 709
Beach, Sylvia, 591
Beagle, H. M. S. (ship), 2, 3
"Bear, The" (Faulkner), 705
Beard, Charles Austin, 320
Beautiful and the Damned, The (Fitzgerald), 695
Beaux Arts, Ecole des, 151, 170, 420
Becquerel, Henri, 373, 375
Beer, Thomas, 445
Beerbohm, Max, 551
Beethoven, Ludwig van, 13, 249, 303, 529, 553
Being and Non-Being (Sartre), 743
Belinsky, Vissarion, 83
Bell, Alexander Graham, 223
Beloved Returns, The (Thomas Mann), 512
Ben Hur (Wallace), 643
Benedict XV (Pope), 175
Benét, Stephen Vincent, 585
Benito Cereno (Melville), 56
Bennett, Harry, 326, 328
Bennett, James Gordon, 481
Benson, Frank, 525
Beowulf, 750
Berceuses du Chat (Stravinsky), 600
Berger, Arthur, 601
Bergson, Henri, 217, 281-286, 426, 431
Berlioz, Hector, 16
Bernays, Martha, 239; *see also* Freud, Martha
Bernstein, Aline, 728
Bernstein, Joseph M., 68
Bers, Sonya, 125; *see also* Tolstaya, Sonya
Bertrand Russell, O.M. (Leggett), 453
Besant, Annie, 253
Bethel Merriday (Lewis), 623
Beuret, Rose, 171, 176
Bewitched Parsonage, The (Braithwaite), 136
Beyond Good and Evil (Nietzsche), 214
Beyond the Horizon (O'Neill), 663
Bezzi-Scali, Countess Maria Cristina, 482
Bhagavad-Gita, 391
Bianchi, Martha Dickinson, 134
Bible, 36, 54, 74, 80, 82, 84, 210, 230, 339, 353, 756
"Biblical Landscape" (Rouault), 423
Big Money, The (Dos Passos), 262
Billings, Josh (pseudonym of Henry Wheeler Shaw), 142

Billy Budd, Foretopman (Melville), 50, 57
Binyon, Laurence, 757
"Birches" (Frost), 473
"Birth of a Nation, The" (motion picture), 671
Birth of Tragedy from the Spirit of Music, The (Nietzsche), 211
Bishop, John Peale, 692
Bismarck, Otto von, 455
Bizet, Georges, 214, 426
Bizet-Straus, Mme. Geneviève; *see* Straus, Mme. Geneviève
Björnson, Björnstjerne, 118
Black, Dora Winifred, 453; *see also* Russell, Dora
Black Riders and Other Lines, The (Crane), 447, 448
Black Swan, The (Thomas Mann), 512
Blake, William, 137, 338, 342, 388, 572
Blankenship, Tom, 139
Blast (periodical), 645
Blavatsky, Elena Petrovna, 337
"Blessed Damozel, The" (Rossetti), 304
Bloy, Léon, 421
"Blue and the Gray, The" (Dresser), 436
"Blue Danube, The" (Strauss), 527, 528
Blunt, Wilfrid Scawen, 276
"Boating Party Luncheon" (Renoir), 180
Boer War, 392, 489-490, 576
Bogan, Louise, 474, 520
Bohème, La (Puccini), 445
Bohemian (periodical), 438
Bohr, Niels, 274, 608
"Bolero" (Ravel), 714
Bolitho, William, 527, 532, 626
Bonnat, Léon, 330
Bonne Chanson, La (Verlaine), 199
Book of Common Prayer, The, 656
Book of Hours, The (Rilke), 517
Book of Pictures, The (Rilke), 515
Book of Prefaces, A (Mencken), 438
Bookbinder, Hilarius (pseudonym of Kierkegaard), 8
Books and Characters (Strachey), 552
Boon (Wells), 196
Borodin, Alexander, 303
Bossuet, Jacques Bénigne, 105
Boston Intelligencer, 37
Bouguereau, Adolphe William, 152, 405
Bouilhet, Louis, 91, 94, 96, 97, 100
Boulton, Agnes, 665
Bound East for Cardiff (O'Neill), 663
Bouvard and Pécuchet (Flaubert), 100, 101
Bowen, Elizabeth, 641
"Bowery, The" (Dresser), 436
Boy in the Bush, The (Lawrence), 638

Boy's Will, A (Frost), 470
Bradley, Captain Alva, 218-219
Brand (Ibsen), 9, 115
Brandeis, Louis D., 189
Brandes, Georg, 118
Branly, Edouard, 479
Braque, Georges, 461, 462, 568, 598
Braithwaite, William Stanley, 136-137
Braun, Eva, 687, 690
Bresslau, Helene, 502; *see also* Schweitzer, Helene
Breton, Jules, 229, 235
Brewer, Griffith, 364
Brewsie and Willie (Gertrude Stein), 466
Bridges, Robert, 205, 206, 207
Brill, Dr. Abraham Arden, 239, 242
Brinnin, John Malcolm, 754
Brisbane, Albert, 314
British Journal of Experimental Pathology, 561
British Museum, 29, 248, 345, 525
Broadway Magazine, 438
Brod, Max, 613, 614, 616
Brontë, Emily, 137
Brooke, Rupert, 470
Brooklyn Daily Times, 39
Brooklyn Eagle, 35
Brooks, Cleanth, 343
Brooks, Van Wyck, 196, 466
Brothers Karamazov, The (Dostoevsky), 84, 87, 88, 89
Brown, John, 287
Brown, John Mason, 665, 667
Browne, Charles Farrar, 142
Browning, Elizabeth Barrett, 63, 133, 517
Browning, Robert, 168, 644
Bruant, Aristide, 331
Bruno, Giordano, 594
Bryan, George S., 225
Bryan, William Jennings, 5, 316, 319, 443
Buch der Bilder, Das (Rilke), 515
Bucke, Dr. Richard M., 43
Buddenbrooks (Thomas Mann), 507-508
Bülow, Cosima Liszt von, 21, 22
Bülow, Hans von, 21, 22
Bullock, Alan, 680, 684
Bulpington of Blup, The (Wells), 350
Bulwark, The (Dreiser), 442
Bunyan, John, 458
Buonanni (Italian scientist), 104
Buoyant Billions (Shaw), 259
"Burgher of Calais, The" (Rodin), 173
Burkholder, Paul, 563
Burns, Robert, 559
Burroughs, John, 43
Burton, Robert, 219
Butterick, Ebenezer, 438

Bynner, Witter, 641
"Byzantium" (Yeats), 343

C

C Major Symphony (Wagner), 13
Cabanel, Alexandre, 152
Cabell, James Branch, 623
Caesar and Cleopatra (Shaw), 254, 255
Caillavet, Mme. Arman de, 426, 427
Caillavet, Gaston de, 426
Cakes and Ale (Maugham), 167
"Calamus" (Whitman), 43
Calhoun, Eleanor, 317
Calhoun, John, 317
Callot, Jacques, 420
Campbell, Mrs. Patrick, 254, 258
Canby, Henry S., 641
Candida (Shaw), 251
Cantlie, Sir James, 354, 355
Cantos (Pound), 646, 647, 648
Canzoni (Pound), 644
Capital (Marx), 30, 31, 32, 33; *see also Kapital, Das*
Captain Brassbound's Conversion (Shaw), 255
Captain Craig (Robinson), 401
Captive, The (Proust), 430
Carnegie, Andrew, 377
Carmen (Bizet), 214
Carolina Folk Songs, 727
Carrier-Belleuse, Albert Ernest, 171
Carroll, Lewis, 594, 629
Carswell, Catherine, 638, 640
Case Against Psychoanalysis, The (Salter), 245
Case of Wagner, The (Nietzsche), 214
Cass Timberlane (Lewis), 623
Castle, The (Kafka), 615, 616, 617
"Cathédrale Engloutie, La" (Debussy), 308
Cather, Willa, 623
Cathleen ni Houlihan (Yeats), 338
Catiline (Ibsen), 114
Cavalcanti, Guido, 655
Cavender's House (Robinson), 402
Cellini, Benvenuto, 316
Cervantes Saavedra, Miguel de, 572
Cézanne, Louis-Auguste, 149, 153
Cézanne, Marie, 149
Cézanne, Paul, 149-155, 156, 157, 158, 159, 161, 174, 178, 179, 406, 408, 420, 568
Cézanne, Paul (*fils*), 151
Chain, Dr. Ernst Boris, 562, 563
Chamber Music (Joyce), 588
Chamberlain, Neville, 494, 686
Chambers, Jessie, 632, 634, 638, 640
Chambers, Robert, 3
"Champion" (Lardner), 628
Chant, Mrs. Ormiston, 487

Chant Funèbre (Stravinsky), 598
Chanute, Octave, 362
Chapelle du Rosaire des Dominicaines, 409
Chaplin, Charles (the elder), 669, 670
Chaplin, Charles Spencer, 666, 669-677
Chaplin, Charles Spencer, Jr., 673
Chaplin, Hannah, 669, 670
Chaplin, Lita Grey, 673
Chaplin, Mildred (*née* Harris), 672
Chaplin, Oona (*née* O'Neill), 674
Chaplin, Sidney, 669, 670
Chaplin, Sydney Earle, 673
Charcot, Jean Marie, 239
Charigot, Aline, 179-180
Charles and Henry (ship), 50
Charles Darwin (Sears), 5
Charlie Chaplin (Huff), 671
Chase, Jack, 50, 52
Chase, Richard, 58
Chase, Stuart, 264
Chekhonte, Antoshe (pseudonym of Anton Chekhov), 295, 296
Chekhov, Alexander, 294, 295
Chekhov, Anton Pavlovich, 113, 121, 257, 294-301
Chekhov, Michael, 295
Chekhov, Nicholas, 294, 295
Chekhov, Pavel, 294
Chekhov: A Life (Magarshack), 296
Chekhova, Olga (*née* Knipper), 299, 300
Chen Chiung-ming, 358
Cheney, Mrs. Mamah Bouton Borthwick, 384
Cherry Orchard, The (Chekhov), 300
Chertkov, V. G., 130, 131
Chiang Kai-shek, 354, 355, 358, 359, 737, 738
Chiang Kai-shek, Mme.; *see* Soong, Mayling
Chicago Record-Herald, 316
Chicago Tribune, 327, 626
Childhood (Tolstoy), 123-124
"Children of Adam" (Whitman), 43
Children of the Night, The (Robinson), 401, 402
Children's Corner (Debussy), 307, 309
Chipman, Alice, 287; *see also* Dewey, Alice
"Choose Something Like a Star" (Frost), 475
Chopin, Frédéric, 303, 528, 598, 712
Christian Examiner, 37
Christian Science Association, 79
Christian Science Monitor, 80
Church of St. Bunco, The (tract), 73
Churchill, Diana, 492
Churchill, Lady Jennie (*née* Jerome); *see* Jerome, Jennie
Churchill, John (1st Duke of Marlborough), 484, 491

Churchill, Mary, 492
Churchill, Randolph, 492
Churchill, Lord Randolph, 484, 491
Churchill, Sarah, 492
Churchill, Sir Winston Leonard Spencer, 252, 484-499, 542, 545, 547, 582, 583, 677
Churchill By His Contemporaries, 498
Churchill Reader, A, 498
"Circus, The" (Toulouse-Lautrec), 334
Cisneros, Evangelina, 315
Cities of the Plain (Proust), 430
"City Lights" (Chaplin), 674, 675
Civil War (U.S.), 39-40, 56, 63, 141, 191, 220, 445, 702
Civil War, Spanish; *see* Spanish Civil War
Civilization and Its Discontents (Freud), 243, 244
Cladel, Judith, 173, 176
Clair de Lune (Debussy), 305
"Clair de Lune" (Verlaine), 199
Clarel (Melville), 56
Clark, James Beauchamp (Champ), 319
Clark, Vernon, 571
Claudel, Paul, 305
Clausewitz, General Karl von, 544
"Clean, Well-Lighted Place, A" (Hemingway), 721
Clemens, Clara, 144
Clemens, Henry, 140
Clemens, Jane Lampton, 139, 140
Clemens, Jean, 144
Clemens, John Marshall, 139, 140
Clemens, Olivia (*née* Langdon), 144
Clemens, Orion, 140, 141-142, 144
Clemens, Samuel Langhorne, 42, 139-142; *see also* Twain, Mark
Clemens, Susie, 143
Clemo Uti, the Water Lilies (Lardner), 629
Climacus, Johannes (pseudonym of Kierkegaard), 9
"Closed for Good" (Frost), 475
Closing the Ring (Churchill), 497
Clotis, Josette, 739
Cocktail Party, The (Eliot), 659
Cocteau, Jean, 597, 599, 602, 604
"Code, The" (Frost), 471
Colburne, Maurice, 253
Colet, Louise, 93 f.
Collected Poems (Crane), 449
Collected Poems (Frost), 472, 474, 477
Collected Poems (Robinson), 402
Collected Poems (Thomas), 754
Collected Poems (Yeats), 340
Collected Poetry (Auden), 748
Collins, Joseph, 592
"Colloque Sentimental" (Verlaine), 199
"Come In" (Frost), 475
Comédie Humaine (Balzac), 161

Coming of Democracy, The (Thomas Mann), 511

Commanville, Mme. (niece of Flaubert), 93, 100

Communication to My Friends, A (Wagner), 16

Communist Manifesto (Marx), 28, 29, 30

Complete Poems (Dickinson), 136

Complete Poems of Robert Frost, 473, 476

Complete Works of Stephen Crane, 449

Conan Doyle, Sir Arthur, 655

Concept of Dread, The (Kierkegaard), 8

Concept of Irony, The (Kierkegaard), 8

"Concerto in F" (Gershwin), 714, 715

Confession, A (Tolstoy), 127

Confessions de Claude (Zola), 159-160

Confessions of St. Augustine, 127

Confidence-Man, The (Melville), 56

Confidential Clerk, The (Eliot), 659

Confucius, 354

Congressional Record, 458

Connecticut Yankee in King Arthur's Court, A (Twain), 147-148

Conquerors, The (Malraux), 737

Conquest of Mexico (Prescott), 469

Conrad, Joseph, 447, 449

"Considerable Speck, A" (Frost), 474

Constantius, Constantin (pseudonym of Kierkegaard), 9

Contemporary (periodical), 123

Contes à Ninon (Zola), 159

Coogan, Jackie, 672

Cooley, Donald G., 562

Coolidge, Calvin, 578

Coolidge, Elizabeth Sprague, 603

Coppée, François, 400

Cora, or Fun at a Spa (Lardner), 629

Corbière, Edouard Joachim, 651

Corbin, John, 252

Corke, Helen, 638

Cormon, Fernand, 330

Cortot, Alfred, 308

Cosmopolitan (magazine), 316

Côté de Guermantes, Le (Proust), 430

"Count, The" (motion picture), 672

Count of Darkness, The (Fitzgerald), 699

Count of Monte Cristo, The (Dumas), 147

Count of Monte Cristo, The (play), 662

"Counterpart" (Joyce), 588

"Countess Kathleen, The" (Yeats), 338

Courbet, Gustave, 68, 420

Cousin, Victor, 93, 94

Couzens, James, 322, 325

Couzens, Rosetta, 322

Coward, Noel, 750

Cowles, Virginia, 490

Cowley, Malcolm, 403, 660, 707

Cox, James M., 578

Coxey, Jacob Sechler, 400

Crack-Up, The (Fitzgerald), 699, 700

Craig, Gordon, 528-529

Crane, Jonathan Townley, 444

Crane, Mary Helen (*née* Peck), 444

Crane, Stephen, 314, 444-449

Craven, Thomas, 180, 331, 573

"Crazy Sunday" (Fitzgerald), 699

Creative Evolution (Bergson), 282

Crime and Punishment (Dostoevsky), 86

Cripps, Sir Stafford, 397

"Cuban Overture" (Gershwin), 714

Curie, Dr. ——— (father of Pierre Curie), 372

Curie, Eve, 371, 376, 377

Curie, Irène, 377

Curie, Jacques, 372

Curie, Marie (*née* Sklodowska), 368-378, 534, 536

Curie, Pierre, 371-376, 534, 536

D

Daisy Miller (Henry James), 193

Dakin, Edwin Franden, 73, 79

Daly, Augustin, 523, 524

Damrosch, Walter, 714

"Dans le Restaurant" (Eliot), 655

Dante Alighieri, 58, 88, 173, 572, 647, 652, 655

"Dark-Eyed Gentleman, The" (Hardy), 169

"Darkling Thrush, The" (Hardy), 169

Darrow, Clarence, 5

Darwin, Charles, 1-6, 29, 168, 185, 238, 245, 283, 287, 450

Darwin, Erasmus, 1

Darwin, Dr. Robert Waring, 1, 2

Darwin, Marx, Wagner (Barzun), 5, 32

Daughters of Temperance, 62

Daumier, Honoré, 68, 333, 420

Davenport, Herbert, 265

Davies, Marion, 317, 318, 320

Davis, Elmer, 677

Davis, Richard Harding, 314

Dawn of Day, The (Nietzsche), 214

"Day in the Country, A" (Chekhov), 301

"Day With Conrad Green, A" (Lardner), 628

Days of Wrath (Malraux), 738

Days Without End (O'Neill), 666

De Forest, Lee, 482

De Gaulle, Charles, 739

De la Noy (Delano) Philippe, 575

De Mille, Cecil B., 671

De Rerum Natura (Lucretius), 1

De Voto, Bernard, 141, 144, 732
"Dead, The" (Joyce), 588
Death in the Afternoon (Hemingway), 718, 720
"Death in the Schoolroom" (Whitman), 35
Death in Venice (Thomas Mann), 508-509
Death of Ivan Ilyich (Tolstoy), 127
"Death of the Hired Man, The" (Frost), 471
Débâcle, Le (Zola), 162
Deburau, Jean Gaspard, 677
Debussy, Claude Achille, 25, 302-310, 598, 602, 712
Debussy, Claude-Emma, 307
Debussy, Emma; *see* Bardac, Mme. Emma
Debussy, "Lily"; *see* Texier, Rosalie
Debussy, Manuel, 302
Decline and Fall of the Roman Empire (Gibbon), 219, 488
Decline of the West, The (Spengler), 217, 553, 554, 558
Dedalus, Stephen (pseudonym of Joyce), 589
Defoe, Daniel, 351
Degas, Hilaire Germain Edgar, 178
"Déjeuner sur l'Herbe" (Manet), 161
Delano, Sara, 575; *see also* Roosevelt, Sara Delano
Delaunay, Dr., 97
Delineator (periodical), 438
Democracy and Education (Dewey), 289
Democratic Vistas (Whitman), 41, 45
Demoiselle Elue, La (Debussy), 304
"Demoiselles d'Avignon, Les" (Picasso), 568
Derain, André, 422, 567, 598
Descent of Man, The (Darwin), 5
Designer (periodical), 438
Desire Under the Elms (O'Neill), 665
Désossé, Valentin le, 331
Desperate Remedies (Hardy), 166
"Desserte, La" (Matisse), 406
Destructive Element, The (Spender), 197, 660
Detroit Free Press, 220
Development of Capitalism in Russia (Lenin), 412
Devil in the Belfry, The (Poe), 308
Devil's Disciple, The (Shaw), 254
Dewey, Evelyn, 289
Dewey, John, 125, 287-293
Dewey, Mrs. John; *see* Chipman, Alice; Grant, Roberta
Dewey, Thomas E., 583
D. H. Lawrence: A Personal Record (Chambers), 640
D. H. Lawrence: An Unprofessional Study (Nin), 638

D. H. Lawrence: Portrait of a Genius But . . . (Aldington), 640
D. H. Lawrence and Maurice Magnus (Douglas), 640
D. H. Lawrence and Susan His Cow (Tindall), 641
d'Humy, Fernand Emil, 73
Diaghilev, Sergei, 570, 598, 599, 600, 603
Dial, The, 266
"Dialogue of Self and Soul, A" (Yeats), 342
"Diamond as Big as the Ritz, The" (Fitzgerald), 696
Dickens, Charles, 230, 248, 346, 351, 435, 625, 627
Dickinson, Edward, 133, 135
Dickinson, Emily, 132-138
Dickinson, Lavinia, 132, 136
Dickinson, William Austin, 132, 134
"Dictionary of Abuse" (Archer), 117
Dictionary of Sciences, 219
Dinggedichte (Rilke), 516
Diodorus, 99
Dionysus in Doubt (Robinson), 402
"Directive" (Frost), 475
Disenchanted, The (Schulberg), 700-701
Divan Japonais (cabaret), 331
Divine Comedy, The (Dante), 652
Dixon, Richard Watson, 205
Djugashvili, Joseph Vissarionovich, 542; *see also* Stalin, Joseph
Dluski, Dr., 370, 371
Dluski, Bronya (*née* Sklodowska), 370-371, 377
Dobson, Austin, 404
"Doctor, The" (Chekhov), 301
Doctor Faustus (Thomas Mann), 512
Dr. Martino and Other Stories (Faulkner), 707
Doctor's Dilemma, The (Shaw), 256-257
Dodsworth (Lewis), 622
Doll's House, A (Ibsen), 113, 116, 117
Don Juan in Hell (Shaw), 256
Donatello, 174
Donizetti, Gaetano, 35
Donne, John, 207, 722
Données Immédiates de la Conscience, Les (Bergson), 282
Dorr, Rheta Childe, 64
Dos Passos, John, 262, 328
Dostoevskaya, Anna, 87
Dostoevskaya, Maria Dmitrievna, 85
Dostoevsky, Fyodor Mikhailovich, 82-90, 237, 618, 709, 737
Dostoevsky, Mikhail Mikhailovich, 82, 84, 85
Double, The (Dostoevsky), 83
Double Dealer, The (magazine), 704
Double Man, The (Auden), 749

Douglas, Norman, 640
Douras, Marion, 318
Dowden, Edward, 42
Doyle, Peter, 41, 43
Dramshop, The (Zola), 162
Dreadful Freedom (Grene), 743
Dream-Crowned (Rilke), 515
Dreiser, Helen; *see* Richardson, Helen Parks
Dreiser, John Paul, 434-435
Dreiser, Mrs. John Paul, 434-435
Dreiser, Paul, 434, 435, 436; *see also* Dresser, Paul
Dreiser, Rome, 434
Dreiser, Sally (*née* White), 441
Dreiser, Theodore, 434-443, 445, 623
Dreiser Looks at Russia, 441
Dresser, Paul (*né* Dreiser), 436, 437, 655
Dreyfus, Captain Alfred, 163-164, 186
Drum-Taps (Whitman), 40, 41
Drunken Boat, The (Rimbaud), 200
Dryden, John, 252, 651
Du Camp, Maxime, 91, 92, 94, 96, 97, 100
Du Côté de Chez Swann (Proust), 440
du Maurier, George, 435
Dubliners (Joyce), 588
"Duel, The" (Chekhov), 301
Düsseldorf, 553
Dufy, Raoul, 405
Duggar, Benjamin, 563
Duineser Elegien (Rilke), 518
Duino Elegies (Rilke), 517, 518-519, 520
Dukas, Paul, 310
Dumas, Alexandre, 109
Dumas, Jean Baptiste, 103
Dunbar, Paul Laurence, 361
Duncan, Mrs. (mother of Isadora Duncan), 522, 523, 524, 525
Duncan, Deirdre, 529, 530
Duncan Elizabeth, 524, 525, 528
Duncan, Isadora, 403, 522-523
Duncan, Patrick, 530
Duncan, Raymond, 524, 525, 526, 527
Duo Concertant (Stravinsky), 603
Dunlap, Orrin, 479
Dupee, F. W., 738, 739
Dupont, Gabrielle, 305
Durant, Will, 188
Dusk of the Gods (Wagner), 20
Duval, Jeanne, 67
Dymant, Dora, 615
Dynasts, The (Hardy), 167

E

Eastman, Max, 288, 669
"Easy Street" (motion picture), 672
Eberhart, Richard, 647
Ecce Homo (Nietzsche), 214
Ecole des Beaux Arts; *see* Beaux Arts, Ecole des

Ecole National des Arts Décoratifs, 420
Ecole Normale (Paris), 103, 741
Ecole Normale Supérieure (Paris), 281, 282
Eddington, Arthur Stanley, 605-611
Eddy, Gilbert, 78
Eddy, Mary Baker, 73-81
Edel, Leon, 191
Edison, Charles, 225
Edison, Madeline, 225
Edison, Marion, 222
Edison, Mary (*née* Stillwell), 225
Edison, Mina (*née* Miller), 226
Edison, Nancy (*née* Elliott), 219
Edison, Samuel, 218
Edison, Theodore, 225
Edison, Thomas Alva, 218-227, 327
Edison, Thomas Alva, Jr., 222
Edison, William, 222
Edison: The Man and His Work (Bryan), 225
Edman, Irwin, 289, 457
Education and the Good Life (Russell), 453
Edward VII (England); *see* Albert Edward
Edward VIII (England), 494
Egmont (Beethoven), 13
Egoist, The (periodical), 580
Eighteen Poems (Thomas), 754
Einem, Gottfried von, 616
Einstein, Albert, 244, 273, 274, 533-541, 607, 608, 749
Einstein, Elsa (*née* Einstein), 537
Einstein, Hans Albert, 540
Einstein, Milova (*née* Marec), 537
Either-Or (Kierkegaard), 8, 9
El Greco, 237
"Elegy" (Gray), 726
Elias, Robert H., 437
Eliot, George, 63, 166
Eliot, George Fielding, 583
Eliot, Thomas Stearns, 196, 423, 592, 602, 645, 650-661, 697, 702, 706, 749, 750
Eliot, Vivienne (*née* Haigh), 650, 659
Elizabeth II (England), 498
Elizabeth and Essex (Strachey), 551
Elliott, Nancy, 218
Ellmann, Richard, 337, 341
Elmer Gantry (Lewis), 622
Elysée-Montmartre (cabaret), 331
Emerson, Ralph Waldo, 38, 44, 45, 59, 139, 325, 533, 597, 731
Emile Zola (Wilson), 159
Emily (Jenkins), 136
Emily Dickinson: The Human Background (Pollitt), 134
Emily Dickinson Face to Face (Bianchi), 134
Eminent Victorians (Strachey), 550

Emperor and Galilean (Ibsen), 116
Emperor Jones, The (O'Neill), 664
Empire of the Air (Mouillard), 362
Emporia Gazette, 320
Encyclopaedia Britannica, 73, 80, 351
Encyclopedia Americana, 73
Encyclopedia of the Social Sciences, 162
Enemy of the People, An (Ibsen), 118
Enfant Prodigue, L' (Debussy), 304
Engels, Friedrich, 28, 29, 31, 32
Enter-Eller (Kierkegaard), 8
Eremitus, Victor (pseudonym of Kierke-
  gaard), 8
*Ernest Hemingway: The Man and His
  Work* (McCaffery, editor), 724
Ernte Seit Goethe, Die (Vesper), 520
Essanay Company (motion pictures),
  671, 672
Essays (Yeats), 340
Essays of Three Decades (Thomas
  Mann), 512
Essenin, Serge, 531
Eternal Husband, The (Dostoevsky), 87
Etudes (Debussy), 309
Euclid, 450, 533, 608
Eugénie Grandet (Balzac), 82
Euripides, 659
"Eveline" (Joyce), 588
Evénement, L' (Paris), 160
Evening Item (Dayton, Ohio), 361
Expanding Universe, The (Eddington),
  607
Experience and Nature (Dewey), 292
Experiment in Autobiography (Wells),
  345-346
Experiments in Aerodynamics (Lang-
  ley), 362
"Extracts from Doctor P. P. Quimby's
  Writings," 77
Exultations (Pound), 644

F

Fabian Essays, 250
Fabian Society, 250, 451
Fabius Maximus (Cunctator), Quintus,
  250
Fable, A (Faulkner), 709-710
Fabre, Jean Henri, 431
Face of a Nation, The (Wolfe), 733
Fainsod, Merle, 548
Fairies, The (Wagner), 14
Fairy's Kiss, The (Stravinsky), 602
Fall of the House of Usher (Poe), 308
Falla, Manuel de, 309, 598
Family Reunion, The (Eliot), 659
Fanny's First Play (Shaw), 257
Far from the Madding Crowd (Hardy),
  166
Farewell to Arms, A (Hemingway), 720,
  722

Farr, Florence, 253
Fate of Man, The (Wells), 350
Faulkner, Jill, 705
Faulkner, William, 449, 702-711, 733
Faulkner, William Cuthbert, 702
"Faulkner: Sorcerer or Slave" (Hamil-
  ton), 709
Faure, Félix, 163
Faust (Goethe), 14
"Fear, The" (Frost), 471
Fear and Trembling (Kierkegaard), 8
Fécondité (Zola), 164
Feen, Die (Wagner), 14; *see also Fairies,
  The*
"Fern Hill" (Thomas), 757
Festspielhaus (Bayreuth), 23
Fêtes Galantes (Debussy), 305
Fêtes Galantes (Verlaine), 199
Fidelio Overture (Beethoven), 13
Fielding, Henry, 458
Fifth Column, The (Hemingway), 721
*Fifth Column and the First Forty-Nine
  Stories, The* (Hemingway), 721
"Fifty Grand" (Hemingway), 721
Figaro, Le, 427
"Figure in the Carpet, The" (Henry
  James), 194
"Fille aux Cheveux de Lin, La" (De-
  bussy), 308
Fils Prodigue, Le (ballet), 422
Financier, The (Dreiser), 439
Finch, Edith, 456
Finnegans Wake (Joyce), 590, 593-596
Fiquet, Hortense, 151
"Fire and Ice" (Frost), 473
Firebird, The (Stravinsky), 598
Fireworks (Stravinsky), 598
First National (motion picture com-
  pany), 672
First Principles (Spencer), 281
Fischer, Louis, 393, 394, 395
Fitts, Dudley, 751
Fitzgerald, Edward, 275, 647, 655
Fitzgerald, F. Scott, 461, 691-701
Fitzgerald, Frances, 694
Fitzgerald, Zelda (*née* Sayre), 694-698
Fitzroy, Captain Robert, 2
Flanner, Janet, 739
Flappers and Philosophers (Fitzgerald),
  695
Flaubert, Mme. (mother of Gustave
  Flaubert), 91, 96, 97
Flaubert, Achille, 91
Flaubert, Dr. Achille-Cléophas, 91, 93,
  94, 97
Flaubert, Gustave, 91-101, 159-160, 161,
  192, 461, 703, 730
Flaubert and Madame Bovary (Steeg-
  muller), 95
Fleming, Alexander, 559-564
Fleming, Hugh, 559

Fleming, John, 560, 561
Fleming, John Ambrose, 482
Fleming, Robert, 560
Fleming, Dr. Thomas, 560
Fleurs du Mal, Les (Baudelaire), 66, 69,
    71, 99
Flies, The (Sartre), 743
Flight Into History (Freudenthal), 362
"Floorwalker, The" (motion picture),
    672
Florey, Dr. Howard W., 562, 563
Flug (Heinrich Adams), 364
Flying Dutchman, The (Wagner), 15,
    16
For the Time Being (Auden), 749
For Whom the Bell Tolls (Heming-
    way), 721-722
Forain, Jean Louis, 333, 334
Ford, Ford Madox, 467, 718, 724
Ford, Henry, 227, 321, 328
Ford, James L., 314
Forster, Edward Morgan, 625
Fort, Charles, 440
Fortnightly Review, 587
Foster, Stephen C., 327
Four Gospels, The (Zola), 164
Four Prophets of Our Destiny (Hub-
    ben), 11, 215
Four Quartets (Eliot), 423, 658, 749
Four Saints in Three Acts (Gertrude
    Stein), 466
Fourier, François Marie Charles, 83,
    190
Fra Angelico, 421
"Fragments From a Writing Desk"
    (Melville), 48
"Frame-Up, A" (Lardner), 628
France, Anatole, 164, 202, 426, 427
Francis of Assisi, St., 504
Franco, General Francisco, 685, 738
Franco-Prussian War, 100, 106, 151,
    171, 199, 213
Frank, Waldo, 618, 745
Frankel, Charles, 746
Franklin, Benjamin, 317
Franklin, Estelle Oldham, 705
Franklin Evans, or The Inebriate
    (Whitman), 35
Franz Kafka—Pre-Fascist Exile (Slo-
    chower), 617
Frapier, E., 422
Frazer, James, 594, 655
Free Air (Lewis), 620-621
"Free Will" (Renouvier), 184
Freedom and Organization (Russell),
    454, 455
Freeman, 35
Freeman, John, 58
Freischütz (Weber), 13
French Academy, 109, 110, 202, 282,
    592

French Revolution (Michelet), 230
Freud, Martha (*née* Bernays), 242
Freud, Sigmund, 25, 89, 238-246, 594,
    635, 640, 685, 749, 754, 756
Freud, Goethe, Wagner (Thomas
    Mann), 512
Freudenthal, Elsbeth E., 362
Friesz, Emile Othon, 422
From Lenin to Malenkov (Seton-Wat-
    son), 548
From Ritual to Romance (Weston), 655
Frost, Elinor (*née* White), 469, 470
Frost, Robert, 468-477
Frost, William Prescott, 468
Frühen Gedichte, Die (Rilke), 517
*F. Scott Fitzgerald: The Man and His
    Work* (Kazin, editor), 700
Fuehrer, Der (Heiden), 682
Fueloep-Miller, René, 86, 87
Further Range, A (Frost), 468, 474
Future of an Illusion (Freud), 243, 244
Fyodor Dostoevsky (Fueloep-Miller), 86

G

Gabrilowitsch, Ossip, 144
Gachet, Dr., 236
Gaelic League, 338
Gage, Matilda Joslyn, 64
Galileo, 555
Gallant Festivals (Verlaine), 199
Gambler, The (Dostoevsky), 86
Gandhi, Harilal, 390, 396
Gandhi, Manilal, 392
Gandhi, Mohandas Karamchand, 129,
    389-398, 418
Gannett, Lewis, 595, 625
Gansevoort, Maria, 47
Gansevoort, Peter, 56
Gansevoort, General Peter, 47
Garbedian, H. Gordon, 222
Garden, Mary, 307
"Gardens in the Rain" (Debussy), 308
Gardner, Helen, 656
Garland, Hamlin, 445
Garnett, David, 638
Garrett, Garet, 328
"Gate of Hell, The" (Rodin), 173, 175
Gathering Storm, The (Churchill), 493,
    497
Gauguin, Eugène Henri Paul, 232, 233-
    235, 408, 566
Gaulle, Charles de; *see* De Gaulle,
    Charles
Gautier, Théophile, 71
Geisha, The (musical comedy), 524
Geismar, Maxwell, 439, 629, 699
Gellhorn, Martha, 724
Genauer, Emily, 175
Genealogy of Morals, The (Nietzsche),
    214

Geneva (Shaw), 259
'Genius,' The (Dreiser), 439, 440
Genthe, Arnold, 524
"Gentle Lena, The" (Gertrude Stein), 461
Geography and Plays (Gertrude Stein), 465
George V (England), 397
George VI (England), 494
George, Henry, 248
Georges Roualt: Paintings and Prints (Soby), 420
Germinal (Zola), 162
Gershwin, George, 712-716
Gershwin, Ira, 712, 716
Gershwin, Morris, 712
Gershwin, Rose Bruskin, 712
Gertrude Stein: A Biography of Her Work (Sutherland), 462
Gertrude Stein: Form and Sensibility (Miller), 462
Geschichten Jaakobs, Die (Thomas Mann), 511
Geschichten vom Lieben Gott (Rilke), 515
Geyer, Cäcelie, 12
Geyer, Ludwig, 12
Ghosts (Ibsen), 116, 117
"Ghosts and Gibberings" (Archer), 117
Gibbens, Alice Howe, 184
Gibbon, Edward, 219, 488
Gide, André, 217, 305, 616
Gideon Planish (Lewis), 623
Gifford, Emma, 165; *see also* Hardy, Emma
"Gift Outright, The" (Frost), 475
Gilbert, Cass, 364
Gilbert, Stuart, 590
Gilbert and Sullivan, 659
Gilchrist, Mrs. Anne, 43
"Girl with Flaxen Hair, The" (Debussy), 308
Gladstone, William Ewart, 487
"Gleaners" (Millet), 230
Gleyre, Charles Gabriel, 177
Glory of the Nightingales, The (Robinson), 402
Glover, George Washington, Jr., 75, 81
Glover, George Washington, Sr., 74-75
Gluck, Christoph Willibald, 249, 526, 529
God-Seeker, The (Lewis), 624
Goddard, Paulette, 673
Godse, Nathuram, 398
Godwin, William, 338
Goebbels, Paul Joseph, 684
Goering, Hermann, 684
Goethe, Johann Wolfgang von, 14, 25, 238, 504, 507, 511, 512, 514, 613
Götterdämmerung (Wagner), 20, 22; *see also Dusk of the Gods*

Gogh, Theo van, 228, 230, 231, 232, 233, 236, 237
Gogh, Vincent van, 154, 228-237, 330, 333, 420, 503, 566
Gogh, Vincent van (the elder), 228
Gogol, Nikolai Vasilevich, 83
Gokhale, Gopal, 396
"Gold Rush, The" (motion picture), 674
Golden Bough, The (Frazer), 655
Golden Bowl, The (Henry James), 190, 193
"Golden Honeymoon, The" (Lardner), 629
"Goldfish" (Debussy), 308
Goldmark, Rubin, 714
Goldschmidt, Clara, 736, 739
Goldwyn, Sam, 671
"Goldwyn Follies, The" (motion picture), 716
"Golliwog's Cake-Walk" (Debussy), 309
Gomulka, Wladslaw, 548
Gonne, Maude, 338, 341, 342
"Good Anna, The" (Gertrude Stein), 461
"Good Gray Poet, The" (O'Connor), 41
Good Housekeeping (magazine), 316
Good Song, The (Verlaine), 199
Gorky, Maxim, 300, 414, 418, 737
Gorman, Herbert, 595
Gosse, Edmund, 42, 592
Gould, George, 134
Goulue, La, 331
Gounod, Charles, 177
Goupil and Company (art dealers), 228, 229
Graham, Tom (pseudonym of Sinclair Lewis), 620
Grand Alliance, The (Churchill), 497
Grande Revue, La, 408
Grant, Roberta L., 291
Grattan, C. Hartley, 698
Graves, John Temple, 319
Graves, Robert, 207
Gray, Thomas, 726
"Great Dictator, The" (Chaplin), 675
Great Gatsby, The (Fitzgerald), 697, 701
Great God Brown, The (O'Neill), 664, 667
Great God Pan, The (Payne), 677
Great Novelists and Their Novels (Maugham), 58
Great Philosophers of the Western World, The (Tomlin), 11, 28, 285
Greeley, Horace, 64
Green Hills of Africa, The (Hemingway), 145, 720
Gregory, Horace, 639, 641, 660
Grene, Marjorie, 743, 745
Grey, Lita, 673
Griffith, David Wark, 671

Grimaldi, Joseph, 677
Grofe, Ferde, 714
Gropius, Walter, 385
Guermantes Way, The (Proust), 430
"Guernica" (Picasso), 571-572, 573
Guernsey, Otis, 676
Guilbert, Yvette, 331, 332
Guillemet, Antoine, 152
Gullible's Travels (Lardner), 627
Gunther, John, 576, 584
Gurvotch, Georges, 745
Guy Domville (Henry James), 193

H

Haas, Charles, 429
Hachette, Louis, 159
Hackett, Francis, 466
Hagedorn, Hermann, 402
Hahn, Emily, 354, 356
Haigh, Vivienne, 650; *see also* Eliot, Vivienne
"Haircut" (Lardner), 627
Hairy Ape, The (O'Neill), 664
Haldane, Charlotte, 428, 430
Hale, Edward Everett, 38
Hambitzer, Charles, 712
Hamilcar, 99
Hamilton, Edith, 709
Hamlet (Shakespeare), 13, 665
Hamlet, The (Faulkner), 707
Hamsun, Knut, 120
Hand of the Potter, The (Dreiser), 440
Handel, George Frederick, 249, 603, 604
Hannibal, 250
Hanslick, Dr. Eduard, 22
Hapgood, Hutchins, 460
"Happiness Makes Up in Weight for What It Lacks in Length" (Frost), 475
Harding, Warren G., 377, 578
Hardy, Emma (*née* Gifford), 167
Hardy, Thomas, 56, 165-169, 196, 206, 277
Harland, James, 41
Harper, Ida Husted, 64
Harpers Ferry Raid, 287
Harper's Monthly, 447
Harris, Frank, 249, 253
Harris, Mildred, 672
Harte, Bret, 143
Harvard *Advocate*, 651
Harvard *Crimson*, 576
Harvard *Lampoon*, 312
Harvard Monthly, 400
Harvest Since Goethe, The (Vesper), 520
"Has Gertrude Stein a Secret?" (Skinner), 459
Hattingberg, Magda von, 514, 519
Haufniensis, Virgilius (pseudonym of Kierkegaard), 8

Hawthorne, Nathaniel, 52, 55, 59, 139, 191, 435
Hawthorne, Sophia, 53
Heard, Gerald, 751
"Hearing of harvests rotting in the valleys" (Auden), 748
Hearst, George, 311, 312-313
Hearst, Millicent (*née* Willson), 318; *see also* Willson, Millicent
Hearst, Phoebe Apperson, 311, 317
Hearst, William Randolph, 259, 311-320, 326, 446, 765
Hearst: An American Phenomenon (Winkler), 315
Heartbreak House (Shaw), 257
Heath, Willie, 427
Hedda Gabler (Ibsen), 119
Hedgehog and the Fox, The (Berlin), 126
Hegel, Georg Wilhelm, 26, 27, 29
Hegger, Grace, 620
Heidegger, Martin, 745
Heiden, Konrad, 682
Heilbroner, Robert L., 30, 32, 418
Heine, Heinrich, 15, 201, 507, 514, 685
Heisenberg, Werner, 273, 274, 608
Helmholtz, Hermann Ludwig von, 270-271
Helmont, Jan Baptista van, 104
Hemingway, Ernest, 145, 449, 461, 654, 698, 717-725, 737
Hemingway, Hadley (*née* Richardson), 717, 720
Hemingway, Mary (*née* Welsh), 724
Hemingway, Pauline (*née* Pfeiffer), 720, 724
Henderson, Philip, 737
Henley, W. E., 470
Henry James: The Untried Years (Edel), 191
Henry James and the Almighty Dollar (Arvin), 196
Hepburn, Katherine, 258
Heraclitus, 1, 281, 553
Heredia, José María de, 198
Hergesheimer, Joseph, 445
Herman Melville (Arvin), 53
Herman Melville (Mumford), 50
Herman Melville: Mariner and Mystic (Weaver), 57
Hermetic Students of the Golden Dawn, 337
Herodotus, 99
Hertz, Heinrich Rudolph, 478
Hey Rub-a-Dub-Dub (Dreiser), 441
Heyward, DuBose, 715
H. G. Wells: Prophet of Our Day (Valentin), 348
H. H. (pseudonym of Kierkegaard), 9
"Hiawatha" (Longfellow), 69

Higginson, Thomas Wentworth, 134, 136
Higher Learning in America, The (Veblen), 265
Hike and the Aeroplane (Lewis), 220
"Hills Like White Elephants" (Hemingway), 721
Hindenburg, Paul von, 684
Hinge of Fate, The (Churchill), 497
Hisgen, Thomas L., 319
Histoire du Soldat, L' (Stravinsky), 601
History of England (Macaulay), 488
History of Impressionism, The (Rewald), 178
History of Modern China, A (Latourette), 359
History of Modern Philosophy, A (Mayer), 414
History of Russian Literature, A (Mirsky), 84, 125, 301
History of Woman Suffrage (Anthony), 64, 65
Hitler, Adolf, 24, 215, 217, 244, 319, 442, 493 f., 510, 538, 546, 547, 553, 677, 678-690
Hitler, Alois, 678, 679
Hitler: A Study in Tyranny (Bullock), 680
Hochzeit, Die (Wagner), 14; see also *Wedding, The*
Hoffman, Malvina, 171
Hoffman, E. T. A., 93
Hogarth, William, 603, 625
Holiday, Mrs., 140
"Hollow Men, The" (Eliot), 656, 706
Holmes, Oliver Wendell (essayist), 42
Holmes, Oliver Wendell (jurist), 189
Holthusen, Hans Egon, 516
"Home Burial" (Frost), 471
Homer, 13, 506, 572, 590
Hoosier Holiday, A (Dreiser), 442
Hoover, Herbert, 580
Hope for Poetry, A (Lewis), 207
Hopkins, Gerard Manley, 137, 204-208, 521, 755
Hopkins, Harry, 545
Horace, 276
Hospital Visits (Whitman), 40
Hour of Decision, The (Spengler), 557
House of Ellis, The (Skinner), 638
House of the Dead (Dostoevsky), 84
"House on the Hill, The" (Robinson), 400
"Housekeeper, The" (Frost), 471
Housman, Alfred Edward, 206, 275-280
Housman, Laurence, 275, 277
How Russia Is Ruled (Fainsod), 548
"How to Make Our Ideas Clear" (Peirce), 186
How to Write Short Stories (Lardner), 627, 629

How We Think (Dewey), 289
Howe, Irving, 708
Howe, Quincy, 557
Howells, William Dean, 191, 445, 446
Hozier, Clementine, 491
Hubben, William, 11, 215
Huckleberry Finn, The Adventures of (Twain), 139-140, 142, 145, 146-147
Huff, Theodore, 669, 671, 672
Hugh Selwyn Mauberley (Pound), 646
Hughes, Charles Evans, 319
Hughes, H. Stuart, 556
Hugo, Victor, 156, 174, 230
Human, All-too Human (Nietzsche), 214
Human Immortality: The Varieties of Religious Experience (William James), 185
Human Knowledge: Its Scope and Limits (Russell), 456
"Humoresque" (Eliot), 651
Humphrey, Leonard, 133-134
"Hunchback in the Park, The" (Thomas), 757
"Hundred Collars, A" (Frost), 471
Huneker, James, 172, 189, 331
Hungry Gulliver (P. H. Johnson), 731
Hunt, Edward, 134
Hunt, Helen; see Jackson, Helen Hunt
Hunt, William, 183
Huxley, Julian, 349
Huxley, Thomas, 4, 337, 346
Huysmans, Joris Karl, 202
Hyde, Douglas, 338
Hyde-Lees, Georgie, 341
Hyde Park (N. Y.), 575, 577, 578

I

I Gaspiri, the Upholsterers (Lardner), 629
"I Got Rhythm" (Gershwin), 713
Ibéria (Debussy), 309
Ibsen, Henrik, 9, 113-120, 248, 249, 587, 745
Ibsen: An Approach (Lavrin), 117
"Ibsen's New Drama" (Joyce), 587
Iceman Cometh, The (O'Neill), 666
Idiot, The (Dostoevsky), 87
Ile (O'Neill), 663
Illuminations (Rimbaud), 200
"Immigrant, The" (motion picture), 672
Impact of Science on Society, The (Russell), 456
Imperial Germany and the Industrial Revolution (Veblen), 266
Imperial Hearst (Lundberg), 320
Imperial Hotel (Tokyo), 384-385
In Country Sleep (Thomas), 755
"In Memory of Ann Jones" (Thomas), 757

"In Memory of W. B. Yeats" (Auden), 752
In Our Time (Hemingway), 718, 720
In Praise of Idleness (Russell), 455
In Search of Time Lost (Proust), 431; see also *Remembrance of Things Past*
"In the Wake of the News" (Lardner), 626
Inchiquin, Lucius O'Brien, 15th Baron, 482
Independent, The (periodical), 469
"Infant Christ Among the Doctors, The" (Rouault), 423
Inferno (Dante), 647, 653
Ingersoll, Robert, 522
Ingres, Jean Auguste Dominique, 151
Innocents, The (Lewis), 620, 621
Innocents Abroad (Twain), 143
Inquiry into the Nature of Peace and the Terms of Its Perpetuation, An (Veblen), 266
Instigations (Pound), 648
Instinct of Workmanship, The (Veblen), 266
Insulted and Injured, The (Dostoevsky), 84
Inter et Inter (pseudonym of Kierkegaard), 9
Internal Constitution of the Stars, The (Eddington), 609
International Cyclopedia of Music and Musicians, The (Thompson), 306
International Woman Suffrage Alliance, 65
Interpretation of Dreams, The (Freud), 241, 594
Introduction to Mathematical Philosophy (Russell), 453
Intruder in the Dust (Faulkner), 707
Invisible Man, The (Wells), 348
Ion (Euripides), 659
"Iphigenia" (Gluck), 529
Irish Homestead, The (periodical), 589
Irish Literary Theater, 338
Irvine, William, 250
Irving, Washington, 321, 346
Is Christian Science a Humbug? (tract), 73
Isadora Duncan School (Grünewald), 528
Isayeva, Maria Dmitrievna, 84; see also Dostoevskaya, Maria
Iskra (periodical), 412, 413, 543
"It Ain't Necessarily So" (Gershwin), 715
It Can't Happen Here (Lewis), 623
Ivanov (Chekhov), 296

J

"J'Accuse" (Zola), 163
Jackson, Helen Hunt, 134

Jackson, Thomas (Stonewell), 723
Jacobs, William Wymark, 195
James, Alice, 190
James, Garth Wilkinson, 190
James, Henry, 98, 182, 183, 185, 188, 190-197, 655, 697, 749
James, Henry (the elder), 182, 183, 190
James, Mary Robertson Walsh, 182, 190
James, Robertson, 190
James, William, 182-189, 190, 194, 195, 287, 292, 458, 459, 469, 558
James Joyce: A Critical Introduction (Levin), 589-590
James Joyce: His Way of Interpreting the Modern World (Tindall), 590
James Joyce's Ulysses (Gilbert), 590-591
"Jardins sous la Pluie" (Debussy), 308
Jarrell, Randall, 474-475
Jaspers, Karl, 745
Jefferson, Thomas, 648
Jenkins, Kathleen, 662; see also O'Neill, Kathleen
Jenkins, MacGregor, 136
Jennie Gerhardt (Dreiser), 438, 439
Jerome, Jennie, 484
Jesus, 500 f.
Joan and Peter (Wells), 349
Joan of Arc, 74
Joan of Arc (Twain), 144
Job, The (Lewis) 620
Jockey Club (Paris), 20, 21
John Dewey: The Reconstruction of the Democratic Life (Nathanson), 293
John Gabriel Borkman (Ibsen), 113, 119
John Marr and Other Sailors (Melville), 57
Johnson, Alvin, 291
Johnson, Lionel, 644
Johnson, Pamela Hansford, 731, 732
Johnson, Dr. Samuel, 729
Johnson, Thomas H., 136
"Jolly Corner, The" (Henry James), 194
Joliot, Frédéric, 377
Jolson, Al, 712
Jones, Ernest, 242
Jones, P. Mansell, 69
Joseph and His Brothers (Thomas Mann), 511, 512
Joseph in Egypt (Thomas Mann), 511
Joseph the Provider (Thomas Mann), 511
Josephson, Matthew, 163
Jourdain, Francis, 334
"Journal of an Airman" (Auden), 748
Journal of My Other Self, The (Rilke), 517
Journal of Researches into the Geology and Natural History of the Various

Countries visited by H. M. S. Beagle (Darwin), 3
"Journey of the Magi" (Eliot), 423, 656
Journey to Athens (Winckelmann), 524
Journey with Genius (Binner), 641
Joyce, James, 197, 431, 432, 506, 586-596, 728, 733, 754
Joyce, Lucia, 593, 595
Joyful Science, The (Nietzsche), 214
"Judaism in Music" (Wagner), 15, 18, 24
Jude the Obscure (Hardy), 166-167
"Judenthum in der Musik, Das" (Wagner), 15; *see also* "Judaism in Music"
June Moon (Lardner), 628
Jung, Dr. Carl, 242, 244, 649
"Just Tell Them That You Saw Me" (Dresser), 436
Justice (Zola), 164

K

Kafka, Franz, 11, 237, 612-618
Kafka, Herman, 612, 617
Kafka, Julie (*née* Loewy), 612
Kallman, Chester, 604
Kamenev, Lev Borisovich, 544
Kapital, Das (Marx), 30, 248; *see also* *Capital*
Karno, Fred, 670
"Kashtanka" (Chekhov), 301
Kasturbai (Mme. Gandhi), 390
Kaufman, George S., 715
Kaufmann, Edgar J., 386
Kaufmann, Edgar, Jr., 382
Kaufmann, W., 534
Kazin, Alfred, 449, 700, 722
Keats, John, 187, 472, 703, 722
Kelly, Fred C., 365, 366
Kerensky, Alexander, 416
Kerr, Orpheus C. (pseudonym of Robert H. Newell), 142
Kerr, Walter F., 298
Key, Ellen, 384
Key, Francis Scott, 691
Keystone Films, 670, 671
"Kid, The" (motion picture), 672
Kierkegaard, Michael Pedersen, 7
Kierkegaard, Søren Aabye, 7-11, 115, 215, 614, 617, 618, 741, 744, 749
"Killers, The" (Hemingway), 721
King, Ginevra, 692, 693
King Jasper (Robinson), 476
King Lear (Shakespeare), 308
King Solomon's Mines (Haggard), 485
Kingdom of God Is Within You, The (Tolstoy), 129, 391
Kingsblood Royal (Lewis), 623
Kingsmill, Hugh, 640
Kipps (Wells), 346, 348
Kirchhoff, Gustav, 271

Kirov, Sergei Mironovich, 545
"Kiss, The" (Rodin), 173
Kitchener, Sir Herbert, 488
Kleine Herr Friedemann, Der (Thomas Mann), 507
Knight, Arthur, 676
Knipper, Olga, 299; *see also* Chekhova, Olga
Königliche Hoheit (Thomas Mann), 508
Koklova, Olga, 570
Kolodin, Irving, 604
Koo, Dr. Wellington, 359
Kornilov, General Lavr, 416
Kostov, Traicho, 548
Kreusi, John, 223, 224
Kreutzer Sonata, The (Tolstoy), 127
Kronenberger, Louis, 280, 552
Kruger, Paul, 489
Krupskaya, Nadezhda Konstantinovna, 412, 413, 414, 416
Krutch, Joseph Wood, 665
Kung, H. H., 354

L

La La Lucille (musical comedy), 712
La Rochefoucauld, François de, 215
Labor (Zola), 164
Lady Chatterley's Lover (Lawrence), 591, 632, 639, 640, 641
Lady from the Sea, The (Ibsen), 119
"Lady Hester Stanhope" (Strachey), 552
Lady of the Lake, The (Scott), 346
Laforgue, Jules, 651
Lahey, G. F., 207
Lamarck, Jean Baptiste de Monet, Chevalier de, 3
Lamartine, Alphonse de, 156, 174
Lambaréné (French Equatorial Africa), 502-504
Lambert, Constant, 715
Lancet, 107
Landon, Alfred M., 320, 581
Langdon, Olivia, 143; *see also* Clemens, Olivia
Langley, Samuel Pierpont, 362, 367
Lapparent, Paul de, 334
Lardner, David, 627
Lardner, James, 627
Lardner, John, 627
Lardner, Ring, 626-631
Lardner, Ring, Jr. (Bill), 627
Lasky, Jesse, 671
Last Billionaire, The (Richards), 324, 328
Last Chance, The (Sartre), 743
Last of the Provincials, The (Geismar), 699
Last Poems (Housman), 277, 278, 279-280
Last Tycoon, The (Fitzgerald), 700

Latourette, Kenneth Scott, 359
Laughlin, J. Laurence, 263
Launcelot (Robinson), 402
Laurence, William L., 539
Laurencin, Marie, 598
Laurent (father of Marie Laurent), 103, 104
Laurent, Marie, 103, 104; *see also* Pasteur, Marie
Laussot, Jessie, 18
Lavignac, Albert, 20
Lavrin, Janko, 117, 127, 129
Law of Civilization and Decay, The (Brooks Adams), 556-557
"Law, Say the Gardeners, Is the Sun" (Auden), 748
Lawrence, David Herbert, 58, 245, 453, 591, 632-642
Lawrence, Frieda (*née* Von Richthofen), 634, 636, 638, 639, 641
Lawrence American, 469
Lawrence Sentinel, 469
Laxdaela Saga, 266
Lazarus Laughed (O'Neill), 664
Lazovich, Olga, 386
Lazovich, Svetanna, 386
Le Mure, Pierre, 332
Le Poittevin, Alfred, 91
League of Nations, 494, 578, 685
Lear, Edward, 550, 629, 657, 749
Leaves of Grass (Whitman), 34 f., 644
Leben und Lieder (Rilke), 515
Leblanc, Georgette, 307
Leclerc, André, 572
Leconte de Lisle, Charles Marie, 198
Lederman, Minna, 601
"Lees of Happiness, The" (Fitzgerald), 696
Leggett, H. W., 453
Lehman, Herbert, 579
Leibnitz, Baron Gottfried Wilhelm von, 452
Leishman, J. B., 517, 520
Lenin, Nikolai, 410-419, 496, 543, 544, 549, 557
Leo Tolstoy (Simmons), 126
Leopold III (Belgium), 495
Lerner, Max, 267
Let 'Em Eat Cake (musical comedy), 715
"Letter That Never Came, The" (Dresser), 436
"Letter to My Father" (Kafka), 612, 614
Letters from the Underworld (Dostoevsky), 86
Leubald und Adelaide (Wagner), 13
Levant, Oscar, 713, 715
Levin, Harry, 589, 591
Levinson, Katherine, 281
Lévy-Bruhl, Lucien, 594
Lewis, C. Day, 207

Lewis, Michael, 620
Lewis, Sinclair, 619-625, 664, 666
Lewis, Wells, 620
Lewis, Wyndham, 644, 645
Liebesverbot, Das (Wagner), 14; *see also Love Ban, The*
Liebold, Ernest, 326
Life (magazine), 456, 604, 657
Life and Good Times of William Randolph Hearst, The (Trebel), 315
Life and Lyrics (Rilke), 515
Life and Mind of Emily Dickinson, The (Taggard), 133
Life and Work of Wilbur Wright, The (Brewer), 364
Life and Works of D. H. Lawrence, The (Moore), 641
Life of D. H. Lawrence, The (Kingsmill), 640
Life of Mahatma Gandhi, The (Fischer), 393
Life of Pasteur (Vallery-Radot), 107
Life of the Virgin Mary, The (Rilke), 517
Life on the Mississippi (Twain), 140-141
Light in August (Faulkner), 706
Light Shines in Darkness, The (Tolstoy), 127
Lilienthal, Otto, 362
"Limelight" (Chaplin), 677
Lincoln, Abraham, 42, 63, 317, 327
Linebarger, Paul, 357
"Lines on the Death of Dr. P. P. Quimby" (Eddy), 77
Lippincott's Magazine, 400, 447
Lipschitz, Jacques, 174
Lister, Joseph, 107, 110, 111
Liszt, Cosima, 19; *see also* Bülow, Cosima von
Liszt, Franz, 17, 18, 19, 22, 24
Literary Evolution of the Nations, 542
Little Brick Church, The (William Cuthbert Faulkner), 702
Little Eyolf (Ibsen), 119
"Little Gidding" (Eliot), 658
Little Mister Friedemann (Thomas Mann), 507
Little Review, The, 591, 646
Living Age, 345
Living Corpse, The (Tolstoy), 127
Lloyd George, David, 492
Lloyd-Jones, Anna, 379
Locke, David Ross, 142
Locke, John, 245
Lodge, Sir Oliver, 480, 482
Loeb, Jacques, 263
Loewy, Julie, 612
Lohengrin (Wagner), 17, 25
London Critic, 38
London Times, 22, 167, 457

Long Day's Journey Into Night (O'Neill), 666
Long Island Star, 35
Long Islander, 35
Long Voyage Home, The (O'Neill), 663
Longfellow, Henry Wadsworth, 59, 69, 139, 327, 470, 643
Look Homeward, Angel (Wolfe), 728-729, 734
Look! We Have Come Through! (Lawrence), 634
Lord, Judge, 136
Lorenzo in Taos (Luhan), 640
Lorrain, Claude, 173
Lotte in Weimar (Thomas Mann), 512
Louys, Pierre, 305
Love and Ethics (Key), 384
Love Ban, The (Wagner), 14
Love Nest, The (Lardner), 627, 628
Love Poems (Lawrence), 634
"Love Song of J. Alfred Prufrock, The" (Eliot), 645, 651-652, 654
"Lovely Shall Be Choosers, The" (Frost), 476
Love's Comedy (Ibsen), 114
Lowell, Amy, 646
Lowell, James Russell, 191
Lowrie, Walter, 10
Lucretius, 1, 104
Lucy Ann (ship), 49
Lucy Church Amiably (Gertrude Stein), 465
Ludwig II (Bavaria), 21, 22
Ludwig, Emil, 241, 245
Luhan, Mabel Dodge, 637, 638, 640
Lundberg, Ferdinand, 320
"Lune de Miel" (Eliot), 655
Lycée Bonaparte (Paris), 198
Lycée Condorcet (Paris), 329, 425, 736
Lycée St. Louis (Paris), 102, 157
Lyon, Mary, 133
Lyrics of Lowly Life (Dunbar), 361

M

Macaulay, Thomas Babington, 488
Macbeth (Shakespeare), 665
Mack, Gerstle, 331-332, 334
Macnamara, Caitlin, 753
Madame Bovary (Flaubert), 97, 98, 99, 159
Madame Curie (Eve Curie), 371
Maeterlinck, Maurice, 306, 307
Magarshack, David, 296, 299
Maggie: A Girl of the Streets (Crane), 444
Magic Mountain, The (Thomas Mann), 509-510
Mahler, Gustav, 175
Maier, Mathilde, 21

Main Street (Lewis), 621, 622
Major Barbara (Shaw), 256-257
Make It New (Pound), 648
Making of Americans, The (Gertrude Stein), 461, 462, 463
Malinovsky (police agent), 543
Mallarmé, Stéphane, 305, 306
Malory, Sir Thomas, 339
Malraux, André, 736-740
Malraux, Clara (*née* Goldschmidt); *see* Goldschmidt, Clara
Malraux, Claude, 740
Malraux, Josette (*née* Clotis); *see* Clotis, Josette
Malraux, Marie-Madeleine, 739
Malraux, Roland, 740
Malte Laurids Brigge, Die Aufzeichnungen des (Rilke), 517
Malthus, Thomas Robert, 3, 4, 455
Man and Superman (Shaw), 251, 255, 256
Man Against the Sky, The (Robinson), 402
"Man Awakening to Nature" (Rodin), 172
Man of Destiny, The (Shaw), 251
"Man Walking" (Rodin), 172
Man Who Died Twice, The (Robinson), 402
Man Who Knew Coolidge, The (Lewis), 622
"Man with a Broken Nose" (Rodin), 171
"Man with the Hoe" (Millet), 230
Man Without a Country, The (Hale), 38
Mandoline (Debussy), 304
"Mandoline" (Verlaine), 199
Manet, Edouard, 161, 178, 420
Manilius, Marcus (poet), 276
Mann, Erika, 508, 747
Mann, Heinrich, 506, 507, 510
Mann, Klaus, 508
Mann, Thomas, 11, 217, 245, 506-510
Manon (Massenet), 317
Man's Fate (Malraux), 737, 738
Man's Hope (Malraux), 738
Mansfield, Katherine, 300
Manual of Design, 230
Mao Tse-tung, 359
Marcel Proust (Haldane), 428
Marconi, Elettra, 482
Marconi, Guglielmo, 478-483
Marcu, Valeriu, 414, 416
Mardi (Melville), 51, 52, 54
Marec, Mileva, 533; *see also* Einstein, Mileva
Marienleben, Das (Rilke), 517
Marlborough, Duke of; *see* Churchill, John; Spencer Churchill, John Winston

Marlborough: His Life and Times (Churchill), 484, 493
Marmion (Scott), 346
Marriage and Morals (Russell), 454, 455
Martin, John, 525
Marx, Jenny, 28, 31
Marx, Karl, 26-33, 162, 244, 248, 267, 396, 411, 413, 418, 442, 455, 543, 680
Mary, Queen (England), 397
Mary Baker Eddy in a New Light (d'Humy), 73
"Massacre in Korea" (Picasso), 573
Massenet, Jules Emile, 308, 317
Master Builder, The (Ibsen), 119
Materialism and Empirio-Criticism (Lenin), 414
Mathilde, Princesse (sister of Napoleon III), 429
Matisse, Henri Emile Benoît, 181, 405-409, 422, 461, 465, 567
Matisse, Jean, 405
Matisse, Marguerite, 405
Matisse, Pierre, 405
Matter and Memory (Bergson), 282, 284
Matthew, St., 442
Matthews, T. S., 657, 699
Matthias at the Door (Robinson), 403
Matthiessen, F. O., 653
Maugham, W. Somerset, 58, 89, 97, 167
Maupassant, Guy de, 100, 159
Mauritius, 67
Mauté de Fleurville, Mme., 303
Mauté de Fleurville, Mathilde, 199; *see also* Verlaine, Mathilde
Mauve, Anton, 231, 232
Maxwell, James Clerk, 478
"May Day" (Fitzgerald), 696
"Maybe" (Gershwin), 713
Mayer, Frederick, 414, 744
"Maysville Minstrel, The" (Lardner), 628
MacArthur, General Douglas, 320
McBride, Henry, 407
McCaffery, John K. M., 724
McCormack, John, 587
MacDonald, Ramsay, 491
McElroy, Sarah Marion, 561
McGeehan, John, 455
McGranery, James Patrick, 677
McGuffey, William Holmes, 327
MacIntyre, C. F., 516, 520
McMurry, Lolita, 673
MacNeice, Louis, 654
McTeague (Norris), 437
Meaning of Relativity, The (Einstein), 539
Meaning of Truth, The (William James), 185
Measure for Measure (Shakespeare), 14
Meck, Nadejda von, 303

"Mediterranean Landscape" (Picasso), 573
Meier-Graefe, Julius, 234, 236
Mein Kampf (Hitler), 494, 679, 680, 683
Meissonier, Jean Louis Ernest, 235
Meister, Joseph, 110
Meistersinger, Die (Wagner), 21, 24
"Melanctha" (Gertrude Stein), 461
Mellon, Andrew, 649
Melville, Allen, 47
Melville, Elizabeth, 57
Melville, Elizabeth Shaw; *see* Shaw, Elizabeth
Melville, Gansevoort, 48
Melville, Herman, 47-59, 710
Melville, Malcolm, 52, 56
Melville, Stanwix, 55, 56
Memoirs of Schnabelewopski (Heine), 15
Memoirs of U. S. Grant, 143
Men of Art (Craven), 180
Men Without Women (Hemingway), 720, 725
Mencken, Henry L., 213, 215, 438, 442, 627, 693, 697
Mendelssohn, Felix, 16, 24, 249, 523 f.
"Mending Wall" (Frost), 471
Mental Assassination or Christian Science: A Physical, Intellectual, Moral and Spiritual Peril, 74
Mer, La (Debussy), 308
Meredith, George, 165, 655
Merlin (Robinson), 402
Merrild, Knud, 641
Mes Haines (Zola), 161
Mesley, Alexandrine, 160; *see also* Zola, Alexandrine
Metternich, Prince Klemens von, 455
Mexican War, 702
Meyer, Friederike, 21
Meyerbeer, Giacomo, 14, 15, 24
Michelangelo, 173, 175, 179, 740
Michelet, Jules, 230
Michelson, Albert, 263, 534
Midcentury Journey (Shirer), 291
Middle Years, The (Henry James), 195
Midget, The (periodical), 361
Midsummer Night's Dream, A (Mendelssohn), 524
Midsummer Night's Dream, A (Shakespeare), 525
Mill, John Stuart, 281
Miller, Dickinson, 185
Miller, Francis Trevelyan, 224
Miller, Lewis, 225
Miller, Mina, 225; *see also* Edison, Mina
Miller, Rosalind S., 462, 464
Millet, Jean François, 230, 236
Millionairess, The (Shaw), 258
Milton, John, 58, 206, 238

Mind at the End of Its Tether (Wells), 350

Mirabeau, Octave, 172

Mirliton, Le (cabaret), 331

Mirsky, D. S., 84, 125, 301

Misalliance (Shaw), 257

Miserere et Guerre (Suarès), 422

"Mr. and Mrs. Fixit" (Lardner), 628

Mrs. Eddy (Dakin), 79

Mrs. Warren's Profession (Shaw), 251

Mizener, Arthur, 692, 696, 701

Moby Dick (Melville), 49 f.

Modern Art (Craven), 331, 573

"Modern Times" (Chaplin), 675

Molière, 551

"Moment Musical" (Schubert), 529

Monet, Claude, 177, 178

Monsieur Croche: Anti-Dilettante (Debussy), 308

"Monsieur Verdoux" (Chaplin), 676

Monterey, Carlotta, 665

Montesquiou, Count Robert de, 429

Moon for the Misbegotten, A (O'Neill), 666

Moon of the Caribbees, The (O'Neill), 663

Moore, Harry T., 641

Moore, Henry, 174

Moore, Vera, 485

More Poems (Housman), 277

Moreau, Gustave, 405, 406, 420, 421

Moreau-Sainti, Mme., 304

Morley, Edward W., 534

Morning Call (San Francisco), 143

Morning Post, 489

Mornings in Mexico (Lawrence), 637

Morris, Lloyd, 189

Morris, May, 253

Morris, Robert, 644

Morris, William, 253

Moscow Art Theater, 298, 299

Moses and Monotheism (Freud), 244

Mosquitoes (Faulkner), 704

Mott, Lucretia, 62

Mouillard, Louis Pierre, 362

Moulin Rouge (cabaret), 331

Moulin Rouge (Le Mure), 332

Moulson, Deborah, 61

"Mountain, The" (Frost), 471

Mountain Interval (Frost), 468, 473

Mourning Becomes Electra (O'Neill), 664-665, 667

Moussorgsky, Modest Petrovich, 99, 305

Mozart, Wolfgang Amadeus, 13, 199, 249, 533, 604

Müller, Hermann, 270

Muir, Edwin, 618, 657

Mumford, Lewis, 50, 52, 58, 264, 379

Murder in the Cathedral (Eliot), 657

Murger, Henri, 305

Murry, John Middleton, 640

Music Dramas of Richard Wagner, The (Lavignac), 20

Music for the Ballet (Berger), 601

Musset, Alfred de, 156

Mussolini, Benito, 648, 683, 689, 738

Mutual Company (motion pictures), 671, 672

"My Brother Paul" (Dreiser), 436

My Early Life (Churchill), 486

My Father Who Is on Earth (John Wright), 381

"My Favorite Hero" (Joyce), 586

"My Gal Sal" (Dresser), 436

My Hates (Zola), 161

"My Life" (Chekhov), 301

My Life (Duncan), 522

My Life (Wagner), 12, 19

My Life and Work (Ford), 322

"My Lost Youth" (Longfellow), 470

"My Platonic Sweetheart" (Twain), 148

My Struggle (Hitler), 679; *see also Mein Kampf*

Mysterious Stranger, The (Twain), 147

N

Name and Nature of Poetry, The (Housman), 276-277

Nana (Zola), 162

Napoleon I, 102, 111, 122, 198, 356

Napoleon III, 157, 681

"Narcissus" (Nevin), 524

Nasby, Petroleum Vesuvius (pseudonym of David Ross Locke), 142

Nathan, George Jean, 693

Nathanson, Jerome, 293

Nation, The, 461

National American Woman Suffrage Association, 64, 65

National Institute of Arts and Letters, 387, 473

Natural History of Invertebrates (Lamarck), 3

Nature of the Physical World, The (Eddington), 607

Nausea (Sartre), 743

Negri, Pola, 673

Nekrasov, Nikolai, 83

Neuberger, Mlle., 286, 426

Neue Gedichte (Rilke), 517, 520

Nevin, Ethelbert, 524, 525

New British Poets (Rexroth), 751, 754

New Hampshire (Frost), 468, 474

New Hopes for a Changing World (Russell), 456

New Idea Woman's Magazine, 438

New London Telegraph, 663

New Monthly Magazine, The, 55

New Orleans Daily Crescent, 35

New Pathways in Science (Eddington), 607

New Republic, The (magazine), 699
New School for Social Research (New York), 266, 291
New World Order, The (Wells), 350
New York Criterion, 37
New York Herald, 110, 366, 481, 577
New York Herald Tribune, 175, 298, 676
New York Journal, 314, 315, 446
New York Press, 57
New York State Teachers' Association, 62
New York Times, The, 4, 32, 38, 40, 88, 146, 188, 218, 251-252, 292, 298, 351, 539, 545, 592, 635, 664-665, 704
New York Tribune, 444
New York Society for the Prevention of Vice, 440
New York World, 63, 312, 313, 314, 436
New Yorker, The, 300, 385
Newcomb, Simon, 360, 367
Newell, Robert H., 142
Newman, Ernest, 17
Newman, John Henry, Cardinal, 204
Newton, Benjamin Franklin, 134-135
Newton, Byron, 366
Newton, Isaac, 273, 533, 534, 536, 608
Nicholas II (Russia), 314, 413 f.
Nicodemus (Robinson), 403
Niebuhr, Reinhold, 11
Nietzsche, Friedrich Wilhelm, 22, 23, 209-217, 508, 515, 553, 554, 555
Nietzsche, Josef, 209
Nietzsche, Therese Elisabeth, 209, 210, 215
Nietzsche Contra Wagner (Nietzsche), 23, 214
"Night Cafe, The" (Van Gogh), 234
Nightmares of Eminent Persons (Russell), 457
Nimet Eloui Bey, 520
Nin, Anaïs, 638
Nine Plays by Eugene O'Neill (Krutch), 665
No Exit (Sartre), 743
Noces, Les (Stravinsky), 600-601
Noel, Miriam, 385
Nones (Auden), 751
"Normal Motor Automatism" (Stein and Solomon), 459
Norris, Frank, 437
North American Review, 191
North of Boston (Frost), 468, 470-471, 473
Northrop, F. S. C., 245
Norton, Charles Eliot, 38, 191
Not I, But the Wind (Frieda Lawrence), 641
Notabene, Nicholas (pseudonym of Kierkegaard), 8

Notebooks of Malte Laurids Brigge, The (Rilke), 517
Notes of a Son and Brother (Henry James), 195
Notes from Underground (Dostoevsky), 86
"Notorious Jumping Frog of Calaveras County, The" (Twain), 143
Novels and Stories of Henry James, The, 195
Novels and Tales (Henry James), 194
Noyes, Alfred, 592
Nuits d'Etoiles (Debussy), 304

O

O'Brien, Hon. Beatrice, 482
"Observations on a Remarkable Bacteriolytic Substance (Lysozyme) Found in Secretions and Tissues" (Fleming), 561
O'Casey, Sean, 260
O'Connor, William Douglas, 41, 43
"Ode: To My Pupils" (Auden), 747
Of the Knowledge of God and of Self (Bossuet), 105
Of Thee I Sing (musical comedy), 715
Of Time and the River (Wolfe), 727, 729, 730, 733
Oedipus (Sophocles), 665
Oedipus Rex, 602
Oeuvre, L' (Zola), 153
O'Hara, John, 691
Oiseau de Feu, L' (Stravinsky), 598
"Old Man" (Faulkner), 707
Old Man and the Sea, The (Hemingway), 732
"Old Man's Winter Night, An" (Frost), 473
Old Possum's Book of Practical Cats (Eliot), 657
"Old Times on the Mississippi" (Twain), 140
Older, Mrs. Fremont, 312
O'Leary, John, 338
Olivier, Fernande, 566
Olsen, Regine, 7, 8
Olson, Elder, 755
Omar Khayyám, 275
Omnibus (Crane), 449
Omoo (Melville), 51, 54
O'Neill, Agnes (*née* Boulton), 665
O'Neill, Carlotta (*née* Monterey), 665
O'Neill, Ella Quinlan, 662
O'Neill, Eugene Gladstone, 245, 662-668, 727
O'Neill, Eugene, Jr., 662, 666
O'Neill, James, 662, 663
O'Neill, Kathleen (*née* Jenkins), 662, 665

O'Neill, Oona, 665, 666, 674; *see also* Chaplin, Oona
O'Neill, Shane, 665, 666
"On Symmetry in Physical Phenomena" (Pierre Curie), 372
"On the Banks of the Wabash" (Dresser and Dreiser), 436, 437
"On the Electrodynamics of Moving Bodies" (Einstein), 534
"On the Feminine in Human Nature" (Wagner), 24
On the Origin of Species By Means of Natural Selection, or the Preservation of Favored Races in the Struggle for Life (Darwin), 4; *see also Origin of Species*
"On the Radiative Equilibrium of Stars" (Eddington), 607
On This Island (Auden), 748
"One Wicked Impulse" (Whitman), 35
Onnen, Frank, 604
Open Boat and Other Tales of Adventure, The (Crane), 446
"Opera and Drama" (Wagner), 18
"Ophelia" (Nevin), 524
Origin of Species (Darwin), 1, 4, 5, 287
Orpen, Sir William, 173
Osler, Sir William, 107
Oswald Spengler: A Cultural Estimate (Hughes), 556
"Our Love Is Here to Stay" (Gershwin), 713
Our Mr. Wrenn (Lewis), 620
Our Native Grounds (Kazin), 722
Out of My Later Life (Einstein), 538
Out of My Life and Thought (Schweitzer), 503
Outline of History, The (Wells), 349
Outlook, The, 402
Ovid, 104
Oxford, Lord, 493

P

Pach, Walter, 180
Packard, Frederick C., Jr., 664
Paine, Tom, 227
"Painter's Notes, A" (Matisse), 408
Pair of Blue Eyes, A (Hardy), 166
Pall Mall Gazette, 117
Pansies (Lawrence), 640
Paolo and Francesca, 306
"Parade" (Satie), 570
Paradiso (Dante), 647
Paris Conservatoire, 303, 304, 317
Parker, Judge Alton B., 318
Parker, Dorothy, 318, 700
Parnasse Contemporain, Le, 198
Parnell, Charles Stewart, 586
Parsifal (Wagner), 23, 35, 214

Partisan Review, The, 738
Passage to India (Whitman), 41
Past Recaptured, The (Proust), 430, 431
Pasteur, Camille, 105
Pasteur, Cécile, 105
Pasteur, Jeanne, 105
Pasteur, Louis, 102-112, 559, 561
Pasteur Institute, 110, 111, 377
"Pasting It Together" (Fitzgerald), 700
Pater, Walter, 204
Paterson, Jenny, 253
Patterson, Dr. Daniel, 75-76, 78
Patterson, Rebecca, 136
Paul, St., 503
Pauker, Anna, 548
Pausanias, 99
Pavannes and Divisions (Pound), 648
Payare, Amélie, 405
Payne, Robert, 677
Payne-Townshend, Charlotte, 254
Paysages Légendaires (Rouault), 422
Peer Gynt (Ibsen), 115
Pegler, Westbrook, 674
Péguy, Charles Pierre, 286
Peirce, Charles, 186
Pelléas et Mélisande (Debussy), 305-308
Perfect Wagnerite, The (Shaw), 24, 249
Pergolesi, Giovanni Battista, 602
Perkins, Maxwell, 693, 728, 730, 734
Permanence of Yeats, The (essays), 343
Perry, Bliss, 43
Perséphone (Stravinsky), 603
Personae (Pound), 644
Personal Papers of Anton Chekhov, The, 299
Pétain, Henri Philippe, 687
Peter and Paul Fortress, 83
Peter the Great, 121
Petrouchka (Stravinsky), 599, 600
Pfeiffer, Pauline, 720; *see also* Hemingway, Pauline
Philanderer, The (Shaw), 251
Phillips, William, 89
Philostratus, 99
Philosopher's Holiday (Edman), 289
Philosophy of Civilization (Schweitzer), 503
Philosophy of Friedrich Nietzsche, The (Mencken), 213
Philosophy of Physical Science, The (Eddington), 607
Philosophy of Poverty, The (Proudhon), 29
Piazza Tales, The (Melville), 56
Picasso, Claude, 573
Picasso, Pablo Ruiz y, 460, 461, 462, 465, 565-574, 598, 602, 604, 740
Picasso, Paloma, 573
Picasso, Paul, 570
Picasso: Fifty Years of His Art (Barr), 568

Picasso and His Friends (Olivier), 566
"Picnic on the Grass" (Manet), 161
Pierné, Gabriel, 303
Pierre, or The Ambiguities (Melville), 55
Pierre-Quint, Léon, 426, 432
Pilgrim of the Apocalypse (Gregory), 639, 641
Pillars of Society (Ibsen), 116, 117
Pirandello, Luigi, 113
Pisan Cantos (Pound), 646, 649
Pissarro, Camille, 150, 152, 178, 232
Plaisirs et les Jours, Les (Proust), 427
Planck, Erwin, 274
Planck, Karl, 274
Planck, Max, 270-274, 538
Planer, Minna; *see* Wagner, Minna Planer
Plato, 488
Plays Unpleasant (Shaw), 250
Plays of the Natural and Supernatural (Dreiser), 440
Plekhanov, George, 412, 415
Pliny, 99, 104
Plumed Serpent, The (Lawrence), 637
Pluralistic Universe, A (James), 185
Poe, Edgar Allen, 59, 68, 69, 92, 308, 364, 400, 401, 710
Poèmes Saturniens (Verlaine), 198
Poems and Ballads (Thomas), 754
Poems of Emily Dickinson, 136
Poems of Gerard Manley Hopkins, 205
Poems of the Past and Present (Hardy), 167
Poems of Things (Rilke), 516
Poet and Two Painters, A (Merrild), 641
Poetry (magazine), 645
Poetry and the Age (Jarrell), 474
Poetry of Dylan Thomas, The (Olson), 755
Poiret, Paul, 529
"Poissons d'Or" (Debussy), 308
Polite Essays (Pound), 648
Political Equality League, 65
Pollitt, Josephine, 134
Pomes Penyeach (Joyce), 588
Poor Folk (Dostoevsky), 83
Poor Man and the Lady, The (Hardy), 165
Pope (Strachey), 551
Pope, Alexander, 256, 551, 749
Porgy and Bess (music drama), 715
Portable Faulkner, The, 707
Portable F. Scott Fitzgerald, The, 700
Portable Ring Lardner, The, 630
Portable Veblen, The, 267
"Portrait d'une Femme" (Pound), 645
"Portrait of a Lady" (Eliot), 645
Portrait of a Lady (Henry James), 190, 192

Portrait of the Artist as a Young Dog (Thomas), 753
Portrait of the Artist as a Young Man, A (Joyce), 587, 589, 590, 591
Portraits and Miniatures (Strachey), 552
Possessed, The (Dostoevsky), 87
Poulenc, Francis, 598
Pound, Ezra Loomis, 471, 643-649, 717
Pouquet, Jeanne Maurice, 426
Poverty of Philosophy, The (Marx), 29
Power of Darkness (Tolstoy), 127
Pradier, James, 93
Praed, Winthrop Mackworth, 404
Prag-Strasschnitz (Czechoslovakia), 615
Pragmatism (William James), 185
Pravda, 543
Prefaces (Kierkegaard), 8
Prélude à l'Après-midi d'un Faune (Debussy), 305-306
Préludes (Debussy), 309
Prescott, William H., 469
Priboutki (Stravinsky), 600
Priestley, John Boynton, 247, 732
Prince and the Pauper, The (Twain), 144
Princeteau, René, 330
Principia Mathematica (Russell and Whitehead), 452
Principles of Psychology (William James), 185
Principles of Psychology (Spencer), 1
Pringsheim, Katia, 508
Printemps (Debussy), 304
Prisonnière, La (Proust), 430
"Private History of a Campaign that Failed" (Twain), 141
Problem of Flying and Practical Experiments in Soaring, The (Lilienthal), 362
Problems of Men (Dewey), 291
Prodigal Parents (Lewis), 624
Prodigal Son, The (ballet), 422
Progress in Flying Machines (Chanute), 362
Prokofiev, Sergei, 302, 422, 598
Proses Lyriques (Debussy), 305
Prospects of Industrial Civilization (Dora and Bertrand Russell), 453
"Protocols of Zion" (forged tract), 325
Proudhon, Pierre Joseph, 29, 256
Proust, Dr. Adrien, 424, 428
Proust, Jeanne (*née* Weill), 424-425, 427, 428
Proust, Marcel, 197, 286, 424, 433, 462, 506, 618, 733
Proust, Dr. Robert, 424, 432
"Provide, Provide" (Frost), 476
Provincetown Players, 663
Prufrock and Other Observations

(Eliot), 653; *see also* "Love Song of J. Alfred Prufrock, The"
Prussian Officer, The (Lawrence), 635
Psychological Review, 459
Psychology (William James), 459
Psychology of Art, The (Malraux), 740
Psychopathology of Everyday Life, The (Freud), 238, 594
Ptolemy, 608
Pulcinella (Stravinsky), 602
Pulitzer, Joseph, 175, 311, 312, 314, 315
Purgatorio (Dante), 647
Purviance, Edna, 672
Pushkin, Alexander, 82
Putnam, James, 242
Pu-yi, Henry (Ch'ing), 356
Pygmalion (Shaw), 254, 257

Q

"Quarry" (Rouault), 421
Quatres Evangiles, Les (Zola), 164
Queen Victoria (Strachey), 551
Quest of the Historical Jesus, The (Schweitzer), 501
Quimby, Phineas P., 76 f.
Quintessence of Ibsenism, The (Shaw), 115, 118, 249

R

Rabelais, 54, 596, 733
Radium Institute (Warsaw), 377
"Ragtime" (Stravinsky), 570, 601
Rainbow, The (Lawrence), 635, 636
Rainer Maria Rilke (Holthusen), 516
Rajk, Laszlo, 548
Rake's Progress, The (Stravinsky), 603
Ramona (Jackson), 134
Rank, Otto, 242
Ransom, John Crowe, 343
Raphael, 179
Rasputin, Grigori, 415
Raubal, Angela (*née* Hitler), 678
Raubal, Geli, 678, 686
Rauschning, Hermann, 688
Ravel, Maurice, 302, 310, 598, 714
Raynal, Maurice, 567, 568
Read, Herbert, 572
Read, Lucy, 60
Readers (McGuffey), 327
Rebels and Ancestors (Geismar), 439
Reconstruction in Philosophy (Dewey), 289, 292
Red Badge of Courage, The (Crane), 444, 445-446
Redburn (Melville), 52, 54
Redemption (Tolstoy), 127
Rée, Paul, 213
Reflections of an Unpolitical Man (Thomas Mann), 509
Régnier, Henri de, 305
Rehan, Ada, 524

Reik, Theodore, 242
Reinach, Joseph, 174
Réincarnations du Père Ubu, Les (Vollard), 422
Reinhardt, Max, 674
Relativity, The Special and General Theory (Einstein), 534
Relativity Theory of Protons and Electrons (Eddington), 609-610
Rembrandt van Rijn, 230, 235, 237, 420
Remembrance of Things Past (Proust), 424, 429, 430, 432
Remington, Frederic, 315
Renan, Ernest, 282
Renard (Stravinsky), 600
Renoir, Auguste, 177-181, 420, 565
Renoir, Jean, 180
Renouvier, Charles Bernard, 184
"Report on the Relativity Theory" (Eddington), 607
Reprieve, The (Sartre), 743
Republic (Plato), 488
Republic of Silence, The (Sartre), 742
Requiem for a Nun (Faulkner), 707
Respectful Prostitute, The (Sartre), 743
Responsibilities (Yeats), 340
Resurrection (Tolstoy), 127
"Return of Buck Gavin, The" (Wolfe), 726
Retrospection and Introspection (Eddy), 74
"Revenge and Requital: A Tale of a Murderer Escaped" (Whitman), 35
Revolution (newspaper), 64
Revolution of 1848 (France), 68; (Russia), 83
Revolutionary War, 47, 218, 575
Revue des Deux-Mondes, 592
Rewald, John, 178
Rexroth, Kenneth, 750-751, 754
"Rhapsody in Blue" (Gershwin), 714, 715
"Rhapsody in Blue" (motion picture), 712
Rheingold, Das (Wagner), 20
Rheinische Zeitung (periodical), 28
Rhinegold, The (Wagner), 20
Rhymers' Club, 336
Rhyming Picture Guide to Ayot Saint Lawrence (Shaw), 259
Rhys, Ernest, 336
Rich, Daniel Catton, 237
"Rich Boy, The" (Fitzgerald), 697
Richards, William C., 324, 328
Richardson, Hadley, 717; *see also* Hemingway, Hadley
Richardson, Helen Parks, 441
Richthofen, Baron Manfred von, 636
Riddle of Emily Dickinson, The (Patterson), 136
Riding, Laura, 207

Rienzi (Wagner), 14 f.
Rigni, Augusto, 479
Rilke, Jaroslav, 515
Rilke, Rainer Maria, 172, 173, 447, 514-521, 567, 618, 749
Rilke, Ruth, 516
Rimbaud, Arthur, 66, 199-201, 651
Rimsky-Korsakov, Nikolai, 303, 598
Ring of the Nibelungs (Wagner), 18, 19, 23, 24, 25, 249
Ripostes (Pound), 644
Rites of Spring, The (Stravinsky), 597
River War, The (Churchill), 488-489
Robbins, Amy Catherine, 347
Robbins, Rossell Hope, 660
Robinson, Dean, 399, 400
Robinson, Edwin Arlington, 399-404, 471, 476
Robinson, Herman, 399, 400
Robinson, Mrs. Herman, 401
Rochefoucauld, François de La; *see* La Rochefoucauld, François de
Rock, The (Eliot), 657
"Rocking Horse Winner, The" (Lawrence), 640
Roderick Hudson (Henry James), 192
Rodin, Auguste, 170-176, 516, 525, 526
Rodrigue et Chimène (Debussy), 305
Roentgen, Wilhelm, 373
Rolfe, Ellen, 263; *see also* Veblen, Ellen
Roman Bartholow (Robinson), 402
Romances Sans Paroles (Verlaine), 201
Romances Without Words (Verlaine), 201
Romantic Egoist, The (Fitzgerald), 693
Romeo and Juliet (Shakespeare), 527
Rommel, General Erwin, 689
Roosevelt, Anna Eleanor, 495, 576, 584
Roosevelt, Franklin Delano, 189, 442, 495, 536, 575-585, 648, 677, 687
Roosevelt, Isaac, 575
Roosevelt, James (I), 575
Roosevelt, James (II), 575
Roosevelt, Sara Delano, 575, 576
Roosevelt, Theodore, 189, 402, 575, 576, 577
Roosevelt in Retrospect (Gunther), 576
Roqui, Jeanne Etiennette, 102
"Rose for Emily, A" (Faulkner), 707
Rosmersholm (Ibsen), 119
Rossetti, Dante Gabriel, 304
Rossini, Gioacchino, 249
Rouault, Georges, 405, 420-423, 565, 567, 598
Roughing It (Twain), 142
Rougon-Macquart novels (Zola), 161-162
Round Up (Lardner), 629
Rousseau, Jean Jacques, 267
Roussel, Albert Charles Paul Marie, 310

Rowlandson, Thomas, 625
Royal Highness (Thomas Mann), 508
Royal Institute of British Architects, 165, 167, 387
Royal Society (London), 110, 563, 605
Royal Way, The (Malraux), 737
Rozerot, Jeanne, 163
Rubáiyát (Omar Khayyám), 168, 275, 278
Rubens, Peter Paul, 181
Ruiz Blasco, José, 565
Ruiz y Picasso, Pablo, 565; *see also* Picasso, Pablo Ruiz y
Ruskin, John, 391, 392, 393
Russell, Alys (*née* Smith), 453, 454
Russell, Bertrand (3d Earl Russell), 450-457
Russell, Dora (*née* Black), 454
Russell, Lady Edith; *see* Finch, Edith
Russell, George (Æ), 398, 589
Russell, Lady Helen (*née* Spence), 456
Russell, John (1st Earl Russell), 450
Russian Assignment (Stevens), 548
Russian Messenger (periodical), 126
Russian Revolution, 358, 416, 543, 600
Russo-Japanese War, 414
Russo-Turkish War, 124
Rutherford, Ernest (1st Baron Rutherford), 274, 608
Ryskind, Morrie, 715

S

Sachs, Hanns, 242
Sacre du Printemps, Le (Stravinsky), 597, 599, 600
Sacred River; An Approach to James Joyce, The (Strong), 594
Sacred Wood, The (Eliot), 654
Sagesse (Verlaine), 202
Saint Joan (Shaw), 258
"St. John the Baptist" (Rodin), 172
St. Lawrence (ship), 48
Saint-Simon, Claude de Rouvroy, Comte de, 425
Sainte-Beuve, Charles Augustin, 71
Saison en Enfer, Un (Rimbaud), 200
Salammbô (Flaubert), 99, 100
Salomé, Lou, 213, 515
Salter, Andrew, 245
Saltus, Edgar, 314
Salut Public (journal), 68
San Francisco Bulletin, 468
San Francisco Examiner, 312-314
Sanctuary (Faulkner), 706
Sand, George, 93, 98
Sanderson, Sybil, 317
Sapiro, Aaron, 325
Sardou, Victorien, 249
Sargeant, Winthrop, 152, 604
Sartoris (Faulkner), 704
Sartre, Jean Paul, 11, 217, 741-746

Sassoon, Siegfried, 168
Satan in the Suburbs (Russell), 456
Satie, Erik, 302, 570
"Satires of Circumstance" (Hardy), 169
Saturday Evening Post, The, 626, 693
Saturday Press (New York), 143
Saturday Review, The, 249, 676, 746
Saturday Review of Literature, 288
Savage Pilgrimage, The (Carswell), 638, 640
Savonarola, Girolamo, 650
Savrola, a Tale of the Revolution in Laurania (Churchill), 484, 488
Sayre, Zelda, 693, 694; *see also* Fitzgerald, Zelda
Scarfe, Francis, 749, 751
Scheherazade (Rimsky-Korsakov), 598
Schicklgruber, Alois, 678
Schicklgruber, Maria, 678
Schiller, Johann Christoph Friedrich von, 507
Schillinger, Joseph, 714
Schlesinger, Elisa, 92, 93, 99, 100
Schoenberg, Arnold, 302
School and Society, The (Dewey), 288
Schools of Tomorrow (Dewey), 289
Schopenhauer, Arthur, 211, 508
Schubert, Franz, 308, 529
Schulberg, Budd, 700
Schumann, Robert, 16
Schuschnigg, Kurt von, 686
Schweitzer, Albert, 500-505
Schweitzer, Helene (*née* Bresslau), 503
Schwimmer, Rosika, 325
Science and Health (Eddy), 76, 78, 79
Science and Society (Clark), 571
Science Book of Wonder Drugs, The, 562
Science of Life, The (Wells and Huxley), 349
Scientific American, 366
Scopes, John Thomas, 5
Scott, Sir Walter, 346, 458
"Sea and the Mirror, The" (Auden), 749
Sea Gull, The (Chekhov), 297, 298, 299
Sears, Paul B., 5
Season in Hell, A (Rimbaud), 200, 201
Second World War, The (Churchill), 484
"Second Rhapsody" (Gershwin), 714, 715
"Secular Masque, The" (Dryden), 651
Sedgwick, Ellery, 58
"Seeing Things in Double Focus" (Frankel), 746
Seldes, Gilbert, 252, 630, 669
Select Conversations with an Uncle (Wells), 347
Selected Papers (Russell), 451
Selected Poems (Pound), 645
Selected Short Stories (Lewis), 621

Selected Writings of Dylan Thomas, The, 755
Self-Help (Smiles), 105
Self-Portrait (Freud), 239
Sennett, Mack, 671
Sense of the Past, The (Henry James), 195
Sentimental Education (Flaubert), 96, 99
"Servant to Servants, A" (Frost), 471
Seton-Watson, Hugh, 548
Seurat, Georges, 232, 568
"Sevastopol Tales" (Tolstoy), 124
Seventh Symphony (Beethoven), 529
Shakespear, Dorothy, 644
Shakespeare, William, 13, 14, 51, 54, 89, 227, 238, 252, 255, 308, 458, 466, 555, 655, 666, 668, 726, 749
Shape of Things to Come, The (Wells), 349
Shaw, Charlotte (*née* Payne-Townshend); *see* Payne-Townshend, Charlotte
Shaw, Elizabeth, 51
Shaw, George Bernard, 24, 33, 113, 115, 118, 119, 175, 182, 247-261, 283, 451, 469, 498, 666, 668, 676, 773
Shaw, George Carr, 247, 248
Shaw, Henry Wheeler, 142
Shaw, Lemuel, 51, 56
Shaw, Lucinda Elizabeth Gurley, 247, 248
Shchukine, Sergei, 567
Sheean, Vincent, 550
Shelley, Persy Bysshe, 248, 336, 338, 753
Sheridan, Clare, 673
Sherman, Stuart P., 440
Shewing Up of Blanco Posnet, The (Shaw), 257
Shirer, William H., 291
"Short Happy Life of Francis Macomber, The" (Hemingway), 721
Short Stories of Dostoevsky, The (Phillips), 89
Shostakovich, Dmitri, 302
"Shoulder Arms" (motion picture), 672
Shropshire Lad, A (Housman), 275, 277
Siegfried (Wagner), 20
Siegfried's Death (Wagner), 17, 19
Signac, Paul, 232
Silentio, Johannes de (pseudonym of Kierkegaard), 8
Simmons, Ernest J., 126, 129, 130
Simonds, Frank, 581
"Simple Heart, A" (Flaubert), 100, 461
Singer, Paris ("Lohengrin"), 529-530
Sinclair, Upton, 619
Sisley, Alfred, 177
Sister Carrie (Dreiser), 436-437, 438, 445
Sitter, Willem de, 607
Sketch of My Life, A (Thomas Mann), 511

Skeleton Key to Finnegans Wake, A (Robinson and Campbell), 596
Skinner, B. F., 459
Skinner, M. L., 638
Slansky, Max, 548
Sklodovska, Bronislava (Bronya), 368, 369, 370; *see also* Dluski, Bronya
Sklodovska, Helen (Hela), 368, 370
Sklodovska, Marya (Marie), 368-372; *see also* Curie, Marie
Sklodovska, Sophie (Zosia), 368
Sklodovski, Dr. Ladislas, 368, 369, 370
Sklodovski, Joseph (Jozio), 368
Slochower, Harry, 617
Small Boy and Others, A (Henry James), 195
Smart Set (magazine), 663, 693
Smattering of Ignorance, A (Levant), 715
Smiles, Samuel, 105
Smith, Alfred E., 579
Smith, Alys Whitall Pearsall, 451; *see also* Russell, Alys
Smith, Clifford P., 73
Smith, Johnston (pseudonym of Stephen Crane), 445
Smith, Logan Pearsall, 451
Smith, Sydney, 226
Smith, General Walter Bedell, 545
Smithsonian Institution, 362, 367
Smollett, Tobias, 458
Smuts, General Jan Christiaan, 394
Snap-Shots (periodical), 361
Snitkin, Anna Grigorievna, 86; *see also* Dostoevskaya, Anna
"Snows of Kilimanjaro, The" (Hemingway), 721
Soby, James Thrall, 420, 423, 574
Socrates, 212, 262, 455
Social Credit: An Impact (Pound), 648
Société Anonyme des Artistes, Peintres, Sculpteurs et Graveurs ("Impressionists"), 178
Society of Men of Letters (France), 164, 174
Society for Psychical Research, 188
Sodom et Gomorrhe (Proust), 430
Soldier's Pay (Faulkner), 704
Solomon, Leon, 459
"Some Like Them Cold" (Lardner), 628
"Somebody Loves Me" (Gershwin), 713
Son of Woman (Murry), 640
"Song for Simeon, A" (Eliot), 656
"Song of Myself" (Whitman), 39, 43, 640
"Song of the Exposition" (Whitman), 44
"Song of Wandering Aengus, The" (Yeats), 339
Sonnete an Orpheus, Die (Rilke), 519
Sonnets from the Portuguese (Elizabeth Barrett Browning), 517

Sonnets to Orpheus (Rilke), 519
Sons and Lovers (Lawrence), 632, 634-635, 638
Soong, Charlie (Yao-ju), 354
Soong, Chingling, 354, 356, 357, 358
Soong, Eling, 354
Soong, Mayling, 354
Soong Sisters, The (Hahn), 354
Sophocles, 635
Sorenson, Charles, 326
Soulima, Nadejda, 603
Sound and the Fury, The (Faulkner), 704
Sousa, John Philip, 712
South Bend (Ind.) *Times*, 626
"Sower, The" (Millet), 230
Space, Time, and Gravitation (Eddington), 607
Spanish-American War, 186, 314-316, 446, 447
Spanish Civil War, 56, 571-572, 627, 685, 721-722, 738, 747
Spark, The (periodical), 543; *see also Iskra*
Specimen Days (Whitman), 45
Spectator (periodical), 550
Spence, Helen Patricia, 454; *see also* Russell, Lady Helen
Spencer, Herbert, 1, 281, 534
Spencer Churchill, John Winston (7th Duke of Marlborough), 485
Spender, Stephen, 197, 204, 521, 660, 748, 749
Spengler, Oswald, 217, 553-558, 773
Spenser, Edmund, 655
Spinoza, Baruch, 533, 541
Spirit of Romance, The (Pound), 648
"Spleen" (Eliot), 651
Spofford, Daniel H., 79
"Spring Song" (Mendelssohn), 523
Spring Storm (periodical), 507
Squaw Woman (play), 671
Stages on Life's Road (Kierkegaard), 8
Stalin, Jacob, 546
Stalin, Joseph, 290, 414, 496, 542-549, 583, 739
Stalin, Svetlana, 546
Stalin, Vassily, 546
Stalin: An Appraisal of the Man and His Influence (Trotsky), 544
Stanislavsky, Constantin, 298, 528
Stanton, Elizabeth Cady, 62, 64
Starkie, Enid, 70
"Starry Night, The" (Van Gogh), 236
Stars and Atoms (Eddington), 607
Steegmuller, Francis, 95
Steeple Bush (Frost), 468
Steeplejack (Huneker), 331
Stein, Amelia Keyser, 458
Stein, Daniel, 458
Stein, Gertrude, 406, 407, 458-467, 567, 717, 718

Stein, Leo, 407, 458, 460
Steiner, Dr. Rudolph, 613
Stekel, Wilhelm, 242
Stephen Hero (Joyce), 589
Stevens, Leslie C., 548
Stevenson, Robert Louis, 288, 559
Stewart, Cora Howarth, 446, 447
Stillwell, Mary, 222; *see also* Edison, Mary
Stockholm speech (Faulkner), 707-708
Stoddard, Charles Warren, 143
"Stoic, The" (Dreiser), 439
"Stoker, The" (Kafka), 614
Stone, Geoffrey, 737-738
Stone, A Leaf, A Door, A (Wolfe), 734
Stories About God (Rilke), 515
Stories for Ninon (Zola), 159
Stories of Three Decades (Thomas Mann), 512
Story of a Novel, The (Wolfe), 728
Story of a Wonderman, The (Lardner), 629
Story of Art, The (Reinach), 174
Story of Philosophy, The (Durant), 188
Story of the Malakand Field Force, The (Churchill), 488
Story of Temple Drake, The (Faulkner), 706
Stowe, Harriet Beecher, 230
Strachey, Lady Jane, 550
Strachey, John, 550
Strachey, Lytton, 550-552
Strachey, General Sir Richard, 550
Strachey, St. Loe, 550
Strange Interlude (O'Neill), 664
Strauss, Mme. Geneviève, 426, 427
Strauss, Johann, 527, 528
Strauss, Richard, 217, 302
Stravinsky, Feodor, 598
Stravinsky, Igor, 25, 302, 570, 597-604, 754
Stravinsky, Milene, 603
Stravinsky, Nadejda (*née* Soulima), 603
Stravinsky, Sviatoslav (Soulima), 603
Stravinsky, Theodore, 603
Stravinsky, Vera (*née* Sudeikine), 603
Strike Up the Band (musical comedy), 715
Strindberg, August, 663
Strong, Leonard Alfred George, 594, 595
Stundenbuch, Das (Rilke), 517
Suarès, André, 307, 422
Sudeikine, Vera, 603
Sue, Eugène, 98
Suite Bergamesque (Debussy), 305
Sullivan, Louis, 380, 381
"Summertime" (Gershwin), 715
Sun Ah Mei, 353
Sun Also Rises, The (Hemingway), 654, 719
Sun Tat-sung, 352

Sun Yat-sen, 352-357, 737
Sun Yat-sen, Mme.; *see* Soong, Ching-ling
Sun Yat-sen and the Chinese Republic (Linebarger), 357
"Sunken Cathedral, The" (Debussy), 308
Suppliants, The (Aeschylus), 528
"Sur l'Herbe" (Verlaine), 199
Survey of Modern Poetry, A (Graves and Riding), 207
Susan B. Anthony: The Woman Who Changed the Mind of a Nation (Dorr), 64
Suslova, Polina, 85, 86
Sutherland, Donald, 462, 464
Suvorin, Alexei, 296
Svanidze, Ekaterina, 546
Swan, Michael, 192
"Swanee" (Gershwin), 712-713
Swann's Way (Proust), 424, 430
Swedenborg, Emanuel, 182, 190
Sweet Cheat Gone, The (Proust), 430
Swift, Jonathan, 596, 630
Swinburne, Charles Algernon, 71, 168, 207, 279, 644
Swinnerton, Frank, 551
Symbolist Movement in Literature (Symons), 651
Symons, Arthur, 69, 651
Symphony in C (Wagner), 24
Symphony of Psalms (Stravinsky), 603
Synge, John Millington, 338, 469, 592

T

Tables of the Law, The (Thomas Mann), 512
Taciturnus, Frater (pseudonym of Kierkegaard), 9
Taft, William Howard, 319
Taggard, Genevieve, 133
Taine, Hippolyte, 161, 282
Taiping Rebellion, 352
Tale of Possessors Self-Dispossessed (O'Neill), 665
Tales of Jacob, The (Thomas Mann), 511
Tales of Space and Time (Wells), 348
Tales of the Jazz Age (Fitzgerald), 696
Taliesin, 384, 385
Taliesin West, 386
Talifer (Robinson), 403
Talmadge, Constance, 697
Tannhäuser (Wagner), 17, 20, 22, 528, 597
Taps at Reveille (Fitzgerald), 699
Tarver, John Charles, 99
Tattler, The (periodical), 361
Taxidea Americana (Lardner), 629
Taylor, Edward, 136

Taylor, Francis Henry, 571
Taylor, Robert Lewis, 484
Tchaikovsky, Peter Ilich, 303, 602, 604
Tebel, John, 315
Teheran (conference), 547, 583
Temple, Mary, 193
Tempest, The (Shakespeare), 749
Temps Retrouvé, Le (Proust), 430
Temptation of St. Anthony (Flaubert), 96, 97, 100
Tender Buttons (Gertrude Stein), 459, 463, 465
Tender is the Night (Fitzgerald), 698, 699
Teresa, St., 93
Terre, La (Zola), 162
Territorial Enterprise (periodical), 142, 143
Terry, Ellen, 253, 254, 525, 528
Tess of the d'Urbervilles (Hardy), 166
Testament, Le (Pound), 648
"Testimony Against Gertrude Stein" (Matisse *et al.*), 465
Texier, Rosalie, 307
Thaïs (Massenet), 317
"That Evening Sun" (Faulkner), 707
Their Finest Hour (Churchill), 497
Theocritus, 525
Theodore Dreiser: Apostle of Nature (Elias), 437
Theory of Business Enterprise, The (Veblen), 264
Theory of the Leisure Class, The (Veblen), 263, 268-269
Thérèse Raquin (Zola), 161
These Thirteen (Faulkner), 707
"Thinker, The" (Rodin), 176
Thirst and Other Plays (O'Neill), 663
This Side of Paradise (Fitzgerald), 693, 694
This Side of Paradise (Mizener), 701
This Was a Poet (Whicher), 134
Thode, Heinrich, 528
Thomas, St., 604
Thomas, Airon, 753
Thomas, Caitlin (*née* Macnamara); *see* Macnamara, Caitlin
Thomas, Colm, 753
Thomas, Dylan Marlais, 204, 753-757
Thomas, Edward, 470
Thomas, Llewelyn, 753
Thomas A. Edison: Benefactor of Mankind (Miller), 224
Thomas Alva Edison (Garbedian), 222
Thomas Mann Reader, The, 509
Thompson, Dorothy, 581, 620, 624
Thompson, Oscar, 306, 310
Thomson, Virgil, 466
Thoreau, Henry David, 50, 139, 391, 394, 449
Thoreson, Susanna, 114

Three Contributions to the Theory of Sex (Freud), 242
Three Lives (Gertrude Stein), 461, 463
Three Stories, The (Chekhov), 300
Three Stories and Ten Poems (Hemingway), 718
Three Taverns, The (Robinson), 402
Thurn und Taxis-Hohenlohe, Princess Marie von, 518
Thus Spake Zarathustra (Nietzsche), 214, 216
Time (magazine), 351, 667
Time and Free Will (Bergson), 282
Time Machine, The (Wells), 347
Time Regained (Proust), 431; *see also Past Recaptured, The*
Tindall, William York, 590, 641
Titan, The (Dreiser), 439
Tito, 547-548
To Have and Have Not (Hemingway), 721
Tobin, Catherine, 381
Todd, Mabel Loomis, 136
Toklas, Alice B., 460
Tolstaya, Alexandra, 129, 130
Tolstaya, Sonya (*née* Mers), 128, 130, 131
Tolstoy, Count Leo Nikolayevich, 85, 121-131, 296, 391, 516, 730
Tolstoy, Count Nikolai Ilich, 121-122
Tolstoy, Nikolai Nikolayevich, 123
Tolstoy, Peter Andreyevich, 121
Tolstoy: An Approach (Lavrin), 127
Tom Sawyer, The Adventures of (Twain), 142, 146, 147
Tomlin, E. W. F., 11, 28, 31, 283, 284
Tonio Kröger (Thomas Mann), 506, 508
Tono-Bungay (Wells), 346, 348
Torrent and the Night Before, The (Robinson), 400
Torrents of Spring, The (Hemingway), 719
Totem and Taboo (Freud), 243, 244
Toulouse-Lautrec, Henri de, 232, 329-335, 566
Toulouse-Lautrec-Monfa, Countess Adèle de, 329, 330, 331
Toulouse-Lautrec-Monfa, Count Alphonse de, 329, 330
Tower, The (Yeats), 342
Town Down the River, The (Robinson), 402
"Tradition and the Individual Talent" (Eliot), 657
Trail of the Hawk, The (Lewis), 620
Tramp Abroad, A (Twain), 142
Transposed Heads, The (Thomas Mann), 512
Traumgekrönt (Rilke), 515
Travail (Zola), 164
Traveler at Forty, A (Dreiser), 439

Treasure Island (Stevenson), 485
"Treat 'Em Rough" (Lardner), 627
Trespasser, The (Lawrence), 638
Trial, The (Kafka), 615, 616, 617
Triangle Club (Princeton), 692
Tristan und Isolde (Wagner), 19, 20, 22, 248, 304, 309
Tristram (Robinson), 402, 403
Triumph and Tragedy (Churchill), 497-498
Trois Nocturnes (Debussy), 308
Trotsky, Leon, 290, 413, 414, 496, 543 f., 737, 739
Truth (periodical), 118
T. S. Eliot Myth, The (Robbins), 660
Turgenev, Ivan, 100, 192
"Turn of the Screw" (Henry James), 194
Turner, Joseph Mallord, 336
Twain, Mark, 73, 80, 139-148, 314, 490, 630; *see also* Clemens, Samuel Langhorne
Tweedmouth, Edward Marjoribanks, 2d Baron, 486
Twelve Against the Gods (Bolitho), 527
Twilight of the Gods, The (Nietzsche), 214
"Two Gallants" (Joyce), 588
Tyndall, John, 227, 337
Typee (Melville), 49 f.

U

Ulianov, Alexander Ilich, 410
Ulianov, Dmitri Ilich, 410
Ulianov, Ilya Nicolaevich, 410
Ulianov, Vladimir Ilich, 410-411; *see also* Lenin, Nikolai
Ulianova, Anna Ilevna, 410
Ulianova, Manyasha Ilevna, 410
Ulianova, Maria Alexandrovna, 410
Ulianova, Olga Ilevna, 410
Ulysses (Joyce), 587, 590-594, 728
Uncle Tom's Cabin (Stowe), 702
Uncle Vanya (Chekhov), 299
"Undefeated, The" (Hemingway), 721
Under Milk Wood (Thomas), 756
Under the Greenwood Tree (Hardy), 166
United States (frigate), 50, 52
Universe and Dr. Einstein, The (Barnett), 537
Universe of G.B.S., The (Irvine), 250
Unpopular Essays (Russell), 456
Untimely Thoughts (Nietzsche), 214
Unto This Last (Ruskin), 391
Unvanquished, The (Faulkner), 707
U.S.A. (Dos Passos), 328
"Use of Poetry, The" (Eliot), 654
Useful Knowledge (Gertrude Stein), 465

V

Valentin, Antonina, 348
Valkyrie, The (Wagner), 20, 25
Vallery-Radot, René, 106, 107, 109
Van Doren, Mark, 470
Van Dyck, Sir Anthony, 427
Van Gogh, Vincent; *see* Gogh, Vincent van
Van Vechten, Carl, 461, 529, 597
Vanbrugh, Sir John, 484
Varieties of Religious Experience (William James), 188
Vasnier, Mme., 304, 305
Veblen, Ellen (*née* Rolfe), 265
Veblen, Thorstein Bunde, 262-269
Vega, Lope de, 643
Vegetable, The (Fitzgerald), 696
Verdi, Giuseppe, 99, 249
Vérité (Zola), 164
Verlaine, Mathilde (*née* Maute), 199, 201
Verlaine, Nicolas Auguste, 198
Verlaine, Paul, 71, 198-203, 303, 651
"Very Short Story, A" (Hemingway), 720
Vested Interests and the State of the Industrial Arts, The (Veblen), 266
Vestiges of Creation, The (Chambers), 3
Vico, Giambattista, 556, 594
Victoria, Queen (England), 314, 551
Vie de Bohème, La (Murger), 305
"Villanelle: The Psychological Hour" (Pound), 645
Villon, François, 202, 648
Vincent: A Life of Vincent van Gogh (Meier-Graefe), 234
Vinci, Leonardo da, 360, 427, 555
Virgil, 104
Vision, A (Yeats), 341, 343
Vlaminck, Maurice de, 567
Voice of Destruction, The (Rauschning), 688
Voices of Silence, The (Malraux), 736, 740
Volga Boatman's Song (Stravinsky), 600
Volkonski, Princess Marya Nikolayevna, 122
Vollard, Ambroise, 153, 155, 406, 422
"Voyage, Le" (Baudelaire), 72
"Voyage à Cythère, Un" (Baudelaire), 69
Vremya (periodical), 84
Vuillermoz, Emile, 600

W

Wadsworth, Rev. Charles, 135
Wagner, Albert, 14
Wagner, Clara, 13

Wagner, Cosima, 22, 23; *see also* Bülow, Cosima Liszt von
Wagner, Eva, 22
Wagner, Isolde, 22
Wagner, Karl Friedrich, 12
Wagner, Minna Planer, 14 f.
Wagner, Richard, 12-25, 210 f., 248 f., 302 f., 597, 655, 687, 776
Wagner, Siegfried, 22
Wagner, Wieland, 25
Wagner As Man and Artist (Newman), 17
Waksman, Dr. Selman A., 563
Walküre, Die (Wagner), 20; *see also Valkyrie, The*
Wallace, Alfred Russel, 4
Wallace, Henry, 675
Wallace, Lew, 643
Walpole, Hugh, 196, 622
War and Peace (Tolstoy), 125-126, 710, 720, 730
War Is Kind (Crane), 447, 448
War of the Worlds, The (Wells), 348
Ward, A. C., 251
Ward, Artemus (pseudonym of Charles F. Browne), 142, 143
"Ward Number Six" (Chekhov), 301
Wars I Have Seen (Gertrude Stein), 466
Washington, George, 582
Waste Land, The (Eliot), 423, 645, 654 f., 698, 749
Watt, Homer, 727
Watteau, Jean Antoine, 199
We Never Called Him Henry (Bennett), 328
Weaver, Raymond M., 57
Web and the Rock, The (Wolfe), 731, 732
Webb, Beatrice, 254, 451
Webb, Sidney, 248, 254, 451
Weber, Karl Maria von, 13
Wedding, The (Wagner), 14
Wedgwood, Emma, 3
Wedgwood, Josiah, 1
Weekley, Professor Ernest, 633
Weekley, Frieda von Richthofen, 634; *see also* Lawrence, Frieda
Weil, Jeanne, 424; *see also* Proust, Jeanne
Weinlig, Theodor, 13
Wells, Herbert George, 106, 345-351, 444, 670
Wells, Isabel Mary, 347
Wells, Jane, 347-348; *see also* Robbins, Amy Catherine
Welsh, Mary, 724
Werfel, Franz, 614
Wesendonck, Mathilde, 18, 19, 21
Wesendonck, Otto, 18, 19
Wesleyan, The, 356
Wessex Poems (Hardy), 167

West, Mae, 317
West, Rebecca, 639
Western Society for the Prevention of Vice, 440
Western Union, 221, 223
Westhoff, Clara, 516
Weston, Jessie, 655
Westphalen, Jenny von, 27; *see also* Marx, Jenny
Weyler, General Valeriano, 315
"What Happened" (Gertrude Stein), 465
What Is Art? (Tolstoy), 127
What Is Man? (Twain), 144
"When Lilacs Last in the Dooryard Bloom'd" (Whitman), 42
When the Sleeper Wakes (Wells), 348
When We Dead Awaken (Ibsen), 119
Whicher, George Frisbie, 134
Whilomville Stories (Crane *et al.*), 447
Whistler, James M., 152
White, Elinor, 469
White, Sara (Sallie), 435; *see also* Dreiser, Sallie
White, William Allen, 320
White-Jacket, or The World in a Man-of-War (Melville), 52, 54
White Peacock, The (Lawrence), 633
White Rose of Memphis, The (William Cuthbert Faulkner), 702, 709
Whitehead, Alfred North, 452
Whiteman, Paul, 713-714
Whitman, Andrew, 34
Whitman, Edward, 34
Whitman, George, 34, 40, 41, 43, 44
Whitman, Hannah, 34
Whitman, Jeff, 34, 35
Whitman, Jesse, 34
Whitman, Walt, 34-46, 59, 139, 172, 289, 523, 640, 644, 726, 731
Whittier, John Greenleaf, 139
Widor, Charles Marie, 500, 502
Widowers' Houses (Shaw), 250-251, 252
Wild Duck, The (Ibsen), 113, 119
"Wild Frank's Return" (Whitman), 35
Wild Palms, The (Faulkner), 707
Wild Swans at Coole, The (Yeats), 340
Wild Wheel, The (Garrett), 328
Wilde, Oscar, 333, 640
Will to Believe, The (William James), 185
Will to Power, The (Nietzsche), 214
William Faulkner: A Critical Study (Irving Howe), 708
Willson, Millicent, 317-318
Wilson, Angus, 159
Wilson, Edmund, 276, 343, 461, 655, 692, 700
Wilson, Woodrow, 5, 189, 319, 557, 577, 578
Winckelmann, Johann Joachim, 524

Wind Among the Reeds, The (Yeats), 339
Winding Stair, The (Yeats), 342
Windsor, Claire, 673
Wings of the Dove, The (Henry James), 190, 193
Winkler, John K., 315
Winner Take Nothing (Hemingway), 720
Winston Churchill: An Informal Study of Greatness (Taylor), 484
Winston Churchill: The Era and the Man (Cowles), 490
"Winter Dreams" (Fitzgerald), 697
Winter Notes on Summer Impressions (Dostoevsky), 85
Wisdom (Verlaine), 202
"Witch of Coös" (Frost), 471
Within a Budding Grove (Proust), 430
Witness Tree, A (Frost), 474
Wolfe, Thomas, 506, 726-735
Wolff, Albert, 178
"Woman in White" (Picasso), 570
"Woman Is a Sometime Thing, A" (Gershwin), 715
"Woman of Paris" (motion picture), 674
Woman Suffrage: the Reform Against Nature, 63
Woman's State Temperance Society (N.Y.), 62
Women in Love (Lawrence), 636
Wood Demon, The (Chekhov), 297, 299
Woolf, Virginia, 88
Woollcott, Alexander, 385
Woolsey, Judge John M., 591-592
Wordsworth, William, 168, 458
Work of Art (Lewis), 623
World As I See It, The (Einstein), 538
World As Will and Idea, The (Schopenhauer), 211
World Between Two Wars, The (Quincy Howe), 557
World Crisis, The (Churchill), 493
World I Breathe, The (Thomas), 754
World of William Clissold (Wells), 349
World Set Free, The (Wells), 349
World So Wide (Lewis), 624
Worldly Philosophers, The (Heilbroner), 30, 418
Wright, Almoth, 560
Wright, Anna (*née* Lloyd-Jones), 379, 380
Wright, Catherine, 381
Wright, Catherine (*née* Tobin), 381, 384, 385
Wright, David, 381
Wright, Frances, 381
Wright, Frank Lloyd, 379-388
Wright, Iovanna, 386

Wright, Jennie, 379
Wright, John, 381
Wright, Katherine, 361
Wright, Lloyd, 381
Wright, Lorin, 361
Wright, Maginel, 379
Wright, Milton, 361
Wright, Miriam (*née* Noel), 385, 386
Wright, Olga, 386
Wright, Orville, 360-367
Wright, Reuchlin, 361
Wright, Robert Llewellyn, 381
Wright, Wilbur, 360-366
Wright, William Russell Cary, 379, 380
Wright Brothers, The (Kelly), 365
Writers in Crisis (Geismar), 629

Y

Yacco, Sada, 525
Yalta (conference), 547, 583, 584
Yasnaya Polyana (estate), 121 f.
Yeats, Georgie, (*née* Hyde-Lees), 341
Yeats, Jack, 336
Yeats, John Butler, 336
Yeats, William Butler, 336-344, 520, 587, 588, 592, 648, 749, 752
Yeats: The Man and the Masks (Ellmann), 337
"Yeats and His Symbols" (Ransom), 343
Yellow Book, The (periodical), 427
Yerkes, Charles T., 439
You Can't Go Home Again (Wolfe), 731, 733, 734
You Know Me, Al (Lardner), 627
You Never Can Tell (Shaw), 251
Young, Stark, 703
Young Art (periodical), 566
"Young Immigrunts, The" (Lardner), 629
Young Joseph (Thomas Mann), 511
Yuan Shih-k'ai, 356, 357

Z

Zayas, Marius de, 569
Zeno, 281
Zervos, Christian, 568
Zilboorg, Gregory, 244
Zinoviev, Grigori, 544, 545
Zola, Alexandrine (*née* Mesley), 163
Zola, Emile, 100, 150, 152, 153, 156-164, 192, 230, 438, 745
Zola, Francesco, 156
Zola, François-Emilie (*née* Aubert), 157, 160
Zola and His Time (Josephson), 163
"Zone of Quiet" (Lardner), 628
Zweig, Stefan, 243

About the Author

An outstanding poet, biographer, and essayist, Louis Untermeyer is also America's best-known and most creative anthologist. His Treasury of Great Poems, *now in its eighth printing, was followed by the highly successful* A Treasury of Laughter. *His collections of* Modern American Poetry *and* Modern British Poetry, *revised and amplified, have sold over a million copies and are standard textbooks in schools and colleges. He is said to have introduced more poets to readers and more readers to poetry than any other American.*

Born in New York City and, as he says, miseducated there, he was unable to comprehend a single geometry problem and consequently failed to graduate from high school. For twenty years he acquired culture by ear and taught himself music, art, and literature while earning his living in the family's manufacturing jewelry establishment. Nearing forty, he quit his desk at the factory, went to Europe, lived for a while in England, Austria, and Italy, and returned home to divide his time writing, lecturing, and farming. (His lecture fees barely paid for his farm losses.) He became "poet in residence" at various universities, writer for the Office of War Information, editor of the Armed Services Editions and, after the war, editor for a leading record company. By the time he was sixty, he was the author or compiler of some sixty volumes, including a novel, Moses, *several travel books and stories for young people—two of which he illustrated—and a quasi-autobiography,* From Another World.

His existence is neatly split between an office in New York and a two-hundred-year-old cottage in Connecticut, where he raises odd-color day lilies and outsize iris. His wife is Bryna Ivens, magazine fiction editor, and his three sons have made him eight times a grandfather. Since none of his widely separated sons is over twenty-seven, he foresees a great future for himself as a peripatetic patriarch.

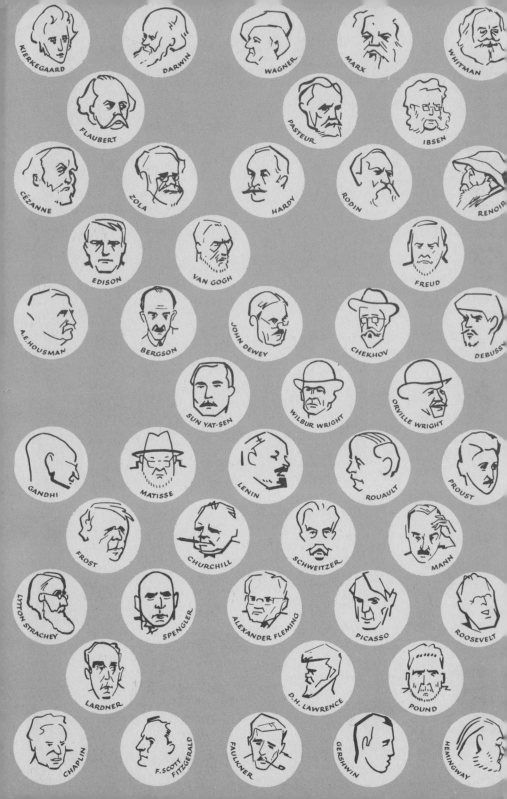